Visit classzone.com and get connected

Online resources provide instruction, practice, and learning support correlated to your text.

- **Guided Web activities** introduce students to real-world Spanish.
- **Audio flashcards** provide review of vocabulary and pronunciation.
- **Self-scoring quizzes** help students assess comprehension.
- **Writing workshops** invite students to share their creations online.
- **Teaching resources** offer answer keys and other support.

You have immediate access to *ClassZone's* teacher resources.

MCDTSHUDEESZ

Use this code to create your own username and password.

Also visit *ClassZone* to learn more about these innovative online resources.

- eEdition Plus Online
- Online Workbook
- eTest Plus Online
- EasyPlanner Plus Online

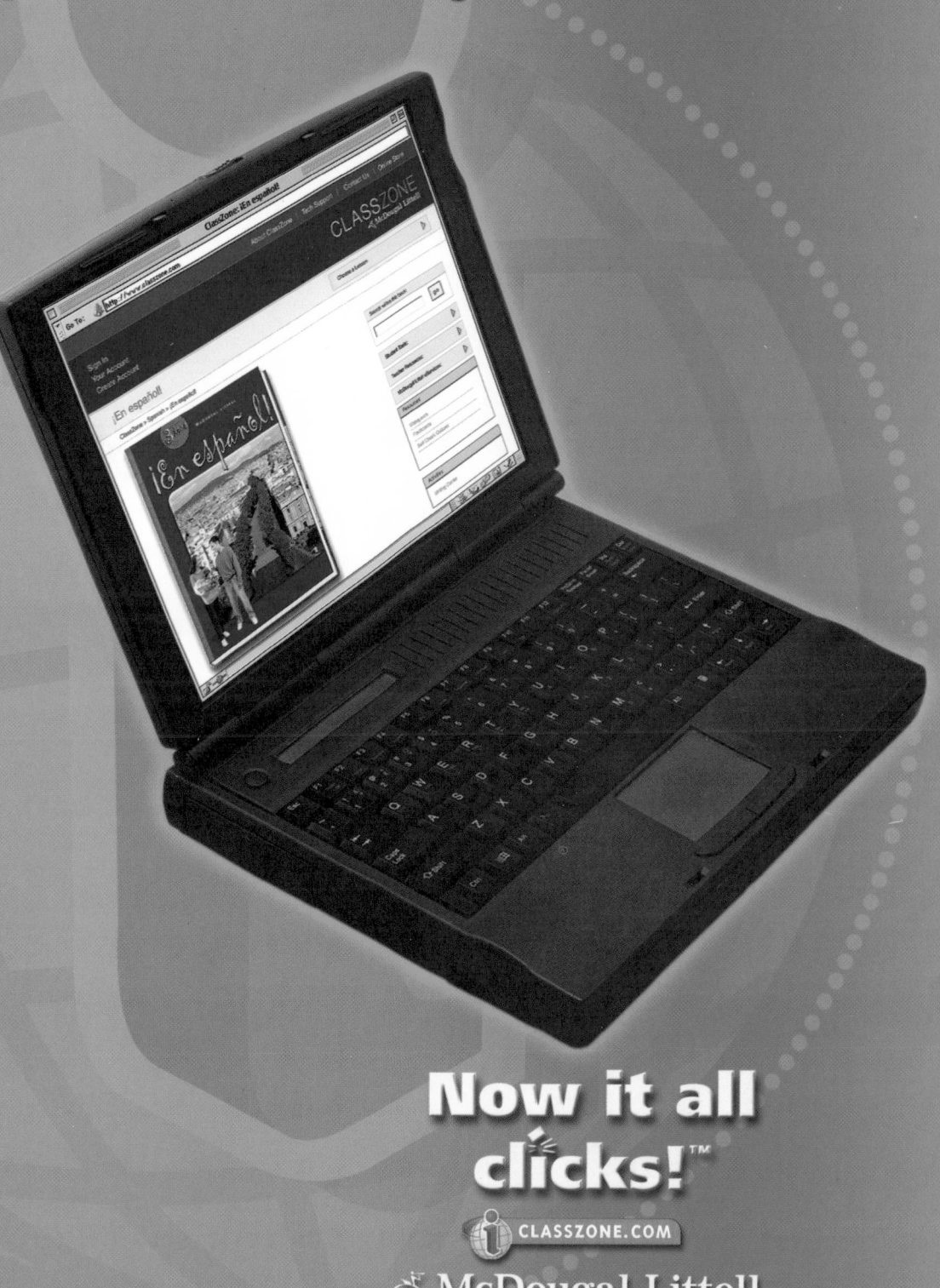

Now it all clicks!™

CLASSZONE.COM

McDougal Littell

3 tres

McDOUGAL LITTELL

¡En español!

Teacher's Edition

AUTHORS

Estella Gahala

Patricia Hamilton Carlin

Audrey L. Heining-Boynton

Ricardo Otheguy

Barbara J. Rupert

CULTURE CONSULTANT

Jorge A. Capetillo-Ponce

McDougal Littell

A HOUGHTON MIFFLIN COMPANY

Evanston, Illinois • Boston • Dallas

Cover Photography

Foreground: Photo by Martha Granger/EDGE Productions.

Background: Aerial view of Las Ramblas, Barcelona, Spain, age fotostock (also appears on spine).

Back cover, top: Peruvian instrument, Wood River Gallery/PNI; from left to right: El Morro Castle, San Juan, Puerto Rico, Bruce Adams/Corbis; Quito, Ecuador, Joseph F. Viesti/The Viesti Collection; Pyramid of the Sun at Teotihuacán, Mexico City, Michael T. Sedam/Corbis; View of Arenal Volcano from Tabacón Hot Springs, Costa Rica, Kevin Schafer; Aerial view of Las Ramblas, Barcelona, Spain, age fotostock; Machu Picchu, Urubamba Valley, Peru, Robert Fried.

Photography

T5 *top right* Leon-Leo Dugast/Panos Pictures, *center right* Jay Ireland & Georgienne E. Bradley/Earth Images, *bottom right* Robert Frerck/Odyssey Productions; **T6** RMIP Richard Haynes; **T19** *left & right* School Division, Houghton Mifflin Co., *center* E.R. Degginger/Photo Researchers; **T48** *left* Leroy Simon/Visuals Unlimited, *second from left* Jo Prater/Visuals Unlimited, *third from left* "The Persistence of Memory" (1939), Salvador Dalí. Oil on canvas, 9 1/2" x 13" (24.1 cm x 33 cm). The Museum of Modern Art, New York. Given anonymously. Photograph © 1998 The Museum of Modern Art, New York; **T49** *left to right* Robert Frerck/Odyssey Productions, Barry Barker/Odyssey Productions, School Division, Houghton Mifflin Co.; **T50** *fish* Jay Ireland & Georgienne E. Bradley/Earth Images, *flag* Tom Stack & Associates, *right & second from right* Robert Frerck/Odyssey Productions; **T51** *left* "New Chicago Athletic Club" (1937), Antonio Berni. Oil on canvas, 6' 3/4" x 9' 10 1/4" (184.9 cm x 600.1 cm). The Museum of Modern Art, New York. Inter-American Fund. Photograph © 1998 The Museum of Modern Art, New York, *second from left* Kim Esterberg, *third from left* School Division, Houghton Mifflin Co., *right* Elsa Hasch/Allsport; **31A** *top* Courtesy of Miami Mensual, *center* RMIP/Richard Haynes, *bottom* T.C. Reiner/ SuperStock; **31F, 53D** RMIP/Richard Haynes; **75B** Telegraph Colour Library; **75D** RMIP/Richard Haynes; **105A** *top* Gail Shumway/Getty Images, *bottom* Jay Ireland & Georgienne E. Bradley/Earth Images; **105B** *top left* Roy Morsch/Corbis, *right* PictureQuest, *bottom left* Gary Antonetti/Ortelius Design; **105F** Unicorn Stock Photos; **149B** Leroy Simon/Visuals Unlimited; **149D** Bob Firth/eStock; **179A** *top* Bill Bachmann/Photo Network/PictureQuest, *bottom* Tom & Therisa Stack; **179B** *top left* Kevin Estrada/Retna, Ltd., *bottom left* Tom & Therisa Stack, *right* Suzanne Murphy-Larronde; **179D** Tom & Therisa Stack; **201B** Torleif Svensson/Corbis; **201D** James P. Dwyer/Stock Boston; **223B** Tony Perrottet/Omni Photo Communications; **223D** Suzanne Murphy-Larronde; **253A** *top* School Division, Houghton Mifflin Co., *center* Steve Niedorf/Getty Images; **253B** *top* Courtesy of Gloria & Claudio Otero/Jim Kelm, *bottom* Tony Morrison/South American Pictures; **253F** Ulrike Welsch; **275D** David Young-Wolff/Getty Images; **297B** Mike Reagan; **297D** Jason P. Howe/South American Pictures; **327A** *bottom* Courtesy of Camino Real Hotel, Cancun, Mexico; 327B *top* Fin Ribar/Stock South/PictureQuest, *bottom* Robert Fried; **327F** Peter Menzel/Stock Boston; **349B** Robert Frerck/Odyssey Productions; **349D** Liba Taylor/Panos Pictures; **401A** Jeff Greenberg/Index Stock; **401B** *left & right* TJ Collection/Shooting Star, *bottom* Barry Barker/Odyssey Productions; **423B** Mark E. Gibson/Visuals Unlimited; **423D** RMIP/Richard Haynes

All other photography Martha Granger/EDGE Productions.

ISBN: 0-618-25069-7   1 2 3 4 5 6 7 8 9 - VJM - 07 06 05 04 03

Internet: www.mcdougallittell.com

In Memoriam

ROGER COULOMBE
(1940–2001)

We would like to dedicate this edition of *¡En español!* to the memory of Roger Coulombe. For over twenty-five years, his hard work, leadership, intelligence, and creativity enriched the world of language education through the creation of outstanding teaching materials. We who have had the privilege to work with him continue to be inspired by his ideas and commitment to excellence.

About the Authors

Estella Gahala holds a Ph.D. in Educational Administration and Curriculum from Northwestern University. A career teacher of Spanish and French, she has worked with a wide range of students at the secondary level. She has also served as foreign language department chair and district director of curriculum and instruction, and has coauthored nine basal textbooks.

Patricia Hamilton Carlin completed her M.A. in Spanish at the University of California, Davis, and a Master of Secondary Education with specialization in foreign languages from the University of Arkansas. She currently teaches Spanish and foreign language/ESL methodology at the University of Central Arkansas, where she coordinates the second language teacher education program.

Audrey L. Heining-Boynton received her Ph.D. in Curriculum and Instruction from Michigan State University. She is a Professor of Education and Romance Languages at The University of North Carolina at Chapel Hill, where she is a second language teacher educator and Professor of Spanish. She has also taught Spanish, French, and ESL at the K–12 level.

Ricardo Otheguy received his Ph.D. in Linguistics from the City University of New York, where he is currently Professor of Linguistics at the Graduate School and University Center. He has written extensively on topics related to Spanish grammar as well as on bilingual education and the Spanish of the United States.

Barbara J. Rupert has taught Level 1 through A.P. Spanish and has implemented a FLES program in her district. She completed her M.A. at Pacific Lutheran University and is the president of the Washington Association for Language Teaching. In 1996 Barbara received the Christa McAuliffe Award for Excellence in Education.

Jorge A. Capetillo-Ponce
Culture Consultant is currently Assistant Professor of Sociology at University of Massachusetts, Boston, and Researcher at the Mauricio Gastón Institute for Latino Community Development and Public Policy. His graduate studies include an M.A. and a Ph.D. in Sociology from the New School for Social Research in New York City, and an M.A. in Area Studies at El Colegio de México in Mexico City.

For further information about the authors see page xxv.

Contributing Writers

Carol Barnett
New York Institute of Technology
Queensborough Community College
Baldwin, NY

Jane M. Govoni
Eckerd College
Shorecrest Preparatory School
St. Petersburg, FL

Sandra Martín Arnold
Palisades Charter High School
Pacific Palisades, CA

Sharon Montoya
New York, NY

Pennie Nichols Alem
Baton Rouge, LA

Cynthia Prieto
Mount Vernon High School
Fairfax, VA

Mayanne Wright
Austin, TX

Reviewers

Lavonne Berry
Oak Grove High School
North Little Rock, AR

Rebecca Carr
William G. Enloe High School
Raleigh, NC

Carol Rechel Espinoza
Boulder High School
Boulder, CO

Kathleen Gliewe
Helena Middle School
Helena, MT

Maureen Rehusch
Palatine High School
Hoffman Estates, IL

Pamela Ross
North Allegheny
    Intermediate High School
Pittsburgh, PA

Consulting Authors

Dan Battisti

Patty Murguía Bohannan

Dr. Teresa Carrera-Hanley

Bill Lionetti

Lorena Richins Layser

CONTENTS

¡En español!

Building Confidence for Communication

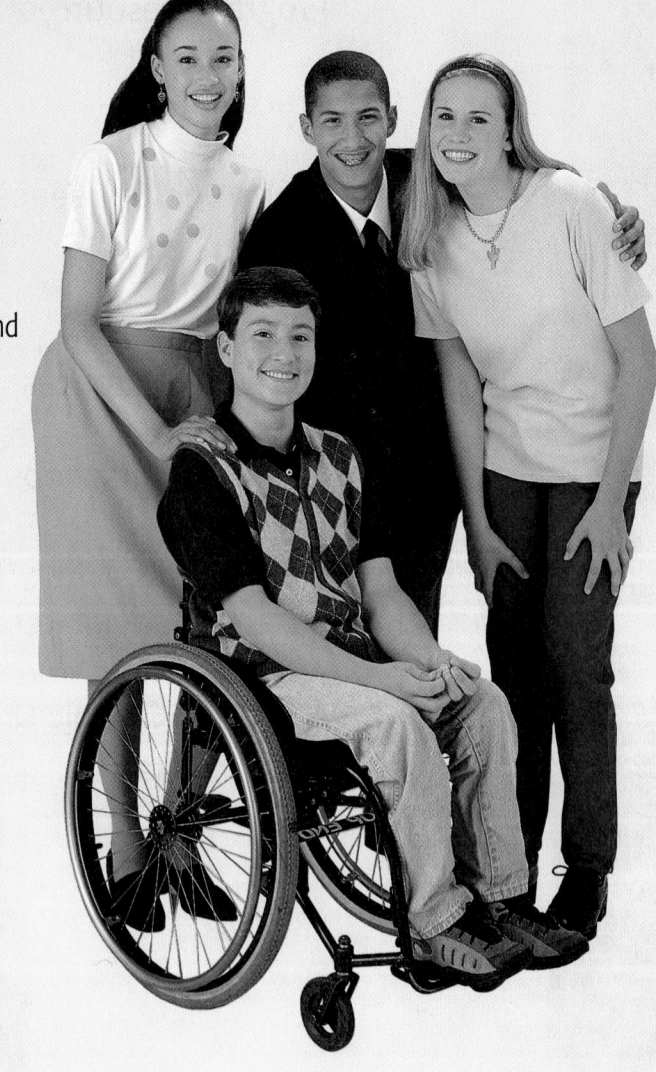

● Boosts vocabulary development

- Real-life context in *En contexto* provides a purpose for communication.

- Two stages of vocabulary presentation—*En contexto* and *En vivo*—build comprehension.

- Additional vocabulary is presented in usable chunks.

Clarifies grammar

- Grammar is taught visually, with rules, through examples, and in context so that all learners can understand.

- Activities progress from controlled to transitional to open-ended to assure development of accurate communication.

● Supports access for all learners

- Strategies for developing listening, speaking, reading, and writing skills plus comparing cultures are included in each *etapa*. Test-taking strategies help prepare students for assessments in all curriculum areas.

- Appealing characters in the integrated video/DVD program make Spanish come alive for students.

- Clear activity models assure success for all learners.

- A variety of activity types (individual, pair, and group) differentiate practice.

- eEdition Plus Online and eEdition CD-ROM provide accessible support.

- Take-Home Tutor CD-ROM and Online Workbook offer individualized review and leveled practice.

Program Resources

Extensive resources tailored to the needs of today's students!

TEACHER'S RESOURCE PACKAGE

- **Unit Resource Books**

  Includes resources for each unit:
  - *Más práctica (cuaderno)* TE
  - *Actividades para todos* TE
  - *Cuaderno para hispanohablantes* TE
  - Information Gap Activities
  - Family Letters
  - Absent Student Copymasters
  - Family Involvement
  - Video Activities
  - Videoscripts
  - Audioscripts
  - Overhead Transparencies

  Assessment Program
  - Vocabulary Quizzes
  - Grammar Quizzes
  - Etapa Exams, Forms A & B
  - *Exámenes para hispanohablantes*
  - Unit Comprehensive Tests
  - *Pruebas comprensivas para hispanohablantes*
  - Multiple Choice Test Questions
  - Portfolio Assessment

- **Block Scheduling Copymasters**

- **Easy Planner CD-ROM/Easy Planner Plus Online**
- **Test Generator CD-ROM/eTest Plus Online**

ADDITIONAL RESOURCES

ESPAÑA Y LAS AMÉRICA

ARTES EN ESPAÑA Y LAS AMÉRICAS

Tradiciones españolas

El Nuevo Mundo

Lo mejor de dos mundos

Churros y chocolate
son una merienda española típica. p. 324

STUDENT WORKBOOKS

- *Más práctica (cuaderno)*
- *Actividades para todos*
- *Cuaderno para hispanohablantes*

- **Posters**
- **Visual Grammar™ Word Tiles**
- **Back to School Pack**
  Family Letter
  TE Workbooks, Etapa preliminar
  Information Gap Activities
  Absent Student Copymasters
  Family Involvement
  Audioscripts/Audio CD
  Assessment
  Overhead Transparencies

Visual Grammar™
Word Tile Overhead Transparencies

Back to School Pack
Etapa preliminar

TECHNOLOGY

ClassZone.com
- A wide range of activities and resources
- eEdition Plus Online
- Online Workbook

Audio Program
- Completely integrated with the text and ancillaries
- Available on audio CD

Canciones
- Two audio CDs with authentic songs

Video Program
- Completely integrated video program provides comprehensible input and cultural information
- Available on videocassette and DVD

CD-ROM
- eEdition
- Take-Home Tutor
- *Intrigas y aventuras*

GRAMMAR ACROSS LEVELS

LEVEL 1

Unit 5

Etapa 1
- Reflexive verbs (p. 330)
- Irregular affirmative *tú* commands (p. 332)
- Negative *tú* commands (p. 334)
- Pronoun placement with commands (p. 335)

Etapa 2
- Pronoun placement with the present progressive tense (p. 352)
- *deber* (p. 355)
- Adverbs with *-mente* (p. 357)

Etapa 3
- Superlatives (p. 374)
- Regular *-ar* preterite verbs (p. 376)
- *-car, -gar, -zar* preterite verbs (p. 378)

Unit 6

Etapa 1
- Regular *-er, -ir* preterite verbs (p. 404)
- Preterite verbs with *i* to *y* spelling change (p. 406)
- Preterite forms of *ir, hacer, ser* (p. 407)

Etapa 2
- Adverbs of location (p. 426)
- Demonstrative adjectives and pronouns (p. 428)
- Ordinals (p. 430)
- Irregular preterite verbs (p. 431)

Etapa 3
- All review

LEVEL 2

Unit 1

Etapa 1
- Regular preterite verbs (p. 38)
- Preterite with *-car, -gar,* and *-zar* spelling changes (p. 40)
- Preterite of *ir, ser, hacer, dar, ver* (p. 42)

Etapa 2
- Irregular preterite verbs (p. 63)

Etapa 3
- Demonstrative adjectives and pronouns (p. 84)
- Preterite verbs with *i* to *y* spelling change (p. 87)

Unit 2

Etapa 1
- Reflexive pronouns and verbs (p. 114)

Etapa 2
- Progressive tenses (p. 134)
- Ordinal number agreement (p. 140)

Unit 3

Etapa 1
- *Deber* (p. 185)
- Pronoun placement (p. 186)

Etapa 2
- Affirmative *tú* commands, regular and irregular (p. 208)
- Negative *tú* commands (p. 210)
- Adverbs ending in *-mente* (p. 212)

REVIEW OF ALL GRAMMAR

LEVEL 4

Unit 1

Lecciones
1: *Ser* vs. *estar*, Adjectives
2: Stem-changing and Irregular Verbs
3: Demonstratives, Comparatives, Superlatives

Unit 2

Lecciones
1: Preterite Tense, Object Pronouns
2: Irregular Preterite Verbs, *gustar*
3: Imperfect Tense

Unit 3

Lecciones
1: Preterite vs. Imperfect, Possessives
2: Affirmative and Negative Words
3: *Para* vs. *por*

Easy Articulation

¡En español! addresses the challenges of articulation between levels by providing a unique instructional overlap. All the grammar and vocabulary taught in Units 5 and 6 of Levels 1 and 2 are covered again in the following level, so teachers can choose how far into the grammatical and functional sequence they wish to go. Students' study of Spanish can continue seamlessly! Level 4 provides a review of all grammar.

Unit 4

Etapa 2
- Prepositions/adverbs of location (p. 285)

Etapa 3
- Comparisons and superlatives (p. 304)
- *deber* (saving and spending money) (p. 308)

Unit 5

Etapa 1
- Future tense (p. 334)
- Using *por* (p. 336)
- *Nosotros* commands (p. 338)

Etapa 2
- Irregular future tense (p. 356)
- Using *para* (p. 360)

Etapa 3
- *Por* vs. *para* (p. 378)
- Conditional tense (p. 380)

Unit 6

Etapa 1
- Impersonal *se* (p. 411)
- Past participles as adjectives (p. 413)

Etapa 2
- Using the preterite and imperfect tenses (p. 430)
- Present perfect tense (p. 432)
- Irregular verbs in the present perfect tense (p. 435)

Etapa 3
- Reported speech (p. 456)

LEVEL 3

Unit 1

Etapa 1
- Preterite/imperfect tenses contrasted (p. 43)
- Present/past perfect tenses, regular/irregular, including past participles (p. 46)

Etapa 2
- *Por* vs. *para* (p. 63)
- Future tense, regular and irregular (p. 65)
- Impersonal *se* (p. 89)

Unit 2

Etapa 1
- *Nosotros* commands (p. 116)
- Conditional tense (p. 119)

Unit 4

Etapa 1
- Present progressive, regular and irregular (p. 264)

Unit 6

Etapa 1
- Reported speech (p. 414)

Unit 4

Lecciones
1: Past Participles, Passive Construction
2: Present Subjunctive, Commands
3: Subjunctive with Desires and Suggestions

Unit 5

Lecciones
1: Relative Pronouns, Subjunctive in Adjectival Clauses
2: Subjunctive in Adverbial Clauses: Conjunctions
3: Subjunctive in Adverbial Clauses: Temporal Conjunctions

Unit 6

Lecciones
1: Future Tense
2: Conditional Tense
3: Imperfect Subjunctive: *si* Clauses

Unit 7

Lecciones
1: Imperfect Subjunctive: Noun and Adjectival Clauses
2: Imperfect Subjunctive: Adverbial Clauses
3: Present Perfect: Indicative and Subjunctive

Unit 8

Lecciones
1: Perfect Tenses
2: Sequence of Tenses: Indicative
3: Sequence of Tenses: Indicative and Subjunctive

¡En español!

Level 1 • Scope & Sequence

		COMMUNICATION	GRAMMAR	CULTURE	RECYCLING	STRATEGIES
PRELIMINAR	**Etapa preliminar** p. 1 *¡Hola, bienvenidos!*	• Greet people • Introduce yourself • Say where you are from • Exchange phone numbers • Say which day it is	**Grammar is presented lexically here** • *Me llamo, te llamas* • *Soy, eres, es + de* **NOTAS** *encantado / encantada; sí* and *no*	**NOTAS CULTURALES** • Greetings • Variations on good-bye • Articles before country names		
UNIDAD 1 Mi mundo • Estados Unidos	**Etapa 1** p. 26 **Miami** *¡Bienvenido a Miami!* **UNIT OPENER CULTURE NOTES** • *Fajitas* • *Murales* • *El Álamo* • *Cascarones* • *Sándwich cubano* • Jon Secada	• Greet others • Introduce others • Say where people are from • Express likes	• Familiar and formal greetings • Subject pronouns and *ser* • *Ser + de* • *Gustar + infinitive: me, te, le* **NOTAS** plurals; *le presento a / te presento a; vivo en*	**EN VOCES** *Los latinos de Estados Unidos* **CONEXIONES** *Los estudios sociales:* compare communities **NOTAS CULTURALES** • Miami: international city • Architectural influences • Last names	Vocabulary from *Etapa preliminar*	**LISTENING:** Listen to intonation **SPEAKING:** Practice; Understand, then speak **READING:** Preview graphics
	Etapa 2 p. 48 **San Antonio** *Mis buenos amigos*	• Describe others • Give others' likes and dislikes • Describe clothing	• Definite articles • Indefinite articles • Noun–adjective agreement: gender • Noun–adjective agreement: number **NOTAS** *¿Qué lleva?; llevo;* shortened forms of adjectives; *cómo + ser; tiene*	**EN COLORES** *El conjunto tejano* (video) **CONEXIONES** *La música:* music styles **NOTAS CULTURALES** • *La charreada*	Activity 3: *gustar* + infinitive Activity 6: professions	**LISTENING:** Listen to stress **SPEAKING:** Trust your first impulse; Think, plan, then speak **CULTURE:** Recognize regional music **READING:** Skim
	Etapa 3 p. 70 **Los Ángeles** *Te presento a mi familia*	• Describe family • Ask and tell ages • Talk about birthdays • Give dates • Express possession	• *Tener* • Possession using *de* • Possessive adjectives • Giving dates **NOTAS** *¿De quién es…?, Es de…; ¿Quién es?, ¿Quiénes son?; hay*	**EN VOCES** *Las celebraciones del año* **EN COLORES** *La quinceañera* **TÚ EN LA COMUNIDAD** **NOTAS CULTURALES** • The oldest house in L.A. • Street names • Writing the date	Activity 4: physical descriptions Activity 6: personal characteristics Activity 10: clothing Activity 13: clothing Activity 14: *ser* Activity 15: clothing	**LISTENING:** Visualize; Get the main idea **SPEAKING:** Rehearse; Practice speaking smoothly **READING:** Look for cognates **WRITING:** Use different kinds of descriptive words **CULTURE:** Compare rites of passage

		COMMUNICATION	**GRAMMAR**	**CULTURE**	**RECYCLING**	**STRATEGIES**
UNIDAD 2 Una semana típica • Ciudad de México	**Etapa 1** p. 100 *Un día de clases* **UNIT OPENER** **CULTURE NOTES** • *Tortillas* • Diego Rivera • *El Palacio de Bellas Artes* • *El Ballet Folklórico* • *El metro* • Lázaro Cárdenas	• Describe classes and classroom objects • Say how often you do something • Discuss obligations	• Present tense of regular -ar verbs • Adverbs of frequency • *Tener que, hay que* **NOTA** Use of articles with titles	**EN VOCES** *Una encuesta escolar* **CONEXIONES** Las matemáticas: take a survey **NOTAS CULTURALES** • *Universidad Autónoma de México* • The origin of *pluma*	Activity 3: hay, colors Activity 4: hay, numbers	**LISTENING:** Listen for feelings **SPEAKING:** Develop more than one way of expressing an idea; Expand the conversation **READING:** Use context clues
	Etapa 2 p. 122 *¡Un horario difícil!*	• Talk about schedules • Ask and tell time • Ask questions • Say where you are going • Request food	• *Ir* • Telling time • *Estar* + location • Interrogative words **NOTAS** *¿Quieres comer…?* and *¿Quieres beber…?*; al; "on" + days of the week	**EN COLORES:** *¿Quieres comer una merienda mexicana?* **CONEXIONES** *La salud:* nutrition **NOTAS CULTURALES** • *torta, bocadillo, pastel* • Mexican school schedules	Activity 3: -ar verbs, school terms Activity 7: days of the week	**LISTENING:** Listen for the main idea **SPEAKING:** Take risks; Help your partner **CULTURE:** Compare snack foods
	Etapa 3 p. 144 *Mis actividades*	• Discuss plans • Sequence events • Talk about places and people you know	• *Ir a* + infinitive • Present tense: regular -er and -ir verbs • Irregular yo forms: *hacer, conocer;* personal *a* • *Oír* **NOTA** *tener sed, tener hambre*	**EN VOCES** *México y sus jóvenes* **EN COLORES** *El Zócalo: centro de México* (video) **TÚ EN LA COMUNIDAD** **NOTAS CULTURALES** • *Museo Nacional de Antropología* • Mexican mealtimes	Activity 3: estar + location, places Activity 6: snacks Activity 7: telling time Activity 11: gustar + infinitive, tener que Activity 13: adverbs of frequency Activity 17: friends and family Activity 19: places	**LISTENING:** Listen and observe **SPEAKING:** Use all you know; Ask for clarification **READING:** Skim **WRITING:** Organize information chronologically and by category **CULTURE:** Compare places
UNIDAD 3 El fin de semana • San Juan, Puerto Rico	**Etapa 1** p. 174 *¡Me gusta el tiempo libre!* **UNIT OPENER** **CULTURE NOTES** • Gigi Fernández • *Pasta de guayaba* • *El Morro* • Luis Muñoz Marín • *Taínos* • *El loro puertorriqueño*	• Extend invitations • Talk on the phone • Express feelings • Say where you are coming from • Say what just happened	• *Estar* + adjectives • *Acabar de* + infinitive • *Venir* • *Gustar* + infinitive: nos, os, les **NOTAS** *cuando; del; conmigo, contigo*	**EN VOCES** *Bomba y plena* **CONEXIONES** *La música:* songs **NOTAS CULTURALES** • The name *Puerto Rico* • Ricky Martin	Activity 3: gustar + infinitive Activity 4: activities, sequencing Activity 9: activities Activity 13: ir a… Activity 14: places Activity 17: activities Activity 19: interrogatives	**LISTENING:** Listen for a purpose **SPEAKING:** Personalize; Use your tone to convey meaning **READING:** Scan
	Etapa 2 p. 196 *¡Deportes para todos!*	• Talk about sports • Express preferences • Say what you know • Make comparisons	• *Jugar* • Stem-changing verbs: e →ie • *Saber* • Comparatives	**EN COLORES** *Béisbol: el pasatiempo nacional* **TÚ EN LA COMUNIDAD** **NOTAS CULTURALES** • *La Fortaleza* • Puerto Rico and the U.S. • Roberto Clemente	Activity 12: activities Activity 16: descriptions Activity 19: interrogatives	**LISTENING:** Listen for "turn-taking" tactics **SPEAKING:** Monitor yourself; Give reasons for your preferences **CULTURE:** Reflect on sports traditions
	Etapa 3 p. 218 *El tiempo en El Yunque*	• Describe the weather • Discuss clothing and accessories • State an opinion • Describe how you feel • Say what is happening	• *Tener* expressions • Weather expressions • Direct object pronouns • Present progressive **NOTAS** *llevar; creer*	**EN VOCES:** *El coquí* **EN COLORES** *Una excursión por la isla* (video) **CONEXIONES** *Las ciencias:* temperature **NOTAS CULTURALES** • *El Yunque*	Activity 3: colors, clothing Activity 8: stem-changing verbs: e →ie Activity 9: ir a…, llevar Activity 11: tener, activities Activity 14: sports Activity 19: activities	**LISTENING:** Sort and categorize details **SPEAKING:** Say how often; Get specific information **READING:** Distinguish details **WRITING:** Appeal to the senses **CULTURE:** Define travel and tourism

		COMMUNICATION	GRAMMAR	CULTURE	RECYCLING	STRATEGIES
UNIDAD 4 ¡De visita! • Oaxaca, México	**Etapa 1** p. 248 *¡A visitar a mi prima!* UNIT OPENER CULTURE NOTES • *Animalitos* • *Pesos* • *Mole negro* • Rufino Tamayo • Benito Juárez • *Monte Albán*	• Identify places • Give addresses • Choose transportation • Request directions • Give instructions	• *Decir* • Prepositions of location • Regular affirmative *tú* commands NOTAS *por; salir;* numbers in addresses; *enfrente de*	EN VOCES *¡Visita Oaxaca! Un paseo a pie* CONEXIONES *La educación física:* Mexican folk dances NOTAS CULTURALES • *Guelaguetza* • The name *Oaxaca*	**Activity 3:** *hay* **Activity 5:** seasons **Activity 13:** activities **Activity 14:** direct object pronouns **Activity 15:** sequencing **Activity 16:** direct object pronouns	LISTENING: Listen and follow directions SPEAKING: Recognize and use set phrases; Use variety to give directions READING: Combine strategies
	Etapa 2 p. 270 *En el mercado*	• Talk about shopping • Make purchases • Talk about giving gifts • Bargain	• Stem-changing verbs: *o→ue* • Indirect object pronouns • Indirect object pronoun placement NOTAS *para; dar; ¿Cuánto cuesta(n)?*	EN COLORES *El Mercado Benito Juárez* CONEXIONES: *Las matemáticas: un mercado* NOTAS CULTURALES • Monte Albán jewelry • Benito Juárez	**Activity 5:** numbers **Activity 7:** places **Activity 8:** time **Activity 9:** places, time **Activity 10:** transportation	LISTENING: Observe as you listen SPEAKING: Express emotion; Disagree politely CULTURE: Compare bargaining customs
	Etapa 3 p. 292 *¿Qué hacer en Oaxaca?*	• Order food • Request the check • Talk about food • Express extremes • Say where you went	• *Gustar* + nouns • Affirmative and negative words • Stem-changing verbs: *e→i* NOTAS *fui/fuiste; ningunos(as); traer;* superlatives; *poner; desayunar*	EN VOCES *Andrés, joven aprendiz de alfarero* (video) EN COLORES *Monte Albán: ruinas misteriosas* TÚ EN LA COMUNIDAD NOTAS CULTURALES • Oaxaca's cuisine • Oaxaca's artistic heritage • Zapotec traditions	**Activity 5:** prepositions of location **Activity 6:** stores **Activity 9:** clothing **Activity 19:** direct object pronouns	LISTENING: Integrate your skills SPEAKING: Vary ways to express preferences; Borrow useful expressions READING: Gather and sort information as you read WRITING: Tell who, what, where, when, why, and how CULTURE: Analyze and recommend
UNIDAD 5 Preparaciones especiales • Barcelona, España	**Etapa 1** p. 322 *¿Cómo es tu rutina?* UNIT OPENER CULTURE NOTES • *Las Ramblas* • Joan Miró • *Aceitunas* • Cervantes • *La Sagrada Familia* • Cristóbal Colón	• Describe daily routine • Talk about grooming • Tell others to do something • Discuss daily chores	• Reflexive verbs • Irregular affirmative *tú* commands • Negative *tú* commands • Pronoun placement with commands	EN VOCES *Una exhibición especial de Picasso* CONEXIONES *El arte:* paintings NOTAS CULTURALES • *Catalán* • *Rock con raíces* • Pablo Picasso	**Activity 3:** time **Activity 16:** restaurant phrases, direct object pronouns	LISTENING: Listen for a mood or a feeling SPEAKING: Sequence events; Use gestures READING: Scan for crucial details
	Etapa 2 p. 344 *¿Qué debo hacer?*	• Say what people are doing • Persuade others • Describe a house • Negotiate responsibilities	• Pronoun placement with present progressive • *Deber* • Adverbs with *-mente* NOTAS *si;* reflexive pronouns	EN COLORES *Las tapas: una experiencia muy española* TÚ EN LA COMUNIDAD NOTAS CULTURALES • *Tortilla*	**Activity 3:** *poner* **Activity 8:** reflexive verbs **Activity 13:** irregular affirmative *tú* commands **Activity 17:** restaurant phrases **Activity 19:** interrogatives, daily chores	LISTENING: Note and compare SPEAKING: Negotiate; Detect misunderstandings CULTURE: Predict reactions about restaurants
	Etapa 3 p. 366 *¡Qué buena celebración!*	• Plan a party • Describe past activities • Express extremes • Purchase food	• Superlatives • Regular *-ar* preterite verbs • *-car, -gar, -zar* preterite NOTAS *¿A cuánto está(n)…?*	EN VOCES *Los favoritos de la cocina española* EN COLORES *Barcelona: joya de arquitectura* (video) CONEXIONES *La salud:* favorite foods NOTAS CULTURALES: • The euro • *Paella* • Gothic Quarter	**Activity 7:** furniture, adjective agreement **Activity 10:** chores	LISTENING: Listen and take notes SPEAKING: Say what is the best and worst; Maintain conversational flow READING: Reorganize information to check understanding WRITING: Engage the reader by addressing him or her personally CULTURE: Make a historical time line

UNIDAD 6 La ciudad y el campo • Quito, Ecuador

	COMMUNICATION	GRAMMAR	CULTURE	RECYCLING	STRATEGIES
Etapa 1 p. 396 *La vida de la ciudad* **UNIT OPENER CULTURE NOTES** • *La casa de Sucre* • *Papas* • *La Mitad del Mundo* • *Atahualpa* • *Tapices* • *Rondador*	• Tell what happened • Make suggestions to a group • Describe city buildings • Talk about professions	• Regular *-er, -ir* preterites • Preterite verbs with *i → y* spelling change • Preterite of *ir, hacer, ser* **NOTAS** *Vamos a* + infinitive; *estar de acuerdo; ver*	**EN VOCES** *Saludos desde Quito* **TÚ EN LA COMUNIDAD NOTAS CULTURALES** • Quito • Dollarization • *Colonia/colonial*	**Activity 7:** superlatives **Activity 10:** time expressions	**LISTENING:** Distinguish between what is said and not said **SPEAKING:** Exaggerate and react to exaggerations; Relate details **READING:** Recognize place names
Etapa 2 p. 418 *A conocer el campo*	• Point out specific people and things • Tell where things are located • Talk about the past	• Location words • Demonstrative adjectives and pronouns • Ordinals • Irregular preterite **NOTAS** *darle(s) de comer*	**EN COLORES** *Los otavaleños* (video) **CONEXIONES** *Las ciencias:* regional animals **NOTAS CULTURALES** • *Quichua*	**Activity 5:** professions **Activity 7:** prepositions of location, school and personal items **Activity 10:** clothing, sports equipment **Activity 11:** school objects, comparisons **Activity 17:** places, preterite	**LISTENING:** Listen for implied statements **SPEAKING:** Recall what you know; Use words that direct others' attention **CULTURE:** Research cultural groups
Etapa 3 p. 440 *¡A ganar el concurso!*	• Talk about the present and future • Give instructions to someone • Discuss the past	• Review: present progressive, *ir a…* • Review: affirmative *tú* commands • Review: regular preterite • Review: irregular preterite	**EN VOCES** *Un paseo por Ecuador* **EN COLORES** *Cómo las Américas cambiaron la comida europea* **CONEXIONES** *La salud:* typical food **NOTAS CULTURALES** • Galápagos • Ecuador's diverse regions		**LISTENING:** Listen and take notes **SPEAKING:** Use storytelling techniques; Rely on the basics **READING:** Reflect on journal writing **WRITING:** Support a general statement with informative details **CULTURE:** Identify international foods

¡En español!

Level 2 · Scope & Sequence

		COMMUNICATION	GRAMMAR	CULTURE	RECYCLING	STRATEGIES
PRELIMINAR	**Etapa preliminar** p. 1 **Northeastern U.S.** *Día a día*	• Exchange greetings • Discuss likes and dislikes • Describe people and places • Ask for and give information • Talk about school life • Talk about the new school year	NOTAS *Gustar* and indirect object pronouns; *preguntar;* expressions of frequency; *venir, decir*	NOTAS CULTURALES • *En Nueva York y New Jersey* • *La población latina* • *De Connecticut* • City Year	• Use adjectives to describe • The verb *tener* • *ser* vs. *estar* • Interrogative words • Tell time • Regular present tense verbs • The verb *ir* • Stem-changing verbs: *e→ie, o→ue* • Irregular *yo* verbs	SPEAKING: Give and get personal information
UNIDAD 1 ¿Qué pasa? • Estados Unidos	**Etapa 1** p. 30 **Los Ángeles** *Pasatiempos* UNIT OPENER CULTURE NOTES • *La misión San Fernando Rey de España* • *Hispanos en Hollywood* • *Tostones* • *Artistas y la comunidad* • *Televisión* • Gloria Estefan • Jorge Ramos y María Elena Salinas	• Talk about where you went and what you did • Discuss leisure time • Comment on airplane travel	All grammar presented in this *etapa* is listed in the recycling category.	EN VOCES *¿Cuánto sabes?* TÚ EN LA COMUNIDAD NOTAS CULTURALES • *La calle Olvera* • *Los murales*	• Regular preterite • Preterite with *-car, -gar,* and *-zar* spelling changes • Irregular preterite: *ir, ser, hacer, dar, ver* Ya sabes: Preterite with *-car, -gar,* and *-zar*	LISTENING: Identify key words SPEAKING: Encourage others; Get more information READING: Read, don't translate; Use visuals and titles to predict the general idea; Scan for cognates
	Etapa 2 p. 52 **Chicago** *¿Qué prefieres?*	• Comment on food • Talk about the past • Express activity preferences • Discuss fine art	• Irregular preterite verbs NOTA *estar de acuerdo*	EN COLORES: *El arte latino de Chicago:* murals (video) CONEXIONES *El arte:* artists' inspirations NOTAS CULTURALES • *El Centro Museo de Bellas Artes Mexicanas* • *La cena*	• Stem-changing verbs: *e→i, jugar* Activity 3: *¡A viajar!* (travel) Activity 14: *¿Cuántas veces?* (expressions of frequency) Ya sabes: *jugar; pedir, servir*	LISTENING: Identify the main idea SPEAKING: Use all you know; Give reasons why CULTURE: Learn about other cultures; Describe the nature of murals
	Etapa 3 p. 74 **Miami** *¿Viste las noticias?*	• Discuss ways to communicate • React to news • Ask for and give information • Talk about things and people you know	• Demonstrative adjectives and pronouns • Stem-changing preterite NOTAS *estar bien informado;* adjectives of nationality; *saber* vs. *conocer; hubo; i→y* with preterite	EN VOCES *¿Leíste el periódico hoy?* EN COLORES *Miami: Puerta de las Américas* CONEXIONES *Las matemáticas:* calculate percentages of television viewing NOTAS CULTURALES • *A la fiesta* • *Periódicos por computadora*	Activity 3: *¡Qué reunión!* (irregular preterite) Ya sabes: stem-changing verbs; *saber, conocer*	LISTENING: Listen with a purpose SPEAKING: Present findings; Provide additional information READING: Skim for the general idea; Scan for specific information WRITING: Bring your event to life CULTURE: Identify characteristics of neighborhoods

		COMMUNICATION	GRAMMAR	CULTURE	RECYCLING	STRATEGIES
UNIDAD 2 Ayer y hoy • Ciudad de México	**Etapa 1** p. 104 *De pequeño* UNIT OPENER CULTURE NOTES • *Los tamales* • *La piñata* • *Hoy no circula* • *El Popocatépetl* • Cristian Castro • Frida Kahlo • Padre Miguel Hidalgo y Costilla	• Describe childhood experiences • Express personal reactions • Discuss family relationships	• Possessive adjectives and pronouns • Imperfect tense NOTAS *dentro de; fuera de;* expressions with *tener (tener hambre, tener sed, etc.); había*	EN VOCES *El monte de nuestro alimento:* legend CONEXIONES *Los estudios sociales:* Aztec calendar NOTAS CULTURALES • *Las marionetas* • *El Bosque de Chapultepec*	• Reflexive pronouns and verbs **Activity 3:** *¡Los conoce!* (nationalities)	LISTENING: Listen for related details SPEAKING: Tell when you were always or never (im)perfect; Add variety to your conversation READING: Analyze folkloric traditions
	Etapa 2 p. 126 *Había una vez...*	• Narrate in the past • Discuss family celebrations • Talk about activities in progress	• Progressive tenses • Preterite vs. imperfect NOTAS *sorpresa, sorprender;* ordinal numbers	EN COLORES *¡Temblor!:* the earthquake of 1985 CONEXIONES: *El arte: El muralista Diego Rivera* NOTAS CULTURALES • *La piñata* • *El Museo Nacional de Antropología*	**Activity 4:** *Una reunión escolar* (imperfect) **Activity 5:** *Reacciones* (reflexives)	LISTENING: Listen for a series of events SPEAKING: Brainstorm to get ideas; Interact by expressing approval, disapproval, or astonishment CULTURE: Observe and generalize
	Etapa 3 p. 148 *Hoy en la ciudad*	• Order in a restaurant • Ask for and pay a restaurant bill • Talk about things to do in the city	• Double object pronouns NOTAS indirect object pronouns with verbs like *gustar; dar una vuelta; ofrecer*	EN VOCES: *Teotihuacán: Ciudad misteriosa* (video) EN COLORES *¡Buen provecho!: La comida mexicana* TÚ EN LA COMUNIDAD NOTAS CULTURALES • *El baile folklórico* • *Las telenovelas*	• Direct object pronouns • Indirect object pronouns **Activity 3:** *¡A divertirse en la ciudad!* (preterite vs. imperfect)	LISTENING: Listen for useful expressions SPEAKING: Personalize responses; Resolve misconceptions READING: Identify gaps in knowledge WRITING: Develop your story CULTURE: Compare meals and mealtimes
UNIDAD 3 Sol y sombra • Puerto Rico	**Etapa 1** p. 178 *¿Estás en forma?* UNIT OPENER CULTURE NOTES • *El observatorio de Arecibo* • *Los pasteles* • *Piratas* • *La ceiba de Ponce* • *El Yunque* • Marc Anthony	• Discuss ways to stay fit and healthy • Make suggestions • Talk about daily routine and personal care	• *Usted/Ustedes* commands • Commands and pronoun placement NOTA *deber*	EN VOCES *Puerto Rico: Lugar maravilloso* CONEXIONES *Las ciencias:* phosphorescence NOTAS CULTURALES • *El béisbol* • *El Viejo San Juan*	• Pronoun placement **Activity 4:** *¿Siempre o nunca?* (expressions of frequency, double object pronouns) Ya sabes: *las preparaciones*	LISTENING: Listen and sort details SPEAKING: Use gestures to convey meaning; React to daily routines READING: Observe organization of ideas
	Etapa 2 p. 200 *Preparaciones*	• Discuss beach activities • Tell someone what to do • Talk about chores • Say if something has already been done	NOTA *acabar de* + infinitive	EN COLORES *El Yunque: Bosque Nacional* (video) TÚ EN LA COMUNIDAD NOTAS CULTURALES • *Después de las clases* • *El manatí*	• Affirmative *tú* commands • Negative *tú* commands • Adverbs ending in *-mente* **Activity 3:** *Por la mañana* (daily routine) Ya sabes: *los quehaceres*	LISTENING: Listen and categorize information SPEAKING: Improvise; Encourage or discourage certain behaviors CULTURE: Recognize unique natural wonders
	Etapa 3 p. 222 *¿Cómo te sientes?*	• Describe time periods • Talk about health and illness • Give advice	• *Hacer* with expressions of time • Subjunctive with impersonal expressions NOTA *doler* with indirect object pronouns; subjunctive after impersonal expressions	EN VOCES *El estatus político de Puerto Rico* EN COLORES *Una voz de la tierra* CONEXIONES *La historia:* pirates NOTAS CULTURALES • *Los huracanes* • *La celebración de Carnaval* • *La cultura de los jíbaros*	**Activity 3:** *Los quehaceres en tu casa* (chores)	LISTENING: Listen sympathetically SPEAKING: Give feedback; Use language for problem-solving READING: Activate associated knowledge WRITING: Compare and contrast to make strong descriptions CULTURE: Discover many cultures inside one country

		COMMUNICATION	GRAMMAR	CULTURE	RECYCLING	STRATEGIES
UNIDAD 4 Un viaje • Madrid, España	**Etapa 1** p. 252 *En la pensión* UNIT OPENER CULTURE NOTES • *El Prado* • *La guitarra* • *Paella* • *El rey y la reina de España* • *don Quijote* • El Greco	• Talk about travel plans • Persuade others • Describe rooms, furniture, and appliances	• Subjunctive to express hopes and wishes • Irregular subjunctive forms	EN VOCES *Felices sueños:* hotel descriptions CONEXIONES *El arte:* Spanish artists NOTAS CULTURALES • *La Plaza de la Cibeles* • *Alojamiento*	Activity 4: *Es mejor que…* (subjunctive) Activity 15: *El metro de Madrid* (commands) Ya sabes: expressing hopes and wishes	LISTENING: Listen and check details SPEAKING: Persuade; Make and express decisions READING: Compare related details
	Etapa 2 p. 274 *Conoce la ciudad*	• Describe your city or town • Make suggestions • Ask for and give directions	• Subjunctive stem changes: *-ar, -er* verbs • Stem-changing *-ir* verbs in the subjunctive • Subjunctive vs. infinitive NOTAS: *ni;* words such as *cuando* and *donde* as bridges mid-sentence	EN COLORES *Vamos a bailar:* Gipsy Kings CONEXIONES: *La tecnología:* creating a webpage NOTAS CULTURALES • *La Plaza Mayor* • *El paseo* • *Los gitanos y el flamenco*	Activity 3: *Una lección* (giving advice using the subjunctive)	LISTENING: Listen and distinguish SPEAKING: Ask for and give directions; Work cooperatively CULTURE: Identify characteristics of successful musical groups
	Etapa 3 p. 296 *Vamos de compras*	• Talk about shopping for clothes • Ask for and give opinions • Make comparisons • Discuss ways to save and spend money	• Subjunctive with expressions of doubt • Subjunctive with expressions of emotion NOTA subjunctive vs. indicative	EN VOCES *Nos vemos en Madrid:* highlights of the city EN COLORES: *¿En qué te puedo atender?:* shopping (video) TÚ EN LA COMUNIDAD NOTAS CULTURALES • *¿Qué talla usas?* • *El euro*	• Comparatives and superlatives Activity 4: *¿Qué me sugieres?* (making suggestions using the subjunctive) Ya sabes: equal/unequal comparisons, expressions of emotion	LISTENING: Listen and infer SPEAKING: Interpret the feelings or values of others; Observe courtesies and exchange information READING: Categorize details WRITING: Persuade your reader CULTURE: Analyze and draw conclusions about shopping as a cultural activity
UNIDAD 5 La naturaleza • San José, Costa Rica	**Etapa 1** p. 326 *En el bosque tropical* UNIT OPENER CULTURE NOTES • José Figueres Ferrer • *Gallo pinto* • Francisco Zúñiga • *El quetzal* • *La cerámica de Nicoya* • *El fútbol*	• Describe geographic characteristics • Make future plans • Talk about nature and the environment	• Future tense • Expressions with *por* • *Nosotros* commands	EN VOCES *El Parque Nacional de Volcán Poás* CONEXIONES *La geografía:* tropical forest locations NOTAS CULTURALES • *El 18 de septiembre de 1502* • *Los saludos*	Activity 3: *En el zoológico* (expressions of doubt)	LISTENING: Organize and summarize environmental information SPEAKING: Share personal plans and feelings; Anticipate future plans READING: Confirm or deny hearsay with reliable information
	Etapa 2 p. 348 *Nuestro medio ambiente*	• Discuss outdoor activities • Describe the weather • Make predictions • Talk about ecology	• Irregular future • Expressions with *para*	EN COLORES *Costa Rica, ¡la pura vida!* (video) TÚ EN LA COMUNIDAD NOTAS CULTURALES • *Los parques nacionales* • *Navegar los rápidos*	• Weather expressions Activity 5: *¿Qué vas a hacer este verano?* (future tense)	LISTENING: Observe relationships between actions and motives SPEAKING: Find alternate ways to communicate; Make recommendations CULTURE: Predict appeal to ecotourists
	Etapa 3 p. 370 *¿Cómo será el futuro?*	• Comment on conservation and the environment • Talk about how you would solve problems	• *Por* or *para* • Conditional tense NOTA *Si estuviera… o Si pudieras…*	EN VOCES: *La cascada de la novia:* legend EN COLORES: *Cumbre ecológica centroamericana: Se reúnen jóvenes en San José* CONEXIONES: *Los estudios sociales:* advertising about the environment NOTAS CULTURALES • *Los campamentos* • *La economía* • *Las leyendas*	Activity 5: *¿Cómo será?* (future tense) Activity 6: *¿Por o para?* (camping vocabulary)	LISTENING: Propose solutions SPEAKING: Identify problems and your commitment to solving them; Hypothesize about the future READING: Recognize characteristics of legends WRITING: Present a thorough and balanced review CULTURE: Prioritize

		COMMUNICATION	GRAMMAR	CULTURE	RECYCLING	STRATEGIES
UNIDAD 6 El mundo del trabajo • Quito, Ecuador	**Etapa 1** p. 400 *Se busca trabajo* UNIT OPENER CULTURE NOTES • *Llapingachos* • *Las islas Galápagos* • *La música andina* • *Andar en bicicleta de montaña* • *La toquilla* • Antonio José de Sucre	• Discuss jobs and professions • Describe people, places, and things • Complete an application	• Impersonal *se* • Past participles used as adjectives	EN VOCES *Bienvenidos a la isla Santa Cruz:* Galapagos Islands (video) CONEXIONES *La geografía:* equatorial regions NOTAS CULTURALES • *Quito* • *La ocarina*	• Present and present progressive **Activity 5:** *Una cápsula del tiempo* (conditional)	LISTENING: Evaluate a plan SPEAKING: Participate in an interview; Check comprehension READING: Use context to find meaning
	Etapa 2 p. 422 *La entrevista*	• Prepare for an interview • Interview for a job • Evaluate situations and people	• Present perfect • Irregular present perfect	EN COLORES *Ciberespacio en Quito* CONEXIONES *La música:* pan flute NOTAS CULTURALES • *Los grupos indígenas* • *Las empresas del mundo hispano*	• Preterite and imperfect **Activity 3:** *¿Qué está dibujado?* (past participle)	LISTENING: Evaluate behavior SPEAKING: Give advice; Refine interview skills CULTURE: Assess use of e-mail
	Etapa 3 p. 444 *¡A trabajar!*	• Talk on the telephone • Report on past, present, and future events • Describe duties, people, and surroundings	• Reported speech	EN VOCES Jorge Carrera Andrade, «*Pasajero del planeta*» EN COLORES *Música de las montañas:* Andean music TÚ EN LA COMUNIDAD NOTAS CULTURALES • *Guayaquil* • *Los festivales*	• Future tense • Conditional tense **Activity 3:** *¿Nunca?* (present perfect) **Activity 4:** *¿Quién lo ha hecho?* (irregular present perfect)	LISTENING: Report what others said SPEAKING: Persuade or convince others; Report on events READING: Observe characteristics of poems WRITING: State your message using a positive tone CULTURE: Reflect on music

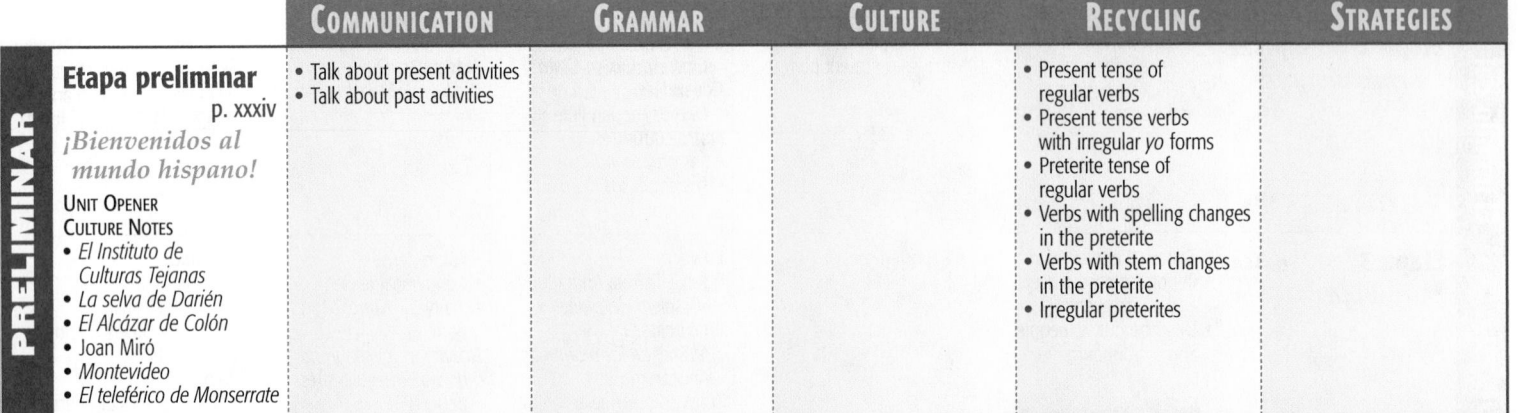

¡En español!

Level 3 Scope & Sequence

		COMMUNICATION	GRAMMAR	CULTURE	RECYCLING	STRATEGIES
PRELIMINAR	**Etapa preliminar** p. xxxiv *¡Bienvenidos al mundo hispano!* **UNIT OPENER** **CULTURE NOTES** • *El Instituto de Culturas Tejanas* • *La selva de Darién* • *El Alcázar de Colón* • Joan Miró • Montevideo • *El teleférico de Monserrate*	• Talk about present activities • Talk about past activities			• Present tense of regular verbs • Present tense verbs with irregular *yo* forms • Preterite tense of regular verbs • Verbs with spelling changes in the preterite • Verbs with stem changes in the preterite • Irregular preterites	
UNIDAD 1 Así somos • Estados Unidos	**Etapa 1** p. 32 *¿Cómo soy?* **UNIT OPENER** **CULTURE NOTES** • Oscar de la Hoya • *La comida mexicana* • *Repertorio Español* • Ellen Ochoa • *La Prensa*	• Describe people • Talk about experiences • List accomplishments	• Present and past perfect	**EN VOCES** Cristina García, *Soñar en cubano* **CONEXIONES** *El arte:* self-portrait **NOTAS CULTURALES** • Concept of *barrio* • *Los apodos* • Spanish-speaking immigrants and identity	• *Ser* vs. *estar* • Imperfect tense • Preterite vs. imperfect **Ya sabes:** *Características*	**LISTENING:** Recognize descriptions **SPEAKING:** Add details to descriptions; Describe personal characteristics and actions **READING:** Observe how verb tenses reveal time
	Etapa 2 p. 54 *¿Cómo me veo?*	• Describe fashions • Talk about pastimes • Talk about the future • Predict actions	• Future tense • Future of probability	**EN COLORES** *Un gran diseñador:* Oscar de la Renta **CONEXIONES** *Las matemáticas:* create an annual budget **NOTAS CULTURALES** • Araceli Segarra, climber of Mt. Everest • Pet sounds and names	• Verbs like *gustar* • *Por* and *para* **Activity 4:** *De compras* (clothing) **Activity 15:** *¿Dónde estarán?* (wondering about location) **Ya sabes:** *¿De qué es?*	**LISTENING:** Distinguish admiring and critical remarks **SPEAKING:** Use familiar vocabulary in a new setting; Brainstorm to get lots of ideas **CULTURE:** Examine the cultural role of fashion
	Etapa 3 p. 76 *¡Hay tanto que hacer!*	• Talk about household chores • Say what friends do • Express feelings	• Reflexives used reciprocally **NOTA** *saber/conocer*	**EN VOCES** Sandra Cisneros, *La casa en Mango Street* **EN COLORES** *El legendario rey del mambo:* Tito Puente **TÚ EN LA COMUNIDAD** **NOTAS CULTURALES** • *El compadrazgo* • Sammy Sosa • Greater Eastside, LA	• Reflexive verbs • Impersonal constructions with *se* **Activity 2:** *¡Hazlo!* (say what you have to do) **Activity 5:** *Un día desastroso* (reflexive verbs) **Activity 9:** *Mi padrino* (imperfect)	**LISTENING:** Make an argument for and against hiring others to maintain a home **SPEAKING:** Identify feelings important in a friendship **READING:** Chart contrasts between dreams and reality **WRITING:** Use details to enrich a description **CULTURE:** Interview, report, and value musical influences

	COMMUNICATION	GRAMMAR	CULTURE	RECYCLING	STRATEGIES
UNIDAD 2 ¡El mundo es nuestro! • México y América Central **Etapa 1** p. 106 *Pensemos en los demás* **UNIT OPENER CULTURE NOTES** • María Izquierdo • *¡Protege la selva tropical!* • *Tejidos guatemaltecos* • *Ruinas de Copán* • *Cebiche mixto* • Oscar Arias	• Say what you want to do • Make requests • Make suggestions	**NOTA** pronoun placement with commands	**EN VOCES** Elizabeth Burgos, *Me llamo Rigoberta Menchú* **TÚ EN LA COMUNIDAD** **NOTAS CULTURALES** • Youth groups in Mexico and C.A. • Young people addressing adults • *Castellano*	• Command forms • *Nosotros* commands • Speculating with the conditional **Activity 2:** *¿Qué vas a hacer?* (say what you are going to do) • **Activity 5:** *La clase de ejercicio (tú, usted o ustedes)* • **Activity 12:** *Costa Rica* (conditional)	**LISTENING:** Anticipate, compare, and contrast **SPEAKING:** Name social problems, then propose solutions; Identify the general ideas, then delegate responsibilities **READING:** Comprehend complex sentences
Etapa 2 p. 128 *Un planeta en peligro*	• Say what should be done • React to the ecology • React to others' actions	• Present perfect subjunctive **NOTA** *-uir* verbs add a *y* in subjunctive form	**EN COLORES:** *Unidos podemos hacerlo:* literacy in Nicaragua **CONEXIONES** *Las ciencias:* recycling **NOTAS CULTURALES** • Currencies in C.A. and Mexico • *Grupo de los Cien:* international conservation	• Present subjunctive **Activity 2:** *El horario de Ángela* (describe schedules) **Activity 5:** *La ecóloga* (subjunctive) **Ya sabes:** *Es bueno que…* etc.	**LISTENING:** Inventory efforts to save the environment **SPEAKING:** Consider the effect of words and tone of voice; Express support (or lack of) **CULTURE:** Gather and analyze information about literacy
Etapa 3 p. 150 *La riqueza natural*	• React to nature • Express doubt • Relate events in time	• Subjunctive with *cuando* and other conjunctions of time **NOTA** *-cer* verbs add a *z* in the subjunctive	**EN VOCES** Juan José Arreola, *Baby H.P.* **EN COLORES** *Un país de encanto:* Costa Rican rainforests **CONEXIONES** *Las ciencias:* the products of a rainforest **NOTAS CULTURALES** • *Isla de Ometepe, Lago Nicaragua* • *Reservas naturales en Centroamérica*	• Subjunctive with expressions of emotion • Subjunctive to express doubt and uncertainty **Activity 3:** *¿Has visto…?* (animals) • **Activity 7:** *El mundo de hoy* (expressing emotion) • **Activity 9:** *No te creo* (expressing doubt) • **Activity 12:** *Tan pronto como* • **Activity 13:** *Los quehaceres* (conjunctions of time) **Ya sabes:** Expressions of emotion and doubt	**LISTENING:** Determine your purpose for listening **SPEAKING:** Gain thinking time before speaking; Reassure others **READING:** Recognize uses of satire, parody, and irony **WRITING:** Persuade by presenting solutions to problems **CULTURE:** Analyze advantages and disadvantages of ecotourism
UNIDAD 3 Celebración de mi mundo • Caribe **Etapa 1** p. 180 *¡Al fin la graduación!* **UNIT OPENER CULTURE NOTES** • *Los Muñequitos de Matanzas* • *Maracas* • *Frutas tropicales* • Rosario Ferré • Juan Luis Guerra • *Parque ceremonial Taíno, Utuado*	• Describe personal celebrations • Say what people want • Link events and ideas	• Subjunctive with conjunctions • Imperfect subjunctive **NOTA** *-ger* verbs change *g* to *j* in subjunctive	**EN VOCES** Nicolás Guillén, *Ébano real* **TÚ EN LA COMUNIDAD** **NOTAS CULTURALES** • Graduation ceremony in the Dominican Republic • *Fiesta de graduación*	• Subjunctive for expressing wishes **Activity 5:** *Pedro* (subjunctive with impersonal expressions) **Activity 13:** *Los chismes* (expressions of doubt) **Activity 14:** *Permiso* (recreation) **Ya sabes:** *otros verbos, conjunciones, el futuro*	**LISTENING:** Recognize major transitions **SPEAKING:** Accept or reject advice; Give advice and best wishes **READING:** Interpret metaphors
Etapa 2 p. 202 *¡Próspero Año Nuevo!*	• Talk about holidays • Hypothesize • Express doubt and disagree • Describe ideals	• Subjunctive with nonexistent and indefinite antecedents • Conditional sentences **NOTA** *sembrar, recoger, educar* spelling changes in subjunctive	**EN COLORES** *Una tradición de Puerto Rico:* masks **CONEXIONES:** *El arte:* art of the Caribbean **NOTAS CULTURALES** • *Salsa* • *Chayanne* • Holidays in Puerto Rico	• Subjunctive for disagreement and denial **Activity 5:** *En la comunidad* (nonexistent and indefinite) **Activity 14:** *Las profesiones* (subjunctive) **Ya sabes:** *dar las gracias, dudar que…,* etc.	**LISTENING:** Observe interview techniques **SPEAKING:** Socialize as host or guest; Encourage participation **CULTURE:** Recognize and describe uses of disguise
Etapa 3 p. 224 *Celebraciones de patria*	• Describe historic events • Make suggestions and wishes • Express emotion and doubt • State cause and effect	• Subjunctive vs. indicative **NOTA** *-cer* verbs change to *z* in subjunctive; *-gar* verbs change to *gu* in subjunctive	**EN VOCES:** José Martí, *de Versos sencillos: I.* **EN COLORES:** *Una historia única:* celebrations in the D.R. **CONEXIONES:** *Los estudios sociales:* independence days **NOTAS CULTURALES** • *El naufragio de la Santa María* • *El Himno Nacional de la R.D.* • *Guantanamera*	• Summary of the subjunctive **Activity 4:** *Las costumbres* (holidays) **Activity 7:** *¡Santo Domingo!* (subjunctive) **Activity 9:** *La comunidad* (subjunctive) **Ya sabes:** *dudar, creer,* etc.	**LISTENING:** Listen and take notes **SPEAKING:** Describe celebrations; Express yourself **READING:** Observe what makes poetry **WRITING:** Use transitions to make text flow smoothly **CULTURE:** Analyze national celebrations

	COMMUNICATION	GRAMMAR	CULTURE	RECYCLING	STRATEGIES
Etapa 1 p. 254 *El próximo paso* **UNIT OPENER CULTURE NOTES** • Antonio Berni • Rafael Guarga • *El arpa andina* • *Mate* • *La bolsa* • *La Universidad de Chile*	• Describe your studies • Ask questions • Say what you are doing • Say what you were doing	• Progressive with *ir, andar,* and *seguir* • Past progressive	**EN VOCES** Jorge Luis Borges, *Borges y yo* **TÚ EN LA COMUNIDAD** **NOTAS CULTURALES** • Hand gestures • Professional titles • First name usage • Borges' blindness	• Interrogative words • Present progressive **Activity 8:** *Las llamadas* (present progressive, reflexives) **Activity 9:** *La limpieza* (present progressive, household chores) **Ya sabes:** question words	**LISTENING:** Evaluate recommendations **SPEAKING:** Establish closer relationships; Extend a conversation **READING:** Analyze the role of identity and fantasy
Etapa 2 p. 276 *¿Cuál será tu profesión?*	• Talk about careers • Confirm and deny • Express emotions • Hypothesize	• Past perfect subjunctive • Conditional perfect **NOTA** placement of object pronouns	**EN COLORES:** *Los jóvenes y el futuro:* career choices **CONEXIONES** *Los estudios sociales:* what professions interest you **NOTAS CULTURALES** • Getting into a university • Popular professions in Spanish-speaking world	• Affirmative and negative expressions **Activity 6:** *Necesitas saber* (affirmative/negative) **Activity 8:** *La celebración* (past perfect subjunctive) **Ya sabes:** negatives/ affirmatives	**LISTENING:** Identify key information for careers **SPEAKING:** Anticipate what others want to know; Conduct an interview **CULTURE:** Formulate plans for the future
Etapa 3 p. 298 *Un mundo de posibilidades*	• Learn about Latin American economics • Clarify possession • Express possession • Express past probability	• Future perfect	**EN VOCES** Isabel Allende, *Paula* **EN COLORES:** *Se hablan... ¡muchos idiomas!:* Spanish language origins **CONEXIONES** *Los estudios sociales:* ONU / OEA **NOTAS CULTURALES** • Job-hunting process in South America • Saving money	• Subject and stressed object pronouns • Possessive pronouns **Activity 3:** *Internet* (numbers) **Activity 5:** *¿Quién?* (subject/ stressed object pronouns) **Activity 9:** *¿De Argentina o Chile?* (possessive pronouns) **Ya sabes:** *comparaciones numéricas,* possessive pronouns, subject/object pronouns	**LISTENING:** Use statistics to evaluate predictions **SPEAKING:** Guess cognates; Speculate about the past **READING:** Speculate about the author **WRITING:** Use cause and effect to demonstrate ability **CULTURE:** Observe how language reflects culture
Etapa 1 p. 328 *Tradiciones españolas* **UNIT OPENER CULTURE NOTES** • Fernando Botero • *Chocolate y churros* • *La reina Isabel* • *Los cantos gregorianos* • Salvador Dalí • *Teatro Colón*	• Identify and specify • Request clarification • Express relationships • Discuss art forms	• *¿Qué? vs. ¿cuál?* • Relative pronouns	**EN VOCES** Miguel de Unamuno and Ana María Matute **CONEXIONES** *Los estudios sociales:* create a time line of the Spanish Civil War **NOTAS CULTURALES** • *El Museo del Prado*	• Demonstrative adjectives and pronouns **Activity 7:** *Las respuestas* (*¿qué? vs. ¿cuál?*) **Activity 14:** *Los artistas* (relative pronouns, literature) **Ya sabes:** *La pintura, la literatura*	**LISTENING:** Use advance knowledge of the topic **SPEAKING:** Discuss a painting; Organize ideas for research **READING:** Compare famous authors
Etapa 2 p. 350 *El Nuevo Mundo*	• Refer to people and objects • Express relationships • Make generalizations • Describe arts and crafts	• Relative pronouns • *Lo que*	**EN COLORES** *Un arquitecto y sus obras:* Mexican architect **CONEXIONES:** *Las matemáticas:* Mayan numerals **NOTAS CULTURALES** • *Bailes típicos* • *El inca Garcilaso de la Vega* • *Las ruinas de Tikal*	• Direct object pronouns • Indirect object pronouns **Activity 4:** *¿Lo conoces?* (direct object pronouns) **Activity 7:** *Después de la entrevista* (indirect object pronouns, work) **Activity 8:** *El viaje* (indirect object pronouns)	**LISTENING:** Improve your auditory memory **SPEAKING:** Maintain a discussion; Discuss Latin American dance **CULTURE:** Use architecture as a cultural text
Etapa 3 p. 372 *Lo mejor de dos mundos*	• Talk about literature • Talk about film • Avoid redundancy	• Nominalization • Nominalization	**EN VOCES:** Federico García Lorca, *La casa de Bernarda Alba* **EN COLORES** *Tres directores:* Spanish-speaking film directors **TÚ EN LA COMUNIDAD** **NOTAS CULTURALES** • Movie titles in Spanish and English • Rosario Ferré	• Double object pronouns **Activity 5:** *El (La) presidente* (double object pronouns) **Activity 12:** *Clarificaciones* (nominalization)	**LISTENING:** Evaluate discussions **SPEAKING:** Discuss a novel; Critique a film **READING:** Interpret a drama **WRITING:** Support an opinion with facts and examples **CULTURE:** Reflect on the international appeal of movies

UNIDAD 4 Un Futuro brillante • Cono Sur

UNIDAD 5 Artes en España y las Américas • España

		COMMUNICATION	GRAMMAR	CULTURE	RECYCLING	STRATEGIES
UNIDAD 6 ¡Ya llegó el futuro! • Bolivia, Colombia, Ecuador, Perú, Venezuela	**Etapa 1** p. 402 *¿Qué quieres ver?* **UNIT OPENER: CULTURE NOTES** • *Parque Maloka* • Machu Picchu • Simón Bolívar • Armando Reverón • *El teléfono celular* • *Plátanos fritos*	• Narrate in the past • Express doubt and certainty • Report what others say • Talk about television	• Sequence of tenses	**EN VOCES** *Brillo afuera, oscuridad en casa:* Spanish-language soap operas **TÚ EN LA COMUNIDAD** **NOTAS CULTURALES** • Invitation implies inviter pays • *Telenovelas*	• Preterite vs. imperfect • Indicative vs. subjunctive • Reported speech **Activity 1:** *¿Por qué no...?* (movies) **Activity 9:** *¡Es dudoso!* (subjunctive with doubt) **Activity 14:** *Abuelo* (reported speech)	**LISTENING:** Keep up with what is said and agreed **SPEAKING:** Negotiate; Retell memories **READING:** Distinguish facts from interpretations
	Etapa 2 p. 424 *Aquí tienes mi número...*	• Talk about technology • State locations • Make contrasts • Describe unplanned events	• *Pero* vs. *sino* • *Se* for unplanned occurrences	**EN COLORES** *¿Un aparato democrático?:* cell phones, Latin America **CONEXIONES** *El arte:* electronics **NOTAS CULTURALES** • Game shows in Spanish	• Conjunctions • Prepositions and adverbs of location **Activity 2:** *¡Voy a ElectroMundo!* (electronics)	**LISTENING:** Analyze the appeal in radio ads **SPEAKING:** Make excuses; Consider the factors for and against an electronic purchase **CULTURE:** Survey technology in daily life
	Etapa 3 p. 446 *¡Un viaje al ciberespacio!*	• Compare and evaluate • Express precise relationships • Navigate cyberspace	• Verbs with prepositions	**EN VOCES** Gabriel García Márquez **EN COLORES** *Bolivia en la red* **CONEXIONES** *La tecnología:* evaluate computer configurations **NOTAS CULTURALES** • Spread of computer technology in Latin America • Searching for websites	• Summary of prepositions • Comparatives and superlatives **Activity 4:** *Comparaciones* (comparatives) **Activity 5:** *Marcos* (comparatives, computers) **Ya sabes:** verbs with prepositions	**LISTENING:** Computer vocabulary **SPEAKING:** Compare and evaluate films, computer configurations **READING:** Monitor comprehension **WRITING:** Prioritize information **CULTURE:** Evaluate the Internet as a means of developing cultural knowledge

	COMMUNICATION	GRAMMAR	CULTURE
Level 4 **Scope & Sequence**	**Unidades** 1: Giving advice (p. 54) 2: Making plans (p. 107) 3: Debating (p. 149) 4: Discussing and deciding (p. 177) 5: Expressing feelings (p. 247) 6: Making requests (p. 282) 7: Proposing a theory (p. 353) 8: Supporting a point of view (p. 407)	**Unidades** 1: Present Tense (pp. G14–G31) 2: Preterite and Imperfect Tenses (pp. G32–G47) 3: Possessives, Affirmative and Negative Words (pp. G48–G60) 4: Passive Construction (pp. G61–G76) 5: Present Subjunctive (pp. G77–G88) 6: Future and Conditional Tenses (pp. G89–G98) 7: Imperfect Subjunctive, Present Perfect (pp. G99–G105) 8: Perfect Tenses, Sequence of Tenses (pp. G106–G116)	**Unidades** 1: Latinos in the U.S. (pp. 22–73) 2: Spain (pp. 74–119) 3: Mexico and Guatemala (pp. 120–163) 4: The Caribbean (pp. 164–213) 5: Central America (pp. 214–267) 6: Colombia, Panama, Venezuela (pp. 268–321) 7: The Andes (pp. 322–373) 8: The Southern Cone (pp. 374–425)

Setting the Stage for Communication

BOOST·CONFIDENCE

Each unit is set in different Spanish-speaking places to excite students about the new places and new things they're going to learn.

● **Unit Standards** preview for the students what they will learn in the unit.

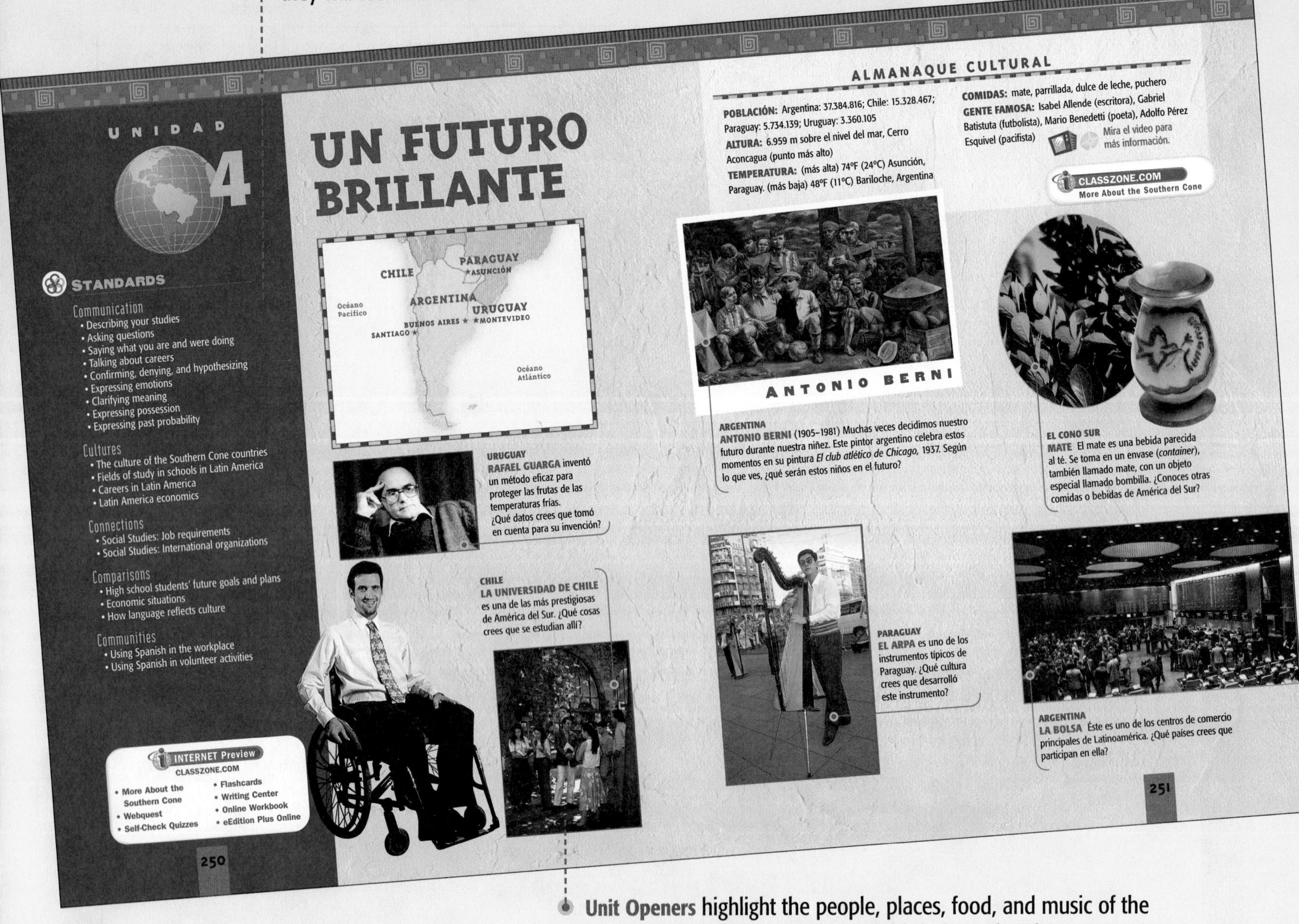

UNIDAD 4

UN FUTURO BRILLANTE

STANDARDS

Communication
- Describing your studies
- Asking questions
- Saying what you are and were doing
- Talking about careers
- Confirming, denying, and hypothesizing
- Expressing emotions
- Clarifying meaning
- Expressing possession
- Expressing past probability

Cultures
- The culture of the Southern Cone countries
- Fields of study in schools in Latin America
- Careers in Latin America
- Latin America economics

Connections
- Social Studies: Job requirements
- Social Studies: International organizations

Comparisons
- High school students' future goals and plans
- Economic situations
- How language reflects culture

Communities
- Using Spanish in the workplace
- Using Spanish in volunteer activities

INTERNET Preview
CLASSZONE.COM
- More About the Southern Cone
- Webquest
- Self-Check Quizzes
- Flashcards
- Writing Center
- Online Workbook
- eEdition Plus Online

250

CHILE
PARAGUAY
ASUNCIÓN
Océano Pacífico
ARGENTINA
URUGUAY
SANTIAGO
BUENOS AIRES ★ ★MONTEVIDEO
Océano Atlántico

URUGUAY
RAFAEL GUARGA inventó un método eficaz para proteger las frutas de las temperaturas frías. ¿Qué datos crees que tomó en cuenta para su invención?

CHILE
LA UNIVERSIDAD DE CHILE es una de las más prestigiosas de América del Sur. ¿Qué cosas crees que se estudian allí?

ALMANAQUE CULTURAL

POBLACIÓN: Argentina: 37.384.816; Chile: 15.328.467; Paraguay: 5.734.139; Uruguay: 3.360.105
ALTURA: 6.959 m sobre el nivel del mar, Cerro Aconcagua (punto más alto)
TEMPERATURA: (más alta) 74°F (24°C) Asunción, Paraguay. (más baja) 48°F (11°C) Bariloche, Argentina

COMIDAS: mate, parrillada, dulce de leche, puchero
GENTE FAMOSA: Isabel Allende (escritora), Gabriel Batistuta (futbolista), Mario Benedetti (poeta), Adolfo Pérez Esquivel (pacifista)

Mira el video para más información.

CLASSZONE.COM
More About the Southern Cone

ANTONIO BERNI

ARGENTINA
ANTONIO BERNI (1905–1981) Muchas veces decidimos nuestro futuro durante nuestra niñez. Este pintor argentino celebra estos momentos en su pintura *El club atlético de Chicago*, 1937. Según lo que ves, ¿qué serán estos niños en el futuro?

EL CONO SUR
MATE El mate es una bebida parecida al té. Se toma en un envase (*container*), también llamado mate, con un objeto especial llamado bombilla. ¿Conoces otras comidas o bebidas de América del Sur?

PARAGUAY
EL ARPA es uno de los instrumentos típicos de Paraguay. ¿Qué cultura crees que desarrolló este instrumento?

ARGENTINA
LA BOLSA Éste es uno de los centros de comercio principales de Latinoamérica. ¿Qué países crees que participan en ella?

251

● **Unit Openers** highlight the people, places, food, and music of the new culture so students learn Spanish in its authentic context.

● **A focus on the standards** helps students strategize about language learning.

> "Everything ties nicely together. The unit has a good introductory theme so that students can take vocabulary and structures and apply them to talk about themselves."
>
> Elizabeth Torosian
> Doherty Middle School
> Andover, MA

UNIDAD

4 UN FUTURO BRILLANTE

- Comunicación
- Culturas
- **Conexiones**
- Comparaciones
- Comunidades

Webquest
CLASSZONE.COM

Explore connections in the Southern Cone through guided Web activities.

C@FE INTERNET
e-mail web irc

Conexiones

Al estudiar español, aprendemos más de otras materias, como el arte, las ciencias, las matemáticas, la música y los estudios sociales. ¿Cuál es tu materia favorita? ¿Qué has aprendido de esa materia por medio del español?

Conexiones en acción Identifica la materia representada por cada foto y explica cómo podrías usar el español para aprender más.

Comparaciones

Es fascinante comparar los idiomas que se hablan en el mundo. ¿Conoces estas palabras? ¿Sabes cuál es su origen?

chocolate
papa
maíz
llama
huracán

Comunicación

Usamos varias formas de comunicación todos los días. Por ejemplo, nos comunicamos por teléfono y por medio de los anuncios. ¿Cuántas formas de comunicación puedes identificar en la foto?

Culturas

La cultura distinta de los países del Cono Sur se refleja en sus productos, costumbres y perspectivas. ¿Cuánto sabes ya de la cultura de Chile, Argentina, Paraguay y Uruguay? ¿Sabes algo de su economía?

Comunidades

En esta unidad conocerás a Toño, un alumno que usa el español en su comunidad. ¿Cómo puede Toño ayudar a una estudiante hispanohablante que no comprende su tarea?

Fíjate

¿Esperas tener un futuro brillante? Explica la relación que puede tener una de las fotos de estas páginas con tu futuro. Si no encuentras una foto adecuada, haz un dibujo que represente tus planes para el futuro.

252

253

MOTIVATE TO COMMUNICATE
¡En español!

Strengthen proficiency through meaningful communicative contexts

Stunning location photos with activating questions immerse students in the cultural context.

• **Etapa Openers** remind students of the communicative objectives.

• **¿Qué ves?** reviews language for application in the new cultural context.

UNIDAD 4

ETAPA

3

Un mundo de posibilidades

OBJECTIVES

• Learn about Latin American economics

• Clarify meaning

• Express possession

• Express past probability

¿Qué ves?

Mira la foto. Contesta las preguntas.

1. ¿Qué cosas ves en la foto?

2. ¿Crees que es un lugar divertido o serio? ¿Cómo lo sabes?

3. ¿Por qué iría alguien a un lugar como éste?

4. ¿Cuáles son algunos(as) profesionales que podrían trabajar aquí?

298

"I could do so much with this in my classroom... it's a fantastic tool and all wonderfully integrated with grammar and vocabulary."

Marco García
Lincoln Park High School
Chicago, IL

MOTIVATE
TO COMMUNICATE
¡En español!

Build vocabulary for success from recognition to production

Two stages of vocabulary introduction better prepare students for recognition and comprehension.

IMPROVE · COMPREHENSION

- **En contexto** visually preteaches active vocabulary in a relevant context.

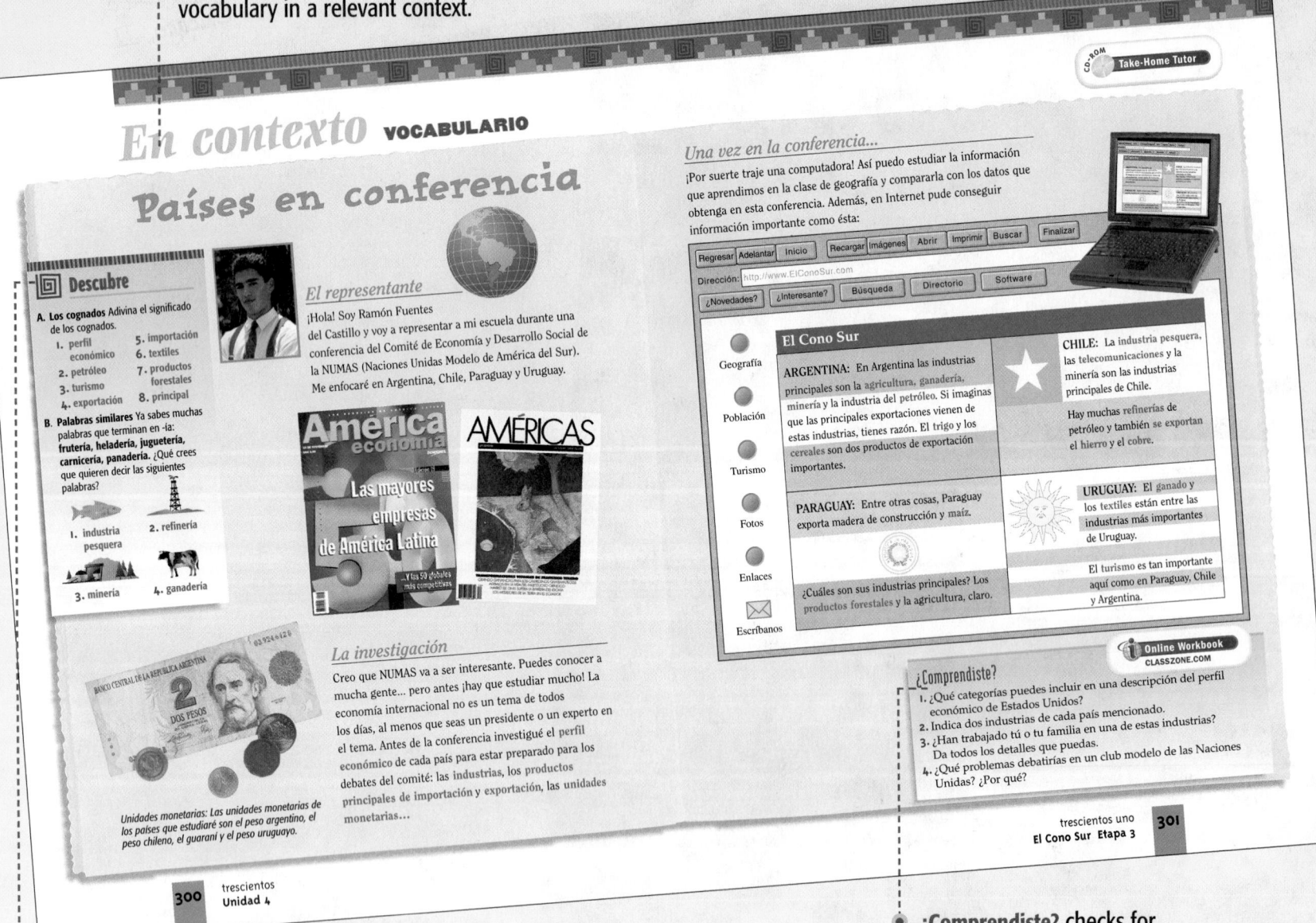

- **Descubre** highlights key words and phrases to prepare students for what they are about to learn.

- **¿Comprendiste?** checks for understanding and prompts students to think critically.

Listening strategies provide a starting point and focus to help comprehension.

"The Descubre box is a great idea. It helps the students to be confident about tackling new vocabulary: 'Oh, I know this.'"

Norma Coto
Bishop Moore High School
Orlando, FL

En vivo
AUDIO
SITUACIONES

PARA ESCUCHAR

STRATEGY: LISTENING

Pre-listening Predict what countries are the largest producers of the world's resources. Do you think these are also favorites with tourists? Think of countries in each category and write your predictions.

Use statistics to evaluate predictions Write down the countries as directed in **Escuchar**, then evaluate your predictions. How well did you identify the countries where major world producers and industries are located? Discuss your insights with your classmates.

Alimentos	Minerales	Turismo
1.		
2.		
3.		

¡Encuéntralo por Internet!

Tienes que escribir un informe sobre la producción mundial (*worldwide*) de varios productos. Encuentras información en Internet. Primero ves la información en la página-web. Luego escuchas más información por audio.

❶ Leer

Encontraste esta página en Internet. Lee la página para saber qué tipo de información tiene.

| Regresar | Adelantar | Inicio | Recargar | Imágenes | Abrir | Imprimir | Buscar | Finalizar |

Dirección: http://www.mundial.com

| ¿Novedades? | ¿Interesante? | Búsqueda | Directorio | Software |

LA PRODUCCIÓN MUNDIAL

Agricultura
Minería
Telecomunicaciones
Ganadería
Petróleo
Textiles
Maderas
Industria pesquera
Turismo

❷ Escuchar

Tienes que informarle a la clase cuáles países del mundo son los que producen la mayor cantidad de ciertos productos. Escucha la información de la página-web «La producción mundial» y escribe los países en el orden correcto.

AGRICULTURA: maíz
País #1: _____
País #2: _____
País #3: _____
País #4: _____
País #5: _____

GANADERÍA: vacas
País #1: _____
País #2: _____
País #3: _____
País #4: _____
País #5: _____

MINERÍA: cobre
País #1: _____
País #2: _____
País #3: _____
País #4: _____
País #5: _____

PETRÓLEO CRUDO
País #1: _____
País #2: _____
País #3: _____
País #4: _____
País #5: _____

INDUSTRIA PESQUERA
País #1: _____
País #2: _____
País #3: _____
País #4: _____
País #5: _____

TURISMO
País #1: _____
País #2: _____
País #3: _____
País #4: _____
País #5: _____

❸ Hablar/Escribir

En grupos de dos o tres, conversen sobre el perfil económico de su ciudad, estado o país. ¿Cuál es la industria más importante de su estado o región? ¿Conocen a alguien que trabaje en esa industria? Entrevisten a esa persona o busquen datos por Internet o en la biblioteca. Escriban un informe en español que explique la importancia de esa industria en su región. También incluyan ideas sobre el desarrollo futuro de sus regiones.

MOTIVATE TO COMMUNICATE
¡En español!

Follow a clear lesson progression to build in success

A well-organized lesson structure with clearly stated objectives takes the guesswork out of practice.

● **The systematic overlap of grammar concepts** provides a seamless connection between Levels 2 and 3. The grammar taught in the latter part of Level 2 is comprehensively reviewed in Level 3. See pp. T10–T11 for details.

Práctica del vocabulario continuación

En acción

PARTE A — Práctica del vocabulario

Objectives for Activities 1–4
• Learn about Latin America economics

1 Las compañías

Hablar/Escribir Tu compañero(a) quiere saber a qué se dedican varias compañías de Buenos Aires. Como sabes un poco de Argentina, tú le contestas sus preguntas.

modelo

Compañero(a): ¿A qué se dedica esa compañía?

Tú: Esa compañía se dedica a la industria pesquera.

1.

2.

3.
4.

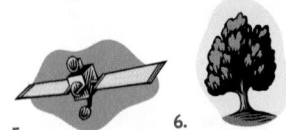
5.
6.

2 Los productos

Escribir En tu clase de geografía, tienes que hacer una tabla que indica los productos que van bajo cada categoría. Copia la tabla y complétala.

Agricultura	cereales		
Ganadería			
Minería			
Industria pesquera			
Textiles			

aceitunas	lana
algodón	maíz
arroz	oro
atún	ovejas (sheep)
caballos	pieles de cuero
cabras (goats)	plata
café	ropa
calamares	seda
cereales	suéteres
cobre	toallas
frutas	trigo
gallinas	trucha (trout)
hierro	vacas

3 Internet

Leer/Hablar Conversa con tu compañero(a) sobre las estadísticas sobre los visitantes a las páginas web de cada país.

modelo

Tú: Este año, la página de Paraguay recibió un millón doscientos mil visitantes.

Compañero(a): De esos visitantes, casi la mitad fue hispanohablante.

Estadísticas sobre los visitantes

Paraguay: 1.200.000 visitantes
Edad promedio: 32
Hispanohablantes: 50%
Inglés: 25%
Otros idiomas: 25%

Chile: 1.500.800 visitantes
Edad promedio: 25
Hispanohablantes: 33%
Inglés: 33%
Otros idiomas: 33%

Argentina: 2.350.700 visitantes
Edad promedio: 22
Hispanohablantes: 20%
Inglés: 40%
Otros idiomas: 40%

Uruguay: 850.000 visitantes
Edad promedio: 45
Hispanohablantes: 70%
Inglés: 10%
Otros idiomas: 20%

Vocabulario

Comparaciones numéricas

comparar *to compare*
las estadísticas *statistics*
mil millones *a billion*
un millón de millones *a trillion*
la mitad de *one half of*
el por ciento *percent*
el porcentaje *percentage*
el promedio *average*
el quinto *one fifth*

sumar *to add*
el tercio *one third*

Ya sabes

un cuarto
un décimo
la mayoría
medio(a)

▶ ¿Puedes usar estas palabras para hablar sobre tu ciudad o estado?

4 Tu estado

STRATEGY: SPEAKING
Guess cognates Spanish and English share many words derived from Latin. Try adding a Spanish ending to an English word and it might be a correct word in Spanish. Look at these cognates for discussing your state's industries: **construcción, cinematografía, energía nuclear, radiodifusión, fuerzas armadas.**

Hablar Tú y tu compañero(a) tienen que preparar un reporte sobre tu estado para la clase de estudios sociales. Antes de ir a la biblioteca tienen que decidir qué tipo de información económica necesitan buscar.

modelo

Tú: La agricultura es muy importante para la economía de Texas.

Compañero(a): Tienes razón. También necesitamos información sobre la ganadería.

● **Repaso grammar boxes** reteach Level 2 grammar concepts so students are wholeheartedly prepared to approach Level 3 concepts.

"I find it very cohesive. I could follow the progression without difficulty. The unit theme is well represented throughout."

Jim Rudy
Glen Este High School
Cincinnati, OH

PARTE B

Práctica: gramática y vocabulario

Objectives for Activities 5–15
• Clarify meaning • Express possession • Express past probability

REPASO   Subject and Stressed Object pronouns

Most of the time you do not use subject pronouns in Spanish, because the verb ending shows who the subject is. When you do include them it is because you wish to add emphasis, clarify, or make a contrast.

• to show emphasis

Yo le di las estadísticas, no Roberto.
I gave him the statistics, not Roberto.

• to make a comparison or clarify

Él salió. Ella se quedó en casa.
He went out. She stayed home.

You use the prepositional **a** + subject pronouns to clarify who the object of a preposition is, except in the case of yo and tú. Here special object pronouns are used (mí, ti).

El profesor les dio el reportaje **a** ellos.
The teacher gave the report to them.

No me lo dio **a** mí.
He didn't give it to me.

Vocabulario

🌀 **Ya sabes**

Subject	a + Pronoun
yo	a mí
tú	a ti
usted	a usted
él	a él
ella	a ella
nosotros	a nosotros
vosotros	a vosotros
ustedes	a ustedes
ellos	a ellos
ellas	a ellas

Practice: Actividades 5 6 7

Más práctica cuaderno pp. 109–110
Para hispanohablantes cuaderno p. 107

Online Workbook CLASSZONE.COM

---

5 ¿Quién?

Escuchar/*Escribir* Estás en una reunión familiar. Contesta las preguntas de tu tío sobre los intereses de todos.

modelo
¿Quién es abogado? él
¿Quién es médica? ella

1. ¿Quién estudió ingeniería?
2. ¿Quién quiere ser veterinario? _____ ¿Y bombero? _____
3. ¿Quién fue a la Universidad de Buenos Aires? _____ ¿Quién fue a la Universidad de Chile? _____
4. ¿Quién estudió para ser arquitecto? _____ ¿E ingeniera? _____
5. ¿A quién le interesa el mercadeo? _____ ¿A quién le interesa la publicidad?
6. ¿Quién es bailarina? _____ ¿Quién es deportista?

También se dice

Trabajar y trabajo son términos universales en todo el mundo de habla española. Pero en México y Colombia se dice también chambear y chamba para referirse al trabajo. En Argentina se usa la palabra changa y en Puerto Rico chiripa para referirse a un trabajo pequeño.

---

6 Ganándose la vida

Hablar/*Escribir* Conversa con tu compañero(a) sobre las profesiones de las personas de la lista y de otras personas que conocen. ¿Cómo se ganan la vida?

Buenos días, Buon giorno, Guten Tag

modelo
la Sra. Martínez
Tú: *¿Cómo se gana la vida la Sra. Martínez?*
Compañero(a): *Ella es intérprete.*

1. el Sr. Martínez

2. Ángel

3. el Sr. Beltrán

4. Susana

5. los Sres. Gutiérrez

6. el Sr. Henares

7. un(a) amigo(a)

8. un(a) pariente

9. un(a) vecino(a)

10. tú

Vocabulario

Carreras con el español

el (la) académico(a) *academic*
el (la) agente de ventas *sales agent*
el (la) banquero(a) *banker*
el (la) bibliotecario(a) *librarian*
el (la) corresponsal *correspondent*
el (la) diplomático(a) *diplomat*
el (la) financiero(a) *financial expert*
el (la) intérprete *interpreter*
el (la) trabajador(a) social *social worker*
el (la) traductor(a) *translator*

¿Conoces a alguien que trabaje en una de estas profesiones?

MOTIVATE TO COMMUNICATE
¡En español!

Walkthrough   T31

Present grammar concepts visually to improve comprehension & retention

Illustrated grammar makes it easier for students to understand, remember, and apply new concepts.

Visual grammar concepts help students see how the language works.

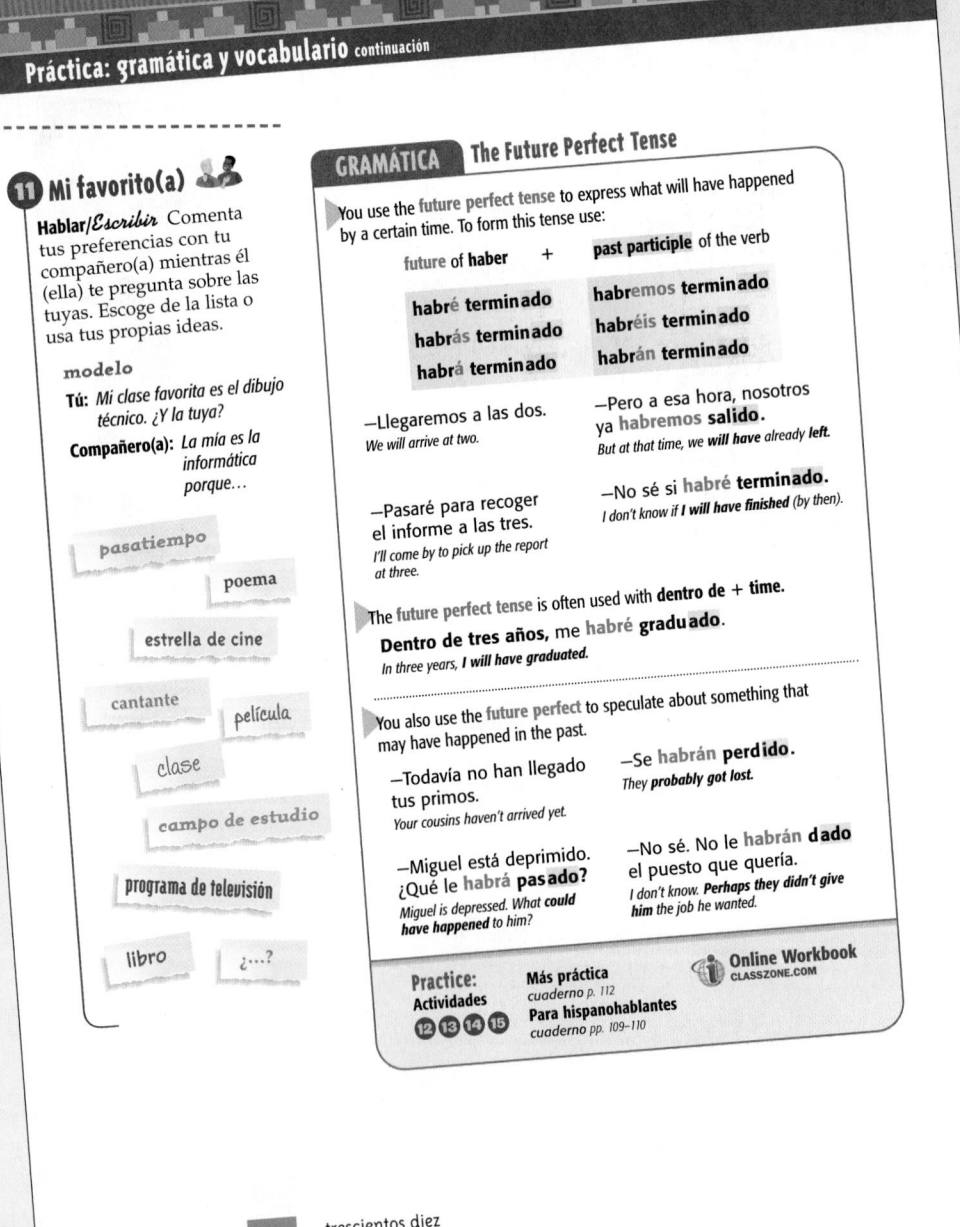

11 Mi favorito(a)

Hablar/Escribir Comenta tus preferencias con tu compañero(a) mientras él (ella) te pregunta sobre las tuyas. Escoge de la lista o usa tus propias ideas.

modelo
Tú: *Mi clase favorita es el dibujo técnico. ¿Y la tuya?*
Compañero(a): *La mía es la informática porque…*

pasatiempo

poema

estrella de cine

cantante   película

clase

campo de estudio

programa de televisión

libro   ¿…?

GRAMÁTICA   The Future Perfect Tense

You use the **future perfect tense** to express what will have happened by a certain time. To form this tense use:

future of **haber**   +   **past participle** of the verb

habré terminado	habremos terminado
habrás terminado	habréis terminado
habrá terminado	habrán terminado

—Llegaremos a las dos.
We will arrive at two.

—Pero a esa hora, nosotros ya **habremos salido**.
*But at that time, we **will have** already **left**.*

—Pasaré para recoger el informe a las tres.
I'll come by to pick up the report at three.

—No sé si **habré terminado**.
*I don't know if **I will have finished** (by then).*

The **future perfect tense** is often used with **dentro de + time**.
Dentro de tres años, me **habré graduado**.
*In three years, **I will have graduated**.*

You also use the **future perfect** to speculate about something that may have happened in the past.

—Todavía no han llegado tus primos.
Your cousins haven't arrived yet.

—Se **habrán perdido**.
*They **probably got lost**.*

—Miguel está deprimido. ¿Qué le **habrá pasado**?
*Miguel is depressed. What **could have happened** to him?*

—No sé. No le **habrán dado** el puesto que quería.
*I don't know. **Perhaps they didn't give him** the job he wanted.*

Practice: Actividades
12 13 14 15

Más práctica
cuaderno p. 112
Para hispanohablantes
cuaderno pp. 109–110

Online Workbook
CLASSZONE.COM

● **The activity sequence,** from controlled to open-ended activities, guides students through a solid progression that builds vocabulary and grammar skills.

● **Clear models** make it easier for students to understand what they are supposed to do.

"I like the fact that there seems to be a good balance between activities that practice new structures and activities that require more creative uses of language in communicative situations."

Vickie Mike
Horseheads High School
Horseheads, NY

Práctica: gramática y vocabulario continuación

14 ¿Qué habrá pasado?

Hablar/Escribir Imagina qué habrá pasado en el mundo económico y profesional al final del día. Contesta las siguientes preguntas.

modelo

¿Cómo se comunicaron?

No sé. ¿Se habrán comunicado por Internet?

1. ¿Qué pasó hoy con la bolsa de valores?
2. ¿Descubrieron algo los científicos?
3. ¿Cuántos boletos vendió el agente de viajes?
4. ¿Quién tradujo las conversaciones diplomáticas?
5. ¿Qué manejaron los banqueros?
6. ¿A quiénes ayudaron los trabajadores sociales?
7. ¿Qué inventaron en el laboratorio?
8. ¿Qué hicieron en la fábrica?
9. ¿Qué tradujo el traductor del periódico?
10. ¿Qué vendió la compañía multinacional?

15 El año 2025

Hablar/Escribir En grupos de tres o cuatro, hablen sobre el futuro. ¿Pueden imaginar cómo será la vida entonces? ¿Cómo será tu rutina diaria? ¿Cómo será tu trabajo? ¿Cómo será tu familia? ¿Tu trabajo?

modelo

Tú: Para el año 2025, habremos construido casas en el planeta Marte.

Compañero(a) 1: No, yo no lo creo. Para el año 2025, habremos curado todas las enfermedades.

Compañero(a) 2: No, yo no lo creo. Lo que yo creo es que para el año 2025, habrán inventado carros que pueden volar.

Amigo(a) 3: No, yo no lo creo. Lo que yo creo es que para el año 2025…

Activity 16 brings together all concepts p...

16 Los bosques

Leer/Escribir Lee la tabla sobre los bosques de Latinoamérica (Iberoamérica) y contesta las preguntas.

1. ¿Qué porcentaje de la tierra paraguaya está cubierta de bosques?
2. ¿Cuál es el área de tu país?
3. Tienes un amigo panameño. ¿Cuál es la tasa anual de cambio de su país?
4. ¿Cuántas especies de árboles tiene Paraguay que son comercialmente explotables? ¿Cuántas de ésas se exportan?
5. PNB quiere decir «Producto Nacional Bruto».¿Sabes cómo se dice eso en inglés?

Fuente de divisas

Un tercio de la tierra paraguaya es boscosa. Hasta 1959, la madera fue el principal producto de exportación del país, y aunque actualmente su contribución al PNB es pequeña, representa una fuente importante de divisas. Unas cuarenta y cinco especies de árboles de los bosques de Paraguay son comercialmente explotables y siete se exportan.

BOSQUES DE IBEROAMÉRICA

PAÍS	ÁREA (1000 Ha)	TASA ANUAL DE CAMBIO
Costa Rica	1.456	2.44
El Salvador	127	1.85
Guatemala	4.253	1.58
Honduras	4.608	1.94
México	48.695	1.21
Nicaragua	6.027	1.69
Panamá	3.123	1.70
Cuba	1.960	0.19
Rep. Dominicana	1.084	2.43
Argentina	34.436	0.57
Chile	8.033	0.07
Uruguay	813	0.12
Bolivia	49.345	1.12
Brasil	566.007	0.58
Colombia	54.190	0.62
Ecuador	12.007	1.65
Paraguay	12.868	2.38
Perú	68.090	0.37
Venezuela	45.943	1.13

More Practice: Más comunicación p. R14

🖥 **Online Workbook** CLASSZONE.COM

Nota cultural

En muchos países de Latinoamérica, la gente tiene una forma especial de ahorrar dinero. Van a una casa de cambio o a un banco y compran dólares estadounidenses. Cuando necesitan usar el dinero, cambian los dólares nuevamente.

Refrán

Promete poco y haz mucho.

¿Qué quiere decir el refrán? En tu opinión, ¿por qué es mejor decir poco y dejar que tus acciones muestren tus intenciones?

«Prometo que lo hago más tarde.»

«¡Gracias! ¡Qué sorpresa magnífica!»

● **Refranes** make learning Spanish and its embedded cultural beliefs both memorable and fun.

MOTIVATE TO COMMUNICATE
¡En español!

Improve students' reading skills with a variety of high-interest selections

Engaging reading selections, which are read and summarized on audio, provide students a tremendous advantage to increase their literacy in Spanish and exposure to AP authors.

- **Reading strategies** develop students' skills by emphasizing different ways to approach a variety of readings and genres.

En voces
LECTURA
AUDIO

PARA LEER
STRATEGY: READING
Analyze the role of identity and fantasy Movies and television often tell stories about people who are uncertain about their identity. Think about a T.V. story or movie where you have seen this theme. What elements does the character see as fact? Which ones does she or he see as fiction? After the reading, list the elements from Borges' life that he uses in his works. Why do you think he chose those? Would you choose the same? Explain.

EL AUTOR

el hogar	lugar donde uno vive
el tigre	gato salvaje
mudarse	cambiarse de casa
por su cuenta	por sí mismo
paterno(a)	del padre
materno(a)	de la madre
reconocido(a)	famoso(a)

Nota cultural
Borges pasó los últimos años de su vida casi ciego, pero su ceguera (blindness) no le impidió seguir escribiendo. Contó con el apoyo de su esposa, María Kodama, quien lo ayudó mucho. Ella hacía los trabajos que él no podía.

270 doscientos setenta
Unidad 4

Jorge Luis Borges

Los laberintos y sueños¹, la fantasía, las identidades misteriosas y la suspensión del tiempo… todos son temas importantes en las obras de Jorge Luis Borges, uno de los autores latinoamericanos más reconocidos del siglo XX.

Borges nació en Buenos Aires en 1899 y vivió allí hasta 1914. Comenzó a escribir a la edad de nueve años, cuando publicó una traducción al español del cuento The Happy Prince de Oscar Wilde. Muchas de sus primeras lecturas fueron en inglés porque su hogar era bilingüe, ya que su abuela era inglesa. A los trece años, publicó su primer cuento original sobre tigres. Desde entonces, los tigres fueron un símbolo importante en la obra de Borges.

En 1914, su familia se mudó a Suiza y en 1919, se trasladó² a España, donde Borges publicó «Himno al mar», su primer poema en español. Regresó a Buenos Aires en 1921, fundó revistas y publicó su primera colección de poemas, Fervor de Buenos Aires (1923). Publicó poesía a lo largo de³ su vida.

---

¹dreams   ²moved   ³throughout

Elogio de la sombra (1969), El oro de los tigres (1972) y La rosa profunda (1975) son otros libros de poemas conocidos. En estos libros, Borges trata los temas de la historia de su familia, una que participó en varias etapas de la historia de Argentina. Su abuelo paterno participó en la guerra civil de Argentina; su abuelo materno también fue soldado. Borges se veía muy distinto a ellos, como dice en «Soy», un poema de La rosa profunda:

❝ Soy… el que no fue una espada⁴ en la guerra. ❞

Borges no luchó con una espada de verdad, pero libró batallas de la imaginación⁵ que resultaron en una obra voluminosa. Además de poemas, publicó varias colecciones de cuentos. Entre las más importantes se encuentran Ficciones (1944) y El Aleph (1949). En sus cuentos, Borges explora el límite entre la realidad y la fantasía y cómo a veces estas cosas se confunden en nuestras vidas.

El sentido del ser—quiénes somos y cómo formamos nuestra identidad—es otro de los temas importantes en la obra de Borges. Él veía su identidad como escritor aparte de su identidad como hombre. Pero Borges el escritor es el que captura finalmente la esencia de Borges el hombre. Hablando de sí mismo como escritor dijo:

❝ …todas las cosas quieren perseverar en su ser⁶; la piedra eternamente quiere ser piedra y el tigre un tigre. Yo he de quedar en Borges, no en mí (si es que alguien soy)… ❞

---

⁴sword
⁵fought battles of the imagination
⁶persevere in being themselves

 Online Workbook
CLASSZONE.COM

¿Comprendiste?
1. ¿Cómo comenzó la carrera literaria de Borges? ¿Qué lo hizo famoso?
2. ¿Cuáles son unos temas importantes de sus obras?
3. ¿Qué tipos de obras literarias escribió Borges? ¿Cómo es el estilo de Borges?

¿Qué piensas?
1. ¿Cómo crees que la historia de la familia de Borges influyó sus escritos?
2. ¿Por qué crees que la naturaleza forma una parte importante de la obra de Borges?

Hazlo tú
Piensa en las personas y cosas que hacen que tú seas la persona que eres: tu familia, el lugar donde vives, tus intereses, las cosas que has estudiado y tus sueños para el futuro. Luego, escribe un poema o cuento que incluya aspectos importantes de tu relación con estas personas o cosas. También puedes buscar otro poema o cuento de Borges y escribir una opinión corta.

doscientos setenta y uno **271**
El Cono Sur Etapa I

- **¿Comprendiste?** checks students' basic understanding of what they've read.

"The strategy boxes will be useful. I'm a true believer in the metacognitive focus of teaching strategies."

Bill Heller
Perry Jr./Sr. High School
Perry, NY

En voces

AUDIO
LECTURA

PARA LEER · STRATEGY: READING

Speculate about the author From your reading, what do you think was the age and professional status of Isabel Allende during her career? What other qualities does she reveal? Do you think it is better to read a piece of literature with or without knowledge about the author? Explain your answer.

EL TRABAJO

a cargo de tener responsabilidad por algo
asomar tras un vidrio verse por un cristal
el canal la compañía de televisión
el guión las palabras de un programa
las orejas una manera de decir "personas"
la pantalla por donde se ve la televisión
puntual a tiempo
el vacío donde no hay nadie

Sobre la autora

Isabel Allende, novelista chilena, nació en Lima, Perú, en 1942. Su familia tuvo que exiliarse de Chile cuando su tío Salvador Allende, el presidente del país, fue vencido por una junta militar en 1973. Isabel Allende empezó a escribir a la edad de diecisiete años y escribió su primera novela, *La casa de los espíritus*, en 1982. También ha trabajado como periodista y en la televisión.

Introducción

Allende comenzó a escribir su libro autobiográfico *Paula* mientras su hija estaba muy enferma. Es una historia que ofrece mucha información y varias anécdotas sobre la familia de Allende y sobre la historia y la política de Chile. En la selección que vas a leer, Allende le habla a su hija sobre su trabajo en Chile.

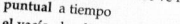

314 trescientos catorce
Unidad 4

Paula

A comienzo de los años sesenta mi trabajo había progresado de las estadísticas forestales a unos tambaleantes inicios[1] en el periodismo, que me condujeron por casualidad a la televisión.

....

Fue así como terminé a cargo de un programa en el cual me tocaba hacer desde el guión hasta los dibujos de los créditos. El trabajo en el Canal consistía en llegar puntual, sentarme ante una luz roja y hablar al vacío; nunca tomé conciencia de que al otro lado de la luz un millón de orejas esperaban mis palabras y de ojos juzgaban mi peinado[2], de ahí mi sorpresa[3] cuando desconocidos[4] me saludaban por la calle. La primera vez que me viste aparecer en la pantalla, Paula, tenías un año y medio y el susto[5] de ver la cabeza decapitada de tu mamá asomando tras un vidrio, te dejó un buen rato[6] en estado catatónico... Me convertí en la persona más conspicua del barrio, los vecinos me saludaban con respeto y los niños me señalaban[7] con el dedo... (Michael y yo) conseguimos un par de becas[8], partimos a Europa y llegamos a Suiza contigo de la mano, tenías casi dos años y eras una mujer en miniatura.

[1] shaky beginning
[2] judged my hairdo
[3] surprise
[4] strangers
[5] shock, fright
[6] quite a while
[7] gestured to me
[8] scholarships

Online Workbook
CLASSZONE.COM

¿Comprendiste?

1. ¿En qué campos trabajaba Isabel Allende?
2. ¿En qué consistía su trabajo en la televisión?
3. ¿Por qué se fue la escritora de Chile?
4. ¿De qué se trata el libro *Paula*?

¿Qué piensas?

1. ¿Cómo se explica la reacción de Paula al ver a su madre en la televisión?
2. ¿Por qué crees que Isabel Allende comenzó a escribir su autobiografía en 1992 a la edad de 50 años?

Hazlo tú

¿Te parece interesante trabajar en la televisión? Si pudieras trabajar en la televisión, ¿qué harías — noticias, pronóstico del tiempo, telenovelas, o programas para niños? Explica tu preferencia.

trescientos quince
El Cono Sur Etapa 3 315

● **¿Qué piensas?** asks students to think critically about the reading selection.

MOTIVATE TO COMMUNICATE
¡En español!

Encourage students to experience different cultures

Focused cultural strategies improve students' ability to understand and appreciate the target culture.

- **Cultural strategies** help students understand their own culture and other cultures to broaden their worldview.

En colores
CULTURA Y COMPARACIONES

PARA CONOCERNOS
STRATEGY: CONNECTING CULTURES
Formulate plans for the future Think about your future after high school, then write down what you need to do to meet your goals: **escribir, estudiar, ganar, preparar, solicitar, tomar decisiones**, etc. Also acknowledge your feelings: **alegre, dudoso(a), frustrado(a), nervioso(a), preocupado(a), seguro(a)** about each task.

Mis metas:

Para hacer	Lo que siento
1.	
2.	
3.	

With which person in *Los jóvenes y el futuro* do you most identify?

Los jóvenes y el futuro

Chile

Ana María Ibáñez, 16 años

Yo estudio en un colegio de monjas[1]. Es un internado — eso significa que las chicas viven allí. Ahora estoy cursando[2] mi último año y preparándome para la Prueba de Aptitud Académica, que también se llama la P.A.A. Quiero estudiar en la Universidad Católica, pero para eso necesito sacar más de 740 en la P.A.A. Me interesa estudiar ingeniería comercial. Pero me da un poco de miedo dejar el colegio. ¡Creo que voy a echarlo de menos[3]!

[1] nuns
[2] I'm enrolled in, I'm taking
[3] to miss it

Paraguay

Alfredo Zubizarreta, 17 años

Estoy en el último año de colegio y pienso mucho en el futuro. Quiero ir a la universidad, pero tengo que pasar el examen de ingreso[4]. Tengo buenas notas, sobre todo en castellano y en literatura, pero dicen que ese examen es muy difícil. Hay pocos puestos en la universidad y muchos estudiantes que quieren estudiar. Por eso algunos salen del país. Si me aceptan en la universidad aquí, voy a estudiar derecho[5], ¡porque los abogados ganan un buen sueldo!

[4] entrance, admission
[5] law

Uruguay

Miguel Corteggiani, 15 años

Estudio en un colegio público. El año que viene será el último año de secundaria. Mis padres quieren que vaya a la universidad pero yo dudo que vaya. Preferiría estudiar en una escuela técnica. Me fascinan los carros y me interesa mucho ser mecánico. Algún día quisiera tener mi propio taller. Yo creo que uno tiene que seguir sus intereses. ¿No estás de acuerdo?

CLASSZONE.COM
More About the Southern Cone

¿Comprendiste?
1. ¿En qué tipo de colegio estudia Ana María Ibáñez?
2. ¿Por qué no sabe Alberto Zubizarreta si podrá estudiar en la universidad?
3. ¿Qué campo le interesa a Miguel Corteggiani? ¿Qué piensan sus padres?

¿Qué piensas?
Estos estudiantes no están completamente seguros de sus decisiones. ¿Por qué?

Hazlo tú
Compara las dudas y los miedos de estos jóvenes sudamericanos con los de los jóvenes norteamericanos. ¿Comprendes estos sentimientos? ¿Los tienes también? Escribe un ensayo sobre tus planes para el futuro.

doscientos noventa y tres
El Cono Sur Etapa 2 293

doscientos noventa y dos
Unidad 4 292

- **¿Qué piensas?** helps students to think critically about the target culture as well as their own culture.

- **¿Comprendiste?** asks students to recall the information in the selection.

"Teaching culture is a real challenge but so important. You have done more with culture than any other series that I have seen."

Deborah Hagen
Ionia High School
Ionia, MI

En colores

CULTURA Y COMPARACIONES

PARA CONOCERNOS

STRATEGY: CONNECTING CULTURES

Observe how language reflects culture Each language reveals the background of the people who speak it. For example, arithmetic is derived from Latin and mathematics from Greek. There is not one English language but several, including Australian, Canadian, British, and American versions. Think about these examples and conjecture what events and experiences cause language to evolve. Organize your ideas in a chart.

Cosas que cambian un idioma
1.
2.
3.

Which of your ideas are represented in *Se hablan... ¡muchos idomas!*?

Se hablan... ¡muchos idiomas!

Galicia **GALLEGO**
País Vasco **VASCUENCE**
Cataluña **CATALÁN**
ESPAÑA

El español o castellano es el idioma oficial de los países hispanohablantes, pero también se hablan otros idiomas. ¡A ver cuáles son!

España

El castellano, que también se conoce como español, se originó en España. En el este de España también se habla el **catalán** y en el noroeste, el **gallego**. El **euskera**, o **vascuence**, se habla en el País Vasco desde antes que llegaran los romanos a España en 202 antes de Cristo¹.

¹before the Christian era

México
NÁHUATL

Algunas palabras del náhuatl son:
aguacate
cacahuete
chocolate
nopal

TAÍNO

palabras ... taíno son:
canoa
hamaca
huracán
maíz
tiburón

Mar Caribe
Costa Rica
Panamá

Guatemala
El Salvador
Honduras
Nicaragua

Venezuela
Colombia
Ecuador
Río Amazonas
Perú
Brasil
QUECHUA
Bolivia

Algunas palabras del quechua son:
cóndor
llama
pampa
papa

Paraguay
Río de la Plata
Uruguay
Chile
Argentina

Océano Pacífico
Océano Atlántico

que nos ha... as ... Latinoamérica. En el mapa ... y otras palabras que pasaron al español ... íno, **náhuatl** y **quechua**, algunos de los idiomas que hablaban los habitantes de América al llegar los españoles? Algunos de estos idiomas todavía se hablan en Latinomérica.

El taíno era el idioma de los indígenas ² del Caribe, también llamados taínos. En México y en Centroamérica los aztecas hablaban el náhuatl y los mayas el **maya-quiché**. El **miskito** se hablaba en Nicaragua. En la capital del Imperio Inca en Cuzco, Perú, se usaba el quechua.

El náhuatl, el maya-quiché y el quechua todavía se hablan hoy en día en México, Guatemala y Perú respectivamente. El país donde mejor se ha conservado un idioma indígena es el Paraguay, donde el **guaraní** es tan oficial como el español.

² indigenous, indigenous peoples

CLASSZONE.COM
More About the Southern Cone

¿Comprendiste?
1. ¿Qué otros idiomas se hablan en España?
2. ¿Qué idiomas indígenas se hablaban en las Américas al llegar los españoles? ¿Cuáles se hablan todavía?
3. Da ejemplos de diez palabras indígenas. Menciona el idioma del cual viene cada palabra.

¿Qué piensas?
Observa las palabras que pasaron al español. ¿Qué categorías hay? ¿En qué situaciones crees que los españoles aprendieron estas palabras?

Hazlo tú
Busca palabras de origen español en inglés. ¿Por qué crees que tenemos estas palabras?

● **Hazlo tú** offers an expansion activity for students to try out the new cultural concepts.

MOTIVATE
TO COMMUNICATE
¡En español!

Follow up with diagnostic review

The comprehensive review, correlated to the Etapa objectives, thoroughly reviews and prepares students to be successful for assessment.

● **The side column learning channel** helps students self-diagnose and review what they can do and where they can go to get help.

ETAPA 3

En uso
REPASO Y MÁS COMUNICACIÓN

OBJECTIVES
- Learn about Latin American economics
- Clarify possession
- Express possession
- Express past probability

Now you can...
- discuss Latin American economics.

❶ La población

Estás creando una encuesta para buscar unas estadísticas demográficas. Primero escribe preguntas y luego contéstalas con la información indicada.

modelo
porcentaje de la población (¿habla español?): $\frac{1}{5}$
Compañero(a): ¿Qué porcentaje de la población habla español?
Tú: Un quinto de la población habla español.

1. porcentaje de la población (¿de habla hispana?): $\frac{1}{3}$
2. edad promedio: 25
3. porcentaje de la población (¿vivir en la ciudad?): 50%
4. porcentaje de la población (¿vivir en el campo?): 50%
5. parte de la población (¿graduarse de la universidad?): la mayoría
6. parte de la población (¿trabajar en la ganadería?): la menor parte

Now you can...
- avoid redundancy.

To review
- subject and stressed object pronouns see p. 306.

❷ ¿Él o ella?

Conoces a varias parejas que trabajan en industrias diferentes. Di en qué trabaja él y en qué trabaja ella.

modelo
Los Sres. Mendoza: una compañía multinacional de turismo / una compañía multinacional de petróleo
Él trabaja en una compañía multinacional que se dedica al turismo. Ella trabaja en una compañía multinacional de petróleo.

1. Los Sres. Moré: un laboratorio / una agencia de viajes para ejecutivos
2. Los Sres. Valdés: una fábrica de textiles / una compañía de telecomunicaciones
3. Los Sres. Puente: una compañía de exportaciones / un banco
4. Los Sres. Colón: un taller de artesanías / la bolsa de valores
5. Los Sres. Prado: un laboratorio / una refinería de petróleo

---

Now you can...
- express possession.
- clarify possession.

To review
- possessive pronouns see p. 308.

Now you can...
- express past probability.

To review
- the future perfect see p. 310.

Self-Check Quiz
CLASSZONE.COM

❸ ¡No!

Estás en una fiesta y ahora tú y tus amigos se están despidiendo de la anfitriona. Ella trata de devolverte cosas que no son tuyas. También trata de devolverles cosas a tus amigos que no son suyas. ¿Cómo le respondes?

modelo
tu paraguas: negro
Anfitriona: Ten, aquí está tu paraguas.
Tú: No, ése no. El mío es negro.

1. tu abrigo: azul
2. la mochila de Hernán: verde
3. la bolsa de Mariluz: amarilla
4. el sombrero de Juan: rojo
5. los platos de Minerva: nuevos
6. los zapatos de tenis de Arnoldo: viejo
7. tu chaqueta: de cuero

❹ Para ese entonces

Tu abuelo(a) está pensando en el futuro de su familia. ¿Qué cree que va a pasar en veinte años? Sigue el modelo.

modelo
(tú) comprar una casa
Para ese entonces, habrás comprado una casa.

1. (nosotros) viajar a Argentina
2. (tú) empezar tu carrera en la industria del petróleo
3. (Enrique y Elena) casarse
4. (Anilú) graduarse de la universidad
5. (Rudi y Luisa) empezar una familia
6. (Felipe) hacerse banquero
7. (ustedes) ahorrar mucho dinero
8. (tú) realizar tus sueños

• **Speaking strategies** help students become better communicators by expanding their repertoire of expressions through tone of voice, personalization, gestures, etc.

"The review sections are very helpful."

Pamela Ross
North Allegheny
Intermediate High School
Pittsburgh, PA

• **En tu propia voz** prompts students with a short writing assignment to sharpen their language skills.

---

5 **¿Dónde está Gerardo?**

STRATEGY: SPEAKING

Speculate about the past When the unexpected occurs, it is natural to express opinions about what may have happened. Your conjecture about Gerardo's absence can be humorous, pleasant, logical or illogical: **¿Por qué no vino Gerardo? Se habrá perdido en el parque zoológico.** Be inventive!

Hablar/*Escribir* Gerardo prometió que iba a venir a la reunión del consejo estudiantil. ¡Pero no llegó! Todos tienen ideas de por qué no vino. Dramaticen esta situación.

modelo

Tú: *¿Pero dónde está Gerardo? Dijo que iba a venir.*
Compañero(a) 1: *Se le habrá olvidado.*
Compañero(a) 2: *Se habrá acostado muy tarde y no se despertó a tiempo.*
Compañero(a) 3: *No, no es eso. Yo creo que…*

---

6 **El mío es de…**

En grupos de dos o tres, conversen sobre las cosas que tengan y de qué tienda son.

modelo

Tú: *Yo compré mi chaqueta de piel en Ropafina.*
Compañero(a) 1: *¿Ah, sí? La mía es de Ropafina también.*
Compañero(a) 2: *Yo no tengo una chaqueta de piel, pero mi collar de oro es de la tienda en la plaza.*
Tú: *El mío es de la misma tienda.*

---

7 **En tu propia voz**

ESCRITURA Escribe un informe sobre el perfil económico de tu estado. Destaca el producto de más importancia. Las siguientes categorías pueden ayudarte a comenzar. Si quieres, incluye fotos en tu informe.

Mi estado:	El petróleo:
Capital:	Los productos forestales:
Unidad monetaria:	La minería:
Perfil económico:	El turismo:
Productos de exportación:	La industria pesquera:
La agricultura:	Las telecomunicaciones:
La ganadería:	Los textiles:

CONEXIONES

Los estudios sociales ¿Qué sabes de la ONU (Organización de las Naciones Unidas)? ¿Has oído alguna vez de la OEA (Organización de los Estados Americanos)? ¿Cuál es el propósito de estas dos organizaciones internacionales? ¿Quiénes son los miembros? Busca la información por Internet o en la biblioteca y escribe un reporte. Comparte tu reporte con la clase.

En resumen
REPASO DE VOCABULARIO

Flashcards CLASSZONE.COM

LEARN ABOUT LATIN AMERICAN ECONOMICS

Careers in Spanish

el (la) académico(a)	academic
el (la) agente de ventas	sales agent
el (la) banquero(a)	banker
el (la) bibliotecario(a)	librarian
el (la) corresponsal	correspondent
el (la) diplomático(a)	diplomat
el (la) financiero(a)	financial expert
el (la) intérprete	interpreter
el (la) trabajador(a) social	social worker
el (la) traductor(a)	translator

Industries

la agricultura	agriculture
los cereales	grains
el cobre	copper
la exportación	export
exportar	to export
la ganadería	livestock industry
el ganado	livestock
el hierro	iron
la importación	import
la industria	industry
la industria pesquera	fishing industry
el maíz	corn
la minería	mining
el perfil económico	economic profile
el petróleo	petroleum
principal	principal
los productos forestales	forestry products
la refinería	refinery
las telecomunicaciones	telecommunications
los textiles	textiles
el trigo	wheat
el turismo	tourism
la unidad monetaria	currency

Statistics

comparar	to compare
las estadísticas	statistics
mil millones	billion
un millón de millones	trillion
la mitad de	one half of
por ciento	percent
el porcentaje	percentage
el promedio	average
el quinto	one fifth
sumar	to add
el tercio	one third

♻ **Ya sabes**

un cuarto	one fourth
un décimo	one tenth
la mayoría	majority
medio(a)	half

Types of companies

la bolsa de valores	stock exchange
la fábrica	factory
el laboratorio	laboratory
multinacional	multinational
la sociedad anónima (S.A.)	corporation (Inc.)

AVOID REDUNDANCY

♻ **Ya sabes**

a mí	to me
a ti	to you
yo	I
tú	you (fam.)
usted	you (for.)
él	he
ella	she
nosotros(as)	we
vosotros(as)	you (fam. pl.)
ustedes	you (for. pl.)
ellos	they
ellas	they (fem.)

EXPRESS POSSESSION

♻ **Ya sabes**

mi/mío(a)	my/mine
tu/tuyo(a)	your (fam.)/yours (fam.)
su/suyo(a)	your (for.), his, her/yours (for.), his, hers, its
nuestro(a)	our/ours
vuestro(a)	your (pl. fam.)/yours (pl. fam.)
su/suyo(a)	your (pl.), their/yours (pl.), theirs

EXPRESS PAST PROBABILITY

The future perfect tense

No sé dónde está Élmer. Fue a la oficina. Habrá encontrado más trabajo allí.

Juego

¿Cuál es tu profesión?

¿Puedes encontrar en el dibujo dos profesiones cuyos nombres empiecen con la letra a?

MOTIVATE TO COMMUNICATE
¡En español!

Cultivate better writers through the writing process

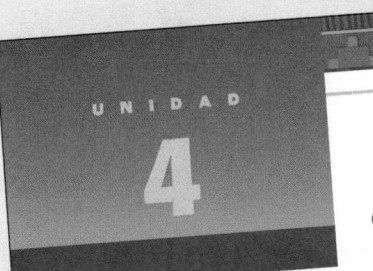

The writing process, at the end of each unit, works as a tutor-in-the-book to teach students how to improve their writing step by step.

- **Writing strategies** offer a variety of prewriting strategies to improve students' writing skills.

- **Student models** show students what to watch out for, and how the assignment is supposed to look.

UNIDAD
4

En tu propia voz
ESCRITURA

Una carrera: ¿Dónde empezar?

Una empresa local busca internos para su programa de entrenamiento. El conocimiento del español es esencial y también una familiaridad con administración de empresas, economía, humanidades o matemáticas. Tu carta adjunta (*cover letter*) debe resumir tus experiencias escolares.

Función: Describirse a sí mismo

Contexto: Informar al Jefe de personal

Contenido: Relación entre tu educación, experiencia y habilidad

Tipo de texto: Carta adjunta

PARA ESCRIBIR · STRATEGY: WRITING

Use cause and effect to demonstrate ability A good cover letter highlights the relationship between your education and experiences (cause) and your ability to do the job (effect). You must impress the potential employer and show that you can handle the position by applying your knowledge to the work.

Modelo del estudiante

A salutation in a business letter is formal, using **Estimado(a)** and the person's title, and ending with a colon.

Estimado Licenciado Ramírez:

El motivo de la presente es solicitar el puesto de interno en su compañía. Actualmente estoy tomando cursos en mercadeo y economía en mi escuela secundaria. También estoy estudiando español y pienso participar en un programa de estudios en el extranjero el año que viene. Tengo buenas notas en estos cursos

The phrase **por eso** indicates the connection between the writer's coursework and her ability to contribute to the company.

y por eso creo que tengo la educación y las habilidades necesarias para contribuir al éxito de su distinguida compañía.

El verano pasado trabajé en el departamento de ventas y mercadeo de una compañía multinacional. Estaba trabajando directamente con el gerente del departamento, así que entiendo bien las responsabilidades de un interno internacional. El gerente me escribió una carta de recomendación diciendo que siempre desempeñé todos mis cargos de una manera excelente.

Adjunto mi currículum vitae. Espero que me encuentre bien capacitada para servirle.

The expression **así que** points out the relationship between the writer's previous experience and her understanding of the needs for the current position.

Atentamente,

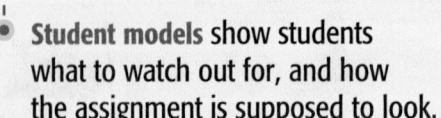
Karen Willis

Typical closings to business letters include **Atentamente** and **Le saluda muy atentamente.**

trescientos veintidós
Unidad 4

322

"I love it!! It is very practical and students are able to learn the material because of the variety of activities."

Lucy García
Pueblo East High School
Pueblo, CO

strategias para escribir

antes de escribir...
Piensa en las calificaciones que necesita un(a) candidato(a) para un trabajo que conoces. Considera la educación, experiencia y las habilidades que se requieren. Inventa un(a) candidato(a) perfecto(a) y crea su perfil. Crea una tabla como la de la derecha para analizar la calificación del (de la) candidato(a).

Writing Center
CLASSZONE.COM

Causa		Resultado
1. Educación: clases de mercadeo, administración de empresas	→	Capacitado (a)
2. Experiencia: multinacional, trabajo con profesionales	→	
3. Habilidades especiales: español	→	

Revisiones
Después de escribir el primer borrador de la carta adjunta, trabajen en grupos de cuatro para intercambiar las cartas y leerlas en voz alta. Decidan qué aspectos de cada carta son más efectivos. Revisen cada carta en grupo para incorporar las técnicas más eficientes y convincentes.

- ¿Qué expresiones usaron para demostrar la conexión entre las calificaciones y la capacidad de hacer el trabajo?
- ¿Qué datos mencionaron para indicar lo que ha hecho el (la) candidato(a) y lo que está haciendo para desarrollar sus habilidades?

La versión final
Para completar tu carta, léela de nuevo y repasa los siguientes puntos:

- ¿Usé bien el **presente continuo** (present progressive) o el **presente perfecto** (present perfect)?

Haz lo siguiente: Subraya los verbos en estos tiempos. ¿Usaste la forma correcta de **estar**? ¿Del presente participio?

- ¿Usé bien el **potencial compuesto** (conditional perfect) o el **pluscuamperfecto de subjuntivo** (past perfect subjunctive)?

Haz lo siguiente: Repasa las conjugaciones de **haber** en estos tiempos. Haz un círculo alrededor de estos verbos. ¿Está conjugado correctamente **haber** y está seguido por un participio pasado correcto?

Sr. Gerente:

Le escribo para solicitar un puesto de trabajo en su compañía editorial. Acabo de terminar mis estudios de periodismo y quisiera trabajar para usted. Además, estoy tomando clases de francés e italiano. Habría estudiando alemán si no habría tenido que viajar a Europa a hacer una entrevista. He trabajado en algunos periódicos y revistas y quisiera tener una entrevista con usted para ofrecerle mis servicios.

hubiera

● **The Internet connection** will offer more writing support. The best written submissions will be posted on the McDougal Littell website.

MOTIVATE
TO COMMUNICATE
¡En español!

Implement ideas and lesson plans easily and effectively

The Ampliación and Etapa Overview in the Teacher's Edition offer outstanding support to make teaching Spanish adaptable to every situation.

● **Ampliación** features multi-modal activities that spark students' excitement with new ways to learn language and culture.

Planning Ahead...

Ampliación

These activities may be used at various points in the Unit 4 sequence.

■ For Block Schedule, you may find that these projects will provide a welcome change of pace while reviewing and reinforcing the material presented in the unit. See the **Block Scheduling Copymasters.**

PROJECTS

Make mobiles of **Southern Cone** countries. Divide the class into 4 groups and assign each group a **Southern Cone** country. Have groups research and collect pictures and realia related to their country that can be used to make a mobile. The images should represent the essence of the country. For example, students creating the Argentina mobile might use a picture of the flag, a **mate** calabash and **bombilla, gaucho** articles, etc. The mobiles should be accompanied by a written report that explains the meaning of the symbols. Hang the mobiles in the classroom and discuss them as you cover the unit.

PACING SUGGESTION: Have students begin research at the beginning of the unit. Final projects are completed at the end of Unit 4.

Film or record an audiovisual guide for career opportunities and training. Divide the class into groups and assign each group a field of study, type of profession, etc. Groups prepare a promotional ad that might be part of a campaign to attract new applicants or employees.

PACING SUGGESTION: Upon completion of Etapa 3.

STORYTELLING

Nuestro futuro After reviewing the vocabulary on professions and fields of study, model a mini-story (using student actors or photos from the text) that students will revise, retell, and expand:

Guillermo y Daniel hablan de sus planes para el futuro y las profesiones que les interesan. Guillermo dice: «Estoy tan confundido. No sé qué estudiar. No tengo talento en ningún campo de estudio». Daniel responde: «No te preocupes. Muchos estudiantes no saben qué campo de estudio o carrera quieren seguir cuando entran a la universidad. Después de uno o dos semestres, vas a descubrir qué carrera te interesa».

Pause as the story is being told so that students may fill in words and act out gestures. Students then write, narrate, and read aloud a longer main story. This new version should include vocabulary from Unit 4.

Vamos a hablar con el consejero Have students tell a story about talking to a school counselor as part of preparing to enter college or train for a career. They can role-play the scene between the counselor and 1 or more students.

PACING SUGGESTION: Upon completion of Etapa 3.

BULLETIN BOARD/POSTERS

Bulletin Board Have students collect information on various professions in which a knowledge of Spanish would be helpful. To arrange the bulletin board, have them create headings for grouping the professions, e.g., **educación, psicología, tecnología, medicina, ciencias**, etc. Students decorate the board with information and images related to the professions.

Posters Have students create •**Country** posters for each of the Southern Cone countries •**Career** posters with information about specific careers •**Industry** posters for promoting good public relations between an industry and the community

SPANET
DISEÑADOR GRÁFICO WEB

☞ *Empresa líder en Internet SPANET requiere personas con conocimientos sobre Internet.*
☞ *Experiencia en diseño y páginas Web.*
☞ *Plataforma Mac o PC.*

Llamar a Raúl Corrales, tel. 1/788-9140, fax 1/788-9158

GAME

¿Cuál es mi profesión?
Have each student prepare 5 descriptive clues about a profession, e.g., (1) **Hay muchas especialidades entre las cuales se puede elegir en mi profesión,** (2) **Mi profesión exige un título de universidad,** etc. Divide the class into 2 teams. Teams take turns giving clues about the professions. The fewer clues the other team needs to guess the profession, the more points it wins.

Each clue is worth 10 points. If a team guesses the profession after the first clue, they earn 50 points. If they need a second clue, they only get 40. If they need a third clue, 30 points, and so on. If the team does not guess the profession after 5 clues, they receive no points. Set a time limit for guessing after hearing a clue, e.g., 5 seconds. The team with the most points at the end wins.

PACING SUGGESTION: Upon completion of Etapa 2.

MUSIC

Tango is a dance of 2 slow, gliding steps, followed by 2 quick steps, then a slow step. The music for this dance requires 4/4 time measure. Carlos Gardel (1887–1935), from Argentina, composed music that was popular for this dance step. Play 1 or more Gardel compositions. If students from the class can demonstrate the tango steps, encourage them to do so. Several movies have tango scenes, including *Evita*, starring Madonna and Antonio Banderas.

HANDS-ON CRAFTS

Point out that **mate,** an herbal drink, is consumed from a container called a **mate** as well. To make a decorative one, roll out a clay pancake (1/2" thick and 8" in diameter), and shape the clay around the bottom of a round glass. Trim excess clay from the top, leaving the sides about 3" high. Carve designs into the wet clay with a toothpick. Run a butter knife around the edge to slide the clay off the glass. Dry 24 hours, then sand smooth. Remove dust, then paint inside and out with acrylic paint. Use a paper straw as a **bombilla.** NOTE: This is for decorative use only.

RECIPE

Sopa paraguaya Sopa paraguaya sounds like soup, but it's corn bread. **Sopa paraguaya,** popular throughout Paraguay, can be prepared using corn meal, fresh corn, or a combination of both. It's normally served with **Só o-Yosopy,** Guaraní for beef soup, the national dish of Paraguay. Beef is a dietary staple in Paraguay, Argentina, Uruguay, and Chile.

Receta

Sopa paraguaya
1/2 taza de cebolla picada fina
2 cucharadas de mantequilla
1 taza de maíz (raspada de la mazorca o congelada)
3/4 taza de harina de maíz
3/4 taza de requesón

3/4 taza de queso Münster rallado
1/2 taza de leche agria (añada unas gotas de vinagre)
1/2 cucharadilla de sal
3 huevos separados

Fría la cebolla en la mantequilla hasta que se ablande. Pase el maíz por el procesador de comidas y mézclalo bien con la harina de maíz, la cebolla frita, el requesón, el queso Münster, la leche agria y la sal. Bata las yemas de huevo hasta que se espesen. Mezcle las yemas y las claras cuidadosamente. Añada 1/3 de la mezcla de huevos a la mezcla de maíz. Mezcle todo bien. Añada el resto de los huevos, mezclándolos con cuidado. Ponga la masa en una fuente (8" x 8" x 2") y hornéela a 400° por 30 minutos. Sírvala a temperatura de ambiente con mantequilla.

● **Easy-to-prepare recipes** give students a delicious opportunity to experience new cultural cuisines.

OCÉANO PACÍFICO

PARAGUAY
★ ASUNCIÓN

OCÉANO ATLÁNTICO

ARGENTINA

URUGUAY
★ MONTEVIDEO

BUENOS AIRES ★

SANTIAGO ★

CHILE

● **At-a-glance overview** outlines the objectives, strategies, and program resources for time-saving support.

"I believe you have an excellent program. The multimedia approach, with the use of articulated video, audio, etc. is well thought out."

Roberto E. del Valle
Shorecrest High School
Shoreline, WA

UNIDAD 4 **ETAPA 3** UN MUNDO DE POSIBILIDADES
pages 298–323

Planning Guide CLASSROOM MANAGEMENT

OBJECTIVES

Communication
• Learn about Latin American economics pp. 300–301, 302–303
• Avoid redundancy p. 314–315
• Express possession pp. 308–310
• Express past probability p. 316–317

Grammar
• Review: Use subject and stressed object pronouns p. 306–308
• Review: Use possessive pronouns pp. 308–310
• Use the future perfect tense pp. 310–312

Culture
• Regional vocabulary pp. 306, 311
• Job hunting in Latin America p. 308
• Saving money in Latin America p. 312
• Isabel Allende, Chilean novelist pp. 314–315
• Languages in Spanish-speaking countries pp. 316–317

♻ Recycling
• Numbers p. 305
• Professions vocabulary p. 306
• Clothing and furniture p. 309

STRATEGIES

Listening Strategies
• Pre-listening p. 302
• Use statistics to evaluate predictions p. 302

Speaking Strategies
• Guess cognates p. 305
• Speculate about the past p. 320

Reading Strategies
• Speculate about the author p. 314
• Activate associated knowledge TE p. 316

Writing Strategies
• Organize information by category TE p. 320
• Use cause and effect to demonstrate ability pp. 322–323

Connecting Cultures Strategies
• Recognize variations in vocabulary pp. 306, 311
• Understand job hunting in Latin America p. 308
• Learn about saving money in Latin America p. 312
• Learn about Isabel Allende, Chilean novelist pp. 314–315
• Observe how language reflects culture pp. 316–317
• Connect and compare what you know about languages in your community to help you learn about languages in a new community pp. 316–317

PROGRAM RESOURCES

🖨 Print
• Más práctica Workbook PE pp. 105–112
• Actividades para todos Workbook PE pp. 121–130
• Block Scheduling Copymasters pp. 97–104
• Unit 4 Resource Book
  Más práctica Workbook TE pp. 141–148
  Actividades para todos Workbook TE pp. 149–158
  Cuaderno para hispanohablantes TE pp. 159–166
  Information Gap Activities pp. 167–170
  Family Letter p. 171
  Absent Student Copymasters pp. 172–178
  Family Involvement pp. 179–180
  Audioscript pp. 181–184
  Assessment Program, Unit 4 Etapa 3 pp. 185–234
  Answer Keys pp. 242–246

🔊 Audiovisual
• Audio Program CD 12
• Canciones CD
• Overhead Transparencies M1–M5; GO1–GO5; 4, 33–46
• Word Tiles U4E3

💻 Technology
• eEdition Plus Online/eEdition CD-ROM
• Easy Planner Plus Online/Easy Planner CD-ROM
• eTest Plus Online/Test Generator CD-ROM
• Online Workbook
• Take-Home Tutor CD-ROM
• 🌐 www.classzone.com

✓ Assessment Program Options
• Unit 4 Resource Book
  Vocabulary Quizzes
  Grammar Quizzes
  Etapa Exam Forms A and B
  Examen para hispanohablantes
  Portfolio Assessment
  Unit 4 Comprehensive Test
  Prueba comprensiva para hispano-hablantes, Unit 4
  Multiple Choice Test Questions
• Audio Program CD 20
• eTest Plus Online/Test Generator CD-ROM

Native Speakers
• Cuaderno para hispanohablantes PE pp. 105–112
• Cuaderno para hispanohablantes TE (Unit 4 Resource Book)
• Examen para hispanohablantes (Unit 4 Resource Book)
• Prueba comprensiva para hispano-hablantes, Unit 4 (Unit 4 Resource Book)
• Audio Program (Para hispanohablantes) CD 12, 20
• Audioscript (Unit 4 Resource Book)

Student Text Listening Activity Scripts

🎧 Situaciones pages 302–303

• CD 12

La producción mundial

Agricultura
En la producción de maíz, Estados Unidos está en primer lugar. Le siguen China, Brasil, México y Argentina. En sexto lugar está la antigua Unión Soviética, seguida por India.

Ganado
La industria ganadera de Argentina es la quinta en el mundo occidental. Alemania está en el cuarto lugar, Brasil en tercer lugar, la antigua Unión Soviética está en segundo y Estados Unidos en primer lugar.

Minería de cobre
Chile es el país que más cobre produce. Luego sigue Estados Unidos, Canadá, Indonesia y finalmente Perú.

Petróleo crudo
Arabia Saudita es el país que produce el más petróleo crudo. Estados Unidos, China, Irak y México le siguen en esta categoría.

Industria pesquera
China es el primer país en la industria pesquera, seguido por Perú, Chile, Japón y Estados Unidos.

Turismo
¿Qué país es el más visitado del mundo? ¡Francia! ¿Parlez vous français? En segundo lugar, está Estados Unidos. España le sigue en tercer lugar. Italia está en cuarto lugar, seguido por el Reino Unido o Inglaterra.

🎧 5 ¿Quién? page 306

Modelo:
Tío: ¿Quién es abogado?
Chico: Él.
Tío: ¿Quién es médica?
Chico: Ella.
1. Tío: ¿Estudiaron ustedes ingeniería?
   Chica: Nosotros sí. Ella no.
2. Tío: ¿Quieren ser veterinarios?
   Chico: Él sí. Yo no. Yo quiero ser bombero.
3. Tío: ¿Fueron a la Universidad de Buenos Aires?
   Mujer: Él fue a la Universidad de Buenos Aires pero ella fue a la Universidad de Chile.
4. Tío: ¿Estudiaste para ser arquitecto?
   Hombre: Yo sí, pero ella no. Ella estudió para ser ingeniera.
5. Tío: ¿Les interesa el mercadeo?
   Mujer: A ella le interesa el mercadeo, pero a él le interesa más la publicidad.
6. Tío: ¿Quién de ustedes es bailarina?
   Chica: Yo soy bailarina. Él es deportista.

🎧 12 ¡Pobre Carlos! page 311

Modelo:
Chica: Carlos tiene hambre.
Chico: No habrá comido bien.
1. Chica: Carlos está enojado.
   Chico: No le dieron el puesto.
2. Chica: Carlos se siente mal.
   Chico: Habrá comido algo que le hizo daño.
3. Chica: Carlos tiene mucho sueño.
   Chico: Se habrá acostado muy tarde.
4. Chica: Carlos está muy triste.
   Chico: Vio a su ex-novia con otro chico.
5. Chica: Carlos dijo que iba a traer los discos compactos y no los trajo.
   Chico: Se le habrán olvidado.
6. Chica: ¿Dónde está Carlos?
   Chico: Se habrá ido.

● **Listening scripts** in the Teacher's Edition provide practical information needed for easier lesson preparation.

MOTIVATE TO COMMUNICATE ¡En español!

Suggests practical teaching ideas for lesson planning

FLEXIBLE AND EXCEPTIONAL

The comprehensive Teacher's Edition and resource materials provide the support you need to introduce, explain, and expand your lessons.

- **Time-saving lessons** present sequenced teaching suggestions and ideas.

UNIDAD 4 ETAPA 3 Pacing Guide

Sample Lesson Plan - 50 Minute Schedule

DAY 1

Etapa Opener
- Quick Start Review (TE, p. 298) 5 MIN.
- Have students look at the *Etapa* Opener and answer the questions. 5 MIN.

En contexto: Vocabulario
- Quick Start Review (TE, p. 300) 5 MIN.
- Present *Descubre*, p. 300. Have students use context and pictures to learn *Etapa* vocabulary. Use the Situational OHTs for additional practice. 15 MIN.

En vivo: Situaciones
- Quick Start Review (TE, p. 302) 5 MIN.
- Present the Listening Strategy, p. 302. Have students read section 1, p. 302. Play the audio for section 2. Have students work in groups to complete section 3. 15 MIN.

Homework Option:
- Have students write answers to *¿Comprendiste?*, p. 303.

DAY 2

En acción: Vocabulario y gramática
- Check homework. 5 MIN.
- Quick Start Review (TE, p. 304) 5 MIN.
- Have students complete *Actividad* 1 in pairs. 5 MIN.
- Have students do *Actividad* 2 in writing. Go over answers orally. 5 MIN.
- Present the *Vocabulario*, p. 305. Then have students read and do *Actividad* 3 in pairs. 10 MIN.
- Present the Speaking Strategy, p. 305. Then have students do *Actividad* 4 in pairs. 5 MIN.
- Present *Repaso:* Subject and Stressed Object Pronouns and the *Vocabulario*, p. 306. 10 MIN.
- Play the audio; do *Actividad* 5. 5 MIN.

Homework Option:
- *Más práctica* Workbook, pp. 109–110. *Cuaderno para hispanohablantes*, p. 107.

DAY 3

En acción (cont.)
- Check homework. 5 MIN.
- Present the *Vocabulario*, p. 307. Then do *Actividad* 6 in pairs. 10 MIN.
- Have students complete *Actividad* 7 in pairs. Expand using Information Gap Activities, *Más comunicación*, p. R14. 15 MIN.
- Quick Start Review (TE, p. 308) 5 MIN.
- Present *Repaso:* Possessive Pronouns and the *Vocabulario*, p. 308. 10 MIN.
- Have students complete *Actividad* 8 in pairs. 5 MIN.

Homework Option:
- *Más práctica* Workbook, p. 111. *Cuaderno para hispanohablantes*, p. 108.

DAY 4

En acción (cont.)
- Check homework. 5 MIN.
- Do *Actividad* 9 orally. 5 MIN.
- Have students complete *Actividad* 10 in groups. 10 MIN.
- Have students complete *Actividad* 11 in pairs. 5 MIN.
- Present *Gramática:* The Future Perfect Tense, p. 310. 10 MIN.
- Play the audio; do *Actividad* 12. 5 MIN.
- Present the *Vocabulario*, p. 311. Then do *Actividad* 13 orally. 10 MIN.

Homework Option:
- Have students complete *Actividad* 9 in writing. *Más práctica* Workbook, p. 112. *Cuaderno para hispanohablantes*, pp. 109–110.
- *Actividades para todos* Workbook, pp. 121–130.

DAY 5

En acción (cont.)
- Check homework. 5 MIN.
- Do *Actividad* 14 orally. 5 MIN.
- Do *Actividad* 15 in groups. 5 MIN.
- Have students read and complete *Actividad* 16 in writing. Expand using Information Gap Activities, Unit 4 Resource Book, p. 168; *Más comunicación*, p. R14. 15 MIN.

Refrán
- Present the *Refrán*, p. 313. 5 MIN.

En voces: Lectura
- Present the Reading Strategy, p. 314. Call on volunteers to read the *Lectura* aloud. Have students answer the *¿Comprendiste?/¿Qué piensas?* questions, p. 315. 15 MIN.

Homework Option:
- Have students complete *Hazlo tú*, p. 315.

DAY 6

En colores: Cultura y comparaciones
- Check homework. 5 MIN.
- Quick Start Review (TE, p. 316) 5 MIN.
- Present the Connecting Cultures Strategy, p. 316. Call on volunteers to read the article aloud. Have students answer the *¿Comprendiste?/¿Qué piensas?* questions, p. 317. 20 MIN.

En uso: Repaso y más comunicación
- Have students do *Actividades* 1 and 3 in pairs and *Actividades* 2 and 4 orally. 20 MIN.

Homework Option:
- Have students complete *Hazlo tú*, p. 317. Review for *Etapa* 3 Exam.

DAY 7

En uso (cont.)
- Check homework. 5 MIN.
- Present the Speaking Strategy, p. 320, and have students do *Actividades* 5 and 6 in groups. 15 MIN.

En tu propia voz: Escritura
- Have students begin their research for *Actividad* 7. 5 MIN.

En resumen: Repaso de vocabulario
- Review grammar questions, etc., as necessary. 5 MIN.
- Complete *Etapa* 3 Exam. 20 MIN.

Homework Option:
- Have students complete their reports for *Actividad* 7, p. 320. Review for Unit 4 Comprehensive Test.

DAY 8

Conexiones
- Check homework. 5 MIN.
- Discuss *Los estudios sociales*, p. 320. 5 MIN.

Unit 4 Comprehensive Test
- Review grammar questions, etc., as necessary. 5 MIN.
- Complete Unit 4 Comprehensive Test. 30 MIN.

En tu propia voz: Escritura
- Present the Writing Strategy, p. 322. Do the writing activity, pp. 322–323. 5 MIN.

Ampliación
- Optional: Use a suggested project, game, or activity. (TE, pp. 253A–253B)

Homework Option:
- Have students complete the assignment for *Conexiones*. Preview *Unidad 5* Opener. Have students read and study pp. 324–3??

● **Block Scheduling Lesson Plans** offer options for pacing and variety.

"There is a step-by-step sequence. The whole unit is structured around a topic and each etapa contributes meaningful elements to the whole."

M. Mercedes Stephenson
Hazelwood Central High School
Florissant, MO

Sample Lesson Plan - Block Schedule (90 mi...

DAY 1

Etapa Opener
• Quick Start Review (TE, p. 298) 5 MIN.
• Have students look at the *Etapa* Opener and answer the questions. 5 MIN.
• Use Block Scheduling Copymasters. 5 MIN.

En contexto: Vocabulario
• Quick Start Review (TE, p. 300) 5 MIN.
• Present *Descubre*, p. 300. Have students use context and pictures to learn *Etapa* vocabulary. Use the Situational OHTs for additional practice. 15 MIN.

En vivo: Situaciones
• Quick Start Review (TE, p. 302) 5 MIN.
• Present the Listening Strategy, p. 302. Have students read section 1, p. 302. Play the audio for section 2. Have students work in groups to complete section 3. 15 MIN.

En acción: Vocabulario y gramática
• Quick Start Review (TE, p. 304) 5 MIN.
• Have students complete *Actividad 1* in pairs. 5 MIN.
• Have students do *Actividad 2* in writing. Go over answers orally. 5 MIN.
• Present the *Vocabulario*, p. 305. Then have students read and do *Actividad 3* in pairs. 10 MIN.
• Present the Speaking Strategy, p. 305. Then have students do *Actividad 4* in pairs. 10 MIN.

Homework Option:
• Have students write answers to *¿Comprendiste?*, p. 301.

DAY 2

En acción (cont.)
• Check homework. 5 MIN.
• Quick Start Review (TE, p. 306) 5 MIN.
• Present *Repaso*: Subject and Stressed Object Pronouns and the *Vocabulario*, p. 306. 10 MIN.
• Play the audio; do *Actividad 5*. 5 MIN.
• Present the *Vocabulario*, p. 307. Then do *Actividad 6* in pairs. 10 MIN.
• Have students complete *Actividad 7* in pairs. Expand using Information Gap Activities, Unit 4 Resource Book, p. 167; *Más comunicación*, p. R14. 20 MIN.
• Quick Start Review (TE, p. 308) 5 MIN.
• Present *Repaso*: Possessive Pronouns and the *Vocabulario*, p. 308. 10 MIN.
• Have students complete *Actividad 8* in pairs. 5 MIN.
• Do *Actividad 9* orally. 5 MIN.
• Have students complete *Actividad 10* in groups. 10 MIN.

Homework Option:
• *Más práctica* Workbook, pp. 109–111. *Cuaderno para hispanohablantes*, pp. 107–108.

DAY 3

En acción (cont.)
• Check homework. 5 MIN.
• Have students complete *Actividad 11* in pairs. 5 MIN.
• Quick Start Review (TE, p. 310) 5 MIN.
• Present *Gramática*: The Future Perfect Tense, p. 310. 10 MIN.
• Play the audio; do *Actividad 12*. 5 MIN.
• Present the *Vocabulario*, p. 311. Then do *Actividad 13* orally. 10 MIN.
• Do *Actividad 14* orally. 5 MIN.
• Do *Actividad 15* in groups. 5 MIN.
• Have students read and complete *Actividad 16* in writing. Expand using Information Gap Activities, Unit 4 Resource Book, p. 168; *Más comunicación*, p. R14. 20 MIN.

Ampliación
• Use a suggested project, game, or activity. (TE, pp. 253A–253B) 15 MIN.

Refrán
• Present the *Refrán*, p. 313. 5 MIN.

Homework Option:
• Have students complete *Actividad 9* in writing. *Más práctica* Workbook, p. 112. *Cuaderno para hispanohablantes*, pp. 109–110.
• *Actividades para todos* Workbook, pp. 121–130.

DAY 4

En voces: Lectura
• Check homework. 5 MIN.
• Quick Start Review (TE, p. 314) 5 MIN.
• Present the Reading Strategy, p. 314. Call on volunteers to read the *Lectura* aloud. Have students answer the *¿Comprendiste?/¿Qué piensas?* questions, p. 315. 15 MIN.

En colores: Cultura y comparaciones
• Quick Start Review (TE, p. 316) 5 MIN.
• Present the Connecting Cultures Strategy, p. 316. Call on volunteers to read the article aloud. Have students answer the *¿Comprendiste?/¿Qué piensas?* questions, p. 317. 15 MIN.

En uso: Repaso y más comunicación
• Quick Start Review (TE, p. 318) 5 MIN.
• Do *Actividades 1–4*. 20 MIN.
• Present the Speaking Strategy, p. 320, and do *Actividades 5* and *6* in groups. 15 MIN.
• Have students begin their research for *Actividad 7*. 5 MIN.

Homework Option:
• Have students complete their reports for *Actividad 7*, p. 320. Review for *Etapa 3* Exam and Unit 4 Comprehensive Test.

DAY 5

En resumen: Repaso de vocabulario
• Check homework. 5 MIN.
• Quick Start Review (TE, p. 321) 5 MIN.
• Review grammar questions, etc., as necessary. 5 MIN.
• Complete *Etapa 3* Exam. 20 MIN.

Conexiones
• Discuss *Los estudios sociales*, p. 320. 5 MIN.

Unit 4 Comprehensive Test
• Review grammar questions, etc., as necessary. 5 MIN.
• Complete Unit 4 Comprehensive Test. 30 MIN.

En tu propia voz: Escritura
• Present the Writing Strategy, p. 322. Do the writing activity, pp. 322–323. 15 MIN.

Homework Option:
• Have students complete the assignment for *Conexiones*. Preview *Unidad 5* Opener: Have students read and study pp. 324–325.

▼ Buscar y conseguir trabajo no es fácil.

...ing Guide • UNIDAD 4 · Etapa 3 **297D**

MOTIVATE
TO COMMUNICATE
¡En español!

Support students' varied learning styles and ability levels

EASILY ADAPTABLE

The Teacher's Edition and ancillaries offer strategies that address the multiple intelligences, different ability levels, and native-speaker needs.

- **Quick Start Reviews** set up short student-directed activities that review and reinforce previously learned vocabulary and grammar concepts.

- **Classroom Community** provides paired, group, and cooperative learning activities to help build your classroom community of Spanish speakers.

UNIDAD 4 Etapa 3
Vocabulary/Grammar

Teaching Resource Options

Print
Más práctica Workbook PE, p. 111
Cuaderno para hispanohablantes PE, p. 108
Block Scheduling Copymasters
Unit 4 Resource Book
Más práctica Workbook TE, p. 147
Cuaderno para hispanohablantes TE, p. 162
Information Gap Activities, p. 167
Absent Student Copymasters, pp. 174–175

Audiovisual
OHT 41 (Quick Start), 45 (Grammar)

Technology
Online Workbook, U4E3
Take-Home Tutor CD-ROM, U4E3

ACTIVIDAD 7 Objective: Open-ended practice
Subject and stressed object pronouns in conversation

Answers will vary.

Quick Start Review
♻ Subject and stressed object pronouns
Use OHT 41 or write on the board:
Rewrite the sentences to emphasize the subject and/or object.
Modelo: Es ingeniero. Soy arquitecta.
Él es ingeniero. Yo soy arquitecta.
1. Somos académicas. Son financieros.
2. Me gustan los animales. Te gusta leer.
3. Mis padres le dieron un carro. Mis padres me dieron una bicicleta.
4. Eres profesor. Es ingeniera.

Answers
1. Nosotras somos académicas. Ellos (Ustedes) son financieros.
2. A mí me gustan los animales. A ti te gusta leer.
3. Mis padres le dieron un carro a él (ella). Mis padres me dieron una bicicleta a mí.
4. Tú eres profesor. Ella (usted) es ingeniera.

Práctica: gramática y vocabulario *continuación*

7 ¿Los conoces?
Hablar/Escribir Un alumno nuevo acaba de llegar a tu escuela. Te toca informarle sobre la escuela y los otros alumnos. Están en la clase de español y él te pregunta sobre los alumnos y el (la) maestro(a).

modelo
Compañero(a): ¿Quién es él?
Tú: Él es el maestro de español.
Compañero(a): ¿Y aquellos muchachos allí?
Tú: Él es Toño y ella es Ryoko.

More Practice:
Más comunicación *p. R14*

Nota cultural
En Latinoamérica, buscar y conseguir trabajo no es tan fácil como en Estados Unidos. Si se encuentra un anuncio interesante en el periódico, se debe ir a una entrevista para presentar el currículum personalmente. Frecuentemente hay muchas personas esperando turno y es necesario esperar mucho. Luego se espera la confirmación telefónica y puede haber otra entrevista antes de obtener el trabajo.

REPASO · Possessive Pronouns
You use possessive adjectives and pronouns to express possession.

Possessive adjective:
Aquí están **mis** datos.
Here are my facts.

Aquí está **mi** reportaje.
Here is my report.

Allí está **tu** reportaje.
There is your report.

Possessive pronoun:
Los **míos** están en el libro.
Mine are in the book.

El **mío** está en la mesa.
Mine is on the table.

Ese reportaje es **el tuyo**.
That report is yours.

Note that possessive adjectives are used with **nouns**, while possessive pronouns replace them:

replaced with

Tu carrera es interesante.
Your career is interesting.

Sí, pero **la tuya** es más interesante que **la mía**.
Yes, but yours is more interesting than mine.

Vocabulario
♻ Ya sabes

mi	mío(a)
tu	tuyo(a)
su	suyo(a)
nuestro(a)	nuestro(a)
vuestro(a)	vuestro(a)
su	suyo(a)

Practice: Actividades 8 9 10 11
Más práctica cuaderno p. 111
Para hispanohablantes cuaderno p. 108
 Online Workbook CLASSZONE.COM

308 trescientos ocho
Unidad 4

308 Vocabulary/Grammar • UNIDAD 4 Etapa 3

Classroom Community

Group Activity Divide the class into groups of 4. Have each group use possessive adjectives and pronouns to talk about things people own and relationships among people. Each group should write a summary of the discussion to present to the class.

Learning Scenario Divide the class into groups of 5–6. Have students imagine that they have found a treasure chest filled with CDs, music videos, money, jewelry, hats, etc. Tell students to have a discussion over whose items are whose. For example: **Es mi disco compacto de Gloria Estefan. No es el tuyo.**

"This incorporates many positive features: relevant context, much exposure to culture, strategy development, recycling, and meaningful practice."

Pam Urdal Silva
East Lake High School
Tarpon Springs, FL

Los productos de América Latina

Hablar/Escribir Tú y tu compañero(a) compraron varios productos y comidas de América Latina. Compara tus productos con los de tu compañero(a).

modelo
Tú: Mi anillo es de oro. ¿Y el tuyo?
Compañero(a): El mío es de plata.

oro/plata

 1. Colombia/Oaxaca  2. cuero/lana

 3. cobre/plata 4. Perú/México

 5. cuero  6. madera

9 ¿De Argentina o de Chile?
Hablar/Escribir Entre tus amigos, todos compraron estas cosas en Argentina o en Chile. ¿De qué país son las cosas que compraron?

modelo
la chaqueta (yo: Argentina; tú: Chile)
La mía es de Argentina.
La tuya es de Chile.

1. los zapatos (yo: Argentina; ella: Chile)
2. el collar (ella: Argentina; tú: Chile)
3. los muebles (nosotros: Argentina; tú: Chile)
4. la camisa (él: Argentina; ella: Chile)
5. las sillas (nosotros: Argentina; ellos: Chile)
6. ¿...?

10 ¿Y el tuyo?
Hablar/Escribir Tú y tus compañeros tienen que hacer un informe sobre la economía latinoamericana, pero nadie puede escoger el mismo tema. En grupos de tres o cuatro, hablen del tema que va a tratar el reporte de cada uno.

modelo
Tú: El informe de Ricardo es sobre la ganadería en Argentina. ¿Y los suyos?
Compañero(a): El mío es sobre el turismo en Chile...

UNIDAD 4
Vocabulary/G

Teaching Suggestions
Reviewing Poss...
- Stress that possessive adjectives and pronouns agree in gender and number with the nouns they modify.
- Remind students that possessive pronouns are usually preceded by the definite article.

ACTIVIDAD 8 **Objective:** Controlled practice
Possessive pronouns in conversation

Answers
1. A: Mi café es de Colombia. ¿Y el tuyo?
   B: El mío es de Oaxaca.
2. A: Mis guantes son de cuero. ¿Y los tuyos?
   B: Los míos son de lana.
3. A: Mi pulsera es de cobre. ¿Y la tuya?
   B: La mía es de plata.
4. A: Mi collar es de Perú. ¿Y el tuyo?
   B: El mío es de México.
5. A: Mi chaqueta es de cuero. ¿Y la tuya?
   B: La mía es de cuero también.
6. A: Mi silla es de madera. ¿Y la tuya?
   B: La mía es de madera también.

ACTIVIDAD 9 **Objective:** Transitional practice
Possessive pronouns
♻ Clothing and furniture

Answers
1. Los míos son de Argentina.
   Los suyos son de Chile.
2. El suyo es de Argentina.
   El tuyo es de Chile.
3. Los nuestros son de Argentina.
   Los tuyos son de Chile.
4. La suya es de Argentina.
   La suya es de Chile.
5. Las nuestras son de Argentina.
   Las suyas son de Chile.
6. Answers will vary.

ACTIVIDAD 10 **Objective:** Open-ended practice
Possessive pronouns in conversation

Answers will vary.

Block Schedule
Change of Pace Have students work in groups of 5–6 and play a round robin of "el mío/el tuyo/el suyo." One student turns to another and begins with **Mi cuaderno es [amarillo]. ¿Y el tuyo?** The next student responds as he/she turns to the next student: **El mío es [verde]. El suyo es [amarillo]. ¿Y el tuyo?** The group completes the round robin. Then another student starts the next round with a new item of his/her choosing. (For additional activities, see **Block Scheduling Copymasters.**)

Vocabulary/Grammar • UNIDAD 4 Etapa 3 309

● **Block Scheduling Suggestions** at point-of-use help teachers vary and streamline their lessons.

Teaching All Students

Extra Help Have students expand **Actividades 8** and **9** by comparing what they are wearing or carrying today. For example. **Mi suéter es de Perú. El tuyo es de Estados Unidos.**

Native Speakers Ask students to prepare a simple explanation of possessive pronouns to help students having difficulty. They may also prepare a short worksheet to accompany the explanation.

Multiple Intelligences
Visual Have students draw cartoons to illustrate the possessive pronouns. For example: a scene with 3 or more people—the closest person is pointing to his/her red book; someone next to him/her is pointing to his/her green book; a person in the background is pointing to his/her black book. Display the drawings and have students take turns talking about them.

● **Teaching All Students** features numerous creative ideas to address different types of students.

Cultural References

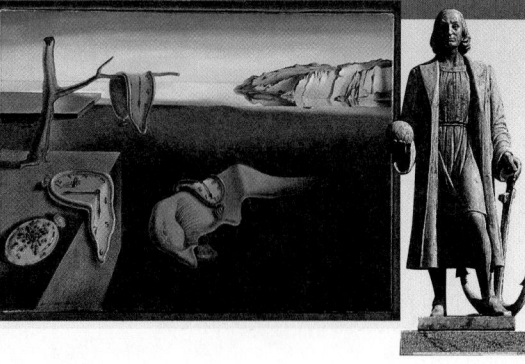

Note: *Page numbers in bold type refer to the Teacher's Edition.*

Parque Nacional Corcovado   *Costa Rica*

Antonio Berni, *New Chicago Athletic Club* (1937)

Points of Interest

Social Customs

Spanish-Speakers in the United States

Spanish-Speaking Places

Technology

INSERVICE WORKSHOPS

This section of your Teacher's Edition contains professional development materials for reference throughout the school year. You may also access www.classzone.com for additional information.

Brain-based Learning and World Languages

Estella Gahala
Albuquerque, NM

Experienced teachers intuitively know **what** is working (as well as who **is** and who **isn't**). This knowledge comes as a result of the repeated meshing of lesson plans, learners, and adjustments made through accumulated experience. Now technology looks inside the brain; neuroscientists and cognitive psychologists interpret observations and their meaning about how the mind and language develop. In other words, current brain research not only confirms **what** works, but also indicates **how** and **why** it happens.

Basic Brain Functions

Teachers should be aware of two aspects of basic brain functions. First, learning takes place in the frontal lobe or cortex where knowing, thinking, and understanding occur. The cortex turns off and no learning occurs when there are threats to survival or lack of emotional readiness. Events on the way to school may turn off the learning part of the brain. Second, the brain's source of input is through the senses (touch/movement, vision, hearing, tasting, smelling) and is stored in different locations. Whatever the topic, shopping or exploring one's feelings, engaging the senses to teach, learn, practice, use, and perform language increases the learner's chances of remembering what was learned.

A first step toward brain-compatible instruction involves understanding what the brain considers important: emotion, attention, and meaning. Robert Sylwester succinctly reminds us that emotion drives attention, attention drives learning, and learning is the search for meaning.[1] How can we use these three driving forces in brain function to lead our students in learning a foreign language?

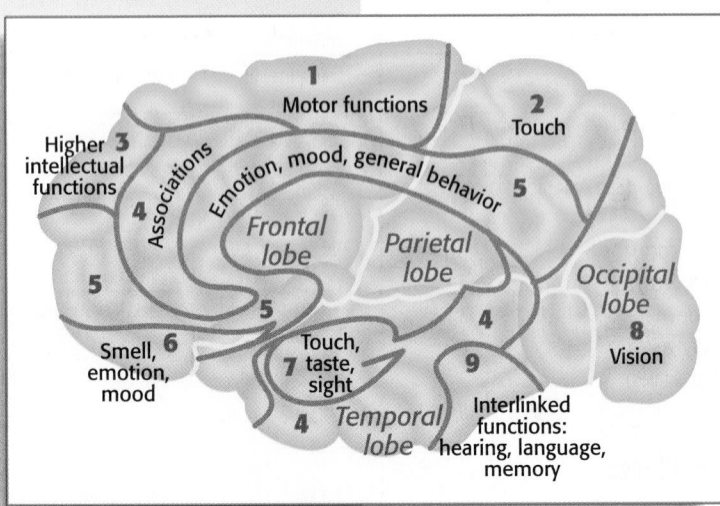

Figure labels: Motor functions (1); Touch (2); Higher intellectual functions (3); Associations (4); Emotion, mood, general behavior; Frontal lobe; Parietal lobe; Occipital lobe; Vision (8); Smell, emotion, mood (6); Touch, taste, sight (7); Temporal lobe; Interlinked functions: hearing, language, memory (9)

Emotion

The brain is always active even in deepest sleep, processing stimuli that bombard it through the senses. Sensory input triggers an emotional response before it is passed to the learning brain. Negative emotions (anger, sadness, fear, disgust, shame, chronic stress) close down readiness for learning and cognitive alertness. Positive emotions (enjoyment, trust, acceptance, friendliness, kindness) get the brain's attention to learn.

How can positive emotions be activated in the classroom? Music can be a passage from the outside to inside the class. An enriched environment that is a visual cultural experience and a gallery of students' work helps. Instructionally, *¡En español!* offers abundant activities that engage emotions and activate the mind. Students express their own and observe others' emotions: *Mi mejor amiga está deprimida. Soy comprensivo. Cuando saco buenas notas, mis padres…, Me alegro de que…* Active learning includes working cooperatively in pair and group activities; performing charades, role play, and scenarios; and doing individual projects. Choices lead learners to use their different intelligences. Strategies lead them to explore different learning processes, and they become more self-directed. Assessments provide many ways of demonstrating progress and achievement and encouraging personal pride in success.

Attention

Emotions tell the brain what merits attention. "If you don't pay attention, you won't learn," the first teacher probably reminded the first student back in the mists of time. There are two kinds of attention: a stable system not under the student's control and an adaptable system which is. Outside conscious control are ninety-minute attention cycles. Classes on a 90-minute block schedule will experience both a peak and a valley of attention; shorter class periods may have one, but not the other. The teaching challenge is to read when vitality is the highest and introduce new concepts then. Save recycling and personal applications of familiar content for low vitality periods. What captures students' adaptable attention? Novelty! Perhaps a video about teenagers' lives in Miami, Madrid, and Mexico, D.F., . . . Or checking into specially prepared websites for learners . . . Even a CD-ROM simulates real-world language experiences. However, where does this leave us with the nitty-gritty of vocabulary, verb conjugations, spelling, and other routine aspects of language? This is where the Teacher's Edition shows how to add emotional overtones to routine learning: challenge activities and rapid action games that help students overlearn and develop automatic responses en español. Undoubtedly the greatest attention-getting event is when the learner receives positive stimulation, encouragement, reinforcement, and reassurance of personal value.

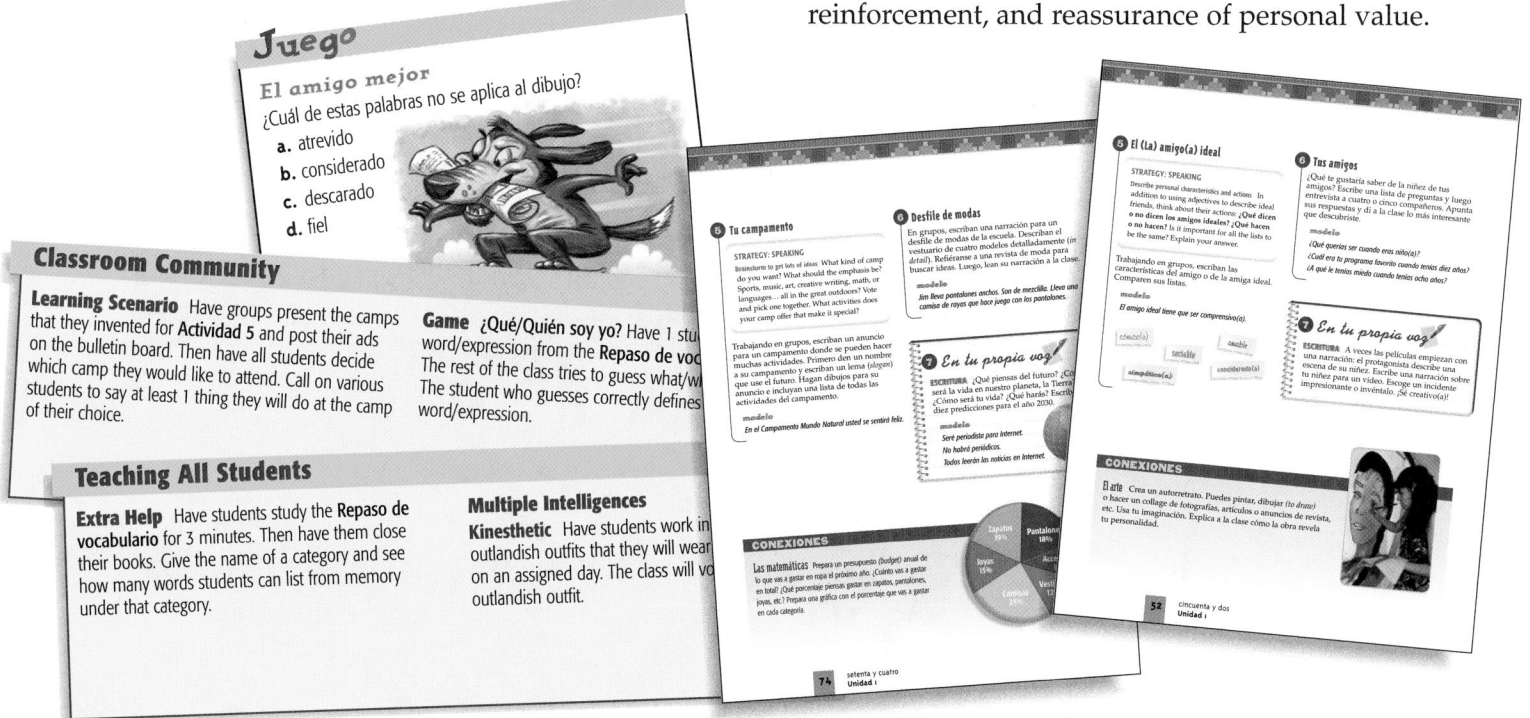

Meaning

The fundamental function of the brain is to make sense of things. Learning is the search for meaning. So to help the brain construct meaning, the content (curriculum) must have these features:

• Storytelling as the base of enriched and abundant input (listening, seeing, reading, receiving the language in cultural contexts and situations).

• Presentation and use of language as means of interacting with people of another culture as well as understanding oneself in one's own culture.

• A process that allows learners to focus on language as a whole before focusing on its parts. Learners then examine the parts of language and reassemble them in varied opportunities for self-expression.

• Real-world connections to reinforce the need, usefulness, and relevance of learning Spanish.

• Lessons that contextualize the building blocks of vocabulary and grammar inside themes and communicative functions, so that learners *experience* the interconnectedness of their learning.

• Varied approaches to learning, practicing, and applying language and cultural concepts that maintain the right balance between the extremes of anxiety and boredom.

• Assessments that provide different ways for students to demonstrate learning.

• Metacognition or strategic thinking about learning, so that the learner connects the content and processes of language learning to other disciplines and becomes more self-directed in learning.

These ingredients build learner confidence and success.

Figure 2 below shows how the various factors influencing cognition and learning interact and lead to meaning.

FIGURE 2: A Brain-based Model for Foreign Language Learning

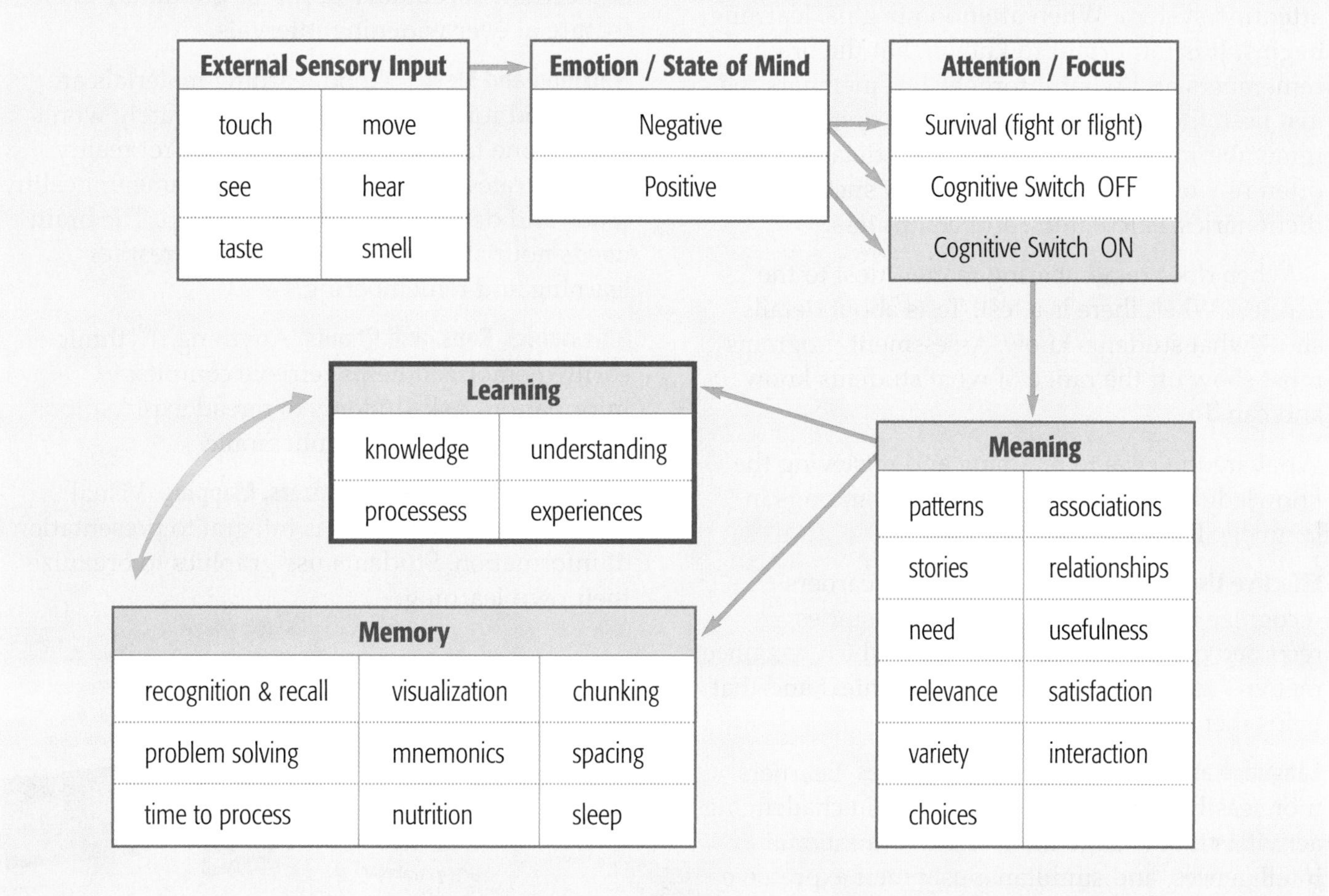

External Sensory Input
touch
move
see
hear
taste
smell
Emotion / State of Mind
Negative
Positive
Attention / Focus
Survival (fight or flight)
Cognitive Switch OFF
Cognitive Switch ON
Learning
knowledge
understanding
processess
experiences
Meaning
patterns
associations
stories
relationships
need
usefulness
relevance
satisfaction
variety
interaction
choices
Memory
recognition & recall
visualization
chunking
problem solving
mnemonics
spacing
time to process
nutrition
sleep

En vivo
SITUACIONES
¡Viva el medio ambiente!
En vivo
SITUACIONES
La graduación de Rosanna
PROGRAMA
Centro de Estudios José Reyes
Diploma

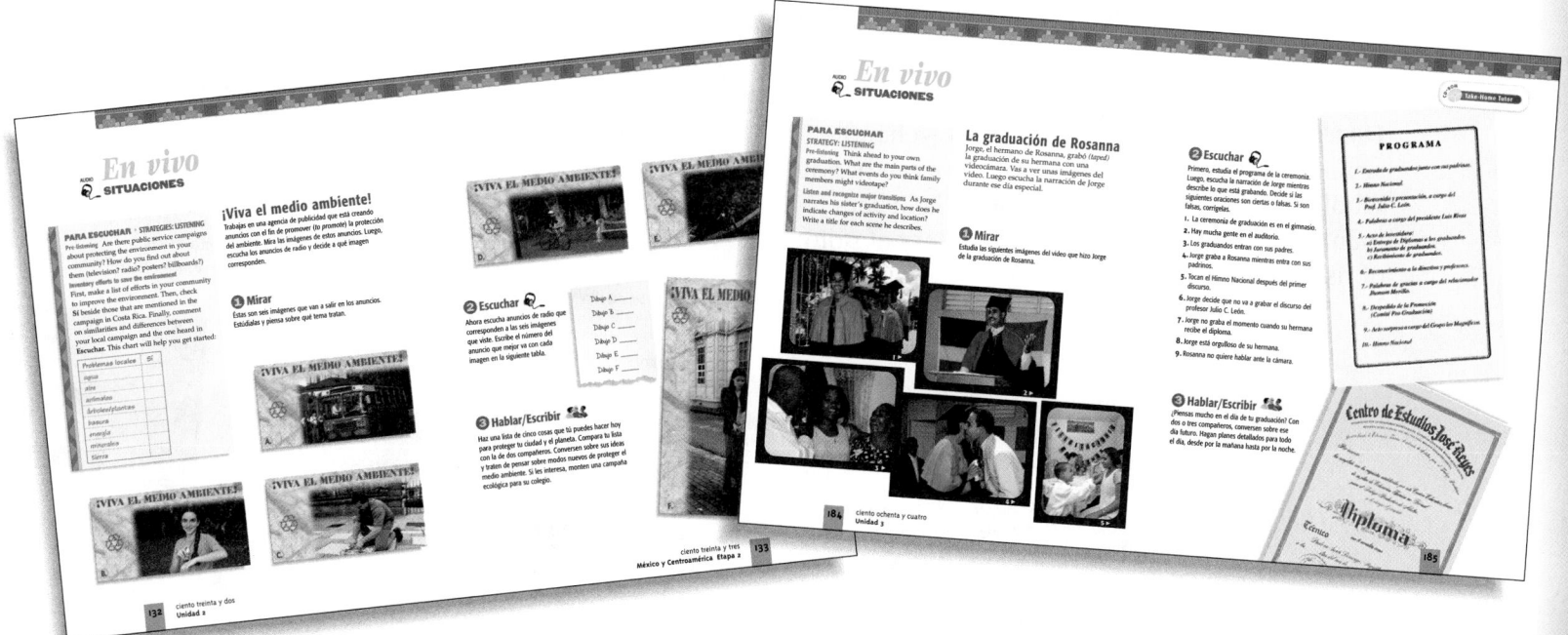

Memory

Let's retrace the steps of what the brain has been doing while learning Spanish. Sensory input hooks the emotions and gains entry into the attention system. When attention begins, learning begins. It is important to know what the brain remembers and what it forgets. It remembers the gist best, the general context. It is worst at remembering details. To remember details we often rely on technological memory such as dictionaries, calculators, and computers.

When does remembering matter most to the learner? When there is a test! Tests about details show what students know. Assessment programs must show off the range of what students know and can **do**.

What are the keys to retaining and retrieving the knowledge, experiences, and understandings in language learning from memory?

Effective Use of Recognition and Recall Learners recognize familiar language through stories, recorded conversations, and video, which reconnect memory to the original emotional context and that helps them recall language.

Language and Problem-solving Experiences Learners more easily access and use language in challenging activities that engage their verbal and rational intelligences, and simultaneously their expressive intelligences (visual-spatial, bodily-kinesthetic, musical-rhythmic). The interpersonal and introspective intelligences are the backdrop for interactive learning.

Chunking New Material Most people can handle seven pieces of new information; few can handle whole telephone books. *¡En español!* clusters manageable thematic sets of vocabulary at point of use throughout each etapa.

Spacing and Time to Process New concepts are intensively practiced and used in the etapa of presentation. In the next etapa they are reentered for use. Then begins a pattern of regular recycling of a certain vocabulary group or grammatical feature at ever widening intervals.

Nutrition and Sleep "Good learning materials are truly food for thought, and they definitely won't put anyone to sleep," one might say. Yet reality demonstrates that our students consume unhealthy foods and deprive themselves of sleep. The brain needs nourishing food and sufficient rest for learning and remembering.

Mnemonics, Raps, and Chants Anything rhythmic or easily memorized helps retrieve complex information. Ask students to reread explanations and make up their own mnemonic.

Visualization, Graphic Organizers, Mapping Visual organization of concepts is integral to presentation of information. Students use graphics to organize their own learning.

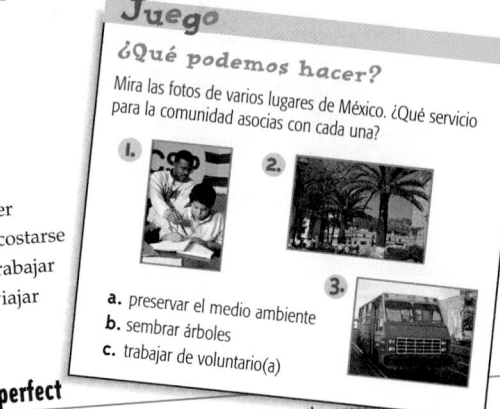

Juego

¿Qué podemos hacer?

Mira las fotos de varios lugares de México. ¿Qué servicio para la comunidad asocias con cada una?

1. descansar
2. levantarse
3. ir
4. ponerse
5. ver
6. acostarse
7. trabajar
8. viajar

a. preservar el medio ambiente
b. sembrar árboles
c. trabajar de voluntario(a)

REPASO **Preterite vs. Imperfect**

¿RECUERDAS? p. 42 You already know two tenses that refer to past time, the preterite and the imperfect. You use each of these tenses to talk about **past** actions in a different way.

- Use the preterite tense to describe an action or series of actions completed in the past.

  Aquel día, Pedro salió del colegio y caminó hasta el café.
  *That day, Pedro **left** school and **walked** to the café.*

- Use the imperfect to describe ongoing actions or conditions in the past, without focusing on their beginning or end.

  Yo siempre salía del colegio y caminaba hasta el café.
  *I always **used to leave** school and **walk** to the Café.*

Sometimes you will need to use the imperfect and preterite in the same sentence.

Use the imperfect to ... Use the preterite to describe the interrupting or main event.

... éfono.

TÚ EN LA COMUNIDAD

James es alumno en Washington. Él trabaja de voluntario con un optómetra en una misión médica en México. Da instrucciones a los pacientes, habla sobre los problemas que tienen y comunica al médico información importante. Cuando está en Washington, habla español con alumnos de otras escuelas.

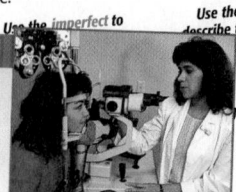

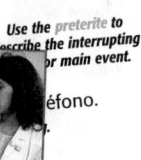

Summary

Foreign language learning built on brain-compatible learning includes:

Curriculum organized around cross-disciplinary, thematic content and experiences reflecting the real world.

Instruction based on holistic approaches that are developmentally and socio-culturally appropriate; creative approaches connecting with emotions, meaning, and reason; active processing; individually distinctive learning opportunities; attention maintaining activities; techniques for remembering.

Assessments such as performance, projects, and portfolios, to reveal deep knowledge, not just discrete surface knowledge.

Classroom management in an enriched, challenging, non-threatening environment that promotes relaxed alertness, cooperative learning and discussion of one's own learning processes.

These provide all the right ingredients to build the learner's confidence for communication.

[1]Sylwester, Robert. (1995) *A Celebration of Neurons: An Educator's Guide to the Human Brain.* Alexandria, VA: Association for Supervision and Curriculum Development.

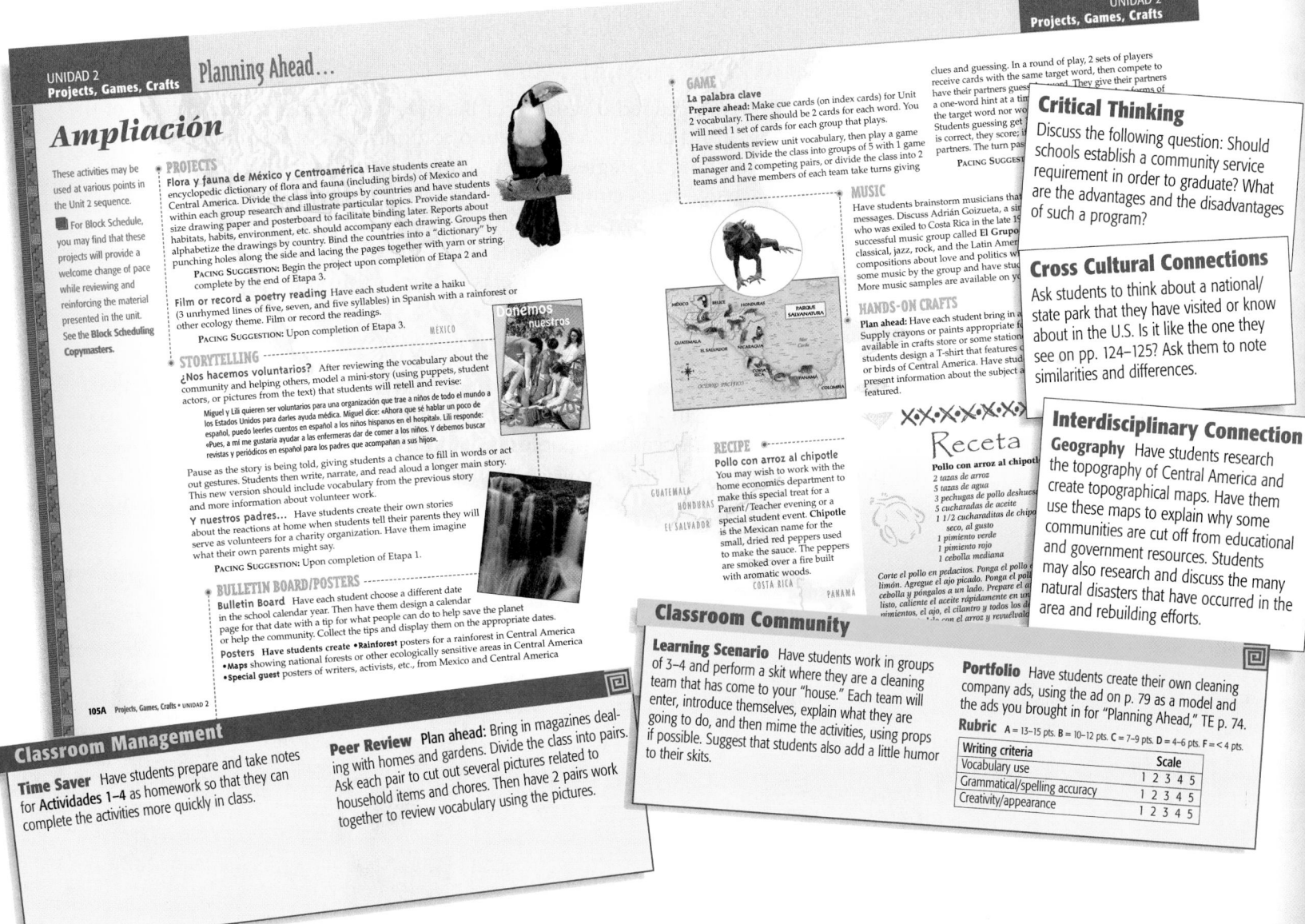

UNIDAD 2
Projects, Games, Crafts

Planning Ahead...

Ampliación

These activities may be used at various points in the Unit 2 sequence.

■ For Block Schedule, you may find that these projects will provide a welcome change of pace while reviewing and reinforcing the material presented in the unit. See the **Block Scheduling Copymasters.**

● PROJECTS

Flora y fauna de México y Centroamérica Have students create an encyclopedic dictionary of flora and fauna (including birds) of Mexico and Central America. Divide the class into groups by countries and have students within each group research and illustrate particular topics. Provide standard-size drawing paper and posterboard to facilitate binding later. Reports about habitats, habits, environment, etc. should accompany each drawing. Groups then alphabetize the drawings by country. Bind the countries into a "dictionary" by punching holes along the side and lacing the pages together with yarn or string.
PACING SUGGESTION: Begin the project upon completion of Etapa 2 and complete by the end of Etapa 3.

Film or record a poetry reading Have each student write a haiku (3 unrhymed lines of five, seven, and five syllables) in Spanish with a rainforest or other ecology theme. Film or record the readings.
PACING SUGGESTION: Upon completion of Etapa 3.

● STORYTELLING

¿Nos hacemos voluntarios? After reviewing the vocabulary about the community and helping others, model a mini-story (using puppets, student actors, or pictures from the text) that students will retell and revise:

Miguel y Lili quieren ser voluntarios para una organización que trae a niños de todo el mundo a los Estados Unidos para darles ayuda médica. Miguel dice: «Ahora que sé hablar un poco de español, puedo leerles cuentos en español a los niños hispanos en el hospital. Lili responde: «Pues, a mí me gustaría ayudar a las padres que acompañan a sus hijos».

Pause as the story is being told, giving students a chance to fill in words or act out gestures. Students then write, narrate, and read aloud a longer main story. This new version should include vocabulary from the previous story and more information about student volunteer work.

Y nuestros padres... Have students create their own stories about the reactions at home when students tell their parents they will serve as volunteers for a charity organization. Have them imagine what their own parents might say.
PACING SUGGESTION: Upon completion of Etapa 1.

● BULLETIN BOARD/POSTERS

Bulletin Board Have each student choose a different date in the school calendar year. Then have them design a calendar page for that date with a tip for what people can do to help save the planet or help the community. Collect the tips and display them on the appropriate dates.
Posters Have students create •**Rainforest** posters for a rainforest in Central America •**Maps** showing national forests or other ecologically sensitive areas in Central America •**Special guest** posters of writers, activists, etc., from Mexico and Central America

105A Projects, Games, Crafts • UNIDAD 2

● GAME

La palabra clave
Prepare ahead: Make cue cards (on index cards) for Unit 2 vocabulary. There should be 2 cards for each word. You will need 1 set of cards for each group that plays.

Have students review unit vocabulary, then play a game of password. Divide the class into groups of 5 with 1 game manager and 2 competing pairs, or divide the class into 2 teams and have members of each team take turns giving

clues and guessing. In a round of play, 2 sets of players receive cards with the same target word, then compete to have their partners guess the word. They give their partners a one-word hint at a time [...] the target word nor wo[...] Students guessing get [...] is correct, they score; [...] partners. The turn pas[...]
PACING SUGGEST[...]

● MUSIC

Have students brainstorm musicians that [...] messages. Discuss Adrián Goizueta, a si[...] who was exiled to Costa Rica in the late 19[...] successful music group called **El Grupo** [...] classical, jazz, rock, and the Latin Amer[...] compositions about love and politics w[...] some music by the group and have stud[...] More music samples are available on yo[...]

● HANDS-ON CRAFTS

Plan ahead: Have each student bring in a [...] Supply crayons or paints appropriate f[...] available in crafts store or some station[...] students design a T-shirt that features o[...] or birds of Central America. Have stud[...] present information about the subject a[...] featured.

● RECIPE

Pollo con arroz al chipotle
You may wish to work with the home economics department to make this special treat for a Parent/Teacher evening or a special student event. **Chipotle** is the Mexican name for the small, dried red peppers used to make the sauce. The peppers are smoked over a fire built with aromatic woods.
COSTA RICA

Receta

Pollo con arroz al chipotl[...]
2 tazas de arroz
5 tazas de agua
3 pechugas de pollo deshues[...]
5 cucharadas de aceite
1 1/2 cucharaditas de chipo[...]
    seco, al gusto
1 pimiento verde
1 pimiento rojo
1 cebolla mediana

Corte el pollo en pedacitos. Ponga el pollo [...] limón. Agregue el ajo picado. Ponga el pol[...] cebolla y póngalos a un lado. Prepare el a[...] listo, caliente el aceite rápidamente en un [...] nimientos, el ajo, el cilantro y todos los [...] [...]la con el arroz y revuelva[...]

Critical Thinking

Discuss the following question: Should schools establish a community service requirement in order to graduate? What are the advantages and the disadvantages of such a program?

Cross Cultural Connections

Ask students to think about a national/state park that they have visited or know about in the U.S. Is it like the one they see on pp. 124–125? Ask them to note similarities and differences.

Interdisciplinary Connection

Geography Have students research the topography of Central America and create topographical maps. Have them use these maps to explain why some communities are cut off from educational and government resources. Students may also research and discuss the many natural disasters that have occurred in the area and rebuilding efforts.

Classroom Management

Time Saver Have students prepare and take notes for **Actividades 1–4** as homework so that they can complete the activities more quickly in class.

Peer Review Plan ahead: Bring in magazines dealing with homes and gardens. Divide the class into pairs. Ask each pair to cut out several pictures related to household items and chores. Then have 2 pairs work together to review vocabulary using the pictures.

Classroom Community

Learning Scenario Have students work in groups of 3–4 and perform a skit where they are a cleaning team that has come to your "house." Each team will enter, introduce themselves, explain what they are going to do, and then mime the activities, using props if possible. Suggest that students also add a little humor to their skits.

Portfolio Have students create their own cleaning company ads, using the ad on p. 79 as a model and the ads you brought in for "Planning Ahead," TE p. 74.
Rubric A = 13–15 pts. B = 10–12 pts. C = 7–9 pts. D = 4–6 pts. F = < 4 pts.

Writing criteria	Scale
Vocabulary use	1 2 3 4 5
Grammatical/spelling accuracy	1 2 3 4 5
Creativity/appearance	1 2 3 4 5

Incorporating Culture

Jorge Capetillo-Ponce
New York, NY

UNIDAD 1
Cultural Opener

Unit Theme

Discussing Spanish-speaking communities in the United States; describing people; and talking about past, present, and future actions

Communication
- Describing people
- Talking about life experiences and accomplishments
- Describing fashions
- Talking about pastimes
- Predicting future actions
- Talking about household chores
- Expressing feelings

Cultures
- The influence of Spanish speakers in the United States
- The cultural role of fashion
- Musical influences

Connections
- Art: Creating a self-portrait
- Math: Preparing an annual clothing budget

Comparisons
- Childhood experiences
- Geography, climate, and customs and how they influence choice of clothing
- Musical instruments and influences

Communities
- Using Spanish in the workplace
- Using Spanish in Spanish-speaking communities for personal enjoyment

When students learn a new language like Spanish, they not only encounter new words, sounds, and grammatical structures, but also a cultural vehicle for presenting the distinctiveness of communities and the drawing of cultural boundaries. Cultures are embedded in languages, and languages constitute reflections of cultural attitudes. Through a common language, the idea of belonging to a group, a community, or a nation is conceived.

A Guided Discovery of Culture

¡En español! offers a guided discovery of the diverse cultures and traditions of the Spanish-speaking world and Hispanic/Latino communities in the United States. A wide range of teaching strategies for both language and culture offers students a framework to achieve cross-cultural understanding. *¡En español!* presents culture in both implicit, embedded forms (authentic documents, photographs, maps, illustrations), and explicit cultural presentations (most notably in the *Cultural Openers, En colores* and *En voces* sections, and in *Notas culturales* throughout the program).

Increasing Understanding of Cultural Diversity

Global interdependence and economic integration among regions is a trend that continues to grow. For this reason, *¡En español!* offers a presentation and analysis of the cultures of Spanish-speaking peoples in Latin America and Spain, as well as Hispanic heritage in the United States. As students progress through the program, critical thinking and cultural process skills are developed, increasing understanding of cultural diversity.

Horizontal and Vertical Levels of Culture

The *¡En español!* program uses text, visuals, audio, and video to immerse students in culture at both horizontal and vertical levels. The horizontal level includes contextual situations, such as what happens in a market in Oaxaca, a restaurant in Madrid, or at a Dominican high school graduation in Santo Domingo or a visit to El Alamo in San Antonio. It is also topical, because it explores diverse national, regional, and communal perspectives on universal themes such as friendship, family, work, leisure, education, schooling, and youth and adult roles, as well as conceptions about the future and the past, celebrations surrounding birth and death, technology, moderns types of communication, and global concerns such as ecology, democracy, and civic duty. These perspectives, related to personal and cultural identities, are presented both from an "outsider" and an "insider" angle to further and widen the discussion about cultural/linguistic differences and similarities.

The movement in the vertical level shifts from popular culture to high culture artifacts. Popular culture examples from diverse nations and regions are presented, such as articles from magazines, newspaper ads, cartoons, and realia from original restaurant menus, high school diplomas, and Internet information. On the other hand, it consists of the presentation of works of the high-culture exponents from Spanish-speaking countries and Latinos in the United States in the fields of poetry, prose, and painting. These words and images of cultural icons reflect the importance of individual perspectives within each cultural space, and demonstrate the union of thought, word (particularly the expressive beauty of the Spanish language), and works of art.

Developing Cultural Process Skills

This horizontal and vertical axis, together with the cultural process skills, which includes the reading of cultural notes at home or in class and the discussion between teacher and students of the cultural content, will aid students in understanding similarities and differences between the nations and communities in the Spanish-speaking world. Understanding another culture depends on the ability to observe and analyze. As students read texts, hear audio material, and watch videos especially designed to portray particular cultural and linguistic situations, they should be encouraged to become keen observers of behavior patterns. The *En colores* sections of *¡En español!* focus on connecting students' prior personal cultural experiences with those of the target culture, engaging students in an ongoing cultural dialog. Additional cultural information is also presented in the *En voces* reading sections, although the pedagogical focus differs. These two sections work together to complement and expand students' cultural knowledge and awareness. In the case of Spanish native speakers, the texts, audio and video will show them that while they are important in the United States, they are also part of a wider cultural heritage.

¡En español! Connecting Cultures

Gaining knowledge and understanding of other cultures, developing insights into one's own culture, and becoming lifelong learners through communication in Spanish underscores the importance of incorporating culture into the language classroom. Communication, Cultures, Connections, Comparisons, Communities: the teaching of culture celebrates the depth and variety of the Hispanic cultural heritage.

Professional Bibliography and Additional Resources

Audrey L. Heining-Boynton
University of North Carolina
Chapel Hill, NC

Part of being a dedicated teacher is committing to life-long learning, keeping abreast of the latest trends and issues. It is helpful to have a synthesis of types and genres of sources and resources where you can find further information on a given topic. What follows is a synthesis of a variety of texts and articles that will provide you with a starting point to explore pertinent issues and "hot topics." If you have other favorite sources that are not listed here, contact the *¡En español!* website to share your suggestions.

There are several journals or yearly reports that will provide you with an excellent choice of articles. They are *Modern Language Journal, Foreign Language Annals, The ACTFL Foreign Language Education Series, Dimensions, Hispania, the TESOL Quarterly, Educational Leadership, The Phi Delta Kappan,* and publications from regional and local educational groups, including *Central States Reports* and *Northeast Conference Reports* and publications from SWCOLT, SCOLT, and PacNW.

What follows are selected articles or texts that deal with eight areas of foreign language teaching and learning: *At-risk Students, Assessment, Content-based Instruction, Culture and Multiculturalism, Foreign Language Standards, General Educational Issues, Second Language Acquisition, Block Scheduling,* and *Technology.*

At-risk Students

• *Readings from Educational Leadership: Students At Risk.* Edited by Ronald S. Brandt (1990). Alexandria, VA: Association for Supervision and Curriculum Development.

For anyone who wants a thorough overview of the problem of at-risk students, this collection of readings is the place to begin. *Educational Leadership,* one of the finest journals for all K-12 teachers, compiles books that are collections of articles from previous editions, and this edition combines over forty articles on this compelling topic.

• Heining-Boynton, A. (1994). "The At-Risk Student in the Foreign Language Classroom." In *Meeting New Challenges in the Foreign Language Classroom.* Edited by Gale K. Crouse. Lincolnwood, IL: National Textbook Company.

This article provides a review of the literature regarding at-risk students, and then provides teaching techniques on how best to meet the needs of these special students. Also listed at the end of the volume is an annotated bibliography with other references dealing with the at-risk learner.

Assessment

• Herman, J.L., Aschbacher, P.R. and Winters, L. (1992). *A Practical Guide to Alternative Assessment.* Alexandria, VA: Association for Supervision and Curriculum Development.

This text is useful because it provides teachers with ways to determine the purpose of assessment, select the tasks and set the criteria, ensure reliable scoring, and incorporate interdisciplinary factors in the equation.

• Marzano, R.J., Pickering, D. and McTighe, J. (1993). *Assessing Student Outcomes: Performance Assessment Using the Dimensions of Learning Model.* Alexandria, VA: Association for Supervision and Curriculum Development.

Beginning with a definition of how assessment standards are linked to the five dimensions of learning, the text offers suggestions on how teachers can assess and keep track of student performance. The authors share an extensive rubric to be used in the process.

• Moeller, A. (1994). "Portfolio Assessment: A Showcase for Growth and Learning in the Foreign Language Classroom." In *Meeting New Challenges in the Foreign Language Classroom.* Edited by Gale K. Crouse. Lincolnwood, IL: National Textbook Company.

This article offers a rationale for the process of portfolio assessment and provides a step-by-step method for foreign language teachers to include this as a holistic component to their instruction and assessment.

• *Teaching, Testing, and Assessment: Making the Connection.* (1994). Northeast Conference Reports. Editor, Charles Hancock. Lincolnwood, IL: National Textbook Company.

Besides an overview of conceptualization that connects teaching, testing, and assessment, the chapters offer ideas for assessing all language skills in a variety of ways.

Content-based Instruction

- Anderson, Karen C. (1993). *Kid's Giant Book of Games*. New York, NY: Times Books, Inc.

  Karen Anderson has published a series of game books. Her ideas lend themselves to adaptation to include higher-order thinking in a content-based context.

- Anderson, Karen C., and Cumbaa, Stephen. (1993). *The Bones and Skeleton Game Book.* New York, NY: Workman Publishing Company.

  Particularly appealing for second language teachers/students are the critical thinking activities/puzzles in this book. The activities practice basic concepts such as genetics in an engaging way that help students learn language in context while employing higher-order thinking.

- Cantoni-Harvey, Gina. (1987). *Content-Area Language Instruction: Approaches and Strategies.* New York, NY: Addison-Wesley Publishing Company.

  This text gives an overview of what content-based instruction is and how to incorporate it in a curriculum.

- Heining-Boynton, Audrey L. & Sonia Torres-Quiñones. (1996). *¡Anímate! Focus on Science and Math. Introductory Spanish.* Addison-Wesley Publishing Company, 1996: White Plains, NY.

  This text and teacher's guide provide Spanish teachers with necessary vocabulary on the environment, endangered species, and other science terms that can be used to make connections with other content areas. Also available are activities that can be age-adjusted.

- Kenda, Margaret, and Williams, Phyllis S. (1992). *Science Wizardry for Kids.* Hauppage, NY: Barron's Educational Series, Inc.

  This series has activity after activity that foreign language teachers can adapt for their classrooms. This and the other books in the series are also non-threatening to the non-science individual.

- Kenda, Margaret, and Williams, Phyllis S. (1995). *Math Wizardry for Kids.* Hauppage, NY: Barron's Educational Series, Inc.

  This text affords a multitude of activities that teachers can adapt for the foreign language classroom. These activities reinforce mathematics in fun, "magic" ways.

- Petreshene, Susan S. (1994) *Brain Teasers!* The Center for Applied Research in Education, Inc.

  Over 180 quick higher order thinking activities are available in this book that can easily be adapted for the foreign language classroom.

- Petreshene, Susan S. *Mind Joggers!* (1985) The Center for Applied Research in Education, Inc.

  As with *Brain Teasers!*, this book offers a multitude of activities that take from five to fifteen minutes.

- Ruiz, José Curbelo; Hernandez, María Teresa; and Zuazo, Prudencio. *La Ciencia 1, 2, 3 y 4.* SM Ediciones. (1985).

  This series from Puerto Rico helps teachers with needed vocabulary and concepts to incorporate science in the language classroom.

- Short, Deborah J. *How to Integrate Language and Content Instruction: A Training Manual.* Center for Applied Linguistics, Washington DC. (1991).

  This practical, how-to manual gives step-by-step instructions on how to incorporate content-based, content-related instruction in the foreign language instruction.

Culture and Multiculturalism

- Noble, J. and Lacasa, J. (1995). *The Hispanic Way.* Lincolnwood, IL: Passport Books.

  This small book provides cultural/sociological information on a variety of topics that encompass the attitudes, behavior, and customs of the Spanish-speaking world.

- Richard-Amato, P. and Snow, M. (1992). *The Multicultural Classroom.* White Plains, NY: Longman.

  Although it is important for foreign language teachers to share target-culture specific information with their students, it is also important for teachers to see the big picture in terms of why we are teaching culture. This text provides that overview.

- *Newsweek en español, People en español, etc.*

  A number of weekly and monthly publications exist to help Spanish teachers maintain a current knowledge of what is happening throughout the Spanish-speaking world. Publications like *Newsweek en español, People en español*, and daily newspapers from the countries that can be accessed on the Internet are filled with news from Spanish-speaking countries. Another excellent resource is *National Geographic*.

- *Teaching Tolerance*

  This free biannual publication available from the Southern Poverty Law Center is an outstanding resource for teachers. Activities abound that can be adapted for the foreign language classroom to help students learn about other cultures and at the same time appreciate, understand and respect students and community members at home. Write to: Teaching Tolerance, Order Dept., 400 Washington Ave., Montgomery, AL 36104.

Foreign Language Standards

- *National Standards: A Catalyst for Reform.* Edited by Robert C. Lafayette. (1996). Lincolnwood, IL: National Textbook Company.

  This compendium looks at the foreign language standards and how they impact all aspects of foreign language teaching. This volume is a good overview of where the profession is headed, from teacher training to classroom implications for the standards.

- *Standards for Foreign Language Learning: Preparing for the 21st Century.* (1996). American Council on the Teaching of Foreign Languages, 6 Executive Plaza, Yonkers, NY.

  Foreign language teaching and learning is now organized by five principles known as the five C's of foreign language education: communication, cultures, connections, comparisons, and communities.

General Educational Issues

Block Scheduling

- Canady, R.L. & Rettig, M.D. (1995). *Block Scheduling: A Catalyst for Change in High Schools.* Larchmont, NY: Eye on Education.

- Canady, R.L. & Rettig, M.D. (1996). *Teaching in the Block: Strategies for Engaging Active Learners.* Larchmont, NY: Eye on Education.

- Cunningham, R. David. Jr. & Nogle, Sue Ann. (December 1996). "Six Keys to Block Scheduling." *The High School Magazine*, 29-32.

- Elkins, G. (Spring 1996). "Making Longer Better: Staff Development for Block Scheduling." Arlington, VA: ASCD Professional Development Newsletter.

- Gerking, Janet L. (April 1995). "Building Block Schedules: A Firsthand Assessment of Restructuring the School Day." *The Science Teacher*, 23–27.

- Hottenstein, D.S. (Winter 1996). "Supporting Block Scheduling: A Response to Critics." *Alliance* 1(2), 11. Reston, VA: The National Alliance of High Schools, a division of the National Association of Secondary School Principals.

- Wisconsin Association of Foreign Language Teachers. (1995). *Redesigning High School Schedules: A Report of the Task Force on Block Scheduling by the Wisconsin Association of Foreign Language Teachers.* Madison, WI: WAFLT (can be found on ERIC on the Internet).

Classroom Management

- Johnson, D. and Johnson, R. (1995). *Reducing School Violence Through Conflict Resolution.* Alexandria, VA: Association for Supervision and Curriculum Development.

  This text offers guidance to teachers on how to teach conflict resolution and actually create an environment that prevents conflict and violence.

- Jones, F. (1987). *Positive Classroom Discipline.* New York, NY: McGraw Hill.

  Dr. Jones spoke at the Central States Conference several years ago, and was a hit. Why? Because everyone could relate to what he was saying! Jones has foolproof ways to have the discipline and classroom management we all want and deserve.

- Kohn, A. (1996). *Beyond Discipline: From Compliance to Community.* Alexandria, VA: Association for Supervision and Curriculum Development.

  This text takes a new approach to classroom management/discipline.

Multiple Intelligences

- Armstrong, Thomas. (1991). *Awakening Your Child's Natural Genius.* Los Angeles, CA: Jeremy P. Tarcher, Inc.

- Armstrong, Thomas. (1987). *Discovering and Encouraging Your Child's Personal Learning Style.* Los Angeles, CA: Jeremy P. Tarcher, Inc., Distributed by St. Martin's Press.

- Armstrong, Thomas. (1994). *Multiple Intelligences in the Classroom.* Alexandria, VA: Association for Supervision and Curriculum Development.

- Gardner, Howard. (1983). *Frames of Mind: The Theory of Multiple Intelligences.* New York, NY: Basic Books.

- Kline, Peter. (1988). *The Everyday Genius: Restoring Children's Natural Joy of Learning, and Yours Too.* Arlington, VA: Great Ocean Publishers.

- Lazear, David. (1994) *Seven Pathways of Learning: Teaching Students and Parents about Multiple Intelligences.* Tucson, AZ: Zephyr Press.

  This text gives a good overview of multiple intelligences and provides suggested activity types to include in any kind of classroom.

Second Language Acquisition

- Krashen, S.D. and Terrell, T.D. (1983) *The Natural Approach: Language Acquisition in the Classroom.* Englewood Cliffs, NJ: Prentice-Hall.

  This text provides the philosophy and approach to teaching second language based on research in linguistics, psychology, and psycholinguistics. Its major concepts are the Input Hypothesis and the Affective Filter Hypothesis.

- Larsen-Freeman, D. and Long, M.H. (1992). *An Introduction to Second Language Acquisition Research.* New York, NY: Longman.

  A complete overview of second language theories, this is a sophisticated text that provides a lengthy bibliography and set of references for further investigation.

- *Research in Language Learning: Principles, Processes and Prospects.* (1993) Editor, Alice Omaggio Hadley. Lincolnwood, IL: National Textbook Company.

  This text, one of the series of ACTFL Foreign Language Education Series, is dedicated to research in language learning. Articles such as "Second Language Production: SLA Research in Speaking and Writing" by Susan Gass and Sally Sieloff Magnan offer a variety of perspectives on language acquisition research and how it applies to the classroom.

- *TESOL Quarterly*

  This journal provides research articles on second language acquisition. Foreign language educators have gained much from the research conducted by second language acquisition researchers whose primary function is working with the English to Speakers of Other Languages (ESOL) student population. We continue to benefit from their research.

- Omaggio Hadley, A. (1993) *Teaching Language in Context.* Boston, MA: Heinle & Heinle.

  Omaggio Hadley's text sets the standard for a thorough exploration of the teaching of the four skills. At the end of each chapter she offers an extensive list of sources for additional consultation.

Technology

- Blyth, C.S. (1998). *Untangling the Web.* New York, NY: St. Martin's Press.

  This no-nonsense, easy to read text demystifies using the World Wide Web. Easy illustrations that show how the computer screen should appear at each step walk beginners and intermediate Internet users through the jungle of terms to achieve positive results when surfing the web.

- Bush, M.D. & Terry, R.M. (Eds.). (1997). *Technology-Enhanced Language Learning.* Illinois: National Textbook Company.

  This ACTFL Foreign Language Education Series volume explores multiple uses of technology in the foreign language classroom. Chapter titles include "Hypermedia Technology for Teaching Reading," "Teaching Listening: How Technology Can Help," and "Learning Language and Culture with Internet Technologies."

- *Educational Leadership* Volume 54, No. 3, November 1996.

  This volume, entitled "Networking," begins, as usual, with a point/counterpoint regarding technology and in particular, the use of the Internet. Articles such as "How Schools Can Create Their Own Web Pages" and "Online Mentors: Experimenting in Science Class" offer excellent ideas for second/foreign language teachers to incorporate in their instruction.

- *Educational Leadership* Volume 53, No. 2, October 1995.

  This issue entitled "How Technology Is Transforming Teaching" explores global issues of technology such as "Selling a School Technology Budget" and "How to Fund Technology Projects." And, as in all issues of this journal, there exists an international section that looks at what is occurring outside the United States. One such article from New Zealand, "Computers Empower Students with Special Needs," reports on successful practices with at-risk students.

- *PC Computing*

  This general magazine on microcomputers provides interesting information for both the novice and the computer devoté and expert. Periodic issues list, for example, the editors' picks on the 1,000 best free WWW downloads. Also provided are evaluations and comparisons of technology products and gadgets.

- *Technological Horizons in Education Journal.* 150 El Camino Real, Suite 112, Tustin CA 92680-8670

  The Journal reports school-based research projects and lists successful ideas that incorporate technology in the classroom. For example, in the December 1995 issue there appeared an article entitled "Maya Mythology & Multimedia: Using Each to Teach the Other."

Additional Resources

There are many organizations that can provide a wealth of additional information and support for Spanish teachers. The list below will help you to expand your classroom resources and contact other teachers. Remember, however, that addresses and telephone numbers often change; it is advisable to verify them before sending inquiries.

Professional Organizations

The American Council on
the Teaching of Foreign
Languages (ACTFL)
6 Executive Plaza
Yonkers, NY 10701
(914) 963-8830
http://www.actfl.org/

American Association of
Teachers of Spanish
and Portuguese (AATSP)
423 Exton Commons
Exton, PA 19341-2451
(610) 363-7005
http://www.aatsp.org

Cultural Offices/Embassies/Consulates/Tourist Offices

Consult the telephone listings in most major cities for a listing of the embassies and consulates of Spanish-speaking countries closest to you.

Tourist Office of Spain
666 Fifth Avenue, 35th Floor
New York, NY 10022
(212) 265-8822
http://www.okspain.org/

Mexican Government Tourist Office
2707 N. Loop West, Suite 450
Houston, TX 77008
(713) 880-5153
http://www.mexico-travel.com

Pen Pal Exchanges

CIEE
633 Third Avenue, 20th Floor
New York, NY 10017-6706
1-800-40-STUDY

World Pen Pals
P.O. Box 337
Saugerties, NY 12477
(845) 246-7828

Travel/Cultural Exchange

STA Travel
205 East 42nd St.
New York, NY 10017
(212) 822-2700
http://www.counciltravel.com/

AFS International
71 West 23rd St., 17th Floor
New York, NY 10010
(212) 807-8686
http://www.afs.org/usa/

Periodicals/Films

Subscriptions may be purchased for the school through the companies listed below, or through others in your local area:

EBSCO Subscription Services
P.O. Box 1943
Birmingham, AL 35201-1943

Continental Book Company
8000 Cooper Avenue Bldg. 29
Glendale, NY 11385
(718) 326-0572

Online Contacts

Many organizations now maintain websites. Since, again, these are subject to change, it is advisable to check before contacting. We encourage you to visit the McDougal Littell website for materials specific to the *¡En español!* program. In addition, FLTEACH provides a discussion forum for teacher exchange of ideas and information:

 www.mcdougallittell.com

FLTEACH
To subscribe or obtain information:
LISTSERV@listserv.buffalo.edu

In your message, put the following:
SUBSCRIBE FLTEACH, first name, last name
(to unsubscribe, send UNSUB FLTEACH,
first name, last name)

To send messages to all FLTEACH subscribers:
FLTEACH@listserv.buffalo.edu

3 tres

McDOUGAL LITTELL

¡En español!

AUTHORS

Estella Gahala

Patricia Hamilton Carlin

Audrey L. Heining-Boynton

Ricardo Otheguy

Barbara J. Rupert

CULTURE CONSULTANT

Jorge A. Capetillo-Ponce

McDougal Littell

A HOUGHTON MIFFLIN COMPANY

Evanston, Illinois • Boston • Dallas

McDougal Littell

¡En español!

CONTENIDO

OBJECTIVES

- Talk about present activities
- Talk about past activities

UNIDAD

ETAPA 1

OBJECTIVES

- Describe people
- Talk about experiences
- List accomplishments

ASÍ SOMOS

Hablamos con hispanohablantes en Estados Unidos sobre la identidad personal, el estilo individual y las responsabilidades diarias.

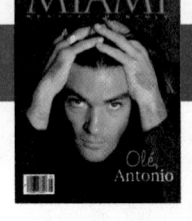

ETAPA
2

OBJECTIVES

- Describe fashions
- Talk about pastimes
- Talk about the future
- Predict actions

ETAPA
3

¡Hay tanto que hacer! 76

2

ETAPA

1

¡EL MUNDO ES NUESTRO!

Visitamos México y América Central, donde hablamos sobre las responsabilidades sociales, el medio ambiente y la riqueza natural.

OBJECTIVES

- Say what you want to do
- Make requests
- Make suggestions

Donemos nuestros esfuerzos

UNIDAD 2

ETAPA 2

OJECTIVES

• Say what should be done
• React to the ecology
• React to others' actions

ETAPA
3

- React to nature
- Express doubt
- Relate events in time

La riqueza natural 150

UNIDAD 3

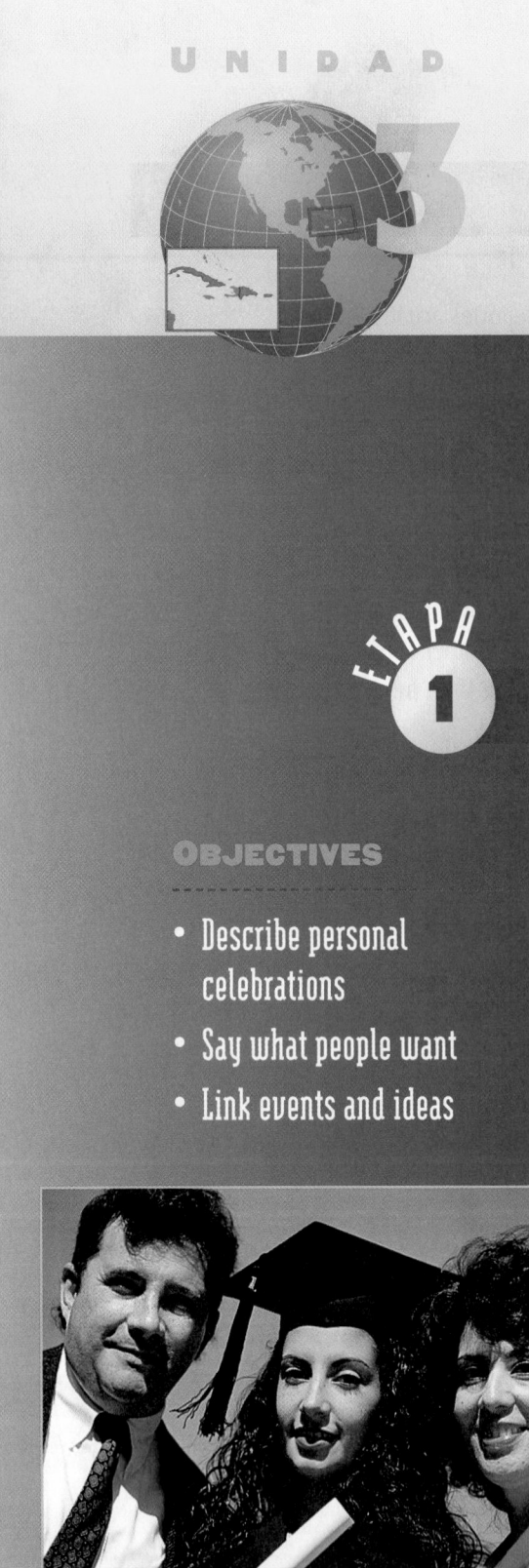

ETAPA **1**

OBJECTIVES

• Describe personal celebrations

• Say what people want

• Link events and ideas

CELEBRACIÓN DE MI MUNDO

¡Celebremos! En Puerto Rico, República Dominicana y Cuba hablamos de las celebraciones personales, los días festivos y las conmemoraciones históricas.

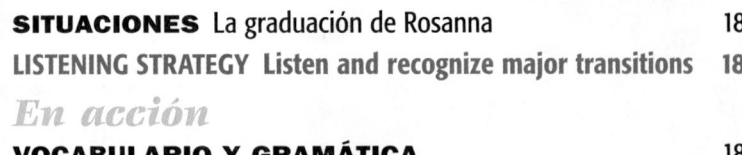

UNIDAD 3

ETAPA 2

OBJECTIVES

- Talk about holidays
- Hypothesize
- Express doubt and disagree
- Describe ideals

¡Próspero Año Nuevo! 202

UNIDAD 3

ETAPA 3

Celebraciones de patria 224

OBJECTIVES

- Describe historic events
- Make suggestions and wishes
- Express emotion and doubt
- State cause and effect

UNIDAD 4

ETAPA 1

xv

ETAPA
2

OBJECTIVES

- Talk about careers
- Confirm and deny
- Express emotions
- Hypothesize

UNIDAD 4

ETAPA 3

Un mundo de posibilidades 298

OBJECTIVES

- Learn about Latin American economics
- Clarify meaning
- Express possession
- Express past probability

xvii

UNIDAD

ARTES EN ESPAÑA Y LAS AMÉRICAS

Pasamos desde España por todo el mundo hispanohablante para explorar las artes y la creatividad.

ETAPA 1

OBJECTIVES

- Identify and specify
- Request clarification
- Express relationships
- Discuss art forms

UNIDAD 5

ETAPA 2

El Nuevo Mundo

OBJECTIVES

- Refer to people and objects
- Express relationships
- Make generalizations
- Describe arts and crafts

UNIDAD 5

ETAPA 3

UNIDAD

6

¡YA LLEGÓ EL FUTURO!

En Bolivia, Colombia, Ecuador, Perú y Venezuela investigamos ¡desde los programas de televisión hasta las computadoras e Internet!

ETAPA

1

OBJECTIVES

- Narrate in the past
- Express doubt and certainty
- Report what others say
- Talk about television

UNIDAD 6

ETAPA 2

OBJECTIVES

- Talk about technology
- State locations
- Make contrasts
- Describe unplanned events

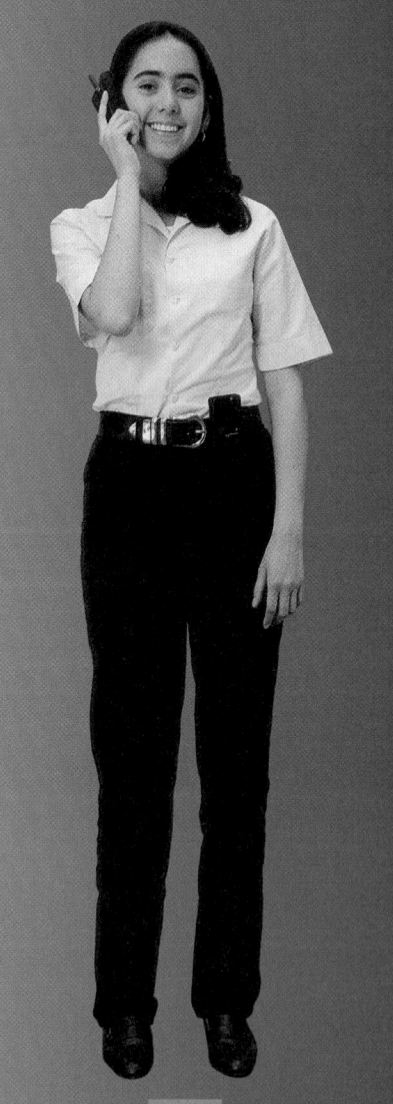

xxii

ETAPA

3

About the Authors

Estella Gahala holds a Ph.D. in Educational Administration and Curriculum from Northwestern University. A career teacher of Spanish and French, she has worked with a wide range of students at the secondary level. She has also served as foreign language department chair and district director of curriculum and instruction. Her workshops at national, regional, and state conferences as well as numerous published articles draw upon the current research in language learning, learning strategies, articulation of foreign language sequences, and implications of the national Standards for Foreign Language Learning upon curriculum, instruction, and assessment. She has coauthored nine basal textbooks.

Patricia Hamilton Carlin completed her M.A. in Spanish at the University of California, Davis, where she also taught as a lecturer. Previously she had earned a Master of Secondary Education with specialization in foreign languages from the University of Arkansas and had taught Spanish and French at levels K–12. Her secondary programs in Arkansas received national recognition. A coauthor of the *iDIME! UNO* and *iDIME! DOS* secondary textbooks, Patricia currently teaches Spanish and foreign language/ESL methodology at the University of Central Arkansas, where she coordinates the second language teacher education program. In addition, Patricia is a frequent presenter at local, regional, and national foreign language conferences.

Audrey L. Heining-Boynton received her Ph.D. in Curriculum and Instruction from Michigan State University. She is a Professor of Education and Romance Languages at The University of North Carolina at Chapel Hill, where she is a second language teacher educator and Professor of Spanish. She has also taught Spanish, French, and ESL at the K–12 level. Dr. Heining-Boynton was the president of the National Network for Early Language Learning, has been on the Executive Council of ACTFL, and involved with AATSP, Phi Delta Kappa, and state foreign language associations. She has presented both nationally and internationally, and has published over forty books, articles, and curricula.

Ricardo Otheguy received his Ph.D. in Linguistics from the City University of New York, where he is currently Professor of Linguistics at the Graduate School and University Center. He has written extensively on topics related to Spanish grammar as well as on bilingual education and the Spanish of the United States. He is coauthor of *Tu mundo: Curso para hispanohablantes,* a Spanish high school textbook for Spanish speakers, and of *Prueba de ubicación para hispanohablantes,* a high school Spanish placement test.

Barbara J. Rupert has taught Level 1 through A.P. Spanish and has implemented a FLES program in her district. She completed her M.A. at Pacific Lutheran University. Barbara is the author of CD-ROM activities for the *¡Bravo!* series and has presented at local, regional, and national foreign language conferences. She is the president of the Washington Association for Language Teaching. In 1996, Barbara received the Christa McAuliffe Award for Excellence in Education, and in 1999, she was selected Washington's "Spanish Teacher of the Year" by the Juan de Fuca Chapter of the AATSP.

Culture Consultant

Jorge A. Capetillo-Ponce is currently Assistant Professor of Sociology at University of Massachusetts, Boston, and Researcher at the Mauricio Gastón Institute for Latino Community Development and Public Policy. His graduate studies include an M.A. and a Ph.D. in Sociology from the New School for Social Research in New York City, and an M.A. in Area Studies at El Colegio de México in Mexico City. He is the editor of the book *Images of Mexico in the U.S. News Media* and has published essays on a wide range of subjects such as media, art, politics, religion, international relations, and cultural theory. Dr. Capetillo's geographical areas of expertise are Latin America, the United States, and the Middle East. During the years 2000 and 2001 he was the Executive Director of the Mexican Cultural Institute of New York. He has also worked as an advisor to politicians and public figures, as a researcher and an editor, and as a university professor and television producer in Mexico, the United States, and Central America.

Consulting Authors

Dan Battisti
Dr. Teresa Carrera-Hanley
Bill Lionetti
Patty Murguía Bohannan
Lorena Richins Layser

Senior Reviewers

O. Lynn Bolton
Dr. Jane Govoni
Elías G. Rodríguez
Ann Tollefson

Contributing Writers

Ronni L. Gordon
Christa Harris
Debra Lowry
Sylvia Madrigal Velasco
Sandra Rosenstiel
David M. Stillman
Jill K. Welch

Regional Language Reviewers

Dolores Acosta (Mexico)
Jaime M. Fatás Cabeza (Spain)
Grisel Lozano-Garcini (Puerto Rico)
Isabel Picado (Costa Rica)
Juan Pablo Rovayo (Ecuador)

Teacher Reviewers

Linda Amour
Highland High School
Bakersfield, CA

Susan Arbuckle
Mahomet-Seymour High School
Mahomet, IL

Dawne Ashton
Sequoia High School
Redwood City, CA

Sheila Bayles
Rogers High School
Rogers, AR

Warren Bender
Duluth East High School
Duluth, MN

Gail Block
Daly City, CA

Amy Brewer
Stonewall Jackson Middle School
Mechanicsville, VA

William Brill
Hollidaysburg Area Junior High School
Hollidaysburg, PA

Adrienne Chamberlain-Parris
Mariner High School
Everett, WA

Norma Coto
Bishop Moore High School
Orlando, FL

Roberto del Valle
Shorecrest High School
Shoreline, WA

Art Edwards
Canyon High School
Santa Clarita, CA

Rubén D. Elías
Roosevelt High School
Fresno, CA

José Esparza
Curie Metropolitan High School
Chicago, IL

Lorraine A. Estrada
Cabarrus County Schools
Concord, NC

Vincent Fazzolari
East Boston High School
East Boston, MA

Alberto Ferreiro
Harrisburg High School
Harrisburg, PA

Judith C. Floyd
Henry Foss High School
Tacoma, WA

Valarie L. Forster
Jefferson Davis High School
Montgomery, AL

Michael Garber
Boston Latin Academy
Boston, MA

Becky Hay de García
James Madison Memorial High School
Madison, WI

Lucy H. García
Pueblo East High School
Pueblo, CO

Marco García
Lincoln Park High School
Chicago, IL

Raquel R. González
Odessa High School
Odessa, TX

Linda Grau
Shorecrest Preparatory School
St. Petersburg, FL

Myriam Gutiérrez
John O'Bryant School
Roxbury, MA

Deborah Hagen
Ionia High School
Ionia, MI

Sandra Hammond
St. Petersburg High School
St. Petersburg, FL

Bill Heller
Perry Junior/Senior High School
Perry, NY

Joan Heller
Lake Braddock Secondary School
Burke, VA

Paula Hirsch
Windward School
Los Angeles, CA

Ann Hively
Orangevale, CA

Robert Hughes
Martha Brown Middle School
Fairport, NY

Janet King
Long Beach Polytechnic High School
Long Beach, CA

Jody Klopp
Oklahoma State Department
   of Education
Edmond, OK

Richard Ladd
Ipswich High School
Ipswich, MA

Carol Leach
Francis Scott Key High School
Union Bridge, MD

Maria Lienenweber
Cresenta Valley High School
La Cresenta, CA

Sandra Martín
Palisades Charter High School
Pacific Palisades, CA

Laura McCormick
East Seneca Senior High School
West Seneca, NY

Karen McDowell
Aptos, CA

Sue McKee
Tustin, CA

Rafaela McLeod
Southeast Raleigh High School
Raleigh, NC

Kathleen L. Michaels
Palm Harbor University High School
Palm Harbor, FL

Vickie A. Mike
Horseheads High School
Horseheads, NY

Robert Miller
Woodcreek High School
Roseville, CA

Barbara Mortanian
Tenaya Middle School
Fresno, CA

Patty Murray
Cretin-Derham Hall High School
St. Paul, MN

Linda Nanos
West Roxbury High School
West Roxbury, MA

Terri Nies
Mannford High School
Mannford, OK

María Emma Nunn
John Tyler High School
Tyler, TX

Leslie Ogden
Nordhoff High School
Ojai, CA

Teri Olsen
Alameda High School
Alameda, CA

Lewis Olvera
Hiram Johnson West Campus
   High School
Sacramento, CA

Judith Pasco
Sequim High School
Sequim, WA

Anne-Marie Quihuis
Paradise Valley High School
Phoenix, AZ

Rita Risco
Palm Harbor University High School
Palm Harbor, FL

James J. Rudy, Jr.
Glen Este High School
Cincinnati, OH

Kathleen Solórzano
Homestead High School
Mequon, WI

Margery Sotomayor
Ferndale, CA

Carol Sparks
Foothill Middle School
Walnut Creek, CA

Sarah Spiesman
Whitmer High School
Toledo, OH

M. Mercedes Stephenson
Hazelwood Central High School
Florissant, MO

Teacher Reviewers (cont.)

Carol Thorp
East Mecklenburg High School
Charlotte, NC

Elizabeth Torosian
Doherty Middle School
Andover, MA

Pamela Urdal Silva
East Lake High School
Tarpon Springs, FL

Dana Valverde
Arroyo Grande High School
Arroyo Grande, CA

Connie Vargas
Granite Hills High School
Apple Valley, CA

Wendy Villanueva
Lakeville High School
Lakeville, MN

Helen Webb
Arkadelphia High School
Arkadelphia, AR

Jena Williams
Jonesboro High School
Jonesboro, AR

Janet Wohlers
Weston Middle School
Weston, MA

Teacher Panel

Linda Amour
Highland High School
Bakersfield, CA

Jeanne Aréchiga
Northbrook High School
Houston, TX

Dena Bachman
Lafayette Senior High School
St. Joseph, MO

Sharon Barnes
J. C. Harmon High School
Kansas City, KS

Ben Barrientos
Calvin Simmons Junior High School
Oakland, CA

Paula Biggar
Sumner Academy of Arts & Science
Kansas City, KS

Hercilia Breton
Highlands High School
San Antonio, TX

Gwen Cannell
Cajon High School
San Bernardino, CA

Edda Cárdenas
Blue Valley North High School
Leawood, KS

Joyce Chow
Crespi Junior High School
Richmond, CA

Laura Cook
Evans Junior High School
Lubbock, TX

Mike Cooperider
Truman High School
Independence, MO

Judy Dozier
Shawnee Mission South High School
Shawnee Mission, KS

Maggie Elliott
Bell Junior High School
San Diego, CA

Dana Galloway-Grey
Ontario High School
Ontario, CA

Nieves Gerber
Chatsworth Senior High School
Chatsworth, CA

April Hansen
Livermore High School
Livermore, CA

Janet King
Long Beach Polytechnic High School
Long Beach, CA

Susanne Kissane
Shawnee Mission Northwest
   High School
Shawnee Mission, KS

Ann López
Pala Middle School
San Jose, CA

Beatrice Marino
Palos Verdes Peninsula High School
Rolling Hills, CA

Anna Marxson
Laguna Creek High School
Elk Grove, CA

Rudy Molina
McAllen Memorial High School
McAllen, TX

Barbara Mortanian
Tenaya Middle School
Fresno, CA

Vickie Musni
Pioneer High School
San Jose, CA

Teri Olsen
Alameda High School
Alameda, CA

Rodolfo Orihuela
C. K. McClatchy High School
Sacramento, CA

Montserrat Rey
Hightower High School
Fort Bend, TX

Terrie Rynard
Olathe South High School
Olathe, KS

Beth Slinkard
Lee's Summit High School
Lee's Summit, MO

Rosa Stein
Park Hill High School
Kansas City, MO

Melanie Tate
McLean Middle School
Fort Worth, TX

Marianne Villalobos
Modesto High School
Modesto, CA

Shannon Zerby
North Garland High School
Garland, TX

Urban Panel

Rebecca Carr
William G. Enloe High School
Raleigh, NC

Norha Franco
East Side High School
Newark, NJ

Kathryn Gardner
Riverside University High School
Milwaukee, WI

Eula Glenn
Remtec Center
Detroit, MI

Jeana Harper
Detroit Fine Arts High School
Detroit, MI

Guillermina Jauregui
Los Angeles Senior High School
Los Angeles, CA

Lula Lewis
Hyde Park Career Academy
    High School
Chicago, IL

Florence Meyers
Overbrook High School
Philadelphia, PA

Vivian Selenikas
Long Island City High School
Long Island City, NY

Sadia White
Spingarn Stay Senior High School
Washington, DC

Block Scheduling Panel

Barbara Baker
Wichita Northwest High School
Wichita, KS

Patty Banker
Lexington High School
Lexington, NC

Beverly Blackburn
Reynoldsburg Senior High School
Reynoldsburg, OH

Henry Foust
Northwood High School
Pittsboro, NC

Gloria Hawks
A. L. Brown High School
Kannapolis, NC

Lois Hillman
North Kitsap High School
Poulsbo, WA

Nick Patterson
Central High School
Davenport, IA

Sharyn Petkus
Grafton Memorial High School
Grafton, MA

Cynthia Prieto
Mount Vernon High School
Alexandria, VA

Julie Sanchez
Western High School
Fort Lauderdale, FL

Marilyn Settlemyer
Freedom High School
Morganton, NC

Student Review Board

Andrea Avila
Fannin Middle School
Amarillo, TX

Maya Beynishes
Edward R. Murrow High School
Brooklyn, NY

James Dock
Guilford High School
Rockford, IL

Richard Elkins
Nevin Platt Middle School
Boulder, CO

Kathryn Finn
Charles S. Pierce Middle School
Milton, MA

Robert Foulis
Stratford High School
Houston, TX

Lorrain García
Luther Burbank High School
Sacramento, CA

Katie Hagen
Ionia High School
Ionia, MI

Steven Hailey
Davis Drive School
Apex, NC

Eli Harel
Thomas Edison Intermediate School
Westfield, NJ

Cheryl Kim
Dr. Leo Cigarroa High School
Laredo, TX

Jennifer Kim
Kellogg Middle School
Seattle, WA

Jordan Leitner
Scripps Ranch High School
San Diego, CA

Courtney McPherson
Miramar High School
Miramar, FL

Zachary Nelson
Warsaw Community High School
Warsaw, IN

Diana Parrish
Oak Crest Junior High School
Encinitas, CA

Kimberly Robinson
Perryville Senior High School
Perryville, AR

John Roland
Mountain Pointe High School
Phoenix, AZ

Nichole Ryan
Bermudian Springs High School
York Springs, PA

Ryan Shore
West Miami Middle School
Miami, FL

Tiffany Stadler
Titusville High School
Titusville, FL

Michael Szymanski
West Seneca East High School
West Seneca, NY

Anela Talic
Soldan International Studies
    High School
St. Louis, MO

Gary Thompson
Fort Dorchester High School
Charleston, SC

Bethany Traynor
Glen Este High School
Cincinnati, OH

Gerard White
Paramount High School
Paramount, CA

Nichols Wilson
Waubonsie Valley High School
Aurora, IL

Amy Wyron
Robert Frost Intermediate School
Rockville, MD

Karina Zepeda
West Mecklenburg High School
Charlotte, NC

El español en Estados Unidos

Un resumen
Desde la llegada de los exploradores europeos hasta nuestros días, los pueblos hispanohablantes han constituido una parte integral de la historia y cultura de Estados Unidos. Éstas son algunas de las importantes maneras en que los hispanohablantes han contribuido con la identidad de nuestro país.

1565

El explorador español **Pedro Menéndez de Avilés** funda **San Agustín,** la colonia europea más antigua en lo que hoy es el territorio de Estados Unidos. En 1821 los españoles cedieron su territorio cuando **Florida** pasó a ser parte de Estados Unidos.

1500　　　**1600**　　　**1700**　　　**1800**

1609–1610

Los españoles fundan la ciudad de **Santa Fe** en lo que hoy es el territorio de **Nuevo México.** Santa Fe perteneció a México y más tarde a Estados Unidos. Allí se encuentra **el Palacio de los Gobernadores**, el edificio de gobierno más antiguo que se conoce en Estados Unidos.

1797

Se termina de construir **la misión San Xavier del Bac** cerca de **Tucson, Arizona.** La arquitectura de su iglesia muestra la influencia de los estilos morisco, bizantino y mexicano.

2000

Todos los años, en el mes de septiembre, se celebra en la ciudad de **Chicago** el **Día de la Independencia de México.** Durante este desfile se puede disfrutar de un gran colorido, ropas típicas y música tradicional mexicana. La comunidad mexicana de Chicago se formó cuando los trabajadores migraron al norte para

trabajar en esta importante zona industrial. Año tras año y hasta el día de hoy, este festival representa el orgullo que los mexicanos tienen por su cultura.

1962–1972

En 1962, **César Chávez** funda el sindicato "United Farm Workers" con el objeto de mejorar las condiciones de trabajo de los campesinos. En 1965 organiza una importante huelga que benefició a los trabajadores de **California.** Gracias a su trabajo por los derechos civiles se convirtió en uno de los líderes chicanos más respetados.

1900

2000

1969

Se funda **el Museo del Barrio** a cargo de personalidades puertorriqueñas. Este museo no sólo presenta el arte de Puerto Rico sino también de otros países latinoamericanos. Se encuentra ubicado en la Quinta Avenida de la ciudad de **Nueva York.**

1938

Se realizan los primeros **Días del Charro** en **Brownsville, Texas,** celebrando a los vaqueros mexicanos. En la actualidad, este festival incluye desfiles, danzas, mariachis y rodeos. También se reúnen los alcaldes de Brownsville y de Matamoros (México).

Cómo estudiar el español

Puedes usar lo que ya sabes y aprender cosas nuevas con estas partes de tu libro.

Estrategias
Tu libro te da la oportunidad de practicar estas estrategias:

Para escuchar: te preparan para escuchar y entender.

Para conversar: te ayudan a expresarte en español.

Para leer: te ayudan a leer los pasajes del libro.

Para escribir: son para mejorar tu habilidad de escribir.

Para comparar: te ayudan a comparar culturas.

STRATEGY: SPEAKING

Gain thinking time before speaking Sometimes ideas do notcome to us as quickly as we would like. One way to gain time is to restate what was just said which may in turn trigger a fresh idea. Example: **Sí, es una lástima. Espero que se proteja la selva también.**

El Apoyo para estudiar
Esta sección te sugiere ideas para estudiar el español más efectiva y eficientemente.

Apoyo para estudiar

Negative command
Remember that in a negative command, object pronouns precede the verb. So you can advise against an action (**¡No se la compre!**), but you should give a reason why (**porque ella prefiere la poesía**).

Siente más seguridad
Recuerda y aprende información nueva mediante **Repaso** y **Gramática**. **Repaso** presenta lo que aprendiste en los Niveles 1 y 2 y **Gramática** es información nueva. La combinación de palabras y gráficas facilitan el aprendizaje de todos los estudiantes.

REPASO — Preterite vs. Imperfect

 ¿RECUERDAS? *p. 42* You already know two tenses that refer to past time, the preterite and the imperfect. You use each of these tenses to talk about **past** actions in a different way.

- Use the preterite tense to describe an action or series of actions completed in the past.

   Aquel día, Pedro salió del colegio y caminó hasta el café.

   *That day, Pedro **left** school and **walked** to the café.*

Practice:
Actividades
12 13 14 15

Más práctica
cuaderno pp. 19
Para hispanohablantes
cuaderno pp. 15–16

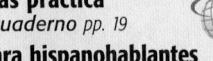 **Online Workbook** CLASSZONE.COM

GRAMÁTICA — The Imperfect Subjunctive

You already know the present and present perfect **subjunctive.** There are also past forms of the subjunctive. Use the imperfect subjunctive instead of the present subjunctive when the context of the sentence is in the past. Compare the following pairs of sentences.

Present context
   Los padrinos quieren que felicitemos al graduando.

   *The godparents **want** us to **congratulate** the graduate.*

Past context
   Los padrinos querían que felicitáramos al graduando.

   *The godparents **wanted** us to **congratulate** the graduate.*

Practice:
Actividades
11 12 13 14

Más práctica
cuaderno pp. 71–72
Para hispanohablantes
cuaderno pp. 69–70

Online Workbook CLASSZONE.COM

Leer y escuchar el español

Lee para aprender palabras nuevas en español.

La sección **En contexto** presenta
vocabulario nuevo en un contexto
real e interesante.

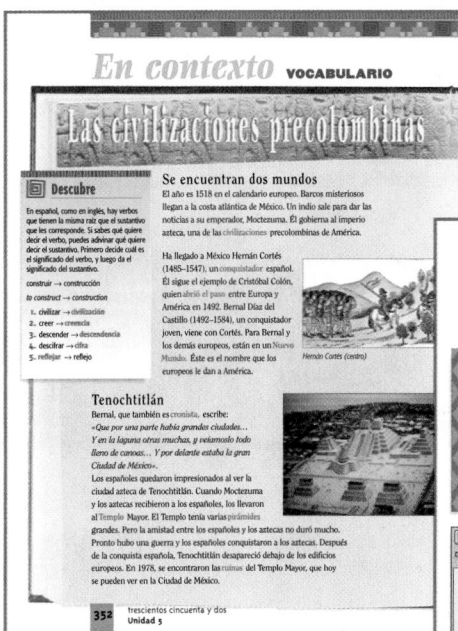

Escucha el español para aprender palabras
nuevas y aplicarlas a un contexto real.
En vivo te prepara para escuchar y entender
un pasaje oral con actividades que aparecen
antes, durante y después de escuchar.

La sección **Descubre** te
enseña palabras y expresiones
nuevas a través de claves
gráficas y textuales.

Descubre

En español, como en inglés, hay verbos
que tienen la misma raíz que el sustantivo
que les corresponde. Si sabes qué quiere
decir el verbo, puedes adivinar qué quiere
decir el sustantivo. Primero decide cuál es
el significado del verbo, y luego da el
significado del sustantivo.

construir → construcción

to construct → construction

1. civilizar → **civilización**
2. creer → **creencia**
3. descender → **descendencia**
4. descifrar → **cifra**
5. **reflejar** → reflejo

¡Diviértete!

Aprender otro idioma puede ser divertido e interesante. Como ya
sabes mucho español, puedes expresarte mejor y comunicarte con
tus compañeros de clase a través de las actividades de tu libro.
Tienes todas las herramientas que necesitas; ¡aprende y disfruta!

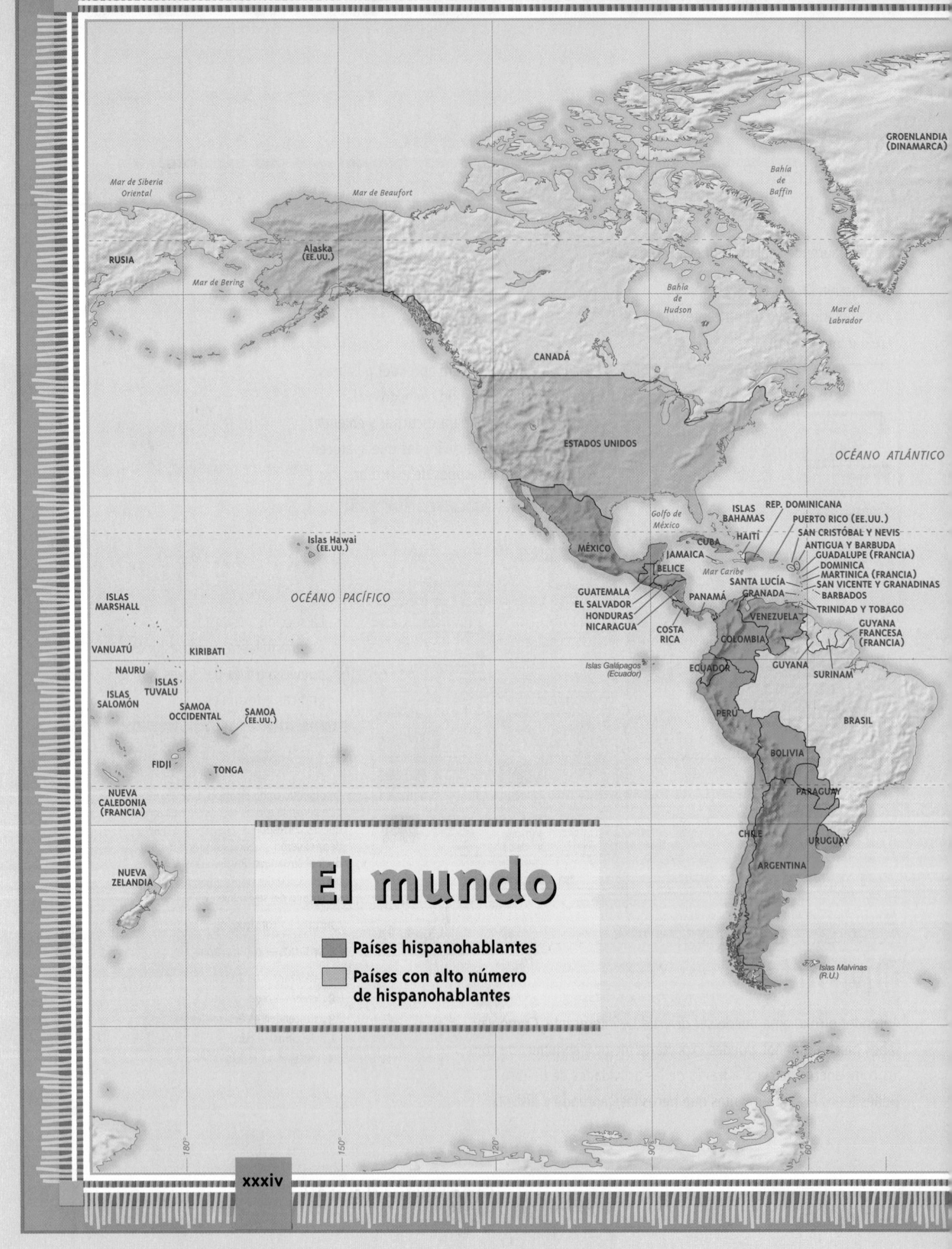

RUSIA

Mar de Siberia Oriental

Mar de Beaufort

Alaska (EE.UU.)

Mar de Bering

GROENLANDIA (DINAMARCA)

Bahía de Baffin

CANADÁ

Bahía de Hudson

Mar del Labrador

ESTADOS UNIDOS

OCÉANO ATLÁNTICO

Golfo de México

Islas Hawai (EE.UU.)

MÉXICO

ISLAS BAHAMAS

CUBA

HAITÍ

REP. DOMINICANA

PUERTO RICO (EE.UU.)

SAN CRISTÓBAL Y NEVIS

ANTIGUA Y BARBUDA

GUADALUPE (FRANCIA)

DOMINICA

MARTINICA (FRANCIA)

SAN VICENTE Y GRANADINAS

BARBADOS

TRINIDAD Y TOBAGO

JAMAICA

BELICE

Mar Caribe

SANTA LUCÍA

GRANADA

GUATEMALA

EL SALVADOR

HONDURAS

NICARAGUA

COSTA RICA

PANAMÁ

VENEZUELA

COLOMBIA

GUYANA

GUYANA FRANCESA (FRANCIA)

SURINAM

Islas Galápagos (Ecuador)

ECUADOR

PERÚ

BRASIL

BOLIVIA

PARAGUAY

CHILE

URUGUAY

ARGENTINA

Islas Malvinas (R.U.)

OCÉANO PACÍFICO

ISLAS MARSHALL

VANUATÚ

KIRIBATI

NAURU

ISLAS TUVALU

ISLAS SALOMÓN

SAMOA OCCIDENTAL

SAMOA (EE.UU.)

FIDJI

TONGA

NUEVA CALEDONIA (FRANCIA)

NUEVA ZELANDIA

El mundo

◼ Países hispanohablantes

◼ Países con alto número de hispanohablantes

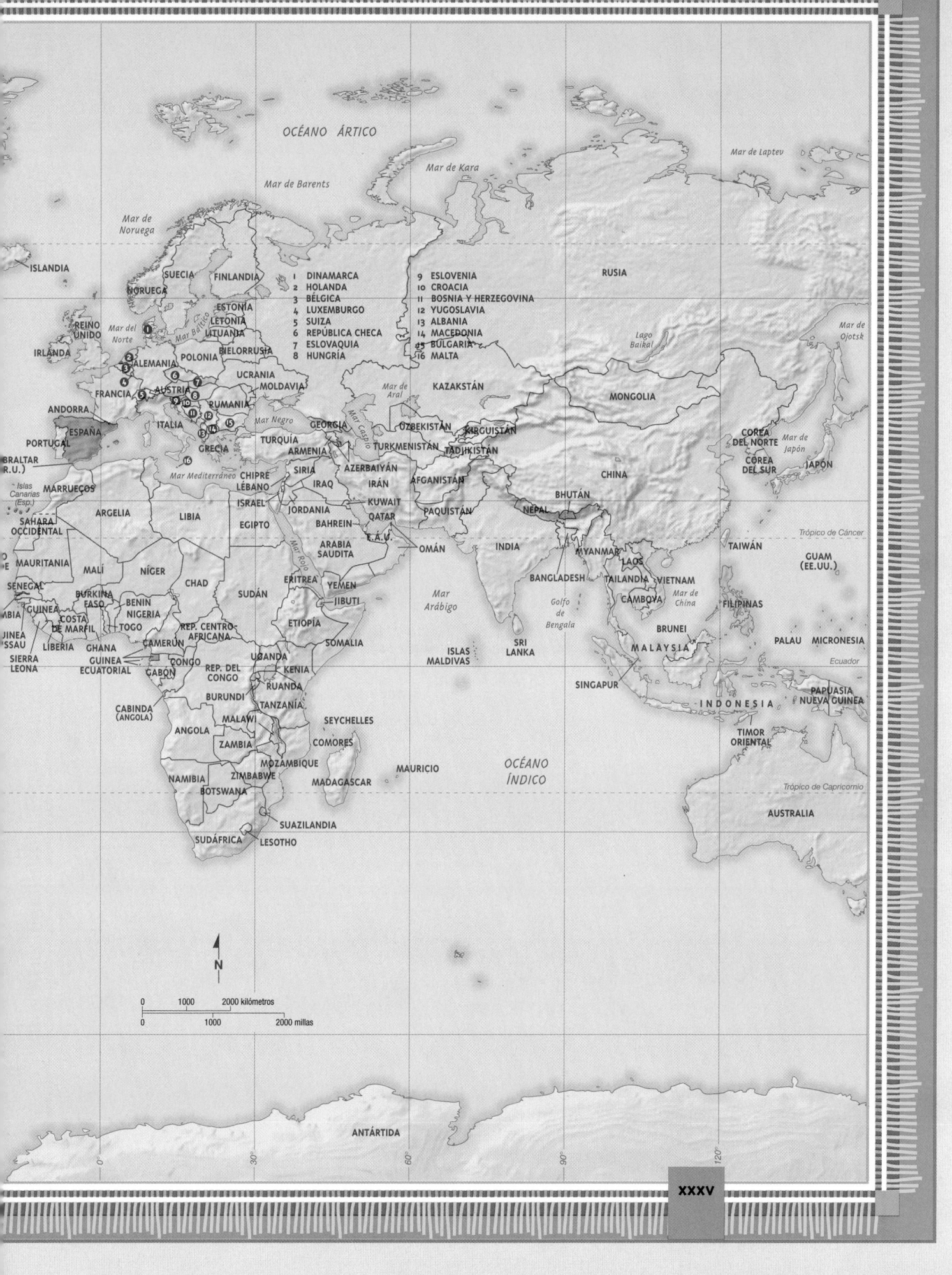

OCÉANO ÁRTICO

Mar de Laptev

Mar de Kara

Mar de Barents

Mar de Noruega

ISLANDIA

SUECIA   FINLANDIA   1 DINAMARCA   9 ESLOVENIA
NORUEGA   2 HOLANDA   10 CROACIA   RUSIA
                               3 BÉLGICA   11 BOSNIA Y HERZEGOVINA
              ESTONIA   4 LUXEMBURGO   12 YUGOSLAVIA
REINO   LETONIA   5 SUIZA   13 ALBANIA
UNIDO   Mar del LITUANIA   6 REPÚBLICA CHECA 14 MACEDONIA   Mar de
         Norte   7 ESLOVAQUIA   15 BULGARIA   Ojotsk
IRLANDA   ALEMANIA POLONIA 8 HUNGRÍA   16 MALTA
                                                          Lago
                  BIELORRUSIA   Baikal
FRANCIA   AUSTRIA UCRANIA
                   MOLDAVIA   Mar de   KAZAKSTÁN   MONGOLIA
ANDORRA   RUMANIA   Aral   COREA
                                        UZBEKISTÁN KIRGUISTÁN   DEL NORTE Mar de
                  ITALIA   Mar Negro GEORGIA TURKMENISTÁN TADJIKISTÁN   Japón
ESPAÑA   COREA JAPÓN
PORTUGAL   GRECIA TURQUÍA ARMENIA   CHINA   DEL SUR
BRALTAR   AZERBAIYÁN AFGANISTÁN
R.U.)   Mar Mediterráneo CHIPRE SIRIA
 Islas   LÍBANO IRAK   IRÁN
Canarias MARRUECOS   ISRAEL   KUWAIT   PAQUISTÁN NEPAL BHUTÁN
(Esp.)   JORDANIA QATAR   Trópico de Cáncer
SAHARA   ARGELIA LIBIA   EGIPTO BAHREIN   TAIWÁN
OCCIDENTAL   E.A.U.   INDIA   MYANMAR   GUAM
MAURITANIA MALÍ NÍGER   ARABIA OMÁN   BANGLADESH LAOS   (EE.UU.)
                          SAUDITA   Mar   TAILANDIA VIETNAM
SENEGAL BURKINA CHAD   ERITREA YEMEN   Arábigo   CAMBOYA Mar de FILIPINAS
         FASO BENIN   SUDÁN   JIBUTI   China
ABIA   NIGERIA   ETIOPÍA   Golfo   BRUNEI
GUINEA COSTA TOGO   de   PALAU MICRONESIA
JINEA   DE MARFIL REP. CENTRO-   SOMALIA   Bengala SRI   MALAYSIA
SSAU   GHANA CAMERÚN AFRICANA   ISLAS   LANKA   Ecuador
SIERRA GUINEA   UGANDA   MALDIVAS   PAPUASIA
LEONA   ECUATORIAL GABÓN KENIA   NUEVA GUINEA
LIBERIA   REP. DEL RUANDA   SINGAPUR   INDONESIA
        CABINDA   CONGO   BURUNDI   TIMOR
        (ANGOLA)   TANZANÍA   ORIENTAL
        ANGOLA MALAWI   SEYCHELLES
                ZAMBIA   COMORES
        NAMIBIA ZIMBABWE MOZAMBIQUE MAURICIO   OCÉANO
                BOTSWANA MADAGASCAR   ÍNDICO   Trópico de Capricornio
                                                                      AUSTRALIA
                SUAZILANDIA
        SUDÁFRICA LESOTHO

N

0   1000   2000 kilómetros
0   1000   2000 millas

ANTÁRTIDA

30°   60°   90°   120°

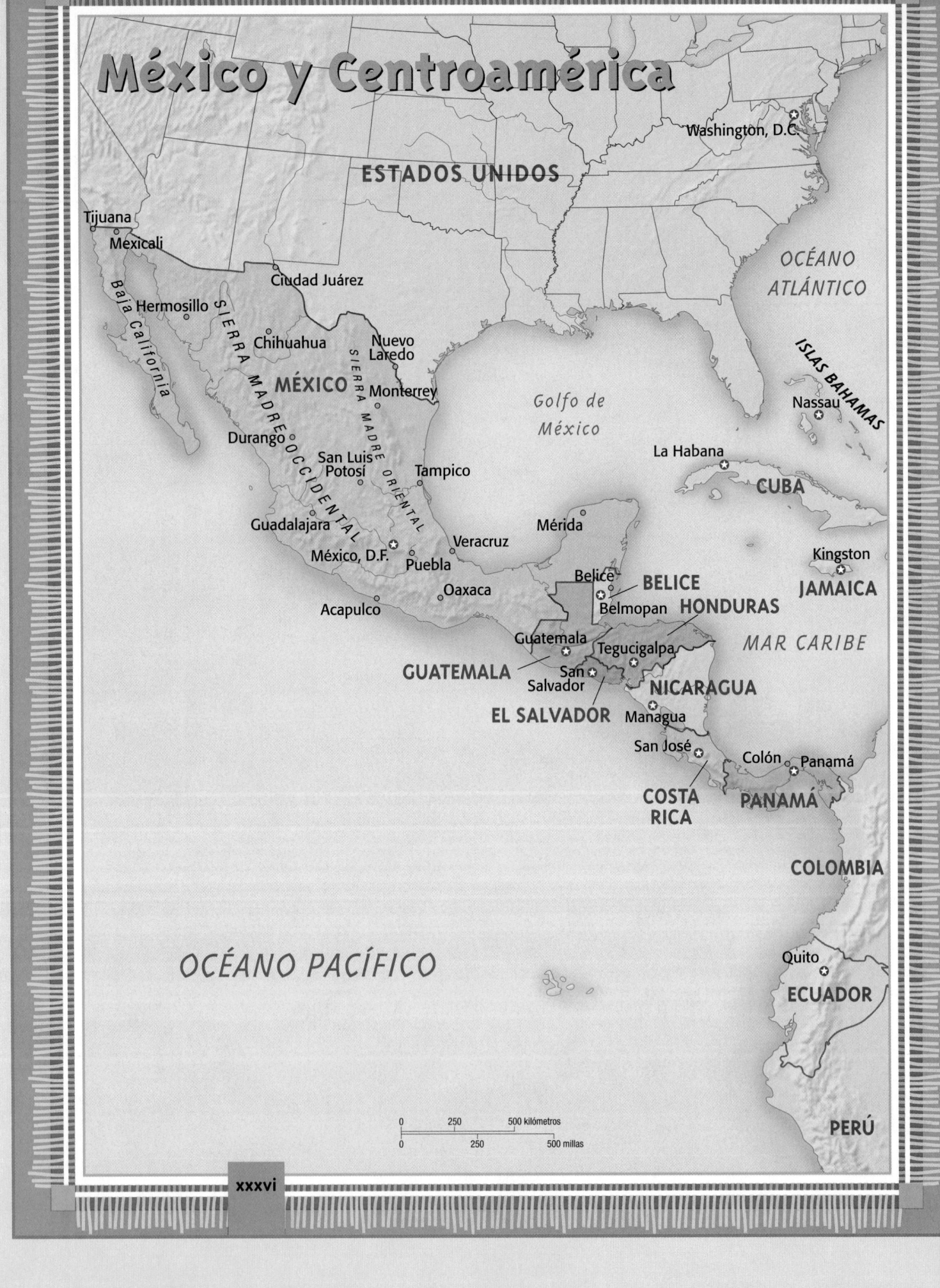

México y Centroamérica

ESTADOS UNIDOS

Washington, D.C.

Tijuana
Mexicali
Ciudad Juárez
Hermosillo
SIERRA MADRE OCCIDENTAL
Chihuahua
Nuevo Laredo
MÉXICO
Monterrey
SIERRA MADRE ORIENTAL
Durango
Baja California
San Luis Potosí
Tampico
Guadalajara
Veracruz
México, D.F.
Puebla
Oaxaca
Acapulco

OCÉANO ATLÁNTICO

Golfo de México

ISLAS BAHAMAS
Nassau

La Habana
CUBA

Mérida

Kingston
JAMAICA

Belice
BELICE
Belmopan
HONDURAS
Guatemala
GUATEMALA
Tegucigalpa
San Salvador
EL SALVADOR
Managua
San José
COSTA RICA

MAR CARIBE

NICARAGUA

Colón
Panamá
PANAMÁ

COLOMBIA

OCÉANO PACÍFICO

Quito
ECUADOR

PERÚ

0   250   500 kilómetros
0   250   500 millas

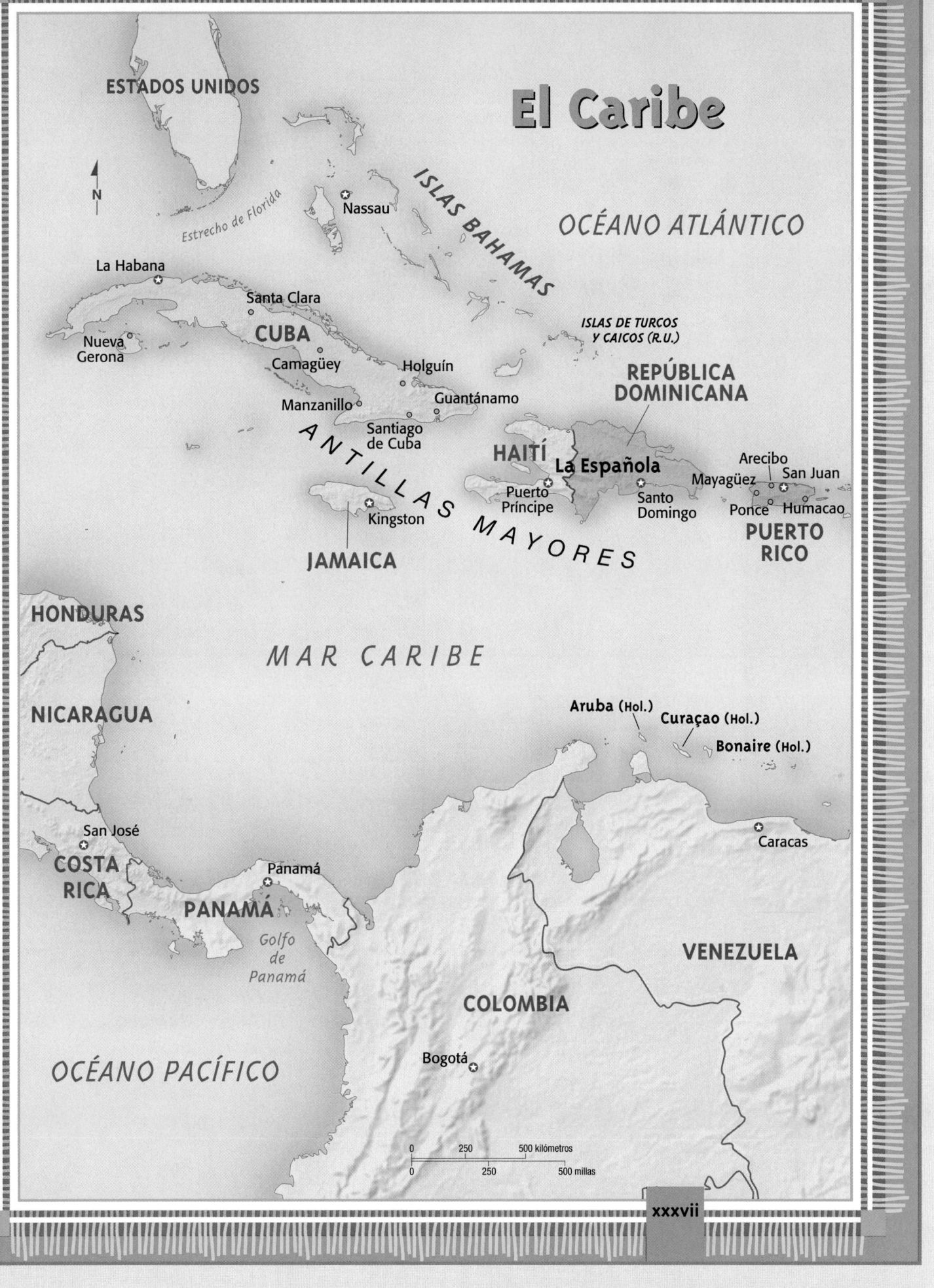

El Caribe

ESTADOS UNIDOS

Estrecho de Florida

Nassau

ISLAS BAHAMAS

OCÉANO ATLÁNTICO

La Habana

Santa Clara

CUBA

Nueva Gerona

Camagüey

Holguín

Manzanillo

Guantánamo

Santiago de Cuba

ISLAS DE TURCOS Y CAICOS (R.U.)

REPÚBLICA DOMINICANA

HAITÍ

La Española

Arecibo

San Juan

Mayagüez

Puerto Príncipe

Santo Domingo

Ponce

Humacao

PUERTO RICO

ANTILLAS MAYORES

Kingston

JAMAICA

HONDURAS

MAR CARIBE

NICARAGUA

Aruba (Hol.)

Curaçao (Hol.)

Bonaire (Hol.)

San José

Caracas

COSTA RICA

Panamá

PANAMÁ

Golfo de Panamá

VENEZUELA

COLOMBIA

Bogotá

OCÉANO PACÍFICO

| 0 | 250 | 500 kilómetros |
| 0 | 250 | 500 millas |

xxxvii

xxxvii

Sudamérica

MAR CARIBE

OCÉANO ATLÁNTICO

Barranquilla
Cartagena
Maracaibo
Lago Maracaibo
Caracas
TRINIDAD Y TOBAGO
Puerto España

VENEZUELA

Medellín
Manizales
Bogotá
COLOMBIA
Cali

Georgetown
Paramaribo
GUYANA
SURINAM
Cayena
GUYANA FRANCESA (FRANCIA)

Ecuador

Otavalo
Quito
ECUADOR
Guayaquil
Cuenca

Río Negro
Río Amazonas

Río Madeira
Río Tapajóz
Río Xingú
Río Tocantins

PERÚ

Trujillo
Lima
Callao

CORDILLERA

BRASIL

Río São Francisco

Lago Titicaca
BOLIVIA
La Paz
Cochabamba
Santa Cruz
Sucre

Brasilia

GRAN CHACO
PARAGUAY
Asunción

Trópico de Capricornio

Salta
San Miguel de Tucumán
Resistencia

CHILE

Córdoba

Valparaíso
Mendoza
Rosario
URUGUAY

Santiago
Buenos Aires
La Plata
Montevideo

OCÉANO PACÍFICO

ARGENTINA

Concepción

PAMPAS

Bahía Blanca
Mar del Plata

Temuco

ANDES

PATAGONIA

OCÉANO ATLÁNTICO

Estrecho de Magallanes

Tierra del Fuego

Islas Malvinas (R.U.)

Cabo de Hornos

Inset map:

Islas Galápagos (Ecuador)

Bogotá
COLOMBIA
Quito
ECUADOR
PERÚ

OCÉANO PACÍFICO

0   250 kilómetros
0   250 millas

Scale:

0   250   500 kilómetros
0   250   500 millas

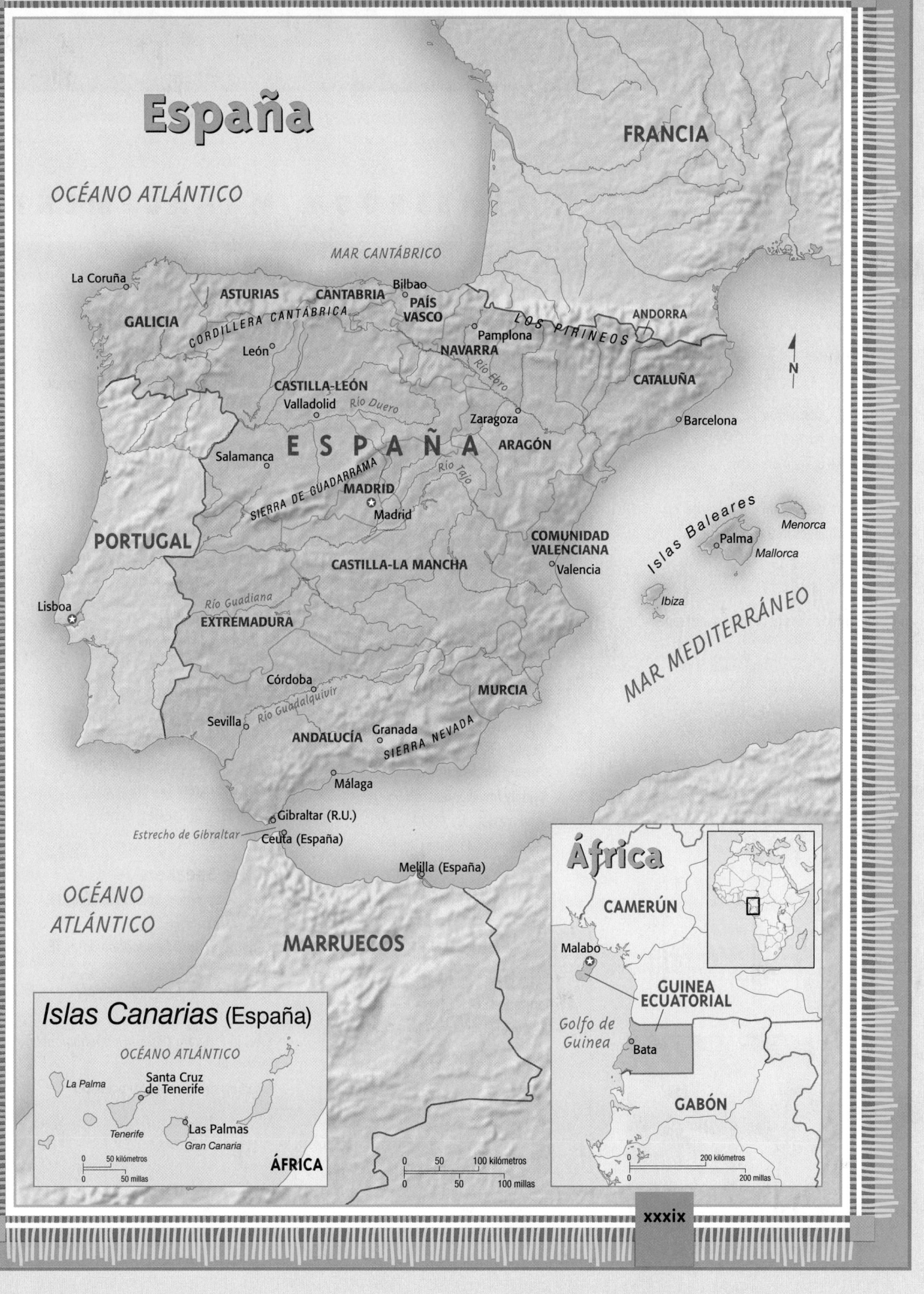

España

FRANCIA

OCÉANO ATLÁNTICO

MAR CANTÁBRICO

La Coruña

ASTURIAS   CANTABRIA   Bilbao
GALICIA   PAÍS
                         VASCO
                                        LOS PIRINEOS   ANDORRA
CORDILLERA CANTÁBRICA
                         Pamplona
León   NAVARRA   CATALUÑA
                                    Río Ebro
CASTILLA-LEÓN
Valladolid   Río Duero
                         Zaragoza   Barcelona
Salamanca   E S P A Ñ A   ARAGÓN

                Río Tajo
SIERRA DE GUADARRAMA
            MADRID   Islas Baleares   Menorca
            Madrid   Palma
PORTUGAL   COMUNIDAD   Mallorca
                                            VALENCIANA
                    CASTILLA-LA MANCHA   Valencia
                                                                Ibiza
            Río Guadiana
Lisboa   MAR MEDITERRÁNEO
            EXTREMADURA

            Córdoba
                                            MURCIA
            Río Guadalquivir
Sevilla
            ANDALUCÍA   Granada
                         SIERRA NEVADA
            Málaga

            Gibraltar (R.U.)
Estrecho de Gibraltar
            Ceuta (España)

                    Melilla (España)

OCÉANO
ATLÁNTICO   **África**

            MARRUECOS   CAMERÚN

                                            Malabo
                                                    GUINEA
                                                    ECUATORIAL
                                            Golfo de
                                            Guinea   Bata

Islas Canarias (España)

OCÉANO ATLÁNTICO

La Palma
            Santa Cruz
            de Tenerife

    Tenerife
                Las Palmas
                Gran Canaria

0   50 kilómetros   0   50   100 kilómetros   GABÓN
0   50 millas   ÁFRICA 0   50   100 millas   0   200 kilómetros
                                                       0   200 millas

Planning Guide CLASSROOM MANAGEMENT

OBJECTIVES

Communication
- Talk about present activities *pp. 4–5, 8–9*
- Talk about past activities *pp. 12–13, 16–17, 20–21, 24–25*

Grammar
- Review: Present tense of regular verbs *pp. 4–5*
- Review: Irregular **yo** forms *pp. 8–9*
- Review: The preterite tense of regular verbs *pp. 12–13*
- Review: Verbs with spelling changes in the preterite *pp. 16–17*
- Review: Verbs with stem changes in the preterite *pp. 20–21*
- Review: Irregular preterites *pp. 24–25*

Culture
- The cultural and geographic diversity of the Spanish-speaking world *p. xxxiv–1*
- The Spanish-speaking community in the United States *pp. 2–3*
- Mexico and Central America *pp. 6–7*
- The Spanish-speaking Caribbean *pp. 10–11*
- El Cono Sur *pp. 14–15*
- Spain *pp. 18–19*
- Bolivia, Colombia, Ecuador, Perú y Venezuela *pp. 22–23*

PROGRAM RESOURCES

 Print
- *Más práctica* Workbook PE *pp. 1–10*
- *Actividades para todos* Workbook PE *pp. 1–10*
- Block Scheduling Copymasters *pp. 1–10*
- Back to School Pack,
  Family Letter *p. vii*
  Diagnostic Placement Test *pp. ix–8*
  Practice Activities *pp. 11–34*
  Más práctica Workbook TE *pp. 35–44*
  Actividades para todos Workbook TE *pp. 45–54*
  Cuaderno para hispanohablantes TE *pp. 55–64*
  Information Gap Activities *pp. 65–68*
  Absent Student Copymasters *pp. 69–74*
  Family Involvement *pp. 75–76*
  Audioscript *pp. 77–79*
  Assessment Program, Etapa preliminar *pp. 81–101*
  Answer Keys *pp. 102–106*

 Audiovisual
- Audio Program CD 1
- *Canciones* CD
- Overhead Transparencies M1–M5; 1–21

 Technology
- eEdition Plus Online/eEdition CD-ROM
- Easy Planner Plus Online/Easy Planner CD-ROM
- eTest Plus Online/Test Generator CD-ROM
- Online Workbook
- www.classzone.com

Assessment Program Options
- Back to School Pack
  Diagnostic Placement Test
  Grammar Quizzes
  Etapa Exam Forms A and B
  Examen para hispanohablantes
  Portfolio Assessment
  Multiple Choice Test Questions
- Audio Program CD 19
- eTest Plus Online/Test Generator CD-ROM

Native Speakers
- *Cuaderno para hispanohablantes* PE *pp. 1–10*
- *Cuaderno para hispanohablantes* TE (Back to School Pack)
- *Examen para hispanohablantes* (Back to School Pack)
- Audio Program *(Para hispanohablantes)* CD 1, 19
- Audioscript (Back to School Pack)

Student Text
Listening Activity Scripts

ACTIVIDAD 7 — ¡Pobre Adriana! *page 12*

Ayer tuve un día horrible. Primero, no sonó el despertador así que me desperté muy tarde. No planché la ropa la noche anterior como de costumbre así que me tuve que poner ropa arrugada. Salí de casa como loca. Después de las clases, trabajé dos horas en la tienda de mi tío. Porque tenía prisa, perdí la tarea. Regresé a casa tan cansada que no cené. Cuando revisé la mochila, vi que no tenía el libro, así que no estudié para el examen de hoy. Me acosté temprano. Espero que hoy vaya mejor, después de comprar el café.

ACTIVIDAD 19 — Irma y Javier *page 25*

Irma:	Anduve por todo el centro comercial buscándote. ¿Adónde fuiste?
Javier:	Estuve en la tienda de música un rato y entonces fui a la tienda de deportes.
Irma:	Nos pusimos de acuerdo, ¿no te acuerdas? Íbamos a encontrarnos a las doce en la cafetería.
Javier:	¡Perdona! Se me olvidó. ¿Hiciste las compras que querías hacer?
Irma:	Sí. Pude encontrar todo lo que tenía en la lista.
Javier:	Yo tuve que ir al banco. Se me acabó todo el dinero.
Irma:	¿No trajiste tu tarjeta de crédito?
Javier:	No, no la traje.
Irma:	¿Sabes a quién vi?
Javier:	No, ¿a quién?
Irma:	A tus amigos Marín y Lupita.
Javier:	¿Ah, sí? ¿Qué hacían?
Irma:	Dijeron que vinieron a comprar una computadora.
Javier:	¿De veras? Qué bueno. Necesitan una nueva.

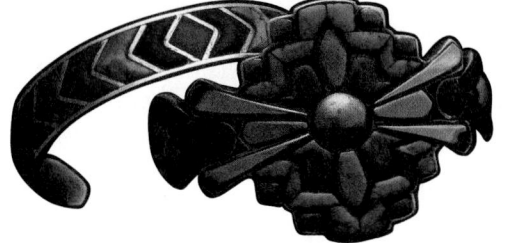

Pacing Guide

Sample Lesson Plan - 50 Minute Schedule

DAY 1

Etapa Opener
- Quick Start Review (TE, p. xl) 5 MIN.
- Use OHT P2 to present the culture notes. Use Map OHTs as needed. 5 MIN.

Estados Unidos
- Quick Start Review (TE, p. 2) 5 MIN.
- Have students read and discuss *Nuestra cultura e historia* on pp. 2–3. 15 MIN.

En acción: Vocabulario y gramática
- Quick Start Review (TE, p. 4) 5 MIN.
- Present *Repaso:* Present Tense of Regular Verbs, p. 4. 5 MIN.
- Have students complete *Actividades* 1 and 2 in pairs. 10 MIN.

Homework Option:
- Have students write 10 true/false statements on the *Etapa* Opener and *Estados Unidos.*

DAY 2

En acción (cont.)
- Check homework. 5 MIN.
- Have students complete *Actividad* 3 in groups. 5 MIN.

México y Centroamérica
- Quick Start Review (TE, p. 6) 5 MIN.
- Have students read and discuss *México y Centroamérica* on pp. 6–7. 15 MIN.

En acción: Vocabulario y gramática
- Present *Repaso:* Irregular *yo* Forms, p. 8. 5 MIN.
- Have students complete *Actividad* 4 orally. 5 MIN.
- Have students complete *Actividad* 5 in writing. Go over answers orally. 5 MIN.
- Have students complete *Actividad* 6 in pairs. 5 MIN.

Homework Option:
- *Más práctica* Workbook, pp. 1–3. *Cuaderno para hispanohablantes,* pp. 1–3.

DAY 3

El Caribe
- Check homework. 5 MIN.
- Quick Start Review (TE, p. 10) 5 MIN.
- Have students read and discuss *El Caribe* on pp. 10–11. 15 MIN.

En acción: Vocabulario y gramática
- Quick Start Review (TE, p. 12) 5 MIN.
- Present *Repaso:* The Preterite Tense of Regular Verbs, p. 12. 5 MIN.
- Play the audio; do *Actividad* 7. 5 MIN.
- Have students complete *Actividad* 8 orally. 5 MIN.
- Have students complete *Actividad* 9 in pairs. 5 MIN.

Homework Option:
- Have students complete *Actividades* 8 and 9 in writing.
- *Más práctica* Workbook, p. 4. *Cuaderno para hispanohablantes,* p. 4.

DAY 4

En acción (cont.)
- Check homework. 5 MIN.
- Have students complete *Actividad* 10 in pairs. Expand using Information Gap Activities, Back to School Pack, p. 65; *Más comunicación,* p. R2. 10 MIN.

El Cono Sur
- Quick Start Review (TE, p. 14) 5 MIN.
- Have students read and discuss *El Cono Sur* on pp. 14–15. 15 MIN.

En acción: Vocabulario y gramática
- Quick Start Review (TE, p. 16) 5 MIN.
- Present *Repaso:* Verbs with Spelling Changes in the Preterite, p. 16. 5 MIN.
- Have students complete *Actividad* 11 in pairs. 5 MIN.

Homework Option:
- Have students complete *Actividad* 11 in writing. *Más práctica* Workbook, pp. 5–6. *Cuaderno para hispanohablantes,* pp. 5–6.

DAY 5

En acción (cont.)
- Check homework. 5 MIN.
- Have students complete *Actividades* 12 and 13 in writing. Have students exchange papers for peer correction. 10 MIN.
- Do *Actividad* 14 in pairs. 5 MIN.

España
- Have students read and discuss *España* on pp. 18–19. 10 MIN.

En acción: Vocabulario y gramática
- Quick Start Review (TE, p. 20) 5 MIN.
- Present *Repaso:* Verbs with Stem Changes in the Preterite, p. 20. 5 MIN.
- Have students complete *Actividad* 15 in writing and *Actividad* 16 in pairs. 10 MIN.

Homework Option:
- *Más práctica* Workbook, pp. 7–8. *Cuaderno para hispanohablantes,* pp. 7–8.

DAY 6

En acción (cont.)
- Check homework. 5 MIN.
- Have students complete *Actividades* 17 and 18 in pairs. 10 MIN.

Bolivia, Colombia,...
- Quick Start Review (TE, p. 22) 5 MIN.
- Have students read and discuss *Bolivia, Colombia,...* on pp. 22–23. 10 MIN.

En acción: Vocabulario y gramática
- Quick Start Review (TE, p. 24) 5 MIN.
- Present *Repaso:* Irregular Preterites, p. 24. 5 MIN.
- Play the audio; do *Actividad* 19. 5 MIN.
- Have students complete *Actividad* 20 in pairs. 5 MIN.

Homework Option:
- *Más práctica* Workbook, pp. 9–10. *Cuaderno para hispanohablantes,* pp. 9–10.

DAY 7

En acción (cont.)
- Check homework. 5 MIN.
- Have students complete *Actividad* 21 in groups. *Más comunicación,* p. R2. 15 MIN.

En uso: Repaso y más comunicación
- Quick Start Review (TE, p. 26) 5 MIN.
- Present the *Repaso y más comunicación* using the Teaching Suggestions (TE, p. 26). 5 MIN.
- Have students do *Actividad* 1 in pairs. 10 MIN.
- Do *Actividad* 2 in pairs or groups. 10 MIN.

Homework Option:
- Review for *Etapa preliminar* Exam.
- *Actividades para todos Workbook,* pp. 1–10.

DAY 8

En tu propia voz: Escritura
- Check homework. 5 MIN.
- Do *Actividad* 3 in writing. Ask volunteers to present their descriptions. 10 MIN.

En resumen: Repaso de vocabulario
- Quick Start Review (TE, p. 27) 5 MIN.
- Review grammar questions, etc., as necessary. 10 MIN.
- Administer *Etapa preliminar* Exam. 20 MIN.

Homework Option:
- Preview *Unidad 1* Opener. Have students jot down their observations.

Sample Lesson Plan - Block Schedule (90 minutes)

DAY 1

Etapa Opener
- Quick Start Review (TE, p. xl) 5 MIN.
- Use OHT P2 to present the culture notes. Use Map OHTs as needed. 10 MIN.
- Use Block Scheduling Copymasters. 10 MIN.

Estados Unidos
- Quick Start Review (TE, p. 2) 5 MIN.
- Have students read and discuss *Nuestra cultura e historia* on pp. 2–3. 15 MIN.

En acción: Vocabulario y gramática
- Quick Start Review (TE, p. 4) 5 MIN.
- Present *Repaso:* Present Tense of Regular Verbs, p. 4. 5 MIN.
- Have students complete *Actividades* 1 and 2 in pairs. 10 MIN.
- Have students complete *Actividad* 3 in groups. 5 MIN.

México y Centroamérica
- Quick Start Review (TE, p. 6) 5 MIN.
- Have students read and discuss *México y Centroamérica* on pp. 6–7. 15 MIN.

Homework Option:
- *Más práctica* Workbook, p. 1. *Cuaderno para hispanohablantes,* p. 1.

DAY 2

En acción: Vocabulario y gramática
- Check homework. 5 MIN.
- Quick Start Review (TE, p. 8) 5 MIN.
- Present *Repaso:* Irregular *yo* Forms, p. 8. 5 MIN.
- Have students complete *Actividad* 4 orally. 5 MIN.
- Have students complete *Actividad* 5 in writing. Go over answers orally. 5 MIN.
- Have students complete *Actividad* 6 in pairs. 5 MIN.

El Caribe
- Quick Start Review (TE, p. 10) 5 MIN.
- Have students read and discuss *El Caribe* on pp. 10–11. 15 MIN.

En acción: Vocabulario y gramática
- Quick Start Review (TE, p. 12) 5 MIN.
- Present *Repaso:* The Preterite Tense of Regular Verbs, p. 12. 5 MIN.
- Play the audio; do *Actividad* 7. 5 MIN.
- Have students complete *Actividad* 8 orally. 5 MIN.
- Have students complete *Actividad* 9 in pairs. 5 MIN.
- Have students complete *Actividad* 10 in pairs. Expand using Information Gap Activities, Back to School Pack, p. 65; *Más comunicación,* p. R2. 15 MIN.

Homework Option:
- Have students complete *Actividad* 8 in writing. *Más práctica* Workbook, pp. 2–4. *Cuaderno para hispanohablantes,* pp. 2–4.

DAY 3

El Cono Sur
- Check homework. 5 MIN.
- Quick Start Review (TE, p. 14) 5 MIN.
- Have students read and discuss *El Cono Sur* on pp. 14–15. 15 MIN.

En acción: Vocabulario y gramática
- Quick Start Review (TE, p. 16) 5 MIN.
- Present *Repaso:* Verbs with Spelling Changes in the Preterite, p. 16. 5 MIN.
- Have students complete *Actividad* 11 in pairs. 5 MIN.
- Have students complete *Actividades* 12 and 13 in writing. Have students exchange papers for peer correction. 10 MIN.
- Do *Actividad* 14 in pairs. 5 MIN.

España
- Quick Start Review (TE, p. 18) 5 MIN.
- Have students read and discuss *España* on pp. 18–19. 15 MIN.

En acción: Vocabulario y gramática
- Quick Start Review (TE, p. 20) 5 MIN.
- Present *Repaso:* Verbs with Stem Changes in the Preterite, p. 20. 5 MIN.
- Have students complete *Actividad* 15 in writing. 5 MIN.

Homework Option:
- *Más práctica* Workbook, pp. 5–6. *Cuaderno para hispanohablantes,* pp. 5–6.

DAY 4

En acción (cont.)
- Check homework. 5 MIN.
- Have students complete *Actividades* 16, 17, and 18 in pairs. 15 MIN.

Bolivia, Colombia,...
- Quick Start Review (TE, p. 22) 5 MIN.
- Have students read and discuss *Bolivia, Colombia,...* on pp. 22–23. 15 MIN.

En acción: Vocabulario y gramática
- Quick Start Review (TE, p. 24) 5 MIN.
- Present *Repaso:* Irregular Preterites, p. 24. 5 MIN.
- Play the audio; do *Actividad* 19. 5 MIN.
- Have students complete *Actividad* 20 in pairs. 5 MIN.
- Have students complete *Actividad* 21 in groups. Expand using Information Gap Activities, Back to School Pack, p. 66; *Más comunicación,* p. R2. 20 MIN.

En uso: Repaso y más comunicación
- Quick Start Review (TE, p. 26) 5 MIN.
- Present the *Repaso y más comunicación* using the Teaching Suggestions (TE, p. 26). 5 MIN.

Homework Option:
- *Más práctica* Workbook, pp. 7–10. *Cuaderno para hispanohablantes,* pp. 7–10. Review for *Etapa preliminar* Exam.
- *Actividades para todos* Workbook, pp. 1–10.

DAY 5

En uso (cont.)
- Check homework. 10 MIN.
- Have students do *Actividad* 1 in pairs. 10 MIN.
- Do *Actividad* 2 in pairs or groups. 10 MIN.

En tu propia voz: Escritura
- Do *Actividad* 3 in writing. Ask volunteers to present their descriptions. 20 MIN.

En resumen: Repaso de vocabulario
- Quick Start Review (TE, p. 27) 5 MIN.
- Review grammar questions, etc., as necessary. 15 MIN.
- Administer *Etapa preliminar* Exam. 20 MIN.

Homework Option:
- Preview *Unidad* 1 Opener. Have students jot down their observations.

Etapa Theme
Talking about present and past activities

Objectives
- Reviewing the use of the present tense of regular verbs
- Reviewing the use of present-tense verbs with irregular **yo** forms
- Reviewing the preterite tense of regular verbs
- Reviewing verbs with spelling changes in the preterite
- Reviewing the use of verbs with stem changes in the preterite
- Reviewing the use of irregular preterites

Teaching Resource Options

Print
Block Scheduling Copymasters
Preliminary Resource Book
  Family Letter, p. vii
  Diagnostic Placement Test, pp. ix–8
  Audioscript, p. 78
  Absent Student Copymasters, p. 69

Audiovisual
OHT M1–M5; 1 (Quick Start), 3
Audio Program CD 19, Track 1
Canciones CD

Quick Start Review
♻ **What do you already know?**
Use OHT 1 or write on the board:
Write 1 fact you know about each of the following Spanish-speaking places:

- Texas
- Panamá
- La República Dominicana
- España
- Colombia
- Uruguay

Answers will vary.

Teaching Suggestions
Previewing the Etapa
- Ask students to study the pictures on pp. xxxiv–1 (1 min.). Ask them to make statements about what they saw: **Describan lo que vieron.**
- Have individual students read the culture notes. Ask yes/no questions.
- Go over students' answers to the Quick Start Review. Compile a class list of facts.

¡Bienvenidos al mundo hispano!

OBJECTIVES

- **Talk about present activities**
- **Talk about past activities**

¡A EXPLORAR!

¡**L**a diversidad cultural y geográfica de los países hispanohablantes es impresionante! En esta etapa preliminar, vas a conocer las seis regiones del mundo hispano que corresponden a las seis unidades de tu libro. Además, vas a practicar el español que ya sabes para prepararte a aprender más... ¡y a explorar nuestro mundo de posibilidades!

UNIDAD 1

ESTADOS UNIDOS
EL INSTITUTO DE CULTURAS TEJANAS Este museo de San Antonio, Texas, ofrece exhibiciones sobre las diferentes culturas que forman la población del estado de Texas. En la Unidad 1, vas a aprender más sobre la identidad y el estilo personal de los hispanohablantes de EE.UU.

UNIDAD 2

La selva de Darién

PANAMÁ
LA SELVA DE DARIÉN Esta selva tropical es muy famosa. Los viajeros tienen que pasar por la selva a pie o tomar un barco desde la costa para seguir su viaje. En la Unidad 2, vas a aprender más sobre la naturaleza y la ecología y cómo podemos preservarlas.

Classroom Management

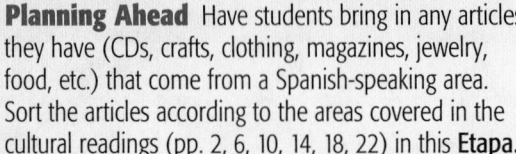

Planning Ahead Have students bring in any articles they have (CDs, crafts, clothing, magazines, jewelry, food, etc.) that come from a Spanish-speaking area. Sort the articles according to the areas covered in the cultural readings (pp. 2, 6, 10, 14, 18, 22) in this **Etapa.**

Peer Review Ask students to review what they covered last year in Spanish class and state their goals for this school year.

Organizing Paired/Group Work Assign students to pairs/groups and arrange classroom locations for group work early in the year. Post this information to facilitate students' work. Monitor pairs/groups to encourage on-task interactions and good habits.

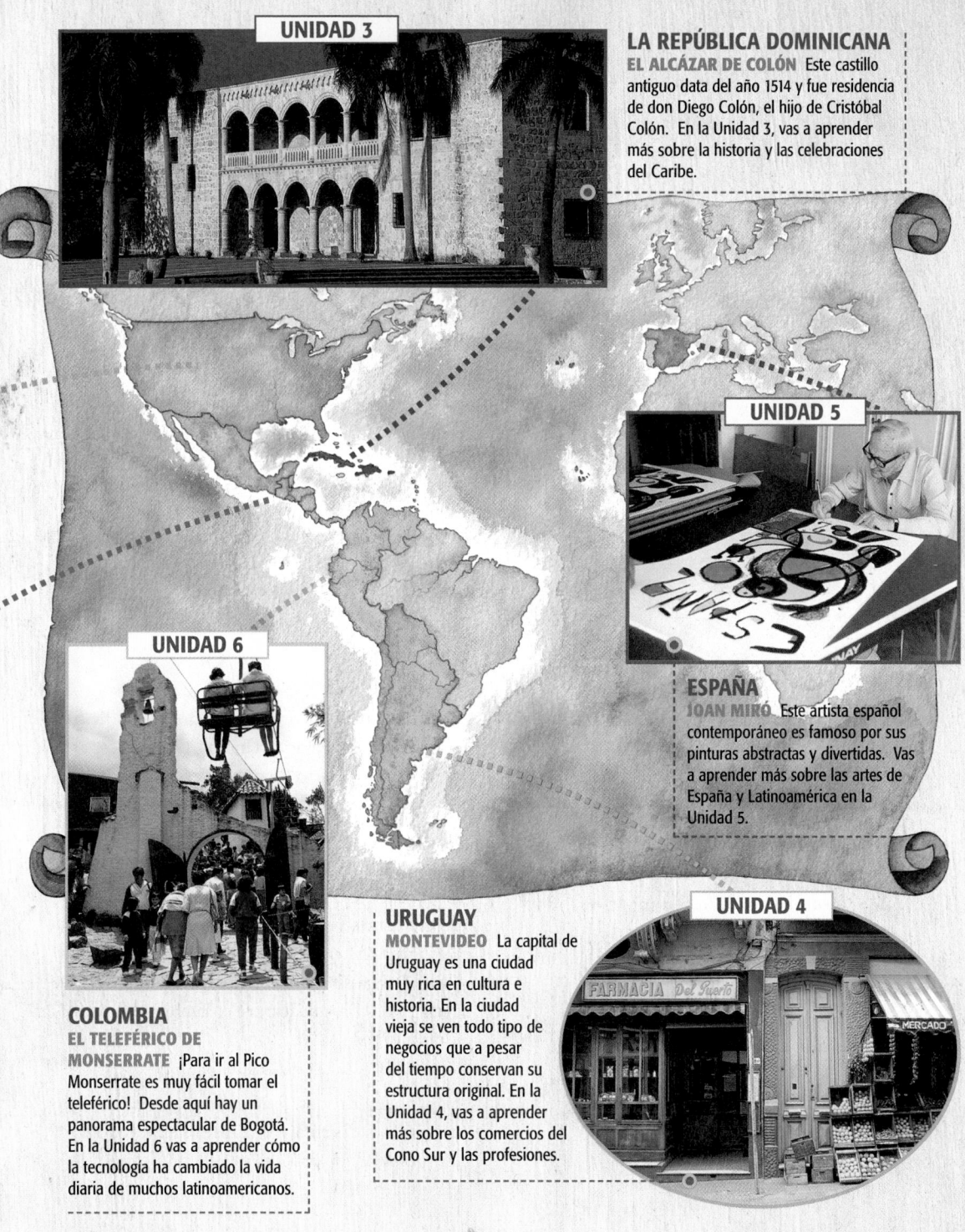

UNIDAD 3

LA REPÚBLICA DOMINICANA

EL ALCÁZAR DE COLÓN Este castillo antiguo data del año 1514 y fue residencia de don Diego Colón, el hijo de Cristóbal Colón. En la Unidad 3, vas a aprender más sobre la historia y las celebraciones del Caribe.

UNIDAD 5

ESPAÑA

JOAN MIRÓ Este artista español contemporáneo es famoso por sus pinturas abstractas y divertidas. Vas a aprender más sobre las artes de España y Latinoamérica en la Unidad 5.

UNIDAD 6

COLOMBIA

EL TELEFÉRICO DE MONSERRATE ¡Para ir al Pico Monserrate es muy fácil tomar el teleférico! Desde aquí hay un panorama espectacular de Bogotá. En la Unidad 6 vas a aprender cómo la tecnología ha cambiado la vida diaria de muchos latinoamericanos.

URUGUAY

MONTEVIDEO La capital de Uruguay es una ciudad muy rica en cultura e historia. En la ciudad vieja se ven todo tipo de negocios que a pesar del tiempo conservan su estructura original. En la Unidad 4, vas a aprender más sobre los comercios del Cono Sur y las profesiones.

UNIDAD 4

I

Cross Cultural Connections

Have students make comparisons and contrasts among the 6 regions pictured on pp. xl–1.

Teaching Suggestion

Ask students the following activating questions: ¿Qué cosas son parte de tu identidad y estilo personal? ¿Qué otras selvas conoces en Latinoamérica? ¿Qué celebraciones son importantes para ti? ¿Qué tecnología usas todos los días? ¿Qué piensas hacer después de la escuela superior?

Culture Highlights

● **ESTADOS UNIDOS** Los hispanohablantes son la minoría que está creciendo más rápido en EE.UU. Para el año 2035, se estima que la población hispanohablante va a ser el doble de lo que es ahora.

● **PANAMÁ** Varios países en América Latina tienen ecoturismo. Entre ellos están Panamá, Costa Rica y Ecuador.

● **LA REPÚBLICA DOMINICANA** Cristóbal Colón estableció la primera colonia española en las Américas en el país que hoy se conoce como la República Dominicana.

● **ESPAÑA** La obra de Joan Miró es una de las más originales del siglo XX. Algunas personas consideran que sus cuadros representan poemas surrealistas.

● **COLOMBIA** Colombia es el único país en Sudamérica que tiene costas en los Océanos Pacífico y Atlántico.

● **URUGUAY** Montevideo, la capital de Uruguay, es el centro económico, político y cultural del país.

Teaching All Students

Extra Help Ask students to list (in Spanish) at least 1 item that they see in each photo. Then have them work in small groups to compare lists. Finally, have groups present their information and make a class list.

Native Speakers Have native speakers create a culture note similar to the ones here for their countries of origin. Have them present them to the class.

Multiple Intelligences

Musical/Rhythmic Bring in examples of **cumbia**, **merengue**, and **Tejano** music. Have students compare the selections to their favorite music. Additional music samples are available on your **Canciones** CD.

Block Schedule

Variety For one week, have students notice and write down (and bring in, if possible) all instances of the Spanish language that they encounter. Discuss each instance to find out why Spanish was used and by whom. (For additional activities, see **Block Scheduling Copymasters**.)

Teaching Resource Options

Print

Block Scheduling Copymasters
Back to School Pack
Absent Student Copymasters, p. 69

Audiovisual

OHT M1; 1 (Quick Start), 4
Canciones CD

Quick Start Review

♻ Etapa opener review

Use OHT 1 or write on the board:
Answer the following questions:

1. ¿En qué ciudad está el Instituto de Culturas Tejanas?
2. ¿En qué país está la selva de Darién?
3. ¿Quién era don Diego Colón?
4. ¿Quién era Joan Miró?
5. ¿Qué se ve desde el teleférico de Monserrate?
6. ¿Cómo se llama la capital de Uruguay?

Answers
1. San Antonio
2. Panamá
3. el hijo de Cristóbal Colón
4. un artista español contemporáneo
5. un panorama espectacular de Bogotá
6. Montevideo

Teaching Suggestions

- Ask students to look at the photos on pp. 2–3 and the culture note headings in order to predict what the reading is about: **Miren las fotos en las páginas 2–3 y los nombres de las notas culturales. ¿Puedes predecir de qué se trata la lectura?**
- Have students scan the reading and make a list of words they don't understand.
- Call on individual students to read each paragraph and culture note.
- Have students look at the list of words they wrote and try to guess their meanings from context.
- Ask the Comprehension questions on TE p. 3.

Estados Unidos

VIDEO   DVD

NUESTRA
cultura e historia

Robert Castro

¡Hola! Yo soy Robert Castro. Soy actor y hago el papel de Francisco García Flores en el video de los niveles 1 y 2 de ¡En español! En la unidad 1 del video para el nivel 3, hablo sobre mi vida y experiencias: la identidad y el estilo personal, mi familia y los latinos en Estados Unidos.

¡Pero eso viene más tarde! Ahora vamos a conocer un poco de la historia y cultura de los hispanohablantes que viven en Estados Unidos.

¡Nos vemos!

Robert

Los hispanohablantes de Estados Unidos somos un grupo diverso con una larga historia. ¿Sabías que ya existían pueblos españoles en el sur y oeste de EE.UU. cuando los ingleses llegaron en el Mayflower para establecer sus propias colonias?

Llegamos al este y noreste del país a fines de los 1800. Como resultado de conflictos entre España y Estados Unidos, Cuba se separó de España y Puerto Rico pasó a ser parte de EE.UU. Después, muchos cubanos y puertorriqueños emigraron a Estados Unidos.

Al empezar el año 1900, la mayoría de los hispanohablantes estadounidenses eran de descendencia española-mexicana y caribeña. Desde entonces han llegado otros grupos étnicos, incluso salvadoreños, nicaragüenses, guatemaltecos, mexicanos, colombianos y dominicanos.

Nos unen la lengua y las tradiciones hispanoamericanas. Pero cada grupo representa una cultura distinta y una historia particular. ¡Representamos una gran variedad de culturas y experiencias!

2 dos
Etapa preliminar

Classroom Community

Cooperative Learning Divide the class into groups of 3 to read the 4 paragraphs on p. 2. Student 1 reads the first paragraph. Student 2 gives a one-sentence summary; Student 3 writes the sentence down. Student 2 begins the next round. The group continues until all paragraphs are done. The group checks the 4 summary sentences and submits them for a grade.

Portfolio Based on Robert's photo and note on p. 2, have students write a description of him, imagining details as necessary. They should include a description of his personality, his likes, and his family.

Rubric **A** = 13–15 pts. **B** = 10–12 pts. **C** = 7–9 pts. **D** = 4–6 pts. **F** = < 4 pts.

Writing criteria	Scale
Grammar/spelling accuracy	1 2 3 4 5
Vocabulary usage	1 2 3 4 5
Creativity/presentation	1 2 3 4 5

Ask students the following activating questions: MURAL: ¿Cómo crees que la cultura latina ha influido la cultura en San Francisco? DESFILE: ¿Por qué es importante que la gente celebre su cultura en EE.UU.? INDEPENDENCIA: ¿Por qué es importante que la gente recuerde su historia? LA CALLE OCHO: ¿Conoces una celebración como ésta? GUAYABERA: ¿Por qué crees que la guayabera es tan popular en el Caribe?

DESFILE Cada año se reúnen miles de personas en Nueva York para celebrar la comunidad puertorriqueña con el «Puerto Rican Pride Parade». ¡No te lo pierdas!

INDEPENDENCIA Para recordar el día de su independencia, los dominicanos de la Ciudad de Nueva York celebran el 27 de febrero con fiestas, música y baile.

MURAL El barrio conocido como el «Mission District», en la ciudad de San Francisco, es un oasis de la cultura mexicano-americana, famoso por sus taquerías, tiendas latinas, cultura y arte.

LA CALLE OCHO La cultura cubana es importante en la ciudad de Miami, que celebra un carnaval cada año. Los mejores artistas hispanohablantes participan en este carnaval, llamado el Carnaval de la Calle Ocho.

GUAYABERA La guayabera es una camisa tradicional de las islas del Caribe. En Miami, La Casa de las Guayaberas es el lugar preferido para comprarse una.

tres
Etapa preliminar | **3**

Comprehension Questions

1. ¿Existían pueblos españoles en EE.UU. cuando los ingleses llegaron en el Mayflower? (Sí)
2. A fines de los 1800, ¿pasó Puerto Rico a ser parte de Cuba o de EE.UU.? (de EE.UU.)
3. En el año 1900, ¿de dónde eran la mayoría de los hispanohablantes estadounidenses? (de México y del Caribe)
4. ¿Qué une a los hispanoamericanos? (la lengua y las tradiciones)
5. ¿Dónde está el «Mission District»? (en San Francisco)
6. ¿Por qué es famoso el «Mission District»? (por sus taquerías, tiendas latinas, cultura y arte)
7. ¿Cómo se celebra la comunidad puertorriqueña en Nueva York? (con el «Puerto Rican Pride Parade»)
8. ¿Qué celebran los dominicanos de Nueva York el 27 de febrero? (el día de su independencia)
9. ¿Dónde puede probarse una guayabera en Miami? (en La Casa de las Guayaberas)
10. ¿Qué se celebra cada año en Miami? (el Carnaval de la Calle Ocho)

Block Schedule

Change of Pace Have students create crossword puzzles for the information in the culture notes on p. 3. Cues should be either definitions or sentences with blanks for the necessary words. Students may then exchange puzzles with a partner and complete each other's puzzles. (For additional activities, see **Block Scheduling Copymasters**.)

Teaching All Students

Extra Help Ask students to write 1 question about each culture note on p. 3. Then have them exchange questions with a partner and write an answer.

Native Speakers Have students write and present a list of Hispanic influences in the U.S., such as in the music industry, place names, food, etc.

Multiple Intelligences

Visual Have the class create a classroom mural depicting some aspect of the history and influence of Spanish-speakers in the U.S.

Teaching Resource Options

Print 📖

Más práctica Workbook PE, p. 1

Cuaderno para hispanohablantes
PE, p. 1

Block Scheduling Copymasters
Back to School Pack
Practice Activities, pp. 12–14
Más práctica Workbook TE, p. 35
Cuaderno para hispanohablantes
TE, p. 55
Absent Student Copymasters, p. 69

Audiovisual 🖥️

OHT 2 (Quick Start) 8 (Grammar)

Technology 💻

Online Workbook, Preliminary

 Quick Start Review

♻️ **Estados Unidos**

Use OHT 2 or write on the board:
Write a sentence about each of the
following:

1. Mission District
2. Puerto Rican Pride Parade
3. la guayabera
4. el Carnaval de la Calle Ocho

Answers will vary.

Teaching Suggestions
**Reviewing Present Tense of
Regular Verbs**

• Remind students that there is no way
of predicting which verbs are stem-
changing. They must be learned.

• Point out that with all stem-changing
verbs in the present tense, the
nosotros and **vosotros** forms keep the
vowel of the infinitive.

• Have students write out the
conjugations of the verbs on index
cards. Add to the cards as verbs are
presented in the **Etapa.** Use the cards
for drill and practice.

• Help students brainstorm a list of
regular verbs, including stem-
changing verbs.

En acción
VOCABULARIO Y GRAMÁTICA

REPASO **Present Tense of Regular verbs**

You use the present tense to talk about what you are doing now and
what you plan to do in the immediate future.

Veo la tele.
I'm watching T.V.

Veo una película
por semana.
I see one movie a week.

Veo a Carmen esta noche.
I'm seeing (I'll see) Carmen
this evening.

Regular verbs

	-ar hablar	-er comer	-ir vivir
yo	hablo	como	vivo
tú	hablas	comes	vives
él, ella, usted	habla	come	vive
nosotros(as)	hablamos	comemos	vivimos
vosotros(as)	habláis	coméis	vivís
ellos, ellas, ustedes	hablan	comen	viven

Remember that in **stem-changing verbs** you change the vowel of the
stem in all the forms of the singular and in the third-person plural of
the present tense.

Stem-changing verbs

	e → ie pensar	o → ue dormir	e → i pedir
yo	pienso	duermo	pido
tú	piensas	duermes	pides
él, ella, usted	piensa	duerme	pide
nosotros(as)	pensamos	dormimos	pedimos
vosotros(as)	pensáis	dormís	pedís
ellos, ellas, ustedes	piensan	duermen	piden

Practice:
Actividades
① ② ③

Más práctica
cuaderno p. 1
Para hispanohablantes
cuaderno p. 1

🖱️ **Online Workbook**
CLASSZONE.COM

---

① Tu rutina

Hablar/*Escribir* Un(a) nuevo(a)
estudiante hispanohablante
quiere saber más sobre
tu rutina. Primero, tu
compañero(a) hace el papel del
(de la) estudiante. Luego,
cambien de papel.

modelo

estudiar (todas las tardes en casa)

Compañero(a): *¿Cuándo estudias?*
o ¿Dónde estudias?

Tú: *Estudio todas las tardes en
casa.*

1. correr en el parque
(tres veces por semana)

2. visitar a tus amigos
(los fines de semana)

3. escribir correo electrónico
(antes de acostarme)

4. leer el periódico estudiantil
(en el colegio)

5. almorzar (a las doce)

6. jugar al tenis (después
de clases)

7. trabajar (en la tienda
de deportes)

8. regresar a casa (a las seis
para la cena)

9. dormir (en mi habitación)

10. estudias (en la biblioteca)

4

cuatro
Etapa preliminar

Classroom Community

Paired Activity Using the list of stem-changing
verbs that students compiled in the "Teaching
Suggestions" on TE p. 4, have students work in pairs to
categorize them according to the vowel change. Then
have them write original present tense sentences using
2 verbs from each category.

Group Activity Have students work in groups of
3–4 to write and act out a scene that takes place in
school. As they act, students describe what they are
doing and talk to each other. Check that students use
stem-changing verbs in their scenes.

2 La playa

Hablar/Escribir Imagina que tú y tu compañero(a) viven en Los Ángeles y van a la playa a menudo. Tú quieres saber qué hacen tu compañero(a) y los miembros de su familia allí. Él (Ella) quiere saber lo mismo de tu familia. Busquen ideas en el dibujo.

modelo

Tú: *¿Qué haces cuando vas a la playa?*

Compañero(a): *¿Yo? Generalmente, tomo el sol o nado. ¿Y tú?*

Tú: *Pues yo llevo mis patines y patino todo el día. ¿Y tu hermano?*

Compañero(a): *A mi hermano no le gusta nadar. Así que generalmente escucha la radio o juega al voleibol.*

3 Los fines de semana

Hablar/Escribir Entrevista a cuatro compañeros(as) de clase. Quieres saber qué hacen los fines de semana. Haz una gráfica (*chart*) y escribe cómo responden.

modelo

Tú: *¿Qué haces los fines de semana?*

Compañero(a): *Generalmente, los sábados por la mañana me levanto temprano y desayuno. Luego, alquilo un video o tomo el sol en la playa.*

Tú: *¿Y los domingos?*

Compañero(a): *…*

Nombre	Sábado	Domingo

Teaching All Students

Extra Help Give students a list of verbs. Have them classify the verbs as regular or stem-changing. Then have them write the **yo** and the **nosotros** form for each verb.

Native Speakers Have Spanish speakers describe an event in their Latino communities here, using regular and stem-changing present tense verbs.

Multiple Intelligences

Kinesthetic Ask students to cut out photos from magazines or make drawings to create scenes similar to the picture in **Actividad 2**. Then have them present their scenes and describe what the people are doing.

ACTIVIDAD 1 **Objective:** Controlled practice Present tense of regular verbs in conversation

Answers
1. A: ¿Cuándo corres en el parque?
   B: Corro en el parque tres veces por semana.
2. A: ¿Dónde visitas a tus amigos?
   B: Visito a mis amigos los fines de semana.
3. A: ¿Cuándo escribes correo electrónico?
   B: Escribo correo electrónico antes de acostarme.
4. A: ¿Dónde lees el periódico estudiantil?
   B: Leo el periódico estudiantil en el colegio.
5. A: ¿A qué hora almuerzas?
   B: Almuerzo a las doce.
6. A: ¿Cuándo juegas al tenis?
   B: Juego al tenis después de clases.
7. A: ¿Dónde trabajas?
   B: Trabajo en la tienda de deportes.
8. A: ¿Cuándo regresas a casa?
   B: Regreso a casa a las seis para la cena.

ACTIVIDAD 2 **Objective:** Transitional practice Present tense of regular verbs in conversation

Answers will vary.

ACTIVIDAD 3 **Objective:** Open-ended practice Present tense of regular verbs in conversation

Answers will vary.

Block Schedule

FunBreak Prepare ahead: Put names of activities expressed by stem-changing verbs on index cards. For example: **dormir hasta las doce este fin de semana, pedir pizza en un restaurante, volver temprano a casa el sábado.** Make at least 3 cards for each activity. Distribute all the cards (students may have more than 1 card). Tell students: **Hay 3 personas que tienen cada actividad. Uds. tienen que buscar a las otras dos personas que comparten su actividad.** Students go around the room asking questions with **poder** to find out who has the same cards as they do: **¿Puedes dormir hasta las doce este fin de semana?** After a set time limit, students return to their seats and present their findings. (For additional activities, see **Block Scheduling Copymasters**.)

Teaching Resource Options

Print 📖
Block Scheduling Copymasters
Back to School Pack
  Absent Student Copymasters, p. 70

Audiovisual 🎧
OHT M2; 2 (Quick Start), 5
Canciones CD

🔔 Quick Start Review

♻ **Present tense of regular verbs**
Use OHT 2 or write on the board:
Write sentences in the present tense
using the following elements:

1. nosotros / trabajar
2. yo / querer
3. tú / vivir
4. mi amigo / llegar
5. Susana / pensar
6. Pablo y yo / escribir
7. las chicas / almorzar
8. tú / dormir

Answers
*Answers will vary, but should include the
following verb forms:*

1. trabajamos	5. piensa
2. quiero	6. escribimos
3. vives	7. almuerzan
4. llega	8. duermes

Teaching Suggestions

• Have students look at the photos on
  pp. 6–7 (1 min.) and say what they
  noticed: ¿Qué notaron?
• Have students scan the reading and
  culture notes for answers to the
  following information: (1) dos
  **lenguas antiguas de México y
  Centroamérica; (2) los nombres de
  los picos del volcán cerca de San
  Salvador; (3) el nombre del
  huracán que destruyó muchos
  pueblos en Honduras; (4) dónde se
  puede ver todo tipo de animales
  acuáticos.**
• Have volunteers read the paragraphs
  and culture notes. Then have the
  class provide a title for each one.
• Ask the Comprehension questions on
  TE p. 7.

Guadalupe
González

México y Centroamérica

VIDEO DVD

TRADICIONES
del pasado

¿Sabes quién soy?

Tal vez me conoces como Isabel Palacios
del video de los niveles 1 y 2. Pero soy
actriz y me llamo Guadalupe González.
En el video de la unidad 2 de este libro,
vamos a hablar de nuestras comunidades,
la naturaleza y los problemas que las
pueden afectar.

Ahora quiero mostrarte los países
en la unidad 2: México, Guatemala,
Honduras, Nicaragua, El Salvador, Costa
Rica y Panamá. ¡Es una región
interesante y bellísima a la vez!

¡Hasta luego! *Guadalupe*

En realidad, ¡el «Nuevo Mundo» de
los conquistadores era tan viejo como Europa!
Grandes civilizaciones, como la maya,
la azteca y la tolteca, ya existían cuando los
conquistadores llegaron aquí por primera vez.
Nuestra cultura tiene estas dos historias.

A principios de los 1800 estos países
se separaron de España. Luego, formaron un
imperio desde Costa Rica hasta el suroeste
de los Estados Unidos. Pero gradualmente,
diferencias étnicas, culturales y políticas
formaron los países que conocemos hoy.

La influencia de los españoles ha sido
grande, pero hoy encontramos millones de
personas que todavía hablan lenguas antiguas
como el maya y el náhuatl. También mantienen
vivas las costumbres y tradiciones que vienen
de la época antes de la llegada de los europeos.
¡Estas tradiciones son parte de nuestra
identidad contemporánea!

6 seis
Etapa preliminar

Classroom Community

Storytelling Have pairs or small groups of students
write and present a story (in the present tense) that
takes place in one of the areas shown on p. 7. Students
should be encouraged to use their imagination and
sense of humor. When presenting the stories, they
should use appropriate expressions and gestures.

Portfolio Have students record themselves reading
all or part of the reading on pp. 6–7.

Rubric A = 13–15 pts. B = 10–12 pts. C = 7–9 pts. D = 4–6 pts. F = < 4 pts.

Interview criteria	Scale
Accuracy of pronunciation	1 2 3 4 5
Fluency	1 2 3 4 5
Expression	1 2 3 4 5

BAJA CALIFORNIA Personas de todo el mundo visitan el estado mexicano de Baja California para ver todo tipo de animales acuáticos que pasan por aquí durante su migración anual.

HONDURAS El huracán Mitch ha sido el peor desastre natural del hemisferio occidental en los últimos doscientos años. Más de un millón de personas perdieron sus casas, familiares y amigos. El huracán destruyó muchos pueblos y vecindades. Más de 20 años pasarán antes de que Honduras pueda reconstruir su infraestructura.

EL SALVADOR Aunque es el país más pequeño de Centroamérica, El Salvador tiene una gran variedad geográfica. Cerca de la capital, San Salvador, se encuentra este volcán de dos picos. El más grande se llama Picacho y el más pequeño Boquerón.

COSTA RICA ¿Un jardín de mariposas? Lo puedes encontrar en San José, Costa Rica. Este país es conocido por la naturaleza que se encuentra allí.

Cross Cultural Connections

Prepare ahead: Collect books, magazines, newspapers, brochures, and maps of Mexico and Central America. Create a classroom Reference Table. Groups of students take turns investigating similarities between the U.S. and other countries. Compile lists on the board.

Teaching Suggestion

Ask the following activating questions:
EL SALVADOR: ¿Es bueno el suelo en El Salvador para la agricultura? ¿Por qué?
HONDURAS: ¿Qué cosas se pueden hacer para ayudar a las víctimas de un huracán? BAJA CALIFORNIA: ¿Por qué hay que proteger las ballenas? COSTA RICA: ¿Qué piensas sobre la actitud de los costarricenses hacia la naturaleza?

Comprehension Questions

1. ¿Era el «Nuevo Mundo» de los conquistadores más viejo que Europa? (No)
2. ¿Cuándo se separaron los países del «Nuevo Mundo» de España—a fines de los 1800 o a principios de los 1800? (a principios de los 1800)
3. ¿Cuáles son dos lenguas antiguas del «Nuevo Mundo»? (el maya y el náhuatl)
4. ¿Cuántas personas perdieron sus hogares a causa del huracán Mitch? (más de un millón)
5. ¿Cuántos años van a pasar antes de que Honduras pueda reconstruir su infraestructura? (20)
6. ¿Cuál es el país más pequeño de Centroamérica? (El Salvador)
7. ¿Qué ven muchas personas en Baja California? (animales acuáticos)
8. ¿Cuándo pasan animales acuáticos por Baja California? (durante su migración anual)
9. ¿Dónde se puede encontrar un jardín de mariposas en Costa Rica? (en San José)
10. ¿Por qué es conocido Costa Rica? (por la naturaleza que se encuentra allí)

Block Schedule

(For additional activities, see **Block Scheduling Copymasters**.)

Teaching All Students

Extra Help Have students make a list of the verbs used on pp. 6–7. Have them put "R" next to those that are regular in the present tense, "S-C" next to those that are stem-changing, and "O" next to all other verbs.

Multiple Intelligences

Verbal Have various students describe something about one of the countries/areas. The rest of the class tries to guess the place. Students may also want to include areas in the U.S. from pp. 2–3.

Logical/Mathematical Have students calculate the distance from their town/city to the capital cities of Mexico and the 6 Central American countries.

Teaching Resource Options

Print

Más práctica Workbook PE, pp. 2–3
Cuaderno para hispanohablantes
 PE, pp. 2–3
Block Scheduling Copymasters
Back to School Pack
 Practice Activities, pp. 15–18
Más práctica Workbook TE,
 pp. 36–37
Cuaderno para hispanohablantes
 TE, pp. 56–57
Absent Student Copymasters, p. 70

Audiovisual

OHT 6 (Quick Start), 9 (Grammar)

Technology

Online Workbook, Preliminary

Quick Start Review

 México y Centroamérica

Use OHT 6 or write on the board:
Write 2 facts about each of the
following countries:

1. México
2. Costa Rica
3. El Salvador
4. Honduras

Answers will vary.

Teaching Suggestions
Reviewing Irregular yo Forms

• Point out other verbs that are
 conjugated like **conocer: traducir,**
 producir, reducir, ofrecer,
 pertenecer, crecer.
• You may wish to point out that there
 are only 5 verbs that do not end in **o**
 in the **yo** form of the present: **doy,**
 sé, estoy, voy, soy.
• Say a subject pronoun and an
 infinitive, while tossing a soft ball to a
 student. The student must give the
 correct present tense verb form. If the
 form is correct, he/she tosses the ball
 back to you. If incorrect, he/she
 tosses the ball to another student.
 Continue with more pronouns and
 infinitives.

En acción
VOCABULARIO Y GRAMÁTICA

REPASO   Irregular **yo** Forms

▶ Remember that some verbs are irregular in the
present tense only in the first person singular (yo)
form. Compare the **yo** and **tú** forms of these verbs.

	yo	tú

• Verbs like **hacer**

caer	caigo	**caes**
hacer	hago	**haces**
poner	pongo	**pones**
salir	salgo	**sales**
traer	traigo	**traes**
valer	valgo	**vales**

• Verbs with a spelling change: c → zc

conocer	conozco	**conoces**

• Other verbs irregular in the yo form

dar	doy	**das**
saber	sé	**sabes**
ver	veo	**ves**

▶ Other irregular verbs that you have already learned
(estar, ir, ser, tener, venir) are conjugated for you
on pp. R33–R35.

Practice:
Actividades ❹ ❺ ❻

Online Workbook
CLASSZONE.COM

Más práctica *cuaderno pp. 2, 3*
Para hispanohablantes *cuaderno pp. 2, 3*

---

❹ La encuesta

Hablar/*Escribir* Estás de vacaciones en Costa
Rica y ves esta encuesta (*survey*) en una revista
para jóvenes. La revista quiere saber más de los
hábitos de los jóvenes. Contesta las preguntas.

modelo

¿Cuándo haces la tarea?

☑ *después de clases* ❑ *después de la cena* ❑ *¿...?*

Hago la tarea después de clases.

Encuesta

1. ¿Con qué frecuencia sales con tus
 amigos? ❑ todos los días
 ❑ los fines de semana ❑ ¿...?
2. ¿Cuándo ves televisión? ❑ después
 de clases ❑ después de la cena
 ❑ ¿...?
3. ¿Conoces la música de Maná?
 ❑ sí ❑ no
4. ¿Quién pone la mesa en tu casa?
 ❑ yo ❑ hermano o hermana ❑ ¿...?
5. ¿Conduces al colegio o tomas el
 autobús? ❑ conducir ❑ tomar el
 autobús ❑ ¿...?
6. ¿Haces tu cama todos los días?
 ❑ sí ❑ no
7. ¿Sabes usar Internet?
 ❑ sí ❑ no

---

8   ocho
 Etapa preliminar

Classroom Community

Storytelling Have students work in groups to create
chain stories using regular and irregular verbs in the
present. The first student gives a sentence to begin the
story. The next student adds to the topic. Students
continue until the story is complete. One student
should be the recorder and write down the sentences.
Have groups read their stories to the class and vote on
the most creative story.

Paired Activity Have students work in pairs to
create their own 5-question **Encuesta**, similar to the one
in **Actividad 4**. Students should make up different
questions, but must use the verbs from the **Repaso** on
p. 8. Have pairs then survey their classmates and tally
the results to present to the class.

5 Correo electrónico

Escribir Escribe una carta por correo electrónico a un(a) amigo(a) nicaragüense. Usa por lo menos cinco palabras de cada columna para describir tu vida.

modelo

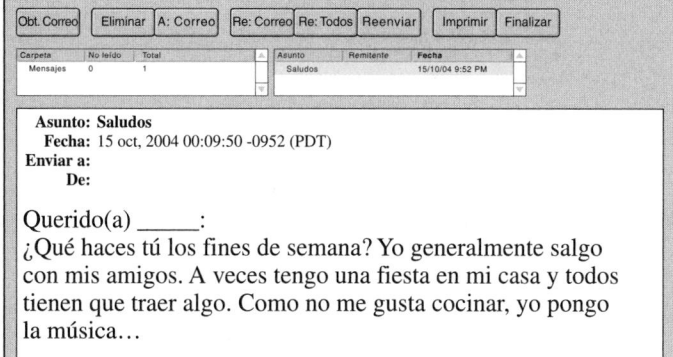

Asunto: Saludos
Fecha: 15 oct, 2004 00:09:50 -0952 (PDT)
Enviar a:
De:

Querido(a) _____:
¿Qué haces tú los fines de semana? Yo generalmente salgo con mis amigos. A veces tengo una fiesta en mi casa y todos tienen que traer algo. Como no me gusta cocinar, yo pongo la música…

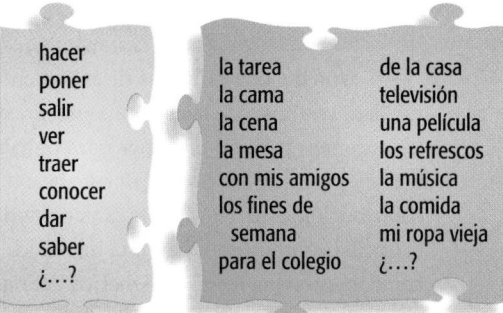

hacer	la tarea	de la casa
poner	la cama	televisión
salir	la cena	una película
ver	la mesa	los refrescos
traer	con mis amigos	la música
conocer	los fines de	la comida
dar	semana	mi ropa vieja
saber	para el colegio	¿…?
¿…?		

6 ¿Lo conoces?

Hablar Acabas de conocer a tu compañero(a) mexicano(a). Quieres saber si él (ella) conoce varias cosas y personas. Hazle varias preguntas. Luego, cambien de papel.

modelo

Tú: *¿Conoces el museo de Frida Kahlo en Coyoacán?*

Compañero(a): *No, no lo conozco, pero sí conozco sus pinturas.*

Tú: *¿De veras? ¿Qué piensas de ellas?*

Compañero(a): …

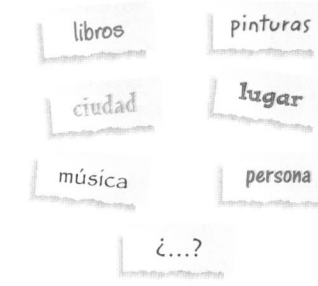

libros   pinturas
ciudad   lugar
música   persona

¿…?

ACTIVIDAD 4 Objective: Controlled practice Irregular **yo** forms

Answers
Answers will vary. Answers could include:
1. Salgo con mis amigos los fines de semana.
2. Veo televisión después de la cena.
3. No, no conozco la música de Maná.
4. Yo pongo la mesa en mi casa.
5. Conduzco al colegio.
6. No, no hago mi cama todos los días.
7. Sí, sé usar Internet.

ACTIVIDAD 5 Objective: Transitional practice Irregular **yo** forms in writing

Answers will vary.

ACTIVIDAD 6 Objective: Open-ended practice Irregular **yo** forms in conversation

Answers will vary.

Supplementary Vocabulary
You may want to present the following expressions for circumlocution:

Es como	*It's like*
Es lo opuesto de	*It's the opposite of*
Es lo mismo que	*It's the same as*
Es un sinónimo de	*It's a synonym of*
Es parecido a	*It's similar to*
Se parece a	*It looks like*
Se usa para	*You use it for*
Significa	*It means*

Teaching All Students

Extra Help Have students complete the following phrase: **Soy buen(a) estudiante porque...** Students must write at least 3 endings, using the verbs listed in the **Repaso** on p. 8.

Native Speakers Have students bring in Spanish-language magazines. Have them show the magazines to the class, explain what types of magazines they are, and say which might be of interest to young people.

Multiple Intelligences

Interpersonal Have students work in pairs to discuss their answers to **Actividad 4.**

Verbal Have students create tongue twisters, using any of the verbs in the **Repaso** on p. 8.

Block Schedule
Expansion Expand on **Actividad 5** by having students write a letter as if they were a famous person of their own choosing. Collect the letters, read them aloud, and have the class guess which famous people "wrote" the letters. (For additional activities, see **Block Scheduling Copymasters.**)

Teaching Resource Options

Print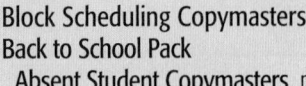

Block Scheduling Copymasters
Back to School Pack
  Absent Student Copymasters, p. 71

Audiovisual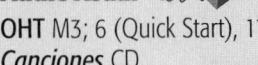

OHT M3; 6 (Quick Start), 11
Canciones CD

🔔 Quick Start Review

♻ Irregular **yo** forms

Use OHT 6 or write on the board:
Write the **yo** form of the present of
each of the following verbs:

1. estar	5. saber
2. ir	6. ver
3. poner	7. caer
4. dar	8. hacer

Answers

1. estoy	5. sé
2. voy	6. veo
3. pongo	7. caigo
4. doy	8. hago

Teaching Suggestions

• Use OHT M3 and have students
locate Cuba, Puerto Rico, and the
Dominican Republic.
• The passage on p. 10 contains 10
sentences. Assign each sentence to a
different student. Then have the
students take charge of reading the
passage while you and the rest of the
class listen.
• Have 4 more students read the
culture notes on p. 11.
• Ask the Comprehension questions on
TE p. 11.

Critical Thinking

Ask students: ¿Por qué piensan que
todos querían controlar las islas del
Caribe? ¿Por qué son importantes?

Nilka Desirée

El Caribe

VIDEO   DVD

UNA HISTORIA
dramática

¡Bienvenidos al Caribe!
Me llamo Nilka Desirée y soy actriz.
En el video del nivel 1 hago el papel de
Diana Ortiz Avilés. Vas a verme otra
vez en el video de la unidad 3 de este
libro, donde hablo un poco sobre las
celebraciones y los festivales del Caribe.

Antes de tratar estos temas, quiero
darte un poco de la historia de los países
que forman el Caribe hispanohablante:
Puerto Rico, la República Dominicana
y Cuba.

¡Hasta pronto!

Nilka

Cuando Cristóbal Colón llegó al Caribe
en 1492, la vida de sus habitantes cambió
dramáticamente. La mayoría de éstos eran de
origen taíno, una tribu de indios que vivían en
Puerto Rico y el este de Cuba.

Los europeos conquistaron a los taínos y
usaron las islas para la conquista de otros
imperios, como el azteca y el inca. El Caribe fue
un teatro de conflicto entre las naciones europeas
y los piratas de todo el mundo. Todos querían
controlar estas islas.

Uno de los resultados de estos conflictos
fue la destrucción de la cultura taína. En su lugar,
los europeos trajeron africanos para trabajar la
tierra y producir el azúcar. Por este hecho, la
contribución de la cultura africana es evidente en
el Caribe, aunque aquí hay una mezcla de culturas
como en otras regiones de América Latina.

Gradualmente, Cuba y la República
Dominicana se separaron de España y Puerto
Rico pasó a ser parte de EE.UU. Hoy en día, estos
países celebran su historia y diversidad cultural,
mostrando un aprecio por las tres culturas que
son parte de ellos.

10 diez
Etapa preliminar

Classroom Community

Learning Scenario Working in pairs, have students
prepare a mini-skit about a person who wants to travel
to one of the Spanish-speaking areas discussed so far
in the **Etapa.** One student plays the tourist and the
other person plays the travel agent.

Paired Activity Assign pairs of students an area to
research: Puerto Rico, Cuba, or the Dominican
Republic. Pairs must research 10 facts about their area
to present to the class. The facts should be presented
with visuals.

PUERTO RICO Las ferias de artesanía en Puerto Rico son una celebración de la cultura e historia popular de las regiones distintas de la isla.

PUERTO RICO En 1508, el explorador Juan Ponce de León conquistó la isla de Borinquen (hoy Puerto Rico). Construyó una casa donde puedes encontrar parte de la historia de los gobernantes de Puerto Rico.

LA HABANA La Habana fue fundada en 1519, en Cuba. Esta sección de la capital cubana se conoce como «La Habana Vieja». Conserva el estilo colonial, incluso calles estrechas y palacios.

REPÚBLICA DOMINICANA Cerca de la capital dominicana de Santo Domingo se encuentra el Parque de los Tres Ojos. Los «ojos» se refieren a lagunas pequeñas de agua azul que «miran» desde las cuevas del parque.

once
Etapa preliminar ll

Teaching Suggestion
Ask students the following activating questions: FERIA DE ARTESANÍA: ¿Qué cosas crees que celebran los artesanos? PUERTO RICO: ¿Qué otras cosas te pueden decir los edificios históricos de un lugar? LA HABANA: Si encuentras edificios coloniales en la Habana Vieja, ¿qué tipos de edificios crees que encontrarás en la Habana? REPÚBLICA DOMINICANA: ¿Conoces otros lugares que tengan nombres asociados con personas o animales?

Comprehension Questions
1. ¿Eran la mayoría de los habitantes del Caribe de origen azteca? (No)
2. ¿Quiénes eran los taínos—unos piratas o una tribu de indios? (una tribu de indios)
3. ¿Cuál fue uno de los resultados de los conflictos en el Caribe? (la destrucción de la cultura taína)
4. ¿Por qué trajeron los europeos africanos al Caribe? (para trabajar la tierra y producir el azúcar)
5. ¿Cuántas culturas forman parte de Cuba, Puerto Rico y la República Dominicana? (3)
6. ¿Quién conquistó la isla de Borinquen? (Juan Ponce de León)
7. ¿Cómo se llama Borinquen hoy? (Puerto Rico)
8. ¿Cuándo fue fundada La Habana? (en 1519)
9. ¿Dónde se encuentra el Parque de los Tres Ojos? (cerca de Santo Domingo)
10. ¿A qué se refieren los «ojos»? (a lagunas pequeñas de agua azul)

Teaching All Students

Extra Help Have students write 5 statements about the 3 countries, some true and some false. Then pairs of students exchange papers, determine whether statements are true or false, and correct the false statements.

Multiple Intelligences
Musical/Rhythmic Have students research the names of musicians from Puerto Rico, Cuba, and the Dominican Republic. Suggest that they visit music stores or use the Internet. If possible, play some music selections. Music samples are available on your **Canciones** CD.

Visual Have students draw the flags of Puerto Rico, Cuba, and the Dominican Republic, then research the significance of the colors and symbols.

Block Schedule
Research Have students research the history of Puerto Rico and create a time line of major events. Also have them look up any recent information concerning the status of Puerto Rico as part of the U.S. (For additional activities, see **Block Scheduling Copymasters**.)

Teaching Resource Options

Print

Más práctica Workbook PE, p. 4
Cuaderno para hispanohablantes
  PE, p. 4
Block Scheduling Copymasters
Back to School Pack
  Practice Activities, pp. 19–22
  Más práctica Workbook TE, p. 38
  Cuaderno para hispanohablantes
  TE, p. 58
  Information Gap Activities, p. 66
  Absent Student Copymasters, p. 71
  Audioscript, pp. 77–78

Audiovisual

OHT 7 (Quick Start), 10 (Grammar)
Audio Program CD 1, Track 1, Actividad 7

Technology

Online Workbook, Preliminary

🔔 Quick Start Review

♻ **El Caribe**

Use OHT 7 or write on the board:
Match the countries with the information.
Some items have more than one answer:

1. ___ Cuba
2. ___ Puerto Rico
3. ___ la República Dominicana
   a. Borinquen
   b. el Parque de los Tres Ojos
   c. Juan Ponce de León
   d. La Habana
   e. Santo Domingo

Answers
1. d   2. a, c   3. b, e

Teaching Suggestions

Reviewing The Preterite Tense of Regular Verbs

• Point out that **-ar** and **-er** stem-changing verbs in the present tense have no stem change in the preterite tense.

• Emphasize that the first- and third-person singular conjugations of the preterite require accents. For example, it is important to differentiate between **hablo** (I speak) and **habló** (he/she spoke) or **¡Hable!** (Speak!) and **hablé** (I spoke).

En acción
VOCABULARIO Y GRAMÁTICA

REPASO   The Preterite Tense of Regular Verbs

▶ You use the **preterite** to talk about actions that you or others completed in the past.

Escribí cartas por una hora.
I wrote letters for an hour.

Bailamos toda la noche.
We danced all night.

> Remember that -er and -ir verbs have the same endings in the preterite.

Regular Preterite Verbs

	-ar hablar	-er comer	-ir vivir
yo	habl**é**	com**í**	viv**í**
tú	habl**aste**	com**iste**	viv**iste**
usted, él, ella	habl**ó**	com**ió**	viv**ió**
nosotros(as)	habl**amos**	com**imos**	viv**imos**
vosotros(as)	habl**asteis**	com**isteis**	viv**isteis**
ustedes, ellos, ellas	habl**aron**	com**ieron**	viv**ieron**

Practice: Actividades ⑦ ⑧ ⑨ ⑩

Más práctica *cuaderno p. 4*
Para hispanohablantes *cuaderno p. 4*

 **Online Workbook** CLASSZONE.COM

---

⑦ **¡Pobre Adriana!**

Escuchar/*Escribir* Adriana está contando lo que le pasó ayer. Escúchala y escribe oraciones para describir su día.

modelo
despertarse
Adriana se despertó muy tarde.

1. planchar   3. trabajar   5. regresar   7. revisar
2. salir   4. perder   6. cenar   8. comprar

---

⑧ **La isla de Puerto Rico**

Hablar/*Escribir* Marcela fue a Puerto Rico durante el verano. ¿Qué hicieron ella y su familia?

modelo
(yo) mandar muchas tarjetas postales
Mandé muchas tarjetas postales.

1. (yo) visitar el Centro Ceremonial Indígena de Tibes
2. (mi familia y yo) comer comida puertorriqueña muy sabrosa
3. (mi hermano) comprar unos discos compactos de salsa
4. (mi familia y yo) caminar por el Viejo San Juan
5. (mi hermana y yo) tomar el sol en la playa de Luquillo
6. (yo) escribir un poema sobre la belleza de la isla
7. (mi hermana) recibir un regalo de su amigo puertorriqueño
8. (yo) comprender por qué llaman a Puerto Rico «la Isla del Encanto»

Classroom Community

Paired Activity As a class, brainstorm a list of verbs that are school-related activities. Have students check the ones that are regular in the preterite. Then have students work in pairs and write 10 things they did in various classes, using the checked verbs. Finally, have 2 pairs work together, read each other their sentences, and have the other pair guess what class is being described.

Game As a class, brainstorm a list of activities that students like to do (**escuchar música, recibir regalos**, etc.). Be sure all verbs are regular in the preterite. Then divide the class into 2 teams. One student thinks of an activity from the list that he/she has done in the past week. Students from the other team ask questions until they guess the activity. Teams switch roles. The team that guesses correctly with the fewest questions wins.

9 La familia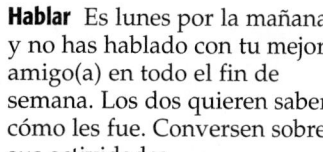

Hablar/*Escribir* El sábado pasado todos los miembros de tu familia hicieron cosas diferentes. Tu amigo(a) te pregunta qué pasó. Mira los dibujos y dile qué hizo cada persona (por lo menos dos cosas). ¡Usa tu imaginación!

modelo

Compañero(a): *¿Qué hizo tu hermano el sábado pasado?*

Tú: *Primero limpió su cuarto y luego alquiló un video.*

Compañero(a): *¡Qué divertido! Y tu mamá, ¿qué hizo?*

Tú: *Pues,…*

1. yo

2. mi abuelo

3. mis primos

4. mi prima

5. mi mamá

6. mi tía

7. mi hermanito

8. mi hermana

9. mi tío

10 El fin de semana

Hablar Es lunes por la mañana y no has hablado con tu mejor amigo(a) en todo el fin de semana. Los dos quieren saber cómo les fue. Conversen sobre sus actividades.

modelo

Tú: *¿Cómo pasaste el sábado?*

Compañero(a): *¿Yo? Pues el sábado por la tarde llamé a Juan. Alquilamos un video y compramos una pizza para comer en casa. Después…*

Tú: *Y el domingo, ¿qué pasó?*

Compañero(a): *…*

More Practice: **Más comunicación** *p. R2*

Teaching All Students

Extra Help Prepare ahead: Make a worksheet containing present tense sentences. Have students change the sentences to the preterite, then exchange papers with a partner for peer correction.

Native Speakers Have students read a short magazine or newspaper article (in English or Spanish) about a recent event. Then have them summarize what happened for the class.

Multiple Intelligences

Verbal Narrate a past event, real or imaginary, to students. Ask students to summarize what you told them.

Interpersonal Have each student create 4 additional drawings/items for **Actividad 9.** Then have students use the new drawings/items to practice with a partner.

ACTIVIDAD 7 **Objective:** Controlled practice Listening comprehension/preterite tense of regular verbs

Answers (See script, p. xxxiiiB.)
1. Adriana no planchó la ropa.
2. Adriana salió de casa como loca.
3. Adriana trabajó dos horas en la tienda de su tío después de las clases.
4. Adriana perdió la tarea.
5. Adriana regresó a casa muy cansada.
6. Adriana no cenó.
7. Adriana revisó su mochila.
8. Adriana compró café.

ACTIVIDAD 8 **Objective:** Controlled practice Preterite tense of regular verbs

Answers
1. Visité el Centro Ceremonial Indígena de Tibes.
2. Comimos comida puertorriqueña muy sabrosa.
3. Compró unos discos compactos de salsa.
4. Caminamos por el Viejo San Juan.
5. Tomamos el sol en la playa de Luquillo.
6. Escribí un poema sobre la belleza de la isla.
7. Recibió un regalo de su amigo puertorriqueño.
8. Comprendí por qué llaman a Puerto Rico «la Isla del Encanto».

ACTIVIDAD 9 **Objective:** Transitional practice Preterite tense of regular verbs in conversation

Answers will vary.

ACTIVIDAD 10 **Objective:** Open-ended practice Preterite tense of regular verbs in conversation

Answers will vary.

Dictation

Using the Listening Activity Script for **Actividad 7** on TE p. xxxixB, dictate selected sentences to students. You may want to have students peer correct the sentences.

Block Schedule

Change of Pace Using the following list of verbs, have students make up a story about someone's day: **comer, beber, comprar, tomar, mirar, preparar, salir, cenar.** Students may add other verbs, provided they are regular in the preterite. (For additional activities, see **Block Scheduling Copymasters.**)

Etapa preliminar • Vocabulary/Grammar **13**

Teaching Resource Options

Print

Block Scheduling Copymasters
Back to School Pack
  Absent Student Copymasters, p. 72

Audiovisual

OHT M4; 7 (Quick Start), 14
Canciones CD

Quick Start Review

♻ **Preterite of regular verbs**

Use OHT 7 or write on the board:
Write preterite sentences using the
following expressions:

1. estudiar para un examen
2. comer en casa
3. escribir cartas
4. salir de la casa
5. regresar a casa

Answers will vary.

Teaching Suggestions

- Use OHT M4 and have students
  locate the **Southern Cone** countries.
- Have students skim pp. 14–15, noting
  clues that indicate the central theme
  of the reading: **¿Qué claves indican
  el tema central de la lectura?**
- If there are any words that students
  do not understand, their classmates
  should help them use context to
  guess the meanings.
- Ask the Comprehension questions on
  TE p. 15.

Culture Highlights

● **PLAYAS** Uruguay y Argentina tienen
playas magníficas en Punta del Este y Mar
del Plata. Turistas de todo el mundo visitan
estos lugares en noviembre y diciembre.

● **EL ESQUÍ** El equipo de esquí de
Estados Unidos se entrena en Chile y
Argentina en junio y julio. ¡Allí es invierno
en estos meses!

El Cono Sur

VIDEO   DVD

VECINOS
hispanohablantes

Marcelo Abramo

Ahora estamos en el Cono Sur:
los países de Argentina, Chile, Uruguay y
Paraguay. ¿Sabes que también se dice
«el Uruguay», «la Argentina» y «el
Paraguay»? Me llamo Marcelo Abramo
y soy de Argentina. ¿Tal vez me reconoces
del video del nivel 1 de ¡En español ?
Hago el papel del arquitecto González.
En el video para la unidad 4 de este libro,
hablo un poco sobre mis experiencias en
el colegio y el mundo del trabajo. Pero
ya es hora de aprender algo sobre este
grupo de países sudamericanos.
¡Hablaremos después!

Marcelo

El Cono Sur es la región que ocupan
Argentina, Uruguay, Paraguay y Chile. Si miras
el mapa, verás que estos forman una especie de
cono en el extremo sur del continente americano.
Tienen una geografía muy variada. La Cordillera
de los Andes pasa por Chile y Argentina. Chile
está en la costa del Pacífico y Argentina y Uruguay
están en la costa del Atlántico. Paraguay está al
noreste de Argentina.

El Cono Sur comparte historia, idioma, y
geografía. Santiago, una de las primeras ciudades
españolas, se convirtió en la capital de Chile. Con
el tiempo, crecieron Buenos Aires, Montevideo y
Asunción, las capitales de Argentina, Uruguay y
Paraguay. Los indígenas huyeron con la llegada
de los europeos, menos en Paraguay, donde hoy la
cultura guaraní es tan importante como la europea.

España dominó esta región, mientras que
Portugal controló el Brasil. En los años 1800, estos
países se separaron de España, bajo líderes como
José de San Martín y Bernardo O'Higgins. Luego,
inmigrantes de Italia, Francia y Alemania vinieron
en la década de 1850. Hoy estos países forman
parte del comercio internacional.

14 catorce
Etapa preliminar

Classroom Community

Paired Activity Have pairs of students choose one
of the **Southern Cone** countries. Using library or
Internet sources, have them research a place of interest
to them and create a tourist poster advertising why
people should visit that place.

Learning Scenario Using the information they
researched for the "Paired Activity," have students write
and present skits. One student plays a tourist visiting
the place advertised in the poster, and the other
student plays a person from the area. The tourist asks
questions about the sites and the local person provides
helpful information.

Ask students the following activating questions: CHILE: ¿Qué minerales crees que hay en Chile? Investiga tus respuestas. URUGUAY: ¿Qué negocios crees que hay en un lugar como Punta del Este? LOS ANDES: ¿Qué característica distingue a los Andes de otras cadenas de montañas? ACONCAGUA: Mira un mapa topográfico de Argentina. ¿Por qué crees que es un paraíso para deportistas? BUENOS AIRES: Según las fotos que ves en esta página, ¿qué clase de compañías crees que hacen negocios en el Cono Sur?

Comprehension Questions

1. ¿El Cono Sur es una región en el extremo sur del continente americano? (Sí)
2. ¿Está Chile en la costa atlántica o pacífica? (pacífica)
3. ¿Cuál es la capital de Chile? (Santiago)
4. ¿Cuál es una cultura indígena importante en Paraguay? (la cultura guaraní)
5. ¿Quiénes fueron líderes en la lucha por la independencia de España? (José de San Martín y Bernardo O'Higgins)
6. ¿Qué mineral precioso se encuentra en Chile? (el lapislázuli)
7. ¿Cómo puedes pasar el Año Nuevo en Punta del Este? (tomar el sol en la playa)
8. ¿Cuáles son dos instalaciones de esquí en el Cono Sur? (Portillo en Chile y Bariloche en Argentina)
9. ¿Qué altura tiene el volcán Aconcagua? (6.959 metros)
10. ¿Por qué es importante Buenos Aires? (Tiene un importante centro financiero.)

CHILE Chile tiene una de las industrias mineras más grandes del mundo. Además de otros minerales, el país tiene minerales preciosos como el lapislázuli, del cual se hacen bellas artesanías.

URUGUAY Si la nieve y el frío te molestan, ¿por qué no visitas el famoso destino turístico de Punta del Este en Uruguay? ¡Aquí puedes pasar el Año Nuevo tomando el sol en la playa!

LOS ANDES Si estás cansado(a) del sol en el verano del hemisferio norte, ¿por qué no vienes al hemisferio sur para esquiar en la nieve durante su invierno? Aquí hay excelentes instalaciones para este deporte, como Portillo en Chile y Bariloche en Argentina.

ARGENTINA El famoso e impresionante Aconcagua, el volcán más alto del continente americano, tiene una altura de 6.959 metros. Es un paraíso para los deportistas de todo el mundo.

ARGENTINA Buenos Aires es una de las ciudades más importantes de las Américas. Tiene un importante centro financiero. Se ha convertido en un centro para muchas compañías internacionales.

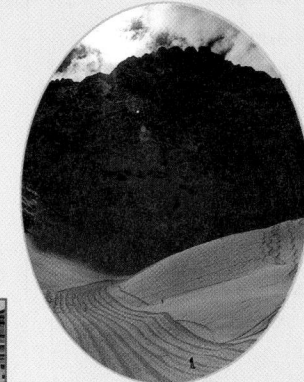

quince
Etapa preliminar **15**

Teaching All Students

Extra Help Check comprehension by making true/false statements about the reading. If the statement is false, students must correct it.

Multiple Intelligences

Intrapersonal Have students write 5 reasons why they would like to visit the countries of the **Southern Cone.**

Kinesthetic Display OHT M4 or a map of the **Southern Cone** countries. As students read each culture note on p. 15, have a volunteer point out the place on the map.

Block Schedule

Variety Ask each student to research 1 recipe from a **Southern Cone** country. Have students present the recipes to the class. Determine which recipes might be easy to make. If possible, make the recipes in school. If not, have volunteers make the recipes to share with the class. (For additional activities, see **Block Scheduling Copymasters.**)

Teaching Resource Options

Print
Más práctica Workbook PE, pp. 5–6
Cuaderno para hispanohablantes
  PE, pp. 5–6
Block Scheduling Copymasters
Back to School Pack
  Practice Activities, pp. 23–26
  Más práctica Workbook TE,
    pp. 39–40
  Cuaderno para hispanohablantes
    TE, pp. 59–60
  Absent Student Copymasters, p. 72

Audiovisual
OHT 12 (Quick Start), 18 (Grammar)

Technology
Online Workbook, Preliminary

Quick Start Review

 El Cono Sur

Use OHT 12 or write on the board:
Identify the following:

1. Aconcagua
2. Punta del Este
3. el lapislázuli
4. Bariloche
5. Buenos Aires

Answers
Answers will vary, but could include:
1. el volcán más alto del continente
   americano
2. un destino turístico en Uruguay
3. un mineral precioso
4. una instalación de esquí en Argentina
5. un importante centro financiero

Teaching Suggestions
Reviewing Verbs with Spelling Changes in the Preterite
• You may want to point out that the **c**
  becomes **qu** to maintain the /k/ sound
  and the **g** become **gu** to maintain the
  /g/ sound before the **-é** ending.
• Ask students what **llegué** and
  busqué would sound like if there
  were no spelling change.
• Have students brainstorm a list of
  other verbs with spelling changes in
  the preterite:
  -car: explicar, marcar, practicar,
    pescar, sacar, secar(se), tocar
  -gar: apagar, jugar, pagar
  -zar: cruzar, comenzar, empezar

En acción
VOCABULARIO Y GRAMÁTICA

REPASO   Verbs with Spelling Changes in the Preterite

Certain verbs change the spelling of their **yo forms** in the **preterite**.
The rest of the preterite forms are regular.

Verbs with Spelling Changes in the Preterite

c → qu	g → gu	z → c
bus**car**	lle**gar**	almor**zar**
bus**qu**é	lle**gu**é	almor**c**é
busc**aste**	lleg**aste**	almorz**aste**
busc**ó**	lleg**ó**	almorz**ó**
busc**amos**	lleg**amos**	almorz**amos**
busc**asteis**	lleg**asteis**	almorz**asteis**
busc**aron**	lleg**aron**	almorz**aron**

Practice:
Actividades
11 12 13 14

Más práctica
cuaderno pp. 5, 6
Para hispanohablantes
cuaderno pp. 5, 6

Online Workbook
CLASSZONE.COM

11 **¡Tantas preguntas!**

Hablar/*Escribir* Tu hermanito(a)
siempre te hace muchas
preguntas. Como no estaba
en casa cuando llegaste del
partido de fútbol ayer, ahora
quiere saber más sobre
el partido. Primero, tu
compañero(a) hará el papel del
(de la) hermanito(a). Luego,
cambien de papel.

modelo
Compañero(a): *¿Jugaste en el partido*
de fútbol?
Tú: *Sí, (No, no) jugué en el partido*
de fútbol.

1. ¿Practicaste antes del
   partido?
2. ¿Sacaste fotos del equipo?
3. ¿Almorzaste con el equipo
   después del partido?
4. ¿Pagaste la cuenta para todo
   el equipo?
5. ¿Llegaste tarde a casa?
6. ¿Le explicaste a papá por
   qué llegaste tarde?
7. ¿Buscaste los libros de
   historia?
8. ¿Visitaste a tus abuelos?
9. ¿Hablaste con el profesor
   de español?
10. ¿Comiste en tu casa ayer?

16 dieciséis
Etapa preliminar

Classroom Community

Paired Activity Write the following list of verbs on
the board: aprender, escuchar, empezar, olvidar,
jugar, tocar, participar, llegar, comprar, practicar,
mirar, buscar, comer, regresar, perder, comprender,
escribir, alquilar, salir, pasar. Then have students
work in pairs and use the list to tell each other at least
3 things they did last week and 3 things they didn't do.

Storytelling Using the list of verbs from the "Paired
Activity," have students write and present humorous
stories about an imaginary person's disastrous week.
Students may also use other verbs that are regular or
have spelling changes in the preterite.

⑫ Buenos Aires

Escribir Caminas por la Avenida 9 de Julio en Buenos Aires y escuchas las siguientes conversaciones. Usa el pretérito.

«_____ (llegar) al mercado con mucho dinero. Después de que _____ (pagar) la comida, ¡no me quedó nada!»

«_____ (sacar) la cámara. _____ (empezar) a sacar fotos. Un turista se enojó.»

«_____ (almorzar) en un restaurante. _____ (salir) a la calle pero no vi que estaba lloviendo. Cuando lo vi, _____ (comenzar) a correr.»

⑬ Ayer

Escribir Escribe una descripción de todo lo que hiciste ayer. Usa los verbos de la lista.

modelo

Ayer jugué al fútbol. Luego fui a mi clase de piano. Después…

buscar	llegar	jugar
cruzar	almorzar	empezar
sacar	pagar	tocar

⑭ De vacaciones

Hablar Fuiste de vacaciones a la República Dominicana. Tu compañero(a) quiere saber más de tu viaje. Luego cambien de papel.

modelo

Tú: *Fui de vacaciones a la República Dominicana.*

Compañero(a): *¿De veras? ¿Sacaste fotos?*

Tú: *Sí, claro. Saqué muchas fotos.*

Compañero(a): *¿Qué más hiciste?*

Tú: *…*

Teaching All Students

Extra Help Have students write answers to the following questions:

1. ¿Qué deporte practicaste la semana pasada?
2. ¿Dónde almorzaste el domingo?
3. ¿A qué hora llegaste a casa ayer?
4. ¿Qué buscaste en tu mochila?
5. ¿A qué hora empezaste la tarea ayer?

Multiple Intelligences

Verbal Call out verbs with spelling changes in the preterite. Have one student provide the **yo** form of the present and another student provide the **él** form of the preterite to hear the difference. For example: **buscar** (yo busco vs. él buscó), **llegar** (yo llego vs. él llegó), **sacar** (yo saco vs. él sacó), **pagar** (yo pago vs. él pagó).

 Objective: Controlled practice
11 Verbs with spelling changes in the preterite in conversation

Answers
1. Sí, (No, no) practiqué antes del partido.
2. Sí, (No, no) saqué fotos del equipo.
3. Sí, (No, no) almorcé con el equipo después del partido.
4. Sí, (No, no) pagué la cuenta para todo el equipo.
5. Sí, (No, no) llegué tarde a casa.
6. Sí, (No, no) le expliqué a papá por qué llegué tarde.

 Objective: Controlled practice
12 Verbs with spelling changes in the preterite in writing

Answers
Conversación #1
Llegué / pagué

Conversación #2
Saqué / Empecé

Conversación #3
Almorcé / Salí / comencé

 Objective: Transitional practice
13 Verbs with spelling changes in the preterite in writing

Answers will vary.

 Objective: Open-ended practice
14 Verbs with spelling changes in the preterite in conversation

Answers will vary.

Teaching Suggestion

To remind students of the regular preterite forms of these verbs, have them also do **Actividad 12** using **él/ella** forms.

▆ Block Schedule

Change of Pace Have students expand on **Actividad 11** and write a sports-related story that either happened to them or to someone else. They must use at least 1 example of each type of spell-changing verb in the preterite. (For additional activities, see **Block Scheduling Copymasters**.)

Teaching Resource Options

Print
Block Scheduling Copymasters
Back to School Pack
  Absent Student Copymasters, p. 73

Audiovisual
OHT M5; 13 (Quick Start), 15
Canciones CD

Quick Start Review

♻ Verbs with spelling changes in the preterite

Use OHT 13 or write on the board: Write preterite sentences using the following verbs in the **yo** form:

1. sacar   4. explicar
2. pagar   5. jugar
3. empezar

Answers
Answers will vary, but will include the following verb forms:
1. saqué   2. pagué   3. empecé
4. expliqué   5. jugué

Teaching Suggestions

• Use OHT M5 and have students locate the regions of Spain and the major cities.
• Have students skim the reading silently, then have volunteers read it aloud.
• Emphasize that within Spain, there are many cultures that differ in dress, music, customs, and language.
• Ask the Comprehension questions on TE p. 19.

Interdisciplinary Connection

Art Tell students that one of the most visible reminders of the Arabic presence in Spain is the architecture. Show them pictures of the Alhambra in Granada as an example of the style. Then have students research other examples of Arabic architecture in Spain and present them to the class.

Culture Highlights

● **GALICIA** Además del castellano, la mayoría de la gente en Galicia habla gallego, un idioma parecido al portugués.

● **TOLEDO** Las iglesias de Toledo tienen unas de las obras más impresionantes de España, como las del pintor El Greco.

España VIDEO DVD

UN PAÍS DE
múltiples culturas

Javier Morcillo

Ahora llegamos

a mi patria: España. Permítanme presentarme... En el video del nivel 1 hago el papel de Luis Paz Villarreal. En realidad soy Javier Morcillo y soy actor. En la unidad 5 de este libro vamos a ver cómo las artes y la arquitectura de España influyeron en los países del Nuevo Mundo ¡y viceversa! También voy a dar mis opiniones sobre las bellas artes.

Antes de empezar, vamos a aprender un poco de la historia de España.

¡Adiós!

Javier

Cuando estudiamos las historias de otros países hispanohablantes, aprendimos cómo España los conquistó y trajo su propia cultura. ¿Pero sabías que hace muchos años la misma cosa ocurrió en España?

La región que hoy es España fue conquistada por varios grupos durante su larga historia — los romanos, los visigodos y los árabes, entre otros. Su nombre viene de los romanos, quienes la llamaron «Hispania». Todavía existen ruinas en España que datan de esta época.

Los árabes llegaron en el año 711 d.C. y estuvieron hasta 1492, cuando las fuerzas de los monarcas Fernando e Isabel los expulsaron de España. Estos reyes unificaron las regiones y culturas diversas del país y establecieron una lengua común, el castellano, como también se llama al español.

La España de hoy es un país muy diverso. Las diferentes influencias culturales se ven en regiones donde se hablan una multitud de lenguas además del español. Entre ellas están el catalán, el vasco y el gallego. Vivimos en un período de libertad cultural. Somos parte de la comunidad europea, ¡pero también mantenemos nuestro estilo propio!

18   dieciocho
Etapa preliminar

Classroom Community

Group Activity Have small groups of students brainstorm and write a list of facts that they already know about Spain. Then have them research and write at least 5 current events in Spain. Have groups present their information to the class. Create a class fact booklet about Spain.

Portfolio Have students research the history of either Madrid, Barcelona, Sevilla, Toledo, Bilbao, Valencia, Granada, Santiago de Compostela, or Pamplona. Have them create time lines that show different events, cultures, etc., that relate to the development of the city.

Rubric **A** = 13–15 pts. **B** = 10–12 pts. **C** = 7–9 pts. **D** = 4–6 pts. **F** = < 4 pts.

Writing criteria	Scale
Accuracy	1 2 3 4 5
Details/organization	1 2 3 4 5
Creativity/presentation	1 2 3 4 5

GALICIA En Galicia existen costumbres celtas muy antiguas. Su instrumento musical, la gaita, se parece al *bagpipe* celta. Y su baile folklórico, la muñeira, es muy similar a las danzas típicas de Irlanda y Escocia.

BARCELONA

TOLEDO Un ejemplo excelente de la fusión de varias culturas es la ciudad de Toledo. Cada parte de esta ciudad evoca su pasado formidable y sus influencias cristianas, árabes y judías.

CATALUÑA El Palau de la Música Catalana es una obra creativa difícil de olvidar. Su arquitecto, Domènech i Montaner, la construyó entre 1905 y 1908. Es muy famoso por su bella y espectacular cúpula.

BILBAO Uno de los edificios más interesantes es el nuevo Museo Guggenheim, en Bilbao. ¡Esta construcción del arquitecto Frank Gehry ya es una de las más famosas del planeta!

diecinueve
Etapa preliminar 19

Teaching Suggestion

Ask students the following activating questions: GALICIA: ¿Con qué otros países comparte Galicia la cultura celta? TOLEDO: ¿En qué otros países de Europa crees que se encuentran culturas múltiples? BILBAO: ¿Crees que tener un museo es importante en una ciudad? CATALUÑA: ¿Qué otros adjetivos puedes asociar con la cúpula?

Comprehension Questions

1. ¿Fue conquistada España por los romanos, los visigodos y los árabes? (Sí)
2. ¿Llegaron los árabes en el año 711 o en·el año 1492? (en el año 711)
3. ¿Quiénes expulsaron a los árabes? (los monarcas Fernando e Isabel)
4. ¿Cuál es el otro nombre de la lengua española? (el castellano)
5. ¿Cuáles son algunas otras lenguas que se hablan en España? (el catalán, el vasco y el gallego)
6. ¿A qué se parece el instrumento musical la gaita? (al *bagpipe* celta)
7. ¿Cómo se llama el baile folklórico de Galicia? (la muñeira)
8. ¿Qué influencias se ven el la ciudad de Toledo? (las influencias cristianas, árabes y judías)
9. ¿Por qué es famoso El Palau de la Música Catalana? (por su bella y espectacular cúpula)
10. ¿Dónde se encuentra el nuevo Museo Guggenheim? (en Bilbao)

Block Schedule

Challenge Have pairs of students first create outline maps of Spain that show the various regions. Then have them research folk dances that represent at least 2 of the regions. Using library or Internet sources, have them draw pictures of typical dancers for each dance and situate them in or near the appropriate regions on the map. (For additional activities, see **Block Scheduling Copymasters**.)

Teaching All Students

Extra Help Provide students with a copy of the Comprehension Questions on TE p. 19. First, have them locate the paragraph where they will find each answer. Then have them write answers to the questions.

Challenge Have students find out how to say *Good morning* in **catalán** and **gallego**. In both languages, it is **Bon dia**.

Multiple Intelligences

Intrapersonal Have students write a brief paragraph explaining which city/region pictured on p. 19 interests them the most.

Logical/Mathematical Have students research the price of an airline ticket from your region to Madrid. Have them calculate the price in **euros**.

Teaching Resource Options

Print 📖

Más práctica Workbook PE, pp. 7–8
Cuaderno para hispanohablantes
 PE, pp. 7–8
Block Scheduling Copymasters
Back to School Pack
 Practice Activities, pp. 27–30
 Más práctica Workbook TE,
 pp. 41–42
 Cuaderno para hispanohablantes
 TE, pp. 61–62
 Absent Student Copymasters, p. 73

Audiovisual 🎧

OHT 13 (Quick Start), 19 (Grammar)

Technology 🎧💻

Online Workbook, Preliminary

Quick Start Review

🔄 España

Use OHT 13 or write on the board:
Match the following items:

1. ___ el Museo Guggenheim
2. ___ el español
3. ___ El Palau de la Música Catalana
4. ___ Galicia
5. ___ Fernando e Isabel
 a. Doménech i Montaner
 b. Bilbao
 c. el castellano
 d. monarcas
 e. la gaita

Answers
1. b 2. c 3. a 4. e 5. d

Teaching Suggestions

Reviewing Verbs with Stem Changes in the Preterite

• Point out that in the preterite there are only 2 types of stem changes: e → i and o → u. These stem changes occur only in the third-person singular and plural forms. Verbs ending in **ar/er** do not have stem changes in the preterite.

• Other verbs conjugated like **sentir** in the preterite are **servir**, **seguir**, and **requerir**. The only verb students know that is conjugated like **dormir** in the preterite is **morir**.

En acción
VOCABULARIO Y GRAMÁTICA

REPASO   **Verbs with Stem Changes in the Preterite**

▶ Remember that **-ir** verbs that have a change in the stem in the present tense also have a stem change (**e → i** or **o → u**) in the **preterite**.

▶ Other verbs like **sentir**:

 despedirse, divertirse, pedir, preferir, repetir, sugerir, vestirse.

-ir Verbs with Stem Changes in the Preterite

	sentir	**dormir**
yo	**sent**í	**dorm**í
tú	**sent**iste	**dorm**iste
usted, él, ella,	**s**i**nt**ió	**d**u**rm**ió
nosotros(as)	**sent**imos	**dorm**imos
vosotros(as)	**sent**isteis	**dorm**isteis
ustedes, ellos, ellas	**s**i**nt**ieron	**d**u**rm**ieron

Practice: **Actividades** 15 16 17 18   **Más práctica** *cuaderno pp. 7, 8*   **Para hispanohablantes** *cuaderno pp. 7, 8*   **Online Workbook** CLASSZONE.COM

---

15 Al día siguiente

Escribir Al día siguiente, Mariana decidió escribirle a su mejor amiga para describir la fiesta de su prima Ángela. Completa su carta con el pretérito de los verbos entre paréntesis.

Nota: Gramática

Remember to use the pronouns **me, te, se, nos** and **os** with reflexive verbs like **vestirse**, **dormirse** and **despedirse**.

Querida Ileana,

 Anoche fui a la fiesta de Ángela. Ella __1__ (sugerir) que llegáramos antes de las seis. Mi hermano Ricardo __2__ (preferir) no ir porque no se sentía bien. Yo decidí ir con Gustavo. Él __3__ (vestirse) con un traje muy elegante.

 Gustavo no sabía llegar, así que le __4__ (pedir) direcciones a un policía que estaba en la esquina. El policía le __5__ (repetir) las direcciones varias veces pero como quiera nos perdimos.

 Por fin llegamos. Ángela __6__ (servir) comida muy sabrosa: tortilla española y otras tapas. Todos los invitados __7__ (divertirse) mucho en la fiesta. Gustavo estaba tan cansado que ¡ __8__ (dormirse) en el sofá! Los invitados __9__ (despedirse) muy tarde. ¡Qué noche más divertida!

Abrazos,

Mariana

20   veinte
 Etapa preliminar

Classroom Community

Game Play Bingo by providing students with a list of 25 verb infinitives reviewed so far in this **Etapa.** Students write the verbs in any order in rows of 5 across and 5 down. Then state sentences using the verbs in the preterite tense. Students check off the infinitives of the verbs they hear. The first person to get 5 in a row wins.

Storytelling In groups of 5, have students tell stories using the stem-changing verbs listed on p. 20. Each student is responsible for incorporating 2 of the verbs into the story.

16 ¡Qué colores!

Hablar/Escribir Tu amigo español, Juan Felipe, invitó a todos sus amigos a una fiesta con una condición: tenían que vestirse de colores brillantes. ¿Cómo se vistieron todos?

Mario

modelo

Tú: ¿Cómo se vistió Mario en la fiesta?

Compañero(a): No sé, ¡pero dicen que se vistió de jeans morados y camiseta roja!

1. Marta y Mariana

2. Álvaro

3. Anita

4. Daniel y Donaldo

17 El desayuno

Hablar Tú y tu familia desayunaron en el Hotel Prisma. Tu amigo(a) quiere saber qué pidieron todos. ¿Qué te pregunta y cómo le contestas?

> **Hotel Prisma**
>
> *Desayuno*
>
> Café con leche
> Bollos de pan
> Chocolate y churros
> Zumo de naranja
> Cereales

modelo

Compañero(a): ¿Qué pediste para el desayuno?

Tú: Yo pedí huevos revueltos con jamón.

Compañero(a): Y papá, ¿qué pidió?…

18 ¿Cómo estuvo?

Hablar Tú y tu compañero(a) hablan sobre fiestas distintas con los verbos de la lista.

modelo

Tú: ¿Se divirtieron todos en la fiesta de Elena?

Compañero(a): ¡Bailamos y comimos! ¿Y en tu fiesta?

Tú: También. Bailamos música del grupo…

despedirse	seguir	preferir	repetir
divertirse	servir	sugerir	vestirse

ACTIVIDAD 15 **Objective:** Controlled practice
Verbs with stem changes in the preterite in writing

Answers
1. sugirió
2. prefirió
3. se vistió
4. pidió
5. repitió
6. sirvió
7. se divirtieron
8. se durmió
9. se despidieron

ACTIVIDAD 16 **Objective:** Transitional practice
Verbs with stem changes in the preterite in conversation

Answers
Answers will vary. Answers could include:
1. A: ¿Cómo se vistieron Marta y Mariana en la fiesta?
   B: No sé, ¡pero dicen que se vistieron de faldas amarillas y blusas de rayas!
2. A: ¿Cómo se vistió Álvaro en la fiesta?
   B: No sé, ¡pero dicen que se vistió de shorts negros, camiseta blanca y chaqueta amarilla!
3. A: ¿Cómo se vistió Anita en la fiesta?
   B: No sé, ¡pero dicen que se vistió de jeans de cuadros y camiseta anaranjada!
4. A: ¿Cómo se vistieron Daniel y Donaldo en la fiesta?
   B: No sé, ¡pero dicen que se vistieron de jeans verdes, camisas rojas y gafas de sol!

ACTIVIDAD 17 **Objective:** Transitional practice
Verbs with stem changes in the preterite in conversation

Answers will vary.

ACTIVIDAD 18 **Objective:** Open-ended practice
Verbs with stem changes in the preterite in conversation

Answers will vary.

Teaching All Students

Extra Help Before doing **Actividad 17**, brainstorm a list of breakfast foods in Spanish with the class.

Native Speakers Have students create menus similar to the one in **Actividad 17**, using dishes that are popular in their countries of origin. Students may use these menus for their conversation.

Multiple Intelligences
Verbal Have each student say how someone they know dressed yesterday.

Block Schedule

Variety Using **Actividad 15** as a model, have students write their own version of a letter to a Spanish-speaking friend where they describe an event that took place. (For additional activities, see **Block Scheduling Copymasters**.)

Teaching Resource Options

Teaching Resource Options

Print 🕮

Block Scheduling Copymasters
Back to School Pack
 Absent Student Copymasters, p. 74

Audiovisual 🎧

OHT M4; 16 (Quick Start), 21
Canciones CD

🔔 Quick Start Review

♻ **Verbs with stem changes in the preterite**
Use OHT 16 or write on the board:
Complete the paragraph with the preterite of the verbs in parentheses:

¿Sabes por qué Amelia nunca ___ (volver) a ese restaurante? Porque ella ___ (pedir) un refresco y ___ (repetir) muchas veces, **Muy frío,** pero el mesero lo ___ (servir) caliente.

Answers
volvió, pidió, repitió, sirvió

Teaching Suggestions

• Use OHT M4 and have students locate the Andes and these countries.
• Have the class brainstorm what they already know about these 5 countries: **¿Qué saben ya sobre estos 5 países?**
• Have students read pp. 22–23 silently. Have students write down unfamiliar words.
• Tell students to use context to guess the meaning of the unfamiliar words.
• Have volunteers reread the selection aloud.
• Ask the Comprehension questions on TE p. 23.

✺ Culture Highlights

● **CUZCO** En Cuzco quedan restos del Templo del Sol, la muralla de la ciudad, paredes, puertas y arcos.

● **EL LAGO TITICACA** El lago Titicaca se extiende desde el sur de Perú hasta el oeste de Bolivia. Mide 110 millas de largo y alrededor de 35 de ancho.

Bolivia, Colombia, Ecuador, Perú y Venezuela 📺 VIDEO 💿 DVD

VISTAS de los Andes

¡**Hola!** ¡Volvemos a Sudamérica otra vez! Yo me llamo Ximena Barros, pero en el video del nivel 1, me conoces como Patricia López Carrera. También estoy en el video de este libro. En la unidad 6 hablo de la tecnología personal y cómo nos ha cambiado la vida.

Pero vamos a dejar ese tema hasta más tarde y hablar sobre los países que vas a conocer al empezar la unidad 6: Perú (o el Perú), Colombia, Bolivia, Venezuela y Ecuador (o el Ecuador).

¡Hasta pronto! *Ximena*

La Cordillera de los Andes pasa por todos estos países. Con la excepción de Bolivia, que no tiene costa, los divide en tres regiones: la montaña, la costa y la selva amazónica. Como puedes ver, ¡es una geografía muy diversa!

También son muy diversas las culturas que se encuentran en estas regiones. Cuando los españoles llegaron aquí en los años 1500, descubrieron una multitud de civilizaciones indígenas, incluso el famoso imperio inca. Por lo general, en la región montañosa la población es europea, mestiza e indígena. En la costa se ve mucho la influencia africana. Y en la selva tropical todavía existen sociedades indígenas.

Simón Bolívar, el «Libertador de América», dirigió los movimientos de independencia de España en esta región. Hoy estos países son un grupo de naciones unidas por diversos elementos naturales y culturales. Sin embargo cada país mantiene su identidad individual y su propia historia económica, social y política.

22 veintidós
Etapa preliminar

Classroom Community

Cooperative Learning Divide the class into 5 groups. Assign 1 of the 5 countries to each group. Groups research interesting information about their countries. Then they design a collage of pictures and facts on a large piece of posterboard. Collect all the posterboards to create a class bulletin board of these Andean countries.

Learning Scenario Have pairs of students role-play an interview. One student is a reporter and the other is a tourist who has just returned from these countries. The reporter asks questions about the trip and about the history, the sights, and life in these countries. Then have students reverse roles.

COLOMBIA Artefactos y objetos de arte de todo tipo forman las exhibiciones en el Museo de Oro en Bogotá. Aquí se puede ver una impresionante colección de joyería de oro que data desde antes de la conquista española.

VENEZUELA El parque nacional Canaima es uno de los más grandes del mundo. Aquí puedes explorar más de 11.500 millas cuadradas de naturaleza protegida.

BOLIVIA/PERÚ El lago Titicaca es el lago navegable más elevado del mundo, a una altura de 3.810 metros. Aquí se pueden ver pueblos y costumbres que nos recuerdan cómo era el mundo americano antes de la llegada de los españoles.

PERÚ Cuzco fue la capital del imperio inca, que dominaba una extensa región de Sudamérica antes de la llegada de los españoles.

ECUADOR En Ecuador, como en los demás países andinos, las antiguas costumbres coexisten con la tecnología. Un ejemplo son las hermosas granjas de flores que exportan plantas al mundo entero.

veintitrés
Etapa preliminar   **23**

Cross Cultural Connections

Have students compare each photo on p. 23 with a place with which they are familiar.

Teaching Suggestion

Ask students the following activating questions: COLOMBIA: ¿Para qué crees que los indígenas utilizaban estas máscaras? VENEZUELA: ¿Cómo crees que se puede usar la tecnología para proteger la naturaleza? PERÚ: Mira la foto. ¿Crees que Cuzco está en un valle o en una montaña? ¿Por qué? LAGO TITICACA: ¿Por qué crees que los indígenas y luego los españoles establecieron ciudades cerca de este lago? ECUADOR: ¿Qué tecnologías pueden utilizar las granjas de flores para su negocio?

Comprehension Questions

1. ¿Tiene costa Bolivia? (No)
2. ¿Llegaron los españoles a esta región en los 1400 o en los 1500? (en los 1500)
3. ¿Qué civilización famosa descubrieron los españoles? (el imperio inca)
4. ¿Cómo es la población en la región montañosa? (europea, mestiza e indígena)
5. ¿Qué todavía existen en la selva tropical? (sociedades indígenas)
6. ¿Quién dirigió los movimientos de independencia de España en esta región? (Simón Bolívar)
7. ¿Dónde se encuentra Canaima? (en Venezuela)
8. ¿A qué altura está el lago Titicaca? (a una altura de más de 3.810 metros)
9. ¿Cuál fue la capital del imperio inca? (Cuzco)
10. ¿Qué exportan muchas granjas en Ecuador? (flores)

Teaching All Students

Extra Help Have students work in pairs and take turns rereading the paragraphs on pp. 22–23. To ensure comprehension, they should stop after each paragraph and ask each other one question.

Multiple Intelligences

Naturalist Have students research and present a brief report on either the ecological reserve Canaima or Lake Titicaca. They should present the report as if the class were on a walking tour of the area.

■ Block Schedule

Variety Have students create maps showing different aspects of the countries: topography, agriculture, landmarks, etc., and decorate them with drawings and objects. (For additional activities, see **Block Scheduling Copymasters**.)

Teaching Resource Options

Print

Más práctica Workbook PE, pp. 9–10
Cuaderno para hispanohablantes
  PE, pp. 9–10
Actividades para todos Workbook PE,
  pp. 1–10
Block Scheduling Copymasters
Back to School Pack
  Practice Activities, pp. 31–34
  Más práctica Workbook TE,
    pp. 43–44
  Actividades para todos Workbook
    TE, pp. 45–54
  Cuaderno para hispanohablantes
    TE, pp. 63–64
  Information Gap Activities, p. 67
  Absent Student Copymasters, p. 74
  Audioscript, pp. 77–78

Audiovisual

OHT 16 (Quick Start), 20 (Grammar)
Audio Program CD 1, Track 2, Actividad 19

Technology

Online Workbook, Preliminary

Quick Start Review

 The Andes countries
Use OHT 16 or write on the board:
Identify each of the following:

1. Simón Bolívar
2. el Lago Titicaca
3. el Museo de Oro en Bogotá
4. Canaima
5. Cuzco

Answers
Answers will vary, but could include:
1. el «Libertador de América»
2. el lago navegable más elevado de mundo
3. donde se puede ver una colección de
   joyería de oro
4. parque nacional de Venezuela
5. la capital del imperio inca

Teaching Suggestions
Reviewing Irregular Preterites
• Point out that all of these verbs form
  the preterite on an irregular stem and
  that they do not have an accent on
  the final syllable.
• Have students create mnemonic
  devices for remembering the verbs
  that are irregular in the preterite.

En acción
VOCABULARIO Y GRAMÁTICA

REPASO   Irregular Preterites

▶ A number of verbs have **irregular preterite** forms.
These verbs are grouped by similar stem changes or other like forms.

	ser and **ir**
yo	**fui**
tú	**fuiste**
usted, él, ella	**fue**
nosotros(as)	**faos**
vosotros(as)	**fuisteis**
ustedes, ellos, ellas	**fueron**

tener	**estar**	**andar**
t**uve**	est**uve**	and**uve**
t**uviste**	est**uviste**	and**uviste**
t**uvo**	est**uvo**	and**uvo**
t**uvimos**	est**uvimos**	and**uvimos**
t**uvisteis**	est**uvisteis**	and**uvisteis**
t**uvieron**	est**uvieron**	and**uvieron**

poder	**po**ner	**sa**ber
p**ude**	p**use**	s**upe**
p**udiste**	p**usiste**	s**upiste**
p**udo**	p**uso**	s**upo**
p**udimos**	p**usimos**	s**upimos**
p**udisteis**	p**usisteis**	s**upisteis**
p**udieron**	p**usieron**	s**upieron**

hacer	**ve**nir	**que**rer
h**ice**	v**ine**	qu**ise**
h**iciste**	v**iniste**	qu**isiste**
h**izo**	v**ino**	qu**iso**
h**icimos**	v**inimos**	qu**isimos**
h**icisteis**	v**inisteis**	qu**isisteis**
h**icieron**	v**inieron**	qu**isieron**

decir	**traer**	**produ**cir
d**ije**	tra**je**	produ**je**
d**ijiste**	tra**jiste**	produ**jiste**
d**ijo**	tra**jo**	produ**jo**
d**ijimos**	tra**jimos**	produ**jimos**
d**ijisteis**	tra**jisteis**	produ**jisteis**
d**ijeron**	tra**jeron**	produ**jeron**

dar	**ver**
di	**vi**
diste	**viste**
dio	**vio**
dimos	**vimos**
disteis	**visteis**
dieron	**vieron**

Practice: **Actividades** ⑲ ⑳ ㉑   **Más práctica** *cuaderno* pp. 9, 10
Para hispanohablantes *cuaderno* pp. 9, 10

 **Online Workbook**
CLASSZONE.COM

Classroom Community

Group Activity Divide the class into small groups.
Using the theme of last summer's vacation, groups
choose to do one of the following activities: perform a
short skit, present a rap or chant, or create a
poster/collage. Groups must use verbs in the preterite.

Learning Scenario Planning ahead: Bring in
magazine pictures that show people in various scenes.
Distribute the pictures to students and have them make
up an explanation of what happened in the pictures.
They must use at least 2 verbs that are irregular in the
preterite.

19 Irma y Javier

Escuchar/*Escribir* Irma y Javier fueron al centro comercial. Escucha su conversación y luego completa las siguientes oraciones con el pretérito del verbo correcto.

modelo

Irma anduvo *por todo el centro comercial buscando a Javier.*

1. Javier _____ en la tienda de música un rato.
2. Entonces _____ a la tienda de deportes.
3. Irma y Javier _____ de acuerdo en dónde se iban a encontrar.
4. Irma _____ las compras que quería hacer.
5. Irma _____ encontrar todo lo que estaba en su lista.
6. Javier _____ que ir al banco.
7. Javier no _____ su tarjeta de crédito.
8. Marín y Lupita _____ que iban a comprar una computadora nueva.

20 ¿Adónde fueron?

Hablar/*Escribir* Tú y tu compañero(a) conversan sobre sus vacaciones. Imagínense que fueron a unos de los países andinos.

modelo

Tú: *¿Adónde fueron de vacaciones este verano?*

Compañero(a): *Fuimos a Ecuador.*

Tú: *¿Ah, sí? ¿Cuánto tiempo estuvieron en Ecuador?*

Compañero(a): *Estuvimos allá dos semanas.*

adónde cuánto tiempo regalos

cambiar dinero la excursión de...

monumentos por el centro ¿ ?

21 ¿Quién dijo qué?

Hablar En grupos de cinco o seis, jueguen a «¿Quién dijo qué»? Inventen un personaje como la María del modelo. Cada persona añade algo más sobre María a la oración. ¡Sean originales!

modelo

Tú: *¿Qué dijo Miguel?*

Compañero(a) 1: *Miguel dijo que María no hizo la tarea. ¿Qué dijo Arturo?*

Compañero(a) 2: *Arturo dijo que María no hizo la tarea y llegó tarde a clase.*

More Practice: **Más comunicación** *p. R2*

veinticinco
Etapa preliminar   **25**

ACTIVIDAD 19 Objective: Controlled practice Listening comprehension/irregular preterites

Answers (See script, p. xxxiiiB.)
1. estuvo
2. fue
3. se pusieron
4. hizo
5. pudo
6. tuvo
7. trajo
8. dijeron

ACTIVIDAD 20 Objective: Transitional practice Irregular preterites in conversation

Answers will vary.

ACTIVIDAD 21 Objective: Open-ended practice Irregular preterites in conversation

Answers will vary.

Dictation

Using the Listening Activity Script for **Actividad 19** on TE p. xxxixB, dictate selected sentences to students. You may want to use this dictation for a quiz grade.

Quick Wrap-up

Ask students to list each region presented in the **Etapa,** as well as the countries included in each one (where applicable).

Teaching All Students

Extra Help Have students work in pairs. Using the list of verbs on p. 24, one student states a subject pronoun and a verb in the infinitive. The other student gives the present tense form and the preterite form. For example: **yo / saber → yo sé, yo supe.** Students should take turns. Set a time limit.

Multiple Intelligences

Verbal Have students present a one-minute speech on one of the following topics: a special occasion in their lives, a fun time, a scary time, or a challenging time.

Block Schedule

Peer Review Have students review their last week's activities. Then have them write 2 sentences describing what they did each day. Have pairs of students exchange papers and peer correct. They should check for correct preterite forms. (For additional activities, see **Block Scheduling Copymasters.**)

ETAPA PRELIMINAR

En uso
REPASO Y MÁS COMUNICACIÓN

ⓘ Self-Check Quiz
CLASSZONE.COM

Now you can…

• talk about present
  activities.

To review

• the present tense
  see pp. 4, 8.

❶ ¿Con qué frecuencia?

Tu compañero(a) quiere saber con qué frecuencia haces
varias cosas. ¿Qué te pregunta y cómo le respondes?

modelo

¿alquilar un video?

Compañero(a): ¿Con qué frecuencia alquilas un video?

Tú: *Alquilo un video una vez por semana.*

1. ¿patinar en el parque?
2. ¿escribir en la computadora?
3. ¿correr?

4. ¿leer una novela?
5. ¿salir con tus amigos?
6. ¿hacer la tarea?

Now you can…

• talk about past
  activities.

To review

• the preterite
  see pp. 12, 16,
  20, 24.

❷ Mis últimas vacaciones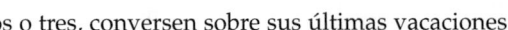

En grupos de dos o tres, conversen sobre sus últimas vacaciones.
Digan adónde fueron, qué hicieron, qué
compraron, qué vieron y si se divirtieron.

modelo

Tú: *¿Adónde fuiste para tus vacaciones?*

Compañero(a) 1: *Fui con mi familia a
Buenos Aires, Argentina.*

Compañero(a) 2: *¿Ah, sí? ¿Qué hicieron? …*

❸ *En tu propia voz*

ESCRITURA Piensa en un evento cómico de tu pasado, o inventa
uno si prefieres. Escribe una descripción del evento. (Si prefieres,
escríbelo como un diálogo.) Luego, lee tu diálogo a la clase.

modelo

*Un día, decidí cortarme el pelo yo mismo(a). Saqué las tijeras y fui al baño
para usar el espejo. Empecé a cortarme el pelo de atrás…*

En resumen

🔄 YA SABES

Flashcards
CLASSZONE.COM

TALK ABOUT PRESENT ACTIVITIES

Common -ar verbs

acampar	to camp
alquilar	to rent
ayudar	to help
bailar	to dance
cambiar	to change
caminar	to walk
cantar	to sing
cenar	to eat dinner
cocinar	to cook
comprar	to buy
desayunar	to have breakfast
descansar	to rest
desear	to desire
enseñar	to teach, to show
escuchar	to listen
esperar	to wait for, to hope
estudiar	to study
ganar	to win
hablar	to talk, to speak
lavar	to wash
limpiar	to clean
llamar	to call
llevar	to take along, to wear, to carry
mandar	to send
mirar	to look at, to watch
nadar	to swim
pasar	to pass, to happen
patinar	to skate
planchar	to iron
quedar	to be (in a specific place), to agree (on)
terminar	to finish
tomar	to take, to eat or drink
trabajar	to work

Common -er verbs

aprender	to learn
beber	to drink
comer	to eat
comprender	to understand
correr	to run
deber	should, ought to
leer	to read
vender	to sell

Common -ir verbs

abrir	to open
compartir	to share
escribir	to write
insistir	to insist
recibir	to receive
vivir	to live

Common stem-changing verbs

cerrar (e→ie)	to close
contar (o→ue)	to tell, to count
encontrar (o→ue)	to find, to meet
entender (e→ie)	to understand
llover (o→ue)	to rain
pensar (e→ie)	to think
perder (e→ie)	to lose
recordar (o→ue)	to remember
sentarse (e→ie)	to sit down
volver (o→ue)	to return, to come back

Common reflexive verbs

acostarse (o→ue)	to go to bed, to lie down
afeitarse	to shave
bañarse	to bathe
despertarse	to wake up
ducharse	to take a shower
lavarse	to wash oneself
levantarse	to get up
maquillarse	to put on makeup
peinarse	to comb one's hair
ponerse	to put on

Common verbs with irregular yo form

caer	to fall
conocer	to know
oír	to hear
salir	to leave
valer	to be worth

TALK ABOUT PAST ACTIVITIES

Common preterite stem-changing verbs

caer	to fall
competir	to compete
conducir	to drive
despedirse	to say goodbye
divertirse	to have fun
dormir	to sleep
pedir	to ask for, to order
preferir	to prefer
repetir	to repeat
sentir	to feel
sugerir	to suggest
vestirse	to dress oneself

Common spelling-change preterite verbs

almorzar	to have lunch
apagar	to turn off
buscar	to look for
comenzar	to start
cruzar	to cross
empezar	to begin
explicar	to explain
jugar	to play (a game)
llegar	to arrive
pagar	to pay
practicar	to practice
sacar	to take
tocar	to play (an instrument)

Common irregular preterite verbs

andar	to walk
dar	to give
decir	to say, to tell
estar	to be
hacer	to do, to make
ir	to go
poder	to be able, can
poner	to put
querer	to want
saber	to know
ser	to be
tener	to have
traer	to bring
venir	to come
ver	to see

veintisiete
Etapa preliminar 27

Rubric: Speaking

Criteria	Scale	
Sentence structure	1 2 3	A = 11–12 pts.
Vocabulary use	1 2 3	B = 9–10 pts.
Originality	1 2 3	C = 7–8 pts.
Fluency	1 2 3	D = 4–6 pts.
		F = < 4 pts.

ACTIVIDAD **3**

En tu propia voz

Rubric: Writing

Criteria	Scale	
Vocabulary use	1 2 3 4 5	A = 14–15 pts.
Accuracy	1 2 3 4 5	B = 12–13 pts.
Creativity, appearance	1 2 3 4 5	C = 10–11 pts.
		D = 8–9 pts.
		F = < 8 pts.

🔔 **Quick Start Review**

🔄 Present tense review

Use OHT 17 or write on the board:
Escribe 5 oraciones para describir tu día típico. Usa verbos de esta etapa, presentados en la sección **En resumen.**

Answers will vary.

Teaching Suggestions
Vocabulary Review

• Have students study the **En resumen** on p. 27.

• Play selections from the **Canciones** CD while students study their vocabulary lists.

• Write 4 or 5 words on the board at a time and have students form present and past tense sentences using all the words.

Teaching All Students 🔲

Extra Help For **Actividad 3,** have students check each other's writing for errors and suggest improvements. Have students save the corrected writing samples in their portfolios. Use the Writing Rubric for grading.

Multiple Intelligences
Musical/Rhythmic Provide students with an outline map of Mexico, Central America, the Caribbean, and South America. Have them research the names of music, dances, and instruments from these areas and locate them on the map. For example: **merengue, salsa, cha-cha-cha, bolero, tango, rumba, cueca, la quena, el arpa andina.**

🔳 **Block Schedule**
FunBreak Have students work in pairs and play hangman with the words in **En resumen.** (For additional activities, see **Block Scheduling Copymasters.**)

Unit Theme
Discussing Spanish-speaking communities in the United States; describing people; and talking about past, present, and future actions

Teaching Resource Options

Print

Block Scheduling Copymasters
Unit 1 Resource Book
  Absent Student Copymasters, p. 39

Audiovisual

OHT M1, M2; 1
Canciones CD
Video Program Videotape 0:00 / DVD,
  Unit 1

Technology

eEdition Plus Online/eEdition CD-ROM
Easy Planner Plus Online/Easy Planner
  CD-ROM
 www.classzone.com

U N I D A D 1

✿ STANDARDS

Communication
- Describing people
- Talking about life experiences and accomplishments
- Describing fashions
- Talking about pastimes
- Predicting future actions
- Talking about household chores
- Expressing feelings

Cultures
- The influence of Spanish speakers in the United States
- The cultural role of fashion
- Musical influences

Connections
- Art: Creating a self-portrait
- Math: Preparing an annual clothing budget

Comparisons
- Childhood experiences
- Geography, climate, and customs and how they influence choice of clothing
- Musical instruments and influences

Communities
- Using Spanish in the workplace
- Using Spanish in Spanish-speaking communities for personal enjoyment

INTERNET Preview
CLASSZONE.COM

- More About Latinos
- Webquest
- Self-Check Quizzes
- Flashcards
- Writing Center
- Online Workbook
- eEdition Plus Online

28

ASÍ SOMOS

SAN ANTONIO
LA PRENSA Éste es el periódico bilingüe que se ha publicado por más tiempo. Lo fundó el Sr. Durán en 1914. ¿Hay un periódico bilingüe en tu comunidad? ¿Cómo se llama?

Classroom Community

Paired Activity Divide the class into pairs. Have each student write 1 question about each culture note. Then have partners ask and answer each other's questions.

Group Activity Working in groups of 3–4, have students compile a list of as many cities in the U.S. as they can think of that have a Spanish name. Have them also list the states where the cities are located. Then have them answer the following questions: Where are most of the cities located? Why?

ALMANAQUE CULTURAL

POBLACIÓN: Porcentaje latino de la población de Estados Unidos: 12,5%

GENTE FAMOSA: Tito Puente (músico), Oscar de la Renta (diseñador), Cristina García (escritora), Sandra Cisneros (escritora)

LUGARES CON NOMBRES DEL ESPAÑOL: Los Ángeles, San Antonio, El Paso, Colorado, Florida, Calle Ocho

VIDEO   DVD   Mira el video para más información.

CLASSZONE.COM
More About Latinos

LOS ÁNGELES
OSCAR DE LA HOYA Este campeón del boxeo ayuda a su comunidad construyendo lugares como el Resurrection Gym donde los atletas jóvenes pueden entrenarse. ¿Piensas que los deportes son buenos para la juventud? ¿Por qué?

CHICAGO
COMIDA MEXICANA El burrito, el taco y la tostada son comidas muy populares en la comunidad mexicana de Chicago. ¿Por qué crees que la comida mexicana también es popular con otros grupos?

NUEVA YORK
REPERTORIO ESPAÑOL Desde 1968, este grupo de teatro presenta obras en español. ¿Alguna vez viste una obra o función en español?

MIAMI
ELLEN OCHOA La Dra. Ellen Ochoa es una astronauta muy conocida y recibió varios premios por su trabajo. Ella investiga los efectos del sol en el clima de la tierra. ¿Qué supones que la Dra. Ochoa estudió para prepararse?

Flamenco & Spanish Dance

PILAR RIOJA

A SALUTE TO GARCÍA LORCA ON HIS CENTENNIAL

August 26 thru October 4

REPERTORIO ESPAÑOL
138 East 27th Street, NYC
(between Lexington & Third Ave.)
(212) 889-2850

29

UNIDAD 1
Cultural Opener

Standards for Foreign Language Learning
Introduction to All Five Standards for Foreign Language Learning

The National Standards are comprised of goals focused on the 5 Cs: Communication, Cultures, Connections, Comparisons, and Communities. Each **Unidad** and **Etapa** of *¡En español!* contains material that introduces students to these goals and then gives them the opportunity to practice and master them. The 5 Cs are five parts of an interconnected whole that represents the consensus of the language teaching profession regarding the goals of language study.

Communication
Communicate in a language other than English.

Cultures
Gain knowledge and understanding of other cultures.

Connections
Connect with other disciplines and acquire information.

Comparisons
Develop insight into the nature of language and culture.

Communities
Participate in multilingual communities at home and around the world.

Teaching Resource Options

Print
Block Scheduling Copymasters

Audiovisual
Poster

Technology
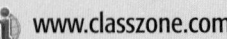 www.classzone.com

Teaching Note
You may wish to explain to students that **Fíjate** means "Take a look."

UNIDAD  1

ASÍ SOMOS

Al seguir estudiando con ¡En español!, vas a desarrollar nuevas habilidades en cinco áreas importantes:

- Comunicación
- Culturas
- Conexiones
- Comparaciones
- Comunidades

Webquest
CLASSZONE.COM

Guided Web-based activities help you explore how Spanish is used in the United States.

Comunicación
Comunícate en otra lengua.

¿Cómo nos comunicamos los unos con los otros? Describimos, preguntamos, explicamos; en fin, nos expresamos. También escuchamos. En la foto, ¿quién habla y quiénes escuchan? ¿Qué tipo de conversación crees que tienen?

Comparaciones
Compara el español con el inglés: las culturas y las lenguas.

Al comparar el español con el inglés aprendes a identificar y a apreciar las semejanzas y las diferencias entre las culturas y las lenguas. ¿Qué semejanzas y diferencias ya conoces? ¿Cuáles se encuentran en este anuncio?

30

Classroom Community

Group Activity Working in groups of five, students make a list of the main points covered in the 5 Cs. Each student within a group may want to cover one of the Cs, recording what they remember from Levels 1 and 2. Have students use the information on pp. 30–31 to help them organize their thoughts. Then, within their groups, have them review the topics and concepts with each other.

Class Activity Write the 5 Cs on the board, creating five columns. Then have students brainstorm what they would like to learn in Level 3 that they have not learned already. Write each of their ideas in the appropriate column. Since some students will list topics presented in earlier levels, this activity will serve as a review. Refer to this list throughout the year, checking off concepts when they are introduced.

Conexiones

Haz conexiones con otras materias.

El español te ayuda a aprender más de otras materias, como el arte, las ciencias y las matemáticas. ¿Qué materias crees que están representadas en la gráfica y en la foto?

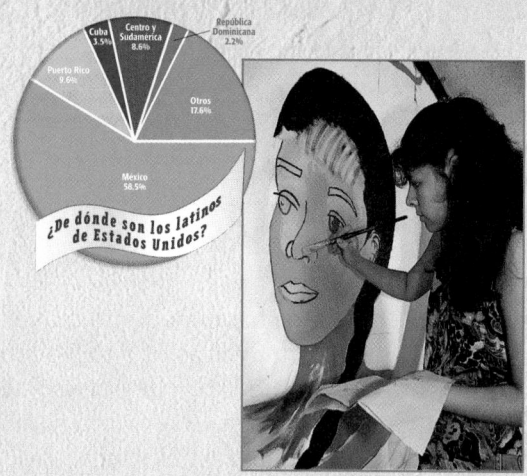

¿De dónde son los latinos de Estados Unidos?

Culturas

Aprende de otras culturas.

Cuando estudiamos las costumbres y los productos de otra cultura, descubrimos las perspectivas que caracterizan a la gente de esa cultura. ¿Qué piensas descubrir al conocer la música de Tito Puente?

Comunidades

Usa el español en tu comunidad.

El español se habla en muchas comunidades del mundo. ¿Se habla español en tu comunidad? Esta alumna usa el español en un hospital. ¿Qué piensas que les pregunta a los pacientes?

Fíjate

¿A cuál de las cinco áreas corresponde cada una de las siguientes situaciones?

1. Estudias y escuchas música hispana para aprender más de la cultura.

2. Buscas en Internet información en español sobre los muralistas hispanos para una presentación en la clase de arte.

3. Trabajas en un lugar donde puedes hablar español.

4. Comparas los anuncios de un periódico hispano con los anuncios del periódico que lees normalmente.

5. En un mensaje electrónico le describes a un(a) amigo(a) tu ropa nueva y le pides su opinión.

31

Teaching Suggestion
Previewing the Standards
- Ask students to list where and when they have either used Spanish or heard it spoken. Then have them share how they might use Spanish after high school. Ask them why they are studying Spanish this year.
- Unit 1, **Así somos**, begins by focusing on the diverse natures of our families and the locales in which we live. After the students describe their worlds, have them compare their lives to those of the actors presented in the Etapa preliminar.

Culture Highlights

● **CONGAS** Los instrumentos de percusión, como las congas de la foto de la página 30, son el alma de muchos ritmos latinos.

Fíjate
Answers
1. Culturas
2. Conexiones
3. Comunidades
4. Comparaciones
5. Comunicación

Teaching All Students

Extra Help Have students bring in pictures of themselves now and in the past. Then have them write five sentences describing themselves now and five sentences describing themselves at the time the picture was taken.

Native Speakers Have the students review the pages in the **Etapa preliminar** that relate to the region of their heritage. Ask students to expand on the information or explain important information they feel has been omitted. Have them use the Internet and create a presentation of their information using an electronic slideshow format or by presenting other visuals to the class.

Block Schedule

Variety Assign groups to research the regions that will be featured in *¡En español!* Level 3. (See the **Etapa preliminar**.) Then have them decide which regions of the United States have been most impacted by the regions they researched and why.

Ampliación

These activities may be used at various points in the Unit 1 sequence.

For Block Schedule, you may find that these projects will provide a welcome change of pace while reviewing and reinforcing the material presented in the unit. See the **Block Scheduling Copymasters.**

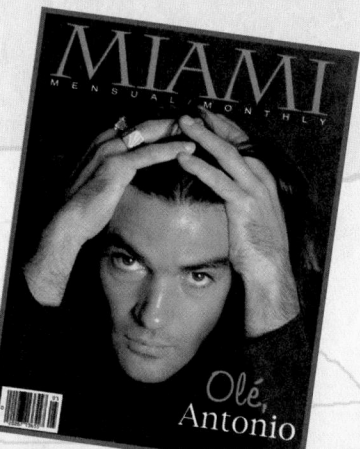

● PROJECTS

Hispanics in the U.S. Make or have students make a large map of the U.S. Have students work in groups of 5 to research Hispanic populations in different parts of the U.S. They can focus on an area (West Coast, Midwest, Southeast, East Coast) or a state. They should find out the origins of the largest Hispanic groups in their area. They can use census reports to find percentages. Have each group use color codes or icons to display the different Hispanic countries of origin on the large map. They also can find information about Hispanic neighborhoods and Hispanic-owned businesses on the Internet.

> PACING SUGGESTION: Display the map and have students begin research at the beginning of the unit. Add to the map until the end of Unit 1.

Hispanic heritage presentations Have students work in pairs to research and present contributions made to the U.S. by the Hispanic community. Each pair should focus on a different contribution (art, music, foods, government, etc.)

> PACING SUGGESTION: Upon completion of Etapa 2.

● STORYTELLING

Mis quehaceres After reviewing the vocabulary for household chores, model a mini-story (using puppets, student actors, or photos from the text) that students will retell and revise:

> Javier y Rosita hablan de sus quehaceres y responsabilidades en casa. Javier dice: «Corté el césped el sábado. También limpié mi habitación y planché toda la ropa. Mi hermana no hace nada en casa. Los chicos tienen que hacer mucho más que las chicas en casa.» Rosita responde: «¡No es verdad! Yo también corté el césped la semana pasada. Y desyerbé el jardín y limpié toda la cocina y la sala.»

Pause as the story is being told, giving students a chance to fill in words or act out gestures. Students then write, narrate, and read aloud a longer main story. This new version should include vocabulary from the previous story.

Otras responsabilidades Ask students to create their own stories about chores and responsibilities at home. They can compare what they do now to what they used to do when they were younger.

> PACING SUGGESTION: Upon completion of Etapa 3.

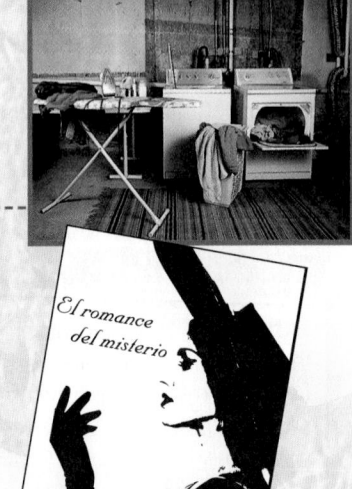

● BULLETIN BOARD/POSTERS

Bulletin Board **Plan ahead:** Have students bring in photos of themselves at different ages. Have them write captions using the imperfect tense to describe how old they were, what they were doing, etc. Create a collage using the photos and captions.

Posters **Have students create** •**Fashion** posters featuring a new look for a new year •**Chile** posters featuring different kinds and uses of peppers •**Hispanic heritage** posters featuring individuals who have made significant contributions to the U.S.

CANADÁ

GAMES

¡A dibujar!

Plan ahead: 2–4 large drawing pads (and easels, if available), 2–4 sets of color markers. Create several descriptions of people, ranging from average to outlandish. Include vocabulary for physical appearance and for clothing. Divide the class into 2–4 teams. Members from each team take turns drawing what they hear as you read descriptions. After each description, compare drawings to see which team came closest to the description. After playing, have volunteers describe some of the drawings.

PACING SUGGESTION: Upon completion of Etapa 2.

Simón dice

Play a game of **Simón dice** using chores as the commands. Say **Simón dice** followed by a formal command to do a household chore. Students use TPR to act out the chore. If you tell them to do a chore without saying **Simón dice,** they should not respond. Students who do the wrong chore or act out chores when they should not are out of the game. You can divide the class into teams, if desired.

PACING SUGGESTION: Upon completion of Etapa 3.

MUSIC

Point out that Tito Puente is most often associated with the birth of **salsa** and that **salsa** originated in **el Barrio** in New York City. Have students make some homemade percussion instruments (plastic eggs or containers filled with rice or beans; coffee cans and drum sticks, etc.). Play some **salsa** selections. Have students accompany the music with their instruments. Point out the importance of percussion in most Hispanic music. Caribbean music samples are available on your *Canciones* CD.

HANDS-ON CRAFTS

Plan ahead: Bring in: chile peppers (of different colors and shapes), toothpicks, fabric scraps, buttons, sequins, glue. **WARNING:** When handling the peppers, students should avoid contact with their eyes and should wash hands thoroughly. They might also wear rubber gloves. Have students create **chicos(as) chile(s)** (chile people) by decorating the peppers using the materials brought in. Variation: Make photocopies of pictures of peppers and have students decorate the photocopies.

MIAMI

RECIPE

Leche quemada is a Mexican dessert that Texans like to serve. It is easy to make and great for **fiestas.** Prepare ahead and serve in class.

Receta

Leche quemada
1/2 galón de leche
1 libra de azúcar

En una olla, combine la leche con el azúcar. Caliente la leche sobre un fuego moderado hasta que hierva y se haga espesa. Baje el fuego y cocine a fuego lento por dos horas. Remueva la leche hasta que no se pegue a los bordes de la olla y se ponga dorada y sin grumos (granules). Vierta la mezcla en una cacerola ligeramente engrasada y déjela enfriar. Cuando se enfríe, córtela en pedazos. Puede decorarlos con una nuez encima.

Planning Guide CLASSROOM MANAGEMENT

OBJECTIVES

Communication
- Describe people *pp. 34–35, 36–37*
- Talk about experiences *pp. 48–49*
- List accomplishments *pp. 36–37*

Grammar
- Review: Use **ser** and **estar** *pp. 40–41*
- Review: Use the imperfect tense *pp. 42–43*
- Review: Use the preterite and imperfect *pp. 43–45*
- Use the present and past perfect tenses *pp. 46–47*

Culture
- Spanish-speaking communities in the U.S. *pp. 30–31, 40*
- Well-known Spanish-speakers in the U.S. *pp. 30–31*
- Variations in vocabulary *p. 38*
- Spanish nicknames *p. 45*
- The life of Spanish-speakers in the U.S. *pp. 48–49*

♻ Recycling
- **Ser** vs. **estar** *pp. 40–41*
- The imperfect tense *pp. 42–43*
- Preterite vs. imperfect *pp. 43–45*

STRATEGIES

Listening Strategies
- Recognize descriptions *p. 36*

Speaking Strategies
- Add details to descriptions *p. 39*
- Describe personal characteristics and actions *p. 52*

Reading Strategies
- Observe how verb tenses reveal time *p. 48*

Writing Strategies
- Appeal to the senses in storytelling *TE p. 52*

Connecting Cultures Strategies
- Learn about Spanish-speaking communities and well-known Spanish speakers in the U.S. *pp. 30–31, 40*
- Recognize variations in vocabulary *p. 38*
- Learn about Spanish nicknames *p. 45*
- Create a historical time line *TE p. 49*
- Connect and compare what you know about your own community to help you learn about a new community *pp. 30–31, 40, 48–49*

PROGRAM RESOURCES

 Print
- *Más práctica* Workbook PE *pp. 11–20*
- *Actividad para todos* Workbook PE *pp. 11–20*
- Block Scheduling Copymasters *pp. 9–16*
- Unit 1 Resource Book
  Más práctica Workbook TE *pp. 3–12*
  Actividades para todos Workbook TE *pp. 13–22*
  Cuaderno para hispanohablantes TE *pp. 23–32*
  Information Gap Activities *pp. 33–36*
  Family Letters *pp. 37–38*
  Absent Student Copymasters *pp. 39–45*
  Family Involvement *pp. 46–47*
  Audioscript *pp. 48–51*
  Assessment Program, Unit 1 Etapa 1 *pp. 53–75; 242–244*
  Answer Keys *pp. 258–261*

Audiovisual
- Audio Program CD 1
- *Canciones* CD
- Overhead Transparencies M1–M5; 2, 5–19
- Word Tiles U1E1

 Technology
- eEditing Plus Online/eEdition CD-ROM
- Easy Planner Plus Online/Easy Planner CD-ROM
- eTest Plus Online/Test Generator CD-ROM
- Online Workbook
- Take-Home Tutor CD-ROM
- www.classzone.com

✓ Assessment Program Options
- Unit 1 Resource Book
  Vocabulary Quizzes
  Grammar Quizzes
  Etapa Exam Forms A and B
  Examen para hispanohablantes
  Portfolio Assessment
  Multiple Choice Test Questions
- Audio Program CD 19
- eTest Plus Online/Test Generator CD-ROM

Native Speakers
- *Cuaderno para hispanohablantes* PE *pp. 11–20*
- *Cuaderno para hispanohablantes* TE (Unit 1 Resource Book)
- *Examen para hispanohablantes* (Unit 1 Resource Book)
- Audio Program (*Para hispanohablantes*) CD 1, 19
- Audioscript (Unit 1 Resource Book)

Student Text
Listening Activity Scripts

 **Situaciones** *pages 36–37*

CD 1

Llamada número 1:

¡Hola! Habla Ricardo Miguel Rodríguez. Soy estudiante de teatro. El otro día cuando estaba en casa de una amiga, vi su anuncio en el periódico buscando actores para la película. He actuado en algunas obras de teatro, así que tengo alguna experiencia. Ah, sí, en el anuncio pidió nuestros datos: Tengo dieciocho años. Soy alto y delgado. Tengo el pelo negro ondulado, y lo llevo en cola de caballo. Tengo los ojos negros. Mamá dice que tengo la cara muy triangular. A ver, ¿qué más? Soy muy trabajador. Creo que es todo. Mi número es el 3-22-34-89. Muchas gracias.

Llamada número 2:

No sé porque estoy llamando. Nunca me escogen. Pero soy actor, y ¡tengo que actuar! Soy un poco grueso. También soy calvo. Tengo bigote y barba pero puedo afeitarme si lo requiere el papel. Soy de estatura mediana. ¡Soy muy buen actor! Déme la oportunidad de demostrárselo. Ay, ¡se me olvidó! Cumplo treinta y siete años este mes. Muchísimas gracias. Habla Pedro Álvarez Soto, a sus órdenes. El número es el 5-31-87-04.

Llamada número 3:

¡Buenas tardes! Estoy llamando porque me gustaría hacer una audición para su película. ¿Qué pidió? A sí, descripción física. Pues, soy baja y tengo el pelo un poco rojizo. En este momento no llevo flequillo, pero puedo cortármelo si no le gusta. Mi cara está llena de pecas... Tengo diecisiete años. He actuado en obras pequeñas aquí en el colegio. Me encantaría ser actriz de cine algún día. ¿Ésta parece la oportunidad perfecta! Me llamo Luci Benita Santos. Me puede llamar por la noche en el 4-36-98-27. ¡Gracias!

Llamada número 4:

Cenábamos en casa de mi mamá, cuando sonó el teléfono. Era mi tía Consuelo. Llamaba porque había visto su anuncio en Internet. ¿Cómo soy yo? Mi familia siempre ha dicho que tengo cuerpo de modelo. Soy alta y esbelta y tengo el pelo largo y negro como la noche. Tengo un lunar en la cara. ¿Experiencia? Muy poca, en realidad. He estudiado ballet toda mi vida, pero en actuación no he tenido la oportunidad. Tengo treinta y cinco años. 2-25-33-94. Espera su llamada... la señorita Estrella Luz Bello.

ACTIVIDAD 7  **La actriz Anilú Pardo** *page 41*

Entrevistador:	Dinos un poco sobre ti, quién eres, de dónde eres...
Anilú:	Me llamo Anilú Pardo. Originalmente soy de la Ciudad de México, soy mexicana.
Entrevistador:	¿Cuál es tu profesión, Anilú?
Anilú:	Soy actriz.
Entrevistador:	¿Qué haces aquí en Nueva York?
Anilú:	Estoy aquí para hacer una película.
Entrevistador:	¿Con quién estás trabajando?
Anilú:	Mi esposo es el director de la película. Él es de Brasil. Los otros actores también son latinoamericanos.
Entrevistador:	¿Cuándo empezaron la filmación?
Anilú:	Estamos en el tercer día de la filmación.
Entrevistador:	¿Y cómo te sientes?
Anilú:	¡Estoy muy nerviosa!
Entrevistador:	Gracias y buena suerte, Anilú.
Anilú:	De nada.

ACTIVIDAD 14 **¡Acción!** *page 45*

Ayer vi una película nueva. ¡Me gustó mucho! La película fue de mucha acción. Lola Díaz, el personaje principal, era una detective alta, esbelta y muy atrevida. Un día, unos hombres malos capturaron a su compañero. Ella tenía que salvarlo sin pedir ayuda. Si pedía ayuda, los ladrones lo iban a matar. Eran muy desagradables. Al fin ella salvó a su compañero. ¡Qué emoción! La actriz es muy buena–ganó un premio por su actuación en esta película. Tienes que verla.

Quick Start Review Answers

p. 40 Ser/estar
1. es
2. son
3. están
4. es
5. está
6. eres
7. estoy
8. está

p. 43 The imperfect tense
1. A las dos, María siempre estaba en la biblioteca.
2. La profesora siempre escribía mucho en el pizarrón.
3. Nosotros íbamos siempre a la playa.
4. Siempre me acostaba temprano.
5. Los viernes ellos siempre comían en el restaurante.

Pacing Guide

Sample Lesson Plan - 50 Minute Schedule

DAY 1

Unit Opener
- Anticipate/Activate prior knowledge: Present the *Almanaque* and the cultural notes. Use Map OHTs as needed. **15 MIN.**

Etapa Opener
- Quick Start Review (TE, p. 32) **5 MIN.**
- Have students look at the *Etapa* Opener and answer the questions. **5 MIN.**

En contexto: Vocabulario
- Quick Start Review (TE, p. 34) **5 MIN.**
- Present *Descubre* (TE, p. 34) **5 MIN.**
- Have students use context and pictures to learn *Etapa* vocabulary, then answer the *¿Comprendiste?* questions, p. 35. Use the Situational OHTs for additional practice. **15 MIN.**

Homework Option:
- Have students create vignettes of themselves on index cards, with a photo or drawing on one side and characteristics on the other.

DAY 2

En vivo: Situaciones
- Check homework. **5 MIN.**
- Quick Start Review (TE, p. 36) **5 MIN.**
- Present the Listening Strategy, p. 36. **5 MIN.**
- Have students read sections 1 and 2, pp. 36–37. Play the audio for section 3. Then have students discuss the questions in section 4. **15 MIN.**

En acción: Vocabulario y gramática
- Quick Start Review (TE, p. 38) **5 MIN.**
- Have students complete *Actividad* 1 in writing, then go over answers orally. **5 MIN.**
- Have students do *Actividad* 2 orally. **5 MIN.**
- Present the Speaking Strategy, p. 39. Do *Actividad* 3 in pairs. **5 MIN.**

Homework Option:
- Have students make a drawing and description similar to those on p. 36. Have them complete *Actividad* 2 in writing.

DAY 3

En acción (cont.)
- Check homework. **5 MIN.**
- Present the *Vocabulario*, p. 39. Then have students complete *Actividad* 4 in pairs. **10 MIN.**
- Quick Start Review (TE, p. 40) **5 MIN.**
- Present *Repaso: Ser* vs. *Estar*, p. 40. **5 MIN.**
- Have students complete *Actividad* 5 in writing, then exchange papers for peer correction. **5 MIN.**
- Have students read and complete *Actividad* 6 in writing. Go over answers orally. **5 MIN.**
- Play the audio; do *Actividad* 7. **5 MIN.**
- Have students read and complete *Actividad* 8 in writing. Go over answers orally. **10 MIN.**

Homework Option:
- *Más práctica* Workbook, pp. 15–16. *Cuaderno para hispanohablantes*, p. 13.

DAY 4

En acción (cont.)
- Check homework. **5 MIN.**
- Quick Start Review (TE, p. 42) **5 MIN.**
- Present *Repaso:* The Imperfect Tense, p. 42. **5 MIN.**
- Have students do *Actividades* 9 and 10 orally. **10 MIN.**
- Have students complete *Actividad* 11 in pairs. **5 MIN.**
- Present *Repaso:* Preterite vs. Imperfect, p. 43. **10 MIN.**
- Present the *Vocabulario*, p. 44. Then have students complete *Actividad* 12 in writing. Go over answers orally. **10 MIN.**

Homework Option:
- Have students complete *Actividades* 9 and 10 in writing. *Más práctica* Workbook, pp. 17–18. *Cuaderno para hispanohablantes*, p. 14.

DAY 5

En acción (cont.)
- Check homework. **5 MIN.**
- Have students do *Actividad* 13 orally. **5 MIN.**
- Play the audio; do *Actividad* 14. **5 MIN.**
- Present the *Vocabulario*, p. 45. Then have students complete *Actividad* 15 in writing. Expand using Information Gap Activities, Unit 1 Resource Book, p. 35; *Más comunicación*, p. R3. **15 MIN.**
- Quick Start Review (TE, p. 46) **5 MIN.**
- Present *Gramática:* Present and Past Perfect Tenses, p. 46. **15 MIN.**

Homework Option:
- Have students complete *Actividad* 13 in writing. *Más práctica* Workbook, p. 19. *Cuaderno para hispanohablantes*, pp. 15–16.
- *Actividades para todos* Workbook, pp. 11–20.

DAY 6

En acción (cont.)
- Check homework. **5 MIN.**
- Review *Gramática:* Present and Past Perfect Tenses, p. 46. **5 MIN.**
- Do *Actividad* 16 orally. **5 MIN.**
- Do *Actividad* 17 in pairs. **5 MIN.**
- Do *Actividad* 18 in groups. **10 MIN.**

Refrán
- Present the *Refrán*, p. 47. **5 MIN.**

En voces: Lectura
- Quick Start Review (TE, p. 48) **5 MIN.**
- Present the Reading Strategy, p. 48. Call on volunteers to read the *Lectura* aloud. Have students answer the *¿Comprendiste?* questions, p. 49. **10 MIN.**

Homework Option:
- Have students do *Actividad* 16 in writing. Have them complete *¿Qué piensas?* and *Hazlo tú*, p. 49.

DAY 7

En uso: Repaso y más comunicación
- Check homework. **5 MIN.**
- Quick Start Review (TE, p. 50) **5 MIN.**
- Present the *Repaso y más comunicación* using the Teaching Suggestions (TE, p. 50) **5 MIN.**
- Do *Actividades* 1 and 2 orally. **5 MIN.**
- Have students write *Actividades* 3 and 4, then check answers with the whole class. **10 MIN.**
- Present the Speaking Strategy, p. 52, and have students do *Actividades* 5 and 6 in groups. **10 MIN.**

En tu propia voz: Escritura
- Do *Actividad* 7 in writing. Have volunteers present their narrations to the class. **10 MIN.**

Homework Option:
- Review for *Etapa* 1 Exam.

DAY 8

Conexiones
- Read *El arte*, p. 52. Have students complete their self-portraits. **15 MIN.**

En resumen: Repaso de vocabulario
- Quick Start Review (TE, p. 53) **5 MIN.**
- Review grammar questions, etc., as necessary. **10 MIN.**
- Complete *Etapa* 1 Exam. **20 MIN.**

Ampliación
- Optional: Use a suggested project, game, or activity. (TE, pp. 31A–31B)

Homework Option:
- Preview *Etapa* 2 Opener.

Sample Lesson Plan - Block Schedule (90 minutes)

DAY 1

Unit Opener
- Anticipate/Activate prior knowledge: Present the *Almanaque* and the cultural notes. Use Map OHTs as needed. 15 MIN.

Etapa Opener
- Quick Start Review (TE, p. 32) 5 MIN.
- Have students look at the *Etapa* Opener and answer the questions. 5 MIN.
- Use Block Scheduling Copymasters, pp. 9–10. 10 MIN.

En contexto: Vocabulario
- Quick Start Review (TE, p. 34) 5 MIN.
- Present *Descubre* (TE, p. 34) 5 MIN.
- Have students use context and pictures to learn *Etapa* vocabulary, then answer the *¿Comprendiste?* questions, p. 35. Use the Situational OHTs for additional practice. 15 MIN.

En vivo: Situaciones
- Quick Start Review (TE, p. 36) 5 MIN.
- Present the Listening Strategy, p. 36. 5 MIN.
- Have students read sections 1 and 2, pp. 36–37. Play the audio for section 3. Then have students discuss the questions in section 4. 20 MIN.

Homework Option:
- Have students choose 1 option: (1) create vignettes of themselves on an index card, with a photo or drawing on one side and characteristics on the other, or (2) make a drawing and description similar to those on p. 36.

DAY 2

En acción: Vocabulario y gramática
- Check homework. 5 MIN.
- Quick Start Review (TE, p. 38) 5 MIN.
- Have students complete *Actividad* 1 in writing, then go over answers orally. 5 MIN.
- Have students do *Actividad* 2 orally. 5 MIN.
- Present the Speaking Strategy, p. 39. Do *Actividad* 3 in pairs. 5 MIN.
- Present the *Vocabulario*, p. 39. Then have students complete *Actividad* 4 in pairs. 10 MIN.
- Quick Start Review (TE, p. 40) 5 MIN.
- Present *Repaso: Ser* vs. *Estar*, p. 40. 5 MIN.
- Have students complete *Actividad* 5 in writing, then exchange papers for peer correction. 5 MIN.
- Have students read and complete *Actividad* 6 in writing. Go over answers orally. 5 MIN.
- Play the audio; do *Actividad* 7. 5 MIN.
- Have students read and complete *Actividad* 8 in writing. Go over answers orally. Expand using Information Gap Activities, Unit 1 Resource Book, p. 34; *Más comunicación*, p. R3. 15 MIN.
- Quick Start Review (TE, p. 42) 5 MIN.
- Present *Repaso:* The Imperfect Tense, p. 42. 5 MIN.
- Have students do *Actividad* 9 orally. 5 MIN.

Homework Option:
- Have students complete *Actividades* 2 and 9 in writing. *Más práctica* Workbook, pp. 15–18. *Cuaderno para hispanohablantes*, pp. 13–14.

DAY 3

En acción (cont.)
- Check homework. 5 MIN.
- Have students do *Actividad* 10 orally. 5 MIN.
- Have students complete *Actividad* 11 in pairs. 5 MIN.
- Quick Start Review (TE, p. 43) 5 MIN.
- Present *Repaso:* Preterite vs. Imperfect, p. 43. 10 MIN.
- Present the *Vocabulario*, p. 44. Then have students complete *Actividad* 12 in writing. Go over answers orally. 10 MIN.
- Have students do *Actividad* 13 orally. 5 MIN.
- Play the audio; do *Actividad* 14. 5 MIN.
- Present the *Vocabulario*, p. 45. Then have students complete *Actividad* 15 in writing. Have a few volunteers present their paragraphs. Expand using Information Gap Activities, Unit 1 Resource Book, p. 35; *Más comunicación*, p. R3. 20 MIN.
- Quick Start Review (TE, p. 46) 5 MIN.
- Present *Gramática:* Present and Past Perfect Tenses, p. 46. 10 MIN.
- Do *Actividad* 16 orally. 5 MIN.

Homework Option:
- Have students complete *Actividades* 10 and 13 in writing. *Más práctica* Workbook, p. 19. *Cuaderno para hispanohablantes*, pp. 15–16.

DAY 4

En acción (cont.)
- Check homework. 5 MIN.
- Review *Gramática:* Present and Past Perfect Tenses, p. 46. 5 MIN.
- Do *Actividad* 17 in pairs and *Actividad* 18 in groups. 10 MIN.

Refrán
- Present the *Refrán*, p. 47. 5 MIN.

En voces: Lectura
- Quick Start Review (TE, p. 48) 5 MIN.
- Present the Reading Strategy, p. 48. Call on volunteers to read the *Lectura* aloud. Have students answer the *¿Comprendiste?/¿Qué piensas?* questions, p. 49. 20 MIN.

En uso: Repaso y más comunicación
- Quick Start Review (TE, p. 50) 5 MIN.
- Do *Actividades* 1 and 2 orally. 10 MIN.
- Have students write *Actividades* 3 and 4, then check answers with the whole class. 15 MIN.
- Present the Speaking Strategy, p. 52, and do *Actividad* 5 in groups. 10 MIN.

Homework Option:
- Have students complete *Hazlo tú*, p. 49. Review for *Etapa* 1 Exam.

DAY 5

En acción (cont.)
- Check homework. 5 MIN.
- Do *Actividad* 6 in groups. 10 MIN.

En tu propia voz: Escritura
- Do *Actividad* 7 in writing. Have volunteers present their narrations to the class. 10 MIN.

Conexiones
- Read *El arte*, p. 52. Have students complete their self-portraits. 15 MIN.

En resumen: Repaso de vocabulario
- Quick Start Review (TE, p. 53) 5 MIN.
- Review grammar questions, etc., as necessary. 10 MIN.
- Complete *Etapa* 1 Exam. 20 MIN.

Ampliación
- Use a suggested project, game, or activity. (TE, pp. 31A–31B) 15 MIN.

Homework Option:
- Preview *Etapa* 2 Opener.
- *Actividaes para todos* Workbook, pp. 11–20

▼ Estudiamos en la biblioteca.

Etapa Theme
Describing people; talking about your experiences; listing accomplishments

Grammar Objectives
- Reviewing the use of **ser** and **estar**
- Reviewing the use of the imperfect tense
- Reviewing the use of the preterite and imperfect
- Using the present and past perfect tenses

Teaching Resource Options

Print

Block Scheduling Copymasters
Unit 1 Resource Book
  Family Letters, pp. 37–38
  Absent Student Copymasters, p. 39

Audiovisual

OHT 2, 11 (Quick Start)

Quick Start Review

 Spanish-speaking communities in the U.S.

Use OHT 11 or write on the board:
Give 2 facts about each of the following cities:

- **Los Ángeles**
- **Chicago**
- **San Antonio**
- **Nueva York**
- **Miami**

Answers will vary.

Teaching Suggestion
Previewing the Etapa
- Ask students to study the picture on pp. 32–33 (1 min.).
- Call on volunteers to name 3 things they notice: **Nombra 3 cosas que notas acerca de la foto.**
- Have them look at the picture again. Call on volunteers: **Nombra 3 detalles más.**
- Use the **¿Qué ves?** questions to focus the discussion.

UNIDAD 1

ETAPA 1

¿Cómo soy?

OBJECTIVES

- Describe people

- Talk about experiences

- List accomplishments

¿Qué ves?

Mira la foto y contesta las preguntas.

1. ¿Dónde están estas personas?

2. ¿Qué cosas te dicen dónde están?

3. ¿Crees que son amigos? ¿Por qué?

4. ¿Qué te dice la revista sobre la cultura de Miami?

32

Classroom Management

Planning Ahead Ask students to each bring in at least 10 magazine/newspaper pictures of different people. These pictures will be used for the TPR activity on TE p. 34. They may also be used for reviewing the verb **ser.**

Student Self-checks Review students' knowledge of descriptions. Call on several students to stand up and describe themselves, using physical and personality characteristics. If students prefer, they may describe a famous person. On an OHT, draw different figures and ask students to describe them.

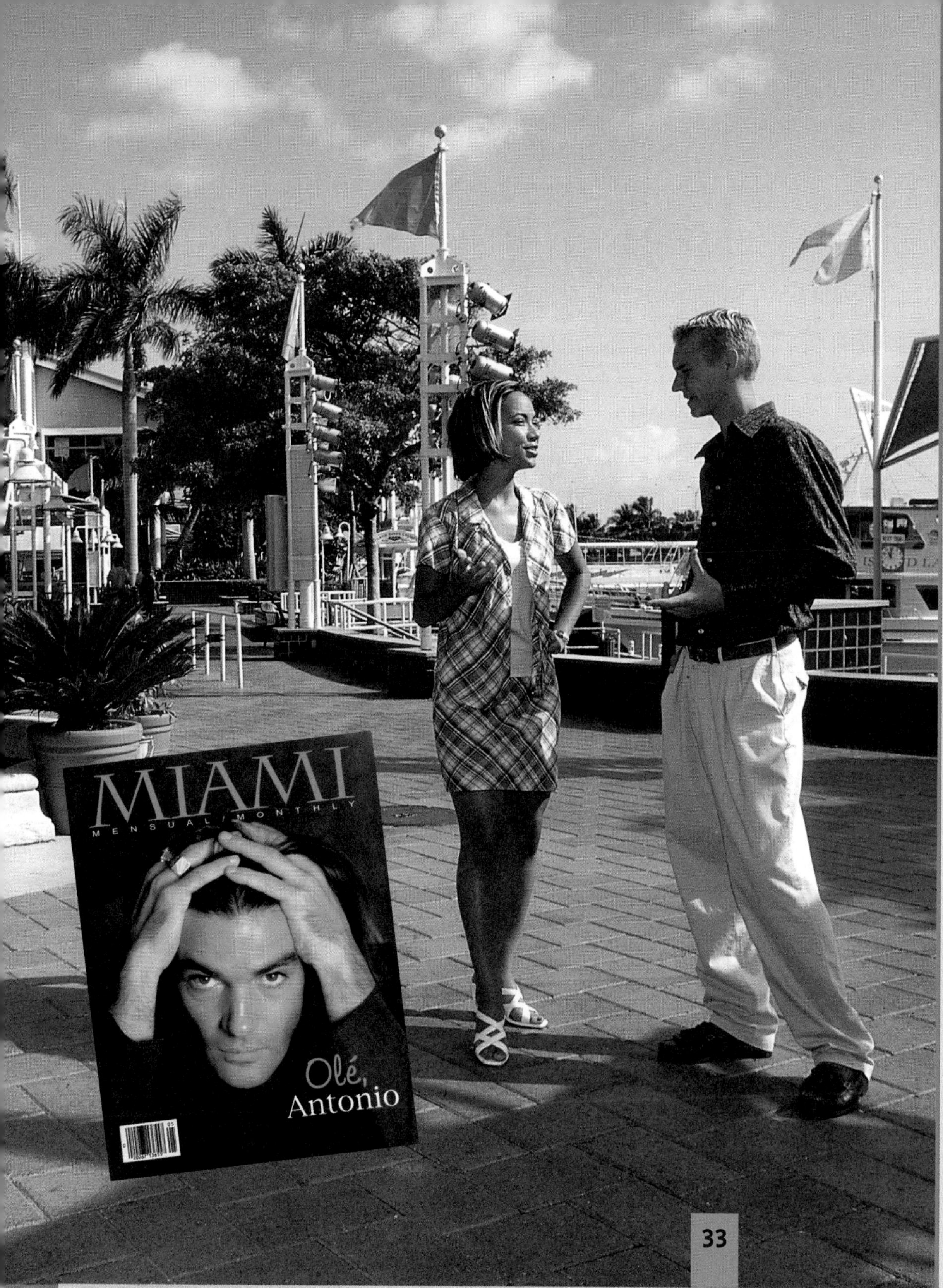

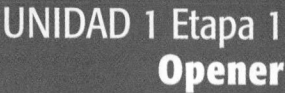

Cross Cultural Connections

You might point out to students that: **Miami es una de las ciudades en Estados Unidos donde hay mucho comercio internacional.** Invite them to think about why this is so and to think of other U.S. cities where there is international commerce. **¿Por qué creen que en Miami hay más comercio internacional que en otras ciudades? ¿En qué otras ciudades hay comercio internacional?** You might have students locate these cities on a map. Ask them to think about what these cities have in common, such as location and population. **¿Qué cosas tienen estas ciudades en común? ¿Dónde están? ¿Viven personas de muchos lugares allí? ¿De qué lugares?** List student responses on the board.

Culture Highlights

● **ANTONIO BANDERAS** Antonio Banderas nació en Málaga, España, en 1960. Comenzó su carrera exitosa durante su adolescencia. Las películas que hizo con el director español Pedro Almodóvar le trajeron reconocimiento internacional. Su primer papel en una película en Estados Unidos fue en la película *The Mambo Kings,* basada en la novela del escritor Oscar Hijuelos, quien es de origen cubano.

Supplementary Vocabulary

la bandera	flag
la estatua	statue
la fuente	fountain
la palma, la palmera	palm tree
el pasillo de ladrillo	brick walkway

MIAMI
MENSUAL/MONTHLY

Olé, Antonio

33

Teaching All Students

Extra Help Have students write 3 questions about the photo. Then have them exchange papers with a partner and answer each other's questions.

Multiple Intelligences

Naturalist Have students look at the photo and list elements that indicate what kind of physical environment is shown. Ask them to also find indicators of the general weather in the photo. Have students list at least 2 similarities or differences between the area shown and the students' local area.

Block Schedule

Research Have students research additional information on Antonio Banderas or another well-known Spanish-speaking entertainer (Jennifer López, Enrique Iglesias, Marc Anthony, etc.). (For additional activities, see **Block Scheduling Copymasters.**)

Teaching Resource Options

Print 📖
Block Scheduling Copymasters
Unit 1 Resource Book
  Absent Student Copymasters, p. 39

Audiovisual 🎧
OHT 5, 6, 7, 7A, 8, 8A, 11 (Quick Start)

Technology 💻
Online Workbook, U1E1
Take-Home Tutor CD-ROM, U1E1

Quick Start Review

♻ **People descriptions**

Use OHT 11 or write on the board:
List 5 words/expressions for each
category to describe people:
• características físicas
• características de personalidad

Answers
Answers will vary. Answers could include:
• características físicas: alto(a), guapo(a),
delgado(a), ojos verdes, pelo largo
• características de personalidad: cómico(a),
inteligente, tímido(a), aburrido(a), amable

Teaching Suggestions
Introducing Vocabulary
• Have students look at pages 34–35.
  Use OHT 5 and 6 to present the
  vocabulary.
• Ask the Comprehension Questions
  on TE p. 35 in order of yes/no
  (questions 1–3), either/or (questions
  4–6), and simple word or phrase
  (questions 7–10). Expand by adding
  similar questions.
• Use the TPR activity to reinforce the
  meaning of individual words.

En contexto VOCABULARIO

Todos somos *diferentes*

🔲 Descubre

A. Palabras dentro de las palabras

A veces hay palabras dentro de las
palabras que ya conoces. Estudia las
palabras a continuación y descubre
su significado.

La forma de la cara

1. ovalado	=	óvalo	
2. cuadrado	=	cuadro	
3. triangular	=	triángulo	

B. Sinónimos y antónimos

A veces ya sabes el sinónimo (una
palabra que tiene el mismo significado)
o el antónimo (una palabra que tiene el
significado opuesto) de una palabra.

La forma del cuerpo

1. grueso	sinónimo = gordo
	antónimo = delgado
2. esbelto	sinónimo = delgado
	antónimo = gordo
3. redondo	sinónimo = circular
	antónimo = cuadrado

Hay tipos de personas que son fáciles de reconocer...
¿Conoces algunos?

Cola de caballo porque no quiere el pelo
en la cara cuando juega al fútbol.

Usa lentes de contacto en vez de gafas,
¡claro!, todo para el deporte.

Siempre tiene el balón a la mano.

La deportista

Edad: 15
Talla: de estatura mediana
Cuerpo: ni gorda ni delgada
Ojos: cafés (y usa lentes de contacto)
Pelo: cabello largo en cola de caballo,
color castaño
Cara: ovalada
Característica: lunar bajo el ojo
Uniforme: shorts, camiseta «polo» y balón
Frase favorita: «¡Te gano!»

El rebelde

Edad: 16
Talla: alto
Cuerpo: delgado
Ojos: azules
Pelo: ¡teñido de naranja!
Cara: triangular
Característica: anteojos redondos
Uniforme: camiseta de los sesenta
Frase favorita: «¡Al contrario!»

Tiene el pelo teñido de
¡naranja!, para distinguirse
del resto del mundo.

Sus anteojos redondos le
dan ese «look» individual.

Camiseta de los sesenta
porque le gusta ser
diferente — hace lo
opuesto de lo que
hacen los otros.

34 treinta y cuatro
Unidad 1

Classroom Community

TPR Use the magazine/newspaper pictures of
different people that students brought in; see TE p. 32.
Make descriptive statements using the vocabulary
words. For example, **Esta persona tiene el pelo
castaño.** Students whose pictures fit the description
stand up, show their pictures, and repeat the
description.

Paired Activity Have students work in pairs to
answer the ¿**Comprendiste?** questions, p. 35. First, they
should ask each other the questions. Then, they should
each make up 2 more questions to ask their partner.
You may also want to have them write answers to the
questions.

El caballero

Edad: 20
Talla: de estatura mediana
Cuerpo: grueso
Ojos: negros
Pelo: calvo (¡no tiene pelo!)
Cara: redonda
Característica: bigote, barba
Uniforme: toda su ropa es de color negro
Frase favorita: «Tú primero.»

Aquí y ahora

¡Es calvo! Se afeita la cabeza porque cree que es un «look» más sofisticado.

Cree que el bigote y la barba le dan un aire misterioso.

Siempre elegante, ¡de pies a cabeza! Y ¿su color preferido? Negro, ¡por supuesto!

Tiene el pelo rojizo y ondulado y lo lleva con flequillo para verse más atractiva.

Tiene un espejo siempre a la mano para admirarse frecuentemente.

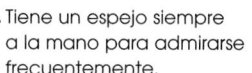

La vanidosa

Edad: 16
Talla: baja
Cuerpo: esbelta
Ojos: verdes
Pelo: rojizo y ondulado, con flequillo
Cara: cuadrada
Característica: pecas
Uniforme: vestido nada convencional
Frase favorita: «¿Cómo me veo?»

Lleva un vestido nada convencional para llamar la atención.

Online Workbook
CLASSZONE.COM

¿Comprendiste?

1. ¿Conoces a personas como éstas?
2. ¿Crees que son tipos verdaderos o estereotipos?
3. ¿Quién te cae bien? ¿Quién te cae mal?
4. ¿Cómo eres tú? Descríbete. Menciona tus ojos, pelo, cara y alguna característica particular.
5. ¿Cuál es tu «uniforme» preferido?
6. ¿Cuál es tu «frase favorita»?

treinta y cinco
Estados Unidos Etapa 1 | 35

Comprehension Questions

1. ¿Somos todos diferentes? (Sí.)
2. ¿Tiene la deportista cola de caballo? (Sí.)
3. ¿Tiene el rebelde anteojos cuadrados? (No.)
4. ¿Lleva el rebelde camiseta «polo» o camiseta de los sesenta? (camiseta de los sesenta)
5. ¿Es calvo el caballero o tiene el pelo teñido de verde? (Es calvo.)
6. ¿Qué dice la deportista, «¿Cómo me veo?» o «¡Te gano!»? (¡Te gano!)
7. ¿Cuál es la característica del caballero? (bigote y barba)
8. ¿Cómo es el pelo de la vanidosa? (rojizo y ondulado, con flequillo)
9. ¿Quién dice «Tú primero»? (el caballero)
10. ¿Qué hace el rebelde? (lo opuesto de lo que hacen los otros)

Quick Wrap-up

Have students write 5 true/false sentences: **Escriba 5 oraciones ciertas o falsas acerca de las personas en la presentación del vocabulario.** Then have pairs exchange papers and correct.

Block Schedule

FunBreak Prepare ahead: Collect pictures of famous people and put them in a box. Divide the class into groups of 4–5. Have each group select 1 student to go to the front of the class. Choose a picture and tape it on the student's back. The other members of the student's group take turns providing descriptive sentences for the student, who must guess the name of the famous person. (For additional activities, see **Block Scheduling Copymasters**.)

Teaching All Students

Extra Help Have students sketch drawings of people similar to those on pp. 34–35 and label them. Then have them work with a partner to ask and answer questions about the people.

Native Speakers Have students write descriptions of well-known personalities in the Spanish-speaking world, then present their descriptions to the class.

Multiple Intelligences

Interpersonal Have students work in pairs. Each student names a well-known person that fits one of the personality types. The pairs then ask and answer questions about the particular characteristics of each person. Ask students to think about the process of stereotyping, then discuss the individual characteristics of each person.

Teaching Resource Options

Print

Block Scheduling Copymasters
Unit 1 Resource Book
  Absent Student Copymasters, p. 40
  Audioscript, p. 48

Audiovisual

OHT 9, 10, 12 (Quick Start)
Audio Program CD 1, Track 3

Technology

Take-Home Tutor CD-ROM, U1E1

Quick Start Review

♻ People descriptions

Use OHT 12 or write on the board:
Write 1 descriptive sentence about each
personality type:

- la deportista
- el caballero
- el rebelde
- la vanidosa

Answers

Answers will vary. Answers could include:
- La deportista siempre tiene el balón a la mano.
- El rebelde tiene el pelo teñido de naranja.
- El caballero es siempre elegante de pies a cabeza.
- La vanidosa tiene un espejo siempre a la mano.

Teaching Suggestions
Presenting Situations

- Present the Listening Strategy, p. 36, and have students jot down characteristics for identifying someone.
- Use OHT 9 and 10 to present the two **Leer** sections. Ask simple yes/no, either/or, or short-answer questions.
- Use Audio CD 1 (see Script TE p. 31D) and have students do the **Escuchar** section. Then have students complete the Listening Strategy exercise.
- Have students work in groups to answer the questions in the **Hablar** section. The groups should then present their conclusions to the class.

AUDIO *En vivo*
SITUACIONES

PARA ESCUCHAR • STRATEGY: LISTENING

Pre-listening How do you recognize someone that you are going to meet but have never seen? List what will help you.

Recognize descriptions Jot down the physical characteristics that best help you identify someone you don't know. Then, after listening to the descriptions, compare that list with yours. How are they the same? How are they different? Would you revise yours?

¡Eres director o directora!

Vas a filmar una película de misterio. Tienes que escoger los actores para los cuatro personajes principales.

1 Leer

Tienes los siguientes dibujos y descripciones de los cuatro personajes principales de la película para ayudarte a seleccionar a los actores.

Dolores MalaGente

Alta, esbelta, siempre lleva gafas negras y ropa elegante. Tiene el pelo largo, negro y liso. Tiene la cara ovalada y los ojos negros. Tiene un lunar bajo el ojo izquierdo. Tiene unos treinta años.

Eduardo Vanidoso

De estatura mediana, el señor Vanidoso es grueso y calvo. Tiene bigote y barba porque cree que así puede esconder su cara redonda. También usa lentes de contacto porque cree que se ve mejor sin anteojos. Viste siempre de trajes italianos muy caros. Es un tipo poco agradable. Tiene entre treinta y cuarenta años.

Marcos Deportista

Marcos tiene el cuerpo de deportista: alto, delgado y sin un kilo de más. Lleva el pelo castaño en cola de caballo que va muy bien con su cara triangular. Es atlético de pie a cabeza: va siempre en ropa cómoda. Tiene entre dieciséis y diecisiete años.

Celia Simpática

Celia es baja. Tiene el pelo rojizo y ondulado, con flequillo. Su cara es un poco cuadrada y tiene pecas. Es la mejor clase de amiga que uno pueda encontrar. Tiene entre dieciséis y diecisiete años.

36 treinta y seis
Unidad 1

Classroom Community

Paired Activity Use the magazine/newspaper pictures that students brought in; see TE p. 32. Have students work in pairs. Each student gets a picture of a person, but doesn't show it to the partner. Students take turns asking questions about the other person's photo until they can describe the type of person in the picture. Students may start with yes/no questions and progress to more specific detailed questions.

Cooperative Learning Divide the class into groups of 4. Each group will do a telephone interview of a famous person of their choosing, asking questions about the person's physical description. Student 1 plays the famous person. Student 2 is the interviewer. Student 3 is the recorder who takes notes on the interview. Student 4 is the spokesperson for the group and will report to the class about the famous person.

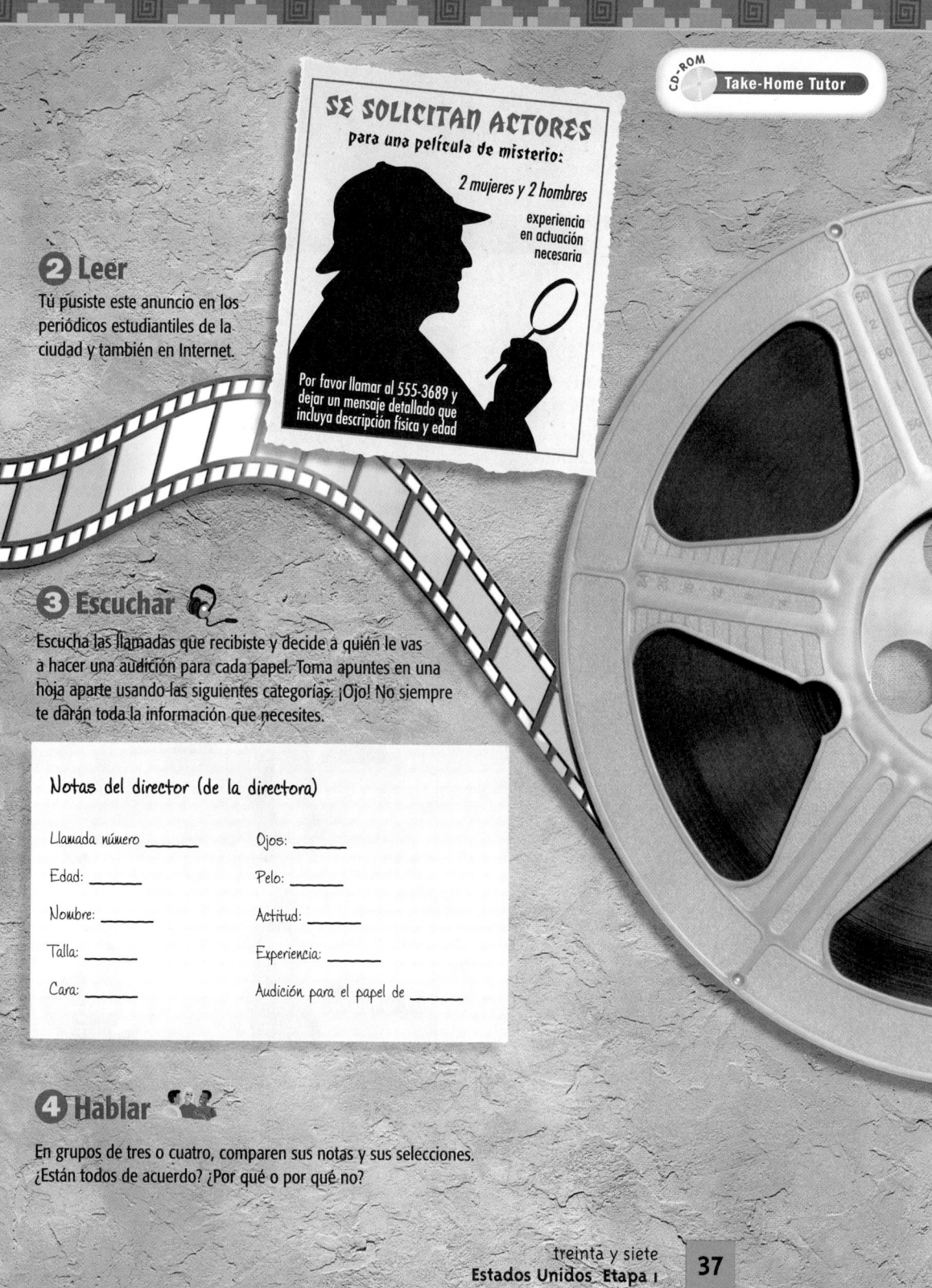

CD-ROM
Take-Home Tutor

SE SOLICITAN ACTORES
para una película de misterio:

2 mujeres y 2 hombres

experiencia
en actuación
necesaria

Por favor llamar al 555-3689 y
dejar un mensaje detallado que
incluya descripción física y edad

❷ Leer

Tú pusiste este anuncio en los
periódicos estudiantiles de la
ciudad y también en Internet.

❸ Escuchar 🎧

Escucha las llamadas que recibiste y decide a quién le vas
a hacer una audición para cada papel. Toma apuntes en una
hoja aparte usando las siguientes categorías. ¡Ojo! No siempre
te darán toda la información que necesites.

Notas del director (de la directora)

Llamada número _____	Ojos: _____
Edad: _____	Pelo: _____
Nombre: _____	Actitud: _____
Talla: _____	Experiencia: _____
Cara: _____	Audición para el papel de _____

❹ Hablar 👥

En grupos de tres o cuatro, comparen sus notas y sus selecciones.
¿Están todos de acuerdo? ¿Por qué o por qué no?

treinta y siete
Estados Unidos Etapa 1   **37**

Escuchar (See script, p. 31D.)

Answers
• Llamada número 1
Edad: 18
Nombre: Ricardo Miguel Rodríguez
Talla: alto
Cara: triangular
Ojos: negros
Pelo: negro ondulado, cola de caballo
Actitud: trabajador
Experiencia: algunas obras de teatro
Audición para el papel de Marcos Deportista

• Llamada número 2
Edad: 37
Nombre: Pedro Álvarez Soto
Talla: de estatura mediana
Cara: No se sabe / No dice
Ojos: No se sabe / No dice
Pelo: calvo, bigote y barba
Actitud: *Answers will vary.* defensivo, vanidoso
Experiencia: es actor
Audición para el papel de Eduardo Vanidoso

• Llamada número 3
Edad: 17
Nombre: Luci Benita Santos
Talla: baja
Cara: llena de pecas
Ojos: No se sabe / No dice
Pelo: un poco rojizo, flequillo
Actitud: *Answers will vary.* nerviosa
Experiencia: obras pequeñas en el colegio
Audición para el papel de Celia Simpática

• Llamada número 4
Edad: 35
Nombre: Estrella Luz Bello
Talla: alta
Cara: tiene lunar
Ojos: No se sabe / No dice
Pelo: largo y negro
Actitud: *Answers will vary.* vanidosa, dramática
Experiencia: muy poca
Audición para el papel de Dolores MalaGente

■ Block Schedule

Change of Pace Divide the class into
groups of 5. One person plays the role
of the director; the others play the 4
characters on p. 36. Have students write
and perform original skits that include
these characters. Groups present their
skits to the class. You may want to
videotape the skits for students to
critique. (For additional activities, see
Block Scheduling Copymasters.)

Teaching All Students

Extra Help Name various characteristics of the 4
people on p. 36 at random. Students must say whom
that characteristic describes.

Native Speakers Ask students to provide synonyms
for the characteristics presented in the **Vocabulario** and
Situaciones, for example, **bajo = chaparro.** Have
students add these to a Supplementary Vocabulary list.

Multiple Intelligences

Kinesthetic Tell students to stand up and group
themselves according to one of various characteristics:
age, height, face shape, hair style, etc. Choose one
characteristic at a time. Students will need to talk to
each other (in Spanish!) in order to find the group they
belong to. Once they are grouped, a spokesperson
explains the group characteristic.

Teaching Resource Options

Print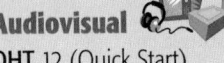

Block Scheduling Copymasters
Unit 1 Resource Book
   Absent Student Copymasters, p. 41

Audiovisual

OHT 12 (Quick Start)

🔔 Quick Start Review

♻ **Descriptions**

Use OHT 12 or write on the board:
Complete the following:

1. Miguel no tiene un kilo de más.
   Él es ___ .
2. Mi hermana no usa anteojos. Usa
   ___ .
3. Tres formas de cara son ___ ,
   ___ y ___ .
4. Un sinónimo de gordo es ___ .
5. El señor García no tiene pelo.
   Es ___ .

Answers
1. delgado
2. lentes de contacto
3. ovalada, cuadrada, triangular
4. grueso
5. calvo

Teaching Suggestions
Comprehension Check

With books closed, ask students to name the 4 people from the **Situaciones** and give words associated with them.

ACTIVIDAD 1 **Objective:** Controlled practice
Vocabulary

Answers

1. c	3. e	5. f	7. d
2. h	4. b	6. a	8. g

En acción

Práctica del vocabulario

Objectives for Activities 1–4
• Describe people

1 Mi amigo es...

Escribir Francisco está describiendo a sus amigos y parientes. Completa su descripción con las frases en la segunda columna.

1. Mi amigo Armando es pelirrojo.
2. A mi amiga Susana no le gusta como se ve con anteojos.
3. El color del cabello de mi tío no es natural.
4. ¡Papá se acaba de afeitar!
5. Mi amiga Alma siempre tiene el pelo en la cara.
6. El pelo de Marcos no es lacio.
7. Mi prima no tiene la cara redonda. ¡Es todo lo opuesto!
8. ¡Mi abuelo no tiene pelo!

a. Es ondulado.
b. Ya no tiene ni bigote ni barba.
c. Tiene el pelo rojizo.
d. Tiene la cara muy cuadrada.
e. Está teñido.
f. Debe usar cola de caballo.
g. Es calvo.
h. Prefiere usar lentes de contacto.

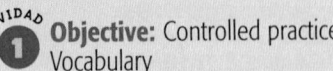

También se dice

Hay muchas maneras de decir que alguien es atractivo:

• **majo(a)**, España;
• **galán**, México
• **buen mozo(a)**, varios países;
• **bien parecido(a)**, varios países.

2 ¿Cómo son?

Hablar/Escribir Describe a las personas de los dibujos. Nombra por lo menos dos características físicas de cada persona.

modelo
Ana es esbelta. Tiene la cara ovalada.

Ana

Sally   1.

Enrique   2.

Sr. Sandoval   3.

Olivia   4.

Classroom Management

Organizing Paired Work Try to provide as much speaking practice as possible. Build in a paired speaking task in every day's lesson plan, perhaps at the beginning of each class. For example, students talk about the last class, homework, last night's activities, current events, etc.

Time Saver Prepare copies of the answers to **Actividades 1** and **2** to allow students to correct their own work.

3 ¿Conoces a Arturo?

> **STRATEGY: SPEAKING**
>
> **Add details to descriptions** Use these categories to help you focus on different aspects of appearance. (1) **castaño, corto, largo, moreno, rubio, pelirrojo;** (2) **alto, bajo, grande, pequeño;** (3) **la boca, la nariz, las orejas, los ojos, los anteojos, los lentes de contacto;** (4) **gordo, delgado, fuerte.**

Hablar/*Escribir* En pares, comenten sobre el aspecto de las siguientes personas. Luego, cambien de papel.

modelo

Arturo

Compañero(a): *¿Conoces a Arturo?*

Tú: *Sí, Arturo tiene el pelo ondulado.*

1. el (la) profesor(a) de inglés
2. mi mejor amigo(a)
3. el (la) director(a)
4. el señor [nombre]
5. mi amigo(a) [nombre]
6. el (la) profesor(a) de español
7. mi papá
8. el chofer del autobús
9. mi hermano(a)
10. el (la) profesor(a) de matemáticas

4 En la cafetería

Hablar Un(a) alumno(a) nuevo(a) llegó a tu escuela. Ustedes están en la cafetería y él(ella) te hace preguntas sobre los otros alumnos y los profesores. Tú los describes con todos los detalles que puedas.

modelo

muchacho

Compañero(a): *¿Quién es el muchacho alto con pelo lacio?*

Tú: *Es mi amigo Héctor. Es muy buen futbolista, pero es modesto. También es muy cómico.*

1. muchacho
2. profesor
3. muchacha
4. muchacho
5. muchacha
6. profesora

Vocabulario

Características	**Ya sabes**
atrevido(a) *daring*	amable
comprensivo(a) *understanding*	cómico(a)
considerado(a) *considerate*	impaciente
desagradable *unpleasant*	obediente
descarado(a) *insolent, shameless*	paciente
fiel *faithful*	sociable
mimado(a) *spoiled*	tímido(a)
modesto(a) *modest*	
vanidoso(a) *vain*	

▶ *¿Conoces a algunas personas con estas características?*

Teaching All Students

Extra Help Before doing **Actividad 3,** have the class compile lists of descriptive words for hair, eyes, facial characteristics, height, body type, clothing, etc. They should refer to these lists when doing this and other activities in the **Etapa.**

Multiple Intelligences

Visual Send artistic volunteers to the board to draw their own interpretations of the people in the vocabulary (pp. 34–35). Have another group of students go to the board and write the names under each drawing. Have a third group go to the board and write one thing about each person.

UNIDAD 1 Etapa 1
Vocabulary/Grammar

ACTIVIDAD 2 Objective: Transitional practice Vocabulary

Answers

Answers will vary.
1. Sally es esbelta. Tiene el pelo rojizo. Tiene pecas.
2. Enrique es alto. Tiene la cara cuadrada. Es un poco grueso.
3. El Sr. Sandoval es calvo. Tiene la cara triangular. Tiene barba y bigote.
4. Olivia es baja. Tiene la cara ovalada. Tiene un lunar bajo el ojo.

ACTIVIDAD 3 Objective: Open-ended practice Vocabulary

Answers will vary.

Teaching Suggestions
Presenting Vocabulary

• Write the new words on an OHT. Point to each word and explain it by using a synonym, antonym, or expression that students already know. For example: **Marco no es tímido. Es atrevido. Mi amiga es amable. No es desagradable.**

• Read the question at the end of the **Vocabulario.** Have each student name a famous person with 1 of the characteristics.

ACTIVIDAD 4 Objective: Open-ended practice Vocabulary

Answers will vary.

Variation: Have students draw pictures from their partner's descriptions.

Block Schedule

Variety Have students draw a picture depicting a person with one of the characteristics in the **Vocabulario,** p. 39. The picture can be a caricature or a realistic scene. Below the picture they should write a short paragraph describing the typical actions of that person. (For additional activities, see **Block Scheduling Copymasters.**)

Teaching Resource Options

Print 📖

Más práctica Workbook PE, pp. 15–16
Cuaderno para hispanohablantes PE, p. 13
Block Scheduling Copymasters
Unit 1 Resource Book
  Más práctica Workbook TE, pp. 7–8
  Cuaderno para hispanohablantes TE, p. 25
  Information Gap Activities, p. 33
  Absent Student Copymasters, p. 41
  Audioscript, p. 49

Audiovisual 🎧

OHT 13 (Quick Start) 16 (Grammar)
Audio Program CD 1, Track 4, Actividad 7

Technology 💻

Online Workbook, U1E1
Take-Home Tutor CD-ROM, U1E1

🔔 Quick Start Review

♻ **Ser/estar**

Use OHT 13 or write on the board: Complete the following with the present tense of **ser** or **estar**:

1. Julio ___ vanidoso.
2. Las mujeres ___ de España.
3. Sus hermanos ___ en Miami.
4. Hoy ___ sábado.
5. ¿Cómo ___ usted?
6. Tú ___ estudiante.
7. Yo ___ muy preocupado.
8. ¿Dónde ___ mi libro?

Answers *See p. 29D.*

Teaching Suggestions
Reviewing Ser vs. Estar

You may wish to give students additional examples contrasting the use of **ser** to tell where or when an event takes place and the use of **estar** to express location.

La fiesta es en casa de Adolfo. The party is taking place at Adolfo's house.

La casa de Adolfo está en la esquina. Adolfo's house is (located) on the corner.

PARTE B Práctica: gramática y vocabulario

Objectives for Activities 5–15
• Describe people • Talk about experiences • List accomplishments

REPASO Ser vs. Estar

Remember that in Spanish you can use two different verbs to mean **to be**:

    ser   and   estar

Use ser...

• to identify people and things.	El señor Ortega **es** profesor. *Mr. Ortega is a professor.*
• to express possession.	Esos libros **son** de Pablo. *Those are Pablo's books.*
• with **de** to express origin and to say what something is made of.	**Es** de oro y **es** de Perú. *It is gold and it is from Perú.*
• to express time and date.	**Son** las doce. Hoy **es** lunes. *It is twelve. Today is Monday.*
• to tell where or when an event takes place.	El concierto **es** en el estadio. *The concert is in the stadium.*
• to describe unchanging characteristics, such as color, nationality, size, physical characteristics, personality.	Tus primos **son** muy simpáticos. *Your cousins are very likable.*

Use estar...

• to express location.	Los Ángeles **está** en California. *Los Angeles is in California.*
• to express a state or condition, such as health, emotions, and feelings.	Mi hermano **está** enfermo. *My brother is sick.* **Estoy** triste y preocupado. *I am sad and worried.*
You also use **estar** to form the **present progressive**.	**Estoy** escuchando. *I am listening.*

You can often use **ser** and **estar** with the same **adjectives**, but with a difference in meaning:

Francisco **es** nervioso.
Francisco is nervous. (He is a nervous person.)

Francisco **está** nervioso hoy porque tiene exámenes.
Francisco is nervous today because he has exams. (He is nervous today.)

Practice: Actividades ❺❻❼❽

Más práctica *cuaderno pp. 15–16*
Para hispanohablantes *cuaderno p. 13*

Online Workbook CLASSZONE.COM

---

40 cuarenta
Unidad 1

---

❺ ¿Soy o estoy?

Escribir Completa las oraciones con la forma correcta de **ser** o **estar**.

modelo

Yo soy de Estados Unidos. Soy estadounidense.

1. Yo _____ estudiante. Ahora _____ en la escuela.
2. Él _____ mi tío. _____ profesor de matemáticas.
3. Ella _____ actriz. _____ en California.
4. Yo _____ del barrio Washington Heights que _____ en Nueva York.
5. ¡_____ las cinco! ¿Dónde _____ los niños?
6. _____ muy preocupada. Tengo un examen.
7. Los niños _____ tristes. Su perrito _____ enfermo.
8. Tú _____ simpático. Siempre _____ de buen humor.

Nota cultural

En algunas ciudades de Estados Unidos, se le da el nombre de **barrio** a zonas urbanas donde hay una gran población latina. La gente allí mantiene vivos las tradiciones y el idioma de su país de origen.

Classroom Community

TPR Prepare ahead: slips of paper containing phrases using **ser** and **estar**. Call students to the front of the class one at a time. Give each student 1 of the slips of paper. The student must act out the phrase. The class tries to make a statement describing what the student is doing. For example: Sara acts very busy (she's reading a book and taking notes). The class guesses: **Sara está muy ocupada.**

Portfolio Have students write a paragraph about a friend including the following information: profession, place of birth, physical characteristics, personality, where the person is now.

Rubric A = 13–15 pts. B = 10–12 pts. C = 7–9 pts. D = 4–6 pts. F = < 4 pts.

Writing criteria	Scale
Vocabulary use	1 2 3 4 5
Correct use of **ser** and **estar**	1 2 3 4 5
Spelling accuracy	1 2 3 4 5

6 ¡Hola, Futbolista29!

Leer/Escribir Completa la carta electrónica de Atleta37 usando la forma correcta de **ser** o **estar**.

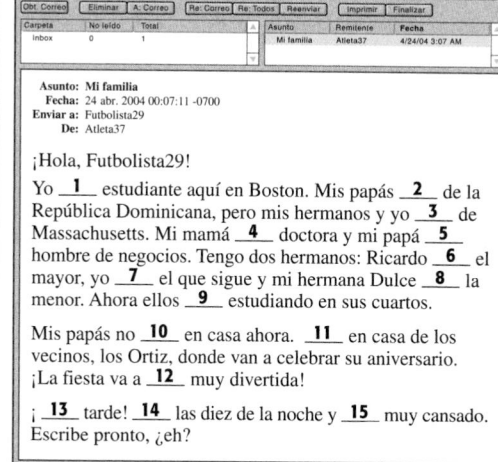

| Obt. Correo | Eliminar | A: Correo | Re: Correo | Re: Todos | Reenviar | Imprimir | Finalizar |

| Carpeta | No leído | Total | | Asunto | Remitente | Fecha |
| Inbox | 0 | 1 | | Mi familia | Atleta37 | 4/24/04 3:07 AM |

Asunto: Mi familia
Fecha: 24 abr. 2004 00:07:11 -0700
Enviar a: Futbolista29
De: Atleta37

¡Hola, Futbolista29!

Yo __1__ estudiante aquí en Boston. Mis papás __2__ de la República Dominicana, pero mis hermanos y yo __3__ de Massachusetts. Mi mamá __4__ doctora y mi papá __5__ hombre de negocios. Tengo dos hermanos: Ricardo __6__ el mayor, yo __7__ el que sigue y mi hermana Dulce __8__ la menor. Ahora ellos __9__ estudiando en sus cuartos.

Mis papás no __10__ en casa ahora. __11__ en casa de los vecinos, los Ortiz, donde van a celebrar su aniversario. ¡La fiesta va a __12__ muy divertida!

¡ __13__ tarde! __14__ las diez de la noche y __15__ muy cansado. Escribe pronto, ¿eh?

7 La actriz Anilú Pardo

Escuchar/Escribir Escucha la entrevista con Anilú Pardo. Luego, contesta en oraciones completas.

1. ¿Quién es?
2. ¿De dónde es?
3. ¿Cuál es su nacionalidad?
4. ¿Cuál es su profesión?
5. ¿Quién es el director de la película?
6. ¿Quiénes son los otros actores?
7. ¿Cómo se siente Anilú?

8 ¡Mi página-web!

Leer/Escribir Navegando por Internet, encontraste un sitio donde jóvenes de todo el mundo ponen anuncios para buscar amigos por correspondencia electrónica. Lee el anuncio de una joven puertorriqueña. Luego escribe tu propio anuncio.

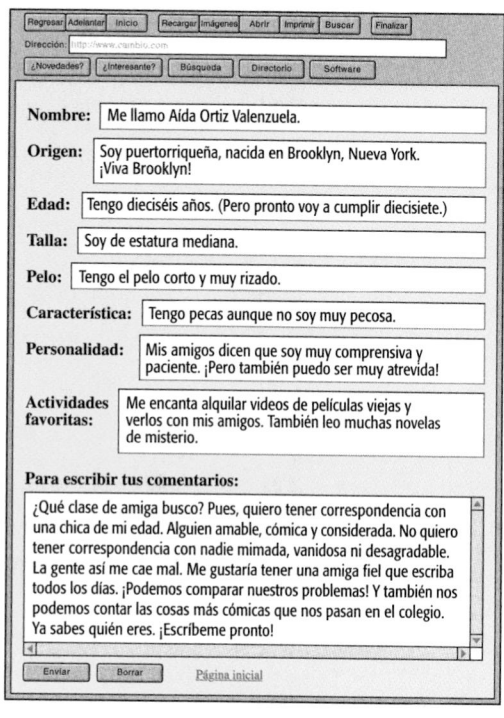

| Regresar | Adelantar | Inicio | Recargar | Imágenes | Abrir | Imprimir | Buscar | Finalizar |

Dirección: http://www.cumbiu.com

| ¿Novedades? | ¿Interesante? | Búsqueda | Directorio | Software |

Nombre: Me llamo Aída Ortiz Valenzuela.

Origen: Soy puertorriqueña, nacida en Brooklyn, Nueva York. ¡Viva Brooklyn!

Edad: Tengo dieciséis años. (Pero pronto voy a cumplir diecisiete.)

Talla: Soy de estatura mediana.

Pelo: Tengo el pelo corto y muy rizado.

Característica: Tengo pecas aunque no soy muy pecosa.

Personalidad: Mis amigos dicen que soy muy comprensiva y paciente. ¡Pero también puedo ser muy atrevida!

Actividades favoritas: Me encanta alquilar videos de películas viejas y verlos con mis amigos. También leo muchas novelas de misterio.

Para escribir tus comentarios:

¿Qué clase de amiga busco? Pues, quiero tener correspondencia con una chica de mi edad. Alguien amable, cómica y considerada. No quiero tener correspondencia con nadie mimada, vanidosa ni desagradable. La gente así me cae mal. Me gustaría tener una amiga fiel que escriba todos los días. ¡Podemos comparar nuestros problemas! Y también nos podemos contar las cosas más cómicas que nos pasan en el colegio. Ya sabes quién eres. ¡Escríbeme pronto!

| Enviar | Borrar | Página inicial |

More Practice: Más comunicación *p. R3*

ACTIVIDAD 5 Objective: Controlled practice
Ser vs. estar

Answers

1. soy, estoy
2. es, Es
3. es, Está
4. Soy, está
5. Son, están
6. Estoy
7. están, está
8. eres, estás

ACTIVIDAD 6 Objective: Controlled practice
Ser vs. estar

Answers

1. soy
2. son
3. somos
4. es
5. es
6. es
7. soy
8. es
9. están
10. están
11. Están
12. ser
13. Es
14. Son
15. estoy

ACTIVIDAD 7 Objective: Transitional practice
Listening comprehension/ser vs. estar

Answers (See script, p. 31D.)
1. Es Anilú Pardo.
2. Es de la Ciudad de México.
3. Es mexicana.
4. Es actriz.
5. Su esposo es el director de la película.
6. Los otros actores son latinoamericanos.
7. Está muy nerviosa.

ACTIVIDAD 8 Objective: Open-ended practice
Ser vs. estar

Answers will vary.

🔔 Quick Wrap-up

Ask students questions using **ser** and **estar**. For example: ¿De dónde es Oscar de la Hoya? ¿Quién es Ellen Ochoa? ¿Dónde está tu casa? ¿Cómo estás hoy?

Dictation

Using the Listening Activity Script for **Actividad 12** on TE p. 31D, dictate selected sentences to students. You may want to use this dictation for a quiz grade.

Block Schedule

Research Have students research a well-known Spanish-speaking person. Using this information, have them create a Web page for the person, using **Actividad 8** as models. Note: Tell students that they will need to use their research for another activity on TE p. 43. (For additional activities, see **Block Scheduling Copymasters**.)

Teaching All Students

Extra Help To reinforce the difference between the use of **ser** and **estar**, have students describe themselves, distinguishing between characteristics and conditions. ¿Cómo eres? *What are you like?* ¿Cómo estás hoy? *How are you today?*

Native Speakers Give students pictures from magazines and have them write brief descriptions using **ser** and **estar**. Ask students to give examples using **ser** and **estar** with the same adjectives to show differences in meaning.

Multiple Intelligences

Intrapersonal Have students draw a picture and write a description of the person they would like to be in 10 years.

Práctica: gramática y vocabulario continuación

Teaching Resource Options

Print 📖

Más práctica Workbook PE, pp. 17–18
Cuaderno para hispanohablantes
PE, p. 14
Block Scheduling Copymasters
Unit 1 Resource Book
  Más práctica Workbook TE, pp. 9–10
  Cuaderno para hispanohablantes
  TE, p. 26
  Absent Student Copymasters, p. 42

Audiovisual 🎧

OHT 13 (Quick Start), 14 (Quick Start)
17–18 (Grammar)

Technology 💻

Online Workbook, U1E1
Take-Home Tutor CD-ROM, U1E1

🔔 Quick Start Review

♻ **Ser** vs. **estar**

Use OHT 13 or write on the board:
Complete the following with the correct
form of **ser** or **estar**:

1. Marcos ____ alto y delgado.
2. ¿Dónde ____ el director?
3. Mis padres ____ de Costa Rica.
4. Tú ____ atrevido.
5. Barcelona ____ en España.
6. Yo ____ un poco triste.
7. Nosotros no ____ mimados.
8. Los chicos ____ filmando un video.

Answers

1. es	2. está	3. son
4. eres	5. está	6. estoy
7. somos	8. están	

Teaching Suggestions
Reviewing The Imperfect Tense

• Review the imperfect tense endings of
regular verbs. Name an infinitive and a
subject pronoun and have a student
supply the imperfect tense form; for
example, **tú / tener = tenías**.
• Review the verbs that are irregular in
the imperfect. Give verb forms and
have students name the infinitive; for
example, **era = ser**.
• Have students supply original
sentences for ongoing actions, habitual
actions, and incomplete actions in the
past, as well as telling time in the past.

REPASO   The Imperfect Tense

▶ You can use the **imperfect tense** in Spanish to talk about ongoing,
habitual, or incomplete actions in the past. You also use the **imperfect**
to tell time in the past, and for descriptions in the past.

▶ Use the **endings** shown below to form the **imperfect tense** of regular
verbs.

	-ar hablar	-er comer	-ir vivir
yo	hablaba	comía	vivía
tú	hablabas	comías	vivías
usted, él, ella,	hablaba	comía	vivía
nosotros(as)	hablábamos	comíamos	vivíamos
vosotros(as)	hablabais	comíais	vivíais
ustedes, ellos, ellas	hablaban	comían	vivían

▶ Only three verbs are **irregular** in the imperfect: **ir**, **ser**, and **ver**.

	ir to go	ser to be	ver to see
yo	iba	era	veía
tú	ibas	eras	veías
usted, él, ella,	iba	era	veía
nosotros(as)	íbamos	éramos	veíamos
vosotros(as)	ibais	erais	veíais
ustedes, ellos, ellas	iban	eran	veían

Mi abuela **era** esbelta y baja y **llevaba** anteojos.
*My grandmother **was** slender and short and **wore** eyeglasses.*

Practice:
Actividades

Más práctica
cuaderno pp. 17–18
Para hispanohablantes
cuaderno p. 14

🌐 **Online Workbook**
CLASSZONE.COM

---

42   cuarenta y dos
Unidad 1

---

9 ¿Dónde estabas? 👥

Hablar/Escribir Tu amigo(a) te
llamó varias veces por teléfono
pero no estabas. Contesta su
pregunta diciéndole dónde
estabas y qué hacías.

modelo

en mi cuarto (hacer la tarea)

Compañero(a): *¿Dónde estabas
cuando te llamé
anoche?*

Tú: *Estaba en mi cuarto. Hacía
la tarea.*

1. en el centro comercial
(comprar discos compactos)
2. en la biblioteca (escribir
la tarea)
3. en la sala (ver la
televisión)
4. en el café (hablar con
mis amigos)
5. en el parque (andar
en bicicleta)
6. en la tienda de videos
(alquilar un video)
7. en el cine (ver una
película)
8. en el gimnasio (levantar
pesas)
9. la fiesta de Adrián (tocar
la guitarra)
10. la casa de mi tía (comer
pastel)

Classroom Community

Paired Activity After presenting the preterite vs.
the imperfect (p. 43), have students work in pairs.
Students tell each other what they did or were doing
yesterday morning, noon, afternoon, and evening. Have
them take notes on what their partner says and report
their findings to the class.

Storytelling After presenting the preterite vs. the
imperfect (p. 43), tell students a story about what you
did last week, using verbs in the preterite and in the
imperfect. Have students raise their right hand when
they hear a verb in the preterite. Have them stand up
when they hear a verb in the imperfect. Then divide
the class into groups and have each group tell a chain
story.

10 El verano

Hablar/*Escribir* Hacías cosas durante el verano que ya no puedes hacer durante el año escolar. ¿Qué cosas hacías que ya no puedes hacer?

modelo

navegar por Internet

Yo siempre navegaba por Internet durante el día, pero ahora no puedo.

1. descansar
2. levantarse
3. ir
4. ponerse
5. ver
6. acostarse
7. trabajar
8. viajar

11 La apariencia ayer y hoy

Hablar Habla con un(a) compañero(a) de clase de cómo se veían hace diez años y cómo se ven hoy. ¿Qué diferencias hay?

modelo

Tú: *Cuando tenía seis años, siempre llevaba el pelo en cola de caballo.*

Compañero(a): *Pues, yo usaba anteojos y estaba muy delgado(a). No me vestía muy bien.*

Tú: *Bueno, ¡ahora eres muy elegante!*

REPASO **Preterite vs. Imperfect**

 ¿RECUERDAS? *p. 42* You already know two tenses that refer to past time, the preterite and the imperfect. You use each of these tenses to talk about **past** actions in a different way.

- Use the preterite tense to describe an action or series of actions completed in the past.

  Aquel día, Pedro salió del colegio y caminó hasta el café.
  *That day, Pedro **left** school and **walked** to the café.*

- Use the imperfect to describe ongoing actions or conditions in the past, without focusing on their beginning or end.

  Yo siempre salía del colegio y caminaba hasta el café.
  *I always **used to leave** school and **walk** to the Café.*

Sometimes you will need to use the **imperfect** and preterite in the same sentence.

Use the imperfect to tell what was going on in the background.

Use the preterite to describe the interrupting action or main event.

Yo hacía la tarea cuando sonó el teléfono.
*I **was doing** my homework when the telephone **rang**.*

Practice: **Actividades** 12 13 14 15 | **Más práctica** *cuaderno p. 19* | **Para hispanohablantes** *cuaderno pp. 15–16* |  **Online Workbook** CLASSZONE.COM

Answers
1. Estaba en el centro comercial. Compraba discos compactos.
2. Estaba en la biblioteca. Escribía la tarea.
3. Estaba en la sala. Veía la televisión.
4. Estaba en el café. Hablaba con mis amigos.
5. Estaba en el parque. Andaba en bicicleta.
6. Estaba en la tienda de videos. Alquilaba un video.
7. Estaba en el cine. Veía una película.
8. Estaba en el gimnasio. Levantaba pesas.
9. Estaba en la fiesta de Adrián. Tocaba la guitarra.
10. Estaba en la casa de mi tía. Comía pastel.

ACTIVIDAD 10 **Objective:** Transitional practice
The imperfect tense

Answers will vary.

ACTIVIDAD 11 **Objective:** Open-ended practice
The imperfect tense

Answers will vary.

🔔 Quick Start Review

♻ The imperfect tense

Use OHT 14 or write on the board: Write sentences using the following elements to say what the people used to do last year. Add any necessary words and make any necessary changes.

1. a las dos / María / estar / siempre / biblioteca
2. profesora / siempre / escribir / mucho / pizarrón
3. nosotros / ir / siempre / playa
4. siempre / acostarme / temprano
5. los viernes / ellos / siempre / comer / restaurante

Answers *See p. 31D.*

Teaching All Students

Extra Help Before working in pairs to do **Actividad 9,** have students give the **yo** form of the imperfect of the verbs in items 1–6.

Native Speakers Have students write a 1-paragraph description of the most important day they can remember. They should tell what the day was like, whom they were with, and what was going on.

Multiple Intelligences

Musical/Rhythmic Have students work in pairs to make up 2 raps/chants. One should illustrate the use of the preterite and the other the use of the imperfect.

▌Block Schedule

Change of Pace Using the research they carried out on a well-known Spanish-speaking person on TE p. 41, have students write a paragraph on the person's earlier life. (For additional activities, see **Block Scheduling Copymasters**.)

Teaching Resource Options

Print
Más práctica Workbook PE, p. 19
Cuaderno para hispanohablantes
  PE, pp. 15–16
Block Scheduling Copymasters
Unit 1 Resource Book
  Más práctica Workbook TE, p. 11
  Cuaderno para hispanohablantes
  TE, pp. 27–28
  Information Gap Activities, p. 34
  Absent Student Copymasters, p. 43
  Audioscript, p. 49

Audiovisual
Audio Program CD 1, Track 5, Actividad 14

Teaching Suggestions
Presenting Vocabulary

- Have students make quick sketches to illustrate each of the new vocabulary words.
- Discuss the question at the end of the vocabulary. In what ways do students have these interactions with their friends?

Objective: Controlled practice
Preterite vs. imperfect

Answers

1. era	12. pareció
2. se llamaba	13. sabía
3. era	14. podía
4. andábamos	15. estaban
5. gustaba	16. repitió
6. gustaba	17. convenció
7. gustaba	18. vimos
8. compartía	19. fue
9. influía	20. llamó
10. estaba	21. estaba
11. dijo	22. resolví

---

12 Yoli la atrevida

Escribir Cristina escribió una composición sobre una amiga de su niñez. Complétala con las formas correctas de los verbos entre paréntesis para leer sus aventuras.

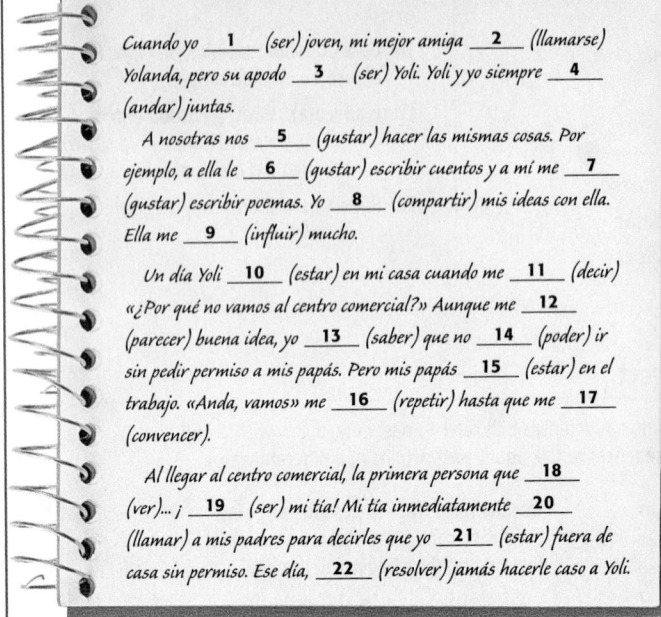

> Cuando yo __1__ (ser) joven, mi mejor amiga __2__ (llamarse) Yolanda, pero su apodo __3__ (ser) Yoli. Yoli y yo siempre __4__ (andar) juntas.
>
> A nosotras nos __5__ (gustar) hacer las mismas cosas. Por ejemplo, a ella le __6__ (gustar) escribir cuentos y a mí me __7__ (gustar) escribir poemas. Yo __8__ (compartir) mis ideas con ella. Ella me __9__ (influir) mucho.
>
> Un día Yoli __10__ (estar) en mi casa cuando me __11__ (decir) «¿Por qué no vamos al centro comercial?» Aunque me __12__ (parecer) buena idea, yo __13__ (saber) que no __14__ (poder) ir sin pedir permiso a mis papás. Pero mis papás __15__ (estar) en el trabajo. «Anda, vamos» me __16__ (repetir) hasta que me __17__ (convencer).
>
> Al llegar al centro comercial, la primera persona que __18__ (ver)... ¡ __19__ (ser) mi tía! Mi tía inmediatamente __20__ (llamar) a mis padres para decirles que yo __21__ (estar) fuera de casa sin permiso. Ese día, __22__ (resolver) jamás hacerle caso a Yoli.

Vocabulario

Interacciones

compartir *to share*
discutir *to argue*
hacerle caso a *to obey, pay attention to*
influir *to influence*

resolver (o→ue) *to resolve*
respetar *to respect*
tener en común *to have in common*

▶ ¿Tienes estas interacciones con tus amigos?

---

13 Mi abuelo

Hablar/Escribir Hablas con tu abuelo sobre las cosas que él hacía cuando era joven. Hace pocos días que tú hiciste las mismas cosas que él hacía hace años. Sigue el modelo.

modelo
ir al museo / los domingos

Abuelo: *Cuando era joven, yo iba al museo los domingos.*

Tú: *¿De veras? Yo fui al museo el domingo pasado.*

1. ir al cine / los sábados
2. salir a pasear con mis amigos / los viernes
3. jugar al fútbol / los fines de semana
4. ir a conciertos / una vez al mes
5. levantar pesas / los lunes
6. estudiar en la biblioteca / los domingos
7. hacer la limpieza / los fines de semana
8. visitar a mis tíos / todas las semanas
9. cocinar pasta / los viernes
10. nadar en la piscina / los jueves

Classroom Community

Paired Activity Working in pairs, have students tell each other about a childhood friend. They should describe what the person looked like, what they used to do together regularly, and an interesting event that took place. Students should ask each other questions about these friends as well.

Storytelling Have students work in groups of 4 to tell a story describing a horrible day. The story should begin with a description in the imperfect tense that sets the scene of a nice day. Then students should use sentences in the preterite to describe an event that interrupts the nice scene. Have groups present their stories to the class.

14 ¡Acción!

Escuchar/Escribir Escucha a Luci Pérez. Ella describe una película que vio ayer. Luego, escribe oraciones basadas en su descripción.

modelo

Luci (ver)

Luci vio una película ayer.

1. la película (tener)
2. Lola (ser)
3. los hombres malos (capturar)
4. ella (tener que)
5. los hombres malos (ser)
6. ella (salvar)
7. la actriz (ganar)

Nota cultural

Los apodos *(nicknames)* son comunes en la cultura latina. Muchas veces el apodo viene del nombre de la persona. Algunos ejemplos son:

Chicos

Antonio = Toño, Toni

Guillermo = Memo

Roberto = Beto

Chicas

Graciela = Chela

Isabel = Chabela

Mercedes = Mercha, Meche

[imagen: placa de California que dice BETO, FEB]

15 Cuando era niño(a)...

Escribir Escribe dos párrafos sobre tu niñez, usando expresiones de la lista de vocabulario.

modelo

Cuando era niño(a), yo era muy trabajador(a), a diferencia de mi hermano(a) que era muy perezoso(a). Me gustaba estudiar y jugar con mis amigos. ¡Pero no me gustaba jugar con mi hermano(a)! Por un lado quería…

- ¿Cómo eras?
- ¿Qué te gustaba hacer? ¿Qué no te gustaba?
- ¿Qué querías ser?
- ¿Qué te interesaba?
- ¿Cómo era tu mejor amigo(a)?
- ¿Qué hacían juntos?
- ¿Puedes describir un incidente en particular?
- ¿…?

Vocabulario

Comparaciones

a diferencia de *as contrasted with*

al contrario *on the contrary*

lo bueno/malo *the good thing/bad thing*

lo más/menos *the most/least*

lo mejor/peor *the best/worst*

por otro lado *on the other (hand)*

por un lado *on the one hand*

semejante a *similar to*

▶ ¿Qué dices si quieres comparar dos cosas?

Teaching All Students

Extra Help Have students make verb flashcards with a subject pronoun and preterite form of a verb on one side and the corresponding imperfect form on the other. Then have students work in pairs and quiz each other.

Native Speakers Have students ask a friend or relative what he/she was like when he/she was a child. Then have them write a 1-paragraph description.

Multiple Intelligences

Kinesthetic First, have the class compile a list of 10 activities they used to do when they were 6–7 years old. Then, have them write a sentence for each activity **(Yo jugaba videojuegos.)** on large pieces of paper and post them around the room. Ask students to line up in front of the activity they did the most often. Have students count how many are in each group and graph the results.

---

13 **Objective:** Controlled practice
Preterite vs. imperfect

Answers

1. Abuelo: Cuando era joven, yo iba al cine los sábados. / Tú: ¿De veras? Yo fui al cine el sábado pasado.
2. Abuelo: Cuando era joven, yo salía a pasear con mis amigos los viernes. / Tú: ¿De veras? Yo salí a pasear con mis amigos el viernes pasado.
3. Abuelo: Cuando era joven, yo jugaba al fútbol los fines de semana. / Tú: ¿De veras? Yo jugué al fútbol el fin de semana pasado.
4. Abuelo: Cuando era joven, yo iba a conciertos una vez al mes. / Tú: ¿De veras? Yo fui a un concierto el mes pasado.
5. Abuelo: Cuando era joven, yo levantaba pesas los lunes. / Tú: ¿De veras? Yo levanté pesas el lunes pasado.
6. Abuelo: Cuando era joven, yo estudiaba en la biblioteca los domingos. / Tú: ¿De veras? Yo estudié en la biblioteca el domingo pasado.
7. Abuelo: Cuando era joven, yo hacía la limpieza los fines de semana. / Tú: ¿De veras? Yo hice la limpieza el fin de semana pasado.
8. Abuelo: Cuando era joven, yo visitaba a mis tíos todas las semanas. / Tú: ¿De veras? Yo visité a mis tíos la semana pasada.
9. Cuando era joven, yo cocinaba pasta todos los viernes. / Tú: ¿De veras? Yo cociné pasta el viernes pasado.
10. Cuando era joven, yo nadaba en la piscina todos los jueves. / Tú: ¿De veras? Yo nadé en la piscina el jueves pasado.

14 **Objective:** Transitional practice
Listening comprehension/preterite vs. imperfect

Answers (See script, p. 31D.)
1. La película tuvo mucha acción.
2. Lola era alta, esbelta y muy atrevida.
3. Los hombres malos capturaron a su compañero.
4. Ella tenía que salvar a su compañero.
5. Los hombres malos eran muy desagradables.
6. Al fin ella salvó a su compañero.
7. La actriz ganó un premio por su actuación.

15 **Objective:** Open-ended practice
Preterite vs. imperfect

Answers will vary.

Block Schedule

Variety Using **Actividad 14** as a model, ask students to write film summaries. Have volunteers read their summaries to the class, without giving the film's name. The class guesses what film is being described. (For additional activities, see **Block Scheduling Copymasters**.)

Teaching Resource Options

Print

Más práctica Workbook PE, pp. 11–14, 20

Cuaderno para hispanohablantes PE, pp. 11–12, 17–18

Block Scheduling Copymasters

Unit 1 Resource Book

  Más práctica Workbook TE, pp. 3–6, 12

  Cuaderno para hispanohablantes TE, pp. 23–24, 29–30

  Absent Student Copymasters, p. 44

Audiovisual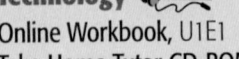

OHT 14 (Quick Start), 19 (Grammar) Word Tiles, U1E1

Technology

Online Workbook, U1E1
Take-Home Tutor CD-ROM, U1E1

🔔 Quick Start Review

♻ **The imperfect tense**

Use OHT 14 or write on the board: Write 3 things you used to do when you were a child and 3 things you did yesterday:

• Cuando era niño(a), yo...
• Ayer yo...

Answers

Answers will vary. Answers could include:
• ...me acostaba a las ocho, iba al parque todos los días, visitaba a mis abuelos los domingos
• ...me levanté a las seis, fui a la escuela, jugué al tenis

Teaching Suggestions
Presenting Present and Past Perfect Tenses

• Practice formation of past participles. Say a verb infinitive and toss a soft ball to a student. If the student gives the correct past participle, he/she tosses the ball back to you. If he/she gives an incorrect answer, he/she tosses the ball to another student.

• Have students provide sample sentences in the present perfect tense, describing what they have already done today.

• Present and practice the imperfect tense forms of **haber**. Then have students provide sample sentences in the past perfect tense.

GRAMÁTICA   **Present and Past Perfect Tenses**

To express the idea that someone has or had already done something, you use the **present perfect** and **past perfect tenses**.

The **present perfect** tense consists of the **present** tense of the auxiliary verb **haber**, *to have*, plus the **past participle** of the verb. To form regular **past participles**, drop the ending from the **infinitive** and add the following endings.

hablar ▸ habl**ado**   comer ▸ com**ido**   vivir ▸ viv**ido**

present perfect of hablar

he **hablado**	hemos **hablado**
has **hablado**	habéis **hablado**
ha **hablado**	han **hablado**

Here are some **irregular past participles:**

abrir → **abierto**, cubrir → **cubierto**, decir → **dicho**, escribir → **escrito**, hacer → **hecho**, morir → **muerto**, poner → **puesto**, resolver → **resuelto**, romper → **roto**, ver → **visto**, volver → **vuelto**.

You use the **present perfect** tense to talk about events or actions that have already occurred.

¿**Has** com**ido**?   No, todavía no **he** com**ido** nada.
Have you eaten?   *No, I still haven't eaten anything.*

The **past perfect** refers to an action that had already occurred when something else happened. Both actions are in the past, one occurring before the other.

past perfect of hablar

había **hablado**	habíamos **hablado**
habías **hablado**	habíais **hablado**
había **hablado**	habían **hablado**

> You form the **past perfect** almost the same way as the **present perfect**, but you use the **imperfect** form of **haber** instead.

Todavía no **había** com**ido** cuando llegó Luis.
*I still **hadn't eaten** when Luis arrived.*

In both the **present perfect** and **past perfect**, you place **object pronouns before** the forms of the verb **haber**.

                           before

Marta ya tenía el libro.   ¿Se **lo había** prest**ado** usted?
Marta already had the book.   *Had you lent it to her?*

Practice: **Actividades** 16 17   **Más práctica** *cuaderno p. 20*   **Para hispanohablantes** *cuaderno pp. 17–18*    **Online Workbook** CLASSZONE.COM

Classroom Community

Group Activity   Have students work in groups of 3. Each group chooses 1 of the characters described on pp. 34–35 and writes interview questions using the present perfect. The groups present their interviews, with 1 student playing the character and the other 2 students asking the questions.

Learning Scenario   Working in pairs or small groups, have students make up a scene depicting an awful day. They should use the following sentence as a model: **Todavía no había comido cuando llegó Luis.** In their scene they must use the past perfect tense at least 5 times.

16 Los quehaceres

Hablar/*Escribir* Haz una lista para tus papás describiendo quién ha hecho cada cosa.

modelo

yo / pasar la aspiradora

Yo he pasado la aspiradora.

1. yo / poner la mesa
2. tú / lavar los platos
3. mis hermanos / hacer las camas
4. mi hermanita / barrer el piso
5. nosotros / abrir las ventanas

17 No sabía que...

Hablar/*Escribir* Le preguntas a tu compañero(a) qué te perdiste antes de que llegaras a la fiesta.

modelo

la fiesta empezar

Tú: *Yo no sabía que la fiesta había empezado.*

Compañero(a): *Ya había empezado cuando tú llegaste.*

1. los músicos tocar
2. la profesora de español bailar
3. Elisa tocar la guitarra
4. los estudiantes comer el pastel
5. los padres de Elisa hablar
6. el hermano de Elisa entrar
7. los abuelos de Elisa salir
8. la fiesta terminar

Activity **18** brings together all concepts presented.

18 ¿Lo has hecho?

Hablar Haz una encuesta o añade cosas a la siguiente lista. Luego, pregúntales a varios compañeros si han hecho las cosas de tu lista. Pídeles que cuenten detalles de las cosas que han hecho.

	Sí	No
¿Siempre viviste en la misma casa?		
¿Estuviste en la casa de una persona vanidosa?		
¿Eras mimado(a) cuando eras más joven?		
¿Has dicho mentiras?		
¿Has resuelto un problema difícil?		
¿Habías estudiado español antes?		

More Practice:
Más comunicación *p. R3*

Online Workbook
CLASSZONE.COM

Refrán

Cada cabeza es un mundo.

¿Qué quiere decir el refrán? ¿Crees que cada persona es un individuo? ¿Cómo puedes describir tu «mundo interior»?

cuarenta y siete
Estados Unidos Etapa 1   47

ACTIVIDAD 16 **Objective:** Controlled practice Present perfect tense

Answers
1. Yo he quitado la mesa.
2. Tú has lavado los platos.
3. Mis hermanos han hecho las camas.
4. Mi hermanita ha barrido el piso.
5. Nosotros hemos abierto las ventanas.

ACTIVIDAD 17 **Objective:** Transitional practice Past perfect tense

Answers
1. A: Yo no sabía que los músicos habían tocado.
   B: Ya habían tocado cuando tú llegaste.
2. A: Yo no sabía que la profesora de español había bailado.
   B: Ya había bailado cuando tú llegaste.
3. A: Yo no sabía que Elisa había tocado la guitarra.
   B: Ya había tocado la guitarra cuando tú llegaste.
4. A: Yo no sabía que los estudiantes habían comido el pastel.
   B: Ya habían comido el pastel cuando tú llegaste.
5. A: Yo no sabía que los padres de Elisa habían hablado.
   B: Ya habían hablado cuando tú llegaste.
6. A: Yo no sabía que el hermano de Elisa había entrado.
   B: Ya había entrado cuando tú llegaste.
7. A: Yo no sabía que los abuelos de Elisa habían salido.
   B: Ya habían salido cuando tú llegaste.
8. A: Yo no sabía que la fiesta había terminado.
   B: Ya había terminado cuando tú llegaste.

ACTIVIDAD 18 Objective: Open-ended practice Present and past perfect tenses

Answers will vary.

Refrán

Introduce the idea of metaphors. Ask students if they can think of any metaphors in English.

Block Schedule

Process Time Allow students time to look back through the **Etapa** and review the vocabulary and grammatical concepts that have been covered. Ask them to share what they found interesting, helpful, easy, difficult, etc. For grammatical concepts, have students who found a particular concept easy explain it to those who found it difficult. (For additional activities, see **Block Scheduling Copymasters**.)

Teaching All Students

Extra Help Have students make flashcards with verb infinitives on 1 side and past participles on the other. Then have them work in pairs and quiz each other.

Multiple Intelligences

Verbal Expand on **Actividad 16**. As a class, brainstorm a list of home-related and school-related chores that need to be done every day. Write the list on the board. Then have each student say which chore(s) they have already done today.

Teaching Resource Options

Print
Actividades para todos Workbook PE,
  pp. 17–19
Block Scheduling Copymasters
Unit 1 Resource Book
  Actividades para todos Workbook
    TE, pp. 18–21
  Absent Student Copymasters, p. 45
  Audioscript, p. 49

Audiovisual
OHT M2, 15 (Quick Start)
Audio Program CD 1, Tracks 6–7
Canciones CD

Technology
Online Workbook, U1E1
Take-Home Tutor CD-ROM, U1E1

Quick Start Review
🔔 Past participles
Use OHT 15 or write on the board:
Write the past participle of the
following verbs:

1. respetar   5. tener
2. morir   6. poner
3. compartir   7. ver
4. hacer   8. decir

Answers
1. respetado   5. tenido
2. muerto   6. puesto
3. compartido   7. visto
4. hecho   8. dicho

Teaching Suggestions
• **Prereading** Present the Culture
  Highlight, TE p. 49, then read and
  discuss the **Nota cultural**, p. 48.
• **Strategy: Observe how verb
  tenses reveal time** Present the
  Reading Strategy, p. 48, for students
  to keep in mind as they read the
  passage.
• **Reading** Have students skim the
  text to get the general idea. Also have
  them look at the **¿Comprendiste?**
  and **¿Qué piensas?** questions. Then
  call on volunteers to read the text
  aloud.
• **Post-reading** Have students
  complete the task outlined in the
  Reading Strategy.

AUDIO
En voces
LECTURA

PARA LEER · STRATEGY: READING
Observe how verb tenses reveal time Verb tenses
show when different events occur in time.
Read Pilar's story of her memories of the
past and her plans for the future. Then select
at least five major events and place them on
a time line. Notice the verb tense of each
event. Are the events scattered on the time
line or clustered together? Can you say why?

LA NIÑEZ

acariciar	hacer un gesto cariñoso a alguien
agarrarse	hacer que una persona no se mueva
escurrirse a hurtadillas	irse de un lugar sin ser visto
gritar a todo pulmón	hablar a todo volumen
la cría	un(a) niño(a) pequeño(a)
sentar en la falda	sentarse sobre las rodillas de alguien que está sentado

Nota cultural
Según el Servicio de Inmigración y Naturalización,
cada año llegan más de 500.000 personas
hispanohablantes a Estados Unidos. Estos grupos
pueden asimilarse dentro de la nueva cultura, pero
sienten mucha nostalgia por su país natal. Es muy
común que un(a) inmigrante de un país
hispanohablante conserve su identidad, no importa
cuántos años viva fuera del país.

Sobre la autora
Cristina García nació en La
Habana, Cuba, en 1958 y se crió
en Nueva York. Asistió a Barnard
College y a la Escuela de Estudios
Internacionales Avanzados de
Johns Hopkins University. Ha trabajado como periodista
en Miami, San Francisco y Los Ángeles, donde vive
actualmente con su esposo. *Soñar en cubano* es su
primera novela.

Introducción
Soñar en cubano es una novela que narra la
historia de una familia cubana. Celia, la abuela,
Lourdes, su hija, y Pilar, su nieta, son los tres
personajes principales. Ellas hablan de los sueños
y el dolor de la familia que vive en Cuba, y de
Lourdes y Pilar. En esta selección habla la nieta,
Pilar Puente.

48 cuarenta y ocho
Unidad 1

Classroom Community

Paired Activity Working with a partner, 1 student
reads several sentences of the reading. The other
student paraphrases what has been read. Then each
student writes a question and exchanges it with the
partner and answers it. Pairs continue until they have
finished the reading.

Portfolio Have students write a diary page as if they
were Abuela Celia the day that she saw Pilar for the last
time.

Rubric A = 13–15 pts. B = 10–12 pts. C = 7–9 pts. D = 4–6 pts. F = < 4 pts.

Writing criteria	Scale
Vocabulary use	1 2 3 4 5
Grammatical/spelling accuracy	1 2 3 4 5
Creativity	1 2 3 4 5

Soñar en cubano

Eso es. Ya lo entiendo. Regresaré a Cuba. Estoy harta[1] de todo. Saco todo mi dinero del banco, 120 dólares, el dinero que he ahorrado esclavizada en la pastelería de mi madre, y compro un billete de autocar para irme a Miami. Calculo que una vez allí, podría gestionar[2] mi viaje a Cuba, alquilando un bote, o consiguiendo un pescador que me lleve. Imagino la sorpresa de Abuela Celia cuando me escurriera a hurtadillas por detrás de ella. Estaría sentada en su columpio de mimbre[3] mirando al mar, y olería a[4] sal y a agua de violetas. Habría gaviotas[5] y cangrejos[6] en la orilla del mar. Acariciaría mis mejillas[7] con sus manos frías, y cantaría silenciosamente en mis oídos.

Cuando salí de Cuba tenía sólo dos años, pero recuerdo todo lo que pasó desde que era una cría, cada una de las conversaciones, palabra por palabra. Estaba sentada en la falda de mi abuela jugando con sus pendientes de perlas, cuando mi madre le dijo que nos iríamos de la isla. Abuela Celia le acusó de haber traicionado la revolución. Mamá trató de separarme de la abuela, pero yo me agarré a ella y grité a todo pulmón. Mi abuelo vino corriendo y dijo: «Celia, deja que la niña se vaya. Debe estar con Lourdes.» Ésa fue la última vez que la vi.

---

[1] to be fed up with
[2] to arrange
[3] wicker rocking chair
[4] she would smell of
[5] seagulls
[6] crabs
[7] cheeks

Online Workbook
CLASSZONE.COM

¿Comprendiste?

1. ¿Por qué quiere regresar a Cuba Pilar?
2. ¿Cómo piensa llegar?
3. ¿A quién va a ver Pilar?
4. ¿Cuántos años tenía Pilar cuando salió de Cuba?
5. ¿Qué cosas asocia Pilar con su abuela?

¿Qué piensas?

En tu opinión, ¿qué sentimientos tiene Pilar hacia la vida que abandonaron ella y su mamá? ¿Por qué quiere regresar?

Hazlo tú

¿Cómo era tu abuela (abuelo) cuando tenías dos años? Busca una foto de esa época y escribe una descripción de ella (él). También puedes describir a otra persona mayor de tu niñez.

Teaching Resource Options
Print 📖
Cuaderno para hispanohablantes
  PE, pp. 19–20
Block Scheduling Copymasters
Unit 1 Resource Book
  Cuaderno para hispanohablantes
    TE, pp. 31–32
  Information Gap Activities, pp. 35–36
  Family Involvement, pp. 46–47

Audiovisual 💻
OHT 15 (Quick Start)

Technology 💿
eTest Plus Online/Test Generator
  CD-ROM
🌐 www.classzone.com

🔔 Quick Start Review
♻ Descriptions
Use OHT 15 or write on the board:
**Escribe por lo menos 8 palabras para
describir la personalidad de una
persona.**

Answers
Answers will vary. Answers could include:
deportista, rebelde, caballero, vanidoso(a),
misterioso(a), sofisticado(a), atrevido(a),
comprensivo(a), considerado(a), modesto(a),
desagradable, descarado(a), fiel, mimado(a)

✓ Teaching Suggestions
What Have Students Learned?
Have students look at the "Now you
can…" notes listed in the left margin
of pages 50–51. Point out that if they
need to review material before doing
the activities or taking the test, they
should consult the pages indicated in
the "To review" notes.

ACTIVIDAD 1 Answers
Answers will vary.
El señor Monsevalles tiene la cara redonda. Tiene
  bigote y barba. Es un poco desagradable.
Sonia tiene la cara triangular. Tiene el pelo rubio
  y largo. Es muy amable.
La profesora Quiñones tiene el pelo rojizo en cola
  de caballo. Es alta y esbelta. Es muy paciente.
Daniel tiene el pelo negro en cola de caballo.
  Tiene el cuerpo de deportista. Es atrevido.
Yolanda tiene la cara cuadrada. Tiene el pelo
  corto y ondulado. Es muy tímida.

ETAPA 1

En uso
REPASO Y MÁS COMUNICACIÓN

OBJECTIVES
• Describe people
• Talk about experiences
• List accomplishments

Now you can...
• describe people.

To review
• **ser** and **estar**,
  see p. 40.

1 Descripciones
Tú le describes las siguientes personas a tu compañero(a).

Martín

modelo
Martín tiene la cara triangular. Usa lentes de contacto.
¡Es muy vanidoso!

PARADA
el señor Monsevalles   Sonia   la profesora Quiñones   Daniel   Yolanda

Now you can...
• describe people.

To review
• **ser** and **estar**,
  see p. 40.

2 El equipo de fútbol
Escribe oraciones con la forma correcta de **ser** o **estar**.

modelo
los chicos / estudiantes Los chicos son estudiantes.

1. ellos / futbolistas
2. el equipo / de Chicago
3. sus uniformes / lana
4. ellos / no / listos
5. el partido / las tres de la tarde
6. ellos / descansar / en el hotel

50 cincuenta
Unidad 1

Classroom Community

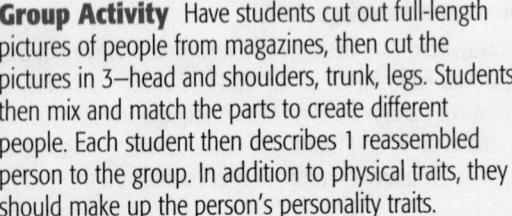

Group Activity Have students cut out full-length
pictures of people from magazines, then cut the
pictures in 3—head and shoulders, trunk, legs. Students
then mix and match the parts to create different
people. Each student then describes 1 reassembled
person to the group. In addition to physical traits, they
should make up the person's personality traits.

Learning Scenario Have students pretend that they
were witnesses to a bank robbery. The police are
looking for a description of the robber. Have students
work in pairs; 1 student is the police officer and the
other is the witness. They then ask and answer
questions about the robber. The officer draws a picture
based on the description.

Now you can...
• talk about experiences.

To review
• the preterite and the imperfect see p. 43.

Self-Check Quiz
CLASSZONE.COM

3 ¡Qué desastre!

Ángel describe un día desastroso de su niñez. Para saber qué le pasó, completa el párrafo usando el pretérito o imperfecto de los verbos entre paréntesis.

Yo ___1___ (tener) diez años. ___2___ (Ser) el día de mi fiesta de cumpleaños. Mamá me ___3___ (decir) que todo ___4___ (estar) listo. La piñata ___5___ (ser) un burro. El pastel ___6___ (ser) de chocolate. Mis amigos y yo ___7___ (estar) muy felices. Nos ___8___ (organizar) para tratar de romper la piñata. Como yo ___9___ (ser) el que ___10___ (cumplir) años, yo ___11___ (ir) a ser el primero. Alguien me ___12___ (poner) un pañuelo en los ojos. Justamente cuando ___13___ (ir) a romper la piñata, ___14___ (empezar) a llover — ¡un aguacero tremendo! Todos ___15___ (correr) hacia la casa. ¡Yo no! ¡Yo ___16___ (querer) seguir con el juego!

Now you can...
• list accomplishments.

To review
• the present and past perfect tenses see p. 46.

4 ¿Qué has hecho?

Tu compañero(a) quiere saber qué han hecho tú y varias personas de tu familia esta semana y la semana pasada.

modelo

tú (trabajar mucho)

Compañero(a): *¿Has trabajado mucho?*

Tú: *Sí, (No, no) he trabajado mucho aunque había trabajado mucho la semana pasada.*

1. tú y tus hermanos (tener mucha tarea)
2. tu padre (viajar mucho)
3. tú (ir al parque)
4. tus primas (comprar muchas cosas)
5. tú y tus hermanos (ver mucha televisión)
6. tú (hablar mucho por teléfono)
7. tú y tus amigos (bailar mucho)
8. tu hermana (visitar a tus abuelos)
9. tú (organizar una fiesta)
10. tú (estudiar español)

cincuenta y uno
Estados Unidos Etapa 1 | **51**

ACTIVIDAD 2 Answers

1. Ellos son futbolistas.
2. El equipo es de Chicago.
3. Sus uniformes son de lana.
4. Ellos no están listos.
5. El partido es a las tres de la tarde.
6. Ellos están descansando en el hotel.

ACTIVIDAD 3 Answers

1. tenía
2. Era
3. dijo
4. estaba
5. era
6. era
7. estábamos
8. organizamos
9. era
10. cumplía
11. iba
12. puso
13. iba
14. empezó
15. corrieron
16. quería

ACTIVIDAD 4 Answers

1. —¿Han tenido mucha tarea tú y tus hermanos? / —Sí, (No, no) hemos tenido mucha tarea, aunque (no) habíamos tenido mucha tarea la semana pasada.
2. —¿Ha viajado mucho tu padre? / —Sí, (No, no) ha viajado mucho, aunque (no) había viajado...
3. —¿Has ido al parque? / —Sí, (No, no) he ido al parque, aunque (no) había ido...
4. —¿Han comprado muchas cosas tus primas? / —Sí, (No, no) han comprado muchas cosas, aunque (no) habían comprado...
5. —¿Han visto mucha televisión tú y tus hermanos? / —Sí, (No, no) hemos visto mucha televisión, aunque (no) habíamos visto...
6. —¿Has hablado mucho por teléfono? / —Sí, (No, no) he hablado mucho por teléfono, aunque (no) había hablado...
7. —¿Han bailado mucho tú y tus amigos? / —Sí, (No, no) hemos bailado mucho, aunque (no) habíamos bailado...
8. —¿Ha visitado tu hermana a tus abuelos? / —Sí, (No, no) ha visitado a mis abuelos, aunque (no) había visitado...
9. —¿Has organizado una fiesta? / —Sí, (No, no) he organizado una fiesta, aunque (no) había organizado...
10. —¿Has estudiado español? / —Sí, (No, no) he estudiado español, aunque (no) había estudiado...

Teaching All Students

Extra Help If students are having difficulty with one particular exercise in the **Repaso**, tell them to review the grammar noted in the "To review" section and redo the related exercises. Then have them explain the concept to you in their own words.

Multiple Intelligences

Visual For a fun expansion of **Actividad 3**, have students make simple **piñatas**. To do this, cover a blown-up balloon with papier-mâché, creating an animal or other object. Let the piece dry for a few days, then paint it and pop the balloon. You may want to have students make a small hole in their **piñatas**, fill them with candy, and then hold a party and break the **piñatas**.

Block Schedule

Peer Review Have students form groups of 3 or 4. Each group should come up with a 10-question **pruebita** that tests information from this **Etapa**. Groups then exchange their **pruebitas**, respond, and do peer corrections. (For additional activities, see **Block Scheduling Copymasters**.)

Teaching Resource Options

Print 📖

Block Scheduling Copymasters
Unit 1 Resource Book
  Audioscript, p. 51
  Vocabulary Quizzes, pp. 54–56
  Grammar Quizzes, pp. 57–58
  Etapa Exam, Forms A and B,
    pp. 59–68
  Examen para hispanohablantes,
    pp. 69–73
  Portfolio Assessment, pp. 74–75
  Multiple Choice Test Questions,
    pp. 242–244

Audiovisual 📺

OHT 15 (Quick Start)
Audio Program CD 19, Track 3

Technology 💻

eTest Plus Online/Test Generator
  CD-ROM
🌐 www.classzone.com

 **and**

Rubric: Speaking

Criteria	Scale	
Sentence structure	1 2 3	A = 11–12 pts.
Vocabulary use	1 2 3	B = 9–10 pts.
Originality	1 2 3	C = 7–8 pts.
Fluency	1 2 3	D = 4–6 pts.
		F = < 4 pts.

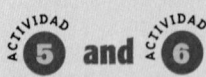 **En tu propia voz**

Rubric: Writing

Criteria	Scale	
Vocabulary use	1 2 3 4 5	A = 14–15 pts.
Accuracy	1 2 3 4 5	B = 12–13 pts.
Creativity, appearance	1 2 3 4 5	C = 10–11 pts.
		D = 8–9 pts.
		F = < 8 pts.

Teaching Note: En tu propia voz

Writing Strategy Suggest that students implement the writing strategy "Appeal to the senses in storytelling" in order to make their narrations memorable. They should do this by using sensory details in their writing.

---

5 El (La) amigo(a) ideal

STRATEGY: SPEAKING

Describe personal characteristics and actions In addition to using adjectives to describe ideal friends, think about their actions: **¿Qué dicen o no dicen los amigos ideales? ¿Qué hacen o no hacen?** Is it important for all the lists to be the same? Explain your answer.

Trabajando en grupos, escriban las características del amigo o de la amiga ideal. Comparen sus listas.

modelo

El amigo ideal tiene que ser comprensivo(a).

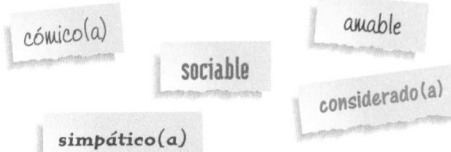

cómico(a)

amable

sociable

considerado(a)

simpático(a)

6 Tus amigos

¿Qué te gustaría saber de la niñez de tus amigos? Escribe una lista de preguntas y luego entrevista a cuatro o cinco compañeros. Apunta sus respuestas y di a la clase lo más interesante que descubriste.

modelo

¿Qué querías ser cuando eras niño(a)?

¿Cuál era tu programa favorito cuando tenías diez años?

¿A qué le tenías miedo cuando tenías ocho años?

7 *En tu propia voz* ✏️

ESCRITURA A veces las películas empiezan con una narración: el protagonista describe una escena de su niñez. Escribe una narración sobre tu niñez para un video. Escoge un incidente impresionante o invéntalo. ¡Sé creativo(a)!

CONEXIONES

El arte Crea un autorretrato. Puedes pintar, dibujar *(to draw)* o hacer un collage de fotografías, artículos o anuncios de revista, etc. Usa tu imaginación. Explica a la clase cómo la obra revela tu personalidad.

Classroom Community

Game Have a student describe a well-known person in the community to the class, using both physical and personality characteristics. Students should raise their hands when they think they know the person being described. If a student's answer is correct, that student then describes another well-known person.

Learning Scenario Have students work in pairs to write and present a dialog about the new exchange student from Argentina that 1 partner has just met. Students first ask and answer questions about a description of the exchange student. They then talk about how they will interact with him/her.

En resumen
REPASO DE VOCABULARIO

DESCRIBE PEOPLE

Personality

atrevido(a)	daring
comprensivo(a)	understanding
considerado(a)	considerate
desagradable	unpleasant
descarado(a)	insolent, shameless
fiel	faithful
mimado(a)	spoiled
modesto(a)	modest
vanidoso(a)	vain

Physical appearance

los anteojos	glasses
el balón	soccer ball
la barba	beard
el bigote	mustache
el cabello	hair
calvo(a)	bald
la cola de caballo	ponytail
cuadrado(a)	square
esbelto(a)	slender
el flequillo	bangs
grueso(a)	heavy
los lentes de contacto	contact lenses
el lunar	beauty mark
ondulado(a)	wavy
opuesto(a)	opposite
ovalado(a)	oval
las pecas	freckles
redondo(a)	round
rojizo(a)	reddish
teñido(a)	dyed
triangular	triangular
verse	to look, to appear

♻ **Ya sabes**

amable	nice
cómico(a)	funny
impaciente	impatient
obediente	obedient
paciente	patient
sociable	sociable
tímido(a)	shy

TALK ABOUT EXPERIENCES

Comparisons

a diferencia de	as contrasted with
al contrario	on the contrary
lo bueno/lo malo	the good thing/ bad thing
lo más/menos	the most/least
lo mejor/peor	the best/worst
por un lado	on the one hand
por otro lado	on the other hand
semejante a	similar to

Interactions

compartir	to share
discutir	to discuss, to argue
hacerle caso a	to obey, to pay attention to
influir	to influence
resolver (o→ue)	to resolve
respetar	to respect
tener en común	to have in common

LIST ACCOMPLISHMENTS

Present and Past Perfect Tenses

Ya **hemos resuelto** el problema.
Ellos **habían discutido** mucho.

Juego

El mejor amigo
¿Cuál de estas palabras no se aplica al dibujo?
- **a.** atrevido
- **b.** considerado
- **c.** descarado
- **d.** fiel

Teaching All Students

Extra Help Have students create crossword puzzles containing 10 words from the **Repaso de vocabulario.** The clues must be in Spanish. Then have them exchange their puzzles with a partner for completing.

Multiple Intelligences

Logical/Mathematical Have students research the current total population and Hispanic population of Los Angeles, San Antonio, Chicago, Miami, and New York. Have them calculate the percentage of the Hispanic population to each city's total population. Variation: Students may also find these figures for 20 years ago and see how the numbers have changed.

UNIDAD 1 Etapa 1
Review

Interdisciplinary Connection
Art Work with the art department to discuss self-portraits, especially those done by Spanish-speaking artists (for example, Frida Kahlo or Pablo Picasso). Why would an artist create a self-portrait?

🔔 Quick Start Review
♻ **Etapa vocabulary**
Use OHT 15 or write on the board.
Escribe 3 oraciones en que describes a una persona que conoces. Tienes que usar por lo menos 9 palabras del Repaso de vocabulario.
Answers will vary.

Teaching Suggestions
Vocabulary Review
Write several vocabulary words on the board. Divide the class into 2 groups. Give 1 student from each group a fly swatter (or similar object). When you say a vocabulary word, the 2 students look for the word and "swat" it. The winner gets a point. Continue with other words, giving each student a chance to play.

Dictation
Dictate the following sentences to review the **Etapa:**
1. Cuando yo tenía 10 años, llevaba el pelo en cola de caballo y usaba anteojos.
2. Mi abuelo era muy comprensivo y considerado.

Juego
Answer: c. descarado

■ Block Schedule
Retention Have students, working in pairs, return to the **Etapa** opener on pp. 32–33 and choose 1 of the couples pictured. They then write a conversation between the 2 people, using vocabulary and grammatical structures covered in the **Etapa,** especially the present and past perfect tenses. Have pairs present their conversations, using appropriate gestures. (For additional activities, see **Block Scheduling Copymasters.**)

Planning Guide CLASSROOM MANAGEMENT

OBJECTIVES

Communication
- Describe fashions *pp. 56–57, 58–59, 70–71*
- Talk about pastimes *p. 67*
- Talk about the future *p. 65*
- Predict actions *p. 65*

Grammar
- Review: Use of verbs like **gustar** *pp. 62–63*
- Review: Use of **por** and **para** *pp. 63–64*
- Use the future tense *pp. 65–67*
- Use the future of probability *pp. 68–69*

Culture
- Araceli Segarra, mountain climber *p. 67*
- Pets *p. 68*
- Regional vocabulary *p. 69*
- Oscar de la Renta, fashion designer *pp. 70–71*

♻ Recycling
- Clothing *p. 61*
- Direct object pronouns *p. 68*

STRATEGIES

Listening Strategies
- Pre-listening *p. 58*
- Listen and distinguish admiring and critical remarks *p. 58*

Speaking Strategies
- Use familiar vocabulary in a new setting *p. 61*
- Brainstorm to get lots of ideas *p. 74*
- Use words of transition *TE p. 74*

Reading Strategies
- Use context clues *TE p. 70*

Writing Strategies
- Tell who, what, where, when, why, and how *TE p. 75*

Connecting Cultures Strategies
- Learn about Araceli Segarra, a Spanish mountain climber *p. 67*
- Learn about pets, common names and the sounds they make *p. 68*
- Recognize regional vocabulary *p. 69*
- Connect and compare what you know about the cultural role of fashion in your community to help you learn about the cultural role of fashion in a new community *pp. 70–71*

PROGRAM RESOURCES

 Print
- *Más práctica* Workbook PE *pp. 21–30*
- *Actividades para todos* Workbook PE *pp. 21–30*
- Block Scheduling Copymasters *pp. 9–16*
- Unit 1 Resource Book
  Más práctica Workbook TE *pp. 79–88*
  Actividades para todos Workbook TE *pp. 89–98*
  Cuaderno para hispanohablantes TE *pp. 99–108*
  Information Gap Activities *pp. 109–112*
  Family Letter *p. 113*
  Absent Student Copymasters *pp. 114–120*
  Family Involvement *pp. 121–122*
  Audioscript *pp. 123–125*
  Assessment Program, Unit 1 Etapa 2 *pp. 127–150; 245–247*
  Answer Keys *pp. 258–261*

 Audiovisual
- Audio Program CD 2
- *Canciones* CD
- Overhead Transparencies M1–M5; 3, 20–34
- Word Tiles, U1 E2

 Technology
- eEdition Plus Online/eEdition CD-ROM
- Easy Planner Plus Online/Easy Planner CD-ROM
- eTest Plus Online/Test Generator CD-ROM
- Online Workbook
- Take-Home Tutor CD-ROM
- ⓘ www.classzone.com

Assessment Program Options
- Unit 1 Resource Book
  Vocabulary Quizzes
  Grammar Quizzes
  Etapa Exam Forms A and B
  Examen para hispanohablantes
  Portfolio Assessment
  Multiple Choice Test Questions
- Audio Program CD 19
- eTest Plus Online/Test Generator CD-ROM

Native Speakers
- *Cuaderno para hispanohablantes* PE *pp. 21–30*
- *Cuaderno para hispanohablantes* TE (Unit 1 Resource Book)
- *Examen para hispanohablantes* (Unit 1 Resource Book)
- Audio Program *(Para hispanohablantes)* CD 2, 19
- Audioscript (Unit 1 Resource Book)

Student Text Listening Activity Scripts

 Situaciones *pages 58–59*

• CD 2

Ana: Hola televidentes de ¡Modas Modernas! Habla Ana Beatriz Castillo desde los Premios de Música en Nueva York.

Javier: Y yo soy Javier Villanueva. Hoy estamos aquí para ver cómo visten los músicos más celebrados del año.

Ana: ¡Qué emoción! Se puede sentir la tensión en el aire.

Javier: Acaba de llegar Carson, el hombre que dio el concierto fabuloso en Central Park. ¿Y cómo va vestido? De negro, por supuesto. Carson siempre lleva un solo color.

Ana: Su medalla de oro es un regalo de su mamá. Siempre la lleva en momentos importantes.

Javier: Ahí viene Ana Luisa. Qué mujer más impresionante. Ahora está en un vestido de color pastel.

Ana: Lo que yo noto son sus pendientes. ¿Dónde los comprará? Y sus zapatos de tacón... no sé cómo camina sin caerse.

Javier: Ahora vemos a Luis Marcos. Aunque tiene voz de ángel, no sé por qué este chico no se compra unos trajes más elegantes. Siempre anda en sudaderas, como si fuera atleta.

Ana: Ay, ¡los Jaguares! Los cuatro, vestidos ¡igualitos! Serán cuádruples. O les darán mejor precio si compran los cuatro trajes iguales.

Javier: Tienen que ser de Texas. Sombreros, jeans, botas de piel.

Ana: ¡Armando Iglesias! ¡Qué visión! Chaleco de color oscuro, pantalones un poco anchos; ¡su pañuelo hace juego con sus calcetines! ¡Qué perfección!

Javier: Pues no lo compares con Carson. Nada lo enoja más.

Ana: Por fin, aquí viene Joya, la mujer más joven y más adorada del mundo. Canta como una sirena pero viste...

Javier: ¡Muy mal! Necesita ayuda ¡pero de emergencia! Su blusa no hace juego con su falda, sus zapatos son de otra época, su joyería parece de jueguito, y su ropa, por lo general, le queda muy floja.

Ana: No seas tan malo. Es joven. No sabe todavía de la moda de Nueva York.

Javier: ¿Dónde comprará su ropa? ¿En otro planeta? Esos lunares no son de este mundo.

Ana: Pero ahí viene Elena. La mujer que sabe más de la moda que nadie. Lleva un traje sencillo de pantalones y saco. Un color oscuro. Pendientes discretos. Esta mujer sabe vestir.

Javier: Estoy de acuerdo. La elegancia de Elena no se puede comparar... ¿Vendrá a hablar con nosotros? Espero que sí...

9 ¿Adónde vas? *page 64*

Miguel: ¿Adónde vas?

María: Voy a la tienda.

Miguel: ¿Para qué?

María: Tengo que comprarle un regalo a mi papá. Es su cumpleaños. Pienso comprarle una guayabera nueva.

Miguel: ¿Tienes dinero para el regalo?

María: Sí, trabajo tres días por semana.

Miguel: ¿Dónde trabajas?

María: Hace tres años que trabajo para la señora Ontiveros, en su oficina de diseño en el centro.

Miguel: ¿Cómo vas a llegar a la tienda?

María: Voy por autobús.

Miguel: ¿No tienes tarea para mañana?

María: Sí, pero ya la hice. Estudié por tres horas después de mis clases.

12 San Antonio *page 66*

¡Hijos! Qué bonito es San Antonio, ¿no? ¿Les gustó el Paseo del Río? Espero que sí. Y el Álamo fue muy interesante también, ¿no? Mañana iremos al Mercado. Allí compraremos algunos regalitos para sus amigos, ¿está bien? Pero, saben qué? También tengo muchas ganas de visitar el Instituto de Culturas Tejanas. Podremos ir allí mañana después del almuerzo. A propósito, ¿qué tal si vamos al concierto de música tejana esta tarde? Se divertirán, estoy segura. ¿Qué más tenemos que hacer antes de volver a casa? Ah, cenaremos en casa de sus primos. Les prometí que veremos a su nueva bebé antes de irnos. Volveremos a casa mañana después de la cena. ¡Qué lástima! Todavía nos quedan tantas cosas que hacer y tan pocas horas para hacerlas. Tendremos que volver a San Antonio muy pronto.

Sample Lesson Plan - 50 Minute Schedule

DAY 1

Etapa Opener
• Quick Start Review (TE, p. 54) 5 MIN.
• Have students look at the *Etapa* Opener and answer the questions. Expand using one of the activities on TE p. 55. 10 MIN.

En contexto: Vocabulario
• Quick Start Review (TE, p. 56) 5 MIN.
• Present *Descubre*, p. 56. 5 MIN.
• Have students use context and pictures to learn *Etapa* vocabulary, then answer the *¿Comprendiste?* questions, p. 57. Use the Situational OHTs for additional practice. 25 MIN.

Homework Option:
• Have students cut out 2 magazine pictures of people, 1 male and 1 female, and write a critique of what the people are wearing.

DAY 2

En vivo: Situaciones
• Check homework. 5 MIN.
• Quick Start Review (TE, p. 58) 5 MIN.
• Present the Listening Strategy, p. 58. 5 MIN.
• Have students read section 1, pp. 58–59. Play the audio for section 2. Then have students complete section 3 in writing. 20 MIN.

En acción: Vocabulario y gramática
• Quick Start Review (TE, p. 60) 5 MIN.
• Have students read and complete *Actividad* 1 in writing, then go over answers orally. 5 MIN.
• Have students do *Actividad* 2 in pairs. 5 MIN.

Homework Option:
• Have students complete *Actividad* 2 in writing.

DAY 3

En acción (cont.)
• Check homework. 5 MIN.
• Present the *Vocabulario*, p. 61. 5 MIN.
• Present the Speaking Strategy, p. 61. Do *Actividades* 3 and 4 in pairs. 10 MIN.
• Present *Repaso:* Verbs Like *gustar*, p. 62. 5 MIN.
• Do *Actividad* 5 orally. 5 MIN.
• Have students complete *Actividad* 6 in pairs. 5 MIN.
• Present the *Vocabulario*, p. 63. Then have students complete *Actividad* 7 in pairs. Have a few pairs present their conversations. 15 MIN.

Homework Option:
• Have students complete *Actividades* 5 and 6 in writing. *Más práctica* Workbook, pp. 25–27. *Cuaderno para hispanohablantes*, pp. 23–25.

DAY 4

En acción (cont.)
• Check homework. 5 MIN.
• Quick Start Review (TE, p. 63) 5 MIN.
• Present *Repaso: Por* and *Para*, p. 63. 10 MIN.
• Have students complete *Actividad* 8 in writing. Go over answers orally. 5 MIN.
• Play the audio; do *Actividad* 9. 5 MIN.
• Have students complete *Actividad* 10 in pairs. 5 MIN.
• Present *Gramática:* The Future Tense, p. 65. 10 MIN.
• Have students complete *Actividad* 11 orally. 5 MIN.

Homework Option:
• Have students complete *Actividad* 11 in writing. *Más práctica* Workbook, pp. 28–29. *Cuaderno para hispanohablantes*, pp. 25–27.
• *Actividades para todos* Workbook, pp. 21–30.

DAY 5

En acción (cont.)
• Check homework. 5 MIN.
• Play the audio; do *Actividad* 12. 5 MIN.
• Do *Actividad* 13 in pairs. 5 MIN.
• Present the *Vocabulario*, p. 67. Then have students read the realia and complete *Actividad* 14 in groups. Expand using Information Gap Activities, Unit 1 Resource Book, p. 109; *Más comunicación*, p. R4. 20 MIN.
• Quick Start Review (TE, p. 68) 5 MIN.
• Present *Gramática:* Future Tense to Express Probability, p. 68. 5 MIN.
• Do *Actividad* 15 orally. 5 MIN.

Homework Option:
• Have students complete *Actividad* 15 in writing. *Más práctica* Workbook, p. 30. *Cuaderno para hispanohablantes*, p. 27.

DAY 6

En acción (cont.)
• Check homework. 5 MIN.
• Do *Actividad* 16 orally. 5 MIN.
• Have students do *Actividad* 17 in pairs. Expand using Information Gap Activities, Unit 1 Resource Book, p. 110; *Más comunicación*, p. R4. 15 MIN.

Refrán
• Present the *Refrán*, p. 69. 5 MIN.

En colores: Cultura y comparaciones
• Quick Start Review (TE, p. 70) 5 MIN.
• Present the Connecting Cultures Strategy, p. 70. Call on volunteers to read the selection aloud. Have students answer the *¿Comprendiste?/¿Qué piensas?* questions, p. 71. 15 MIN.

Homework Option:
• Have students complete *Hazlo tú*, p. 71.

DAY 7

En uso: Repaso y más comunicación
• Check homework. 5 MIN.
• Quick Start Review (TE, p. 72) 5 MIN.
• Have students do *Actividad* 1 in pairs. 5 MIN.
• Do *Actividades* 2 and 3 orally. 5 MIN.
• Have students do *Actividad* 4 in pairs. 5 MIN.
• Present the Speaking Strategy, p. 74, and have students do *Actividad* 5 or 6 in groups. 15 MIN.

En tu propia voz: Escritura
• Do *Actividad* 7 in writing. Have volunteers present their predictions to the class. 10 MIN.

Homework Option:
• Review for *Etapa* 2 Exam.

DAY 8

Conexiones
• Read *Las matemáticas*, p. 74. Have students complete their budgets and graphs. 15 MIN.

En resumen: Repaso de vocabulario
• Quick Start Review (TE, p. 75) 5 MIN.
• Review grammar questions, etc., as necessary. 10 MIN.
• Complete *Etapa* 2 Exam. 20 MIN.

Ampliación
• Optional: Use a suggested project, game, or activity. (TE, pp. 31A–31B)

Homework Option:
• Preview *Etapa* 3 Opener.

Sample Lesson Plan - Block Schedule (90 minutes)

DAY 1

Etapa Opener
- Quick Start Review (TE, p. 54) 5 MIN.
- Have students look at the Etapa Opener and answer the questions. 5 MIN.
- Use Block Scheduling Copymasters, pp. 17–18. 10 MIN.

En contexto: Vocabulario
- Quick Start Review (TE, p. 56) 5 MIN.
- Present Descubre (TE, p. 56) 5 MIN.
- Have students use context and pictures to learn Etapa vocabulary, then answer the ¿Comprendiste? questions, p. 57. Use the Situational OHTs for additional practice. 20 MIN.

En vivo: Situaciones
- Quick Start Review (TE, p. 58) 5 MIN.
- Present the Listening Strategy, p. 58. 5 MIN.
- Have students read section 1, pp. 57–58. Play the audio for section 2. Then have students complete section 3 in writing. 20 MIN.
- Quick Start Review (TE, p. 60) 5 MIN.
- Have students read and complete Actividad 1 in writing, then go over answers orally. 5 MIN.

Homework Option:
- Have students cut out 2 magazine pictures of people, 1 male and 1 female, and write a critique of what the people are wearing.

DAY 2

En acción: Vocabulario y gramática
- Check homework. 5 MIN.
- Have students do Actividad 2 in pairs. 5 MIN.
- Present the Vocabulario, p. 61. 5 MIN.
- Present the Speaking Strategy, p. 61. Do Actividades 3 and 4 in pairs. 10 MIN.
- Quick Start Review (TE, p. 62) 5 MIN.
- Present Repaso: Verbs Like gustar, p. 62. 5 MIN.
- Do Actividad 5 orally. 5 MIN.
- Have students complete Actividad 6 in pairs. 5 MIN.
- Present the Vocabulario, p. 63. Then have students complete Actividad 7 in pairs. Have a few pairs present their conversations. 15 MIN.
- Quick Start Review (TE, p. 63) 5 MIN.
- Present Repaso: Por and Para, p. 63. 10 MIN.
- Have students complete Actividad 8 in writing. Go over answers orally. 5 MIN.
- Play the audio; do Actividad 9. 5 MIN.
- Have students complete Actividad 10 in pairs. 5 MIN.

Homework Option:
- Have students complete Actividades 3 and 5 in writing. Más práctica Workbook, pp. 25–28. Cuaderno para hispanohablantes, pp. 23–25.

DAY 3

En acción (cont.)
- Check homework. 5 MIN.
- Quick Start Review (TE, p. 65) 5 MIN.
- Present Gramática: The Future Tense, p. 65. 10 MIN.
- Have students complete Actividad 11 orally. 5 MIN.
- Play the audio; do Actividad 12. 5 MIN.
- Do Actividad 13 in pairs. 5 MIN.
- Present the Vocabulario, p. 67. Then have students read the realia and complete Actividad 14 in groups. Expand using Information Gap Activities, Unit 1 Resource Book, p. 109; Más comunicación, p. R4. 20 MIN.
- Quick Start Review (TE, p. 68) 5 MIN.
- Present Gramática: Future Tense to Express Probability, p. 68. 5 MIN.
- Do Actividad 15 orally. 5 MIN.
- Do Actividad 16 orally. 5 MIN.
- Have students do Actividad 17 in pairs. Expand using Information Gap Activities, Unit 1 Resource Book, p. 110; Más comunicación, p. R4. 15 MIN.

Homework Option:
- Have students complete Actividades 11 and 15 in writing. Más práctica Workbook, pp. 29–30. Cuaderno para hispanohablantes, pp. 26–28.
- **Actividades para todos** Workbook, pp. 21–30.

DAY 4

Refrán
- Check homework. 5 MIN.
- Present the Refrán, p. 69. 5 MIN.

En colores: Cultura y comparaciones
- Quick Start Review (TE, p. 70) 5 MIN.
- Present the Connecting Cultures Strategy, p. 70. Call on volunteers to read the selection aloud. Have students answer the ¿Comprendiste?/¿Qué piensas? questions, p. 69. 25 MIN.

En uso: Repaso y más comunicación
- Quick Start Review (TE, p. 72) 5 MIN.
- Have students do Actividad 1 in pairs, Actividades 2 and 3 orally, and Actividad 4 in pairs. 25 MIN.
- Present the Speaking Strategy, p. 74, and have students do Actividades 5 and 6 in groups. 20 MIN.

Homework Option:
- Have students complete Hazlo tú, p. 71. Review for Etapa 2 Exam.

DAY 5

En tu propia voz: Escritura
- Check homework. 5 MIN.
- Do Actividad 7 in writing. Have volunteers present their predictions to the class. 15 MIN.

Conexiones
- Read Las matemáticas, p. 74. Have students complete their budgets and graphs. 20 MIN.

En resumen: Repaso de vocabulario
- Quick Start Review (TE, p. 75) 5 MIN.
- Review grammar questions, etc., as necessary. 10 MIN.
- Complete Etapa 2 Exam. 20 MIN.

Ampliación
- Use a suggested project, game, or activity. (TE, pp. 31A–31B) 15 MIN.

Homework Option:
- Preview Etapa 3 Opener.

▼ ¿Dedicas mucho tiempo a pensar en tu «look» individual?

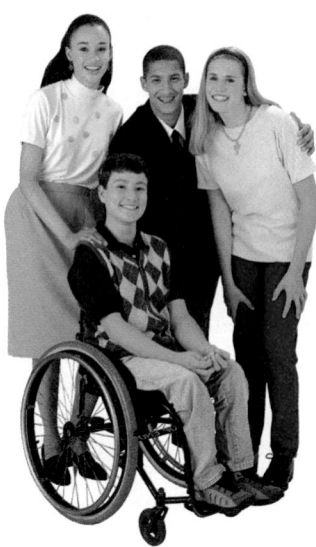

Etapa Theme
Talking about fashion and discussing future actions

Grammar Objectives
- Review using verbs like **gustar**
- Review using **por** and **para**
- Using the future tense
- Using the future of probability

Teaching Resource Options

Print

Block Scheduling Copymasters
Unit 1 Resource Book
  Family Letters, p. 113
  Absent Student Copymasters, p. 114

Audiovisual

OHT 3, 26 (Quick Start)

Quick Start Review

♻ Spanish-speaking population of the U.S.

Use OHT 26 or write on the board:
Write the following:

• 5 ciudades en Estados Unidos con una población hispanohablante

• El porcentaje latino de la población de Estados Unidos

Answers
Answers will vary. Answers could include:
- San Antonio, Miami, Los Ángeles, Nueva York, Chicago
- 12%

Teaching Suggestions
Previewing the Etapa
- Ask students to study the picture on pp. 54–55 (1 min.).
- Have them talk about their initial impressions of the setting. Ask: **¿Cuáles son tus impresiones iniciales del ambiente de la foto— el tiempo, los edificios, las actividades, etc.?**
- Ask volunteers to give 1-sentence descriptions of the scene and what the people are doing.
- Use the **¿Qué ves?** questions to focus the discussion.

UNIDAD 1

ETAPA 2

¿Cómo me veo?

OBJECTIVES

- Describe fashions

- Talk about pastimes

- Talk about the future

- Predict actions

¿Qué ves?

Mira la foto. Contesta las preguntas.

1. ¿Qué cosas en la foto te dicen dónde están estas personas?
2. ¿Qué relación tienen? ¿Por qué crees esto?
3. ¿Crees que la opinión de los chicos es igual? ¿Por qué?
4. ¿Por qué crees que este lugar se llama La Villita?

54

La Villita →

Classroom Management

Planning Ahead Bring in fashion magazines and clothing catalogs showing a variety of fashions for men and women. Set the stage for the **Etapa** vocabulary and grammar by preparing students to observe and talk about fashion trends and their personal likes and dislikes in clothing. Show them the photos and have them say **Sí, me gusta** or **No, no me gusta**. Then have students add a comment explaining why or why not.

Time Saver Have students look at the list of objectives on p. 54. Then have them brainstorm a list of related vocabulary words and phrases they already know that can be used for reference throughout this **Etapa**.

Cross Cultural Connections

Ask students if there is an original or older section to their town/city. What are the buildings like there? Are there any other historical buildings in their town/city? Do any of these buildings have plaques on them noting when they were constructed?

Culture Highlights

● **LA VILLITA** La Villita significa «pequeño pueblo» y es el poblado original del viejo San Antonio. Hoy en día es una comunidad de artesanos que tienen 26 tiendas en edificios históricos. Los estilos de arquitectura de La Villita varían desde las estructuras sencillas de adobe hasta las casas victorianas muy decoradas. Es un lugar muy agradable para ir de compras y cenar.

● **SAN ANTONIO** Esta ciudad ha tenido una fuerte presencia hispana desde su fundación en 1718.

Critical Thinking

Students should note that the girl in the photo is showing the boys a pair of earrings she has just bought. From this information, what can they deduce about the section of San Antonio called **La Villita**?

Supplementary Vocabulary

la bandera	flag
la cerca de hierro forjado	wrought iron fence
la flecha	arrow
el letrero	sign
el porche, el portal	porch

55

Teaching All Students

Extra Help Have each student write 3 sentences describing the picture, 2 of which are true and 1 that is false. Then have them exchange papers with a partner and determine which sentence is false.

Multiple Intelligences

Interpersonal Have students work in groups of 3 to prepare and present a mini-dialog among the 3 people in the photo.

Block Schedule

Research Have students do an Internet or library search for information on **La Villita** and other tourist sites in San Antonio. Have them choose 1 site that they would especially want to visit and explain why. (For additional activities, see **Block Scheduling Copymasters**.)

Teaching Resource Options

Print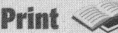

Block Scheduling Copymasters
Unit 1 Resource Book
　Absent Student Copymasters, p. 114

Audiovisual

OHT 20, 21, 22, 22A, 23, 23A, 26
　(Quick Start)

Technology

Online Workbook, U1 E2
Take-Home Tutor CD-ROM, U1 E2

Quick Start Review

♻ Clothing/colors/jewelry

Use OHT 26 or write on the board:
List 5 items for each category:
- ropa
- colores
- joyería

Answers

Answers will vary. Answers could include:
- ropa: una camiseta, un vestido, unos jeans, un suéter, unos zapatos
- colores: rojo, azul, verde, blanco, amarillo
- joyería: un anillo, unos aretes, un collar, una pulsera, un reloj

Teaching Suggestions
Introducing Vocabulary

- Have students look at pages 56–57. Use OHT 20 and 21 to present the vocabulary.
- Ask the Comprehension Questions on TE p. 57 in order of yes/no (questions 1–3), either/or (questions 4–6), and simple word or phrase (questions 7–10). Expand by adding similar questions.
- Use the TPR activity to reinforce the meaning of individual words.

Descubre

Answers

llaves = *keys;* llavero = *keychain*
monedas = *change;* monedero = *change purse*
billetes = *bills;* billetera = *wallet (billfold)*
prender = *to pin;* prendedor = *pin*
sudar = *to sweat;* sudaderas = *sweats*

En contexto VOCABULARIO

LOS ESTILOS DE LAS ESTRELLAS

🔲 Descubre

Busca las palabras dentro de las palabras. ¿Te da alguna idea de qué quieren decir?

llavero: llaves =

monedero: monedas =

billetera: billetes =

prendedor: prender =

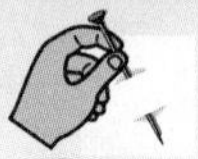

sudaderas: sudar =

C: Esa **cadena** de oro tiene inspiración en los años setenta. ¿No sabe que es el siglo 21? ¡Y esa **medalla**!

R: A mí me impresiona el chaleco **estampado**. ¿Dónde lo compró? En 'Nosotros-Somos-Hippies'?

C: ¡Ese **bolso**! ¿Qué llevará adentro? Esos **pendientes** parecen adornos para el árbol de Navidad.

R: ¡Por favor! Ese vestido **suelto** de **lunares** es algo extraterrestre. ¿De dónde es su **diseñador**—del planeta Marte?

C: Pobre chico. Gran actor y no tiene dinero para comprar pantalones. Siempre anda en **sudaderas**.

R: Las sudaderas no me molestan. ¡Pero ese **color brillante**! Necesito mis gafas de sol para mirarlo.

Los críticos

Carlota Jáuregui
Esta venezolana reconocida es la diseñadora que Hollywood más adora. Ha vestido a algunas de las personas más prestigiosas del mundo.

Raúl Montenegro
Después de 15 años de tomarles fotos a las estrellas, se puede decir que este fotógrafo famoso sabe algo de **moda**.

RAÚL

CARLOTA

56 cincuenta y seis
Unidad 1

Classroom Community

TPR Assign an item of clothing or an accessory to each student and have them draw a picture of the item. Be sure to specify color and design when appropriate. Then tell students you are having a fashion show. Have 2 students alternate calling out the names of the items. The student who has the item parades in front of the class. Call on other students to describe the item. This activity may also be done with actual articles of clothing.

Paired Activity Have students work in pairs to ask each other the **¿Comprendiste?** questions. Also have them draw a picture to accompany their answers to question #6. Then have them report 1 of their partner's answers to the class.

CD-ROM
Take-Home Tutor

C: Elegantísimo. El pañuelo de **seda**. El traje de **color oscuro**. **Se destaca** por su elegancia de pie a cabeza.

R: Este chico es **único**. Para él, **poliéster** es una mala palabra.

C: Parece ángel en ese **color claro**. ¿Y ves el **prendedor**? ¡Sus accesorios tienen más estilo que tú y yo juntos!

R: ¿Dónde comprará sus joyas esta mujer? ¿Será amiga de la reina de Inglaterra?

C: ¡Y ese traje!

R: Me encanta su traje **de un solo color**. Dice «elegante», dice «no necesito llamar la atención». Si quieres saber cuál es la moda de **la temporada**, es suficiente ver su **vestuario**.

Online Workbook
CLASSZONE.COM

¿Comprendiste?

1. ¿Lees revistas de moda? ¿Cuáles?
2. ¿Te interesa saber cómo se visten las estrellas de cine? ¿Por qué?
3. Da un ejemplo en el que estás de acuerdo con los críticos y uno en el que no lo estás.
4. ¿Dedicas mucho tiempo a pensar en tu «look» individual o no te importa mucho?
5. ¿Hablas mucho con tus amigos sobre la moda más popular y aceptada en la escuela?
6. ¿Cómo te vistes tú? Describe tu propio estilo.
7. ¿Crees que la moda es importante o que la gente le da demasiada importancia? Explica.

cincuenta y siete
Estados Unidos Etapa 2
57

Comprehension Questions

1. ¿Es venezolana Carlota Jáuregui? (Sí.)
2. ¿Es diseñador Raúl Montenegro? (No.)
3. ¿Es de plata la cadena del primer chico? (No.)
4. ¿Es el vestido de la muchacha apretado o suelto? (suelto)
5. Y sus pendientes, ¿son adornos para el árbol de Navidad o para llevar en las orejas? (para llevar en las orejas)
6. ¿Lleva el segundo chico jeans o sudaderas? (sudaderas)
7. ¿De qué es el pañuelo del primer hombre? (de seda)
8. ¿Por qué se destaca el traje de color oscuro? (por su elegancia)
9. ¿De qué color es el vestido de la mujer? (de color claro)
10. ¿Cómo puedes saber cuál es la moda de la temporada? (Es suficiente ver el vestuario del segundo hombre.)

Supplementary Vocabulary

el corbatín, la corbata de lazo	bow tie
el esmoquin	tuxedo
el vestido sin mangas	sleeveless dress

Cross Cultural Connections

Ask students if they know of any magazines in the U.S. that are published both in English and Spanish. **¿Conoces revistas en Estados Unidos que se publican en inglés y español?** (Some are **People en español** and **Newsweek en español**.) Have students think about the markets that the publishers will reach. **¿En qué lugares pueden vender estas revistas?** Students should think about places in the U.S. and outside it.

Teaching All Students

Extra Help Describe the 6 people from this section one at a time, ask **¿Quién es?**, and have students respond.

Native Speaker Have students write a detailed description of the clothing they would wear to participate in their favorite activity. Then have them present their descriptions to the class as if they were narrating a fashion show.

Multiple Intelligences

Verbal Have students look through the fashion magazines and clothing catalogs brought in for "Planning Ahead," TE p. 54, for a model wearing an outfit they think is interesting. Then ask volunteers to stand in front of the class and describe the clothing in the picture in the same style as **Los críticos**.

Block Schedule

Change of Pace Have students draw cartoons of characters wearing outrageous outfits. Under their cartoons, they should write a description of the character, including name, physical appearance, personality, and clothing. (For additional activities, see **Block Scheduling Copymasters**.)

Teaching Resource Options

Print

Block Scheduling Copymasters
Unit 1 Resource Book
    Absent Student Copymasters, p. 115
    Audioscript, p. 123

Audiovisual

OHT 24, 25, 27 (Quick Start)
Audio Program CD 2, Track 1

Technology

Take-Home Tutor CD-ROM, U1 E2

🔔 Quick Start Review

♻ Clothing vocabulary

Use OHT 27 or write on the board:
Write what you would typically wear to
these places:

• la escuela
• un restaurante elegante
• una fiesta
• un partido de baloncesto

Answers

Answers will vary. Answers could include:
• la escuela: una camiseta, unos jeans
• un restaurante elegante: un vestido/un traje
• una fiesta: una falda y una camisa/una
  camisa y unos pantalones
• un partido de baloncesto: una camiseta y
  unos shorts

Teaching Suggestions
Presenting Situations

• Present the Listening Strategy, p. 58,
  and have students make a copy of
  the chart to fill out.
• Use OHT 24 and 25 to present the
  Leer section. Ask simple yes/no,
  either/or, or short-answer questions.
• Use Audio CD 2 (see Script TE
  p. 53B) and have students listen to
  the **Escuchar** section. Then have
  them listen again and complete the
  Listening Strategy exercise.
• Have students work in pairs to complete
  the **Escribir** section. The pairs should
  then present their answers to the class.

AUDIO En vivo
🎧 SITUACIONES

PARA ESCUCHAR
STRATEGY: LISTENING

Pre-listening Have you watched award
ceremonies? What comments does the master
or mistress of ceremonies usually make? How
are they said?

Distinguish admiring and critical remarks What do
they admire or criticize about the artists? Listen
for the general idea.

Artista	Admiran	Critican
Carson		
Ana Luisa		
Luis Marcos		
Los Jaguares		
A. Iglesias		
Joya		
Elena		

¡Persigue la moda!

Eres reportero(a) en los Premios de Música en
Nueva York y estás ahí para oír todos los detalles
que pueden interesar a los lectores de tu revista,
Modas Modernas. Escucha los últimos chismes de
la moda para que tus lectores puedan encontrar
lo último del vestir en estas tiendas.

① Leer

Estudia los anuncios de las tiendas de moda.

Para los que saben....

EL HOMBRE FINO

La elegancia está en los detalles

Joyería y Accesorios de Hoy

58   cincuenta y ocho
Unidad 1

Classroom Community

Group Activity Have students work in groups of
5–6 to plan and present a skit similar to the one they
heard on the audio CD. One student plays the reporter
and the others play the celebrities. Have each group
present their skit to the class. Vote on the most
interesting skit.

Game Have 1 student think of a famous actor or
singer. He/she then describes that person, while the
class tries to guess the identity. Whoever guesses
correctly gets to give the next description.

Escuchar (See script, TE p. 53B.)

Answers

Answers will vary.

Carson	vestido de negro, medalla de oro
Ana Luisa	vestido de color pastel, pendientes, zapatos de tacón
Luis Marcos	siempre en sudaderas
Los Jaguares	vestidos igualitos; sombreros, jeans, botas de piel
A. Iglesias	chaleco de color oscuro, pantalones un poco anchos, pañuelo hace juego con calcetines
Joya	viste muy mal; blusa no hace juego con falda, zapatos de otra época, joyería de jueguito, ropa le queda muy floja
Elena	sabe vestir; traje sencillo de pantalones y saco, color oscuro, pendientes discretos

Escribir

Answers will vary.

Cross Cultural Connections

Plan ahead: Bring in fashion magazines from Spanish-speaking countries and from the U.S. Have students cut out ads from the Spanish-language magazines and the U.S. magazines for similar products. Then have them compare and contrast the ads. Do the advertisers use the same approach? Do they try to appeal to the same senses? the same audience?

2 Escuchar 🎧

En los Premios ves a tus viejos amigos, los reporteros Ana Beatriz Castillo y Javier Villanueva. Ellos describen el vestuario de cada persona famosa que pasa y ¡no se les escapa nada! Comentan sobre la ropa, los zapatos, los accesorios, ¡todito! Escucha y haz apuntes en una hoja aparte.

3 Escribir

Después de escuchar el comentario de los locutores, escribe dónde crees que estos músicos compraron su ropa.

Carson	Los Jaguares
Ana Luisa	Armando Iglesias
Elena	Luis Marcos
Joya	

Block Schedule

Variety Have students write the names of favorite celebrities on slips of paper. Put the slips in a box, and draw two for each group. Have students work in groups of 4. Groups then design two outfits for their celebrities. Finally, have the groups describe their outfits to the class. The class votes on the two best outfits. (For additional activities, see **Block Scheduling Copymasters.**)

Teaching All Students

Extra Help Use the fashion magazines and clothing catalogs brought in for "Planning Ahead," TE p. 54. Hold up the magazine/catalog photos of people wearing various articles of clothing and accessories. Point out the items and have students give the names.

Native Speakers Have students bring in a photo of a family member or friend. Students say who is in the picture and describe the person.

Multiple Intelligences

Intrapersonal Using the **Escuchar** dialog as a model, have students write a description of themselves in their notebooks.

Teaching Resource Options

Print

Block Scheduling Copymasters
Unit 1 Resource Book
  Absent Student Copymasters, p. 116

Audiovisual

OHT 27 (Quick Start)

Quick Start Review

 Vocabulary

Use OHT 27 or write on the board:
Which word does not belong to the
group, based on meaning?

1. cadena   estampado   medalla
2. sudaderas pendientes prendedor
3. chaleco   billetera   camisa
4. seda   poliéster   diseñador
5. oscuro   vestuario   brillante
6. monedero temporada   billetera

Answers

1. estampado
2. sudaderas
3. billetera
4. diseñador
5. vestuario
6. temporada

Teaching Suggestions
Comprehension Check

Use **Actividades 1–4** to assess
retention. For **Actividad 1,** have each
student write 1 additional item. Write
the items on the board or on an OHT
for the class to answer.

 Objective: Controlled practice
Vocabulary

Answers
1. a   2. b   3. a   4. a   5. b

Objective: Transitional practice
Vocabulary in conversation

Answers

Answers will vary.
1. A: Mercedes lleva una blusa de lunares.
   B: También lleva unos pendientes.
2. A: Gerardo lleva un traje de color oscuro.
   B: También lleva una camisa de un solo color.
3. A: Joaquín lleva un chaleco estampado.
   B: También lleva una camiseta de color oscuro.
4. A: Belisa lleva una cadena.
   B: También lleva una camiseta de color claro.

En acción

PARTE A — Práctica del vocabulario

Objectives for Activities 1–4
• Describe fashions

1 ¿Con qué va?

Leer/*Escribir* Andrea describe
el uso de algunos accesorios y
otras cosas relacionadas con
la moda. Completa sus
comentarios.

1. Para no perder mis llaves,
   las pongo todas en un
   _____.
   a. llavero
   b. monedero

2. No me gusta tener
   monedas sueltas en mi
   bolsillo. Las pongo todas
   en un _____.
   a. bolso
   b. monedero

3. Papá pone sus billetes en
   una _____.
   a. billetera
   b. cadena

4. Cuando voy al colegio, uso
   mi mochila. Pero cuando
   salgo el fin de semana,
   prefiero usar mi _____.
   a. bolso
   b. prendedor

5. Me gusta mucho la moda.
   Sueño con ser _____.
   a. arquitecto(a)
   b. diseñador(a)

2 Estilos diferentes

Hablar/*Escribir* ¿Cómo se visten las personas siguientes?
Con un(a) compañero(a), digan por lo menos dos cosas
sobre el vestuario de cada una.

modelo

Tú: *Julia lleva unas sudaderas de un solo color.*

Compañero(a): *También lleva una camiseta de
color brillante.*

Julia

1. Mercedes
2. Gerardo
3. Joaquín
4. Belisa

60 sesenta
Unidad 1

Peer Review Have students work in pairs and
sketch the characters on pp. 56–57. Then have them
ask and answer questions about the people.

Time Saver Have students complete **Actividades 2,
3,** and **4** for homework with a "study buddy." Have
various pairs present some of their answers the next
day in class.

3 La moda de hoy

STRATEGY: SPEAKING

Use familiar vocabulary in a new setting While learning new words about clothing and fashion, use some that you have already learned: **bufanda, collar, anillo, pulsera, aretes, sandalias, a rayas, a cuadros,** as well as old friends like **blusa, calcetín, camisa, camiseta, falda, jeans, pantalones, suéter, vestido, zapato,** and of course, the colors: **amarillo, anaranjado, azul, blanco, marrón, morado, negro, rojo, verde.**

Hablar/*Escribir* Tú y tu compañero(a) encontraron una revista de modas. Tu compañero(a) quiere saber si te gustan ciertas cosas. Di lo que piensas de cada artículo.

modelo

chaleco

Compañero(a): *¿Te gusta el chaleco de rayas?*

Tú: *¡Sí! Hace juego con los pantalones de mezclilla.*
o No, prefiero el chaleco de cuero.

1. falda
2. traje
3. blusa
4. sudaderas

5. pantalones
6. suéter
7. vestido
8. chaqueta

4 De compras

Hablar Tú y tu compañero(a) están de compras en una tienda de modas. Tú te pones varias cosas y le preguntas a tu compañero(a) si te quedan bien. Él (Ella) te responde y te hace otra sugerencia. Luego, cambien de papel.

modelo

Tú: *¿Cómo me veo? ¿Te gusta esta chaqueta de lana?*

Compañero(a): *¡Uy, no! ¡Te queda muy floja! Mejor cómprate la chaqueta de seda. Es más elegante.*

Vocabulario

¿De qué es?

el algodón *cotton*
el cuero *leather*
el fleco *fringe*
la lana *wool*
la lentejuela *sequin*
la mezclilla *denim*

 Ya sabes

ancho(a)
apretado(a)
estrecho(a)
flojo(a)
hacer juego con…
oscuro(a)
un par de
las rayas
sencillo(a)

▶¿Puedes describir tu vestuario con estas palabras?

Teaching Suggestions
Presenting Vocabulary

- **Plan ahead:** Bring in articles made from the various materials. Use these articles to present the new vocabulary.
- Have volunteers present the review vocabulary using props and gestures.
- Have each student name and describe 1 article in their closet using the vocabulary.

ACTIVIDAD 3 **Objective:** Open-ended practice
Vocabulary in conversation

Answers will vary.

ACTIVIDAD 4 **Objective:** Open-ended practice
Vocabulary in conversation
♻ Clothing

Answers will vary.

Quick Wrap-up

Ask students to describe what various students in the class are wearing: **Describe la ropa que lleva un(a) estudiante de la clase.** The class guesses who is being described.

Teaching All Students

Extra Help Have students make flashcards for old and new vocabulary for clothing, colors, fabrics, and descriptions. They should put the Spanish word on one side and a picture on the other side. Then have them use the cards to quiz each other.

Multiple Intelligences

Visual Plan ahead: Have volunteers bring in doll clothing. Place all the clothing in a box. As you remove each item, have students name it and describe it completely (color, design, fabric). Then repack the items. Have students list all the clothing items they remember. Keep the doll clothing on hand for "Multiple Intelligences: Verbal," TE p. 63.

Block Schedule

Variety Have students bring in pictures of their favorite musicians and actors and describe them to the class. Encourage them to describe not only their clothing, but also their physical characteristics and personality.
(For additional activities, see **Block Scheduling Copymasters.**)

Teaching Resource Options

Print

Más práctica Workbook PE, pp. 25–26
Cuaderno para hispanohablantes
PE, pp. 23–24
Block Scheduling Copymasters
Unit 1 Resource Book
  Más práctica Workbook TE,
  pp. 113–114
  Cuaderno para hispanohablantes
  TE, pp. 121–122
  Absent Student Copymasters, p. 116

Audiovisual

OHT 27, 28 (Quick Start) 31–32
  (Grammar)
Word Tiles, U1E2

Technology

Online Workbook, U1E2
Take-Home Tutor CD-ROM, U1E2

Quick Start Review

♻ Vocabulary

Use OHT 27 or write on the board:
A. Give the opposite:

1. apretado   3. de un solo color
2. ancho   4. de color oscuro

B. List 3 clothing fabrics.

Answers: A. 1. suelto/flojo   2. estrecho
3. estampado/a rayas/a cuadros   4. de color
claro B. *Answers will vary. Answers could*
include: la seda, el algodón, el cuero, la lana.

Teaching Suggestions
Reviewing Verbs Like gustar

• Review indirect object pronouns.
• Remind students that with **gustar** the
  indirect object refers to the person
  doing the liking. The subject of
  gustar usually comes at the end of
  the sentence; it determines a singular
  or plural form of the verb.

ACTIVIDAD
5 **Objective:** Controlled practice
Gustar

Answers

1. A ti te gustan las botas de cuero.
2. A Hernán le gusta el sombrero negro.
3. A Érica y Laurita les gusta la ropa suelta.
4. A nosotros nos gustan los zapatos de tenis.
5. A usted le gusta el bolso de rayas.
6. A mí me gustan los pantalones de lana.

PARTE B   **Práctica: gramática y vocabulario**

Objectives for Activities 14–15
• Describe fashions • Talk about pastimes • Talk about the future • Predict actions

REPASO   **Verbs Like gustar**

▸ You most often use verbs like gustar
with the **indirect object pronouns**
me, te, le, nos, os, and les to express
your and others' reactions to things.

Me gusta tu **prendedor.**
I like your pin.

Gracias. ¡Y a mí **me gustan** tus **zapatos!**
Thanks. And I like your shoes!

▸ You already know many verbs that are used like gustar.

encantar	interesar
faltar	quedarle bien
fascinar	quedarle mal
molestar	importar

Me encantan los **deportes.**
I love sports.

¡Qué **bien te queda** ese **sombrero!**
*That hat **looks good** on you!*

A Marta **le molestan** los **anteojos** nuevos.
*Marta's new glasses **are bothering** her.*

*Notice that the form of these verbs matches **deportes**, not **me**.*

Practice: **Actividades** ⑤ ⑥   *Más práctica* cuaderno pp. 25–27
Para hispanohablantes cuaderno pp. 23–25

 **Online Workbook** CLASSZONE.COM

---

⑤ Gustos

Hablar/*Escribir* Todos tenemos gustos
diferentes. Di qué le gusta a cada persona.

modelo
a mí: las blusas sencillas
A mí me gustan las blusas sencillas.

1. a ti: las botas de cuero
2. a Hernán: el sombrero negro
3. A Érica y a Laurita: la ropa suelta
4. a nosotros: los zapatos de tenis
5. a usted: el bolso de rayas
6. a mí: los pantalones de lana

---

⑥ ¡Me fascina!

Hablar/*Escribir* Tu compañero te pregunta
si te gustan las siguientes cosas. Contéstale
usando uno de estos verbos: **gustar, encantar,
fascinar** o **interesar.**

modelo
las películas románticas
Compañero(a): *¿Te gustan las películas románticas?*
Tú: *No, no me interesan (o) Sí, me interesan.*

1. la ropa de moda   5. las obras de teatro
2. las telenovelas   6. la historia maya
3. la música clásica   7. los videojuegos
4. la música «rap»   8. los patines en línea

---

62   sesenta y dos
Unidad 1

Classroom Community

Paired Activity Have students work in pairs and
expand on **Actividad 6**. Each student adds 4 more
items to ask their partner about. Then have pairs ask
another pair about these items.

Portfolio Have students write an essay about their
clothing likes and dislikes, using verbs like **gustar** and
the **Vocabulario** on p. 63.

Rubric   A = 13–15 pts. B = 10–12 pts. C = 7–9 pts. D = 4–6 pts. F = < 4 pts.

Writing criteria	Scale
Vocabulary use	1 2 3 4 5
Correct use of **gustar** construction	1 2 3 4 5
Spelling accuracy	1 2 3 4 5

7 ¿De veras?

Hablar ¿Conoces los gustos de tu compañero(a)? Dile cinco cosas que detestas o que te fascinan. ¿Cómo reacciona? Luego, cambien de papel.

modelo

Tú: *No me cae bien la música de los sesenta.*

Compañero(a): *¿De veras? Yo creo que es genial.*

Compañero(a): *Me fascina la moda de los sesenta.*

Tú: *¿De veras? Yo creo que es muy incómoda.*

Vocabulario

¿Cómo es?

caer bien/mal *to like, dislike*

cómodo(a) *comfortable*

detestar *to hate*

formidable *great*

genial *wonderful*

horrible *horrible*

incómodo(a) *uncomfortable*

pesado(a) *boring, heavy*

▸ ¿Puedes describir tus pasatiempos o actividades con estas palabras?

REPASO   **Por and Para**

▸ You already know the prepositions **por** and **para**. Both words can mean *for* in English, but the meaning can change depending on how it is used. Look at these examples.

▸ Use **por** to indicate…

• the idea of passing through.
Esta carretera pasa **por** Tejas.
*This highway goes **through** Texas.*

• general rather than specific location.
No sé si hay una piscina **por** aquí.
*I don't know if there is a pool **around** here.*

• how long something lasts.
Vivimos en Puerto Rico **por** muchos años.
*We lived in Puerto Rico **for** many years.*

• the cause of something.
No podemos acampar **por** la tormenta.
*We can't camp **because of** the storm.*

• an exchange.
Cecilia pagó mucho **por** sus anteojos.
*Cecilia paid a lot **for** her glasses.*

• doing something in place of or instead of someone else.
No puedo ir. ¿Puedes ir **por** mí?
*I can't go. Can you go **in my place**?*

• a means of transportation.
Viajamos **por** barco.
*We traveled **by** boat.*

▸ Use **para** to indicate…

• for whom something is done.
Compraremos un regalo **para** Silvia.
*We will buy a gift **for** Silvia.*

• destination.
Francisco tomó el avión **para** San Juan.
*Francisco took the plane **to** San Juan.*

• the purpose for which something is done.
Compré anteojos **para** ver mejor.
*I bought glasses **in order to** see better.*

• to express an opinion.
Para mí, el montañismo es maravilloso.
***To** me, mountaineering is marvelous.*

• to contrast or compare.
Para programador, no sabe mucho de computadoras.
***For** a programmer, he doesn't know much about computers.*

• to express the idea of a deadline.
Hay que terminar la tarea **para** mañana.
*The assignment has to be finished **by** tomorrow.*

Practice:
Actividades
8 9 10

Más práctica
cuaderno p. 28
Para hispanohablantes
cuaderno p. 25

 **Online Workbook**
CLASSZONE.COM

sesenta y tres   **63**
Estados Unidos Etapa 2

 Objetive: Transitional practice
Verbs like **gustar** in conversation

Answers will vary.

 Objetive: Open-ended practice
Verbs like **gustar** in conversation

Answers will vary.

Quick Start Review

♻ Verbs like **gustar**

Use OHT 28 or write on the board: Make sentences using the following elements. Add any necessary words and make any necessary changes.

1. Mamá / molestar / lana
2. nosotros / fascinar / los vestidos de lentejuela
3. Rosa y Raúl / encantar / deportes de invierno
4. yo / gustar / colores brillantes
5. tú / quedar bien / ese chaleco estampado

Answers *See p. 53B.*

Teaching Suggestions
Presenting Por and Para

• Point out that in general **por** is used to express reason or cause behind an action (having done something), while **para** refers to the underlying goal, purpose, or use.
• Have students write a personal sentence for each use of **por** and **para**.

Block Schedule

FunBreak Have groups of 4 design 3 outfits for a particular place or special occasion (school, wedding, theater, mall, etc.). Students draw the clothes and write a script for their segment. Then 3 students play the models and carry the drawings down the "catwalk" while the other student reads the script. Play Spanish music in the background. (For additional activities, see **Block Scheduling Copymasters**.)

Teaching All Students

Extra Help Have students refer back to the **En contexto**, pp. 56–57, and comment on the clothing using verbs like **gustar** and the **Vocabulario** on p. 61.

Multiple Intelligences

Verbal Reuse the doll clothing that students brought in for "Multiple Intelligences," TE p. 61. This time, have students say how they feel about the clothing items, using **gustar** and verbs like **gustar**.

Teaching Resource Options

Print

Más práctica Workbook PE, pp. 27–28
Cuaderno para hispanohablantes PE, p. 25
Block Scheduling Copymasters
Unit 1 Resource Book
  Más práctica Workbook TE, pp. 85–86
  Cuaderno para hispanohablantes TE, p. 103
  Absent Student Copymasters, p. 117
  Audioscript, p. 123

Audiovisual

OHT 28 (Quick Start) 33 (Grammar)
Audio Program, CD 2, Track 2, Actividad 9

Technology

Online Workbook, U1 E2
Take-Home Tutor CD-ROM, U1 E2

ACTIVIDAD 8 Objective: Controlled practice
Por and **para** In writing

Answers

#1: 1. por 2. para 3. para 4. para 5. para

#2: 6. por 7. por 8. para 9. para 10. para

#3: 11. por 12. para 13. por 14. para 15. por

#4: 16. Por

ACTIVIDAD 9 Objective: Transitional practice
Listening comprehension/**por** and **para**

Answers (See script, p. 53B.)

1. para, para; 2. para; 3. para; 4. por; 5. para;
6. por; 7. para; 8. por

ACTIVIDAD 10 Objective: Open-ended practice
Por and **para** in conversation

Answers will vary.

Dictation

Using the Listening Activity Script for **Actividad 9** on TE p. 53D, dictate selected sentences to students. You may want to use this dictation for a quiz grade.

Culture Highlights

● **LA GUAYABERA** Una guayabera es una camisa de hombre de algodón o de seda. Usualmente tiene diseños bordados. Es popular en México y el Caribe. Se usa en vez de traje y corbata.

64 Vocabulary/Grammar • UNIDAD 1 Etapa 2

---

8 El diario de Maité

Escribir Maité escribió este pasaje en su diario. Complétalo con **para** o **por** para saber más de su viaje a Los Ángeles.

3 de julio

Nos vamos de vacaciones ___1___ un mes. Salimos ___2___ Los Ángeles pasado mañana. Primero voy a la agencia de viajes ___3___ los boletos. Luego voy al centro ___4___ comprar una maleta. La maleta que tengo es demasiada pequeña ___5___ toda la ropa que quiero llevar.

He hablado ___6___ teléfono ___7___ dos horas con Carmela, la prima que vamos a visitar. Ella estudia ___8___ ser abogada. Carmela es muy inteligente ___9___ su edad. Siempre me dice «Tienes que ahorrar dinero ___10___ ir a la universidad. ¡Es muy importante!»

Yo le dije que me gustaría viajar ___11___ todo California. No sé si vamos a tener tiempo ___12___ hacer todo lo que quiero. Me prometió que íbamos a dar un paseo ___13___ la playa en cuanto lleguemos. Compré un traje de baño nuevo ___14___ llevar. Pagué treinta dólares ___15___ él.

¡Qué dicha! ¡ ___16___ fin voy a conocer California!

9 ¿Adónde vas?

Escuchar/Escribir Escucha la conversación entre María y Miguel. Luego completa las oraciones con **por** o **para.**

1. María va a la tienda _____ comprar una guayabera _____ su papá.
2. El regalo es _____ su papá.
3. María tiene dinero _____ el regalo.
4. María trabaja en esa oficina _____ tres años.
5. María trabaja _____ la señora Ontiveros.
6. María va a la tienda _____ autobús.
7. María tiene tarea _____ mañana.
8. María estudió _____ tres horas después de clases.

10 La fiesta de cumpleaños

Hablar Tú y tu compañero(a) van a una fiesta de cumpleaños. Usen las palabras **para** y **por** para hablar sobre la persona festejada, el regalo que le darán, cómo van a llegar y cuánto tiempo durará la fiesta.

modelo

Tú: *¿Vas a comprar algo para Miguel para su cumpleaños?*

Compañero(a): *Creo que sí, pero no puedo pagar mucho por el regalo.*

Classroom Community

Storytelling Have students work in small groups and make up a humorous story using **por** and **para** at least 5 times each. Some story themes might be a vacation trip, a school day, a shopping trip, or a party. Have groups present their stories to the class. Vote on the most outrageous/funny story.

Portfolio Have students write a personal version of a diary entry, using **Actividad 8** as a model.

Rubric A = 13–15 pts. B = 10–12 pts. C = 7–9 pts. D = 4–6 pts. F = < 4 pts.

Writing criteria	Scale
Vocabulary use	1 2 3 4 5
Correct use of **por** and **para**	1 2 3 4 5
Spelling accuracy	1 2 3 4 5

GRAMÁTICA The Future Tense

You have already learned two ways to talk about the **future.**

- You can use: **ir + a + infinitive**

  Vamos a estudiar en la biblioteca.
  We'll study (We're going to study) in the library.

- You can use the present tense when the **context** makes it clear that you are talking about the future.

  Mañana alquilamos una película.
  Tomorrow we're renting a film.

You can also use the future tense. You form the future tense by adding a special set of **endings** to the **infinitive.**

comer *to eat*

comeré	**comer**emos
comerás	**comer**éis
comerá	**comer**án

> **All** verbs have the same endings in the future tense.

Nosotros **llegar**emos a las siete.
*We **will arrive** at seven.*

With some verbs, you have to change the form of their infinitive slightly before adding the future tense endings.

infinitive	future stem
decir	dir-
hacer	har-
poner	pondr-
salir	saldr-
tener	tendr-
valer	vald-
venir	vendr-
poder	podr-
querer	querr-
saber	sabr-

> You still use the same future tense endings.

The future of **hay** is **habrá.**

Apoyo para estudiar

Express future plans or events

Generally you will use **ir + a + infinitive** or the present tense to express the future where intention is strong and the event will happen soon. The future tense is often associated with plans, predictions, or events that are less certain. Which of the following two sentences is more certain? **Voy a México en julio. Algún día iré a Madrid.**

Practice: **Actividades** 11 12 13 14   **Más práctica** *cuaderno p. 29*   **Para hispanohablantes** *cuaderno p. 26*   **Online Workbook** CLASSZONE.COM

Teaching All Students

Extra Help Working in pairs, have each student write 4 sentences, 2 that require **por** and 2 that require **para,** leaving a blank where the word should be. Have partners exchange papers and write the answers on a separate sheet of paper. Then have pairs exchange with another pair and complete the sentences.

Multiple Intelligences

Musical/Rhythmic Have students write a song/rap about clothing and shopping that uses **por** at least 3 times and **para** at least 3 times.

Naturalist Have students write 8–10 sentences describing a trip through the forest, jungle, desert, countryside, or mountains. Each sentence must use **por** or **para.**

♻ **Future with ir a + infinitive**

Use OHT 28 or write on the board: Complete the following sentences using **ir a** + infinitive to say what these people are going to do on Saturday.

1. Mi mejor amigo(a)...
2. Nosotros...
3. Yo...
4. Tú...
5. Mis padres...

Answers
Answers will vary. Answers could include:
1. Mi mejor amigo(a) va a esquiar.
2. Nosotros vamos a ver una película.
3. Yo voy a ir de compras.
4. Tú vas a trabajar.
5. Mis padres van a dar un paseo.

Teaching Suggestions
Teaching The Future Tense

Make flashcards of infinitives, the stems of verbs that are irregular in the future, and future tense endings. Use different colors for infinitives, irregular stems, and endings. Have a group of 4 students come to the front of the class. Give a verb infinitive or irregular stem card to each student. Then assign a subject noun/pronoun to each student. Students must find the card with the correct ending, then hold up the 2 cards together and repeat the subject noun/pronoun and verb form. Continue with other groups of students.

Block Schedule

Process Time Allow students 5 minutes to read **Gramática: The Future Tense** to themselves before you present the information. Then ask them to try to do #1–5 in **Actividad 11** by themselves. They will complete this exercise after you have thoroughly gone over the **Gramática** with them. (For additional activities, see **Block Scheduling Copymasters.**)

Teaching Resource Options

Print

Más práctica Workbook PE, p. 29
Cuaderno para hispanohablantes
  PE, p. 26
Block Scheduling Copymasters
Unit 1 Resource Book
  Más práctica Workbook TE, p. 87
  Cuaderno para hispanohablantes
    TE, p. 104
  Information Gap Activities, p. 109
  Absent Student Copymasters, p. 118
  Audioscript, p. 124

Audiovisual

Audio Program CD 2, Track 3,
  Actividad 12

Objective: Controlled practice
Future tense

Answers
1. Su papá le prestará su carro nuevo.
2. Ismael llegará a las siete.
3. Yo estaré lista.
4. Me pondré el nuevo vestido de lunares.
5. Él me traerá flores.
6. Cenaremos en un restaurante francés.
7. Él podrá leer el menú en francés.
8. Bailaremos toda la noche.
9. Hablará sobre su futuro.
10. Yo contaré chistes.
11. Nuestros amigos nos verán.
12. Me divertiré muchísimo.
13. Haremos otra cita.

Objective: Controlled practice
Listening comprehension/Future
tense

Answers (See script, p. 53B.)
1. a
2. a
3. b
4. b
5. b

Objective: Transitional practice
Future tense in conversation

Answers will vary.

---

11 La cita ideal

Hablar/*Escribir* Ana Bárbara va a salir con Ismael el sábado. Ella imagina cómo va a ser su primera cita con él. ¿Qué dice?

modelo

yo / salir / con Ismael / sábado por la noche

Saldré con Ismael el sábado por la noche.

1. su papá / prestarle / su carro nuevo
2. Ismael / llegar / a las siete
3. yo / estar / lista
4. yo / ponerse / el nuevo vestido de lunares
5. él / traer [a mí] / flores
6. nosotros / cenar / en un restaurante francés
7. él / poder leer / el menú en francés
8. nosotros / bailar / toda la noche
9. él / hablar / sobre su futuro
10. yo / contar / chistes
11. nuestros amigos / ver [a nosotros]
12. yo / divertirse / mucho
13. nosotros / hacer / otra cita

12 San Antonio

Escuchar/*Escribir* Julia está en San Antonio con su familia por dos días. Al final del primer día, su mamá cuenta lo que hicieron ese día y los planes para el otro día. ¿Qué hicieron ayer y qué van a hacer mañana? Escoge la respuesta correcta.

1. **a.** Fueron al Paseo del Río.
   b. Irán al Paseo del Río.
2. **a.** Fueron a El Álamo.
   b. Irán a El Álamo.
3. **a.** Fueron al Mercado.
   b. Irán al Mercado.
4. **a.** Compraron regalitos para sus amigos.
   b. Comprarán regalitos para sus amigos.
5. **a.** Asistieron a un concierto de música tejana.
   b. Asistirán a un concierto de música tejana.

13 El año que viene

Hablar/*Escribir* Pregunta a un(a) compañero(a) si hará las siguientes actividades el año que viene. Luego, cambien de papel.

modelo

Tú: *¿Trabajarás el año que viene?*

Compañero(a): *Sí, trabajaré en la tienda de música el año que viene.*

trabajar...   hacer...   dar...   acampar...

viajar a ...   estudiar...   ver...

ir a   volver a...   comprar...   competir...

jugar a...   salir...   celebrar...   ¿...?

Classroom Community

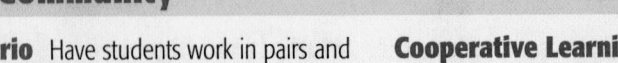

Learning Scenario Have students work in pairs and play "fortune teller." Each student takes a turn at telling the future of his/her partner. Have volunteers present their predictions to the class.

Cooperative Learning Have students work in groups of 4 to practice the **Vocabulario** on p. 67. Student 1 acts out an expression; student 2 guesses the expression; student 3 makes a sentence using the expression; student 4 records the sentence; the group evaluates the sentence and makes necessary corrections. Student 2 acts on the next expression, and so on. Finally, groups submit their sentences for a quiz grade.

14 El Campamento MonteVerde

Hablar Vas a ir al Campamento MonteVerde con dos amigos. Conversen sobre qué les gustaría hacer allí. Hablen de todas las posibilidades y digan por qué les gustan o no las actividades del Campamento.

modelo

Tú: ¿Qué harás tú en el Campamento MonteVerde?

Amigo 1: ¿Yo? Yo haré alpinismo. Me encanta estar al aire libre y ver las flores y los animales.

Amigo 2: Ay, a mí no. No me interesa la naturaleza. Yo navegaré por Internet.

More Practice: **Más comunicación** p. R4

Vocabulario

Los pasatiempos

acampar to camp

coleccionar to collect

escalar montañas to mountain climb

esquiar en el agua to waterski

hacer alpinismo to go hiking

hacer montañismo to go mountaineering

navegar en tabla de vela to windsurf

navegar por Internet to surf the Internet

pescar en alta mar to go deep-sea fishing

pilotar una avioneta
  to fly a single-engine plane

volar en planeador to hang-glide

¿Has hecho una de estas actividades alguna vez?

¡Disfruta de la naturaleza! Ven al

Campamento Monteverde

Aquí podrás...

esquiar en el agua

escalar montañas

acampar bajo la luna

hacer alpinismo

volar en planeador

remar en una canoa

y también podrás...
¡navegar por Internet!

Ya verás cuánto te divertirás aquí en
Campamento Monteverde
Una semana aquí y nunca querrás regresar a casa.

Nota cultural

Araceli Segarra es la primera mujer española en escalar el famoso monte Everest. Este pico formidable tiene más de 29.000 pies de altura. Los alpinistas que tratan de conquistar el Everest tienen que entrenarse por mucho tiempo para acostumbrarse a la falta de oxígeno que existe en las altitudes muy elevadas.

Teaching All Students

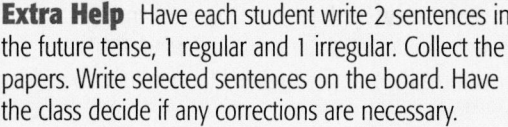

Extra Help Have each student write 2 sentences in the future tense, 1 regular and 1 irregular. Collect the papers. Write selected sentences on the board. Have the class decide if any corrections are necessary.

Multiple Intelligences

Logical/Mathematical Have students choose the pastime from the **Vocabulario** that interests them the most. Then have them research the costs involved in the pastime: equipment, fees, rentals, etc.

Teaching Suggestions
Presenting Vocabulary
Present the vocabulary by miming the activities, where possible. Then have students create icons for each activity, similar to those used in the realia on p. 67. Use these to practice the vocabulary and ask personal questions about the activities.

14 Objective: Open-ended practice
The future tense in conversation

Answers will vary.

Critical Thinking
After reading the list of activities available at **Campamento Monteverde,** ask students where they think this camp might be. Students may want to look at a topographical map of the Western Hemisphere for support.

Culture Highlights

● **ARACELI SEGARRA** Araceli Segarra, de Cataluña, España, es una alpinista versátil. Tenía 26 años cuando llegó a la cima del Monte Éverest. Este logro *(accomplishment)* aparece en la película *Everest,* que se ha mostrado mundialmente en teatros IMAX. La película también puede alquilarse en una tienda de videos.

Block Schedule

Research Ask students to choose a Spanish-speaking city or vacation area and plan a trip there. They will first need to research, either in the library or on the Internet, the activities/sites available. They then write 10–12 sentences using the future tense explaining what they will do. Each sentence should also be accompanied by a visual. Have students present their itineraries and visuals to the class. (For additional activities, see **Block Scheduling Copymasters.**)

Teaching Resource Options

Print

Más práctica Workbook PE,
pp. 21–24, 30

Actividades para todos Workbook PE,
pp. 21–30

Cuaderno para hispanohablantes
PE, pp. 21–22, 27–28

Block Scheduling Copymasters

Unit 1 Resource Book

  Más práctica Workbook TE,
  pp. 79–82, 88

  Actividades para todos Workbook TE,
  pp. 89–98

  Cuaderno para hispanohablantes
  TE, pp. 99–100, 105–106

  Information Gap Activities, p. 110

  Absent Student Copymasters, p. 119

  Audioscript, p. 137

Audiovisual

OHT 29 (Quick Start) 34 (Grammar)

Technology

Online Workbook, U1 E2
Take-Home Tutor CD-ROM, U1 E2

Quick Start Review

🔄 Future tense

Use OHT 29 or write on the board:
Give the **tú** form of the future for each
of the following verbs:

1. leer	2. tener
3. estar	4. venir
5. hacer	6. viajar
7. poner	8. ir

Answers

1. leerás	2. tendrás
3. estarás	4. vendrás
5. harás	6. viajarás
7. pondrás	8. irás

Teaching Suggestions
Presenting Future Tense to Express Probability

• Point out to students that to convey
the idea of "probably" they should
use a verb in the future tense. Tell
them that this usage is common and
probably the one they will hear most
often in conversational Spanish.

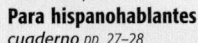

GRAMÁTICA **Future Tense to Express Probability**

▶ You can use the **future tense** to speculate about what might occur or
what others are doing. When used this way, the **future tense** implies
that you are **wondering about an event** or **guessing whether or not
it has occurred.**

Marcos ya no quiere jugar fútbol los sábados.
¿Por qué **será**?
Marcos doesn't want to play soccer on Saturdays any more.
What could be *the reason for that?*

Tendrá novia.
He **probably has** *a girlfriend.*

¿De veras? ¿Quién **será**?
Really? **I wonder** *who* **it might be**?

Practice:
Actividades
15 **16**

Más práctica
cuaderno p. 30
Para hispanohablantes
cuaderno pp. 27–28

 **Online Workbook**
CLASSZONE.COM

Nota cultural

Cuando hablamos de las mascotas,
es importante saber algunas
diferencias entre el mundo en inglés
y el hispanohablante. En inglés nos
referimos al **sonido** (sound) que
hacen los perros como *bow-wow*,
pero en español es guau-guau.
Otra diferencia es que los gatos
«hispanohablantes» dicen miau en vez de *meow* y los pájaros pío-pío en
vez de *tweet-tweet*. Algunos nombres típicos para mascotas son Colita,
Mancha y Pelusa para los perros, y Michi o Michifús para los gatos.

---

15 **¿Dónde estarán?**

Hablar/*Escribir* Nunca sabes
dónde están tus cosas, tu
familia, tus mascotas (*pets*), tus
amigos. Expresa tu frustración.

modelo

mis libros (sala)

*¿Dónde estarán mis libros? ¿Estarán
en la sala? Tendré que buscarlos.*

1. mi gato (debajo de
la cama)
2. mi hermano (afuera)
3. mis zapatos (en el clóset)
4. mi perro (en el jardín)
5. mi mamá (en su
habitación)
6. mi raqueta de tenis (en
el carro)
7. mis discos compactos (en
el cuarto de mi hermano)
8. mi gorro (en mi
habitación)
9. mis carpetas (en mi
mochila)
10. mi cámara (en casa de
mi amiga Delia)
11. Hernán (en la biblioteca)
12. Delia (en el gimnasio)

---

68   sesenta y ocho
Unidad 1

Classroom Community

Group Activity Have students work in groups of 4
to discuss what they will probably do next summer.
They must continue talking until they find 3 things that
they are all planning to do. Have the groups present
these 3 things to the class.

Paired Activity Have students work in pairs and
create 5–8 additional items for **Actividad 16**. The new
items must be questions related to them and their lives.

16 No sé exactamente

Hablar/Escribir Tu compañero(a) te hace muchas preguntas. No estás seguro(a) de la respuesta, pero tratas de contestarle. Sigue el modelo.

modelo

¿Dónde está Ricardo? (en su cuarto)

Compañero(a): *¿Dónde estará Ricardo?*

Tú: *No sé exactamente. Estará en su cuarto.*

1. ¿Cuándo vienen los primos? (la semana que viene)
2. ¿Cuántos años tiene esa señora? (unos ochenta años)
3. ¿Qué hora es? (las diez o las once de la noche)
4. ¿Qué es esa cosa en la calle? (una bolsa de basura)
5. ¿Qué dice la profesora si le dices que no hiciste la tarea? (que no hay problema)
6. ¿Hay suficiente comida para todos? (más en el refrigerador)
7. ¿Dónde están mis sudaderas? (en tu cuarto)
8. ¿Cuándo traen los pasteles? (después del almuerzo)

También se dice

Aunque en la mayoría de los países latinoamericanos se dice **sudadera**, en España se usa la palabra **chándal**.

17 La fiesta

Hablar Tú y tu compañero(a) van a dar una fiesta. Tu compañero(a) siempre se pone nervioso(a) pensando en lo que puede pasar. Te hace muchas preguntas. Contéstale para que se quede tranquilo(a). Luego cambien de papel.

modelo

Compañero(a): *¿Lloverá durante la fiesta?*

Tú: *¡No te preocupes! No va a llover durante la fiesta. Hará mucho calor y vendrá mucha gente.*

Compañero(a): *¿Les gustará la música?*

Tú: *Sí, les encantará.*

llover
venir los invitados
haber suficiente comida
tocar muy mal los músicos
ser aburrido
irse demasiado temprano los invitados
gustar la música

Activity 17 brings together all concepts presented.

More Practice:
Más comunicación *p. R4*

 Online Workbook
CLASSZONE.COM

Refrán

Aunque la mona se vista de seda, mona se queda.

¿Qué quiere decir el refrán? ¿Crees que es posible poner demasiado énfasis en la apariencia personal? ¿Por qué?

cuarenta y nueve **69**
Estados Unidos Etapa 2

Teaching All Students

Extra Help For **Actividad 16,** have students first locate the verb in each sentence, give its infinitive, and then give the appropriate future tense form.

Native Speakers Have students ask Spanish-speaking friends, neighbors, or relatives for other **refranes.** Have each student present at least 1 new **refrán** to the class and explain its meaning.

Multiple Intelligences

Kinesthetic Call on a student to come to the front of the class to act out an activity of his/her choosing. Ask the class: **¿Qué hará?** Students must answer using the future to express probability. The student who answers correctly acts out the next activity.

Teaching Resource Options

Print 📖

Actividades para todos Workbook PE, pp. 27–29

Block Scheduling Copymasters

Unit 1 Resource Book
  Actividades para todos Workbook TE, pp. 95–97
  Absent Student Copymasters, p. 120

Audiovisual

OHT 29 (Quick Start)

Technology

  ⓘ www.classzone.com

Quick Start Review

♻ Clothing

Use OHT 29 or write on the board: Complete the following sentences with items of clothing:

1. Cuando hace calor me gusta llevar...
2. En el invierno me encanta llevar...
3. En la primavera me fascina llevar...
4. En el otoño me gusta llevar...

Answers will vary.

Teaching Suggestions

Presenting Cultura y comparaciones

• Present the Connecting Cultures Strategy and have students complete the task.

• Have students look at the pictures on pp. 70–71 and make observations about the content of the reading. Ask: **Basándote en esta foto, ¿qué puedes determinar acerca del contenido de la lectura?**

• After a student reads each paragraph, ask yes/no, either/or, or simple answer questions.

Reading Strategy

Use context clues Remind students to use context clues to guess the meanings of unfamiliar words. Also point out that pictures often contribute to understanding.

En colores
CULTURA Y COMPARACIONES

Un gran diseñador

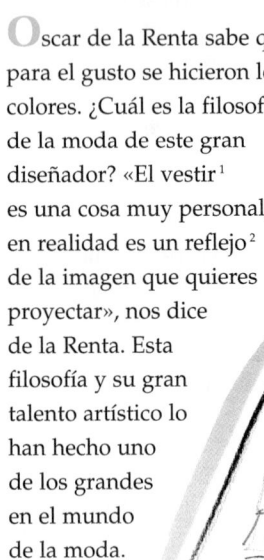

PARA CONOCERNOS
STRATEGY: CONNECTING CULTURES
Examine the cultural role of fashion How do fads, personal style, and high style influence your decisions when you buy clothing? Imagine you are packing for a trip to another country, another culture. How might geography, climate, or local customs influence your choice of clothing? Name an article of clothing you would take and the characteristic that influenced your choice.

Country_____

	Característica	Ropa
Geografía		
Clima		
Costumbres		
Otro		

O scar de la Renta sabe que para el gusto se hicieron los colores. ¿Cuál es la filosofía de la moda de este gran diseñador? «El vestir[1] es una cosa muy personal; en realidad es un reflejo[2] de la imagen que quieres proyectar», nos dice de la Renta. Esta filosofía y su gran talento artístico lo han hecho uno de los grandes en el mundo de la moda.

———
[1] dressing
[2] reflection

70 setenta
Unidad 1

Classroom Community

Paired Activity Have students work in pairs to create and conduct an interview. One student plays the reporter and the other plays Oscar de la Renta. The reporter must ask at least 5 questions. Have pairs present their interviews to the class.

Portfolio Have students write a fashion review of the 2 fashion models on p. 69. They should use the reviews on pp. 54–55 as examples.

Rubric A = 13–15 pts. B = 10–12 pts. C = 7–9 pts. D = 4–6 pts. F = < 4 pts.

Writing criteria	Scale
Vocabulary use	1 2 3 4 5
Grammatical/spelling accuracy	1 2 3 4 5
Creativity, presentation	1 2 3 4 5

Oscar de la Renta ha hecho mucho por la niñez de Santo Domingo. Ha ayudado a construir una escuela y un orfelinato³ para 350 niños, a quienes visita en las Navidades.

De la Renta nació en la República Dominicana y allí estudió pintura en la Escuela de Bellas Artes de Santo Domingo. A la edad de 18 años fue a Madrid, donde conoció al diseñador Cristóbal Balenciaga y se convirtió en su ilustrador. En 1963 fue a Nueva York. Desde entonces, de la Renta ha iniciado muchas tendencias de la moda.

«Lo que se quiere es que alguien te vea a ti primero y que te encuentre bien, y que después se fije⁴ en tu ropa. Lo contrario, yo creo que es negativo».

³ orphanage
⁴ to look at

CLASSZONE.COM
More About Latinos

¿Comprendiste?

1. ¿Qué piensa de la Renta del vestir?
2. ¿Cuándo comenzó de la Renta su carrera como diseñador en Estados Unidos?
3. Según el diseñador, ¿cómo debe uno vestirse?
4. ¿Cómo ha ayudado Oscar de la Renta a los dominicanos?

¿Qué piensas?

1. ¿Qué hay que hacer para ser diseñador de alta moda?
2. ¿Estás de acuerdo con la filosofía de la moda de Oscar de la Renta? ¿Por qué?

Hazlo tú

Muchos diseñadores hispanos han influenciado la moda, como Carolina Herrera, Paloma Picasso y Narciso Rodríguez. Busca datos y escribe un párrafo sobre uno de ellos. Si es posible, incluye en tu composición una foto o un dibujo de uno de sus modelos.

setenta y uno
Estados Unidos Etapa 2   **71**

Culture Highlights

● **CRISTÓBAL BALENCIAGA** El famoso diseñador español Cristóbal Balenciaga (1895–1972) fue un maestro de la alta costura entre los años treinta y los sesenta. Fue uno de los pocos diseñadores que podía diseñar, cortar y coser sus diseños. Hizo el traje de negocios más femenino y el vestido estilo chemise en 1955. Tenía casas de moda en Barcelona, Madrid y París.

Cross Cultural Connections

Have students investigate the influence of Spanish-speaking designers and Spanish fashion on fashion in the U.S. and the world today and in the past. For example, toreador pants were popular in the 50s and Mexican peasant blouses were popular in the 70s.

¿Comprendiste?

Answers
1. Piensa que es una cosa muy personal, que es un reflejo de la imagen que quieres proyectar.
2. Comenzó su carrera en Estados Unidos en 1963.
3. Uno debe vestirse de manera que alguien te vea a ti primero y que te encuentre bien, y que después se fije en tu ropa.
4. Ha ayudado a construir una escuela y un orfelinato para 350 niños, a quienes visita en las Navidades.

Teaching All Students

Extra Help In groups of 5, have students write each sentence of the reading on a separate slip of paper. Have them mix up the slips, then reorganize them in proper order. Have students take turns reading the sentences to retell the story.

Multiple Intelligences

Verbal Have a classroom discussion about clothing styles of the future. Will styles for men and women be similar? What will influence these styles?

Block Schedule

FunBreak Have students do the Hands-On Crafts activity (**chile chicos**) on TE p. 29B of the **Ampliación**. (For additional activities, see **Block Scheduling Copymasters**.)

Teaching Resource Options

Print 📖

Cuaderno para hispanohablantes PE, pp. 29–30
Block Scheduling Copymasters
Unit 1 Resource Book
  Cuaderno para hispanohablantes
  TE, pp. 107–108
  Information Gap Activities,
  pp. 111–112
  Family Involvement, pp. 121–122

Audiovisual 🎧

OHT 30 (Quick Start)

Technology 💻

eTest Plus Online/Test Generator
CD-ROM

🔖 www.classzone.com

🔔 Quick Start Review

♻ Clothing

Use OHT 30 or write on the board:
Escribe una descripción completa de la ropa que llevas hoy.

Answers will vary.

✓ Teaching Suggestions
What Have Students Learned?

Have students look at the "Now you can..." notes listed on the left side of pages 72–73. Point out that if they feel they need to review material before doing the activities, they should consult the "To review" notes.

 **Answers**

Answers will vary.

ETAPA 2

En uso
REPASO Y MÁS COMUNICACIÓN

OBJECTIVES
- Describe fashions
- Talk about pastimes
- Talk about the future
- Predict actions

Now you can...
- describe fashions.

To review
- verbs like **gustar**
  see p. 62.

1 ¿Qué lleva?

Hablas por teléfono con un(a) amigo(a). Te pregunta qué llevan varias personas. Contesta y añade tu propio comentario con el verbo indicado.

modelo

Martín/quedar

Compañero(a): *¿Qué lleva Martín?*

Tú: *Martín lleva una camisa de un solo color.*

Compañero(a): *¿Le queda bien?*

Tú: *Sí, le queda bien. Hace juego con sus pantalones.*

Martín / quedar

la profesora García / gustar

Raquel / encantar

Guillermo / gustar

Patricia / quedar

Sabrina / gustar

Gustavo /importar

setenta y dos
Unidad 1

Classroom Community

Group Activity Divide the class into 4 groups. Assign each group a "Now you can..." / "To review" section. Each group reviews the concepts and presents a short overview with examples to the class.

Paired Activity Have students write 5 sentences using **por** and 5 sentences using **para**. Then have them work in pairs, exchange sentences, and explain the use of **por/para** in each of their partner's sentences.

Now you can...

• talk about pastimes.

To review

• **por** and **para**
  see p. 63.

② Nueva York

Usa **por** y **para** y completa la nota que te escribió un amigo sobre sus planes.

¡Hola! Salgo _____ Nueva York el mes que viene. Voy a viajar _____ tren. Pagué cuarenta dólares _____ el boleto. Voy a visitar a mi hermano que estudia _____ ser doctor. Ha vivido en Nueva York _____ dos años. Me gustaría pasear _____ el Parque Central. También quiero ir al Museo del Barrio _____ ver la exposición de arte taíno. ¡Pero no creas que voy sólo _____ divertirme! Trabajaré _____ mi tío. Ya sabes que necesito ahorrar dinero _____ ir a la universidad. ¡Te mando una postal!

Now you can...

• talk about the future.

To review

• the future tense
  see p. 65.

③ El club de español

El club de español va a tener su reunión anual. ¿Qué harán todos?

modelo

A Mireya le gusta preparar comida dominicana.

Mireya preparará comida dominicana.

1. A todos les gusta divertirse.
2. A Susana le gusta bailar salsa.
3. A ellos les gusta sacar fotos.
4. A ti te interesa traer los refrescos.
5. A David le gusta hablar.
6. A nosotros nos gusta comer.

Now you can...

• predict actions.

To review

• the future of probability
  see p. 68.

④ ¡Haces demasiadas preguntas!

Tu hermanito(a) quiere saber cosas sobre tus vacaciones con tu amigo(a).

modelo

ir de compras solo(a) o con su amiga

Hermanito(a): *¿Crees que irás de compras solo(a) o con tu amiga?*

Tú: *No sé. Tal vez iré solo(a).*

1. comprar el equipo de acampar o navegar en tabla de vela
2. volar en planeador o hacer alpinismo
3. pescar en alta mar o nadar en la piscina
4. alquilar un video o ir al cine

setenta y tres
Estados Unidos Etapa 2   **73**

 **Answers**

para / por / por / para / por / por / para / para / para / para

 **Answers**

1. Todos se divertirán.
2. Susana bailará salsa.
3. Ellos sacarán fotos.
4. Tú traerás los refrescos.
5. David hablará.
6. Comeremos.

 **Answers**

Answers will vary.

Teaching All Students

Extra Help Have students return to pp. 72–73 and find examples of each of the structures listed under the "To review" notes.

Multiple Intelligences

Kinesthetic First, have students add 6 more activities (#7–12) to **Actividad 4**. Then, have various students act out the activities. The class guesses which number is being mimed. This activity may also be done in small groups.

■ Block Schedule

Change of Pace Have each student draw a pair of people. The people must be wearing some similar clothing/ accessories and some different clothing/ accessories. Students then exchange papers with a partner. They must write 3 sentences describing similarities and 3 sentences describing differences. (For additional activities, see **Block Scheduling Copymasters**.)

Teaching Resource Options

Print

Unit 1 Resource Book
  Vocabulary Quizzes, pp. 129–131
  Audioscript, p. 125
  Grammar Quizzes, pp. 132–133
  Etapa Exam, Forms A and B,
    pp. 134–143
  Examen para hispanohablantes,
    pp. 146–148
  Portfolio Assessment, pp. 149–150.
  Multiple Choice Test Questions,
    pp. 248–250

Audiovisual

OHT 30 (Quick Start)
Audio Program CD 19, Track 4

Technology

eTest Plus Online/Test Generator
CD-ROM

  www.classzone.com

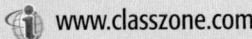

Rubric: Speaking

Criteria	Scale	
Sentence structure	1 2 3	A = 11–12 pts.
Vocabulary use	1 2 3	B = 9–10 pts.
Originality	1 2 3	C = 7–8 pts.
Fluency	1 2 3	D = 4–6 pts.
		F = < 4 pts.

  **En tu propia voz**

Rubric: Writing

Criteria	Scale	
Vocabulary use	1 2 3 4 5	A = 14–15 pts.
Accuracy	1 2 3 4 5	B = 12–13 pts.
Creativity, appearance	1 2 3 4 5	C = 10–11 pts.
		D = 8–9 pts.
		F = < 8 pts.

PARA CONVERSAR
STRATEGY: SPEAKING

Use words of transition As you narrate the fashion show, use expressions of transition to maintain focus and interest. For ideas, review **En vivo,** pp. 58–59. Other ideas include: expressions of sequence (**primero, entonces, luego, por fin**); questions or commands to focus attention (¿Qué lleva... ? ¿Qué vemos ahora? ¡Mira... !); or personal reactions (¡Qué emoción! ¡Muy mal! ¡Qué horror!).

---

5 Tu campamento

> **STRATEGY: SPEAKING**
>
> **Brainstorm to get lots of ideas** What kind of camp do you want? What should the emphasis be? Sports, music, art, creative writing, math, or languages… all in the great outdoors? Vote and pick one together. What activities does your camp offer that make it special?

Trabajando en grupos, escriban un anuncio para un campamento donde se pueden hacer muchas actividades. Primero den un nombre a su campamento y escriban un lema (*slogan*) que use el futuro. Hagan dibujos para su anuncio e incluyan una lista de todas las actividades del campamento.

modelo

En el Campamento Mundo Natural usted se sentirá feliz.

6 Desfile de modas

En grupos, escriban una narración para un desfile de modas de la escuela. Describan el vestuario de cuatro modelos detalladamente (*in detail*). Refiéranse a una revista de moda para buscar ideas. Luego, lean su narración a la clase.

modelo

Jim lleva pantalones anchos. Son de mezclilla. Lleva una camisa de rayas que hace juego con los pantalones.

7 En tu propia voz

ESCRITURA ¿Qué piensas del futuro? ¿Cómo será la vida en nuestro planeta, la Tierra? ¿Cómo será tu vida? ¿Qué harás? Escribe diez predicciones para el año 2030.

modelo

Seré periodista para Internet.

No habrá periódicos.

Todos leerán las noticias en Internet.

CONEXIONES

Las matemáticas Prepara un presupuesto (*budget*) anual de lo que vas a gastar en ropa el próximo año. ¿Cuánto vas a gastar en total? ¿Qué porcentaje piensas gastar en zapatos, pantalones, joyas, etc.? Prepara una gráfica con el porcentaje que vas a gastar en cada categoría.

Zapatos 19%
Pantalones 18%
Accesorios 10%
Vestidos 12%
Camisas 25%
Joyas 15%

Classroom Community

Learning Scenario Have groups present the camps that they invented for **Actividad 5** and post their ads on the bulletin board. Then have all students decide which camp they would like to attend. Call on various students to say at least 1 thing they will do at the camp of their choice.

Game ¿Qué/Quién soy yo? Have 1 student define a word/expression from the **Repaso de vocabulario** list. The rest of the class tries to guess what/who it is. The student who guesses correctly defines the next word/expression.

En resumen
REPASO DE VOCABULARIO

DESCRIBE FASHIONS

Fashion

destacarse	to stand out
el (la) diseñador(a)	designer
la moda	fashion, style
suelto(a)	loose
la temporada	season, period of time
único(a)	unique, only
el vestuario	wardrobe

Items

la billetera	wallet
el bolso	shoulder bag
la cadena	chain
el llavero	keychain
la medalla	medallion
el monedero	change purse
los pendientes	dangling earrings
el prendedor	pin
las sudaderas	sweats

Likes and dislikes

caer bien/mal	to like/dislike
cómodo(a)	comfortable
detestar	to hate
formidable	great
genial	wonderful
horrible	horrible
incómodo(a)	uncomfortable
pesado(a)	boring, heavy

Materials

el algodón	cotton
el color brillante	bright color
el color claro	pastel
el color oscuro	dark color
el cuero	leather
de un solo color	solid color
estampado(a)	print
el fleco	fringe
la lana	wool
la lentejuela	sequin
los lunares	polka-dots
la mezclilla	denim
el poliéster	polyester
la seda	silk

♻ **Ya sabes**

ancho(a)	wide
apretado(a)	tight
estrecho(a)	narrow
flojo(a)	loose
hacer juego con	to match with
oscuro(a)	dark
un par de	a pair of
las rayas	stripes
sencillo(a)	simple

TALK ABOUT PASTIMES

acampar	to camp
coleccionar	to collect
escalar montañas	to mountain climb
esquiar en el agua	to water-ski
hacer alpinismo	to go hiking
hacer montañismo	to go mountaineering
navegar en tabla de vela	to windsurf
navegar por Internet	to surf the Internet
pescar en alta mar	to go deep-sea fishing
pilotar una avioneta	to fly a single-engine plane
volar en planeador	to hang–glide

TALK ABOUT THE FUTURE

Future tense

Iré a la fiesta.

PREDICT ACTIONS

Future of probability

¿Dónde estará?

Juego

Sopa de letras

Pon en orden estas letras para saber qué no cambia pero sí da cambio:

REDONOME

setenta y cinco
Estados Unidos Etapa 2 75

Teaching All Students

Extra Help Have students study the **Repaso de vocabulario** for 3 minutes. Then have them close their books. Give the name of a category and see how many words students can list from memory under that category.

Multiple Intelligences

Kinesthetic Have students work in pairs to plan outlandish outfits that they will wear and describe on an assigned day. The class will vote on the most outlandish outfit.

Teaching Note: En tu propia voz
Writing Strategy Tell students to use the writing strategy "Tell who, what, where, when, why, and how" when writing their predictions. Following these guidelines will help them cover all details.

Interdisciplinary Connection
Mathematics Once students have determined their total budget and the percentage for each expense, have them calculate the exact amount of money for each expense.

Quick Start Review
♻ Etapa vocabulary
Use OHT 30 or write on the board: Write 3 complete sentences. Each sentence must contain 1 word from each of the following categories: "Items," "Likes and dislikes," and "Materials."
Answers will vary.

Teaching Suggestions
Vocabulary Review
Have students work in pairs and play hangman with the vocabulary words. Variation: Students can compose short sentences and use these for playing hangman.

Juego
Answer: monedero

Block Schedule
Variety In small groups, have students write and then present a short dialog or conversation that incorporates 10–15 vocabulary words.

Planning Guide CLASSROOM MANAGEMENT

OBJECTIVES

Communication
- Talk about household chores *pp. 78–79, 80–81*
- Say what friends do *pp. 78–79*
- Express feelings *pp. 92–93*

Grammar
- Review: Use reflexive verbs *pp. 84–85*
- Use reflexive verbs reciprocally *pp. 86–88*
- Review: Use impersonal constructions with **se** *pp. 89–91*

Culture
- Regional vocabulary *pp. 79, 83*
- **El compadrazgo** *p. 87*
- Sammy Sosa *p. 88*
- Los Angeles *p. 91*
- Life in a **barrio latino** *pp. 92–93*
- Tito Puente, the king of mambo *pp. 94–95*

♻ Recycling
- Affirmative **tú** commands *p. 82*
- Future tense *p. 82*
- Reflexive verbs *p. 85*
- Imperfect tense *p. 87*

STRATEGIES

Listening Strategies
- Pre-listening *p. 80*
- Make an argument for and against hiring others *p. 80*

Speaking Strategies
- Use associated vocabulary *TE p. 83*
- Identify feelings important in a friendship *p. 98*

Reading Strategies
- Chart contrasts between dreams and reality *p. 92*
- Observe organization of ideas *TE p. 94*

Writing Strategies
- Persuade your reader *TE p. 98*
- Use details to enrich a description *pp. 100–101*

Connecting Cultures Strategies
- Recognize regional vocabulary *p. 79, 83*
- Learn about **el compadrazgo** *p. 87*
- Learn about a famous Hispanic baseball player *p. 88*
- Learn about Hispanic communities *pp. 91, 92–93*
- Identify characteristics of neighborhoods *TE p. 93*
- Research, report, and value musical influences *p. 94*
- Connect and compare what you know about musical influences *pp. 94–95*

PROGRAM RESOURCES

Print
- *Más práctica* Workbook PE *pp. 31–40*
- *Actividades para todos* Workbook PE *pp. 31–40*
- Block Scheduling Copymasters *pp. 25–32*
- Unit 1 Resource Book
  - *Más práctica* Workbook TE *pp. 153–162*
  - *Actividades para todos* Workbook TE *pp. 163–172*
  - *Cuaderno para hispanohablantes* TE *pp. 173–182*
  - Information Gap Activities *pp. 183–186*
  - Family Letter *p. 187*
  - Absent Student Copymasters *pp. 188–194*
  - Family Involvement *pp. 195–196*
  - Audioscript *pp. 197–200*
  - Assessment Program, Unit 1 Etapa 1 *pp. 201–241; 248–250*
  - Video Activities *pp. 251–254*
  - Videoscript *pp. 255–257*
  - Answer Keys *pp. 258–261*

Audiovisual
- Audio Program CD 3
- *Canciones* CD
- Video Program Videotape 0:00 / DVD, Unit 1
- Overhead Transparencies M1–M5; GO1–GO5; 3, 35–49
- Word Tiles U1E3

Technology
- eEdition Plus Online/eEdition CD-ROM
- Easy Planner Plus Online/Easy Planner CD-ROM
- eTest Plus Online/Test Generator CD-ROM
- Online Workbook
- Take-Home Tutor CD-ROM
- 🌐 www.classzone.com

Assessment Program Options
- Unit 1 Resource Book
  - Vocabulary Quizzes
  - Grammar Quizzes
  - Etapa Exam Forms A and B
  - *Examen para hispanohablantes*
  - Portfolio Assessment
  - Unit 1 Comprehensive Test
  - *Prueba comprensiva para hispanohablantes,* Unit 1
  - Multiple Choice Test Questions
- Audio Program CD 19
- eTest Plus Online/Test Generator CD-ROM

Native Speakers
- *Cuaderno para hispanohablantes* PE *pp. 31–40*
- *Cuaderno para hispanohablantes* TE (Unit 1 Resource Book)
- *Examen para hispanohablantes* (Unit 1 Resource Book)
- *Prueba comprensiva para hispanohablantes,* Unit 1 (Unit 1 Resource Book)
- Audio Program *(Para hispanohablantes)* CD 3, 19
- Audioscript (Unit 1 Resource Book)

Student Text
Listening Activity Scripts

 **Situaciones** *pages 80–81*

• CD 3

¡Buenos días! Usted se ha comunicado con el servicio de limpieza CasaLimpia.

¿Qué es lo que usted necesita? En CasaLimpia se hace de todo:

¿Muchos platos sucios en la cocina? Se los lavamos.

¿Ventanas sucias? ¡No se preocupe! También lavamos ventanas.

¿Mucho polvo en la sala? No hay problema. ¡Quitamos el polvo de todos los muebles!

Pasamos la aspiradora por toda la casa. Y barremos y lavamos esos pisos sucios.

¿Hay algunos gabinetes en el sótano que están desorganizados?

¡Fácil! Organizamos y limpiamos sus gabinetes bajo su dirección.

Y por último, en el jardín podemos cortar el césped y regar las plantas.

Aquí en CasaLimpia, le garantizamos una casa limpia...

Si quiere hablar con un agente, por favor marque el cero.

¡Gracias! Y que pase buen día.

ACTIVIDAD 5  Un día desastroso *page 85*

¡Qué día horroroso! Me acosté muy tarde anoche porque tenía mucha tarea. No puse el despertador, así que no sonó por la mañana. Me desperté ¡muy tarde!–a las diez. Me levanté como loco y corrí hacia el baño. Quería ducharme pero mi hermanita estaba en el baño. ¡Se duchó por media hora! Por fin salió y yo me duché. Quería secarme el pelo pero la secadora de pelo no funcionaba. No me peiné. Me vestí rápidamente. Cuando llegué al colegio, me di cuenta que ¡no me había puesto calcetines!

ACTIVIDAD 13 Mundo de Autos *page 90*

Buenas tardes, señoras y señores. ¡Vengan hoy a Mundo de Autos! Se venden carros de todo tipo: nuevos, usados, domésticos, japoneses... Durante la rebaja de este mes, se ofrecen precios increíbles. ¡No lo va a creer! Jamás ha visto precios tan bajos. Si sale con un carro nuevo, va a salir súper-feliz. Pero no lo olvide–la rebaja se termina a finales de este mes.

En Mundo de Autos se habla español, se habla inglés y también se habla japonés. Los vendedores son fantásticos. Se dice que son los mejores vendedores de la ciudad. Y si no quiere comprar un carro nuevo, traiga su carro usado cuando necesite reparaciones. Aquí se reparan carros el mismo día. ¡Venga a Mundo de Autos hoy!

▲ Quick Start Review Answers

p. 80 Vocabulary review

1. Mamá quiere que limpie los gabinetes.
2. Voy a esconderme en el desván.
3. Debo desyerbar el jardín.
4. También tengo que vaciar el basurero.
5. Enchufé el televisor y voy a encenderlo.

Sample Lesson Plan - 50 Minute Schedule

DAY 1

Etapa Opener
- Quick Start Review (TE, p. 76) 5 MIN.
- Have students look at the *Etapa* Opener and answer the questions. 5 MIN.

En contexto: Vocabulario
- Quick Start Review (TE, p. 78) 5 MIN.
- Present *Descubre*, p. 78. 5 MIN.
- Have students use context and pictures to learn *Etapa* vocabulary. Use the Situational OHTs for additional practice. 10 MIN.

En vivo: Situaciones
- Quick Start Review (TE, p. 80) 5 MIN.
- Present the Listening Strategy, p. 80. 5 MIN.
- Have students look at and read sections 1 and 2, pp. 80–81. Play the audio for section 3. 10 MIN.

Homework Option:
- Have students write answers to *¿Comprendiste?*, p. 79, and *Escribir*, p. 81.

DAY 2

En acción: Vocabulario y gramática
- Check homework. 5 MIN.
- Quick Start Review (TE, p. 82) 5 MIN.
- Have students read and complete *Actividad* 1 in writing, then go over answers orally. 5 MIN.
- Have students do *Actividad* 2 in pairs. 5 MIN.
- Present the *Nota*, then do *Actividad* 3 in pairs. 10 MIN.
- Have students do *Actividad* 4 in pairs. 5 MIN.
- Present *Repaso:* Reflexive Verbs and the *Vocabulario*, p. 84. 10 MIN.
- Play the audio; do *Actividad* 5. 5 MIN.

Homework Option:
- Have students complete *Actividad* 2 in writing. *Más práctica* Workbook, pp. 35–36. *Cuaderno para hispanohablantes*, pp. 33–34.

DAY 3

En acción (cont.)
- Check homework. 5 MIN.
- Do *Actividad* 6 orally. 5 MIN.
- Have students complete *Actividad* 7 in pairs. Have a few pairs present their conversations. 10 MIN.
- Quick Start Review (TE, p. 86) 5 MIN.
- Present *Gramática:* Reflexive Verbs Used Reciprocally and the *Vocabulario*, p. 86. 10 MIN.
- Have students read and complete *Actividad* 8 in writing, then go over answers orally. 5 MIN.
- Have students complete *Actividad* 9 in writing. 5 MIN.
- Have students complete *Actividad* 10 in pairs. 5 MIN.

Homework Option:
- Have students complete *Actividad* 6 in writing. *Más práctica* Workbook, pp. 37–38. *Cuaderno para hispanohablantes*, pp. 35–36.

DAY 4

En acción (cont.)
- Check homework. 5 MIN.
- Do *Actividad* 11 orally. Expand using Information Gap Activities, Unit 1 Resource Book, p. 183; *Más comunicación*, p. R5. 20 MIN.
- Quick Start Review (TE, p. 89) 5 MIN.
- Present *Repaso:* Impersonal Constructions with *se*, p. 89. 10 MIN.
- Have students complete *Actividad* 12 in writing, then go over answers orally. 5 MIN.
- Play the audio; do *Actividad* 13. 5 MIN.
- Do *Actividad* 14 in pairs. 5 MIN.

Homework Option:
- Have students complete *Actividad* 11 in writing. *Más práctica* Workbook, pp. 39–40. *Cuaderno para hispanohablantes*, pp. 37–38.

DAY 5

En acción (cont.)
- Check homework. 5 MIN.
- Have students do *Actividad* 15 in groups. Expand using *Más comunicación*, p. R5. 15 MIN.

Refrán
- Present the *Refrán*, p. 91. 5 MIN.

En voces: Lectura
- Quick Start Review (TE, p. 92) 5 MIN.
- Present the Reading Strategy, p. 92. Call on volunteers to read the *Lectura* aloud. Have students answer the *¿Comprendiste?/ ¿Qué piensas?* questions, p. 93. 20 MIN.

Homework Option:
- Have students complete *Hazlo tú*, p. 93.
- *Actividades para todos* Workbook, pp. 31–40

DAY 6

En colores: Cultura y comparaciones
- Check homework. 5 MIN.
- Quick Start Review (TE, p. 94) 5 MIN.
- Present the Connecting Cultures Strategy, p. 94. Call on volunteers to read the article aloud. Have students answer the *¿Comprendiste?/¿Qué piensas?* questions, p. 95. 20 MIN.

En uso: Repaso y más comunicación
- Have students do *Actividades* 1, 2, 3 orally and *Actividad* 4 in pairs. 20 MIN.

Homework Option:
- Have students complete *Hazlo tú*, p. 95. Review for *Etapa* 3 Exam.

DAY 7

En uso (cont.)
- Check homework. 5 MIN.
- Present the Speaking Strategy, p. 98, and have students do *Actividades* 5 and 6 in groups. 15 MIN.

En resumen: Repaso de vocabulario
- Quick Start Review (TE, p. 99) 5 MIN.
- Review grammar questions, etc., as necessary. 5 MIN.
- Complete *Etapa* 3 Exam. 20 MIN.

Homework Option:
- Have students complete their ads for *Actividad* 7, p. 98. Review for Unit 1 Comprehensive Test.

DAY 8

Tú en la comunidad
- Check homework. 5 MIN.
- Read and discuss *La'Donna*, p. 98. 5 MIN.

En tu propia voz: Escritura
- Present the Writing Strategy, p. 100. Do the writing activity, pp. 100–101. 10 MIN.

Unit 1 Comprehensive Test
- Complete Unit 1 Comprehensive Test. 30 MIN.

Ampliación
- Optional: Use a suggested project, game, or activity. (TE, pp. 31A–31B)

Homework Option:
- Preview *Unidad 2* Opener: Have students read and study pp. 102–103.

Sample Lesson Plan - Block Schedule (90 minutes)

DAY 1

Etapa Opener
- Quick Start Review (TE, p. 76) 5 MIN.
- Have students look at the *Etapa* Opener and answer the questions. 5 MIN.
- Use Block Scheduling Copymasters, p. 25. 5 MIN.

En contexto: Vocabulario
- Quick Start Review (TE, p. 78) 5 MIN.
- Present *Descubre* (TE, p. 78) 5 MIN.
- Have students use context and pictures to learn *Etapa* vocabulary. Use the Situational OHTs for additional practice. 10 MIN.

En vivo: Situaciones
- Quick Start Review (TE, p. 80) 5 MIN.
- Present the Listening Strategy, p. 80. 5 MIN.
- Have students look at and read sections 1 and 2, pp. 80–81. Play the audio for section 3. 15 MIN.
- Quick Start Review (TE, p. 82) 5 MIN.
- Have students read and complete *Actividad* 1 in writing, then go over answers orally. 5 MIN.
- Have students do *Actividad* 2 in pairs. 5 MIN.
- Present the *Nota,* then do *Actividad* 3 in pairs. 10 MIN.
- Have students do *Actividad* 4 in pairs. 5 MIN.

Homework Option:
- Have students write answers to *¿Comprendiste?,* p. 79, and *Escribir,* p. 81. Have students complete *Actividad* 2 in writing.

DAY 2

En acción: Vocabulario y gramática
- Check homework. 10 MIN.
- Quick Start Review (TE, p. 84) 5 MIN.
- Present *Repaso:* Reflexive Verbs and the *Vocabulario,* p. 84. 15 MIN.
- Play the audio; do *Actividad* 5. 5 MIN.
- Do *Actividad* 6 orally. 5 MIN.
- Have students complete *Actividad* 7 in pairs. Have a few pairs present their conversations. 10 MIN.
- Quick Start Review (TE, p. 86) 5 MIN.
- Present *Gramática:* Reflexive Verbs Used Reciprocally and the *Vocabulario,* p. 86. 15 MIN.
- Have students read and complete *Actividad* 8 in writing, then go over answers orally. 5 MIN.
- Have students complete *Actividad* 9 in writing, then exchange papers for peer correction. 10 MIN.
- Have students complete *Actividad* 10 in pairs. 5 MIN.

Homework Option:
- Have students complete *Actividad* 6 in writing. *Más práctica* Workbook, pp. 35–38. *Cuaderno para hispanohablantes,* pp. 33–36.

DAY 3

En acción (cont.)
- Check homework. 10 MIN.
- Do *Actividad* 11 orally. Expand using Information Gap Activities, Unit 1 Resource Book, p. 183; *Más comunicación,* p. R5. 20 MIN.
- Quick Start Review (TE, p. 89) 5 MIN.
- Present *Repaso:* Impersonal Constructions with *se,* p. 89. 10 MIN.
- Have students complete *Actividad* 12 in writing, then go over answers orally. 5 MIN.
- Play the audio; do *Actividad* 13. 5 MIN.
- Have students do *Actividad* 14 in pairs. 5 MIN.
- Have students do *Actividad* 15 in groups. Expand using Information Gap Activities, Unit 1 Resource Book, p. 184; *Más comunicación,* p. R5. 20 MIN.
- Use an expansion activity from TE pp. 90–91 for reinforcement and variety. 5 MIN.

Refrán
- Present the *Refrán,* p. 91. 5 MIN.

Homework Option:
- Have students complete *Actividad* 11 in writing. *Más práctica* Workbook, pp. 39–40. *Cuaderno para hispanohablantes,* pp. 37–38.
- *Actividades para todos* Workbook, pp. 31–40

DAY 4

En voces: Lectura
- Check homework. 5 MIN.
- Quick Start Review (TE, p. 92) 5 MIN.
- Present the Reading Strategy, p. 92. Call on volunteers to read the *Lectura* aloud. Have students answer the *¿Comprendiste?/¿Qué piensas?* questions, p. 93. 15 MIN.

En colores: Cultura y comparaciones
- Quick Start Review (TE, p. 94) 5 MIN.
- Present the Connecting Cultures Strategy, p. 94. Have volunteers read the article aloud, then answer the *¿Comprendiste?/¿Qué piensas?* questions, p. 95. 15 MIN.

En uso: Repaso y más comunicación
- Quick Start Review (TE, p. 96) 5 MIN.
- Do *Actividades* 1, 2, 3 orally and *Actividad* 4 in pairs. 15 MIN.
- Present the Speaking Strategy, p. 98, and do *Actividades* 5 and 6 in groups. 15 MIN.
- Do *Actividad* 7 in writing. 10 MIN.

Homework Option:
- Have students complete *Hazlo tú,* pp. 93 and 95. Review for *Etapa* 3 Exam and Unit 1 Comprehensive Test.

DAY 5

En resumen: Repaso de vocabulario
- Check homework. 5 MIN.
- Quick Start Review (TE, p. 99) 5 MIN.
- Review grammar questions, etc., as necessary. 5 MIN.
- Complete *Etapa* 1 Exam. 20 MIN.

Tú en la comunidad
- Read and discuss *La'Donna,* p. 98. 5 MIN.

En tu propia voz: Escritura
- Present the Writing Strategy, p. 100. Do the writing activity, pp. 100–101. 15 MIN.

Unit 1 Comprehensive Test
- Review grammar questions, etc. as necessary. 5 MIN.
- Complete Unit 1 Comprehensive Test. 30 MIN.

Ampliación
- Optional: Use a suggested project, game, or activity. (TE, pp. 31A–31B) 15 MIN.

Homework Option:
- Preview *Unidad* 2 Opener: Have students read and study pp. 102–103.

▼ ¿Qué cosas hacen los vecinos para cuidar el jardín?

Etapa Theme
Talking about chores and what people do and expressing feelings

Grammar Objectives
- Reviewing the use of reflexive verbs
- Using reflexive verbs reciprocally
- Reviewing the use of impersonal constructions with **se**

Teaching Resource Options

Print

Block Scheduling Copymasters
Unit 1 Resource Book
  Family Letter, p. 187
  Absent Student Copymasters, p. 188

Audiovisual

OHT 4, 41 (Quick Start)
Canciones CD

Quick Start Review
♻ Household chores

Use OHT 41 or write on the board:

Escribe por lo menos 5 quehaceres.

Answers
Answers will vary. Answers could include:
sacar la basura, quitar el polvo, limpiar mi habitación, lavar los platos, poner la mesa, pasar la aspiradora, barrer el piso, hacer la cama

Teaching Suggestions
Previewing the Etapa
- Ask students to study the picture on pp. 76–77 (1 min.).
- Close books; ask students to name at least 3 things they remember.
- Reopen books and have students describe the people and the setting: **Describe las personas y el ambiente de la foto.**
- Use the **¿Qué ves?** questions to focus the discussion.

UNIDAD 1
ETAPA 3

¡Hay tanto que hacer!

OBJECTIVES

- Talk about household chores
- Say what friends do
- Express feelings

¿Qué ves?

Mira la foto. Contesta las preguntas.

1. ¿Qué hacen estas personas?
2. ¿A qué grupo crees que pertenecen?
3. ¿Crees que todos toman decisiones sobre el jardín? ¿Qué más pueden hacer?
4. Mira el póster. ¿Qué cosas hacen los vecinos para cuidar el jardín?

76

Classroom Management

Planning Ahead Prepare to introduce the theme of household chores by bringing in ads from cleaning services to use as models for students to create their own ads (see "Portfolio," TE p. 80). Also bring in want ads from Spanish-language newspapers to demonstrate the impersonal **se** (see "Extra Help," TE p. 91).

Organizing Paired Work One method for pairing students involves picking cards. Students must locate the person with the matching card. For example, half the cards would have countries on them and half would have the capital cities. Other possibilities are sports and sports equipment, vocabulary synonyms or antonyms, or a word and its picture.

Celebra El día del jardín en el
jardín comunitario de

Jamaica
Plain

Siembra, cosecha y comparte

con familiares,

amigos y vecinos.

¡Más de 27 sembrados de flores y verduras!

77

Cross Cultural Connections

Have students compare the garden they see in this photo with gardens they might have at home or have seen in their neighborhoods. Do more people have flower gardens or vegetable gardens? Who usually takes care of the gardens?

Culture Highlights

● **HISPANOS EN EL NORESTE DE ESTADOS UNIDOS** Más del 15% de la población hispanohablante de Estados Unidos vive en el noreste. La mayoría es del Caribe o de Centroamérica, aunque hay personas de Sudamérica también. El mayor número de hispanohablantes vive en Filadelfia, Nueva York, Nueva Jersey y Massachusetts.

Critical Thinking

The photo on pp. 76–77 shows a community garden in a neighborhood of Boston, Massachusetts. Ask students why they think having a community garden is important: **¿Por qué crees que es importante tener jardines para la comunidad?**

Supplementary Vocabulary

el clavel	carnation
el geranio	geranium
el girasol	sunflower
la margarita	daisy
el pensamiento	pansy
la petunia	petunia
la violeta	violet

Teaching All Students

Extra Help Give students a list of 6 sentences describing the photo: 3 are true and 3 are false. Students determine which are true and correct the ones that are false.

Native Speaker Have students make up a simple scenario to go with the photo. They can give the people names and make up a short story about what they are doing and why.

Multiple Intelligences

Naturalist Have students research the names of trees, plants, and flowers in Spanish. Then have them make a bulletin board of pictures of the items with labels.

Block Schedule

Process Time Have students spend 1 minute looking at the photo. They should then write 3 sentences about the photo and how it relates to them (what they do, what they like, etc.). Have volunteers share their sentences. (For additional activities, see **Block Scheduling Copymasters.**)

Teaching Resource Options

Print

Block Scheduling Copymasters

Unit 1 Resource Book
Absent Student Copymasters, p. 188

Audiovisual

OHT 35, 36, 37, 37A, 38, 38A, 41

Technology

Online Workbook, U1E3
Take-Home Tutor CD-ROM, U1E3

Quick Start Review

🔄 Rooms in the house

Use OHT 41 or write on the board:
Haz una lista de 5 habitaciones en una casa y 1 artículo en esa habitación.

Answers
Answers will vary. Answers could include:
la cocina: el frigorífico
el comedor: la mesa
la sala: el sofá
la habitación: la cama
el baño: la bañera
el garaje: el carro

Teaching Suggestions
Introducing Vocabulary

• Have students look at pages 78–79. Use OHT 35 and 36 to present the vocabulary.
• Ask the Comprehension Questions on TE p. 79 in order of yes/no (questions 1–3), either/or (questions 4–6), and simple word or phrase (questions 7–10). Expand by adding similar questions.
• Use the TPR activity to reinforce the meaning of individual words.

Descubre

Answers
desorganizado = *disorganized*
desconectar = *to disconnect*
desenchufar = *to unplug*
desarmar = *to disassemble; to take apart*

En contexto VOCABULARIO

Descubre

A. **El prefijo** Cuando una palabra empieza con el prefijo **des-**, esa palabra significa lo opuesto de la misma palabra sin el prefijo **des-**. Trata de descubrir el sentido de las siguientes palabras.

organizado = *organized*
desorganizado = _____
conectar = *to connect*
desconectar = _____
enchufar = *to plug in*
desenchufar = _____
armar = *to assemble*
desarmar = _____

B. **La casa** Ya sabes los nombres de los cuartos de la casa. Aquí hay dos más. ¿Tiene **sótano** tu casa? ¿**desván**?

el desván

el sótano

Manolo el imposible

Fian Arroyo es un artista de Surfside, Florida. Él dibuja una tira cómica sobre el personaje de Manolo, un niño que siempre causa problemas por todo el mundo. Aquí tienes un episodio de sus aventuras.

Debo cambiar la bombilla de la lámpara.

También tengo que vaciar el basurero.

Mamá quiere que limpie los gabinetes. Están muy desorganizados.

¡Pero no tengo ganas! Mejor voy al jardín.

78 setenta y ocho
Unidad 1

Classroom Community

TPR Plan ahead: Have students make drawings of the various chores presented and collect them. Give commands to students to do certain chores. Students must come up, show the appropriate pictures, and mime the activities as well.

Paired Activity Have pairs of students draw house plans and label the rooms and furniture. In addition, they should write 1 sentence for each room to describe an activity/chore done there.

CD-ROM Take-Home Tutor

En el jardín

Tengo que regar las plantas.

¡Necesito reparar el cortacésped. ¡No funciona! Para repararlo, lo tengo que desarmar.

Debo desyerbar el jardín. ¡Pero hay tantas malas hierbas! ¡Va a tomarme horas!

¡No tengo ganas! Mejor voy a la oficina de mis padres.

En la oficina

Debo pasar la aspiradora, pero no quiero. ¡Voy a desenchufarla!

Si desconecto el teléfono, puedo ver la televisión sin interrupciones.

¡Enchufé el televisor y voy a encenderlo!

¡Oigo que vienen mis padres! ¡Voy a esconderme en el desván!

También se dice

In Latin America, a potato is **una papa,** but in Spain it is **una patata. Papas fritas** and **patatas fritas** are both french fries and potato chips.

Online Workbook
CLASSZONE.COM

¿Comprendiste?

1. ¿Haces quehaceres en tu casa?
2. ¿Cuántas veces por semana tienes que ayudar en tu casa?
3. ¿Qué quehaceres te tocan a ti?
4. ¿Hay quehaceres que te gustan hacer? ¿que no te gustan hacer? ¿Por qué?
5. ¿Crees que es importante tener responsabilidades en la casa? ¿O tienes suficientes responsabilidades de la escuela?
6. Imagina que eres el jefe o la jefa de tu casa. ¿Cómo compartirías los quehaceres de tu casa?

setenta y nueve
Estados Unidos Etapa 3
79

Comprehension Questions

1. ¿Debe Manolo cambiar la bombilla de la lámpara? (Sí.)
2. ¿Tiene Manolo que llenar el basurero? (No.)
3. ¿Limpia Manolo los gabinetes? (No.)
4. ¿Va Manolo al jardín o limpia los gabinetes? (Va al jardín.)
5. ¿En el jardín hay bombillas o plantas? (plantas)
6. ¿Tiene Manolo que reparar o romper el cortacésped? (reparar el cortacésped)
7. ¿Qué otra cosa tiene que hacer Manolo en el jardín? (desyerbar el jardín)
8. ¿Qué hace Manolo con la aspiradora? (La desenchufa.)
9. ¿Qué desconecta Manolo? (el teléfono)
10. ¿Dónde se esconde Manolo? (en el desván)

Supplementary Vocabulary

la alfombra	carpet
la escoba	broom
la manguera	water hose
la plancha	iron
el trapo	dust rag

Teaching All Students

Extra Help Make statements about the various cartoon frames. Have students point to the scene in the book.

Multiple Intelligences

Visual Have students draw a 2–3 frame cartoon of themselves doing chores at home. They should write something about what they are doing in speech bubbles.

Block Schedule

Change of Pace Have students write a list of chores they do at home and how often. Then have them rank the chores from 1–5 in order of which they prefer to do the most (5) to the least (1). (For additional activities, see **Block Scheduling Copymasters.**)

Teaching Resource Options

Print 📖

Block Scheduling Copymasters
Unit 1 Resource Book
  Absent Student Copymasters, p. 189
  Audioscript, p. 197

Audiovisual 🎧

OHT 39, 40, 42 (Quick Start)
Audio Program CD 3, Track 1

Technology 💻

Take-Home Tutor CD-ROM, U1E3

Quick Start Review

 Vocabulary review

Use OHT 42 or write on the board:
Unscramble the words to make
sentences from **Manolo el imposible.**

1. gabinetes / que / los / Mamá /
   limpie / quiere
2. en / voy / esconderme / el /
   desván / a
3. el / debo / desyerbar / jardín
4. tengo / también / vaciar / que /
   basurero / el
5. a / el / voy / enchufé / y /
   encenderlo / televisor

Answers *See p. 75B.*

Teaching Suggestions
Presenting Situations

• Present the Listening Strategy, p. 80,
  and have students jot down the list of
  chores for inside and outside the home.
• Use OHT 39 and 40 to present the
  Mirar and **Leer** sections. Ask yes/no,
  either/or, or short-answer questions.
• Use Audio CD 3 (see Script TE p.
  75B) and have students do the
  Escuchar section. Then have students
  complete the Listening Strategy
  exercise.
• Have students write answers to the
  Escribir section.

AUDIO
En vivo
SITUACIONES

PARA ESCUCHAR

STRATEGY: LISTENING

Pre-listening Most of us like to live in a clean
and orderly place, although not all of us like
to do the necessary work. Make a list of what
is necessary to do both inside and outside
your home to maintain it.

**Make an argument for and against hiring others to
maintain a home** How does your list compare
with the services of Casa Limpia? Do you
think those who live in the home should do
the work? Do you think it's o.k. to pay others
to do it? What are the reasons for and against
either option?

¡Qué desastre!

Acabas de regresar de las vacaciones.
Cuando vuelves, ves que tu casa es un
desastre. Hay muchos quehaceres. Primero
identifica lo que tienes que hacer. Luego
llama a un servicio de limpieza para saber
si te pueden ayudar.

① Mirar

Mira las fotos de los cuartos de esta casa desorganizada.
Escribe una lista de todas las cosas que deben hacerse.

En la cocina

En la lavandería

En la sala

80 ochenta
Unidad 1

Classroom Community

Learning Scenario Have students work in groups
of 3–4 and perform a skit where they are a cleaning
team that has come to your "house." Each team will
enter, introduce themselves, explain what they are
going to do, and then mime the activities, using props
if possible. Suggest that students also add a little humor
to their skits.

Portfolio Have students create their own cleaning
company ads, using the ad on p. 81 as a model and
the ads you brought in for "Planning Ahead," TE p. 76.

Rubric A = 13–15 pts. B = 10–12 pts. C = 7–9 pts. D = 4–6 pts. F = < 4 pts.

Writing criteria	Scale				
Vocabulary use	1	2	3	4	5
Grammatical/spelling accuracy	1	2	3	4	5
Creativity/appearance	1	2	3	4	5

En el jardín

En el sótano

CD-ROM
Take-Home Tutor

② Leer

¡Qué suerte! Ves el anuncio a la derecha en el periódico. Claro, llamas inmediatamente.

③ Escuchar

Antes de escuchar el mensaje de CasaLimpia, copia este formulario en otro papel. A la izquierda, escribe la lista de quehaceres que ya escribiste. Mientras escuchas el mensaje, marca «sí» en tu formulario si ofrecen el servicio que necesitas y marca «no» si no lo ofrecen.

SERVICIO DE LIMPIEZA

CasaLimpia

¡Hacemos de todo!

¡Relájese!

Limpiamos su casa, su oficina o su apartamento mientras usted descansa.

Llame al 555-3489 para informarse sobre nuestros servicios.

¡Llame hoy! y pronto tendrá...
CasaLimpia

Quehaceres	Servicio de limpieza CasaLimpia		Quehaceres	Servicio de limpieza CasaLimpia	
	Sí	No		Sí	No
En la cocina			**En el jardín**		
___			___		
___			___		
___			___		
En el sótano			**En la sala**		
___			___		
___			___		
En la lavandería			___		
___					
___					

④ Escribir

¿Qué tengo que hacer yo? Ahora haz una lista de los quehaceres que tendrás que hacer porque el servicio CasaLimpia no ofrece esos servicios.

Teaching All Students

Extra Help Point to each of the 5 photos on pp. 80–81 and ask yes/no questions. For example: **En la sala, ¿hay que pasar la aspiradora? En el sótano, ¿hay que cortar el césped?**

Multiple Intelligences

Verbal Have students give complete descriptions of the photos on pp. 80–81, including name of the room/area, items in the room/area, colors of items, activities done in the room/area, chores necessary to keep the room/area maintained.

Logical/Mathematical Have students research the average cost of cleaning a house in your area.

Escuchar (See script, p. 75B.)

Answers

Answers will vary.

Quehaceres	Servicio de limpieza
En la cocina	
•lavar los platos	Sí
•lavar las ventanas	Sí
•barrer el piso	Sí
•sacar la basura	No
En el sótano	
•limpiar los gabinetes	Sí
En la lavandería	
•lavar la ropa	No
•planchar la ropa	No
En el jardín	
•cortar el césped	Sí
•regar las plantas	Sí
•reparar el cortacésped	No
•desyerbar	No
En la sala	
•quitar el polvo	Sí
•pasar la aspiradora	Sí
•cambiar las bombillas	No

Escribir

Answers
sacar la basura
cambiar las bombillas
lavar la ropa
planchar la ropa
reparar el cortacésped
desyerbar

Block Schedule

Variety Have students work in pairs to write 10 sentences describing items and chores for rooms/areas of the home. Half of the sentences should be true and half should be false. Then have pairs exchange papers and determine which sentences are true and which are false. They should correct any false statements. (For additional activities, see **Block Scheduling Copymasters**.)

Teaching Resource Options

Print

Block Scheduling Copymasters
Unit 1 Resource Book
  Absent Student Copymasters, p. 190

Audiovisual
OHT 42 (Quick Start)

Quick Start Review

♻ Activities at home

Use OHT 42 or write on the board:
Does the activity *generally* takes place
in the indicated room/area? Write **sí** or
no.

1. cocina: limpiar los gabinetes
2. jardín: regar las plantas
3. comedor: desyerbar
4. sala: pasar la aspiradora
5. jardín: enchufar el televisor
6. sótano: cambiar la bombilla

Answers
1. sí 2. sí 3. no 4. sí 5. no 6. sí

Teaching Suggestions
Comprehension Check

Use **Actividades 1–4** to assess
retention after the **Vocabulario** and
Situaciones. Before doing **Actividad 2,**
you may wish to review the formation
of affirmative **tú** commands.

ACTIVIDAD 1
Objective: Controlled practice
Vocabulary in reading

Answers
1. a
2. b
3. c
4. c
5. b

En acción

PARTE A

Práctica del vocabulario

Objectives for Activities 1–4
• Talk about households chores • Say what friends do

1 Manolo el bueno

Leer/*Escribir* ¿Qué pasa? ¡Parece que
Manolo ha cambiado de personalidad!
Ahora quiere hacer todas las cosas que no
hizo el otro día. ¿Qué dice? Completa sus
oraciones con la respuesta correcta.

1. «No ha llovido en tres semanas.
   Necesito _____».
   a. regar las plantas
   b. desyerbar el jardín
   c. cortar el césped

2. «No puedo encender el televisor. ¡Ah!
   Es porque no está _____».
   a. desenchufado
   b. enchufado
   c. desconectado

3. «La lámpara no funciona; no da luz.
   Probablemente necesito _____».
   a. desarmar la lámpara
   b. reparar el cortacésped
   c. cambiar la bombilla

4. «Tuvimos una fiesta anoche y hoy
   tenemos mucha basura. Tengo que
   _____».
   a. organizar los gabinetes
   b. planchar la ropa
   c. vaciar el basurero

5. «Quiero cortar el césped pero no
   puedo porque _____ no funciona.
   Necesito repararlo».
   a. el televisor
   b. el cortacésped
   c. el gabinete

2 ¡Hazlo! ♻ 👥

Hablar/*Escribir* Hay muchas cosas que hacer.
Dile a tu compañero(a) que las haga. Luego,
cambien de papel.

modelo

vaciar

Tú: *¡Por favor! Vacía el basurero.*

Compañero(a): *Está bien. Lo haré
inmediatamente.*

1. enchufar

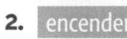
2. encender

3. desconectar

4. cambiar

5. desyerbar

6. reparar

Classroom Management

Time Saver Have students prepare and take notes
for **Actividades 1–4** as homework so that they can
complete the activities more quickly in class.

Peer Review **Plan ahead:** Bring in magazines
dealing with homes and gardens. Divide the class into
pairs. Ask each pair to cut out several pictures related to
household items and chores. Then have 2 pairs work
together to review vocabulary using the pictures.

3 **¿Sabes?**

Hablar/*Escribir* Hay quehaceres que no sabes hacer. Tú y tu compañero(a) conocen a varias personas que los pueden ayudar. Conversen sobre la situación.

modelo

reparar el cortacésped

Tú: *¿Sabes reparar el cortacésped?*

Compañero(a): *No, no sé hacerlo.*

Tú: *¿Conoces a Arturo?*

Compañero(a): *Sí, sí lo conozco.*

Tú: *Él sabe repararlo. Vamos a pedirle ayuda.*

> **Nota: Gramática**
>
> Remember that you use both **saber** and **conocer** to mean *to know*. Use **saber** when someone knows facts or information. Use **conocer** to express familiarity and acquaintance with people and places.

1. desarmar el televisor
2. reparar la computadora
3. encender las luces en el desván
4. reparar la lámpara
5. apagar la calefacción
6. desarmar el lavaplatos
7. desyerbar el jardín
8. desenchufar la nevera

También se dice

Además de la palabra **césped,** hay muchas otras palabras que significan la misma cosa. Puedes usar también **hierba, pasto, zacate** o **grama** en otras partes del mundo hispanohablante.

4 **No puedo**

Hablar Quieres invitar a tu mejor amigo(a) a salir. Pero él (ella) te dice que no puede porque tiene algo que hacer en la casa. Conversen sobre la situación. Luego le toca a tu compañero(a) hacerte las preguntas.

modelo

Tú: *¿Quieres ir conmigo al cine? Hay una película nueva en el Cineplex.*

Compañero(a): *Me gustaría, ¡pero no puedo! Tengo que cortar el césped.*

Tú: *¿Por qué no lo haces mañana?*

Compañero(a): *...*

Teaching All Students

Extra Help Have students review the conjugations of **saber** and **conocer** before completing **Actividad 3.** Then have them each contribute 1 original sentence using each verb.

Native Speakers Ask students which of the terms given in **También se dice** they use. Have them give any other variations they use for other vocabulary words.

Multiple Intelligences

Kinesthetic In groups of 3–4, have students present skits dealing with a parent who wants his/her children to help prepare the house and yard for company coming this weekend. The parent gives commands and the children either agree to do as asked or make excuses for not doing as asked.

ACTIVIDAD 2 **Objective:** Transitional practice Vocabulary in conversation

♻ Affirmative **tú** commands/ future tense

Answers
1. A: ¡Por favor! Enchufa la computadora.
   B: Está bien. Lo haré inmediatamente.
2. A: ¡Por favor! Enciende el televisor.
   B: Está bien. Lo haré inmediatamente.
3. A: ¡Por favor! Desconecta el teléfono.
   B: Está bien. Lo haré inmediatamente.
4. A: ¡Por favor! Cambia la bombilla.
   B: Está bien. Lo haré inmediatamente.
5. A: ¡Por favor! Desyerba el jardín.
   B: Está bien. Lo haré inmediatamente.
6. A: ¡Por favor! Repara el cortacésped.
   B: Está bien. Lo haré inmediatamente.

PARA CONVERSAR
STRATEGY: SPEAKING

Use associated vocabulary Learning words in pairs, especially opposites, expands your vocabulary more easily. Which of these are opposites of words you used in **Actividad 2:** apagar, conectar, desenchufar, llenar, quitar, plantar, desarmar? Redo the activity using these words to emphasize the command. **Vacía el basurero. No debes llenarlo más.**

ACTIVIDAD 3 **Objective:** Transitional practice Vocabulary in conversation

Answers will vary.

ACTIVIDAD 4 **Objective:** Open-ended practice Vocabulary in conversation

Answers will vary.

Block Schedule

Change of Pace Have students work in pairs and pretend that they are planning a party. They should come up with a list of at least 10 chores to be done in preparation for the party and 5 chores to be done after the party. They must also decide who will do each chore. Pairs then present their preparations to the class. (For additional activities, see **Block Scheduling Copymasters.**)

Teaching Resource Options

Print

Más práctica Workbook PE, pp. 35–36
Cuaderno para hispanohablantes
  PE, pp. 33–34
Block Scheduling Copymasters
Unit 1 Resource Book
  Más práctica Workbook TE,
  pp. 157–158
  Cuaderno para hispanohablantes
  TE, pp. 175–176
  Absent Student Copymasters, p. 190
  Audioscript, p. 197

Audiovisual

OHT 43 (Quick Start), 47 (Grammar)
Audio Program CD 3, Track 2, Actividad 5

Technology

Online Workbook, U1E3
Take-Home Tutor CD-ROM, U1E3

Quick Start Review

🔔 **Reflexives**

Use OHT 43 or write on the board:
Choose a verb to complete each of the
following sentences:

> se seca / se lava / se levanta /
> se acuesta / se maquilla

1. José ____ a las siete de la mañana.
2. Estela siempre ____ a las diez de la noche.
3. Olivia ____ el pelo con una toalla.
4. Pablo ____ los dientes después del desayuno.
5. Ana se peina y luego ____.

Answers

1. se levanta   4. se lava
2. se acuesta   5. se maquilla
3. se seca

Teaching Suggestions
Reviewing Reflexive Verbs

- Review reflexive verbs using magazine pictures or drawings of daily routine activities.
- Review and practice the present tense, preterite, imperfect tense, and future tense conjugations of reflexive verbs.
- Present the **Vocabulario**. Have volunteers use the words in sentences about their own lives.

Objectives for Activities 5–13
- Talk about households chores • Say what friends do • Express feelings

REPASO   Reflexive Verbs

▶ Remember that you use reflexive verbs to describe a person doing something that involves himself or herself. These verbs use **reflexive pronouns** that refer to the person doing the action. Reflexive pronouns are: **me, te, se, nos** and **os**.

Andrés **se** lastimó.	Lucía **se** despertó.
Andrés hurt himself.	*Lucía woke up.*

▶ You can also use most of these verbs nonreflexively.

nonreflexive	reflexive *matches*
Desperté a mi hermanito a las siete y media.	Me despert**é** a las siete y media.
I woke my little brother up at seven thirty.	*I woke up at seven thirty.*

> Remember that the **reflexive pronoun** and the **verb** always match.

▶ You will often use reflexive verbs to refer to:

- emotions • feelings • reactions.

▶ When using a reflexive verb, put the **reflexive pronoun** before the **conjugated verb**.

¿Cuándo **se levantó** Marcos?	Todavía no **se ha levantado**.
When did Marcos get up?	*He hasn't gotten up yet.*

▶ When you use a reflexive verb in the infinitive, you can put the **reflexive pronouns** either:

- before the **conjugated verb** …

  No **te debes** preocupar.
  You shouldn't worry.

- or attach it to the end of the infinitive.

  No **debes** preocupar**te**.

Vocabulario

Las emociones

animarse *to become encouraged, get interested*
dedicarse a *to apply oneself to something*
desanimarse *to get discouraged*
entusiasmarse *to get excited*
oponerse a *to oppose*
ponerse nervioso(a) *to get nervous*
sentirse (e→ie) frustrado(a) *to feel frustrated*

▶ ¿Cuándo te sientes así?

Practice: **Actividades** ⑤ ⑥ ⑦
Más práctica *cuaderno pp. 35–36*
Para hispanohablantes *cuaderno pp. 33–34*

🛈 **Online Workbook**
CLASSZONE.COM

84 ochenta y cuatro
  Unidad 1

Classroom Community

Storytelling Have students work in small groups to make up a story using at least 3 of the new reflexive verbs from the **Vocabulario**, p. 84. Groups then present their stories to the class using props and gestures if possible.

Group Activity First, have students brainstorm a class list of all reflexive verbs they can remember. Display the list on the board or an OHT. Call on various students to act out the meanings of the verbs. The class guesses the activity.

5 Un día desastroso

Escuchar/Escribir ¡Manolo tuvo un día horroroso! ¿Qué le pasó? Escucha y escribe oraciones que describen su día desastroso.

modelo

Manolo / despertarse

Manolo se despertó muy tarde.

1. Manolo / acostarse
2. Manolo / levantarse
3. la hermanita de Manolo / ducharse
4. Manolo / secarse el pelo
5. Manolo / vestirse
6. Manolo / ponerse calcetines

6 Un sábado en Los Ángeles

Hablar/Escribir Beatriz describe un sábado en su casa cuando todos tuvieron que ayudar con la limpieza.

modelo

Yo tuve que planchar la ropa. Me aburrí al planchar la ropa. (aburrirse)

1. Mamá entró a la casa. _____ al ver la casa tan sucia. (desanimarse)
2. Nuestros primos vinieron a ayudarnos. Nosotros _____ cuando los vimos. (animarse)
3. Mi hermano cortó el césped. _____ mucho. (cansarse)
4. Mi hermana no nos ayudó. Papá _____ con ella. (enojarse)
5. Yo desenchufé la computadora. Mamá _____ cuando vio que la computadora no funcionaba. (ponerse nerviosa)
6. Natalia fue la primera que terminó con sus quehaceres. _____ después de acabarlos. (divertirse)

7 ¿Cómo te sentiste?

STRATEGY: SPEAKING

Express feelings You already know many adjectives like **contento(a), nervioso(a), tímido(a)** to express feelings. Add to your "emotional" vocabulary with verbs or their past participles like **cansarse: me cansé, estaba cansado(a), me sentí cansado(a).** What other verbs express how you feel on different occasions?

Hablar Pregúntale a tu compañero(a) cómo se sintió en estas ocasiones. Luego, cambien de papel.

modelo

Tú: *¿Cómo te sentiste cuando sacaste mala nota en álgebra?*

Compañero(a): *Pues me sentí muy frustrado(a) porque estudié mucho y no pensé que iba a sacar mala nota.*

> sacar mala nota en...
> tener examen final en...
> salir con tus amigos...
> perder el partido de ...
> ¿...?

ACTIVIDAD 5

Objective: Controlled practice Listening comprehension

 Reflexive verbs

Answers (See script, p. 75B.)
1. Manolo se acostó muy tarde.
2. Manolo se levantó como loco.
3. La hermanita de Manolo se duchó por media hora.
4. Manolo quería secarse el pelo [pero la secadora de pelo no funcionaba]. *o:* Manolo no se secó el pelo.
5. Manolo se vistió rápidamente.
6. Manolo no se puso calcetines. [Manolo no se había puesto calcetines.]

ACTIVIDAD 6

Objective: Transitional practice Reflexive verbs of emotion

Answers
1. Se desanimó
2. nos animamos
3. Se cansó
4. se enojó
5. se puso nerviosa
6. Se divirtió

ACTIVIDAD 7

Objective: Open-ended practice Reflexive verbs in conversation

Answers will vary.

Dictation

Using the Listening Activity Script for **Actividad 5** on TE p. 75B, dictate selected sentences to students. You may want to use this dictation for a quiz grade.

Block Schedule

Variety Have students work in pairs to write a letter to an advice columnist. They must use at least 4 of the reflexive verbs of emotion on p. 84. Students must also write an answer to the letter. Display the letters on the bulletin board. (For additional activities, see **Block Scheduling Copymasters.**)

Teaching All Students

Extra Help Have students work in pairs and ask each other the following questions:

- ¿Prefieres bañarte o ducharte?
- ¿A qué hora te despiertas durante la semana?
- ¿Cómo te sientes hoy?
- ¿Cuándo te pones nervioso(a)?
- ¿Cuándo te sientes frustrado(a)?

Multiple Intelligences

Kinesthetic Have students write down at what time they do the following activities: **despertarse los martes, acostarse los sábados, levantarse los domingos, ducharse los días de clase.** Then have them circulate and find classmates who do these things at the same time.

Teaching Resource Options

Print

Más práctica Workbook PE, pp. 37–38
Cuaderno para hispanohablantes
  PE, pp. 35–36
Block Scheduling Copymasters
Unit 1 Resource Book
  Más práctica Workbook TE,
    pp. 159–160
  Cuaderno para hispanohablantes
    TE, pp. 177–178
  Absent Student Copymasters, p. 191

Audiovisual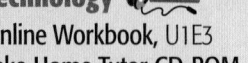

OHT 43 (Quick Start), 48 (Grammar)
Word Tiles, U1E3

Technology

Online Workbook, U1E3
Take-Home Tutor CD-ROM, U1E3

Quick Start Review

♻ **Reflexive verbs**
Use OHT 43 or write on the board:
Complete each sentence with the
preterite form of the verb:

1. El perro ___ a las siete.
   (despertarse)
2. ___ cuando vio a Carlos.
   (entusiasmarse)
3. ___ cuando no recibió su
   desayuno inmediatamente.
   (desanimarse)
4. ___ cuando por fin Carlos le dio
   su alimento. (animarse)
5. ___ cuando alguien llamó a la
   puerta. (ponerse nervioso)

Answers
1. se despertó
2. Se entusiasmó
3. Se desanimó
4. Se animó
5. Se puso nervioso

Teaching Suggestions
Teaching Reflexive Verbs Used Reciprocally

• Have students provide their own
  examples in Spanish of reciprocal
  actions.
• Present the **Vocabulario**. Have pairs
  of students act out the verbs.

GRAMÁTICA Reflexive Verbs Used Reciprocally

▶ You can also use **reflexive verbs** to express the idea
of *each other.*

> **Alicia** y **yo nos** conocemos muy bien.
> *Alicia and I know each other very well.*

> **Mis hermanitos se** pelean mucho.
> *My little brothers fight with each other a lot.*

> **Ustedes** deben ayudar**se**.
> *You ought to help each other.*

▶ You can also add the phrase el uno al otro (la una
a la otra) to emphasize the reciprocal meaning:

> **Mauricio** y **Sara**   **To each other**
> **se** saludaron.   is implied, but
> *Mauricio and Sara said hello.*   not stated.

> **Mauricio** y **Sara**
> **se** saludaron el uno a la otra.
> *Mauricio and Sara said hello to each other.*

Vocabulario

Las interacciones

apoyarse *to support each other*

ayudarse *to help each other*

conocerse bien/mal
  to know each other well/not very well

contarse (o→ue) *secretos/chismes*
  to tell each other secrets/gossip

llevarse bien/mal (con) *to get along well/badly (with)*

odiarse *to hate each other*

pelearse/no pelearse frecuentemente
  to fight/not to fight often

perdonarse *to forgive each other*

quejarse *to complain*

saludarse *to greet, say hello to each other*

telefonearse *to phone each other*

▶ ¿Con quién haces estas cosas?

Practice: **Actividades** ⑧ ⑨ ⑩ ⑪   **Más práctica** *cuaderno pp. 37–38*    **Online Workbook** CLASSZONE.COM
   Para hispanohablantes *cuaderno pp. 35–36*

 Apoyo para estudiar

Reflexive verbs used reciprocally

Read these examples of reciprocal use: **Tú y yo nos ayudamos el uno al
otro. Tú y Mauricio se entienden bien. Nuestras hermanas no se
conocen bien.** Why will reciprocal verbs always have a plural ending
and never a singular ending?

86 ochenta y seis
Unidad 1

Classroom Community

Cooperative Learning Have students complete
Actividad 9 in groups of 4. Student 1 answers items
1 and 2, Student 2 answers items 3 and 4, and so on.
The group then checks each others' answers and
submits their work for a quiz grade.

Storytelling Have small groups of students write a
short love story that includes the verbs presented in the
Vocabulario on p. 86. Have groups present their stories
to the class. One member of the group should sketch
the scene on the board as the other members present
the story.

8 Se llevan muy bien

Leer/*Escribir* Tienes un(a) amigo(a) que es muy chismoso(a). Lee sus descripciones de varias personas en la primera columna. Luego, escoge la frase de la segunda columna que mejor complete su descripción.

1. Paco y Lola son amigos desde el primer grado.
2. Chela y Juan siempre andan juntos.
3. Mari y Ana hablan todas las noches, no importa dónde están.
4. Pepe y José se mandan cartas a menudo.
5. Pedro y Alicia se hablan cuando se ven en la calle.
6. A Nando y a Berta les gusta hablar de lo que pasa en sus vidas.
7. Tomás y Chepa se pelean, pero luego se piden disculpas.
8. Quique y Rosa siempre están de acuerdo.

a. Se telefonean.
b. Se conocen muy bien.
c. No se pelean.
d. Se escriben.
e. Se saludan.
f. Se llevan muy bien.
g. Se perdonan.
h. Se cuentan todo.

Nota cultural

El compadrazgo Una persona se considera el compadre o la comadre de una familia al compartir la responsabilidad de criar *(to raise)* a un niño o una niña con los padres. El compadre o la comadre es **el padrino** o **la madrina** delniño(a), que se llama **ahijado(a)**.Generalmente, los padrinos van a todas las celebraciones importantes de su ahijado(a), incluso la graduación y la boda.

9 Mi padrino ♻

Escribir Tu padrino es el mejor amigo de tu papá. Para saber cómo era su relación cuando eran jóvenes, completa las oraciones de tu papá con el imperfecto del verbo entre paréntesis.

modelo
Nos apoyábamos en momentos difíciles. (apoyarse)

1. _____ con todo. (ayudarse)
2. _____ muy bien. (entenderse)
3. _____ secretos. (contarse)
4. _____ muy bien. (conocerse)
5. _____ todos los días. (hablarse)
6. _____ muy bien. (llevarse)
7. No _____ frecuentemente. (pelearse)
8. Y cuando nos peleábamos, _____. (perdonarse)
9. _____ para ir a pasear. (telefonearse)
10. _____ si no podíamos vernos. (quejarse)

Teaching All Students

Extra Help Have students complete the following sentence using the verbs in parentheses and giving a reason: **Mis amigos y yo (ayudarse, contarse chismes, escribirse, pelearse, telefonearse) cuando...**

Native Speakers Have students talk about their **padrino** or **madrina** and the role that person plays in their life.

Multiple Intelligences

Intrapersonal Have students write a 1-paragraph diary entry about their relationships with friends and/or family members. They should use the **Vocabulario** on p. 86.

ACTIVIDAD **8** **Objective:** Controlled practice Reflexive verbs used reciprocally in reading

Answers
1. b
2. f
3. a
4. d
5. e
6. h
7. g
8. c

ACTIVIDAD **9** **Objective:** Controlled practice Reflexive verbs used reciprocally in writing
♻ **Imperfect tense**

Answers
1. Nos ayudábamos
2. Nos entendíamos
3. Nos contábamos
4. Nos conocíamos
5. Nos hablábamos
6. Nos llevábamos
7. nos peleábamos
8. nos perdonábamos
9. Nos telefoneábamos
10. Nos quejábamos

Block Schedule

Peer Teaching Have students imagine that they are teachers. Half the class will have to explain the use of reflexive verbs to describe a person doing something that involves himself/herself. The other half will have to explain the reciprocal use of reflexives. Have them prepare a short lesson that includes examples and a short 3-item exercise. Then pair up students from each half to present their lesson and exercise to their partner. (For additional activities, see **Block Scheduling Copymasters**.)

Teaching Resource Options

Print

Block Scheduling Copymasters
Unit 1 Resource Book
 Information Gap Activities, p. 183
 Absent Student Copymasters, p. 191

Audiovisual

OHT 44 (Quick Start), 49 (Grammar)

Technology

Online Workbook, U1E3
Take-Home Tutor CD-ROM, U1E3

10 Objective: Transitional practice
Reflexive verbs used reciprocally
in conversation

Answers will vary.

11 Objective: Open-ended practice
Reflexive verbs used reciprocally

Answers will vary.

Quick Wrap-up

Draw stick figures on the board or on
an OHT to demonstrate various
reflexive verbs from pp. 84 and 86.
Have students guess the verb and
make a sentence for each picture.

---

10 Entre nosotros

Hablar/Escribir Tú y tu
compañero(a) comentan
sobre las relaciones entre
varios amigos y compañeros
de clase. ¿Qué dicen?

> **modelo**
>
> *Están en comunicación constante.
> (telefonearse)*
>
> **Tú:** *¿Sabías que Juan y Olga están
> en comunicación constante?*
>
> **Compañero(a):** *Sí, se telefonean
> todos los días.*

1. A veces se pelean por algo
   muy tonto. (perdonarse)
2. Nos conocemos desde
   muy pequeñas.
   (entenderse)
3. Son amigos por
   correspondencia de
   Internet. (escribirse)
4. Casi nunca se hablan.
   (odiarse)
5. No somos buenos amigos.
   (llevarse mal)
6. Salen juntos los fines de
   semana. (verse)
7. No vemos las cosas de la
   misma manera. (pelearse)
8. Cuando necesito ayuda, yo
   lo llamo a él. (apoyarse)

---

11 Las relaciones

Hablar/Escribir Las relaciones son muy importantes en la
vida. ¿Cómo se sienten algunas personas en tu vida hacia
otras? Di cómo se sienten cuatro pares de personas y luego
explica por qué se sienten así.

> **modelo**
>
> *Mi prima y yo nos entendemos muy bien. Somos de la misma edad.*
>
> *Mis hermanos se pelean frecuentemente. Siempre quieren usar
> la computadora al mismo tiempo.*

nombre y yo
nombre y nombre

ayudarse
entenderse
escribirse
conocerse bien/mal
pelearse/no pelearse
 frecuentemente
quererse
telefonearse
¿...?

More Practice: **Más comunicación** *p. R5*

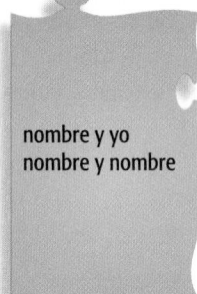

Nota cultural

Sammy Sosa es un beisbolista dominicano. Al
igual que Mark McGwire, se ha destacado por romper
récords y anotar un sinnúmero de jonrones. A pesar de
jugar en diferentes equipos, los dos son buenos amigos.
Sammy Sosa además creó la Fundación que lleva su
nombre para ayudar a los niños necesitados de
Chicago y de la República Dominicana. En
1999 fue reconocido como el Hombre del
Año durante los Players Choice Awards.

---

88 ochenta y ocho
Unidad 1

Classroom Community

Paired Activity Have the students who are working
in pairs for **Actividad 10** write 4 more items to continue
the activity. Tell pairs to exchange items with another
pair and complete the new items orally.

Portfolio Have students write a paragraph about
their best friend or a favorite family member. They
should use as many words as possible from the
Vocabulario on pp. 84 and 86.

Rubric A = 13–15 pts. **B** = 10–12 pts. **C** = 7–9 pts. **D** = 4–6 pts. **F** = < 4 pts.

Writing criteria	Scale
Vocabulary use	1 2 3 4 5
Correct use of reflexive pronouns	1 2 3 4 5
Spelling accuracy	1 2 3 4 5

REPASO Impersonal Constructions with **se**

You can use the pronoun **se** in order to avoid specifying the person who is doing the action of the **verb**.

For example, when you say:

Se alquila apartamento.
*Apartment **for rent**.*

you are indicating that *someone* is renting an apartment, but that you either don't know who that person is or don't choose to identify him or her.

When you use **se**, the verb is always in the third person.

* If the noun that follows the verb is singular, the verb is in the **él/ella** form.

singular

Aquí **se habla** español.
*Spanish **is spoken** here.*

¿Cómo **se apaga** la aspiradora?
*How **do you** (do we, does one) **turn off** the vacuum cleaner?*

* If the noun that follows the verb is plural, you use the **ellos/ellas** form of the verb.

plural

Aquí **se reparan** carros.
*Cars **are repaired** here.*

You can use this construction with **se** in all tenses. For example:

Se hizo mucho.
*A lot **was done**.*

Se había hecho mucho.
*A lot **had been done**.*

Se hará mucho.
*A lot **will be done**.*

Practice: **Actividades** 12 13 14   **Más práctica** *cuaderno pp. 39–40*   **Para hispanohablantes** *cuaderno pp. 37–38*   **Online Workbook** CLASSZONE.COM

Teaching All Students

Extra Help Have students correct the sentences that are false:
1. Se habla español en Brasil. (Se habla portugués.)
2. Se comen tacos en México.
3. En España se cena después de las nueve.
4. Se puede esquiar en Argentina en julio.
5. Se ve una película en la biblioteca. (... en el cine.)
6. Los tacos se preparan con tortillas.

Multiple Intelligences
Logical/Mathematical Have students research additional statistics for Sammy Sosa and present them to the class. They may also research statistics for other well-known Spanish-speaking baseball players.

Quick Start Review

♻ **Reflexive verbs used reciprocally**
Use OHT 44 or write on the board: Write 5 sentences using items from each column:

mis padres	verse	algunas
mis amigos	escribirse	veces
mis primos	saludarse	siempre
mis profesores	llevarse bien	mucho
mis hermanos	apoyarse	casi
		nunca

Answers will vary.

Teaching Suggestions
Reviewing Impersonal Constructions with se
* Write the sentence ¿**Cómo se dice... en español?** on the board. Remind students that they have heard this sentence many times. Point out the pronoun **se** and explain its meaning.
* Show the class ads from Spanish newspapers, or make your own, showing examples of impersonal constructions with **se**. Ask students to explain the meanings.

Block Schedule

Variety Have students work in pairs to create a list of things that are and are not permitted in school. For example: **Se permite hacer las tareas en la biblioteca. No se permite llevar sombrero.** Have students make signs for the things that are not permitted and post them in the classroom or around the school. Then have a class discussion about these rules. Would students like to see these rules changed? (For additional activities, see **Block Scheduling Copymasters**.)

Teaching Resource Options

Print

Más práctica Workbook PE,
  pp. 31–34, 39–40
Cuaderno para hispanohablantes PE,
  pp. 31–32, 37–38
Unit 1 Resource Book
  Más práctica Workbook TE,
    pp. 153–156, 161–162, 165–166
  Cuaderno para hispanohablantes
    TE, pp. 173–174, 179–180
  Information Gap Activities, p. 184
  Absent Student Copymasters, p. 192
  Audioscript, p. 197

Audiovisual

Audio Program CD 3, Track 3,
  Actividad 13

Technology

Online Workbook, U1E3
Take-Home Tutor CD-ROM, U1E3

Language Note

A change is occurring in the use of the impersonal **se** in want ads in Spanish-speaking newspapers. It used to be common to see the more formal **Se solicitan vendedores** or **Se alquila apartamento**, where it is not specified who is looking for salespeople or who is renting an apartment. Recent newspapers use the more informal **yo** form in the present tense, as in **Solicito vendedores** or **Alquilo apartamento** or **Vendo carro.**

 Objective: Controlled practice Impersonal constructions with **se** in writing

Answers
1. Se alquila
2. Se reparan
3. Se necesitan
4. Se busca
5. Se habla
6. Se ofrecen
7. Se arreglan
8. Se sirve

---

12 Chicago

Escribir Cuando caminas por el barrio (*neighborhood*) Pilsen de Chicago, ves los siguientes letreros. Completa los letreros.

modelo
vender

1. alquilar

2. reparar

3. necesitar

4. buscar

5. hablar

6. ofrecer

7. arreglar

8. servir

13 Mundo de Autos

Escuchar/*Escribir* Escucha el anuncio de la radio para Mundo de Autos. Luego, di si las siguientes oraciones son ciertas o falsas. Si la oración es falsa, corrígela.

1. En Mundo de Autos, sólo se venden carros nacionales.
2. Se ofrecen precios baratos.
3. La rebaja se termina en dos meses.
4. En Mundo de Autos sólo se habla inglés.
5. Se dice que los vendedores de Mundo de Autos son los mejores de la ciudad.
6. En Mundo de Autos se reparan carros.
7. No se reparan carros en el mismo día.
8. También se habla ruso y francés.
9. En Mundo de Autos se venden carros usados.
10. Se invita a la gente a ir a Mundo de Autos la semana que viene.

90 noventa
Unidad 1

Classroom Community

Learning Scenario Have students work in pairs. One student is new to your town/city and needs information. The other student is working at the visitors' center. The newcomer asks various questions about the town/city using impersonal constructions with **se**. The other student answers the questions and offers other helpful information.

Paired Activity Have students work in pairs to make at least 4 helpful signs about school life. For example: **Se venden lápices en la tienda de los estudiantes.** They should decorate the signs and post them in the classroom.

14 Turista

Hablar/*Escribir* Estás en Los Ángeles en un hotel donde se habla español. Le preguntas al (a la) recepcionista varias cosas. Dramatiza la conversación con un(a) compañero(a) y luego cambien de papel.

modelo

¿cómo? / llegar al banco desde el hotel

Tú: *¿Cómo se llega al banco desde el hotel?*

Compañero(a): *Salga del hotel y doble a la derecha…*

1. ¿a qué hora? / servir el desayuno
2. ¿a qué hora? / abrir el gimnasio
3. ¿a qué hora? / abrir las tiendas
4. ¿a qué hora? / cerrar las tiendas
5. ¿dónde? / comprar discos compactos mexicanos
6. ¿dónde? / alquilar videos en español
7. ¿dónde? / escuchar música mexicana tradicional
8. ¿dónde? / cambiar cheques de viajero

Nota cultural

Los Ángeles Una de las comunidades latinas más importantes de Estados Unidos se encuentra en el Este de Los Ángeles. La población de **Greater Eastside** es mayormente de origen mexicano. En las décadas de los setenta y ochenta, el Eastside creció mucho cuando vinieron muchos inmigrantes no sólo de México, sino también de países de Centroamérica como El Salvador, Guatemala y Nicaragua. En esta comunidad también viven grupos del Medio Oriente y de Asia. Es actualmente una de las zonas manufactureras e industriales más importantes de todo el país.

15 DiscoLandia

Hablar En grupos de tres o cuatro, hablen sobre las tiendas en su ciudad. Expresen sus opiniones.

modelo

Tú: *¿Se venden discos compactos buenos en Música Moderna?*

Amigo(a) 1: *No. Se venden discos muy tradicionales allí.*

Tú: *¿En qué tienda te gusta comprar discos compactos?*

Amigo(a) 2: *En DiscoLandia.*

Tú: *¿Te prestas los discos con tus amigos?*

Amigo(a) 3: *Sí, nos los prestamos.*

More Practice:
Más comunicación *p. R5*

Online Workbook
CLASSZONE.COM

Refrán

La ocupación constante previene las distracciones.

¿Qué te sugiere el refrán sobre las veces cuando sientes aburrimiento? ¿Qué debes hacer para no aburrirte?

noventa y uno
Estados Unidos Etapa 3

91

Objective: Controlled practice
Listening comprehension/impersonal
constructions with **se**

ACTIVIDAD 13
Objective: Controlled practice Listening comprehension/impersonal constructions with **se**

Answers (See script, p. 75B.)
1. Falso. En Mundo de Autos, también se venden carros japoneses.
2. Cierto.
3. Falso. La rebaja se termina a finales de este mes.
4. Falso. Se habla español, inglés y japonés.
5. Cierto.
6. Cierto.
7. Falso. Se reparan carros en el mismo día.
8. Falso.
9. Cierto.
10. Falso. Se invita a la gente hoy mismo.

ACTIVIDAD 14
Objective: Transitional practice Impersonal constructions with **se** in conversation

Answers

*Answers for **Compañero(a)** will vary.*
1. Tú: ¿A qué hora se sirve el desayuno?
2. Tú: ¿A qué hora se abre el gimnasio?
3. Tú: ¿A qué hora se abren las tiendas?
4. Tú: ¿A qué hora se cierran las tiendas?
5. Tú: ¿Dónde se compran discos compactos mexicanos?
6. Tú: ¿Dónde se alquilan videos en español?
7. Tú: ¿Dónde se escucha música mexicana tradicional?
8. Tú: ¿Dónde se puede cambiar cheques de viajero?

ACTIVIDAD 15
Objective: Open-ended practice Impersonal constructions with **se** in conversation

Answers will vary.

Teaching All Students

Extra Help Give students want ads from Spanish-language newspapers (see "Planning Ahead," TE p. 76). Have students cut out at least 1 ad with the impersonal **se,** show it to the class, and explain it.

Multiple Intelligences

Interpersonal Have students work in pairs to ask and answer questions about what kinds of things one does in other classes. For example: **¿Se leen obras de Shakespeare en la clase de inglés?** Ask students to notice each other's activities in other classes and try to continue the conversation by asking additional appropriate personalized questions.

Block Schedule

FunBreak Have students review the cultural information in the Unit Opener and in all the **Notas culturales** and create crossword puzzles that summarize the names and places mentioned. Then have them exchange puzzles with a partner and complete their partner's puzzle.

🔔 Quick Start Review

♻ **The house**
Use OHT 44 or write on the board:
Write 1 room/area of the home where you might find the following items:

1. el cortacésped   5. la computadora
2. la lámpara   6. los gabinetes
3. el basurero   7. las malas hierbas
4. el televisor   8. la ropa vieja

Answers
Answers will vary. Answers could include:
1. el garaje   5. la habitación
2. la sala   6. la cocina
3. la cocina   7. el jardín
4. la sala   8. el desván

Teaching Suggestions

• **Prereading** Have students look at the 2 drawings on pp. 92 and 93 and write down observations about them. What do they think the reading will be about?

• **Reading** Before reading, have students skim the ¿Comprendiste? and ¿Qué piensas? questions to focus their reading.

• **Post-reading** Have students complete the charts as outlined in the Reading Strategy.

AUDIO *En voces*
🎧 LECTURA

PARA LEER
STRATEGY: READING
Chart contrasts between dreams and reality in a personal narrative Maintaining a balance between dreams and reality is an important part of our growth. Do you have in your imagination a dream house or a dream room? How would you describe it? Set up two charts to compare the author's **casa de sus sueños** *(dreams)* and **la casa de Mango Street**. Consider each one from these points of view:

Interior	Exterior
Habitaciones	Patio
Tamaño	Jardín
Otro	Otro

What do both houses have in common?

LAS CASAS

la cerca	marca el límite de una propiedad
el escalón	parte de una escalera
el agua corriente	agua en casa
el ladrillo	material de construcción
mudarse	cambiar de casa
el pasto	el césped
el tubo	conductor para agua en forma de cilindro

Sobre la autora

Sandra Cisneros, la autora de *La casa en Mango Street*, nació en Chicago en 1954. Escribe ficción y poesía y vive en San Antonio, Texas.

Introducción

*L*a casa en Mango Street es una novela que narra las experiencias de Esperanza Cordero, una chica que vive en un barrio latino de Chicago. Ella quiere tener una casa y escribir cuentos. En prosa sencilla y colorida, Sandra Cisneros describe los pensamientos de esta joven. Elena Poniatowska, una escritora mexicana famosa, tradujo esta selección del inglés al español.

noventa y dos
Unidad 1

Classroom Community

Learning Scenario Have pairs of students write a dialog between Esperanza and a friend in which she expresses her disappointment with the house on Mango Street. The friend asks questions as to why Esperanza does and does not like the house.

Storytelling Have students retell each paragraph of the story in their own words. They may add imaginary details as well. Then have them add additional paragraphs, dealing with things such as what everyone does in the house, how people feel, etc.

La casa en Mango Street

Siempre decían que algún día nos mudaríamos a una casa, una casa de verdad, que fuera nuestra para siempre, de la que no tuviéramos que salir cada año, y nuestra casa tendría agua corriente y tubos que sirvieran[1]. Y escaleras interiores propias como las de la tele. Y tendríamos un sótano, y por lo menos tres baños para no tener que avisarle[2] a todo el mundo cada vez que nos bañáramos. Nuestra casa sería blanca, rodeada[3] de árboles, un jardín enorme y el pasto creciendo sin cerca. Ésa es la casa de la que hablaba Papá cuando tenía un billete de lotería y ésa es la casa que Mamá soñaba[4] en los cuentos que nos contaba antes de dormir.

Pero la casa de Mango Street no es de ningún modo como ellos la contaron. Es pequeña y roja, con escalones apretados al frente y unas ventanitas tan chicas que parecen guardar su respiración. Los ladrillos se hacen pedazos[5] en algunas partes y la puerta del frente se ha hinchado[6] tanto que uno tiene que empujar[7] fuerte para entrar. No hay jardín al frente sino cuatro olmos[8] chiquititos que la ciudad plantó en la banquera.

Afuera, atrás hay un garaje chiquito para el carro que no tenemos todavía, y un patiecito que luce[9] todavía más chiquito entre los edificios de los lados. Nuestra casa tiene escaleras pero son ordinarias, de pasillo, y tiene solamente un baño. Todos compartimos recámaras, Mamá y Papá, Carlos y Kiki, yo y Nenny.

---

[1] that work
[2] to announce
[3] surrounded
[4] dreamed about
[5] to fall apart
[6] has swollen
[7] to push
[8] elms
[9] appears

Online Workbook
CLASSZONE.COM

¿Comprendiste?

1. ¿Cómo es la casa que imaginaba Esperanza?
2. ¿Cómo es la casa de Mango Street?
3. ¿Dónde vivió Esperanza antes de mudarse a Mango Street?
4. ¿Quiénes son los miembros de la familia Cordero?

¿Qué piensas?

En tu opinión, ¿qué sentimientos tiene la narradora hacia la casa de Mango Street? Explica tus razones.

Hazlo tú

Eres novelista. Escribe los tres primeros párrafos de tu novela. Narra cómo es tu vida en la casa donde vives ahora y cómo era tu vida en la casa donde vivías antes. Luego describe a tu familia y habla un poco de tus planes e ilusiones. ¡Puedes escribir una combinación de autobiografía y ficción!

noventa y tres
Estados Unidos Etapa 3 **93**

Culture Highlights

● **ELENA PONIATOWSKA** Elena Poniatowska, la traductora de esta selección, es una escritora mexicana que escribe biografías, ensayos políticos y artículos periodísticos. Ha publicado muchos libros, incluyendo *Hasta no verte Jesús mío* y *La noche de Tlatelolco,* este último sobre el movimiento de protesta estudiantil en México en 1968. Poniatowska vive en la Ciudad de México y se considera una de las personas más prominentes de este país.

Cross Cultural Connections

Strategy Have students identify characteristics of neighborhoods. Discuss how the house on Mango Street and its neighborhood might contribute to the unique flavor of the city.

Critical Thinking

Ask students if they have ever suffered a disappointment similar to Esperanza's. Do they think it is possible to learn from a disappointment or become a stronger individual? How can a person take a disappointment and turn it around to be a positive event?

¿Comprendiste?

Answers

1. La casa que imaginaba tiene agua corriente, tubos que sirven, escaleras interiores propias, un sótano y por lo menos tres baños; es blanca, rodeada de árboles, con un jardín enorme y el pasto creciendo sin cerca.
2. La casa de Mango Street es pequeña y roja, con escalones apretados al frente y unas ventanitas; los ladrillos se hacen pedazos y la puerta del frente se ha hinchado; no hay jardín sino cuatro olmos chiquititos; hay un garaje chiquito y un patiecito; las escaleras son ordinarias; hay un baño.
3. Vivió en un apartamento.
4. Son Mamá, Papá, Carlos, Kiki, Nenny y Esperanza.

■ Block Schedule

Time Saver Have students prepare the **Lectura** as homework to allow extra time for class discussion. Give students 5 min. to review and summarize the reading in class, then do the ¿Comprendiste? and ¿Qué piensas? questions. (For additional activities, see **Block Scheduling Copymasters**.)

Teaching All Students

Extra Help Have students write down any words they don't understand. Then have them try to use context and visuals to make an educated guess.

Native Speakers Plan ahead: Bring in copies of **La casa en Mango Street.** Have students read additional sections and summarize them for the class.

Multiple Intelligences

Visual Have students design a book jacket for **La casa en Mango Street.** Display the jackets on the bulletin board. Discuss students' interpretations of the story.

Teaching Resource Options

Print 📖

Unit 1 Resource Book
  Absent Student Copymasters, p. 194
  Video Activities, pp. 251–254
  Videoscript, pp. 255–257

Audiovisual 🎧💿

OHT 45 (Quick Start)
Canciones CD
Video Program Videotape 0:00 / DVD,
  Unit 1

🔔 Quick Start Review

♻ **Music**

Use OHT 45 or write on the board:
List 3 items in each category:
• instrumentos musicales
• tipos de música
• cantantes hispanohablantes

Answers
Answers will vary. Answers could include:
• la guitarra, el piano, el saxofón
• música tejana, música clásica, rock,
• Enrique Iglesias, Gloria Estefan, Selena

Teaching Suggestions

Presenting Cultura y comparaciones

• Have students look at the pictures on
  pp. 94–95 and make observations.
  They should especially note the
  instruments pictured.
• Have students make a copy of the
  chart to fill out with information
  about Tito Puente.

Reading Strategy

Have students use the Reading Strategy
"Observe organization of ideas." Remind
them that the number of paragraphs is
often a clue to the number of main ideas
in the reading. Have students read the 4
paragraphs quickly to get the main ideas,
then read each paragraph again and give a
title to each one.

En colores
CULTURA Y
COMPARACIONES

PARA CONOCERNOS
STRATEGY: CONNECTING CULTURES
Interview, report, and value musical influences
Do you know someone who has his or her
own musical group? Interview that person.
Take notes about instruments, influences, and
the type of music they play. After reading «En
colores» fill in the same information about
Tito Puente.

Músico	T. Puente
Instrumentos	
Influencias	
Tipo de música	
Comentario	

El legendario rey del *mambo*

Tito Puente pasó casi medio siglo[1] uniendo[2] diferentes estilos y
culturas musicales y produciendo música de constante calidad.
Fue un experto compositor y autor de arreglos[3] musicales como
los clásicos «Ran Kan Kan» y «Mambo diablo». Fue también un
excelente saxofonista y un experto ejecutante de muy distintos
instrumentos de percusión. Además fue el mejor timbalero del
mundo, el patriarca de los timbales, esos tambores[4] metálicos
cubanos que son el alma[5] de muchos ritmos latinos.

---

[1] century   [3] arrangements   [5] soul
[2] uniting   [4] drums

94   noventa y cuatro
        Unidad 1

Classroom Community

Paired Activity Have students use the library and
the Internet to research a Spanish-speaking musical
artist or group. The report should include country of
origin, type of music, instruments used, some well-
known songs, musical awards, etc. If possible, students
might play some sample music (libraries often loan
CDs) or present the words to a song (often available
on the Internet).

Group Activity Have students work in small groups
to create a collage of ads from newspapers and
magazines promoting Spanish-speaking concerts,
musicians, or CDs. The groups then present their ads
and comment on each one, trying to convince other
class members that they should go to the concert or
buy the CD.

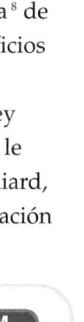

Ernest Anthony Puente Jr. nació en 1923 en la ciudad de Nueva York, hijo de puertorriqueños recién emigrados a los Estados Unidos. En East Harlem, «El Barrio» de la ciudad de Nueva York, «Ernestito» creció[6] en un mundo de boleros y rumbas que se mezclaban[7] con los grandes conjuntos de swing de la época y la creciente tendencia a la improvisación en el jazz.

Con el tiempo fue reclutado por la Marina[8] de Estados Unidos y esto le dio algunos beneficios muy positivos. Una de las decisiones más acertadas[9] de su vida fue aprovechar[10] la ley de ayuda a los veteranos de guerra[11], que le permitió asistir a la Escuela de Música Juilliard, de Nueva York. Allí estudió teoría, orquestación y dirección.

Tito Puente Jr., el hijo de Tito Puente, también es músico. Sus versiones de «Oye como va» y «Azúcar» se oyen en discos alrededor del mundo.

La carrera de Tito Puente fue una larga lista de éxitos[12]. Además, Tito Puente les dio oportunidades a los jóvenes, otorgándoles becas para continuar sus estudios de música. En esos jóvenes músicos Tito Puente vio la continuación de la forma de arte que él comenzó. Este músico genial falleció en la ciudad de Nueva York el 1 de junio del 2000.

[6] grew up	[9] right	[12] successes
[7] mixed	[10] to take advantage of	[13] scholarships
[8] Navy	[11] war	

CLASSZONE.COM
More About Latinos

¿Comprendiste?

1. ¿Qué instrumentos musicales tocaba Tito Puente?
2. ¿De dónde era Tito Puente? ¿Y su familia?
3. ¿Dónde estudió Puente música? ¿Qué clases tomó?

¿Qué piensas?

1. ¿Cómo contribuyó la vida de El Barrio a la formación musical de Tito Puente?
2. Para ti, ¿cuáles son los aspectos más admirables de la vida de Tito Puente?

Hazlo tú

Busca información sobre un(a) músico que te guste. Escribe un breve artículo sobre la vida y la carrera del músico usando como modelo el artículo sobre Tito Puente.

noventa y cinco
Estados Unidos Etapa 3   95

● **CELIA CRUZ** Se considera que Tito Puente es el rey del mambo y Celia Cruz es la reina de la salsa. Ella comenzó a cantar durante la década de 1950 en Cuba, donde nació. Celia Cruz ha vivido en Estados Unidos desde 1959. Hoy en día es una estrella internacional.

Cross Cultural Connections

Ask a few volunteers to bring in samples of their favorite music. Then have them compare this music to samples of Tito Puente's music and other music samples from the *Canciones* CD. Students should listen for differences in rhythm and types of instruments.

Interdisciplinary Connection

Music First, have students research a traditional musical instrument used in a Spanish-speaking country. Then have them create a facsimile of the instrument.

¿Comprendiste?

Answers
1. Tocaba el saxofón y varios instrumentos de percusión.
2. Tito Puente era de Nueva York. Su familia es de Puerto Rico.
3. Estudió en la Escuela de Música Juilliard de Nueva York. Tomó clases de teoría, orquestación y dirección.

Quick Wrap-up

Call on students at random to give 1 fact about Tito Puente and his music: **Digan un hecho acerca de Tito Puente y su música.**

Teaching All Students

Extra Help Have students write a 4-sentence summary of the reading.

Native Speakers Ask students to bring in some of their favorite music by Hispanic musicians. Have them present the singer/group and explain the type of music and what instruments are used.

Multiple Intelligences

Musical/Rhythmic Play some samples of Tito Puente's music and music samples provided on the *Canciones* CD. Have students compare and contrast those samples with Tito Puente's music. You might also offer students opportunities to demonstrate their own instruments and rhythms that are unique to Latin jazz, pop, and traditional music.

Block Schedule

FunBreak Bring in a karaoke machine and have a karaoke hour in class, using Hispanic songs. If a karaoke machine is not available, play CDs of Hispanic music and have students sing along. Have volunteers come to the front of the room and "perform" the music.

Teaching Resource Options

Print

Cuaderno para hispanohablantes PE, pp. 39–40

Block Scheduling Copymasters

Unit 1 Resource Book

Cuaderno para hispanohablantes TE, pp. 220–221

Information Gap Activities, pp. 185–186

Family Involvement, pp. 195–196

Audiovisual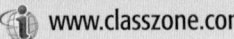

OHT 45 (Quick Start)

Technology

eTest Plus Online/Test Generator CD-ROM

www.classzone.com

Quick Start Review

♻ Reflexive verbs

Use OHT 45 or write on the board: Answer the following questions about your best friend in complete sentences:

1. ¿Cuánto tiempo hace que tú y tu mejor amigo(a) se conocen?
2. ¿Cuándo se ven?
3. ¿Cuántas veces al día (a la semana) se llaman por teléfono?
4. ¿Se pelean a veces? ¿a menudo? ¿nunca?
5. ¿Se ayudan con la tarea?

Answers will vary.

✓ Teaching Suggestions
What Have Students Learned?

Have students look at the "Now you can…" notes listed on the left side of pages 96–97. Point out that if they need to review material before doing the activities or taking the test, they should consult the "To review" notes.

Answers

Answers will vary.
1. Tienes que vaciar el basurero.
2. Tienes que desconectar el teléfono.
3. Tienes que enchufarlo.
4. Tienes que limpiar el gabinete. Está muy desorganizado.
5. Tienes que desyerbar el jardín.
6. Tienes que reparar el cortacésped.
7. Tienes que regar las plantas.

ETAPA **3**

En uso
REPASO Y MÁS COMUNICACIÓN

OBJECTIVES
• Talk about household chores
• Say what friends do
• Express feelings

Now you can...
• talk about household chores.

To review
• vocabulary for chores see p. 76.

① ¡Ayúdame!

Tu amigo(a) está en ciertas situaciones. Ayúdalo a resolver los problemas.

modelo

La lámpara no funciona.

Tienes que cambiar la bombilla.

1. Tuvimos una fiesta ayer y hoy hay mucha basura.
2. Me voy a volver loco. El teléfono ha estado sonando *(ringing)* todo el día.
3. El televisor no enciende. No sé por qué.
4. Mira este gabinete. ¡Qué desastre!
5. El jardín está lleno de malas hierbas.
6. Tengo que cortar el césped, pero el cortacésped no funciona.
7. ¡Las plantas están muy secas! No ha llovido en dos semanas.

Now you can...
• express feelings.

To review
• reflexive verbs see p. 84.

② Un día en la casa de Alma

Alma describe cómo se sintieron varias personas de su familia el otro día. Usa los verbos de la lista.

aburrirse   cansarse   desanimarse   entusiasmarse   sentirse frustrado(a)

animarse   divertirse   enojarse   ponerse nervioso   preocuparse

modelo

Mi hermanito no tenía nada que hacer. (él)   *Se aburrió.*

1. Papá hizo quehaceres todo el día. (él)
2. La profesora me dijo que había hecho un buen trabajo. (yo)
3. Por la tarde, fuimos a ver una película muy divertida. (nosotros)
4. Ricardo no hizo lo que le pidió mamá. (mamá)
5. Mi mamá tenía mucho trabajo y la computadora no funcionaba. (ella)
6. Mi hermano estudió mucho y de todas maneras sacó una mala nota. (él)
7. Cuando papá dijo que íbamos a salir, nos dio mucho gusto. (nosotros)

96 noventa y seis
Unidad 1

Classroom Community

Game Divide the class into groups of 4–5. Give each group an envelope that contains a 2–sentence description using reflexive verbs. For example: **Mis hermanos se pelean frecuentemente. Siempre quieren usar el teléfono al mismo tiempo.** The first student reads the message and whispers it to a second student. That student then whispers the message to a third student and so on, trying to pass on the message correctly. The group's last person says the message aloud; the group closest to its original message wins.

Paired Activity Have students work in pairs to complete **Actividades 1–4**. Students take turns completing the items.

Self-Check Quiz
CLASSZONE.COM

Now you can...
• say what friends do.

To review
• reflexives used as reciprocals see p. 86.

3 La telenovela

Una telenovela le encanta a tu abuela y ella te cuenta sobre los personajes. Completa su descripción con los verbos de la lista. Se puede repetir el verbo.

pelearse	conocerse	hablarse	escribirse
telefonearse	odiarse	perdonarse	saludarse
contarse chismes	entenderse	llevarse muy mal	quererse
	verse		ayudarse

Érica y Olivia siempre __1__ cuando tienen problemas. __2__ con todo, con el trabajo de la casa y de la oficina. __3__ muy bien porque han sido amigas desde pequeñas. Casi nunca __4__. Cuando __5__, __6__ de todos los vecinos.

Hay un vecino que no les gusta para nada. Se llama José. José y Érica __7__. __8__ frecuentemente sobre cosas muy tontas. Un día __9__ porque el perro de José corrió por el jardín de Érica y destruyó todas las plantas.

Olivia y José también __10__. Unos años antes, Olivia y José eran novios en la universidad y __11__ mucho. Entonces __12__ todos los días por Internet. __13__ muy bien porque los dos eran atletas y pasaban los días entrenándose. Ahora no __14__, imagínate, ¡ni una palabra! No __15__ desde que rompieron como novios. __16__ muy poco, y cuando se ven, ni __17__. ¡Ay, la juventud!

4 Se hace así

Now you can...
• say what friends do.

To review
• impersonal constructions with **se** see p. 89.

Tu amigo(a) quiere saber cosas sobre tus vacaciones con tu primo(a). ¿Qué te pregunta y cómo le contestas?

modelo

¿a qué hora? / servir el almuerzo (a las doce)

Tú: *¿A qué hora se sirve el almuerzo en la casa de tu primo?*

Compañero(a): *En su casa se sirve el almuerzo a las doce.*

1. ¿a qué hora? / apagar el televisor (a las ocho)
2. ¿cuándo? / hacer los quehaceres (los domingos)
3. ¿cuáles? / hablar idiomas (inglés y español)
4. ¿qué clase? / escuchar música (música clásica)
5. ¿cuándo? / hacer la tarea (temprano)
6. ¿a qué hora? / servir la cena (a las siete)

noventa y siete
Estados Unidos Etapa 3   **97**

Answers

Answers may vary.
1. Se cansó.
2. Me animé.
3. Nos divertimos.
4. Se enojó.
5. Se desanimó.
6. Se sintió frustrado.
7. Nos entusiasmamos.

Teaching Note

For **Actividad 3**, remind students that it is important to have a coherent story that makes effective use of reciprocals.

Answers

Answers will vary. Answers could include:
1. se ayudan
2. Se ayudan
3. Se conocen
4. se pelean
5. se telefonean
6. se cuentan chismes
7. se odian
8. Se pelean
9. se pelearon
10. se llevan muy mal
11. se querían
12. Se escribían
13. se entendían
14. se hablan
15. se han perdonado
16. Se ven
17. se saludan

Answers

1. A: ¿A qué hora se apaga el televisor en la casa de tu primo?
   B: En su casa se apaga el televisor a las ocho.
2. A: ¿Cuándo se hacen los quehaceres en la casa de tu primo?
   B: En su casa se hacen los quehaceres los domingos.
3. A: ¿Qué idiomas se hablan en la casa de tu primo?
   B: En su casa se hablan inglés y español.
4. A: ¿Qué clase de música se escucha en la casa de tu primo?
   B: En su casa se escucha música clásica.
5. A: ¿Cuándo se hace la tarea en la casa de tu primo?
   B: En su casa se hace la tarea temprano.
6. A: ¿A qué hora se sirve la cena en la casa de tu primo?
   B: En su casa se sirve la cena a las siete.

Teaching All Students

Extra Help Have students do a variation of **Actividad 4** and give answers based on what happens in their household.

Native Speakers Have students write their own version of **Actividad 3**, possibly based on a current TV program.

Multiple Intelligences

Visual Have students draw pictures to illustrate household chores. Below each picture they must write a sentence describing the scene and a sentence saying whether or not they do that activity or like that activity.

Block Schedule

Retention Have students do **Actividades 1–3** as homework to allow more class time for questions and review before the test. (For additional activities, see **Block Scheduling Copymasters**.)

Teaching Resource Options

Print

Unit 1 Resource Book
Audioscript, p. 200
Vocabulary Quizzes, p. 202–204
Grammar Quizzes, pp. 205–206
Etapa Exam, Forms A and B,
  pp. 207–216
Examen para hispanohablantes,
  pp. 217–221
Portfolio Assessment, pp. 222–223
Unit 1 Comprehensive Test,
  pp. 226–233
*Prueba comprensiva para
hispanohablantes,* Unit 1,
  pp. 234–241
Multiple Choice Test Questions,
  pp. 248–250

Audiovisual

OHT 46 (Quick Start)
Audio Program CD 19, Tracks 5-9

Technology

eTest Plus Online/Test Generator
CD-ROM
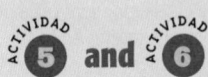 www.classzone.com

 and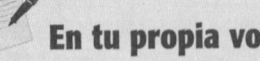

Rubric: Speaking

Criteria	Scale	
Sentence structure	1 2 3	A = 11–12 pts.
Vocabulary use	1 2 3	B = 9–10 pts.
Originality	1 2 3	C = 7–8 pts.
Fluency	1 2 3	D = 4–6 pts.
		F = < 4 pts.

En tu propia voz

Rubric: Writing

Criteria	Scale	
Vocabulary use	1 2 3 4 5	A = 14–15 pts.
Accuracy	1 2 3 4 5	B = 12–13 pts.
Creativity, appearance	1 2 3 4 5	C = 10–11 pts.
		D = 8–9 pts.
		F = < 8 pts.

---

5 ¿Qué te anima?

STRATEGY: SPEAKING

Identify feelings important in a friendship
Before beginning your interview, identify
for yourself those feelings you consider
important in a friend. Then review the
vocabulary for talking about friendship.
Finally, write down the questions you really
want to ask to know your classmates better,
then conduct your interviews.

Quieres saber qué inspira ciertos sentimientos
en tus amigos. Escribe una lista de preguntas
para conocerlos mejor. Luego, haz las
preguntas a cuatro o cinco compañeros.
Anota sus respuestas y haz un resumen
de los resultados para la clase.

modelo

Preguntas
*¿Qué te pone nervioso(a)? ¿Qué te aburre? ¿Qué te
anima?*

Resultados
*Cuatro personas se ponen nerviosas cuando tienen un
examen. Tres personas se aburren en la clase de
biología. Dos personas se animan cuando sacan
buenas notas.*

6 ¡Se odian!

Trabajando en grupos, inventen cuatro personajes
que viven en un pueblito y que tienen muchos
sentimientos entre sí. Expliquen por qué se
sienten así el uno hacia el otro. Escriban por lo
menos seis frases que describan estas relaciones
complicadas.

modelo

*Marcos y Marcelo se odian porque los dos quieren a
Gloria. Marcos y Marcelo se pelean frecuentemente.*

7 En tu propia voz

ESCRITURA ¡Vas a empezar tu propia compañía!
Primero decide qué clase de compañía es y qué
servicios va a ofrecer. Dale un nombre a tu
compañía y luego escribe un anuncio para
poner en el periódico.

modelo

La compañía DiseñoNet

Se ofrecen clases de Internet.

Se diseñan páginas iniciales.

TÚ EN LA COMUNIDAD

La´Donna es alumna en New Jersey. Trabaja de voluntaria en un hospital. Ella habla español con los
pacientes para saber si tienen hambre, cómo llegaron al hospital, cuántos años tienen, si viven solos,
etc. También habla español con su tía y a veces con sus amigos.

Classroom Community

Cooperative Learning Divide the class into 4
groups. Assign each group one of the **Repaso de
vocabulario** sections and have them create flashcards
of the words. Each group then comes to the front of the
room and uses the flashcards to quiz the class. Student
1 presents the card to the class. Student 2 decides if the
answer from the class is correct. Student 3 gives the
correct answer. Student 4 writes it on the board.

Portfolio Have students expand on **Actividad 7** by
also creating the visuals for the ad. Then have them
include the ad in their portfolio.

Rubric A = 13–15 pts. B = 10–12 pts. C = 7–9 pts. D = 4–6 pts. F = < 4 pts.

Writing criteria	Scale
Vocabulary use	1 2 3 4 5
Grammar/spelling accuracy	1 2 3 4 5
Creativity/appearance	1 2 3 4 5

En resumen
REPASO DE VOCABULARIO

TALK ABOUT HOUSEHOLD CHORES

Tasks

conectar	to connect
desarmar	to take apart
desconectar	to disconnect, to turn off
desenchufar	to unplug
desyerbar	to weed
encender (e→ie)	to turn on
enchufar	to plug in
esconderse	to hide
regar (e→ie)	to water
reparar	to repair
vaciar	to empty

Objects

el basurero	trash can, wastebasket
la bombilla	lightbulb
el cortacésped	lawnmower
desorganizado(a)	disorganized
el desván	attic
el gabinete	cabinet
las malas hierbas	weeds
el sótano	basement

EXPRESS FEELINGS

animarse	to get encouraged, interested
dedicarse a	to apply oneself to something
desanimarse	to get discouraged
entusiasmarse	to get excited
oponerse a	to oppose
ponerse nervioso(a)	to get nervous
sentirse (e→ie) frustrado(a)	to feel frustrated

OTHER WORDS

 Ya sabes

armar	to assemble
organizado	organized
el televisor	television set

SAY WHAT FRIENDS DO

apoyarse	to support each other
ayudarse	to help each other
conocerse bien/mal	to know each other well/ not very well
contarse (o→ue) chismes	to tell each other gossip
contarse secretos	to tell each other secrets
llevarse bien/mal con	to get along well/badly (with)
odiarse	to hate each other
pelearse/no pelearse frecuentemente	to fight/not to fight often
perdonarse	to forgive each other
quejarse	to complain
saludarse	to greet, to say hello to each other
telefonearse	to phone each other

Impersonal se

Se habla español.
Se venden libros.

Juego

¡Tanto que hacer!

Escribe los quehaceres indicados. Luego pon en orden las letras en los círculos para saber cuál es la última cosa que todavía queda por hacer.

1. _ ◯ _ _ _ ◯ _ EL CORTACÉSPED.
2. ◯ _ _ _ _ _ _ _ ◯ _ EL JARDÍN.
3. _ _ _ ◯ _ _ ◯ EL BASURERO.

noventa y nueve
Estados Unidos Etapa 3   99

Teaching All Students

Extra Help If a student is having difficulty with a particular concept, have him/her redo the related activities in the text. Have a student who understands the concept work with him/her to help explain the concept and correct the activities.

Multiple Intelligences

Interpersonal Have pairs of students imagine that they have to clean a house. Each student has a different idea as to what needs to be done and where to begin. Have students create and present a mini-skit in which the problem is resolved, using **Etapa** vocabulary as much as possible.

Community Connections

Ask students to find out what volunteer opportunities are available in your local area where knowing Spanish would be helpful. If this is not possible, have them brainstorm a list of businesses/agencies that might need Spanish speakers.

Quick Start Review

♻ Vocabulary review

Use OHT 46 or write on the board: Write 3 personalized sentences, 1 for each of the vocabulary categories:
- Talk about household chores
- Express feelings
- Say what friends do

Answers will vary.

Teaching Suggestions
Vocabulary Review

Divide the class into groups of 3–4. In 3 minutes, see how many sentences students can make using 3 vocabulary words per sentence. The team with the largest number of grammatically correct sentences wins.

Dictation

Dictate the following sentences to review the **Etapa**:

1. Tengo que vaciar el basurero y desyerbar el jardín.
2. ¿Cómo se desconecta la computadora?
3. Nuestros hermanos no se conocen bien.
4. José se desanima cuando no saca buenas notas.

Juego

Answers
1. reparar   2. desyerbar   3. vaciar
descansar

Block Schedule

Change of Pace Have students work in pairs to create a poster entitled **El mejor amigo/La mejor amiga.** The poster should include written descriptions, using reflexive verbs as much as possible, and visuals.

Teaching Resource Options

Print
Block Scheduling Copymasters

Audiovisual
OHT GO1–GO5, 46 (Quick Start)

Technology
www.classzone.com

Quick Start Review

🔄 Verbs like **gustar**

Use OHT 46 or write on the board:
Write sentences using the following verbs:

1. encantar
2. interesar
3. fascinar
4. importar
5. molestar

Answers will vary.

Teaching Strategy
Prewriting

- Have students generate (in Spanish) a list of categories of things they like and a list of words that describe themselves.
- Ask students to imagine how another person might describe them. Have them add any new words to the list.
- Demonstrate how students should transfer information from their lists to their word webs.

Post-writing

- Have students practice proofreading skills. Have them read their drafts aloud in order to hear as well as see any errors, then use proofreading symbols to show corrections. Remind them that they used these symbols in Level 2.
- Have pairs exchange drafts and offer suggestions to improve the profiles.

UNIDAD 1

En tu propia voz!
ESCRITURA

Presentaciones personales

Vas a representar a tu club de español en una reunión nacional de clubes en Estados Unidos. Cada participante debe mandar una foto y preparar una descripción personal para presentarse ante los otros delegados. Tienes que escribir una descripción personal para el programa.

Función: Describirse a sí mismo

Contexto: Presentarse ante los delegados de la reunión

Contenido: Información sobre tu personalidad e intereses

Tipo de texto: Cuadro personal

> **HABLA**
> **Conferencia anual de estudiantes de español**
> Los Ángeles, California
> 14 al 17 de marzo
>
> ¡Bienvenido a *HABLA*!
>
> HABLA es una conferencia para que los estudiantes de español practiquen, aprendan y disfruten juntos al compartir sus experiencias de aprendizaje y las excursiones y eventos de HABLA, nuestra organización.
>
> Agradecemos al alcalde y la ciudad de Los Ángeles por brindarnos su hospitalidad.

PARA ESCRIBIR • STRATEGY: WRITING

Use details to enrich a description Include in your profile a complete description with specific details and facts that communicate personality, interests, and activities. Each paragraph should begin with a clear topic sentence supported by facts and details. Others want information that shows your uniqueness!

Modelo del estudiante

> The writer included a **specific anecdote** to support his more generalized statement.

> Each paragraph is introduced by a **concise topic sentence** that defines its content.

> The author indicates a **personal preference** to add depth to his description and to support the topic sentence.

Mi descripción personal

🔵 ¡Hola! Mi nombre es Javier Gutiérrez, pero mis parientes y amigos me llaman «Hooper» porque me encanta el baloncesto. Me puse un poco nervioso durante los partidos importantes, pero ¡todo resultó bien el año pasado cuando mi equipo ganó el campeonato del estado!

🔵 Además de participar activamente en el club de español, soy miembro del club de ajedrez y toco el violín en la orquesta. 🔵 Me encanta la música clásica, especialmente la de Beethoven, mi compositor favorito.

Aunque tengo muchos intereses académicos y extracurriculares, lo que más me importa es mi relación con mi familia y mis amistades. El verano pasado mis amigos y yo fuimos a las montañas para acampar. Nos divertimos pescando, haciendo montañismo y volando en planeador. Nos sentimos más unidos por la experiencia y yo los aprecio aun más que antes.

Classroom Community

Paired Activity Have pairs read each other's profiles, then role-play meeting their partner at the conference. Have them ask each other questions about points made in their profiles to initiate their conversation. They may also talk about what they expect to do at the conference.

Portfolio Have students save this description for their portfolios. Subsequent writing projects will show their progress in Spanish.

Group Activity Divide the class into 3 or 4 groups. Have group members put their profiles in a pile, then have each student take one profile. Students take turns reading profiles aloud without saying the writer's name. Group members guess who wrote each piece.

Writing Center
CLASSZONE.COM

Estrategias para escribir

Antes de escribir …

Para crear una descripción completa, es necesario pensar en los detalles que debes incluir para hacerla más específica. Haz una lista de categorías, usando la lista de abajo como ejemplo. Luego usa tu lista para crear una «red de palabras» como la de la derecha. Usa el gráfico para organizar tu información en párrafos lógicos con datos interesantes y reveladores.

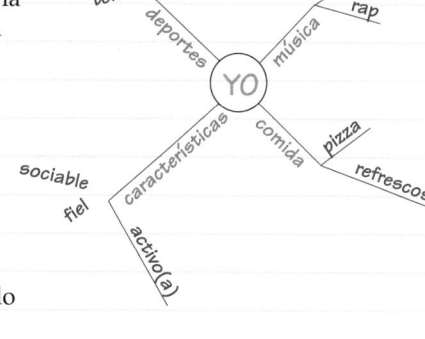

Música:	Me gusta la música clásica
Deportes:	Mis favoritos son…
Comida:	Prefiero comer…
Características:	Soy… pero no soy…

Revisiones

Después de escribir el primer borrador (draft), compártelo con un(a) compañero(a) de clase. Pregúntale:

- ¿Qué otras ideas o datos específicos debo incluir?
- ¿Cómo puedo mejorar la organización de las ideas?
- ¿Cómo refleja la descripción mi personalidad, intereses y actividades?

La versión final

Antes de crear tu versión final, léela de nuevo y repasa los siguientes puntos:

- ¿Usé **ser** y **estar** correctamente?

Haz lo siguiente: Subraya (Underline) estos verbos y verifica que escogiste el verbo correcto y que la forma concuerda (agrees) con el sujeto.

- ¿Están correctas las formas de los verbos **gustar, encantar, interesar, importar** y otros parecidos?

Haz lo siguiente: Subraya el sustantivo (noun) y el verbo para ver si concuerdan. Haz un círculo alrededor del pronombre para ver si se refiere a la persona correcta.

PROOFREADING SYMBOLS

∧ Add letters, words, or punctuation marks.

≡ Capitalize a letter.

/ Make a capital letter lowercase.

∼ Switch the position of letters or words.

⌐ Take out letters or words.

Me llamo Martina Ibañez.
Soy Estoy de Denver, Colorado y soy estudiante. Me gustan la nieve y gusta me encanta esquiar. Soy muy Estoy contenta cuando estoy en las montañas…

el anuario	yearbook
el club de teatro	drama club
el coro	chorus
el hockey sobre hierba	field hockey
trabajar de voluntario(a)	to volunteer
vitorear	to cheer

Rubric: Writing

Let students know ahead of time which elements of their writing you will be evaluating. A global evaluation is more helpful to students than a correction of every mistake made. Consider the following in scoring compositions:

Sentences	
1	Most not logical
2	Somewhat logical
3	In logical order
4	Logical with some flow
5	Flow purposefully

Details	
1	Few details
2	Some basic details
3	Sufficient basic details
4	Substantial details
5	Clear and vivid detail

Organization	
1	Very little organization
2	Poorly organized
3	Some organization
4	Sufficiently organized
5	Strong organization

Accuracy	
1	Errors prevent comprehension
2	Comprehensible, yet many errors
3	Some spelling and agreement errors throughout
4	A few errors
5	Very few errors

Criteria	Scale	
Logical sentence order	1 2 3 4 5	A = 17–20 pts.
Clear and vivid detail	1 2 3 4 5	B = 13–16 pts.
Organization	1 2 3 4 5	C = 9–12 pts.
Accuracy	1 2 3 4 5	D = 5–8 pts.
		F = < 5 pts.

Teaching All Students

Extra Help Review structures with students before writing:
- Use of **ser** vs. **estar**.
- Use of **gustar** and related verbs.
- Subject/verb agreement.
- Subject/adjective agreement.

Native Speakers Have Spanish speakers present their descriptions to the class as models for other students.

Multiple Intelligences

Intrapersonal Have students write a poem to express or describe themselves. Have volunteers turn in their poems to be read for the class. The class should try to identify the poet.

Block Schedule

Variety Have students compose a list of questions they would ask other conference delegates. (For additional activities, see **Block Scheduling Copymasters**.)

Unit Theme
Helping others and helping to preserve our planet and its natural resources

Teaching Resource Options

Print
Block Scheduling Copymasters
Unit 2 Resource Book
   Absent Student Copymasters, p. 34

Audiovisual
OHT M1, M2; 1–3
Canciones CD
Video Program Videotape 08:30 /
   DVD, Unit 2

Technology
eEdition Plus Online/eEdition
   CD-ROM
Easy Planner Plus Online/Easy
   Planner CD-ROM
   www.classzone.com

UNIDAD 2

¡EL MUNDO ES NUESTRO!

STANDARDS

Communication
• Saying what you want to do
• Making requests and suggestions
• Saying what should be done
• Reacting to ecology and nature
• Reacting to others' actions
• Expressing doubt
• Relating events in time

Cultures
• Influential people from Mexico and Central America
• Literacy in the Spanish-speaking world
• Volunteer opportunities
• Natural reserves in Costa Rica

Connections
• Science: Charting recycling efforts
• Science: Promoting the preservation of rainforests

Comparisons
• Ethnic groups in Central America and in the U.S.
• Literacy rates in the Spanish-speaking world and in the U.S.
• Ecotourism in the Spanish-speaking world and in the U.S.

Communities
• Using Spanish in volunteer activities
• Using Spanish with other students

MÉXICO
MÉXICO, D.F.

GUATEMALA   HONDURAS
GUATEMALA   TEGUCIGALPA
             NICARAGUA
SAN SALVADOR   MANAGUA
EL SALVADOR
             SAN JOSÉ   PANAMÁ
             COSTA RICA   PANAMÁ

MÉXICO
MARÍA IZQUIERDO (1902–1955)
Es una de las artistas más importantes de México. Sus pinturas tratan costumbres y escenas rurales. ¿Qué temas de la comunidad se ven en esta pintura?

INTERNET Preview
CLASSZONE.COM
• More About Mexico   • Flashcards
  and Central America   • Writing Center
• Webquest   • Online Workbook
• Self-Check Quizzes
        • eEdition Plus Onine

102

Classroom Community

Group Activity Have groups of students draw a large outline map of Mexico and Central America. Then have them display information from pp. 102–103 on the map. They can use flags, drawings, etc., but the information should point to specific places on the map. Students can add other information they already know, and continue to add information as they work through the unit.

Game As a class, brainstorm additional information students know about Mexico and Central America. Topics may include politics, sports, arts, literature, or music. Then divide the class into 4 teams. Have students study the information in the **Almanaque** and the additional information. Then ask questions. The first student to raise his/her hand gets to answer. The team with the most points wins. Have a prize for the winning team.

ALMANAQUE CULTURAL

POBLACIÓN: México: 101.879.171, Centroamérica: 37.240.008

ALTURA: 4211m sobre el nivel del mar, Volcán Tajumulco, Guatemala (punto más alto)

CLIMA: (más alta) 82°F (28°C) Panamá, Panamá, (más baja) 63°F (18°C) Ciudad de México, México

COMIDA TÍPICA: Tamales, pupusas, cebiche

GENTE FAMOSA DE MÉXICO Y CENTROAMÉRICA:
María Izquierdo (artista), Óscar Arias (político), Juan José, Arreola (escritor), Rigoberta Menchu (activista)

 VIDEO DVD Mira el video para más información.

 CLASSZONE.COM
More About Mexico and Central America

RUINAS DE COPÁN

HONDURAS
RUINAS DE COPÁN En el siglo XX, la O.N.U *(U.N.)* declaró que las Ruinas de Copán son «patrimonio universal de la humanidad». ¿Por qué crees que esta declaración es importante?

¡Protege la selva tropical!

CENTROAMÉRICA
¡PROTEGE LA SELVA TROPICAL! Animales como éste y árboles bellos viven en la selva tropical. ¿Cómo puedes protegerlos?

COSTA RICA
ÓSCAR ARIAS ganó un premio por trabajar para proteger el medio ambiente. ¿Qué otras personas famosas protegen el medio ambiente?

GUATEMALA
TEJIDOS GUATEMALTECOS Los tejidos de Guatemala se hacen desde hace cientos de años. ¿Qué aspecto de la cultura indígena crees que represente este tejido?

MÉXICO Y CENTROAMÉRICA
CEBICHE MIXTO El cebiche es un plato de camarones y pescado en salsa de limón. Mira el mapa. ¿Por qué crees que el cebiche es popular en México y Centroamérica?

103

UNIDAD 2
Cultural Opener

Teaching Suggestion
Previewing the Unit
Tell students that this unit centers on Mexico City and Central America. Ask students to scan these two pages for 15 seconds, then close their books and tell you what they remember. The cultural video is available for expansion.

Culture Highlights

● **MARÍA IZQUIERDO** En 1930, María Izquierdo fue la primera mujer mexicana en tener una exposición en Nueva York. Su pintura en la página 100 muestra los temas de la devoción familiar y la armonía con la naturaleza.

● **¡PROTEGE LA SELVA TROPICAL!** Según World Conservation Monitoring Centre, el **oso hormiguero** está en peligro de extinción en Centroamérica.

● **TEJIDOS GUATEMALTECOS** La mayoría de los tejedores en Guatemala son mujeres. Muchos de sus tejidos muestran animales simbólicos. Los diseños más abstractos a menudo indican el pueblo o la tribu de origen.

● **RUINAS DE COPÁN** Esta ciudad maya en el oeste de Honduras floreció desde 300 d.C. hasta el 900 d.C. Las ruinas incluyen la Escalera Jeroglífica, con casi 2.000 glifos.

● **CEBICHE MIXTO** El cebiche mixto incluye varios tipos de pescado. Generalmente se hace de pescado de carne suave que se deja marinar en una mezcla de limón, ajo, sal y pimienta. A veces se le añade cebollas.

● **OSCAR ARIAS** Oscar Arias fue el presidente de Costa Rica de 1986 a 1990. Ganó el Premio Nóbel de la Paz en 1987 por sus esfuerzos a favor de la paz en Centroamérica en un momento de guerra.

Block Schedule
Reference Lists Have students compile lists of facts about Mexico and Central America, especially facts about ecology and conservation. Use these lists for projects and discussion. (For additional activities, see **Block Scheduling Copymasters**.)

Teaching All Students

Extra Help Have students work in pairs to read the culture notes and guess meanings of words they don't understand based on context and photos.

Native Speakers Have students write a complete description of the painting by María Izquierdo or the ruins of Copán. Then have them present the descriptions to the class, explaining words that other students might not know.

Multiple Intelligences

Visual Ask students to draw a picture in the style of María Izquierdo. The theme should be that of family life, traditions, or harmony with nature.

Standards for Foreign Language Learning
The Communication standard is the focus for this unit.

Communication

Standard 1.1 Students engage in conversations, provide and obtain information, express feelings and emotions, and exchange opinions.

Standard 1.2 Students understand and interpret written and spoken language on a variey of topics.

Standard 1.3 Students present information, concepts, and ideas to an audience of listeners or readers on a variety of topics.

Teaching Resource Options

Print
Block Scheduling Copymasters

Audiovisual
Poster

Technology
www.classzone.com

U N I D A D

2

¡EL MUNDO ES NUESTRO!

- Comunicación

- Culturas

- Conexiones

- Comparaciones

- Comunidades

Webquest
CLASSZONE.COM

Explore communication in Mexico and Central America through guided Web activities.

104

Comunicación en acción Estas personas están discutiendo un tema importante. ¿Crees que están de acuerdo? ¿Por qué?

Comunicación

¿Te gusta expresar tus opiniones? ¿Cómo reacciones al oír opiniones opuestas a las tuyas? ¿Te interesa hacer sugerencias y buscar soluciones a los problemas del mundo?

Leer es poder

Campaña Nacional de Alfabetización, Ministerio Nicaragüense de Educación

Comunidades

En esta unidad hablaremos de nuestras oportunidades para servir a la comunidad. Conoceremos a un alumno de Washington que sirve a la comunidad usando el español en su trabajo de voluntario. ¿Cómo ayudan los alumnos de las fotos?

Classroom Community

Paired Activity The title of this unit is **¡El mundo es nuestro!** With a partner have the students share three things that are positive about where they live (either their home or their community) and three things they would like to improve in their personal world.

Group Activity Divide the class into several groups. As a preview of this unit, have students make a list of world topics that they feel need our attention. Then have them suggest actions that can be taken to help with those issues. Have them prioritize their initiatives. Where appropriate, they can mark on a world map with pushpins where global efforts are needed, such as the rain forest in Brazil.

EL RIO ES FUENTE DE VIDA
NO CONTAMINE

joven, ¡participa!
concierto de rock al aire libre

El grupo internacional de artistas
voces del mundo

presenta un concierto
para hacer de la Ciudad de
México un mejor lugar para
vivir y unir la comunidad.

¿Cuándo?
El sábado 20 de junio
a las 8:00

¿Dónde?
Ciudad de México, D.F.

NOS VEMOS ALLÍ

Comparaciones

En tu opinión, ¿cómo se comparan las
preocupaciones de los jóvenes hispanos
con las de los jóvenes estadounidenses?
¿Son semejantes o diferentes? ¿Expresan
sus opiniones de la misma manera?

Culturas

México y Centroamérica
representan su cultura
con muchos colores.
¿Piensas que eso está
relacionado con su alegría
o con la naturaleza?
Explica tu opinión.

Conexiones

El español te ayuda a
investigar y presentar
información relacionada
con las ciencias naturales.
¿Qué sabes ya de las
selvas tropicales?

Fíjate

Observa las fotos de estas
dos páginas. ¿Puedes
identificar algunos de los
problemas del mundo
que vamos a tratar en esta
unidad? Haz una lista.

105

Teaching Suggestion
Previewing the Standard
Communication is the first of the 5
Cs. It includes both oral and written
communication and encourages the
learner to be able to communicate in
interpretive, interpersonal, and
presentational modes.

Unit 2 and Communication
¡El mundo es nuestro! encourages students
to think about the interconnectivity of our
lives on this planet. The featured national
standard of this unit is Communication, but
students should notice that the unit is also
directly related to Connections with the
environmental sciences. As you progress
through the unit, encourage your students
to begin with their own world to determine
what can be done to protect the planet.
Help them incorporate the Communication
standard in creative ways, such as through
e-mails, oral presentations, or visual
presentations to demonstrate their learning.

Culture Highlights

● **TEJIDOS DE GUATEMALA**
Guatemala es conocida por sus
maravillosos tejidos, como el de la foto
de la página 104.

● **MARÍA IZQUIERDO** La pintura de la
página 105 de la artista mexicana María
Izquierdo se encuentra en el Museo de
Arte Moderno de la Ciudad de México.

● **RIGOBERTA MENCHÚ** Menchú (la
mujer de la foto de la página 105) luchó
por la emancipación de los indios
guatemaltecos.

Fíjate
Answers
*Answers will vary, and may include ecología,
contaminación, el medio ambiente, los derechos
humanos, etc.*

Block Schedule
Variety Have the class select
endangered species and list information
about them and what can be done to
help them.

Teaching All Students

Extra Help Have students write two things about
each of the images on pp. 104-105. They may describe
an image or give an opinion about it. Then, have them
speak with a partner to share their comments.

Native Speakers Have native speakers create a
presentation regarding ecological issues in the region of
their heritage. They can use any media they wish, such
as video, slide show, or hand-held visuals. They should

include maps and images that depict what is being
done and what needs to be done. These presentations
can then be used as an organizer for the unit.

Challenge Have students imagine that they are
developers in their neighborhood who are designing
the ideal house or town. They must create a poster
persuading prospective buyers to live there. The class
should vote on the most convincing one.

Ampliación

These activities may be used at various points in the Unit 2 sequence.

For Block Schedule, you may find that these projects will provide a welcome change of pace while reviewing and reinforcing the material presented in the unit. See the **Block Scheduling Copymasters.**

• PROJECTS

Flora y fauna de México y Centroamérica Have students create an encyclopedic dictionary of flora and fauna (including birds) of Mexico and Central America. Divide the class into groups by countries and have students within each group research and illustrate particular topics. Provide standard-size drawing paper and posterboard to facilitate binding later. Reports about habitats, habits, environment, etc. should accompany each drawing. Groups then alphabetize the drawings by country. Bind the countries into a "dictionary" by punching holes along the side and lacing the pages together with yarn or string.

PACING SUGGESTION: Begin the project upon completion of Etapa 2 and complete by the end of Etapa 3.

Film or record a poetry reading Have each student write a haiku (3 unrhymed lines of five, seven, and five syllables) in Spanish with a rainforest or other ecology theme. Film or record the readings.

PACING SUGGESTION: Upon completion of Etapa 3.

MÉXICO

• STORYTELLING

¿Nos hacemos voluntarios? After reviewing the vocabulary about the community and helping others, model a mini-story (using puppets, student actors, or pictures from the text) that students will retell and revise:

Miguel y Lili quieren ser voluntarios para una organización que trae a niños de todo el mundo a los Estados Unidos para darles ayuda médica. Miguel dice: «Ahora que sé hablar un poco de español, puedo leerles cuentos en español a los niños hispanos en el hospital». Lili responde: «Pues, a mí me gustaría ayudar a las enfermeras dar de comer a los niños. Y debemos buscar revistas y periódicos en español para los padres que acompañan a sus hijos».

Pause as the story is being told, giving students a chance to fill in words or act out gestures. Students then write, narrate, and read aloud a longer main story. This new version should include vocabulary from the previous story and more information about volunteer work.

Y nuestros padres... Have students create their own stories about the reactions at home when students tell their parents they will serve as volunteers for a charity organization. Have them imagine what their own parents might say.

PACING SUGGESTION: Upon completion of Etapa 1.

• BULLETIN BOARD/POSTERS

Bulletin Board Have each student choose a different date in the school calendar year. Then have them design a calendar page for that date with a tip for what people can do to help save the planet or help the community. Collect the tips and display them on the appropriate dates.

Posters Have students create •**Rainforest** posters for a rainforest in Central America •**Maps** showing national forests or other ecologically sensitive areas in Central America •**Special guest** posters of writers, activists, etc., from Mexico and Central America

GAME

La palabra clave

Prepare ahead: Make cue cards (on index cards) for Unit 2 vocabulary. There should be 2 cards for each word. You will need 1 set of cards for each group that plays.

Have students review unit vocabulary, then play a game of password. Divide the class into groups of 5 with 1 game manager and 2 competing pairs, or divide the class into 2 teams and have members of each team take turns giving clues and guessing. In a round of play, 2 sets of players receive cards with the same target word, then compete to have their partners guess the word. They give their partners a one-word hint at a time and may not use other forms of the target word nor words that contain the target word. Students guessing get 1 guess after each hint. If the guess is correct, they score; if not, play passes to the other set of partners. The turn passes until someone guesses the word.

PACING SUGGESTION: Upon completion of Etapa 3.

MUSIC

Have students brainstorm musicians that use political, social, or ecological messages. Discuss Adrián Goizueta, a singer-songwriter born in Argentina who was exiled to Costa Rica in the late 1970s. Today he heads an internationally successful music group called **El Grupo Experimental.** The band combines classical, jazz, rock, and the Latin American new song movement in poetic compositions about love and politics with messages of hope. If possible, play some music by the group and have students listen for the group's messages. More music samples are available on your *Canciones* CD.

HANDS-ON CRAFTS

Plan ahead: Have each student bring in a plain, white cotton T-shirt. Supply crayons or paints appropriate for decorating clothing, available in crafts store or some stationery stores. Have students design a T-shirt that features one of the flora, fauna, or birds of Central America. Have students also research and present information about the subject and country they featured.

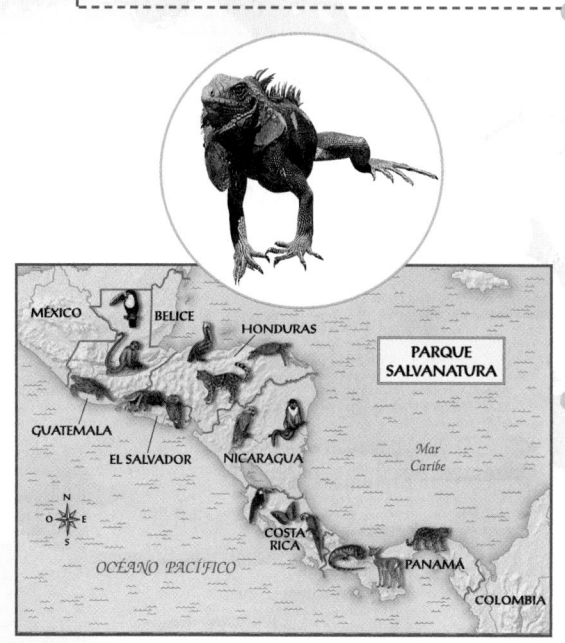

RECIPE

Pollo con arroz al chipotle

You may wish to work with the home economics department to make this special treat for a Parent/Teacher evening or a special student event. **Chipotle** is the Mexican name for the small, dried red peppers used to make the sauce. The peppers are smoked over a fire built with aromatic woods.

Receta

Pollo con arroz al chipotle

2 tazas de arroz
5 tazas de agua
3 pechugas de pollo deshuesadas
5 cucharadas de aceite
1 1/2 cucharaditas de chipotle seco, al gusto
1 pimiento verde
1 pimiento rojo
1 cebolla mediana

4 dientes de ajo
1 cucharadita de comino molido
1 cucharada de sal, al gusto
1/4 cucharadita de chile molido
1/8 cucharadita de pimienta de chile molida
1/8 taza de jugo de limón
1/4 taza de cilantro picado fresco

Corte el pollo en pedacitos. Ponga el pollo en un recipiente y mézclelo con el jugo de limón. Agregue el ajo picado. Ponga el pollo a un lado. Pique los pimientos y la cebolla y póngalos a un lado. Prepare el arroz con agua. Cuando el arroz esté casi listo, caliente el aceite rápidamente en una sartén y fría el pollo, la cebolla, los pimientos, el ajo, el cilantro y todos los demás ingredientes. Cuando el pollo esté cocido, mézclelo con el arroz y revuélvalos. Sirva caliente. Para 6 personas.

Planning Guide CLASSROOM MANAGEMENT

OBJECTIVES

Communication
- Say what you want to do *pp. 110–111*
- Make requests *pp. 108–109*
- Make suggestions *pp. 108–109*

Grammar
- Review: Use command forms *pp. 114–115*
- Review: Use **nosotros** commands *pp. 116–118*
- Review: Speculating with the conditional *pp. 119–121*

Culture
- México: its history and culture *pp. 102–103*
- Central America: its history and culture *pp. 102–103*
- Regional vocabulary *p. 112*
- Community help in Mexico *p. 118*
- Respect for elders *p. 120*
- **Hablar castellano** *p. 122*
- Rigoberta Menchú, an international figure *pp. 122–123*

♻ Recycling
- **Ir a** + infinitive *p. 112*
- Command forms *p. 115*
- Preterite tense *p. 120*

STRATEGIES

Listening Strategies
- Pre-listening *p. 110*
- Anticipate, compare, and contrast election issues *p. 110*

Speaking Strategies
- Name social problems then propose solutions *p. 121*
- Identify the general ideas, then delegate responsibilities *p. 126*

Reading Strategies
- Comprehend complex sentences *p. 122*

Writing Strategies
- Persuade your reader *TE p. 126*

Connecting Cultures Strategies
- Learn about the history and culture of Mexico and Central America *pp. 102–103*
- Recognize variations in vocabulary *p. 112*
- Learn about community help in Mexico *p. 118*
- Understand respect for elders *p. 120*
- Learn about Rigoberta Menchú, an international figure *pp. 122–123*
- Connect and compare what you know about your own community to help you learn about a new community *TE pp. 123*

PROGRAM RESOURCES

 Print
- *Más práctica* Workbook PE *pp. 41–48*
- *Actividades para todos* Workbook PE *pp. 41–50*
- Block Scheduling Copymasters *pp. 33–40*
- Unit 1 Resource Book
  Más práctica Workbook TE *pp. 3–10*
  Actividades para todos Workbook TE *pp. 11–20*
  Cuaderno para hispanohablantes TE *pp. 21–28*
  Information Gap Activities *pp. 29–32*
  Family Letter *p. 33*
  Absent Student Copymasters *pp. 34–39*
  Family Involvement *pp. 40–41*
  Audioscript *pp. 42–45*
  Assessment Program, Unit 2 Etapa 1 *pp. 47–70; 226–228*
  Answer Keys *pp. 242–246*

 Audiovisual
- Audio Program CD 4
- *Canciones* CD
- Overhead Transparencies M1–M5; 2, 5–18
- Word Tiles U2E1

 Technology
- eEdition Plus Online/eEdition CD-ROM
- Easy Planner Plus Online/Easy Planner CD-ROM
- eTest Plus Online/Test Generator CD-ROM
- Online Workbook
- Take-Home Tutor CD-ROM
- www.classzone.com

Assessment Program Options
- Unit 2 Resource Book
  Vocabulary Quizzes
  Grammar Quizzes
  Etapa Exam Forms A and B
  Examen para hispanohablantes
  Portfolio Assessment
  Multiple Choice Test Questions
- Audio Program CD 19
- eTest Plus Online/Test Generator CD-ROM

Native Speakers
- *Cuaderno para hispanohablantes* PE *pp. 41–48*
- *Cuaderno para hispanohablantes* TE (Unit 2 Resource Book)
- *Examen para hispanohablantes* (Unit 2 Resource Book)
- Audio Program *(Para hispanohablantes)* CD 4, CD 19
- Audioscript (Unit 2 Resource Book

Student Text
Listening Activity Scripts

 **Situaciones** *pages 110–111*

• CD 4

Sra. Chávez:	Mi campaña se centra en los servicios sociales. Creo que es muy importante dedicar la mayoría de los fondos al problema de la gente sin hogar y de los ancianos sin familia para cuidarlos.
Sr. Herrera:	Y, ¿no cree usted que mantener limpia nuestra ciudad es un problema?
Sra. Chávez:	Sí, señor Herrera, pero no es un problema grave.
Sr. Herrera:	No estoy de acuerdo, señora Chávez. Tener una ciudad limpia y bella es muy importante para los ciudadanos. Yo estoy a favor de la campaña para embellecer la ciudad.
Sra. Chávez:	No es que yo esté en contra de esa campaña, Sr. Herrera, pero creo que la gente es más importante que ¡los árboles!
Sr. Herrera:	Usted quiere usar todos los fondos municipales para los centros de la comunidad y los comedores de beneficencia. ¡Hay otras cosas que importan también!
Sra. Chávez:	¿Cómo qué, señor Herrera?
Sr. Herrera:	Hay negocios que necesitan dinero. Podemos ayudar a esos negocios, dándoles el dinero para crear más trabajos en la ciudad. Si hay más trabajos, entonces la gente sin hogar no necesitaría los comedores de beneficencia.
Sra. Chávez:	¡Esos negocios pueden pedirle el dinero a los bancos!
Sr. Herrera:	Ayudar a los negocios y cortar los servicios sociales es un mejor uso de los fondos.
Sra. Chávez:	En eso nunca vamos a estar de acuerdo. Estoy totalmente en contra de eliminar los servicios sociales.
Sr. Herrera:	Eso está claro, señora Chávez.
Sra. Chávez:	El otro problema serio en nuestra comunidad es el prejuicio. Yo creo que debemos educar al público y poner fin al prejuicio. Tenemos que aprender a convivir con nuestros vecinos de otras culturas.
Sr. Herrera:	Sus intenciones son honorables, señora Chávez, pero le digo que hay mejor usos para los fondos. Lo que necesitamos es más trabajos...
Moderador:	Se nos ha acabado el tiempo, señora Chávez y señor Herrera. Muchas gracias por sus opiniones.

5  La clase de ejercicio *page 115*

1. Haga ejercicio tres veces a la semana. Se sentirá mejor.
2. Manténganse sanos. Es importante para la salud.
3. Estire las piernas antes de hacer ejercicio.
4. No te acuestes tan tarde. Necesitas dormir más.
5. Relájate, Víctor. Estás muy tenso.
6. No levante pesas hoy, Sr. García.
7. Corran una milla por día por lo menos.

12 Costa Rica *page 120*

¡Me encanta este campo! Hay tanto que hacer. En todos los años que hemos venido aquí, no hemos tenido la oportunidad de hacer todo lo que queremos hacer.

1. Yo dije que este año, acamparía junto al mar.
2. El año pasado, mi hermana y yo navegamos en tabla de vela.
3. Mi primo Juan dijo que él haría surfing.
4. Mamá dijo que ella haría alpinismo.
5. Mis padres dijeron que este año escalarían montañas.
6. El año pasado, mis hermanas esquiaron en el agua. ¡Les gustó mucho!
7. Mi prima Ana levantó pesas todos los días la última vez que estuvimos aquí.
8. Papá dijo que si había tiempo, pescaría en alta mar.

Quick Start Review Answers

p. 110 Vocabulary review
Answers will vary.
Answers could include:
1. Los árboles embellecen la ciudad.
2. Debemos pasar tiempo con los ancianos.
3. La gente sin hogar necesita nuestra ayuda.
4. Podemos juntar fondos para la gente sin hogar.
5. Hay mucho prejuicio contra la gente sin hogar.

p. 127 Etapa vocabulary
Answers will vary.
Answers could include:
1. votar
2. juntar fondos
3. educar el público
4. comedor de beneficencia
5. enfermos

Sample Lesson Plan - 50 Minute Schedule

DAY 1

Unit Opener
- Anticipate/Activate prior knowledge: Present the *Almanaque* and the cultural notes. Use Map OHTs as needed. 15 MIN.

Etapa Opener
- Quick Start Review (TE, p. 106) 5 MIN.
- Have students look at the *Etapa* Opener and answer the questions. 5 MIN.

En contexto: Vocabulario
- Quick Start Review (TE, p. 108) 5 MIN.
- Present *Descubre*, p. 108. 5 MIN.
- Have students use context and pictures to learn *Etapa* vocabulary, then answer the *¿Comprendiste?* questions, p. 109. Use the Situational OHTs for additional practice. 15 MIN.

Homework Option:
- Have students create a poster similar to the one on p. 108, dealing with issues relevant to your school.

DAY 2

En vivo: Situaciones
- Check homework. 5 MIN.
- Quick Start Review (TE, p. 110) 5 MIN.
- Present the Listening Strategy, p. 110. 5 MIN.
- Have students read section 1, p. 110. Play the audio for section 2. Then have students write answers to the questions in section 3. 15 MIN.

En acción: Vocabulario y gramática
- Quick Start Review (TE, p. 112) 5 MIN.
- Have students complete *Actividad* 1 in writing, then go over answers orally. 5 MIN.
- Have students do *Actividades* 2 and 3 in pairs. 10 MIN.

Homework Option:
- Have students complete *Actividades* 2 and 3 in writing.

DAY 3

En acción (cont.)
- Check homework. 5 MIN.
- Present the *Vocabulario*, p. 113. Then have students complete *Actividad* 4 in pairs. Have a few pairs present their conversations. 15 MIN.
- Quick Start Review (TE, p. 114) 5 MIN.
- Present *Repaso:* Command Forms, p. 114. 5 MIN.
- Play the audio; do *Actividad* 5. 5 MIN.
- Have students complete the exercise in *Apoyo para estudiar*, p. 114. 5 MIN.
- Have students do *Actividad* 6 orally. 5 MIN.
- Present the *Nota* and have students complete *Actividad* 7 in pairs. 5 MIN.

Homework Option:
- Have students complete *Actividades* 6 and 7 in writing. *Más práctica* Workbook, p. 45. *Cuaderno para hispanohablantes*, pp. 43–44.

DAY 4

En acción (cont.)
- Check homework. 5 MIN.
- Quick Start Review (TE, p. 116) 5 MIN.
- Present *Repaso: Nosotros* Commands, p. 116. 5 MIN.
- Have students do *Actividad* 8 in pairs 5 MIN.
- Present the *Vocabulario*, p. 117. Then have students complete *Actividad* 9 orally. 10 MIN.
- Have students complete *Actividad* 10 in pairs. 5 MIN.
- Have students complete *Actividad* 11 in writing. Go over answers orally. Expand using Information Gap Activities, Unit 2 Resource Book, p. 29; *Más comunicación*, p. R6. 15 MIN.

Homework Option:
- Have students complete *Actividades* 8 and 9 in writing. *Más práctica* Workbook, p. 46. *Cuaderno para hispanohablantes*, p. 45.

DAY 5

En acción (cont.)
- Check homework. 5 MIN.
- Quick Start Review (TE, p. 119) 5 MIN.
- Present *Repaso:* Speculating with the Conditional, p. 115. 10 MIN.
- Play the audio; do *Actividad* 12. 10 MIN.
- Do *Actividad* 13 orally. 5 MIN.
- Present the Speaking Strategy, p. 121. Have students do *Actividad* 14 in pairs. 10 MIN.
- Use an expansion activity from TE pp. 120–121 for variety. 5 MIN.

Homework Option:
- Have students complete *Actividad* 13 in writing. *Más práctica* Workbook, pp. 47–48. *Cuaderno para hispanohablantes*, p. 46.

DAY 6

En acción (cont.)
- Check homework. 5 MIN.
- Have students complete *Actividad* 15 in groups. Expand using Information Gap Activities, Unit 2 Resource Book, p. 30; *Más comunicación*, p. R6. 20 MIN.

Refrán
- Present the *Refrán*, p. 121. 5 MIN.

En voces: Lectura
- Present the Reading Strategy, p. 122. Call on volunteers to read the *Lectura* aloud. Have students answer the *¿Comprendiste?/¿Qué piensas?* questions, p. 123. 20 MIN.

Homework Option:
- Have students complete *Hazlo tú*, p. 123.
- *Actividades para todos* Workbook, pp. 41–50.

DAY 7

En uso: Repaso y más comunicación
- Check homework. 5 MIN.
- Quick Start Review (TE, p. 124) 5 MIN.
- Do *Actividades* 1 and 2 orally. 5 MIN.
- Have students do *Actividad* 3 in pairs. 5 MIN.
- Have students write *Actividad* 4, then check answers with the whole class. 5 MIN.
- Present the Speaking Strategy, p. 126. Do *Actividades* 5 and 6 in groups. 15 MIN.

En tu propia voz: Escritura
- Have students do *Actividad* 7 in writing. 5 MIN.

Homework Option:
- Review for *Etapa* 1 Exam.

DAY 8

En tu propia voz (cont.)
- Have volunteers present their products to the class. 10 MIN.

Tú en la comunidad
- Present and discuss *James*, p. 126. 5 MIN.

En resumen: Repaso de vocabulario
- Quick Start Review (TE, p. 127) 5 MIN.
- Review grammar questions, etc., as necessary. 10 MIN.
- Complete *Etapa* 1 Exam. 20 MIN.

Ampliación
- Optional: Use a suggested project, game, or activity. (TE, pp. 105A–105B)

Homework Option:
- Preview *Etapa* 2 Opener.

Sample Lesson Plan - Block Schedule (90 minutes)

DAY 1

Unit Opener
- Anticipate/Activate prior knowledge: Present the *Almanaque* and the cultural notes. Use Map OHTs as needed. 15 MIN.

Etapa Opener
- Quick Start Review (TE, p. 106) 5 MIN.
- Have students look at the *Etapa* Opener and answer the questions. 5 MIN.
- Use Block Scheduling Copymasters. 10 MIN.

En contexto: Vocabulario
- Quick Start Review (TE, p. 108) 5 MIN.
- Present *Descubre* (TE, p. 108) 5 MIN.
- Have students use context and pictures to learn *Etapa* vocabulary, then answer the *¿Comprendiste?* questions, p. 109. Use the Situational OHTs for additional practice. 15 MIN.

En vivo: Situaciones
- Quick Start Review (TE, p. 110) 5 MIN.
- Present the Listening Strategy, p. 110. 5 MIN.
- Have students read section 1, p. 110. Play the audio for section 2. Then have students write answers to the questions in section 3. 20 MIN.

Homework Option:
- Have students create a poster similar to the one on p. 108, dealing with issues relevant to your school.

DAY 2

En acción: Vocabulario y gramática
- Check homework. 5 MIN.
- Quick Start Review (TE, p. 112) 5 MIN.
- Have students complete *Actividad* 1 in writing, then go over answers orally. 5 MIN.
- Have students do *Actividades* 2 and 3 in pairs. 10 MIN.
- Present the *Vocabulario*, p. 113. Then have students complete *Actividad* 4 in pairs. Have a few pairs present their conversations. 15 MIN.
- Quick Start Review (TE, p. 114) 5 MIN.
- Present *Repaso:* Command Forms, p. 114. 10 MIN.
- Play the audio; do *Actividad* 5. 5 MIN.
- Have students complete the exercise in *Apoyo para estudiar,* p. 114. 5 MIN.
- Have students do *Actividad* 6 orally. 5 MIN.
- Present the *Nota* and have students complete *Actividad* 7 in pairs. 5 MIN.
- Quick Start Review (TE, p. 116) 5 MIN.
- Present *Repaso: Nosotros* Commands, p. 116. 5 MIN.
- Have students do *Actividad* 8 in pairs. 5 MIN.

Homework Option:
- Have students complete *Actividades* 2, 6, and 8 in writing. *Más práctica* Workbook, p. 45. *Cuaderno para hispanohablantes,* pp. 43–44.

DAY 3

En acción (cont.)
- Check homework. 5 MIN.
- Present the *Vocabulario,* p. 117. Then have students complete *Actividad* 9 orally. 15 MIN.
- Have students complete *Actividad* 10 in pairs. 5 MIN.
- Have students complete *Actividad* 11 in writing. Go over answers orally. Expand using Information Gap Activities, Unit 2 Resource Book, p. 29; *Más comunicación,* p. R6. 15 MIN.
- Quick Start Review (TE, p. 119) 5 MIN.
- Present *Repaso:* Speculating with the Conditional, p. 119. 10 MIN.
- Play the audio; do *Actividad* 12. 5 MIN.
- Do *Actividad* 13 orally. 5 MIN.
- Present the Speaking Strategy, p. 121. Have students do *Actividad* 14 in pairs. 10 MIN.
- Have students complete *Actividad* 15 in groups. Expand using Information Gap Activities, Unit 2 Resource Book, p. 30; *Más comunicación,* p. R6. 15 MIN.

Homework Option:
- Have students complete *Actividades* 9 and 13 in writing. *Más práctica* Workbook, pp. 46–48. *Cuaderno para hispanohablantes,* pp. 45–46.
- *Actividades para todos* Workbook, pp. 41–50.

DAY 4

Refrán
- Check homework. 10 MIN.
- Present the *Refrán,* p. 121 5 MIN.

En voces: Lectura
- Quick Start Review (TE, p. 122) 5 MIN.
- Present the Reading Strategy, p. 122. Call on volunteers to read the *Lectura* aloud. Have students answer the *¿Comprendiste?/¿Qué piensas?* questions, p. 123. 25 MIN.

En uso: Repaso y más comunicación
- Quick Start Review (TE, p. 124) 5 MIN.
- Do *Actividades* 1 and 2 orally. 10 MIN.
- Have students do *Actividad* 3 in pairs. 5 MIN.
- Have students write *Actividad* 4, then check answers with the whole class. 5 MIN.
- Present the Speaking Strategy, p. 126. Do *Actividades* 5 and 6 in groups. 20 MIN.

Homework Option:
- Have students complete *Hazlo tú,* p. 123. Review for *Etapa* 1 Exam.

DAY 5

En tu propia voz: Escritura
- Have students do *Actividad* 7 in writing. Have volunteers present their products to the class. 20 MIN.

Tú en la comunidad
- Present and discuss *James,* p. 126. 5 MIN.

En resumen: Repaso de vocabulario
- Quick Start Review (TE, p. 127) 5 MIN.
- Review grammar questions, etc., as necessary. 15 MIN.
- Complete *Etapa* 1 Exam. 20 MIN.

Ampliación
- Use one or more suggested projects, games, or activities. (TE, pp. 105A–105B) 25 MIN.

Homework Option:
- Preview *Etapa* 2 Opener.

▼ Participamos en una campaña para embellecer el centro.

Etapa Theme
Making requests and suggestions for what you want to do

Grammar Objectives
• Reviewing the use of command forms
• Reviewing the use of **nosotros** commands
• Reviewing the use of the conditional tense

Teaching Resource Options

Print

Block Scheduling Copymasters
Unit 2 Resource Book
  Family Letter, p. 33
  Absent Student Copymasters, p. 34

Audiovisual

OHT 2, 11 (Quick Start)
Canciones CD

Quick Start Review

♻ Music and concerts

Use OHT 11 or write on the board:
Answer the following questions:

1. ¿Te gusta ir a conciertos?
2. ¿Cuántas veces por año vas a conciertos?
3. ¿Cómo se llama tu cantante favorito?
4. ¿Cómo se llama tu conjunto favorito?
5. ¿Adónde vas para asistir a un concierto?

Answers will vary.

Teaching Suggestion
Previewing the Etapa
• Ask students to study the picture on pp. 106–107 (1 min.).
• Have students brainstorm a list of words they already know to describe the photo: **¿Qué palabras ya saben para describir la foto?** Give them the Supplementary Vocabulary list on TE p. 107.
• Use the **¿Qué ves?** questions to focus the discussion.

UNIDAD 2

ETAPA 1

Pensemos en los demás

OBJECTIVES

• Say what you want to do

• Make requests

• Make suggestions

¿Qué ves?

Mira la foto. Contesta las preguntas.

1. ¿Desde qué punto de vista piensas que se tomó esta foto?
2. ¿Qué clase de evento crees que es éste?
3. ¿Cómo crees que se conecta con la comunidad?
4. Lee el póster. ¿Conoces a otros artistas que hagan lo mismo?

106

Classroom Management

Planning Ahead Collect materials related to community improvement, volunteer opportunities, and elections to bring in to class. Look for the following: brochures; magazine or newspaper photos, articles, or advertisements; and campaign literature. The Internet may be helpful in finding information in Spanish.

Organizing Group Work Create several ecology stations in the classroom with labels, such as **las selvas tropicales, la basura, el agua,** etc. At each station, provide a sheet to list problems and issues, and another sheet to list solutions. Students can also use these stations to practice vocabulary, give each other commands and suggestions, and talk about what they would do as they review the conditional tense.

joven, ¡participa!

concierto de rock al aire libre

El grupo internacional de artistas

voces del mundo

presenta un concierto para hacer de la Ciudad de México un mejor lugar para vivir y unir la comunidad.

¿Cuándo?
El sábado 20 de junio a las 8:00

¿Dónde?
Ciudad de México, D.F.

nos vemos allí

107

Connecting Cultures

Point out that many musical events in the U.S. have been held to benefit specific groups such as farmers or to raise money for world hunger. Have students brainstorm to recall specific events. They might also use the Internet to find out about past and future events.

Culture Highlights

● **EL ROCK** Dos lugares populares para conciertos en la ciudad de México son el Estadio Azteca y el Auditorio Nacional. Dos grupos populares de rock son Timbiriche y Maná.

Supplementary Vocabulary

los altavoces	speakers
el alumbrado	lighting
los efectos especiales	special effects
el escenario	stage
la gente	crowd
el público	audience

Teaching All Students

Extra Help Ask students a series of simple questions about the photo. For example: ¿Qué hora es? ¿Qué día es? ¿Qué tiempo hace? ¿Dónde es el concierto?

Native Speakers Have students name other popular Hispanic bands and musicians they know. Are any of them socially conscious artists? If possible, play some of their music. Use the lyrics to develop vocabulary and cloze activities.

Multiple Intelligences

Naturalist Have students look at the photo and list elements that describe the environment and activities. Have them compare the location in the photo to their own community, and list possible consequences of holding large, outdoor events on the environment.

Block Schedule

Process Time Allow students time to look at the photo and read the ¿Qué ves? questions to themselves before discussing the Etapa opener. (For additional activities, see **Block Scheduling Copymasters**.)

Teaching Resource Options

Print
Block Scheduling Copymasters
Unit 2 Resource Book
  Absent Student Copymasters, p. 34

Audiovisual
OHT 5, 6, 7, 7A, 8, 8A, 11 (Quick Start)

Technology
Online Workbook, U2 E1
Take-Home Tutor CD-ROM, U2 E1

🔔 Quick Start Review

♻ Environment vocabulary
Use OHT 11 or write on the board:
Enumera por lo menos 5 verbos que asocias con proteger el medio ambiente (los verbos pueden ser afirmativos o negativos).

Answers
Answers will vary. Answers could include:
reciclar, limpiar, conservar, proteger etc.

Teaching Suggestions
Introducing Vocabulary

• Have students look at pages 108–109. Use OHT 5 and 6 to present the vocabulary.
• Ask the Comprehension Questions on TE p. 109 in order of yes/no (questions 1–3), either/or (questions 4–6), and simple words or phrases (questions 7–10). Expand by adding similar questions.
• Use the TPR activity to reinforce the meaning of individual words.

Descubre

Answers

A.
1. campaign
2. solution
3. to educate the public
4. social service
5. to donate
6. to participate
7. to vote
8. community center
9. volunteer

B.
1. to beautify
2. poverty
3. citizen
4. to live together

En contexto VOCABULARIO

EL CIUDADANO
el periódico estudiantil

Participa en la campaña para embellecer la ciudad. Puedes...

🔲 Descubre

A. **Cognados** Los cognados son palabras que se escriben más o menos igual en español y en inglés. ¿Puedes decir qué significan los siguientes cognados?

1. campaña
2. solución
3. educar al público
4. servicio social
5. donar
6. participar
7. votar
8. centro de la comunidad
9. voluntario

B. **Palabras dentro de palabras** A veces las palabras contienen parte de su significado. ¿Qué significan las siguientes palabras?

1. embellecer (bello = *beautiful*)
2. pobreza (pobre = *poor*)
3. ciudadano (ciudad = *city*)
4. convivir (vivir = *to live*)

recoger basura

sembrar árboles

juntar fondos

Expresa tu opinión. ¡Vota!

¿Estás a favor de…?   ¿Estás en contra de…?

Sí
• comprar uniformes nuevos para el equipo de fútbol
• tener una fiesta a fines del año

No
• construir un parque pequeño al lado de la escuela
• ayudar a eliminar la pobreza

¿Cómo vamos a usar el dinero que juntamos este año?

¡Mantengamos nuestra ciudad limpia!

¡No seas parte del problema!

¡Sé parte de la solución!

108 ciento ocho
Unidad 2

Classroom Community

TPR **Plan ahead:** Make signs that include the new words and tape them around the room. For example: **Centro de la Comunidad, Comedor de Beneficencia, Sembrar árboles, Juntar fondos,** etc. Then ask each student: **¿Qué vas a hacer para la comunidad?** The student must go stand under the sign of what he/she wants to do and make a statement about it.

Storytelling Have students work in pairs to write and present a story about 2 young people—1 who does his/her part to help the community and the other who does not. Each student must explain his/her actions or inactions. Students may also make posters of "do's" and "don'ts."

CD-ROM Take-Home Tutor

En esta edición:

- Participa en la campaña para embellecer la ciudad.
- ¡Vota!
- Oportunidades para trabajar de voluntario(a)
- Opinión
- Discusión sobre las diferencias culturales

Éstas son las opiniones de dos estudiantes. ¿Qué piensas tú?

«Yo creo que los jóvenes no participamos mucho en la comunidad. Como parte de nuestros estudios, debemos hacer veinte horas de servicio social al mes para ser buenos ciudadanos».

«Estoy muy ocupado, con el fútbol, la tarea, los quehaceres en casa... No quiero usar mi tiempo libre para las causas de la comunidad. ¡Ésas son cosas de adultos!»

Oportunidades para trabajar de voluntario(a): ¿Cuál es tu talento? Puedes trabajar de voluntario(a) en...

El Centro de la Comunidad

Los ancianos valoran tu tiempo y tus atenciones. Puedes conversar, pasear, leer o jugar al ajedrez con ellos.

El Comedor de Beneficencia

La gente sin hogar también valora tu tiempo. Puedes servir la cena, donar ropa o dar clases de inglés.

Vamos a educar al público sobre: la importancia de luchar contra el prejuicio y cómo convivir con otras culturas.

¡TODOS SOMOS IGUALES!

Online Workbook
CLASSZONE.COM

¿Comprendiste?

1. ¿Cómo usarías el dinero que juntaron estos estudiantes?
2. ¿Es importante hacer algo para embellecer tu ciudad?
3. ¿Hay un centro de la comunidad donde vives?
4. ¿Qué puedes hacer en el centro de beneficencia de tu comunidad?
5. ¿Qué harías para cambiar los prejuicios contra otra cultura?
6. ¿Crees que los jóvenes deben ser voluntarios unas horas al mes?

Comprehension Questions

1. Para embellecer la ciudad, ¿puedes juntar fondos? (Sí.)
2. Para embellecer la ciudad, ¿puedes echar la basura en el parque? (No.)
3. Para expresar tu opinión, ¿puedes votar? (Sí.)
4. Para mantener la ciudad, ¿es mejor ser parte del problema o ser parte de la solución? (ser parte de la solución)
5. ¿Los ancianos valoran tu ropa o tu tiempo? (tu tiempo)
6. Para ayudar a la gente sin hogar, ¿puedes donar ropa o sembrar árboles? (donar ropa)
7. ¿Cómo se llama la gente entre 12 y 25 años? (los jóvenes)
8. ¿Dónde puedes ir para ayudar a los ancianos? (al Centro de la Comunidad)
9. ¿Dónde puedes servir la cena a la gente sin hogar? (en el Comedor de Beneficencia)
10. ¿Qué tenemos que hacer para convivir con otras culturas? (luchar contra el prejuicio)

Quick Wrap-up

Play a word association game. Say a word and have students give an associated word. For example:
sembrar → árboles, jóvenes → ancianos, dinero → pobreza

Critical Thinking

Discuss the following question: Should schools establish a community service requirement? What are the advantages and the disadvantages of such a program?

Block Schedule

Retention Have students make a list of ecological and social issues presented on pp. 108–109. Then have them write 5 original sentences associated with the issues. They should put each sentence on a separate piece of paper and decorate it. Make a **Pensemos en los demás** bulletin board display using a selection of the sentences, or develop a short TV "spot." (For additional activities, see **Block Scheduling Copymasters**.)

Teaching All Students

Extra Help Have students make a list of the words written in blue on pp. 108–109. Then, working in pairs, each student takes a turn defining a word in Spanish. The partner must guess which word is being defined.

Native Speakers Have students contact a local organization such as the United Way or the Red Cross and ask for information in Spanish. Then have them present and explain the information to the class.

Multiple Intelligences

Intrapersonal Have students write a short paragraph describing a few things that they do to help the community or the planet. As they work through the **Etapa,** they can add to this paragraph other things they would like to do. Students may also research and explore careers in ecology.

Teaching Resource Options

Print

Block Scheduling Copymasters
Unit 2 Resource Book
  Absent Student Copymasters, p. 35
  Audioscript, p. 42

Audiovisual

OHT 9, 10, 12 (Quick Start)
Audio Program CD 4, Track 1

Technology

Take-Home Tutor CD-ROM, U2 E1

Quick Start Review

♻ Vocabulary review

Use OHT 12 or write on the board:
Write a sentence with each of the
following:

1. embellecer
2. los ancianos
3. la gente sin hogar
4. juntar fondos
5. el prejuicio

Answers *See p. 105D.*

Teaching Suggestions
Presenting Situations

• Present the Listening Strategy, p. 110,
  and have students make a list of the
  candidates' issues.

• Use OHT 9 and 10 to present the
  Leer section. Ask simple yes/no,
  either/or, or short-answer questions.

• Use Audio CD 4 and have students
  do the **Escuchar** section (see Script
  TE p. 105D). Then have students
  complete the Listening Strategy
  exercise.

• Have students write answers to the
  Escribir section.

• Have students complete the Listening
  Strategy activity.

AUDIO
En vivo
🎧 **SITUACIONES**

PARA ESCUCHAR

STRATEGY: LISTENING

Pre-listening Think back
to a recent local election.
How did the candidates
try to capture public
interest? What issues did
they identify? Make a list.
Were they complex issues
or emotional issues?

**Anticipate, compare and
contrast election issues** Scan
your list as you listen to
the candidates' promises.
If they mention one on
your list, place a check
mark beside it. How
would you describe the
differences between your
local campaign and the
one you listened to?

¡Los candidatos!

Lee sobre dos candidatos para alcalde (*mayor*). Luego escucha un debate
entre los dos y decide por quién vas a votar.

❶ Leer

Lee sobre los candidatos para alcalde de tu ciudad.

Eduardo Herrera Garza

• *Es hombre de negocios.*

• *Sabe juntar fondos y
  aumentarlos.*

• *Ha servido como presidente
  de la organización para
  embellecer la ciudad.*

Vote por
Eduardo Herrera Garza
y tendrá

• **una ciudad limpia y bella**

• **mejor uso de los fondos municipales**

• **un trabajo para cada individuo**

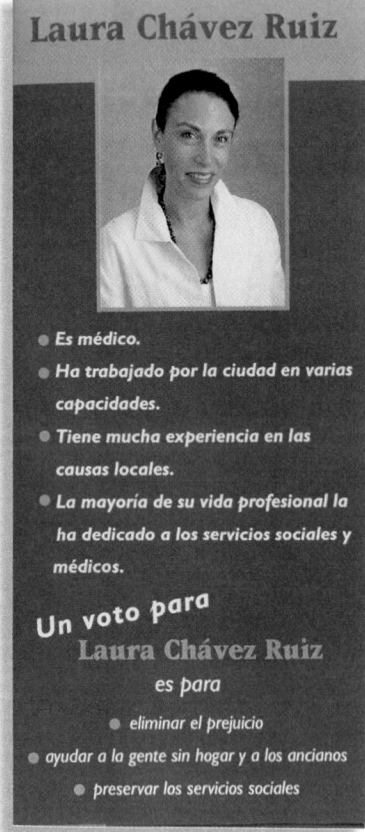

Laura Chávez Ruiz

● *Es médico.*

● *Ha trabajado por la ciudad en varias
  capacidades.*

● *Tiene mucha experiencia en las
  causas locales.*

● *La mayoría de su vida profesional la
  ha dedicado a los servicios sociales y
  médicos.*

Un voto para
Laura Chávez Ruiz
es para

● *eliminar el prejuicio*

● *ayudar a la gente sin hogar y a los ancianos*

● *preservar los servicios sociales*

110   ciento diez
Unidad 2

Classroom Community

Paired Activity Give pairs of students 5 minutes to
discuss and write a list of things that can be done in
their school or community to improve it. Have pairs
share their lists with the class.

Learning Scenario After completing the **Escuchar**
section, have students work in pairs and act out their
own version of 2 candidates running for office. They
might focus on a school or a local campaign. Students
could individually present their campaigns, act out a
debate, a press interview, or do a crowd hand-shaking
scene.

② Escuchar

Ahora escucha un debate entre la señora Chávez Ruiz y el señor Herrera Garza. En una hoja aparte, anota las posiciones de los candidatos: ¿De qué cosas están a favor? y ¿de qué cosas están en contra?

Laura Chávez Ruiz

Está a favor de…   Está en contra de…

_____   _____

_____   _____

Eduardo Herrera Garza

Está a favor de…   Está en contra de…

_____   _____

_____   _____

③ Escribir

¿Por quién quieres votar? ¿Por qué? De las causas que se mencionan en el debate, ¿por cuáles estás a favor? ¿y en contra? Escribe dos cosas por las cuales estás a favor y dos cosas por las cuales estás en contra.

Escuchar (See script, p. 105D.)

Answers

Answers will vary.

Laura Chávez Ruiz

Está a favor de…
• los servicios sociales
• educar al público y poner fin al prejuicio

Está en contra de…
• ayudar a los negocios
• eliminar los servicios sociales

Eduardo Herrera Garza

Está a favor de…
• la campaña para embellecer la ciudad
• ayudar a los negocios con dinero para crear más trabajos

Está en contra de…
• los servicios sociales
• los comedores de beneficencia

Escribir

Answers will vary.

Teaching Note

You might explain to students that **votar por** is used to express that they are voting for someone, **votar por el (la) candidato(a)**, and **votar para** when they are voting for a specific cause, **votar para embellecer la ciudad.**

Supplementary Vocabulary

el asunto electoral	election issue
el botón	button
el debate	debate
el lema	slogan
el papeleta	ballot
el podio	podium
el (la) votante	voter

▨ Block Schedule

Change of Pace Have pairs of students create a one-page pamphlet for a third candidate for mayor. The pamphlets should include the reasons why the public should vote for the particular candidate, what the candidate will accomplish, and a catchy phrase. (For additional activities, see **Block Scheduling Copymasters.**)

Teaching All Students

Extra Help For students having trouble with the **Escuchar** section, break the listening into smaller sections. Have students rephrase each section using their own words. Correct mistakes only if they impede comprehension.

Multiple Intelligences

Verbal Have students prepare and present a television ad for a candidate running for governor of your state. Students might want to videotape their ads and present them to the class.

Musical/Rhythmic Have students create and present a musical jingle for the campaign of Eduardo Herrera Garza or Laura Chávez Ruiz.

Teaching Resource Options

Print

Block Scheduling Copymasters
Unit 2 Resource Book
  Absent Student Copymasters, p. 36

Audiovisual

OHT 12 (Quick Start)

Quick Start Review

♻ Vocabulary review

Use OHT 12 or write on the board:
Complete the sentences with words
from the following list:

**convivir / donar / embellecer /
pobreza / sembrar**

1. Es importante ___ árboles.
2. Es una campaña para ___ la
   ciudad.
3. Los artistas pueden ___ su
   tiempo o dinero a la campaña.
4. Necesitamos ___ con los
   animales.
5. La ___ es un problema social
   grave.

Answers
1. sembrar   4. convivir
2. embellecer   5. pobreza
3. donar

Teaching Suggestions
Comprehension Check

Use **Actividades 1–4** to assess retention
after the **Vocabulario** and **Situaciones.**
After completing **Actividad 1,** have
students exchange papers with a
partner for peer correction.

 Objective: Controlled practice
Vocabulary in writing

Answers
1. sembrar árboles
2. votar
3. convivir
4. gente sin hogar
5. comedores de beneficencia
6. trabajar de voluntario(a)

En acción

PARTE A **Práctica del vocabulario**

Objectives for Activities 2-4
• Say what you want to do • Make requests

1 Las campañas

Escribir Las campañas siempre tienen un
lema (*slogan*) publicitario. Escoge frases de
la lista para completar los siguientes lemas.

> gente sin hogar
> trabajar de voluntario(a)
> sembrar árboles
> votar
> convivir
> comedores de beneficencia

1. Para embellecer la ciudad, hay que _____ .
2. Para ser buen(a) ciudadano(a), hay que
   _____ en las elecciones.
3. Para combatir el prejuicio, hay que _____
   con vecinos de todas las culturas.
4. Para luchar contra la pobreza, hay que
   ayudarle a la _____ .
5. Para luchar contra el hambre, hay que
   construir más _____ .
6. Para apoyar al centro de la comunidad,
   hay que _____ .

También se dice

Aunque la palabra **anciano** se usa en todo el mundo
hispanohablante, también se utilizan las siguientes
expresiones:

• **gente grande** (Argentina)

• **abuelitos** (México), aun para personas que no sean
  familiares

2 ¿Qué vas a hacer?

Hablar/*Escribir* Tu compañero(a) quiere
saber qué vas a hacer hoy para mejorar la
comunidad. Basándote en los dibujos, dile
lo que vas a hacer. Luego,
cambien de papel.

¡VOTA HOY!

modelo

Compañero(a): *¿Qué vas a hacer hoy?*

Tú: *Voy a votar.*

1.

2.

3.

4.

5.

6.

Classroom Management

Time Saver Prepare answer keys for **Actividades
1–3** and distribute them to students so that they may
check their own work.

Peer Teaching After completing the activities, divide
the class into groups of 4–5 and assign 1 student in
each group to be the "teacher." The "teacher" helps the
students to review vocabulary and then gives them a
short oral quiz to test comprehension. A practice
dictation to enhance listening, pronunciation, and
spelling is also useful.

3 **¿Estás a favor de...?**

Hablar/Escribir Tú quieres saber si tu compañero(a) está a favor o en contra de estas cosas. ¿Qué le preguntas?

modelo

¿a favor de? / la campaña para embellecer la ciudad

Tú: *¿Estás a favor de la campaña para embellecer la ciudad?*

Compañero(a): *Sí, (No, no) estoy a favor de la campaña para embellecer la ciudad.*

1. ¿a favor de? / construir un parque
2. ¿a favor de? / tener menos horas de clase
3. ¿en contra de? / tener una sola comida en el menú de la cafetería
4. ¿en contra de? / usar uniformes para la escuela
5. ¿en contra de? / recoger basura todos los sábados por la mañana
6. ¿a favor de? / reciclar vidrio, plástico y papel
7. ¿en contra de? / luchar contra el hambre
8. ¿...? / ¿...?

4 **Voluntarios**

Hablar/Escribir Escribe dos cosas que quieres hacer en la comunidad. Luego, pide ayuda a tu compañero(a). Después, cambien de papel.

modelo

Tú: *¿Puedes hacerme un favor?*

Compañero(a): *Sí, con mucho gusto.*

Tú: *¿Podrías darme una mano con esta ropa? Voy a llevarla al centro de la comunidad.*

Compañero(a): *Lo siento mucho, pero no puedo. Hoy voy a participar en la campaña para embellecer la ciudad.*

Tú: *…*

Vocabulario

Para pedir ayuda y responder

¿Cómo puedo ayudarte(lo, la)? *How can I help you?*

¿Podría(s) darme una mano? *Could you give me a hand?*

¿Puede(s) ayudarme? *Can you help me?*

¿Puede(s) hacerme un favor? *Can you do me a favor?*

Estoy agotado(a). *I'm exhausted.*

Lo siento mucho, pero… *I'm sorry, but…*

Me es imposible. *It's just not possible for me.*

No, de veras, no puedo. *No, really, I can't.*

¿Por qué no? *Sure, why not?*

Sí, con mucho gusto. *Yes, gladly.*

Si pudiera, lo haría. *If I could, I would.*

▶ ¿Cómo pides ayuda y cómo respondes?

ACTIVIDAD 2

Objective: Transitional practice
Vocabulary in conversation

♻ **Ir a** + infinitive

Answers
1. A: ¿Qué vas a hacer hoy?
   B: Voy a sembrar árboles.
2. A: ¿Qué vas a hacer hoy?
   B: Voy a recoger basura.
3. A: ¿Qué vas a hacer hoy?
   B: Voy a donar ropa.
4. A: ¿Qué vas a hacer hoy?
   B: Voy a juntar fondos.
5. A: ¿Qué vas a hacer hoy?
   B: Voy a trabajar en un comedor de beneficencia.
6. A: ¿Qué vas a hacer hoy?
   B: Voy a servir de voluntario(a).

ACTIVIDAD 3

Objective: Transitional practice
Vocabulary in conversation

Answers
1. A: ¿Estás a favor de construir un parque?
   B: Sí, (No, no) estoy a favor de construir un parque.
2. A: ¿Estás a favor de tener menos horas de clase?
3. A: ¿Estás en contra de tener una sola comida en el menú de la cafetería?
4. A: ¿Estás en contra de usar uniformes para la escuela?
5. A: ¿Estás en contra de recoger basura todos los sábados por la mañana?
6. A: ¿Estás a favor de reciclar vidrio, plástico y papel?
7. A: ¿Estás en contra de luchar contra el hambre?
8. *Answers will vary.*

Teaching Suggestions
Presenting Vocabulary

• Ask individual students the questions in the **Vocabulario.**
• Have pairs of students present **Actividad 4** to the class.

ACTIVIDAD 4

Objective: Open-ended practice
Vocabulary in conversation

Answers will vary.

Teaching All Students

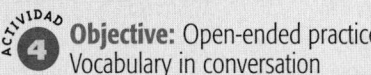

Extra Help Working in pairs, have students list ways to fulfill a community service requirement. Have pairs share lists, correct errors, and discuss ideas.

Challenge Have students gather names and resources of specific community agencies and draft a sample letter volunteering their services.

Multiple Intelligences

Visual Have students create buttons dealing with community service or conservation efforts. The buttons should include a graphic design and a slogan.

Teaching Resource Options

Print

Más práctica Workbook PE, p. 45
Cuaderno para hispanohablantes
PE, pp. 43–44
Block Scheduling Copymasters
Unit 2 Resource Book
Más práctica Workbook TE, p. 7
Cuaderno para hispanohablantes
TE, pp. 23–24
Absent Student Copymasters, p. 36
Audioscript, p. 42

Audiovisual

OHT 13 (Quick Start), 15 (Grammar)
Audio Program CD 4, Track 2, Activity 5
Word Tiles, U2E1

Technology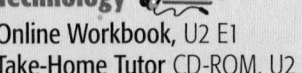

Online Workbook, U2 E1
Take-Home Tutor CD-ROM, U2 E1

Quick Start Review

♻ Irregular present tense

Use OHT 13 or write on the board:
Give the present tense **yo** form of the
following verbs:

1. caer	6. salir
2. tener	7. traer
3. hacer	8. saber
4. poner	9. ofrecer
5. decir	10. venir

Answers

1. caigo	6. salgo
2. tengo	7. traigo
3. hago	8. sé
4. pongo	9. ofrezco
5. digo	10. vengo

Teaching Suggestions
Reviewing Command Forms

• Remind students that only the
following 4 verbs have irregular
negative **tú** command forms:
**dar, no des; estar, no estés;
ir, no vayas; ser, no seas.**
• Practice affirmative command forms.
Say a verb infinitive and either **tú, usted,**
or **ustedes** while throwing a soft ball
to a student. If he/she gives the correct
form, he/she tosses the ball back.

PARTE B — Práctica: gramática y vocabulario

Objectives for Activities 5–13
• Say what you want to do • Make suggestions • Make requests

REPASO Command Forms

One of the ways to tell someone to do or not to do something is to use command forms.
The **Ud.** and **Uds. command forms** are all formed by taking the **yo form** of a verb,
dropping the **-o** and adding the appropriate endings.

• For **Ud.** commands add:
  -e for **-ar** verbs
  -a for **-er** or **-ir** verbs

• For **Uds.** commands add:
  -en for **-ar** verbs
  -an for **-er** or **-ir** verbs

El Sr. Arroyuelo **cambia** la bombilla en el desván.
*Mr. Arroyuelo **is changing** the lightbulb in the attic.*

Sr. Arroyuelo, por favor **cambie** la bombilla.
*Mr. Arroyuelo, please **change** the lightbulb!*

> Regular
> **tú commands** look just
> like the third person
> indicative.

The **tú** command has a different form for **negative** commands.

• For **negative tú** commands add:
  -es for **-ar** verbs
  -as for **-er** or **-ir** verbs

No **comas** ese dulce.
*Don't **eat** that candy.*

If the stem of a verb is **irregular** in the **yo form**, it will be irregular in the command form.
The endings will be the same as regular commands.

infinitive	yo form indicative	command form
seguir →	si**g**o →	¡Si**g**a!

Other verbs like this are: **caer, hacer, oír, poner,
salir, venir, tener, traer, ofrecer.**

Remember that verbs ending in
-**c**ar, -**g**ar, and -**z**ar require
spelling changes to keep the
pronunciation consistent.

c	→	qu
g	→	gu
z	→	c

changes before an -e

yo bus**c**o → ¡Bus**qu**e Ud.! ¡Bus**c**a tú!

no change before an -a

Apoyo para estudiar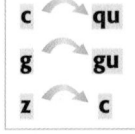

Here is an auditory way to help you
remember all these commands.
Tape record yourself as you carefully
say each of the commands with
pauses between each one. Then,
using the form in Actividad 5, replay
the tape. As you hear each
command, check the correct form
and say it. This reinforces your
visual, kinesthetic, and auditory
memory.

Practice:

Actividades 5 6 7	*Más práctica* cuaderno p. 45	Online Workbook CLASSZONE.COM
	Para hispanohablantes cuaderno pp. 43–44	

Classroom Community

Cooperative Learning Write the following list on
the board: **votar, donar ropa, educar, luchar, eliminar
la pobreza, convivir, recoger basura, sembrar
árboles.** Divide the class into groups of 3. Student 1
writes and says the **tú** command of the first verb, then
passes the paper to the next student. Student 2 writes
and says the **Ud.** form of the verb, then passes the
paper to the next student. Student 3, writes and says
the **Uds.** form. Group members should correct on the
paper any mistakes they hear. Student 2 begins the
next round.

Storytelling Working in pairs, have students write
and present a skit about an eccentric inventor who
creates a robot that does everything he/she says.
Students should use as many command forms as
possible.

5 La clase de ejercicio

Escuchar/Escribir El instructor de la clase de ejercicio aconseja a personas de varias edades. Escucha sus consejos. Primero, decide si el mandato es afirmativo o negativo. Luego, decide si él usa **tú, usted** o **ustedes.**

modelo

afirmativo <u>X</u> negativo _____ tú _____ usted _____ ustedes <u>X</u>

1. afirmativo _____ negativo _____	tú _____ usted _____ ustedes _____
2. afirmativo _____ negativo _____	tú _____ usted _____ ustedes _____
3. afirmativo _____ negativo _____	tú _____ usted _____ ustedes _____
4. afirmativo _____ negativo _____	tú _____ usted _____ ustedes _____
5. afirmativo _____ negativo _____	tú _____ usted _____ ustedes _____
6. afirmativo _____ negativo _____	tú _____ usted _____ ustedes _____
7. afirmativo _____ negativo _____	tú _____ usted _____ ustedes _____

6 Tu amigo(a)

Hablar/Escribir Tienes un(a) amigo(a) que siempre te dice lo que tienes que hacer. Usa los siguientes verbos para expresar lo que te dice. Sigue el modelo.

modelo

ir   *Ve al centro de la comunidad.*

1. votar
2. donar
3. ayudar
4. recoger
5. tirar

6. reciclar
7. convivir
8. gastar
9. sembrar
10. educar

7 Tráemelo

Hablar/Escribir Usa los verbos a continuación para hacer preguntas a tu compañero(a). Sigue el modelo.

modelo

traer

Tú: *¿Traigo los libros?*

Compañero(a): *Sí, tráelos.* o
                 No, no los traigas.

> **Nota: Gramática**
>
> Remember that pronouns are attached to the end of affirmative commands. In negative commands they come before the verb.
>
> —**Dime**, papá. ¿Traigo el periódico?
>
> —No, gracias. **No lo traigas. Déjalo** en la sala.

llevar	vender
comprar	dar
traer	regalar
preparar	prestar

ciento quince

México y Centroamérica Etapa 1

115

Práctica: gramática y vocabulario continuación

Teaching Resource Options

Print

Más práctica Workbook PE, p. 46
Cuaderno para hispanohablantes
  PE, p. 45
Block Scheduling Copymasters
Unit 2 Resource Book
  Más práctica Workbook TE, p. 8
  Cuaderno para hispanohablantes
    TE, p. 25
  Absent Student Copymasters, p. 37

Audiovisual

OHT 13 (Quick Start), 17 (Grammar)

Technology

Online Workbook, U2 E1
Take-Home Tutor CD-ROM, U2 E1

Quick Start Review

♻ Present tense forms

Use OHT 13 or write on the board:
Write the **yo** and **nosotros** forms of the
present tense of the following verbs:

1. decir   5. ir
2. pedir   6. conocer
3. dormir   7. sentir
4. hacer   8. ser

Answers
1. digo, decimos   5. voy, vamos
2. pido, pedimos   6. conozco, conocemos
3. duermo, dormimos 7. siento, sentimos
4. hago, hacemos   8. soy, somos

Teaching Suggestions
Reviewing Nosotros Commands

• Point out that **nosotros** commands
  are more frequently used to suggest
  than to command.
• Emphasize that if the **yo** form of the
  present tense ends in -**go** or –**zco**, the
  g or **zc** appears in the **nosotros**
  command. You may want to suggest
  that students use the **Apoyo** on p. 114.
• You might point out to students that
  -**ar** and -**er** stem-changing verbs do
  not require a stem change in the
  nosotros command, and that **ir** stem-
  changing verbs alternate between **i**
  and **ie** and **u** and **ue**.

Práctica: gramática y vocabulario continuación

REPASO Nosotros Commands

When you want to say *let's do something* or *let's not do something* you use nosotros
commands. Remember to start with the **yo form** of the verb, drop the -**o** and add the
appropriate ending.

• -**ar** verbs end in -**emos**   • -**er** and -**ir** verbs end in -**amos**

Participemos en la campaña para mejorar nuestra ciudad.
Let's participate in the campaign to improve our city.

If a verb has an irregular **yo form** it also appears in the nosotros command.

Irregular yo form: Nosotros command:

Yo siempre **dig**o la verdad sobre   **Dig**amos la verdad sobre los
los problemas en nuestra ciudad.   problemas en nuestra ciudad.
*I always **tell** the truth about the problems in our city.*   *Let's **tell** the truth about the problems in our city.*

Some verbs are **irregular** in the nosotros command form and are
not created using the **yo form**.

Use the present subjunctive of the nosotros form for
stem-changing verbs.

dar	demos
estar	estemos
saber	sepamos
ser	seamos

When you want to say *let's go*, use: **vamos**   To say *let's not go*, use: **no vay**amos

Besides the command form, you already   To say *let's not do something*
know another way to say *let's do something*:   you must use:

  vamos a + **infinitive**   **no** + nosotros command

Vamos a luchar contra el prejuicio   **No olvid**emos a los ancianos
en nuestra sociedad.   ni a los enfermos.
*Let's **fight** against prejudice in our society.*   *Let's **not forget** the elderly and the sick.*

With **reflexive verbs**, you drop the final **s** of the command form
before attaching the reflexive pronoun **nos** :

                                                    Notice the **accent.**
levantemo~~s~~ + **nos** ➡ **Levantémonos**   It is added to keep
              Let's get up.   the pronunciation
                                                    consistent.

Practice: Actividades   **Más práctica** *cuaderno p. 46*   **Online Workbook**
                8 9 10 11   **Para hispanohablantes** *cuaderno p. 45*   CLASSZONE.COM

116   ciento dieciséis
          Unidad 2

Classroom Community

Group Activity Have students work in groups and
imagine that they are tour guides taking travelers to a
very exotic part of the universe. They should create a
5-day itinerary, using **nosotros** commands. For example:
**El lunes levantémonos temprano y visitemos el
bosque morado. El martes vayamos a la selva de
algodón,** etc. Encourage students to use their
imagination and be as outrageous as they want.

Portfolio Have students create brochures or posters
to incite interest in the local community or school
involvement, using **nosotros** commands.

Rubric A = 13–15 pts. B = 10–12 pts. C = 7–9 pts. D = 4–6 pts. F = < 4 pts.

Writing criteria	Scale
Correct use of **nosotros** commands	1 2 3 4 5
Details and organization	1 2 3 4 5
Creativity/appearance	1 2 3 4 5

8 Hagamos algo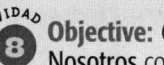

Hablar/Escribir Pasas el fin de semana con un(a) amigo(a). El (Ella) quiere hacer varias cosas, pero a ti no te gustan sus ideas. Sugiere que hagan otra cosa.

modelo

ver la película romántica (la película de acción)

Compañero(a): *¿Por qué no vemos la película romántica?*

Tú: *No, mejor veamos la película de acción.*

1. ir al museo (centro comercial)
2. comprar el helado de chocolate (de fresa)
3. jugar al tenis (al fútbol)
4. visitar a mis primos (a mis amigos)
5. preparar hamburguesas (salchichas)
6. andar por el parque (por la playa)
7. salir por la tarde (por la noche)
8. votar a Eduardo Herrera (a Laura Chávez)
9. pasear por la ciudad (por el campo)
10. donar videos (ropae)

9 El club de voluntarios

Hablar/Escribir Estás en una reunión del club de voluntarios. Todos tienen ideas diferentes de lo que deben hacer. ¿Qué dicen?

modelo

luchar contra el hambre

Luchemos contra el hambre.

1. convivir con nuestros vecinos
2. preservar los derechos humanos
3. resolver el problema de la gente sin hogar
4. consumir menos
5. conservar más
6. cuidar de los ancianos
7. hacer un esfuerzo para unir al pueblo
8. trabajar de voluntarios en el centro de rehabilitación
9. acabar con el racismo
10. crear soluciones realísticas para nuestros problemas

Vocabulario

En la comunidad

colaborar con *collaborate with*
conservar más *to conserve more*
consumir menos *to consume less*
crear *to create*
cuidar de *to take care of*
hacer un esfuerzo *to make an effort*
permitir *to permit*
pertenecer *to belong*
preservar *to preserve*
resolver *to resolve*

el centro de rehabilitación *rehabilitation center*
los derechos humanos *human rights*
el desarrollo *development*
la discriminación *discrimination*
los enfermos *the sick*
los minusválidos *the physically challenged*
el ser humano *human being*

 ¿Cómo puedes usar estas palabras para describir tus actividades?

Teaching All Students

Extra Help Pair students with a native speaker or a more advanced student. Have them write **nosotros** command sentences using the following verbs: **cuidar, resolver, preservar, mantener, colaborar con, consumir menos, pertenecer, crear.**

Multiple Intelligences

Verbal Working in pairs, have students create and present public service announcements. Each student takes a turn giving a simple statement, then a **nosotros** command; for example, **Es nuestra ciudad. Mantengámosla.** Pairs should present at least 6 statements.

Answers

1. A: ¿Por qué no vamos al museo?
   B: No, mejor vayamos al centro comercial.
2. A: ¿Por qué no compramos el helado de chocolate?
   B: No, mejor compremos el helado de fresa.
3. A: ¿Por qué no jugamos al tenis?
   B: No, mejor juguemos al fútbol.
4. A: ¿Por qué no visitamos a mis primos?
   B: No, mejor visitemos a mis amigos.
5. A: ¿Por qué no preparamos hamburguesas?
   B: No, mejor preparemos salchichas.
6. A: ¿Por qué no andamos por el parque?
   B: No, mejor andemos por la playa.
7. A: ¿Por qué no salimos por la tarde?
   B: No, mejor salgamos por la noche.
8. A: ¿Por qué no votamos por Eduardo Herrera?
   B: No, mejor votemos por Laura Chávez.
9. A: ¿Por qué no paseamos por la ciudad?
   B: No, mejor paseemos por el campo.
10. A: ¿Por qué no donamos videos?
    B: No, mejor donemos ropa.

Teaching Suggestions
Presenting Vocabulary

On an OHT, sketch activities that demonstrate the vocabulary words and ask questions. For example, sketch a large car and a small car and ask, **¿Cuál consume menos gasolina?**

Teaching Note

Remind students that **resolver** is a **ue** stem-changing verb.

ACTIVIDAD 9 Objective: Controlled practice **Nosotros** commands, vocabulary

Answers

1. Convivamos con nuestros vecinos.
2. Preservemos los derechos humanos.
3. Resolvamos el problema de la gente sin hogar.
4. Consumamos menos.
5. Conservemos más.
6. Cuidemos de los ancianos.
7. Hagamos un esfuerzo para unir al pueblo.
8. Trabajemos de voluntarios en el centro de rehabilitación.
9. Acabemos con el racismo.
10. Creemos soluciones realísticas para nuestros problemas.

Teaching Resource Options

Print

Block Scheduling Copymasters
Unit 2 Resource Book
  Information Gap Activities, p. 29
  Absent Student Copymasters, p. 37

Audiovisual

OHT 14 (Quick Start), 18 (Grammar)

Technology

Online Workbook, U2 E1
Take-Home Tutor CD-ROM, U2 E1

Teaching Note

Remind students that **educar** is a spell-changing verb conjugated like **buscar**. **Embellecer** is a spell-changing verb conjugated like **conocer**. See p. R32.

Objective: Transitional practice **Nosotros** commands, vocabulary in conversation

Answers

*Answers will vary, but should use these verb forms in the **Compañero(a)** response.*
1. luchemos
2. hagamos
3. donemos
4. colaboremos
5. trabajemos
6. cuidemos
7. acabemos
8. eduquemos
9. votemos
10. embellezcamos
11. participemos
12. convivamos

Objective: Open-ended practice **Nosotros** commands in writing

Answers will vary.

Quick Wrap-up

Give sentences that use various command forms. Ask students whether the command is a **tú** command, **nosotros** command, **Ud.** command, or **Uds.** command: **¿Qué tipo de mandato es: tú, nosotros, Ud. o Uds.?** For example: **Siembren árboles.** (Uds.); **Conserva energía.** (tú); **Reciclemos las botellas.** (nosotros)

10 ¿Qué haremos?

Hablar/*Escribir* Tú y tu compañero(a) son buenos ciudadanos. Conversen sobre sus planes para servir a la comunidad.

modelo

trabajar de voluntarios

Tú: *¿Dónde debemos trabajar de voluntarios?*

Compañero(a): *Trabajemos en el centro de la comunidad.*

Tú: *No, no trabajemos en el centro de la comunidad. Mejor trabajemos en el comedor de beneficencia.*

1. luchar contra
2. hacer un esfuerzo
3. donar
4. colaborar con
5. trabajar de voluntarios
6. cuidar de
7. acabar con
8. educar al público
9. votar
10. embellecer
11. participar
12. convivir con

Nota cultural

En México se han formado grupos de jóvenes para ayudar a la comunidad. Se conocen como asociaciones de segundo piso y su propósito es establecer relaciones con hombres y mujeres de negocios para recolectar desechos (*scrap material*) y basura industriales. Luego estos grupos venden los materiales y juntan fondos para programas sociales dirigidos a los ancianos, niños y minusválidos, entre otros.

11 La publicidad

Escribir Estás a cargo de la publicidad para tu club de voluntarios. Escribe tres lemas publicitarios para un folleto (*brochure*) que describa los propósitos de tu club.

modelo

More Practice: **Más comunicación** *p. R6*

Classroom Community

Paired Activity Have students work in pairs to discuss what they want to do this weekend, using **nosotros** commands. Student 1 makes a suggestion and Student 2 agrees or disagrees. Then Student 2 makes a suggestion, and so on. Pairs should come up with a list of at least 5 activities that they agree on to present to the class.

Cooperative Learning Have students work in groups of 4. Each student writes 3 **tú** commands on a piece of paper, then passes the paper to the left. Students change the command to the negative **tú** form, and pass the paper to the left. Then students change the command to the **usted** form and pass the paper. Finally students change the command to the **nosotros** form. The group then checks all forms for accuracy. This can also be done as a relay race.

REPASO Speculating with the Conditional

To talk about what you *should, could,* or *would do,* use the **conditional tense.**

The conditional:

- helps you to talk about what would happen under certain conditions.
- is used to make polite requests.

> Yo no **me quejaría** tanto. Yo **me llevaría** bien con todos.
> *I **wouldn't complain** so much. I **would get along** well with everyone.*

Verbs ending with **-ar, -er** and **-ir** all have the same endings in the **conditional.** You add the endings directly to the **infinitive.**

conditional ending

infinitive +		
	-ía	-íamos
	-ías	-íais
	-ía	-ían

> Yo **estaría** a favor de comprar árboles y flores para embellecer el centro de la comunidad.
> *I **would be** in favor of buying trees and flowers to beautify the community center.*

If a verb has an **irregular stem** in the **future,** you use that same stem to form the conditional. The endings are the **same endings** as in the above chart.

infinitive	irregular future stem	conditional
decir	→ diré	→ diría

Note: The conditional of **hay** is always **habría.**

infinitive	irregular stem
decir	dir-
hacer	har-
poder	podr-
poner	pondr-
querer	querr-
saber	sabr-
salir	saldr-
tener	tendr-
valer	valdr-
venir	vendr-

Practice: Actividades  **Más práctica** *cuaderno pp. 47–48*
Para hispanohablantes *cuaderno p. 46*  **Online Workbook** CLASSZONE.COM

Teaching All Students

Extra Help Write the following list of verbs on the board. Have students provide the **tú** and **nosotros** forms of the conditional: **donar, embellecer, querer, convivir, educar, recoger, tener, poder, sembrar, luchar, poder.**

Multiple Intelligences

Verbal Call on various students to say what the following people said they would do about problems in the community/country: **el alcalde, la alcaldesa** (mayor), **el (la) gobernador(a), el (la) candidato(a), el (la) presidente(a), un(a) artista de cine.**

Quick Start Review

♻ Verbs with irregular stems in the future

Use OHT 14 or write on the board: Write the future tense forms for the following verbs:

1. tú: saber   5. Uds.: poder
2. yo: ser   6. él: querer
3. Ud.: tener   7. yo: decir
4. nosotros: salir   8. ellas: hacer

Answers

1. sabrás   5. podrán
2. seré   6. querrá
3. tendrá   7. diré
4. saldremos   8. harán

Teaching Suggestions
Reviewing Speculating with the Conditional

- Point out that the conditional endings are the same as those of **-er** and **-ir** verbs in the imperfect tense.
- You may want to review the future tense before presenting the conditional.
- Remind students that the conditional is often used to make polite requests: **¿Podrías ayudarme?**

Block Schedule

Change of Pace Have students work in pairs and imagine that they have been given the opportunity to visit Mexico or Central America. They should first decide where they would go and then decide on at least 5 things that they would do in that country. Students may need time to research their chosen countries. Have pairs present their lists to the class. (For additional activities, see **Block Scheduling Copymasters.**)

Teaching Resource Options

Print

Más práctica Workbook PE,
  pp. 41–44, 47–48
Actividades para todos Workbook PE,
  pp. 41–46
Cuaderno para hispanohablantes
  PE, pp. 41–42, 46
Block Scheduling Copymasters
Unit 2 Resource Book
  Más práctica Workbook TE,
    pp. 3–6, 9–10
  Actividades para todos Workbook
  TE, pp. 11–16
  Cuaderno para hispanohablantes
    TE, pp. 21–22, 26
  Information Gap Activities, p. 30
  Absent Student Copymasters, p. 38
  Audioscript, p. 42

Audiovisual

Audio Program CD 4, Track 3, Activity 12

Technology

Online Workbook, U2 E1
Take-Home Tutor CD-ROM, U2 E1

ACTIVIDAD 12 Objective: Controlled practice
Listening comprehension/
speculating with the conditional
♻ Preterite tense

Answers (See script, p. 105D.)
1. Acamparía.
2. Navegaron en tabla de vela.
3. Haría surfing.
4. Haría alpinismo.
5. Escalarían montañas.
6. Esquiaron en el agua.
7. Levantó pesas.
8. Pescaría en alta mar.

ACTIVIDAD 13 Objective: Controlled practice
Speculating with the conditional

Answers
1. Iría a las pirámides de Teotihuacán.
2. Compraría regalos en la Zona Rosa.
3. Escucharía música de mariachi.
4. Asistiría a un concierto de Luis Miguel.
5. Comería en el restaurante del San Ángel Inn.
6. Mandaría tarjetas postales a todos mis amigos.
7. Buscaría el museo de Frida Kahlo.
8. Me pasearía por el Parque de Chapultepec.

Práctica: gramática y vocabulario continuación

12 Costa Rica

Escuchar/Escribir Cada año, la familia de Fausto va al mismo campo en Costa Rica. Escucha su descripción de las vacaciones anteriores y las de este año. Decide si cada persona en su familia ya participó en una actividad, o si participaría en esa actividad durante el próximo viaje.

modelo

Joaquín: volar en planeador

△ Ya voló en planeador.   ✗ Volaría en planeador.

1. Fausto	5. los padres de Fausto
△ Acampó.	△ Escalaron montañas.
△ Acamparía.	△ Escalarían montañas.
2. Fausto y su hermana	6. las hermanas de Fausto
△ Navegaron en tabla de vela.	△ Esquiaron en el agua.
△ Navegarían en tabla de vela.	△ Esquiarían en el agua.
3. Juan	7. Ana
△ Hizo surfing.	△ Levantó pesas.
△ Haría surfing.	△ Levantaría pesas.
4. la mamá de Fausto	8. el papá de Fausto
△ Hizo alpinismo.	△ Pescó en alta mar.
△ Haría alpinismo.	△ Pescaría en alta mar.

13 La Ciudad de México

Hablar/Escribir Imagínate que vas de viaje a la Ciudad de México. ¿Qué harías allí?

modelo

visitar el Palacio de Bellas Artes
Visitaría el Palacio de Bellas Artes.

1. ir a las pirámides de Teotihuacán
2. comprar regalos en la Zona Rosa
3. escuchar música de mariachi
4. asistir a un concierto de Luis Miguel
5. comer en el restaurante del San Ángel Inn
6. mandar tarjetas postales a todos mis amigos
7. buscar el museo de Frida Kahlo
8. pasearme por el Parque de Chapultepec

Nota cultural

En América Latina y España normalmente se habla a la gente mayor con mucho respeto. Sería mal educado (*impolite*) decir a alguien mayor «¡Tráigamelo!» Es más cortés decir «Por favor don Ramón, ¿puede traérmelo?» o «Don Ramón, ¿me hace usted el favor de traerlo?»

Classroom Community

Learning Scenario Working in pairs, have students create and present a skit about what they would do if they bought a lottery ticket together and won the jackpot. How would they divide the shared earnings and how would they spend the money?

Paired Activity Have students interview a classmate about an imaginary vacation he/she would take. They may use the following questions as guidelines: ¿Cuándo serían tus vacaciones? ¿Cuánto tiempo tendrías? ¿Adónde te gustaría ir? ¿Por qué? ¿Qué harías? ¿Quién te acompañaría?

Activities **14–15** bring together all concepts presented.

14 Mi comunidad

STRATEGY: SPEAKING

Name social problems, then propose solutions
Here are a few words to help you get started.
Issues include **pobreza, discriminación, crimen.** People who need help include **ancianos, gente sin hogar, jóvenes, refugiados.** Organizations that can help include **centros de la comunidad, escuelas, servicios sociales.** One can always give **ayuda, dinero, consejos.** Add your own ideas for being a good citizen.

Hablar/*Escribir* Eres el (la) presidente(a) de una organización que cuida el medio ambiente. En tu discurso, le dices a la gente lo que debe hacer.

modelo

trabajar de voluntarios en...

Tú: *Trabajen de voluntarios en un programa de reciclaje.*

1. votar por la campaña para…
2. estar a favor de…
3. estar en contra de…
4. participar en…
5. hacer el esfuerzo para…
6. colaborar con…
7. conservar…
8. valorar…
9. cuidar de…
10. resolver…
11. ¿….?

15 En mis sueños

Hablar Imagínate que puedes hacer lo que quieras: que no tienes límites ni de dinero ni de tiempo. ¿Sabes lo que harías? En grupos de tres o cuatro, expresen tres cosas que harían.

modelo

Tú: *Yo pasaría más tiempo con mis amigos y mi familia.*

Amigo(a) 1: *Yo compraría una casa cerca de la playa.*

Amigo(a) 2: *Yo viajaría por toda Latinoamérica.*

Amigo(a) 3: *Yo donaría mucho dinero a las causas de mi comunidad.*

More Practice: **Más comunicación** *p. R6*

 **Online Workbook**
CLASSZONE.COM

Refrán

Haz bien y no mires a quién.

¿Qué quiere decir el refrán? ¿Qué harías tú para «hacer bien» sin «mirar a quién»?

Teaching All Students

Challenge Have students say or write that they would do the following, but can't because of some reason (… **pero no puedo porque…**) : (1) **conservar agua**, (2) **recoger basura**, (3) **votar en las elecciones**, (4) **juntar fondos para el equipo de fútbol**, (5) **servir la cena a la gente sin hogar**, (6) **trabajar de voluntario(a) en el centro de la comunidad.**

Multiple Intelligences

Logical/Mathematical Do a variation of **Actividad 15.** Give students a set amount of play money. Have them calculate how they would spend the money and include this information in their conversations.

 Objective: Transitional practice
Speculating with the conditional in conversation

Answers will vary but should use the following verb forms.

1. votaría(s)	6. colaboraría(s)
2. estaría(s)	7. conservaría(s)
3. estaría(s)	8. valoraría(s)
4. participaría (s)	9. cuidaría(s)
5. haría(s)	10. resolvería(s)

 Objective: Open-ended practice Speculating with the conditional in conversation

Answers will vary.

Dictation

Using the Listening Activity Script for **Actividad 12** on TE p. 105D, dictate selected sentences to students. You may want to use this dictation for a quiz grade.

Quick Wrap-up

List all the boldfaced words presented in the Speaking Strategy on p. 121 on the board. Point to a word and call on a student to explain in Spanish the meaning of the word: **¿Qué quiere decir esta palabra?**

Block Schedule

Variety Have students work in groups of 4–5 and imagine that they are coordinating volunteer efforts for a community service organization. First, have them make a list of at least 10 activities. Then have them list at least 10 people who have volunteered. For example: **un cantante de 20 años, una doctora de 40 años, el club de español,** etc. Then have them match each activity with an appropriate person/group. Groups then present to the class who would do what for their organization. For example: **La doctora cuidaría a los ancianos.** (For additional activities, see **Block Scheduling Copymasters.**)

Teaching Resource Options

Print
Actividades para todos Workbook
  PE, p. 47–49
Block Scheduling Copymasters
Unit 2 Resource Book
Actividades para todos Workbook
  PE, p. 17–19
  Absent Student Copymasters, p. 39
  Audioscript, p. 43

Audiovisual
OHT 14 (Quick Start)
Audio Program CD 4, Tracks 4–5

Technology
Online Workbook, U2 E1
Take-Home Tutor CD-ROM, U2 E1

Quick Start Review

♻ **Biographical information**

Use OHT 14 or write on the board:
Answer the following questions about
yourself:

1. ¿Dónde naciste?
2. ¿Cuántas personas hay en tu familia?
3. ¿Cómo fue tu primer día de escuela primaria?
4. ¿Qué hacías con tus amigos(as) en la escuela primaria?

Answers will vary.

Teaching Suggestions

- **Prereading** Have students scan the reading and look for cognate words. Ask students: ¿Qué pueden determinar sobre la lectura basándose en los cognados (palabras afines)?

- **Strategy: Comprehend complex sentences** Ask students what might help them determine the smaller units within a long sentence (conjunctions, commas, semicolons).

- **Reading** Have students skim the 2 excerpts on p. 123. Then have them work on determining the meaningful units inside the longer sentences.

En voces
AUDIO
LECTURA

PARA LEER
STRATEGY: READING

Comprehend complex sentences
Rigoberta Menchú is an admirable international figure. When she writes or speaks, she usually combines several ideas in one paragraph. For example, here are the meaningful units inside one of her sentences:

Tenemos el reto / de construir y consolidar la democracia y la paz, / resolviendo los problemas internos y privilegiando el diálogo.

Focus first on the small units of meaning rather than on the entire sentence. Read the sections aloud. What words connect the units of meaning? Try this technique with other sentences so that you can understand them more easily.

Nota cultural

Rigoberta Menchú habla de **construir la democracia.** Guatemala, al igual que muchos países de Latinoamérica, sufrieron fuertes dictaduras. Al establecerse de nuevo la democracia, todas las personas vuelven a tener derechos.

122

Rigoberta Menchú

Rigoberta Menchú cuenta una historia tan extraordinaria como su vida. Ella se escapó de la represión del gobierno de Guatemala durante las décadas de los 70 y los 80, cuando muchas personas murieron, incluyendo miembros de la familia de Rigoberta.

Una de las razones de la represión fue la discriminación de la clase alta y la clase media contra los indios, quienes viven en las montañas, lejos de la ciudad, y con muy pocos recursos.

---

[1] Nobel Peace Prize

Classroom Community

Group Activity Working in groups, have students describe Rigoberta Menchú's clothing. Have them discuss why her clothing is important and why she continues to dress that way. Ask them what other cultures are connected to particular types of clothing. Have a representative from each group report their discussions to the class.

Portfolio Have students research important events in Guatemalan history and create a timeline. Then have students research Rigoberta Menchú's life and add these events to the timeline.

Rubric A = 13–15 pts. B = 10–12 pts. C = 7–9 pts. D = 4–6 pts. F = < 4 pts.

Writing criteria	Scale
Accuracy/completeness of information	1 2 3 4 5
Grammar/spelling accuracy	1 2 3 4 5
Appearance	1 2 3 4 5

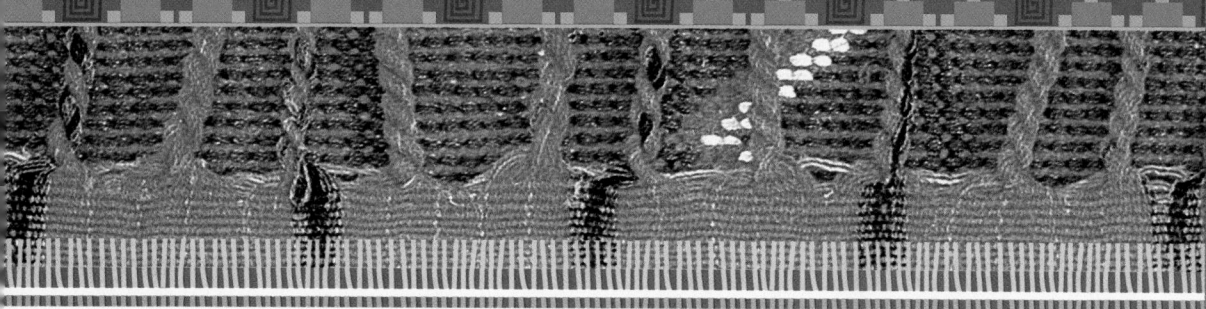

Rigoberta Menchú decidió organizar a los indios para que se defendieran contra la violencia del gobierno, pero luego tuvo que irse de su país. Fue a París, donde Elizabeth Burgos, una activista de nacionalidad francesa y venezolana, la ayudó a escribir su historia. Por los esfuerzos para mejorar las condiciones de su pueblo, Rigoberta Menchú ganó el Premio Nóbel de la Paz[1] en 1992. Ella habla frecuentemente sobre la paz.

> 66 El tesoro más grande que tengo en la vida es la capacidad de soñar. En las situaciones más duras y complejas, he sido capaz de soñar con un futuro más hermoso. 99

En su testimonio personal, *Me llamo Rigoberta Menchú y así me nació la conciencia*, Rigoberta Menchú cuenta cómo fue una de las víctimas del prejuicio de pertenecer a un pueblo indígena, donde casi todos hablan su propia lengua, el quiché. Además, en sus entrevistas siempre hace referencia a la unión de los pueblos.

> 66 La utopía de la interculturalidad debe convertirse en el motor que guíe las relaciones entre pueblos y culturas. 99

Online Workbook
CLASSZONE.COM

¿Comprendiste?
1. ¿Cuál es el sueño más grande de Rigoberta Menchú?
2. ¿De qué habla en su libro?
3. ¿De qué habla en sus entrevistas?

¿Qué piensas?
Para Rigoberta, ¿existen esperanzas de que su pueblo sea aceptado por otras culturas? ¿Con qué palabras expresa ella esta relación?

Hazlo tú
En un mapa de Guatemala busca el Departamento de El Quiché. Estudia los nombres de los pueblos. ¿Cuáles parecen ser de origen indígena y cuáles son nombres castellanos?

ciento veintitrés
México y Centroamérica Etapa 1
123

Culture Highlights

● **RIGOBERTA MENCHÚ** Menchú no es la única guatemalteca en haber recibido el Premio Nóbel. En 1967, Miguel Ángel Asturias, un escritor guatemalteco, recibió el Premio Nóbel de Literatura.

Cross Cultural Connections
Strategy Ask students to research cultural groups. Have them choose an indigenous people from Guatemala and from the U.S. to compare and contrast. They might use the following questions to help them gather information: ¿Quién? ¿Qué? ¿Cuándo? ¿Dónde? ¿Por qué?

Interdisciplinary Connection
Social Studies Have students research the names of the various people of indigenous background in Guatemala and the proportion of these people within the total population. Students might also research the same information for Mexico and other Central American countries.

¿Comprendiste?
Answers
1. Lograr un futuro más hermoso.
2. Habla sobre su pueblo indígena.
3. Habla sobre la unión de los pueblos.

■ Block Schedule
Change of Pace Have each student prepare 1 or 2 biographical or autobiographical paragraphs similar to the second one on p. 123. Students may wish to focus on a personal situation that caused some kind of conflict. You may have students exchange papers and peer edit. (For additional activities, see **Block Scheduling Copymasters**.)

Teaching All Students

Extra Help Have students work in pairs to reread the **Lectura**. After reading each paragraph, have them write 1–3 key words. After reading the entire **Lectura**, they should work together to provide a 2–3 sentence summary.

Native Speakers Have students read more selections from **Me llamo Rigoberta Menchú y así me nació la conciencia** and present a report to the class.

Students may also select a writer from another Spanish-speaking country.

Multiple Intelligences

Verbal Have students role play an interview with Rigoberta Menchú. One student plays Rigoberta Menchú and the other plays a reporter who asks questions after Menchú has won the Nobel Peace Prize.

Teaching Resource Options

Print

Cuaderno para hispanohablantes
  PE, pp. 47–48
Unit 2 Resource Book
  Cuaderno para hispanohablantes
   TE, pp. 27–28
  Information Gap Activities, pp. 29–30
  Family Involvement, pp. 40–41

Audiovisual

OHT 15 (Quick Start)

Technology

eTest Plus Online/Test Generator
  CD-ROM
  www.classzone.com

Quick Start Review

♻ **Command forms**

Use OHT 15 or write on the board:
Give the affirmative **tú, Ud., Uds.,** and
nosotros command forms for each of
the following verbs:

1. conocer
2. dormir
3. educar
4. preservar
5. resolver

Answers
1. conoce, conozca, conozcan, conozcamos
2. duerme, duerma, duerman, durmamos
3. educa, eduque, eduquen, eduquemos
4. preserva, preserve, preserven, preservemos
5. resuelve, resuelva, resuelvan, resolvamos

✓ Teaching Suggestions
What Have Students Learned?

Point out the Objectives at the top of
the page. Ask students what they most
need to review, and how they plan to
review and practice (making flashcards,
studying with a partner in a question/
answer session, etc.).

ETAPA 1

Now you can...
• make requests.

To review
• command forms
  see p. 114.

Now you can...
• make suggestions.

To review
• **nosotros**
  commands
  see p. 116.

En uso
REPASO Y MÁS COMUNICACIÓN

OBJECTIVES
• Say what you want
  to do
• Make requests
• Make suggestions

1 En el centro de la comunidad

Trabajas de voluntario(a) en el centro de la comunidad. Hay
letreros que tienen reglas para los estudiantes voluntarios y para
las personas que viven allí. ¿Qué dicen?

modelo

a los residentes: no perder sus cosas.

al estudiante: ayudar con el almuerzo

a los dos: escuchar estos anuncios

1. al residente: acostarse antes de la medianoche
2. a la estudiante: llegar antes de las diez
3. a los dos: ver el video sobre el centro
4. al residente: no olvidarse de tomar su medicina
5. a los dos: salir al parque para los ejercicios
6. al estudiante: ir a la cafetería para servir el almuerzo
7. al residente: tener cuidado con el equipo deportivo
8. al estudiante: no hacer tu tarea aquí

2 La reunión municipal

Varias personas en la reunión municipal expresan sus opiniones
sobre temas que afectan la ciudad. ¿Qué dice cada persona?

modelo

limpiar nuestra ciudad

Limpiemos nuestra ciudad. o ¡No limpiemos nuestra ciudad!

1. abrir los brazos a la gente sin hogar
2. eliminar la discriminación
3. colaborar con los demás
4. apoyar a nuestros líderes
5. eliminar el hambre
6. participar en las actividades
   de la comunidad
7. ayudar a la gente sin hogar

Classroom Community

Game Write a list of people on the board; for
example, **padre/madre, director(a) de la escuela,**
director(a) de una organización voluntaria, etc. Then
give a command that one of the people might give.
Have students guess who would say that command.
For additional practice, you may also have students
brainstorm additional commands these people might
give.

Learning Scenario Have students imagine that
they have to give a very brief speech at a town meeting
to incite community involvement. They should write a
speech that is about 10 sentences long. Ask volunteers
to give their speeches to the class. Have the class
decide if the students gave convincing speeches.

Self-Check Quiz
CLASSZONE.COM

Now you can...
- say what you want to do.

To review
- the conditional
  see p. 119.

3 Servicio a la comunidad

Usa la frase indicada para empezar una conversación con tu compañero(a) sobre los servicios a la comunidad.

modelo

participar en…

Compañero(a): *¿Participarías en una campaña para embellecer el centro?*

Tú: *Sí, ¿por qué no? Participaría en una campaña para embellecer el centro. o No, lo siento mucho pero no podría hacerlo.*

1. trabajar de voluntario(a)
2. embellecer la ciudad
3. donar ropa
4. juntar fondos para…
5. estar a favor de…
6. estar en contra de…

Now you can...
- say what you want to do.

To review
- the conditional
  see p. 119.

4 Reacciones

¿Qué harían las siguientes personas con una gran cantidad de dinero?

modelo

Tú: *vender tu carro viejo y comprar un carro nuevo*

Venderías tu carro viejo y comprarías un carro nuevo.

1. yo: poner el dinero en el banco y vivir como siempre
2. tú: gastar todo el dinero y quedarte con nada
3. él: salir todos los días y no preocuparse de nada
4. ella: empacar sus maletas y viajar a Europa
5. usted: construir una casa nueva e invitar a sus amigos
6. ustedes: seguir con sus estudios e ir a la universidad
7. nosotros: divertirnos y también tener tiempo para trabajar de voluntarios

 **Answers**

1. Acuéstese antes de la medianoche.
2. Llega antes de las diez.
3. Vean el video sobre el centro.
4. No se olvide de tomar su medicina.
5. Salgan al parque para los ejercicios.
6. Ve a la cafetería para servir el almuerzo.
7. Tenga cuidado con el equipo deportivo.
8. No hagas tu tarea aquí.

 **Answers**

1. Abramos los brazos a la gente sin hogar. *o:* ¡No abramos... !
2. Eliminemos la discriminación. *o:* ¡No eliminemos... !
3. Colaboremos con los demás. *o:* ¡No colaboremos... !
4. Apoyemos a nuestros líderes. *o:* ¡No apoyemos ... !
5. Eliminemos el hambre. *o:* ¡No eliminemos...
6. Participemos en las actividades de la comunidad. *o:* ¡No participemos... !
7. Ayudemos a la gente sin hogar. *o:* ¡No ayudemos... !

3 Answers

Answers will vary.

4 Answers

1. Pondría el dinero en el banco y viviría como siempre.
2. Gastarías todo el dinero y te quedarías sin nada.
3. Saldría todos los días y no se preocuparía de nada.
4. Ella empacaría *(would pack)* sus maletas y viajaría a Europa.
5. Usted construiría una casa nueva e invitaría a sus amigos.
6. Ustedes seguirían con sus estudios e irían a la universidad.
7. Nos divertiríamos y también tendríamos tiempo para trabajar de voluntarios.

Block Schedule

Personalizing Have students brainstorm things they would do to improve their school. Start them out and elicit the conditional by asking yes/no questions. For example, **¿Pintarían ustedes las salas de clase? ¿Sembrarían ustedes árboles en el patio de la escuela?**, etc. Students can express what they would do in the **yo** or **nosotros** forms of the conditional.

Teaching All Students

Extra Help For students having trouble with command forms, have them make a chart with **tú**, **usted**, **ustedes**, and **nosotros** across the top. Give them a list of verbs to put along the side. Then have them complete the chart with the correct command forms of the verbs, both affirmative and negative.

Multiple Intelligences

Logical/Mathematical Have pairs of students imagine that they have been given a $20,000 grant to address a school or community problem. Instruct pairs to decide on the problem, plan how to solve it, and itemize how the grant would be spent. Pairs should submit their plans for an extra credit grade.

Teaching Resource Options

Print 📖

Unit 2 Resource Book
 Audioscript, p. 26
 Vocabulary Quizzes, pp. 49–51
 Grammar Quizzes, pp. 52–53
 Etapa Exam, Forms A and B,
  pp. 54–63
 Examen para hispanohablantes,
  pp. 64–68
 Portfolio Assessment, pp. 69–70
 Multiple Choice Test Questions,
  pp. 226–228

Audiovisual 💻

OHT 15 (Quick Start)
Audio Program CD 19, Track 10

Technology 💻

eTest Plus Online/Test Generator
CD-ROM
🌐 www.classzone.com

ACTIVIDAD 5 and ACTIVIDAD 6

Rubric: Speaking

Criteria	Scale	
Sentence structure	1 2 3	A = 11–12 pts.
Vocabulary use	1 2 3	B = 9–10 pts.
Originality	1 2 3	C = 7–8 pts.
Fluency	1 2 3	D = 4–6 pts.
		F = < 4 pts.

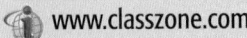

ACTIVIDAD 7 ✏️ En tu propia voz

Rubric: Writing

Criteria	Scale	
Vocabulary use	1 2 3 4 5	A = 14–15 pts.
Accuracy	1 2 3 4 5	B = 12–13 pts.
Creativity, appearance	1 2 3 4 5	C = 10–11 pts.
		D = 8–9 pts.
		F = < 8 pts.

Teaching Note: En tu propia voz

Writing Strategy Suggest that students implement the writing strategy "Persuade your reader" when writing their ads. They should offer simple, direct information and give the reader strong verbal images to make an impression on the reader's mind.

---

5 El club

> **STRATEGY: SPEAKING**
> **Identify the general ideas, then delegate responsibilities**
> Before delegating the responsibilities, it is good to decide what they are. Agree on a list of things to be done (infinitives). Then decide who is to do them (commands). You can also decide what not to

Tú y dos amigos han decidido que van a empezar un club de voluntarios. Quieren tener la primera reunión en tu casa. Todos tienen ideas de qué se debe hacer.

modelo

Tú: *Enrique, haz una lista de las personas que vamos a invitar.*

Amigo(a) 1: *Sandra, tú y Hernán empiecen a llamar a todos en la lista.*

Amigo(a) 2: …

6 En tu lugar 👥

Imagina que tu amigo(a) es famoso(a)—puede ser actor o actriz, artista, escritor(a), atleta, presidente(a) de un país, ¡lo que sea! Trabajen en grupos de tres o cuatro. Primero decidan quién del grupo es famoso(a) y por qué. Luego, los demás dan consejos a la persona famosa empezando con la frase «En tu lugar».

modelo

escritora famosa

Amigo(a) 1: *En tu lugar, yo escribiría una novela de ciencia-ficción.*

Amigo(a) 2: *En tu lugar, yo pediría más dinero por la próxima novela.*

Amigo(a) 3: *En tu lugar, yo descansaría un rato antes de escribir otra novela.*

7 En tu propia voz ✏️

ESCRITURA Inventa un producto y escribe un anuncio para venderlo. Los anuncios frecuentemente usan las formas de **usted** o **ustedes** al dar mandatos. Tu anuncio va a salir en Internet, así que asegura que sea ¡interesante y atractivo!

modelo

¡Piense en el futuro de sus hijos! ¡Compre la computadora SúperRápida!

 **TÚ EN LA COMUNIDAD**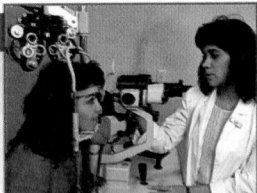

James es alumno en Washington. Él trabaja de voluntario con una optómetra en una misión médica en México. Da instrucciones a los pacientes, habla sobre los problemas que tienen y comunica al médico información importante. Cuando está en Washington, habla español con alumnos de otras escuelas.

Classroom Community

Storytelling Call on a student to begin telling a story using words from the **Repaso de vocabulario** on p. 127. Call on another student to repeat the first sentence and supply the next sentence. Continue adding sentences until the story is complete. This may also be done with pictures of vocabulary words; students tell a story according to the order of the illustrations.

Group Activity Have students work in groups of 4 to research tourist information about Mexico or a Central American country. They may use library sources and/or the Internet. Have them use this information to create a travel brochure that includes a map, a few places of interest, and interesting activities.

Flashcards
CLASSZONE.COM

En resumen
REPASO DE VOCABULARIO

SAY WHAT YOU WANT TO DO

Actions

colaborar con	to collaborate with
conservar más	to conserve more
consumir menos	to consume less
convivir	to live together, to get along
crear	to create
cuidar de	to take care of
donar	to donate
educar al público	to educate the public
embellecer	to beautify
estar a favor de	to be for
estar en contra de	to be against
hacer un esfuerzo	to make an effort
juntar fondos	to fundraise
luchar contra	to fight against
participar	to participate
permitir	to permit
pertenecer	to belong
preservar	to preserve
recoger	to pick up
resolver (o→ue)	to resolve
sembrar (e→ie)	to plant
trabajar de voluntario(a)	to volunteer
valorar	to value
votar	to vote

People, places, and things

los ancianos	the elderly
el árbol	tree
la basura	garbage
la campaña	campaign
el centro de la comunidad	community center
el centro de rehabilitación	rehabilitation center
el (la) ciudadano(a)	citizen
el comedor de beneficencia	soup kitchen
los derechos humanos	human rights
el desarrollo	development
la discriminación	discrimination
los enfermos	the sick
la gente sin hogar	the homeless
los jóvenes	young people
los minusválidos	the physically challenged
la pobreza	poverty
el prejuicio	prejudice
el ser humano	human being
el servicio social	social service
la solución	solution

MAKE REQUESTS

Questions

¿Cómo puedo ayudarte(lo, la)?	How can I help you?
¿Podría(s) darme una mano?	Could you give me a hand?
¿Puede(s) ayudarme?	Can you help me?
¿Puede(s) hacerme un favor?	Can you do me a favor?

Responses

Estoy agotado(a).	I'm exhausted.
Lo siento mucho, pero…	I'm sorry, but…
Me es imposible.	It's just not possible for me.
No, de veras, no puedo.	No, really, I can't.
¿Por qué no?	Sure, why not?
Sí, con mucho gusto.	Yes, gladly.
Si pudiera, lo haría.	If I could, I would.

MAKE SUGGESTIONS

***Nosotros* commands**

Trabajemos de voluntarios.
Ayudemos a los demás.

Juego
¿Qué podemos hacer?

Mira las fotos de varios lugares de México. ¿Qué servicio para la comunidad asocias con cada una?

1.    **2.**

3.

a.   preservar el medio ambiente
b.   sembrar árboles
c.   trabajar de voluntario(a)

Teaching All Students

Extra Help Have students study the **Repaso de vocabulario** for 2 minutes, then close their books. They then write down as many vocabulary words as they can remember. Next students exchange papers with a partner and circle any misspelled words. They then return the papers and correct mistakes.

Multiple Intelligences

Musical/Rhythmic Ask students to write a simple song encouraging others to do volunteer work. The song may be in the form of a rap.

Community Connections

Have students research the names of medical facilities in your area. Ask a student to contact each place to see if they have volunteer opportunities available for Spanish speakers. Invite a volunteer to come speak to the class.

🔔 Quick Start Review

♻ Etapa vocabulary

Use OHT 15 or write on the board: Write the vocabulary word/expression that you associate with each of the following:

1. las elecciones
2. el dinero
3. los anuncios públicos
4. la sopa
5. el hospital

Answers *See p. 105D.*

Teaching Suggestions
Vocabulary Review

Have students work in small teams to come up with as many commands as possible, using at least 1 word from the vocabulary in each. The team with the most correct commands at the end of a given time limit wins.

Dictation

Dictate the following sentences to review the **Etapa**:

1. Educa al público sobre los derechos humanos.
2. Trabaja de voluntario en un centro de la comunidad.
3. Quizás habrían más personas si la comida fuera mejor.

Juego

Answers: 1. c   2. b   3. a

📋 Block Schedule

FunBreak Have students work in small groups to create their own **Juegos** similar to the one on p. 127. They may draw the pictures or use cut-outs from magazines. When complete, display the new **Juegos** so that other students can guess the answers.

Planning Guide CLASSROOM MANAGEMENT

OBJECTIVES

Communication
- Say what should be done *pp. 136–140*
- React to the ecology *pp. 130–131, 132–133*
- React to others' actions *pp. 141–142*

Grammar
- Review: Use the present subjunctive (regular, irregular, stem-changing verbs) *pp. 136–140*
- Use the present perfect subjunctive *pp. 141–143*

Culture
- Regional vocabulary *p. 136*
- Monetary units *p. 140*
- The ecological movement in Mexico *p. 142*
- Literacy in Nicaragua *pp. 144–145*

♻ Recycling
- **Ir a** + infinitive *p. 134*
- mpersonal expressions *p. 137*

STRATEGIES

Listening Strategies
- Inventory local efforts to save the environment *p. 132*

Speaking Strategies
- Consider the effect of words and tone of voice *p. 137*
- Express support or lack of support *p. 148*

Reading Strategies
- Scan for details *TE p. 144*

Writing Strategies
- State your message using a positive tone *TE p. 148*

Connecting Cultures Strategies
- Recognize regional vocabulary *p. 136*
- Learn about monetary units *p. 140*
- Learn about the ecological movement in Mexico *p. 142*
- Gather and analyze information about literacy *pp. 144–145*
- Connect and compare what you know about literacy in your community to help you learn about literacy in a new community *pp. 144–145*

PROGRAM RESOURCES

 Print
- *Más práctica* Workbook PE *pp. 49–56*
- *Actividades para todos* Workbook PE *pp. 51–60*
- Block Scheduling Copymasters *pp. 41–48*
- Unit 2 Resource Book
  Más práctica Workbook TE *pp. 72–79*
  Actividades para todos Workbook TE *pp. 80–89*
  Cuaderno para hispanohablantes TE *pp. 90–97*
  Information Gap Activities *pp. 98–101*
  Family Letter *p. 102*
  Absent Student Copymasters *pp. 103–109*
  Family Involvement *pp. 110–111*
  Audioscript *pp. 112–114*
  Assessment Program, Unit 2 Etapa 1 *pp. 115–138; 229–231*
  Answer Keys *pp. 242–246*

 Audiovisual
- Audio Program CD 5
- Overhead Transparencies M2; 3; 19–33
- Word Tiles U2E2

 Technology
- eEdition Plus Online/eEdition CD-ROM
- Easy Planner Plus Online/Easy Planner CD-ROM
- eTest Plus Online/Test Generator CD-ROM
- Online Workbook
- Take-Home Tutor CD-ROM
- www.classzone.com

Assessment Program Options
- Unit 2 Resource Book
  Vocabulary Quizzes
  Grammar Quizzes
  Etapa Exam Forms A and B
  Examen para hispanohablantes
  Portfolio Assessment
  Multiple Choice Test Questions
- Audio Program CD 19
- eTest Plus Online/Test Generator CD-ROM

Native Speakers
- *Cuaderno para hispanohablantes* PE *pp. 49–56*
- *Cuaderno para hispanohablantes* TE (Unit 2 Resource Book)
- *Examen para hispanohablantes* (Unit 2 Resource Book)
- Audio Program CD 5, 19
- Audioscript (Unit 2 Resource Book

Student Text Listening Activity Scripts

Situaciones *pages 132–133*

• CD 5

Trabajas en una agencia de publicidad que está creando anuncios con el fin de promover la protección del ambiente. Mira las imágenes de estos anuncios. Luego, escucha los anuncios de radio y decide a qué imagen corresponden.

Ahora escucha anuncios de radio que corresponden a las seis imágenes que viste. Escribe el número del anuncio que mejor va con cada imagen en la siguiente lista.

Anuncio número 1

¡No te subas a ese carro!
Mejor ve en el metro...
o en el autobús.
O camina si puedes.

¿Sabías que cada vez que te subes a tu carro echas contaminantes al aire?

Anuncio número 2

Si no vas a ir muy lejos, ¿por qué no vas en bicicleta? Las bicicletas son un modo ideal de transportación. Economizan espacio y no utilizan combustible, que envía gases dañinos a la capa de ozono. ¡Ir en bicicleta ayuda a mantener el aire limpio!

Anuncio número 3

¡No eches eso a la basura!
¡Recíclalo!
En el programa de reciclaje de San José,
puedes reciclar
todas las latas
las botellas de vidrio
los productos de plástico
el cartón y todos los productos de papel.

¿Sabías que cada vez que echas algo que se puede reciclar a la basura, contribuyes al desperdicio?

Anuncio número 4

¡No compres ese aerosol!
Usa otro producto más natural.

¿Sabías que cada vez que usas un aerosol, estás destruyendo la capa de ozono?

Anuncio número 5

¡Conserva los árboles! Junta los periódicos que leen en tu casa y recíclalos.

Anuncio número 6

San José es tu ciudad. Costa Rica es tu país. Nosotros como costarricenses tenemos que crear conciencia en la sociedad para conservar las riquezas naturales de nuestro país. Así podemos compartir y disfrutar de la naturaleza hoy y mañana.

ACTIVIDAD 5 La ecóloga *page 136*

Es triste que nosotros los seres humanos no respetemos el medio ambiente. Miren a su alrededor: en las calles, en los parques, en las playas: ¡basura por todas partes! Es una lástima que la gente no comprenda la importancia de proteger nuestro planeta. Pero no vine aquí para dar sermones. Vine para darles ideas de qué podemos hacer hoy.

¡Hay muchas cosas que podemos hacer! Es importante que cada comunidad instituya programas de reciclaje. En vez de echar todo a la basura, es mejor que tú recicles los productos de plástico, papel y vidrio.

¡No tienes que usar el carro todos los días! Es malo que contamines el aire con combustibles. ¡Camina o usa el transporte público! Es lógico que en el futuro los científicos desarrollen otras formas de energía. Pero por ahora debemos tratar de usar los carros sólo cuando no hay otro modo de llegar.

¡Es necesario que protejamos la Tierra! No se te olvide que es nuestro único hogar. Gracias por escuchar la estación WXFM hoy.

ACTIVIDAD 15 El club de ecología *page 142*

1. Juan recicló los periódicos y las revistas.
2. Esperanza y Arnoldo compartieron el carro toda la semana.
3. Usted no usó el transporte público.
4. Ustedes echaron las botellas de plástico a la basura.
5. Nosotros trabajamos como voluntarios en el programa de reciclaje.
6. Tú compraste un aerosol el otro día.

Quick Start Review Answers

p. 138 Present subjunctive: regular verbs
1. Es necesario que yo separe la basura.
2. Es una lástima que tú no recicles.
3. Es importante que todos protejan/ protejamos las especies.
4. Es bueno que Ana tenga más ayuda.
5. Es peligroso que nosotros consumamos tanta energía.

p. 139 Present subjunctive: irregular verbs
Answers will vary.
Answers could include:
1. Es raro que Teresa diga la verdad.
2. Es probable que yo salga esta noche.
3. Es ridículo que vayamos al cine cuando tenemos mucha tarea.
4. Es lógico que pongas la leche en el frigorífico.
5. Es una lástima que no tengas tu pasaporte.

p. 141 Present subjunctive: stem-changing verbs
1. Es importante que nosotros pidamos dinero.
2. Es una lástima que ustedes mientan.
3. Es necesario que él duerma ocho horas.
4. Es peligroso que tú vuelvas tarde.
5. Es raro que ella cierre las ventanas.

p. 149 Etapa vocabulary
1. contaminación del aire
2. aerosol
3. desperdicio
4. contaminante
5. petróleo
6. smog
Mensaje: Protege el planeta.

Sample Lesson Plan - 50 Minute Schedule

DAY 1

Etapa Opener
- Quick Start Review (TE, p. 128) **5 MIN.**
- Have students look at the *Etapa* Opener and answer the questions. Expand using one of the activities on TE p. 129. **10 MIN.**

En contexto: Vocabulario
- Quick Start Review (TE, p. 130) **5 MIN.**
- Present *Descubre*, p. 130. **5 MIN.**
- Have students use context and pictures to learn *Etapa* vocabulary, then answer the *¿Comprendiste?* questions, p. 131. Use the Situational OHTs for additional practice. **15 MIN.**
- Use an expansion activity from TE pp. 130–131 for variety. **10 MIN.**

Homework Option:
- Have students write sentences explaining activities that they do to help preserve the planet.

DAY 2

En vivo: Situaciones
- Check homework. **5 MIN.**
- Quick Start Review (TE, p. 132) **5 MIN.**
- Present the Listening Strategy, p. 138. **5 MIN.**
- Have students look at section 1, pp. 132–133. Play the audio for section 2. Then have students complete section 3 in groups. **15 MIN.**

En acción: Vocabulario y gramática
- Quick Start Review (TE, p. 134) **5 MIN.**
- Have students complete *Actividad* 1 in writing, then go over answers orally. **5 MIN.**
- Have students do *Actividad* 2 in pairs. **10 MIN.**

Homework Option:
- Have students complete *Actividad* 2 in writing.

DAY 3

En acción (cont.)
- Check homework. **5 MIN.**
- Have students do *Actividad* 3 in pairs. **5 MIN.**
- Present the *Vocabulario*, p. 135. Then do *Actividad* 4 in pairs. **10 MIN.**
- Present *Repaso:* The Present Subjunctive of Regular Verbs, p. 136. **5 MIN.**
- Play the audio; do *Actividad* 5. **5 MIN.**
- Present the *Nota* and have students complete *Actividad* 6 orally. **5 MIN.**
- Present the *Vocabulario*, p. 137. **5 MIN.**
- Present the Speaking Strategy, p. 137. Have students do *Actividad* 7 in pairs. **10 MIN.**

Homework Option:
- Have students complete *Actividad* 3 in writing. *Más práctica* Workbook, p. 53. *Cuaderno para hispanohablantes*, p. 51.

DAY 4

En acción (cont.)
- Check homework. **5 MIN.**
- Quick Start Review (TE, p. 138) **5 MIN.**
- Present *Repaso:* The Present Subjunctive of Irregular Verbs, p. 138. **10 MIN.**
- Do *Actividades* 8 and 9 orally. **10 MIN.**
- Have students complete *Actividad* 10 in pairs. **5 MIN.**
- *Repaso:* The Present Subjunctive of Stem-Changing Verbs, p. 139. **10 MIN.**
- Have students complete *Actividad* 11 in pairs. **5 MIN.**

Homework Option:
- Have students complete *Actividades* 8 and 9 in writing. *Más práctica* Workbook, pp. 54–55. *Cuaderno para hispanohablantes*, pp. 52–53.

DAY 5

En acción (cont.)
- Check homework. **5 MIN.**
- Do *Actividad* 12 orally. **5 MIN.**
- Have students do *Actividad* 13 in pairs. Expand using *Más comunicación*, p. R7. **15 MIN.**
- Quick Start Review (TE, p. 141) **5 MIN.**
- Present *Gramática:* The Present Perfect Subjunctive, p. 141. **10 MIN.**
- Have students do *Actividad* 14 in pairs. **5 MIN.**
- Play the audio; do *Actividad* 15. **5 MIN.**

Homework Option:
- Have students complete *Actividad* 12 in writing. *Más práctica* Workbook, p. 56. *Cuaderno para hispanohablantes*, p. 54.
- *Actividades para todos* Workbook, pp. 51–56.

DAY 6

En acción (cont.)
- Check homework. **5 MIN.**
- Have students read and complete *Actividad* 16 in pairs. **5 MIN.**
- Present the *Vocabulario*, p. 143. Do *Actividad* 17 in groups. Expand using *Más comunicación*, p. R7. **15 MIN.**

Refrán
- Present the *Refrán*, p. 143. **5 MIN.**

En colores: Cultura y comparaciones
- Quick Start Review (TE, p. 144) **5 MIN.**
- Present the Connecting Cultures Strategy, p. 144. Call on volunteers to read the selection aloud. Have students answer the *¿Comprendiste?/¿Qué piensas?* questions, p. 145. **15 MIN.**

Homework Option:
- Have students complete *Hazlo tú*, p. 145.

DAY 7

En uso: Repaso y más comunicación
- Check homework. **5 MIN.**
- Quick Start Review (TE, p. 146) **5 MIN.**
- Have students do *Actividad* 1 in pairs. **5 MIN.**
- Do *Actividades* 2 and 3 orally. **5 MIN.**
- Have students do *Actividad* 4 in writing. Go over answers orally. **5 MIN.**
- Present the Speaking Strategy, p. 148, and have students do *Actividades* 5 and 6 in groups. **15 MIN.**

En tu propia voz: Escritura
- Do *Actividad* 7 in writing. Have volunteers present their brochures to the class. **10 MIN.**

Homework Option:
- Review for *Etapa* 2 Exam.

DAY 8

Conexiones
- Read *Las ciencias*, p. 148. Have students prepare their charts. **5 MIN.**

En resumen: Repaso de vocabulario
- Quick Start Review (TE, p. 149) **5 MIN.**
- Review grammar questions, etc., as necessary. **10 MIN.**
- Complete *Etapa* 2 Exam. **20 MIN.**

Ampliación
- Use a suggested project, game, or activity. (TE, pp. 105A–105B) **10 MIN.**

Homework Option:
- Have students complete the assignment for *Conexiones*. Preview *Etapa* 3 Opener.

Sample Lesson Plan - Block Schedule (90 minutes)

DAY 1

Etapa Opener
- Quick Start Review (TE, p. 128) 5 MIN.
- Have students look at the Etapa Opener and answer the questions. 5 MIN.
- Use Block Scheduling Copymasters. 10 MIN.

En contexto: Vocabulario
- Quick Start Review (TE, p. 130) 5 MIN.
- Present Descubre, p. 130. 5 MIN.
- Have students use context and pictures to learn Etapa vocabulary, then answer the ¿Comprendiste? questions, p. 131. Use the Situational OHTs for additional practice. 15 MIN.

En vivo: Situaciones
- Quick Start Review (TE, p. 132) 5 MIN.
- Present the Listening Strategy, p. 132. 5 MIN.
- Have students look at section 1, pp. 132–133. Play the audio for section 2. Then have students complete section 3 in groups. 20 MIN.

En acción: Vocabulario y gramática
- Quick Start Review (TE, p. 134) 5 MIN.
- Have students complete Actividad 1 in writing, then go over answers orally. 5 MIN.
- Have students do Actividad 2 in pairs. 5 MIN.

Homework Option:
- Have students write sentences explaining activities that they do to help preserve the planet. Have them complete Actividad 2 in writing.

DAY 2

En acción (cont.)
- Check homework. 5 MIN.
- Have students do Actividad 3 in pairs. 5 MIN.
- Present the Vocabulario, p. 135. Then do Actividad 4 in pairs. 10 MIN.
- Quick Start Review (TE, p. 136) 5 MIN.
- Present Repaso: The Present Subjunctive of Regular Verbs, p. 136. 5 MIN.
- Play the audio; do Actividad 5. 10 MIN.
- Present the Nota and have students complete Actividad 6 orally. 5 MIN.
- Present the Vocabulario, p. 137. 5 MIN.
- Present the Speaking Strategy, p. 137. Have students do Actividad 7 in pairs. 10 MIN.
- Quick Start Review (TE, p. 138) 5 MIN.
- Present Repaso: The Present Subjunctive of Irregular Verbs, p. 138. 10 MIN.
- Do Actividades 8 and 9 orally. 10 MIN.
- Have students complete Actividad 10 in pairs. 5 MIN.

Homework Option:
- Have students complete Actividades 6, 8, and 9 in writing. Más práctica Workbook, pp. 53–54. Cuaderno para hispanohablantes, pp. 51–52.

DAY 3

En acción (cont.)
- Check homework. 10 MIN.
- Quick Start Review (TE, p. 139) 5 MIN.
- Repaso: The Present Subjunctive of Stem-Changing Verbs, p. 139. 10 MIN.
- Have students complete Actividad 11 in pairs. 5 MIN.
- Do Actividad 12 orally. 5 MIN.
- Have students do Actividad 13 in pairs. Expand using Information Gap Activities, Unit 2 Resource Book, p. 98; Más comunicación, p. R7. 20 MIN.
- Quick Start Review (TE, p. 141) 5 MIN.
- Present Gramática: The Present Perfect Subjunctive, p. 141. 10 MIN.
- Have students do Actividad 14 in pairs. 5 MIN.
- Play the audio; do Actividad 15. 10 MIN.
- Have students read and complete Actividad 16 in pairs. 5 MIN.

Homework Option:
- Have students complete Actividad 12 in writing. Más práctica Workbook, pp. 55–56. Cuaderno para hispanohablantes, pp. 53–54.
- Actividades para todos Workbook, pp. 51–56

DAY 4

En acción (cont.)
- Check homework. 10 MIN.
- Present the Vocabulario, p. 143. Do Actividad 17 in groups. Expand using Information Gap Activities, Unit 2 Resource Book, p. 99; Más comunicación, p. R7. 20 MIN.

Refrán
- Present the Refrán, p. 139. 5 MIN.

En colores: Cultura y comparaciones
- Quick Start Review (TE, p. 144) 5 MIN.
- Present the Connecting Cultures Strategy, p. 144. Call on volunteers to read the selection aloud. Have students answer the ¿Comprendiste?/¿Qué piensas? questions, p. 145. 20 MIN.

En uso: Repaso y más comunicación
- Quick Start Review (TE, p. 146) 5 MIN.
- Do Actividad 1 in pairs and Actividades 2 and 3 orally. 15 MIN.
- Do Actividad 4 in writing. Go over answers orally. 10 MIN.

Homework Option:
- Have students complete Hazlo tú, p. 145. Review for Etapa 2 Exam.

DAY 5

En uso (cont.)
- Check homework. 5 MIN.
- Present the Speaking Strategy, p. 148, and have students do Actividades 5 and 6 in groups. 15 MIN.

En tu propia voz: Escritura
- Do Actividad 7 in writing. Have volunteers present their brochures to the class. 15 MIN.

Conexiones
- Read Las ciencias, p. 148. Have students prepare their charts. 5 MIN.

En resumen: Repaso de vocabulario
- Quick Start Review (TE, p. 149) 5 MIN.
- Review grammar questions, etc., as necessary. 5 MIN.
- Complete Etapa 2 Exam. 20 MIN.

Ampliación
- Use a suggested project, game, or activity. (TE, pp. 105A–105B) 20 MIN.

Homework Option:
- Have students complete the assignment for Conexiones. Preview Etapa 3 Opener.

▼ ¡Viva el medio ambiente!

Etapa Theme
Reacting to the ecology and saying what should be done

Grammar Objectives
• Reviewing the use of the present subjunctive (regular, irregular, stem-changing verbs)
• Using the present perfect subjunctive

Teaching Resource Options

Print
Block Scheduling Copymasters
Unit 2 Resource Book
    Family Letter, p. 102
    Absent Student Copymasters, p. 103

Audiovisual
OHT 3, 25 (Quick Start)

Quick Start Review
♻ Rainforest vocabulary
Use OHT 25 or write on the board:
Escribe por lo menos 8 palabras que asocias con las selvas tropicales.

Answers
Answers will vary. Answers could include:
agua, animales, árboles, calor, ciencias, indios, llover, medicina, plantas, ríos

Teaching Suggestions
Previewing the Etapa
• Ask students to study the picture on pp. 128–129 (1 min.).
• Have them close their books and give their initial impressions of the scene—the people, weather, clothing, activities, etc.
• Ask students what other textbooks this photo might appear in (science, geography). ¿En qué otros libros de texto podría aparecer esta foto?
• Use the ¿Qué ves? questions to focus the discussion.

UNIDAD 2

ETAPA

2

Un planeta en peligro

OBJECTIVES

• Say what should be done

• React to ecology

• React to others' actions

¿Qué ves?

Mira la foto. Contesta las preguntas.

1. ¿Qué cosas llevan los jóvenes? ¿En qué lugar las están usando?

2. ¿Qué hacen? ¿Crees que llevan el equipo correcto?

3. ¿Llevarías otras cosas? ¿Por qué?

4. ¿Crees que sería útil un libro como *El manejo de la iguana verde*? ¿Por qué?

128

Classroom Management

Planning Ahead Ask students to bring in books with information on Costa Rica, rainforests in Latin America, and other related topics. Many can be found in school and local libraries. Science teachers may have some as well. Students can use these books to look up information and enhance discussion.

Peer Review Have students work in small groups and review vocabulary from **Etapa 1** (refer them to p. 127). Have them use this vocabulary to write at least 5 sentences that could pertain to what they see in the photo on pp. 128–129.

El Manejo de la
Iguana Verde
TOMO VIII

La Iguana Verde
en áreas
de amortiguamiento

129

Cross Cultural Connections

Ask students to think about a national/
state park that they have visited or know
about in the U.S. Is it like the one they see
on pp. 128–129? Ask them to note
similarities and differences.

Culture Highlights

● **MONTEVERDE** El pueblo de
Monteverde está situado en las Montañas
Tilarán de Costa Rica. En él se encuentran
algunos de los bosques tropicales más
famosos del país y del mundo. Entre ellos
se hallan el Bosque Nuboso Monteverde,
la Reserva Forestal Santa Elena y la
Reserva Sendero Tranquilo. Se han visto
más de 450 especies de pájaros en esta
área.

Supplementary Vocabulary

los binoculares	binoculars
la botella de agua	water bottle
la enredadera	vine
un helecho	fern
el lente de zoom	zoom lens

Quick Wrap-up

Provide students with a list of items,
some of which are shown in the photo
and some of which are not. With books
closed, have students check the items
they recall seeing: **Verifiquen los
artículos que se acuerdan haber
visto.** Then have students open their
books and check their answers.

Teaching All Students

Extra Help Ask students about the photo using
yes/no or either/or questions. For example: ¿**Están en
una selva tropical? ¿Los chicos están de vacaciones o
en clase? ¿Hay plantas y flores?**

Multiple Intelligences

Verbal Have students make a list of adjectives they
could use to describe the rainforest. Creative students
can use the words to make short poems or haikus.

Musical/Rhythmic Point out that rainforest sounds
are often recorded on CD. Play some sample music
and have students discuss how the sounds affect them.

Block Schedule

Variety Have students research the
role of rainforests in the ecology of the
earth and why they are worth saving.
Have them also find out how rainforests
are being destroyed, by whom, and at
what rate. (For additional activities, see
Block Scheduling Copymasters.)

Teaching Resource Options

Print

Block Scheduling Copymasters
Unit 2 Resource Book
 Absent Student Copymasters, p. 103

Audiovisual

OHT 19, 20, 21, 21A, 22, 22A, 25 (Quick Start)

Technology

Online Workbook, U2E2
Take-Home Tutor CD-ROM, U2E2

Quick Start Review

♻ **Conditional**

Use OHT 25 or write on the board:
Escribe 3 oraciones describiendo lo que harías en una selva. Usa el condicional.

Answers
Answers will vary. Answers could include:
Caminaría por la selva.
Vería muchos animales.
Escucharía los pájaros.
Estudiaría las plantas.

Teaching Suggestions
Introducing Vocabulary

• Have students look at pages 130–131. Use OHT 49 and 50 to present the vocabulary.
• Ask the Comprehension Questions on TE p. 131 in order of yes/no (questions 1–3), either/or (questions 4–6), and simple words or phrases (questions 7–10). Expand by adding similar questions.
• Use the TPR activity to reinforce the meaning of individual words.

Descubre

Answers
1. c
2. f
3. a
4. e
5. b
6. d

En contexto VOCABULARIO

Descubre

¿Puedes adivinar el significado de las siguientes frases? Escoge de la lista de abajo. ¡Fácil!

1. la capa de ozono
2. el desperdicio
3. el derrame de petróleo
4. los recursos naturales
5. las zonas de reserva ecológica
6. la contaminación del aire

 a. *oil spill*
 b. *conservation land*
 c. *ozone layer*
 d. *air pollution*
 e. *natural resources*
 f. *waste*

Nuestro Planeta

¡Es el único que tenemos!

130

Classroom Community

TPR Have small groups of students take turns acting out the solutions to the problems on p. 131. The rest of the class identifies the solution.

Paired Activity Have students work in pairs to ask and answer the **¿Comprendiste?** questions on p. 131. Have the pairs write out the answers together and submit them for a classwork grade.

A nivel personal

Problema ecológico:
la contaminación del aire
¿Qué puedes hacer tú?
➤ Compartir el carro con amigos y colegas.
➤ ¡Caminar!
➤ Usar el transporte público.

Problema ecológico:
la destrucción de la capa de ozono
¿Qué puedes hacer tú?
➤ Limitar el uso de **aerosoles**.

Problema ecológico:
el desperdicio
¿Qué puedes hacer tú?
➤ ¡No **eches** los siguientes productos a la basura!
➤ ¡Recíclalos! **Instituye** programas de **reciclaje**.

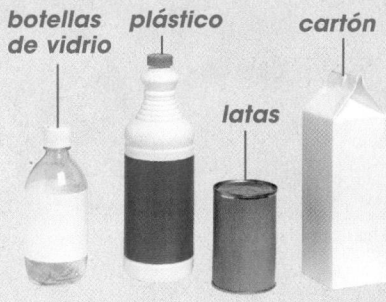

botellas de vidrio   **plástico**   **cartón**
latas

A nivel oficial

Problema ecológico:
los derrames de petróleo
Soluciones posibles:
➤ **Desarrollar** otras formas de energía.

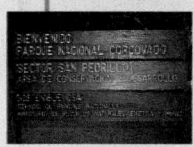

Problema ecológico:
la destrucción de los recursos naturales
Soluciones posibles:
➤ Declarar **zonas de reserva ecológica**.

➤ **Prohibir** el uso de **contaminantes**
➤ No comprar productos que usan **químicos dañinos**.

¡A todos nos toca proteger el medio ambiente! ¡No contamines tu planeta!

Online Workbook
CLASSZONE.COM

¿Comprendiste?
1. ¿Hay un programa de reciclaje en tu ciudad?
2. En tu casa, ¿se reciclan todos los productos de aluminio, vidrio y papel? ¿Quién lo hace? ¿Qué tienen que hacer: llevar los productos a un sitio específico o poner los productos con la basura?
3. ¿Cómo llegas al colegio? ¿Tratas de caminar o ir en bicicleta cuando puedes?
4. ¿Crees que nos toca a todos cuidar del medio ambiente?
5. ¿Crees que el gobierno está haciendo su parte para la conservación del medio ambiente? ¿Qué más crees que debe hacer?

ciento treinta y uno
México y Centroamérica Etapa 2   **131**

Comprehension Questions
1. ¿Hay zonas de reserva ecológica en Estados Unidos? (Sí.)
2. Para evitar la destrucción de la capa de ozono, ¿debemos limitar el uso de aerosoles? (Sí.)
3. ¿Debemos echar plásticos a la basura? (No)
4. Para evitar derrames de petróleo, ¿debemos desarrollar otras formas de energía o usar más petróleo? (desarrollar otras formas de energía)
5. Para evitar la destrucción de los recursos naturales, ¿debemos usar químicos dañinos o declarar zonas de reserva ecológica? (declarar zonas de reserva ecológica)
6. ¿Debemos prohibir el uso de contaminantes o permitir que se usen? (prohibir el uso de contaminantes)
7. ¿Cómo puedes evitar la contaminación del aire? *(Answers will vary.)*
8. ¿Qué productos no debes echar a la basura? (botellas de vidrio, plástico, latas y cartón)
9. ¿Cómo puedes evitar la destrucción de la capa de ozono? (limitar el uso de aerosoles)
10. ¿Cómo puedes evitar la destrucción de los recursos naturales? (declarar zonas de reserva ecológica, no comprar productos que usan químicos dañinos, prohibir el uso de contaminantes)

Supplementary Vocabulary
la cascada	waterfall
la energía acuática	water energy
la energía solar	solar energy
el molino	windmill
el nivel hidrostático	water table
el panel solar	solar panel

Block Schedule
Research Have students work in small groups to research **El Yunque** rainforest in Puerto Rico and **Piedras Blancas** national park in Costa Rica. The reports should compare and contrast the weather, flora and fauna, and protection efforts. Reports should be accompanied by illustrations. (For additional activities, see **Block Scheduling Copymasters**.)

Teaching All Students

Extra Help Pair students needing extra help with more advanced students and have them write 5 questions using the vocabulary words. Then have 2 pairs work together and ask and answer each other's questions.

Multiple Intelligences

Visual Have students design posters saying things students can do to protect the environment. Display the posters on the bulletin board.

Intrapersonal Have students tell which ecological problem seems the most serious to them and why. What do they do, if anything, to remedy this problem?

Teaching Resource Options

Print

Block Scheduling Copymasters
Unit 2 Resource Book
  Absent Student Copymasters, p. 104
  Audioscript, p. 112

Audiovisual

OHT 23, 24, 26 (Quick Start)
Audio Program CD 5, Track 1

Technology

Take-Home Tutor CD-ROM, U2E2

Quick Start Review

 Environment vocabulary

Use OHT 26 or write on the board:
**Enumera 3 problemas ecológicos y
1 solución para cada uno.**

Answers

Answers will vary. Answers could include:
La contaminación del aire: usar el transporte
  público.
El desperdicio: instituir un programa de
  reciclaje.
La destrucción de los recursos naturales:
  prohibir el uso de contaminantes.

Teaching Suggestions
Presenting Situations

• Present the Listening Strategy, p. 132,
  and have students make a chart
  to inventory efforts to save the
  environment. They can complete the
  charts for homework.
• Use OHT 53 and 54 to present the
  Mirar section. Ask simple yes/no,
  either/or, or short-answer questions.
• Use Audio CD 5 and have students
  do the **Escuchar** section (see Script
  TE p. 127B). Then have students
  complete the Listening Strategy
  exercise.
• Have students work in groups to
  write and discuss answers to the
  Hablar/Escribir section.

AUDIO *En vivo*
SITUACIONES

PARA ESCUCHAR • STRATEGIES: LISTENING

Pre-listening Are there public service campaigns
about protecting the environment in your
community? How do you find out about
them (television? radio? posters? billboards?)

Inventory efforts to save the environment
First, make a list of efforts in your community
to improve the environment. Then, check
Sí beside those that are mentioned in the
campaign in Costa Rica. Finally, comment
on similarities and differences between
your local campaign and the one heard in
Escuchar. This chart will help you get started:

Problemas locales	Sí
agua	
aire	
animales	
árboles/plantas	
basura	
energía	
minerales	
tierra	

¡Viva el medio ambiente!

Trabajas en una agencia de publicidad que está creando
anuncios con el fin de promover (*to promote*) la protección
del ambiente. Mira las imágenes de estos anuncios. Luego,
escucha los anuncios de radio y decide a qué imagen
corresponden.

① Mirar

Éstas son seis imágenes que van a salir en los anuncios.
Estúdialas y piensa sobre qué tema tratan.

132   ciento treinta y dos
Unidad 2

Classroom Community

Paired Activity Have students work in pairs to
describe the 6 posters on pp. 132–133, using as much
detail as possible. Each pair should write up a
description of one of their posters to present to the
class.

Cooperative Learning Have students work in
groups to design an ad campaign to improve the
community. Each group should focus on a different
aspect: the environment, natural resources, pollution,
recycling, the elderly, the needy, etc. As a group, they
should develop a general slogan, then work individually
to create announcements linked to the slogan. Each
group can present their campaign to the class.

D.

E.

2 Escuchar

Ahora escucha anuncios de radio que corresponden a las seis imágenes que viste. Escribe el número del anuncio que mejor va con cada imagen en la siguiente tabla.

Dibujo A _____

Dibujo B _____

Dibujo C _____

Dibujo D _____

Dibujo E _____

Dibujo F _____

3 Hablar/Escribir

Haz una lista de cinco cosas que tú puedes hacer hoy para proteger tu ciudad y el planeta. Compara tu lista con la de dos compañeros. Conversen sobre sus ideas y traten de pensar sobre modos nuevos de proteger el medio ambiente. Si les interesa, monten una campaña ecológica para su colegio.

F.

Answers
Dibujo A: Anuncio 1
Dibujo B: Anuncio 4
Dibujo C: Anuncio 5
Dibujo D: Anuncio 2
Dibujo E: Anuncio 6
Dibujo F: Anuncio 3

Escribir

Answers will vary.

Quick Wrap-up

Write 10 sentences on the board dealing with preserving the environment. Half of the sentences should make sense, the other half should not. Have students name the illogical sentences and correct them. **¿Qué oraciones son ilógicas? ¿Cómo las corregirían?**

Culture Highlights

● **EL MEDIO AMBIENTE** La preservación del medio ambiente es una tarea que las comunidades comparten en América Latina. Los miembros de la comunidad comparten sus conocimientos acerca de la naturaleza y hablan sobre sus necesidades para explorar las mejores alternativas de conservación. En países como Belice y Costa Rica, los científicos y los agricultores dialogan sobre cómo administrar los recursos naturales. En El Salvador, los jóvenes construyen hábitats naturales para pájaros y demás animales.

Pídales a los estudiantes que piensen en los conocimientos sobre la flora y la fauna de la zona donde viven que contribuirían a preservar el ambiente. ¿Cuáles de estos conocimientos tienen? ¿Cuáles quisieran investigar?

Block Schedule

FunBreak Many ad campaigns are accompanied by a jingle. Have students work in small groups, choose a simple, familiar tune, and write a jingle in Spanish to support environmental protection efforts. Have volunteers perform their jingle for the class. (For additional activities, see **Block Scheduling Copymasters.**)

Teaching All Students

Extra Help Before listening to the audio for **Escuchar,** have students write affirmative and negative **tú** commands that correspond to each photo on pp. 132–133.

Multiple Intelligences

Visual Point out that the recycling icon is recognized throughout the world. Have students design other icons that correspond to environmental protection efforts. Display the icons without words and have students try to guess the meanings.

Teaching Resource Options

Print

Block Scheduling Copymasters
Unit 2 Resource Book
  Absent Student Copymasters, p. 105

Audiovisual

OHT 26 (Quick Start)

Quick Start Review

♻ **Nosotros commands**

Use OHT 26 or write on the board:
Write 3 **nosotros** command sentences that promote environmental activism, using the following verbs:

1. conservar
2. preservar
3. recoger
4. prohibir
5. echar

Answers
Answers will vary. Answers could include:
1. Conservemos energía.
2. Preservemos las selvas.
3. Recojamos la basura.
4. Prohibamos el uso de aerosoles.
5. No echemos las botellas de vidrio a la basura.

Teaching Suggestions
Comprehension Check
Use **Actividades 1–4** to assess retention after the **Vocabulario** and **Situaciones**. After completing **Actividad 1**, have students exchange papers with a partner for peer correction.

Objective: Controlled practice
Vocabulary

Answers
1. desperdicio	9. medio ambiente
2. echar	10. contaminación del aire
3. reciclar	11. petróleo
4. latas	12. químicos dañinos
5. vidrio	13. destrucción
6. plástico	14. capa de ozono
7. cartón	15. desarrollen
8. reciclaje	

En acción

PARTE A — **Práctica del vocabulario**

For Activities 1–4
• Say what should be done • React to ecology • React to others' actions

1 La composición

Escribir Andrés tuvo que escribir una composición sobre el medio ambiente. Completa su composición usando las palabras de la lista.

plástico	cartón
destrucción	contaminación del aire
reciclaje	botellas
latas	desarrollen
desperdicio	medio ambiente
químicos dañinos	reciclar
echar	vidrio
petróleo	capa de ozono

Hay mucho __1__ en el mundo. No deberíamos __2__ todo a la basura. Hay muchas cosas que podemos __3__: las __4__, las botellas de __5__, los productos de __6__, el __7__, los periódicos y las revistas. Si no hay un programa de __8__ en tu ciudad, debes ayudar a empezar uno.

Es importante conservar el __9__. La __10__ se puede controlar. El __11__ que usamos cuando viajamos en nuestros carros echa __12__ al aire. Esos químicos contribuyen a la __13__ de la __14__. Tenemos que pedirles a nuestros políticos y científicos que __15__ otras formas de energía.

2 El horario de Ángela ♻ 👥

Hablar/*Escribir* Ángela vio un documental sobre el medio ambiente y decidió que tenía que hacer algo cada día para conservarlo. Con un(a) compañero(a), conversen sobre su horario.

modelo

usar el metro

Tú: *¿Cuándo va a usar Ángela el metro?*

Compañero(a): *Ángela va a usar el metro para ir al colegio el lunes y el miércoles.*

lunes	
8:00	usar el transporte público para ir al colegio
martes	
4:00	trabajar de voluntaria en el programa de reciclaje
miércoles	
8:00	usar el transporte público para ir al colegio
jueves	
7:00	caminar al colegio
5:00	juntar y recoger las latas para llevarlas a reciclar
viernes	
4:00	llevar cartón, periódicos y revistas a reciclar
sábado	
10:00	pedir a los vecinos que no usen sus carros hoy
2:00	participar en la limpieza del parque municipal
domingo	
10:00	sembrar árboles en el centro
2:00	investigar la política de los candidatos sobre el medio ambiente

1. caminar	4. hablar con los vecinos
2. reciclar	5. participar en la limpieza
3. investigar	6. trabajar de voluntaria

Classroom Management

Organizing Pair Work For **Actividades 2–4**, match up pairs of students with a third student. This student will play the part of "teacher reviewer," helping out when necessary and correcting when necessary.

Planning Ahead Prepare flashcards of subjunctive trigger phrases (**Es importante que,** etc.) to be used when reviewing the subjunctive and to elicit creative sentences.

3 La perezosa

Hablar/*Escribir* Antes, Luci no hacía mucho para cuidar del medio ambiente. Describe lo que ocurre en cada dibujo. ¿Cambió Luci su modo de pensar o no?

modelo

Tú: *Había muchas cosas en su casa que podía reciclar, pero antes Luci no lo quería hacer.*

Compañero(a): *¡Sí! Había botellas de plástico y de vidrio…*

Antes

Ahora

4 ¿Qué podemos hacer?

Hablar Tú y tu compañero(a) hablan sobre problemas ecológicos. ¿Qué soluciones hay?

modelo

Tú: *¿Cómo podemos eliminar la contaminación del aire?*

Compañero(a): *Pues, es muy complicado. Si cada familia usa su carro sólo tres veces por semana…*

destrucción de la capa de ozono
contaminación del aire
extinción de las especies
los derrames de petróleo
los combustibles

Vocabulario

El medio ambiente

el combustible *fuel*	por todas partes *all around*
complicado(a) *complicated*	proteger las especies *to protect the species*
descubrir *to discover*	reducir *to reduce*
los efectos *effects*	respetar *to respect*
increíble *incredible*	separar *to separate*
inútil *useless*	el smog *smog*
¡Qué lío! *What a mess!*	la tierra *land*
el permiso *permission*	
la población *population*	

¿Cómo puedes usar estas palabras para describir un problema ecológico en tu región?

Teaching All Students

Extra Help Ask students to choose 10 words from the **Vocabulario** on p. 135. Have them write a sentence for each word that will help them remember the meanings.

Native Speakers Ask students to talk at length about the environment of your community and how it can be protected.

Multiple Intelligences

Kinesthetic Have pairs of students create and act out short skits based on a vocabulary word or phrase. Pairs can say what their word or phrase is or have the class guess. Students should use props and gestures.

Objective: Transitional practice
Vocabulary in conversation

♻ **Ir a** + infinitive

Answers
1. A: ¿Cuándo va a caminar Ángela?
   B: Ángela va a caminar al colegio el jueves.
2. A: ¿Cuándo va a reciclar Ángela?
   B: Ángela va a reciclar el jueves y el viernes.
3. A: ¿Cuándo va a investigar Ángela?
   B: Ángela va a investigar la política de los candidatos sobre el medio ambiente el domingo.
4. A: ¿Cuándo va a hablar Ángela con los vecinos?
   B: Ángela va a hablar con los vecinos el sábado.
5. A: ¿Cuándo va a participar Ángela en la limpieza del parque municipal?
   B: Ángela va a participar en la limpieza del parque municipal el sábado.
6. A: ¿Cuándo va a trabajar de voluntaria Ángela?
   B: Ángela va a trabajar de voluntaria en el programa de reciclaje el martes.

Objective: Transitional practice
Vocabulary in conversation

Answers will vary.

Teaching Suggestions
Teaching Vocabulary
After presenting the vocabulary, call on volunteers to mime or sketch one of the words/expressions. The rest of the class tries to guess what is being illustrated.

Objective: Open-ended practice
Vocabulary in conversation

Answers will vary.

Block Schedule

Change of Pace Have students write a newspaper headline and lead-in sentence for an article dealing with each of the following:
• an oil spill
• air pollution
• polluted rivers
• a recycling program
• a new system of public transportation
(For additional activities, see **Block Scheduling Copymasters**.)

Teaching Resource Options

Print 📖

Más práctica Workbook PE, p. 53
Cuaderno para hispanohablantes
 PE, p. 51
Block Scheduling Copymasters
Unit 2 Resource Book
 Más práctica Workbook TE, p. 76
 Cuaderno para hispanohablantes
  TE, p. 92
 Absent Student Copymasters, p. 106
 Audioscript, p. 112

Audiovisual 🎧📺

OHT 27 (Quick Start), 30 (Grammar)
Audio Program CD 5, Track 2, Activity 5

Technology 🎧💻

Online Workbook, U2E2
Take-Home Tutor CD-ROM, U2E2

Quick Start Review

 Usted commands

Use OHT 27 or write on the board:
Write the **usted** command form for the following verbs:

1. sacar   4. usar
2. recoger   5. cuidar
3. eliminar   6. reducir

Answers
1. saque   3. elimine   5. cuide
2. recoja   4. use   6. reduzca

Teaching Suggestions
Reviewing the Present Subjunctive of Regular Verbs

• Remind students that you use the subjunctive to express emotion, doubt, opinion, point of view, and indirect command.
• The *main clause* uses the main verb expressing emotion, doubt, etc., in the *indicative,* and the *dependent clause* uses the verb in the *subjunctive.*
• **Que** usually appears before the subjunctive, and joins the main and dependent clauses.

PARTE B **Práctica: gramática y vocabulario**

Objetivos for Activities 5–15
• Say what should be done • React to ecology • React to others' actions

REPASO The Present Subjunctive of Regular Verbs

♻ **¿RECUERDAS?** *pp. 114, 116*
Remember when you learned to tell someone not to do something using **negative command forms?**

¡No **habl**es mucho!
¡No **habl**e mucho!
¡No **habl**emos mucho!

The same endings are used when you want to express your opinion or point of view using the subjunctive.

Es importante que uses el transporte público.
It's important that you use public transportation.

The present subjunctive

	-ar hablar	-er comer	-ir escribir
yo	hable	coma	escriba
tú	hables	comas	escribas
él, ella, usted	hable	coma	escriba
nosotros(as)	hablemos	comamos	escribamos
vosotros(as)	habléis	comáis	escribáis
ellos, ellas, ustedes	hablen	coman	escriban

Remember that you have to change the spelling for some verbs to keep the pronunciation the same.

bus**c**ar → bus**qu**e   pa**g**ar → pa**gu**e

cru**z**ar → cru**c**e   reco**g**er → reco**j**a

Practice: **Actividades** 5 6 7

Más práctica *cuaderno p. 53*
Para hispanohablantes *cuaderno p. 51*

🌐 **Online Workbook** CLASSZONE.COM

---

5 La ecóloga ♻ 🎧

Escuchar/*Escribir* Escucha lo que dice la ecóloga en la radio sobre el medio ambiente y qué podemos hacer para protegerlo. Empieza tus oraciones con las siguientes frases.

modelo
Es triste que...
Es triste que nosotros no respetemos el medio ambiente.

1. Es una lástima que…
2. Es importante que…
3. Es mejor que…
4. Es malo que…
5. Es lógico que…
6. Es necesario que…

También se dice
¡Hay muchos ambientes! Cuando hables del **ambiente,** especifica a cual te refieres.
• Si le preguntas a un(a) amigo(a) **¿cómo está el ambiente?** te refieres a la onda de un lugar.
• Ambiente también significa **atmósfera.**

Classroom Community

Storytelling Have students work in pairs or small groups to write short stories for children about protecting the environment. They should incorporate the phrases in the **Vocabulario** on p. 137. Have pairs/groups present their stories to the class.

Portfolio Have students choose an environmental issue and write a paragraph describing the problem (**Es una lástima que...**) and suggesting possible actions (**Es mejor que...**).

Rubric A = 13–15 pts. B = 10–12 pts. C = 7–9 pts. D = 4–6 pts. F = < 4 pts.

Writing criteria	Scale
Correct use of subjunctive	1 2 3 4 5
Other grammar/spelling accuracy	1 2 3 4 5
Vocabulary usage	1 2 3 4 5

6 Protejamos el medio ambiente

Hablar/Escribir Los expertos quieren que hagamos ciertas cosas para proteger el medio ambiente. ¿Qué quieren que hagamos?

modelo

no contaminar el medio ambiente

Quieren que no contaminemos el medio ambiente.

> **Nota: Gramática**
>
> Don't forget that verbs that end in **-uir**, like **contribuir**, include a **y** in their subjunctive form: **contribuya, contribuyas**, etc.

1. reciclar los productos de plástico
2. usar el transporte público
3. compartir el carro con amigos y colegas
4. no contribuir al desperdicio
5. andar en bicicleta
6. respetar el medio ambiente
7. no echar las botellas de vidrio a la basura
8. no contaminar el aire con químicos dañinos

7 Tu amigo(a) perezoso(a)

> **STRATEGY: SPEAKING**
>
> **Consider the effect of words and tone of voice**
> What is your purpose: to persuade, irritate, prompt action, work on sense of responsibility? What is a probable response to these two sentences: **¡Es ridículo que no recicles los periódicos!** and **Es una lástima que no recicles los periódicos.** Choose your words and tone of voice to fit your purpose.

Hablar/Escribir Quieres convencer a tu amigo(a) de que debería proteger el medio ambiente. Usa las siguientes expresiones impersonales para empezar un diálogo. Luego, cambien de papel.

modelo

Tú: *¡Es ridículo que no recicles los periódicos!*

Compañero(a): *Sí, lo sé.*

Tú *¡Es importante que los recicles hoy!*

Compañero(a) *Está bien. Más tarde voy al programa de reciclaje.*

> ### Vocabulario
>
> **Ya sabes**
>
> | | |
> |---|---|
> | es bueno que… | es posible que … |
> | es importante que… | es probable que … |
> | es lógico que… | es raro que … |
> | es malo que … | es ridículo que … |
> | es mejor que … | es triste que … |
> | es necesario que … | es una lástima que … |
> | es peligroso que … | |
>
> ¿Qué otras opiniones puedes expresar?

ACTIVIDAD 5 **Objective:** Controlled practice
Listening comprehension/Present subjunctive of regular verbs

♻ Impersonal expressions

Answers (See script, p. 127B.)

1. Es una lástima que la gente no comprenda la importancia de proteger nuestro planeta.
2. Es importante que cada comunidad instituya programas de reciclaje.
3. Es mejor que tú recicles los productos de plástico, papel y vidrio.
4. Es malo que contamines el aire con combustibles.
5. Es lógico que en el futuro los científicos desarrollen otras formas de energía.
6. Es necesario que protejamos la Tierra.

ACTIVIDAD 6 **Objective:** Transitional practice
Present subjunctive of regular verbs

Answers

1. Quieren que reciclemos los productos de plástico.
2. Quieren que usemos el transporte público.
3. Quieren que compartamos el carro con amigos y colegas.
4. Quieren que no contribuyamos al desperdicio.
5. Quieren que andemos en bicicleta.
6. Quieren que respetemos el medio ambiente.
7. Quieren que no echemos las botellas de vidrio a la basura.
8. Quieren que no contaminemos el aire con químicos dañinos.

Teaching Suggestions
Teaching Vocabulary
Remind students that these expressions require the subjunctive in the dependent clause because they refer to an opinion or point of view held by the speaker.

ACTIVIDAD 7 **Objective:** Open-ended practice
Present subjunctive of regular verbs in conversation/impersonal expressions

Answers will vary.

▣ Block Schedule
Variety Have students work in pairs to discuss "How to succeed…" + a topic of their choosing (in school, in football, in politics, in the theater, etc.). They should use the phrases in the **Vocabulario** on p. 137. Each pair should should also write down at least 8 sentences to present to the class. (For additional activities, see **Block Scheduling Copymasters**.)

Teaching All Students

Extra Help Have students make flashcards of the following verbs: **compartir, contaminar, desarrollar, descubrir, echar, prohibir, proteger, respetar, reciclar.** They should put the infinitive on one side and the complete subjunctive conjugation on the other side. Then have them work in pairs to quiz each other.

Multiple Intelligences

Interpersonal Have students work in pairs to ask and answer questions about any issues (school, friends, politics, ecology) that matter to them. They should use the phrases in the **Vocabulario** on p. 137 as starting points.

Teaching Resource Options

Print

Más práctica Workbook PE, p. 54
Cuaderno para hispanohablantes
  PE, p. 52
Block Scheduling Copymasters
Unit 2 Resource Book
  Más práctica Workbook TE, p. 77
  Cuaderno para hispanohablantes
    TE, p. 93
  Absent Student Copymasters, p. 107

Audiovisual

OHT 27 (Quick Start), 28 (Quick Start),
31 (Grammar), 32 (Grammar)

Technology

Online Workbook, U2E2
Take-Home Tutor CD-ROM, U2E2

Quick Start Review

🔄 **Present subjunctive: regular verbs**
Use OHT 27 or write on the board:
Write sentences using the following
elements:

1. es necesario / yo / separar /
   la basura
2. es una lástima / tú / no reciclar
3. es importante / todos / proteger /
   las especies
4. es bueno / Ana / tener / más ayuda
5. es peligroso / nosotros /
   consumir / tanta energía

Answers *See p. 127B.*

Teaching Suggestions
Reviewing The Present Subjunctive of Irregular Verbs

On the board or an OHT, write the list
of verbs from the bottom of p. 138. For
each one, call on one student to write
the **yo** form, then on another student
to supply the present subjunctive forms.

 Objective: Controlled practice
Present subjunctive of irregular verbs

Answers
1. Es importante que tengas...
2. salgas
3. estés
4. sepas
5. oigas
6. seas
7. traigas
8. conozcas
9. leas
10. vengas

REPASO — **The Present Subjunctive of Irregular Verbs**

♻️ **¿RECUERDAS?** *p.136* You have already learned to form the
subjunctive of regular verbs to express your opinion or
point of view.

> **Es importante que** uses el transporte público.
> *It's important that you use public transportation.*

▶ Some verbs have **irregular forms** in the **subjunctive**.

dar	estar	ir	saber	ser
dé	esté	vaya	sepa	sea
des	estés	vayas	sepas	seas
dé	esté	vaya	sepa	sea
demos	estemos	vayamos	sepamos	seamos
deis	estéis	vayáis	sepáis	seáis
den	estén	vayan	sepan	sean

> **Es bueno que** vayas a la escuela en autobús.
> *It's good that you go to school by bus.*

> **Es malo que no** estén de acuerdo.
> *It's too bad that they don't agree.*

The subjunctive of **haber** is haya.

> **Hay** mucha basura.
> *There is a lot of trash.*

> **Es malo que** haya mucha basura.
> *It's bad that there is a lot of trash.*

▶ Verbs with **yo forms** that end in **-go** or **-zco** in the present indicative use
the same **irregular stem** in the subjunctive.

decir → digo		conocer → conozco	
diga	digamos	conozca	conozcamos
digas	digáis	conozcas	conozcáis
diga	digan	conozca	conozcan

Other verbs like these are:

caer, hacer, oír, poner, salir, venir, tener, traer, ofrecer

Practice:
Actividades
8 9 10

Más práctica
cuaderno p. 54
Para hispanohablantes
cuaderno p. 52

 **Online Workbook**
CLASSZONE.COM

138 ciento treinta y ocho
Unidad 2

---

8 **Un viaje a Honduras**

Hablar/Escribir Vas a ir a
visitar a tus abuelos en
Tegucigalpa, Honduras.
Tu abuelita te da consejos.
¿Qué te dice?

> **modelo**
> *hacer las reservaciones*
> *Es importante que hagas las
> reservaciones.*

1. tener tu pasaporte
2. salir temprano para
   el aeropuerto
3. estar en el mostrador dos
   horas antes de la salida
4. saber el número de
   tu vuelo
5. oír los anuncios para
   los vuelos
6. ser cortés con los otros
   pasajeros
7. traer suficiente ropa
   para dos semanas
8. conocer la ciudad
   de Tegucigalpa
9. leer sobre la historia de
   Honduras
10. ¡venir a vernos!

Classroom Community

Learning Scenario Your visitors have arrived in
Honduras but don't know what to see or do. Have
students research places of interest in Honduras, then
make recommendations to their guests.

Game Have students work in groups of 5. On a single
sheet of paper, have the first student write a phrase
that triggers the subjunctive. The second student writes
a completion. The third student writes another phrase.
The fourth student writes a completion, and so on.
Group members continue passing the paper around for
a set period of time. At the end of the time, the group
with the most correct completions wins.

9 El guía turístico

Hablar/*Escribir*** Un grupo de tu colegio ha viajado a Guatemala con su profesor(a) de español. El guía turístico les recomienda diferentes cosas a todos. ¿Qué les recomienda?

modelo

tú / ir al museo

Es mejor que tú vayas al museo.

1. yo/ver las pirámides
2. nosotros/ser turistas responsables
3. usted/dar una donación al pueblo
4. ustedes/estar en el hotel a las siete
5. tú/traer tu cámara para sacar fotos

10 Los consejos

Hablar/*Escribir*** Dale consejos a tu amigo(a) usando los verbos en la lista y una expresión impersonal de la página 137. ¡Trata de dar consejos útiles! Luego cambien de papel.

modelo

conocer

Tú: *Es importante que conozcas los problemas ecológicos.*

Compañero(a): *Tienes razón. Buscaré información.*

1. poner
2. ir
3. dar
4. ver
5. tener
6. salir
7. hacer
8. escribir

REPASO   The Present Subjunctive of Stem-Changing Verbs

When you use the present subjunctive of -ar and -er **stem-changing verbs,** remember to make the same stem-changes as in the present indicative.

cerrar *to close*
e → ie

cierre	cerremos
cierres	cerréis
cierre	cierren

volver *to return*
o → ue

vuelva	volvamos
vuelvas	volváis
vuelva	vuelvan

Notice that -ir verbs change their stems differently. The stem of **mentir** alternates between **ie** and **i**, and **dormir** alternates between **ue** and **u**.

The verb **pedir** also has a stem change. The stem changes from **e** to **i** in all forms in the subjunctive.

mentir *to lie*
(e → ie and i)

mienta	mintamos
mientas	mintáis
mienta	mientan

dormir *to sleep*
(o → ue and u)

duerma	durmamos
duermas	durmáis
duerma	duerman

pedir *to ask for, to order*
(e → i)

pida	pidamos
pidas	pidáis
pida	pidan

Practice:
Actividades 11 12 13
Más práctica *cuaderno p. 55*
Para hispanohablantes *cuaderno p. 53*

Online Workbook CLASSZONE.COM

ciento treinta y nueve
México y Centroamérica Etapa 2   **139**

Teaching All Students

Extra Help Have students add to their flashcards (see "Extra Help," TE p. 137), this time using **empezar, recomendar, contar, entender, poder, resolver.** Again, they should put the infinitive on one side and the complete subjunctive conjugation on the other side. Then have them work in pairs to quiz each other.

Multiple Intelligences

Verbal Have students choose a location (**en la playa, en las montañas, en la selva,** etc.). Then have them write sentences about the location, using the subjunctive.

Naturalist Have students research the origins and growth of the issue of environmental awareness. Variation: Students might interview someone in the forest service or a comparable organization about this topic.

ACTIVIDAD 9 **Objective:** Transitional practice
Present subjunctive of irregular verbs

Answers *Answers may vary.*
1. Es mejor que yo vea las pirámides. 2. Es mejor que nosotros seamos turistas responsables. 3. Es mejor que usted dé una donación al pueblo. 4. Es mejor que ustedes estén en el hotel a las siete. 5. Es mejor que tú traigas tu cámara para sacar fotos.

ACTIVIDAD 10 **Objective:** Open-ended practice
Present subjunctive of irregular verbs in conversation

Answers
Answers will vary, but should use these verb forms in the tú statements.
1. pongas   3. des   5. tengas   7. hagas
2. vayas   4. veas   6. salgas   8. escribas

Quick Start Review

♻ **Present subjunctive: irregular verbs**
Use OHT 28 or write on the board: Complete the expressions with one of the following verbs:
dar / ir / poner / decir / salir / tener
1. Es raro que…
2. Es probable que…
3. Es ridículo que…
4. Es lógico que…
5. Es una lástima que…

Answers *See p. 127B.*

Teaching Suggestions
Reviewing The Present Subjunctive of Stem-Changing Verbs

Brainstorm a list of stem-changing verbs that students have learned. Then use the flashcards prepared for "Planning Ahead," TE p. 134. Show a flashcard, name a stem-changing verb infinitive, and have a student provide a sentence.

Block Schedule

Change of Pace Have pairs of students write 5–8 sentences using subjunctive phrases that they can represent with an icon or simple drawing (for example, a pillow could represent **Es importante que durmamos 8 horas.**). Have pairs display their drawings. Then the pairs read their sentences at random. The class must match the sentences with the images. (For additional activities, see **Block Scheduling Copymasters.**)

Teaching Resource Options

Print

Más práctica Workbook PE, p. 55
Cuaderno para hispanohablantes
  PE, p. 53
Block Scheduling Copymasters
Unit 2 Resource Book
  Más práctica Workbook TE, p. 78
  Cuaderno para hispanohablantes
  TE, p. 94
  Information Gap Activities, p. 98
  Absent Student Copymasters, p. 107

Audiovisual

OHT 28 (Quick Start), 33 (Grammar)
Word Tiles, U2E2

Technology

Online Workbook, U2E2
Take-Home Tutor CD-ROM, U2E2

ACTIVIDAD 11

Objective: Controlled practice
Present subjunctive of stem-changing
verbs in conversation

Answers

1. A: Es lógico que piense en su novia(o) todo el
tiempo. B: Es malo que piense en su novia(o)
todo el tiempo. *Rest varies.* 2. A: Es lógico que
te vistas de estilo *grunge.* B: Es malo que te
vistas de estilo *grunge. Rest varies.* 3. A: Es
lógico que vuelvan tarde a casa. B: Es malo
que vuelvan tarde a casa. *Rest varies.* 4. A: Es
lógico que sirva la cena antes de las ocho. B:
Es malo que sirva la cena antes de las ocho.
Rest varies. 5. A: Es lógico que jueguen
videojuegos todo el día. B: Es malo que
jueguen videojuegos todo el día. *Rest varies.*
6. A: Es lógico que nos acostemos temprano.
B: Es malo que nos acostemos temprano.
Rest varies.

ACTIVIDAD 12

Objective: Transitional practice
Present subjunctive of stem-changing
verbs

Answers

*Answers will vary, but should begin with the
following:*
1. Es importante que empieces...
2. Es bueno que pienses...
3. Es necesario que entiendas...
4. Es lógico que resuelvas...
5. Es mejor que pidas...
6. Es peligroso que pierdas...
7. Es posible que quieras...
8. *Answers will vary.*

---

11 ¿Es bueno o malo?

Hablar/*Escribir* Tú y tu compañero(a) no
siempre están de acuerdo. ¿Qué dicen? Sigan
el modelo.

> **modelo**
>
> *nosotros: pedir dinero a nuestros padres*
>
> **Tú:** *Es lógico que pidamos dinero a nuestros padres.*
>
> **Compañero(a):** *Es malo que les pidamos dinero. Es
> importante que ganemos nuestro
> propio dinero.*

1. él/ella: pensar en su novia(o) todo
   el tiempo
2. tú: vestirte de estilo *grunge*
3. ustedes: volver tarde a casa
4. usted: servir la cena antes de las ocho
5. los niños: jugar videojuegos todo el día
6. nosotros: acostarnos temprano

Nota cultural

Muchas de las unidades monetarias de Centroamérica
muestran personas o cosas históricas. En Guatemala la
moneda oficial es el **quetzal**, también nombre de un
pájaro nativo de Centroamérica que tenía gran significado
para los mayas. En Costa Rica y El Salvador se usa el
colón, nombrado así en honor al famoso explorador
Cristóbal Colón. El **balboa** es la
moneda oficial de Panamá. Su
nombre se refiere a Vasco Núñez
de Balboa, uno de los primeros
exploradores de esa región. Las
otras monedas de esta región
son el **peso** (México), la
córdoba (Nicaragua) y el
lempira (Honduras).

---

12 Consejos para proteger el planeta

Hablar/*Escribir* Hablas con tu primo(a) que
es menor que tú. Quieres darle buenos
consejos para que comience a proteger el
planeta. ¿Qué le dices?

> **modelo**
>
> *importante / empezar*
>
> *Es importante que empieces a pensar en el ambiente.*

1. importante/
   empezar
2. bueno/ pensar
3. necesario/
   entender
4. lógico/ resolver
5. mejor / pedir
6. peligroso/ perder
7. posible / querer
8. ¿...?

13 Recomendaciones

Hablar Tú y tu compañero(a) conversan
sobre el medio ambiente. Hablen sobre los
problemas que vean y algunas soluciones
posibles.

> **modelo**
>
> **Tú:** *Es necesario que resolvamos el problema de la
> contaminación del aire. ¿No crees?*
>
> **Compañero(a):** *Sí, claro. Por eso es importante que
> busquemos otras formas de energía.
> El petróleo es malo para el medio
> ambiente.*

More Practice: **Más comunicación** *p. R7*

Classroom Community

Group Activity Students work in groups of 3, and
write their solutions to protect the environment using
the expression **Es necesario que** + subjunctive. Have
students compile their solutions and rank them in order
of importance. Have groups present their solutions to
the class.

Game **Plan ahead:** Prepare a set of situation cards;
for example, **Hay mucha basura en el parque.** Divide
the class into teams. In turn, each team picks a card.
The team should respond within a time limit, using a
subjunctive phrase; for example, **Es mejor que
recojamos la basura.** The team with the most
grammatically correct sentences wins.

GRAMÁTICA   The Present Perfect Subjunctive

 ¿RECUERDAS? *p. 46* You have already learned how to form the **present perfect** in the **indicative.**

present tense of the auxiliary verb **haber,** *to have*   +   **past participle** of the verb.

The subjunctive also has a present perfect tense. To form it you use:

present subjunctive of **haber**   +   **past participle** of the verb.

haya **lleg**ado	**hay**amos **lleg**ado
hayas **lleg**ado	**hay**áis **lleg**ado
haya **lleg**ado	**hay**an **lleg**ado

You use the present perfect subjunctive to indicate that the action of the subordinate clause took place in the past. Compare these sentences.

present subjunctive

Es posible que Juan **visit**e Mitla.
*It's possible that Juan is **visiting/will visit** Mitla.*

present perfect subjunctive

Es posible que Juan **hay**a **visit**ado Mitla.
*It's possible that Juan **has visited/visited** Mitla.*

present subjunctive

Es bueno que **hag**as eso.
*It's good that **you're doing/will do** that.*

present perfect subjunctive

Es bueno que **hay**as **hecho** eso.
*It's good that **you've done/you did** that.*

Las ruinas de Mitla

Notice how the meanings of two subjunctives contrast with each other.

Practice:

 Actividades 14 15

Más práctica *cuaderno p. 56*
Para hispanohablantes *cuaderno p. 54*

 **Online Workbook**
CLASSZONE.COM

ciento cuarenta y uno
México y Centroamérica Etapa 2   **141**

Teaching All Students

Extra Help List verbs with irregular past participles on the board and have students provide the past participles.

Native Speakers Have students write a brief composition about what is necessary to do in their country of origin to protect the environment.

Multiple Intelligences

Interpersonal Have students work in pairs to role play an interview. The interviewer should begin with questions such as **¿Qué has hecho en la clase de matemáticas este año?** The other student responds.

Logical/Mathematical Have students make a chart of countries in Latin America, the names of their currencies, and the denominations of bills and coins.

Answers will vary.

Culture Highlights

● **UNIDADES MONETARIAS** El lempira de Honduras se nombró por un líder indígena, Lempira (1497–1537), que murió luchando contra los conquistadores españoles.

El peso nuevo comenzó a circular en México a principio de los noventa y se escribía N\$. Después de 1996, se dejó de utilizar «nuevo». El peso es la moneda actual de México.

Quick Start Review

Present subjunctive: stem-changing verbs

Use OHT 28 or write on the board: Write sentences using the following elements:

1. es importante / nosotros / pedir / dinero
2. es una lástima / Uds. / mentir
3. es necesario / él / dormir / ocho horas
4. es peligroso / tú / volver / tarde
5. es raro / ella / cerrar / ventanas

Answers *See p. 127B.*

Teaching Suggestions
Presenting The Present Perfect Subjunctive

- Review the present perfect tense by asking questions; for example: ¿Has comido hoy? ¿Has hecho la tarea? ¿Has visto la película *Frida*?
- You may wish to point out that the English equivalent of the present perfect subjunctive can be expressed as a simple or as a compound tense. **Es bueno que hayas comido.** = It's good that you ate/have eaten.

Teaching Resource Options

Print

Más práctica Workbook PE,
pp. 49–52, 56

Actividades para todos Workbook PE,
pp. 51–56

Cuaderno para hispanohablantes
PE, pp. 49–50, 54

Block Scheduling Copymasters

Unit 2 Resource Book

Más práctica Workbook TE,
pp. 72–75, 79

Actividades para todos Workbook
TE, pp. 80–85

Cuaderno para hispanohablantes
TE, pp. 90–91, 95

Information Gap Activities, p. 99

Absent Student Copymasters, p. 108

Audioscript, pp. 112

Audiovisual

Audio Program CD5, Track 3, Activity 15

Technology

Online Workbook, U2E2

Take-Home Tutor CD-ROM, U2E2

ACTIVIDAD 14 Objective: Controlled practice
Present perfect subjunctive in
conversation

Answers

1. A: Marta y Martín no hicieron la tarea. B: Es
increíble que (Marta y Martín) no hayan hecho la
tarea. 2. A: Pedro no fue a la biblioteca todavía. B:
Es posible que (Pedro) no haya ido a la biblioteca
todavía. 3. A: Tú trabajaste toda la noche. B: Es
bueno que (tú) hayas trabajado toda la noche. 4.
A: Nosotros olvidamos el examen. B: Es malo que
(nosotros) hayamos olvidado el examen. 5. A:
Arturo comprendió la tarea. B: Es importante que
(Arturo) haya comprendido la tarea. 6. A: Fumiko
y Kai no entendieron el capítulo. B: Es posible
que (Fumiko y Kai) no hayan entendido el
capítulo.

ACTIVIDAD 15 Objective: Controlled practice
Listening comprehension/present
perfect subjunctive

Answers (See script, p. 127B.)

1. Es bueno que Juan haya reciclado los periódicos
y las revistas. 2. Es bueno que Esperanza y Arnoldo
hayan compartido el carro toda la semana. 3. Es
malo que usted no haya usado el transporte
público. 4. Es malo que ustedes hayan echado las
botellas de plástico a la basura. 5. Es bueno que
nosotros hayamos trabajado como voluntarios en
el programa de reciclaje. 6. Es malo que tú hayas
comprado un aerosol el otro día.

14 El colegio

Hablar/Escribir Todos tienen mucho que
hacer para sus clases en el colegio. Tú y tu
compañero(a) conversan sobre qué han hecho
y no han hecho los estudiantes de su clase. ¿
Qué dicen?

> **modelo**
>
> *yo: estudiar para el examen toda la noche (es importante)*
>
> **Tú:** *Yo estudié para el examen toda la noche.*
>
> **Compañero(a):** *Es importante que (tú) hayas estudiado para el examen toda la noche.*

1. Marta y Martín: no hacer la tarea (es increíble)
2. Pedro: no ir a la biblioteca todavía (es posible)
3. tú: trabajar toda la noche (es bueno)
4. nosotros: olvidar el examen (es malo)
5. Arturo: comprender la tarea (es importante)
6. Fumiko y Kai: no entender el capítulo (es posible)

Nota cultural

El movimiento ecológico mexicano empezó
en serio a principios de los años ochenta, con
la constitución del **Grupo de los Cien**. Este
grupo incluyó a los artistas, intelectuales,
académicos y políticos más famosos de
México. Actualmente existen diversos grupos
ambientalistas como **Biodiversidad** y **Red
Ambiental Joven de México**.

15 El club de ecología

Escuchar/Hablar/Escribir Escucha lo que dice el
presidente del club de ecología sobre lo que
hizo cada miembro esta semana. Luego, di si
lo que han hecho es bueno o malo. Sigue el
modelo.

> **modelo**
>
> *Armando y Laura (es bueno que)*
>
> *Es bueno que Armando y Laura hayan participado en la campaña para embellecer la ciudad.*

1. Juan (es bueno que)
2. Esperanza y Arnoldo (es bueno que)
3. usted (es malo que)
4. ustedes (es malo que)
5. nosotros (es bueno que)
6. tú (es malo que)

Vocabulario

Nuestro planeta

la altura *height, altitude*

el bosque *forest*

el cielo *sky*

el clima *climate*

la colina *hill*

diverso(a) *diverse*

el ecosistema *ecosystem*

la fauna silvestre *wild animal life*

la flora silvestre *wild plant life*

la naturaleza *nature*

la piedra *rock*

la selva *jungle, forest*

la sequía *drought*

el valle *valley*

> ¿Qué palabras usarías para describir la región donde vives?

Classroom Community

Learning Scenario Give students a variety of
situations and have them respond logically to each,
using the present perfect subjunctive. For example:
Eva tiene muchas fotos de Costa Rica. → **Es posible
que haya visitado Costa Rica.**

Storytelling Have pairs or small groups of students
make up stories that incorporate at least 2 examples of
the present perfect subjunctive and 8 of the words
from the **Vocabulario** on p. 143. Encourage them to be
creative. Have pairs/groups present their stories using
props, gestures, or visuals, as appropriate.

Activities 16–17 bring together all concepts presented.

16 Sierra Madre

Hablar/Leer Tú y tu compañero(a) ven este anuncio para la empresa Sierra Madre en una revista. Léanlo y juntos contesten las siguientes preguntas.

1. ¿Para qué trabaja el grupo Sierra Madre?
2. ¿Dónde tiene programas?
3. ¿Qué hace el grupo Sierra Madre en la sociedad?
4. ¿De qué depende en gran parte el futuro de los mexicanos?
5. Según lo que aprendiste en este capítulo, ¿qué clase de grupo es Sierra Madre?
6. ¿Qué te gustaría hacer si trabajaras en Sierra Madre?

SIERRA MADRE

TRABAJAMOS POR LA CONSERVACIÓN DE LA NATURALEZA

Crear Conciencia en la sociedad para un manejo inteligente y duradero de los recursos naturales mexicanos, de los cuales depende en gran medida nuestro futuro.

17 La naturaleza

Hablar En grupos de tres o cuatro, conversen sobre la naturaleza de su pueblo. Mencionen los efectos del clima y todo lo que se relaciona con la conservación de la naturaleza.

modelo

Tú: *Por fin llovió este mes.*

Amigo(a) 1: *Sí. Es bueno que la sequía se haya acabado.*

Amigo(a) 2: *Tienes razón. El mes pasado los ríos habían bajado.*

Amigo(a) 3: *Y las plantas silvestres se estaban muriendo.*

More Practice: **Más comunicación** *p. R7*

 Online Workbook CLASSZONE.COM

Refrán

El que planta árbolesama a otros además de a sí mismo.

¿Qué quiere decir el refrán? En tu opinión, ¿por qué es sembrar árboles un acto de beneficencia? ¿Puedes pensar en otras actividades que benefician a la comunidad y a sus ciudadanos?

Teaching All Students

Extra Help Have each student write a sentence that includes 3 words from the **Vocabulario** and an example of the use of the present perfect subjunctive. Call on individual students to write their sentences on the board. Have the class make any necessary corrections.

Challenge Have students write poems entitled **La Naturaleza,** using words from the **Vocabulario,** or a brief dialog (pro-conservation/pro-development).

Multiple Intelligences

Visual Have students draw and label a scene that includes at least 10 words from the **Vocabulario.**

Musical/Rhythmic Have students create a rap or chant that includes at least 5 words from the **Vocabulario.**

 16 Objective: Transitional practice Present perfect subjunctive in conversation

Answers
1. Trabaja para la conservación de la naturaleza.
2. Tienen programas en México.
3. El grupo crea conciencia.
4. El futuro de los mexicanos depende del manejo inteligente y duradero de los recursos naturales.
5. *(Possible answer)* Es un grupo que protege el medio ambiente.
6. *Answers will vary.*

Teaching Suggestions
Teaching Vocabulary
Present the words/expressions using drawings and gestures. Ask for examples of appropriate words, such as **la fauna silvestre** or **el clima [de Florida].** Then discuss the question at the end.

 17 Objective: Open-ended practice Present perfect subjunctive/ vocabulary in conversation

Answers will vary.

Dictation
Using the Listening Activity Script for **Actividad 15** on TE p. 127B, dictate selected sentences to students. You may want to have students peer correct the sentences.

Critical Thinking
Tell students that as countries become more developed, this development endangers the environment. Have students discuss why this is true. Do they see any way that development and protecting the environment can be reconciled?

Block Schedule
Change of Pace Have students create crossword puzzles using words from the **Vocabulario** on pp. 130–131 and p. 143. Clues may be definitions in Spanish or sentences with the target words missing. Have students exchange and solve puzzles. (For additional activities, see **Block Scheduling Copymasters.**)

Teaching Resource Options

Print 📖

Actividades para todos Workbook
PE, pp. 57–59
Block Scheduling Copymasters
Unit 2 Resource Book
 Actividades para todos Workbook
 TE, pp. 86–88
 Absent Student Copymasters, p. 109

Audiovisual 🎧

OHT 29 (Quick Start)
Canciones CD

Technology 💻

🌐 www.classzone.com

🔔 Quick Start Review

♻ Central America

Use OHT 29 or write on the board:
• Escribe los nombres de los 7 países de Centroamérica.
• ¿En cuál no se habla el español?

Answers
• Guatemala, El Salvador, Honduras, Nicaragua, Costa Rica, Panamá, Belize
• Belize (Note: many Spanish speakers live in Belize)

Teaching Suggestions
Presenting Cultura y comparaciones

• Have students look at the pictures on pp. 144–145 and guess the topic of the reading. Write the list of possibilities on the board.
• Ask various students for their observations on the photos: ¿Qué observas en las fotos?

Reading Strategy

Scan for details Have students scan the text to find answers to these questions: ¿Dónde pasa el verano Rafaela Dávila? ¿Con quién vive? ¿Cuál es la profesión del señor Rodríguez? ¿Cuántos años tiene la anciana?

En colores
CULTURA Y COMPARACIONES

UNIDOS podemos hacerlo

PARA CONOCERNOS
STRATEGY: CONNECTING CULTURES Gather and analyze information about literacy Look up the word literacy. Then use the word **alfabetización** to add to that definition. Below is a chart showing literacy rates in three countries. In the library, look up two or three other countries and add them to the chart. What do you think accounts for differences among countries?

País	Por ciento
Argentina	96%
E.E.U.U.	97%
Honduras	73%

Nicaragua es uno de los países más hermosos de América Central, pero ha tenido que hacer muchos cambios para avanzar su desarrollo económico. A principios de los años 80, casi 50% de los nicaragüenses no sabían leer ni escribir. Desde entonces, Nicaragua ha organizado campañas de alfabetización para enseñar a leer y escribir a sus ciudadanos. Ahora, cerca del 65% de estos saben leer.

Vas a leer una página del diario de Rafaela Dávila, una estudiante que ayudó a la comunidad sirviendo como profesora en la campaña de alfabetización[1] en Nicaragua. Ella era estudiante de preparatoria[2] en Masaya cuando pasó el verano en el pueblo de Santo Tomás del Norte, situado en las montañas cerca de Honduras.

---

[1] literacy
[2] preparatory school

144 ciento cuarenta y cuatro
Unidad 2

Classroom Community

Paired Activity Have students work in pairs to answer the **¿Comprendiste?** questions on p. 141 before reviewing them in class.

Portfolio Have students work in pairs to write and record or videotape an interview. One partner plays the role of Rafaela. The other plays one of her friends and asks questions about her experiences.

Rubric A = 8–9 pts. B = 6–7 pts. C = 4–5 pts. D = 2–3 pts. F = < 2 pts.

Interview criteria	Scale
Accuracy of pronunciation	1 2 3
Accuracy/completeness of content	1 2 3
Creativity/interest	1 2 3

Santo Tomás del Norte, martes 30 de junio

Ya llevo una semana en Santo Tomás del Norte y me encuentro muy a gusto[3] aquí. Vivo en casa de los Rodríguez, una familia que tiene cinco hijos. La señora Rodríguez, Doña Rosa, sabe leer un poco, pero el señor Rodríguez, Don Mario, no sabe ni una letra del abecedario[4]. Es carpintero y él y los otros hombres del pueblo se han juntado para reparar una vieja casa abandonada que nos servirá de[5] escuela.....

Noto que hay mucho entusiasmo en el pueblo. Esta gente nunca ha tenido la oportunidad de estudiar nada y tiene muchas ganas de aprender. Un caso en especial me pareció muy conmovedor[6]. Ayer en la calle me habló una anciana. Dicen en el pueblo que tiene ochenta y cinco años. Ella me mostró su lápiz y su cuaderno y me preguntó que si las clases comenzaban ese mismo día. Le dije que hoy no, que pasado mañana. —Bueno, me contestó con una sonrisa, —hace más de ochenta años que espero. Puedo esperar dos días más.

[3] comfortable, happy
[4] alphabet
[5] will be used as
[6] moving

Leer es poder

Campaña Nacional de Alfabetización,
Ministerio Nicaragüense de Educación

CLASSZONE.COM
More About Central America

¿Comprendiste?

1. ¿Quién es Rafaela Dávila?
2. ¿Qué hace en Santo Tomás?
3. ¿Qué hacen los hombres de Santo Tomás del Norte para ayudar a Rafaela?
4. ¿Qué quería saber la anciana que habló con Rafaela?

¿Qué piensas?

¿Por qué están tan entusiasmados por aprender los residentes de Santo Tomás del Norte?

Hazlo tú

Piensa en lo que significa ser voluntario(a). ¿Qué conocimientos y cualidades personales debe tener esa persona? Elige un campo en el cual te interese ser voluntario(a) (la alfabetización, el servicio a la comunidad, la política, u otro). Haz un póster o escribe un anuncio para atraer a otros voluntarios.

Culture Highlights

● **NICARAGUA** Nicaragua es la nación más grande de Centroamérica. Se conoce como «la Tierra de lagos y volcanes» porque tiene los dos lagos más grandes de Centroamérica y numerosos volcanes activos.

Managua, la capital de Nicaragua, tiene muy pocos edificios históricos debido a los terremotos de 1931 y 1972 que prácticamente destruyeron la ciudad.

● **EL HURACÁN MITCH** A finales de octubre de 1998, el Huracán Mitch azotó a Centroamérica. Algunos dicen que posiblemente este desastre natural es el más devastador de la historia. Murieron más de 10.000 personas y más de un millón quedaron sin hogar. En Nicaragua hubo 4.300 muertos o perdidos y 725.000 personas que quedaron sin hogar.

Interdisciplinary Connection

Geography Have students research the topography of Central America and create topographical maps. Have them use these maps to explain why some communities are cut off from educational and government resources. Students may also research and discuss the many natural disasters that have occurred in the area, and rebuilding efforts.

¿Comprendiste?

Answers
1. Rafaela Dávila es estudiante de preparatoria en Masaya, Nicaragua.
2. Sirve como profesora en la campaña de alfabetización en Nicaragua.
3. Reparan una vieja casa abandonada para que sirva de escuela.
4. Quería saber si las clases comenzaban el mismo día.

Block Schedule

Peer Teaching Have students work in pairs to think about how they would present the Spanish alphabet and a beginning reading lesson to a community that has never had a school. Have volunteers try out their presentations with the class. (For additional activities, see **Block Scheduling Copymasters**.)

Teaching All Students

Extra Help Encourage students to read the passage more than once and to make use of cognates. Have students make a list of cognates and their meanings.

Native Speakers Ask students to talk about schools in Latin America. At what age do students start school? How many grades are there? Do students have to pass a test to graduate?

Multiple Intelligences

Logical/Mathematical Have students research the literacy rates of Mexico and all 7 Central American countries. Have them also research the total population of each country. Then have them calculate the number of people who know how to read and write.

Teaching Resource Options
Print
Cuaderno para hispanohablantes PE,
  pp. 55–56
Unit 2 Resource Book
  Cuaderno para hispanohablantes
  TE, pp. 96–97
  Information Gap Activities,
  pp. 100–101
  Family Involvement, pp. 110–111

Audiovisual
OHT 29 (Quick Start)

Technology
eTest Plus Online / Test Generator
CD-ROM
  www.classzone.com

🔔 **Quick Start Review**
♻ Protecting the environment
Use OHT 29 or write on the board:
Haciendo uso del presente del subjuntivo, escribe 5 oraciones en que expliques cómo te sientes acerca de proteger el medio ambiente.
Answers will vary.

✓ **Teaching Suggestions**
What Have Students Learned?
Have students look at the "Now you can…" notes listed on the left side of pages 146–147. Tell them to think about which areas they might not be sure of and consult those "To review" notes.

Now you can...
• say what should be done.

To review
• the present subjunctive of regular verbs see p. 136.
• the present subjunctive of irregular verbs see p. 138.

Now you can...
• say what should be done.

To review
• the present subjunctive of regular verbs see p. 136.
• the present subjunctive of stem-changing verbs see p. 139.

En uso
REPASO Y MÁS COMUNICACIÓN

OBJECTIVES
• Say what should be done
• React to the ecology
• React to others' actions

1 ¿Crees que...?

Tu compañero(a) quiere hacerte algunas preguntas sobre el medio ambiente. ¿Qué te pregunta y cómo le respondes?

modelo

nosotros / proteger el planeta
Compañero(a): *¿Debemos proteger el planeta?*
Tú: *Sí, es importante que protejamos el planeta.*

1. nosotros / ir en autobús
2. yo / reciclar las botellas de vidrio
3. las comunidades / limitar el uso de aerosoles
4. nosotros / no echar todo a la basura
5. las ciudades / instituir un programa de reciclaje
6. nosotros / no destruir la capa de ozono
7. yo / saber más sobre el medio ambiente
8. los políticos / declarar zonas de reserva ecológica

2 ¡Un robo!

Dos personas vieron un robo. ¿Qué es necesario que hagan?

modelo

ayudar a las víctimas
Es necesario que ayuden a las víctimas.

1. llamar a la policía
2. pedir información de las víctimas
3. volver a la escena del crimen
4. contar lo que pasó a la policía
5. describir a los criminales
6. recordar qué pasó

146 ciento cuarenta y seis
Unidad 2

Classroom Community

Paired Activity After working in pairs to complete **Actividad 1,** have students use the answers to create a flier for an environmental awareness campaign. When possible, the answers should be expanded to explain why the action is necessary. For example: **Es importante que compartamos el carro con amigos y colegas para evitar la contaminación del aire.**

Learning Scenario Some community members don't want to do anything to help protect the environment. Have students convince them that there are simple ways in which they can help, and that every effort counts.

Now you can...

- react to the ecology.

To review

- the present subjunctive of regular verbs see p. 136.
- the present subjunctive of irregular verbs see p. 138.

3 Una entrevista

Tú eres el (la) nuevo(a) presidente(a) del club para proteger el medio ambiente. Te hacen una entrevista para el periódico de la escuela sobre tus opiniones.

modelo

¿Es necesario hacer todo lo posible para preservar nuestro planeta?

¡Claro! Es necesario que hagamos todo lo posible para preservar nuestro planeta.

1. ¿Es posible reducir la contaminación del aire?
2. ¿Es bueno reciclar los productos de plástico?
3. ¿Es importante buscar otras formas de energía?
4. ¿Es malo contaminar el aire con combustibles?
5. ¿Es lógico limitar el uso de aerosoles?
6. ¿Es malo no respetar el medio ambiente?
7. ¿Es triste no comprender la importancia de proteger la fauna silvestre?
8. ¿Es una lástima no saber conservar los recursos naturales?

EL RIO ES FUENTE DE VIDA NO CONTAMINE

Now you can...

- react to others' actions.

To review

- the present perfect subjunctive see p. 141.

4 Mi reacción

¿Qué piensas de las actividades de los demás? Escribe una oración que describa tu reacción.

modelo

bueno: Los científicos desarrollaron otras formas de energía.

Es bueno que los científicos hayan desarrollado otras formas de energía.

1. bueno: Tú reciclaste las latas.
2. lógico: Mis vecinos participaron en la limpieza del parque.
3. malo: Mi amigo no fue a la reunión del club de ecología.
4. lástima: Nosotros destruimos la capa de ozono.
5. triste: Ustedes contribuyeron a la contaminación del aire.
6. bueno: Las ciudades prohibieron el uso de contaminantes.
7. lógico: Los políticos instituyeron un programa de reciclaje.
8. malo: Tú echaste las revistas a la basura.

ciento cuarenta y siete
México y Centroamérica Etapa 2 **147**

ACTIVIDAD 1 Answers

1. A: ¿Crees que nosotros debemos ir en autobús? / B: Sí, es importante que vayamos en autobús.
2. A: ¿Crees que yo debo reciclar las botellas de vidrio? / B: Sí, es importante que recicles las botellas de vidrio.
3. A: ¿Crees que las comunidades deben limitar el uso de aerosoles? / B: Sí, es importante que limiten el uso de aerosoles.
4. A: ¿Crees que nosotros no debemos echar todo a la basura? / B: Sí, es importante que no echemos todo a la basura.
5. A: ¿Crees que las ciudades deben instituir un programa de reciclaje? / B: Sí, es importante que instituyan un programa de reciclaje.
6. A: ¿Crees que nosotros no debemos destruir la capa de ozono? / B: Sí, es importante que no destruyamos la capa de ozono.
7. A: ¿Crees que yo debo saber más sobre el medio ambiente? / B: Sí, es importante que sepas más sobre el medio ambiente.
8. A: ¿Crees que el gobierno debe declarar zonas de reserva ecológica? / B: Sí, es importante que declare zonas de reserva ecológica.

ACTIVIDAD 2 Answers

1. Es necesario que llamen a la policía. 2. Es necesario que pidan información de las víctimas. 3. Es necesario que vuelvan a la escena del crimen. 4. Es necesario que no digan mentiras a la policía. 5. Es necesario que describan a los criminales. 6. Es necesario que recuerden qué pasó.

ACTIVIDAD 3 Answers

1. Es posible que reduzcamos la contaminación del aire. 2. Es bueno que reciclemos los productos de plástico. 3. Es importante que busquemos otras formas de energía. 4. Es malo que contaminemos el aire con combustibles. 5. Es lógico que limitemos el uso de aerosoles. 6. Es malo que no respetemos el medio ambiente. 7. Es triste que no comprendamos la importancia de proteger la fauna silvestre. 8. Es una lástima que no sepamos conservar los recursos naturales.

ACTIVIDAD 4 Answers

1. Es bueno que hayas reciclado las latas.
2. Es lógico que hayan participado en la limpieza del parque.
3. Es malo que no haya ido a la reunión del club de ecología.
4. Es una lástima que hayamos destruido la capa de ozono.
5. Es triste que hayan contribuido a la contaminación del aire.
6. Es bueno que hayan prohibido el uso de contaminantes.
7. Es lógico que hayan instituido un programa de reciclaje.
8. Es malo que hayas echado las revistas a la basura.

Teaching All Students

Extra Help Working in pairs, have students scramble the word order for the questions in **Actividad 3**. They should then exchange papers and re-order the words.

Multiple Intelligences

Interpersonal Have students write a letter to the editor of your school newspaper explaining why and how students should become more involved in protecting the environment. Have them propose the establishment of a new environmental club.

Naturalist Have students develop a visual, chart, or mind map that shows the interrelated cause and effect of environmental or ecological issues.

Teaching Resource Options

Print

Unit 2 Resource Book
Audioscript, p. 71
Vocabulary Quizzes, pp. 117–119
Grammar Quizzes, pp. 120–121
Etapa Exam, Forms A and B,
  pp. 122–131
Examen para hispanohablantes,
  pp. 132–136
Portfolio Assessment, pp. 137–138
Multiple Choice Test Questions,
  pp. 229–231

Audiovisual

OHT 29 (Quick Start)
Audio Program CD 19, Track 11

Technology

eTest Plus Online / Test Generator
CD-ROM

www.classzone.com

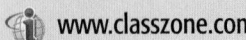 **5** and **6**

Rubric: Speaking

Criteria	Scale	
Sentence structure	1 2 3	A = 11–12 pts.
Vocabulary use	1 2 3	B = 9–10 pts.
Originality	1 2 3	C = 7–8 pts.
Fluency	1 2 3	D = 4–6 pts.
		F = < 4 pts.

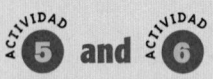 **7** En tu propia voz

Rubric: Writing

Criteria	Scale	
Vocabulary use	1 2 3 4 5	A = 14–15 pts.
Accuracy	1 2 3 4 5	B = 12–13 pts.
Creativity, appearance	1 2 3 4 5	C = 10–11 pts.
		D = 8–9 pts.
		F = < 8 pts.

Teaching Note: En tu propia voz

Writing Strategy Suggest that students implement the writing strategy "State your message using a positive tone" in order to make their brochures more effective. They should begin with a strong opening statement and provide details. They should end by reemphasizing their message.

---

5 Y yo, ¿qué puedo hacer?

STRATEGY: SPEAKING
Express support or lack of support Listen to your group member's plans and decide if you want to support their efforts. Use impersonal expressions (p. 133) to state your position or to ask for clarification from your classmates.

En grupos de dos o tres, conversen sobre lo que pueden hacer hoy para proteger el medio ambiente.

modelo

Tú: *Yo voy a caminar al colegio.*

Amigo(a) 1: *Yo voy a reciclar mis revistas.*

Amigo(a) 2: …

6 ¿Cuál es el problema?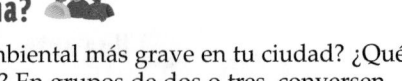

¿Cuál es el problema ambiental más grave en tu ciudad? ¿Qué sugieres para resolverlo? En grupos de dos o tres, conversen sobre los problemas en su comunidad y las soluciones posibles.

modelo

Amigo 1: *Yo creo que el desperdicio es el problema más grave que tenemos.*

Amigo 2: *Es importante que reciclemos todos los productos de plástico, papel y vidrio.*

Amigo 3: *Yo creo que la contaminación del aire es el problema más grave.*

Amigo 1: …

---

7 *En tu propia voz*

ESCRITURA Te han elegido para escribir y diseñar un folleto (*brochure*) que se va a distribuir en tu colegio. El propósito del folleto es educar a los estudiantes sobre el medio ambiente y cómo protegerlo. Escribe dos o tres oraciones que expliquen la importancia de proteger el medio ambiente. Ilustra tus ideas si quieres.

modelo

¿Tienes bicicleta? ¡Úsala! Las bicicletas no echan combustibles al aire. Cada vez que te subes a un carro, estás destruyendo la capa de ozono. ¿Lo sabías?

CONEXIONES

Las ciencias Haz una investigación sobre el reciclaje en tu comunidad. ¿Quién recicla y cuánto? Haz una gráfica de lo que reciclas tú y lo que reciclan tu familia, tu escuela y tu comunidad en una semana. Incluye la cantidad. Haz un reportaje de lo que aprendas. Compara el porcentaje de lo que echan a la basura y lo que reciclan. ¿Es necesario que tu escuela y comunidad hagan más? ¿Es posible que tú puedas hacer más?

El reciclaje de...	el papel/el cartón	el vidrio	las latas	el plástico
mi casa			10 latas	2 botellas de jugo
mi escuela	papel de computadora			
mi comunidad	periódicos/revistas		latas de sopa	

148 ciento cuarenta y ocho
Unidad 2

Classroom Community

TPR Ask students the following questions. If the answer is yes, students stand up and act out the activity; if it is no, students remain seated or sit down. ¿Reciclas periódicos? ¿Compras aerosoles? ¿Caminas a la escuela? ¿Compras productos que usan químicos dañinos? ¿Usas el transporte público durante el fin de semana? ¿No echas a la basura botellas de vidrio? ¿Usas contaminantes? etc.

Game Divide the class into 2 teams. Have a member of 1 team come to the board. Give that student a card with a phrase on it (**la destrucción de la capa de ozono**), which he/she must communicate to the team by drawing on the board (without speaking or writing words). The team must guess the phrase within a time limit. If the team guesses, they get a point and the other team goes. If the team does not guess, the card passes to the other team. Teams should rotate artists.

Flashcards
CLASSZONE.COM

En resumen
REPASO DE VOCABULARIO

REACT TO THE ECOLOGY

Environment

el combustible	fuel
los efectos	effects
el medio ambiente	environment
el planeta	planet
la población	population
por todas partes	all around
los recursos naturales	natural resources
la tierra	land

Problems

el aerosol	aerosol
la capa de ozono	ozone layer
complicado(a)	complicated
la contaminación del aire	air pollution
el contaminante	pollutant
dañino(a)	damaging
el derrame de petróleo	oil spill
el desperdicio	waste
la destrucción	destruction
echar	to throw away
inútil	useless
¡Qué lío!	What a mess!
el químico	chemical
el smog	smog

Solutions

¡A todos nos toca!	It's up to all of us!
la botella	bottle
el cartón	cardboard
desarrollar	to develop
descubrir	to discover
increíble	incredible
instituir	to institute
la lata	can
el permiso	permission
el plástico	plastic
el programa de reciclaje	recycling program
prohibir	to prohibit

Solutions (continued)

proteger	to protect
reducir	to reduce
respetar	to respect
separar	to separate
el vidrio	glass
las zonas de reserva ecológica	conservation land

Nature

la altura	altitude
el bosque	forest
el cielo	sky
el clima	climate
la colina	hill
diverso(a)	diverse
el ecosistema	ecosystem
las especies	species
la fauna silvestre	wild animal life
la flora silvestre	wild plant life
la naturaleza	nature
la piedra	rock
la selva	jungle, forest
la sequía	drought
el valle	valley

SAY WHAT SHOULD BE DONE

♻ **Ya sabes**

Es...

bueno que	It's good that
importante que	It's important that
lógico que	It's logical that
malo que	It's bad that
mejor que	It's better that
necesario que	It's necessary that
peligroso que	It's dangerous that
posible que	It's possible that
probable que	It's probable that
raro que	It's rare that
ridículo que	It's ridiculous that
triste que	It's sad that
una lástima que	It's a pity that

SAY WHAT SHOULD BE DONE

Subjunctive with regular verbs

Es malo que **contaminemos** el aire y el agua.

Subjunctive with irregular verbs

Es bueno que **sepas** más sobre el medio ambiente.

Subjunctive with stem-changing verbs

Es importante que **recuerden** que el planeta es para todos.

REACT TO OTHERS' ACTIONS

Present perfect subjunctive

Es lógico que **hayas empezado** un programa de reciclaje.

Juego

Sopa de letras

Pon en orden las letras siguientes para saber qué es lo que no se puede ver, pero que nos protege todos los días. (¡Ojo! Son cuatro palabras enteras.)

O E D A N P D A C O A L O Z

Teaching All Students

Extra Help Have students create simple word search puzzles using 5–10 words from the **Vocabulario** on p. 149. Have them exchange puzzles with a partner for completion.

Challenge Have students create a political cartoon dealing with protecting the environment. You may want to bring in examples in English from local or national newspapers.

Native Speakers Have students investigate if local, state, or federal agencies have environmental information written in Spanish. If so, they should obtain the information and present it to the class, helping other students with vocabulary.

Interdisciplinary Connection

Science Work with the science department to find out what a recycling plant does to recycle paper, glass, metal, and plastic. Students might also look at products at home to see if any of them say that they are made from recycled products.

🔔 Quick Start Review

♻ **Etapa vocabulary**

Use OHT 29 or write on the board:
Fill in the missing letters for each word. Then unscramble these letters to discover a message.

1. cont _ minación de _ ai _ e
2. _ _ rosol
3. d _ s _ _ rdicio
4. con _ amina _ t _
5. _ e _ ró _ eo
6. sm _ _

Mensaje:

_ _ _ _ _ _ _   _ _   _ _ _ _ _ _ _

Answers *See p. 127B.*

Teaching Suggestions
Vocabulary Review

Have students create tongue twisters using **Etapa** vocabulary.

Dictation

Dictate the following sentences to review the **Etapa:**

1. La niña descubre la fauna silvestre.
2. Es una lástima que no hayan empezado un programa de reciclaje.
3. Es bueno que hayan visitado tantas zonas de reserva ecológica.

Juego

Answer: la capa de ozono

Block Schedule

Research Have students choose a Spanish-speaking country and investigate what natural reserves have been created and what other measures that country is taking to protect the environment.

Planning Guide CLASSROOM MANAGEMENT

OBJECTIVES

Communication
- React to nature *pp. 152–153, 154–155, 168–169*
- Express doubt *pp. 160–162*
- Relate events in time *pp. 162–166*

Grammar
- Review: Use the subjunctive with expressions of emotion *pp. 158–159*
- Review: Use the subjunctive to express doubt and uncertainty *pp. 160–162*
- Use the subjunctive with **cuando** and other conjunctions of time *pp. 162–164*

Culture
- Regional vocabulary *p. 156*
- **La Isla de Ometepe** *p. 158*
- Nature reserves in Central America *p. 161*
- Juan José Arreola, a Mexican storywriter *pp. 166–167*
- Costa Rica's national parks *pp. 168–169*

♻ Recycling
- Ecology vocabulary *p. 159*
- Pastimes *p. 161*
- Future tense *p. 163*
- Household chores *p. 164*

STRATEGIES

Listening Strategies
- Determine your purpose for listening *p. 154*

Speaking Strategies
- Gain thinking time before speaking *p. 159*
- Reassure others *p. 172*

Reading Strategies
- Recognize uses of satire, parody, and irony *p. 166*
- Compare related details *TE p. 168*

Writing Strategies
- Use details to enrich a description *TE p. 172*
- Persuade by presenting solutions to problems *p. 174*

Connecting Cultures Strategies
- Recognize variations in vocabulary *p. 156*
- Learn about **La Isla de Ometepe** *p. 158*
- Learn about nature reserves in Central America *p. 161*
- Judge homogenization of culture *TE p. 166*
- Analyze the advantages and disadvantages of ecotourism *p. 168*
- Connect and compare what you know about ecotourism in your community to help you learn about ecotourism in a new community *pp. 168–169*

PROGRAM RESOURCES

 Print
- *Más práctica* Workbook PE *pp. 57–64*
- *Actividades para todos* Workbook PE *pp. 61–70*
- Block Scheduling Copymasters *pp. 49–56*
- Unit 2 Resource Book
  - *Más práctica* Workbook TE *pp. 141–148*
  - *Actividades para todos* Workbook TE *pp. 149–158*
  - *Cuaderno para hispanohablantes* TE *pp. 159–166*
  - Information Gap Activities *pp. 167–170*
  - Family Letter *p. 171*
  - Absent Student Copymasters *pp. 172–178*
  - Family Involvement *pp. 179–180*
  - Audioscript *pp. 181–184*
  - Assessment Program, Unit 2 Etapa 3 *pp. 185–225; 232–234*
  - Video Activities *pp. 235–238*
  - Videoscript *pp. 239–241*
  - Answer Keys *pp. 242–246*

 Audiovisual
- Audio Program CD 6
- *Canciones* CD
- Video Program Videotape 08:30 / DVD, U2
- Word Tiles U2E3
- Overhead Transparencies M1–M5; GO1–GO5; 4, 34–49

 Technology
- eEdition Plus Online/eEdition CD-ROM
- Easy Planner Plus Online/Easy Planner CD-ROM
- eTest Plus Online/Test Generator CD-ROM
- Online Workbook
- Take-Home Tutor CD-ROM
- www.classzone.com

Assessment Program Options
- Unit 2 Resource Book
  - Vocabulary Quizzes
  - Grammar Quizzes
  - Etapa Exam Forms A and B
  - *Examen para hispanohablantes*
  - Portfolio Assessment
  - Unit 2 Comprehensive Test
  - *Prueba comprensiva para hispanohablantes,*
  - Multiple Choice Test Questions
- Audio Program CD 19
- eTest Plus Online/Test Generator CD-ROM

Native Speakers
- *Cuaderno para hispanohablantes* PE *pp. 57–64*
- *Cuaderno para hispanohablantes* TE (Unit 2 Resource Book)
- *Examen para hispanohablantes* (Unit 2 Resource Book)
- *Prueba comprensiva para hispanohablantes,* Unit 2 (Unit 2 Resource Book)
- Audio Program *(Para hispanohablantes)* CD 6, 19
- Audioscript (Unit 2 Resource Book)

Student Text
Listening Activity Scripts

 **Situaciones** *pages 154–155*

• CD 6

¡Hola, amigos! Soy el capitán Carlos Camacho. Es un placer llevarlos por el Parque SalvaNatura y darles una breve introducción a la flora y fauna de cada país centroamericano.

Empecemos en la sección guatemalteca. Guatemala es un país fabuloso para la conservación de la vida silvestre. En la colección de SalvaNatura, tenemos dos tipos de pájaros guatemaltecos: los loros y los tucanes. En nuestro parque también incluimos los monos araña que son tan curiosos, y las tortugas, que también dan gran placer con sus movimientos calculados. Aunque Guatemala también tiene muchas serpientes, no las hemos incluido en nuestra colección.

Ahora pasemos a la sección hondureña. Honduras es un país lleno de sorpresas. Para nuestra colección, hemos traído desde Honduras algunos jaguares y boas constrictoras. Nos fascinan las tortugas de río y de mar, así que tenemos unas pocas de ellas y para no perder de la vida costeña, también hemos incluido algunos pelícanos.

Sigamos con la sección salvadoreña. ¿Cómo podemos abrir una sección sobre El Salvador y no incluir esos encantadores osos hormigueros? También verán algunos zorrillos. ¿Y los pájaros? En SalvaNatura hay para todos: tucanes, picaflores, búhos y quetzales. ¡Que no se les olviden los binoculares!

Ahora estamos en la sección nicaragüense. ¿Sabían que los únicos tiburones de agua dulce en el mundo residen en el Lago de Nicaragua? Claro, no pudimos traerlos a nuestra reserva pero sin embargo hay otros animales de Nicaragua que pueden presenciar aquí: los monos y los loros verdes.

La sección costarricense es una de nuestras secciones más visitadas por los EcoTuristas. ¿Por qué será? Costa Rica es famosa por tantos animales que nos fue muy difícil decidir cuáles traer. Tenemos mariposas de las cuales hay 1000 especies. Y los pájaros. En Costa Rica se han registrado 850 especies de pajáros. En SalvaNatura tenemos las quince especies de loros, seis diferentes tipos de tucanes, el quetzal y muchos más.

Y para terminar, tenemos la sección panameña. De Panamá hemos incluido en nuestra colección los venados, algunos jaguares y las iguanas verdes. Panamá tiene una variedad rica de pájaros, pero no las hemos incluido porque la sección costarricense incluye muchos de los mismos pájaros.

Gracias por visitar el Parque SalvaNatura. Esperamos que hayan disfrutado su visita.

ACTIVIDAD 6  **Juan** *page 159*

Modelo: Adriana, espero que vayas conmigo a la fiesta.
1. Papá, siento que estés enfermo.
2. Hermanito, me alegro de que estudies tanto.
3. Martín, tengo miedo de que te enojes conmigo.
4. Hermanita, siento que no puedas ir al cine con nosotros.
5. Adriana, me alegro de que me invites al baile.
6. Felipe, espero que te sientas mejor mañana.

ACTIVIDAD 13  **Los quehaceres** *page 164*

Modelo: Cortaré el césped en cuanto pueda.
1. Plancharé la ropa hasta que me canse.
2. Corté el césped hasta que anocheció.
3. Limpiaré el cuarto en cuanto llegue a casa.
4. Barrí el piso hasta que acabé.
5. Pasaré la aspiradora en cuanto acabe de lavar los platos.
6. Regué las plantas hasta que oscureció.
7. Haré la cena tan pronto como llegue a casa.
8. Sacaré las malas hierbas hasta que no quede ninguna.

Quick Start Review Answers

p. 162 Expressions of doubt/uncertainty
1. Es verdad que yo pago mil dólares por las vacaciones.
2. Es cierto que tú sales mañana de vacaciones.
3. Dudo que él pueda nadar con tubo de respiración.
4. Quizás el ecoturismo sea bueno para los animales salvajes.
5. No es seguro que los monos vivan en el bosque.

p. 173 Word association
Answers will vary. Answers could include:
1. el saco de dormir
2. el aguacero
3. el anochecer
4. el agua dulce
5. la mariposa
6. la linterna

Sample Lesson Plan - 50 Minute Schedule

DAY 1

Etapa Opener
- Quick Start Review (TE, p. 150) 5 MIN.
- Have students look at the *Etapa* Opener and answer the questions. 5 MIN.

En contexto: Vocabulario
- Quick Start Review (TE, p. 152) 5 MIN.
- Present *Descubre*, p. 152. Have students use context and pictures to learn *Etapa* vocabulary. Use the Situational OHTs for additional practice. 15 MIN.

En vivo: Situaciones
- Quick Start Review (TE, p. 154) 5 MIN.
- Present the Listening Strategy, p. 154. Have students read section 1, p. 154. Play the audio for section 2. Have students work in groups to complete section 3. 15 MIN.

Homework Option:
- Have students write answers to *¿Comprendiste?*, p. 153.

DAY 2

En acción: Vocabulario y gramática
- Check homework. 5 MIN.
- Quick Start Review (TE, p. 156) 5 MIN.
- Have students complete *Actividad* 1 orally. 5 MIN.
- Have students do *Actividad* 2 in pairs. 5 MIN.
- Have students do *Actividades* 3 and 4 in pairs. 10 MIN.
- Quick Start Review (TE, p. 158) 5 MIN.
- Present *Repaso:* The Subjunctive with Expressions of Emotion and the *Vocabulario*, p. 158. 10 MIN.
- Do *Actividad* 5 orally. 5 MIN.

Homework Option:
- Have students complete *Actividad* 5 in writing. *Más práctica* Workbook, p. 61. *Cuaderno para hispanohablantes*, p. 59.

DAY 3

En acción (cont.)
- Check homework. 5 MIN.
- Play the audio; do *Actividad* 6. 5 MIN.
- Present the Speaking Strategy, p. 159. Then have students complete *Actividad* 7 in pairs. 15 MIN.
- Quick Start Review (TE, p. 160) 5 MIN.
- Present *Repaso:* The Subjunctive to Express Doubt and Uncertainty and the *Vocabulario*, p. 160. 10 MIN.
- Have students complete *Actividad* 8 orally. 5 MIN.
- Have students complete *Actividad* 9 in pairs. Have volunteer pairs present various items. 5 MIN.

Homework Option:
- Have students complete *Actividad* 8 in writing. *Más práctica* Workbook, p. 62. *Cuaderno para hispanohablantes*, p. 60.

DAY 4

En acción (cont.)
- Check homework. 5 MIN.
- Have students complete *Actividad* 10 in pairs. 5 MIN.
- Quick Start Review (TE, p. 162) 5 MIN.
- Present *Gramática:* The Subjunctive with *cuando* and Other Conjunctions of Time and the *Vocabulario*, pp. 162 and 163. 10 MIN.
- Present the *Nota*, then do *Actividad* 11 orally. 5 MIN.
- Have students complete *Actividad* 12 in pairs. 5 MIN.
- Play the audio; do *Actividad* 13. 5 MIN.
- Present the *Vocabulario*, p. 164. Then do *Actividad* 14 in pairs. 10 MIN.

Homework Option:
- Have students complete *Actividad* 11 in writing. *Más práctica* Workbook, pp. 63–64. *Cuaderno para hispanohablantes*, pp. 61–62.

DAY 5

En acción (cont.)
- Check homework. 5 MIN.
- Have students work in groups to read and complete *Actividad* 15. Expand using Information Gap Activities, Unit 2 Resource Book, p. 168; *Más comunicación*, p. R8. 20 MIN.

Refrán
- Present the *Refrán*. 5 MIN.

En voces: Lectura
- Quick Start Review (TE, p. 166) 5 MIN.
- Present the Reading Strategy, p. 166. Call on volunteers to read the *Lectura* aloud. Have students answer the *¿Comprendiste?/¿Qué piensas?* questions, p. 167. 15 MIN.

Homework Option:
- Have students complete *Hazlo tú*, p. 167.
- *Actividades para todos* Workbook, pp. 61–66.

DAY 6

En colores: Cultura y comparaciones
- Check homework. 5 MIN.
- Quick Start Review (TE, p. 170) 5 MIN.
- Present the Connecting Cultures Strategy, p. 168. Call on volunteers to read the article aloud. Have students answer the *¿Comprendiste?/¿Qué piensas?* questions, p. 169. 20 MIN.

En uso: Repaso y más comunicación
- Quick Start Review (TE, p. 170) 5 MIN.
- Have students do *Actividades* 1–4 orally. 15 MIN.

Homework Option:
- Have students complete *Hazlo tú*, p. 169. Review for *Etapa* 3 Exam.

DAY 7

En uso (cont.)
- Check homework. 5 MIN.
- Present the Speaking Strategy, p. 172, and have students do *Actividades* 5 and 6 in groups. 10 MIN.

En tu propia voz: Escritura
- Have students brainstorm ideas for *Actividad* 7. 5 MIN.

En resumen: Repaso de vocabulario
- Quick Start Review (TE, p. 173) 5 MIN.
- Review grammar questions, etc., as necessary. 5 MIN.
- Complete *Etapa* 3 Exam. 20 MIN.

Homework Option:
- Have students complete their compositions for *Actividad* 7, p. 172. Review for Unit 2 Comprehensive Test.

DAY 8

En tu propia voz: Escritura
- Check homework. 5 MIN.
- Present the Writing Strategy, p. 174. Do the writing activity, pp. 174–175. 10 MIN.

Unit 2 Comprehensive Test
- Review grammar questions, etc., as necessary. 5 MIN.
- Complete Unit 2 Comprehensive Test. 30 MIN.

Ampliación
- Optional: Use a suggested project, game, or activity. (TE, pp. 105A–105B)

Homework Option:
- Have students complete the assignment for *Conexiones*. Preview *Unidad* 3 Opener. Have students read and study pp. 176–177.

Sample Lesson Plan - Block Schedule (90 minutes)

DAY 1

Etapa Opener
- Quick Start Review (TE, p. 150) 5 MIN.
- Have students look at the *Etapa* Opener and answer the questions. 5 MIN.
- Use Block Scheduling Copymasters. 10 MIN.

En contexto: Vocabulario
- Quick Start Review (TE, p. 152) 5 MIN.
- Present *Descubre*, p. 152. Have students use context and pictures to learn *Etapa* vocabulary. Use the Situational OHTs for additional practice. 15 MIN.

En vivo: Situaciones
- Quick Start Review (TE, p. 154) 5 MIN.
- Present the Listening Strategy, p. 154. 5 MIN.
- Have students read section 1, p. 154. Play the audio for section 2. Have students work in groups to complete section 3. 15 MIN.

En acción: Vocabulario y gramática
- Quick Start Review (TE, p. 156) 5 MIN.
- Have students complete *Actividad* 1 orally. 5 MIN.
- Have students do *Actividad* 2 in pairs. Have several pairs present their mini-conversations. 5 MIN.
- Have students do *Actividades* 3 and 4 in pairs. 10 MIN.

Homework Option:
- Have students write answers to *¿Comprendiste?*, p. 153. Have students complete *Actividades* 3 and 4 in writing.

DAY 2

En acción (cont.)
- Check homework. 5 MIN.
- Quick Start Review (TE, p. 158) 5 MIN.
- Present *Repaso:* The Subjunctive with Expressions of Emotion and the *Vocabulario*, p. 158. 10 MIN.
- Do *Actividad* 5 orally. 5 MIN.
- Play the audio; do *Actividad* 6. 10 MIN.
- Present the Speaking Strategy, p. 159. Then have students complete *Actividad* 7 in pairs. Expand using Information Gap Activities, Unit 2 Resource Book, p. 167; *Más comunicación*, p. R8. 20 MIN.
- Quick Start Review (TE, p. 160) 5 MIN.
- Present *Repaso:* The Subjunctive to Express Doubt and Uncertainty and the *Vocabulario*, p. 160. 10 MIN.
- Have students complete *Actividad* 8 orally. 5 MIN.
- Have students complete *Actividad* 9 in pairs. Have volunteer pairs present various items. 10 MIN.
- Have students complete *Actividad* 10 in pairs. 5 MIN.

Homework Option:
- Have students complete *Actividades* 5 and 8 in writing. *Más práctica* Workbook, pp. 61–62. *Cuaderno para hispanohablantes*, pp. 59–60.

DAY 3

En acción (cont.)
- Check homework. 10 MIN.
- Quick Start Review (TE, p. 162) 5 MIN.
- Present *Gramática:* The Subjunctive with *cuando* and Other Conjunctions of Time and the *Vocabulario*, p. 162. 10 MIN.
- Present the *Vocabulario*, p. 163. 5 MIN.
- Present the *Nota,* then do *Actividad* 11 orally. 5 MIN.
- Have students complete *Actividad* 12 in pairs. 5 MIN.
- Use an expansion activity from TE pp. 160–161 for variety. 5 MIN.
- Play the audio; do *Actividad* 13. 10 MIN.
- Present the *Vocabulario*, p. 164. Then do *Actividad* 14 in pairs. 10 MIN.
- Have students work in groups to read and complete *Actividad* 15. Expand using Information Gap Activities, Unit 2 Resource Book, p. 168; *Más comunicación*, p. R8. 20 MIN.

Refrán
- Present the *Refrán*. 5 MIN.

Homework Option:
- Have students complete *Actividad* 11 in writing. *Más práctica* Workbook, pp. 63–64. *Cuaderno para hispanohablantes*, pp. 61–62.
- *Actividades para todos* Workbook, pp. 61–66.

DAY 4

En voces: Lectura
- Check homework. 5 MIN.
- Quick Start Review (TE, p. 166) 5 MIN.
- Present the Reading Strategy, p. 166. Call on volunteers to read the *Lectura* aloud. Have students answer the *¿Comprendiste?/¿Qué piensas?* questions, p. 167. 15 MIN.

En colores: Cultura y comparaciones
- Quick Start Review (TE, p. 168) 5 MIN.
- Present the Connecting Cultures Strategy, p. 168. Call on volunteers to read the article aloud. Have students answer the *¿Comprendiste?/¿Qué piensas?* questions, p. 169. 15 MIN.

En uso: Repaso y más comunicación
- Quick Start Review (TE, p. 170) 5 MIN.
- Do *Actividades* 1–4 orally. 15 MIN.
- Present the Speaking Strategy, p. 172, then do *Actividades* 5 and 6 in groups. 10 MIN.
- Do *Actividad* 7 in writing. 15 MIN.

Homework Option:
- Have students complete *Hazlo tú*, pp. 167 and 169. Review for *Etapa* 3 Exam and Unit 2 Comprehensive Test.

DAY 5

En resumen: Repaso de vocabulario
- Check homework. 5 MIN.
- Quick Start Review (TE, p. 173) 5 MIN.
- Review grammar questions, etc., as necessary. 5 MIN.
- Complete *Etapa* 3 Exam. 20 MIN.

Conexiones
- Discuss *Las ciencias*, p. 172. 5 MIN.

Unit 2 Comprehensive Test
- Review grammar questions, etc., as necessary. 5 MIN.
- Complete Unit 2 Comprehensive Test. 30 MIN.

En tu propia voz: Escritura
- Present the Writing Strategy, p. 174. Do the writing activity, pp. 174–175. 15 MIN.

Ampliación
- Optional: Use a suggested project, game, or activity. (TE, pp. 105A–105B)

Homework Option:
- Have students complete the assignment for *Conexiones*. Preview *Unidad 3* Opener. Have students read and study pp. 176–177.

▼ Vamos a acampar en un parque nacional.

Etapa Theme
Reacting to nature; expressing doubt; and relating events in time

Grammar Objectives
- Reviewing the use of the subjunctive with expressions of emotion
- Reviewing the use of the subjunctive to express doubt and uncertainty
- Using the subjunctive with **cuando** and other conjunctions of time

Teaching Resource Options

Print

Block Scheduling Copymasters
Unit 2 Resource Book
  Family Letter, p. 171
  Absent Student Copymasters, p. 172

Audiovisual

OHT 3, 40 (Quick Start)
Canciones CD
Video Program Videotape 08:30 / DVD, U2

Quick Start Review

♻ **Capital cities**

Use OHT 40 or write on the board:
Write the capital city of each country:

1. Guatemala	4. Nicaragua
2. El Salvador	5. Costa Rica
3. Honduras	6. Panamá

Answers

1. Guatemala	4. Managua
2. San Salvador	5. San José
3. Tegucigalpa	6. Panamá

Teaching Suggestions
Previewing the Etapa
- Ask students to study the picture on pp. 150–151 (1 min.).
- Close books; have students name at least 3 things that they noticed.
- Ask students to speculate on what the **Etapa** is about and what type of vocabulary they may be learning. **¿De qué piensan que se trata esta Etapa? ¿Qué tipo de vocabulario piensan que van a aprender?**
- Use the **¿Qué ves?** questions to focus the discussion.

UNIDAD 2

ETAPA 3

La riqueza natural

OBJECTIVES

- React to nature
- Express doubt
- Relate events in time

¿Qué ves?

Mira la foto. Contesta las preguntas.

1. ¿Qué cosas ven los turistas?
2. ¿Dónde se encuentran?
3. ¿Cómo crees que se sentirán el chico de la mochila azul y el chico de la gorra? ¿Cómo te sentirías tú?
4. ¿Sabes de qué país viene la foto pequeña? ¿Cómo podrías averiguarlo?

150

Classroom Management

Planning Ahead Collect and bring in travel brochures, posters, photos, postcards, etc. from the Central American countries. Also bring in samples of ecotour brochures from travel agencies.

Peer Review Before beginning this **Etapa**, have students work in pairs to review the present subjunctive and present perfect subjunctive forms. They can use flashcards created in **Etapa 2** to quiz each other orally.

Culture Highlights

● **PARQUE NACIONAL VOLCÁN POÁS**
El Parque Poás es el más popular de Costa Rica. El Volcán Poás tiene 8.884 pies de altura. Su cráter activo emite vapor tóxico continuamente. Es uno de los pocos volcanes activos accesibles de las Américas.

● **LOS MAYAS** Los mayas, los habitantes que vivían en América Central antes de que llegara Cristóbal Colón, pensaban que aspectos de la naturaleza como el sol y la luna eran dioses. El volcán también era un dios y los mayas llamaban Masaya a la diosa de los volcanes. Otras civilizaciones, como los aztecas, compartían la creencia de que los volcanes eran divinos.

Cross Cultural Connections

Ask students to research **El Volcán Poás** in Costa Rica and Mount Saint Helens in the state of Washington, then compare and contrast the two.

Supplementary Vocabulary

la chimenea volcánica	volcanic vent
hacer erupción	to erupt
el río de lava	lava stream
el volcán activo	active volcano
el volcán inactivo	inactive volcano

151

Block Schedule

Research Point out that volcanoes on the west coast of the Americas are part of what is called the Pacific Ring of Fire. Have students research the Ring of Fire and identify the Spanish-speaking countries included in that ring. Also have them identify which volcanoes in those countries are active. (For additional activities, see **Block Scheduling Copymasters.**)

Teaching All Students

Extra Help Ask yes/no or either/or questions about the photo. For example: ¿Están en la selva tropical? ¿Hace frío o calor? ¿La camisa del chico de la gorra es de muchos colores?

Challenge Have students write a paragraph describing the picture. Ask individual students to write their paragraphs on the board. Correct as a whole class.

Multiple Intelligences
Verbal Have students write out a dialog, then dramatize a conversation among the people in the photo.
Naturalist Have students research information about the different kinds of volcanoes, the structure of volcanoes, or myths within communities that live around volcanoes. Many Web sites are dedicated to volcanoes and provide interesting facts and activities.

Teaching Resource Options

Print 📖
Block Scheduling Copymasters
Unit 2 Resource Book
  Absent Student Copymasters, p. 172

Audiovisual 🎧
OHT 34, 35, 36, 36A, 37, 37A, 40
  (Quick Start)

Technology 💻
Online Workbook, U2E3
Take-Home Tutor CD-ROM, U2E3

🔔 Quick Start Review

♻ **Animals**

Use OHT 40 or write on the board:
Escribe por lo menos 6 animales que conozcas.

Answers
Answers will vary. Answers could include:
el loro, la rana, el pez, el perro, el gato, el pollo, el caballo, el cerdo, el león, la llama, la vaca, el mono

Teaching Suggestions
Introducing Vocabulary

• Have students look at pages 152–153. Use OHT 59 and 60 to present the vocabulary.

• Ask the Comprehension Questions on TE p. 153 in order of yes/no (questions 1–3), either/or (questions 4–6), and simple words or phrases (questions 7–10). Expand by adding similar questions.

• Use the TPR activity to reinforce the meaning of individual words.

Descubre

Answers
1. b
2. c

En contexto VOCABULARIO

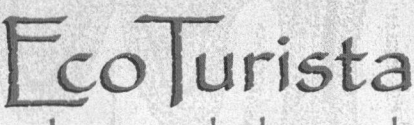

EcoTurista
Lo mejor de dos mundos: la ecología y el turismo

Seis recomendaciones para el EcoTurista que quiere conocer CENTROAMÉRICA.

📦 Descubre

Lee cada oración y decide qué quiere decir la frase en **azul**.

1. Manejar un coche cuando tienes sueño es **peligroso**.
   a. *safe*
   b. *dangerous*
   c. *intelligent*
2. Los lagos y ríos son de **agua dulce**; los mares son de agua salada.
   a. *saltwater*
   b. *ice water*
   c. *freshwater*

En COSTA RICA
Los ríos Sarapiquí, Corobicí y Pacuare Costa Rica cuenta con buenos ríos para la **navegación por rápidos**. Este deporte, a veces **peligroso**, es una aventura. El que esté atento verá iridiscentes **mariposas** azules y los colores llamativos de los **tucanes**.

En EL SALVADOR
Parque Nacional Montecristo
Si tienes suerte, aquí verás monos, **zorrillos** y **osos hormigueros**. Hay 87 especies de pájaros como los **picaflores** y los **búhos**.

En GUATEMALA
Biotopo Cerro Cahuí
Aquí verás los colores brillantes de las muchas variedades de tucanes, **loros** y **halcones**. En la selva hay más de 20 especies de animales, tales como los **monos araña**, los **venados** y los **ocelotes**. En el agua hay **tortugas** y **serpientes**.

152

Classroom Community

TPR Draw or cut out pictures from magazines of the birds and animals on pp. 152–153. Display the pictures in the room. Ask individual students to do various things with the pictures, such as the following: **Toca la mariposa. Describe el mono araña. Llévale el ocelote a Rosa. Dale los animales del agua a Alejandro.**

Group Activity Divide the class into 6 groups and assign a Central American country to each group. Have the groups research another natural reserve/geographical feature in their assigned countries. They should find information on location, flora, fauna, geography, and preservation efforts. Have each group present its reserve to the class, showing the location on a map.

En PANAMÁ

El Refugio de Vida Silvestre Isla Iguana

Este refugio es famoso no sólo por las **iguanas** que le dan su nombre, pero también por las **ballenas jorobadas** que visitan sus mares de junio a noviembre. En Isla Iguana puedes **bucear** y **nadar con tubo de respiración** si quieres ver los **peces** tropicales, pescar o solamente descansar en la playa.

En HONDURAS

Refugio de Vida Silvestre Cuero y Salado

En este refugio encontrarás una selva llena de animales **salvajes:** monos, **jaguares** y **boas constrictoras**. Entre las 196 especies de pájaros hay tucanes, loros y **pelícanos**.

En NICARAGUA

Isla de Ometepe

Esta isla es la más grande del mundo en un lago **de agua dulce**. Los únicos **tiburones** de agua dulce del mundo viven en el Lago de Nicaragua. ¡Atrévete!

Online Workbook CLASSZONE.COM

¿Comprendiste?

1. ¿Has ido alguna vez a una reserva ecológica? ¿Cuál?
2. ¿Has visto algunos de los animales mencionados en la revista EcoTurista? ¿Cuáles?
3. ¿Te gustaría conocer uno de los lugares recomendados por la revista EcoTurista? ¿Cuál? ¿Por qué?
4. ¿Crees que serías un(a) buen(a) EcoTurista? ¿Por qué o por qué no?
5. ¿Piensas que es importante que los países protejan su flora y fauna? ¿Crees que el ecoturismo es una buena idea para realizar eso?

Teaching All Students

Extra Help Have students go through the **En contexto** and list the words under the following categories: **pájaro, pez, otro animal.** Then have them sort and organize the words according to other categories (size, color, habitat, etc.).

Native Speakers Ask students to narrate a more complete description of a visit to one of the reserves, including transportation, accommodations, and activities.

Multiple Intelligences

Kinesthetic Have students work in pairs to create a postcard for 1 of the ecological reserves/geographical locations. They should create a drawing on the front of the card, and write a brief note home describing their experience on the back. Have pairs present their postcards and read their notes. The science department may have additional resources to share.

Comprehension Questions

1. ¿Son los mares de agua dulce? (No.)
2. En Costa Rica, ¿hay buenos ríos para la navegación por rápidos? (Sí.)
3. ¿Es peligrosa la navegación por rápidos? (Sí.)
4. ¿Los zorrillos son blancos y negros o azules y negros? (blancos y negros)
5. En el agua, ¿hay loros y halcones o tortugas y serpientes? (tortugas y serpientes)
6. ¿Las iguanas son reptiles o pájaros? (reptiles)
7. ¿Con qué puedes nadar para ver los peces tropicales? (con tubo de respiración)
8. ¿Cuáles son algunos animales salvajes? (jaguares, boas constrictoras, monos)
9. ¿En qué clase de lago está la Isla de Ometepe? (en un lago de agua dulce)
10. ¿Qué animales viven en el Lago de Nicaragua? (tiburones de agua dulce)

Culture Highlights

● **EL RÍO PACUARE** El río Pacuare está actualmente amenazado con la posible construcción de una represa para la generación de electricidad. Si se construye, se verán amenazados el ecosistema del bosque y las tierras de los indios cabecar, una tribu que vive al sureste de Costa Rica.

● **EL BIOTOPO CERRO CAHUÍ** El Biotopo Cerro Cahuí, al lado del lago Petén Itzá, tiene muchos senderos desde los cuales se puede ver el lago completo.

● **EL REFUGIO DE VIDA SILVESTRE ISLA IGUANA** Hay más de 200 especies de peces y 13 de las 20 especies de corales que habitan el Pacífico oriental.

● **LA ISLA DE OMETEPE** En la Isla de Ometepe se encuentran los volcanes Concepción y Maderas.

Block Schedule

Change of Pace Have pairs of students design a poster for an ecotour to 1 of the reserves/geographical locations. Remind them to use the strategy "Appeal to the senses" **(la vista, el oído, el tacto, el gusto, el olfato)** to entice people to visit the reserve. (For additional activities, see **Block Scheduling Copymasters**.)

Teaching Resource Options

Print
Block Scheduling Copymasters
Unit 2 Resource Book
  Absent Student Copymasters, p. 173
  Audioscript, p. 181

Audiovisual
OHT 38, 39, 41 (Quick Start)
Audio Program CD 6, Track 1

Technology
Take-Home Tutor CD-ROM

Quick Start Review

 Natural reserves

Use OHT 41 or write on the board:
Match each country with the corresponding information:

1. ___ Costa Rica
2. ___ El Salvador
3. ___ Guatemala
4. ___ Honduras
5. ___ Nicaragua
6. ___ Panamá
   a. Refugio de Vida Silvestre Cuero y Salado
   b. Isla de Ometepe
   c. Sarapiquí, Corobicí, Pacuare
   d. Biotopo Cerro Cahuí
   e. Refugio de Vida Silvestre Isla Iguana
   f. Parque Nacional Monte Cristo

Answers
1. c   2. f   3. d   4. a   5. b   6. e

Teaching Suggestions
Presenting Situations

• Present the Listening Strategy, p. 154, and discuss the Pre-listening questions. Then have students make their list of listening strategies.
• Use OHT 38 and 39 to present the **Leer** section. Ask simple yes/no, either/or, or short-answer questions.
• Use Audio CD 6 and have students do the **Escuchar** section (see Script TE p. 149B). Then have students complete the Listening Strategy exercise.
• Have students work in groups to complete the **Hablar/Escribir** section.

AUDIO
En vivo
SITUACIONES

PARA ESCUCHAR • STRATEGY: LISTENING

Pre-listening What memories do you have of visits to the zoo? What are the pros and cons of taking animals out of their natural habitat?

Determine your purpose for listening You will hear a guide give a tour of a zoological park. Before listening, decide whether you are on a field trip or a visit with friends. Then, make a list of listening strategies you consider most appropriate and use them while listening.

How effective were your purpose and strategies? Would a different purpose and strategies change your understanding and memory?

El Parque SalvaNatura

Estás en el Parque SalvaNatura y escuchas al guía turístico, quien explica las secciones y la vida silvestre del parque.

1 Leer

Cuando llegas al Parque SalvaNatura, la primera cosa que te da el guía turístico es un mapa del parque. El parque tiene seis secciones que representan la flora y fauna de cada país en Centroamérica. Estudia el mapa para ver qué hay en cada uno.

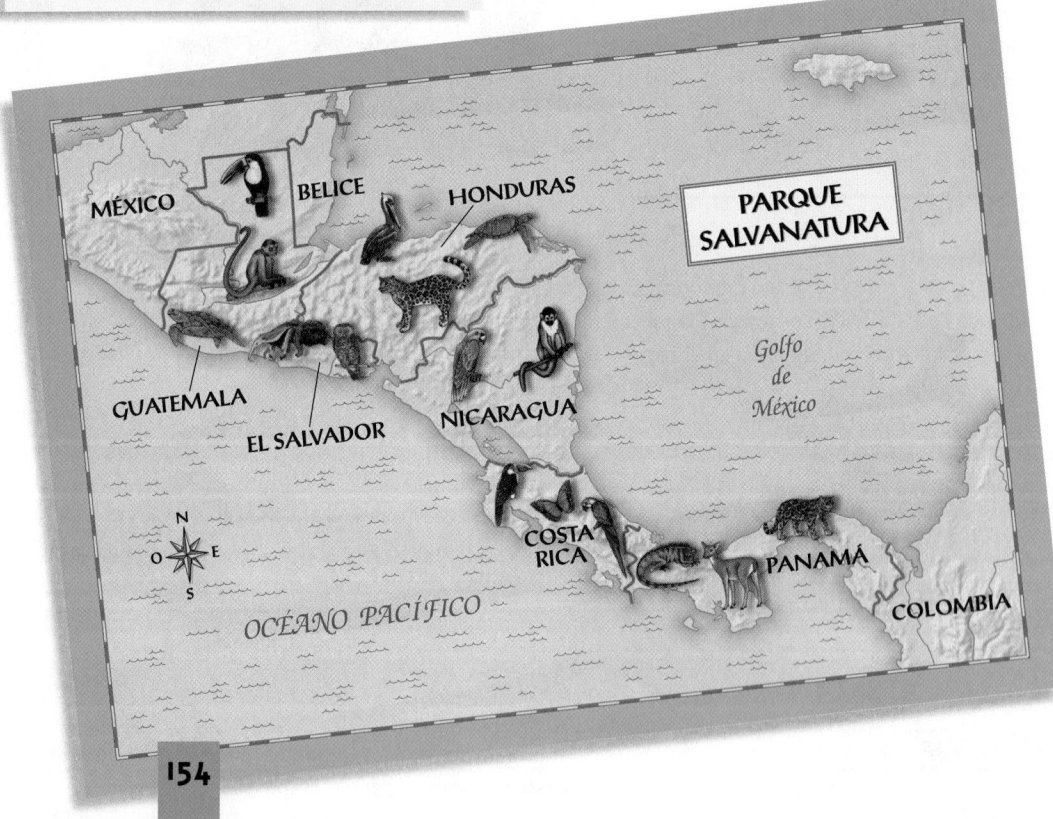

154

Classroom Community

Paired Activity Have students take turns pretending they are various animals. They should describe each animal and mime its activities. The partner guesses the identity. This activity may also be done in written form: **Yo soy... ¿Quién soy?**

Game Plan ahead: Make drawings or have students make drawings of the various animals on pp. 148–149. Make enough pictures for the whole class (some will be duplicates). Have each student choose 1 drawing and write 3 statements about it. Two of the statements are true and 1 is false. Divide the class into 2 teams. One student at a time from each team takes a turn reading his/her statements. Students from the other team take turns guessing the false one. If they guess correctly the team gets a point.

Take-Home Tutor

② Escuchar

El guía turístico te explica qué animales hay en cada sección del parque. Escucha y decide si esos animales están (sí) o no están (no) en cada sección.

En la sección guatemalteca		
• tucanes	Sí	No
• monos araña	Sí	No
• serpientes	Sí	No

En la sección hondureña		
• jaguares	Sí	No
• venados	Sí	No
• tortugas	Sí	No

En la sección salvadoreña		
• boas constrictoras	Sí	No
• mariposas	Sí	No
• osos hormigueros	Sí	No

En la sección nicaragüense		
• tiburones	Sí	No
• monos	Sí	No
• serpientes	Sí	No

En la sección costarricense		
• mariposas	Sí	No
• loros	Sí	No
• jaguares	Sí	No

En la sección panameña		
• iguanas	Sí	No
• venados	Sí	No
• jaguares	Sí	No

③ Hablar/Escribir

Ahora tú eres el (la) guía turístico(a) de un parque zoológico. ¿Qué animales escogerías para tu parque? Con dos o tres compañeros, diseñen un parque, decidan qué animales traerían a su parque y dibujen un mapa para los turistas con el país de origen de cada animal. Den un nombre imaginativo a su parque.

Parque Nacional Corcovado Costa Rica

Teaching All Students

Extra Help For students having difficulty with **Escuchar,** play the audio again in sections. Stop after each section and have students recap what they heard.

Multiple Intelligences

Musical/Rhythmic Musical instruments are often used to represent animals, especially in children's stories. Have students imagine that they are working on a televised narration of a children's story and they need to assign a musical instrument to each animal. Have them choose at least 6 animals from Central America and assign an instrument to each.

Escuchar (See script, p. 149B.)

Answers

En la sección guatemalteca
• tucanes	Sí
• monos araña	Sí
• serpientes	No

En la sección hondureña
• jaguares	Sí
• venados	No
• tortugas	Sí

En la sección salvadoreña
• boas constrictoras	No
• mariposas	No
• osos hormigueros	Sí

En la sección nicaragüense
• tiburones	No
• monos	Sí
• serpientes	No

En la sección costarricense
• mariposas	Sí
• loros	Sí
• jaguares	No

En la sección panameña
• iguanas	Sí
• venados	Sí
• jaguares	Sí

Escribir

Answers will vary.

Block Schedule

Variety Have students use library sources or the Internet to research various zoos in the United States to see if they have animals from Central America. Have them present a list to the class. If necessary, students should look up the Spanish names in a dictionary. Have them add these words to a supplementary vocabulary list. Also have students talk about any animals from Central America that they may have seen in a zoo. (For additional activities, see **Block Scheduling Copymasters**.)

Teaching Resource Options

Print

Block Scheduling Copymasters
Unit 2 Resource Book
   Absent Student Copymasters, p. 174

Audiovisual

OHT 41 (Quick Start)

Quick Start Review

♻ **Animals and birds**

Use OHT 41 or write on the board:
Unscramble the letters to spell the
name of a Central American animal or
bird.

1. ocanplíe   5. brótinu
2. rorilozl   6. lebalna rojodaba
3. átunc   7. noom ñaara
4. lóchna   8. rugaja

Answers
1. pelícano   5. tiburón
2. zorrillo   6. ballena jorobada
3. tucán   7. mono araña
4. halcón   8. jaguar

Teaching Suggestions
Comprehension Check

Use **Actividades 1–4** to assess retention
after the **Vocabulario** and **Situaciones**.
After completing **Actividad 1**, have
students exchange papers with a
partner for peer correction. Have
students expand **Actividad 2** with 4
more items.

 **Objective:** Controlled practice
Vocabulary

Answers
1. d
2. b
3. c
4. a
5. f
6. e

En acción

PARTE A   **Práctica del vocabulario**

Objectives for Activities 1-4
• React to nature

1 Los animales

Hablar/Escribir ¿Qué oración describe a
cada dibujo?

1.

2.

3.

4.

5.

6.  ¡Buenos días!

a. El tucán es un pájaro con un pico de
   muchos colores.

b. Los jaguares son de la familia de los
   gatos.

c. Hay muchas mariposas en esta selva.

d. Dicen que las tortugas son muy lentas.

e. Los loros pueden imitar el habla de la
   gente.

f. ¡Mira la ballena jorobada! ¡Qué
   enorme!

2 El hábitat natural

Hablar/Escribir ¿Cuál es el hábitat natural de
estos animales? Pregúntale a tu compañero(a).

modelo

ballena

   a. río   b. mar   c. tierra

Tú: *¿Cuál es el hábitat natural de la ballena?*

Compañero(a): *Las ballenas viven en el mar.*

1. venado
   a. río   b. mar   c. bosque

2. jaguar
   a. selva   b. mar   c. río

3. tortuga
   a. palmera   b. montañas   c. río

4. mono araña
   a. río   b. mar   c. selva

5. pelícano
   a. mar   b. bosque   c. montañas

6. tiburón
   a. montañas   b. mar   c. río

También se dice

Hay muchas maneras de nombrar los animales.

• **chango**   = mono
• **perico, cotorra** = loro
• **víbora**   = serpiente
• **colibrí**   = picaflor
• **mofeta**   = zorrillo

Classroom Management

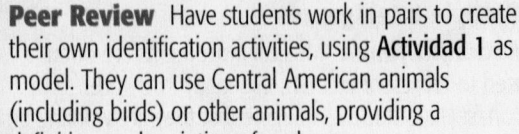

Peer Review Have students work in pairs to create
their own identification activities, using **Actividad 1** as a
model. They can use Central American animals
(including birds) or other animals, providing a
definition or description of each.

Streamlining **Actividades 2–4** can be combined by
having students talk about the animals in **Actividad 2**
and **3** (some are duplicates). Students give each
animal's habitat, say whether or not they have seen the
animal, what they think of it, and where they go to see
the animal.

Práctica del vocabulario continuación

3 ¿Has visto...?

Hablar/Escribir Quieres saber qué animales tu compañero(a) ha visto y qué piensa de ellos. Hazle preguntas sobre los animales en las fotos. Luego cambien de papel.

modelo

Tú: ¿Has visto un mono araña alguna vez?

Compañero(a): Sí, lo vi en el zoológico.

Tú: ¿Qué piensas de los monos?

Compañero(a): Pues, son muy inteligentes y cómicos.

1.

2.

3.

4.

5.

6.

4 ¡Vamos a Costa Rica!

Hablar/Escribir Vas a viajar a Costa Rica. Pregúntale a tu amigo(a) costarricense dónde puedes ver las cosas que te interesan. Usa el mapa como guía. Luego, cambien de papel.

modelo

Tú: Me interesan mucho las tortugas. ¿Adónde debo ir?

Compañero(a): Debes ir al Parque Nacional Tortuguero. Allí hay muchas tortugas.

COSTA RICA

PARQUES NACIONALES DE COSTA RICA

1. Tortuguero
2. Braulio Carrillo
3. Manuel Antonio
4. Río Pacuare
5. Marino Ballena
6. Isla del Coco

Isla del Coco

ciento cincuenta y siete
México y Centroamérica Etapa 3 | **157**

Teaching All Students

Extra Help Ask students questions about the animals. For example, ¿Qué animal te gusta más? ¿Qué animal te gustaría tener en tu casa? ¿Qué come un jaguar?

Native Speakers Have students brainstorm a list of additional animals for the rest of the class to add to their supplementary vocabulary lists.

Multiple Intelligences

Logical/Mathematical Have students divide a sheet of paper into 3 columns. Label the columns: **animales que nadan, animales que caminan, animales que vuelan.** Have students list the animals learned in this **Etapa** and any other animals they know in the appropriate column. Some animals can be written under more than one column.

Side column (right)

ACTIVIDAD 2 Objective: Transitional practice
Vocabulary in conversation

Answers

1. A: ¿Cuál es el hábitat natural del venado?
   B: Los venados viven en el bosque.
2. A: ¿Cuál es el hábitat natural del jaguar?
   B: Los jaguares viven en la selva.
3. A: ¿Cuál es el hábitat natural de la tortuga?
   B: Las tortugas viven en el río.
4. A: ¿Cuál es el hábitat natural del mono araña?
   B: Los monos arañas viven en la selva.
5. A: ¿Cuál es el hábitat natural del pelícano?
   B: Los pelícanos viven a las orillas del mar.
6. A: ¿Cuál es el hábitat natural del tiburón?
   B: Los tiburones viven en el mar.

ACTIVIDAD 3 Objective: Transitional practice
Vocabulary in conversation

♻ **Present perfect tense**

Answers

Answers will vary, but should begin with the following questions:

1. ¿Has visto una ballena alguna vez?
2. ¿Has visto un picaflor alguna vez?
3. ¿Has visto una tortuga alguna vez?
4. ¿Has visto un zorrillo alguna vez?
5. ¿Has visto una boa constrictora alguna vez?
6. ¿Has visto un pelícano alguna vez?

ACTIVIDAD 4 Objective: Open-ended practice
Vocabulary in conversation

Answers will vary.

🔔 **Quick Wrap-up**

Name a habitat (**río, mar, selva, bosque, granja, casa**) and ask students for the names of animals that live there (¿Quién vive en [el río]?).

■ **Block Schedule**

Variety Working in pairs, have students create an ad announcing the arrival of a Central American animal to a local zoo. (For additional activities, see **Block Scheduling Copymasters.**)

Vocabulary/Grammar • UNIDAD 2 Etapa 3 | **157**

Teaching Resource Options

Print

Más práctica Workbook PE, p. 61
Cuaderno para hispanohablantes
 PE, p. 59
Block Scheduling Copymasters
Unit 2 Resource Book
 Más práctica Workbook TE, p. 145
 Cuaderno para hispanohablantes
  TE, p. 161
 Information Gap Activities, p. 167
 Absent Student Copymasters, p. 174
 Audioscript, p. 181

Audiovisual

OHT 42 (Quick Start), 46 (Grammar)
Audio Program CD 6, Track 2, Activity 6

Technology

Online Workbook, U2E3
Take-Home Tutor CD-ROM, U2E3

Quick Start Review

♻ Present subjunctive

Use OHT 42 or write on the board:
Use the following cues to form
sentences with the present subjunctive:

1. bueno / el parque / cuidar
 animales silvestres
2. una lástima / muchos animales /
 estar en peligro
3. importante / las mariposas /
 tener refugios
4. posible / tú / encontrar un mono
 en la selva
5. probable / Carlos / ver tucanes
 en Costa Rica

Answers

1. Es bueno que el parque cuide animales
silvestres. 2. Es una lástima que muchos
animales estén en peligro. 3. Es importante
que las mariposas tengan refugios. 4. Es posible
que tú encuentres un mono en la selva. 5. Es
probable que Carlos vea tucanes en Costa Rica.

PARTE B — Práctica: gramática y vocabulario

Objectives for Activities 5–14
• React to nature • Express doubt • Relate events in time

REPASO — The Subjunctive with Expressions of Emotion

Remember that you use the **subjunctive** after expressions of emotion such as
I'm happy and *I'm sad*.

The vocabulary box at the right lists some **expressions of emotions.**

> **Me alegro de que** te **guste** la naturaleza.
> *I'm happy that you like nature.*

> **Espero que podamos** hacer algo pronto.
> *I hope that we can do something soon.*

You can use either the **present subjunctive** or the
present perfect subjunctive after expressions of emotion.
Just remember that:

- the **present subjunctive** refers to **present** or **future** time.
- the **present perfect subjunctive** refers to the **past**.

> **Es triste que haya** tanta contaminación.
> *It's sad that there is so much pollution.*

> Sí. **Ojalá que puedan** reducirla. **Tengo miedo
> de que sea** muy peligrosa
> *Yes. I hope that they can reduce it. I'm afraid that it is very dangerous.*

> **Siento que** no **haga** buen tiempo.
> *I'm sorry the weather is not good.*

> **Siento que** no **haya hecho** buen tiempo.
> *I'm sorry the weather wasn't good.*

Vocabulario

♻ **Ya sabes**

Es ridículo que...
Es triste que...
Es una lástima que...
Espero que...

Me alegro de que...
Ojalá que...
Siento que...
Tengo miedo de que...

Practice: | Actividades **5 6 7** | **Más práctica** *cuaderno p. 61*
Para hispanohablantes *cuaderno p. 59* |  **Online Workbook** CLASSZONE.COM

Nota cultural

La isla de Ometepe se considera una de las islas más bellas del
mundo, localizada en el Lago de Nicaragua. El lago es casi del mismo
tamaño(*size*) del lago Titicaca en Perú. La isla de Ometepe tiene dos
grandes montañas gemelas. Los aventureros salen de las montañas en
planeadores o avionetas pequeñas para ver la belleza natural de esta
isla, uno de los centros turísticos más bellos de Centroamérica.

Classroom Community

Learning Scenario Divide the class into groups of
4. Each group is trying to decide where to go on
vacation together. One student wants to go to **Biotopo
Cerro Cahuí** in Guatemala, but the other 3 want to go
whitewater rafting in Costa Rica. Have the 3 students
use expressions of emotion and/or doubt to explain to
the first student why they should go to Costa Rica. The
first student tells his/her opinion.

Portfolio Have students write 2 paragraphs. In 1
paragraph they tell what they are happy about and
hope will happen. In the other, they tell what they are
sad or sorry about.

Rubric A = 13–15 pts. B = 10–12 pts. C = 7–9 pts. D = 4–6 pts. F = < 4 pts.

Writing criteria	Scale
Subjunctive and other grammar accuracy	1 2 3 4 5
Organization and clarity of ideas	1 2 3 4 5
Vocabulary usage	1 2 3 4 5

5 Reunión familiar

Hablar/*Escribir* Tu tía llama a toda la familia para hablar de sus esperanzas para la reunión familiar. ¿Qué le dice a cada uno?

modelo

a ustedes (llegar a tiempo)
Espero que lleguen a tiempo.

1. a ti (gustar la comida)
2. a usted (divertirse)
3. a mi prima (invitar a tu novio)
4. a mis papás (bailar mucho)
5. a mí (comer suficiente)
6. a ustedes (vestirse bien)
7. a tu tío (llegar temprano)
8. sus amigas (traer el postre)

6 Juan

Escuchar/*Escribir* Escucha lo que les dice Juan a varios amigos y parientes. Luego escribe cómo se siente Juan en cada situación. Primero escucha el modelo.

modelo

Adriana
Juan espera que Adriana vaya con él a la fiesta.

7 El mundo de hoy

STRATEGY: SPEAKING

Gain thinking time before speaking Sometimes ideas do not come to us as quickly as we would like. One way to gain time is to restate what was just said which may in turn trigger a fresh idea. Example: **Sí, es una lástima. Espero que se proteja la selva también.**

Hablar/*Escribir* Tú y tu compañero(a) hablan sobre el estado del mundo de hoy. Usa las frases de la primera columna para expresar cómo te sientes sobre alguna situación en la segunda columna.

modelo

Tú: *Es una lástima que los jaguares estén en peligro de extinción.*
Compañero(a): *Tienes razón, es muy triste. Espero que…*

Me alegro de que…	países: (no) declarar zonas de reserva ecológicas
Siento que…	jaguares: (no) estar en peligro de extinción
Tengo miedo de que…	ciudades: (no) instituir programas de reciclaje
Es una lástima que…	gente: (no) reciclar el plástico
Ojalá que…	nosotros: (no) proteger las especies
Espero que…	nosotros: (no) destruir la capa de ozono
Es triste que…	gente: (no) respetar el planeta
Es ridículo que…	carros: (no) contaminar el aire (no) haber derrames de petróleo ¿…?

More Practice: **Más comunicación** *p. R8*

Teaching All Students

Extra Help Have students use the **Vocabulario** on p. 158 and the subjunctive to write 3 things they want or don't want their friends to do on their vacation in Central America. For example: **Me alegro de que Julio vaya a Panamá. Espero que se divierta mucho. Ojalá que vaya a Isla Iguana.**

Multiple Intelligences

Musical/Rhythmic Have students use the subjunctive to create jingles that encourage vacationers to visit one of the places mentioned on pp. 152–153. For example: **Espero que le guste el Parque Montecristo, un lugar que tiene que ser visto.** You may want to have students record their jingle to music.

Teaching Suggestions
Reviewing The Subjunctive with Expressions of Emotion

- Have each student write 1 sentence using the present subjunctive and 1 using the present perfect subjunctive.
- Have several students write their sentences on the board. The class checks them for accuracy.

ACTIVIDAD 5 Objective: Controlled practice Subjunctive with expressions of emotion

Answers
1. Espero que te guste la comida.
2. Espero que se divierta.
3. Espero que invites a tu novio.
4. Espero que bailen mucho.
5. Espero que comas suficiente.
6. Espero que se vistan bien.
7. Espero que llegues temprano.
8. Espero que traigan el postre.

ACTIVIDAD 6 Objective: Transitional practice Listening comprehension/subjunctive with expressions of emotion

Answers (See script, p. 149B.)
1. Juan siente que su papá esté enfermo.
2. Juan se alegra de que su hermanito estudie tanto.
3. Juan tiene miedo de que Martín se enoje con él.
4. Juan siente que su hermanita no pueda ir al cine con ellos.
5. Juan se alegra de que Adriana lo invite al baile.
6. Juan espera que Felipe se sienta mejor mañana.

ACTIVIDAD 7 Objective: Open-ended practice Subjunctive with expressions of emotion in conversation

 Ecology vocabulary

Answers will vary.

Block Schedule

Retention Have students close their books. Make a series of announcements, real or imaginary, about upcoming events in class or school (a big exam, a field trip, etc.). Have students react using one of the expressions from the **Vocabulario**, p. 158. For example: **Es triste que haya un examen mañana.** (For additional activities, see **Block Scheduling Copymasters.**)

Teaching Resource Options

Print

Más práctica Workbook PE, p. 62
Cuaderno para hispanohablantes
  PE, p. 60
Block Scheduling Copymasters
Unit 2 Resource Book
  Más práctica Workbook TE, p. 146
  Cuaderno para hispanohablantes
  TE, p. 162
  Absent Student Copymasters, p. 175

Audiovisual

OHT 42 (Quick Start), 47 (Grammar)

Technology

Online Workbook, U2E3
Take-Home Tutor CD-ROM, U2E3

Quick Start Review

♻ Expressions of emotion

Use OHT 42 or write on the board:
Use an element from each column to
form 5 logical sentences:

A	B
me alegro de	hay mucha
ojalá	contaminación
siento	saco buena nota
espero	el viaje es peligroso
tengo miedo de	han reducido la
	contaminación
	hace buen tiempo

Answers

Answers will vary. Answers could include:
Me alegro de que haga buen tiempo, Ojalá
que saque buena nota, etc.

Teaching Suggestions
Reviewing The Subjunctive to Express Doubt and Uncertainty

• You may want to emphasize that
when using **creer** in the negative or
interrogative, the subjunctive is used:
**¿Crees que tus padres te den el
carro?**
• You may want to explain that it is also
possible to use the subjunctive after
affirmative expressions like **Creo
que...**, but that using the subjunctive
introduces an element of doubt to
what is being said.

REPASO   The Subjunctive to Express Doubt and Uncertainty

▶ Remember that you use the **subjunctive** in the dependent clause
after **expressions of doubt** and **uncertainty** such as those in
the vocabulary box.

> **Dudo que** tus primos **quieran** acampar con nosotros.
> *I doubt that your cousins want to camp with us.*

> ¿Quién sabe? **Quizás** les **interese** la idea.
> *Who knows? Maybe the idea will interest them.*

> **No creo que** Pedro **haya visto** un animal salvaje
> en toda su vida.
> *I don't think that Pedro has seen a wild animal in his whole life.*

> **Tal vez quiera** ir con nosotros al refugio de
> vida silvestre.
> *Maybe he would want to come with us to the wildlife preserve.*

> **Vocabulario**
>
> ♻ **Ya sabes**
>
> Dudo que...
> No creo que...
> No es cierto que...
> No es seguro que...
>
> No es verdad que...
> Quizás.../ Quizá...
> Tal vez...

▶ You can use the **present subjunctive** or the **present perfect subjunctive** after
expressions of doubt and **uncertainty.**

• the **present subjunctive** refers to
present or **future** time

> **No es cierto que** Julio y Vera
> **naden** con tubo de respiración.
> *It's not true that Julio and Vera are going
> to snorkel.*

• the **present perfect subjunctive** refers to
the **past**

> **No es cierto que** Julio y Vera **hayan
> nadado** con tubo de respiración.
> *It's not true that Julio and Vera have snorkeled.*

▶ Normally, you don't use the **subjunctive** after the following expressions because
they express **certainty,** not doubt.

↳ *expresses certainty*

> Yo **no dudo que** él ya sabe navegar por rápidos.
> *I don't doubt that he already knows how to white water raft.*

> no dudo que...
> creo que...
> es cierto que...
> es verdad que...
> es seguro que...

Practice: Actividades 8 9 10   **Más práctica** *cuaderno p. 62*   **Para hispanohablantes** *cuaderno p. 60*

 Online Workbook CLASSZONE.COM

ciento sesenta
Unidad 2
160

Classroom Community

Game **Prepare ahead:** Make cards of expressions
that trigger the subjunctive. Have students make bingo
cards with 9 squares (3 columns, 3 rows), and fill them
with 9 of the subjunctive trigger phrases. To play, draw
a card and read it. Students with that phrase should
mark the square. Continue until someone has 3 in a
row. In order to win, that student must read back the
phrases and use 1 in a complete sentence.

Paired Activity Have students write true/false
sentences about geography and wildlife in Central
America. Then have them work in pairs to take turns
reading each other their sentences. When they hear a
sentence, they should react with a subjunctive
sentence. For example: **Las tortugas comen peces.** →
Dudo que las tortugas coman peces.

8 Dudo que...

Hablar/Escribir Tienes algunas dudas sobre los animales de la selva y el mar. Exprésalas.

> *modelo*
>
> (no) dudo que: haber / tiburones en la playa
> *Dudo que haya tiburones en la playa.*

1. (no) creo que: las mariposas / vivir solamente en el bosque
2. (no) dudo que: el ecoturismo / resolver todos los problemas ecológicos
3. (no) es verdad que: los venados / ser peligrosos
4. (no) es seguro que: los monos / entender a los humanos
5. (no) dudo que: los tucanes / poder hablar
6. (no) creo que: las serpientes / comer peces
7. (no) es cierto que: las ballenas / existir sólo en los ríos
8. (no) es cierto que: las tortugas / estar en peligro de extinción
9. (no) es verdad que: la isla de Ometepe / ser muy bella
10. (no) creo que: los osos hormigueros / comer fruta

La tortuga

Es uno de los animales más apreciados por el hombre, de nosotros depende su conservación. No adquiera ni consuma productos de tortuga, ayudemos a preservar con ella la biodiversidad de México.

9 No te creo

Hablar/Escribir Tu amigo(a) siempre exagera y dice que ha hecho cosas increíbles. Tú nunca le crees. ¿Cómo le respondes cuando dice que ha hecho las siguientes cosas?

> *modelo*
>
> *Fui a...*
>
> **Amigo(a):** *Fui a Centroamérica.*
>
> **Tú:** *No creo que hayas ido a Centroamérica.*

1. Hice alpinismo en…
2. Navegué por rápidos en…
3. Vi un jaguar en…
4. Buceé en…
5. Nadé con tubo de respiración en…
6. Pesqué en alta mar…
7. Piloté una avioneta en…
8. Conocí a Rigoberta Menchú…

Nota cultural

Recientemente muchos de los países de Centroamérica, particularmente Guatemala, Honduras, Nicaragua, Costa Rica y Panamá, han designado varias áreas como **reservas naturales** destinadas a la preservación de la fauna y flora de la región.

ACTIVIDAD 8 Objective: Controlled practice Subjunctive to express doubt and uncertainty

Answers

1. No creo que las mariposas vivan solamente en el bosque.
2. Dudo que el ecoturismo resuelva todos los problemas ecológicos.
3. No es verdad que los venados sean peligrosos.
4. No es seguro que los monos entiendan a los humanos.
5. Dudo que los tucanes puedan hablar.
6. No creo que las serpientes coman peces.
7. No es cierto que las ballenas existan sólo en los ríos.
8. No es cierto que las tortugas estén en peligro de extinción.
9. No es verdad que la isla de Ometepe sea muy bella.
10. No creo que los osos hormigueros coman fruta.

Teaching Note

For **Actividad 8,** students might also choose to answer in the indicative.

ACTIVIDAD 9 Objective: Transitional practice Subjunctive to express doubt and uncertainty in conversation

 Pastimes

Answers

Answers will vary, but should begin with the following:

1. No creo que hayas hecho alpinismo en…
2. No creo que hayas navegado por rápidos en…
3. No creo que hayas visto un jaguar en….
4. No creo que hayas buceado en…
5. No creo que hayas nadado con tubo de respiración en…
6. No creo que hayas pescado en alta mar en…
7. No creo que hayas pilotado una avioneta en…
8. No creo que hayas conocido a Rigoberta Menchú.

Block Schedule

Change of Pace Have students work in pairs to make up a story using the following guidelines: you believe that the math teacher is not coming to class tomorrow / you are sure that he/she has been sick / you doubt that he/she has been in the hospital / you don't believe that there is a test tomorrow / you doubt there will be one at the end of the week / you are not sure that the class is prepared for a test. (For additional activities, see **Block Scheduling Copymasters**.)

Teaching All Students

Extra Help For **Actividad 8,** tell students to first focus on the verb. Have them write the present indicative form and the present subjunctive form for each one. Then have them decide which expression they will use and whether it requires the indicative or the subjunctive. Have them cross out the form they do not need. Finally, have them complete the activity.

Multiple Intelligences

Interpersonal Have students work in pairs and choose a well-known personality. One partner makes a statement about the person (**Vive en una casa pequeña.**) and the other reacts using an expression of doubt or uncertainty and/or an expression of certainty (**Dudo que viva en una casa pequeña. Estoy seguro que vive en una casa grande**).

Teaching Resource Options

Print 📖

Más práctica Workbook PE, pp. 63–64
Cuaderno para hispanohablantes
  PE, pp. 61–62
Unit 2 Resource Book
  Más práctica Workbook TE,
    pp. 147–148
  Cuaderno para hispanohablantes
    TE, pp. 163–164
  Absent Student Copymasters, p. 175

Audiovisual

OHT 43 (Quick Start), 49 (Grammar)
Word Tiles, U2E3

Technology

Online Workbook, U2E3
Take-Home Tutor CD-ROM, U2E3

Teaching Note

When doing **Actividad 10,** tell students to
use the expressions from the **Vocabulario**
box on p. 160.

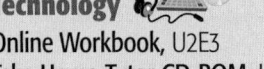

Objective: Open-ended practice
Subjunctive to express doubt and
uncertainty in conversation

Answers will vary.

Quick Start Review

♻ Expressions of doubt/uncertainty

Use OHT 43 or write on the board:
Write complete sentences using the
following elements:

1. es verdad / yo / pagar / mil /
   dólar / por / vacaciones
2. es cierto / tú / salir / mañana /
   vacaciones
3. dudo / él / poder / nadar con
   tubo de respiración
4. quizás / ecoturismo / ser /
   bueno / animales salvajes
5. no es seguro / vivir / monos /
   bosque

Answers *See p. 145B.*

Práctica: gramática y vocabulario *continuación*

10 Conversaciones diarias

Hablar A veces tenemos dudas sobre las situaciones en que nos
encontramos. Con un(a) compañero(a), expresa algunas dudas que
tengas usando las expresiones de la página 156. Tu compañero(a) te
contesta usando *tal vez* o *quizás*. Luego, cambien de papel.

modelo

Tú: *No creo que papá esté en casa.*

Compañero(a): *Tal vez esté en la oficina.*

Compañero(a): *Dudo que mi hermana me preste
    el dinero.*

Tú: *¿Quién sabe? Quizás se sienta generosa.*

comprar	tener
hablar	venir
invitar	¿?

GRAMÁTICA **The Subjunctive with cuando and Other Conjunctions of Time**

You use the **subjunctive** after certain **conjunctions of time** to show
that you are **not sure when** or **if** something will happen.

You use the **indicative** with the same **conjunctions of time**, if the
main clause refers to the present or the past. Using the **indicative**
shows that you are already **certain** about the outcome of the action
described in the subordinate clause.

Vocabulario

El tiempo

cuando *when*
en cuanto *as soon as*
hasta que *until*
tan pronto como *as soon as*

Subjunctive
not sure of outcome

Bucearán **hasta que** anochezca.
They will scuba dive until it gets dark.

Avísame **cuando** sepas.
Let me know when you find something out.

Indicative
certain of outcome

Bucearon **hasta que** anocheció.
They were scuba diving until it got dark.

Siempre me avisas **cuando** sabes.
You always let me know when you find something out.

Practice: **Actividades** ⑪ ⑫ ⑬ ⑭   **Más práctica** *cuaderno pp. 63–64*
    Para hispanohablantes *cuaderno pp.61–62*

Online Workbook
CLASSZONE.COM

---

162   ciento sesenta y dos
    Unidad 2

Classroom Community

Group Activity Have students work in small groups
to create and present a skit about a camping trip in a
nature park. They will need to prepare a vocabulary list
of clothing, supplies, and camping equipment for
ecotourism. Encourage students to use their
imagination and humor. When presenting their stories,
they should use props and gestures as appropriate.

Learning Scenario After completing **Actividad 12,**
tell students that their new job is to write messages for
fortune cookies. Have students work in pairs to write 10
messages on small slips of paper. The messages must
use a conjunction of time and the subjunctive. For
example: **Irás de vacaciones cuando te ganes la lotería.
No recibirás buenas notas hasta que estudies mucho.**
Then put the fortunes in a bowl and have students pick
one, then write a reaction using the subjunctive.

11 El Refugio

Hablar/Escribir Un grupo de tu colegio va al refugio. ¿Qué dicen que van a hacer y hasta cuándo?

modelo

seguir el sendero / acabarse

Vamos a seguir el sendero hasta que se acabe.

> **Nota: Gramática**
>
> Remember that when you form the subjunctive of verbs that end in **-cer** (such as **conocer, oscurecer, anochecer, amanecer,** etc.), the subjunctive forms include a **z: conozca, conozcas, conozca, conozcamos, conozcan.**

1. caminar / no haber luz
2. nadar / oscurecer
3. dormir / amanecer
4. hacer alpinismo / anochecer
5. disfrutar de la naturaleza / (nosotros) cansarse
6. observar la flora y fauna / (nosotros) tener hambre
7. buscar monos / (nosotros) ver uno
8. quedarnos / (ellos) cerrar el refugio

12 Tan pronto como...

Hablar/Escribir Tú y tu hermano(a) menor van a acampar en un parque nacional y él (ella) te hace muchas preguntas. ¿Qué le dices?

modelo

recoger la leña

Tu hermano(a): ¿Por qué no recoges la leña?

Tú: *Recogeré la leña tan pronto como lleguemos al campamento.*

1. hacer el fuego
2. abrir la tienda de campaña
3. acostarte en el saco de dormir
4. darme la manta
5. poner la linterna
6. abrir las latas
7. bajar la almohada del carro
8. traer agua
9. buscar un animal raro
10. cocinar sopa

Vocabulario

Vamos a acampar

el abrelatas *can opener*	**el campamento** *camp*	**la manta** *blanket*
la almohada *pillow*	**descubrir** *to discover*	**la navaja** *jackknife*
(el) amanecer *dawn; to start the day*	**el fósforo** *match*	**oscurecer** *to get dark*
	el fuego *fire*	**la oscuridad** *darkness*
(el) anochecer *nightfall; to get dark*	**la leña** *firewood*	**el saco de dormir** *sleeping bag*
	la linterna *flashlight*	**el sendero** *path*
(el) atardecer *late afternoon; to get dark*	**la luz** *light*	**la tienda de campaña** *tent*

¿Qué objetos necesitas para acampar?

Teaching All Students

Extra Help Have students complete the following sentences with as many items as they can: **Compraré un(a)... cuando... No iré de vacaciones hasta que...** Write some of the sentences on the board and correct.

Multiple Intelligences

Intrapersonal Have students write 5 statements about their future, using the subjunctive with a conjunction of time. For example: **Iré a la universidad tan pronto como tenga el dinero.**

Teaching Suggestions
Teaching Vocabulary

Ask a volunteer to draw a camping scene on the board. Then call on various students to label each item and provide a sentence using that item.

11 Objective: Controlled practice
Subjunctive with conjunctions of time

Answers

1. Vamos a caminar hasta que no haya luz.
2. Vamos a nadar hasta que oscurezca.
3. Vamos a dormir hasta que amanezca.
4. Vamos a hacer alpinismo hasta que anochezca.
5. Vamos a disfrutar de la naturaleza hasta que nos cansemos.
6. Vamos a observar la flora y fauna hasta que tengamos hambre.
7. Vamos a buscar monos hasta que veamos uno.
8. Vamos a quedarnos hasta que cierren el refugio.

12 Objective: Transitional practice
Subjunctive with conjunctions of time

 Future tense

Answers

Answers will vary, but should be similar to the following:

1. A: ¿Por qué no haces el fuego? B: Haré el fuego tan pronto como encuentre los fósforos.
2. A: ¿Por qué no abres la tienda de campaña? B: Abriré la tienda de campaña tan pronto como comamos.
3. A: ¿Por qué no te acuestas en el saco de dormir? B: Me acostaré en el saco de dormir tan pronto como oscurezca.
4. A: ¿Por qué no me das la manta? B: Te daré la manta tan pronto como tengas frío.
5. A: ¿Por qué no pones la linterna? B: Pondré la linterna tan pronto como anochezca.
6. A: ¿ Por qué no abres las latas? B: Abriré las latas tan pronto como encuentre el abrelatas.
7. A: ¿Por qué no bajas la almohada del carro? B: Bajaré la almohada del carro tan pronto como te acuestes.
8. A: ¿Por qué no traes agua? B: Traeré agua tan pronto como pueda.
9. A: ¿Por qué no buscas un animal raro? B: Buscaré un animal raro tan pronto deje de llover.
10. A: ¿Por qué no cocinas sopa? B: Cocinaré sopa tan pronto como encuentre agua.

Block Schedule

Expansion Have students work in pairs to create their own version of **Actividad 12.** Have them take turns suggesting and making excuses, but in a different situation of their choosing. For example, preparing for a party: ¿Por qué no pones la mesa? → Pondré la mesa tan pronto como termine este programa.

Teaching Resource Options

Print

Más práctica Workbook PE, pp. 57–60
Actividades para todos Workbook
PE, pp. 61–66
Cuaderno para hispanohablantes
PE, pp. 57–58
Block Scheduling Copymasters
Unit 2 Resource Book
Más práctica Workbook TE,
pp. 141–144
Actividades para todos Workbook
TE, pp. 149–153
Cuaderno para hispanohablantes
TE, pp. 159–160
Information Gap Activities, p. 168
Absent Student Copymasters, p. 176
Audioscript, p. 181

Audiovisual

Audio Program CD 6, Track 4, Activity
13

Technology

Online Workbook, U2E3
Take-Home Tutor CD-ROM, U2E3

 Objective: Transitional practice
Listening comprehension/subjunctive
with conjunctions of time

 Household chores

Answers (See script, p. 149B.)

1. No ha planchado la ropa. La planchará hasta
que se canse.
2. Cortó el césped. Lo cortó hasta que
anocheció.
3. No ha limpiado el cuarto. Lo limpiará en
cuanto llegue a casa.
4. Barrió el piso. Lo barrió hasta que acabó.
5. No ha pasado la aspiradora. La pasará en
cuanto acabe de lavar los platos.
6. Regó las plantas. Las regó hasta que
oscureció.
7. No ha hecho la cena. La hará tan pronto
como llegue a casa.
8. No ha sacado las malas hierbas. Las sacará
hasta que no quede ninguna.

Teaching Suggestions
Presenting Vocabulary

Bring in pictures from magazines
showing different weather phenomena.
Show the pictures and have students
identify the weather in each scene.

---

13 Los quehaceres

Escuchar/Escribir ¡Pobre
Imelda! Tiene muchos
quehaceres hoy. Escucha lo que
dice. Di si ya hizo el quehacer
que menciona, o si todavía le
falta hacerlo. Luego escribe una
oración usando **en cuanto,
hasta que** o **tan pronto como**.

modelo

*No ha cortado el césped. Lo cortará
en cuanto pueda.*

1. planchar	5. pasar
2. cortar	6. regar
3. limpiar	7. hacer
4. barrer	8. sacar

---

14 El tiempo

Hablar/Escribir Pregúntale a tu compañero(a) si quiere hacer
algo para disfrutar de la naturaleza. Él (Ella) te contesta de
acuerdo a cómo está el tiempo. Luego, cambien de papel.

modelo

quitarse la neblina

Tú: *¿Quieres ir a pescar? o ¿Quieres ir a bucear?*

Compañero(a): *Sí, vamos a pescar (bucear) en cuanto se quite la
neblina*

1. parar los truenos
2. irse el huracán
3. estar soleado
4. terminar el aguacero

5. irse las nubes
6. bajar la temperatura
7. pasar el relámpago
8. parar la llovizna

Vocabulario

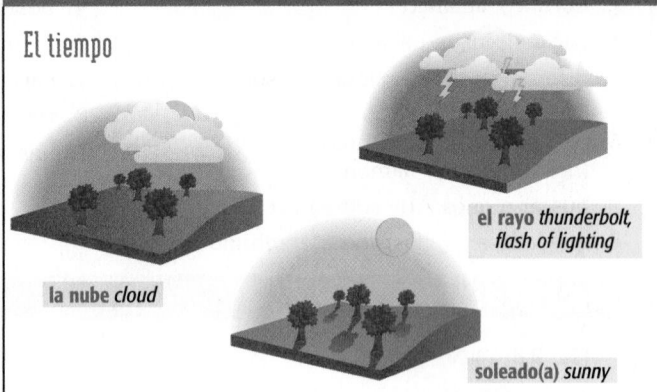

El tiempo

la nube *cloud*

el rayo *thunderbolt,
flash of lighting*

soleado(a) *sunny*

el aguacero *downpour*
centígrado(a) *centigrade*
húmedo(a) *humid, wet*
el huracán *hurricane*

la llovizna *drizzle*
la neblina *fog, mist*
el relámpago *lightning*
el trueno *thunder*

▶ ¿Puedes usar algunas de estas palabras para describir el tiempo hoy?

Classroom Community

Paired Activity Have students work in pairs to
prepare a 5-day weather forecast for a real or an
imaginary Spanish-speaking city. They should use as
many of the words from the **Vocabulario** on p. 160 as
possible. Have them present the forecast as if they
were weather reporters on television.

Storytelling Have students work in pairs to write
and present a weather-related, human interest story.
For example, they might write about a cat that is caught
in a downpour and is saved by a dog. Students may
also present the story in the form of a newscast with
other team members doing weather, sports,
entertainment, etc.

PARTE C
Todo en acción

Activity 15 brings together all concepts presented.

15 La finca de mariposas

Hablar/Leer En grupos de tres o cuatro, hablen sobre este folleto de La Finca de Mariposas en La Guácima de Alajuela, Costa Rica.

modelo

Tú: ¿Te gustan las mariposas?

Amigo(a) 1: Sí. Pero no sé cómo atraerlas a mi jardín.

Amigo(a) 2: Pues, aquí dice que …

Amigo(a) 3: ¿Sabes cuántas especies de mariposas hay…?

Refrán

A cada pájaro le gusta oír su propio canto.

¿Qué quiere decir el refrán? ¿Estás de acuerdo? ¿Crees que preferimos las cosas que conocemos bien a las que no conocemos?

More Practice: Más comunicación p. R8

Online Workbook CLASSZONE.COM

ciento sesenta y cinco
México y Centroamérica Etapa 3 **165**

Objective: Transitional practice
Subjunctive with conjunctions of time in conversation

Answers will vary.

Objective: Open-ended practice
Subjunctive with conjunctions of time in conversation

Answers will vary.

Dictation

Using the Listening Activity Script for **Actividad 13** on TE p. 149B, dictate selected sentences to students. You may want to write answers on the board for students to correct their own work.

Teaching All Students

Extra Help As a class, brainstorm additional weather-related vocabulary words. Then have students work in pairs to play hangman or Pictionary™ with the words.

Multiple Intelligences

Logical/Mathematical Have students research one day's temperature in at least 5 different Spanish-speaking cities around the world. Have them give the temperatures in Fahrenheit and Celsius. Elevations may also be researched and recorded in meters/feet.

Block Schedule

FunBreak Have students do a Bulletin Board/Posters or Hands-On Crafts project on TE pp. 105A–105B. (For additional activities, see **Block Scheduling Copymasters.**)

Teaching Resource Options

Print

Actividades para todos Workbook PE, pp. 67–69

Block Scheduling Copymasters

Unit 2 Resource Book

  Actividades para todos Workbook TE, pp. 155–157

  Absent Student Copymasters, p. 177

  Audioscript, pp. 181–182

Audiovisual

OHT TK (Quick Start)

Audio Program CD 6, Tracks 4–5

Canciones CD

Technology

Online Workbook, U2E3

Take-Home Tutor CD-ROM, U2E3

Quick Start Review

♻ **Weather conditions**

Use OHT TK or write on the board: Write a 5-sentence paragraph about a rainy day, including a description of the weather and what you are doing.

Answers will vary.

Teaching Suggestions

- **Prereading** Have students scan the reading for cognates and list them. What do these words tell them about the reading? ¿Qué pueden determinar sobre la lectura basándose en los cognados (palabras afines)?
- **Strategy: Recognize uses of satire, parody, and irony** Discuss the 3 humor devices. Tell students to keep these in mind as they read.
- **Reading** Ask students: Other than the fact that this story is written in Spanish, are there any indicators that would help place this in a particular place, time, or culture?
- **Post-reading** Have students identify the examples of satire, parody, and irony in the selection. Have them name examples of movies that use the 3 humor devices.

En voces
AUDIO 🎧 LECTURA

PARA LEER

STRATEGY: READING

Recognize uses of satire, parody, and irony What advertisements, TV shows, or movies do you see that use humor about someone or something? Their humor is often based on these three devices:

  Satire: use of sarcasm to make fun of someone or something

  Parody: a satirical imitation of a serious piece of writing

  Irony: use of language whose meaning is the opposite of what is intended

Give examples of satire, parody, or irony in *Baby H.P.*

EN LA CASA

ama de casa	mujer que trabaja en la casa
el agobiante ajetreo	actividad energética
hogareño	de la casa
la rabieta	cuando un niño llora y grita
los vástagos	niños

Sobre el autor

Juan José Arreola, cuentista mexicano, es uno de los escritores más originales y más importantes de su generación. Nació en Ciudad Guzmán en el estado de Jalisco en 1918. Publicó sus primeros cuentos en unas revistas de Guadalajara durante los años 40. Las piezas cortas escritas por Arreola son cuentos, fábulas, viñetas o simplemente piezas cortas. Arreola se sirve del humor para satirizar ciertas características de la sociedad y del ser humano.

Introducción

«Baby H.P.», escrita en 1952, es una pieza satírica que trata del mundo de la publicidad y los anuncios. El autor parodia los anuncios dirigidos a las amas de casa, describiendo un aparato que se pone al niño para conservar su energía y convertirla después en la electricidad.

166 ciento sesenta y seis
Unidad 2

Classroom Community

Paired Activity Have students work in pairs to create and present a television ad for the Baby H.P. device. In their ads they should use drawings, props, and background music.

Cooperative Learning Have students work in groups of 5 and assign 1 paragraph of the reading to each student. In turn, each student reads his/her paragraph to the group and then provides a summary of the paragraph, and points out important vocabulary and cognates. He/She is responsible for being sure that the rest of the group understands the paragraph. When complete, students have a 5-sentence summary to present to the class.

Baby H.P.

Señora ama de casa: convierta usted en fuerza motriz[1] la vitalidad de sus niños. Ya tenemos a la venta[2] el maravilloso Baby H.P., un aparato que está llamado a revolucionar la economía hogareña.

. . . .

El Baby H.P. es una estructura de metal muy resistente y ligera que se adapta con perfección al delicado cuerpo infantil, mediante cómodos cinturones, pulseras, anillos y broches[3]. Las ramificaciones de este esqueleto suplementario recogen[4] cada uno de los movimientos del niño, haciéndolos converger en una botellita de Leyden que puede colocarse en la espalda o en el pecho, según necesidad.

. . . .

De hoy en adelante usted verá con otros ojos el agobiante ajetreo de sus hijos. Y ni siquiera perderá la paciencia ante una rabieta convulsiva, pensando en que es una fuente[5] generosa de energía.

[1] power, moving force
[2] for sale
[3] fasteners, clips
[4] to collect
[5] source
[6] leftover, surplus
[7] storage battery
[8] overflowing

Las familias numerosas pueden satisfacer todas sus demandas de electricidad, instalando un Baby H.P. en cada uno de sus vástagos, y hasta realizar un pequeño y lucrativo negocio, transmitiendo a los vecinos un poco de la energía sobrante[6].

. . . .

Los niños deben tener puesto día y noche su lucrativo H.P. Es importante que lo lleven siempre a la escuela, para que no se pierdan las horas preciosas del recreo, de las que ellos vuelven con el acumulador[7] rebosante[8] de energía.

Online Workbook
CLASSZONE.COM

¿Comprendiste?

1. ¿Cómo son las obras de Arreola?
2. ¿Para qué sirve el aparato Baby H.P.?
3. ¿Cómo es el aparato?
4. ¿Qué ventaja tienen las familias numerosas?

¿Qué piensas?

1. ¿Qué te parece la idea de Arreola? ¿Por qué es buena? ¿Por qué no?
2. ¿Crees que él habla en serio? ¿Por qué? Cita frases del texto en tu respuesta.

Hazlo tú

Inventa un aparato y descríbelo, imitando el estilo de Arreola. Menciona cómo es, para qué sirve y los beneficios que tiene.

ciento sesenta y siete
México y Centroamérica Etapa 3 | **167**

Teaching Resource Options

Print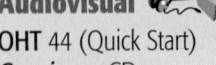

Unit 2 Resource Book
  Absent Student Copymasters, p. 178

Audiovisual

OHT 44 (Quick Start)
Canciones CD
Video Program Videotape 08:30 /
  DVD, Unit 2

Technology

www.classzone.com

Quick Start Review

 Vocabulary review

Use OHT 44 or write on the board:
Match the 2 columns of words:

1. ___ fósforo   a. linterna
2. ___ luz   b. leña
3. ___ bucear   c. saco de dormir
4. ___ nubes   d. pez
5. ___ almohada   e. aguacero

Answers
1. b   2. a   3. d   4. e   5. c

Teaching Suggestions
Presenting Cultura y comparaciones

- Have students make observations about the pictures on pp. 168–169 and predict the topic of the selection.
- Read and discuss the Connecting Cultures Strategy to help students think about the consequences of ecotourism.
- Point out the location of **el Parque Nacional Braulio Carrillo** and **el Parque Nacional Manuel Antonio** on a map of Costa Rica.

Reading Strategy

Compare related details Point out that a travel brochure tells enough to get your interest, but may leave out information you need to know. Have students use a chart to compare the 2 national parks. What else would they like to know before visiting one of them?

En colores
CULTURA Y COMPARACIONES

Un país de encanto

PARA CONOCERNOS

STRATEGY:
CONNECTING CULTURES
Analyze the advantages and disadvantages of ecotourism

This brochure makes ecotourism very appealing by providing new experiences for tourists and economic benefits for local citizens. Analyze the positive and possible negative consequences of ecotourism. Present your findings in a chart that might be used to inform both the Department of Tourism and the Chamber of Commerce. What is your personal position as a result of this analysis?

	ventajas	desventajas
ecoturismo	1.	1.
	2.	2.
	3.	3.

Costa Rica es muy conocido por sus parques nacionales, reservas biólogicas y refugios naturales. Miles de turistas visitan este país para conocer sus ecosistemas y disfrutar de su belleza.

Los aficionados de la naturaleza encontrarán en los bosques de Costa Rica más de 850 especies de aves[1] como halcones, tucanes y pelícanos.

Al norte de San José se encuentra el Parque Nacional Braulio Carrillo, creado para proteger el bosque tropical de la construcción de la carretera que va desde San José a Puerto Limón.

[1] birds

168 ciento sesenta y ocho
Unidad 2

Classroom Community

Paired Activity Have students work in pairs to role-play a conversation between a travel agent and a tourist who wants to visit Costa Rica. Have students incorporate the information in the cultural reading as well as **Etapa** vocabulary and structures.

Game Have students work in groups of 3 to create board games where the players travel around Costa Rica. During their trip, the "travelers" might visit places, run into animals in national parks, encounter weather problems, go camping, etc.

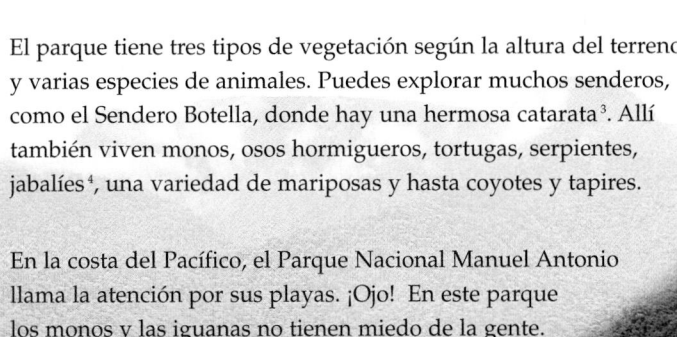

El parque tiene tres tipos de vegetación según la altura del terreno [2] y varias especies de animales. Puedes explorar muchos senderos, como el Sendero Botella, donde hay una hermosa catarata [3]. Allí también viven monos, osos hormigueros, tortugas, serpientes, jabalíes [4], una variedad de mariposas y hasta coyotes y tapires.

En la costa del Pacífico, el Parque Nacional Manuel Antonio llama la atención por sus playas. ¡Ojo! En este parque los monos y las iguanas no tienen miedo de la gente. Suelen acercarse [5] a los turistas en las hermosas playas de Espadilla Sur, Manuel Antonio y Puerto Escondido. Pero no des de comer a los monos porque se ponen muy pesados. ¡Hasta se meten [6] en las bolsas!

[2] altitude of terrain   [4] wild boars   [6] get into
[3] waterfall   [5] they often come up to

CLASSZONE.COM
More About Central America

¿Comprendiste?

1. ¿Qué animales se pueden ver en los parques nacionales de Costa Rica?
2. ¿Cómo es el Parque Nacional Braulio Carrillo?
3. ¿Qué parque nacional tiene playas hermosas?
4. ¿Cuál de los parques tiene una catarata?
5. ¿Qué animales llaman la atención en el Parque Nacional Manuel Antonio? ¿Qué hacen?

¿Qué piensas?

¿Qué piensas de los parques zoológicos en contraste con los refugios de vida silvestre? ¿Cuál prefieres? ¿Por qué?

Hazlo tú

Estudia un mapa de Costa Rica y planea una visita a unos de sus parques nacionales. Indica lo que quieres ver en cada parque.

Teaching All Students

Extra Help Have students create crossword puzzles using details from the reading. Clues may be definitions or sentences with a word missing. Have pairs of students exchange and complete their puzzles.

Multiple Intelligences
Naturalist Have students research the scientific names of the animals. Then have them discuss the purpose of Latin scientific names in communication.

Culture Highlights

● **EL PARQUE NACIONAL BRAULIO CARRILLO** Gran parte de la selva en el Parque Braulio Carrillo no ha sido explorada por seres humanos. Muchas especies en peligro de extinción viven dentro de este parque, incluyendo jaguares, quetzales y tapires.

● **EL PARQUE NACIONAL MANUEL ANTONIO** Un sendero con vistas espectaculares en el Parque Manuel Antonio es el que da la vuelta a la Punta Catedral. También hay muchos cangrejos (crabs) coloridos que salen justo antes de la estación lluviosa del verano.

Critical Thinking

Have students debate the pros and cons of ecotourism. Should people intrude on the habitats of the animals? Does ecotourism help to promote the environment?

Cross Cultural Connection

Have students provide a similar description of a park, national park, or conservation area in their region or one that they have visited in the U.S. Remind students to think about the Culture Strategy as they work.

¿Comprendiste?

Answers
1. Se pueden ver más de 850 especies de aves, monos, osos hormigueros, tortugas, serpientes, jabalíes, mariposas, coyotes y tapires.
2. El parque tiene tres tipos de vegetación según la altura del terreno.
3. El Parque Nacional Manuel Antonio tiene playas hermosas.
4. El Parque Nacional Braulio Carrillo tiene una catarata.
5. Los monos llaman la atención porque se meten en las bolsas.

Block Schedule

Variety Have students visit a travel agency and pick up brochures about Costa Rica. Do the brochures show any of the places described on pp. 168–169? Have students create a collage of the images in their brochures. Students may also use photos or information from nature/travel magazines or information from the Internet.

Teaching Resource Options

Print 📖

Cuaderno para hispanohablantes
PE, pp. 63–64
Block Scheduling Copymasters
Unit 2 Resource Book
Cuaderno para hispanohablantes
TE, pp. 165–166
Information Gap Activities,
pp. 169–170
Family Involvement, pp. 179–180

Audiovisual 🎧

OHT 44 (Quick Start)

Technology 💻

eTest Plus Online/Test Generator
CD-ROM

🌐 www.classzone.com

🔔 Quick Start Review

♻️ **Subjunctive review**

Use OHT 44 or write on the board:
Complete the following to form
sentences about how you feel today:

1. Me alegro que...
2. Tengo miedo de que...
3. Espero que...
4. No creo que...

Answers will vary.

☑️ Teaching Suggestions
What Have Students Learned?

Have students look at the "Now you
can…" notes listed on the left side of
pages 170–171. Point out that if they
need to review material before doing
the activities or taking the test, they
should consult the "To review" notes.

ETAPA 3

Now you can...

• react to nature.

To review

• subjunctive with
expressions
of emotion
see p. 158.

Now you can...

• express doubt.

To review

• the subjunctive
to express doubt
and uncertainty
see p. 160.

OBJECTIVES

• React to nature
• Express doubt
• Relate events
in time

En uso

REPASO Y **MÁS COMUNICACIÓN**

① El fin de semana

Vas al Parque Nacional con tu familia este fin de semana.
Combina las siguientes frases.

modelo

Vamos al Parque Nacional este fin de semana. Me alegro.

Me alegro de que vayamos al Parque Nacional este fin de semana.

1. Mi amigo no viene con nosotros. Es una lástima.
2. Mi hermano no tiene tiempo para acompañarnos. Siento mucho.
3. Siempre llueve durante nuestras vacaciones. Es ridículo.
4. Papá viene con nosotros. Me alegro.
5. Siempre nos perdemos en el parque. Mi hermanita tiene miedo.
6. Hay tantas especies de mariposas en el parque. Me alegro mucho.
7. Nos divertimos mucho. Ojalá.

② El campamento

Tú y tu compañero(a) están en un campamento. Él (Ella) dice
algunas cosas que tú dudas. ¿Qué te dice y cómo le respondes?

modelo

¡Hay serpientes en el campamento! (no es cierto)

Compañero(a): *¡Hay serpientes en el campamento!*

Tú: *No es cierto que haya serpientes en el campamento.*

Compañero(a): *¿Entonces qué hay?*

Tú: *Hay pájaros y hormigas.*

1. Veré un jaguar. (dudo que)
2. Haré un fuego con leña. (no creo que)
3. Tengo fósforos. (no es verdad que)
4. Escucharé un disco compacto. (no es seguro que)
5. Veremos un mono araña. (no creo)
6. Sacaré fotos de los osos hormigueros. (dudo que)
7. Usaré un saco de dormir. (no creo que)

170 ciento setenta
Unidad 2

Classroom Community

Cooperative Learning Have students plan a
Review Fair. Divide the information in the **Etapa** into
categories: subjunctive with verbs of emotion;
subjunctive with expressions of doubt; subjunctive with
conjunctions; flora and fauna vocabulary; weather and
camping vocabulary.
• Have groups sign up for the category they feel most
prepared in. Be sure categories are equally represented.

• Each group will assemble flashcards, review sheets,
information posters, and short quizzes for their booth.
• Each group then sets up a booth for each category
where everyone can visit and practice the materials.
• Students will need to trade off booth duty and visiting
other booths.

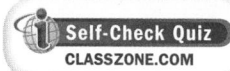
Self-Check Quiz
CLASSZONE.COM

Now you can...

• relate events
  in time.

To review

• the subjunctive
  with **cuando** and
  other expressions
  of time see p. 162.

3 Primera vez

Es la primera vez que Miguel va a acampar. ¿Qué dice que va a hacer? Usa **cuando** en sus oraciones.

modelo

abrir la tienda de campaña (llegar al campamento)
Abriré la tienda de campaña cuando llegue al campamento.

1. juntar leña (necesitar más)
2. empezar el fuego (tener frío)
3. abrir las latas de comida (encontrar el abrelatas)
4. guardar la comida (terminar de comer)
5. acostarme en el saco de dormir (cansarme)
6. despertarme (salir el sol)

Now you can...

• relate events
  in time.

To review

• the subjunctive
  with **cuando** and
  other expressions
  of time see p. 162.

4 Después de clases

Le describes a un(a) amigo(a) qué van a hacer tú y tu hermano(a) hoy después de clases. ¿Qué le dices?

modelo

ir a la biblioteca / en cuanto / salir de la última clase
Iremos a la biblioteca en cuanto salgamos de la última clase.

1. quedarse en el colegio / hasta que / venir mamá por nosotros
2. hacer la tarea / en cuanto / llegar a casa
3. preparar la cena / tan pronto como / terminar la tarea
4. encender el televisor / tan pronto como / lavar los platos
5. ver la tele / hasta que / oscurecer
6. acostarse / en cuanto / apagar el televisor
7. dormirse / tan pronto como / acostarse
8. no despertarse / hasta que / amanecer

Answers

1. Es una lástima que mi amigo no venga con nosotros.
2. Siento mucho que mi hermano no tenga tiempo para acompañarnos.
3. Es ridículo que siempre llueva durante nuestras vacaciones.
4. Me alegro de que papá venga con nosotros.
5. Mi hermanita tiene miedo de que nos perdamos en el parque.
6. Me alegro mucho de que haya tantas especies de mariposas en el parque.
7. Ojalá que nos divirtamos.

Answers

1. Dudo que veas un jaguar.
2. No creo que sepas hacer un fuego con leña.
3. No es verdad que no tengas fósforos.
4. No es seguro que llueva mañana.
5. Quizás veamos un mono araña.
6. Dudo que saques fotos de los osos hormigueros.
7. No creo que duermas bien sin saco de dormir.

Answers

1. Juntaré leña cuando necesite más.
2. Empezaré el fuego cuando tenga frío.
3. Abriré las latas de comida cuando encuentre el abrelatas.
4. Guardaré la comida cuando termine de comer.
5. Me acostaré en el saco de dormir cuando me canse.
6. Me despertaré cuando salga el sol.

Answers

1. Nos quedaremos en el colegio hasta que venga mamá por nosotros.
2. Haremos la tarea en cuanto lleguemos a casa.
3. Prepararemos la cena tan pronto como terminemos la tarea.
4. Encenderemos el televisor tan pronto como lavemos los platos.
5. Veremos la tele hasta que oscurezca.
6. Nos acostaremos en cuanto apaguemos el televisor.
7. Nos dormiremos tan pronto como nos acostemos.
8. No nos despertaremos hasta que amanezca.

Block Schedule

Peer Review Have students write answers for **Actividades 1, 3,** and **4.** Then have students work in pairs to correct each other's sentences. Pairs should work together to help each other make necessary changes. (For additional activities, see **Block Scheduling Copymasters**.)

Teaching All Students

Challenge Have students create a brochure for an ecotourism trip in your state. Include highlights of the trip, lodging or camping sites, animals that travelers will see, and weather conditions.

Native Speakers Have students choose a vacation spot in their country of origin or that of their relatives. Have them describe the place (location, weather, flora, fauna) and tell what travelers see and do there.

Multiple Intelligences

Kinesthetic Have student write sentences using **Es triste, Ojalá, Siento, Me alegro de, Es ridículo,** and **Tengo miedo.** As they read their sentences, they should express the sentiments facially and with gestures. Students might focus on their own future plans/fears/desires.

Verbal Call on each student to say 1 thing they doubt they will do this weekend and 1 thing they hope to do.

Teaching Resource Options

Print

Unit 2 Resource Book
Audioscript, pp. 183–184
Vocabulary Quizzes, pp. 186–188
Grammar Quizzes, pp. 189–190
Etapa Exam, Forms A and B,
pp. 191–200
Examen para hispanohablantes,
pp. 201–205
Portfolio Assessment, pp. 206–207
Unit 2 Comprehensive Test,
pp. 210–217
*Prueba comprensiva para
hispanohablantes,* Unit 2,
pp. 218–225
Multiple Choice Test Questions,
pp. 232–234

Audiovisual

OHT 45 (Quick Start)
Audio Program CD 19, Tracks 12–16

Technology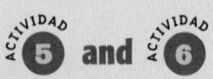

eTest Plus Online/Test Generator
CD-ROM

www.classzone.com

ACTIVIDAD **5** and ACTIVIDAD **6**

Rubric: Speaking

Criteria	Scale	
Sentence structure	1 2 3	A = 11–12 pts.
Vocabulary use	1 2 3	B = 9–10 pts.
Originality	1 2 3	C = 7–8 pts.
Fluency	1 2 3	D = 4–6 pts.
		F = < 4 pts.

ACTIVIDAD **7** **En tu propia voz**

Rubric: Writing

Criteria	Scale	
Vocabulary use	1 2 3 4 5	A = 14–15 pts.
Accuracy	1 2 3 4 5	B = 12–13 pts.
Creativity, appearance	1 2 3 4 5	C = 10–11 pts.
		D = 8–9 pts.
		F = < 8 pts.

Teaching Note: En tu propia voz

Writing Strategy Suggest that students implement the writing strategy "Use details to enrich a description." They should give a variety of details and facts to help the reader get to know their animal better.

---

5 ¡Somos ecoturistas!

STRATEGY: SPEAKING

Reassure others When people are planning an extensive trip together, it is important that they express hopes, feelings, concerns, and doubts. How can you reassure them? Here are some ways: **¡No te pongas triste! ¡No te preocupes! ¡Sé más optimista!** Can you think of other ways?

En grupos de dos o tres, conversen sobre un viaje que van a hacer como ecoturistas en Centroamérica. Primero decidan adónde van, y entonces digan cómo se sienten.

modelo

Tú: *Me alegro de que vayamos a acampar este fin de semana.*

Compañero(a) 1: *Es triste que Carlos no pueda venir con nosotros.*

Compañero(a) 2: *¡Sí, pobrecito! Ojalá que mañana se sienta mejor.*

6 Cuando haga esto...

En grupos de dos o tres, conversen sobre los planes que realizarán cuando terminen otras cosas.

modelo

Amigo(a) 1: *Yo voy a buscar trabajo en cuanto termine este año escolar.*

Amigo(a) 2: *Yo no. Yo voy a viajar por Centroamérica cuando pueda.*

Amigo(a) 3: *Yo no sé qué voy a hacer. Quizás me vaya a Nueva York.*

Amigo(a) 1: ...

7 *En tu propia voz*

ESCRITURA Escoge uno de los animales de Centroamérica y haz una investigación sobre ese animal. Escribe una composición que describa el animal: cuál es su hábitat natural, qué come, cómo es, etc. Si prefieres, escribe un cuento de ficción sobre un animal centroamericano.

modelo

El jaguar vive en la selva. Sólo sale al amanecer...

CONEXIONES

Las ciencias Las selvas tropicales producen una gran parte del oxígeno que necesita el mundo para vivir. Investiga algunos productos que vienen de la selva. ¿Crees que son necesarios? ¿Cuáles son algunos cambios que podrían pasar al medio ambiente si desaparecen las selvas tropicales? Puedes buscar en la biblioteca o en Internet. Comparte tu información en un ensayo o en un póster.

172 ciento setenta y dos
Unidad 2

Classroom Community

Portfolio Have students write a poem about an animal from the **Etapa**, following this model:

• name /adjective	Mono bonito
• 2 verbs in **-ando/-iendo**	corriendo, saltando
• phrase about the subject	de árbol a árbol
• descriptive word	Solo

Rubric A = 13–15 pts. B = 10–12 pts. C = 7–9 pts. D = 4–6 pts. F = < 4 pts.

Writing criteria	Scale
Correct poem form	1 2 3 4 5
Grammar/spelling accuracy	1 2 3 4 5
Creativity	1 2 3 4 5

Flashcards
CLASSZONE.COM

En resumen
REPASO DE VOCABULARIO

REACT TO NATURE

In the wild

el agua dulce	freshwater
(el) amanecer	dawn; to start the day
(el) anochecer	nightfall; to get dark
(el) atardecer	late afternoon; to get dark
bucear	to scuba-dive
el campamento	camp
descubrir	to discover
el (la) ecoturista	ecotourist
la luz	light
nadar con tubo de respiración	to snorkel
navegar por rápidos	to go white-water rafting
oscurecer	to get dark
la oscuridad	darkness
peligroso(a)	dangerous
el refugio de vida silvestre	wildlife refuge
salvaje	wild
el sendero	path

Animals, birds, and insects

la ballena jorobada	humpback whale
la boa constrictora	boa constrictor
el búho	owl
el halcón	falcon
la iguana	iguana
el jaguar	jaguar
el loro	parrot
la mariposa	butterfly
el mono araña	spider monkey
el ocelote	ocelot
el oso hormiguero	anteater
el pelícano	pelican
el pez	fish
el picaflor	hummingbird
la serpiente	snake
el tiburón	shark
la tortuga	turtle
el tucán	toucan
el venado	deer
el zorrillo	skunk

Camping

el abrelatas	can opener
la almohada	pillow
el fósforo	match
el fuego	fire
la leña	firewood
la linterna	flashlight
la manta	blanket
la navaja	jackknife
el saco de dormir	sleeping bag
la tienda de campaña	tent

Weather

el aguacero	downpour
centígrado	centigrade
húmedo(a)	humid, wet
el huracán	hurricane
la llovizna	drizzle
la neblina	fog, mist
la nube	cloud
el rayo	thunderbolt, flash of lightning
el relámpago	lightning
soleado(a)	sunny
el trueno	thunder

♻ **Ya sabes**

Es ridículo que...	It's ridiculous that...
Es triste que...	It's sad that...
Es una lástima que...	It's a shame that...
Espero que...	I hope that...
Me alegro de que...	I'm happy that...
Ojalá que...	I hope that...
Siento que...	I'm sorry that...
Tengo miedo de que...	I'm afraid that...

EXPRESS DOUBT

♻ **Ya sabes**

Dudo que...	I doubt that...
No creo que...	I don't think that...
No es cierto que...	It's not certain that...
No es seguro que...	It's not sure that...
No es verdad que...	It's not true that...
quizás / quizá	maybe
tal vez	perhaps, maybe

RELATE EVENTS IN TIME

cuando	when
en cuanto	as soon as
hasta que	until
tan pronto como	as soon as

Juego

La selva misteriosa

¿Qué hay en la selva? ¿Puedes encontrar dos animales cuyos nombres empiecen con la letra **m**?

ciento setenta y tres
México y Centroamérica Etapa 3   **173**

Teaching All Students

Extra Help Have students return to the **Etapa** opener on pp. 150–151. Have them write 3 sentences that the people in the photo might be saying: 1 sentence using the subjunctive with a verb of emotion, 1 sentence using the subjunctive with an expression of doubt, and 1 sentence using the subjunctive with a conjunction.

Multiple Intelligences

Naturalist Have students cut out 3 photos from magazines that depict scenes from nature. Have them describe the scenes in writing or orally for the class.

Visual Have students draw their own animals, give them a name, and describe them to the class.

Interdisciplinary

Science Have students research and explain the process by which the rainforest provides the world with oxygen.

🔔 Quick Start Review

♻ **Word association**

Use OHT 45 or write on the board: Write 1 word/expression that you associate with each of the following:

1. la manta   4. el río
2. llover   5. volar
3. la noche   6. la luz

Answers See p. 149B.

Teaching Suggestions
Vocabulary Review

Have students make word webs for the following words: **el ecoturista, el aguacero, el refugio de vida silvestre, bucear.** For example: **el ecoturista: el medio ambiente, campamento, tienda de campaña,** etc.

Dictation

Dictate the following sentences to review the **Etapa**:

1. Tengo miedo de que las serpientes salgan al anochecer.
2. No es seguro de que hayan ballenas jorobadas en esa playa.
3. Recogeré la leña tan pronto como lleguemos al campamento.

Juego

Answer: mono, mariposa

📖 Block Schedule

Change of Pace In pairs or groups of 3, have students imagine that they are planning a vacation to Central America. Each student has a different idea as to where he/she would like to go and what he/she would like to do. Have students create and present mini-skits in which the problem is discussed and solved, using vocabulary and structures from the **Etapa**.

Teaching Resource Options

Print
Block Scheduling Copymasters

Audiovisual
OHT GO1–GO5, 45 (Quick Start)

Technology
www.classzone.com

Quick Start Review

♻ **Nosotros** commands

Use OHT 68 or write on the board: Write sentences using the **nosotros** command form of these verbs to encourage your friends to join you in activities:

- ir
- hacer
- limpiar
- practicar
- trabajar

Answers
Answers will vary, but will include the following verb forms:

- vayamos
- hagamos
- limpiemos
- practiquemos
- trabajemos

Teaching Strategy
Prewriting

- Lead the class in brainstorming a list of ecological problems. Then have each student choose several issues for the first column of his/her chart.
- Ask students to recall what they've learned in this unit when completing their charts.

Post-writing

- When students exchange their drafts, have them not only review the points mentioned in the textbook, but also make any additional suggestions that might improve the content or structure of the speeches.

UNIDAD 2

En tu propia voz
ESCRITURA

¡A todos nos toca!

Tu amiga costarricense es candidata para presidenta de su clase. Te pide que le escribas un discurso sobre la preservación del medio ambiente. Tienes que escribir un discurso persuasivo dando tres razones por las cuales los alumnos deben votar por ella.

Función: Persuadir a votar   **Contenido:** La protección del medio ambiente
Contexto: Informar a los alumnos   **Tipo de texto:** Discurso persuasivo

PARA ESCRIBIR · STRATEGY: WRITING

Persuade by presenting solutions to problems A persuasive political speech convinces voters that a candidate can identify important issues, define shared goals, and offer specific solutions to problems. It also highlights the benefits of solving the problems.

Modelo del estudiante

> The writer clearly **identifies the problems** the candidate intends to solve.

> The writer involves listeners in the speech directly by using **nosotros** as opposed to **yo** forms, as well as **nosotros commands.**

> As the speech is developed, the writer **establishes a clear relationship** between the problems, the solutions, and the future benefits.

Estudiantes votantes: ¿Valoran el futuro? ¿Quieren contribuir con nuestra comunidad? Todos deseamos mejorar el mundo en que vivimos.

Sin embargo, día tras día tenemos que confrontar la creciente contaminación de nuestro aire y agua. ¿Podemos evitar los malos efectos de la destrucción de nuestras áreas verdes? ¿Es posible reducir la contaminación, consumir menos y conservar más?

¡Yo creo que sí! Si nuestra clase me elige presidenta, verán lo que puede hacer una líder dedicada a la preservación de la ecología. ¡Trabajemos juntos para luchar contra la degradación de nuestro medio ambiente! ¡Colaboremos desde nuestra escuela para nuestra comunidad!

Como presidenta de la clase, crearé y pondré en práctica programas efectivos. Les prometo organizar una campaña de sembrar árboles y flores alrededor de la escuela para embellecerla y devolver el oxígeno al aire. Lucharé por grupos de estudiantes para recoger basura, para que no se ensucie más nuestra vecindad. Organizaré un programa de reciclaje más completo para conservar papel, latas y plásticos de la escuela.

Su voto por mí es un voto por el futuro. Estar a favor de mi presidencia es estar a favor del medio ambiente. Ojalá que juntos podamos cumplir con mis esperanzas y planes para nuestra clase. ¿Me pueden ayudar? ¡Protejamos los beneficios del aire limpio, de un paisaje bello y de un futuro más seguro! No se olviden... ¡A todos nos toca!

Classroom Community

Paired Activity Have students work in pairs and list other issues they would like a class president to address. Then have them fill out a chart like the one on p. 175. Finally, have groups of 3 pairs meet and compare ideas.

Group Activity In groups of 5, have students take turns reading their speeches while group members listen. The group then votes on the best "candidate."

Portfolio Have students save their speeches for their portfolios. Subsequent writing projects will show their progress in Spanish.

Estrategias para escribir

Antes de escribir…

Piensa en varios problemas ecológicos que se deben mencionar. ¿Qué problemas puedes solucionar con programas en la escuela? Crea una tabla como la de la derecha. Determina qué problemas son más importantes para los alumnos e identifica soluciones generales. Después, piensa en programas que puedan implementar las soluciones de una manera concreta.

Problema general	Solución general	Programas específicos de la candidata
contaminación del aire	devolver el oxígeno	sembrar árboles y plantas
consumo de recursos naturales	conservar	reciclar papel, latas, plástico y más
una vecindad sucia	limpiar	recoger la basura

Revisiones

Después de escribir el primer borrador, pídele a un(a) compañero(a) que lo lea en voz alta. Pregúntale:

- *¿Qué más debo hacer para identificar los problemas de una manera clara?*
- *¿Cómo puedo explicar la relación entre los problemas, las soluciones y los beneficios?*
- *¿Qué más necesito hacer para que los estudiantes tomen un interés personal?*

La versión final

Antes de crear tu versión final, léela de nuevo y repasa los siguientes puntos:

- *¿Usé el subjuntivo con expresiones de duda, emoción o deseo?*

Haz lo siguiente: Subraya todas las expresiones de duda, emoción o deseo. Subraya dos veces los verbos que se usan con estas expresiones. Míralos para ver si debes usar el subjuntivo o el indicativo en cada caso. ¡Ojo! No te olvides de usar el indicativo con expresiones de certeza.

- *¿Incluí mandatos con la forma nosotros en el discurso?*

Haz lo siguiente: Haz un círculo alrededor de todos los mandatos con la forma nosotros. Míralos y corrígelos si es necesario. Recuerda que estos mandatos tienen la misma forma nosotros en el subjuntivo, con la excepción de los irregulares.

La naturaleza es la responsabilidad de todos. ¡Hacemos [*Hagamos*] nuestra parte! Es peligroso que no la hemos [*hayamos*] protegido más y que no hayamos descubierto soluciones para preservarla. ¡Tengo miedo de que la destrucción del medio ambiente va [*vaya*] a ser desastroso [*desastrosa*] para todos! Es evidente que tenemos [*tengamos*] que sacrificar y conservar para mantener el equilibrio ecológico. ¡No contaminamos! ¡Sobrevivamos!

Rubric: Writing

Let students know ahead of time which elements of their writing you will be evaluating. A global evaluation is more helpful to students than a correction of every mistake made. Consider the following in scoring compositions:

Sentences	
1	Most not logical
2	Somewhat logical
3	In logical order
4	Logical with some flow
5	Flow purposefully

Details	
1	Few details
2	Some basic details
3	Sufficient basic details
4	Substantial details
5	Clear and vivid detail

Organization	
1	Very little organization
2	Poorly organized
3	Some organization
4	Sufficiently organized
5	Strong organization

Accuracy	
1	Errors prevent comprehension
2	Comprehensible, yet many errors
3	Some spelling and agreement errors throughout
4	A few errors
5	Very few errors

Criteria	Scale	
Logical sentence order	1 2 3 4 5	A = 17–20 pts.
Clear and vivid detail	1 2 3 4 5	B = 13–16 pts.
Organization	1 2 3 4 5	C = 9–12 pts.
Accuracy	1 2 3 4 5	D = 5–8 pts.
		F = < 5 pts.

Teaching All Students

Extra Help Review structures with students before writing: Use of the subjunctive with expressions of doubt, wishes, and emotion; **Nosotros** commands.

Challenge Have students write to Spanish language students at other schools to find out school and community ecology issues and programs.

Native Speakers Have Spanish speakers read their speeches to the class. Ask others to listen carefully to pronunciation and intonation.

Multiple Intelligences

Visual Have students create posters, flyers, buttons, and/or bumper stickers to support their candidacy.

Block Schedule

Variety Have a candidates' panel, with volunteeers reading their pieces to the class. (For additional activities, see **Block Scheduling Copymasters**.)

Unit Theme

Celebrating personal occasions, holidays, and historic events in the Spanish-speaking Caribbean world

Teaching Resource Options

Print

Block Scheduling Copymasters
Unit 3 Resources Book
  Absent Student Copymasters, p.34

Audiovisual

OHT M1, M3; 1
Canciones CD
Video Program Videotape 18:06 / DVD, Unit 3

Technology

eEdition Plus Online/eEdition CD-ROM
Easy Planner Plus Online/Easy Planner
  CD-ROM
  www.classzone.com

UNIDAD 3

CELEBRACIÓN DE MI MUNDO

 STANDARDS

Communication
• Describing celebrations, holidays, and historic events
• Saying what people want
• Linking events and ideas
• Hypothesizing
• Expressing doubt, disagreement, and emotion
• Making suggestions and wishes
• Stating cause and effect

Cultures
• Regional vocabulary
• Celebrations, holidays, and historic events in the Spanish-speaking Caribbean world
• The history and culture of the Spanish-speaking Caribbean world

Connections
• Art: Caribbean art style
• Social Studies: Investigating independence days in the Spanish-speaking world

Comparisons
• Celebrations, holidays, and historic events in the Spanish-speaking Caribbean world and in the U.S.
• Music in the Spanish-speaking Caribbean world and in the U.S.

Communities
• Using Spanish in the workplace
• Using Spanish with friends at school

INTERNET Preview
CLASSZONE.COM
• More About the Caribbean
• Webquest
• Self-Check Quizzes
• Flashcards
• Writing Center
• Online Workbook
  • eEdition Plus Online

176

EL CARIBE

Estados Unidos — Islas Bahamas — Cuba — Jamaica — Haití — República Dominicana — Puerto Rico — Antillas Menores

FLORIDA — LA HABANA — BAHAMAS — CUBA — REPÚBLICA DOMINICANA — HAITÍ — SAN JUAN — SANTO DOMINGO — PUERTO RICO — MAR CARIBE

Los MUÑEQUITOS DE MATANZAS
LIVE IN NEW YORK

CUBA
LOS MUÑEQUITOS DE MATANZAS
Este grupo de música afrocubana utiliza tradiciones e instrumentos de África. También cantan en yoruba, un lenguaje africano. ¿En cuáles otros países del Caribe se puede ver la influencia africana?

Classroom Community

Group Activity Divide the class into groups. Have half the groups list differences among Cuba, the Dominican Republic, and Puerto Rico. Have the other half of the groups list similarities. Lists may include culture, history, music, government, land, etc.

Paired Activity Give pairs of students an outline map of the Caribbean region. Have them work together to research, then label, the Spanish-speaking countries, capitals, major cities, seas, and oceans.

ALMANAQUE CULTURAL

POBLACIÓN: Puerto Rico: 3.839.810
República Dominicana: 8.581.477
Cuba: 11.184.023

ALTURA: 3175 m sobre el nivel del mar (punto más alto: Pico Duarte, República Dominicana)

CLIMA: 80°F (27°C) San Juan (Temp. más alta); 77°F (25°C) Habana (Temp. más baja)

COMIDA TÍPICA: chicharrones, sancocho, tostones

GENTE FAMOSA DEL CARIBE: José Martí (escritor), Pedro Martínez (atleta), Juan Luis Guerra (músico), Rosario Ferré (escritora)

VIDEO DVD Mira el video para más información.

CLASSZONE.COM
More About the Caribbean

PUERTO RICO
ROSARIO FERRÉ es una de las escritoras más prominentes de América Latina. Ha escrito y publicado libros en inglés y español. ¿Cómo crees que la historia de Puerto Rico ha influido en esto?

EL CARIBE
FRUTAS TROPICALES Las guayabas, quenepas y piñas son algunas de las frutas que se cultivan en el clima tropical del Caribe. Se hacen muchos dulces y refrescos con éstas. ¿Conoces otras frutas que vengan de un clima tropical?

LA REPÚBLICA DOMINICANA
JUAN LUIS GUERRA Este músico es uno de los grandes del merengue. El merengue es la música más popular de la República Dominicana. Es conocida a través del mundo latinoamericano. ¿Sabes qué otra cosa significa **merengue**?

PUERTO RICO
PARQUE CEREMONIAL TAÍNO, UTUADO
Los taínos, las personas que vivían en Puerto Rico cuando llegaron los españoles, celebraban el batey o juego de pelota en este parque ceremonial. Según la foto, ¿a qué deporte crees que se parece este juego?

Utuado, P.R.

EL CARIBE
MARACAS Este instrumento de percusión es muy popular en el Caribe. Es de origen africano. ¿Qué otros instrumentos conoces de origen africano?

177

Standards for Foreign Language Learning

The Cultures standard is the focus for this unit.

Cultures

Standard 2.1 Students demonstrate an understanding of the relationship between the practices and perspectives of the culture studied.

Standard 2.2 Students demonstrate an understanding of the relationship between the products and perspectives of the culture studied.

Teaching Resource Options

Print
Block Scheduling Copymasters

Audiovisual
Poster

Technology
 www.classzone.com

Teaching Suggestion
Previewing the Standard

By the time students reach Level 3, they have been exposed to the diversity of the Spanish-speaking world. It is important that they understand that there is a wide array of individuals speaking Spanish, whose customs are as diverse and unique as their homelands. Focus on the similarities among us and not solely on the differences. You may want to begin this process by having students consider the diversity of cultures within their hometown.

UNIDAD

3

CELEBRACIÓN DE MI MUNDO

- Comunicación

- **Culturas**

- Conexiones

- Comparaciones

- Comunidades

Webquest
CLASSZONE.COM

Explore cultures in the Caribbean through guided Web activities.

178

Culturas

La cultura del Caribe es única. ¿Cómo y por qué se distinguen las culturas de diferentes regiones y países?

Culturas en acción Observa estas tres fotos. ¿Te dicen algo especial sobre el Caribe? ¿Te recuerdan otros países? Explica.

Monumento a Colón, Santo Domingo, República Dominicana

Comunicación

Nos gusta conversar mucho cuando celebramos alguna ocasión especial. Imagina la conversación de esta familia. En tu opinión, ¿qué están diciendo?

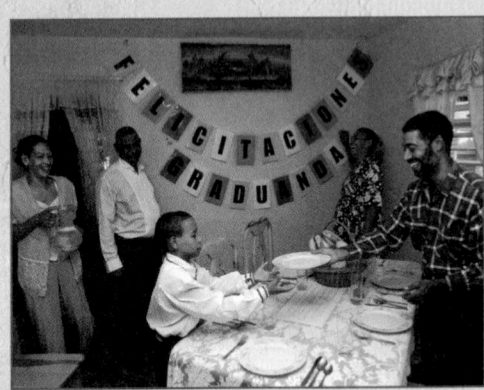

Classroom Community

Paired Activity Ask students to think about their favorite personal celebration and their favorite national one. Have them write how their families celebrate each. Then have them work in pairs and share their responses with each other.

Group Activity Ask students what they think the most interesting information is they have learned about the Spanish-speaking world. Generate a list of opinions, writing their responses on the board. Then have the class rank the top five that they would like to know more about, voting by using a ranking system of 1–5. Assign students to five groups and have each group further investigate one of the five topics.

Comparaciones

En todos los países del mundo se celebran algunos eventos históricos. ¿Cómo se comparan las celebraciones de la foto? ¿En cuál te gustaría participar?

Conexiones

En esta unidad tendrás la oportunidad de investigar el arte caribeño y los días de independencia de varios países. ¿Cuál de estas dos áreas te interesa más? ¿Por qué?

Comunidades

En esta unidad conocerás a un alumno que habla español en el restaurante donde trabaja. ¿Dónde hablas español en tu comunidad?

Fíjate

Hay diferentes tipos de celebraciones. En la siguiente tabla escribe dos celebraciones que compartas con tu familia o amigos, y dos celebraciones que compartas en la escuela.

Celebraciones con familia o amigos	Celebraciones en la escuela
_____	_____
_____	_____

179

Unit 3 and Cultures

Celebración de mi mundo reminds us to start with our own world and environment and appreciate our day-to-day life with its art, music, literature, foods, celebrations and the like. Once students focus on their own culture, they are better able to comprehend that of others.

Culture Highlights

● **MÁSCARAS** El arte de hacer máscaras, como la de la foto de la página 178, es una parte de la tradición histórica y cultural puertorriqueña.

● **FRUTAS TROPICALES** La página 178 muestra una foto con piñas, guayabas (*guavas*) y quenepas (*avocados*).

● **MARACAS** Las maracas, los populares instrumentos caribeños de la foto de la página 178, están hechas de calabazas huecas con semillas sueltas dentro.

● **LA REPÚBLICA DOMINICANA** La República Dominicana logró su independencia de Haití el 27 de febrero de 1844. Los participantes del desfile de la foto de la página 179 están celebrando esta fecha.

● **PUERTO RICO** Un conjunto puertorriqueño celebra El Día de la Abolición de la Esclavitud en la foto del la página 179.

● **JUAN PABLO DUARTE** En 1844 Duarte inició el movimiento independentista de la República Dominicana contra Haití. La página 179 muestra una foto de su estatua.

Fíjate

Answers
Answers will vary.

Block Schedule

Variety Have students research the culture of their heritage. If they are of mixed heritage, they should focus on only one culture. Have them prepare a description that includes the following: country, language(s) spoken, typical food, dress, and music. Then have them compare their description to what they have learned about a Spanish-speaking country.

Teaching All Students

Extra Help Have students select one of the pictures from pp. 178–179 and write three sentences about the picture. Their sentences can include descriptions or opinions.

Native Speakers Ask native speakers to select the characteristic of American culture that they feel is most different from the culture of their country of heritage. Have them present an oral report to the class.

Challenge Ask students to investigate the **taíno** people; where they came from and what happened to them after the arrival of the Spaniards. Have them write a report or give an oral presentation to the class.

Ampliación

These activities may be used at various points in the Unit 3 sequence.

■ For Block Schedule, you may find that these projects will provide a welcome change of pace while reviewing and reinforcing the material presented in the unit. See the **Block Scheduling Copymasters.**

UNA INVITACIÓN ESPECIAL
Querido *Pedro*
Te invito a ti y a tu familia a que vengan a la
FIESTA DE GRADUACIÓN.
DÓNDE: Salón principal,
Hotel Mar Azul, Santo Domingo
CUÁNDO: domingo 13 de mayo
12:00 p.m. a 7:00 p.m.
Habrá baile y comida.
¡Te espero allí!
Un abrazo y felicidades.
Tu amiga, Estefanía

● PROJECTS

Create a festivities guide in Spanish. Have students work in pairs to research holiday celebrations in a Spanish-speaking country of their choice. Give each pair several sheets of heavy paper or posterboard so that all students use the same size and quality of paper. They will use their paper to write descriptions of the holidays in their country, illustrating them with drawings or clippings from magazines or printouts from the Internet. They should include important dates, names, and events associated with the festivals. Encourage them to also include a map to orient readers. Have the class work together to alphabetize and bind the descriptions. Display the guide in class.

PACING SUGGESTION: Have students begin research at the beginning of the unit. Final projects are completed at the end of Unit 3.

Film or record a fortune teller scene Have students work in groups to write and perform a fortune teller scene centering on what students will do after graduation from high school. Encourage humor and creativity.

PACING SUGGESTION: Upon completion of Etapa 1.

CUBA

● STORYTELLING

La graduación de Rosanna After reviewing the vocabulary for graduation, model a mini-story (using student actors or photos from the text) that students will revise, retell, and expand:

La ceremonia de graduación es en dos semanas y Rosanna se siente feliz y ansiosa a la vez. Le dice a su mejor amiga, Nina: «Tengo tantas cosas que hacer para el día de graduación y no sé dónde empezar». Nina le pregunta: «¿Cómo puedo ayudarte?» Rosanna responde: «Es importante que yo escriba un discurso y no tengo ideas». Nina le dice a Rosanna: «¿Quieres que te ayude? Es mejor que hables de las cosas que conoces».

HAITÍ

As you give your model, pause so that students may fill in words and act out gestures. Students then write, narrate, and read aloud a longer main story, using vocabulary from this unit. Students can write, illustrate, and act out new stories based on this storytelling experience.

Mi discurso Have students prepare their own graduation speeches. They can speak as themselves or role-play someone from a real or imaginary school.

PACING SUGGESTION: Upon completion of Etapa 1.

● BULLETIN BOARD/POSTERS

Bulletin Board Plan ahead: Have students bring in old photos of themselves. Make copies of the photos and have students decorate them with caps and gowns. Have them also write superlative captions (**el más atlético,** etc.).

Posters Have students create •**A graduation poster** in Spanish for their graduating class •**Festival** calendars for Spanish-speaking countries •**A festival event** poster for one of the festivals researched for Projects.

GAMES

¿Quién es?

Plan ahead: Have each student write the name of a well-known Spanish-speaking person (living or dead) on a slip of paper and give it to you. Write a complete list of people on the board. Then have each student write a one-sentence description of their person on a slip of paper. Put the slips in a box. Divide the class into 3–4 groups. Each group in turn chooses a slip of paper, reads the description aloud, and guesses to whom it refers. If they guess correctly, they get a point. If not, the team to raise their hands first gets a chance to guess. The team with the most correct guesses wins.

> **PACING SUGGESTION:** Upon completion of Etapa 3.

Peces

Select and write on the board nouns and verbs from **Etapas 1** and **2** related to graduation and celebrations. The nouns/verbs should be ones that students can illustrate. Then have students work in groups of 4 to make decks of cards. Each student in the group makes 1 card for each word on the board. When the groups finish their cards, have them play **Peces** (Go fish!).

> **PACING SUGGESTION:** Upon completion of Etapa 3.

MUSIC

Point out that an important element of **merengue** is the rhythm. Play some **merengue** music and have students follow the rhythm by tapping their hands on their desks (or use drums or other percussion instruments). Then have volunteers demonstrate a typical **merengue** rhythm without the music. More music samples are available on your *Canciones* CD.

REPÚBLICA DOMINICANA

HANDS-ON CRAFTS

Plan ahead: Bring in balloons, old newspaper, wheat flour, aluminum foil, and paints. Have students create masks. Cut strips of newspaper. Mix the flour and water to form a paste. Wet the strips in the paste and layer on the inflated balloons. As students layer the strips, they should shape their masks. Horns, beaks, etc. can be formed with aluminum foil, covered by several wet strips of newspaper. Let the masks dry for at least 24 hours. Then paint and decorate the masks.

PUERTO RICO

RECIPE

Tartas de coco dominicanas

Coconut is used in many sweets in the Dominican Republic and other Caribbean countries. The coconut is actually a tropical seed, and because it is dispersed by ocean currents, its region of origin is uncertain. For all tropical countries, the coconut palm and its seed have many uses, including cooking.

Receta

Tartas de coco dominicanas

2 huevos, ligeramente revueltos	1/4 taza de azúcar
1 1/2 tazas de leche	1/2 taza de coco rallado
1/2 taza de requesón	6 masas de tarta pequeñas

Caliente el horno a 325°. En una olla, caliente la leche a fuego lento hasta hervir. Quítela del fuego. Mezcle la leche con los huevos. Añada el queso, el azúcar y el coco. Ponga la mezcla en las masas de tarta y luego hornee las masas por veinte minutos. Refrésquelas 30 minutos antes de servir.

Planning Guide CLASSROOM MANAGEMENT

OBJECTIVES

Communication
- Describe personal celebrations *pp. 182–183, 184–185*
- Say what people want *pp. 188–189*
- Link events and ideas *pp. 184–185*

Grammar
- Review: Use the subjunctive for expressing wishes *pp. 188–189*
- Use the subjunctive with conjunctions *pp. 190–191*
- Use the imperfect subjunctive *pp. 192–194*

Culture
- History and culture of the Caribbean *pp. 176–177*
- Regional vocabulary *p. 188*
- Graduation celebrations and trips in the Dominican Republic *pp. 190, 193*
- Nicolás Guillén, a Cuban poet *pp. 196–197*

♻ Recycling
- Expressions of doubt and uncertainty *p. 194*
- Recreation vocabulary *p. 194*

STRATEGIES

Listening Strategies
- Pre-listening *p. 184*
- Listen and recognize major transitions *p. 184*

Speaking Strategies
- Accept or reject advice *p. 189*
- Give advice and best wishes *p. 200*

Reading Strategies
- Interpret metaphors *p. 196*

Writing Strategies
- Bring your event to life *TE p. 200*

Connecting Cultures Strategies
- Learn about the history and culture of the Caribbean *pp. 176–177*
- Recognize variations in vocabulary *p. 188*
- Learn about graduation celebrations and trips in the Dominican Republic *pp. 190, 193*
- Learn about Nicolás Guillén, a Cuban poet, and his poetry *pp. 196–197*
- Research African-American writers *TE p. 197*
- Connect and compare what you know about poetry in your community to help you learn about poetry in a new community *pp. 196–197*

PROGRAM RESOURCES

Print

- *Más práctica* Workbook PE *pp. 65–72*
- *Actividad es para todos* Workbook PE *pp. 71–80*
- Block Scheduling Copymasters *pp. 57–64*
- Unit 3 Resource Book
  - *Más práctica* Workbook TE *pp. 3–10*
  - *Actividad es para todos* Workbook TE *pp. 11–20*
  - *Cuaderno para hispanohablantes* TE *pp. 21–28*
  - Information Gap Activities *pp. 29–32*
  - Family Letter *p. 33*
  - Absent Student Copymasters *pp. 34–39*
  - Family Involvement *pp. 40–41*
  - Audioscript *pp. 42–45*
  - Assessment Program, Unit 3 Etapa 1 *pp. 47–69; 226–228*
  - Answer Keys *pp. 250–254*

Audiovisual

- Audio Program CD 7
- *Canciones* CD
- Overhead Transparencies M1–M3; 2, 5–17
- Word Tiles U3E1

Technology

- eEdition Plus Online/eEdition CD-ROM
- Easy Planner Plus Online/Easy Planner CD-ROM
- eTest Plus Online/Test Generator CD-ROM
- Online Workbook
- Take-Home Tutor CD-ROM
- www.classzone.com

✔ Assessment Program Options

- Unit 3 Resource Book
  - Vocabulary Quizzes
  - Grammar Quizzes
  - Ftapa Exam Forms A and B
  - *Fxamen para hispanohablantes*
  - Portfolio Assessment
  - Multiple Choice Test Questions
- Audio Program CD 19
- eTest Plus Online/Test Generator CD-ROM

Native Speakers

- *Cuaderno para hispanohablantes* PE *pp. 65–72*
- *Cuaderno para hispanohablantes* TE (Unit 3 Resource Book)
- *Examen para hispanohablantes* (Unit 3 Resource Book)
- Audio Program (Para hispanohablantes) CD 7, 19
- Audioscript (Unit 3 Resource Book)

Student Text
Listening Activity Scripts

 **Situaciones** *pages 184–185*

• CD 7

Jorge: Aquí estamos en el auditorio del Colegio Nuestra Señora del Rosario de Fátima. ¡Hay mucha gente! Es un día muy importante para mi hermana. ¡Por fin se va a graduar de la secundaria!

Aquí viene el desfile de los graduandos con sus padrinos. ¡Allí está Rosanna! Rosanna, Rosanna, ¡mira la cámara! ¡Ustedes también! ¡Quiero grabar a los padrinos también!

Bueno, voy a buscar mi asiento antes de que toquen el himno nacional. ¡Quiero grabar toda la ceremonia de graduación! Le va a gustar mucho a Rosanna.

Profesor: Señores y señoras. Es un gran placer estar aquí hoy en este día tan especial para nuestros estudiantes...

Jorge: Ay, ¡los discursos! ¡Qué aburrido! No quiero usar toda la cinta grabando este discurso. Siempre dicen lo mismo: «Les deseamos mucho éxito, ¡enhorabuena!, estamos todos muy emocionados, bla, bla». Voy a apagar la cámara hasta que empiecen a dar los diplomas a los graduandos.

¡Ahora sí! Ay, ¡mira a Rosanna recibiendo su diploma! ¡Qué intelectual se ve en su birrete y toga! ¡Casi ni la conozco!

¡Qué bien! Estoy muy orgulloso de mi hermana. Le agradezco mucho que se graduara, porque ¡ahora su cuarto va a ser mío!

Jorge: Rosanna, unas palabras para la cámara ahora que estamos en casa celebrando con la familia.

Rosanna: ¿Qué les puedo decir? Mil gracias a todos ustedes, que me han apoyado durante toda mi carrera. No saben cuánto aprecio su generosidad y su cariño. ¿Qué haría sin ustedes?

Jorge: Aquí terminamos la primera parte de la graduación de Rosanna Lisette Cruz de la Rosa. En otras noticias...

 **ACTIVIDAD 6 Consejos a los graduandos** *page 189*

Modelo: Armando y Nydia, les sugiero que vayan a la universidad.
1. Ana Luisa, te aconsejo que estudies ingeniería.
2. Juan y María, les aconsejo que trabajen durante los veranos.
3. Arturo, recomiendo que no gastes mucho dinero.
4. Martín y Laura, les sugiero que no compren un coche.
5. Eduardo, recomiendo que no salgas mucho.
6. Joaquín, sugiero que estudies todos los días.
7. Marisa y Enedina, les aconsejo que hagan la tarea a tiempo.
8. Rogelio, recomiendo que duermas lo suficiente.

ACTIVIDAD 12 ¿En qué insistían? *page 193*

Modelo: Mi papá insistía en que yo fuera a la universidad.
1. Mi mamá insistía en que mis hermanos y yo continuáramos nuestra educación.
2. Mi papá insistía en que yo estudiara todos los días.
3. Mi mamá insistía en que mis hermanos y yo nos vistiéramos apropiadamente.
4. Mis padres insistían en que mis hermanos y yo trabajáramos en los veranos.
5. Mi papá insistía en que yo guardara mi dinero.
6. Mi mamá insistía en que mis hermanos hicieran la tarea antes de la cena.
7. Mis padres insistían en que mis hermanos y yo respetáramos a nuestros profesores.
8. Mis padres insistían en que mis hermanos se acostaran temprano.
9. Mi papá insistía en que yo no saliera durante la semana.

Sample Lesson Plan - 50 Minute Schedule

DAY 1

Unit Opener
- Anticipate/Activate prior knowledge: Present the *Almanaque* and the cultural notes. Use Map OHTs as needed. **15 MIN.**

Etapa Opener
- Quick Start Review (TE, p. 180) **5 MIN.**
- Have students look at the *Etapa* Opener and answer the questions. **5 MIN.**

En contexto: Vocabulario
- Quick Start Review (TE, p. 182) **5 MIN.**
- Present *Descubre*, p. 182. **5 MIN.**
- Have students use context and pictures to learn *Etapa* vocabulary, then answer the *¿Comprendiste?* questions, p. 183. Use the Situational OHTs for additional practice. **15 MIN.**

Homework Option:
- Have students write answers to the *¿Comprendiste?* questions, p. 183.

DAY 2

En vivo: Situaciones
- Check homework. **5 MIN.**
- Quick Start Review (TE, p. 184) **5 MIN.**
- Present the Listening Strategy, p. 184. **5 MIN.**
- Have students look at section 1, p. 184. Play the audio for section 2. Then have students work in pairs or groups to complete section 3. **15 MIN.**

En acción: Vocabulario y gramática
- Quick Start Review (TE, p. 186) **5 MIN.**
- Have students complete *Actividad* 1 in writing, then go over answers orally. **5 MIN.**
- Have students do *Actividades* 2 and 3 in pairs. **10 MIN.**

Homework Option:
- Have students write out their answers to *Situaciones*, section 3, p. 185.

DAY 3

En acción (cont.)
- Check homework. **5 MIN.**
- Have students complete *Actividad* 4 in pairs. Have a few pairs present their conversations. **10 MIN.**
- Quick Start Review (TE, p. 188) **5 MIN.**
- Present *Repaso:* The Subjunctive for Expressing Wishes and *Vocabulario*, p. 188. **10 MIN.**
- Present the *Nota* and have students complete *Actividad* 5 orally. **5 MIN.**
- Play the audio; do *Actividad* 6. **5 MIN.**
- Present the Speaking Strategy, p. 189, and have students complete *Actividad* 7 in pairs. **10 MIN.**

Homework Option:
- Have students complete *Actividad* 5 in writing. *Más práctica* Workbook, p. 69. *Cuaderno para hispanohablantes*, p. 67.

DAY 4

En acción (cont.)
- Check homework. **5 MIN.**
- Present *Gramática:* The Subjunctive with Conjunctions, p. 190. **10 MIN.**
- Have students do *Actividad* 8 orally. **5 MIN.**
- Have students complete *Actividad* 9 in pairs. **5 MIN.**
- Have students complete *Actividad* 10 in writing. Go over answers orally. Expand using Information Gap Activities, Unit 3 Resource Book, p. 29; *Más comunicación*, p. R9. **15 MIN.**
- Use an expansion activity from TE pp. 190–191 for variety. **10 MIN.**

Homework Option:
- Have students complete *Actividad* 8 in writing. *Más práctica* Workbook, p. 70. *Cuaderno para hispanohablantes*, p. 68.

DAY 5

En acción (cont.)
- Check homework. **5 MIN.**
- Quick Start Review (TE, p. 192) **5 MIN.**
- Present *Gramática:* The Imperfect Subjunctive, p. 192. **10 MIN.**
- Do *Actividad* 11 orally. **5 MIN.**
- Play the audio; do *Actividad* 12. **5 MIN.**
- Have students complete *Actividad* 13 in pairs. **5 MIN.**
- Have students do *Actividad* 14 in groups. Expand using *Más comunicación*, p. R9. **15 MIN.**

Homework Option:
- Have students complete *Actividades* 11 and 13 in writing. *Más práctica* Workbook, pp. 71–72. *Cuaderno para hispanohablantes*, pp. 69–70.
- *Actividades para todas:* Workbook, pp. 71–76.

DAY 6

En acción (cont.)
- Check homework. **5 MIN.**
- Present the *Vocabulario*, p. 195. **5 MIN.**
- Have students read and complete *Actividad* 15 in writing. Go over answers orally. **10 MIN.**

Refrán
- Present the *Refrán*, p. 195. **5 MIN.**

En voces: Lectura
- Quick Start Review (TE, p. 196) **5 MIN.**
- Present the Reading Strategy, p. 196. Call on volunteers to read the *Lectura* aloud. Have students answer the *¿Comprendiste?/¿Qué piensas?* questions, p. 197. **20 MIN.**

Homework Option:
- Have students complete *Hazlo tú*, p. 197.

DAY 7

En uso: Repaso y más comunicación
- Check homework. **5 MIN.**
- Quick Start Review (TE, p. 198) **5 MIN.**
- Do *Actividad* 1 in pairs. **5 MIN.**
- Do *Actividad* 2 in groups. **5 MIN.**
- Have students do *Actividades* 3 and 4 orally. **10 MIN.**
- Present the Speaking Strategy, p. 200. Do *Actividad* 5 in groups. **15 MIN.**

En tu propia voz: Escritura
- Have students do *Actividad* 6 in writing. **5 MIN.**

Homework Option:
- Review for *Etapa* 1 Exam.

DAY 8

En tu propia voz (cont.)
- Have volunteers present their postcards to the class. **10 MIN.**

Tú en la comunidad
- Present and discuss *Jordan*, p. 200. **5 MIN.**

En resumen: Repaso de vocabulario
- Quick Start Review (TE, p. 201) **5 MIN.**
- Review grammar questions, etc., as necessary. **10 MIN.**
- Complete *Etapa* 1 Exam. **20 MIN.**

Ampliación
- Optional: Use a suggested project, game, or activity. (TE, pp. 179A–179B)

Homework Option:
- Preview *Etapa* 2 Opener.

Sample Lesson Plan - Block Schedule (90 minutes)

DAY 1

Unit Opener
- Anticipate/Activate prior knowledge: Present the *Almanaque* and the cultural notes. Use Map OHTs as needed. 15 MIN.

Etapa Opener
- Quick Start Review (TE, p. 180) 5 MIN.
- Have students look at the *Etapa* Opener and answer the questions. 5 MIN.
- Use Block Scheduling Copymasters. 10 MIN.

En contexto: Vocabulario
- Quick Start Review (TE, p. 182) 5 MIN.
- Present *Descubre*, p. 182. 5 MIN.
- Have students use context and pictures to learn *Etapa* vocabulary, then answer the *¿Comprendiste?* questions, p. 183. Use the Situational OHTs for additional practice. 15 MIN.

En vivo: Situaciones
- Quick Start Review (TE, p. 184) 5 MIN.
- Present the Listening Strategy, p. 184. 5 MIN.
- Have students look at section 1, p. 184. Play the audio for section 2. Then have students work in pairs or groups to complete section 3. 20 MIN.

Homework Option:
- Have students write answers to the *¿Comprendiste?* questions, p. 183, and to *Situaciones,* section 3, p. 185.

DAY 2

En acción: Vocabulario y gramática
- Check homework. 5 MIN.
- Quick Start Review (TE, p. 186) 5 MIN.
- Have students complete *Actividad* 1 in writing, then go over answers orally. 5 MIN.
- Have students do *Actividades* 2 and 3 in pairs. 10 MIN.
- Have students complete *Actividad* 4 in pairs. Have a few pairs present their conversations. 5 MIN.
- Quick Start Review (TE, p. 188) 5 MIN.
- Present *Repaso:* The Subjunctive for Expressing Wishes and *Vocabulario,* p. 188. 10 MIN.
- Present the *Nota* and have students complete *Actividad* 5 orally. 5 MIN.
- Play the audio; do *Actividad* 6. 10 MIN.
- Present the Speaking Strategy, p. 189, and have students complete *Actividad* 7 in pairs. 10 MIN.
- Quick Start Review (TE, p. 190) 5 MIN.
- Present *Gramática:* The Subjunctive with Conjunctions, p. 190. 10 MIN.
- Have students do *Actividad* 8 orally. 5 MIN.

Homework Option:
- Have students complete *Actividades* 5 and 8 in writing. *Más práctica* Workbook, pp. 69–70. *Cuaderno para hispanohablantes,* pp. 67–68.

DAY 3

En acción (cont.)
- Check homework. 5 MIN.
- Have students complete *Actividad* 9 in pairs. 5 MIN.
- Have students complete *Actividad* 10 in writing. Go over answers orally. Expand using Information Gap Activities, Unit 3 Resource Book, p. 29; *Más comunicación,* p. R9. 20 MIN.
- Use an expansion activity from TE pp. 190–191 for variety. 10 MIN.
- Quick Start Review (TE, p. 192) 5 MIN.
- Present *Gramática:* The Imperfect Subjunctive, p. 192. 10 MIN.
- Do *Actividad* 11 orally. 5 MIN.
- Play the audio; do *Actividad* 12. 5 MIN.
- Have students complete *Actividad* 13 in pairs. 5 MIN.
- Have students do *Actividad* 14 in groups. Expand using Information Gap Activities, Unit 3 Resource Book, p. 30; *Más comunicación,* p. R9. 20 MIN.

Homework Option:
- Have students complete *Actividades* 11 and 13 in writing. *Más práctica* Workbook, pp. 71–72. *Cuaderno para hispanohablantes,* pp. 69–70.
- *Actividades para todos* Workbook, pp. 71–76.

DAY 4

En acción (cont.)
- Check homework. 5 MIN.
- Present the *Vocabulario,* p. 195. Then have students read and complete *Actividad* 15 in writing. Go over answers orally. 15 MIN.

Refrán
- Present the *Refrán,* p. 195. 5 MIN.

En voces: Lectura
- Quick Start Review (TE, p. 196) 5 MIN.
- Present the Reading Strategy, p. 198. Call on volunteers to read the *Lectura* aloud. Have students answer the *¿Comprendiste?/¿Qué piensas?* questions, p. 197. 20 MIN.

En uso: Repaso y más comunicación
- Quick Start Review (TE, p. 198) 5 MIN.
- Do *Actividad* 1 in pairs and *Actividad* 2 in groups. 10 MIN.
- Have students do *Actividades* 3 and 4 orally. 10 MIN.
- Present the Speaking Strategy, p. 200. Do *Actividad* 5 in groups. 15 MIN.

Homework Option:
- Have students complete *Hazlo tú,* p. 197. Review for *Etapa* 1 Exam.

DAY 5

En tu propia voz: Escritura
- Check homework. 5 MIN.
- Have students do *Actividad* 6 in writing. Have volunteers present their captions to the class. 20 MIN.

Tú en la comunidad
- Present and discuss *Jordan,* p. 200. 5 MIN.

En resumen: Repaso de vocabulario
- Quick Start Review (TE, p. 201) 5 MIN.
- Review grammar questions, etc., as necessary. 15 MIN.
- Complete *Etapa* 1 Exam. 20 MIN.

Ampliación
- Use one or more suggested projects, games, or activities. (TE, pp. 179A–179B) 20 MIN.

Homework Option:
- Preview *Etapa* 2 Opener.

▼ ¡Por fin se va a graduar de la secundaria!

Etapa Theme
Describing personal celebrations; saying what people want; and linking events and ideas

Grammar Objectives
• Reviewing the use of the subjunctive for expressing wishes
• Using the subjunctive with conjunctions
• Using the imperfect subjunctive

Teaching Resource Options

Print

Block Scheduling Copymasters
Unit 3 Resource Book
  Family Letter, p. 33
  Absent Student Copymasters, p. 34

Audiovisual

OHT 2, 11 (Quick Start)
Canciones CD

Quick Start Review
♻ **Celebrations**
Use OHT 11 or write on the board:
¿Cómo piensas celebrar un cumpleaños o una ocasión especial? Escribe 3–5 oraciones.
Modelo: Voy a tener una fiesta grande.
Answers will vary.

Teaching Suggestion
Previewing the Etapa
• Ask students to study the picture on pp. 180–181 (1 min.).
• Close books; ask students to describe at least 3 things that they noticed.
• Reopen books and look at the picture again. Have students brainstorm a list of words to describe the picture (people, clothing, colors, furniture, table setting, foods). Give them the Supplementary Vocabulary list on TE p. 181.
• Ask students to look at the sign hanging on the wall. Is the party for a girl or a boy? How can they tell? **¿Es la fiesta para una niña o un niño? ¿Cómo lo saben?**
• Use the **¿Qué ves?** questions to focus the discussion.

UNIDAD 3

ETAPA **1**

¡Al fin la graduación!

OBJECTIVES
• Describe personal celebrations
• Say what people want
• Link events and ideas

¿Qué ves?
Mira la foto de la celebración. Contesta las preguntas.
1. ¿Qué se está celebrando?
2. ¿Quiénes son las personas en la foto?
3. ¿Dónde es la celebración?
4. Según el diploma, ¿en qué país sucede este evento?

180

Classroom Management

Planning Ahead In preparation for discussing personal celebrations, particularly graduations, bring in related items. For example: photographs, report cards, yearbooks, invitations, programs, diplomas, etc. If possible, bring in items from Spanish-speaking countries.

Student Self-checks Have students work in pairs. Within a 3-minute time limit, each partner lists as many words/expressions related to the photo as possible. Then partners combine lists. The pair with the most correct items on their list gets extra credit points.

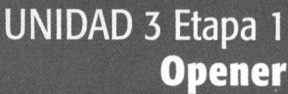
Cross Cultural Connections

Ask students to compare this celebration with one that has taken place in their home. How was the table set? What kind of clothes did people wear? What food was served?

Culture Highlights

● **GRADUACIÓN** Pregúnteles a los estudiantes cuándo se gradúan generalmente los estudiantes en Estados Unidos. En Latinoamérica, los estudiantes tienen casi siempre dos graduaciones: la graduación de escuela primaria *(primary school)* y la graduación de escuela secundaria *(high school)*.

Pídales a los estudiantes que piensen por qué se le da tanta importancia a la graduación de escuela secundaria. ¿Qué cosas representa ese evento? Escriba sus respuestas en el pizarrón. ¿Pueden ver algunas de esas ideas en la foto? ¿Cuáles?

Supplementary Vocabulary

la canasta de frutas	fruit basket
la colgadura	hanging sign
las cortinas	curtains
el jarrón	water pitcher
el mantel de encaje	lace tablecloth

Teaching Note

The term **el (la) graduando(a)** is a regional term used in Puerto Rico to refer to someone who is graduating. This is not typical of most Spanish-speaking countries. The term **el (la) graduado(a)** is more commonly used to refer to a recent graduate.

181

Teaching All Students

Extra Help Ask simple questions about the photo: ¿Cuántas personas hay? ¿Qué hay en la mesa? ¿Qué hay en la pared? ¿Cómo es la camisa del hombre a la derecha? ¿Qué crees que van a comer las personas?

Native Speakers Ask students to describe a graduation party they have been to. Make a list of important vocabulary words they use for the other students to add to a supplementary vocabulary list.

Multiple Intelligences

Verbal Have students work in small groups to write and perform a dialog among the people in the photo.

Intrapersonal Ask students to write whether or not this photo depicts how they envision their graduation party. How will their party be different?

Block Schedule

Expansion Have students write a story about the graduate for whom this party is being held. They should include the name of the graduate, the degree received, what the person will do after graduation, etc. (For additional activities, see **Block Scheduling Copymasters.**)

Teaching Resource Options

Print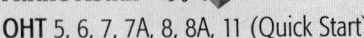
Block Scheduling Copymasters
Unit 3 Resource Book
  Absent Student Copymasters, p. 34

Audiovisual
OHT 5, 6, 7, 7A, 8, 8A, 11 (Quick Start)

Technology
Online Workbook, U3E1
Take-Home Tutor CD-ROM, U3E1

Quick Start Review

♻ School activities

Use OHT 11 or write on the board:
Escribe 5 oraciones que expliquen lo que debe hacer un estudiante para tener éxito y para graduarse de la escuela superior.
Modelo: Tiene que estudiar mucho.

Answers
Answers will vary. Answers could include:
Tiene que leer y escribir mucho.
Tiene que hacer la tarea todos los días.
Hay que escuchar al profesor.
Hay que sacar buenas notas.
Debe pensar en planes para su futuro.

Teaching Suggestions
Introducing Vocabulary

• Have students look at pp. 182–183. Use OHT 5 and 6 to present the vocabulary.
• Ask the Comprehension Questions on TE p. 183 in order of yes/no (questions 1–3), either/or (questions 4–6), and simple word or phrase (questions 7–10).
• Use the TPR activity to reinforce the meaning of individual words.

Descubre

Answers
1. e 2. c 3. a 4 g 5. d 6. b 7. h 8. f

En contexto VOCABULARIO

El día de mi graduación

Descubre

Adivina el significado de las palabras en **azul** según el contexto.

1. Estás en una ceremonia de graduación. Ahora entra el **desfile de graduandos.**
2. En su **discurso** el profesor les dice algunas palabras a los graduandos.
3. Les **desea mucho éxito** a todos los estudiantes.
4. Los padres del graduando están muy **orgullosos** de él.
5. El graduando ha **llevado a cabo** sus estudios.
6. Antes de comer hay un **brindis** por el graduando.
7. El graduando les da las gracias a sus padres y a sus **padrinos** por su ayuda.
8. Les dice «**se la agradezco** mucho».
   a. wishes them success
   b. toast
   c. speech
   d. accomplished
   e. procession of graduates
   f. is grateful to them
   g. proud
   h. godparents

Estamos entrando al auditorio en el desfile de graduandos. ¡Todos estamos muy emocionados! Es un día muy importante para nosotros. ¡Por fin vamos a graduarnos!

Entrada de los graduandos

El profesor Julio Capetillo León dio la bienvenida. Su discurso fue muy inspirador. Sus últimas palabras fueron: «Les deseo mucho éxito a todos los graduandos. Espero que disfruten de la vida y que su educación los lleve a lo mejor que la vida puede ofrecer.»

La ceremonia de graduación

¡Aquí estoy yo con mi diploma! Me veo muy sofisticada en mi toga y birrete. ¡Estoy lista para conquistar el mundo!

El diploma

Classroom Community

TPR Have students act out **En contexto** while you or a volunteer reads the text. Assign roles. Emphasize the vocabulary words as they are read.

Paired Activity Have students scramble the letters of 5 vocabulary items and give them to their partners to unscramble. Students must then write a sentence with the vocabulary. Finally, partners peer correct their sentences.

Take-Home Tutor

Aquí estoy con mis padrinos. Nos damos la enhorabuena. ¡Qué felices estamos, y qué orgullosos! ¡Por fin! En este momento podemos ver que vale la pena trabajar duro y seguir nuestros sueños.

¡Felicitaciones!

Luego todos fuimos a casa para celebrar. En esta foto brindamos por mi graduación y futuro. Yo pude apreciar el apoyo que me ha dado mi familia: «Mil gracias por su generosidad. Se la agradezco mucho. Verdaderamente han sido muy generosos. Por esto voy a poder llevar a cabo mis sueños.»

La celebración entre familia

Online Workbook
CLASSZONE.COM

¿Comprendiste?

1. ¿Alguien en tu familia se ha graduado de la secundaria? ¿Quién?
2. ¿Has ido a una ceremonia de graduación? ¿Dónde fue?
3. ¿Hubo discursos? ¿Qué pensaste de ellos?
4. ¿Hubo una celebración después? ¿Qué hicieron?
5. ¿Cómo se sintieron los padres del graduando?
6. ¿Esperas tu día de graduación con emoción? ¿Cómo crees que te vas a sentir ese día? Explica.

Centro de Estudios José Reyes

Ceremonia de graduación
4 de junio
Auditorio Duarte

ciento ochenta y tres
El Caribe Etapa 1
183

Comprehension Questions

1. ¿Están entrando los graduandos al auditorio? (Sí.)
2. ¿Entran en el desfile de graduandos? (Sí.)
3. ¿Entran los padres con los graduandos? (No.)
4. ¿El discurso del profesor fue aburrido o inspirador? (inspirador)
5. ¿El birrete se lleva en la cabeza o en la mano? (en la cabeza)
6. ¿La muchacha recibe un libro o un diploma? (un diploma)
7. ¿Cómo se sienten los graduandos? (orgullosos)
8. ¿Qué puede apreciar la muchacha? (el apoyo de su familia)
9. ¿Qué dice primero la muchacha a su familia? (mil gracias por su generosidad)
10. ¿Qué va a poder hacer la muchacha? (llevar a cabo sus sueños)

Block Schedule

Change of Pace Have pairs of students create and present a skit between a reporter and a high school graduate. The report asks questions about the student's high school years and about the graduation ceremony. If possible, videotape the skits for students to analyze. (For additional activities, see **Block Scheduling Copymasters**.)

Teaching All Students

Extra Help Point to each picture on pp. 182–183 and ask simple questions. For example: ¿Quién es la muchacha? ¿Qué da el profesor?

Native Speakers Ask students to interview a Spanish-speaking relative or friend about a graduation in their country of origin. Have students present a brief report to the class.

Multiple Intelligences

Visual Ask students to draw pictures as if they were photos of their graduation, then write captions for each.

Logical/Mathematical **Prepare ahead:** Write graduation day events in order on a sheet of paper. Make 5–8 copies. Then cut them into strips, with an event on each strip. Give sets of strips to small groups and have students put the events in order.

Teaching Resource Options

Print 📖

Block Scheduling Copymasters
Unit 3 Resource Book
  Absent Student Copymasters, p. 35
  Audioscript, p. 42

Audiovisual 🎧

OHT 9, 10, 12 (Quick Start)
Audio Program CD 7, Track 1

Technology 💻

Take-Home Tutor CD-ROM, U3E1

🔔 Quick Start Review

♻ Vocabulary review

Use OHT 12 or write on the board:
Write a sentence using each of the
following words:

1. desfile
2. graduando
3. toga
4. enhorabuena
5. generosidad
6. llevar a cabo

Answers
Answers will vary. Answers could include:
1. El desfile de graduandos está entrando.
2. Todos los graduandos están felices hoy.
3. A todos les gusta mucho llevar una toga.
4. Sus padres les dicen «Enhorabuena».
5. Beto va a decir muchas gracias a sus padres por su generosidad.
6. Todos los estudiantes han llevado a cabo su vida escolar.

Teaching Suggestions
Presenting Situations

• Present the Listening Strategy, p. 184, and have students make a list of the parts of a graduation ceremony.
• Use OHT 9 and 10 to present the **Mirar** section. Ask simple yes/no, either/or, or short-answer questions.
• Use Audio CD 7 and have students do the **Escuchar** section (see Script p. 179D). Then have students complete the Listening Strategy exercise.
• Have students work in groups to complete the **Hablar/Escribir** section.

AUDIO
En vivo
🎧 SITUACIONES

PARA ESCUCHAR

STRATEGY: LISTENING

Pre-listening Think ahead to your own graduation. What are the main parts of the ceremony? What events do you think family members might videotape?

Listen and recognize major transitions As Jorge narrates his sister's graduation, how does he indicate changes of activity and location? Write a title for each scene he describes.

La graduación de Rosanna

Jorge, el hermano de Rosanna, grabó *(taped)* la graduación de su hermana con una videocámara. Vas a ver unas imágenes del video. Luego escucha la narración de Jorge durante ese día especial.

① Mirar

Estudia las siguientes imágenes del video que hizo Jorge de la graduación de Rosanna.

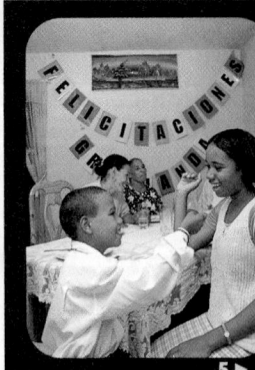

Classroom Community

Storytelling Divide the class into 5 groups. Assign each group 1 of the photos on p. 184. Groups must make up a complete story about their pictures, using their imagination to fill in details and conversations. Have groups present their stories to the class.

Cooperative Learning First, have students decide on a well-known Spanish-speaker to speak at their graduation. Then divide the class into 3 groups. Group 1 writes a letter asking the person to speak at the ceremony. Group 2 prepares the invitations for the ceremony. Group 3 designs a program. Have groups share their work with the class.

② Escuchar 🎧

Primero, estudia el programa de la ceremonia. Luego, escucha la narración de Jorge mientras describe lo que está grabando. Decide si las siguientes oraciones son ciertas o falsas. Si son falsas, corrígelas.

1. La ceremonia de graduación es en el gimnasio.

2. Hay mucha gente en el auditorio.

3. Los graduandos entran con sus padres.

4. Jorge graba a Rosanna mientras entra con sus padrinos.

5. Tocan el Himno Nacional después del primer discurso.

6. Jorge decide que no va a grabar el discurso del profesor Julio C. León.

7. Jorge no graba el momento cuando su hermana recibe el diploma.

8. Jorge está orgulloso de su hermana.

9. Rosanna no quiere hablar ante la cámara.

③ Hablar/Escribir 👥

¿Piensas mucho en el día de tu graduación? Con dos o tres compañeros, conversen sobre ese día futuro. Hagan planes detallados para todo el día, desde por la mañana hasta por la noche.

PROGRAMA

1.- Entrada de graduandos junto con sus padrinos.

2.- Himno Nacional.

3.- Bienvenida y presentación, a cargo del Prof. Julio C. León.

4.- Palabras a cargo del presidente Luis Rivas

5.- Acto de investidura:
 a) Entrega de Diplomas a los graduandos.
 b) Juramento de graduandos.
 c) Recibimiento de graduandos.

6.- Reconocimiento a la directiva y profesores.

7.- Palabras de gracias a cargo del relacionador Jhonson Morillo.

8.- Despedida de la Promoción (Comité Pro-Graduación)

9.- Acto sorpresa a cargo del Grupo los Magníficos.

10.- Himno Nacional

185

Escuchar (See script, p. 179D.)

Answers
1. Falso. La ceremonia de graduación es en el auditorio.
2. Cierto.
3. Falso. Los graduandos entran con sus padrinos.
4. Cierto.
5. Falso. Tocan el Himno Nacional antes del primer discurso.
6. Cierto.
7. Falso. Jorge sí graba el momento cuando su hermana recibe el diploma.
8. Cierto.
9. Falso. Rosanna le da las gracias a su familia ante la cámara.

Hablar/Escribir

Answers will vary.

🔔 Quick Wrap-up

Have students say which photo on p. 184 you are describing.
- Rosanna recibe su diploma. (4)
- Aquí viene el desfile de los graduandos. (1)
- Rosanna habla con su hermano. (5)
- El profesor León da su discurso. (2)
- Los padrinos de Rosanna le felicitan. (3)

Teaching All Students

Extra Help For the **Escuchar** section, play the audio in segments. Have students act out each segment and use their own words.

Multiple Intelligences

Kinesthetic Have students act out each scene from the pictures on p. 184, narrating and conversing as they act it out.

Block Schedule

FunBreak Play a variety of Spanish musical selections for the class and have them choose 1 piece to be their music for graduation from Spanish, Level 3. (For additional activities, see **Block Scheduling Copymasters**.)

Teaching Resource Options

Print
Block Scheduling Copymasters
Unit 3 Resource Book
  Absent Student Copymasters, p. 36

Audiovisual
OHT 12 (Quick Start)

Quick Start Review

♻ Vocabulary review

Use OHT 12 or write on the board:
Match the following definitions/
synonyms to a vocabulary word:

1. un sombrero
2. una charla
3. una celebración del fin de los estudios secundarios
4. caminar uno tras otro
5. una persona que da mucho es así
   a. birrete
   b. desfile
   c. generoso(a)
   d. discurso
   e. ceremonia de graduación

Answers
1. a   2. d   3. e   4. b   5. c

Teaching Suggestions
Comprehension Check

Use **Actividades 1–4** to assess retention after the **Vocabulario** and **Situaciones.** After completing **Actividad 1,** have students exchange papers with a partner for peer correction. Before doing **Actividad 3,** have students act out or define each word in the list.

Objective: Controlled practice
Vocabulary

Answers
1. graduación
2. me gradué
3. toga y birrete
4. se emocionaron
5. diploma
6. desfile
7. graduandos
8. discurso
9. éxito
10. orgulloso
11. Mil gracias
12. generosa
13. aprecio
14. generosidad
15. felicitar
16. llevado a cabo

En acción

Práctica del vocabulario

Objectives for Activities 1-4
Describe personal celebrations

1 ¡Qué emoción!

Escribir Rosanna le escribió esta carta a su prima Cristina en Nueva York para describir su ceremonia de graduación. Completa la carta con las siguientes palabras.

aprecio	toga	graduación
desfile	discurso	generosidad
me gradué	birrete	orgulloso
felicitar	diploma	llevado a cabo
graduandos	generosa	se emocionaron
mil gracias	éxito	

Querida Cristina,

¡Qué emoción! Ayer fue mi ceremonia de __1__. ¿Puedes creerlo? Por fin __2__ de la secundaria. Me hubieras visto en mi __3__. ¡Me veía muy intelectual! Mis padres __4__ mucho al verme recibir mi __5__.

Déjame describirte todo. Primero hicimos el __6__ de __7__. Entonces el profesor León dio un __8__ muy inspirador. Él nos deseó mucho __9__ en nuestras carreras y dijo que estaba muy __10__ de todos los graduandos.

¡__11__ por el regalo que me mandaste! Siempre has sido muy __12__: no sabes cuánto __13__ tu __14__. Por favor escríbeme y dime cómo fue tu graduación. Te quiero __15__ por haber __16__ tu educación secundaria.

Cuídate y muchos abrazos,

tu prima Rosanna

2 ¡Enhorabuena!

Hablar/*Escribir* Tu compañero(a) te lee una oración. Decide qué dibujo está describiendo.

f.
modelo
Tú: «¡Enhorabuena, hija! Te felicitamos».
Compañero(a): Es el dibujo f.

a.    b.    c.

d.    e.

1. «Mis padrinos brindaron porque me gradué segunda en mi clase.»
2. «Los graduandos llevan toga y birrete.»
3. «¡Los discursos me aburren! ¡Qué fatal!»
4. «Fuimos a la ceremonia de graduación de Rosanna. ¡Qué bonito estuvo todo!»
5. «¡Mira! Puse mi diploma en la pared para que lo vieran todos.»

186 ciento ochenta y seis
Unidad 3

Classroom Management

Streamlining Do **Actividades 3** and **4** with the whole class. Ask a few volunteers to write exceptional responses on the board.

Peer Review Ask students to brainstorm words related to school and graduation. Write a master list on an OHT for students to copy. Students should refer to the list when doing activities throughout the **Etapa.**

③ Mi graduación

Hablar/Escribir Imagina que te vas a graduar de la secundaria. Usa las siguientes palabras para dramatizar esta situación con tu compañero(a). Luego, cambien de papel.

modelo

Tú: *Hoy es la ceremonia de mi graduación.*

Compañero(a): *¡Te felicito!*

Tú: *Mil gracias, te lo agradezco.*

graduando
toga y birrete
diploma
generosidad
desfile
felicitar
brindar
graduarse
desfilar
apreciar
enhorabuena
emocionarse
llevar a cabo
mil gracias
ceremonia de graduación
Te lo agradezco.
Te deseo mucho éxito.
¿...?

④ Un día importante

Hablar/Escribir Conversa con un(a) compañero(a) sobre lo que ocurre en cada dibujo. Describan cada escena con todo el detalle que puedan.

modelo

Tú: *Es una ceremonia de graduación.*

Compañero(a): *Sí. Los graduandos llevan togas y birretes.*

Tú: *Están entrando en el desfile de graduandos…*

1.

2.

3.

4.

Objective: Transitional practice
Vocabulary in conversation

Answers
1. e   2. c   3. b   4. a   5. d

Objective: Open-ended practice
Vocabulary in conversation

Answers will vary.

Objective: Open-ended practice
Vocabulary in conversation

Answers will vary.

Quick Wrap-up

Call on students at random to quickly supply 1 sentence that describes graduation from high school:
Dime una oración que describa la graduación de la secundaria.

Teaching All Students

Extra Help Have students write a caption for each drawing on pp. 186 and 187. Then have them exchange papers with a partner for peer correction.

Challenge Have students write Cristina's response to Rosanna's letter in **Actividad 1**.

Multiple Intelligences

Verbal Ask students to describe how their graduation from high school will be different from their graduation from elementary school (if they had one).

Musical/Rhythmic Have students work in pairs to write a graduation song. They may want to put the words to a well-known tune.

Block Schedule

Variety Have students mind map an "ideal" graduation ceremony versus a "traditional" ceremony at your school. Discuss the various "ideal" ceremonies as a class and have students vote on the idea that most students prefer. (For additional activities, see **Block Scheduling Copymasters**.)

Teaching Resource Options

Print

Más práctica Workbook PE, p. 69
Cuaderno para hispanohablantes
 PE, p. 67
Block Scheduling Copymasters
Unit 3 Resource Book
 Más práctica Workbook TE, p. 7
 Cuaderno para hispanohablantes
  TE, p. 23
 Absent Student Copymasters, p. 36
 Audioscript, p. 42

Audiovisual

OHT 13 (Quick Start), 15 (Grammar)
Audio Program CD 7, Track 2, Activity 6

Technology

Online Workbook, U3E1
Take-Home Tutor CD-ROM, U3E1

Quick Start Review

🔄 Graduation vocabulary review

Use OHT 13 or write on the board:
**Ofrece un brindis a un(a)
graduando(a) y dile cómo te sientes.
Escribe 4 cosas que puedes decirle.**

Answers
Answers will vary. Answers could include:
¡Enhorabuena!
¡Felicitaciones!
Estoy muy orgulloso(a) de ti.
Te deseo mucho éxito.

Teaching Suggestions
Reviewing The Subjunctive for Expressing Wishes

• Review the formation of the present
 subjunctive (pp. 138, 140, 141) and
 expressions that take the subjunctive
 (pp. 139, 160, 162, 164).
• Present the **Vocabulario.** Students
 must write one sentence with a
 change of subject (subjunctive) and
 one sentence without a change of
 subject (infinitive).

PARTE B Práctica del vocabulario

Objectives for Activities 5–14
• Say what people want • Link events and ideas

REPASO   The Subjunctive for Expressing Wishes

▶ Remember that you learned to use the **subjunctive** with **impersonal expressions**
such as **es importante que** and **es necesario que.**

You know how to use the subjunctive after verbs like **querer que** and **preferir que**
to indicate that one person wants someone else to do something.

> **Rosanna quiere que** sus padrinos la **acompañen.**
> *Rosanna **wants** her godparents to **accompany** her.*

▶ You also use the **subjunctive** after other verbs, like the
ones below, that express wishes.

> **Rosanna espera que** no **llueva.**
> *Rosanna **hopes** it **doesn't rain.***

▶ You only use the **subjunctive** with these **verbs**
when there is a change of subject.

Compare the following sentences.

> **Yo quiero que tú asistas** a
> la ceremonia.
> *I want **you** to attend the ceremony.*

> **Yo quiero asistir** a la ceremonia.
> *I want to attend the ceremony.*

> When there is
> no change of subject, you
> use the **infinitive** instead
> of the subjunctive.

Vocabulario

Otros verbos	♻ Ya sabes
dejar *to allow*	aconsejar
exigir *to demand*	desear
insistir en *to insist*	esperar
oponerse a *to oppose*	mandar
prohibir *to prohibit*	pedir (e→i)
rogar (o→ue) *to beg*	permitir
suplicar *to ask, plead*	querer (e→ie)
	recomendar (e→ie)
	sugerir (e→ie)

Practice: Actividades **5 6 7**
Más práctica *cuaderno p. 69*
Para hispanohablantes *cuaderno p. 67*

 Online Workbook
CLASSZONE.COM

También se dice

El (la) **graduando(a)** es el (la) estudiante que está en la ceremonia de
graduación y se está graduando. Se dice **graduado(a)** a la persona que ya
se graduó y tiene su diploma de bachiller.

188 ciento ochenta y ocho
Unidad 3

Classroom Community

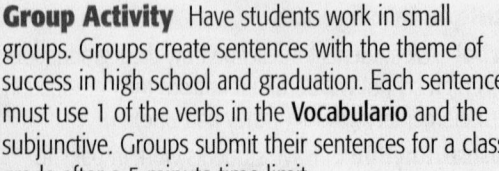

Group Activity Have students work in small
groups. Groups create sentences with the theme of
success in high school and graduation. Each sentence
must use 1 of the verbs in the **Vocabulario** and the
subjunctive. Groups submit their sentences for a class
grade after a 5-minute time limit.

Learning Scenario Have students work in pairs and
do a variation of **Actividad 7.** This time they may
choose their own theme, but must use the expressions
provided. Themes might be after-school plans,
weekend plans, planning a party, planning a vacation,
etc.

5 Pedro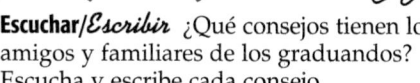

Hablar/Escribir Hoy es el día de graduación de Pedro. Su madre le dice que quiere que haga ciertas cosas. ¿Qué le dice?

modelo

querer que / estar listo a las cinco

Quiero que estés listo a las cinco.

> **Nota: Gramática**
>
> Verbs that end in **-ger** and **-gir** change **g** to **j** in the subjunctive: **exija, exijas,** etc.

1. insistir en que / cortarse el pelo
2. recomendar que / comprar zapatos nuevos
3. sugerir que / recoger tu cuarto
4. esperar que / sentirse orgulloso
5. rogar que / no ponerse esa camisa
6. pedir que / llegar a tiempo

6 Consejos a los graduandos

Escuchar/Escribir ¿Qué consejos tienen los amigos y familiares de los graduandos? Escucha y escribe cada consejo.

modelo

Armando y Nydia   Les sugiero que vayan a la universidad.

1. Ana Luisa
2. Juan y María
3. Arturo
4. Martín y Laura
5. Eduardo
6. Joaquín
7. Lisa y Dina
8. Rogelio

7 Por favor

> **STRATEGY: SPEAKING**
>
> **Accept or Reject Advice** Here are ways to respond to well-meant advice or requests:
>
> **a.** Accept and seek more information or show a positive reaction: **¿Cuándo? Me alegro de que…**
>
> **b.** Indicate uncertainty or a condition: **Dudo que… Puedo salir en cuanto…**
>
> **c.** Reject and give reasons: **No puedo… Es imposible que… No es lógico que…**

Hablar/Escribir Es la última semana antes de la graduación y quieres que tu compañero(a) haga ciertas cosas contigo. ¿Qué le dices y cómo te responde? Usa los verbos de la lista. Luego, cambien de papel.

modelo

querer que

Tú: *Quiero que estudies conmigo para los exámenes finales.*

Compañero(a): *Está bien. ¿Qué vamos a estudiar?*

> desear que
> sugerir que
> suplicar que
> aconsejar
> insistir en que
> mandar que
> rogar que
> recomendar que
> prohibir que
> pedir que

Language Note

You may wish to remind students that many of the verbs for expressing wishes, such as **rogar, pedir, aconsejar,** and **suplicar,** require the use of indirect object pronouns (**me, te, le, nos, os, les**) because they are asking someone to do something: **Te ruego que, Les aconsejo que,** etc.

ACTIVIDAD 5 **Objective:** Controlled practice
Subjunctive for expressing wishes

Answers

1. Insisto en que te cortes el pelo.
2. Recomiendo que compres zapatos nuevos.
3. Sugiero que recojas tu cuarto.
4. Espero que te sientas orgulloso.
5. Te ruego que no te pongas esa camisa.
6. Te pido que llegues a tiempo.

ACTIVIDAD 6 **Objective:** Transitional practice
Listening comprehension/subjunctive for expressing wishes

Answers (See script, p. 179D.)

1. Le aconsejo que estudie ingeniería.
2. Les aconsejo que trabajen durante los veranos.
3. Recomiendo que no gaste mucho dinero.
4. Les sugiero que no compren un coche.
5. Recomiendo que no salga mucho.
6. Le sugiero que estudie todos los días.
7. Les aconsejo que hagan la tarea a tiempo.
8. Recomiendo que duerma lo suficiente.

ACTIVIDAD 7 **Objective:** Open-ended practice
Subjunctive for expressing wishes in conversation

Answers will vary.

Block Schedule

Challenge Using the **Vocabulario** on p. 188, 1 student forms a sentence to begin a story. The next student repeats the first sentence and adds another one. The next student repeats the second sentence and adds a third one. Continue around the room until the story is complete. Assign 1 student to be a recorder and write the sentences as they are added. Present the entire story. (For additional activities, see **Block Scheduling Copymasters.**)

Teaching All Students

Extra Help Prepare a worksheet that scrambles the answers to **Actividad 5** (see Answers on TE p. 189). Have students rewrite the sentences appropriately.

Multiple Intelligences

Kinesthetic **Prepare ahead:** Write out 5 wish prompts (**quiero que,** etc.), 5 subjunctive verbs, and 5 indicative verbs, each on its own index card. Make 5 or 6 sets of cards. Distribute sets to groups. Have students match prompts and verbs, then write complete sentences.

Teaching Resource Options

Print

Más práctica Workbook PE, p. 70
Cuaderno para hispanohablantes
 PE, p. 68
Block Scheduling Copymasters
Unit 3 Resource Book
 Más práctica Workbook TE, p. 8
 Cuaderno para hispanohablantes
  TE, p. 24
 Information Gap Activities, p. 29
 Absent Student Copymasters, p. 37

Audiovisual

OHT 13 (Quick Start), 16 (Grammar)

Technology

Online Workbook, U3E1
Take-Home Tutor CD-ROM, U3E1

Quick Start Review

♻ Subjunctive review

Use OHT 13 or write on the board:
Complete the sentences with the
appropriate form of the verb:

1. En cuanto nosotros ___ , ellos se
   van. (llegar)
2. Estarán aquí hasta que ___ de
   llover. (parar)
3. Tan pronto como ___ la
   graduación, nos vamos.
   (terminarse)
4. Quizás tú ___ a los graduandos.
   (ver)
5. Ojalá que la ceremonia no ___
   muy larga. (ser)

Answers
1. lleguemos   2. pare   3. se termine
4. veas   5. sea

REPASO   The Subjunctive with Conjunctions

 ¿RECUERDAS? *p. 162* Remember that you use the subjunctive with **cuando** and **conjunctions of time** in order to express that you are not sure when or if something will happen.

The following **conjunctions** also express degrees of doubt or certainty about events.

Iremos a la fiesta **a menos que** no nos **inviten.**
*We will go to the party **unless** they **don't invite us.***

Vendrán a la fiesta **con tal de que** bailen.
*They will come to the party **as long as** they **can dance**.*

Trae el mapa **en caso de que** nos perdamos.
*Bring the map in case **we get lost**.*

Acérquense todos **para que** brindemos.
*Come close **so that** we **can make a toast**.*

> **Vocabulario**
>
> **Conjunciones**
>
> a menos que *unless*
> con tal (de) que *provided that,*
> *as long as*
> en caso de que *in case*
> para que *so that*
>
> ♻ **Ya sabes:** antes (de) que

The adverbial expression **antes de que** requires the subjunctive. However, the expression **antes de** requires the infinitive. Compare these sentences.

Yo necesito felicitar al graduando **antes de que** él **salga.**
*I need to congratulate the graduate before **he** leaves.*

Yo necesito felicitar al graduando **antes de salir.**
*I need to congratulate the graduate before **I** leave.*

> One exception is
> **a menos que** which
> always requires the
> subjunctive.

Practice: **Actividades** 8 9 10   **Más práctica** *cuaderno p. 70*
Para hispanohablantes *cuaderno p. 68*

 **Online Workbook**
CLASSZONE.COM

Nota cultural

En la República Dominicana, como en muchos países de Latinoamérica, existe la tradición de que grupos de amigos hagan juntos un viaje de graduación después de la ceremonia formal de la graduación. Por lo regular, si viven en pueblos del interior o de la costa, van a las ciudades principales como Santo Domingo, Santiago o Puerto Plata. Si son de las ciudades, van a la costa o al campo. Para conseguir dinero para el viaje, hacen rifas *(raffles)* y fiestas durante el año escolar.

Classroom Community

Group Activity Divide the class into groups. Each group makes a set of cards with the 5 conjunctions. They make another set with subject nouns and pronouns. Students then combine the 2 sets of cards and write as many sentences as they can based on different card combinations, within a time limit. Then groups exchange papers and correct them.

Learning Scenario Have students work in pairs and imagine that they are on their way to a graduation ceremony, but the car breaks down. Have them discuss the problem and figure out how they are going to get to the graduation on time. They must use the conjunctions in their conversation. Have pairs present their skits to the class.

8 Para que...

Hablar/Escribir Todos van a hacer algo para que otros puedan hacer otra cosa. ¿Qué van a hacer?

modelo

Tú vas a llamar a tus amigos. (ellos venir a tu casa)

Tú vas a llamar a tus amigos para que ellos vengan a tu casa.

1. Yo voy a comprar los boletos. (ustedes ir al concierto)
2. Ricardo va a preparar una paella. (nosotros probarla)
3. Mis hermanos van a salir a jugar. (yo poder estudiar)
4. Nosotros lavaremos el coche. (papá sentirse orgulloso)
5. Pepe va a escribir a sus padres. (ellos saber que está bien)
6. María va a hablar con el profesor. (él explicarle la tarea)

9 ¿Cuándo?

Hablar/Escribir Pregúntale a tu compañero(a) cuándo va a hacer ciertas cosas. Él o ella responde usando **antes de que** o **después de que** con el subjuntivo. Luego, cambien de papel.

modelo

Tú: *¿Cuándo vas a hacer la tarea?*

Compañero(a): *Voy a hacer la tarea antes de que salgamos.*

limpiar	llamar
estudiar	felicitar
cenar	agradecer
comprar	¿...?
salir	

10 Mis opiniones

Escribir Piensa en una celebración personal reciente. ¿Qué opiniones tienes sobre el evento? Escribe cuatro oraciones usando las siguientes frases.

modelo

Me encantan las fiestas de cumpleaños con tal de que pueda comer pastel.

a menos que

con tal de que

en caso de que

para que

More Practice: Más comunicación *p. R9*

ciento noventa y uno
El Caribe Etapa I

191

Teaching All Students

Extra Help Have students work in pairs and write a sentence for each conjunction using the subjunctive. Write several on an OHT for the class to evaluate.

Challenge Have pairs of students exchange papers for **Actividad 10.** Call on various students to restate their partner's responses: **(Julia) dice que...**

Multiple Intelligences

Interpersonal Have pairs of students tell each other 3 things they will do so that their dreams come true. Then have them say what they will do after their dreams come true.

Teaching Suggestions
Teaching The Subjunctive with Conjunctions

• Point out that these conjunctions imply that the actions have not occurred and may not occur.

• You may want to present a mnemonic device for students to remember the expressions: A PACE (**a** menos que, **p**ara que, **a**ntes [de] que, **c**on tal [de] que, **e**n caso de que)

ACTIVIDAD 8 Objective: Controlled practice Subjunctive with conjunctions

Answers

1. Yo voy a comprar los boletos para que ustedes vayan al concierto.
2. Ricardo va a preparar una paella para que nosotros la probemos.
3. Mis hermanos van a salir a jugar para que yo pueda estudiar.
4. Nosotros lavaremos el coche para que papá se sienta orgulloso.
5. Pepe le va a escribir a sus padres para que ellos sepan que está bien.
6. María va a hablar con el profesor para que él le explique la tarea.

ACTIVIDAD 9 Objective: Transitional practice Subjunctive with conjunctions in conversation

Answers will vary.

ACTIVIDAD 10 Objective: Open-ended practice Subjunctive with conjunctions in writing

Answers will vary.

Block Schedule

Change of Pace Have students prepare a speech about their plans after graduation day. They must include each of the conjunctions in the **Vocabulario** on p. 190. Then have them give their speeches to the class. (For additional activities, see **Block Scheduling Copymasters.**)

Teaching Resource Options

Print

Más práctica Workbook PE, pp. 71–72
Cuaderno para hispanohablantes
  PE, pp. 69–70
Block Scheduling Copymasters
Unit 3 Resource Book
  Más práctica Workbook TE,
    pp. 9–10
  Cuaderno para hispanohablantes
    TE, pp. 25–26
  Absent Student Copymasters, p. 38
  Audioscript, p. 42

Audiovisual

OHT 13 (Quick Start), 17 (Grammar)
Audio Program CD 7, Track 3, Activity 12
Word Tiles, U3E1

Technology

Online Workbook, U3E1
Take-Home Tutor CD-ROM, U3E1

Quick Start Review

🔄 **Preterite review**

Use OHT 13 or write on the board:
Give the **ellos/ellas/Uds.** form of the
preterite of the following verbs:

1. decir   7. poner
2. estar   8. querer
3. haber   9. saber
4. hacer   10. ser
5. ir   11. tener
6. poder   12. venir

Answers
1. dijeron   7. pusieron
2. estuvieron   8. quisieron
3. hubieron   9. supieron
4. hicieron   10. fueron
5. fueron   11. tuvieron
6. pudieron   12. vinieron

GRAMÁTICA The Imperfect Subjunctive

▶ You already know the present and present perfect **subjunctive**. There are also past forms of the subjunctive. Use the **imperfect subjunctive** instead of the present subjunctive when the context of the sentence is in the **past**.

Compare the following pairs of sentences.

Present context

Los padrinos quieren **que** felicitemos al graduando.
*The godparents **want** us to **congratulate** the graduate.*

La madre de la graduanda sugiere **que** hagamos un brindis.
*The mother of the graduate **suggests** we **make** a toast.*

Past context

Los padrinos querían **que** felicitáramos al graduando.
*The godparents **wanted** us to **congratulate** the graduate.*

La madre de la graduanda sugirió **que** hiciéramos un brindis.
*The mother of the graduate **suggested** we **make** a toast.*

▶ You form the **imperfect subjunctive** by removing the **-ron** ending of the **ellos/ellas/Uds.** form of the **preterite** and adding a special set of endings. The endings are the same for **-ar, -er,** and **-ir** verbs.

hablar ⟶ habla**ron** ◀— endings

habla**ra**   hablá**ramos**
habla**ras**   habla**rais**
habla**ra**   habla**ran**

*Notice the accent in the **nosotros** form.*

Los padres de la graduanda querían **que** nosotros comié**ramos** con ellos.
*The graduate's parents **wanted** us **to eat** with them.*

Los padrinos querían mucho **que** Rosanna recibie**ra** su diploma.
*The godparents really **wanted** Rosanna **to receive** her diploma.*

▶ If a verb is **irregular** in the **ellos/ellas/Uds.** form of the preterite, like the verb **ir (fueron)**, it will also be **irregular** in the **imperfect subjunctive** (**fue**ra).

Practice: **Actividades** 11 12 13 14
Más práctica *cuaderno pp. 71–72*
Para hispanohablantes *cuaderno pp. 69–70*

Online Workbook
CLASSZONE.COM

---

192 ciento noventa y dos
Unidad 3

Classroom Community

Paired Activity Have students work in pairs to create invitations for a senior prom and for a graduation party. Display the invitations on the bulletin board.

Portfolio Have students write a paragraph describing Cinderella's life before the ball. They should write what Cinderella's stepmother wanted and did not want her to do, using the imperfect subjunctive.

Rubric A = 13–15 pts. B = 10–12 pts. C = 7–9 pts. D = 4–6 pts. F = < 4 pts.

Writing criteria	Scale
Correct use of imperfect subjunctive	1 2 3 4 5
Spelling accuracy	1 2 3 4 5
Creativity	1 2 3 4 5

⑪ Los padres

Hablar/*Escribir* Los padres siempre quieren que los hijos sean perfectos. ¿Qué querían los padres de Alma que hicieran ella y sus hermanos?

modelo

estudiar mucho

Querían que estudiaran mucho.

1. sacar buenas notas en todas las clases
2. no salir mucho
3. llegar temprano
4. limpiar sus cuartos
5. poner su educación ante todo
6. entender la importancia de una buena educación
7. darles las gracias a sus abuelos por su apoyo
8. ser estudiantes modelos
9. comer con toda la familia
10. hablar de su futuro

⑫ ¿En qué insistían?

Escuchar/*Escribir* Estos estudiantes acaban de llegar a la universidad. Están en una reunión y leen apuntes sobre su niñez. ¿En qué insistían sus padres? Completa las oraciones según lo que dicen.

modelo

Mi papá insistía en que yo <u>fuera a la universidad</u> .

1. Mi mamá insistía en que mis hermanos y yo _____.
2. Mi papá insistía en que yo _____.
3. Mi mamá insistía en que mis hermanos y yo _____.
4. Mis padres insistían en que mis hermanos y yo _____.
5. Mi papá insistía en que yo _____.
6. Mi mamá insistía en que mis hermanos _____.
7. Mis padres insistían en que mis hermanos y yo _____.
8. Mis padres insistían en que mis hermanos _____.
9. Mi papá insistía en que yo _____.

Nota cultural

Fiesta de graduación En la República Dominicana, no se celebra la graduación con un baile como el «prom». Generalmente los padres y los padrinos dan una fiesta para el (la) graduando(a). A veces dan una fiesta para un grupo de graduandos que son amigos en la casa de su(s) familias o en un restaurante u hotel.

UNA INVITACIÓN ESPECIAL
Querido ___Pedro___
Te invito a ti y a tu familia a que vengan a la
FIESTA DE GRADUACIÓN.
DÓNDE: Salón principal,
Hotel Mar Azul, Santo Domingo
CUÁNDO: domingo 13 de mayo
12:00 p.m. a 7:00 p.m.
Habrá baile y comida.
¡Te espero allí!
Un abrazo y felicidades.
Tu amiga, Estefanía

Teaching Suggestions
Teaching The Imperfect Subjunctive

- Using the list of irregular verbs in the Quick Start Review, have students create sentences in the imperfect subjunctive.
- A complete list of irregular verbs is available in the verb charts at the back of the book.

⑪ **Objective:** Controlled practice Imperfect subjunctive

Answers
1. Querían que sacaran buenas notas en todas las clases.
2. Querían que no salieran mucho.
3. Querían que llegaran temprano.
4. Querían que limpiaran sus cuartos.
5. Querían que pusieran nuestra educación ante todo.
6. Querían que entendieran la importancia de una buena educación.
7. Querían que les dieran las gracias a sus abuelos por su apoyo.
8. Querían que fueran estudiantes modelos.
9. Querían que comiera con toda la familia.
10. Querían que hablara de su futuro.

⑫ **Objective:** Transitional practice Listening comprehension/imperfect subjunctive

Answers (See script, p. 179D.)
1. ...continuáramos nuestra educación.
2. ...estudiara todos los días.
3. ...nos vistiéramos apropiadamente.
4. ...trabajáramos en los veranos.
5. ...guardara mi dinero.
6. ...hicieran la tarea antes de la cena.
7. ...respetáramos a nuestros profesores.
8. ...se acostaran temprano.
9. ...no saliera durante la semana.

Block Schedule

Variety Ask students to imagine that their graduation is now over. Have them reflect on what they wanted to happen that didn't happen at the graduation ceremony or even in their last year of school. They should write 5 sentences. For example: **Quería que el profesor León hablara menos.** (For additional activities, see **Block Scheduling Copymasters**.)

Teaching All Students

Extra Help Have students work in pairs. Give them the following list of verbs: **cantar, entender, asistir, servir, traducir, repetir, dar, creer.** One student conjugates the verb in the third-person plural of the preterite and the other gives the first person singular of the imperfect subjunctive.

Multiple Intelligences

Intrapersonal Ask students to mind map the wishes and desires of Alma's parents in **Actividad 11** with those of their own parents.

Teaching Resource Options

Print

Más práctica Workbook PE, pp. 65–68
Actividades para todos Workbook
PE, pp. 71–76
Cuaderno para hispanohablantes
PE, pp. 65–66
Block Scheduling Copymasters
Unit 3 Resource Book
Más práctica Workbook TE, pp. 3–6
Actividades para todos Workbook
TE, pp. 11–16
Cuaderno para hispanohablantes
TE, pp. 21–22
Information Gap Activities, p. 30
Absent Student Copymasters, p. 38

Technology

Online Workbook, U3E1
Take-Home Tutor CD-ROM, U3E1

Objective: Transitional practice
Imperfect subjunctive

♻ **Expressions of doubt and
uncertainty**

*Answers will vary, but should include these verb
forms.*

1. A: Me dijo que conoció...
   B: No es cierto que conociera...
2. A: Me dijo que ganó...
   B: No es cierto que ganara...
3. A: Me dijo que fue...
   B: No es cierto que fuera...
4. A: Me dijo que leyó...
   B: No es cierto que leyera...
5. A: Me dijo que escribió...
   B: No es cierto que escribiera...
6. A: Me dijo que actuó...
   B: No es cierto que actuara...
7. A: Me dijo que aprendió...
   B: No es cierto que aprendiera...
8. A: Me dijo que llegó...
   B: No es cierto que llegara...
9. A: Me dijo que hizo...
   B: No es cierto que hiciera...
10. A: Me dijo que asistió...
    B: No es cierto que asistiera...

Objective: Open-ended practice
Imperfect subjunctive in conversation

♻ **Recreation vocabulary**

Answers will vary.

Práctica: gramática y vocabulario continuación

13 Los chismes 🔄 👥

Hablar/*Escribir* Hablas con un(a) amigo(a) y
le cuentas los chismes que otro(a) amigo(a) te
contó la semana pasada. Tu compañero(a)
sabe lo que ocurrió en realidad y te dice la
verdad sobre la situación. Sigue el modelo y
usa las siguientes expresiones.

> **modelo**
>
> comprar un coche nuevo
>
> **Tú:** *Me dijo que se compró un coche nuevo.*
>
> **Compañero(a):** *¡No es cierto que se comprara un
> coche nuevo!*

No es cierto	Dudo que
No creo que	No es verdad que
No es seguro que	

1. conocer a Michael Jordan
2. ganar la lotería
3. ir de viaje a Nepal
4. leer cien libros en una semana
5. escribir una composición de quinientas
   páginas
6. actuar en un programa de televisión
7. aprender a hacer alpinismo en una hora
8. llegar a casa a las siete todos los sábados
9. hacer un brindis con Eva
10. asistir a tu graduación

14 Permiso 🔄 👥

Hablar/*Escribir* Necesitamos el permiso de
nuestros padres para participar en varias
actividades. En grupos de tres o cuatro,
conversen sobre sus planes para la semana
después de la graduación. Digan qué piensan
sus padres.

> **modelo**
>
> **Tú:** ¿Van a poder salir esta noche?
>
> **Amigo(a) 1:** *Mi papá se opuso a que
> yo saliera esta noche.*
>
> **Amigo(a) 2:** *Mi mamá me pidió que
> yo volviera temprano.*
>
> **Amigo(a) 3:** *Mi papá recomendó que
> mejor saliéramos el viernes.*

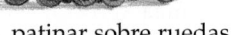

1. patinar sobre ruedas   **2.** remar

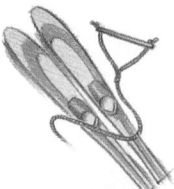

3. esquiar en el agua   **4.** ir al teatro

5. acampar   **6.** hacer alpinismo

194

ciento noventa y cuatro
Unidad 3

Classroom Community

Paired Activity Have students work in pairs and
choose an opener photo from a previous **Etapa.** They
should write at least 5 sentences in the imperfect
subjunctive that describe what was happening in the
photo. For example, pp. 128–129: **La muchacha quería
que los otros esucharan los pájaros.**

Portfolio Have students record the **Refrán.**
Record other pronunciation activities during the year
for students to evaluate improvement in their
pronunciation.

Activity 15 brings together all concepts presented.

 15 Camino al éxito

Leer/*Escribir* Lee la introducción en el programa de la graduación de Rosanna Lisette Cruz de la Rosa. Luego contesta las preguntas.

1. ¿Quién crees que camina hacia el futuro?
2. ¿Importa su posición social o económica?
3. Al avanzar, ¿de qué están seguros los graduandos?
4. ¿Cuáles necesidades vencen siempre?
5. ¿Qué sienten al avanzar?
6. ¿Cuál es la gran satisfacción que obtienen?
7. ¿Cómo siguen adelante?
8. ¿Hacia qué siguen avanzando?
9. ¿Crees que la introducción inspira a los graduandos? ¿Por qué?

Vocabulario

El futuro

avanzar *to advance*   el orgullo *pride*
el camino *path*   el tropiezo *setback*
imponer *to impose*   vencer *to defeat, triumph*

 Ya sabes: la meta

¿Relacionas estas palabras con tu futuro?

More Practice: Más comunicación *p. R9*

 Online Workbook
CLASSZONE.COM

INVITACIÓN Y PROGRAMA
ACTO DE INVESTIDURA
PROMOCIÓN
"EXITUS 00"
"CAMINO AL ÉXITO"

INTRODUCCIÓN

Cuando caminamos hacia el futuro, sin importar nuestra posición social o económica, avanzamos con la seguridad de llegar a nuestras metas, sin importar los tropiezos y obstáculos que encontremos en el camino.
Venciendo siempre las necesidades que nos impone la sociedad y la vida misma, como pago a nuestro esfuerzo y al de nuestros padres; por eso siempre seguiremos adelante sin importar las barreras de la vida, ni los derrumbes de vicios que obstaculizan nuestro camino, avanzando con orgullo y con la frente en alto, para obtener la gran satisfacción que sentimos al llegar a la meta deseada y seguir adelante con respeto, disciplina, trabajo y esfuerzo, para seguir avanzando...camino al éxito.

J. H. M. A.

 **Refrán**

La prosperidad hace amigos, pero la adversidad los prueba.

¿Qué quiere decir el refrán? ¿Crees que si alguien no está a tu lado durante los tiempos difíciles es verdaderamente un(a) amigo(a)? ¿Por qué? ¿Cuáles son algunas características de un(a) buen(a) amigo(a)?

Have students personalize the vocabulary by asking them questions, such as: What makes you proud? How do you overcome a setback?

Objective: Open-ended practice Vocabulary in reading and writing

Answers
1. Los graduandos caminan hacia el futuro.
2. No importa su posición social o económica.
3. Los graduandos avanzan con la seguridad de llegar a sus metas.
4. Los graduandos siempre vencen las necesidades que impone la sociedad y la vida misma.
5. Avanzan con orgullo.
6. Obtienen la gran satisfacción de llegar a la meta deseada.
7. Siguen adelante con respeto, disciplina, trabajo y esfuerzo.
8. Siguen avanzando camino al éxito.
9. *Answers will vary.*

Critical Thinking

Ask students to name a time in their lives when they had to choose between 2 paths (which subjects to choose in school, what to do during the summer). Which path did they take? When faced with 2 options, do they tend to choose the usual option or the unusual?

Block Schedule

FunBreak Have students work in groups to complete the fortune teller scene as outlined in the **Ampliación** on TE p. 179A. (For additional activities, see **Block Scheduling Copymasters**.)

Teaching All Students

Extra Help Have groups expand **Actividad** 14 by adding 3 more activities to discuss.

Native Speakers Ask students to write a composition about a birthday celebration that took place in their family. They should use at least 3 sentences in the imperfect subjunctive.

Multiple Intelligences

Visual Have students create drawings/cartoons to illustrate **el orgullo, el tropiezo,** or **vencer.**

Naturalist Have students imagine that they took a trip to a natural reserve in a Spanish-speaking country. Have them write a short paragraph about what they saw and did there, using the imperfect subjunctive. They may want to refer back to **Unidad 2, Etapa 3** for ideas.

Teaching Resource Options

Print

Actividades para todos Workbook
  PE, pp. 77–79
Block Scheduling Copymasters
Unit 3 Resource Book
  Actividades para todos Workbook
  TE, pp. 17–19
  Absent Student Copymasters, p. 39
  Audioscript, p. 43

Audiovisual

OHT 14 (Quick Start)
Audio Program CD 7, Tracks 4–5
Canciones CD

Technology

Online Workbook, U3E1
Take-Home Tutor CD-ROM, U3E1

Quick Start Review

 Cuba

Use OHT 14 or write on the board:
Escribe por lo menos 5 hechos o cosas informativas sobre Cuba.

Answers
Answers will vary. Answers could include:
Cuba es una isla.
Su capital es La Habana.
Se situa al sur de Florida en el Mar Caribe.
Se habla español en Cuba.
Se toca música afrocubana.

Teaching Suggestions

- **Prereading** Have students study the illustration on pp. 196–197 for 1 min. Based on this information, what do they think the reading is about?

- **Strategy: Interpret metaphors** Have students brainstorm a list of things that a tree represents for them.

- **Reading** Have students scan the poem to find at least 3 things the poet asks the tree to give him. **¿Por qué quiere el poeta estas cosas? ¿Qué podrían ellas representar?**

- **Post-reading** Ask students to summarize the poem in 2 sentences.

En voces
AUDIO LECTURA

PARA LEER • STRATEGY: READING

Interpret metaphors A metaphor is an implicit comparison between two things, such as "a sea of troubles." It may also be a symbol in which one thing represents another. **Ébano** *(Ebony)* is defined as **un árbol cuya madera es dura y negra. Real** can mean both royal and real. Read **"Ébano real"** and listen to it read aloud. What do you think this tree represents to the poet?

EL ÁRBOL

duro	muy denso
el ébano	tipo de árbol de color muy oscuro
la madera	material que viene del árbol
el tronco	parte vertical del árbol

Sobre el autor

Nicolás Guillén tal vez sea el poeta cubano más conocido. Nació en Camagüey, Cuba, en 1902 y viajó a México y luego a España. En aquel entonces estaba prohibido tocar el son, un tipo de música que combina baile y cantos de estilo africano con romances castellanos de España. Guillén adoptó los ritmos[1] del son en sus poemas, creando un estilo nuevo de poesía que honra la cultura de sus compatriotas afroamericanos. Se llama «poesía negra» a la poesía de Guillén y otros poetas del Caribe. Esta poesía se basa en los ritmos y los temas folklóricos de la gente de descendencia africana.

Introducción

En el poema «Ébano real», Guillén describe un árbol viejo y majestuoso. La repetición de las frases y las palabras con sonidos africanos, como **arará** y **sabalú**, contribuyen a la musicalidad del son cubano en los versos.

---

[1] rhythms

196 ciento noventa y seis
Unidad 3

Classroom Community

Storytelling Have students retell the poem in story form. Advanced students may add imagined details.

Portfolio Have students write a poem about a place that they remember from their childhood. They should also create an illustration to accompany the poem. The poem should follow these guidelines:

- **primera línea:** ¿Qué es?
- **segunda línea:** Describe el lugar con dos palabras.
- **tercera línea:** Escribe tres cosas que hacías ahí.
- **cuarta línea:** ¿Dónde está el lugar?
- **quinta línea:** ¿Cómo se llama el lugar?

Rubric A = 13–15 pts. B = 10–12 pts. C = 7–9 pts. D = 4–6 pts. F = < 4 pts.

Writing criteria	Scale
Correct poetic form	1 2 3 4 5
Grammar/spelling accuracy	1 2 3 4 5
Creativity/appearance	1 2 3 4 5

Ébano real

Te vi al pasar, una tarde,
ébano, y te saludé;
duro entre todos los troncos,
duro entre todos los troncos,
tu corazón[2] recordé.
    Arará, cuévano,
    arará, sabalú.
—Ébano real[3], yo quiero un barco,
ébano real, de tu negra madera…
Ahora no puede ser,
espérate, amigo, espérate,
espérate a que me muera.
    Arará, cuévano,
    arará, sabalú.
—Ébano real, yo quiero un cofre[4],
ébano real, de tu negra madera…
Ahora no puede ser,
espérate, amigo, espérate,
espérate a que me muera.
    Arará, cuévano,
    arará, sabalú.
—Ébano real, yo quiero un techo[5],
ébano real, de tu negra madera…
Ahora no puede ser,
espérate, amigo, espérate,
espérate a que me muera.
    Arará, cuévano,
    arará, sabalú.

—Quiero una mesa cuadrada
y el asta[6] de mi bandera[7];
quiero mi pesado lecho[8]
quiero mi lecho pesado,
ébano, de tu madera…
Ahora no puede ser,
espérate, amigo, espérate,
espérate a que me muera.
    Arará, cuévano,
    arará, sabalú.
Te vi al pasar, una tarde,
ébano, y te saludé;
duro entre todos los troncos,
duro entre todos los troncos,
tu corazón recordé.

---

[2] heart	[5] roof	[7] flag
[3] royal	[6] flagpole	[8] heavy bed
[4] chest		

Online Workbook
CLASSZONE.COM

¿Comprendiste?

1. ¿Qué relación tiene la forma musical del son con la poesía de Guillén?
2. ¿Qué protesta la poesía de Guillén?
3. ¿Qué cosas le pide el autor al árbol?

¿Qué piensas?

¿Cuáles son las palabras repetidas del poema? ¿Qué efecto tienen?

Hazlo tú

Piensa en una cosa que ves a menudo. ¿Qué palabras puedes usar para «saludarla»? Describe qué representa este objeto para ti en unos versos.

ciento noventa y siete
El Caribe Etapa 1 **197**

Culture Highlights

● **NICOLÁS GUILLÉN** Nicolás Guillén (1902–1989) fue el poeta nacional de Cuba. Era de descendencia mixta africana y europea. Quiso crear una poesía nacional «negri-blanca» que mezclara la herencia española y africana de Cuba con la musicalidad cubana. Fue el actor principal en el movimiento negrista de Cuba, que glorificaba la cultura e identidad afrocubana. Aunque la poesía de temas africanos ya era popular en Cuba cuando Guillén publicó su primer libro de poesía, él fue el primero en presentar las culturas afrocubanas como algo más que presencia exótica.

Cross Cultural Connections

Strategy Ask students to research poets or writers in the U.S. that promote Afro-American culture and identity (for example, Langston Hughes and Maya Angelou). Have them bring in samples of their works, especially poems.

Interdisciplinary Connections

English/Literature Bring in additional examples of poems by Guillén. Have students work with the English department to discuss the meanings of onomatopoeia, alliteration, and musical metaphors and how they apply to Guillén's poetry.

Science Have student research where ebony grows in the world. Then have them find out what products are made from ebony and why.

¿Comprendiste?

Answers
1. Guillén adoptó los ritmos del son en sus poemas. El son combina baile y cantos de estilo africano con romances castellanos de España.
2. Protesta contra la opresión hacia los afroamericanos.
3. Le pide un barco, un cofre, un techo, una mesa cuadrada, el asta de su bandera y su lecho pesado.

■ Block Schedule

Change of Pace Bring in copies of additional poems by Nicolás Guillén. Distribute them to students to read and make comparisons to **Ébano real**. (For additional activities, see **Block Scheduling Copymasters**.)

Teaching All Students

Extra Help Pair students needing help with a partner who is an advanced student or a native speaker. Have students read the poem aloud in sections while the partner explains the meaning.

Native Speakers Have students research Nicolás Guillén and write a brief biography to present to the class.

Multiple Intelligences

Verbal Have students read the poem in pairs. One student plays the part of the poet, the other plays the part of the tree.

Musical/Rhythmic Have students work in pairs to reread the poem and list the sounds that repeat themselves most often. Have students determine the effect that the repetitive sounds produce.

Teaching Resource Options

Print

Cuaderno para hispanohablantes
  PE, pp. 71–72
Block Scheduling Copymasters
Unit 3 Resource Book
  Cuaderno para hispanohablantes
    TE, pp. 27–28
  Information Gap Activities, pp. 31–32
  Family Involvement, pp. 40–41

Audiovisual

OHT 14 (Quick Start)

Technology

eTest Plus Online/Test Generator
CD-ROM

  www.classzone.com

Quick Start Review

♻ Subjunctive/vocabulary review

Use OHT 14 or write on the board:
First, give the **yo** form of the imperfect
subjunctive for each verb. Then give
the related noun.

1. desfilar   a. _____ b. _____
2. felicitar   a. _____ b. _____
3. emocionar a. _____ b. _____
4. brindar   a. _____ b. _____
5. celebrar   a. _____ b. _____

Answers
1. a. desfilara   b. el desfile
2. a. felicitara   b. la felicidad
3. a. emocionara b. la emoción
4. a. brindara   b. el brindis
5. a. celebrara   b. la celebración

Teaching Suggestions
What Have Students Learned?

Plan time for a Reviewers' Workshop.
Have students work in small groups to
review according to "Now you can.../
To review." If one member of the group
is having trouble with a point, the
others are responsible for clarifying it.

ETAPA 1

En uso
REPASO Y MÁS COMUNICACIÓN

OBJECTIVES
• Describe personal
  celebrations
• Say what people want
• Link events and ideas

Now you can...

• describe personal
  celebrations.

• say what people
  want

To review

• the subjunctive for
  expressing wishes
  see p. 188.

1 Sugiero que...

Tu compañero(a) hace el papel del (de la) graduando(a) en su día
de graduación. Tú haces el papel de su mamá o de su papá.
¿Qué le dices?

modelo

(sugerir que) llegar temprano a la ceremonia de graduación

Tú: *Sugiero que llegues temprano a la ceremonia de graduación.*

Compañero(a): *Está bien, mamá (papá). Llegaré temprano.*

1. (querer que) vestirse bien
2. (querer que) darles las gracias a tus padrinos
3. (recomendar que) dar un discurso inspirador
4. (sugerir que) no emocionarse demasiado
5. (aconsejar que) no ponerse la toga y el birrete antes de la ceremonia
6. (sugerir que) felicitar a tus compañeros
7. (esperar que) disfrutar de la ceremonia

Now you can...

• say what people
  want.

To review

• the subjunctive for
  expressing wishes
  see p. 188.

2 Mi familia

Las familias siempre tienen mucho que decir sobre las
actividades de los familiares jóvenes. Haz oraciones que expresan
estos deseos usando frases de las dos columnas.

modelo

mi madre querer / yo asistir a la ceremonia de graduación
Mi madre quiere que yo asista a la ceremonia de graduación.

1. mis abuelos esperar / mis hermanos saludar a los padrinos
2. mi tío prohibir / mi prima salir con los amigos después de
   la celebración
3. mi padre insistir en / yo agradecer la generosidad de los invitados
4. mis primos pedir / mis hermanos y yo llegar temprano a la fiesta
5. mi madre exigir / yo vestirme muy elegante

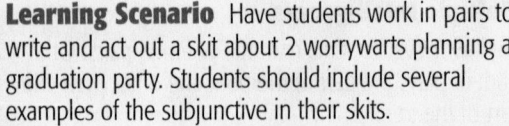

Classroom Community

Learning Scenario Have students work in pairs to
write and act out a skit about 2 worrywarts planning a
graduation party. Students should include several
examples of the subjunctive in their skits.

Paired Activity In pairs, have students create
crossword puzzles. The cues should be sentences
requiring a subjunctive form to be filled in on the grid.
Have pairs exchange and complete puzzles.

Self-Check Quiz
CLASSZONE.COM

3 ¡Ay, abuela!

Hoy es tu día de graduación y tu abuela tiene muchas cosas que decirte. ¿Qué te dice?

modelo

(tú: pensar ir con tus amigos) Ven conmigo a la ceremonia a menos que _____.

Ven conmigo a la ceremonia a menos que pienses ir con tus amigos.

1. (el discurso: ser largo) Voy a hacer un video de toda la ceremonia a menos que _____.
2. (tú: olvidarse) Aquí está tu bolso antes de que _____.
3. (la ceremonia: no terminar muy tarde) Vamos a quedarnos hasta el final con tal de que _____.
4. (tú: ponerse la toga) Péinate antes de que _____.
5. (tú: recibir el diploma) Mira la cámara antes de que _____.
6. (llover) La ceremonia va a ser en el auditorio en caso de que _____.
7. (tú: decidir acompañarme) Voy a esperarte después en caso de que _____.
8. (tú: necesitarme) Voy a estar allí en caso de que _____.
9. (tú: descansar) Siéntate un rato para que _____.

4 El profesor

Tu profesor favorito dio un discurso a la clase de graduandos antes de la ceremonia. ¿Qué les dijo a ustedes?

modelo

no ponerse nerviosos

Nos dijo que no nos pusiéramos nerviosos.

1. disfrutar del tiempo libre
2. brindar con nuestros padres
3. sentirse orgullosos
4. apreciar a nuestros profesores
5. apoyarse el uno al otro
6. dedicarnos a nuestros estudios
7. dar las gracias a nuestra familia
8. felicitar a nuestros compañeros de clase
9. llevar a cabo nuestros sueños
10. avanzar hacia nuestras metas

Now you can...
• link events and ideas.

To review
• the subjunctive with conjunctions see p. 190.

Now you can...
• say what people want.

To review
• the imperfect subjunctive see p. 192.

ciento noventa y nueve
El Caribe Etapa 1 199

Answers

Answers will vary.
1. Quiero que sepas que te vistas bien.
2. Quiero que les des las gracias a tus padrinos.
3. Recomiendo que des un discurso inspirador.
4. Sugiero que no te emociones demasiado.
5. Te aconsejo que no te pongas la toga y el birrete antes de la ceremonia.
6. Sugiero que felicites a tus compañeros.
7. Espero que disfrutes de la ceremonia.

Answers

Answers will vary.

Answers

1. ...el discurso sea aburrido.
2. ...se te olvide.
3. ...la ceremonia no termine muy tarde.
4. ...te pongas la toga.
5. ...recibas el diploma.
6. ...llueva.
7. ...decidas acompañarme.
8. ...me necesites.
9. ...te descanses.

Answers

1. Nos dijo que disfrutáramos del tiempo libre.
2. Nos dijo que brindáramos con nuestros padres.
3. Nos dijo que nos sintiéramos orgullosos.
4. Nos dijo que apreciáramos a nuestros profesores.
5. Nos dijo que nos apoyáramos el uno al otro.
6. Nos dijo que nos dedicáramos a nuestros estudios.
7. Nos dijo que les diéramos las gracias a nuestras familia.
8. Nos dijo que felicitáramos a nuestros compañeros de clase.
9. Nos dijo que lleváramos a cabo nuestros objetivos.
10. Nos dijo que avanzáramos hacia nuestras metas.

Teaching All Students

Extra Help Have students create a 5-item exercise on any grammar or vocabulary studied in the **Etapa**. Have them exchange exercises with a partner, complete them, and correct them.

Multiple Intelligences

Kinesthetic Prepare ahead: Write the answers to **Actividad 4** on separate slips of paper. Then cut the slips into 2 parts: (1) **Nos dijo que** + verb, and (2) rest of sentence. Distribute sentence pieces to students, who must find their "other halves." Write extra sentences if needed.

Block Schedule

Variety Have students create an "Advice" bulletin board. Each student writes and illustrates a sentence using the subjunctive that relays a piece of advice for doing well in school, graduating, and succeeding in life. (For additional activities, see **Block Scheduling Copymasters**.)

Teaching Resource Options

Print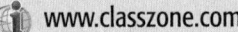

Unit 3 Resource Book
  Audioscript, p. 45
  Vocabulary Quizzes, pp. 48–50
  Grammar Quizzes, pp. 51–52
  Etapa Exam, Forms A and B,
    pp. 53–62
  Examen para hispanohablantes,
    pp. 63–67
  Portfolio Assessment, pp. 68–69
  Multiple Choice Test Questions,
    pp. 226–228

Audiovisual

OHT 14 (Quick Start)
Audio Program CD 19, Track 17

Technology

eTest Plus Online/Test Generator
  CD-ROM

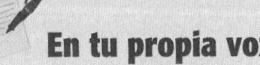 www.classzone.com

ACTIVIDAD 5

Rubric: Speaking

Criteria	Scale	
Sentence structure	1 2 3	A = 11–12 pts.
Vocabulary use	1 2 3	B = 9–10 pts.
Originality	1 2 3	C = 7–8 pts.
Fluency	1 2 3	D = 4–6 pts.
		F = < 4 pts.

ACTIVIDAD 6 En tu propia voz

Rubric: Writing

Criteria	Scale	
Vocabulary use	1 2 3 4 5	A = 14–15 pts.
Accuracy	1 2 3 4 5	B = 12–13 pts.
Creativity, appearance	1 2 3 4 5	C = 10–11 pts.
		D = 8–9 pts.
		F = < 8 pts.

Teaching Note: En tu propia voz

Writing Strategy Suggest that students "Bring their event to life" when writing their captions. They should share how they feel about what is happening in the photos—about the people, places, and events.

Community Connections

For the next week, ask students to list every opportunity they have to hear, speak, or read Spanish outside of class.

---

5 El (La) graduando(a)

STRATEGY: SPEAKING

Give advice and best wishes Think of the different suggestions and recommendations you might make to the graduate. You can offer the usual phrases, be socially correct, or you might capture the graduate's attention by saying something unusual and unorthodox. Use your imagination!

En grupos de tres o cuatro, escojan a una persona que sea el (la) graduando(a). Los demás deben hacer el papel de parientes y felicitarlo(la) y darle consejos.

modelo

Tú: *¡Te felicito en tu graduación!*

El graduando: *Muchas gracias, se lo agradezco.*

Amigo(a) 1: *¡Enhorabuena, hijo! Estamos muy orgullosos de ti.*

Amigo(a) 2: *Te deseo mucho éxito, y sugiero que…*

6 *En tu propia voz*

ESCRITURA Imagina el día de tu graduación. ¿Cómo va a ser? ¿Cómo te vas a sentir? ¿A quiénes vas a invitar? ¿Dónde y cómo van a celebrar? Escribe tres leyendas detalladas para tu álbum de fotos.

TÚ EN LA COMUNIDAD

Jordan es alumno en Arkansas. Su familia vivió en la República Dominicana por diez años y todos aprendieron a hablar español. Jordan trabaja en un restaurante de Arkansas. Habla español con los clientes que no hablan inglés y les ayuda a pedir la comida. También habla español con sus compañeros de la escuela de vez en cuando. ¿Hablas español cuando tienes la oportunidad?

200 doscientos
Unidad 3

Classroom Community

Game Divide the class into small groups and give each a large piece of paper. Each group writes as many sentences as they can using words/expressions from the **Repaso de vocabulario** on p. 201. Give a 5-minute time limit. Display the papers on the board and have the class check for spelling and grammar errors. The team with the most correct sentences wins.

Paired Activity Have students work in pairs to review the **Repaso de vocabulario** on p. 201 One student gives a definition and/or mimes a word/expression. The other students guesses it.

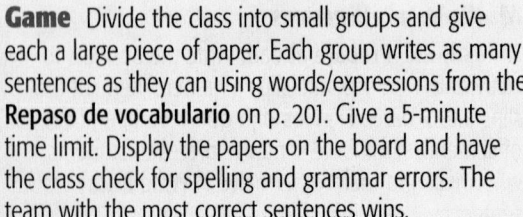

En resumen
REPASO DE VOCABULARIO

Flashcards
CLASSZONE.COM

DESCRIBE PERSONAL CELEBRATIONS

Graduation

agradecer	to thank
el apoyo	support
apreciar	to appreciate
el birrete	cap
brindar	to make a toast
el brindis	toast
la ceremonia de graduación	graduation ceremony
el desfile	parade, procession
el diploma	diploma
el discurso	speech
emocionarse	to be thrilled, touched
la enhorabuena	congratulations
el éxito	success
la generosidad	generosity
generoso(a)	generous
el (la) graduando(a)	graduate
graduarse	to graduate
llevar a cabo	to accomplish
Mil gracias.	Many thanks.
orgulloso(a)	proud
los padrinos	godparents
la toga	gown
valer la pena	to be worthwhile

The future

avanzar	to advance
el camino	path, road
imponer	to impose
el orgullo	pride
el tropiezo	setback
vencer	to defeat, to overcome

SAY WHAT PEOPLE WANT

The subjunctive for expressing wishes

dejar	to allow
exigir	to demand
insistir en	to insist on
oponerse a	to oppose
prohibir	to prohibit
rogar (o→ue)	to beg
suplicar	to ask, to plead

♻ **Ya sabes**

aconsejar	to advise
desear	to want
esperar	to hope, wait
mandar	to order, send
pedir (e→i)	to request
permitir	to permit
querer (e→ie)	to want
recomendar (e→ie)	to recommend
sugerir (e→ie)	to suggest

LINK EVENTS AND IDEAS

Conjunctions

a menos que	unless
con tal de que	provided that, as long as
en caso de que	in case
para que	so that

♻ **Ya sabes**

antes (de) que	before

Juego

Consejos para el graduando

¿Cuál de estas palabras no se aplica al dibujo?

a. emocionados
b. prohibir
c. enhorabuena
d. llevar a cabo

doscientos uno
El Caribe Etapa 1 201

♻ **Etapa vocabulary**

Use OHT 14 or write on the board: Write 2 words/expressions pertaining to graduation for each of the following categories:

1. Lo que vemos
2. Lo que hacemos
3. Lo que sentimos

Answers
Answers will vary. Answers could include:
1. el desfile, las togas
2. agradecer, brindar
3. orgullosos(as), apreciar

Teaching Suggestions
Vocabulary Review

Have students create mnemonic devices or rhymes to help them remember the verbs expressing wishes that elicit the subjunctive and/or conjunctions that require the subjunctive.

Dictation

Dictate the following sentences to review the **Etapa:**

1. Vale la pena que insistas en practicar tu discurso.
2. Sugiero que llegues temprano a la ceremonia de graduación.
3. Llenen los vasos para que brindemos.
4. Los padrinos quieren que le demos la enhorabuena al graduando.

Juego

Answers: b. prohibir

Block Schedule

FunBreak Play Bingo using irregular and stem-changing verbs in the imperfect subjunctive. Write all the possible infinitives on the board. Have students fill out their cards with conjugated forms. Give clues such as: **yo** form of **estar.** When a student has 5 in a row, he/she must recite the full conjugation of that verb.

Teaching All Students

Extra Help Have students place the verbs expressing wishes on a continuum, ranging from gentlest to strongest. For example, **rogar** is on the gentle end and **oponerse** is on the strong end.

Native Speakers Ask students to talk about the occasions when they speak Spanish at home, in school, and in the community. Was there one occasion when speaking Spanish allowed them to help someone else?

Multiple Intelligences

Intrapersonal Have students write a short graduation speech that they might give. They should start with **Espero que...**

Visual Have students create their own version of the **Juego** on p. 201, with a drawing and a choice of words.

Planning Guide CLASSROOM MANAGEMENT

OBJECTIVES

Communication
- Talk about holidays *pp. 204–205, 206–207, 212–213*
- Hypothesize *pp. 214–216*
- Express doubt and disagree *pp. 206–207*
- Describe ideals *pp. 210–211*

Grammar
- Use the subjunctive with nonexistent and indefinite *pp. 210–211*
- Review: Use the subjunctive for disagreement and denial *pp. 212–213*
- Use conditional sentences *pp. 214–217*

Culture
- **Salsa** music *p. 211*
- Holidays in Puerto Rico *p. 212*
- Chayanne, a singer from Puerto Rico *p. 215*
- Regional vocabulary *p. 216*
- The tradition of mask-making in Puerto Rico *pp. 218–219*

♻ Recycling
- Community service vocabulary *p. 210*
- Professions *p. 216*

STRATEGIES

Listening Strategies
- Observe interview techniques *p. 206*

Speaking Strategies
- Socialize as host or guest *p. 209*
- Encourage participation *p. 222*

Reading Strategies
- Observe organization of ideas *TE p. 218*

Writing Strategies
- Tell who, what, where, when, why, and how *TE p. 222*

Connecting Cultures Strategies
- Learn about **salsa** music and musicians *p. 211*
- Learn about holidays in Puerto Rico *p. 212*
- Learn about Chayanne, a singer from Puerto Rico *p. 215*
- Recognize variations in vocabulary *p. 216*
- Recognize and describe uses of disguise *p. 218*
- Connect and compare what you know about art traditions in your community to help you learn about art traditions in a new community *pp. 218–219, 222*

PROGRAM RESOURCES

Print
- *Más práctica* Workbook PE *pp. 73–80*
- *Actividades para todos* Workbook PE *pp. 81–90*
- Block Scheduling Copymasters *pp. 65–72*
- Unit 3 Resource Book
  Más práctica Workbook TE *pp. 73–80*
  Actividades para todos Workbook TE *pp. 81–90*
  Cuaderno para hispanohablantes TE *pp. 91–98*
  Information Gap Activities *pp. 99–102*
  Family Letter *p. 103*
  Absent Student Copymasters *pp. 104–109*
  Family Involvement *pp. 110–111*
  Audioscript *pp. 112–114*
  Assessment Program, Unit 3 Etapa 2 *pp. 115–138; 229–331*
  Video Activities *pp. 243–246*
  Videoscript *pp. 247–249*
  Answer Keys *pp. 250–254*

Audiovisual
- Audio Program CD 8
- *Canciones* CD
- Video Program Videotape 18:06 / DVD, Unit 3
- Overhead Transparencies M1–M3; 3; 18–31
- Word Tiles U3E2

Technology
- eEdition Plus Online/eEdition CD-ROM
- Easy Planner Plus Online/Easy Planner CD-ROM
- eTest Plus Online/Test Generator CD-ROM
- Online Workbook
- Take-Home Tutor CD-ROM
- www.classzone.com

✔ Assessment Program Options
- Unit 3 Resource Book
  Vocabulary Quizzes
  Grammar Quizzes
  Etapa Exam Forms A and B
  Examen para hispanohablantes
  Portfolio Assessment
  Multiple Choice Test Questions
- Audio Program CD 19
- eTest Plus Online/Test Generator CD-ROM

Native Speakers
- *Cuaderno para hispanohablantes* PE *pp. 73–80*
- *Cuaderno para hispanohablantes* TE (Unit 3 Resource Book)
- *Examen para hispanohablantes* (Unit 3 Resource Book)
- Audio Program *(Para hispanohablantes)* CD 8, 19
- Audioscript (Unit 3 Resource Book)

Student Text Listening Activity Scripts

Situaciones *pages 206–207*

• CD 8

Eduardo: ¡Hola, Puerto Rico! ¡Les habla Eduardo Canales desde KQ102! Hoy vamos a entrevistar a la pareja que ganó nuestro concurso de salsa, Emilia Ruedas y Alex Ortiz. ¡Los mejores salseros en todo Puerto Rico!

Buenos días, Emilia, Alex, es el tres de enero y todo el mundo quiere saber cómo les fue. ¿Cómo pasaron el Año Nuevo?

Emilia: ¡Lo pasamos muy bien! ¡De maravilla!

Alex: Hombre, no sabes lo felices que estamos.

Eduardo: Qué gusto me da oír eso. ¿Les gustaron los disfraces?

Emilia: A mí sí, pero Alex se sintió raro vestido de iguana. A mí me encantó mi disfraz de mariposa.

Alex: Es que no acostumbro llevar un disfraz.

Eduardo: El tema era el bosque tropical, ¿no? ¿Estilo El Yunque?

Emilia: Sí, así es. Los diseñadores fueron muy originales, ¡pero me alegro de que no tuviéramos que llevarlos toda la noche!

Eduardo: Bueno, sigamos. ¿Qué pensaron de la orquesta de Gilberto Santa Rosa?

Alex: Ese hombre es un genio. ¡Bailamos sin parar!

Eduardo: Háblenme de la cena.

Emilia: Uy, ¡comimos demasiado! El lechón asado, por supuesto, estuvo delicioso.

Alex: A mí me encantaron los pasteles. Para chuparse los dedos.

Eduardo: Y ¿qué tal los fuegos artificiales?

Emilia: El Morro es un sitio fenomenal. Ver los fuegos artificiales allí, ¡fue un sueño!

Eduardo: ¿Se pudieron comer las uvas a tiempo con cada campanada?

Alex: No fue fácil, pero lo logramos. ¿Eso nos trae buena suerte, o qué?

Emilia: No sé, pero ya tuvimos buena suerte, ¿no?

Eduardo: Y el amanecer, en la playa del Condado, ¿cómo se sintieron? Díganle a nuestros radioyentes.

Emilia: Puerto Rico es único. El amanecer en Puerto Rico no se puede describir.

Alex: Si vinieran aquí, verían el amanecer más espectacular de sus vidas.

Eduardo: Con esas palabras, acabamos nuestra entrevista. Dudo que nuestros radioyentes no sientan la felicidad de Emilia y Alex. Todo hecho posible por la radioemisora KQ102. ¡Hasta mañana, radioyentes de KQ102!

ACTIVIDAD 6 ¿Existe o no? *page 211*

Modelo: Conozco a alguien que sabe reparar computadoras.

1. Conozco a un señor que habla francés.
2. No hay nadie aquí que pueda tocar la guitarra.
3. Necesitamos una orquesta que no cueste mucho.
4. Conozco un músico que canta muy bien.
5. Quiero un apartamento que tenga jardín.
6. Buscamos a unos estudiantes que puedan trabajar los fines de semana.
7. Tenemos amigos que saben bailar salsa.
8. En esta casa, no hay ninguna radio que funcione.

ACTIVIDAD 13 ¿Qué va a hacer? *page 215*

Modelo: Si tuviera dinero, compraría un traje.

1. Iré si hay una gala.
2. Si supiera cómo, prepararía un lechón asado.
3. Empezaría un grupo musical si pudiera tocar un instrumento.
4. Si hubiera un concurso de baile, yo participaría en él.
5. Si hay fuegos artificiales, los veré.
6. Si mis padres me lo permitieran, iría a ver el amanecer en la playa.

Sample Lesson Plan - 50 Minute Schedule

DAY 1

Etapa Opener
- Quick Start Review (TE, p. 202) 5 MIN.
- Have students look at the *Etapa* Opener and answer the questions. Expand using one of the activities on TE pp. 202–203. 10 MIN.

En contexto: Vocabulario
- Quick Start Review (TE, p. 204) 5 MIN.
- Present *Descubre,* p. 204. 5 MIN.
- Have students use context and pictures to learn *Etapa* vocabulary, then answer the *¿Comprendiste?* questions, p. 205. Use the Situational OHTs for additional practice. 25 MIN.

Homework Option:
- Have students write answers to the *¿Comprendiste?* questions, p. 205.

DAY 2

En vivo: Situaciones
- Check homework. 5 MIN.
- Quick Start Review (TE, p. 206) 5 MIN.
- Present the Listening Strategy, p. 206. 5 MIN.
- Have students read section 1, p. 206. Play the audio for section 2. Then have students complete section 3 in pairs or groups. 20 MIN.

En acción: Vocabulario y gramática
- Quick Start Review (TE, p. 208) 5 MIN.
- Do *Actividad* 1 orally. 5 MIN.
- Have students do *Actividad* 2 in pairs. 5 MIN.

Homework Option:
- Have students write a description of a typical New Year's celebration in the U.S.

DAY 3

En acción (cont.)
- Check homework. 5 MIN.
- Present the *Vocabulario,* p. 209. Then have students do *Actividad* 3 in pairs. 10 MIN.
- Present the Speaking Strategy, p. 209. Have students do *Actividad* 4 in groups. 5 MIN.
- Quick Start Review (TE, p. 210) 5 MIN.
- Present *Gramática:* Subjunctive with Nonexistent and Indefinite, p. 210. 10 MIN.
- Present the *Nota* and have students complete *Actividad* 5 in writing. 5 MIN.
- Play the audio; do *Actividad* 6. 5 MIN.
- Have students do *Actividad* 7 in pairs. 5 MIN.

Homework Option:
- *Más práctica* Workbook, p. 77. *Cuaderno para hispanohablantes,* p. 75.

DAY 4

En acción (cont.)
- Check homework. 5 MIN.
- Quick Start Review (TE, p. 212) 5 MIN.
- Present *Repaso:* The Subjunctive for Disagreement and Denial and *Vocabulario,* p. 212. 10 MIN.
- Have students complete *Actividades* 8, 9 and 10 in pairs. 15 MIN.
- Present the *Vocabulario,* p. 213. Then have students do *Actividad* 11 orally. Expand using Information Gap Activities, Unit 3 Resource Book, p. 99; *Más comunicación,* p. R10. 15 MIN.

Homework Option:
- Have students complete *Actividad* 11 in writing. *Más práctica* Workbook, p. 78. *Cuaderno para hispanohablantes,* p. 76.

DAY 5

En acción (cont.)
- Check homework. 5 MIN.
- Quick Start Review (TE, p. 214) 5 MIN.
- Present *Gramática:* Conditional Sentences, p. 214. 10 MIN.
- Have students do *Actividad* 12 orally. 5 MIN.
- Play the audio; do *Actividad* 13. 10 MIN.
- Have students complete *Actividad* 14 in pairs. 5 MIN.
- Have students complete *Actividad* 15 in groups. 10 MIN.

Homework Option:
- Have students complete *Actividad* 12 in writing. *Más práctica* Workbook, pp. 79–80. *Cuaderno para hispanohablantes,* pp. 77–78.
- *Actividades para todos* Workbook, pp. 81–86.

DAY 6

En acción (cont.)
- Check homework. 5 MIN.
- Present the *Vocabulario,* p. 217. 5 MIN.
- Have students read and complete *Actividad* 16 in writing. Expand using Information Gap Activities, Unit 3 Resource Book, p. 100; *Más comunicación,* p. R10. 15 MIN.

Refrán
- Present the *Refrán,* p. 217. 5 MIN.

En colores: Cultura y comparaciones
- Quick Start Review (TE, p. 218) 5 MIN.
- Present the Connecting Cultures Strategy, p. 218. Call on volunteers to read the selection aloud. Have students answer the *¿Comprendiste?/¿Qué piensas?* questions, p. 219. 15 MIN.

Homework Option:
- Have students complete *Hazlo tú,* p. 219.

DAY 7

En uso: Repaso y más comunicación
- Check homework. 5 MIN.
- Quick Start Review (TE, p. 220) 5 MIN.
- Have students do *Actividades* 1 and 2 orally. 10 MIN.
- Do *Actividades* 3 and 4 in writing. 5 MIN.
- Present the Speaking Strategy, p. 222, and have students do *Actividad* 5 in groups. 10 MIN.
- Have students do *Actividad* 6 in pairs. 5 MIN.

En tu propia voz: Escritura
- Do *Actividad* 7 in writing. Have volunteers present their ads to the class. 10 MIN.

Homework Option:
- Review for *Etapa* 2 Exam.

DAY 8

Conexiones
- Read *El arte,* p. 222. Have students prepare their cards. 5 MIN.

En resumen: Repaso de vocabulario
- Quick Start Review (TE, p. 223) 5 MIN.
- Review grammar questions, etc., as necessary. 10 MIN.
- Complete *Etapa* 2 Exam. 20 MIN.

Ampliación
- Use a suggested project, game, or activity. (TE, pp. 179A–179B) 10 MIN.

Homework Option:
- Have students complete the assignment for *Conexiones.* Preview *Etapa* 3 Opener.

Sample Lesson Plan - Block Schedule (90 minutes)

DAY 1

Etapa Opener
- Quick Start Review (TE, p. 202) 5 MIN.
- Have students look at the *Etapa* Opener and answer the questions. 5 MIN.
- Use Block Scheduling Copymasters. 10 MIN.

En contexto: Vocabulario
- Quick Start Review (TE, p. 204) 5 MIN.
- Present *Descubre,* p. 204. 5 MIN.
- Have students use context and pictures to learn *Etapa* vocabulary, then answer the *¿Comprendiste?* questions, p. 205. Use the Situational OHTs for additional practice. 25 MIN.

En vivo: Situaciones
- Quick Start Review (TE, p. 206) 5 MIN.
- Present the Listening Strategy, p. 206. 5 MIN.
- Have students read section 1, p. 206. Play the audio for section 2. Then have students complete section 3 in pairs or groups. 25 MIN.

Homework Option:
- Have students write answers to the *¿Comprendiste?* questions, p. 205. Have students write a description of a typical New Year's celebration in the U.S.

DAY 2

En acción: Vocabulario y gramática
- Check homework. 5 MIN.
- Quick Start Review (TE, p. 208) 5 MIN.
- Do *Actividad* 1 orally. 5 MIN.
- Have students do *Actividad* 2 in pairs. 5 MIN.
- Present the *Vocabulario,* p. 209. Then have students do *Actividad* 3 in pairs. 10 MIN.
- Present the Speaking Strategy, p. 209. Have students do *Actividad* 4 in groups. 5 MIN.
- Quick Start Review (TE, p. 210) 5 MIN.
- Present *Gramática:* Subjunctive with Nonexistent and Indefinite, p. 210. 10 MIN.
- Present the *Nota* and have students complete *Actividad* 5 in writing. Go over answers orally. 10 MIN.
- Play the audio; do *Actividad* 6. 5 MIN.
- Have students do *Actividad* 7 in pairs. 5 MIN.
- Quick Start Review (TE, p. 212) 5 MIN.
- Present *Repaso:* The Subjunctive for Disagreement and Denial and *Vocabulario,* p. 212. 10 MIN.
- Have students do *Actividad* 8 in pairs. 5 MIN.

Homework Option:
- Have students complete *Actividades* 7 and 8 in writing. *Más práctica* Workbook, pp. 77–78. *Cuaderno para hispanohablantes,* pp. 75–76.

DAY 3

En acción (cont.)
- Check homework. 5 MIN.
- Have students complete *Actividades* 9 and 10 in pairs. 10 MIN.
- Present the *Vocabulario,* p. 213. Then have students do *Actividad* 11 orally. Expand using Information Gap Activities, Unit 3 Resource Book, p. 99; *Más comunicación,* p. R10. 25 MIN.
- Quick Start Review (TE, p. 214) 5 MIN.
- Present *Gramática:* Conditional Sentences, p. 214. 10 MIN.
- Have students do *Actividad* 12 orally. 5 MIN.
- Play the audio; do *Actividad* 13. 10 MIN.
- Have students complete *Actividad* 14 in pairs. 10 MIN.
- Have students complete *Actividad* 15 in groups. 10 MIN.

Homework Option:
- Have students complete *Actividades* 11 and 12 in writing. *Más práctica* Workbook, pp. 79–80. *Cuaderno para hispanohablantes,* pp. 77–78.
- *Actividades para todos* Workbook, pp. 81–86.

DAY 4

En acción (cont.)
- Check homework. 5 MIN.
- Present the *Vocabulario,* p. 217. Then have students read and complete *Actividad* 16 in writing. Expand using Information Gap Activities, Unit 3 Resource Book, p. 100; *Más comunicación,* p. R10. 25 MIN.

Refrán
- Present the *Refrán,* p. 217. 5 MIN.

En colores: Cultura y comparaciones
- Quick Start Review (TE, p. 218) 5 MIN.
- Present the Connecting Cultures Strategy, p. 218. Call on volunteers to read the selection aloud. Have students answer the *¿Comprendiste?/¿Qué piensas?* questions, p. 219. 20 MIN.

En uso: Repaso y más comunicación
- Quick Start Review (TE, p. 220) 5 MIN.
- Have students do *Actividades* 1 and 2 orally. 10 MIN.
- Do *Actividades* 3 and 4 in writing. Go over answers orally. 15 MIN.

Homework Option:
- Have students complete *Hazlo tú,* p. 219. Review for *Etapa* 2 Exam.

DAY 5

En uso (cont.)
- Check homework. 5 MIN.
- Present the Speaking Strategy, p. 222, and have students do *Actividad* 5 in groups. 10 MIN.
- Have students do *Actividad* 6 in pairs. 5 MIN.

En tu propia voz: Escritura
- Do *Actividad* 7 in writing. Have volunteers present their ads to the class. 10 MIN.

Conexiones
- Read *El arte,* p. 222. Have students prepare their cards. 5 MIN.

En resumen: Repaso de vocabulario
- Quick Start Review (TE, p. 223) 5 MIN.
- Review grammar questions, etc., as necessary. 10 MIN.
- Complete *Etapa* 2 Exam. 20 MIN.

Ampliación
- Use a suggested project, game, or activity. (TE, pp. 179A–179B) 20 MIN.

Homework Option:
- Have students complete the assignment for *Conexiones.* Preview *Etapa* 3 Opener.

▼ La gente lo está pasando muy bien en la gala.

Etapa Theme

Talking about holidays; hypothesizing, doubting, and disagreeing; and describing ideals

Grammar Objectives

- Reviewing the use of the subjunctive with the nonexistent and the indefinite
- Reviewing the use of the subjunctive for disagreement and denial
- Using conditional sentences

Teaching Resource Options

Print

Block Scheduling Copymasters
Unit 3 Resource Book
  Family Letter, p. 103
  Absent Student Copymasters, p. 104

Audiovisual

OHT 3, 24 (Quick Start)
Canciones CD

Quick Start Review

♻ Holidays/months

Use OHT 24 or write on the board:
Fill in the month of these holiday dates:

1. el 14 de ___
2. el primero de ___
3. el 31 de ___
4. el 4 de ___
5. el 25 de ___

Answers
1. febrero
2. enero (abril)
3. octubre (diciembre)
4. julio
5. diciembre

Teaching Suggestions
Previewing the Etapa

- Ask students to study the picture on pp. 202–203 (1 min.).
- Have them close their books and discuss their initial impressions of the scene—the buildings, geography, weather, activities, etc.
- Ask students if they have ever seen a similar greeting card in the U.S. **¿Han visto alguna vez alguna tarjeta parecida en los Estados Unidos?**
- Use the **¿Qué ves?** questions to focus the discussion.

UNIDAD 3

ETAPA 2

¡Próspero Año Nuevo!

OBJECTIVES

- **Talk about holidays**
- **Hypothesize**
- **Express doubt and disagree**
- **Describe ideals**

¿Qué ves?

Mira la foto. Contesta las preguntas.

1. ¿Qué observas en la foto?
2. ¿Crees que es una noche regular o una noche especial en este lugar? ¿Por qué?
3. ¿Qué época del año es? ¿Cómo te sientes durante esa época del año?
4. ¿Qué otras cosas puede decir la tarjeta?

202

Classroom Management

Planning Ahead Prepare to introduce the theme of celebrating holidays by collecting invitations and ads for celebrations (especially New Year's Eve). If possible, bring in items from Puerto Rico.

Peer Review Have students write 3 additional questions about the photo. Then have them work with a partner to ask and answer each other's questions.

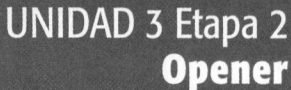
Cross Cultural Connections

Point out that this photo was taken in San Juan, Puerto Rico. Ask students to compare this scene to a New Year's Eve celebration in the U.S., perhaps the one in Times Square in New York City.

Culture Highlights

● **LA FORTALEZA** La Fortaleza, que se ve en el trasfondo de la página 197, es la mansión ejecutiva más antigua del hemisferio occidental. Se utilizó originalmente como casa del gobernador y con propósitos militares. Cuando fue terminada en 1540, los arquitectos se dieron cuenta de que sería difícil defenderla por su posición en la cima de una colina. Por lo tanto se comenzó la construcción del Castillo de San Felipe del Morro, una fortaleza de seis niveles al noroeste del Viejo San Juan, para defender la ciudad de los ataques por mar. El Morro es una de las fortalezas más antiguas en el Nuevo Mundo.

Supplementary Vocabulary

la fortaleza	fortress
el malecón	boardwalk
el muelle	pier, dock
la orilla del mar	seashore

¡Próspero Año Nuevo!

203

Block Schedule

Research Ask students to research the names and dates of major holidays in Cuba, the Dominican Republic, Puerto Rico, and Mexico. Then have them discuss which holidays are the same as in the U.S., which are different, and which the 4 countries have in common. (For additional activities, see **Block Scheduling Copymasters.**)

Teaching All Students

Extra Help As a class, brainstorm a list of all known vocabulary students could use to talk about the photo. Then have them use these words to provide descriptions.

Native Speakers Ask students to look for maps of San Juan on the Internet and download any they find. Have them locate the scene in the photo and discuss what else is found in that area of the city.

Multiple Intelligences

Visual Ask students to sketch a scene similar to the one in the photo. Then have them add at least 2 people to the scene, along with speech bubbles of what they might be saying.

Teaching Resource Options

Print

Block Scheduling Copymasters
Unit 3 Resource Book
  Absent Student Copymasters, p. 104

Audiovisual

OHT 18, 19, 20, 20A, 21, 21A, 24
  (Quick Start)
Canciones CD

Technology

Online Workbook, U3E2
Take-Home Tutor CD-ROM, U3E2

Quick Start Review

♻ **Holidays and celebrations**

Use OHT 24 or write on the board:
Haz una lista de al menos 10
palabras o expresiones que tengan
relación con días feriados y las
celebraciones.

Answers
Answers will vary. Answers could include:
brindar, celebrar, el aniversario, la música,
el cumpleaños, el pastel, las velas, ¡Salud!,
bailar, cantar, los adornos, divertirse

Teaching Suggestions
Introducing Vocabulary

- Have students look at pp. 204–205.
  Use OHT 18 and 19 to present the
  vocabulary.
- Ask the Comprehension Questions
  on TE p. 205 in order of yes/no
  (questions 1–3), either/or (questions
  4–6), and simple word or phrase
  (questions 7–10). Expand by adding
  similar questions.
- Use the TPR activity to reinforce the
  meaning of individual words.

Descubre

Answers

1. c	2. d	3. f	4. a
5. e	6. g	7. b	

En contexto VOCABULARIO

¡Gánate una FIESTA continua!

De KQ 102 y Milton Canales,
el disc-jockey que conoce
tus gustos...

🔲 Descubre

Decide Usa tu intuición y lo que ya sabes
para unir cada palabra en azul con su
significado en la columna derecha.

1. La persona
   que da la fiesta
   es el **anfitrión**
   o la **anfitriona**.
2. La **radioemisora**
   patrocina eventos
   como concursos
   de baile.
3. La **pareja**
   participa en
   el concurso
   de baile.
4. Los amigos se
   juntan para
   festejar.
5. A las doce, la
   campana toca doce
   veces. Cada vez es
   una **campanada**.
6. Los **cohetes** hacen
   mucho **ruido**.
7. Ver los fuegos
   artificiales es una
   experiencia
   inolvidable.

a. to celebrate
b. unforgettable
c. host, hostess
d. radio station
   sponsors
e. bells, tolling
   of the bell
f. couple
g. firecrackers,
   noise

¿Cómo vas a recibir el **Año Nuevo** en San Juan?
KQ **102** quiere ser tu anfitrión. Por ese motivo, ¡KQ **102**
va a patrocinar un concurso de baile! La pareja que gane
el concurso va a festejar la despedida del año en una fiesta
continua por todo San Juan. ¡Van a pasarlo muy bien!

Premios para
la pareja ganadora...

Como huéspedes del Hotel Caribe,
la pareja primero va a disfrutar de
una cena fabulosa con todas las
comidas típicas de Puerto Rico:
lechón asado, arroz con gandules y
pasteles. ¡Buen provecho!

La noche sigue con una
gala en el Hotel Caribe,
donde van a oír la música de
la gran **orquesta** de Gilberto
Santa Rosa. Algunos de los
mejores **músicos** de todo San
Juan tocan en esta orquesta
formidable.

204 doscientos cuatro
Unidad 3

Classroom Community

TPR Have students act out and make comments
about the vocabulary words. Other students guess the
words. For example: the student mimes eating and
says, **Mmm... los puertorriqueños comen esto
durante los días festivos.** The answer would be
comida típica.

Paired Activity Working in pairs, have students
plan what they would consider the perfect New Year's
Eve celebration. Then have pairs present their plans to
the class.

Radioemisora KQ102

¡Donde se oye salsa todo el día!

Lo último   octubre   42

Después una limosina los llevará a El Morro, donde verán un *show* espectacular de **fuegos artificiales**. ¡Qué **ruido** hacen los **cohetes**! Y la gente también, por supuesto.

A la medianoche la pareja se encontrará en el Viejo San Juan. Allí se comerán las doce uvas tradicionales: tienen que comérselas una por una sincronizadas con las **campanadas** de la Catedral. No se olviden de brindar por un ¡**Próspero Año Nuevo**!

En la **madrugada**, la pareja irá a la playa del Condado para ver el espectáculo que es el **amanecer** puertorriqueño.

¡Anímate! ¡Participa en el concurso de baile!

Gánate una despedida de año **inolvidable** cortesía de tu estación favorita, KQ102.

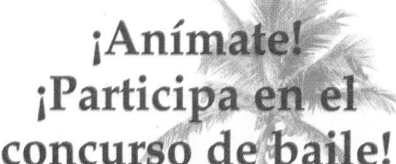

Online Workbook
CLASSZONE.COM

¿Comprendiste?

1. ¿Celebras el Año Nuevo? ¿Cómo? ¿Con quiénes?
2. ¿Hay fuegos artificiales en tu ciudad para el Año Nuevo? ¿Vas a verlos o los ves por la televisión?
3. ¿Te quedas despierto(a) hasta que cambia el año? ¿Por qué?
4. ¿Tienes tradiciones personales para el Año Nuevo? ¿Cuáles son?

doscientos cinco
El Caribe Etapa 2   205

Comprehension Questions

1. ¿El disc-jockey se llama Manuel Costa? (No.)
2. ¿Van a recibir el Año Nuevo en San Juan? (Sí.)
3. ¿KQ102 quiere ser el anfitrión? (Sí.)
4. ¿KQ102 va a patrocinar un concurso de música o un concurso de baile? (un concurso de baile)
5. ¿Los ganadores van a comer hamburguesas o lechón asado? (lechón asado)
6. ¿La noche empieza con una gala o un concierto? (una gala)
7. ¿Quiénes tocan en la orquesta de Gilberto Santa Rosa? (algunos de los mejores músicos de todo San Juan)
8. ¿De qué es el *show*? (de fuegos artificiales)
9. ¿De dónde vienen las campanadas? (de la Catedral)
10. ¿Cuándo irá la pareja a la playa del Condado? (en la madrugada)

Culture Highlights

● **EL CONDADO** El área del Condado está al este de San Juan en la costa norte entre el Océano Atlántico y la Laguna del Condado. Es un área de playas, hoteles, condominios, tiendas, restaurantes y discotecas.

● **LAS DOCE UVAS** La costumbre de comer una uva para cada campanada del reloj a la medianoche en la víspera de Año Nuevo es muy común en países de habla hispana. Se supone que una persona haga un deseo antes de comenzar a hacerlo. Si termina las doce uvas antes de que suene la última campanada, el deseo se hará realidad.

Block Schedule

Change of Pace Have students work in pairs to create their own holiday. Students write a short description of the new holiday (activities, food, etc.) and create an invitation to invite other students to take part in it. For example, the holiday might be **El Día del Alumno(a)**. (For additional activities, see **Block Scheduling Copymasters**.)

Teaching All Students

Extra Help Have students sort and organize the vocabulary under the following headings: **sustantivos, verbos, adjetivos, otros**.

Native Speakers Ask students to present a detailed description of a New Year's Eve celebration in their country of origin. As the students talk, put key words on the board for the rest of the class to add to a supplementary vocabulary list.

Multiple Intelligences

Visual Have students create an ad for a New Year's Eve Party. You may want to have some students focus on a party for young people and the others focus on a party for adults.

Musical/Rhythmic Play Auld Lang Syne for students. Ask them if they think this song would be played in Puerto Rico. Why or why not?

Teaching Resource Options

Print

Block Scheduling Copymasters
Unit 3 Resource Book
  Absent Student Copymasters, p. 105
  Audioscript, p. 112

Audiovisual

OHT 22, 23, 25 (Quick Start)
Audio Program CD 8, Track 1

Technology

Take-Home Tutor CD-ROM, U3E2

Quick Start Review

♻ Vocabulary review

Use OHT 25 or write on the board:
Complete the following with appropriate
vocabulary words:

¿Cómo vas a recibir el ___ ___ ?
KQ102 quiere ser tu ___ y va a ___
un ___ de baile. La ___ que gane el
concurso va a ___ ___ ___ del año
en una fiesta continua.

Answers
Año Nuevo / anfitrión / patrocinar / concurso /
pareja / festejar la despedida

Teaching Suggestions
Presenting Situations

• Present the Listening Strategy, p. 206,
  and discuss the Pre-listening questions.
• Use OHT 22 and 23 to present the
  Leer section. Ask simple yes/no,
  either/or, or short-answer questions.
• Use Audio CD 8 and have students
  do the **Escuchar** section (see Script
  p. 201B). Then have students
  complete the Listening Strategy
  exercise.
• Have students work in groups to
  complete the **Hablar** section.
• Have students complete the Listening
  Strategy activity.

AUDIO

En vivo
SITUACIONES

PARA ESCUCHAR
STRATEGY: LISTENING

Pre-listening Do you listen to or watch talk-
show interviews? How does the host move the
conversation along and keep it interesting?
What kinds of questions does he/she ask?

Observe interview techniques As you listen to the
winners' responses, notice the kinds of questions
Milton Canales asks. Check the frequency with
which he uses these question types:

Tipo de pregunta	Muchas veces	A veces	Casi veces	nunca
sí/no				
dos respuestas				
respuesta corta				
varias respuestas				

Which one elicits the most interesting
information?

RESTAURANTE EL COQUÍ

¡GRACIAS POR SU VISITA!

206   doscientos seis
Unidad 3

¡Próspero Año Nuevo!
Estás en casa y ves un anuncio en el periódico
sobre el concurso de salsa y la pareja ganadora.
Luego, escuchas una entrevista entre ellos y el
disc jockey de KQ102, Milton Canales.

① Leer
Lee el anuncio de KQ102 en el periódico.

*LA PAREJA GANADORA
DEL CONCURSO DE
SALSA DE*

EMILIA RUEDAS
Y
ALEX ORTIZ

¿Cómo pasaron la despedida
de año Emilia y Alex?

*Si quieres saber, pon la radio en tu estación
favorita,* KQ102 *a las doce en punto. Milton
Canales va a entrevistar a la pareja ganadora.*

Classroom Community

Group Activity Working in small groups, have
students create a list of 10 New Year's resolutions that
high school students might make. Then have them rank
them in order of importance and present their top 10
list to the class, beginning with the least important.

Game Have each student write either a true or a false
statement about the interview. Then divide the class in
half and have them face each other. In turn, each team
tries to trick the other. The team guessing **cierto** or
falso correctly gets 1 point. If they can correct a false
statement, they get a bonus point. When all students
have read statements, the team with the most points
wins.

EL MORRO

② Escuchar

Milton Canales, el disc-jockey de KQ102, habla con Emilia Ruedas y Alex Ortiz, la pareja ganadora del concurso de salsa. Escucha y escoge la respuesta correcta.

1. La despedida de año
   a. Lo pasaron muy bien.
   b. Fue una despedida de año horrible para la pareja.
2. La orquesta de Gilberto Santa Rosa
   a. Alex cree que Gilberto Santa Rosa no es buen músico.
   b. Alex cree que Gilberto Santa Rosa es excelente.
3. La cena
   a. La pareja comió muy bien.
   b. La pareja no disfrutó de la cena.
4. Los fuegos artificiales
   a. Emilia dice que El Morro no es un buen sitio para ver los fuegos artificiales.
   b. Emilia dice que no hay otro lugar como el Morro para ver los fuegos artificiales.
5. Las campanadas
   a. Se pudieron comer las uvas a tiempo con cada campanada.
   b. No pudieron comerse las uvas a tiempo con cada campanada.
6. El amanecer
   a. La pareja cree que el amanecer en la playa Condado es ordinario.
   b. La pareja cree que el amanecer en la playa Condado es inolvidable.

③ Hablar

En grupos de dos o tres, conversen sobre la despedida de año ideal. ¿Qué harían? ¿Adónde irían? ¿Dónde cenarían? ¿Les gustaría pasar la despedida de año en Puerto Rico? Comparen las celebraciones en Estados Unidos con la celebración de la pareja ganadora en San Juan, Puerto Rico.

doscientos siete
El Caribe Etapa 2 207

gilberto santa rosa
...de corazón

Answers
1. a 2. b 3. a 4. b 5. a 6. b

Hablar

Answers will vary.

🔔 Quick Wrap-up

Ask students to create a caption for each photo/image on pp. 206–207: **Inventen un subtítulo para cada foto de las páginas 206–207.**

Critical Thinking

Ask students if celebrating on New Year's Eve is important to them and why. What feelings do they associate with New Year's Eve? Why do people feel it is important to make resolutions?

❄ Culture Highlights

● **EL MORRO** El Castillo San Felipe del Morro, conocido como El Morro, es una de las vistas más impresionantes de San Juan. El Castillo en realidad fue utilizado como un fuerte para combatir a los piratas e invasores que querían dominar la ciudad de San Juan. El Morro, que tomó alrededor de 70 años para construirse, está a 140 pies de altura sobre el mar y tiene una vista completa de la Bahía de San Juan. Hoy en día, los visitantes al Morro pueden ver los cañones y armas que utilizaron los españoles para defenderse, además de disfrutar de una vista magnífica.

▦ Block Schedule

Peer Review In small groups, students take turns describing a special holiday/celebration, but they don't say what it is. In the description, they must include the following: where they were, who was with them, what they did to celebrate. The other members of the group try to guess the holiday. (For additional activities, see **Block Scheduling Copymasters**.)

Teaching All Students

Extra Help After listening to the **Escuchar** interview, have students retell it in their own words, using gestures and voice inflection.

Multiple Intelligences

Naturalist Have students list other costumes they would have seen at the **bosque tropical** party. What animals and plants live in El Yunque?

Interpersonal Have pairs of students talk about their most memorable New Year's celebrations. How were the two experiences similar? How were they different?

CD-ROM Take-Home Tutor

Teaching Resource Options

Print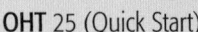

Block Scheduling Copymasters
Unit 3 Resource Book
  Absent Student Copymasters, p. 106

Audiovisual

OHT 25 (Quick Start)

Quick Start Review

♻ Vocabulary review

Use OHT 25 or write on the board:
Match the following words with their
definitions/synonyms:

1. la anfitriona
2. pasar muy bien
3. los músicos
4. la madrugada
5. la campanada
  a. divertirse
  b. una cosa que oyes
  c. muy temprano por la mañana
  d. la persona que da la fiesta
  e. las personas que tocan
    instrumentos

Answers
1. d   2. a   3. e   4. c   5. b

Teaching Suggestions
Comprehension Check

Use **Actividades 1–4** to assess retention
after the **Vocabulario** and **Situaciones**.
Before doing **Actividad 1**, have
students work in pairs. Each student
picks out a few new vocabulary words
that are used and asks his/her partner
what they mean. Then have the pairs
complete the activity.

 Objective: Controlled practice
Vocabulary

Answers
1. invitado
2. anfitrión
3. anfitrión
4. anfitrión o invitado
5. invitado
6. anfitrión
7. anfitrión
8. anfitrión o invitado
9. anfitrión o invitado
10. invitado

En acción

PARTE A

Práctica del vocabulario

Objectives for Activities 1-4
• Talk about holidays

❶ ¿Quién habla?

Hablar/*Escribir* Lee las
oraciones. ¿Quién habla: el
anfitrión de una celebración,
un invitado o cualquiera de
los dos?

modelo

*Bienvenidos, pasen, pasen. Denme
sus abrigos.*

el anfitrión

1. Su casa es bella, señora
  Ruiz.
2. Gracias por venir a festejar
  con nosotros.
3. Un brindis para nuestros
  invitados de honor.
4. La orquesta es buenísima,
  ¿no crees?
5. Le traje un regalito. Espero
  que le gusten las rosas.
6. ¡Buen provecho! Ojalá que
  les guste el lechón asado.
7. ¿Vinieron en auto?
8. Es medianoche. ¡Próspero
  Año Nuevo!
9. ¡Vamos a bailar!
10. Lo pasamos muy bien.
   Gracias por invitarnos.

❷ ¿Cuál es?

Hablar/*Escribir* Léele una oración a tu compañero(a).
Él (Ella) te va a decir qué dibujo describes. Luego,
cambien de papel.

modelo

Tú: *Dicen que ese cantante es increíble.*

Compañero(a): *Estás describiendo el dibujo* **e.**

a.    b.

c.    d.

e.    f.

1. La gente lo está pasando muy bien en la gala.
2. ¡Próspero Año Nuevo!
3. ¡Mira los fuegos artificiales! ¡Qué bonitos!
4. Es la madrugada. ¡No hay nada como el amanecer!
5. Es la orquesta más famosa de San Juan.

208   doscientos ocho
Unidad 3

Classroom Management

Time Saver Do **Actividades 1** and **2** with the whole
class, calling on volunteers to read the items and
answer them. **Actividad 3** can also be done with the
whole class, by calling on 2 volunteers to complete
each item.

Peer Review Have students work in pairs to review
the story line of the **Vocabulario** and the **Situaciones**.
In turn, each student supplies a sentence describing
what took place in correct chronological order.

3 No hay de qué

Hablar/Escribir Habla con tu compañero(a) sobre el año nuevo.

modelo

el Año Nuevo

Tú: *Gracias por venir a celebrar el Año Nuevo con nosotros.*

Compañero(a): *No hay de qué, es un placer para mí.*

Tú: *Espero que lo pases muy bien.*

1. orquesta
2. músico
3. festejar
4. fuegos artificiales
5. pasteles
6. fiesta continua

Vocabulario

Dar las gracias

Muy amable. *That's kind of you.*
No hay de qué. *It's nothing.*

♻ Ya sabes

De nada.
Es un placer…
Gracias.
Mil gracias.
Se lo agradezco.

▶ ¿Cuándo usas estas frases?

4 ¡Bienvenidos!

STRATEGY: SPEAKING

Socialize as host or guest As the host at your own party, you will want to suggest choices of food, drink, or entertainment. **(Tú podrás…, Recomiendo…, Sugiero…, ¿Te gustaría…?, Sería buena idea…, Quizás…)** As a guest you will want to accept or decline by expressing your own preferences. **(Prefiero…, Es posible…, Me gustaría…, Quisiera…, Se puede…)**

Hablar/Escribir Tú eres el (la) anfitrión(a) de una gala para celebrar el Año Nuevo. Con dos o tres compañeros, dramaticen esta situación.

modelo

Tú: *Pasen, pasen. Bienvenidos a mi casa.*

Compañero(a): *Gracias, muy amable.*

Tú: *Hay mucho que hacer. Si tienen ganas de bailar…*

Compañero(a): …

Teaching All Students

Extra Help Ask students to sketch and label the various activities in which the contest winners participated. Then have them briefly describe their sketches to a partner.

Multiple Intelligences

Kinesthetic Discuss what kinds of gestures and facial expressions would be used to do **Actividades 3** and **4.** Ask students to use these gestures and expressions while doing the activities, then report on how they aided their communication.

 2 Objective: Transitional practice
Vocabulary in conversation

Answers
1. dibujo d
2. dibujo c
3. dibujo b
4. dibujo f
5. dibujo a

Teaching Suggestions
Teaching Vocabulary

Have students brainstorm a list of occasions when they would use the expressions for giving thanks. Then have them work in pairs to act out brief skits in which one partner does something and the other thanks him/her.

 3 Objective: Open-ended practice
Vocabulary in conversation

Answers will vary.

4 Objective: Open-ended practice
Vocabulary in conversation

Answers will vary.

🔲 Block Schedule

Variety Have students design and write thank you notes to a friend or relative for something that person did or a gift he/she gave (situations may be real or imaginary). Students should be sure to use expressions from the **Vocabulario** on p. 209. (For additional activities, see **Block Scheduling Copymasters**.)

Teaching Resource Options

Print

Más práctica Workbook PE, p. 77
Cuaderno para hispanohablantes
  PE, p. 75
Block Scheduling Copymasters
Unit 3 Resource Book
  Más práctica Workbook TE, p. 77
  Cuaderno para hispanohablantes
    TE, p. 93
  Absent Student Copymasters, p. 106
  Audioscript, p. 112

Audiovisual

OHT 26 (Quick Start), 29 (Grammar)
Audio Program CD 8, Track 2, Activity 6

Technology

Online Workbook, U3E2
Take-Home Tutor CD-ROM, U3E2

Quick Start Review

♻ **Subjunctive review**

Use OHT 26 or write on the board:
Write complete sentences using the
following elements:

1. yo insisto en que / tú /
   acompañarme / fiesta
2. ellos ruegan que / nosotros / ir /
   celebración
3. nosotros / ir a tener fuegos
   artificiales / a menos que / llover
4. ellas / hacer un gran esfuerzo /
   para que / yo / pasarlo bien
5. por favor / deje que / Alicia y
   Tomás / participar en / concurso

Answers

1. Yo insisto en que tú me acompañes a la
   fiesta.
2. Ellos ruegan que nosotros vayamos a la
   celebración.
3. Nosotros vamos a tener fuegos artificiales a
   menos que llueva.
4. Ellas hacen un gran esfuerzo para que yo lo
   pase bien.
5. Por favor, deje que Alicia y Tomás
   participen en el concurso.

Objectives for Activities 5–15
• Express doubt and disagree • Hypothesize • Describe ideals

GRAMÁTICA — Subjunctive with Nonexistent and Indefinite

▶ If you want to say that something **may not exist,** you use
the subjunctive.

may not exist

No hay orquesta que me **guste.**
There is no orchestra that I like.

may not exist

No conozco a nadie que lo **pase** bien.
I don't know anyone who is having a good time.

> The **thing**
> or **person** probably
> doesn't exist: *there is
> **no** orchestra…*

▶ **Expressions** that trigger this use of the subjunctive include:

No hay… que
No hay nadie que…
No hay nada que…
No hay ningún/ninguna… que…

▶ A related way to use the subjunctive is in
subordinate clauses that are **indefinite**
or **uncertain:**

> **Uncertain:**
> we don't know if
> these musicians exist
> or not.

subordinate clause

Buscamos músicos que **sepan** tocar música bailable.
*We're looking for musicians who **know how** to
play dance music.*

▶ **Words** and **expressions** that trigger this
use of the subjunctive include:

Buscar/Querer/Necesitar… que
¿Hay algo/alguien que… ?
¿Conoces a alguien que… ?
¿Tienes algo que… ?

Practice: Actividades ⑤⑥⑦ | **Más práctica** *cuaderno p. 77*
Para hispanohablantes *cuaderno p. 75* | **Online Workbook** CLASSZONE.COM

---

⑤ En la comunidad ♻

Escribir Quieres saber quién
participa en actividades para
la comunidad. Escribe diez
preguntas que puedes hacerle
a tu clase.

modelo

*participar en la campaña para
embellecer la ciudad*

*¿Hay alguien que participe en la
campaña para embellecer la ciudad?*

> **Nota: Gramática**
>
> Remember that **sembrar** is an
> **e→ie** stem-changing verb.
> **Recoger** and **educar** have
> spelling changes in most of their
> subjunctive forms; **g→j** and
> **c→qu** respectively.

1. trabajar de voluntario(a)
   en un comedor de
   beneficencia
2. juntar fondos para la
   comunidad
3. estar en contra de los
   servicios sociales
4. donar ropa a la gente
   sin hogar
5. sembrar árboles en
   la comunidad
6. recoger basura en
   el vecindario
7. pasar tiempo con ancianos
8. educar al público sobre los
   problemas sociales
9. querer colaborar con
   alimentos
10. conocer un centro de
    reciclaje

Classroom Community

Paired Activity Have students work in pairs to find
people in class that do the things listed below. Students
write the name of the person down. If there isn't
anyone, they write **No hay nadie que…**

Buscamos una persona que… (1) preste servicios a
la comunidad, (2) ayude a otros en la clase (3) estudie
mucho, (4) tenga un hermano, (5) sea miembro de
un equipo de deporte, (6) hable bien el español.

Cooperative Learning Divide the class into groups
of 4. Student 1 chooses a situation. Student 2 chooses
an expression or question from the **Gramática** box.
Student 3 completes the phrase or question. Student 4
records the sentence. Students repeat the round,
changing roles, until all expressions and questions have
been used.

6 ¿Existe o no?

Escuchar/*Escribir* Copia la siguiente tabla y escucha las oraciones de varias personas. Si la persona o cosa indicada existe en la vida de la persona que habla, marca **sí**. Si en este momento esa cosa o persona no existe, marca **no**.

modelo

alguien que sabe reparar computadoras	Sí	No
	x	

¿Existe…?	Sí	No
1. un señor que habla francés		
2. alguien que puede tocar la guitarra		
3. una orquesta que no cuesta mucho		
4. un músico que canta muy bien		
5. un apartamento que tiene jardín		
6. unos estudiantes que pueden trabajar los fines de semana		
7. unos amigos que saben bailar salsa		
8. una radio que funciona		

7 ¿Conoces a alguien…?

Hablar/*Escribir* Pregunta a tu compañero(a) si él (ella) conoce a varias personas que puedan hacer las cosas indicadas. Luego, cambien de papel.

modelo

Tú: *¿Conoces a alguien que celebre el Año Nuevo con sus padres?*

Compañero(a): *Sí, conozco a alguien que celebra el año nuevo con sus padres. o No, no conozco a nadie que celebre el año nuevo con sus padres.*

> bailar muy bien
> tocar en una orquesta
> ser músico
> saber preparar comida puertorriqueña
> tener una limosina
> querer comprar un vestido muy elegante
> dar clases de salsa

Nota cultural

Salsa En Puerto Rico, la música **salsa** tiene muchos entusiastas y grandes exponentes como Tito Puente y Willie Colón. A través de toda la isla, hay salones de baile donde los **salseros** (los entusiastas de la salsa) pueden bailar y divertirse.

doscientos once
El Caribe Etapa 2

211

Teaching Suggestions
Presenting Subjunctive with Nonexistent and Indefinite

Point out that the existence or non-existence of the noun for the subject of the sentence is what determines the indicative or the subjunctive. For example: **Compré una casa que tiene cinco cuartos.** vs. **Quiero una casa que tenga cinco cuartos.** The house is likely to exist, but it has not been experienced by the subject.

ACTIVIDAD 5 Objective: Controlled practice Subjunctive with nonexistent and indefinite in writing

♻ **Community service vocabulary**

Answers
1. ¿Hay alguien que trabaje de voluntario(a) en un comedor de beneficencia? 2. ¿Hay alguien que junte fondos para la comunidad? 3. ¿Hay alguien que esté en contra de los servicios sociales? 4. ¿Hay alguien que done su ropa a la gente sin hogar? 5. ¿Hay alguien que siembre árboles en la comunidad? 6. ¿Hay alguien que recoja basura en el vecindario? 7. ¿Hay alguien que pase tiempo con ancianos? 8. ¿Hay alguien que eduque al público sobre los problemas sociales? 9. ¿Hay alguien que quiera colaborar con alimentos? 10. ¿Hay alguien que conozca un centro de reciclaje?

ACTIVIDAD 6 Objective: Transitional practice Listening comprehension/subjunctive with nonexistent and indefinite

Answers (See script, p. 201B.)
1. sí	3. no	5. no	7. sí
2. no	4. sí	6. no	8. no

ACTIVIDAD 7 Objective: Open-ended practice Subjunctive with nonexistent and indefinite in conversation

Answers
Answers will vary. The following are possible questions:
¿Conoces a alguien que baile muy bien?
¿Conoces a alguien que toque en una orquesta?

Block Schedule

Change of Pace Have students imagine that they are the manager of a company that needs to hire several employees. Ask them to create a list of 5 qualities they are looking for in potential employees and use this information in a want ad that includes **Buscamos un empleado que...** (For additional activities, see **Block Scheduling Copymasters.**)

Teaching All Students

Extra Help Have students answer any 4 of the questions formed in **Actividad 5**. Write selected ones on the board for the class to evaluate and correct if necessary.

Multiple Intelligences
Verbal As a class, extend **Actividad 7** with more activities (**cantar con una orquesta, bailar salsa, esquiar,** etc.). Then ask various students the questions.

Musical/Rhythmic After reading the **Nota cultural** on p. 211, play a song by Tito Puente or Willie Colón. Ask students how the music makes them feel. Does it give them energy or relax them?

Teaching Resource Options

Print 📖

Más práctica Workbook PE, p. 78
Cuaderno para hispanohablantes
PE, p. 76
Block Scheduling Copymasters
Unit 3 Resource Book
Más práctica Workbook TE, p. 78
Cuaderno para hispanohablantes
TE, p. 94
Information Gap Activities, p. 99
Absent Student Copymasters, p. 107

Audiovisual 📺

OHT 25 (Quick Start), 30 (Grammar)

Technology 💻

Online Workbook, U3E2
Take-Home Tutor CD-ROM, U3E2

Quick Start Review

♻ Subjunctive with indefinite
Use OHT 25 or write on the board:
Answer the questions negatively:

1. ¿Hay algo que pueda comprarte?
2. ¿Hay alguien que toque la guitarra?
3. ¿Conoces a un(a) joven que hable 5 idiomas?
4. ¿Existe un(a) estudiante en esta escuela que sepa bailar salsa?

Answers *See p. 201B.*

Teaching Suggestions
Reviewing The Subjunctive for Disagreement and Denial

- Remind students that the indicative is used with expressions of certainty.
- Point out that **no dudar** doesn't require the subjunctive because the **no** negates the meaning of doubt.

Objective: Controlled practice
Subjunctive for disagreement and denial

Answers

1. A: Yo creo que mis papás van a festejar... / B: Dudo que tus papás festejen... 2. A: Yo creo que lo vamos a pasar muy bien... / B: Dudo que lo pasemos muy bien... 3. A: Yo creo que Andrés va a ponerse... / B: Dudo que Andrés se ponga... 4. A: Yo creo que la orquesta va a ser... / B: Dudo que la orquesta sea... 5. A: Yo creo que los fuegos artificiales van a ser... / B: Dudo que los fuegos artificiales sean... 6. A: Yo creo que la fiesta se va a acabar... / B: Dudo que la fiesta se acabe...

Práctica: gramática y vocabulario *continuación*

REPASO   The Subjunctive for Disagreement and Denial

▶ Another way to use the **subjunctive forms** you have already learned isto express **doubt** or **disagreement**. You already know many ways to express doubt or to disagree with someone.

Jorge: ¿Sabes si Mamá invitó a doña Laura?
Do you know if Mom invited doña Laura?

Rosanna: Yo creo que sí, pero **es improbable que** venga. Está enferma.
*I think so, but **it's unlikely that** she **will come**. She's sick.*

Vocabulario

♻ **Ya sabes**

Dudar que...	No es seguro que...
Es imposible que...	No es verdad que...
Es improbable que...	no estar seguro (de) que...
no creer/no pensar (e→ie)	no opinar que...
No es cierto que...	

Practice: Actividades 8 9 10 11

Más práctica *cuaderno* p. 78
Para hispanohablantes *cuaderno* p.76

🖥 **Online Workbook** CLASSZONE.COM

8 Las dudas de Enrique

Hablar/*Escribir* Enrique, tu mejor amigo, siempre duda de lo que dices. ¿Qué le dices y cómo te responde?

> **modelo**
> **los García:** *dar una gala*
> **Tú:** *Yo creo que los García van a dar una gala.*
> **Enrique:** *Dudo que los García den una gala.*

1. mis papás: festejar hasta la madrugada
2. nosotros: pasarlo muy bien en esa fiesta
3. Andrés: ponerse un traje
4. la orquesta: ser muy buena
5. los fuegos artificiales: ser magníficos
6. la fiesta: acabarse a la medianoche

Nota cultural

En Puerto Rico se celebran muchos días festivos. Por ser un Estado Libre Asociado, muchos de esos días son los mismos que se celebran en Estados Unidos, como el Día de la Independencia de Estados Unidos (4 de julio) y el Día del Trabajo (primer lunes de septiembre). Además se celebran fiestas nacionales como el Descubrimiento de Puerto Rico (19 de noviembre), el Día de la Abolición de la Esclavitud (22 de marzo), y el nacimiento de héroes de la independencia puertorriqueña, como Eugenio María de Hostos (10 de enero), y de poetas, como Luis Muñoz Rivera (18 de julio).

212 doscientos doce
Unidad 3

Classroom Community

Paired Activity Working in pairs, have students use expressions of doubt and certainty to write down 10 statements about what beings on another planet might be like. For example: **Creemos que en el Planeta X los niños conducen carros. Dudamos que la gente tenga solamente dos brazos.** Students should accompany their statements with a drawing. Pairs then present their information to the class.

Portfolio Ask students to think about their next birthday and write at least 8 sentences expressing doubt about what will or won't happen.

Rubric A = 13–15 pts. B = 10–12 pts. C = 7–9 pts. D = 4–6 pts. F = < 4 pts.

Writing criteria	Scale
Correct use of subjunctive	1 2 3 4 5
Vocabulary use	1 2 3 4 5
Creativity	1 2 3 4 5

9 No estoy seguro(a)

Hablar/Escribir Tú y tu amigo(a) comentan sobre una fiesta, pero él (ella) no está seguro(a) de lo que tú dices. Dramaticen la situación.

modelo

Tú: *La música es divertida.*

Compañero(a): *No estoy seguro(a) de que la música sea divertida.*

1. Los invitados se divierten.
2. La anfitriona cocina muy bien.
3. La orquesta toca toda la noche.
4. Los fuegos artificiales hacen mucho ruido.
5. Oímos las campanadas de la catedral a la medianoche.
6. ¿...?

10 ¡Es imposible!

Hablar/Escribir Le sugieres ideas a tu padre para celebrar el Año Nuevo. ¿Cómo te responde?

modelo

Tú: *Papá, ¿por qué no damos una gala para despedir el año?*

Papá: *¡Es imposible que demos una gala!*

1. invitar	6. comprar
2. cocinar	7. festejar
3. buscar	8. ir
4. celebrar	9. brindar
5. aprender	10. llamar

11 Los días festivos

Hablar/Escribir Usa palabras de la lista y comenta sobre cómo van a celebrar los días festivos.

modelo

la Navidad

Dudo que celebremos la Navidad en casa de mis tíos.

1. el Día de Acción de Gracias
2. el Día del Trabajo
3. el Día de las Madres o de los Padres
4. el Día de la Amistad
5. el Día de la Raza
6. el Día de la Independencia

no pensar	no es seguro
no es cierto	es improbable
no creer	dudar

Vocabulario

Los días festivos

el Día de Acción de Gracias *Thanksgiving*

el Día de la Amistad *Valentine's Day*

el Día de la Independencia *Independence Day*

el Día de las Madres / los Padres *Mother's / Father's Day*

el Día de la Raza *Columbus Day*

Hanuka *Hanukkah*

la Navidad *Christmas*

las Pascuas *Easter*

la quinceañera *fifteenth birthday*

▶ ¿Cómo celebras estos días festivos en casa?

More Practice: **Más comunicación** *p. R10*

doscientos trece
El Caribe Etapa 2 **213**

ACTIVIDAD
9 **Objective:** Transitional practice Subjunctive for disagreement and denial in conversation

Answers
1. No estoy seguro(a) de que los invitados se diviertan.
2. No estoy seguro(a) de que la anfitriona cocine muy bien.
3. No estoy seguro(a) de que la orquesta toque toda la noche.
4. No estoy seguro(a) de que los fuegos artificiales hagan mucho ruido.
5. No estoy seguro(a) de que oigamos las campanadas de la catedral a la medianoche.
6. *Answers will vary.*

ACTIVIDAD
10 **Objective:** Open-ended practice Subjunctive for disagreement and denial/vocabulary in conversation

Answers
Answers will vary. Answers could include:
1. ¡Es imposible que invitemos a tantas personas!
2. ¡... cocinemos lechón asado y pasteles!
3. ¡... busquemos una orquesta!
4. ¡... celebremos hasta la madrugada!
5. ¡... aprendamos a bailar salsa en tan poco tiempo!
6. ¡... compremos cohetes!
7. ¡... festejemos por tres días!
8. ¡... vayamos a Puerto Rico!
9. ¡... brindemos con leche!
10. ¡... llamemos a un mago!

Teaching Suggestions
Teaching Vocabulary

Create a calendar time line on the board and have students write where each holiday falls. Also add students' birthdays and any other holidays they might want to add.

ACTIVIDAD
11 **Objective:** Open-ended practice Subjunctive for disagreement and denial in conversation

Answers will vary.

Block Schedule

FunBreak Have students create a logo for each holiday listed in the **Vocabulario** on p. 213 and label it. Have them also create one for their birthday. (For additional activities, see **Block Scheduling Copymasters.**)

Vocabulary/Grammar • UNIDAD 3 Etapa 2 **213**

Teaching All Students

Extra Help Ask students to create sentences beginning with the following expressions: **No pienso que, No es cierto que, Es improbable que, Dudamos que, Creen que.** Put selected sentences on the board for the class to evaluate.

Native Speakers Have students present a brief report on how one of the holidays is celebrated in their country of origin.

Multiple Intelligences

Verbal State one of the expressions of doubt in the **Vocabulario** on p. 212. Point to a student and have him/her finish the sentence using the present subjunctive. That student says another expression and points to another student, and so on.

Visual Have students look at pictures in magazines and form sentences of doubt about what they see. Be creative.

Teaching Resource Options

Print

Más práctica Workbook PE, pp. 79–80
Cuaderno para hispanohablantes
  PE, pp. 77–78
Block Scheduling Copymasters
Unit 3 Resource Book
  Más práctica Workbook TE,
    pp. 79–80
  Cuaderno para hispanohablantes
    TE, pp. 95–96
  Absent Student Copymasters, p. 108
  Audioscript, p. 112

Audiovisual

OHT 27 (Quick Start), 31 (Grammar)
Audio Program CD 8, Track 3, Activity 13
Word Tiles, U3E2

Technology

Online Workbook, U3E2
Take-Home Tutor CD-ROM, U3E2

Quick Start Review

♻ Conditional

Use OHT 27 or write on the board:
Change the following to the conditional
form:

1. soy	5. pierdes
2. quiere	6. puedo
3. duermen	7. tienen
4. hacemos	8. decimos

Answers
1. sería 2. querría 3. dormirían 4. haríamos
5. perderías 6. podría 7. tendrían 8. diríamos

Teaching Suggestions
**Presenting Conditional
Sentences**

• Review formation of the conditional
  and imperfect subjunctive.
• You may want to point out that to
  make statements like *He talks as if he
  knew it all,* Spanish uses **como si**
  followed by the imperfect subjunctive.
  **Ella habla francés como si viviera en
  Francia.**

GRAMÁTICA   Conditional Sentences

▶ In Spanish, many sentences are composed of a si-clause *(if-clause)* and a main clause .

To predict a future result based on an initial action, use:
the present tense in the si-clause and the future in the main clause .

present tense	si-clause	main clause	future tense

Si **vienes,** lo **pasarás** bien.
*If you **come,** you **will have** a good time.*

▶ In order to say what things would be like if circumstances were different,
you use:
the imperfect subjunctive in the si-clause and the conditional in the main clause .

imperfect subjunctive	si-clause	main clause	conditional

Si **vinieras,** lo **pasarías** bien.
*If you **came (could come),** you **would have** a good time.*

▶ Compare these two sentences.

In the first example, your friend
might come to the party. So her
future *(having a good time)* will
happen based on her **initial action**
(coming to the party).

Si **vienes,** lo **pasarás** bien.
*If you **come, you will have** a good time.*

In the second, you know that your friend
is probably not coming to the party. If
circumstances were different, *(if she
came)* you want her to know **what it
would be like** *(she'd have a good time).*

Si **vinieras,** lo **pasarías** bien.
*If you **came, you would have** a good time.*

▶ In both of these cases, the order of the clauses can be switched.

Lo **pasarás** bien si **vienes.**   Lo **pasarías** bien si **vinieras.**

Practice: **Actividades**   **Más práctica** *cuaderno pp. 79–80*   🅘 **Online Workbook**
                 ⑫ ⑬ ⑭ ⑮   **Para hispanohablantes** *cuaderno pp. 77–78*   CLASSZONE.COM

Classroom Community

Learning Scenario In groups of 3, have students
discuss 10 things they would do if they won one million
dollars in the lottery: **Si ganara un millón de dólares,
yo...**

Paired Activity Have students work in pairs and
ask each other questions using the following phrases:
**Si te ofrecieran dinero..., Si te pidieran prestado...,
Si te ofrecieran.., Si tuvieras la oportunidad de...**
Have students present one of their partner's answers to
the class.

12 Los sueños

Hablar/Escribir Todos tenemos sueños de qué haríamos bajo ciertas condiciones. ¿Qué dicen las siguientes personas?

modelo

hablar francés (viajar a Francia)

Si hablara francés, viajaría a Francia.

1. ser actor o actriz (irse para Los Ángeles)
2. estar en la universidad (estudiar informática)
3. trabajar (guardar mi dinero)
4. tener mucho dinero (no trabajar)
5. poder hacerlo todo (conocer a Europa)
6. manejar (comprar un carro deportivo)
7. vivir en Puerto Rico (vivir en San Juan)
8. saber tocar un instrumento (tocar en una orquesta)

Nota cultural

Chayanne Nacido en Río Piedras, Puerto Rico, este joven es uno de los cantantes más populares de Latinoamérica. Ganó un premio en el Festival de la Canción de Viña del Mar, en Chile, quizá el concurso más importante de música popular de Latinoamérica.

13 ¿Qué va a hacer?

Escuchar/Escribir Gustavo dice que va a hacer algunas cosas y también dice que haría otras cosas si pudiera. Di bajo qué condiciones haría esas cosas.

modelo

Comprar un traje.

a. Lo va a hacer.

ⓑ *Lo haría si* tuviera dinero .

1. Ir a una gala.
   a. Lo va a hacer.
   b. Lo haría si _____.
2. Preparar un lechón asado.
   a. Lo va a hacer.
   b. Lo haría si _____.
3. Empezar un grupo musical.
   a. Lo va a hacer.
   b. Lo haría si _____.
4. Participar en un concurso de baile.
   a. Lo va a hacer.
   b. Lo haría si _____.
5. Ir a ver los fuegos artificiales.
   a. Lo va a hacer.
   b. Lo haría si _____.
6. Ir a ver el amanecer en la playa.
   a. Lo va a hacer.
   b. Lo haría si _____.

Teaching All Students

Extra Help For **Actividad 13,** replay each sentence from the audio. Tell students to listen for the verb forms. Ask them to tell you what they heard. Discuss what tense the forms require.

Multiple Intelligences

Logical/Mathematical Have pairs of students create conditional sentences with the imperfect subjunctive, then give explanations modeled after the one in the grammar box.

Intrapersonal Have students complete the following with at least 5 sentences: **Si yo pudiera ser cualquier persona en el mundo, yo...**

Culture Highlights

● **CHAYANNE** Chayanne es el nombre de escenario de Elmer Figueroa Arce. Comenzó su carrera artística como roquero. Desde entonces ha expandido su repertorio para incluir baladas románticas. En 1998, protagonizó con Vanessa Williams en la película *Dance with Me.*

ACTIVIDAD 12 Objective: Controlled practice Conditional sentences

Answers

1. Si fuera actor (actriz), me iría para Los Ángeles.
2. Si estuviera en la universidad, estudiaría informática.
3. Si trabajara, guardaría mi dinero.
4. Si tuviera mucho dinero, no trabajaría.
5. Si pudiera hacerlo todo, conocería a Europa.
6. Si manejara, compraría un carro deportivo.
7. Si viviera en Puerto Rico, viviría en San Juan.
8. Si supiera tocar un instrumento, tocaría en una orquesta.

ACTIVIDAD 13 Objective: Transitional practice Listening comprehension/conditional sentences

Answers (See script, p. 201B.)

1. a.
2. b. supiera hacerlo
3. b. pudiera tocar un instrumento
4. b. hubiera un concurso de baile
5. a.
6. b. sus padres se lo permitieran

Dictation

Using the Listening Activity Script for **Actividad 13** on TE p. 201B, dictate selected sentences to students. You may want to have students peer correct the sentences.

Block Schedule

Change of Pace Have students complete one of the following with 6 different phrases. Encourage them to exaggerate: **Si yo fuera presidente de los Estados Unidos, yo..., Si yo pudiera cumplir todos mis sueños, yo..., Si yo participara en las Olimpiadas, yo...** (For additional activities, see **Block Scheduling Copymasters.**)

Teaching Resource Options

Print

Más práctica Workbook PE, pp. 73–76
Actividades para todos Workbook PE,
  pp. 81–86
Cuaderno para hispanohablantes
  PE, pp. 73–74
Block Scheduling Copymasters
Unit 3 Resource Book
  Más práctica Workbook TE,
  pp. 73–76
  Actividades para todos Workbook
  TE, pp. 81–86
  Cuaderno para hispanohablantes
  TE, pp. 91–92
  Information Gap Activities, p. 100
  Absent Student Copymasters, p. 108

Technology

Online Workbook, U3E2
Take-Home Tutor CD-ROM, U3E2

 Objective: Transitional practice
Conditional sentences in conversation
 Professions

Answers will vary.

 Objective: Open-ended practice
Conditional sentences in conversation

Answers will vary.

Quick Wrap-up

Go around the room asking students
for conditional sentences: **¿Qué harías
si tuvieras un millón de dólares?**
Encourage them to be humorous and
creative.

---

14 **Las profesiones**

Hablar/*Escribir* Tú y tu compañero(a)
conversan sobre sus planes para después de
la graduación. Di qué harían si estuvieran en
ciertas profesiones.

modelo

Compañero(a): *Si fuera músico(a), escribiría mis
propias canciones.*

Tú: *Si yo fuera músico(a), escribiría canciones
románticas.*

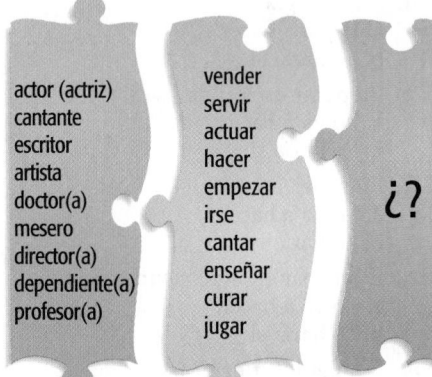

actor (actriz)	vender
cantante	servir
escritor	actuar
artista	hacer
doctor(a)	empezar
mesero	irse
director(a)	cantar
dependiente(a)	enseñar
profesor(a)	curar
	jugar

¿?

También se dice

Puerto Rico también se conoce por el nombre
Borinquen o Boriquén, el nombre taíno de la isla.
Los taínos vivían en la región al llegar los españoles.
Algunos puertorriqueños también usan la palabra
boricua para indicar que son de Puerto Rico.

---

15 **¿Qué harías?**

Hablar/*Escribir* En grupos de tres o cuatro,
conversen sobre qué harían en ciertos días
festivos.

modelo

Tú: *¿Qué harías si fuera la quinceañera
de tu prima?*

Amigo(a) 1: *Si fuera la quinceañera de
mi prima, iríamos a la casa
de mis abuelos.*

Amigo(a) 2: *Nosotros iríamos a una
gala en un hotel elegante.*

Amigo(a) 3: *Mi familia y yo
compraríamos regalos
como….*

1.    2.

3.    4.

5.    6.

7.    8.

216

doscientos dieciséis
Unidad 3

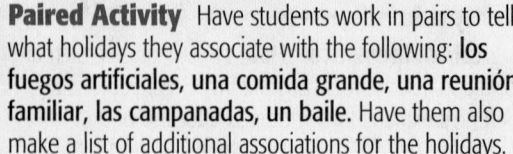

Classroom Community

Paired Activity Have students work in pairs to tell
what holidays they associate with the following: **los
fuegos artificiales, una comida grande, una reunión
familiar, las campanadas, un baile.** Have them also
make a list of additional associations for the holidays.

Group Activity Have students work in groups of 3
to write and perform a skit about 2 customers and a
server in a restaurant in Puerto Rico. One of the
customers is unfamiliar with the foods and asks his/her
companion and the server about them.

Activity **16** brings together all concepts presented.

16 Planes para celebrar

Leer/*Escribir* Piensas celebrar el Año Nuevo con tu familia en el restaurante Casa Borinquen. Mira el menú. Luego explica qué deseos tienes, qué comida pedirías y qué dudas tienes sobre la celebración.

modelo

Me gustaría comer con toda mi familia. Pediría pasteles para todos. Si viniera mi hermano, comería mucho budín. No creo que mis tíos puedan venir.

Vocabulario

Comidas típicas

el arroz con dulce *dessert dish of rice, cinnamon, and coconut milk*

el arroz con gandules *rice and pigeon peas*

el arroz con leche *dessert dish of sweet rice and milk*

el budín *pudding*

el coquito *eggnog with coconut and condensed milk*

los guineítos en escabeche *small green bananas in a garlic, vinegar, and oil sauce with red pepper*

el lechón asado *suckling pig*

los pasteles *tamale-like item of plantain, yuca, and meat*

el pavo *turkey*

el tembleque *coconut-milk custard*

▶ ¿Incluyes algunas de estas comidas en tu dieta?

CASA BORINQUEN

Platos principales
Lechón asado
Pavo
Arroz con gandules
Pasteles
Guineítos

Bebidas
Coquito
Refrescos
Batidos de fruta

Postres
Arroz con dulce
Arroz con leche
Budín
Tembleque

More Practice: **Más comunicación** *p. R10*

Online Workbook
CLASSZONE.COM

Refrán

Este mundo es un fandango y, bien o mal, hay que bailarlo.

En tu opinión, ¿qué dice este refrán sobre la vida y las celebraciones? ¿Crees que si tienes que hacer algo por lo menos debes divertirte? ¿Por qué?

Teaching All Students

Extra Help Describe the ingredients of the foods in the **Vocabulario** and have students guess what you are describing.

Native Speakers Ask students to describe typical dishes from their country of origin and which one is their favorite.

Multiple Intelligences

Naturalist Ask students to determine if the ingredients of each dish in the **Vocabulario** come primarily from plants or animals. Which provide the most protein? Which provide the most carbohydrates?

Teaching Suggestions
Teaching Vocabulary

• Ask students to classify the foods according to **Platos principales**, **Bebidas**, and **Postres**.

• Have students elaborate on answers to the question: **¿Incluyes algunas de estas comidas en tu dieta?** What foods do they include? Do they consciously follow a balanced diet?

ACTIVIDAD 16 **Objective:** Open-ended practice Conditional sentences/vocabulary in reading and writing

Answers will vary.

Culture Highlights

● **COCINA PUERTORRIQUEÑA** Los ingredientes y las sazones de la cocina puertorriqueña son diferentes de las de la tierra del continente americano. Se preparan platos deliciosos usando la cáscara o el jugo de la lima fresca y la naranja agria. Las hierbas favoritas son las hojas del culantro y del orégano seco. También se usan a menudo el adobo y el sofrito. El adobo es una mezcla de pimienta, orégano, ajo, sal, aceite de oliva y vinagre o jugo de lima, mezclado en un pilón. Se le frota al pollo y a las carnes para darles una sazón única. El sofrito es una mezcla de puerco salado, jamón curado, grasa o aceite vegetal, orégano, cebolla, pimiento verde, chile dulce, pimienta, culantro y ajo, lo cual se cocina junto y se usa para darle un sabor distintivo a varios platos locales. El plátano, que nunca se come crudo, se cocina al fuego, o al horno, o se hierve completo o en tajadas, en muchas recetas interesantes. Las hojas del plátano se usan para envolver ciertas comidas que se hierven o se cocinan al horno.

Block Schedule

FunBreak Have students find recipes for Puerto Rican dishes. Present them to the class. Determine which would be easy to make and that the class would enjoy. If possible, prepare the dishes in school. If not, ask for volunteers to prepare the dishes at home to share with the class. (For additional activities, see **Block Scheduling Copymasters**.)

Teaching Resource Options

Print

Actividades para todos Workbook PE, pp. 87–89
Block Scheduling Copymasters
Unit 3 Resource Book
  Actividades para todos Workbook TE, pp. 87–89
  Absent Student Copymasters, p. 109
  Video Activities, p. 243–246
  Videoscript, pp. 247–249

Audiovisual

OHT 27 (Quick Start)
Canciones CD
Video Program Videotape 18:06 / DVD, Unit 3

Technology

  www.classzone.com

Quick Start Review

♻ **Holidays**

Use OHT 27 or write on the board:
Answer the following:

¿Cuáles son 2 actividades que haces durante los siguientes días festivos?
  1. el día de la Independencia
  2. el día de Acción de Gracias
  3. el día de las Madres

Answers
Answers will vary. Answers could include:
1. ir a un desfile, ver fuegos artificiales
2. comer pavo, dar las gracias
3. dar una tarjeta y unas flores a mi mamá, llevar a mi mamá a un restaurante

---

Teaching Suggestions

Presenting Cultura y comparaciones

• Read and discuss the questions in the Connecting Cultures Strategy.

Reading Strategy

Remind students to observe organization of ideas. The number of paragraphs is a clue to the number of key ideas. Have students reread each paragraph and give a title to each one and a 1–2 sentence summary.

En colores

CULTURA Y COMPARACIONES

Una tradición de Puerto Rico

PARA CONOCERNOS

STRATEGY: CONNECTING CULTURES

Recognize and describe uses of disguise As children, did you and your friends like to take on new identities by disguising yourselves? What did you do to change your appearance? How did this change make you feel?

Where in the adult world do you find disguises? Masks are one type of disguise. Think of social events, holidays, characters in literature. Make a list of examples. How long a list can you make?

EVENTOS SOCIALES	FIESTAS	LITERATURA
	carnaval	

En Puerto Rico, la fabricación y el uso de máscaras [1] es una importante tradición que continúa hasta hoy. Según la mayor parte de los antropólogos, el uso de las máscaras en el Puerto Rico de hoy viene de las tradiciones españolas de la Edad Media. Las máscaras se usaban en las fiestas religiosas.

En Puerto Rico la manera de hacer máscaras varía de una ciudad a otra. La ciudad de Ponce, ubicada [2] en la costa sur de la Isla, se conoce por las máscaras de cartón que se fabrican allí. Estas caretas [3] se ponen para Carnaval y se admiran por su brillante colorido.

[1] masks
[2] located
[3] masks

doscientos dieciocho
Unidad 3

Classroom Community

Paired Activity In pairs, have students create and perform 1 of the following skits: (a) One person is a mask maker. The other is a customer who wants to buy a mask. He/She asks the mask maker questions about how and why the masks are made. (b) One person is a mask wearer at a festival and the other is a reporter from a local TV station. The reporter interviews the mask wearer about the mask and its significance.

Storytelling Have students make up a story about a magical mask that brings either good or evil to those who wear it. The story should include some facts taken from the cultural reading to either describe the mask or explain its origins.

para la temporada de Carnaval. Los mascareros aprenden el arte de sus padres y abuelos y transmiten su arte a sus hijos. Hoy día muchos de estos mascareros gozan de[8] prestigio y fama en Puerto Rico y fuera de la Isla. Las máscaras no sólo se usan para Carnaval. También se venden en las galerías de arte, los museos y las tiendas especializadas y turísticas. Se consideran objetos de arte popular que tienen valor histórico y decorativo.

Niñas en el Taller de Máscaras del Residencial Roosevelt, Mayagüez, Puerto Rico

[8] enjoy, have

Los mascareros[4] hacen las caretas del carnaval ponceño con papel, pintura[5] y engrudo. El engrudo es una pasta blanca que se consigue al cocinar harina de trigo[6] con agua.

Pocos artesanos se dedican a la fabricación de estas caretas a tiempo completo[7]. Muchos trabajan en otro oficio y fabrican las máscaras

[4] maskmakers
[5] paint
[6] wheat flour
[7] full time

Máscaras en una tienda en Bayamón

CLASSZONE.COM
More About the Caribbean

¿Comprendiste?
1. ¿Cuál es el origen del uso de las máscaras en Puerto Rico?
2. ¿Para qué se usan las máscaras en Puerto Rico?
3. ¿Es igual la manera de fabricar máscaras en toda la isla? ¿Qué ciudad se conoce por sus máscaras?
4. ¿Ha cambiado el modo de trabajar de los mascareros?

¿Qué piensas?
¿Por qué crees que las máscaras tienen valor histórico y decorativo?

Hazlo tú
¿En qué fiestas norteamericanas se usan máscaras? ¿Qué máscara crearías tú para esa fiesta? ¿Con qué materiales la fabricarías? Dibuja la máscara y explica lo que representa.

doscientos diecinueve
El Caribe Etapa 2 219

Teaching Resource Options

Print

Cuaderno para hispanohablantes
  PE, pp. 79–80
Block Scheduling Copymasters
Unit 3 Resource Book
  Cuaderno para hispanohablantes
    TE, pp. 97–98
  Information Gap Activities, pp. 101–102
  Family Involvement, pp. 110–111

Audiovisual

OHT 28 (Quick Start)

Technology

eTest Plus Online/Test Generator
CD-ROM

www.classzone.com

Quick Start Review

♻ **Conditional sentences**

Use OHT 28 or write on the board:
Rewrite each sentence using the correct
form of the verb in parentheses.

1. Si yo (tener) hambre, (comer) pavo.
2. Si tú (venir) más temprano,
   nosotros (poder) ir a la fiesta con
   José.
3. Si ellos (estar) en la calle, (ver)
   los fuegos artificiales.
4. Si nosotros (ser) los maestros, no
   (dar) mucha tarea.

Answers
1. Si yo tuviera hambre, comería pavo.
2. Si tú vinieras más temprano, nosotros
   podríamos ir a la fiesta con José.
3. Si ellos estuvieran en la calle, verían los
   fuegos artificiales.
4. Si nosotros fuéramos los maestros, no
   daríamos mucha tarea.

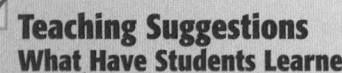

Teaching Suggestions
What Have Students Learned?

Have students look at the "Now you
can…" notes listed on the left side of
pp. 220–221. Tell students to think
about which areas they might not be
sure of. For those areas, they should
consult the "To review" notes.

ETAPA 2

En uso
REPASO Y MÁS COMUNICACIÓN

Now you can...
• describe ideals.

To review
• the subjunctive
with nonexistent
and indefinite
see p. 210.

OBJECTIVES
• Talk about holidays
• Hypothesize
• Express doubt and
  disagree
• Describe ideals

❶ La gala

Todos están haciendo planes para una gala que van a dar para
el Año Nuevo. ¿Qué buscan o necesitan?

modelo

nosotros: buscar unos músicos / saber tocar salsa

Buscamos unos músicos que sepan tocar salsa.

1. nosotros: buscar un lugar / no costar mucho para alquilar
2. yo: necesitar una limosina / ser bastante grande para todos los invitados
3. Marta y Juan: buscar unos cohetes / no ser caros
4. nosotros: necesitar un cocinero / preparar lechón asado
5. yo: necesitar un camarógrafo / hacer un video de la gala
6. Elena: buscar unos fuegos artificiales/ no hacer mucho ruido
7. nosotros: buscar un lugar donde / poderse ver el amanecer
8. yo: buscar un cantante / tener una voz fenomenal

Now you can...
• express doubt and
  disagree.

To review
• the subjunctive for
  disagreement and
  denial
  see p. 212.

❷ ¡Es muy improbable!

Le dices a tu compañero(a) qué harás con otras personas. Él (Ella)
no te cree. ¿Qué le dices y cómo te responde?

modelo

Voy a celebrar el día de Acción de Gracias en San Juan. (dudar que)

Compañero(a): *Dudo que celebres el día de Acción de Gracias en San Juan.*

1. Le voy a comprar un carro a mi novio(a). (es improbable que)
2. Mis hermanos y yo le daremos un viaje a Puerto Rico a nuestro papá.
   (no es seguro que)
3. Mi hermana y yo limpiaremos la casa. (no creer que)
4. Mi familia y yo invitaremos a cien personas a casa. (es imposible que)
5. Yo voy a festejar las Pascuas con mis primos en España. (dudar que)
6. Yo tendré una fiesta para mi cumpleaños. (es improbable que)
7. Mis primos no van al colegio el Día de la Raza. (es imposible que)

220

doscientos veinte
Unidad 3

Classroom Community

Group Activity Have students work in small groups.
Each student completes the following phrases: **Espero
conocer a alguien que...**, **Espero tener amigos que...**,
Prefiero vivir en un lugar que..., **Quiero tener un
carro que...**, **No quiero ver a nadie que...** If someone
has trouble forming a sentence, the others help out.
Students should also write out their answers and
submit them for a group grade.

Paired Activity Working in pairs, one student tells
the other 5 doubts about the other's activities (for
example: **jugar al fútbol, estudiar el francés, bailar la
salsa,** etc.). The other student either confirms or denies
that the doubt is true.

Modelo: A: **Es improbable que estudies el francés.**
        B: **Es verdad. No estudio el francés.** *o:*
           No tienes razón. Estudio el francés.

3 Si fuera verdad

Eres muy imaginativo(a) y estás pensando en una fiesta que quisieras dar. Pero lamentablemente las cosas no son como las sueñas. Di cómo serían las cosas bajo ciertas condiciones.

modelo

Va a haber una fiesta. Yo voy a preparar los pasteles.

Si hubiera una fiesta, yo prepararía los pasteles.

1. Vamos a ser los anfitriones. Vamos a invitar a muchas personas.
2. Tengo que traer un postre. Voy a traer budín.
3. Nydia sabe cocinar. Va a hacer unos guineítos en escabeche.
4. Vamos a invitar a todas las clases de español. Nos vamos a divertir mucho.
5. Mucha gente va a venir a la fiesta. Vamos a comprar mucha comida.
6. Vamos a probar el lechón asado. Probablemente nos va a gustar.
7. Los chicos pueden tocar salsa. Los vamos a invitar a tocar en la fiesta.
8. Las chicas van a festejar hasta la madrugada. Pueden ver el amanecer.

4 Los días festivos

Ya sabes mucho de cómo se celebran los días festivos, pero todavía quieres saber más. Usando frases de las dos columnas, haz oraciones que expresen lo que dudas o lo que te gustaría saber.

modelo

Las Pascuas / organizar un concurso de salsa

No creo que nadie organice un concurso de salsa para las Pascuas. o:
¿Hay alguien aquí que organice un concurso de salsa para las Pascuas?

1. las Pascuas / desyerbar el jardín
2. el día de Acción de Gracias / hacer un viaje en limosina
3. el día de la Amistad / tener una orquesta formal en casa
4. el día de la Independencia / preparar una cena para cien invitados
5. el día de las Madres/ los Padres / volar en planeador sobre el océano
6. el día de la Raza / comer dos lechones asados
7. la quinceañera / cantar una ópera entera con los amigos

Now you can...
• hypothesize.

To review
• conditional sentences see p. 214.

Now you can...
• talk about holidays.

To review
• the subjunctive with nonexistent and indefinite see p. 210.
• the subjunctive with disagreement and denial see p. 212.

ACTIVIDAD **1** **Answers**

1. Buscamos un lugar que no cueste mucho para alquilar.
2. Necesito una limosina que sea bastante grande para todos los invitados.
3. Buscan unos cohetes que no sean caros.
4. Necesitamos un cocinero que prepare lechón asado.
5. Necesito un camarógrafo que haga un video de la gala.
6. Busca unos fuegos artificiales que no hagan mucho ruido.
7. Buscamos un lugar donde se pueda ver el amanecer.
8. Busco una cantante que tenga una voz fenomenal.

ACTIVIDAD **2** **Answers**

1. Es improbable que le compres un carro a tu novio(a).
2. No es seguro que le den un viaje a Puerto Rico a tu papá.
3. No creo que limpien la casa para su madre.
4. Es imposible que inviten a cien personas a casa.
5. Dudo que festejes las Pascuas con tus primos en España.
6. Es improbable que tengas una fiesta para tu cumpleaños.
7. Es imposible que no vayan al colegio el Día de la Raza.

ACTIVIDAD **3** **Answers**

1. Si fuéramos los anfitriones, invitaríamos a muchas personas.
2. Si tuviera que traer un postre, traería budín.
3. Si supiera cocinar, haría unos guineítos en escabeche.
4. Si invitáramos a todas las clases de español, nos divertiríamos mucho.
5. Si viniera mucha gente a la fiesta, compraríamos mucha comida.
6. Si probáramos el lechón asado, probablemente nos gustaría.
7. Si pudieran tocar salsa, los invitaríamos a tocar en la fiesta.
8. Si festejaran hasta la madrugada, podrían ver el amanecer.

ACTIVIDAD **4** **Answers**

Answers will vary.

Teaching All Students

Extra Help Have students work in groups of 3 to do **Actividades 1–4.** Before each activity, they should drill each other on the verb forms they need. Next, they take turns doing items orally. Then everyone writes the activity, they exchange papers for correction, and review items that are incorrect.

Multiple Intelligences

Kinesthetic Write out answers to **Actividad 3** and photocopy them 5 times. Cut the answers into pieces: **si** + verb in the subjunctive / rest of clause / verb in conditional / rest of clause. Divide the class into 5 groups and give each one a set of sentence pieces. Have students put the sentences back together again.

Block Schedule

Variety Have students prepare menus for the holidays listed in **Actividad 4.** They should include items under each course and decorate the menus. Then use the menus for a restaurant role-play activity. (For additional activities, see **Block Scheduling Copymasters.**)

Teaching Resource Options

Print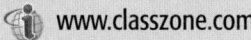

Unit 3 Resource Book
Audioscript, p. 114
Vocabulary Quizzes, pp. 117–119
Grammar Quizzes, pp. 120–121
Etapa Exam, Forms A and B,
pp. 122–131
Examen para hispanohablantes,
pp. 132–136
Portfolio Assessment, pp. 137–138
Multiple Choice Test Questions,
pp. 229–231

Audiovisual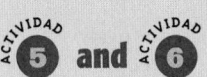

OHT 28 (Quick Start)
Audio Program CD 19, Track 18

Technology

eTest Plus Online/Test Generator
CD-ROM
www.classzone.com

ACTIVIDAD 5 and ACTIVIDAD 6

Rubric: Speaking

Criteria	Scale	
Sentence structure	1 2 3	A = 11–12 pts.
Vocabulary use	1 2 3	B = 9–10 pts.
Originality	1 2 3	C = 7–8 pts.
Fluency	1 2 3	D = 4–6 pts.
		F = < 4 pts.

ACTIVIDAD 7 En tu propia voz

Rubric: Writing

Criteria	Scale	
Vocabulary use	1 2 3 4 5	A = 14–15 pts.
Accuracy	1 2 3 4 5	B = 12–13 pts.
Creativity, appearance	1 2 3 4 5	C = 10–11 pts.
		D = 8–9 pts.
		F = < 8 pts.

Teaching Note: En tu propia voz

Writing Strategy Suggest that students "Tell who, what, where, when, why, and how" when writing their ads. They should provide many details to communicate their information.

---

5 ¿Hay alguien que...?

STRATEGY: SPEAKING

Encourage participation Write the names of two or three classmates and one thing that person can do and one thing he or she probably cannot do. Then pool the papers. Each person selects one paper at random and begins the conversation about what people may or may not be able to do for the class party.

Van a dar una fiesta para celebrar un día festivo en su clase de español. Tienen que decidir cómo van a participar todos. En grupos de tres o cuatro, conversen sobre los varios talentos de todos los estudiantes. Claro, ¡siempre hay personas que dudan de los demás!

modelo

Tú: *¿Hay alguien aquí que sepa cocinar comida puertorriqueña?*

Amigo(a) 1: *Dudo que haya alguien en la clase que sepa hacerlo.*

Amigo(a) 2: *¡Yo sé preparar arroz con gandules!*

Amigo(a) 3: *¡No es cierto que sepas preparar arroz con gandules!*

6 Para celebrar

Pregunta a tu compañero(a) qué hizo para celebrar varios días festivos. Luego pregúntale qué haría si pudiera hacer lo que quisiera. Después, cambien de papel.

modelo

Tú: *¿Qué hiciste para celebrar el Año Nuevo?*

Compañero(a): *Me quedé en casa y vi unos videos.*

Tú: *¿Qué harías si pudieras hacer lo que quisieras?*

Compañero(a): *Si alguien me invitara, iría a una gala.*

7 En tu propia voz

ESCRITURA Imagina que pasaste la semana de Año Nuevo con tus primos. En tu diario, escribe lo que hicieron cada día.

modelo

El lunes fuimos a…
El martes visitamos…
El miércoles celebramos…

CONEXIONES

El arte Crea una tarjeta para desear a un(a) amigo(a) un Próspero Año Nuevo. Investiga el arte del Caribe y haz una tarjeta con arte al estilo caribeño. Explica a la clase cómo tu tarjeta representa el arte caribeño.

222 doscientos veintidós
Unidad 3

Classroom Community

Learning Scenario Working in pairs, have students write and performs skits about preparing for a holiday celebration. Each student has a different idea as to what preparations are necessary and what activities will take place. Have students discuss their ideas and resolve the problem.

Game Divide the class into 2 teams. A member of 1 team (students will take turns) calls out a category (**cosa, persona, acción, expresión, comida, día festivo, expresión de duda**). You choose a word from the **Repaso de vocabulario** and give a synonym, definition, mime, or drawing for the other team to guess. If they guess correctly they get 1 point. If they guess incorrectly, the other team gets a chance to score.

En resumen
REPASO DE VOCABULARIO

TALK ABOUT HOLIDAYS

Actions

festejar	to celebrate
pasarlo bien	to have a good time
patrocinar	to sponsor

Expressions

¡Buen provecho!	Enjoy! (your meal)
¡Próspero Año Nuevo!	Happy New Year!

Give thanks

Muy amable.	That's kind of you.
No hay de qué.	It's nothing.

Foods

el arroz …	
con dulce	rice-coconut milk dessert
con gandules	rice and pigeon peas
con leche	sweet rice-milk dessert
el budín	pudding
el coquito	eggnog
los guineítos en escabeche	small green bananas in garlic vinegar, red pepper, and oil
el lechón asado	roast suckling pig
el pastel	tamale-like mixture of plantain, yuca, and meat
el pavo	turkey
el tembleque	coconut-milk custard

Holidays

El día de …	
Acción de Gracias	Thanksgiving
la Amistad	Valentine's Day
la Independencia	Independence Day
las Madres / de los Padres	Mother's / Father's Day
la Raza	Columbus Day
la Hanuka	Hanukkah
la Navidad	Christmas
las Pascuas	Easter
la quinceañera	fifteenth birthday

People and things

el anfitrión	host
la anfitriona	hostess
el Año Nuevo	New Year
la campana	bell
la campanada	tolling of the bell
el cohete	firecracker
el concurso	contest
la despedida del año	New Year's Eve
la fiesta continua	party in stages
los fuegos artificiales	fireworks
la gala	big, formal party
inolvidable	unforgettable
la madrugada	early morning, dawn
el motivo	purpose
el (la) músico(a)	musician
la orquesta	orchestra
la pareja	couple
la radioemisora	radio station
el ruido	noise
típico(a)	typical, regional

♻ **Ya sabes**

De nada.	You're welcome.
Es un placer…	It's a pleasure…
Gracias.	Thank you.
Mil gracias.	Many thanks.
Se lo agradezco.	It's really appreciated.

EXPRESS DOUBT AND DISAGREE

♻ **Ya sabes**

dudar que	to doubt that
Es imposible que	It's impossible that
Es improbable que	It's improbable that
no creer que	to not think that
no es cierto que	it's not true that
no es verdad que	it's not true that
no estar seguro(a) (de) que	to not be sure that
no opinar que	to not be of the opinion that
no pensar (e→ie) que	to not think that

DESCRIBE IDEALS

♻ **Ya sabes**

buscar	to look for
no hay nada	there is nothing
no hay nadie	there is nobody
¿Hay algo…?	Is there anything…?
¿Hay alguien…?	Is there anyone…?

HYPOTHESIZE

Use conditional sentences

Si vas a la fiesta, te divertirás.
Si fueras a la fiesta, te divertirías.

Juego

¿Qué hay en la mesa? ¿Puedes encontrar dos tipos de comida cuyos nombres empiecen con la letra **p**?

doscientos veintitrés
El Caribe Etapa 2   **223**

Planning Guide CLASSROOM MANAGEMENT

OBJECTIVES

Communication
- Describe historic events *pp. 226–227, 228–229, 242–243*
- Make suggestions and wishes *pp. 232–233*
- Express emotion and doubt *pp. 232–233*
- State cause and effect *pp. 234–237*

Grammar
- Summary of the subjunctive *pp. 232–237*
- Subjunctive vs. indicative *pp. 238–239*

Culture
- Christopher Columbus *pp. 227, 228–229, 234, 242*
- History of the Dominican Republic *pp. 227, 242–243*
- Regional vocabulary *p. 237*
- The Dominican Republic's National Anthem *p. 237*
- José Martí *p. 240*
- **Guantanamera** *p. 240*

♻ Recycling
- Holiday vocabulary *p. 231*
- Community service vocabulary *p. 235*
- Travel vocabulary *p. 233*

STRATEGIES

Listening Strategies
- Listen and take notes *p. 228*

Speaking Strategies
- Describe celebrations *p. 231*
- Express yourself *p. 246*

Reading Strategies
- Observe what makes poetry *p. 240*
- Preview graphics *TE p. 242*

Writing Strategies
- Organize information chronologically and by category *TE p. 246*
- Use transitions to make text flow smoothly *p. 248*

Connecting Cultures Strategies
- Learn about Christopher

Columbus and his voyages *pp. 227, 228–229, 234, 242*
- Recognize variations in vocabulary *p. 237*
- Learn the Dominican Republic's National Anthem *p. 237*
- José Martí: poet, writer and patriot *pp. 240–241*
- Learn about the song **Guantanamera** *p. 240*
- Make a historical time line *TE p. 240*
- Analyze national celebrations *p. 242*
- Connect and compare what you know about the history of your community to help you learn about the history of a new community *pp. 242–243, 246*

PROGRAM RESOURCES

Print
- *Más práctica* Workbook PE *pp. 81–88*
- *Actividades para todos* Workbook PE *pp. 91–100*
- Block Scheduling Copymasters *pp. 73–80*
- Unit 3 Resource Book
  - *Más práctica* Workbook TE *pp. 141–148*
  - *Actividades para todos* Workbook TE *pp. 149–158*
  - *Cuaderno para hispanohablantes* TE *pp. 159–166*
  - Information Gap Activities *pp. 167–170*
  - Family Letter *p. 171*
  - Absent Student Copymasters *pp. 172–178*
  - Family Involvement *pp. 179–180*
  - Audioscript *pp. 181–184*
  - Assessment Program, Unit 3 Etapa 3 *pp. 185–242*
  - Answer Keys *pp. 250–254*

Audiovisual
- Audio Program CD 9
- *Canciones* CD
- Overhead Transparencies M1–M5; GO1–GO5; 4, 32–46
- Word Tiles U3E3

Technology
- eEdition Plus Online/eEdition CD-ROM
- Easy Planner Plus Online/Easy Planner CD-ROM
- eTest Plus Online/Test Generator CD-ROM
- Online Workbook
- Take-Home Tutor CD-ROM
- www.classzone.com

Assessment Program Options
- Unit 3 Resource Book
  - Vocabulary Quizzes
  - Grammar Quizzes
  - Etapa Exam Forms A and B
  - *Examen para hispanohablantes*
  - Portfolio Assessment
  - Unit 3 Comprehensive Test
  - *Prueba comprensiva para hispanohablantes,* Unit 3
  - Midyear Test
  - Multiple Choice Test Questions
- Audio Program CD 19
- eTest Plus Online/Test Generator CD-ROM

Native Speakers
- *Cuaderno para hispanohablantes* PE *pp. 81–88*
- *Cuaderno para hispanohablantes* TE (Unit 3 Resource Book)
- *Examen para hispanohablantes* (Unit 3 Resource Book)
- *Prueba comprensiva para hispanohablantes,* Unit 3 (Unit 3 Resource Book)
- Audio Program *(Para hispanohablantes)* CD 9, 19
- Audioscript (Unit 3 Resource Book)

Student Text Listening Activity Scripts

 **Situaciones** *pages 228–229*

• CD 9

Todo empieza cuando los monarcas de España, Fernando e Isabel, deciden darle dinero a Cristóbal Colón para su viaje a Asia.

El tres de agosto, 1492, Colón sale del Puerto de Palos en España. Colón es el capitán de la expedición que incluye los barcos que se llaman la Niña, la Pinta y la Santa María.

Pasan dos meses más. La expedición de Colón llega a una isla en las Bahamas que se conoce por su nombre taíno: Guanahaní. Ese día, el doce de octubre de 1492, es el día oficial que marca el descubrimiento de las Américas. Colón cree que ha llegado a las Indias.

Colón se va para Cuba. De Cuba, Colón se va para otra isla, que nombra "La Española". Llega a esta isla hermosa el 6 de diciembre de 1492. En una carta a Fernando e Isabel describe la isla como un paraíso sin igual.

La isla le parece a Colón el sitio perfecto para establecer una colonia española. Colón pone la bandera de España en la isla y vuelve a España para dar la noticia de su descubrimiento a Fernando e Isabel.

Después de diez meses, Colón vuelve a La Española, donde construye La Isabela, la primera ciudad española de las Américas. Es el año 1493.

En 1496, el hermano menor de Colón, Bartolomé, funda a Santo Domingo.

En 1506, Cristóbal Colón muere en España, sin saber que ha descubierto el Nuevo Mundo. Muere convencido de que su expedición de 1492 llegó a las Indias.

La isla de La Española hoy se conoce como la República Dominicana y Haití. Por eso el día de la Raza, el 12 de octubre, es un día festivo muy importante en mi país. Honramos a Cristobal Colón con procesiones y desfiles a la zona colonial de Santo Domingo. Allí hay varios monumentos históricos que conmemoran el descubrimiento de las Américas. Es un día solemne y es un día para celebrar.

 **El desfile** *page 232*

Modelo: Quiero que vayas al desfile conmigo.
1. Recomiendo que te pongas ropa de verano porque va a hacer mucho calor.
2. Insisto en que lleguemos al desfile temprano porque va a haber mucha gente.
3. Te aconsejo que traigas una silla porque nos vamos a cansar mucho.
4. Tu papá quiere que invites a dos amigos.
5. Tus papás recomiendan que tus amigos vengan a la casa dos horas antes del desfile.
6. Tus hermanos insisten en que nosotros nos quedemos en el parque todo el día.

 **El (La) dudoso(a)** *page 238*

Modelo: Creo que el presidente es eficiente.
1. Creo que el alcalde tiene mucho poder.
2. Creo que la monarquía existirá en veinte años.
3. Creo que el ejército está listo para una guerra.
4. Creo que el gobernador ganará las elecciones.
5. Creo que el congreso pasará esa ley.
6. Creo que nuestros antepasados sufrieron mucho.

Sample Lesson Plan - 50 Minute Schedule

DAY 1

Etapa Opener
- Quick Start Review (TE, p. 224) 5 MIN.
- Have students look at the *Etapa* Opener and answer the questions. 5 MIN.

En contexto: Vocabulario
- Quick Start Review (TE, p. 226) 5 MIN.
- Present *Descubre,* p. 226. Have students use context and pictures to learn *Etapa* vocabulary. Use the Situational OHTs for additional practice. 15 MIN.

En vivo: Situaciones
- Quick Start Review (TE, p. 228) 5 MIN.
- Present the Listening Strategy, p. 228. Have students look at section 1, p. 228. Play the audio for section 2. Have students work in groups to complete section 3. 15 MIN.

Homework Option:
- Have students write answers to *¿Comprendiste?,* p. 227.

DAY 2

En acción: Vocabulario y gramática
- Check homework. 5 MIN.
- Quick Start Review (TE, p. 230) 5 MIN.
- Have students read and write answers to *Actividad* 1. Go over answers orally. 5 MIN.
- Have students do *Actividad* 2 orally. 5 MIN.
- Present the *Vocabulario,* p. 231. Then do *Actividad* 3 in pairs. 10 MIN.
- Present the Speaking Strategy, p. 231. Then have students do *Actividad* 4 in pairs. 5 MIN.
- Present *Repaso:* Summary of the Subjunctive (Part 1), p. 232. 10 MIN.
- Play the audio; do *Actividad* 5. 5 MIN.

Homework Option:
- Have students write answers to the question at the end of the *Vocabulario,* p. 231.

DAY 3

En acción (cont.)
- Check homework. 5 MIN.
- Present the *Nota.* Then have students do *Actividad* 6 in writing. Go over answers orally. 10 MIN.
- Present the *Nota.* Then have students do *Actividad* 7 in pairs. 5 MIN.
- Have students complete *Actividad* 8 in pairs. 5 MIN.
- Quick Start Review (TE, p. 234) 5 MIN.
- Present *Repaso:* Summary of the Subjunctive (Part 2), p. 234. 5 MIN.
- Have students read and complete *Actividad* 9 in writing. Have volunteers present their answers. 5 MIN.
- Present the *Vocabulario,* p. 236. Then do *Actividad* 10 orally. 10 MIN.

Homework Option:
- Have students complete *Actividad* 10 in writing. *Más práctica* Workbook, p. 85. *Cuaderno para hispanohablantes,* p. 83.

DAY 4

En acción (cont.)
- Check homework. 5 MIN.
- Present the *Nota.* Then do *Actividad* 11 orally. 5 MIN.
- Have students complete *Actividad* 12 in pairs. Expand using *Más comunicación,* p. R11. 15 MIN.
- Quick Start Review (TE, p. 238) 5 MIN.
- Present *Gramática:* Subjunctive vs. Indicative and the *Vocabulario,* p. 238. 10 MIN.
- Have students complete *Actividad* 13 in pairs. 5 MIN.
- Play the audio; do *Actividad* 14. 5 MIN.

Homework Option:
- Have students complete *Actividades* 11 and 13 in writing. *Más práctica* Workbook, p. 86. *Cuaderno para hispanohablantes,* p. 84.
- *Actividades para todos* Workbook, pp. 91–100.

DAY 5

En acción (cont.)
- Check homework. 5 MIN.
- Have students complete *Actividad* 15 in pairs. 5 MIN.
- Have students complete *Actividad* 16 in groups. Expand using Information Gap Activities, Unit 3 Resource Book, p. 168; *Más comunicación,* p. R11. 15 MIN.

Refrán
- Present the *Refrán,* p. 239. 5 MIN.

En voces: Lectura
- Quick Start Review (TE, p. 240) 5 MIN.
- Present the Reading Strategy, p. 240. Call on volunteers to read the *Lectura* aloud. Have students answer the *¿Comprendiste?/ ¿Qué piensas?* questions, p. 241. 15 MIN.

Homework Option:
- Have students complete *Hazlo tú,* p. 241.

DAY 6

En colores: Cultura y comparaciones
- Check homework. 5 MIN.
- Quick Start Review (TE, p. 242) 5 MIN.
- Present the Connecting Cultures Strategy, p. 242. Call on volunteers to read the article aloud. Have students answer the *¿Comprendiste?/¿Qué piensas?* questions, p. 243. 20 MIN.

En uso: Repaso y más comunicación
- Quick Start Review (TE, p. 244) 5 MIN.
- Have students do *Actividades* 1 and 3 in pairs and *Actividades* 2 and 4 orally. 15 MIN.

Homework Option:
- Have students complete *Hazlo tú,* p. 243. Review for *Etapa* 3 Exam.

DAY 7

En uso (cont.)
- Check homework. 5 MIN.
- Present the Speaking Strategy, p. 246, and have students do *Actividades* 5 and 6 in groups. 10 MIN.

En tu propia voz: Escritura
- Have students brainstorm their ideas for *Actividad* 7. 5 MIN.

En resumen: Repaso de vocabulario
- Quick Start Review (TE, p. 247) 5 MIN.
- Review grammar questions, etc., as necessary. 5 MIN.
- Complete *Etapa* 3 Exam. 20 MIN.

Homework Option:
- Have students complete their postcards for *Actividad* 7, p. 246. Review for Unit 3 Comprehensive Test.

DAY 8

Conexiones
- Check homework. 5 MIN.
- Discuss *Los estudios sociales,* p. 246. 5 MIN.

Unit 3 Comprehensive Test
- Review grammar questions, etc., as necessary. 5 MIN.
- Complete Unit 3 Comprehensive Test. 30 MIN.

En tu propia voz: Escritura
- Present the Writing Strategy, p. 248. Do the writing activity, pp. 248–249. 5 MIN.

Ampliación
- Optional: Use a suggested project, game, or activity. (TE, pp. 179A–179B)

Homework Option:
- Have students complete the assignment for *Conexiones.* Preview *Unidad 4* Opener: Have students read and study pp. 250–251.

Sample Lesson Plan - Block Schedule (90 minutes)

DAY 1

Etapa Opener
- Quick Start Review (TE, p. 224) 5 MIN.
- Have students look at the *Etapa* Opener and answer the questions. 5 MIN.
- Use Block Scheduling Copymasters. 10 MIN.

En contexto: Vocabulario
- Quick Start Review (TE, p. 226) 5 MIN.
- Present *Descubre*, p. 226. Have students use context and pictures to learn *Etapa* vocabulary. Use the Situational OHTs for additional practice. 15 MIN.

En vivo: Situaciones
- Quick Start Review (TE, p. 228) 5 MIN.
- Present the Listening Strategy, p. 228. Have students look at section 1, p. 228. Play the audio for section 2. Have students work in groups to complete section 3. 15 MIN.

En acción: Vocabulario y gramática
- Quick Start Review (TE, p. 230) 5 MIN.
- Have students read and write answers to *Actividad* 1. Go over answers orally. 5 MIN.
- Have students do *Actividad* 2 orally. 5 MIN.
- Present the *Vocabulario*, p. 231. Then do *Actividad* 3 in pairs. 10 MIN.
- Present the Speaking Strategy, p. 231. Then have students do *Actividad* 4 in pairs. 5 MIN.

Homework Option:
- Have students write answers to *¿Comprendiste?*, p. 227, and to the question at the end of the *Vocabulario*, p. 231.

DAY 2

En acción (cont.)
- Check homework. 5 MIN.
- Quick Start Review (TE, p. 232) 5 MIN.
- Present *Repaso:* Summary of the Subjunctive (Part 1), p. 232. 10 MIN.
- Play the audio; do *Actividad* 5. 10 MIN.
- Present the *Nota*. Then have students do *Actividad* 6 in writing. Go over answers orally. 10 MIN.
- Present the *Nota*. Then have students do *Actividad* 7 in pairs. 5 MIN.
- Have students complete *Actividad* 8 in pairs. 5 MIN.
- Quick Start Review (TE, p. 234) 5 MIN.
- Present *Repaso:* Summary of the Subjunctive (Part 2), p. 234. 10 MIN.
- Have students read and complete *Actividad* 9 in writing. Have volunteers present their answers. 10 MIN.
- Present the *Vocabulario*, p. 236. Then do *Actividad* 10 orally. 10 MIN.
- Present the *Nota*. Then do *Actividad* 11 orally. 5 MIN.

Homework Option:
- Have students complete *Actividad* 10 in writing. *Más práctica* Workbook, pp. 85–86. *Cuaderno para hispanohablantes*, pp. 83–84.

DAY 3

En acción (cont.)
- Check homework. 5 MIN.
- Have students complete *Actividad* 12 in pairs. Expand using Information Gap Activities, Unit 3 Resource Book, p. 167; *Más comunicación*, p. R11. 20 MIN.
- Quick Start Review (TE, p. 238) 5 MIN.
- Present *Gramática:* Subjunctive vs. Indicative and the *Vocabulario*, p. 238. 10 MIN.
- Have students complete *Actividad* 13 in pairs. 5 MIN.
- Play the audio; do *Actividad* 14. 10 MIN.
- Have students complete *Actividad* 15 in pairs. Have a few pairs present their conversations. 10 MIN.
- Have students complete *Actividad* 16 in groups. Expand using Information Gap Activities, Unit 3 Resource Book, p. 168; *Más comunicación*, p. R11. 20 MIN.

Refrán
- Present the *Refrán*, p. 239. 5 MIN.

Homework Option:
- Have students complete *Actividades* 11 and 13 in writing. *Más práctica* Workbook, pp. 87–88. *Cuaderno para hispanohablantes*, pp. 85–86.
- *Actividades para todos* Workbook, pp. 91–100.

DAY 4

En voces: Lectura
- Check homework. 5 MIN.
- Quick Start Review (TE, p. 240) 5 MIN.
- Present the Reading Strategy, p. 240. Call on volunteers to read the *Lectura* aloud. Have students answer the *¿Comprendiste?/ ¿Qué piensas?* questions, p. 241. 15 MIN.

En colores: Cultura y comparaciones
- Quick Start Review (TE, p. 242) 5 MIN.
- Present the Connecting Cultures Strategy, p. 242. Call on volunteers to read the article aloud. Have students answer the *¿Comprendiste?/¿Qué piensas?* questions, p. 243. 15 MIN.

En uso: Repaso y más comunicación
- Quick Start Review (TE, p. 244) 5 MIN.
- Do *Actividades* 1 and 3 in pairs and 2 and 4 orally. 20 MIN.
- Present the Speaking Strategy, p. 246, and have students do *Actividades* 5 and 6 in groups. 15 MIN.
- Do *Actividad* 7 in writing. 5 MIN.

Homework Option:
- Have students complete *Hazlo tú*, pp. 241 and 243. Review for *Etapa* 3 Exam and Unit 3 Comprehensive Test.

DAY 5

En resumen: Repaso de vocabulario
- Check homework. 5 MIN.
- Quick Start Review (TE, p. 247) 5 MIN.
- Review grammar questions, etc., as necessary. 5 MIN.
- Complete *Etapa* 3 Exam. 20 MIN.

Conexiones
- Discuss *Los estudios sociales*, p. 246. 5 MIN.

Unit 3 Comprehensive Test
- Review grammar questions, etc., as necessary. 5 MIN.
- Complete Unit 3 Comprehensive Test. 30 MIN.

En tu propia voz: Escritura
- Present the Writing Strategy, p. 248. Do the writing activity, pp. 248–249. 15 MIN.

Ampliación
- Optional: Use a suggested project, game, or activity. (TE, pp. 179A–179B)

Homework Option:
- Have students complete the assignment for *Conexiones*. Preview *Unidad 4* Opener: Have students read and study pp. 250–251.

▼ Los dominicanos celebran el día de la Independencia con el Carnaval.

Etapa Theme
Describing historic events; making suggestions and wishes; expressing emotion and doubt; stating cause and effect

Grammar Objectives
• Summary of the subjunctive
• Subjunctive vs. indicative

Teaching Resource Options

Print

Block Scheduling Copymasters
Unit 3 Resource Book
  Family Letter, p. 171
  Absent Student Copymasters, p. 172

Audiovisual

OHT 3, 38 (Quick Start)

Quick Start Review

♻ Holidays

Use OHT 38 or write on the board:
Write the holiday that corresponds to each date:

1. el 4 de julio
2. el 14 de febrero
3. el 12 de octubre
4. el 25 de diciembre
5. el primero de enero

Answers
Answers will vary. Answers could include:
1. el día de la Independencia de EE.UU.
2. el día de la Amistad
3. el día de la Raza
4. la Navidad
5. el Año Nuevo

Teaching Suggestions
Previewing the Etapa
• Ask students to study the picture on pp. 224–225 (1 min.).
• Close books; ask students to name at least 3 items that they noticed.
• Reopen books and ask students how the **Etapa** objectives relate to the photo. **¿Cómo se relacionan los objetivos de la Etapa a la foto?** What else might be included in this **Etapa? ¿Qué más se podría incluir en esta Etapa?**
• Use the **¿Qué ves?** questions to focus the discussion.

U N I D A D   3

ETAPA 3

Celebraciones de patria

OBJECTIVES

• Describe historic events

• Make suggestions and wishes

• Express emotion and doubt

• State cause and effect

¿Qué ves?

Mira la foto. Contesta las preguntas.

1. ¿Quiénes son estas personas? ¿Cómo crees que se sienten?

2. ¿Qué celebración crees que sea? ¿Has estado en celebraciones parecidas?

3. Mira el sello. ¿Cómo puedes averiguar en qué país están?

224

Classroom Management

Planning Ahead Prepare to discuss the theme of historic and patriotic events in the Dominican Republic by asking volunteers to research pertinent information on the Internet or in the library. Ask them to locate pictures of these events to display on the bulletin board. You might also bring in items related to patriotism in the U.S. to compare to those in the Dominican Republic.

Peer Review As a class, brainstorm a list of activities related to Independence Day celebrations. Have students look up any words they might not have learned. Have them add these new words to their supplementary vocabulary lists.

Cross Cultural Connections

Ask students if this photo of Independence Day in the Dominican Republic would be similar to one that might be taken in the U.S. Would this be a typical Independence Day activity in the U.S.? What other activities are typical?

Culture Highlights

● **LA REPÚBLICA DOMINICANA** La República Dominicana logró su independencia el 27 de febrero de 1844. El día se celebra con manifestaciones patrióticas en las que participan niños y adultos.

● **LAS FIESTAS EN LA REPÚBLICA DOMINICANA** Hay muchas ocasiones especiales durante el año en la República Dominicana. En la ciudad de Puerto Plata se da un Festival Cultural en la tercera semana de junio. Cantantes ofrecen conciertos, y grupos de baile muestran bailes tradicionales, desde los espirituales africanos hasta la salsa. También hay exhibiciones de artes manuales de los artesanos locales.

El pueblo playero de Cabarete auspicia varios eventos atléticos cada año. Todos los fines de semana en febrero hay un festival diferente, incluyendo carreras de bicicletas de terreno, competencias de papelotes, competencias de castillos de arena y competencias de *surfing* y de tabla de vela.

Durante la Semana Santa, muchos van al pueblo de Sousa para disfrutar de una semana de voleibol, de comida y de baile.

Supplementary Vocabulary

la bandera	flag
marchar	to march
el uniforme	uniform

Block Schedule

Variety Have students work in pairs to role-play a conversation between a person who has just returned from the parade pictured on pp. 224–225 and another who couldn't go, but wants to know all about it. Students should make up additional details. (For additional activities, see **Block Scheduling Copymasters**.)

Teaching All Students

Extra Help Ask several students to supply a detail to describe the photo. Write the descriptions on the board. Have students then reorganize the details and write a cohesive paragraph.

Native Speakers Ask students to describe a patriotic celebration in their home countries, especially Independence Day.

Multiple Intelligences

Naturalist Ask students to research the names of natural symbols (animals, birds, natural reserves) that the Dominican Republic, Puerto Rico, and Cuba use on their flags, stamps, tourism ads, etc.

Intrapersonal Ask students how they feel when they attend a patriotic celebration. Does it make them feel proud? Happy? Sad? Indifferent?

Teaching Resource Options

Print 📖
Unit 3 Resource Book
  Absent Student Copymasters, p. 172

Audiovisual 📼
OHT 32, 33, 34, 34A, 35, 35A,
  38 (Quick Start)

Technology 💻
Online Workbook, U3E3
Take-Home Tutor CD-ROM, U3E3

Quick Start Review

♻ Holiday vocabulary

Use OHT 38 or write on the board:
¿Cómo celebramos los feriados
nacionales? Escriba al menos 3 modos.

Answers
Answers will vary. Answers could include:
Celebramos con fuegos artificiales.
Asistimos a desfiles.
Comemos comidas especiales.
Tenemos fiestas.
No vamos ni al trabajo ni a la escuela.

Teaching Suggestions
Introducing Vocabulary

• Have students look at pp. 226–227.
  Use OHT 32 and 33 to present the
  vocabulary.
• Ask the Comprehension Questions
  on TE p. 227 in order of yes/no
  (questions 1–3), either/or (questions
  4–6), and simple word or phrase
  (questions 7–10). Expand by adding
  similar questions.
• Use the TPR activity to reinforce the
  meaning of individual words.

Descubre

Answers

1. c	3. b	5. h	7. f	9. j
2. i	4. a	6. d	8. g	10. e

En contexto VOCABULARIO

EL DIARIO 23-30 marzo

Dos ensayos patrióticos

Estos chicos caribeños participaron
en una competencia de ensayos
patrióticos. Tuvieron que escribir un
breve ensayo que describe el día
festivo que tiene más importancia en
su familia.

Descubre

Usa tu intuición y lo que ya sabes para
decidir el significado de cada palabra.
Escoge del segundo grupo de palabras.

1. costumbre	a. fight, struggle
2. acudir	b. ancestors
3. antepasados	c. custom
4. lucha	d. to honor
5. enfrentar	e. essays
6. honrar	f. slaves
7. esclavos	g. to commemorate
8. conmemorar	h. to confront
9. competencia	i. to attend
10. ensayos	j. contest

Día de la Abolición de la Esclavitud en Puerto Rico

22 de marzo

El Día de la Abolición
de la Esclavitud es un
día muy solemne para
mi familia porque
algunos de nuestros
antepasados fueron
esclavos en aquel
entonces. Tenemos varias costumbres
para honrar su memoria. Empezamos
el día con unos momentos de silencio
alrededor de la mesa. Papá dice unas
palabras sobre la injusticia que sufrieron
nuestros antepasados y la lucha que
enfrentaban todos los días contra el
opresor. Este día fue una victoria justa
contra los proponentes de la esclavitud.

Luego vamos al Parque de Bombas para
celebrar. Me gusta ir a la Plaza para oír la
bomba y plena que tocan los conjuntos
afrocaribeños. Allí todos compartimos y
recordamos juntos. Es una ocasión alegre.

Emilio Hernández de la Cruz

Monumento a la
Abolición de la
Esclavitud, Ponce,
Puerto Rico

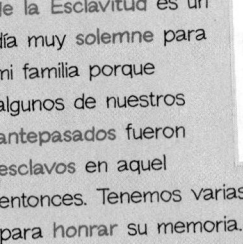

Pleneros celebran el Día de la Abolición

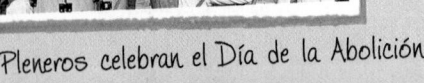

226 doscientos veintiséis
Unidad 3

Classroom Community

TPR Have students create drawings for the vocabulary
words/phrases. Place them around the room. Call on
students to substitute different words for the commands.
(Miguel), levántate. Camina hacia «los antepasados».
Tómalo. Dáselo a (Carolina). Regresa a tu asiento.
(Luisa), toma «el almirante». Camina hacia el
asiento de (Rogelio). Muéstrale «el almirante».
Ahora, pon «el almirante» en mi escritorio.

Paired Activity Make copies of the Comprehension
Questions on TE p. 227. Give copies to pairs of
students. Students take turns asking and answering the
questions. Have each student make up 2 additional
questions to ask his/her partner.

Día de la Raza en la República Dominicana

El día en que Cristóbal Colón descubrió las Américas.

Los dominicanos tienen una relación especial con la familia Colón. El **Almirante** Cristóbal fue el primer europeo que llegó a la isla en diciembre de 1492. El hermano de Cristóbal, Bartolomé, fundó Santo Domingo poco después de la fundación de una colonia española en la isla. Y el hijo de Cristóbal, Diego, se estableció en Santo Domingo por unos años.

En la zona colonial de Santo Domingo hay varios monumentos históricos para **conmemorar** el **descubrimiento** de las Américas. Cada 12 de octubre, miles de estudiantes dominicanos **acuden** a estos monumentos para celebrar el día de la Raza. Hay **procesiones** de estudiantes y **bandas** y **suenan** las campanas de las iglesias. En general, es un día de mucha alegría.

Las escuelas organizan desfiles por la zona colonial de Santo Domingo y en el **Faro** de Colón, con **banderas** dominicanas y con flores de diversos tipos, sobre todo rosas. Es un día que no olvido, no importa en donde esté. En Nueva York o en Santo Domingo, el 12 de octubre será un día en el cual siempre estaré consciente de mi herencia. ¡Dominicana hoy y siempre!

Ángela Beatriz Corona

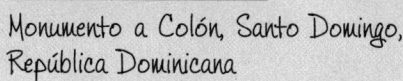
Monumento a Colón, Santo Domingo, República Dominicana

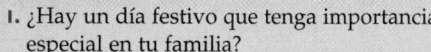
Colón llega al Caribe

Online Workbook
CLASSZONE.COM

¿Comprendiste?

1. ¿Hay un día festivo que tenga importancia especial en tu familia?
2. Algunos días festivos celebran relaciones personales, como el Día de las Madres y de los Padres, o el Día de la Amistad. Pero otros conmemoran días nacionales, como el Día de la Independencia. ¿Cuál prefieres? ¿Por qué?
3. ¿Piensas mucho en tu nacionalidad? ¿Hay días festivos en los cuales piensas más en tu nacionalidad que en otros?
4. ¿Crees que es importante tener días festivos nacionales? ¿Por qué?
5. ¿Qué sabes de Cristóbal Colón? ¿Tienes la misma relación con él y su familia como la que tiene Ángela? ¿Por qué?

doscientos veintisiete
El Caribe Etapa 3 **227**

Comprehension Questions

1. ¿El Día de la Abolición de la Esclavitud es un día muy solemne? (Sí.)
2. ¿Fueron esclavos algunos de los antepasados de Emilio? (Sí.)
3. ¿Empiezan el día con una procesión? (No.)
4. ¿Sufrieron los esclavos justicia o injusticia? (injusticia)
5. ¿Tuvieron los antepasados una lucha o una fiesta contra el opresor? (una lucha)
6. En la Plaza, ¿oyen el himno nacional o la bomba y plena? (la bomba y plena)
7. ¿Quién fue el primer europeo que llegó a la República Dominicana? (el Almirante Cristóbal Colón)
8. ¿Qué conmemoran los monumentos históricos en la zona colonial de Santo Domingo? (el descubrimiento de las Américas)
9. ¿Qué hacen los estudiantes dominicanos cada 12 de octubre? (Acuden a los monumentos históricos para celebrar el día de la Raza.)
10. ¿Qué otras cosas toman lugar el día de la Raza? (Hay procesiones de estudiantes y bandas y suenan las campanas de las iglesias.)

Culture Highlights

● **SANTO DOMINGO** La ciudad colonial de Santo Domingo fue la primera ciudad construida en el Nuevo Mundo por los colonizadores europeos. Es el lugar de varios edificios históricos «primeros» en el Nuevo Mundo: la Catedral Santo Domingo, la primera catedral; las ruinas del hospital Nicolás de Bari, el primer hospital; y la Fortaleza Ozama, la fortaleza más antigua.

Block Schedule

Change of Pace Have students imagine that they are reporting live on television about 1 of the 2 celebrations described here. Have them begin their reports by stating where they are, what is being celebrated, the date, the time of day, what they see, and what people are doing and feeling.

Teaching All Students

Extra Help Working in pairs, have students re-read each paragraph of the **En contexto**. Have them ask each other one question about each paragraph.

Challenge Use the **¿Comprendiste?** questions as a basis for students to create surveys. They may add additional questions. Students then survey at least 5 people and compile the results.

Multiple Intelligences

Interpersonal Have small groups of students discuss **El Día de la Abolición de la Esclavitud.** How would they describe the different customs? Have each group suggest 3 more ways to observe this day. Do they know of any similar observances in the mainland U.S.?

🔔 Quick Start Review

♻ Vocabulary review

Use OHT 39 or write on the board:
Write the word that doesn't belong in each group.

1. la plena, la bomba, la bandera, la cumbia
2. el faro, la banda, el conjunto, la orquesta
3. conmemorar, enfrentar, honrar, celebrar
4. el almirante, la costumbre, el descubrimiento, la bandera
5. los antepasados, el esclavo, la victoria, el opresor

Answers
1. la bandera   2. el faro   3. enfrentar
4. la costumbre   5. la victoria

Teaching Suggestions
Presenting Situations

- Present the Listening Strategy, p. 228, and discuss the Pre-listening question.
- Have students look at a current map of the Caribbean. What countries are on the island of **La Española?**
- Use OHT 36 and 37 to present the **Mirar** section. Ask simple yes/no, either/or, or short-answer questions.
- Use Audio CD 9 and have students do the **Escuchar** section (see Script, TE p. 223B). Then have students complete the Listening Strategy exercise.
- Have students work in pairs or groups to complete the **Hablar/Escribir** section.

AUDIO 🎧
En vivo
SITUACIONES

PARA ESCUCHAR
STRATEGY: LISTENING

Pre-listening Here you will listen to a formal presentation about Columbus. What differences do you anticipate between an oral report and an informal conversation?

Listen and take notes Quick comprehension of numbers is often one of the last listening skills we master. Write down each date when you hear it. Afterward, go back and jot down what happened on that date.

Los viajes del Almirante

Estudias los viajes de Cristóbal Colón en tu clase de historia. Primero vas a mirar un mapa de sus viajes y luego escucharás a un compañero dominicano que da un informe oral sobre Colón.

❶ Mirar

Estudia el mapa que sigue los viajes de Cristóbal Colón en el año 1492.

El Viaje de Colón
Océano Atlántico
Guanahaní
Cuba
La Española

228   doscientos veintiocho
Unidad 3

② Escuchar 🎧

En tu clase de historia, Miguel, un estudiante dominicano, escribió su ensayo sobre Cristóbal Colón. Primero, lee las oraciones a continuación. Luego, escucha mientras Miguel lee su ensayo. Ordena las oraciones según la información que da Miguel.

_____ Colón establece la primera ciudad española y la nombra «La Isabela».

_____ Los monarcas Fernando e Isabel le dieron el dinero a Colón para hacer su viaje.

_____ Colón murió en España, convencido de que su expedición llegó a las Indias.

_____ El tres de agosto, 1492, la expedición de Colón salió de España en la Niña, la Pinta y la Santa María.

_____ Colón llegó a una bella isla que nombró «La Española».

_____ Colón llegó a una isla llamada Guanahaní.

_____ El hermano menor de Colón, Bartolomé, fundó Santo Domingo.

Puerto de Palos

③ Hablar/Escribir 👥

En grupos de dos o tres, conversen sobre la vida de Cristóbal Colón. ¿Creen que su descubrimiento fue importante? ¿Saben algo más sobre sus viajes? ¿Pueden añadir información al ensayo de Miguel? Busquen más información sobre Colón en Internet o en una enciclopedia. Cada persona del grupo debe traer un dato importante sobre el hombre.

Teaching All Students

Extra Help Play the audio again so that students can take notes about dates and events. Then have students use their notes to create a time line of the important events given about Columbus.

Multiple Intelligences

Logical/Mathematical Have students look at a globe and chart on graph paper the routes of each of Columbus' voyages. They should include any major changes in latitude and longitude made during the trips.

Interdisciplinary Connection

Geography Have students create topographical maps of the Dominican Republic. They might research the names of cities and geographic features on a Spanish map and use these on their maps.

Escuchar (See script, p. 223B.)

Answers
5 Colón establece la primera ciudad española y la nombra «La Isabela».
1 Los monarcas Fernando e Isabel le dieron el dinero a Colón para hacer su viaje.
7 Colón murió en España, convencido de que su expedición llegó a las Indias.
2 El tres de agosto, 1492, la expedición de Colón salió de España en la Niña, la Pinta y la Santa María.
4 Colón llegó a una bella isla que nombró «La Española».
3 Colón llegó a una isla llamada Guanahaní.
6 El hermano menor de Colón, Bartolomé, fundó Santo Domingo.

Hablar/Escribir

Answers will vary.

Block Schedule

Variety Divide the class into small groups. Have each group imagine an important discovery for the 21st century. Each group should decide on a discovery, make a sketch of it, and describe it. In addition, they should explain its importance to the community/world. (For additional activities, see **Block Scheduling Copymasters**.)

Teaching Resource Options

Print

Block Scheduling Copymasters
Unit 3 Resource Book
  Absent Student Copymasters, p. 174

Audiovisual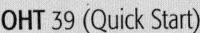

OHT 39 (Quick Start)

Quick Start Review

♻ Dialog review

Use OHT 39 or write on the board:
Create sentences, adding words and
making necessary changes:

1. antepasado / ser / esclavos
2. almirante / descubrir / América
3. ser / victoria justa
4. conjuntos / tocar / música / afrocaribeño
5. haber / procesiones / día de la Raza

Answers.
Answers will vary. Answers could include:
1. Nuestros antepasados fueron esclavos.
2. El almirante Colón descubrió América en 1492.
3. Fue una victoria justa.
4. Los conjuntos tocaron música afrocaribeña.
5. Hay procesiones el día de la Raza.

Teaching Suggestions
Comprehension Check

Use **Actividades 1–4** to assess retention
after the **Vocabulario** and **Situaciones.**
As a homework assignment, have
students create 1 additional item for
Actividad 1 and 2 additional items for
Actividad 2 for the class to complete.

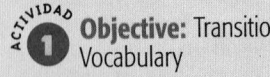
Objective: Transitional practice
Vocabulary

Answers
1. c	3. b
2. d	4. a

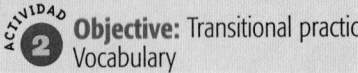
Objective: Transitional practice
Vocabulary

Answers
1. ensayo patriótico	5. honrar
2. banda	6. injusticia
3. costumbres	7. antepasados
4. acuden	

En acción

PARTE
A

Práctica del vocabulario

Objectives for Activities 1-4
• Describe historic events

① Descripciones

Leer/*Escribir* Lee las descripciones. Decide
qué oración mejor describe cada foto.

a.

b.

c.

d.

1. La procesión de los estudiantes a la estatua de Colón es una costumbre del día de la Raza.

2. El día de los Veteranos es un día solemne en el cual honramos la memoria de los soldados de nuestro país.

3. La bandera es un símbolo que representa la historia de un país.

4. Muchas personas acudieron para apoyar su discurso.

② El ensayo patriótico

Hablar/*Escribir* Completa las oraciones con las
palabras de la lista.

acuden   banda   costumbres
antepasados   ensayo patriótico
injusticia   honrar

1. Voy a escribir un _____ sobre la lucha para nuestra independencia.

2. En los desfiles, siempre hay una _____ que toca el himno nacional.

3. En mi familia tenemos varias _____ para celebrar el día de la Raza.

4. Durante el día de la Raza, miles de personas _____ a la plaza central de la ciudad para oír discursos y celebrar el descubrimiento de las Américas.

5. Es importante _____ a los héroes que dieron sus vidas para luchar contra la esclavitud.

6. No debemos tolerar la _____ contra las personas sin hogar.

7. Nuestros _____ lucharon para nuestra independencia, algo que olvidamos fácilmente.

Classroom Management

Time Saver Prepare an answer key for **Actividades
1** and **2** on an overhead transparency. Have students
exchange papers for peer correction.

Peer Review Have partners review the Speaking
Strategy on p. 231. Then have them brainstorm
together to create notes that will help them organize
what they want to say in **Actividad 4.**

3 Conversación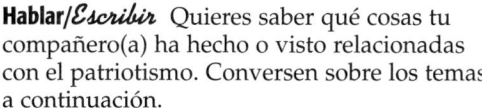

Hablar/Escribir Quieres saber qué cosas tu compañero(a) ha hecho o visto relacionadas con el patriotismo. Conversen sobre los temas a continuación.

modelo

ensayo patriótico

Tú: *¿Has escrito un ensayo patriótico alguna vez?*

Compañero(a): *Sí, lo escribí sobre el día de la Independencia de Estados Unidos.*

procesión patriótica
enfrentar una injusticia
celebrar una victoria
conmemorar antepasados
bailar bomba y plena
una banda en desfile
costumbres de la familia para el día de…

Vocabulario

El orgullo nacional

la patria *mother country*
el (la) patriota *patriot*
patriótico(a) *patriotic*
el patriotismo *patriotism*

▶ *¿Crees que tenemos mucho patriotismo en este país? ¿Por qué?*

4 Las costumbres

STRATEGY: SPEAKING

Describe celebrations There are many aspects in a description of a celebration: **el lugar, la gente, la ropa, la comida, las acciones**. Think also about the time frame you want to use: **Por lo general, vamos a… vemos a…, llevamos…, comemos…, hacemos….** What if you changed the time frame? What tenses would you use if you said: **Pero el año pasado…** or **Cuando era niño(a)**…

♻ **Hablar** Quieres saber si tu compañero(a) tiene algunas costumbres para ciertos días festivos. Conversen sobre dos o tres días festivos de su ciudad, estado o país. Mira la página 213 para repasar los días festivos.

modelo

Tú: *¿Cómo celebran el día de Acción de Gracias en tu familia?*

Compañero(a): *Pues, tenemos varias costumbres. Primero… Y tu familia, ¿cómo celebra el día de… ?*

3 Objective: Transitional practice
Vocabulary in conversation

Answers will vary.

4 Objective: Open-ended practice
Vocabulary in conversation
♻ Holiday vocabulary

Answers will vary.

Teaching Suggestions
Teaching Vocabulary
After presenting the vocabulary for **El orgullo nacional,** have students come up with tongue twisters using the words.

🔔 Quick Wrap-up
Ask simple yes/no questions:
¿Cristóbal Colón salió del Puerto de Palos en España? (Sí) ¿Salió el 20 de agosto de 1492? (No) ¿Los monarcas españoles eran Fernando e Isabel? (Sí) ¿Después de 2 meses Colón llegó a una isla que se llama Guanahaní? (Sí) etc.

Block Schedule
FunBreak Divide the class into groups of 4–5. Put the names of several holidays in a paper bag. Have groups brainstorm descriptions of various holidays. Then 1 member draws a holiday and describes it for his/her group. If the group guesses correctly, it gets a point. If not, the next group gets a chance to guess. After a group guesses correctly, play passes to the next group.

Teaching All Students

Extra Help Focus on a whole-class review of the vocabulary. Divide the class into 2 teams. Write vocabulary words/expressions on slips of paper. Hand 1 slip to 1 student from each team. Students act out the words/expressions or give a synonym or definition. Their respective teams have to guess the word. If the team guesses correctly, they get a point. If not, the other team gets a chance to guess.

Multiple Intelligences
Verbal Have students sketch scenes of a celebration of **el Día de la Abolición de la Esclavitud** in Puerto Rico.
Intrapersonal Have students write a short paragraph about 1 of the following: (a) **Cómo yo soy patriótico(a)**; (b) **Cómo llegué a entender el patriotismo.**

Teaching Resource Options

Print

Más práctica Workbook PE,
   pp. 85–86
Cuaderno para hispanohablantes
   PE, pp. 83–84
Block Scheduling Copymasters
Unit 3 Resource Book
   Más práctica Workbook TE,
      pp. 145–146
   Cuaderno para hispanohablantes
      TE, pp. 161–162
   Absent Student Copymasters, p. 174
   Audioscript, p. 181

Audiovisual

OHT 40 (Quick Start), 44 (Grammar)
Audio Program CD 9, Track 2, Activity 5

Technology

Online Workbook, U3E3
Take-Home Tutor CD-ROM, U3E3

Quick Start Review

🕭 Subjunctive forms

Use OHT 40 or write on the board:
Complete each sentence with the
appropriate present subjunctive form of
the verb:

1. Me aconsejan que ___ mucho.
   (estudiar)
2. Insisto en que tú ___ aquí.
   (dormir)
3. Mariana se alegra de que ustedes
   ___ el día de la Raza. (celebrar)
4. No es cierto que ___ procesión
   de estudiantes mañana. (haber)
5. Sientes que ellos no ___ . (venir)

Answers
1. estudie   4. haya
2. duermas   5. vengan
3. celebren

Objectives for Activities 5–15
• Make suggestions and wishes • Express emotion and doubt • State cause and effect

REPASO   Summary of the Subjunctive (Part 1)

As you have learned, you use the **subjunctive** in Spanish in subordinate
clauses when the **main clause** expresses…

• **wishes:** querer, recomendar, insistir en, aconsejar, etc.

   Queremos que vengas a la procesión.
   We want you to come to the procession.

   ¿Qué **recomienda Ud. que hagamos**?
   What do you recommend that we do?

• **emotion:** alegrarse, sentir, esperar, ojalá, es bueno/malo/
   mejor que, etc.

   Me alegro de que Uds. conozcan la bomba y plena.
   I am happy that you know the bomba and plena.

• **doubt, disagreement,** and **denial:** no creer/pensar, dudar, no
   es cierto/verdad que, etc.

   Dudábamos de que ellos **enfrentaran** el problema.
   We doubted that they would face the problem.

When you have a sentence with a subordinate clause and the subjunctive
is required, the main clause will be in the indicative and the subordinate
clause in the subjunctive. The tense you use in the main clause will help
you determine which tense to use in the subordinate clause.

Main Clause Indicative	Subordinate Clause Subjunctive
if **present, future, present perfect**	use present
	Siento que **termine** la celebración. *I'm sorry that the celebration is ending.*
if **present**	use present perfect (if action has taken place)
	Siento que **se haya terminado** la celebración. *I'm sorry that the celebration has ended.*
if **preterite, imperfect, conditional, past perfect**	use imperfect
	Sentía que **terminara** la celebración. *I was sorry that the celebration was ending.*

Practice:
⑤⑥⑦⑧
Más práctica
cuaderno p. 85
Para hispanohablantes
cuaderno pp. 83–84

Online Workbook
CLASSZONE.COM

---

⑤ El desfile

Escuchar/*Escribir* Tu familia te
habla sobre el desfile que van
a ver hoy. Escucha y di qué
quieren que tú hagas.

modelo

mi abuela / ir al desfile

*Mi abuela quiere que yo vaya al
desfile con ella.*

1. mi abuela / ponerse ropa
   de verano
2. mi abuela / llegar al
   desfile temprano
3. mi abuela / traer una silla
4. mi papá / invitar a dos
   amigos
5. mis papás / venir a la casa
   dos horas antes del desfile
6. mis hermanos / quedarse
   en el parque todo el día

Apoyo para estudiar

Tenses of the subjunctive

This chart will help you
remember what tenses to use:

Main Clause Indicative	Subordinate Subjunctive
present, future, present perfect	present
present	present perfect (if action has taken place)
preterite, imperfect, conditional, past perfect	imperfect

Classroom Community

Paired Activity Have students work in pairs to
complete the following sentences: El/La profesor(a)
de español nos pidió que no… / El/La profesor(a)
de español esperaría que… / El/La profesor(a) de
español quería que… / El/La profesor(a) de español
nos recomendará que… Have pairs write answers on
the board and correct.

Learning Scenario Have students do a variation of
Actividad 7. This time they discuss a holiday of their
own choosing, using the list of expressions given and
adding any others that are necessary.

6 ¡Me alegro!

Escribir Vas a ir a la República Dominicana para celebrar el día de la Raza con tu amiga dominicana Susana. Ella te escribe esta carta. Completa la carta con la forma correcta de los verbos indicados.

> **Nota: Gramática**
>
> Don't forget that verbs that end in **-cer** add a **z** to their subjunctive forms. Verbs that end in **-gar** add a **u** to their subjunctive forms.

Querido(a) amigo(a),

¡No puedo creer que la próxima semana vas a estar aquí en Santo Domingo! Ya sabes que vamos a ir a la celebración del día de la Raza el sábado. Me alegro de que tú __1__ (querer) venir con nosotros. Quiero que tú __2__ (ver) como celebramos nosotros los dominicanos. No es cierto que __3__ (ser) un día solemne. Hay muchas cosas divertidas que hacer. Siento que tu hermana no __4__ (poder) venir contigo. Dudo que (nosotros) __5__ (quedarse) todo el día, porque queremos llegar a casa antes de que __6__ (oscurecer). ¡Espero que __7__ (divertirse)! Recomiendo que tú __8__ (llegar) a nuestra casa como a las diez de la mañana. ¡Qué lindo será verte!

Un abrazo,

Susana

7 Santo Domingo

Hablar Tu compañero(a) va a celebrar el día de la Raza en Santo Domingo. ¿Qué le recomiendas?

modelo

Compañero(a): *Voy a celebrar el día de la Raza en Santo Domingo.*

Tú: *¡Recomiendo que hagas tus reservaciones hoy!*

Compañero(a): *Pienso viajar en avión.*

Tú: *Recomiendo que...*

> **Nota: Gramática**
>
> Remember that verbs that end in **-ger** change the **g** to a **j** in their subjunctive forms.

- hacer tus reservaciones
- comprar tus boletos
- llamar a la agencia de viajes
- escoger un hotel cerca del centro
- llevar ropa de verano
- comprar cheques de viajero
- no ir solo(a)
- visitar los monumentos históricos
- ser parte del desfile estudiantil

Teaching Suggestions
Reviewing Summary of the Subjunctive (Part 1)

- Begin by reviewing subjunctive forms. Point out to students the verb charts beginning on p. R29. Students should refer to these charts when necessary.
- Have students give additional sample sentences for the 3 categories in the subjunctive tense summary chart.

ACTIVIDAD 5 **Objective:** Controlled practice Listening comprehension/subjunctive

Answers (See script, p. 223B.)
1. Mi abuela recomienda que me ponga ropa de verano.
2. Mi abuela insiste en que lleguemos al desfile temprano.
3. Mi abuela me aconseja que traiga una silla.
4. Mi papá quiere que yo invite a dos amigos.
5. Mis papás recomiendan que mis amigos vengan a la casa dos horas antes del desfile.
6. Mis hermanos insisten en que nos quedemos en el parque todo el día.

ACTIVIDAD 6 **Objective:** Transitional practice Subjunctive in writing

Answers
1. quieras   2. veas   3. sea
4. pueda   5. nos quedemos
6. oscurezca   7. te diviertas   8. llegues

ACTIVIDAD 7 **Objective:** Open-ended practice Subjunctive in conversation

 Travel vocabulary

Answers will vary.

Dictation

Using the Listening Activity Script for **Actividad 5** on TE p. 223B, dictate selected sentences to students. You may want to write answers on the board for students to correct their own work.

Block Schedule

Change of Pace Have students design a flier for an all-inclusive vacation in Santo Domingo. They will need to look up information in the library or on the Internet. The flier should include information about the hotel, food, activities, and prices. It should also include a paragraph of recommendations using verbs such as **recomendar, insistir en, aconsejar,** etc. (For additional activities, see **Block Scheduling Copymasters.**)

Teaching All Students

Extra Help Have students write the **tú** present subjunctive forms of all the verbs in the list for **Actividad 7** before completing the activity.

Native Speakers Tell students to imagine they work for a travel magazine. Have them write a magazine article about their countries of origin, giving recommendations for what visitors should bring, see, do, etc.

Multiple Intelligences

Visual Have students use colored pencils or markers to write subjunctive sentences. They should use 3 different colors: 1 for the subjunctive trigger phrase, 1 for the subjunctive form, and 1 for any other words.

Musical/Rhythmic Have students create a rap mnemonic device for remembering the sequence of tenses for the subjunctive.

Teaching Resource Options

Print 📖

Block Scheduling Copymasters
Unit 3 Resource Book
  Absent Student Copymasters,
  pp. 174–175

Audiovisual 🎧

OHT 40 (Quick Start), 45 (Grammar)

Technology 💻

Online Workbook, U3E3
Take-Home Tutor CD-ROM, U3E3

ACTIVIDAD 8 Objective: Open-ended practice
Subjunctive in conversation

Answers will vary.

🔔 Quick Start Review

♻️ **Subjunctive**

Use OHT 40 or write on the board:
Complete the following sentences with
phrases of your choosing:

1. Mi abuela quiere que yo...
2. Yo dudaba que mis hermanos...
3. Ojalá que nosotros...
4. Mis hermanas insistían en que yo...
5. Yo daría una fiesta si ellos....

Answers will vary.

Teaching Suggestions
Reviewing Summary of the Subjunctive (Part 2)

- Ask students to supply sentences for
  the subjunctive after the nonexistent
  or indefinite antecedents that are
  relative to their lives.
- Have students write slogans with the
  themes of holidays and celebrations
  for the conjunctions of time.
- To reinforce the meanings of the
  conjunctions of time, give students
  subjunctive sentences with the
  conjunctions and have them tell what
  happens next. For example: **Iremos al
  parque a menos que llueva. →
  Llueve; no vamos al parque.**

Práctica: gramática y vocabulario *continuación*

8 ¡Vamos a celebrar!

Hablar/*Escribir* Ayer fue el día
de la Raza en Santo Domingo.
¿Qué querían todos que hicieras?

modelo

Compañero(a): *¿Qué querían tus
padres que hicieras?*

Tú: *Mis padres querían que fuera
al desfile con mi hermana.*

tu mejor amigo(a)   tu tío(a)

tu primo(a)

tu profesor(a)

tu hermano(a)

tus amigos(as)

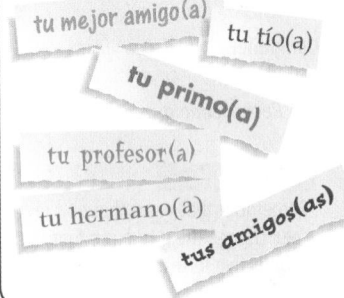

Nota cultural

El naufragio de la Santa María
En diciembre de 1492, la Santa
María, uno de los tres barcos de
Colón, naufragó (*shipwrecked*)
cerca de la isla La Española. Con
la madera y otros materiales
rescatados del naufragio, Colón y
sus acompañantes construyeron
un fuerte al que dieron el nombre
de La Navidad. En su segundo
viaje, en 1493, Colón llegó al
fuerte que encontró vacío.
Abandonó el fuerte y estableció la
colonia de Isabela cerca del Cabo
Isabela en lo que hoy se conoce
como la República Dominicana.

REPASO Summary of the Subjunctive (Part 2)

▸ You have also learned to use the **subjunctive** after the **nonexistent** or
indefinite antecedents:

No hay discurso **que
me interese.**
There's no speech that interests me.

Busco una banda **que sepa
tocar** el himno nacional.
*I'm looking for a band that knows
how to play the national anthem.*

> No hay nada/nadie que...
>
> Busco/Necesito/Quiero...
>   algo/alguien que...
>
> ¿Hay algo/alguien que... ?
>
> ¿Conoces a alguien que... ?

▸ Use the **subjunctive** with these **conjunctions of time,** but only if the
main clause has a **command** or refers to the **future:**

Nos iremos cuando termine
la fiesta.
We'll leave when the party ends.

Quédense aquí **hasta que empiece**
el desfile.
Stay here until the parade begins.

> cuando
> en cuanto
> después (de) que
> tan pronto como
> hasta que

▸ You do not use the subjunctive if the **conjunction** is in a past-tense
context.

Estaba lloviendo cuando empezó el discurso.
It was raining when the speech began..

▸ Use the **subjunctive** with these **conjunctions:**

Te lo digo/Te lo diré **para que** te des
cuenta del problema.
*I'm telling you/I will tell you **so that** you'll **realize**
the problem.*

Te lo dije **para que** te dieras cuenta
del problema.
*I told you **so that** you'd **realize** the problem.*

> antes (de) que
> con tal (de) que
> a menos que
> para que
> en caso (de) que

**Practice:
Actividades**
9 10 11 12

Más práctica
cuaderno p. 86
Para hispanohablantes
cuaderno pp. 83–84

🌐 **Online Workbook**
CLASSZONE.COM

Classroom Community

Learning Scenario Have students imagine that
they are part of Columbus' expedition. Have them
describe what they do and what they see.

Game Divide the class into groups of 6. Have
students make a set of cards with the conjunctions on
p. 234, and the following words: **busco, necesito,
quiero algo, quiero alguien, ¿hay algo?, ¿hay
alguien?** Then have them make a spinner with a piece
of cardboard and a paper clip for a pointer and a pencil
for a pivot. On the spinner have them write the names
of each member of the group. Students spin the
spinner, then take a card and say a sentence that
includes the word written on the card. For example:
**Necesito estudiar esta noche. Necesito que alguien
me ayude a estudiar.**

⑨ La comunidad ♻

Leer/*Escribir* Eres el (la) presidente(a) del comité para mejorar la ciudad. Creas varios pósters que pones por toda la ciudad. Le explicas a un(a) compañero(a) el propósito *(purpose)* de cada cartel. ¿Qué le dices?

modelo

buscar voluntarios / mantener limpia la ciudad

Buscamos voluntarios que mantengan limpia la ciudad.

1. *buscar / músicos hacer audición para...*

2. *necesitar / candidato ser conservador*

3. *querer / voluntarios mantener...*

4. *buscar / personas luchar contra...*

5. *querer / ciudadanos respetar leyes de la ciudad*

6. *necesitar / personas resolver problemas...*

doscientos treinta y cinco
El Caribe Etapa 3 **235**

ACTIVIDAD 9 **Objective:** Controlled practice
Subjunctive in reading and writing

♻ **Community service vocabulary**

Answers

1. Buscamos músicos que hagan una audición para el conjunto de bomba y plena.
2. Necesitamos un candidato que sea conservador.
3. Queremos voluntarios que mantengan limpia la ciudad.
4. Buscamos personas que luchen contra la injusticia.
5. Queremos ciudadanos que respeten las leyes de la ciudad.
6. Necesitamos personas que resuelvan problemas del gobierno.

Critical Thinking

Ask students if they agree with the messages in posters #2–6. Why or why not? What might they include on a community action poster?

Culture Highlights

● **¡VOTA!** En Costa Rica, alrededor de 10.000 niños participan en las elecciones. Los votos no cuentan, por supuesto, pero así los chicos tienen la oportunidad de pensar sobre los temas sobresalientes de cada elección. Para llenar las papeletas *(ballots)*, los niños utilizan crayolas e incluso, sus huellas digitales.

Pida a los estudiantes que piensen sobre los problemas que les interesarían si tuvieran que votar hoy mismo. ¿Por qué son importantes?

Block Schedule

Variety Have students act out wishes while the class forms sentences using the subjunctive. For example: Carlos acts thirsty and the class responds, **Carlos quiere que nosotros le demos una bebida.** Then Carlos falls to the ground, and the class responds, **Necesita que nosotros lo ayudemos.** (For additional activities, see **Block Scheduling Copymasters.**)

Teaching All Students

Extra Help Ask students to talk about their plans for the weekend, using conjunctions of time + subjunctive.

Native Speakers Have students prepare a more detailed report about Columbus' first trip to the Americas to present to the class.

Multiple Intelligences

Naturalist Have students write 5 environmental slogans or warnings using the conjunctions of time listed on p. 234.

Verbal Ask students to prepare a 3–5 sentence speech from the perspective of one of the individuals featured in the posters on p. 235, then present it to the class.

Teaching Resource Options

Print

Más práctica Workbook PE,
 pp. 85–86

Cuaderno para hispanohablantes
 PE, pp. 83–84

Unit 3 Resource Book
 Más práctica Workbook TE,
  pp. 145–146
 Cuaderno para hispanohablantes
  TE, pp. 161–162
 Information Gap Activities, p. 167
 Absent Student Copymasters, p. 175

Objective: Controlled practice
Subjunctive/vocabulary

Answers

1. El pueblo quiere un alcalde que entienda los problemas de la ciudad.
2. La monarquía necesita ciudadanos que respeten las leyes.
3. La gente quiere un gobierno que sea democrático.
4. El país quiere un presidente que tenga una ideología honorable.
5. La gente quiere un líder que sepa tomar decisiones.
6. El alcalde necesita ciudadanos que lo apoyen.
7. El estado quiere un(a) gobernador(a) que no olvide sus responsabilidades.
8. El rey busca un ejército que esté siempre listo.
9. Los ciudadanos quieren elecciones que sean limpias.
10. Los políticos necesitan gente que vote por ellos.

Teaching Suggestions
Teaching Vocabulary

Introduce the vocabulary by comparing the governments of England and the U.S. Give examples that are easily recognizable to reinforce individual words. For example: **La reina de Inglaterra es Elizabeth II. Su hijo Charles va a ser el rey algún día.**

10 El gobierno

Hablar/*Escribir* La política es muy complicada. ¿Qué necesitan los ciudadanos y las personas en el poder?

modelo

 gente / querer / gobierno / escribir leyes justas

 La gente quiere un gobierno que escriba leyes justas.

1. pueblo / querer / alcalde / entender los problemas de la ciudad
2. monarquía / insistir en que / ciudadanos / obedecer las leyes
3. gente / querer / gobierno / ser democrático
4. país / querer / presidente(a) / tener una ideología honorable
5. gente / querer / líder / saber tomar decisiones
6. alcalde / necesitar / ciudadanos / apoyarlo
7. estado / querer / gobernador(a) / no olvidar sus responsabilidades
8. rey / buscar / ejército / estar siempre listo
9. ciudadanos / querer / elecciones / ser limpias
10. políticos / necesitar / gente / votar por ellos

Vocabulario

La política

el (la) alcalde(sa) *mayor*

conservador(a) *conservative*

la constitución *constitution*

la democracia *democracy*

democrático(a) *democratic*

el derecho *the (legal) right*

el ejército *army*

el (la) gobernador(a) *governor*

el gobierno *government*

la ideología *ideology*

la ley *law*

el (la) líder *leader*

liberal *liberal*

la monarquía *monarchy*

el poder *power*

el (la) presidente(a) *president*

la reina *queen*

el rey *king*

¿Qué tipo de gobierno tenemos en este país? En tu opinión, ¿cómo es? ¿Quiénes son los líderes más importantes? ¿Cómo son?

236 doscientos treinta y seis
Unidad 3

Classroom Community

Group Activity Divide the class into groups. Have each group write a plan for what they consider the perfect student/school government. Their plan should begin with **Queremos un gobierno que...**

Portfolio Have students write a paragraph about the type of government in the U.S. and explain who holds the reins of power at the local, state, and national levels.

Rubric A = 13–15 pts. B = 10–12 pts. C = 7–9 pts. D = 4–6 pts. F = < 4 pts.

Writing criteria	Scale				
Vocabulary use	1	2	3	4	5
Grammar/spelling accuracy	1	2	3	4	5
Clear main idea and details	1	2	3	4	5

11 Las celebraciones

Hablar/*Escribir* ¿Qué hacen todos antes y después de la celebración? Combina palabras y frases de las dos columnas para explicarlo. Usa el adverbio **cuando** y los detalles que necesites en tus oraciones.

modelo

Ellos se irán a casa cuando termine la celebración.

> **Nota: Gramática**
>
> Remember that verbs that end in **-zar** change the **z** to a **c** in their subjunctive forms.

yo	terminar la celebración
tú	empezar el desfile
él/ella	subir la bandera
ellos	visitar el monumento
nosotros(as)	tocar el himno nacional
todos	sonar las campanas
	acabarse el discurso

12 ¿Qué van a hacer?

Hablar/*Escribir* Tú quieres saber qué van a hacer tu compañero(a) y sus amigos para celebrar ciertos días festivos. ¿Qué le preguntas y cómo te responde? Conversen sobre todas las posibilidades, usando la frase **con tal de que** y siguiendo el modelo.

modelo

Tú: *¿Van a participar en el desfile?*

Compañero(a): *Sí. Vamos a participar en el desfile con tal de que no tome mucho tiempo.*

More Practice: Más comunicación *p. R11*

También se dice

A los dominicanos también se les llama **quisqueyanos**.

Nota cultural

El Himno Nacional de la República Dominicana fue escrito en 1883. El poeta y educador Emilio Prud'homme compuso la letra y el maestro José Reyes la música. Reyes vio el himno de Argentina en un periódico parisino y decidió escribir uno para la República Dominicana. Invitó a su amigo Prud'homme a escribir la letra. El himno se cantó en febrero de 1884 al llevar a la República los restos de Juan Pablo Duarte, el libertador del país, quien murió en 1876 en Venezuela.

El Himno Nacional

Quisqueyanos valientes,
alcemos Nuestro canto con
viva emoción. Y del mundo
a la faz ostentemos
Nuestro invicto, glorioso perdón.

¡Salve! el pueblo que, intrépido
y fuerte. A la guerra a morir
se lanzó. Cuando en bélico
reto de muerte sus cadenas
de esclavo rompió.

Teaching All Students

Extra Help Have students scramble the letters of 10 words from the **Vocabulario.** Then have them exchange papers with a partner to unscramble his/her words. Finally, students write sentences using 5 of the 10 words for partners to peer correct.

Multiple Intelligences

Musical/Rhythmic Divide the class into small groups and assign each group a Spanish-speaking country. Have groups research the national anthem of their country. They should try to find out who wrote it, something about its history, and the lyrics.

 Objective: Transitional practice
11 Subjunctive

Answers will vary.

 Objective: Open-ended practice
12 Subjunctive

Answers will vary.

Quick Wrap-up

Write the following expressions on the board: **tan pronto como, cuando, en cuanto, después (de) que, con tal (de) que, a menos que, en caso (de) que.** Then call on students at random to use the expressions to say what they plan to do after graduation: **Usa estas frases para decirme lo que piensas hacer después de la graduación.**

Block Schedule

Expansion Have students work in groups to plan their own school patriotic holiday. The holiday should include: name, date, reason for celebrating, how celebrated, what people should think about on that day. In addition, they should write a school song/anthem to be sung to a familiar tune. (For additional activities, see **Block Scheduling Copymasters.**)

Teaching Resource Options

Print

Más práctica Workbook PE,
  pp. 81–84, 87–88
Actividades para todos Workbook
  PE, pp. 91–96
Cuaderno para hispanohablantes PE,
  pp. 81–82, 85–86
Block Scheduling Copymasters
Unit 3 Resource Book
  Más práctica Workbook TE,
    pp. 143–148
  Actividades para todos Workbook
    TE, pp. 149–154
  Cuaderno para hispanohablantes
    TE, pp. 161–164
  Information Gap Activities, p. 168
  Absent Student Copymasters, p. 176
  Audioscript, p. 181

Audiovisual

OHT 41 (Quick Start), 46 (Grammar)
Audio Program CD 9, Track 3, Activity 14
Word Tiles, U3E3

Technology

Online Workbook, U3E3
Take-Home Tutor CD-ROM, U3E3

Quick Start Review

♻ Conjunctions of time

Use OHT 41 or write on the board:
Complete each sentence with 1 of the
following conjunctions:

**tan pronto como / antes de que /
para que / en caso de que /
a menos que**

1. Te lo digo ___ sepas lo que pasa.
2. Empezaremos ___ ellos lleguen.
3. Estoy preparado para dar el
   discurso ___ él no venga.
4. Estará allí ___ esté enfermo.
5. Quiero cortar el césped ___
   llueva.

Answers.
1. para que
2. tan pronto como
3. en caso de que
4. a menos que
5. antes de que

GRAMÁTICA Subjunctive vs. Indicative

Use the **subjunctive**:

- after expressions of **doubt**
  No creo que sepan la respuesta.
  I don't think that they know the answer.

- to make **suggestions** or **recommendations**
  Marta dijo que viéramos fuegos artificiales.
  Marta said we should see the fireworks.

Use the **indicative**:

- to express **certainty**
  Creo que saben la respuesta.
  I think they know the answer.

- to **report** actions
  Marta dijo que vimos fuegos artificiales.
  Marta said we saw the fireworks.

Vocabulario

♻ **Ya sabes**

dudar	pensar
no creer	creer
es dudoso	es cierto
es improbable	es verdad
no estoy seguro(a)	estoy seguro(a)

Practice: Actividades 13 14 15
Más práctica *cuaderno pp. 87–88*
Para hispanohablantes *cuaderno pp. 85–86*
Online Workbook CLASSZONE.COM

---

13 Opiniones opuestas

Hablar/Escribir Di si estás de acuerdo con estas ideas.

modelo
ese candidato: ser liberal
Creo que ese candidato es liberal.
No creo que ese candidato sea liberal.

1. el gobierno: ser democrático
2. el alcalde: tener dinero
3. el desfile: ser solemne
4. el (la) presidente(a): dar un discurso
5. el (la) gobernador(a): venir a la celebración
6. la ley: ser justa
7. el (la) presidente(a): llegar temprano

14 El (La) dudoso(a)

Escuchar/Escribir Escucha las oraciones y di lo que dudas.

modelo
Dudo que el presidente sea eficiente.

Classroom Community

Paired Activity Divide the class into pairs to debate their opposing party platforms. Students should first discuss who will take what basic position: conservative or liberal. Each person then promotes what they plan to do if their party is elected and instills doubt about the opposing party's objectives and practices.

Learning Scenario Have students pretend that they were President For A Day. Each student states 3 things that he/she did during that day. The other students comment on the statements, using expressions of doubt or certainty.

Activity 16 brings together all concepts presented.

15 ¿Qué dijo?

Hablar/*Escribir* Tu hermano fue a una celebración nacional y te contó todo lo que pasó. Ahora le cuentas los eventos a tu compañero(a). Primero habla sobre los discursos de los políticos durante la celebración y luego cuenta qué pasó, según tu hermano. Sigue el modelo.

modelo

el alcalde / ver la bandera

Compañero(a): *¿Qué dijo el alcalde que hicieran?*

Tú: *Dijo que viéramos la bandera.*

Compañero(a): *¿Qué dijo tu hermano que hicieron?*

Tú: *Dijo que vieron la bandera.*

el alcalde	ver la bandera
la gobernadora	celebrar el día de la Raza
el presidente	subir la bandera
el político liberal	tocar el himno nacional
la política conservadora	luchar por la independencia
	ver el desfile del ejército
	sonar las campanas

16 La entrevista

Hablar Tú eres reportero(a) y dos o tres de tus compañeros son candidatos para alcalde de la ciudad. Hazles preguntas sobre sus campañas.

modelo

Tú: *¿Por qué quiere ser alcalde?*

Compañero(a) 1: *Es importante que participemos en la política de la ciudad.*

Compañero(a) 2: *Yo también voy a hacer campaña. Yo creo que es necesario que…*

Compañero(a) 3: *Cuando sea alcalde…*

More Practice: **Más comunicación** *p. R11*

Online Workbook
CLASSZONE.COM

Refrán

El que quiere ser cabeza, que sea puente.

¿Qué quiere decir el refrán?

¿Crees que los políticos pueden juntar varios grupos de gente? En tu opinión, ¿es mejor ser el (la) líder o parte del grupo? ¿Quién debe establecer las metas para todos?

doscientos treinta y nueve
El Caribe Etapa 3 **239**

Teaching All Students

Extra Help Ask students to give their reactions to the following statements:
• El presidente visitará la escuela esta semana.
• Los estudiantes van a recibir una semana adicional de vacaciones.
• En la cafetería van a vender mejor comida.
• Los profesores no van a dar ni tareas ni exámenes.

Multiple Intelligences
Kinesthetic Begin a sentence with 1 of the vocabulary expressions on p. 238. Tell students to slouch in their chairs if doubt is expressed and sit up straight if certainty is expressed. Next, make statements. If the statement is a suggestion or recommendation, students stand up. If it reports an action, students remain in their seats.

Teaching Suggestions
Teaching Subjunctive vs. Indicative
You may wish to point out to students that in questions with **creer**, the indicative or the subjunctive may be used depending on the certainty or uncertainty of the questioner. For example: ¿Crees que él se siente mal hoy? ¿Crees que tengan tiempo?

ACTIVIDAD 13 **Objective:** Controlled practice Subjunctive vs. indicative
Answers
1. Creo que el gobierno es democrático. *o:* No creo que el gobierno sea democrático.
2. Creo que el alcalde tiene mucho dinero. *o:* No creo que el alcalde tenga mucho dinero.
3. Creo que el desfile es solemne. *o:* No creo que el desfile sea solemne.
4. Creo que el (la) presidente(a) dará un discurso. *o:* No creo que el presidente(a) dé un discurso.
5. Creo que el (la) gobernador(a) vendrá a la celebración. *o:* No creo que el gobernador venga a la celebración.
6. Creo que la ley es justa. *o:* No creo que la ley sea justa.
7. Creo que el (la) presidente(a) llegará temprano. *o:* No creo que el (la) presidente(a) llegue temprano.

ACTIVIDAD 14 **Objective:** Transitional practice Listening comprehension/subjunctive vs. indicative
Answers (See script, p. 223B.)
1. Dudo que el alcalde tenga mucho poder.
2. Dudo que la monarquía exista en veinte años.
3. Dudo que el ejército esté listo para una guerra.
4. Dudo que el gobernador gane las elecciones.
5. Dudo que el congreso pase esa ley.
6. Dudo que nuestros antepasados hayan sufrido mucho.

ACTIVIDAD 15 **Objective:** Open-ended practice Subjunctive vs. indicative in conversation
Answers will vary.

ACTIVIDAD 16 **Objective:** Open-ended practice Subjunctive vs. indicative in conversation
Answers will vary.

Critical Thinking
Ask students what leaders (school, local, national, international) they think have exhibited the behavior expressed in the **Refrán** and why.

Teaching Resource Options

Print

Actividades para todos Workbook PE, pp. 97–99
Block Scheduling Copymasters
Unit 3 Resource Book
 Actividades para todos Workbook TE, pp. 155–157
 Absent Student Copymasters, p. 177
 Audioscript, pp. 181–182

Audiovisual

OHT 41 (Quick Start)
Audio Program CD 9, Tracks 4–5
Canciones CD

Technology

Online Workbook, U3E3
Take-Home Tutor CD-ROM, U3E3

Quick Start Review

♻ Descriptions

Use OHT 41 or write on the board:
Escribe 5 finales diferentes a lo siguiente:
Yo soy...
Answers will vary.

Teaching Suggestions

• **Prereading** Point out to students that the **Versos sencillos** were spontaneous outbursts that Martí wrote while recuperating in the mountains during the winter of 1891.

• **Strategy: Observe what makes poetry** Have students complete the activities outlined under each basic characteristic of a poem.

• **Reading** Have individual students read the **Versos sencillos.** Stop after every 4 lines and ask questions, such as: ¿De qué país habla el poeta cuando dice, «De donde crece la palma»? ¿De dónde vienen sus versos?

En voces
AUDIO
LECTURA

PARA LEER
STRATEGY: READING
Observe what makes poetry Poems are meant to be spoken and are often sung. Here is a poem in which the language is simple but the thought and form are complex. Four basic characteristics of a poem are: rhythm, rhyme, metaphor, and inverted word order.

Rhythm Read the poem aloud. Can you tap a steady beat?

Rhyme Scan the sounds of the last word of each line. Is there a pattern?

Metaphor Find a comparison between two things or a person and a thing. For example in line 8, Martí says «**En los montes, monte soy.**» What do you think he means?

Inverted word order To make everything work together, sometimes the poet changes natural word order. Can you find an example?

LA NATURALEZA

las alas	lo que usa el pájaro para volar
el alma	el espíritu
crecer	vivir y florecer
la lumbre	luz
las yerbas	el césped

Nota cultural

El poema «Versos sencillos» fue la inspiración para la famosa canción "Guantanamera". ¿La conoces?

Sobre el autor

José Martí, poeta, escritor y patriota cubano, nació en La Habana en 1853 cuando Cuba era todavía una colonia española. Escribió y habló a favor de la independencia de Cuba y fue exiliado a España por sus actividades revolucionarias. Luego fundó el Partido Revolucionario Cubano en 1892 y murió en una batalla por la independencia de Cuba en 1895. Martí murió como vivió, al servicio de la libertad de su patria.

Introducción

La poesía de Martí es directa y sincera. Entre sus poesías más famosas se destacan los *Versos libres* e *Ismaelillo*, escritos alrededor de 1882. Aquí tienes unos versos de su libro más conocido, *Versos sencillos*, escrito en 1891.

240 doscientos cuarenta
Unidad 3

Classroom Community

Cooperative Learning Divide the class into groups of 3. Each group member is responsible for analyzing 8 lines of the poem and explaining it to the group. The group then compiles the ideas for a complete poem analysis. Groups present their ideas to the class.

Paired Activity Have pairs of students make a list of all nouns in the poem having to do with nature. Then have them decide together what they think each noun symbolizes. Discuss ideas as a class.

de *Versos sencillos: I.*

Yo soy un hombre sincero
De donde crece la palma,
Y antes de morirme quiero
Echar[1] mis versos del alma.

Yo vengo de todas partes,
Y hacia todas partes voy:
Arte soy entre las artes,
En los montes, monte soy.

Yo sé los nombres extraños[2]
De las yerbas y las flores,
Y de mortales engaños[3],
Y de sublimes dolores[4].

Yo he visto en la noche oscura
Llover sobre mi cabeza
Los rayos de lumbre[5] pura
De la divina belleza.

Alas nacer vi en los hombros
De las mujeres hermosas:
Y salir de los escombros[6],
Volando las mariposas.

Todo es hermoso y constante,
Todo es música y razón,
Y todo, como el diamante,
Antes que luz es carbón.

[1] to send out

[2] strange
[3] tricks, deceits
[4] pains
[5] light

[6] rubble, debris

Online Workbook
CLASSZONE.COM

¿Comprendiste?

1. ¿Cómo participó Martí en la lucha para la independencia de Cuba?
2. ¿Cuáles son las imágenes que usa Martí? ¿Qué piensas de ellas?
3. ¿En qué líneas del poema habla Martí de su origen?

¿Qué piensas?

1. ¿Cómo trata Martí los temas de la naturaleza y el patriotismo?
2. ¿Qué significan estos versos en el contexto de la poesía?
   a. Yo vengo de todas partes / Y hacia todas partes voy.
   b. Y todo, como el diamante, / Antes que luz es carbón.

Hazlo tú

Escribe un poema parecido a éste. Empieza con **yo soy…, de donde…, y antes de morirme…**.

doscientos cuarenta y uno
El Caribe Etapa 3 241

Culture Highlights

● **JOSÉ MARTÍ** José Martí escribió poesía que lleva su estampa única: de tono modesto y callado en su apariencia, pero a la vez brillante y llamativo. Además de participar en la revolución que trajo al tiempo la independencia a Cuba, Martí participó como escritor en otra revolución—una que produjo grandes cambios en la literatura hispana. Éste era un movimiento conocido como el modernismo. El modernismo le dio a los escritores de la América Latina una conciencia más intensa de su propio ambiente. Sirvió para unir diversas corrientes europeas y nativas en una estética nueva y entera.

¿Comprendiste?

Answers
1. Martí escribió y habló a favor de la independencia de Cuba.
2. Usa imágenes sencillas, directas y sinceras. *Answers will vary for second question.*
3. Habla de su origen cuando dice «De donde crece la palma».

Cross Cultural Connections

Have students read the lyrics to *The Star Spangled Banner.* What kinds of images are used in this national anthem? What are the song's themes? Have students compare and contrast the images and themes with those of **Versos sencillos.**

Teaching All Students

Extra Help Ask students to practice the poem and recite it for the class, using appropriate intonation and gestures.

Native Speakers Have students read an additional selection from **Versos sencillos** and compare it to this one.

Multiple Intelligences

Visual Have students illustrate the verses of the poem and write the poem's lines beneath the illustrations.

Block Schedule

Expansion Ask students to write and illustrate a short poem using the vocabulary under **La Naturaleza** on p. 240. (For additional activities, see **Block Scheduling Copymasters.**)

Teaching Resource Options

Print

Block Scheduling Copymasters
Unit 3 Resource Book
  Absent Student Copymasters, p. 178

Audiovisual

OHT 42 (Quick Start)

Technology

www.classzone.com

Quick Start Review

♻ Vocabulary review

Use OHT 42 or write on the board: List at least 5 words related to each of the following:

• la independencia
• una celebración

Answers
Answers will vary. Answers could include:
• la libertad, enfrentar, el poder, la lucha, la historia, conmemorar, la victoria
• la fiesta, el desfile, la máscara, la bomba, la banda, la procesión, sonar

Teaching Suggestions
Presenting Cultura y comparaciones

• Have students read the Connecting Cultures strategy and complete the chart.
• Ask students to brainstorm facts they already know about Christopher Columbus and his voyages.
• Ask students to look at the 3 subtitles of the selection. What do they tell them about this reading?

Reading Strategy

Remind students to preview graphics and photos before reading. What difference do they see between the illustrations at the bottom of p. 242 and the photos on p. 243? What does this juxtaposition tell them about the reading?

En colores
CULTURA Y COMPARACIONES

Una historia única

PARA CONOCERNOS
STRATEGY: CONNECTING CULTURES

Analyze national celebrations You have both read about and experienced national celebrations. Pick a particular celebration, perhaps July 4 in the United States. What did the celebration originally represent? What has it become in popular culture? Make a chart to compare your observations:

DÍA DE LA INDEPENDENCIA EE.UU.

Importancia histórica	Cómo lo conmemoramos
1.	1.
2.	2.
Etc.	Etc.

What conclusions would you make about your observations?

Desfiles, disfraces¹, festejos… El día de la Independencia en la República Dominicana es una ocasión especial por su historia única.

Historia

En 1492, Cristóbal Colón llegó a una isla que llamó La Española. Los españoles luego se instalaron en la parte este de la isla, pero en la parte oeste, los franceses crearon la colonia de Haití. En 1804, los haitianos ganaron su independencia de Francia y en 1822 ocuparon la ciudad española de Santo Domingo.

¹ costumes

242 doscientos cuarenta y dos
Unidad 3

Classroom Community

Group Activity Have groups of 4 students plan an independence day celebration. One student will plan the decorations, one will plan the menu, one will plan the activities, and the fourth will design an invitation. Have the groups present their plans.

Storytelling Have pairs or small groups of students write simple children's stories about the life and voyages of Christopher Columbus. They should research necessary information in the library or on the Internet. Plan a "story time" when pairs/groups read their stories to the class.

Independencia

Después de la ocupación, el patriota dominicano Juan Pablo Duarte fundó un movimiento de resistencia. La noche del 27 de febrero de 1844, los dominicanos declararon la independencia de Haití. Poco después, los haitianos tuvieron que irse de la nueva nación, la República Dominicana.

Celebraciones

En la República Dominicana hay eventos oficiales durante este día patriótico y también hay eventos populares. El 27 de febrero, la gente disfruta del comienzo del Carnaval disfrazándose de payaso², animal u otras cosas. En Santo Domingo, orquestas tocan música bailable a lo largo del hermoso malecón³ de la capital. Los dominicanos celebran hasta altas horas de la noche, conmemorando el día de la Independencia con la alegría del Carnaval.

² clown
³ boardwalk

CLASSZONE.COM
More About the Caribbean

¿Comprendiste?

1. ¿Qué dos países colonizaron La Española?
2. ¿Qué día se celebra la independencia dominicana? ¿Qué evento histórico conmemora?
3. ¿Qué hacen los dominicanos en el malecón en la noche del 27 de febrero?

¿Qué piensas?

1. ¿Cuáles son los dos elementos que dan a la celebración del Día de la Independencia de la República Dominicana un aspecto especial?
2. Compara esta celebración con la de Estados Unidos. ¿Qué elementos comparten?¿Cómo son diferentes?

Hazlo tú

Escribe una breve descripción del día de la Independencia de Estados Unidos. ¿Qué eventos históricos conmemora? ¿Cómo celebra el pueblo estadounidense su independencia? ¿Cómo celebran el día tú y tu familia?

doscientos cuarenta y tres
El Caribe Etapa 3 **243**

Culture Highlights

● **EL CARNAVAL** El carnaval de Santo Domingo es la culminación de la celebración de la época antes de la Cuaresma en todo el país. De los pueblos de Santiago y La Vega vienen los participantes con sus magníficas máscaras de características humanas grotescas, y vistiendo largas capas de seda con chaquetas y pantalones en conjunto con los colores del arco iris. Carrozas, grupos de baile y personajes disfrazados desfilan a lo largo del malecón.

Critical Thinking

Ask students for a definition of a colony. Then ask why colonies often end up fighting for independence. How do the government, economy, and life of the residents change once a colony gains independence?

Interdisciplinary Connection

History Have students research the Dominican patriot Juan Pablo Duarte.

¿Comprendiste?

Answers

1. Francia y España colonizaron La Española.
2. Se celebra el 27 de febrero. Conmemora el día en que los dominicanos declararon la independencia de Haití en 1844.
3. Orquestas tocan música bailable a lo largo del malecón.

Teaching All Students

Extra Help In pairs, have students write 5–8 true/false statements about the reading. Then have them work with another pair and determine the validity of each other's statements.

Multiple Intelligences

Intrapersonal Ask students to write a short paragraph on what independence means to them.

Logical/Mathematical Have students outline the important events of Dominican history from colonization to independence from Haiti.

Block Schedule

Research Have students research the holidays of the Dominican Republic. How many are there? What are they? When are they? What do they commemorate? (For additional activities, see **Block Scheduling Copymasters**.)

Teaching Resource Options

Print

Cuaderno para hispanohablantes PE,
  pp. 87–88
Block Scheduling Copymasters
Unit 3 Resource Book
  Cuaderno para hispanohablantes
    TE, pp. 165–166
  Information Gap Activities, pp. 169–170
  Family Involvement, pp. 179–180

Audiovisual

OHT 42 (Quick Start)

Technology

eTest Plus Online/Test Generator
CD-ROM

🌐 www.classzone.com

Quick Start Review

♻ **Subjunctive with doubt and denial**

Use OHT 42 or write on the board:
Complete each sentence with the
appropriate form of the verb in
parentheses:

1. Pienso que él ____ hoy. (venir)
2. Es improbable que nosotros ____
   a las seis. (terminar)
3. No cree que ésa ____ la bandera
   de Puerto Rico. (ser)
4. Están seguras que Francisco ____
   a tiempo. (llegar)
5. Es verdad que ella ____ una A en
   el examen. (sacar)

Answers
Answers will vary. Answers could include:

1. viene	4. llega (llegó)
2. terminemos	5. saca (sacó)
3. sea	

✓ ### Teaching Suggestions
What Have Students Learned?

Have students look at the "Now you
can…" notes listed on the left side of
pp. 244–245. Remind them to review
the material in the "To review" notes
before doing the activities or taking the
test.

ETAPA 3

Now you can...

• describe historic
  events.

• make suggestions
  and wishes.

To review

• the subjunctive,
  see pp. 232, 234.

Now you can...

• make suggestions
  and wishes.

To review

• the subjunctive,
  see pp. 232, 234.

En uso
REPASO Y MÁS COMUNICACIÓN

OBJECTIVES

• Describe historic events
• Make suggestions and wishes
• Express emotion and doubt
• State cause and effect

① La celebración

Vas a tener una celebración para el día de la Raza, pero tienes
muchos problemas. Conversa con un(a) compañero(a) sobre
qué necesitan para la celebración.

modelo

El conjunto no sabe tocar bomba y plena.

Tú: *Tenemos un problema.*

Compañero(a): *¿Qué?*

Tú: *Necesitamos un conjunto que sepa tocar bomba y plena.*

1. La banda no toca el himno nacional.
2. El cocinero no prepara comida dominicana.
3. Los músicos no cantan canciones tradicionales.
4. La candidata no quiere dar un discurso patriótico.
5. Los estudiantes no quieren participar en el desfile.
6. El lugar no es grande.

② Santo Domingo

Piensas visitar a tu amigo(a) dominicano(a). Él te escribe una carta con sus planes.
Complétala con el subjuntivo de los verbos entre paréntesis para saber qué te dice.

> Querido Esteban:
>
> Siento que se ____ (haber terminado) el verano pero me alegro de que ____
> (venir) a visitarme a Santo Domingo. Yo dudaba de que ____ (poder) venir.
> Quiero que ____ (conocer) nuestras playas. Voy a llamar a alguna amiga que
> ____ (saber) bailar merengue para que te ____ (enseñar). No dejaré que ____
> (regresar) a Boston hasta que ____ (aprender). Cuando ____ (bailar) como yo,
> serás casi dominicano. Para que te ____ (dar cuenta), aquí baila todo el mundo.
>
> Hasta pronto,
>
> Rubén

244 doscientos cuarenta y cuatro
Unidad 3

Classroom Community

Cooperative Learning Divide the class into groups
of 3 and do **Actividad 2** as a cooperative learning
activity. Student 1 gives the first answer orally. Student 2
writes it down. Student 3 checks it for accuracy. Student
2 then begins the next round. Continue until all items
are done. Have students recheck all answers and
submit them for a grade.

Portfolio Have students imagine they are TV
newscasters broadcasting from the carnival in Santo
Domingo. Have them record their descriptions.

Rubric A = 13–15 pts. B = 10–12 pts. C = 7–9 pts. D = 4–6 pts. F = < 4 pts.

Writing criteria	Scale
Grammar and vocabulary accuracy	1 2 3 4 5
Fluency	1 2 3 4 5
Originality	1 2 3 4 5

Self-Check Quiz
CLASSZONE.COM

Now you can...
• express emotion and doubt.

To review
• subjunctive vs. indicative, see p. 238.

3 El debate

Estás en una reunión de tu comunidad. Tú y tu vecino siempre tienen opiniones opuestas sobre la política. ¿Qué le dices y cómo te responde?

modelo

alcalde: *ser conservador*

Tú: *Pienso que el alcalde es conservador.*

Compañero(a): *Dudo que el alcalde sea conservador.*

1. la gobernadora: tener mucho poder
2. el presidente: resolver los problemas de los ciudadanos
3. todos los países: necesitar un ejército
4. el rey: colaborar con la gente
5. el gobierno: preservar los derechos humanos
6. la constitución: necesitar cambios
7. la presidenta: apoyar el desarrollo de los países pobres
8. la reina: tener una ideología liberal

Now you can...
• state cause and effect.

To review
• the subjunctive, see pp. 232, 234.

4 Con tal de que...

Tú dices que vas a hacer algo bajo ciertas condiciones. ¿Qué dices?

modelo

Voy a votar por el candidato liberal con tal de que _____ (resolver los problemas de la ciudad)

Voy a votar por el candidato liberal con tal de que resuelva los problemas de la ciudad.

1. Voy a donar mucho dinero a esa organización con tal de que _____ (honrar la memoria de los veteranos)
2. Vamos a visitar a ciertos países con tal de que _____ (tener un gobierno democrático)
3. Vamos a apoyar a ese gobierno con tal de que _____ (colaborar con los gobiernos de otros países)
4. Voy a votar por el candidato liberal con tal de que _____ (organizar a la gente del pueblo)
5. Voy a participar en la campaña para juntar fondos con tal de que _____ (usarse para mantener limpia la ciudad)
6. Voy a trabajar de voluntario(a) para esa organización con tal de que _____ (luchar contra la pobreza)

ACTIVIDAD 1 Answers

1. Necesitamos una banda que toque el himno nacional.
2. Necesitamos un cocinero que prepare comida dominicana.
3. Necesitamos unos músicos que canten canciones tradicionales.
4. Necesitamos una candidata que dé un discurso patriótico.
5. Necesitamos unos estudiantes que quieran participar en el desfile.
6. Necesitamos un lugar que sea grande.

ACTIVIDAD 2 Answers

1. haya terminado
2. vengas
3. pudieras
4. conozcas
5. sepa
6. enseñe
7. regreses
8. aprendas
9. bailes
10. des cuenta

ACTIVIDAD 3 Answers

1. A: Pienso que la gobernadora tiene mucho poder. / B: Dudo que la gobernadora tenga mucho poder.
2. A: Pienso que el presidente resuelve los problemas de los ciudadanos. / B: Dudo que el presidente resuelva los problemas de los ciudadanos.
3. A: Pienso que todos los países necesitan un ejército. / B: Dudo que todos los países necesiten un ejército.
4. A: Pienso que el rey colabora con la gente. / B: Dudo que el rey colabore con la gente.
5. A: Pienso que el gobierno preserva los derechos humanos. / B: Dudo que el gobierno preserve los derechos humanos.
6. A: Pienso que la constitución necesita cambios. / B: Dudo que la constitución necesite cambios.
7. A: Pienso que la presidenta apoya el desarrollo de los países pobres. / B: Dudo que la presidenta apoye el desarrollo de los países pobres.
8. A: Pienso que la reina tiene una ideología bastante liberal. / B: Dudo que la reina tenga una ideología bastante liberal.

ACTIVIDAD 4 Answers

1. Voy a donar mucho dinero a esa organización con tal de que honre la memoria de los veteranos.
2. Vamos a visitar a ciertos países con tal de que tengan un gobierno democrático.
3. Vamos a apoyar a ese gobierno con tal de que colabore con los gobiernos de otros países.
4. Voy a votar por el candidato liberal con tal de que organice a la gente del pueblo.
5. Voy a participar en la campaña para juntar fondos con tal de que se usen para mantener limpia la ciudad.
6. Voy a trabajar de voluntario(a) para esa organización con tal de que luche contra la pobreza.

Teaching All Students

Extra Help Write the following categories on the board: doubt, certainty, action, suggestion or recommendation, emotion, wish, time conjunction, or indefinite. Then call out a verb or expression and have students name the category and state if the subjunctive will follow it.

Multiple Intelligences

Kinesthetic Divide the class into 2 teams. Call out 1 of the items in **Actividad 3** (you will need to write additional items as well). When you say "Go," 1 student from each team runs to the board and writes the indicative response. When finished, they hand off the chalk to a team member who writes the subjunctive response. Other team members should call out any errors to be fixed. The first team done with no mistakes gets a point. Continue until all students participate.

Teaching Resource Options

Print

Block Scheduling Copymasters
Unit 3 Resource Book
  Audioscript, pp. 183–184
  Vocabulary Quizzes, pp. 186–188
  Grammar Quizzes, pp. 189–190
  Etapa Exam, Forms A and B,
    pp. 191–200
  Examen para hispanohablantes,
    pp. 201–205
  Portfolio Assessment, pp. 206–207
  Unit 3 Comprehensive Test,
    pp. 209–217
  *Prueba comprensiva para
    hispanohablantes,* Unit 3
    pp. 218–225
  Multiple Choice Test Questions,
    pp. 232–234
  Midterm Exam, pp. 235–242

Audiovisual

OHT 43 (Quick Start)
Audio Program CD 19, Tracks 19–24

Technology

eTest Plus Online/Test Generator
  CD-ROM
  www.classzone.com

 and

Rubric: Speaking

Criteria	Scale	
Sentence structure	1 2 3	A = 11–12 pts.
Vocabulary use	1 2 3	B = 9–10 pts.
Originality	1 2 3	C = 7–8 pts.
Fluency	1 2 3	D = 4–6 pts.
		F = < 4 pts.

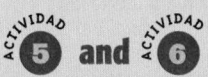  **En tu propia voz**

Rubric: Writing

Criteria	Scale	
Vocabulary use	1 2 3 4 5	A = 14–15 pts.
Accuracy	1 2 3 4 5	B = 12–13 pts.
Creativity, appearance	1 2 3 4 5	C = 10–11 pts.
		D = 8–9 pts.
		F = < 8 pts.

5 Mi comunidad

STRATEGY: SPEAKING

Express yourself In this discussion of politics, express your wishes, hopes, emotions, doubts, uncertainties, and concerns about the actions of your political leaders. How can you use what you have learned in this unit?

En grupos de dos o tres, conversen sobre los políticos de su ciudad, su estado y su país. Si es necesario, lean sobre los políticos en el periódico para saber más de su ideología.

modelo

Tú: *El alcalde de mi ciudad es bastante liberal. Apoya los servicios sociales y …*

Amigo 1: *La gobernadora de mi estado es conservadora…*

Amigo 2: *El presidente de nuestro país es…*

6 Vamos a celebrar

En grupos de dos o tres, planeen una celebración para un día patriótico o histórico. Primero, escojan un día que quieran celebrar. Luego, preparen los planes para la fiesta.

modelo

Tú: *¿Por qué no celebramos el día que fundaron nuestra ciudad?*

Amigo 1: *Buena idea. Podemos buscar datos…*

Amigo 2: *Y luego podemos…*

7 En tu propia voz

ESCRITURA Imagínate que estás en Puerto Rico para el día de la Abolición de la Esclavitud. Escribe una tarjeta postal a tu familia describiendo qué hiciste y qué viste.

CONEXIONES

Los estudios sociales En Estados Unidos celebramos nuestra independencia de Inglaterra el 4 de julio. Escoge tres países hispanohablantes y haz una investigación para descubrir lo siguiente: ¿Celebra el país un día de la independencia? Si lo celebra, ¿de quién ganó la independencia y cuándo se celebra? Si no celebra un día de la independencia, ¿por qué no? Escribe un reportaje y compara los resultados con dos o tres compañeros de la clase.

Classroom Community

Paired Activity Have students work in pairs to research 1 of the following: (a) 2–3 current events about the Dominican Republic; (b) a list of Dominican baseball players in the U.S.; (c) a Dominican recipe.

Learning Scenario Have students work in pairs to perform an interview. One student is a political candidate. The other is a reporter. The reporter prepares a list of questions for the candidate to answer. Then students change roles.

Flashcards
CLASSZONE.COM

En resumen
REPASO DE VOCABULARIO

DESCRIBE HISTORIC EVENTS

Columbus Day

acudir a	*to attend*
el (la) almirante	*admiral*
la banda	*band*
la bandera	*flag*
el descubrimiento	*discovery*
el faro	*lighthouse*
la procesión	*procession*
sonar (o→ue)	*to sound, to ring*

Abolition of slavery

los antepasados	*ancestors*
la bomba	*Afro-Caribbean dance*
el conjunto	*musical group*
conmemorar	*to commemorate*
la costumbre	*custom*
el día de la Abolición de la Esclavitud	*Abolition Day*
enfrentar	*to confront*
el (la) esclavo(a)	*slave*
honrar	*to honor*
la injusticia	*injustice*
justo(a)	*just, fair*
la lucha	*fight*
el (la) opresor(a)	*oppressor*
la plena	*Afro-Caribbean dance*
el (la) proponente	*supporter*
solemne	*solemn*
la victoria	*victory*

Government

conservador(a)	*conservative*
la constitución	*constitution*
la democracia	*democracy*
democrático(a)	*democratic*
el derecho	*the (legal) right*
el ejército	*army*
el gobierno	*government*
la ideología	*ideology*
la ley	*law*
liberal	*liberal*
la monarquía	*monarchy*
el poder	*power*

Leaders

el (la) alcalde(sa)	*mayor*
el (la) gobernador(a)	*governor*
el (la) líder	*leader*
el (la) presidente(a)	*president*
la reina	*queen*
el rey	*king*

Patriotism

la competencia	*competition*
el ensayo	*essay*
la patria	*mother country*
el (la) patriota	*patriot*
patriótico(a)	*patriotic*
el patriotismo	*patriotism*

EXPRESS EMOTION AND DOUBT

♻ **Ya sabes**

dudar	*to doubt*
es cierto	*it's certain*
es dudoso	*it's doubtful*
es improbable	*it's improbable*
es verdad	*it's true*
estoy seguro(a)	*I'm sure*
no estoy seguro(a)	*I'm not sure*
no creer	*to not believe*
creer	*to believe*
pensar (e→ie)	*to think*

STATE CAUSE AND EFFECT

The subjunctive

Vamos a la celebración a menos que no **haya** tiempo.
Podemos quedarnos hasta que la banda **empiece** a tocar.

MAKE SUGGESTIONS AND WISHES

The subjunctive

Busco un conjunto que **sepa** tocar la plena y la bomba.
El gobernador quiere que **participemos** en la procesión.

Juego

Saludo a la gente pero no tengo manos. Me comunico con la gente pero no tengo boca. Soy alto pero no necesito ropa especial. Doy apoyo y protección a la gente. ¿Qué soy?

doscientos cuarenta y siete
El Caribe Etapa 3   **247**

Teaching All Students

Extra Help Have students complete the following: **Si yo fuera director(a) de mi escuela, yo...** Call on volunteers to present their answers. Write them on the board to correct any errors. Then discuss everyone's ideas with the class.

Native Speakers Have students create additional **Juegos** for the class to answer.

Multiple Intelligences

Musical/Rhythmic Have students write a rhyming jingle about Columbus Day, patriotism, or government.

Kinesthetic Have students role play the party they planned in **Actividad 6**.

Teaching Note: En tu propia voz
Writing Strategy Suggest that students implement the writing strategy "Organize information chronologically and by category." A clear organized schedule of holiday activities will help students write their postcards.

🔔 Quick Start Review

🔄 **Vocabulary review**

Use OHT 43 or write on the board: Write down 5 types of leaders in Spanish and the name of a person who fills that job.

Answers
el (la) alcalde(sa), el (la) gobernador(a), el (la) presidente(a), la reina, el rey
Leaders names will vary.

Teaching Suggestions
Vocabulary Review

Have students work in pairs and play hangman with the vocabulary. Have them play until each has guessed 3 words/expressions.

Dictation

Dictate the following sentences to review the **Etapa**:

1. Es importante honrar a los héroes que dieron sus vidas para luchar contra la esclavitud.
2. Busco un conjunto que sepa tocar la plena y la bomba.
3. No hay discurso que me interese.
4. Mis papás recomiendan que mis amigos vengan a la casa dos horas antes de la procesión.

Juego

Answer: el faro

💻 Block Schedule

FunBreak Have students write and illustrate poems using as many words as possible from the **Repaso de vocabulario**. (For additional activities, see **Block Scheduling Copymasters**.)

Teaching Resource Options

Print
Block Scheduling Copymasters

Audiovisual
OHT GO1–GO5, 43 (Quick Start)

Technology

www.classzone.com

Quick Start Review

♻ Subjunctive review

Use OHT 43 or write on the board:
Complete the following sentences:

1. Busco un restaurante que...
2. Creo que...
3. Quiero que...
4. Dudo que...
5. Espero que...
6. Es cierto que...

Answers will vary.

Teaching Strategy
Prewriting

- Have students brainstorm lists of wishes for the teens of the future. Then have each student choose 3 wishes on which to focus.
- Review the function, context, content, and type of text with the class. Be sure students are clear about these elements of the assignment.

Post-writing

- When students exchange papers, be sure they compare the rough drafts with the idea webs. Have partners determine whether the transition words are used correctly to aid the flow of ideas.
- Encourage students to use the proofreading marks they have learned.

Post-writing

-

UNIDAD 3

En tu propia voz
ESCRITURA

¡Les deseamos mucho éxito!

¡Felicitaciones! Te vas a graduar este año y tu clase quiere expresar sus deseos para los estudiantes del futuro. Están preparando una «cápsula de tiempo» donde van a incluir una carta dirigida a estos estudiantes.

Función: Expresar deseos
Contexto: Escribirles a los estudiantes del futuro
Contenido: Experiencias en la escuela
Tipo de texto: Carta personal

PARA ESCRIBIR · STRATEGY: WRITING

Use transitions to make text flow smoothly Using transition words helps you organize the major points of your letter and move logically from one point to another. Some Spanish transition words are **primero, segundo, tercero, al principio, entonces, luego, además, por último,** and **también.**

Modelo del estudiante

> The salutation for a personal letter usually begins with **Querido(a)** and ends with a comma.

Queridos estudiantes del futuro,

Estamos a punto de graduarnos y pensamos en el futuro. ¡Ojalá que pudiéramos ver esta escuela en 100 años y hablar con los estudiantes del siglo veintidós! Tenemos muchas esperanzas para el futuro.

> **Primero** signals a list of ideas.

Primero, ¡sería mejor que en el futuro los estudiantes no tuvieran que pasar tanto tiempo haciendo la tarea! ¿No sería mucho mejor si tuvieran más tiempo para las actividades y para estudiar para exámenes?

Segundo, nos gustaría que hubiera unos cambios en nuestra comunidad. ¿No sería buena idea permitir a los jóvenes conducir un coche a la edad de catorce años en vez de a los dieciséis? ¡Entonces los otros miembros de la familia no tendrían que gastar su tiempo llevándonos a nuestras actividades!

También, esperamos que en el futuro las posibilidades de empleo sean mejores para todos los estudiantes. ¡Necesitamos más oportunidades!

> **Para concluir** indicates that you have reached the concluding paragraph.

Para concluir, ¡les deseamos todo lo bueno de nuestra época y esperamos que todo lo malo haya mejorado al llegar a la suya!

Atentamente,

> Typical closings for a personal letter are **Atentamente, Cordialmente, Un abrazo,** etc., followed by a comma and a signature.

Los estudiantes del siglo veintiuno

248

Classroom Community

Paired Activity Have partners read each other's letters, then comment on whether they think the wishes could come true. If a wish seems unrealistic, have the partner suggest a more realistic modification.

Group Activity In groups of 4, have students list other things they would want to include in a time capsule, such as cultural artifacts, a school newspaper, or a description of their Spanish class.

Portfolio Have students save their letters for their portfolios. Subsequent writing projects will show their progress in Spanish.

Writing Center
CLASSZONE.COM

Estrategias para escribir

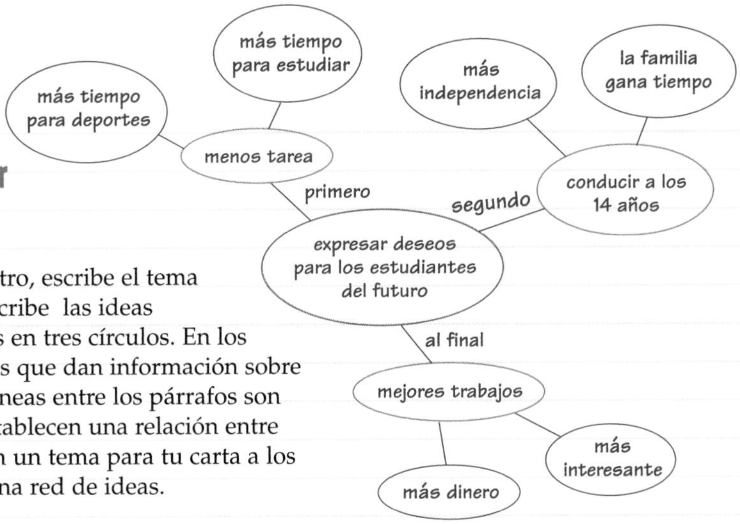
más tiempo para estudiar
más tiempo para deportes
menos tarea
más independencia
la familia gana tiempo
conducir a los 14 años
primero
segundo
expresar deseos para los estudiantes del futuro
al final
mejores trabajos
más interesante
más dinero

Antes de escribir...

Mira la red de ideas. En el centro, escribe el tema principal de la carta. Luego escribe las ideas principales de los tres párrafos en tres círculos. En los otros círculos pon las oraciones que dan información sobre el tema de cada párrafo. Las líneas entre los párrafos son palabras transicionales que establecen una relación entre las ideas principales. Piensa en un tema para tu carta a los estudiantes del futuro y haz una red de ideas.

Revisiones

Después de escribir el primer borrador, pídele a un(a) compañero(a) que la compare con su red de ideas. Pregúntale:

- *¿Cuáles son las palabras y expresiones transicionales que usé para establecer una relación entre los tres párrafos?*
- *¿Cuál es la relación entre cada párrafo y el tema principal?*
- *¿Cómo se relacionan las oraciones de cada párrafo con la idea principal del párrafo?*

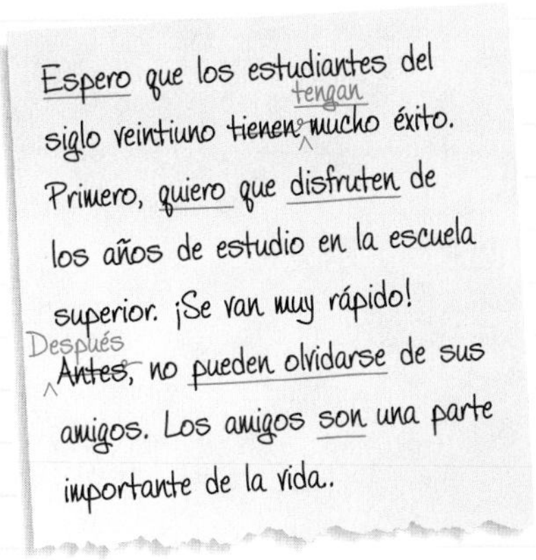
Espero que los estudiantes del siglo veintiuno ~~tienen~~ tengan mucho éxito. Primero, quiero que disfruten de los años de estudio en la escuela superior. ¡Se van muy rápido! ~~Antes,~~ Después no pueden olvidarse de sus amigos. Los amigos son una parte importante de la vida.

La versión final

Para completar tu carta, léela de nuevo y repasa los siguientes puntos:

- *¿Usé alguna expresión de duda, incertidumbre, juicio, no-existencia o emoción que requiere el subjuntivo?*

Haz lo siguiente: Subraya los verbos en el presente del indicativo o en el subjuntivo. Determina por qué el contexto requiere estos tiempos. Corrige los verbos.

- *¿Usé el tiempo verbal condicional correctamente?*

Haz lo siguiente: Confirma la aplicación apropiada del condicional. Haz un círculo alrededor de los verbos y las formas. ¿Está conjugado correctamente el verbo condicional? ¿Deberías usar subjuntivo para expresar una situación hipotética?

Rubric: Writing

Let students know ahead of time which elements of their writing you will be evaluating. A global evaluation is more helpful to students than a correction of every mistake made. Consider the following in scoring compositions:

Sentences	
1	Most not logical
2	Somewhat logical
3	In logical order
4	Logical with some flow
5	Flow purposefully

Details	
1	Few details
2	Some basic details
3	Sufficient basic details
4	Substantial details
5	Clear and vivid detail

Organization	
1	Very little organization
2	Poorly organized
3	Some organization
4	Sufficiently organized
5	Strong organization

Accuracy	
1	Errors prevent comprehension
2	Comprehensible, yet many errors
3	Some spelling and agreement errors throughout
4	A few errors
5	Very few errors

Criteria	Scale	
Logical sentence order	1 2 3 4 5	A = 17–20 pts.
Clear and vivid detail	1 2 3 4 5	B = 13–16 pts.
Organization	1 2 3 4 5	C = 9–12 pts.
Accuracy	1 2 3 4 5	D = 5–8 pts.
		F = < 5 pts.

Teaching All Students

Extra Help Review structures with students before writing:
- Use of the subjunctive
- Conditional sentences

Challenge Ask students to think of 3 wishes they would like to come true for themselves after high school graduation. Have them make an idea web with supporting details.

Native Speakers Ask students to share additional transition words with the class. Encourage them to include more supporting details in their letters.

Block Schedule

Variety Have students share their wishes with the class. Write all the wishes on the board, then have the class vote on their 3 favorite wishes. (For additional activities, see **Block Scheduling Copymasters.**)

Unit Theme

Discussing your studies and your future career plans, and learning about the economics of Latin America

Teaching Resource Options

Print

Block Scheduling Copymasters
Unit 4 Resource Book
  Absent Student Copymasters, p. 34

Audiovisual

OHT M4; 1, 2
Canciones CD
Video Program Videotape 28:36 / DVD, Unit 4

Technology

eEdition Plus Online/eEdition CD-ROM
Easy Planner Plus Online/Easy Planner CD-ROM
 www.classzone.com

UNIDAD 4

UN FUTURO BRILLANTE

 STANDARDS

Communication
- Describing your studies
- Asking questions
- Saying what you are and were doing
- Talking about careers
- Confirming, denying, and hypothesizing
- Expressing emotions
- Clarifying meaning
- Expressing possession
- Expressing past probability

Cultures
- The culture of the Southern Cone countries
- Fields of study in schools in Latin America
- Careers in Latin America
- Latin America economics

Connections
- Social Studies: Job requirements
- Social Studies: International organizations

Comparisons
- High school students' future goals and plans
- Economic situations
- How language reflects culture

Communities
- Using Spanish in the workplace
- Using Spanish in volunteer activities

INTERNET Preview
CLASSZONE.COM

- More About the Southern Cone
- Webquest
- Self-Check Quizzes
- Flashcards
- Writing Center
- Online Workbook
- eEdition Plus Online

250

URUGUAY
RAFAEL GUARGA inventó un método eficaz para proteger las frutas de las temperaturas frías. ¿Qué datos crees que tomó en cuenta para su invención?

CHILE
LA UNIVERSIDAD DE CHILE es una de las más prestigiosas de América del Sur. ¿Qué cosas crees que se estudian allí?

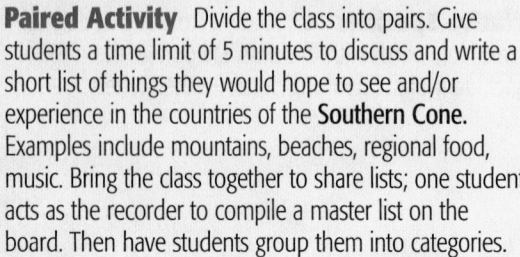

Classroom Community

Paired Activity Divide the class into pairs. Give students a time limit of 5 minutes to discuss and write a short list of things they would hope to see and/or experience in the countries of the **Southern Cone.** Examples include mountains, beaches, regional food, music. Bring the class together to share lists; one student acts as the recorder to compile a master list on the board. Then have students group them into categories.

Group Activity Divide the class into 4 groups and assign each group one of the **Southern Cone** countries. Groups then research at least 10 interesting facts about their countries in the library or on the Internet. They should make posters that include the facts as well as illustrations to be displayed on the bulletin board.

ALMANAQUE CULTURAL

POBLACIÓN: Argentina: 37.384.816; Chile: 15.328.467; Paraguay: 5.734.139; Uruguay: 3.360.105

ALTURA: 6.959 m sobre el nivel del mar, Cerro Aconcagua (punto más alto)

TEMPERATURA: (más alta) 74°F (24°C) Asunción, Paraguay. (más baja) 48°F (11°C) Bariloche, Argentina

COMIDAS: mate, parrillada, dulce de leche, puchero

GENTE FAMOSA: Isabel Allende (escritora), Gabriel Batistuta (futbolista), Mario Benedetti (poeta), Adolfo Pérez Esquivel (pacifista)

Mira el video para más información.

CLASSZONE.COM
More About the Southern Cone

ANTONIO BERNI

ARGENTINA
ANTONIO BERNI (1905–1981) Muchas veces decidimos nuestro futuro durante nuestra niñez. Este pintor argentino celebra estos momentos en su pintura *El club atlético de Chicago,* 1937. Según lo que ves, ¿qué serán estos niños en el futuro?

PARAGUAY
EL ARPA es uno de los instrumentos típicos de Paraguay. ¿Qué cultura crees que desarrolló este instrumento?

EL CONO SUR
MATE El mate es una bebida parecida al té. Se toma en un envase (*container*), también llamado mate, con un objeto especial llamado bombilla. ¿Conoces otras comidas o bebidas de América del Sur?

ARGENTINA
LA BOLSA Éste es uno de los centros de comercio principales de Latinoamérica. ¿Qué países crees que participan en ella?

251

Teaching Suggestion
Previewing the Unit

Tell students that this unit centers on the **Southern Cone** countries: Chile, Argentina, Paraguay, and Uruguay. Ask students to scan these two pages for 15 seconds, then close their books. Then ask them to tell you what they remember.

Culture Highlights

● **ANTONIO BERNI** Antonio Berni nació en Rosario, Argentina. El Museo de Arte Moderno de Nueva York, el Museo de Saint Denis en Francia y muchos museos argentinos y latinoamericanos poseen sus obras.

● **RAFAEL GUARGA** Como decano (*dean*) de la Facultad de Ingeniería de la Universidad de la República Oriental del Uruguay, el Profesor Rafael Guarga quiere que los negocios privados trabajen con la universidad para desarrollar más tecnologías. Pregunte a los estudiantes por qué creen que es importante que el gobierno y la empresa privada trabajen juntos para desarrollar nuevas tecnologías.

● **MATE** El mate se prepara de las hojas secas de un arbusto relacionado al acebo (*holly*). La bebida, de color verdoso, contiene cafeína pero es menos astringente que el té.

● **LA UNIVERSIDAD DE CHILE** La Universidad de Chile cuenta con 14 facultades y el Instituto de Ciencias Políticas. Ofrecen 43 carreras y 23 programas. Fue fundada en Santiago de Chile a mediados del siglo XIX y hoy en día tiene 4 recintos.

● **LA BOLSA ARGENTINA** Casi todos los países principales del mundo participan en la Bolsa argentina.

Block Schedule

Variety Have students write a complete description of Antonio Berni's painting on p. 250. Students may also create their own version of the painting. (For additional activities, see **Block Scheduling Copymasters.**)

Teaching All Students

Native Speakers Ask students to research one of the famous people listed in the **Almanaque** on p. 251 and present a short report to the class. They may also research a person from one of the **Southern Cone** countries of their own choosing.

Multiple Intelligences

Logical/Mathematical Have students compare and contrast the population and geography of the **Southern Cone** countries.

Musical/Rhythmic Bring in a cassette or a CD of tango music. Have students talk about how the music makes them feel. How does the rhythm compare to music they usually listen to?

Standards for Foreign Language Learning

The Connections standard is the focus for this unit.

Connections

Standard 3.1 Students reinforce and further their knowledge of other disciplines through the foreign language.

Standard 3.2 Students acquire information and recognize the distinctive viewpoints that are only available through the foreign language and its cultures.

Teaching Resource Options

Print
Block Scheduling Copymasters

Audiovisual
Poster

Technology
www.classzone.com

Teaching Suggestion
Previewing the Standard

Connections, the third national standard, encourages students and teachers to demonstrate how Spanish relates to other disciplines, and how it can be used in lifetime careers. The national standards encourage us to help our students see the potential for using Spanish outside of the classroom. When students observe a variety of options for language use, they are more likely to continue their use of Spanish, and possibly other languages, as adults.

UNIDAD 4

UN FUTURO BRILLANTE

- Comunicación
- Culturas
- Conexiones
- Comparaciones
- Comunidades

Webquest
CLASSZONE.COM

Explore connections in the Southern Cone through guided Web activities.

Conexiones

Al estudiar español, aprendemos más de otras materias, como el arte, las ciencias, las matemáticas, la música y los estudios sociales. ¿Cuál es tu materia favorita? ¿Qué has aprendido de esa materia por medio del español?

Conexiones en acción Identifica la materia representada por cada foto y explica cómo podrías usar el español para aprender más.

Comparaciones

Es fascinante comparar los idiomas que se hablan en el mundo. ¿Conoces estas palabras? ¿Sabes cuál es su origen?

chocolate
papa
maíz
llama
huracán

252

Classroom Community

Paired Activity Have students share their favorite school subject with a partner. Then have them hypothesize in what career that subject may be useful and how a knowledge of Spanish might further help in that career.

Class Activity Have each student select a review topic related to language or culture and become the class "expert" on that topic. As part of the daily class warm-up, have a student guide the class in a review of their assigned topic. Encourage students to select topics they find challenging so that they improve their understanding.

Comunicación

Usamos varias formas de comunicación todos los días. Por ejemplo, nos comunicamos por teléfono y por medio de los anuncios. ¿Cuántas formas de comunicación puedes identificar en la foto?

Culturas

La cultura distinta de los países del Cono Sur se refleja en sus productos, costumbres y perspectivas. ¿Cuánto sabes ya de la cultura de Chile, Argentina, Paraguay y Uruguay? ¿Sabes algo de su economía?

Fíjate 💡

¿Esperas tener un futuro brillante? Explica la relación que puede tener una de las fotos de estas páginas con tu futuro. Si no encuentras una foto adecuada, haz un dibujo que represente tus planes para el futuro.

Comunidades

En esta unidad conocerás a Toño, un alumno que usa el español en su comunidad. ¿Cómo puede Toño ayudar a una estudiante hispanohablante que no comprende su tarea?

253

Unit 4 and Connections

Un futuro brillante encourages students to think positively about the opportunities available to them where they can put to use the Spanish they have been learning. It affords teachers the opportunity to guide students to consider teaching among the many life careers available. While studying this unit you may want to have community members speak to students regarding the importance of knowing another language within their fields of expertise.

✳ Culture Highlights

● **ANTONIO BERNI** La pintura de la página 252 es del artista argentino Antonio Berni (1905–1981). Se llama *El club atlético de Chicago*.

● **EL ARPA ANDINA** El hombre de la foto de la página 252 está tocando el arpa, un instrumento típico de la música paraguaya.

Fíjate

Answers
Answers will vary.

▣ Block Schedule

Variety Have students list their top three choices for professions. Then have them search the Internet for universities offering courses related to those professions either in the **Cono sur** or another area of the Spanish-speaking world. Have them search university Web sites to find which courses they would need to study for that profession if they lived and studied in that country. (For additional activities, see **Block Scheduling Copymasters**.)

Teaching All Students

Extra Help Have students make a list of what they already know about the **Cono sur** region. They should include at least three things.

Native Speakers Have students investigate more about Rafael Guarga, scientist and engineer from Uruguay. Then have them compare his life with that of a scientist from the region of their heritage.

Challenge Have students research political and economic challenges faced by one of the **Cono sur** countries in recent years and report on their findings.

Ampliación

These activities may be used at various points in the Unit 4 sequence.

■ For Block Schedule, you may find that these projects will provide a welcome change of pace while reviewing and reinforcing the material presented in the unit. See the **Block Scheduling Copymasters.**

● PROJECTS

Make mobiles of **Southern Cone** countries. Divide the class into 4 groups and assign each group a **Southern Cone** country. Have groups research and collect pictures and realia related to their country that can be used to make a mobile. The images should represent the essence of the country. For example, students creating the Argentina mobile might use a picture of the flag, a **mate** calabash and **bombilla, gaucho** articles, etc. The mobiles should be accompanied by a written report that explains the meaning of the symbols. Hang the mobiles in the classroom and discuss them as you cover the unit.

> PACING SUGGESTION: Have students begin research at the beginning of the unit. Final projects are completed at the end of Unit 4.

Film or record an audiovisual guide for career opportunities and training. Divide the class into groups and assign each group a field of study, type of profession, etc. Groups prepare a promotional ad that might be part of a campaign to attract new applicants or employees.

> PACING SUGGESTION: Upon completion of Etapa 3.

● STORYTELLING

Nuestro futuro After reviewing the vocabulary on professions and fields of study, model a mini-story (using student actors or photos from the text) that students will revise, retell, and expand:

> Guillermo y Daniel hablan de sus planes para el futuro y las profesiones que les interesan. Guillermo dice: «Estoy tan confundido. No sé qué estudiar. No tengo mucho talento en ningún campo de estudio». Daniel responde: «No te preocupes. Muchos estudiantes no saben qué campo de estudio o carrera quieren seguir cuando entran a la universidad. Después de uno o dos semestres, vas a descubrir qué carrera te interesa».

Pause as the story is being told so that students may fill in words and act out gestures. Students then write, narrate, and read aloud a longer main story. This new version should include vocabulary from Unit 4.

Vamos a hablar con el consejero Have students tell a story about talking to a school counselor as part of preparing to enter college or train for a career. They can role-play the scene between the counselor and 1 or more students.

> PACING SUGGESTION: Upon completion of Etapa 3.

● BULLETIN BOARD/POSTERS

Bulletin Board Have students collect information on various professions in which a knowledge of Spanish would be helpful. To arrange the bulletin board, have them create headings for grouping the professions, e.g., **educación, psicología, tecnología, medicina, ciencias,** etc. Students decorate the board with information and images related to the professions.

Posters Have students create •**Country** posters for each of the **Southern Cone** countries •**Career** posters with information about specific careers •**Industry** posters for promoting good public relations between an industry and the community

OCÉANO PACÍFICO

PARAGUAY

★ ASUNCIÓN

ARGENTINA

URUGUAY

BUENOS AIRES ★ ★ MONTEVIDEO

★ SANTIAGO

CHILE

GAME

¿Cuál es mi profesión?

Have each student prepare 5 descriptive clues about a profession, e.g., (1) **Hay muchas especialidades entre las cuales se puede elegir en mi profesión,** (2) **Mi profesión exige un título de universidad,** etc. Divide the class into 2 teams. Teams take turns giving clues about the professions. The fewer clues the other team needs to guess the profession, the more points it wins.

Each clue is worth 10 points. If a team guesses the profession after the first clue, they earn 50 points. If they need a second clue, they only get 40. If they need a third clue, 30 points, and so on. If the team does not guess the profession after 5 clues, they receive no points. Set a time limit for guessing after hearing a clue, e.g., 5 seconds. The team with the most points at the end wins.

PACING SUGGESTION: Upon completion of Etapa 2.

OCÉANO
ATLÁNTICO

MUSIC

Tango is a dance of 2 slow, gliding steps, followed by 2 quick steps, then a slow step. The music for this dance requires 4/4 time measure. Carlos Gardel (1887–1935), from Argentina, composed music that was popular for this dance step. Play 1 or more Gardel compositions. If students from the class can demonstrate the tango steps, encourage them to do so. Several movies have tango scenes, including *Evita*, starring Madonna and Antonio Banderas.

HANDS-ON CRAFTS

Point out that **mate,** an herbal drink, is consumed from a container called a **mate** as well. To make a decorative one, roll out a clay pancake (1/2" thick and 8" in diameter), and shape the clay around the bottom of a round glass. Trim excess clay from the top, leaving the sides about 3" high. Carve designs into the wet clay with a toothpick. Run a butter knife around the edge to slide the clay off the glass. Dry 24 hours, then sand smooth. Remove dust, then paint inside and out with acrylic paint. Use a paper straw as a **bombilla.** NOTE: This is for decorative use only.

RECIPE

Sopa paraguaya **Sopa paraguaya** sounds like soup, but it's corn bread. **Sopa paraguaya,** popular throughout Paraguay, can be prepared using corn meal, fresh corn, or a combination of both. It's normally served with **Só o-Yosopy,** Guaraní for beef soup, the national dish of Paraguay. Beef is a dietary staple in Paraguay, Argentina, Uruguay, and Chile.

Receta

Sopa paraguaya

1/2 taza de cebolla picada fina
2 cucharadas de mantequilla
1 taza de maíz (raspada de la mazorca o congelada)
3/4 taza de harina de maíz
3/4 taza de requesón

3/4 taza de queso Münster rallado
1/2 taza de leche agria (añada unas gotas de vinagre)
1/2 cucharadilla de sal
3 huevos separados

Fría la cebolla en la mantequilla hasta que se ablande. Pase el maíz por el procesador de comidas y mézclelo bien con la harina de maíz, la cebolla frita, el requesón, el queso Münster, la leche agria y la sal. Bata las yemas de huevo hasta que se espesen. Mezcle las yemas y las claras cuidadosamente. Añada 1/3 de la mezcla de huevos a la mezcla de maíz. Mezcle todo bien. Añada el resto de los huevos, mezclándolos con cuidado. Ponga la masa en una fuente (8" x 8" x 2") y hornéela a 400° por 30 minutos. Sírvala a temperatura de ambiente con mantequilla.

Planning Guide CLASSROOM MANAGEMENT

OBJECTIVES

Communication
- Describe your studies *pp. 256–257, 258–259*
- Ask questions *pp. 262–263*
- Say what you are doing *pp. 264–267*
- Say what you were doing *pp. 268–269*

Grammar
- Review the use of interrogative words *pp. 262–263*
- Review the use of the present progressive tense *pp. 264–265*
- Use the progressive with **ir, andar,** and **seguir** *pp. 266–267*
- Use the past progressive tense *pp. 268–269*

Culture
- The culture of the countries of **the Southern Cone** *pp. 252–253*
- Gestures *p. 265*
- Regional vocabulary *p. 266*
- Names and professional titles *pp. 266, 267*
- Jorge Luis Borges *pp. 270–271*

♻ Recycling
- Reflexive verbs *p. 264*
- Household chores *p. 265*

STRATEGIES

Listening Strategies
- Pre-listening *p. 258*
- Evaluate recommendations *p. 258*

Speaking Strategies
- Establish closer relationships *p. 263*
- Extend a conversation *p. 274*

Reading Strategies
- Analyze the role of identity and fantasy *p. 270*

Writing Strategies
- Ask who, what, where, when, why, and how *TE p. 274*

Connecting Cultures Strategies
- Learn about the culture of the countries of **the Southern Cone** *pp. 252–253*
- Understand gestures *p. 265*
- Recognize variations in vocabulary *p. 266*
- Recognize names and professional titles *pp. 266, 267*
- Learn about the life and works of Jorge Luis Borges *pp. 270–271*
- Connect and compare what you know about cultural influences on literature in your community to help you learn about cultural influences on literature in a new community *TE p. 271*

PROGRAM RESOURCES

 Print
- *Más práctica* Workbook PE *pp. 89–96*
- *Actividades para todos* Workbook PE *pp. 101–110*
- Block Scheduling Copymasters *pp. 81–88*
- Unit 4 Resource Book
  - *Más práctica* Workbook TE *pp. 3–10*
  - *Actividades para todos* Workbook TE *pp. 11–20*
  - *Cuaderno para hispanohablantes* TE *pp. 21–28*
  - Information Gap Activities *pp. 29–32*
  - Family Letter *p. 33*
  - Absent Student Copymasters *pp. 34–40*
  - Family Involvement *pp. 41–42*
  - Audioscript *pp. 43–46*
  - Assessment Program, Unit 4 Etapa 1 *pp. 47–69; 226–228*
  - Answer Keys *pp. 242–246*

Audiovisual
- Audio Program CD 10
- *Canciones* CD
- Overhead Transparencies M1–M4; 1–2, 5–19
- Word Tiles U4E1

 Technology
- eEdition Plus Online/eEdition CD-ROM
- Easy Planner Plus Online/Easy Planner CD-ROM
- eTest Plus Online/Test Generator CD-ROM
- Online Workbook
- Take-Home Tutor CD-ROM
- www.classzone.com

Assessment Program Options
- Unit 4 Resource Book
  - Vocabulary Quizzes
  - Grammar Quizzes
  - Etapa Exam Forms A and B
  - *Examen para hispanohablantes*
  - Portfolio Assessment
  - Multiple Choice Test Questions
- Audio Program CD 20
- eTest Plus Online/Test Generator CD-ROM

Native Speakers
- *Cuaderno para hispanohablantes* PE *pp. 89–96*
- *Cuaderno para hispanohablantes* TE (Unit 4 Resource Book)
- *Examen para hispanohablantes* (Unit 4 Resource Book)
- Audio Program (*Para hispanohablantes*) CD 10, 20
- Audioscript (Unit 4 Resource Book)

Student Text
Listening Activity Scripts

 **Situaciones** *pages 258–259*

• CD 10

Sra. Cisneros:	Pasa, Emilio, siéntate.
Emilio:	Gracias, señora Cisneros.
Sra. Cisneros:	He estado estudiando tus datos. Siempre has sacado buenas notas en ciencias y matemáticas, pero veo también que te has destacado en la clase de arte.
Emilio:	Sí, señora, me gusta mucho dibujar, especialmente edificios y monumentos.
Sra. Cisneros:	Pues, por qué no repasamos los campos de estudio a ver cuáles te interesan más. Supongo que la agricultura no tiene ninguna atracción especial para ti.
Emilio:	No, señora, estoy de acuerdo.
Sra. Cisneros:	Bueno, como tienes buena cabeza para las matemáticas, podrías estudiar contabilidad...
Emilio:	Emmm... , es que me parece un poco aburrido.
Sra. Cisneros:	Ya veo... O finanzas, o a ver, también en el comercio se necesita saber cómo manejar los números.
Emilio:	Sí, los dos son posibilidades. Pero me gustaría hacer algo con el dibujo.
Sra. Cisneros:	Pues, el dibujo técnico sería perfecto para ti, como te gusta dibujar cosas muy detalladas. Quizás podrías combinar tu talento artístico con estudios en ingeniería civil.
Emilio:	Sí... eso me parece interesante.
Sra. Cisneros:	Con lo poco que he hablado contigo, pienso que no te interesarían campos como el mercadeo o la publicidad, ¿no es así?
Emilio:	Tiene razón, señora, no me llaman la atención.
Sra. Cisneros:	Y, ¿la tecnología?
Emilio:	Pues usted sabe que hay muchos programas de software para facilitar el dibujo. Tengo algún interés en aprender más sobre ellos.
Sra. Cisneros:	¡Muy bien! Creo que hemos aclarado un poco los campos de estudio que deberías considerar.
Emilio:	¡Gracias, señora Cisneros!

ACTIVIDAD 6  **Los datos** *page 263*

Empleado:	Buenas tardes.
Sra. Madrigal:	Buenas tardes.
Empleado:	Primero necesito completar el formulario con sus datos. ¿Cómo se llama?
Sra. Madrigal:	Me llamo Dulce Madrigal Velasco.
Empleado:	¿Cuál es su estado civil?
Sra. Madrigal:	Soy casada.
Empleado:	¿Cuál es su fecha de nacimiento?
Sra. Madrigal:	Nací el siete de septiembre de mil novecientos cincuenta y ocho.
Empleado:	¿En qué se especializó?
Sra. Madrigal:	En administración de empresas.
Empleado:	¿De dónde recibió su licenciatura?
Sra. Madrigal:	Recibí mi licenciatura de la Universidad de Buenos Aires.
Empleado:	¿Y su maestría?
Sra. Madrigal:	También de allí, de la Universidad de Buenos Aires.
Empleado:	¿Y su doctorado?
Sra. Madrigal:	De la Universidad de Santiago de Chile.
Empleado:	¿Cuándo va a enviar su solicitud?
Sra. Madrigal:	Bueno, la mandaré mañana para que llegue pasado mañana, el 25 de febrero.
Empleado:	Muy bien, Sra. Madrigal. Hágame el favor de firmar aquí.

ACTIVIDAD 12  **¿Es cierto?** *page 267*

Modelo: Sí, jefe, Gómez sigue trabajando en la compañía.

1. Sí, sí, claro. Ribeira sigue superándose en su puesto.
2. No sé. No me habla mucho, pero estoy seguro que sigue compartiendo sus ideas con sus compañeros.
3. Prado tiene muy buena cabeza para las finanzas. Según lo que me dice, va ganando mucho dinero.
4. Sí, jefe, Durán sigue estudiando mercadeo y relaciones públicas por las noches en la Universidad.
5. Vega dice que todos los días aprende algo nuevo. Va adaptándose a la vida profesional.
6. No, señor. Silva no es así. Nunca corre riesgos innecesarios.

Sample Lesson Plan - 50 Minute Schedule

DAY 1

Unit Opener
- Anticipate/Activate prior knowledge: Present the *Almanaque* and the cultural notes. Use Map OHTs as needed. 15 MIN.

Etapa Opener
- Quick Start Review (TE, p. 254) 5 MIN.
- Have students look at the *Etapa* Opener and answer the questions. 5 MIN.

En contexto: Vocabulario
- Quick Start Review (TE, p. 256) 5 MIN.
- Present *Descubre*, p. 256. 5 MIN.
- Have students use context and pictures to learn *Etapa* vocabulary, then answer the *¿Comprendiste?* questions, p. 257. Use the Situational OHTs for additional practice. 15 MIN.

Homework Option:
- Have students write answers to the *¿Comprendiste?* questions, p. 257.

DAY 2

En vivo: Situaciones
- Check homework. 5 MIN.
- Quick Start Review (TE, p. 258) 5 MIN.
- Present the Listening Strategy, p. 258. 5 MIN.
- Have students read section 1, p. 258. Play the audio for section 2. Then have students work in pairs or groups to complete section 3. 15 MIN.

En acción: Vocabulario y gramática
- Have students complete *Actividad* 1 in writing, then go over answers orally. 5 MIN.
- Have students do *Actividad* 2 in pairs. 5 MIN.
- Present the *Vocabulario*, p. 261. Then have students complete *Actividad* 3 in pairs. 10 MIN.

Homework Option:
- Have students complete *Actividad* 2 in writing. Have students write sentences using the *Vocabulario*, p. 261.

DAY 3

En acción (cont.)
- Check homework. 5 MIN.
- Have students complete *Actividad* 4 in pairs. 5 MIN.
- Quick Start Review (TE, p. 262) 5 MIN.
- Present *Repaso:* Interrogative Words and *Vocabulario*, p. 262. 5 MIN.
- Do *Actividad* 5 orally. 5 MIN.
- Present the *Vocabulario*, p. 263. Then play the audio and do *Actividad* 6. 10 MIN.
- Present the Speaking Strategy, p. 263. Then have students complete *Actividad* 7 in pairs. Expand using Information Gap Activities, Unit 4 Resource Book, p. 29; *Más comunicación*, p. R12. 15 MIN.

Homework Option:
- Have students complete *Actividad* 5 in writing. *Más práctica* Workbook, p. 94. *Cuaderno para hispanohablantes*, p. 91.

DAY 4

En acción (cont.)
- Check homework. 5 MIN.
- Quick Start Review (TE, p. 264) 5 MIN.
- Present *Repaso:* The Present Progressive, p. 264. 10 MIN.
- Have students complete *Actividad* 8 in pairs. 5 MIN.
- Have students complete *Actividad* 9 in writing, then exchange papers for peer correction. 10 MIN.
- Have students complete *Actividad* 10 in pairs. Expand using *Más comunicación*, p. R12. 15 MIN.

Homework Option:
- *Más práctica* Workbook, p. 93. *Cuaderno para hispanohablantes*, p. 92.

DAY 5

En acción (cont.)
- Check homework. 5 MIN.
- Quick Start Review (TE, p. 266) 5 MIN.
- Present *Gramática:* The Progressive with *ir, andar,* and *seguir*, p. 266. 10 MIN.
- Do *Actividad* 11 orally. 5 MIN.
- Play the audio; do *Actividad* 12. 5 MIN.
- Have students complete *Actividades* 13 and 14 in pairs. 10 MIN.
- Present *Gramática:* The Past Progressive, p. 268. 5 MIN.
- Do *Actividad* 15 orally. 5 MIN.

Homework Option:
- Have students complete *Actividades* 11 and 15 in writing. *Más práctica* Workbook, pp. 95–96. *Cuaderno para hispanohablantes*, pp. 93–94.
- *Actividades para todos* Workbook, pp. 101–110.

DAY 6

En acción (cont.)
- Check homework. 5 MIN.
- Have students complete *Actividad* 16 in pairs. 5 MIN.
- Have students read and complete *Actividad* 17 in writing. Go over answers orally. 15 MIN.

Refrán
- Present the *Refrán*, p. 269. 5 MIN.

En voces: Lectura
- Quick Start Review (TE, p. 270) 5 MIN.
- Present the Reading Strategy, p. 270. Call on volunteers to read the *Lectura* aloud. Have students answer the *¿Comprendiste?/¿Qué piensas?* questions, p. 271. 15 MIN.

Homework Option:
- Have students complete *Hazlo tú*, p. 271.

DAY 7

En uso: Repaso y más comunicación
- Check homework. 5 MIN.
- Quick Start Review (TE, p. 272) 5 MIN.
- Have students do *Actividad* 1 in pairs. 5 MIN.
- Do *Actividades* 2 and 3 orally. 5 MIN.
- Have students do *Actividad* 4 in pairs. 10 MIN.
- Present the Speaking Strategy, p. 274. Do *Actividades* 5 and 6 in groups. 15 MIN.

En tu propia voz: Escritura
- Have students write their interview questions for *Actividad* 7. 5 MIN.

Homework Option:
- Review for *Etapa* 1 Exam.

DAY 8

En tu propia voz (cont.)
- Have students conduct their interviews. 10 MIN.

Tú en la comunidad
- Present and discuss *Toño*, p. 274. 5 MIN.

En resumen: Repaso de vocabulario
- Quick Start Review (TE, p. 275) 5 MIN.
- Review grammar questions, etc., as necessary. 10 MIN.
- Complete *Etapa* 1 Exam. 20 MIN.

Ampliación
- Optional: Use a suggested project, game, or activity. (TE, pp. 253A–253B)

Homework Option:
- Preview *Etapa* 2 Opener.

Sample Lesson Plan - Block Schedule (90 minutes)

DAY 1

Unit Opener
- Anticipate/Activate prior knowledge: Present the *Almanaque* and the cultural notes. Use Map OHTs as needed. **15 MIN.**

Etapa Opener
- Quick Start Review (TE, p. 254) **5 MIN.**
- Have students look at the *Etapa* Opener and answer the questions. **5 MIN.**
- Use Block Scheduling Copymasters. **10 MIN.**

En contexto: Vocabulario
- Quick Start Review (TE, p. 256) **5 MIN.**
- Present *Descubre,* p. 256. **5 MIN.**
- Have students use context and pictures to learn *Etapa* vocabulary, then answer the *¿Comprendiste?* questions, p. 257. Use the Situational OHTs for additional practice. **15 MIN.**

En vivo: Situaciones
- Quick Start Review (TE, p. 258) **5 MIN.**
- Present the Listening Strategy, p. 258. **5 MIN.**
- Have students read section 1, p. 258. Play the audio for section 2. Then have students work in pairs or groups to complete section 3. **20 MIN.**

Homework Option:
- Have students write answers to the *¿Comprendiste?* questions, p. 257.

DAY 2

En acción: Vocabulario y gramática
- Check homework. **5 MIN.**
- Quick Start Review (TE, p. 260) **5 MIN.**
- Have students complete *Actividad* 1 in writing, then go over answers orally. **5 MIN.**
- Have students do *Actividad* 2 in pairs. **5 MIN.**
- Present the *Vocabulario,* p. 261. Then have students complete *Actividad* 3 in pairs. **10 MIN.**
- Have students complete *Actividad* 4 in pairs. **5 MIN.**
- Quick Start Review (TE, p. 262) **5 MIN.**
- Present *Repaso:* Interrogative Words and *Vocabulario,* p. 262. **10 MIN.**
- Do *Actividad* 5 orally. **5 MIN.**
- Present the *Vocabulario,* p. 263. Then play the audio and do *Actividad* 6. **10 MIN.**
- Use an expansion activity from TE, pp. 262–263, for reinforcement and variety. **5 MIN.**
- Present the Speaking Strategy, p. 263. Then have students complete *Actividad* 7 in pairs. Expand using Information Gap Activities, Unit 4 Resource Book, p. 29; *Más comunicación,* p. R12. **20 MIN.**

Homework Option:
- Have students complete *Actividad* 5 in writing. *Más práctica* Workbook, p. 94. *Cuaderno para hispanohablantes,* p. 91.

DAY 3

En acción (cont.)
- Check homework. **5 MIN.**
- Quick Start Review (TE, p. 264) **5 MIN.**
- Present *Repaso:* The Present Progressive, p. 264. **5 MIN.**
- Have students complete *Actividad* 8 in pairs. **5 MIN.**
- Have students complete *Actividad* 9 in writing, then exchange papers for peer correction. **10 MIN.**
- Have students complete *Actividad* 10 in pairs. Expand using Information Gap Activities, Unit 4 Resource Book, p. 30; *Más comunicación,* p. R12. **15 MIN.**
- Quick Start Review (TE, p. 266) **5 MIN.**
- Present *Gramática:* The Progressive with *ir, andar,* and *seguir,* p. 266. **5 MIN.**
- Do *Actividad* 11 orally. **5 MIN.**
- Play the audio; do *Actividad* 12. **5 MIN.**
- Have students complete *Actividades* 13 and 14 in pairs. **10 MIN.**
- Quick Start Review (TE, p. 268) **5 MIN.**
- Present *Gramática:* The Past Progressive, p. 268. **5 MIN.**
- Do *Actividad* 15 orally. **5 MIN.**

Homework Option:
- Have students complete *Actividades* 11 and 15 in writing. *Más práctica* Workbook, pp. 93–95, 96. *Cuaderno para hispanohablantes,* pp. 92–94.
- *Actividades para todos* Workbook, pp. 101–110.

DAY 4

En acción (cont.)
- Check homework. **5 MIN.**
- Do *Actividad* 16 in pairs. **5 MIN.**
- Have students read and complete *Actividad* 17 in writing. Go over answers orally. **15 MIN.**
- Use an expansion activity from TE pp. 268–269 for reinforcement and variety. **10 MIN.**

Refrán
- Present the *Refrán,* p. 269. **5 MIN.**

En voces: Lectura
- Quick Start Review (TE, p. 270) **5 MIN.**
- Present the Reading Strategy, p. 270. Call on volunteers to read the *Lectura* aloud. Have students answer the *¿Comprendiste?/¿Qué piensas?* questions, p. 271. **20 MIN.**

En uso: Repaso y más comunicación
- Quick Start Review (TE, p. 272) **5 MIN.**
- Do *Actividad* 1 in pairs. **5 MIN.**
- Do *Actividades* 2 and 3 orally. **5 MIN.**
- Do *Actividad* 4 in pairs. **10 MIN.**

Homework Option:
- Have students complete *Hazlo tú,* p. 271. Review for *Etapa* 1 Exam.

DAY 5

En uso (cont.)
- Check homework. **5 MIN.**
- Present the Speaking Strategy, p. 274. Do *Actividades* 5 and 6 in groups. **15 MIN.**

En tu propia voz: Escritura
- Have students complete *Actividad* 7. **20 MIN.**

Tú en la comunidad
- Present and discuss *Toño,* p. 274. **5 MIN.**

En resumen: Repaso de vocabulario
- Quick Start Review (TE, p. 275) **5 MIN.**
- Review grammar questions, etc., as necessary. **10 MIN.**
- Complete *Etapa* 1 Exam. **20 MIN.**

Ampliación
- Use a suggested project, game, or activity. (TE, pp. 253A–253B) **10 MIN.**

Homework Option:
- Preview *Etapa* 2 Opener.

▼ Los estudiantes están en el jardín de la Universidad de Chile.

Etapa Theme
Describing your studies, asking questions, and saying what you are doing and were doing

Grammar Objectives
- Reviewing interrogative words
- Reviewing the present progressive tense
- Using the progressive with **ir, andar,** and **seguir**
- Using the past progressive tense

Teaching Resource Options

Print

Block Scheduling Copymasters
Unit 4 Resource Book
  Family Letter, p. 33
  Absent Student Copymasters, p. 34

Audiovisual

OHT 2, 11 (Quick Start)
Canciones CD

Quick Start Review
♻ Classes and professions
Use OHT 11 or write on the board:
Match each profession with a school subject:

1. ingeniero(a)   a. el arte
2. deportista   b. la música
3. cantante   c. la biología
4. artista   d. las matemáticas
5. doctor(a)   e. la educación física

Answers
1. d   2. e   3. b   4. a   5. c

Teaching Suggestion
Previewing the Etapa
- Ask students to study the photo on pp. 254–259 (1 min.).
- Reopen books. Give students the Supplementary Vocabulary on TE p. 255 and ask them to give a complete description of the photo: **Describan la foto.**
- Use the **¿Qué ves?** questions to focus the discussion.

UNIDAD 4

ETAPA 1

El próximo paso

OBJECTIVES

- Describe your studies
- Ask questions
- Say what you are doing
- Say what you were doing

¿Qué ves?

Mira la foto. Contesta las preguntas.

1. ¿En qué clase estarán estos estudiantes? ¿Cómo lo sabes?

2. ¿Tienen esta clase en tu escuela? ¿La has tomado?

3. ¿Cómo crees que se sienten los estudiantes? ¿Por qué?

254

Classroom Management

Planning Ahead In preparation for the vocabulary in this **Etapa**, set up 3–5 different job fair stations. Display the types of professions available at each station. As students work through the **Etapa**, have them add information (a list of school and training requirements, the names of possible companies, places where the jobs are available, etc.).

Time Saver Make copies of the survey cards on p. 258 so that students can fill them out and use them to role-play counseling scenes.

TODOS JUNTOS

Nº10   Revista escolar   marzo

EL
FUTURO
ES
NUESTRO

Dirección General de Escuelas
Escuela 208   Buenos Aires

Cross Cultural Connections

Ask students to compare the photo on pp. 254–255 with what they would see in a photo of a chemistry class in your school. What conclusion can they draw from this comparison?

Culture Highlights

● **LA EDUCACIÓN** En Chile se ofrecen 8 años de educación compulsoria y gratuita, mientras que en Argentina son 7 años. Los adultos de ambos países tienen un índice de alfabetización de 96%, y el 12% de sus poblaciones asisten a la universidad.

Supplementary Vocabulary

el experimento	experiment
la fórmula química	chemical formula
el frasco, la cubeta	flask, beaker
el laboratorio	laboratory
el majadero	pestle
el mortero	mortar
la probeta graduada	graduated cylinder
la solución	solution
el tubo de ensayo, la probeta	test tube

Block Schedule

FunBreak Play a word association game, using fields of study and professions. Begin with a word such as **ciencias** and have the first student give a related Spanish word, such as **doctor.** The next student gives a word related to **doctor,** such as **biología.** Continue until students can no longer find a related word. Then begin a new round. (For additional activities, see **Block Scheduling Copymasters.**)

Teaching All Students

Extra Help Have students brainstorm school subjects and professions they remember. List them on the board. Have students write them in their notebooks for reference throughout this unit.

Native Speakers Have students add and explain the names of school subjects and professions not listed in "Extra Help."

Multiple Intelligences

Interpersonal Have students work in pairs to discuss the classes they have this year, the ones they enjoy the most, and the fields of study or careers that interest them.

Teaching Resource Options

Print 📖

Block Scheduling Copymasters
Unit 4 Resource Book
  Absent Student Copymasters, p. 34

Audiovisual 🎧

OHT 5, 6, 7, 7A, 8, 8A, 11 (Quick Start)

Technology 💻

Online Workbook, U4E1
Take-Home Tutor CD-ROM, U4E1

🔔 Quick Start Review

♻ Vocabulary review

Use OHT 11 or write on the board:
Haz una lista de 5 carreras o profesiones que te interesan.

Answers will vary.

Teaching Suggestions
Introducing Vocabulary

• Have students look at pages 256–257. Use OHT 5 and 6 to present the vocabulary.

• Ask the Comprehension Questions on TE p. 257 in order of yes/no (questions 1–3), either/or (questions 4–6), and simple word or phrase (questions 7–10). Expand by adding similar questions.

• Use the TPR activity to reinforce the meaning of individual words.

Descubre

Answers
1. b
2. f
3. e
4. d
5. g
6. c
7. a

En contexto VOCABULARIO

¿Qué quieres hacer?

Es importante pensar en tu futuro. ¿Qué campo de estudio te interesa después del colegio?

🔲 Descubre

Usa tu intuición y lo que ya sabes para decidir el significado de cada palabra. Escoge de la segunda columna.

1. administración de empresas
2. contabilidad
3. informática
4. mercadeo
5. campo de estudio
6. ventas
7. ingeniería

a. engineering
b. management
c. sales
d. marketing
e. computer science
f. accounting
g. field of study

Administración de empresas

Agronomía
Agronomía

Te interesa cultivar vegetales, frutas, o cualquier producto de la tierra.

Administración de empresas
Te llevas bien con la gente. Crees que podrías manejar el personal de un negocio.

Comercio
Quieres ser un hombre o mujer de negocios para ver cómo funcionan los negocios grandes.

Contabilidad
Tienes gran habilidad para las matemáticas. ¡Lo cuentas todo!

Finanzas
Lo que más te interesa es cómo aumentar fondos.

Informática
¡Quieres hacer que la computadora haga lo que tú quieras!

Mercadeo
Te gustaría saber qué estrategias convierten un producto en un éxito.

Ventas
¡Tienes poder de persuasión! Convences a los consumidores sobre los productos que deben comprar.

256 doscientos cincuenta y seis
Unidad 4

Classroom Community

TPR Assign various students the fields on pp. 256–257. Have students work alone or with a partner to act out scenes (verbal or pantomimic) that take place in these fields. The class guesses the fields.

Group Activity Have students work in groups to expand the descriptions of the type of person suitable for each field listed on pp. 256–257. They should include at least one more personality description/personal interest for each field. As a class, discuss the additional information to see if everyone agrees.

CD-ROM
Take-Home Tutor

Comprehension Questions

1. Si te llevas bien con la gente, ¿estudias administración de empresas? (Sí)
2. Si quieres ser un hombre o una mujer de negocios, ¿estudias biología? (No)
3. Si tienes gran habilidad para las matemáticas, ¿estudias contabilidad? (Sí)
4. Para aumentar fondos, ¿estudias finanzas o informática? (finanzas)
5. Si tienes poder de persuasión, ¿estudias ventas o contabilidad? (ventas)
6. Si te gusta cultivar productos de la tierra, ¿estudias informática o agronomía? (agronomía)
7. Si te gustaría enseñar, ¿qué estudias? (educación)
8. ¿Qué debes estudiar si te gusta crear anuncios? (publicidad)
9. Si te gusta dibujar con mucha precisión, ¿qué estudias? (dibujo técnico)
10. ¿Qué campo se dedica a la producción de las máquinas? (ingeniería mecánica)

Educación

Siempre has querido ser maestro o maestra. Te encantaría enseñar a otros todo lo que sabes.

Humanidades

Te interesa todo lo que tiene que ver con la gente y la cultura: la filosofía, la literatura, las bellas artes.

Educación

Ingeniería civil

Diseño

Eres muy creativo(a) y artístico(a). Ya sean libros o revistas o anuncios, tú los quieres diseñar.

Publicidad

Tú quieres crear los anuncios que atraen la atención del público.

Relaciones públicas

Para tener una buena relación con el público, las compañías emplean a gente que se dedica solamente a eso.

Dibujo técnico

Te gusta dibujar y eres muy exacto(a). Te encanta pasar horas dibujando con mucha precisión.

Ingeniería civil

¿Cómo se construyen las ciudades? Quieres diseñar y construir **carreteras** y puentes.

Ingeniería mecánica

Este campo se dedica a la producción, el diseño y el uso de las máquinas.

Diseño

Online Workbook
CLASSZONE.COM

¿Comprendiste?

1. ¿Qué campo te interesa? ¿Por qué?
2. ¿Qué tienen en común los campos de publicidad, mercadeo y ventas?
3. ¿Te interesa seguir la profesión de alguien que conoces? ¿Por qué?
4. ¿En qué campo de estudio crees que podrías desarrollar tus habilidades y talentos?
5. ¿Explorarás varios campos antes de seguir uno? ¿Sabes cuál vas a seguir? Explica.

Quick Wrap-up

Ask students to write additional descriptive captions for the photos on pp. 256–257.

Teaching All Students

Extra Help Read a description of a field and have students tell you which one you are talking about.

Native Speakers Ask students to investigate and present information to the class about a career of their choosing in their countries of origin. They should include information on type of education necessary, how many years of study, job outlook, salary, etc.

Multiple Intelligences

Naturalist Have students research agriculture in their community. Which crops are cultivated? What livestock is raised? Ask them to generate a list of these words in Spanish. If the presence of agriculture is limited in the community, have students choose one of the **Southern Cone** countries. Distribute the list to the class and use the words as a source of extra credit vocabulary for quizzes and tests.

Block Schedule

Change of Pace Have students work in pairs to discuss the jobs of adults they know well. Have them talk about the people's personalities, dispositions, and interests, and why they probably chose the professions they did. (For additional activities, see **Block Scheduling Copymasters**.)

Teaching Resource Options

Print

Block Scheduling Copymasters
Unit 4 Resource Book
  Absent Student Copymasters, p. 35
  Audioscript, p. 43

Audiovisual

OHT 9, 10, 12 (Quick Start)
Audio Program CD 10, Track 1

Technology

Take-Home Tutor CD-ROM, U4E1

Quick Start Review

♻ **Fields of study**

Use OHT 12 or write on the board:
Write a field of study that you associate
with each of the following:

1. los negocios   4. la cultura
2. las plantas   5. los números
3. los dibujos

Answers
Answers will vary. Answers could include:
1. administración de empresas, comercio,
   finanzas, mercadeo, ventas
2. agronomía
3. diseño, dibujo técnico, ingeniería civil,
   ingeniería mecánica
4. educación, humanidades
5. contabilidad, finanzas

Teaching Suggestions
Presenting Situations

• Present the Listening Strategy, p. 258,
  and have students answer the
  Pre-listening questions.
• Use OHT 9 and 10 to present the
  Leer section. Ask simple yes/no,
  either/or, or short-answer questions.
• Have students complete the Listening
  Strategy exercise. Then use Audio CD
  10 and have students do the
  Escuchar section (see Script p. 253D).
• Have students work in pairs or groups
  to complete the **Hablar** section.

AUDIO
SITUACIONES

PARA ESCUCHAR

STRATEGIES: LISTENING

Pre-listening Scan the fields of study on p. 256.
In addition to knowledge, each one requires
certain personal qualities. Which ones require
the ability to get along with others? Which
ones are best suited for those who think for
themselves and set personal goals?

Evaluate recommendations: Read **Datos
personales** and analyze Emilio's interests and
skills. What courses would you recommend
for him? Then listen to his interview with the
counselor. How does your suggestion compare
with hers? How do you explain the differences?

¡Eso sí me interesa!

Esperas hablar con la consejera del colegio y
ves el formulario de otro estudiante. Luego,
escuchas una entrevista entre este estudiante
y la consejera sobre los planes que él tiene
para el futuro.

1 Leer

Encuentras este formulario en la oficina mientras estás
esperando a la consejera. Estúdialo para saber más sobre
el estudiante que lo dejó.

DATOS PERSONALES

Nombre: _Emilio García Ávila_

Dirección: _____

No. de teléfono: _____ **Fecha de nacimiento** _____

Marca los campos de estudio que te interesan:

☐ Agri~~c~~ultura   *Me parece un poco aburrido...*   ☐ Huma~~n~~idades

☐ Administración de empresas   ☐ Informática   *¡Eso no es para mí!*

☐ Comercio   ☐ Ingeniería civil

☐ Contabilidad   ☐ Ingeniería mecánica

☑ (Dibujo técnico)   ☐ Mercadeo   *Soy demasiado tímido para trabajar con la gente. ¡Olvida Ventas y Relaciones públicas!*

☐ Diseño   ☐ Publicidad

☐ Educación   ☐ Rela~~c~~iones públicas

☐ Finanzas   ☐ ~~Ventas~~

Classroom Community

Game First have each student write the definition of a
different field on an index card. Be sure all careers are
covered. Some may be duplicated. Put all the cards in a
bag. Divide the class into 4–5 groups. Choose a
scorekeeper to keep track of points. A player from
Group 1 picks a card from the bag and reads it aloud.
If he/she can't think of the career, the card is given to
Group 2 to answer. Otherwise, a player from Group 2
selects a new card. The player who guesses the career
wins a point for his/her team. Players return cards to
the bag after each use. When everyone from the class
has had at least one turn, points are tallied to
determine the winning team.

CD-ROM Take-Home Tutor

2 Escuchar 🎧

Emilio está en la oficina de la consejera para hablar con ella de los campos de estudio que le interesan. Escucha la entrevista. Marca **sí** si el campo de estudio le interesa a Emilio. Marca **no** si no le interesa. Marca **no se menciona** si ese campo de estudio no se menciona en la entrevista.

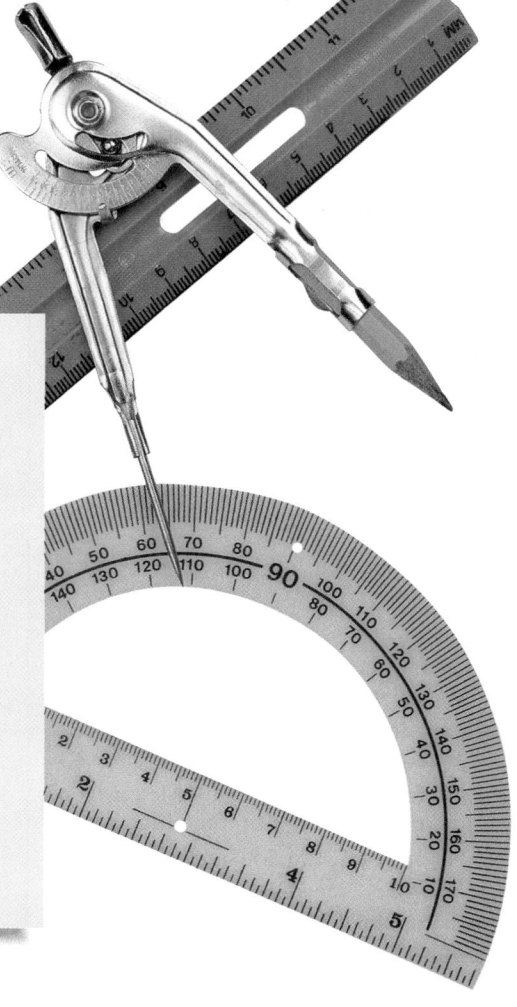

	Sí	No	No se menciona
Agricultura	○	○	○
Comercio	○	○	○
Contabilidad	○	○	○
Dibujo técnico	○	○	○
Diseño	○	○	○
Educación	○	○	○
Finanzas	○	○	○
Humanidades	○	○	○
Ingeniería civil	○	○	○
Ingeniería mecánica	○	○	○
Mercadeo	○	○	○
Publicidad	○	○	○
Relaciones públicas	○	○	○
Tecnología	○	○	○

3 Hablar 👥

En grupos de dos o tres, conversen sobre los campos de estudio que más les interesan. Hablen de sus talentos y habilidades. Escojan dos o tres campos y digan por qué les interesan. Luego escojan otros dos o tres campos y digan por qué no les interesan.

doscientos cincuenta y nueve
El Cono Sur Etapa I

259

Escuchar (See script, p. 253D.)

Answers

Agricultura	No
Comercio	Sí
Contabilidad	No
Dibujo técnico	Sí
Diseño	No se menciona
Educación	No se menciona
Finanzas	Sí
Humanidades	No se menciona
Ingeniería civil	Sí
Ingeniería mecánica	No se menciona
Mercadeo	No
Publicidad	No
Relaciones públicas	No se menciona
Tecnología	Sí

Hablar

Answers will vary.

Critical Thinking

Have students discuss which personality traits they think are best suited to the fields listed in the table on p. 259. After coming up with lists for most or all of the areas, have students decide which field would be most appropriate for them: **¿Qué campo sería más apropiada para ti?**

Teaching All Students

Extra Help Have students write quizzes for matching careers with fields of study or descriptions. Quizzes should have at least 5 items. Then have students exchange quizzes with a partner, complete the quizzes, and peer correct.

Multiple Intelligences

Verbal Have students write and present/record a radio announcement about a university that offers the following courses of study: **agronomía, administración de empresas, comercio,** and **informática.**

Interpersonal Have students think about personality types and how they relate to career choices. For example, an organized person might want to be an accountant.

Block Schedule

Variety Have students make Venn diagrams of 2 or more fields of study to illustrate what they have in common and how they differ. Call on volunteers to present their diagrams. (For additional activities, see **Block Scheduling Copymasters.**)

Teaching Resource Options

Print

Block Scheduling Copymasters
Unit 4 Resource Book
  Absent Student Copymasters, p. 36

Audiovisual

OHT 12 (Quick Start)

🔔 Quick Start Review

Gustar

Use OHT 12 or write on the board:
Use **gustar** and the following elements
to tell what the people like:

Modelo: a Carlos / poesía
A Carlos le gusta la poesía.

1. a Félix / bellas artes
2. a Víctor / matemáticas
3. a Juana y a Tomás / agricultura
4. a nosotros / la Bolsa
5. a mí / ¿?

Answers
1. A Félix le gustan las bellas artes.
2. A Víctor le gustan las matemáticas.
3. A Juana y a Tomás les gusta la agricultura.
4. A nosotros nos gusta la Bolsa.
5. A mí me gusta(n)...

Teaching Suggestions
Comprehension Check

Use **Actividades 1–4** to assess retention
after the **Vocabulario** and **Situaciones**.
After completing **Actividad 1**, read
items 1, 3, 5, and 7 aloud as a dictation
exercise. Have volunteers write the
sentences on the board for class
review and student self-check.

Actividad 1 Objective: Controlled practice
Vocabulary

Answers
1. Educación   5. Comercio
2. Relaciones públicas 6. Finanzas
3. Ingeniería mecánica 7. Publicidad
4. Diseño   8. Informática

En acción

PARTE A — **Práctica del vocabulario**

Objectives for Activities 2–4
• Describe your studies • Ask questions

1 El (La) consejero(a)

Escribir Eres el (la) consejero(a) de un
colegio. Varios estudiantes quieren tu
opinión. Según sus intereses, diles qué
deberían estudiar.

Diseño   Informática   Finanzas

Comercio   Educación   Publicidad

Ingeniería mecánica   Relaciones públicas

1. Quiero ser maestro en una escuela
   secundaria.
2. Soy muy social. Quiero un puesto en
   algo que tenga que ver con la gente.
3. Me fascinan las máquinas. Me gusta
   desarmarlas para ver cómo funcionan.
4. Soy muy artística. Me gustaría diseñar
   libros.
5. El mundo de los negocios me interesa
   mucho.
6. ¡Quiero hacerme rico! Saber invertir el
   dinero es muy importante para vivir
   bien.
7. Soy muy creativa. Creo que puedo
   inventar anuncios para la tele.
8. Tengo tres computadoras. ¡No puedo
   vivir sin mis computadoras!

2 La especialización

Hablar/*Escribir* Quieres saber en qué se
especializaron las siguientes personas.
Sigue el modelo.

hermano mayor

Tú: *¿En qué se especializó tu
hermano(a) mayor?*

Compañero(a): *Se especializó
en dibujo
técnico.*

1.   Luis Pablo

2.   tío Ernesto

3.   prima Aurora

4.   Mercedes

5.   doña Carmen

6.   Rodolfo

Classroom Management

Time Saver Write the answers to **Actividades 1** and
2 on an OHT. When students complete the activities,
show the OHT and have them check their answers.

Peer Review Have each student write 3 questions
using 3 different words from the **Vocabulario** on
p. 261. Pairs then ask each other their questions. Call
on several pairs to present a few questions to the class.

③ La solicitud

Hablar/Escribir Tú y tu compañero van a llenar una solicitud de empleo para los siguientes departamentos de una empresa. Hablen sobre la información que tienen que dar usando expresiones del vocabulario.

modelo

mercadeo

Tú: *En la solicitud preguntan para qué estás capacitado(a).*

Compañero(a): *Me especialicé en mercadeo. Me gusta tomar decisiones. ¿Y tú?…*

1. relaciones públicas   **3.** educación

2. finanzas   **4.** diseño

Vocabulario

Tus habilidades

adaptarse *to adapt oneself*

capacitado(a) *qualified*

correr riesgos *to take risks*

desempeñar un cargo *to carry out a responsibility*

emprendedor(a) *enterprising*

encargarse de *to be in charge of*

especializarse *to specialize*

estar dispuesto(a) a *to be willing to*

la formación *training, education*

superarse *to get ahead, excel*

tomar decisiones *to make decisions*

▶ ¿Qué palabras usarías para describirte?

④ ¿Cuál te interesa?

Hablar/Escribir Quieres saber qué campo de estudio le interesa a tu compañero(a) y cuáles son las habilidades que tiene para ese campo. Luego, él (ella) quiere saber lo mismo sobre ti.

modelo

Tú: *¿Qué campo de estudio te interesa?*

Compañero(a): *Me interesa mucho la ingeniería mecánica.*

Tú: *¿De veras? ¿Por qué?*

Compañero(a): *Desde niño(a) me han fascinado las máquinas. También quiero diseñar equipo mecánico.*

Teaching All Students

Extra Help Have students draw 2 cartoons to represent 2 different fields. They should label each cartoon and present them to a partner or the class.

Multiple Intelligences

Intrapersonal Have students think about 3 adults that they admire most in each of their chosen professions. Have them explain why they admire each person.

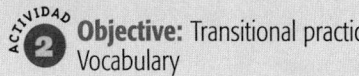

ACTIVIDAD 2 Objective: Transitional practice
Vocabulary

Answers *Answers will vary.*
1. A: ¿En qué se especializó Luis Pablo?
   B: Se especializó en ingeniería civil.
2. A: ¿En qué se especializó tío Ernesto?
   B: Se especializó en mercadeo *(o:* finanzas).
3. A: ¿En qué se especializó tu prima Aurora?
   B: Se especializó en humanidades.
4. A: ¿En qué se especializó Mercedes?
   B: Se especializó en ingeniería mecánica.
5. A: ¿En qué se especializó doña Carmen?
   B: Se especializó en administración de empresas.
6. A: ¿En qué se especializó Rodolfo?
   B: Se especializó en ventas *(o:* comercio).

Teaching Suggestions
Teaching Vocabulary

Model pronunciation of the **Vocabulario**. Then have students write a description of themselves using the words. Ask volunteers to read their descriptions aloud.

ACTIVIDAD 3 Objective: Open-ended practice
Vocabulary

Answers will vary.

ACTIVIDAD 4 Objective: Open-ended practice
Vocabulary

Answers will vary.

Block Schedule

Change of Pace Have students work in pairs to create 2 drawings—one of a child involved in an activity that hints at his/her future, and another of that same person as an adult in his/her profession. Display the drawings and use them to talk about childhood inclinations, personality, etc. and the relationship of those with adulthood professions. (For additional activities, see **Block Scheduling Copymasters**.)

Teaching Resource Options

Print

Más práctica Workbook PE, p. 94
Cuaderno para hispanohablantes
 PE, p. 91
Block Scheduling Copymasters
Unit 4 Resource Book
 Más práctica Workbook TE, p. 8
 Cuaderno para hispanohablantes
  TE, p. 23
 Information Gap Activities, p. 29
 Absent Student Copymasters, p. 36
 Audioscript, p. 43

Audiovisual

OHT 13 (Quick Start), 16 (Grammar)
Audio Program CD 10, Track 2, Activity 6

Technology

Online Workbook, U4E1
Take-Home Tutor CD-ROM, U4E1

Quick Start Review

♻ **Abilities/experience vocabulary**
Use OHT 13 or write on the board:
Match each expression with an
adjective that is opposite in meaning:

1. adaptarse
2. desempeñar un cargo
3. estar dispuesto
4. correr riesgos
5. tomar decisiones
  a. indeciso
  b. prudente
  c. inadaptado
  d. irresponsable
  e. contrario

Answers
1. c 2. d 3. e 4. b 5. a

Teaching Suggestions
Reviewing Interrogative Words

• Ask students questions using each of
 the question words in the **Vocabulario.**
• Say a question word, then call on a
 student to form a question with that
 word. Call on a second student to
 answer the question.

Objectives for Activities 5–16
• Ask questions • Say what you are doing • Say what you were doing

REPASO Interrogative Words

▶ There are many words you can use to ask questions. Many of the ones
you already know are reviewed in the vocabulary box below.

▶ When you ask someone to repeat what
they just said, use **¿Cómo?** rather than
¿Qué? It is more polite.

—Mañana no hay clases.
Tomorrow there are no classes.

—¿Cómo?
What *(did you say)?*

▶ As you know, the meaning of ¿Cómo? changes depending on whether
you use it with **ser** or **estar**:

asks about appearance,   *asks about*
character, and personality   *her health*

¿Cómo es Laura?   **¿Cómo está** Laura?
What *does Laura look like?* **How** *is Laura?*
What *is Laura like?*

Don't forget to write
Spanish question words
with an **accent mark.**

Vocabulario

♻ **Ya sabes**

¿Adónde?   ¿De quién(es)?
¿A quién(es)?   ¿Dónde?
¿Cómo?   ¿Para qué?
¿Cuál(es)?   ¿Por qué?
¿Cuándo?   ¿Qué?
¿Cuánto(s)/Cuánta(s)?   ¿Quién(es)?
¿De dónde?

Practice: **Más práctica**   **Online Workbook**
Actividades cuaderno p. 94   CLASSZONE.COM
5 6 7   **Para hispanohablantes**
                 cuaderno p. 91

---

5 Preguntón

Hablar/*Escribir* Estás
sentado(a) en el jardín de
la Universidad de Chile. Un
estudiante te ve y empieza
a hacerte muchas preguntas.
¿Qué te pregunta? Usa las
palabras interrogativas del
vocabulario para completar
sus preguntas.

modelo

Yo soy de Santiago.
Y tú, ¿de dónde eres?

1. ¿_____ te graduaste de
   la secundaria?
2. ¿_____ es tu clase
   favorita?
3. ¿_____ te gusta la
   ingeniería mecánica?
4. ¿_____ libros necesitas
   comprar para esa clase?
5. ¿_____ es tu profesor de
   dibujo mecánico?
6. ¿_____ aprendiste a
   dibujar tan bien?
7. ¿Ya te vas? ¿_____ vas?
8. ¿_____ está la biblioteca?
9. ¿_____ es esa bicicleta?
10. ¿Tomaste apuntes en
    clase? ¿_____ le prestaste

Classroom Community

Learning Scenario Have students write and
present skits similar to the one in the listening script for
Actividad 6. Students should create their own interview
forms to use as guidance for asking the interview
questions.

Game Divide the class into teams to play a "what is
the question" game. Use information about students
and school. For example, say: **Es de San Antonio,
Texas.** The first team to clap or ring a bell answers,
¿De dónde es Ana?

6 Los datos

Escuchar/*Escribir* Escucha una entrevista entre la señora Madrigal y un empleado de la universidad. Luego completa el formulario.

Solicitud de empleo

Nombre: _____ Fecha de nacimiento: _____

Estado civil: _____ Campo de estudio: _____

Educación:

Licenciatura: _____ Maestría: _____ Doctorado: _____

Fecha de solicitud: _____

Vocabulario

Dar información por escrito

el currículum vitae *resumé*

los datos *facts; information*

el doctorado *doctorate*

el estado civil *civil status (married, divorced, single)*

la estatura *height*

la fecha de nacimiento *date of birth*

la firma *signature*

la licenciatura *university degree*

la maestría *master's degree*

el paquete *package*

el sobre *envelope*

solicitar *to request, to apply for*

la solicitud *application*

▶ ¿Qué información has dado por escrito y para qué?

7 Un(a) nuevo(a) amigo(a)

> **STRATEGY: SPEAKING**
>
> **Establish closer relationships** In developing a new friendship, you not only want to find out biographical information, but also know about that person's plans, hopes, beliefs, and feelings. These verbs will help you: **pensar, esperar, creer, sentirse.**

Hablar/*Escribir* Imagina que tú y tu compañero(a) se acaban de conocer. Hazle preguntas primero. Luego, cambien de papel.

¿Adónde?   ¿Para qué?

¿Cuánto?/¿Cuántos?

¿Dónde?   ¿Cuánta?/¿Cuántas?

¿De dónde?   ¿Por qué?   ¿Qué?

¿Cuál?/¿Cuáles?   ¿Quién?/¿Quiénes?

¿Cómo?   ¿De quién?/¿De quiénes?

¿A quién?/¿A quiénes?   ¿Cuándo?

modelo

Tú: *¡Hola! Yo me llamo… Y tú, ¿cómo te llamas?*

Compañero(a): *Me llamo… ¿De dónde eres tú?*

Tú: *Yo soy de….*

More Practice: Más comunicación *p. R12*

Teaching All Students

Extra Help Have students write 5 sentences using the question words and the words in the **Vocabulario** on p. 263. Call on 2 students at a time to write 1 of their sentences on the board. Have the class correct any errors.

Multiple Intelligences

Visual Have students work in pairs to create cartoons that could be captioned with 1 or more question words (for example, a dog looking for a ball under a chair). Students should write the question word(s) on the back. Then display the cartoons and have the class guess questions for each one.

Teaching Note

Students will receive a complete explanation of ¿**Qué?** vs. ¿**Cuál?** in **Unidad 5, Etapa 1.**

ACTIVIDAD 5 **Objective:** Controlled practice Interrogative words

Answers

1. Cuándo
2. Cuál
3. Por qué
4. Cuántos
5. Quién
6. Cómo
7. Adónde
8. Dónde
9. De quién
10. A quién

Teaching Suggestions
Teaching Vocabulary

Display a résumé and/or a job application on an OHT. Tell students that in Latin America it is common to include one's marital status and age.

ACTIVIDAD 6 **Objective:** Transitional practice Listening comprehension/ interrogative words

Answers (See script, p. 253D.)
Nombre: Dulce Madrigal Velasco
Fecha de nacimiento: 7 de septiembre, 1958
Estado civil: casada
Campo de estudio: Administración de empresas
Educación:
Licenciatura: Universidad de Buenos Aires
Maestría: Universidad de Buenos Aires
Doctorado: Universidad de Santiago de Chile
Fecha de solicitud: 25 de febrero

ACTIVIDAD 7 **Objective:** Open-ended practice Interrogative words in conversation

Answers will vary.

Block Schedule

Expansion Have students research and bring in examples of résumés and job applications. Make overhead transparencies of several of them. Have the class analyze what kind of information is given in résumés and what kind of information is asked for in job applications. Is there any information that cannot be asked on a job application? (For additional activities, see **Block Scheduling Copymasters.**)

Teaching Resource Options

Print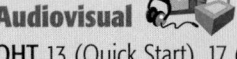

Más práctica Workbook PE, p. 93
Cuaderno para hispanohablantes
  PE, p. 92
Block Scheduling Copymasters
Unit 4 Resource Book
  Más práctica Workbook TE, p. 7
  Cuaderno para hispanohablantes
  TE, p. 24
  Information Gap Activities, p. 30
  Absent Student Copymasters, p. 37

Audiovisual

OHT 13 (Quick Start), 17 (Grammar)

Technology

Online Workbook, U4E1
Take-Home Tutor CD-ROM, U4E1

Quick Start Review

♻ Question words

Use OHT 13 or write on the board:
Complete each question with the
appropriate question word.

1. ¿ ____ estudiantes hay en clase?
2. ¿ ____ va la profesora?
3. ¿ ____ habla con la profesora?
4. ¿ ____ es el examen final, el lunes
   o el miércoles?
5. ¿ ____ estás, bien o mal?

Answers
1. Cuántos   2. Adónde
3. Quién   4. Cuándo
5. Cómo

Teaching Suggestions
Reviewing The Present Progressive

• Emphasize that the present progressive
  is not used as frequently in Spanish
  as in English. It is only used to say
  what is in progress at the moment.
• Point out that no words ever come
  between **estar** and the present
  participle.
• Call out infinitives and have students
  give the present participle.

REPASO   The Present Progressive

The **present progressive** tense is only used for an action that is going on
at the time of the sentence. The present progressive is like the **-ing** form
(gerund) of a verb in English.

  *What are you do**ing**?*
  *I am study**ing**.*

To form the **present progressive tense** use:

  present tense of estar + present participle

You already know the forms of **estar**. To form the **present participle**,
drop the ending of the infinitive and add the appropriate ending.

  -ar verbs   **estudi a̶r̶ + ando** ➡ **estudiando**

  -er, ir verbs   **com e̶r̶ + iendo** ➡ **comiendo**

  leer, oír, creer le e̶r̶ + yendo ➡ **leyendo**

  —Buenas tardes, señora. ¿José Antonio **está comiendo**?
  Good afternoon, Ma'am. Is José Antonio eating (now)?

  —No, ya comió. **Está estudiando**.
  No, he already ate. He's studying (at this moment).

- -

When you have object pronouns or reflexive pronouns with the present
progressive, you can either:

• place the pronouns
  before **estar**
    before
    Los estudiantes **se están adapt**ando
    a la vida universitaria.
    The students are adapting to university life.

• or attach them to the
  present participle.
    attaches
    Los estudiantes **están adaptándo**se
    a la vida universitaria.
    *The students are adapting
    to university life.*

    When you attach
    the pronouns, you add an
    accent mark to the **a** or **e**
    before **-ndo**.

Practice:
Actividades
8 9 10

Más práctica
cuaderno p. 93
Para hispanohablantes
cuaderno p. 92

 **Online Workbook**
CLASSZONE.COM

---

⑧ Las llamadas

Hablar/Escribir Haces unas
llamadas para hablar con
varios amigos. Pero no pueden
hablar contigo porque están
haciendo otra cosa. ¿Qué están
haciendo?

  modelo

  Ariel / ducharse

  Tú: *¿Puedo hablar con Ariel?*

  Compañero(a): *No, lo siento. Se
  está duchando.
  (Está duchándose.)*

  Nota: Gramática

  -ir stem-changing verbs change
  e → i and **o → u** in the
  present participle.
  v**e**stirse → v**i**stiéndose
  d**o**rmir → d**u**rmiendo

1. Esteban: afeitarse
2. Mónica: arreglarse el pelo
3. Arturo: bañarse
4. Marta: correr
5. Cristina: maquillarse
6. Armando: peinarse
7. Raquel: vestirse
8. Beto: secarse el pelo
9. Joaquín: escribir una carta
10. Jimena: acostarse

Classroom Community

Storytelling Prepare ahead: Have students bring in
comic strips that show actions in each frame. In class,
have students cut apart the cartoon frames and put each
cut-up strip into a separate envelope. Divide the class
into groups of 4. Give each group 4 envelopes. Have
students arrange the frames from each envelope on a
piece of paper. The order may or may not be the
original order. Then have students retell the story by

writing sentences describing what the characters are
doing in each frame. Have groups present their stories
to the class.

Paired Activity One student makes a request of
his/her partner and the partner makes an excuse
because he/she is doing something else. For example:
¿Quieres ir a la playa? → **No puedo. Estoy haciendo
la tarea.** Each student should make at least 5 requests.

9 La limpieza ♻

Escribir La familia Márquez está muy ocupada hoy. Es el primer fin de semana de la primavera y ya es hora de hacer la limpieza anual. ¿Qué están haciendo?

modelo

El Sr. Márquez está barriendo el suelo.

10 ¡No puede! 👥

Hablar/Escribir Buscas a varias personas para salir. ¡Pero nadie puede porque todos están ocupados! Pregunta a tu compañero(a) dónde están cinco amigos. Luego, él (ella) te pregunta por otros cinco. Sigue el modelo.

modelo

Tú: *¿Dónde está Miguel? ¿Puede ir al cine con nosotros?*

Compañero(a): *No, no puede. Está estudiando para el examen de español.*

More Practice:

Más comunicación *p. R12*

Nota cultural

Estados Unidos: «¡Excelente!»
Uruguay: «O.K.»

Estados Unidos: «O.K.»

Uruguay: «Lo dudo.»

ACTIVIDAD 8 Objective: Controlled practice
Present progressive in conversation

♻ **Reflexive verbs**

Answers
1. Se está afeitando. (Está afeitándose.)
2. Se está arreglando el pelo. (Está arreglándose el pelo.)
3. Se está bañando. (Está bañándose.)
4. Está corriendo.
5. Se está maquillando. (Está maquillándose.)
6. Se está peinando. (Está peinándose.)
7. Se está vistiendo. (Está vistiéndose.)
8. Se está secando el pelo. (Está secándose el pelo.)
9. Está escribiendo una carta.
10. Se está acostando. (Está acostándose.)

ACTIVIDAD 9 Objective: Transitional practice
Present progressive in writing

♻ **Household chores**

Answers
1. Está pasando la aspiradora.
2. Están desyerbando el jardín.
3. Está vaciando el basurero.
4. Está regando las plantas.
5. Está desarmando (reparando) el cortacésped.
6. Está lavando los platos.
7. Está reciclando las botellas de plástico.
8. Está cambiando la bombilla.
9. Está desconectando (desenchufando) el televisor.

ACTIVIDAD 10 Objective: Open-ended practice
Present progressive in conversation

Answers will vary.

▪ Block Schedule

Variety Have students write what the following people are doing at the time indicated: (1) mi mejor amigo(a) / ahora; (2) mi hermano(a) / en este momento; (3) mi profesor(a) de inglés / ahora; (4) mi primo(a) favorito(a) / ahora mismo. Students may make up answers as necessary. Then have students work in pairs to compare answers. Are there any similarities? Have pairs tell the class the similarities they found. (For additional activities, see **Block Scheduling Copymasters.**)

Teaching All Students

Extra Help Have each student draw someone doing a household chore. Display the drawings and have students take turns telling what the people in the drawings are doing.

Challenge Have students write poems using the present progressive. They might want to use one of the following themes: school, career plans, household chores, daily routine, ecology.

Multiple Intelligences

Kinesthetic Divide the class into groups of 4. Each student has to mime 2 activities and the rest of the group uses the present progressive to say what the person is doing. Then have groups choose 4 activities to mime for the class.

Teaching Resource Options

Print

Más práctica Workbook PE, p. 95
Cuaderno para hispanohablantes
  PE, p. 93
Block Scheduling Copymasters
Unit 4 Resource Book
  Más práctica Workbook TE, p. 9
  Cuaderno para hispanohablantes
    TE, p. 25
  Absent Student Copymasters, p. 38
  Audioscript, p. 44

Audiovisual

OHT 14 (Quick Start), 18 (Grammar)
Audio Program CD 10, Track 3,
  Activity 12
Word Tiles, U4E1

Technology

Online Workbook, U4E1
Take-Home Tutor CD-ROM, U4E1

Quick Start Review

🔔 Present progressive

Use OHT 14 or write on the board:
Use the present progressive to write
what the following people are doing:

1. Julio / afeitarse
2. Anita / descansar
3. yo / escribir la tarea
4. tú / peinarse
5. nosotros / escuchar al profesor

Answers
1. Julio se está afeitando (está afeitándose).
2. Anita está descansando.
3. Yo estoy escribiendo la tarea.
4. Tú te estás peinando (estás peinándote).
5. Nosotros estamos escuchando al profesor.

Teaching Suggestions
**Presenting The Progressive with
ir, andar, and seguir**

• Point out that **seguir** + present
  participle indicates that an action that
  began in the past is still continuing or
  that it happens regularly.
• Tell students that another way to
  express an action that keeps on
  happening is with **continuar** +
  present participle: **José continúa
  buscando trabajo.**

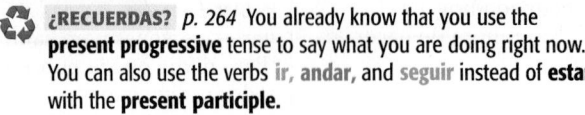

Práctica: gramática y vocabulario continuación

GRAMÁTICA The Progressive with **ir, andar,** and **seguir**

♻️ **¿RECUERDAS?** *p. 264* You already know that you use the
present progressive tense to say what you are doing right now.
You can also use the verbs **ir, andar,** and **seguir** instead of **estar**
with the **present participle.**

▶ Each of these verbs has a special meaning in progressive constructions.

ir + **present participle**

Anita **se va adapt ando** a su puesto.
Anita is (slowly but surely) adjusting to her job.

andar + **present participle**

Isabel **anda busc ando** trabajo.
Isabel is going around looking for work.

seguir + **present participle**

Isabel **sigue busc ando** trabajo.
Isabel is still looking for work.

Practice:
Actividades
11 12 13 14

Más práctica
cuaderno p. 95
Para hispanohablantes
cuaderno p. 93

🔵 **Online Workbook**
CLASSZONE.COM

Nota cultural

En muchos países hispanohablantes se usa el título profesional. Por ejemplo:
Ingeniero Fernández, Arquitecta Herrera Valentín, etc. Recuerda que los
hispanohablantes usan dos apellidos, el del padre y el de la madre. Las
mujeres casadas usan el apellido de su padre y el de su esposo.

SPMNET

Ingeniero Suárez Santini

Calle Mar de Plata
#167890 Unidad 28   tel. 1/788-5468
1040 Buenos Aires   fax 1/788-5788

266 doscientos sesenta y seis
Unidad 4

---

11 Un amigo de Paraguay

Hablar/*Escribir* Ramiro, tu
amigo de Paraguay, está
hablando por teléfono con
sus padres. Les está contando
cosas de su vida en Estados
Unidos. ¿Qué les dice?

modelo

estudiar tres horas al día

Sigo estudiando tres horas al día.

1. trabajar los fines
   de semana
2. aprender más idiomas
3. tocar la guitarra
4. correr por las mañanas
5. hacer ejercicio todos
   los días
6. buscar un carro barato
7. correr riesgos en
   mi trabajo
8. tomar decisiones para
   mi futuro
9. superarse en mi campo
   de estudio
10. adaptarse a las costumbres
    norteamericanas

También se dice

El **mercadeo** también se llama:
• **mercadotecnia**
• **marketing**

Classroom Community

Paired Activity Have students work in pairs and
take turns telling what they used to do when they were
younger. For example: **Jugaba al tenis todos los días.**
The other student asks a question based on the
information. For example: **¿Sigues jugando al tenis
todos los días?** Students must each make at least 5
statements.

Cooperative Learning **Prepare ahead:** Bring in
magazine pictures that show a lot of activity. Divide
students into groups of 3. Distribute several pictures to
each group. Student 1 describes the first picture using
ir, andar, or **seguir** + present participle. Student 2
writes down the sentence. Student 3 checks the
sentence. Then Student 2 describes the second picture,
and so on until all pictures are described. The group
submits their sentences for a grade.

12 ¿Es cierto?

Escuchar/*Escribir* Ruiz, el gerente, habla sobre la vida de sus empleados. Di si las oraciones son ciertas o falsas según Ruiz.

modelo

Gómez trabaja en la compañía.
Cierto.

1. Ribeira sigue superándose en su puesto.
2. Escobar nunca comparte sus ideas con otros compañeros de trabajo.
3. Prado va perdiendo mucho dinero.
4. Durán sigue estudiando mercadeo y relaciones públicas.
5. Vega no se está adaptando bien a la vida profesional.
6. Silva anda corriendo riesgos innecesarios.

Nota cultural
En Estados Unidos es común llamar a alguien por su nombre de pila *(first name)*. En la mayoría de los países hispanohablantes se usa el título y el apellido. Por ejemplo, «Sr. Blázquez, ¿está listo el folleto?» Solamente familia, buenos amigos o niños usan el nombre de pila.

13 ¿Qué sabes de...?

Hablar/*Escribir* Con un(a) compañero(a), hablen sobre amigos que acaban de ver. Haz una lista de cinco amigos. Usa la construcción progresiva con **ir**, **andar** o **seguir**. ¡Sé creativo(a)!

modelo

Tú: *Oye, ¿has hablado con Enrique? ¿Qué sabes de él?*

Compañero(a): *Sí, hablé con él el otro día. Anda disfrutando de las vacaciones. ¿Viste a Marta? Vino a visitar a sus padres ayer.*

Tú: *Sí, la vi. Me dice que está estudiando mucho.*

> acostumbrarse a las tradiciones de…
> adaptarse a su puesto
> buscar trabajo
> correr riesgos sin tener por qué
> darse cuenta de que [campo de estudio] no es nada fácil
> decidir su carrera
> disfrutar de las vacaciones
> inventar proyectos para el verano
> preocuparse más y más sobre…
> prepararse para la universidad
> tomar decisiones sin pensar
> tratar de convencer a sus padres de que…
> vender su carro

14 Verano

Hablar/*Escribir* Conversa con un(a) compañero(a) sobre lo que estás haciendo en el verano. Luego, escribe tus ideas.

modelo

Tú: *¿Sigues buscando trabajo para el verano?*

Compañero(a): *Sí, estoy entrevistándome en varias compañías.*

ACTIVIDAD 11 **Objective:** Controlled practice Progressive with **seguir**

Answers
1. Sigo trabajando los fines de semana.
2. Sigo aprendiendo más idiomas.
3. Sigo tocando la guitarra.
4. Sigo corriendo por las mañanas.
5. Sigo haciendo ejercicio todos los días.
6. Sigo buscando un carro barato.
7. Sigo corriendo riesgos en mi trabajo.
8. Sigo tomando decisiones para mi futuro.
9. Sigo superándome en mi campo de estudio.
10. Sigo adaptándome a las costumbres norteamericanas.

ACTIVIDAD 12 **Objective:** Transitional practice Listening comprehension/progressive with **ir**, **andar**, and **seguir**

Answers (See script, p. 253D.)
1. Cierto   4. Cierto
2. Falso   5. Falso
3. Falso   6. Falso

ACTIVIDAD 13 **Objective:** Transitional practice Progressive with **ir**, **andar**, and **seguir** in conversation

Answers will vary.

ACTIVIDAD 14 **Objective:** Open-ended practice Progressive with **ir**, **andar**, and **seguir** in conversation

Answers will vary.

Dictation
Using the Listening Activity Script for **Actividad 12** on TE p. 253D, dictate selected sentences to students. You may want to use this dictation for a quiz grade.

Teaching All Students

Extra Help Give students a series of situations; for example, **Roberto está en la oficina de la compañía Mendoza.** Students respond with a logical reason for the situation; for example, **Roberto anda buscando trabajo.**

Multiple Intelligences
Visual Have students create 3 cartoons to illustrate each of the progressive constructions. In addition to the characters' speech bubbles, students write a caption that includes **ir**, **andar**, or **seguir** + present participle.

Block Schedule
FunBreak Have students mime activities to solicit sentences such as **Andas quitando polvo.** Encourage humor and creativity. (For additional activities, see **Block Scheduling Copymasters**.)

Teaching Resource Options

Print 📖

Más práctica Workbook PE,
   pp. 89–92, 96
Actividades para todos Workbook PE,
   pp. 101–106
Cuaderno para hispanohablantes
   PE, pp. 89–90, 94
Block Scheduling Copymasters
Unit 4 Resource Book
   Más práctica Workbook TE,
      pp. 3–6, 10
   Actividades para todos Workbook
      TE, pp. 11–16
   Cuaderno para hispanohablantes
      TE, pp. 21–22, 26
   Absent Student Copymasters, p. 39

Audiovisual

OHT 14 (Quick Start), 19 (Grammar)

Technology

Online Workbook, U4E1
Take-Home Tutor CD-ROM, U4E1

Quick Start Review

♻ Present progressive

Use OHT 14 or write on the board:
Write what the following people are
doing:

1. Jaime / andar / buscar trabajo
2. yo / ir / aprender francés
3. Uds. / seguir / estudiar historia
4. tú / andar / perder todo
5. Inés / seguir / escribir la
   composición

Answers
1. Jaime anda buscando trabajo.
2. Yo voy aprendiendo francés.
3. Uds. siguen estudiando historia.
4. Tú andas perdiendo todo.
5. Inés sigue escribiendo la composición.

GRAMÁTICA   Present and Past Perfect Tenses

▸ You use the **past progressive** to emphasize that an action was in progress at a
particular time in the past. It is usually formed by using:

> The action was in progress at a specific time in the past.

imperfect form of estar + **present participle**

—¿Qué estabas **hac**iendo
a las nueve de la mañana?
What were you doing at nine A.M.?

—Estaba desayun**ando** y estudi**ando** para
el examen de mercadeo.
I was eating breakfast and studying for the marketing exam.

▸ You can also use the **past progressive** to emphasize that an action continued in the past for
a specific period of time until it came to an end. To form this use of the past progressive use:

preterite of estar + **present participle**

> It is clear that the action has ended.

Estuvimos **escrib**iendo toda la mañana.
We were writing all morning. (We spent the whole morning writing.)

Practice: Actividades **15** **16**   Más práctica *cuaderno p. 96*   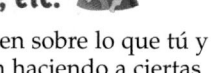 **Online Workbook** CLASSZONE.COM
Para hispanohablantes *cuaderno p. 94*

---

15 Ayer ellos estuvieron...

Hablar/*Escribir* ¿Qué estuvieron haciendo ayer?

modelo

Gabriel: escribir un ensayo para la clase

Gabriel estuvo escribiendo un ensayo para la clase.

1. yo: diseñar un folleto
2. Paula y Carlos: hacer un dibujo mecánico
3. Herlinda: leer para la clase de educación
4. Gustavo: hacer ventas por teléfono
5. Clara: leer la sección de negocios
6. María y Consuelo: estudiar un programa
   de computación
7. Leonardo: buscar trabajo
8. Nosotros: leer artículos periodísticos

16 A las dos, a las tres, etc. 👥

Hablar/*Escribir* Conversen sobre lo que tú y
tu compañero(a) estaban haciendo a ciertas
horas ayer.

modelo

Tú: *Ayer a las dos, yo estaba tomando el examen
de informática. ¿Qué estabas haciendo tú?*

Compañero(a): *Yo estaba estudiando en la biblioteca.*

> tomar el examen de...
> enviar mi solicitud
> llenar el formulario para el puesto de...
> escribir un trabajo para la clase de...
> trabajar en la oficina de...
> hacer la tarea para la clase de...

Classroom Community

TPR Have students work in groups of 4–5. Tell them
that they were baby-sitting 2 mischievous children last
night who were doing everything they were not
supposed to be doing. What was happening when they
lost their patience? Have students take turns miming
what was happening. The rest of the group has to
describe the action using the past progressive.

Group Activity Working in groups of 3, have
students create a skit using the past progressive and
ideas and vocabulary from **Actividades 15** and **16**.
Then have groups present their skits to other groups.

Activity 17 brings together all concepts presented.

17 Paramedia

Leer/*Escribir* Lee el folleto de la compañía Paramedia y contesta las preguntas.

1. ¿Qué clase de compañía es Paramedia?
2. ¿Cuáles son las cuatro áreas en que se especializa Paramedia?
3. ¿Hacen anuncios publicitarios? ¿Para qué medios de comunicación?
4. ¿En qué países tienen contactos?
5. Si fueras artístico(a), ¿en qué área trabajarías?
6. Si te gustara escribir, ¿en qué área trabajarías?
7. Si estudiaras relaciones públicas, ¿dónde crees que te pondrían a trabajar?
8. ¿Qué les dirías de tus habilidades para que te dieran un puesto? ¿En qué lugares estuviste trabajando antes?

AUDIOVISUAL

Especializados en Spots publicitarios de 35 mm. Realizadores nacionales e internacionales. Equipos de producción. Proyectos multimedia. Vídeo interactivo, corporativo e industrial. Posproducciones digitales y grafismo electrónico. Fotografía. Contactos en Francia, Italia, Finlandia, Holanda, Inglaterra y Estados Unidos.

COMUNICACIÓN

Transmita lo que desee, cuando y como precise, a quien usted quiera. Estrategias planificadas. Convocatorias informativas. Presencia en los medios: Prensa, radio, TV... Convenciones y presentaciones. Relaciones públicas. Desde el posicionamiento hasta el target, cuidamos su imagen y su proyección corporativa.

EDITORIAL

De la concepción y gerencia del producto a la entrega del mismo totalmente acabado. Diseño, diagramación, maquetación. Selección de soportes y artes gráficas. Libros, revistas, posters, folletos, catálogos, papelería corporativa. A la vanguardia en la utilización de papeles especiales para todos los sistemas de impresión.

CREATIVIDAD

Manuales de Identidad Corporativa. Logotipos y aplicaciones. Arte publicitario. Bocetos, ilustraciones, grafismo, dibujo. Entorno Macintosh. Artes finales. Maquetas en volumen. Aerografía. Desde el concepto hasta su desarrollo y total ejecución. Contamos con elementos humanos y técnicos para hacer realidad su mejor idea.

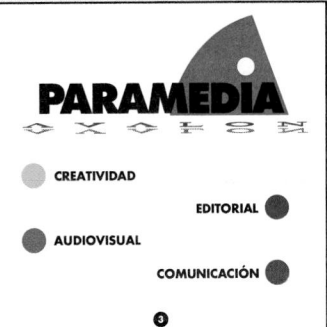

PARAMEDIA
OXFORD

○ CREATIVIDAD
EDITORIAL ●
● AUDIOVISUAL
COMUNICACIÓN ●
❸

More Practice: Más comunicación *p. R12*

 Online Workbook CLASSZONE.COM

Refrán

Con paciencia se gana lo imposible.

¿Qué quiere decir el refrán? ¿Puedes pensar en una situación en que tuviste que tener mucha paciencia? En tu opinión, ¿es importante tener paciencia?

doscientos sesenta y nueve
El Cono Sur Etapa 1
269

Teaching Suggestions
Presenting The Past Progressive

- Point out that the past progressive is most frequently formed with the imperfect form of **estar**.
- You may want to tell students that the preterite and the past progressive are often used together. The preterite is used to describe a specific action with a definitive beginning and end. The imperfect progressive is used to tell of an action happening with no specific beginning or end. For example: **Cuando fui a la ceremonia de graduación, estaba saliendo el sol.**

ACTIVIDAD **15** **Objective:** Controlled practice Past progressive

Answers
1. Yo estuve diseñando un folleto.
2. Paula y Carlos estuvieron haciendo un dibujo mecánico.
3. Herlinda estuvo leyendo para la clase de educación.
4. Gustavo estuvo haciendo ventas por teléfono.
5. Clara estuvo leyendo la sección de negocios.
6. María y Consuelo estuvieron escribiendo un programa.
7. Leonardo estuvo buscando trabajo.
8. Nosotros estuvimos leyendo artículos periodísticos.

ACTIVIDAD **16** **Objective:** Transitional practice Past progressive in conversation

Answers will vary.

ACTIVIDAD **17** **Objective:** Open-ended practice Etapa review in reading and writing

Answers
1. Paramedia es una agencia de publicidad.
2. Las cuatro áreas son audiovisual, comunicación, editorial y creatividad .
3. Sí. Para la prensa, la radio y la televisión.
4. En Francia, Italia, Finlandia, Holanda, Inglaterra y Estados Unidos
5. Creatividad
6. Editorial
7. Comunicación
8. *Answers will vary.*

■ Block Schedule

Change of Pace Give students copies of the social page from any Spanish-language newspaper. Have students find people who use their professional title and women who use their maiden name followed by **de** and the husband's name. (For additional activities, see **Block Scheduling Copymasters**.)

Teaching All Students

Extra Help Have students draw pictures that include people doing different actions. Then have them describe what everyone was doing, using the past progressive.

Native Speakers Have students write the beginning of a mystery story in which they set the scene using the past progressive with the imperfect of **estar**. Then they use the past progressive with the preterite of **estar** to have something happen that will change the situation.

Multiple Intelligences

Interpersonal Have students work in pairs and take turns telling each other what they were doing at specific times during the day. For example: **A las once y media, yo estaba comiendo en la cafetería. A las tres, yo estaba tocando la flauta.** Then have students say why they like or dislike each activity.

Teaching Resource Options

Print 📖

Actividades para todos Workbook PE, pp. 107–109

Unit 4 Resource Book
Audioscript, p. 44
Actividades para todos Workbook
PE, pp. 17–19
Absent Student Copymasters, p. 40

Audiovisual 🎧💻

OHT 14 (Quick Start)
Audio Program CD 10, Tracks 4-5

Technology 🎧💻 CD-ROM

Online Workbook, U4E1
Take-Home Tutor CD-ROM, U4E1

🔔 Quick Start Review

♻ **Past progressive**

Use OHT 14 or write on the board:
Write what these people were doing.

Modelo: Paco estaba en la cafetería
a las doce.
Estaba almorzando.

1. Ana estaba en el gimnasio a las tres.
2. Los amigos estaban en la discoteca a las diez.
3. Andrés estaba en el sofá a las siete.
4. Camila estaba en la biblioteca a las cinco.

Answers
Answers will vary.

Teaching Suggestions

- **Prereading** Present the Culture Highlights on TE p. 271 so that students may better understand Borges and his works.
- **Strategy: Analyze the role of identity and fantasy** Present the strategy and discuss the theme of identity in T.V. and movie stories.
- **Reading** Have a volunteer read each paragraph. Ask students to summarize each paragraph after it is read.
- **Post-reading** Have students complete the Strategy tasks for the reading.

En voces

AUDIO 🎧
LECTURA

PARA LEER
STRATEGY: READING
Analyze the role of identity and fantasy Movies and television often tell stories about people who are uncertain about their identity. Think about a T.V. story or movie where you have seen this theme. What elements does the character see as fact? Which ones does she or he see as fiction? After the reading, list the elements from Borges' life that he uses in his works. Why do you think he chose those? Would you choose the same? Explain.

EL AUTOR

el hogar	lugar donde uno vive
el tigre	gato salvaje
mudarse	cambiarse de casa
por su cuenta	por sí mismo
paterno(a)	del padre
materno(a)	de la madre
reconocido(a)	famoso(a)

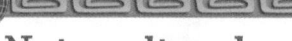

Nota cultural
Borges pasó los últimos años de su vida casi ciego, pero su ceguera *(blindness)* no le impidió seguir escribiendo. Contó con el apoyo de su esposa, María Kodama, quien lo ayudó mucho. Ella hacía los trabajos que él no podía.

270 doscientos setenta
Unidad 4

Jorge Luis Borges

Los laberintos y sueños[1], la fantasía, las identidades misteriosas y la suspensión del tiempo… todos son temas importantes en las obras de Jorge Luis Borges, uno de los autores latinoamericanos más reconocidos del siglo XX.

Borges nació en Buenos Aires en 1899 y vivió allí hasta 1914. Comenzó a escribir a la edad de nueve años, cuando publicó una traducción al español del cuento *The Happy Prince* de Oscar Wilde. Muchas de sus primeras lecturas fueron en inglés porque su hogar era bilingüe, ya que su abuela era inglesa. A los trece años, publicó su primer cuento original sobre tigres. Desde entonces, los tigres fueron un símbolo importante en la obra de Borges.

En 1914, su familia se mudó a Suiza y en 1919, se trasladó[2] a España, donde Borges publicó «Himno al mar», su primer poema en español. Regresó a Buenos Aires en 1921, fundó revistas y publicó su primera colección de poemas, *Fervor de Buenos Aires* (1923). Publicó poesía a lo largo de[3] su vida.

[1]dreams   [2]moved   [3]throughout

Classroom Community

Paired Activity Have students work in pairs to write 10 true/false statements based on the reading. Before writing, have them reread the selection applying different reading skills. They can make a list of cognates, unfamiliar words, write a title for each paragraph, etc. Then have 2 pairs come together to respond to each other's true/false statements.

Portfolio Have students research Borges' life and make a collage representing the important dates and events.

Rubric A = 13–15 pts. B = 10–12 pts. C = 7–9 pts. D = 4–6 pts. F = < 4 pts.

Criteria	Scale				
Appropriateness of images	1	2	3	4	5
Details	1	2	3	4	5
Creativity, appearance	1	2	3	4	5

Elogio de la sombra (1969), *El oro de los tigres* (1972) y *La rosa profunda* (1975) son otros libros de poemas conocidos. En estos libros, Borges trata los temas de la historia de su familia, una que participó en varias etapas de la historia de Argentina. Su abuelo paterno participó en la guerra civil de Argentina; su abuelo materno también fue soldado. Borges se veía muy distinto a ellos, como dice en «Soy», un poema de *La rosa profunda*:

> " Soy… el que no fue una espada[4] en la guerra. "

Borges no luchó con una espada de verdad, pero libró batallas de la imaginación[5] que resultaron en una obra voluminosa. Además de poemas, publicó varias colecciones de cuentos. Entre las más importantes se encuentran *Ficciones* (1944) y *El Aleph* (1949). En sus cuentos, Borges explora el límite entre la realidad y la fantasía y cómo a veces estas cosas se confunden en nuestras vidas.

El sentido del ser—quiénes somos y cómo formamos nuestra identidad—es otro de los temas importantes en la obra de Borges. Él veía su identidad como escritor aparte de su identidad como hombre. Pero Borges el escritor es el que captura finalmente la esencia de Borges el hombre. Hablando de sí mismo como escritor dijo:

> " …todas las cosas quieren perseverar en su ser[6];
> la piedra eternamente quiere ser piedra y el tigre
> un tigre. Yo he de quedar en Borges, no en mí
> (si es que alguien soy)… "

---

[4] sword
[5] fought battles of the imagination
[6] persevere in being themselves

Online Workbook
CLASSZONE.COM

¿Comprendiste?

1. ¿Cómo comenzó la carrera literaria de Borges? ¿Qué lo hizo famoso?
2. ¿Cuáles son unos temas importantes de sus obras?
3. ¿Qué tipos de obras literarias escribió Borges? ¿Cómo es el estilo de Borges?

¿Qué piensas?

1. ¿Cómo crees que la historia de la familia de Borges influyó sus escritos?
2. ¿Por qué crees que la naturaleza forma una parte importante de la obra de Borges?

Hazlo tú

Piensa en las personas y cosas que hacen que tú seas la persona que eres: tu familia, el lugar donde vives, tus intereses, las cosas que has estudiado y tus sueños para el futuro. Luego, escribe un poema o cuento que incluya aspectos importantes de tu relación con estas personas o cosas. También puedes buscar otro poema o cuento de Borges y escribir una opinión corta.

doscientos setenta y uno
El Cono Sur Etapa 1   271

Teaching Resource Options

Print

Cuaderno para hispanohablantes PE, pp. 95–96

Block Scheduling Copymasters
Unit 4 Resource Book
Cuaderno para hispanohablantes
TE, pp. 27–28
Information Gap Activities, pp. 31–32
Family Involvement, pp. 41–42

Audiovisual

OHT 15 (Quick Start)

Technology

eTest Plus Online/Test Generator CD-ROM

www.classzone.com

Quick Start Review

♻ Vocabulary review

Use OHT 15 or write on the board:
Match the words in the 2 columns:

1. la firma
2. datos
3. el curriculum vitae
4. la fecha de nacimiento
5. la estatura
   a. la educación y experiencia
   b. ¿alto o bajo?
   c. el nombre
   d. información
   e. el cumpleaños

Answers
1. c   2. d   3. a   4. e   5. b

✔ Teaching Suggestions
What Have Students Learned?

Have students look at the "Now you can…" notes and give examples of each category. Have them spend extra time reviewing categories they feel they are weak in by consulting the "To review" notes.

 **ACTIVIDAD 1 Answers**

1. Dónde	5. Cuál
2. Qué	6. Quién
3. Por qué	7. Cuántos
4. Cuándo	8. Cuántas

ETAPA 1

En uso
REPASO Y MÁS COMUNICACIÓN

Now you can…
• describe studies.
• ask questions.

To review
• interrogative words see p. 262.

OBJECTIVES
• Describe your studies
• Ask questions
• Say what you are doing
• Say what you were doing

1 Inés

Completa las preguntas para saber más sobre la amiga de tu compañero(a).

modelo

Tú: *¿Quién es tu amiga?*

Compañero(a): *¿Ella? Es Inés de la Cruz.*

1. —¿_____ estudia Inés? —Estudia en la Universidad de Buenos Aires.
2. —¿_____ estudia Inés? —Estudia publicidad.
3. —¿_____ estudia publicidad? —Trabajará en una agencia de publicidad.
4. —¿_____ toma clases? —Toma clases de lunes a viernes.
5. —¿_____ es su clase favorita? —Es «Publicidad para la televisión».
6. —¿_____ es el profesor de esa clase? —El señor Chávez.
7. —¿_____ estudiantes hay en esa clase? —Hay sesenta estudiantes.
8. —¿_____ clases toma por semestre? —Toma seis clases por semestre.

Now you can…
• say what you are doing.

To review
• the present progressive see p. 264.

2 Los estudiantes

En este momento todos los estudiantes están haciendo algo para sus clases. ¿Qué están haciendo?

modelo

Ángela: estudiar para su examen de comercio

Está estudiando para su examen de comercio.

1. Tito: diseñar un folleto publicitario
2. Berta: entrevistar a un candidato
3. Enrique: enviar un paquete
4. Alicia: escribir un ensayo para la clase de humanidades
5. Clara: hablar con su profesor de dibujo técnico
6. Tomás: ver un video para su clase de publicidad
7. Bárbara: tratar de hacer una venta
8. Eliseo: completar la solicitud para el puesto

272 doscientos setenta y dos
Unidad 4

Classroom Community

Paired Activity Have students create a version of their schedule, similar to the one in **Actividad 4**. Then have them work in pairs to ask and answer questions about each other's schedules.

Learning Scenario Have pairs prepare and present a mini-dialog between 2 high school students who will be graduating soon and need to make school and career plans.

Self-Check Quiz
CLASSZONE.COM

Now you can...

• say what you are doing.

To review

• the progressive with **ir**, **andar**, and **seguir** see p. 266.

③ La familia

Algunos miembros de tu familia están en varias situaciones en sus carreras. Explica sus situaciones. Sigue el modelo.

modelo

mi hermana Eugenia: ir / prepararse para la universidad

Mi hermana Eugenia se va preparando para la universidad.

1. mi primo Hernán: seguir / pensar en ser ingeniero
2. mi prima Amelia: ir / adaptarse a su puesto en la agencia de publicidad
3. mi tío: ir / acostumbrarse a la vida de un ingeniero civil
4. mi tía: seguir / trabajar en relaciones públicas
5. mi hermano menor: andar / tratar de decidir en su carrera
6. mi primo Rolando: seguir / enviar solicitudes a varias compañías

Now you can...

• say what you were doing.

To review

• the past progressive see p. 268.

④ ¿Qué estaba haciendo?

Ésta es la agenda de Lorena. Ayer pasó el día investigando varios campos de estudio en la universidad. Di qué estaba haciendo a ciertas horas.

modelo

8:00 / revisar el folleto de la universidad

Tú: *¿Qué estabas haciendo a las ocho de la mañana?*

Compañero(a): *Estaba revisando el folleto de la universidad.*

	miércoles
9:00	llegar a la universidad
10:00	entrevistarse con el profesor de contabilidad
10:30	ver los anuncios publicitarios en la clase de diseño
12:00	almorzar con un estudiante de informática
4:00	leer varios ensayos para la clase de educación
5:00	completar la solicitud para el programa de verano
7:00	visitar la clase de ventas
7:30	regresar a la casa

doscientos setenta y tres
El Cono Sur Etapa 1 273

ACTIVIDAD ② Answers

1. Está diseñando un folleto publicitario.
2. Está entrevistando a un candidato.
3. Está enviando un paquete.
4. Está escribiendo un ensayo para la clase de humanidades.
5. Está hablando con su profesor de dibujo técnico.
6. Está viendo un video para su clase de publicidad.
7. Está tratando de hacer una venta.
8. Está completando la solicitud para el puesto.

ACTIVIDAD ③ Answers

1. Mi primo Hernán sigue pensando en ser ingeniero.
2. Mi prima Amelia se va adaptando (va adaptándose) a su puesto en la agencia de publicidad.
3. Mi tío se va acostumbrando (va acostumbrándose) a la vida de un ingeniero civil.
4. Mi tía sigue trabajando en relaciones públicas.
5. Mi hermano menor anda tratando de decidir en su carrera.
6. Mi primo Rolando sigue enviando solicitudes a varias compañías.

ACTIVIDAD ④ Answers

1. A: ¿Qué estabas haciendo a las nueve de la mañana?
   B: Estaba llegando a la universidad.
2. A: ¿Qué estabas haciendo a las diez de la mañana?
   B: Me estaba entrevistando (Estaba entrevistándome) con el profesor de contabilidad.
3. A: ¿Qué estabas haciendo a las diez y media de la mañana?
   B: Estaba viendo los anuncios publicitarios en la clase de diseño.
4. A: ¿Qué estabas haciendo al mediodía?
   B: Estaba almorzando con un estudiante de informática.
5. A: ¿Qué estabas haciendo a las cuatro de la tarde?
   B: Estaba leyendo varios ensayos para la clase de educación.
6. A: ¿Qué estabas haciendo a las cinco de la tarde?
   B: Estaba completando la solicitud para el programa de verano.
7. A: ¿Qué estabas haciendo a las siete de la tarde?
   B: Estaba visitando la clase de ventas.
8. A: ¿Qué estabas haciendo a las siete y media de la noche?
   B: Estaba regresando a casa.

Teaching All Students

Extra Help Have students write 2 additional items for **Actividades 1, 2,** and **3.** Then have them exchange papers with a partner and complete each other's items. Finally, have them peer correct the papers and help each other understand any errors they made.

Multiple Intelligences

Logical/Mathematical In groups of 4, students take turns thinking of an activity and giving hints, using the present progressive. For example: **Estoy tomando jugo. Estoy comiendo cereal.** Group members guess the activity (**desayunar**).

Interpersonal Ask students to write 5 questions to ask you about your college education and career training. Have volunteers ask you the questions.

Block Schedule

Variety Have students write 5–7 questions that a job applicant would ask an interviewer. For example: **¿Cuándo empezaría a trabajar?** (For additional activities, see **Block Scheduling Copymasters**.)

Teaching Resource Options

Print 📖

Block Scheduling Copymasters
Unit 4 Resource Book
  Audioscript, p. 46
  Vocabulary Quizzes, pp. 48–50
  Grammar Quizzes, pp. 51–52
  Etapa Exam, Forms A and B,
    pp. 53–62
  Examen para hispanohablantes,
    pp. 63–67
  Portfolio Assessment, pp. 68–69
  Multiple Choice Test Questions,
    pp. 226–228

Audiovisual 📼

OHT 15 (Quick Start)
Audio Program CD 20, Track 1

Technology 💻 CD ROM

eTest Plus Online/Test Generator CD-ROM
🌐 www.classzone.com

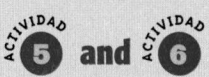 ACTIVIDAD 5 **and** ACTIVIDAD 6

Rubric: Speaking

Criteria	Scale	
Sentence structure	1 2 3	A = 11–12 pts.
Vocabulary use	1 2 3	B = 9–10 pts.
Originality	1 2 3	C = 7–8 pts.
Fluency	1 2 3	D = 4–6 pts.
		F = < 4 pts.

 ACTIVIDAD 7 **En tu propia voz**

Rubric: Writing

Criteria	Scale	
Vocabulary use	1 2 3 4 5	A = 14–15 pts.
Accuracy	1 2 3 4 5	B = 12–13 pts.
Creativity, appearance	1 2 3 4 5	C = 10–11 pts.
		D = 8–9 pts.
		F = < 8 pts.

Teaching Note: En tu propia voz

Writing Strategy Suggest that students answer the questions "who, what, where, when, why, and how" in their interviews. By asking different questions they will get a variety of details.

---

5 A mí me interesa...

STRATEGY: SPEAKING

Extend a conversation By now, you have had lots of experience in brief question-and-answer conversations. Here you can put together all that you know in discussing different areas of study. You can state opinions and preferences, give reasons, ask clarifying questions, give personal or emotional reactions, express doubts or concerns. These are what you have been learning and practicing!

En grupos de dos o tres, conversen sobre los campos de estudio que les interesan y los que no les interesan.

modelo

Tú: *A mí me interesa la finanza. Creo que es importante saber manejar el dinero.*

Amigo(a) 1: *Yo quiero estudiar la publicidad porque me encantaría hacer anuncios para la tele.*

Amigo(a) 2: …

6 Su propia compañía

En grupos de tres, imaginen que van a tener su propia compañía. Primero decidan qué tipo de compañía será. Luego, decidan quién se encarga de cada departamento y por qué.

modelo

Amigo 1: *¿Por qué no hacemos una compañía de publicidad?*

Amigo 2: *Buena idea. Tenemos que darle un nombre.*

Amigo 3: *Y tenemos que decidir quién se encarga de las finanzas…*

7 En tu propia voz

ESCRITURA Imagínate que eres el (la) gerente de una empresa. Vas a tener que entrevistar a varias personas para un puesto en tu compañía. Escribe seis preguntas para los candidatos. Luego, hazles la entrevista a dos compañeros.

modelo

- ¿En qué se especializó?
- ¿Cuáles son sus habilidades?
- ¿Por qué cree que usted sería el mejor candidato para este puesto?
- ¿…?

TÚ EN LA COMUNIDAD

Toño es alumno en Wisconsin. Trabaja en una compañía de equipo médico. A veces se comunica en español con los clientes hispanohablantes. También trabaja de voluntario con niños hispanohablantes. Los ayuda con su tarea y también habla con sus padres, que no hablan inglés. ¿Usas tu español para ayudar a los demás?

274 doscientos setenta y cuatro
Unidad 4

Classroom Community

Paired Activity Give copies of classified ads from a Spanish-language newspaper to pairs of students. Students should look over the ads and find one that interests each of them. Have them discuss why the jobs sound interesting and the qualifications one needs. Also have them explain why they think they would be suited for these jobs.

Portfolio Have students write a description of their interests and abilities and what job they are suited for. The descriptions should be similar to the ones on pp. 256–257, but expanded.

Rubric **A** = 13–15 pts. **B** = 10–12 pts. **C** = 7–9 pts. **D** = 4–6 pts. **F** = < 4 pts.

Writing criteria	Scale
Grammar/spelling accuracy	1 2 3 4 5
Vocabulary use	1 2 3 4 5
Creativity	1 2 3 4 5

En resumen
REPASO DE VOCABULARIO

DESCRIBE YOUR STUDIES

Coursework

la administración de empresas	business administration
la agronomía	agronomy
el campo de estudio	field of study
la carretera	road, highway
el comercio	business
la contabilidad	accounting
el dibujo técnico	technical drawing
el diseño	design
la educación	education
las finanzas	finance
las humanidades	humanities
la informática	computer science
la ingeniería civil	civil engineering
la ingeniería mecánica	mechanical engineering
el mercadeo	marketing
la publicidad	publicity
las relaciones públicas	public relations
las ventas	sales

Abilities and experience

adaptarse	to adapt oneself
capacitado(a)	qualified
correr riesgos	to take risks
desempeñar un cargo	to carry out a responsibility
emprendedor(a)	enterprising
encargarse de	to take charge of
especializarse	to specialize
estar dispuesto(a) a	to be willing to
la formación	training, education
superarse	to get ahead, to excel
tomar decisiones	to make decisions

Written information

el currículum vitae	résumé
los datos	facts, information
el doctorado	doctorate
el estado civil	civil status
la estatura	height
la fecha de nacimiento	date of birth
la firma	signature
la licenciatura	university degree
la maestría	master's degree
el paquete	package
el sobre	envelope
solicitar	to request, to apply for
la solicitud	application

ASK QUESTIONS

♻ **Ya sabes**

¿Adónde?	Where to?
¿Dónde?	Where?
¿De dónde?	From where?
¿Cómo?	How?
¿Cuándo?	When?
¿Cuánto(s)/Cuánta(s)?	How much/many?
¿Cuál(es)?	Which? (choosing items)
¿Para qué?	For what purpose?
¿Por qué?	Why?
¿Qué?	What?
¿Quién(es)?	Who?
¿A quién(es)?	Whom?
¿De quién(es)?	Whose?

SAY WHAT YOU ARE DOING

The Present Progressive Tense

En este momento **estoy estudiando** para el examen.
Mi hermano **sigue buscando** trabajo.

SAY WHAT YOU WERE DOING

The Past Progressive Tense

El viernes a las ocho **estábamos asistiendo** a la clase.

Juego

¡A trabajar!

¿Qué oración va mejor con el dibujo? ¿Por qué?

1. A Magda le gusta trabajar en una oficina.

2. A Magda le gusta correr riesgos.

3. Magda no presta atención a su trabajo.

doscientos setenta y cinco
El Cono Sur Etapa 1 **275**

Community Connections

Have students look in the Help Wanted section of area newspapers or of an on-line newspaper for a metropolitan area. Can they find any jobs that require a knowledge of Spanish?

🔔 Quick Start Review

♻ **Etapa vocabulary**

Use OHT 15 or write on the board: Write a mini-dialog that contains at least 3 words/expressions from each of the following categories:

1. Coursework
2. Abilities and experience
3. Written information
4. Ask questions

Answers
Answers will vary.

Teaching Suggestions
Vocabulary Review

Have students make flashcards of 10 vocabulary words/expressions and quiz each other in groups of 2 or 3. After 5–10 minutes have students give dictations to each other and check spelling.

Dictation

Dictate the following sentences to review the **Etapa:**

1. ¿Dónde está el currículum vitae?
2. Estoy entrevistando a un candidato.
3. Me voy adaptando a mi nuevo puesto.
4. María y Jorge estaban leyendo para el examen.

Juego

Answer: 2. A Magda le gusta correr riesgos.

Teaching All Students

Extra Help For **Actividad 6,** you may want to supply students with the Help Wanted section of a Spanish-language newspaper. The information in the ads may provide additional hints for setting up their companies.

Multiple Intelligences

Visual **Plan ahead:** Ask students to bring in photos or drawings of themselves at different points in their lives. Have students make a collage with the images, then use the past progressive to describe what they were doing. Ask them to elaborate by telling whether or not they still do the activities, using **seguir** + present participle.

▮ Block Schedule

FunBreak Have students create the **mate** as described in "Hands-On Crafts" on TE p. 253B. (For additional activities, see **Block Scheduling Copymasters.**)

Planning Guide CLASSROOM MANAGEMENT

OBJECTIVES

Communication
- Talk about careers *pp. 278–279, 280–281, 292–293*
- Confirm and deny *pp. 284–285*
- Express emotions *pp. 287–288*
- Hypothesize *pp. 289–291*

Grammar
- Review the use of affirmative and negative expressions *pp. 284–285*
- Use the past perfect subjunctive tense *pp. 286–288*
- Use the conditional perfect tense *pp. 289–291*

Culture
- High school diplomas and university entrance in Latin American countries *p. 285*
- Careers in Spanish-speaking countries *p. 288*
- Regional vocabulary *p. 290*
- Future plans of Latin American high school students *pp. 292–293*

♻ Recycling
- Fields of study *p. 285*
- Celebrations vocabulary *p. 287*

STRATEGIES

Listening Strategies
- Identify key information for careers *p. 280*

Speaking Strategies
- Anticipate what others want to know *p. 283*
- Conduct an interview *p. 296*

Reading Strategies
- Gather and sort information as you read *TE p. 292*

Writing Strategies
- Brainstorm details, then organize your information *TE p. 296*

Connecting Cultures Strategies
- Learn about high school diplomas and university entrance in Latin American countries *p. 285*
- Explore careers in Spanish-speaking countries *p. 288*
- Recognize variations in vocabulary *p. 290*
- Formulate plans for the future *p. 292*
- Connect and compare what you know about planning future careers in your community to help you learn about planning future careers in a new community *pp. 292–293, 296*

PROGRAM RESOURCES

 Print
- *Más práctica* Workbook PE *pp. 97–104*
- *Actividades para todos* Workbook PE *pp. 111–120*
- Block Scheduling Copymasters *pp. 89–96*
- Unit 4 Resource Book
  Más práctica Workbook TE *pp. 73–80*
  Actividades para todos Workbook TE *pp. 81–90*
  Cuaderno para hispanohablantes TE *pp. 91–98*
  Information Gap Activities *pp. 99–101*
  Family Letter *p. 103*
  Absent Student Copymasters *pp. 104–109*
  Family Involvement *pp. 110–111*
  Audioscript *pp. 112–114*
  Assessment Program, Unit 4 Etapa 2 *pp. 115–138; 229–231*
  Video Activities *pp. 235–238*
  Videoscript *pp. 239–241*
  Answer Keys *pp. 242–246*

Audiovisual
- Audio Program CD 11
- *Canciones* CD
- Video Program Videotape 28:36 / DVD, Unit 4
- Overhead Transparencies M1–M4; 3, 20–32
- Word Tiles U4E2

 Technology
- eEdition Plus Online/eEdition CD-ROM
- Easy Planner Plus Online/Easy Planner CD-ROM
- eTest Plus Online/Test Generator CD-ROM
- Online Workbook
- Take-Home Tutor CD-ROM
- www.classzone.com

✓ Assessment Program Options
- Unit 4 Resource Book
  Vocabulary Quizzes
  Grammar Quizzes
  Etapa Exam Forms A and B
  Examen para hispanohablantes
  Portfolio Assessment
  Multiple Choice Test Questions
- Audio Program CD 20
- eTest Plus Online/Test Generator CD-ROM

Native Speakers
- *Cuaderno para hispanohablantes* PE *pp. 97–104*
- *Cuaderno para hispanohablantes* TE (Unit 4 Resource Book)
- *Examen para hispanohablantes* (Unit 4 Resource Book)
- Audio Program *(Para hispanohablantes)* CD 11, 20
- Audioscript (Unit 4 Resource Book)

Student Text
Listening Activity Scripts

 **Situaciones** *pages 280–281*

- CD 11

Locutor:

¡Buenos días, Buenos Aires! Habla Manolo Arteaga y es hora para leerles los anuncios clasificados.

Hoy tengo cuatro anuncios nuevos. Todos ustedes que andan buscando trabajo, pongan mucha atención. Supongo que ya tienen un bolígrafo a la mano para apuntar números de teléfono y direcciones. Bueno, empecemos.

El primer anuncio nos viene de la compañía Multinacional 3. Necesitan un abogado con edad 25 a 35 años. Piden su currículum vitae con fotografía. El candidato tiene que estar dispuesto a viajar por todo el país, según las necesidades de la compañía. Llamen al 1/312-3612 para pedir su solicitud.

El segundo anuncio es de la empresa Inbursa. Solicitan auxiliares de contabilidad para el departamento de ventas. Los candidatos tienen que estar licenciados en Contabilidad y tener experiencia mínima de dos años. Excelente oportunidad de desarrollo. Edad de 23 a 28 años. Interesados favor de comunicarse al 1/371-2939 o presentar currículum en las oficinas Inbursa en Lavalle 1444 entre las 8:00 a 14:00 horas.

El tercer anuncio viene de la empresa líder en Internet, SPMNet. Solicitan un diseñador gráfico web con conocimientos en Internet. Experiencia en diseño y publicación de páginas web. Edición y composición de gráficos para Internet. Plataforma Mac o PC. Comunicarse con Raúl Cerviño al teléfono: 1/788-9150 o por fax al 1/788-9158.

El cuarto y último anuncio es para los secretarios. Una empresa internacional solicita secretarios ejecutivos bilingües. El requisito más importante es saber inglés, radioyentes, así que no soliciten el puesto si no se comunican bien en inglés. También requieren que los candidatos sepan manejar correo electrónico, archivos y computadoras ambiente Windows. Experiencia mínima de cinco años. Apunten este número: el 1/806-2433. Excelente presentación, edad de 25 a 30 años.

Es todo por hoy radioyentes. ¡Suerte con sus solicitudes!

SE SOLICITAN

AUXILIARES DE CONTABILIDAD
Departamento de Ventas

Requisitos:
- Licencia en contabilidad
- Mínimo de 2 años de experiencia
- Edad de 23 a 28 años

INBURSA

Por favor comunicarse con el 1/371-2939 o presentarse en Lavalle 1444 con su currículum vitae entre las 8.00-14.00 horas.

 **ACTIVIDAD 5 Preguntas** *page 284*

Modelo:

Mujer:	¿Has conocido a un ingeniero alguna vez?
Hombre:	Sí, hace años conocía a un ingeniero.

1. **Mujer:** ¿Has trabajado en una oficina de ingenieros alguna vez?
   Hombre: No, nunca he trabajado en una oficina de ingenieros.
2. **Mujer:** ¿Sabes algo de ingeniería civil?
   Hombre: No, no sé nada de ingeniería civil.
3. **Mujer:** ¿Conoces a alguien que sea arquitecto en Buenos Aires?
   Hombre: Sí, la verdad es que sí conozco a alguien que es arquitecto en Buenos Aires.
4. **Mujer:** ¿Trabajas los fines de semana?
   Hombre: ¿Yo? Yo siempre trabajo los fines de semana.
5. **Mujer:** ¿Sabes qué? Jamás me ha interesado estudiar para ser ingeniera.
   Hombre: A mí tampoco me interesa estudiar para ser ingeniero.
6. **Mujer:** ¿Tienes alguna idea de qué quieres ser?
   Hombre: Sí, creo que tengo alguna idea, ¡pero no te voy a decir cuál es!

 **ACTIVIDAD 13 ¡Por eso!** *page 290*

Modelo: ¡No sabes hablar español! Por eso no te dieron el puesto.
1. ¡No tienes las destrezas necesarias! Por eso no te llamaron.
2. ¡No llegaste a la entrevista a tiempo! Por eso no te vieron.
3. ¡No llevaste tu currículum vitae! Por eso no te entrevistaron.
4. ¡No pediste recomendaciones! Por eso no pudiste solicitar ese puesto.
5. ¡No estudiaste ingeniería! Por eso no conseguiste el puesto.
6. ¡No te pusiste una corbata! Por eso no hiciste una buena impresión.

Sample Lesson Plan - 50 Minute Schedule

DAY 1

Etapa Opener
- Quick Start Review (TE, p. 276) 5 MIN.
- Have students look at the *Etapa* Opener and answer the questions. 5 MIN.

En contexto: Vocabulario
- Quick Start Review (TE, p. 278) 5 MIN.
- Present *Descubre,* p. 278. 5 MIN.
- Have students use context and pictures to learn *Etapa* vocabulary, then answer the *¿Comprendiste?* questions, p. 279. Use the Situational OHTs for additional practice. 20 MIN.
- Use an expansion activity from TE pp. 278–279 for variety. 10 MIN.

Homework Option:
- Have students write and illustrate a future portrait of themselves for a 10th reunion.

DAY 2

En vivo: Situaciones
- Check homework. 5 MIN.
- Quick Start Review (TE, p. 280) 5 MIN.
- Present the Listening Strategy, p. 280. 5 MIN.
- Have students read section 1, pp. 280–281. Play the audio for section 2. Then have students work in pairs or groups to complete section 3. 20 MIN.

En acción: Vocabulario y gramática
- Quick Start Review (TE, p. 282) 5 MIN.
- Have students complete *Actividad* 1 in pairs. 5 MIN.
- Do *Actividad* 2 orally. 5 MIN.

Homework Option:
- Have students write an additional item for *Actividades* 1 and 2.

DAY 3

En acción (cont.)
- Check homework. 5 MIN.
- Present the *Vocabulario,* p. 283. Then have students do *Actividad* 3 in pairs. 10 MIN.
- Present the Speaking Strategy, p. 283. Then do *Actividad* 4 in pairs. 5 MIN.
- Quick Start Review (TE, p. 284) 5 MIN.
- Present *Repaso:* Affirmative and Negative Expressions and the *Vocabulario,* p. 284. 5 MIN.
- Play the audio; do *Actividad* 5. 5 MIN.
- Have students complete *Actividad* 6 in pairs. 5 MIN.
- Have students do *Actividad* 7 in groups. Expand using Information Gap Activities, Unit 4 Resource Book, p. 94; *Más comunicación,* p. R13. 10 MIN.

Homework Option:
- *Más práctica* Workbook, p. 101. *Cuaderno para hispanohablantes,* p. 99.

DAY 4

En acción (cont.)
- Check homework. 5 MIN.
- Quick Start Review (TE, p. 286) 5 MIN.
- Present *Gramática:* Past Perfect Subjunctive, p. 286. 10 MIN.
- Have students complete *Actividad* 8 in pairs. 5 MIN.
- Present the *Vocabulario,* p. 287. Then do *Actividad* 9 orally. 10 MIN.
- Have students complete *Actividad* 10 in pairs. 5 MIN.
- Have students complete *Actividad* 11 in writing. Go over answers orally. Expand using *Más comunicación,* p. R13. 10 MIN.

Homework Option:
- Have students complete *Actividad* 9 in writing. *Más práctica* Workbook, p. 103. *Cuaderno para hispanohablantes,* pp. 100–101.

DAY 5

En acción (cont.)
- Check homework. 5 MIN.
- Quick Start Review (TE, p. 289) 5 MIN.
- Present *Gramática:* The Conditional Perfect Tense, p. 289. 10 MIN.
- Present the *Vocabulario,* p. 290. Then do *Actividad* 12 orally. 10 MIN.
- Play the audio; do *Actividad* 13. 10 MIN.
- Have students do *Actividad* 14 in pairs. 5 MIN.
- Use one or more expansion activities from TE, pp. 290–291, for reinforcement and variety. 5 MIN.

Homework Option:
- Have students complete *Actividad* 12 in writing. *Más práctica* Workbook, p. 104. *Cuaderno para hispanohablantes,* p. 102.

DAY 6

En acción (cont.)
- Check homework. 5 MIN.
- Have students read and complete *Actividad* 15 in groups. 15 MIN.

Refrán
- Present the *Refrán,* p. 291. 5 MIN.

En colores: Cultura y comparaciones
- Quick Start Review (TE, p. 292) 5 MIN.
- Present the Connecting Cultures Strategy, p. 292. Call on volunteers to read the selection aloud. Have students answer the *¿Comprendiste?/¿Qué piensas?* questions, p. 293. 20 MIN.

Homework Option:
- Have students complete *Hazlo tú,* p. 293.
- *Actividades para todos* Workbook, pp. 111–116.

DAY 7

En uso: Repaso y más comunicación
- Check homework. 5 MIN.
- Quick Start Review (TE, p. 294) 5 MIN.
- Have students do *Actividad* 1 in writing, then exchange papers for peer correction. 10 MIN.
- Do *Actividades* 2 and 3 orally. 10 MIN.
- Present the Speaking Strategy, p. 296, and have students do *Actividad* 4 in groups. 10 MIN.

En tu propia voz: Escritura
- Do *Actividad* 5 in writing. Have volunteers present their ads to the class. 10 MIN.

Homework Option:
- Review for *Etapa* 2 Exam.

DAY 8

Conexiones
- Read *Los estudios sociales,* p. 296. Have students prepare their interview questions. 5 MIN.

En resumen: Repaso de vocabulario
- Quick Start Review (TE, p. 297) 5 MIN.
- Review grammar questions, etc., as necessary. 10 MIN.
- Complete *Etapa* 2 Exam. 20 MIN.

Ampliación
- Use a suggested project, game, or activity. (TE, pp. 253A–253B) 10 MIN.

Homework Option:
- Have students complete the assignment for *Conexiones.* Preview *Etapa* 3 Opener.

Sample Lesson Plan - Block Schedule (90 minutes)

DAY 1

Etapa Opener
- Quick Start Review (TE, p. 276) 5 MIN.
- Have students look at the *Etapa* Opener and answer the questions. 5 MIN.
- Use Block Scheduling Copymasters. 10 MIN.

En contexto: Vocabulario
- Quick Start Review (TE, p. 278) 5 MIN.
- Present *Descubre*, p. 278. 5 MIN.
- Have students use context and pictures to learn *Etapa* vocabulary, then answer the *¿Comprendiste?* questions, p. 279. Use the Situational OHTs for additional practice. 20 MIN.
- Use an expansion activity from TE pp. 278–279 for variety. 10 MIN.

En vivo: Situaciones
- Quick Start Review (TE, p. 280) 5 MIN.
- Present the Listening Strategy, p. 280. 5 MIN.
- Have students read section 1, pp. 280–281. Play the audio for section 2. Then have students work in pairs or groups to complete section 3. 20 MIN.

Homework Option:
- Have students write and illustrate a future portrait of themselves for a 10th reunion.

DAY 2

En acción: Vocabulario y gramática
- Check homework. 5 MIN.
- Quick Start Review (TE, p. 282) 5 MIN.
- Have students complete *Actividad* 1 in pairs. 5 MIN.
- Do *Actividad* 2 orally. 5 MIN.
- Present the *Vocabulario*, p. 283. Then have students do *Actividad* 3 in pairs. 10 MIN.
- Present the Speaking Strategy, p. 283. Then do *Actividad* 4 in pairs. 10 MIN.
- Quick Start Review (TE, p. 284) 5 MIN.
- Present *Repaso:* Affirmative and Negative Expressions and the *Vocabulario*, p. 284. 5 MIN.
- Play the audio; do *Actividad* 5. 5 MIN.
- Have students complete *Actividad* 6 in pairs. 5 MIN.
- Have students do *Actividad* 7 in pairs. Expand using Information Gap Activities, Unit 4 Resource Book, p. 99; *Más comunicación*, p. R13. 15 MIN.
- Present *Gramática:* Past Perfect Subjunctive, p. 286. 10 MIN.
- Have students complete *Actividad* 8 in pairs. 5 MIN.

Homework Option:
- *Más práctica* Workbook, pp. 101–103. *Cuaderno para hispanohablantes*, pp. 99–101.

DAY 3

En acción (cont.)
- Check homework. 5 MIN.
- Quick Start Review (TE, p. 286) 5 MIN.
- Present the *Vocabulario*, p. 287. Then do *Actividad* 9 orally. 10 MIN.
- Have students complete *Actividad* 10 in pairs. 5 MIN.
- Have students complete *Actividad* 11 in writing. Go over answers orally. Expand using Information Gap Activities, Unit 4 Resource Book, p. 95; *Más comunicación*, p. R13. 15 MIN.
- Quick Start Review (TE, p. 289) 5 MIN.
- Present *Gramática:* The Conditional Perfect Tense, p. 289. 10 MIN.
- Present the *Vocabulario*, p. 290. Then do *Actividad* 12 orally. 10 MIN.
- Play the audio; do *Actividad* 13. 10 MIN.
- Have students do *Actividad* 14 in pairs. 5 MIN.
- Use one or more expansion activities from TE, pp. 290–291, for reinforcement and variety. 10 MIN.

Homework Option:
- Have students complete *Actividades* 9 and 12 in writing. *Más práctica* Workbook, p. 104. *Cuaderno para hispanohablantes*, p. 102.
- *Actividades para todos* Workbook, pp. 111–116.

DAY 4

En acción (cont.)
- Check homework. 10 MIN.
- Have students read and complete *Actividad* 15 in groups. 15 MIN.

Refrán
- Present the *Refrán*, p. 291. 5 MIN.

En colores: Cultura y comparaciones
- Quick Start Review (TE, p. 292) 5 MIN.
- Present the Connecting Cultures Strategy, p. 292. Have volunteers read the selection aloud. Have students answer the *¿Comprendiste?/¿Qué piensas?* questions, p. 293. 25 MIN.

En uso: Repaso y más comunicación
- Quick Start Review (TE, p. 294) 5 MIN.
- Have students do *Actividad* 1 in writing, then exchange papers for peer correction. 10 MIN.
- Do *Actividades* 2 and 3 orally. 15 MIN.

Homework Option:
- Have students complete *Hazlo tú*, p. 293. Review for *Etapa* 2 Exam.

DAY 5

En uso (cont.)
- Check homework. 5 MIN.
- Present the Speaking Strategy, p. 296, and have students do *Actividad* 4 in groups. 10 MIN.

En tu propia voz: Escritura
- Do *Actividad* 5 in writing. Have volunteers present their ads to the class. 15 MIN.

Conexiones
- Read *Los estudios sociales*, p. 296. Have students prepare their interview questions. 5 MIN.

En resumen: Repaso de vocabulario
- Quick Start Review (TE, p. 297) 5 MIN.
- Review grammar questions, etc., as necessary. 10 MIN.
- Complete *Etapa* 2 Exam. 20 MIN.

Ampliación
- Use a suggested project, game, or activity. (TE, pp. 253A–253B) 20 MIN.

Homework Option:
- Have students complete the assignment for *Conexiones*. Preview *Etapa* 3 Opener.

▼ La señora Ibáñez es abogada.

Etapa Theme
Making career plans; confirming and denying; expressing emotions; and hypothesizing

Grammar Objectives
- Reviewing the use of affirmative and negative expressions
- Using the past perfect subjunctive tense
- Using the conditional perfect tense

Teaching Resource Options

Print
Block Scheduling Copymasters
Unit 4 Resource Book
  Family Letter, p. 103
  Absent Student Copymasters, p. 104

Audiovisual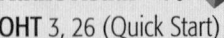
OHT 3, 26 (Quick Start)

Quick Start Review
♻ **Computer vocabulary**

Use OHT 26 or write on the board:
Draw a computer and printer and write the following labels in Spanish: computer, keyboard, mouse, screen, printer.

Answers
Drawings will vary, but should include:
la computadora, el teclado, el ratón, la pantalla, la impresora

Teaching Suggestions
Previewing the Etapa
- Ask students to study the picture on pp. 276–277 (1 min.).
- Have them close their books and describe at least 3 items that they noticed.
- Have them reopen their books. Ask students what they have studied previously that relates to this photo: **¿Qué han estudiado anteriormente que se relaciona a esta foto?**
- Use the **¿Qué ves?** questions to focus the discussion.

UNIDAD 4

ETAPA 2

¿Cuál será tu profesión?

OBJECTIVES
- Talk about careers
- Confirm and deny
- Express emotions
- Hypothesize

¿Qué ves?

Mira la foto. Contesta las preguntas.

1. ¿Qué detalles te dan una clave del lugar donde están estas personas?
2. ¿Crees que son amigos o trabajan juntos? ¿Por qué?
3. ¿Qué cosas crees que hace el chico?
4. ¿Qué conocimientos crees que necesitas para ser un(a) diseñador(a) gráfico(a) web?

276

SPMNET

DISEÑADOR GRÁFICO WEB

☑ *Empresa líder en Internet SPMNET requiere personas con conocimientos sobre Internet.*

☑ *Experiencia en diseño y páginas-Web. Plataforma Mac o PC.*

Llamar a Raúl Cerviño, tel. 1/788-9150, fax 1/788-9158

Classroom Management

Planning Ahead Prepare to introduce the theme of professions by bringing in, or having students bring in, magazine and newspaper articles/ads related to different professions. Also bring in items related to the professions; for example, a toy fire truck, a toy car, a stuffed animal, an envelope, etc.

Peer Review Have students work in pairs to brainstorm a list of professions learned so far. Then, have pairs present their lists to the class. Write the professions on the board and have students make a complete list in their notebooks. They should refer to this list throughout the **Etapa**.

277

Cross Cultural Connections

Ask students if they know of any companies in the U.S. whose headquarters are in a Spanish-speaking country. Have students look in a Spanish-language newspaper for job ads for companies whose headquarters are in the U.S.

Culture Highlights

● **EL AMBIENTE DE TRABAJO**
Recuérdeles sus estudiantes que en América Latina el ambiente de trabajo es más formal que en Estados Unidos. En general, es más propio utilizar títulos profesionales con compañeros y superiores en el trabajo, a no ser que se conozcan por algún tiempo. En algunos países, las personas tienden a llamarse por su primer apellido en vez del nombre aunque trabajen juntos por mucho tiempo.

Supplementary Vocabulary

la carpeta	file folder
el fichero	filing cabinet
la silla giratoria	swivel chair

Block Schedule

Peer Review Have students work in pairs to begin making flashcards with the name of a profession on one side and the principal activity on the other; for example: **profesor(a) / enseñar, ingeniero(a) civil / diseñar y construir carreteras y puentes.** Students should cover the professions they know so far and add to the flash-cards as they move through the **Etapa.** (For additional activities, see **Block Scheduling Copymasters.**)

Teaching All Students

Extra Help Ask students a series of yes/no or simple answer questions about the photo, such as ¿La mujer lleva un vestido? ¿De qué color es su suéter? ¿Cómo es la camisa del hombre sentado? ¿Qué ves en la pared? ¿Cuántas plantas hay?

Multiple Intelligences

Visual Have students design simple ads for professions they know, similar to the one on p. 268. You may want to provide samples from English and Spanish newspapers.

Teaching Resource Options

Print
Block Scheduling Copymasters
Unit 4 Resource Book
  Absent Student Copymasters, p. 104

Audiovisual
OHT 20, 21, 22, 22A, 23, 23A, 26
  (Quick Start)

Technology
Online Workbook, U4E2
Take-Home Tutor CD-ROM, U4E2

Quick Start Review

♻ Coursework

Use OHT 26 or write on the board:
Match the fields of study with the
classes:

1. humanidades	a. matemáticas
2. comercio	b. literatura
3. contabilidad	c. biología
4. agronomía	d. economía

Answers
1. b　2. d　3. a　4.c

Teaching Suggestions
Introducing Vocabulary

• Have students look at pages 278–279.
Use OHT 20 and 21 to present the
vocabulary.

• Ask the Comprehension Questions
on TE p. 279 in order of yes/no
(questions 1–3), either/or (questions
4–6), and simple word or phrase
(questions 7–10). Expand by adding
similar questions.

• Use the TPR activity to reinforce the
meaning of individual words.

Descubre

Answers
1. c 2. a 3. d 4. b

En contexto VOCABULARIO

La décima reunión

¡Qué gusto ver a todos! Dicen que yo—Maité Martínez—lleno el requisito perfecto para escribir un resumen de las noticias—¡Soy la más chismosa de todos!

Descubre

Usa las palabras dentro de las palabras para adivinar las profesiones. Mira los dibujos y escoge el equivalente.

1. **deportista** (deporte)
2. **bailarina** (bailar)
3. **diseñador(a) gráfico(a)** (diseño)
4. **cartero** (carta)

a.　b.　c.　d.

Josefina Álvarez es abogada en un bufete en Buenos Aires. Nos presentó a su esposo que también es abogado. Son empleados en la misma oficina. ¡Felicidades, Josefina!

¡No van a creer quién se hizo bailarín! Jorge Valdez me contó que ahora vive en la gran ciudad de Montevideo donde es miembro del grupo de ballet del Teatro Solís.

¿Qué noticias tenemos de la famosa deportista de nuestra clase? Andrea, la gran tenista de Santiago de Chile, viaja por todo el mundo con su raqueta.

La arquitecta Ramona Díaz me contó que ha diseñado varios edificios comerciales en la ciudad de Bariloche.

Classroom Community

TPR Have students take turns acting out the various professions. For example, a student might hang a backpack on one shoulder and pretend to be delivering mail at different points in the classroom. The class guesses what profession is being demonstrated and describes the activity.

Paired Activity Have students answer the ¿Comprendiste? questions in pairs. Students should ask each other the questions and write down their answers. Have them peer correct each other's papers and hand them in for a writing assignment grade.

Lorenzo Godoy ahora es **agricultor** en su ciudad natal en la pampa argentina. En las Granjas Godoy, se producen todo tipo de vegetales y granos. ¡Qué delicia!

Le pregunté al **cartero** Víctor Benedetti si había notado alguna disminución en el número de cartas a causa de Internet, ¡pero parece que él todavía tiene mucho que hacer!

¿Se acuerdan como Tito Villarreal le cortaba el pelo a todo el mundo? Ahora es **peluquero** con un salón exclusivo en Buenos Aires. ¡Pasen a verlo y saldrán con un elegante corte de pelo!

A Carmen Rossi siempre le han encantado los **coches**, así que no me sorprendió nada saber que ahora es **mecánica** en varios talleres de reparación de autos en la ciudad de Valparaíso. ¡Tiene **conocimiento** de todo tipo de coche!

Elsa Jiménez tiene el **puesto** de **diseñadora gráfica** web. Me parece muy natural... siempre estaba haciendo dibujos en la computadora. ¡Y lo sigue haciendo!

¿Y yo? ¿Qué hago yo? Soy **secretaria** ejecutiva bilingüe para una **empresa** multinacional muy importante. ¡Aprender inglés fue la mejor decisión de mi carrera!

Abrazos y saludos a todos.
¡Hasta la próxima!
Maité

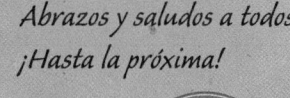

Online Workbook
CLASSZONE.COM

¿Comprendiste?

1. De todas las profesiones, ¿cuál te interesa más? ¿Por qué?
2. ¿Conoces a alguien que esté en una de las profesiones que menciona Maité? ¿Quién? ¿Le gusta su trabajo?
3. ¿Qué habilidades crees que debería tener una persona que quiere ser abogado(a)? ¿deportista? ¿diseñador(a) gráfico(a)? ¿agricultor(a)?
4. ¿Has pensado en tu futuro? ¿Crees que es importante saber cuál profesión te interesa antes de la graduación? ¿Por qué?

doscientos setenta y nueve
El Cono Sur Etapa 2

279

Comprehension Questions

1. ¿Es abogada Josefina Álvarez? (Sí)
2. ¿Ella y su esposo son empleados en la misma oficina? (Sí)
3. Es Jorge Valdez bailarín en Barcelona? (No)
4. ¿Ramona Díaz es arquitecta o deportista? (arquitecta)
5. ¿Lorenzo Godoy es agricultor en Buenos Aires o en la pampa argentina? (en la pampa argentina)
6. ¿El cartero Víctor Benedetti tiene mucho o poco que hacer? (mucho)
7. ¿Qué profesión tiene Tito Villarreal? (Es peluquero.)
8. ¿Qué hace Carmen Rossi? (Es mecánica.)
9. ¿Qué puesto tiene Elsa Jiménez? (Es diseñadora gráfica.)
10. ¿Para quién trabaja la secretaria? (para una empresa multinacional)

Culture Highlights

● **PROFESIONES** Hoy en día en América Latina más mujeres eligen carreras que tradicionalmente eran carreras para hombres.

La posición de secretaria ejecutiva bilingüe tiene mucho prestigio en países de América Latina.

Interdisciplinary Connection
Physical Education Have students research the names and countries of origin of well-known **deportistas** from Spanish-speaking countries.

Block Schedule
FunBreak Have students make simple crossword puzzles, using people's names or job definitions as clues. Have them exchange puzzles with a partner for completion. (For additional activities, see **Block Scheduling Copymasters**.)

Teaching All Students

Extra Help Use the job-related items brought in for "Planning Ahead," TE p. 276. Display the items and have students tell you what profession they relate to and what that person does.

Native Speakers Have students find out what a degreed **agricultor(a)** would do in a Spanish-speaking country.

Multiple Intelligences

Intrapersonal Have students write their own 10-year reunion descriptions, similar to the ones on pp. 278–279.

Quick Start Review

♻ **Profession vocabulary**
Use OHT 27 or write on the board:
Write the profession described:

1. Lleva muchas cartas y paquetes.
2. Diseña edificios.
3. Baila en un grupo de ballet.
4. Repara coches.
5. Arregla el pelo de sus clientes.

Answers
1. el (la) cartero(a)
2. el (la) arquitecto(a)
3. el bailarín, la bailarina
4. el (la) mecánico(a)
5. el (la) peluquero(a)

Teaching Suggestions
Presenting Situations

• Present the Listening Strategy, p. 280. Have students answer the Pre-listening questions and complete the chart.
• Use OHT 24 and 25 to present the **Leer** section. Ask simple yes/no, either/or, or short-answer questions.
• Use Audio CD 11 and have students do the **Escuchar** section (see Script p. 275B). Then have students complete the Listening Strategy exercise.
• Have students work in pairs or groups to complete the **Hablar/Escribir** section.

AUDIO

En vivo

SITUACIONES

PARA ESCUCHAR
STRATEGY: LISTENING

Pre-listening Have you ever applied for a job? What information did the employer want? Write down some key words.

Identify key information for careers Employment ads have two purposes: (1) to encourage qualified applicants, and (2) to discourage unqualified applicants. List the information that should be included to attain those goals.

Información a incluir
1.
2.
3.
etc.

Listen to the radio job bank and decide if the announcements meet your guidelines. Are there major differences?

Y yo, ¿qué quiero ser?
Estás buscando trabajo en Buenos Aires. Vas a ver unos anuncios clasificados y luego escucharás un programa de radio que describe trabajos posibles.

❶ Leer
Ves estos anuncios clasificados en el periódico *La Nación*. Léelos.

SE BUSCA ABOGADO

• Edad de 25 a 35 años

• Dispuesto a viajar por todo el país

Interesados llamar al 1/312-3612 para pedir solicitud y dirección. Deben presentarse con currículum vitae y foto.

MULTINACIONAL

Classroom Community

Paired Activity Have students work in pairs to create 2 more job ads to present in broadcast style. Have all students present a job ad to the class. Students should all choose a job to apply for. Poll the class to see which ones students chose. Was one particular job preferred?

Learning Scenario Have students work in pairs and role-play the follow-up interview for one of the ads in the **Escuchar** section. Have them present the skit to the class, who must decide if the candidate is qualified for the job he/she is applying for.

SE SOLICITAN

AUXILIARES DE CONTABILIDAD

Departamento de Ventas

Requisitos:

• Licencia en contabilidad
• Mínimo de 2 años de experiencia
• Edad de 23 a 28 años

INBURSA

Por favor comunicarse con el 1/371-2939 o presentarse en Lavalle 1444 con su currículum vitae entre las 8.00-14.00 horas.

SPMNET

DISEÑADOR GRÁFICO WEB

☑ *Empresa líder en Internet SPMNET requiere personas con conocimientos sobre Internet.*
☑ *Experiencia en diseño y páginas Web. Plataforma Mac o PC.*

Llamar a Raúl Cerviño, tel. 1/788-9140, fax 1/788-9158

---

2 Escuchar

Después de leer los anuncios en el periódico, pones la radio. Escuchas un programa que se dedica a dar anuncios clasificados para las empresas que buscan empleados. Copia la tabla siguiente. Luego, escucha los anuncios. Para cada uno, completa la tabla con la información que falta. Si el anuncio no da esa información, deja el espacio en blanco.

Anuncio:	
Puesto:	
Compañía:	
Años de experiencia:	
Edad:	
Requisitos:	
Número de teléfono:	

3 Hablar/Escribir

En grupos de dos o tres, conversen sobre las profesiones que les interesan. ¿Tienes alguna idea de qué quieres ser? Pregúntales a tus compañeros si ellos saben a qué profesión quieren entrar. Hagan una lista de posibilidades y comparen sus listas con los otros grupos en la clase. ¿Cuántas personas en su clase quieren ser abogados? ¿secretarios? ¿diseñadores? Den los resultados al (a la) profesor(a).

SECRETARIOS EJECUTIVOS BILINGÜES

Requisitos:

➤ inglés 80%
➤ presencia excelente
➤ manejar computadora ambiente Windows
➤ experiencia mínima de 5 años
➤ carrera comercial

Empresa Internacional

Interesados llamar al 1/806-2433

---

doscientos ochenta y uno **281**
El Cono Sur Etapa 2

Escuchar (See script, p. 275B.)

Answers

Anuncio #1:
Puesto: abogado(a)
Compañía: Multinacional 3
Años de experiencia: ___
Edad: 25 a 35 años
Requisitos: dispuesto(a) a viajar por todo el país
Número de teléfono: 1/312-3612

Anuncio #2
Puesto: auxiliar de contabilidad
Compañía: Inbursa
Años de experiencia: dos años
Edad: 23 a 28 años
Requisitos: licenciado(a) en Contabilidad
Número de teléfono: 1/371-2939

Anuncio #3:
Puesto: diseñador gráfico Web
Compañía: SPMNet
Años de experiencia: ___
Edad: ___
Requisitos: experiencia en Diseño y publicación de páginas Web
Número de teléfono: 1/788-9150 o fax 1/788-9158

Anuncio #4:
Puesto: secretaria ejecutiva bilingüe
Compañía: ___
Años de experiencia: cinco años
Edad: 25 a 30 años
Requisitos: saber inglés; saber manejar correo electrónico, archivos y computadoras ambiente Windows
Número de teléfono: 1/806-2433

Hablar/Escribir

Answers will vary.

Interdisciplinary Connection

Social Studies Have students research the following labor force statistics for the **Southern Cone** countries: unemployment rate, percentage of women in the work force, and percentage of skilled vs. unskilled laborers.

Block Schedule

Change of Pace Have students work in small groups and create a Help Wanted page. Students should write and design a minimum of 8 job ads and lay them out on a large piece of paper. Display the "newspapers" on the bulletin board. (For additional activities, see **Block Scheduling Copymasters**.)

Teaching All Students

Extra Help Replay the **Escuchar,** stopping after each job ad. Ask simple questions to help students find the information that they need to fill out their charts.

Native Speakers Have students find 2 job ads in a Spanish-language newspaper and create an announcement for each one, following the style of the **Escuchar** announcements.

Multiple Intelligences

Interpersonal Point out that some companies require a paragraph explaining why you are interested in their company. Have students write a paragraph explaining why they are interested in one of the companies advertised here.

Teaching Resource Options

Print
Block Scheduling Copymasters
Unit 4 Resource Book
  Absent Student Copymasters, p. 106

Audiovisual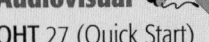
OHT 27 (Quick Start)

🔔 Quick Start Review

♻ **Profession vocabulary**

Use OHT 27 or write on the board:
Complete each word. Then unscramble the
circled letters to spell another work-related
word.

1. de __ orti◯ta
2. ar __ uit◯cta
3. __ m◯re __ a
4. b◯fe __ e
5. c◯no __ i __ i __ n◯o

___ ___ ___ ___ ___ ___

Answers
1. deportista   4. bufete
2. arquitecta   5. conocimiento
3. empresa   puesto

Teaching Suggestions
Comprehension Check

Use **Actividades 1–4** to assess retention
after the **Vocabulario** and **Situaciones**.
After completing **Actividades 1** and **2**,
have students write additional items to
ask a partner.

Objective: Controlled practice
Vocabulary in conversation

Answers
1. Deberías ser bailarín(a).
2. Deberías ser diseñador(a) gráfico.
3. Deberías ser arquitecto(a).
4. Deberías ser deportista.
5. Deberías ser mecánico(a).
6. Deberías ser agricultor(a).

En acción

PARTE A **Práctica del vocabulario**

Objectives for Activities 1–4
• Talk about careers

1 Deberías ser...

Hablar/Escribir Tu compañero(a)
no sabe qué quiere ser. ¿Qué le
dirías si te dijera estas cosas?

> **modelo**
>
> **Compañero(a):** *Me gusta hablar con
> la gente y andar por
> los barrios de la
> ciudad. No me
> importa el
> mal tiempo.*
>
> **Tú:** *Deberías ser cartero(a).*

1. La música me encanta.
   Siempre quiero bailar
   cuando oigo música.

2. Me gusta el arte. También
   me encanta organizar
   elementos visuales para
   crear un concepto total.

3. Me fascinan los edificios:
   las casas, los edificios de
   apartamentos, los edificios
   comerciales.

4. Practico varios deportes:
   el fútbol, el béisbol, el tenis
   y el golf.

5. Me encanta desarmar
   los motores de los carros,
   encontrar el problema
   y armarlos de nuevo.

6. Mi familia ha tenido granjas
   desde hace muchos años.
   Cultivamos vegetales,
   granos y frutas.

2 ¿Cuál es su profesión?

Hablar/Escribir Tus padres tienen amigos en varias
profesiones. ¿Cuáles son sus profesiones?

> **modelo**
> *La señora Ibáñez trabaja en un bufete donde
> protegen los derechos legales de la gente.
> La señora Ibáñez es abogada.*

1. El señor Gómez trabaja
   en una compañía que
   diseña páginas para la red.

2. La señorita Campoy
   hace planos para
   edificios nuevos.

3. La señora Botero
   trabaja en un taller
   donde se reparan
   automóviles.

4. El señor Varo crea
   peinados muy
   modernos. También
   se especializa en
   teñir el pelo.

Classroom Management

Time Saver Have students prepare **Actividades 1–4**
for homework with a "study buddy." Then call on one
pair to present each item to the class.

Peer Review Before completing **Actividad 3,** have
students refer to the list of professions begun in "Peer
Review" on TE p. 276. Students should have also added
new professions from **En contexto.**

Práctica del vocabulario continuación

3 ¿Qué quieres ser?

Hablar/Escribir Habla con un(a) compañero(a) sobre qué les gustaría ser y por qué. Luego, cambien de papel.

modelo

Tú: ¿Qué quieres ser? ¿Por qué?

Compañero(a): ¿Yo? Yo quiero ser abogado(a). Me gustaría ayudar a las personas con problemas legales.

Profesiones	¿Por qué?
abogado(a)	ayudar a las personas con problemas legales
arquitecto(a)	diseñar edificios y supervisar la construcción
niñero(a)	cuidar a los niños pre-escolares
peluquero(a)	saber cortar el pelo al estilo preferido
técnico(a) de sonido	trabajar en una radioemisora
veterinario(a)	trabajar con animales
otra	¿…?

Vocabulario

Más profesiones

el (la) artesano(a) *artisan*
el (la) asistente *assistant*
el bombero *firefighter*
el (la) contador(a) *accountant*
el (la) dueño(a) *owner*
el (la) entrevistador(a) *interviewer*
el (la) gerente *manager*
el (la) ingeniero(a) *engineer*

el (la) jardinero(a) *gardener*
el (la) juez(a) *judge*
el (la) niñero(a) *baby sitter*
el (la) obrero(a) *worker*
el (la) operador(a) *operator*
el (la) taxista *taxi driver*
el (la) técnico(a) *technician*
el (la) veterinario(a) *veterinarian*

¿Conoces a personas que tengan estas profesiones?

4 La agencia de empleos

STRATEGY: SPEAKING
Anticipate what others want to know Rehearse in order to be well-prepared and confident for a job interview. Here are some areas you should be ready to talk about: **intereses, estudios, trabajos, cualidades personales y ambiciones para el futuro.**

Hablar/Escribir Una agencia de empleos te entrevista. Tu compañero(a) hace el papel del agente. Luego, cambien de papel.

modelo

Compañero(a): ¿En qué se especializó?

Tú: En diseño gráfico.

Compañero(a): ¿Qué experiencia tiene?

Tú: He trabajado en una agencia de publicidad por tres años. o No tengo experiencia todavía, pero aprendo rápidamente.

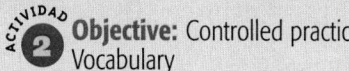

Teaching All Students

Extra Help Give the name of a profession and a job description. Some should be logical and others illogical. Students must say **lógico** or **ilógico**. If the sentence is illogical, students must correct it. For example: **El veterinario trabaja con animales. (lógico) La taxista diseña edificios. (ilógico: La arquitecta diseña edificios.)**

Multiple Intelligences
Logical/Mathematical Have students research average salaries in one of the **Southern Cone** countries for a few of the professions shown here. How do they compare to U.S. salaries for these professions?

2 Objective: Controlled practice Vocabulary

Answers
1. El señor Gómez es diseñador gráfico.
2. La señorita Campoy es arquitecta.
3. La señora Botero es mecánica.
4. El señor Varo es peluquero.

Teaching Suggestions
Presenting Vocabulary
• Present the vocabulary words using the job-related items brought in for "Planning Ahead," TE p. 276, when possible. Make sketches of any other professions.
• Ask students for the names of people they know (personally or a TV/movie character) in each profession.

3 Objective: Transitional practice Vocabulary in conversation
Answers will vary.

4 Objective: Open-ended practice Vocabulary in conversation
Answers will vary.

Quick Wrap-up
Play a game of **¿Quién soy?** in which you describe the activities of various professions. Students must name the professions.

Block Schedule
Variety Have students find examples of Job Fairs in area newspaper Help Wanted sections. Then have them create a similar ad using professions in Spanish. (For additional activities, see **Block Scheduling Copymasters.**)

Teaching Resource Options

Print

Más práctica Workbook PE, p. 101
Cuaderno para hispanohablantes
  PE, p. 99
Block Scheduling Copymasters
Unit 4 Resource Book
  Más práctica Workbook TE, p. 77
  Cuaderno para hispanohablantes
   TE, p. 93
  Information Gap Activities, p. 99
  Absent Student Copymasters, p. 106
  Audioscript, p. 112

Audiovisual

OHT 27 (Quick Start), 30 (Grammar)
Audio Program CD 11, Track 2, Activity 5

Technology

Online Workbook, U4E2
Take-Home Tutor CD-ROM, U4E2

Quick Start Review

♻ Professions vocabulary
Use OHT 27 or write on the board:
Complete the following sentences:

1. El (La) ___ trabaja con los
   números.
2. El (La) ___ cuida a los niños.
3. El (La) ___ lleva a la gente de un
   lugar a otro en su carro.
4. El (La) ___ responde a las
   emergencias, especialmente los
   fuegos.
5. El (La) ___ corta el césped y
   riega las plantas.

Answers
1. contador(a) 2. niñero(a) 3. taxista
4. bombero(a) 5. jardinero(a)

Objectives for Activities 5–14
• Talk about carrers • Confirm and deny • Express emotions • Hypothesise

---

REPASO Affirmative and Negative Expressions

You have learned many words that you can use in negative and
affirmative sentences. Here are some you already know in addition
to a few more.

• Remember that Spanish uses a double negative: when a negative
  word follows the verb, use **no** before the verb.

follows the verb

No estoy haciendo **nada** ahora.
I'm not doing anything now.

• But when you use a negative word before the verb, omit **no**:

before the verb

Nunca trabajo los domingos.
I never work on Sundays.

- -

Affirmative and negative **adjectives** agree with the nouns that they
modify.

agrees
alg**unas** empres**as**

agrees
ning**una** muchach**a**

Alguno and **ninguno** change
to **algún** and **ningún** when
they come before a
masculine singular noun.

Estoy buscando **algún**
trabaj**o**, pero no
encuentro **ninguno**.
*I'm looking for **some kind of**
a job, but I'm **not** finding **one**.*

Vocabulario

Palabras afirmativas y negativas

a menudo, muchas veces *often*
a veces *sometimes*
ni...ni *neither...nor*
o...o *either...or*

♻ **Ya sabes**

algo	nada
alguien	nadie
alguno(a)	ninguno(a)
siempre	nunca, jamás
también	tampoco

**Practice:
Actividades**
⑤ ⑥ ⑦

Más práctica
cuaderno p. 101
Para hispanohablantes
cuaderno p. 99

 Online Workbook
CLASSZONE.COM

---

⑤ Preguntas

Escuchar/*Escribir* Elena, la
nueva amiga argentina de
Jorge, quiere saber más
sobre su pasado. Escucha
sus preguntas y escoge la
palabra o frase que mejor
describe la respuesta de
Jorge.

modelo

Elena: *¿Has conocido a un
  ingeniero alguna vez?*

Jorge: *Sí, hace años conocí a un
  ingeniero.*

☒ *alguna vez*   ❑ *nunca*

1. ❑ alguna vez
   ❑ nunca
2. ❑ algo
   ❑ nada
3. ❑ alguien
   ❑ nadie
4. ❑ siempre
   ❑ nunca
5. ❑ también
   ❑ tampoco
6. ❑ alguna idea
   ❑ ninguna idea

También se dice
Cuando una persona se gradúa
se dice que recibe su **diploma**
o su **título**. En Argentina también
se dice que la persona "se recibe".

Teaching Suggestions
**Reviewing Affirmative and
Negative Expressions**

• Remind students to use the personal
  a before **alguien** and **nadie**.

Classroom Community

Cooperative Learning Divide the class into groups
of 3. Student 1 presents a scenario. Student 2 plays the
optimist. Student 3 plays the pessimist. For example:
Student 1 says, **Se me perdió el permiso de conducir.**
Student 2 would say, **Alguien va a encontrarlo.**
Student 3 would say, **Nunca vas a encontrarlo.**
Student 2 begins the next round. Each student should
present 2 scenarios.

Paired Activity Have students work in pairs to take
turns asking each other what they know, using the
question/answer pattern: **–¿Sabes algo de ___?** –Sí,
sé algo de ___. / No, no sé nada de ___. Students
take notes about what the other person does/does not
know in order to recommend a course of study and/or
profession.

---

6 Necesitas saber

Hablar/Escribir Es tu primer día en la Universidad de Buenos Aires. Le haces muchas preguntas a tu nuevo(a) amigo(a) argentino(a). Conversa con tu compañero(a) sobre los temas en la lista. Luego cambien de papel.

modelo

Tú: ¿Conoces a alguien que estudie diseño?

Compañero(a): No, no conozco a nadie que estudie diseño. o Sí, sí conozco a alguien que estudia diseño.

conocer a alguien que estudia diseño

estudiar finanza alguna vez

saber mucho del mercadeo

tener algún interés en estudiar dibujo técnico

conocer a alguien que estudia ingeniería

saber algo de informática

ver algún anuncio publicitario para la educación

¿...?

7 El día de profesiones

Hablar/Escribir Tú y tus compañeros(as) forman parte de un comité que organizará el día de las profesiones en su escuela. Ustedes van a decidir a quiénes van a invitar. Primero, investiguen las profesiones que les interesan a sus compañeros de clase. Entonces, decidan a qué profesionales van a invitar.

modelo

¿Hay alguien en la clase que quiera ser abogado?

sí_____   no _HH IIII

No hay nadie en la clase que quiera ser abogado.

¿Hay alguien en la clase que sepa algo de informática?

sí _HH I_____   no ____III

Hay seis personas en la clase que saben algo de informática.

More Practice: **Más comunicación** *p. R13*

Nota cultural

La escuela secundaria es el equivalente del *high school* estadounidense. Al finalizar el último año de estudios secundarios, el (la) estudiante recibe un diploma, con el cual puede conseguir trabajo y seguir sus estudios universitarios. En la mayoría de los países latinoamericanos los estudiantes toman un examen de aptitud para poder entrar en la universidad. Algunas escuelas secundarias requieren un año de clases adicionales. De esta manera, los estudiantes aseguran su plaza universitaria sin tener que tomar el examen de aptitud.

Gabriela Columbaro

Calle 9 N° 380, (1900) La Plata, Pcia. de Buenos Aires
Tel./Fax: (021) 89-8783
e-mail: gcolumbaro@edu.com

EXPERIENCIA
• **Médica general,** *Hospital de Emergencias de La Plata* (1996 / Presente)
• **Asistente del Departamento de Psiquiatría,** *Clínica Dr. Eugenio, Necochea* (Abril 1993 / 1996).
• **Asistente médica,** *Seguro de Salud Cruz Azul, Buenos Aires (1990 / 1993)*
• **Empleada administrativa,** *Clínica Yoli, Salto (1988 / 1990)*

ESTUDIOS
• **Universidad de La Plata:** Doctorado en medicina general (1993)
• **Universidad de Belgrano:** Curso: Investigación en psiquiatría (1992)
• **Cruz Roja Argentina:** Curso: Primeros auxilios (1990)

CONOCIMIENTOS
• Computación: procesador de textos y base de datos.
• Idiomas: Inglés, italiano y francés.

PASATIEMPOS
• Lectura, música, turismo.

Referencias disponibles.

ACTIVIDAD 5
Objective: Controlled practice Listening comprehension/affirmative and negative expressions

Answers (See script, p. 275B.)
1. nunca
2. nada
3. alguien
4. siempre
5. tampoco
6. alguna idea

Teaching Note

Remind students that the subjunctive is used with indefinite and non-existent objects.

ACTIVIDAD 6
Objective: Transitional practice Affirmative and negative expressions in conversation
♻ **Fields of study**

Answers will vary.

ACTIVIDAD 7
Objective: Open-ended practice Affirmative and negative expressions in conversation

Answers will vary.

Dictation

Using the Listening Activity Script for **Actividad 5** on TE p. 275B, dictate selected sentences to students. You may want to have students peer correct the sentences.

Teaching All Students

Extra Help Practice the **alguno/ninguno** forms, using classroom object, photos, or drawings to ask questions. For example: –¿Hay algunos libros franceses en esta clase? –No, no hay ningún libro francés.

Native Speakers Have students research and present information about the courses and exams students need to take to graduate from high school in their countries of origin.

Multiple Intelligences

Verbal Have students make up sentences using as many of the affirmative or negative words as possible. For example: **Algún día quiero comprar algo de alguien de algún país hispano.**

Kinesthetic Have students create "puzzle pieces" for the affirmative and negative words, where the affirmative word must join to its negative counterpart.

Block Schedule

Change of Pace Have students use affirmative and negative words to talk about the following: **la comida de la cafetería, la biblioteca, los profesores, las asignaturas.** (For additional activities, see **Block Scheduling Copymasters.**)

Teaching Resource Options

Print

Más práctica Workbook PE,
  pp. 102–103
Cuaderno para hispanohablantes
  PE, pp. 100–101
Block Scheduling Copymasters
Unit 4 Resource Book
  Más práctica Workbook TE, pp. 78–79
  Cuaderno para hispanohablantes
  TE, pp. 94–95
  Absent Student Copymasters, p. 107

Audiovisual

OHT 28 (Quick Start), 31 (Grammar)
Word Tiles, U4E2

Technology

Online Workbook, U4E2
Take-Home Tutor CD-ROM, U4E2

Quick Start Review

♻ Affirmative and negative
expressions
Use OHT 28 or write on the board:
Write sentences using the following:

1. algo / nada
2. alguien / nadie
3. alguno / ninguno
4. siempre / nunca

Answers will vary.

Teaching Suggestions
Presenting Past Perfect Subjunctive

• Stress that the past perfect
  subjunctive refers to actions that have
  been completed before another
  action in the past.
• Ask volunteers to provide sentences
  about their lives using the past
  perfect subjunctive.
• You may want to tell students that
  there is another form of the past
  perfect subjunctive: **hubiese,
  hubieses, hubiese, hubiésemos,
  hubieseis, hubiesen.**

Práctica: gramática y vocabulario continuación

GRAMÁTICA Past Perfect Subjunctive

▶ You can use the past perfect subjunctive to say that you wish that things had happened
differently than they did. For example, use it after **ojalá que** to express a wish about something
that didn't happen:

> **Ojalá que** hubiera **llamado.**
> *I wish I had called. (But I didn't.)*

▶ To form the past perfect subjunctive use:

    past subjunctive   +   **past participle** of the verb.
    of **haber**

hub**iera** **llamado**	hub**iéramos** **llamado**
hub**ieras** **llamado**	hub**ierais** **llamado**
hub**iera** **llamado**	hub**ieran** **llamado**

▶ Here are some **irregular past participles:**
abrir → **abierto,** cubrir → **cubierto,** decir → **dicho,** escribir → **escrito,**
hacer → **hecho,** morir → **muerto,** poner → **puesto,** resolver → **resuelto,**
romper → **roto,** ver → **visto,** volver → **vuelto.**

▶ You can also use the past perfect subjunctive, like the present perfect subjunctive, to say that one
action took place before another action. You use the past perfect subjunctive when the verb of the
main clause is in the **imperfect** or the **preterite**.

Compare these sentences:

> **Espero que** te hayan dado el puesto.
> *I hope they gave you the job.*

(I don't know if they did.)

> **Esperaba que** te hubieran dado el puesto.
> *I hoped they had given you the job.*

(I had hoped they would have given you the job, but they didn't.)

Practice: **Actividades** 8 9 10 11   **Más práctica** *cuaderno pp. 102–103*   **Para hispanohablantes** *cuaderno pp. 100–101*    **Online Workbook** CLASSZONE.COM

286   doscientos ochenta y seis
      Unidad 4

Classroom Community

Game Divide the class into groups of 5. On a single
sheet of paper, the first student writes a question using
the past perfect subjunctive (¿Qué te hubiera gustado
hacer ayer por la tarde?). The second student writes a
response beginning with Ojalá (Ojalá que hubiera ido
al cine). Groups continue passing the paper, writing
questions then responses. At the end of 5 minutes, the
group with the most correct exchanges wins.

Learning Scenario Have students work in pairs to
write and present a skit for the interview in **Actividad 9**.
Pairs who logically work in every word in the
Vocabulario on p. 287 get extra credit points.

8 La celebración

Hablar/Escribir Hubo una celebración para el Año Nuevo. Todos tuvieron experiencias distintas esa noche. Describe qué hicieron según las indicaciones. Luego, tu compañero(a) te contesta. Cambien de papel.

modelo

yo: no ir a la gala

Tú: *No fui a la gala.*

Compañero(a): *Ojalá que hubieras ido.*

1. nosotros: no festejar el Año Nuevo
2. tú y Paulina: no ver los fuegos artificiales
3. nosotros: no dar las gracias a la anfitriona
4. tú: no volver temprano
5. nosotros: no celebrar hasta la madrugada
6. tú y Aída: no pasarlo bien en la fiesta
7. yo: no gustar el lechón asado
8. ustedes: no llamar a su profesor(a)
9. Hilda: no comer pan dulce
10. ellos: no tocar la guitarra

9 Después de la entrevista

Hablar/Escribir Tuviste una entrevista para un puesto que querías conseguir. Estás nervioso(a) después de la entrevista y le cuentas a tu madre cómo te fue. ¿Cómo te responde ella?

modelo

Mamá, no me dijeron los requisitos para el puesto antes de la entrevista.

Esperaba que te los hubieran dicho.

> **Nota: Gramática**
>
> Remember that when you have both **direct** and **indirect object pronouns**, the indirect object pronoun goes first.
>
> Esperaba que te los hubieran dicho.

1. Mamá, no me hicieron muchas preguntas.
2. Mamá, no me pidieron el currículum vitae.
3. Mamá, no me pidieron recomendaciones.
4. Mamá, no me preguntaron sobre mi licenciatura.
5. Mamá, no me ofrecieron entrenamiento.
6. Mamá, no me explicaron los beneficios.
7. Mamá, no me dijeron el resultado de la entrevista.
8. Mamá, no sé si me dieron el puesto.

Vocabulario

Un puesto nuevo

aumentar *to increase*	**jubilarse** *to retire*
los beneficios *benefits*	**la puntualidad** *punctuality*
el contrato *contract*	**requerir** (e→ie) *to require*
el entrenamiento *training*	**el seguro (médico)** *(health) insurance*
las habilidades *capabilities*	**el sueldo** *salary*

ACTIVIDAD 8 **Objective:** Controlled practice
Past perfect subjunctive in conversation

 Celebrations vocabulary

Answers
1. A: No festejamos el Año Nuevo.
   B: Ojalá que lo hubieran (hubiéramos) festejado.
2. A: No vieron los fuegos artificiales.
   B: Ojalá que los hubiéramos visto.
3. A: No le dimos las gracias a la anfitriona.
   B: Ojalá que le hubieran (hubiéramos) dado las gracias a la anfitriona.
4. A: No volviste temprano.
   B: Ojalá que hubiera vuelto temprano.
5. A: No celebramos hasta la madrugada.
   B: Ojalá que hubieran (hubiéramos) celebrado hasta la madrugada.
6. A: No lo pasaron bien en la fiesta.
   B: Ojalá que lo hubiéramos pasado bien.
7. A: No me gustó el lechón asado.
   B: Ojalá que te hubiera gustado el lechón asado.
8. A: No comió pan dulce.
   B: Ojalá que hubiera comido pan dulce.
9. A: No tocaron la guitarra.
   B: Ojalá que hubieran tocado la guitarra.

Teaching Suggestions
Teaching Vocabulary

Model pronunciation of the **Vocabulario**. Have students create sentences that use 2 words in each sentence: **Me dijeron que han aumentado mi sueldo.**

ACTIVIDAD 9 **Objective:** Controlled practice
Past perfect subjunctive

Answers
1. Esperaba que te hubieran hecho muchas preguntas.
2. Esperaba que te hubieran pedido el currículum vitae.
3. Esperaba que te hubieran pedido recomendaciones.
4. Esperaba que te hubieran preguntado sobre tu licenciatura.
5. Esperaba que te hubieran ofrecido entrenamiento.
6. Esperaba que te hubieran explicado los beneficios.
7. Esperaba que te hubieran dicho el resultado de la entrevista.
8. Esperaba que te hubieran dado el puesto.

Teaching All Students

Extra Help Using the job ads on pp. 280–281, have students make statements about them using the **Vocabulario** on p. 287.

Native Speakers Have students prepare a curriculum vitae for themselves.

Multiple Intelligences

Visual Have students create dual drawings to illustrate the items in **Actividad 8**. One side of the drawing shows what they did and the other side shows what they wish they had done. Have pairs use these drawings and present the exercise items to the class.

Teaching Resource Options

Print

Block Scheduling Copymasters
Unit 4 Resource Book
  Information Gap Activities, p. 100
  Absent Student Copymasters, p. 107

Audiovisual

OHT 28 (Quick Start), 32 (Grammar)

Technology

Online Workbook, U4E2
Take-Home Tutor CD-ROM, U4E2

Objective: Transitional practice
Past perfect subjunctive in conversation

Answers

Answers will vary.
A: ¿Supiste que me aumentaron el sueldo?
B: Sí, me alegré muchísimo de que te hubieran aumentado el sueldo.
A: ¿Supiste que me dieron el contrato?
B: Sí, me alegré muchísimo de que te hubieran dado el contrato.
A: ¿Supiste que me dieron recomendaciones positivas?
B: Sí, me alegré muchísimo de que te hubieran dado recomendaciones positivas.
A: ¿Supiste que se jubiló mi jefe?
B: Sí, me alegré muchísimo de que se hubiera jubilado tu jefe.
A: ¿Supiste que me ofrecieron beneficios muy buenos?
B: Sí, me alegré muchísimo de que te hubieran ofrecido beneficios muy buenos.
A: ¿Supiste que me ofrecieron entrenamiento?
B: Sí, me alegré muchísimo de que te hubieran ofrecido entrenamiento.
A: ¿Supiste que me pagaron ayer?
B: Sí, me alegré muchísimo de que te hubieran pagado ayer.

Objective: Open-ended practice
Past perfect subjunctive in writing

Answers will vary.

10 ¿Supiste?

Hablar/*Escribir* Pasaron muchas cosas en el trabajo y se las cuentas a tu compañero(a). Di lo que pasó para que él (ella) te responda. Luego, cambien de papel.

> **modelo**
>
> *dar el contrato*
>
> **Tú:** *¿Supiste que me dieron el contrato?*
>
> **Compañero(a):** *Sí, me alegré muchísimo de que te hubieran dado el contrato.*

aumentar el sueldo
dar el contrato
dar recomendaciones positivas
jubilarse (mi jefe)
ofrecer beneficios muy buenos
ofrecer entrenamiento
pagar ayer
¿…?

11 Las reacciones de la familia

Escribir Andas buscando trabajo y pasas por muchas experiencias buenas y también difíciles. ¿Cómo reacciona tu familia? Primero escribe cinco cosas que te pasaron (te fue bien/mal en la entrevista, te dieron o no te dieron el puesto, etc.). Luego, para cada cosa que te pasó, escribe una oración describiendo las reacciones de tu familia. Usa los verbos de la lista.

> **modelo**
>
> *No me dieron el puesto.*
>
> *Papá dudaba que me hubieran dado el puesto. o Abuela sentía que no me hubieran dado el puesto. o Mi hermana esperaba que me hubieran dado el puesto.*

alegrarse de que   esperar que

sentir que

ojalá que   dudar que

Nota cultural

Las carreras tradicionales en los países hispanos siempre fueron medicina, abogacía y administración de empresas. Por lo general, las carreras humanísticas, como arte o lenguaje, han estado en segundo lugar. En los últimos años, la computación es muy popular y muchas personas se dedican a estudiarla. Es necesaria para conseguir trabajo.

Classroom Community

Paired Activity Have students create their own version of **Actividad 10**, using a list of verbal expressions related to school activities. For example: **sacar una buena nota en matemáticas, ofrecer el papel de Romeo/Julieta**, etc.

Portfolio Have students write a variation of **Actividad 11** in which they talk about events in their school/after-school life and people's reactions to these events.

Rubric A = 13–15 pts. B = 10–12 pts. C = 7–9 pts. D = 4–6 pts. F = < 4 pts.

Writing criteria	Scale
Grammar/spelling accuracy	1 2 3 4 5
Vocabulary use	1 2 3 4 5
Creativity	1 2 3 4 5

GRAMÁTICA   The Conditional Perfect Tense

You use the **conditional perfect** to say that you *would have done* something:

Yo habría **trabajado**.
I would have worked.

Le habría **ofrecido** el puesto.
I would have offered him (her) the job.

To form the **conditional perfect** tense use:

conditional of **haber**   +   **past participle** of the verb.

habría **trabajado**	habríamos **trabajado**
habrías **trabajado**	habríais **trabajado**
habría **trabajado**	habrían **trabajado**

The **conditional perfect** is most commonly used with a **si clause** to say what might have been if things had been different. In these sentences you use the past perfect subjunctive and the **conditional perfect** together.

Si **hubieras** sabido hablar español, **te habrían dado** el puesto.
If you had known how to speak Spanish, they would have given you the job.

Habríamos podido trabajar en finanzas si **hubiéramos estudiado** economía.
We would have been able to work in finance if we had studied economics.

Contrast the meaning of the three types of sentences with **si clauses** that you have learned:

present tense → *future tense*

Si solicitas el empleo, lo conseguirás.
If you apply for the job you will get it.

imperfect subjunctive → *conditional*

Si solicitaras el empleo, lo conseguirías.
If you were to apply for the job (which you aren't), you would get it.

past perfect subjunctive → *conditional perfect*

Si hubieras solicitado el empleo, lo habrías conseguido.
If you had applied for the job you would have gotten it.

Practice: Actividades **12** **13** **14**

Más práctica *cuaderno p. 104*
Para hispanohablantes *cuaderno p. 102*

 **Online Workbook**
CLASSZONE.COM

doscientos ochenta y nueve
El Cono Sur Etapa 2   **289**

Quick Start Review

♻ Present conditional

Use OHT 28 or write on the board: Give the present conditional of the following:

1. yo / aumentar
2. usted / querer
3. nosotros / tener
4. ellos / conseguir
5. tú / requerir

Answers
1. yo aumentaría
2. Ud. querría
3. nosotros tendríamos
4. ellos conseguirían
5. tú requerirías

Teaching Suggestions
Presenting The Conditional Perfect Tense

Stress that the conditional perfect describes an action that did not take place in the past because it depended on some condition that was not met.

Teaching All Students

Extra Help Give students a worksheet containing a paragraph that includes several forms of the conditional perfect tense. Have students find the forms and underline them. Then have them explain in their own words why the conditional perfect is used.

Multiple Intelligences

Logical/Mathematical Have students research information related to the **Nota cultural** on p. 288. They should look for statistics for the **Cono Sur** countries (or other Spanish-speaking countries) that give the proportion of the population for various professions. Students might also make pie charts with the information they find.

Block Schedule

FunBreak Have students play the game ¿Cuál es mi profesión? described on TE p. 253B. (For additional activities, see **Block Scheduling Copymasters**.)

Teaching Resource Options

Print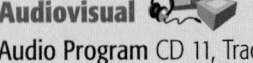

Más práctica Workbook PE,
  pp. 97–100, 104

Actividades para todos Workbook PE,
  pp. 111–116

Cuaderno para hispanohablantes
  PE, pp. 97–98, 102

Block Scheduling Copymasters

Unit 4 Resource Book

  Más práctica Workbook TE,
    pp. 73–76, 80

  Actividades para todos Workbook TE,
    pp. 81–86

  Cuaderno para hispanohablantes
    TE, pp. 91–92, 96

  Absent Student Copymasters, p. 108

  Audioscript, pp. 112–113

Audiovisual

Audio Program CD 11, Track 3,
  Activity 13

Technology

Online Workbook, U4E2

Take-Home Tutor CD-ROM, U4E2

Teaching Suggestions
Teaching Vocabulary

Assign a career to each student. Then
have each student provide information
about his/her career, using at least 2
words from the **Vocabulario**.

---

12 Tampoco o también

Hablar/*Escribir* Muchos de tus amigos están
tomando decisiones en relación a sus carreras.
Di qué habrías o no habrías hecho tú en las
mismas circunstancias. Sigue el modelo.

> **modelo**
>
> *Juan no estudió para ser abogado.*
>
> *Yo tampoco habría estudiado para ser abogado.*

1. María no aceptó el trabajo a tiempo
   parcial.
2. Joaquín cambió de carrera.
3. Arturo no quería un trabajo a tiempo
   completo.
4. Ana buscó trabajo en publicidad.
5. El señor Miranda no se jubiló hasta que
   cumplió setenta años.
6. Hernán llegó a todas sus entrevistas
   a tiempo.

Vocabulario

El trabajo

la carrera *career*

la desventaja *disadvantage*

emplear *to employ*

el empleo *job*

ganarse la vida *to earn a living*

el trabajo a tiempo completo *full-time job*

el trabajo a tiempo parcial *part-time job*

la ventaja *advantage*

> ¿Puedes usar algunas de estas palabras y frases para
> describir tu empleo, si tienes uno?

---

13 ¡Por eso!

Escuchar/*Escribir* El consejero de la agencia
de empleos les habla a varias personas para
explicar por qué no tuvieron éxito en sus
entrevistas. Escucha lo que dice para luego
decir lo mismo de una manera más cortés.

> **modelo**
>
> *¡No sabes hablar español! Por eso no te dieron
> el puesto.*
>
> *Si hubieras sabido hablar español, te habrían dado
> el puesto.*

1. Si hubieras tenido las destrezas
   necesarias, te _____.
2. Si hubieras llegado a la entrevista a
   tiempo, te _____.
3. Si hubieras llevado tu currículum vitae,
   te _____.
4. Si hubieras pedido recomendaciones,
   _____ ese puesto.
5. Si hubieras estudiado ingeniería, _____
   el puesto.
6. Si te hubieras puesto una corbata, _____
   una buena impresión.

También se dice

Aunque **trabajo a tiempo parcial** es la frase más
común en el mundo hispanohablante, también se utilizan
las siguientes expresiones:

• **trabajo de medio tiempo** (Argentina)

• **trabajo de media jornada** (España)

Classroom Community

Paired Activity Have students work in pairs to
discuss what they would have done if there had been
no school today due to bad weather. Have them write
down their ideas and submit them for a grade.

Storytelling Have students work in pairs to write and
illustrate a story about a college graduate who is now
out looking for a job. The graduate thinks back about
what he/she studied, what he/she should have studied,
what he/she is qualified for, and his/her job-search
experience.

14 Cómo prepararse

Hablar/*Escribir* Estudia los dibujos. Con un(a) compañero(a), conversen sobre los chicos de los dibujos. ¿Cómo crees que les va a ir en la entrevista? Den todos los detalles que puedan.

modelo

Tú: *Si el chico se hubiera acostado temprano, habría llegado a la entrevista a tiempo.*

Compañero(a): *Es verdad. Probablemente le van a dar el puesto a la chica porque ella llegó a tiempo.*

Cómo prepararse para la entrevista

Cómo vestirse para la entrevista

Cómo comportarse en la entrevista

15 Operadores telefónicos

Hablar/*Escribir* En grupos pequeños, hablen del siguiente puesto. ¿Les interesa? ¿Por qué sí o por qué no? ¿Qué requisitos se necesitan? ¿Qué les gustaría que pasara en la entrevista?

modelo

Tú: *Ofrecen trabajos a tiempo completo o parcial.*

Compañero(a) 1: *Me interesan los trabajos a tiempo parcial. Así puedo seguir estudiando. Piden conocimiento de PC. Ojalá hubiera encontrado este aviso antes.*

MERKNTEL

Empresa solicita

Operadores
telefónicos

Requisitos
• *Edad mínima de 20 años*
• *Preparatoria o equivalente; aceptamos estudiantes de licenciatura*
• *Buena presentación, excelente ortografía y conocimiento de PC*

Ofrecemos
• *Sueldo base más bonos*
• *Trabajos a tiempo completo o parcial*
• *Ambiente agradable de trabajo*
• *Capacitación desde tu ingreso*

Comunicarse al 2-97765 de 9 a 14 y de 16 a 19 horas o presentarse en:
Rambla O'Higgins 5306, Montevideo

More Practice: **Más comunicación** *p. R13*

 Online Workbook
CLASSZONE.COM

Refrán

El mal obrero culpa las herramientas.

¿Qué quiere decir el refrán? Cuando hay problemas con un proyecto, ¿dónde crees que está la causa del problema?

doscientos noventa y uno
El Cono Sur Etapa 2

291

Answers
1. Yo tampoco habría aceptado el trabajo a tiempo parcial.
2. Yo también habría cambiado de carrera.
3. Yo tampoco habría querido un trabajo a tiempo completo.
4. Yo también habría buscado trabajo en publicidad.
5. Yo tampoco me habría jubilado hasta cumplir setenta años.
6. Yo también habría llegado a todas mis entrevistas a tiempo.

Objective: Controlled practice
Listening comprehension/conditional perfect tense

Answers (See script, p. 275B.)
1. habrían llamado
2. habrían visto
3. habrían entrevistado
4. habrías podido solicitar
5. habrías conseguido
6. habrías hecho

Objective: Transitional practice
Conditional perfect tense in conversation

Answers will vary.

Objective: Open-ended practice
Etapa review in conversation

Answers will vary.

🔔 Quick Wrap-up

Call on various students to complete the following sentences: **Si hubiera escuchado al profesor (a la profesora)... , Si hubiera escuchado a mi madre (padre)... , Si hubiera escuchado a mi mejor amigo(a)...**

▇ Block Schedule

Change of Pace Have students work in pairs to complete a chart dealing with at least 5 professions. The chart should have the heads **ventajas** and **desventajas** at the top, and the names of the professions down the side. Students list at least one item in each column for each profession. Discuss the information as a class. (For additional activities, see **Block Scheduling Copymasters**.)

Teaching All Students

Challenge Have students write 5 more reasons why the people in **Actividad 13** were not successful in their interviews.

Native Speakers Have students imagine that they are retiring from their job and must write a speech for their retirement dinner. They should discuss their early years with the company, their first interview, their qualifications, their starting salary, etc.

Multiple Intelligences

Intrapersonal Have students write about the advantages and disadvantages of working part-time during the school year.

Teaching Resource Options

Print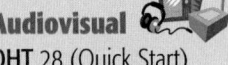

Actividades para todos Workbook
  PE, pp. 117–119
Block Scheduling Copymasters
Unit 4 Resource Book
  Actividades para todos Workbook
    TE, pp. 87–89
  Absent Student Copymasters, p. 109
  Video Activities, pp. 235–238
  Videoscript, pp. 239–241

Audiovisual

OHT 28 (Quick Start)
Canciones CD
Video Program Videotape 28:36 / DVD,
  Unit 4

Technology

  www.classzone.com

Quick Start Review

♻ **Career plans**

Use OHT 28 or write on the board:
Complete the following paragraph with
your own ideas:

Quiero ser___ porque me gusta ___
y ___. Sé que tengo que estudiar
___ por ___ años. Después de la
universidad, voy a ___. Para
conseguir lo que quiero, tengo que
___ . Así tendré éxito en la vida.

Answers

Answers will vary, but should resemble:
veterinario(a), cuidar animales, biología y
medicina, ocho, buscar empleo con una
clínica, trabajar mucho

Teaching Suggestions

Presenting Cultura y comparaciones

• Have students read the Connecting
  Cultures Strategy and complete the
  chart.
• Discuss the photo of the boys working
  on a car engine on p. 293. Would
  such a scene take place in your school?
  If not, where? ¿Tal escena ocurriría
  en esta escuela? Si no, ¿dónde?

Reading Strategy

Gather and sort information As they
read the selection, have students fill out a
chart with the following information for
each student: name, current school, exam
to take (if any), future plans.

En colores

CULTURA Y COMPARACIONES

PARA CONOCERNOS

STRATEGY: CONNECTING CULTURES

Formulate plans for the future Think about your
future after high school, then write down
what you need to do to meet your goals:
**escribir, estudiar, ganar, preparar, solicitar,
tomar decisiones**, etc. Also acknowledge
your feelings: **alegre, dudoso(a), frustrado(a),
nervioso(a), preocupado(a), seguro(a)** about
each task.

Mis metas:

Para hacer	Lo que siento
1.	
2.	
3.	

With which person in *Los jóvenes y el futuro* do
you most identify?

Los jóvenes y el futuro

 Chile

*Ana María Ibáñez,
16 años*

Yo estudio en un colegio de monjas[1]. Es
un internado — eso significa que las chicas
viven allí. Ahora estoy cursando[2] mi último
año y preparándome para la Prueba de
Aptitud Académica, que también se llama
la P.A.A. Quiero estudiar en la Universidad
Católica, pero para eso necesito sacar más
de 740 en la P.A.A. Me interesa estudiar
ingeniería comercial. Pero me da un poco
de miedo dejar el colegio. ¡Creo que voy a
echarlo de menos[3]!

---

[1] nuns
[2] I'm enrolled in, I'm taking
[3] to miss it

Classroom Community

Paired Activity Have students work in pairs and
use the Internet to look up a school in Latin America or
Spain. Many have Web sites. Have students list the
information they find. As a class, compare and contrast
your school with the schools students researched.

Portfolio Have students write a paragraph about
themselves similar to the paragraphs on pp. 292–293.

Rubric A = 13–15 pts. B = 10–12 pts. C = 7–9 pts. D = 4–6 pts. F = < 4 pts.

Writing criteria	Scale
Grammar/spelling accuracy	1 2 3 4 5
Vocabulary use	1 2 3 4 5
Creativity	1 2 3 4 5

Paraguay

Alfredo Zubizarreta,
17 años

Estoy en el último año de colegio y pienso mucho en el futuro. Quiero ir a la universidad, pero tengo que pasar el examen de ingreso[4]. Tengo buenas notas, sobre todo en castellano y en literatura, pero dicen que ese examen es muy difícil. Hay pocos puestos en la universidad y muchos estudiantes que quieren estudiar. Por eso algunos salen del país. Si me aceptan en la universidad aquí, voy a estudiar derecho[5], ¡porque los abogados ganan un buen sueldo!

[4] entrance, admission
[5] law

Uruguay

Miguel Corteggiani,
15 años

Estudio en un colegio público. El año que viene será el último año de secundaria. Mis padres quieren que vaya a la universidad pero yo dudo que vaya. Preferiría estudiar en una escuela técnica. Me fascinan los carros y me interesa mucho ser mecánico. Algún día quisiera tener mi propio taller. Yo creo que uno tiene que seguir sus intereses. ¿No estás de acuerdo?

CLASSZONE.COM
More About the Southern Cone

¿Comprendiste?

1. ¿En qué tipo de colegio estudia Ana María Ibáñez?
2. ¿Por qué no sabe Alberto Zubizarreta si podrá estudiar en la universidad?
3. ¿Qué campo le interesa a Miguel Corteggiani? ¿Qué piensan sus padres?

¿Qué piensas?

Estos estudiantes no están completamente seguros de sus decisiones. ¿Por qué?

Hazlo tú

Compara las dudas y los miedos de estos jóvenes sudamericanos con los de los jóvenes norteamericanos. ¿Comprendes estos sentimientos? ¿Los tienes también? Escribe un ensayo sobre tus planes para el futuro.

Teaching All Students

Extra Help Have students reread the paragraphs and write 2 questions for each one. Then have them work in pairs to ask each other their questions.

Native Speakers Have students investigate a college or university in their country of origin, or another Spanish-speaking country, and find out the entrance requirements.

Multiple Intelligences

Verbal Have students give a piece of information about the students on pp. 292–293, without naming them. The class guesses which student is being referred to.

Naturalist Ask students to discuss career options that involve interaction with some aspect of nature. What type of schooling do they think would be necessary to pursue this career? Does this type of work interest them?

Culture Highlights

● **EL COLEGIO/LA UNIVERSIDAD** En muchos países de América Latina, las universidades no ofrecen electivas. Los estudiantes siguen un curso de estudio determinado. No estudian un currículo general de artes y ciencias. Cada facultad o colegio prepara a los estudiantes para una carrera específica.

Cross Cultural Connections

Ask students to compare and contrast the information the 3 students give about their school life with information about their own school life.

Interdisciplinary Connections

Social Studies Have students find out what is included in the **Prueba de Aptitud Académica** that students who want to attend a university in Chile have to take.

Critical Thinking

Have students think about their anticipated careers. Would studying abroad while in college better prepare them for this career? Are they interested in studying abroad for personal reasons? In which country would they choose to study? Why? Discuss the advantages and disadvantages of their choices.

¿Comprendiste?

Answers

1. Estudia en un colegio de monjas. Es un internado.
2. Porque tiene que pasar un examen de ingreso y porque hay pocos puestos en la universidad.
3. Le interesa ser mecánico. Sus padres quieren que vaya a la universidad.

Block Schedule

Expansion Have students create a survey to find out classmates' plans after high school. Each student will interview 8–10 other students. Have them find out who is going to college or to a trade school, what subjects they will major in, who will get a job right away, etc. Have students summarize their findings and present them to the class. (For additional activities, see **Block Scheduling Copymasters**.)

Teaching Resource Options

Print

Cuaderno para hispanohablantes PE,
   pp. 103–104
Block Scheduling Copymasters
Unit 4 Resource Book
   Cuaderno para hispanohablantes
   TE, pp. 97–98
   Information Gap Activities,
   pp. 101–102
   Family Involvement, pp. 110–111

Audiovisual

OHT 29 (Quick Start)

Technology

eTest Plus Online/Test Generator
CD-ROM

www.classzone.com

Quick Start Review

 Conditional perfect

Use OHT 29 or write on the board:
Complete the following sentences with
the conditional perfect.

1. Si me gustaran los animales, ___
   para veterinario. (estudiar)
2. Si hubiera querido ser contadora
   ___ más clases de matemáticas.
   (tomar)
3. Si supiera cantar muy bien, ___
   cantante profesional. (ser)
4. Si fuera bailarina, ___ muchas
   clases de baile. (tener)

Answers
1. habría estudiado
2. habría tomado
3. habría sido
4. habría tenido

Teaching Suggestions
What Have Students Learned?

Have students look at the "Now you
can…" notes listed on the left side of
pages 294–295. Tell students to think
about which areas they might not be
sure of. For those areas, they should
consult the "To review" notes.

ETAPA 2

En uso
REPASO Y MÁS COMUNICACIÓN

Now you can...
• talk about careers.
• confirm and deny.

To review
• affirmative and
  negative
  expressions
  see p. 284.

OBJECTIVES
• Talk about careers
• Confirm and deny
• Express emotions
• Hypothesize

1 Algún día

Íñigo va a graduarse pronto y no sabe qué quiere estudiar.
Completa esta entrada en su diario con las palabras afirmativas
o negativas apropiadas.

algo   jamás   nada   ni...ni   nunca

alguien   ninguno(a)

algún   algunos(as)   nadie   siempre   tampoco

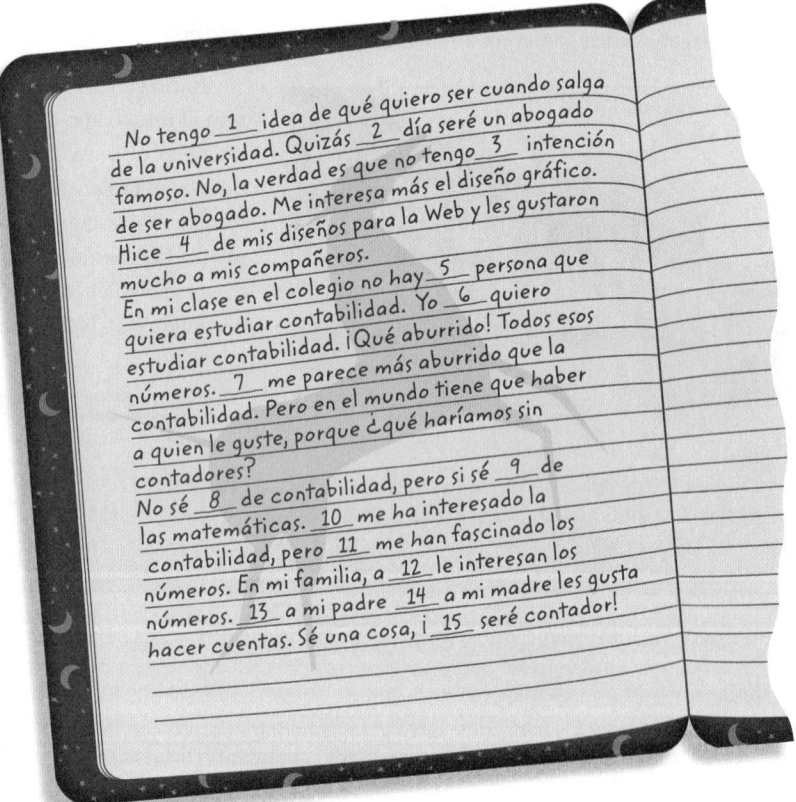

No tengo __1__ idea de qué quiero ser cuando salga
de la universidad. Quizás __2__ día seré un abogado
famoso. No, la verdad es que no tengo __3__ intención
de ser abogado. Me interesa más el diseño gráfico.
Hice __4__ de mis diseños para la Web y les gustaron
mucho a mis compañeros.
En mi clase en el colegio no hay __5__ persona que
quiera estudiar contabilidad. Yo __6__ quiero
estudiar contabilidad. ¡Qué aburrido! Todos esos
números. __7__ me parece más aburrido que la
contabilidad. Pero en el mundo tiene que haber
a quien le guste, porque ¿qué haríamos sin
contadores?
No sé __8__ de contabilidad, pero si sé __9__ de
las matemáticas. __10__ me ha interesado la
contabilidad, pero __11__ me han fascinado los
números. En mi familia, a __12__ le interesan los
números. __13__ a mi padre __14__ a mi madre les gusta
hacer cuentas. Sé una cosa, ¡ __15__ seré contador!

doscientos noventa y cuatro
Unidad 4

Classroom Community

Game Collect or have students collect short facts on
index cards about the 4 **Southern Cone** countries.
Divide the class into 3 teams. One student from each
team takes a turn, and members of each team rotate
after each turn. Read a fact, and allow the first student
from each team to raise his/her hand or ring a bell to
guess. If he/she guesses correctly, the team gets a point.
If not, one of the other two students tries to guess.

Paired Activity Have students work in pairs to
write a variation of the 3 paragraphs in **Actividad 1**.
Then have them exchange papers with another pair
and complete each other's paragraphs.

Self-Check Quiz
CLASSZONE.COM

Now you can...

• express emotions.

To review

• past perfect
subjunctive
see p. 286.

2 Después de la reunión

Vas a una reunión de tu clase y tienes algunas opiniones de la gente que ves allí. Después de la reunión, le escribes a tu mejor amigo sobre cada una de las personas que viste. Cambia los verbos para expresar tus opiniones. Sigue el modelo.

modelo

Yo espero que Felipe haya viajado por todo el mundo.

Yo esperaba que Felipe hubiera viajado por todo el mundo.

1. No estoy seguro(a) de que él haya estudiado arquitectura.
2. Espero que Juan Felipe haya ido a la universidad.
3. No creo que Julia haya sacado su licencia en ingeniería.
4. Ojalá que Teresa y su novio se hayan casado.
5. No creo que Pedro se haya graduado de la universidad.
6. Dudo que Vanessa haya querido hacerse bombero.
7. Espero que Sara se haya preparado para ser veterinaria.
8. Dudo que José Armando haya tenido su propio negocio.

Now you can...

• hypothesize.

To review

• conditional perfect
see p. 289.

3 Las posibilidades

Siempre pensamos en lo que pudo ser pero no fue. Un(a) amigo(a) te dice qué habría pasado si hubieras hecho las cosas de otra manera. ¿Qué te dice?

modelo

No tenía experiencia. No me dieron el puesto.

Si hubieras tenido experiencia, te habrían dado el puesto.

1. No fui a la universidad. No recibí la licenciatura.
2. No estudié finanzas. No he ganado mucho dinero.
3. No trabajé a tiempo parcial. Tuve tiempo para mis estudios.
4. No trabajé a tiempo completo. No recibí un buen sueldo.
5. No leí el contrato. No sé qué beneficios me ofrecían.
6. No recibí el entrenamiento. No pude hacer el trabajo.
7. No tenía el conocimiento necesario. No me gustó el trabajo.

ACTIVIDAD 1 Answers

1. ninguna 2. algún 3. ninguna 4. algunos
5. ninguna 6. tampoco 7. Nada 8. nada
9. algo 10. Nunca 11. siempre 12. nadie
13. Ni 14. ni 15. nunca/jamás

ACTIVIDAD 2 Answers

1. Yo estaba seguro(a) de que él hubiera estudiado arquitectura.
2. Esperaba que Juan Felipe hubiera ido a la universidad.
3. No creía que Julia hubiera sacado su licencia en ingeniería.
4. Ojalá que Teresa y su novio se hubieran casado.
5. No creía que Pedro se hubiera graduado de la universidad.
6. Dudaba que Vanessa hubiera querido hacerse bombero.
7. Esperaba que Sara se hubiera preparado para ser veterinaria.
8. Dudaba que José Armando hubiera tenido su propio negocio.

ACTIVIDAD 3 Answers

1. Si hubieras ido a la universidad, habrías recibido la licenciatura.
2. Si hubieras estudiado finanzas, habrías ganado mucho dinero.
3. Si hubieras trabajado a tiempo parcial, habrías tenido tiempo para tus estudios.
4. Si hubieras trabajado a tiempo completo, habrías recibido un buen sueldo.
5. Si hubieras leído el contrato, habrías sabido qué beneficios te ofrecían.
6. Si hubieras recibido el entrenamiento, habrías podido hacer el trabajo.
7. Si hubieras tenido el conocimiento necesario, te habría gustado el trabajo.

Block Schedule

Variety Have students work in groups of 4–5. Students will prepare a TV talk show. One student will be the TV host and the others will be guests. Each guest represents a different profession. The host will ask the guests about their professions. The guests should answer the host's questions and discuss work in general with the other guests. (For additional activities, see **Block Scheduling Copymasters**.)

Teaching All Students

Extra Help Before completing the activities, have students make lists of the **haber** forms for the conditional perfect and the past perfect subjunctive. Also review past participle forms.

Multiple Intelligences

Visual Have students create posters describing the advantages of pursuing a profession of their choosing.

Musical/Rhythmic Using verbs that express opinion, have pairs of students write lyrics to convey their feelings about something in their lives (school, a hobby, a person, etc.). Then have them find music that expresses this feeling. Ask volunteers to present their songs to the class.

Rubric: Speaking

Criteria	Scale	
Sentence structure	1 2 3	A = 11–12 pts.
Vocabulary use	1 2 3	B = 9–10 pts.
Originality	1 2 3	C = 7–8 pts.
Fluency	1 2 3	D = 4–6 pts.
		F = < 4 pts.

En tu propia voz

Rubric: Writing

Criteria	Scale	
Vocabulary use	1 2 3 4 5	A = 14–15 pts.
Accuracy	1 2 3 4 5	B = 12–13 pts.
Creativity, appearance	1 2 3 4 5	C = 10–11 pts.
		D = 8–9 pts.
		F = < 8 pts.

Teaching Note: En tu propia voz
Writing Strategy Suggest that students brainstorm details, then organize their information in order to write ads. They should evaluate their brainstormed list, determine which ideas to keep, and organize them.

---

4 El cuestionario

STRATEGY: SPEAKING

Conduct an interview How can you handle the social and emotional aspects of an interview? One way is to ask a few open-ended questions that encourage personal expression by the person you are interviewing:

Dígame algo de…

¿Por qué se interesa en…?

¿Qué haría si…?

Si tuviera la oportunidad de…

Remember to use the **usted** form.

En grupos de tres o cuatro, escriban un cuestionario para entrevistar a unos candidatos para un puesto. Primero, decidan cuál es el puesto, los requisitos, etc. Luego, háganse la entrevista. Usen estas ideas.

- puesto
- requisitos
- habilidades
- trabajo a tiempo completo o parcial
- recomendaciones
- sueldo
- beneficios

---

5 En tu propia voz

ESCRITURA Escribe un anuncio clasificado para un puesto. Primero decide qué ofrece tu compañía. Decide cuál es el puesto y escribe una lista de requisitos. También decide lo que ofrece tu compañía para los empleados (sueldo, horas, beneficios, etc.) ¡Sé creativo(a)!

Empresa solicita

TÉCNICO DE COMPUTADORAS

Requisitos:

✓ mínimo de experiencia: 5 años
✓ conocimiento de varios sistemas
✓ buena presencia y habilidad para trabajar con distintos departamentos

Ofrecemos:

✓ beneficios y salario competitivo
✓ horarios flexibles
✓ bonos

*Interesados llamar al 1/495-98710
o enviar su currículo a*

Calle Tapes 98 Montevideo, Uruguay

CONEXIONES

Los estudios sociales ¿Qué profesiones te interesan? En tu escuela, entrevista a tres maestros(as) que enseñan tres materias diferentes. Pregunta sobre las profesiones en las cuales hay que saber mucho de las mátematicas (o el arte, las ciencias, etc.). Pregunta también cómo saber español te ayudaría en esa profesión. Comparte lo que descubras con la clase.

Classroom Community

Storytelling Have students get in groups of 4. A student begins to tell a story using the **Vocabulario** on p. 297. The next student continues with the story by repeating the first sentence and adding another. Continue until the story is complete. Then begin a new story.

Paired Activity Have students work in pairs to perform a skit. One student is an exchange student from one of the **Southern Cone** countries in a U.S. university. The other is a U.S. student. The students meet the first day of classes and talk about what they studied in high school, what classes they are taking now, whether or not they work part-time, etc.

En resumen
REPASO DE VOCABULARIO

Flashcards
CLASSZONE.COM

TALK ABOUT CAREERS

Professions

el (la) abogado(a)	lawyer
el (la) agricultor(a)	farmer
el (la) arquitecto(a)	architect
el (la) artesano(a)	artisan
el (la) asistente	assistant
el bailarín/	dancer
la bailarina	
el (la) bombero(a)	firefighter
el (la) cartero(a)	mail carrier
el (la) contador(a)	accountant
el (la) deportista	athlete
el (la) diseñador(a) gráfico(a)	graphic designer
el (la) dueño(a)	owner
el (la) empleado(a)	employee
el (la) entrevistador(a)	interviewer
el (la) gerente	manager
el (la) ingeniero(a)	engineer
el (la) jardinero(a)	gardener
el (la) juez(a)	judge
el (la) mecánico(a)	mechanic
el (la) niñero(a)	baby sitter
el (la) obrero(a)	worker
el (la) operador(a)	operator
el (la) peluquero(a)	hairstylist
el (la) secretario(a)	secretary
el (la) taxista	taxi driver
el (la) técnico(a)	technician
el (la) veterinario(a)	veterinarian

Personal background

el conocimiento	knowledge
el entrenamiento	training
las habilidades	capabilities
la puntualidad	punctuality

In the workplace

aumentar	to increase
los beneficios	benefits
el bufete	law office
la carrera	career
el coche	car
chismoso(a)	gossipy
el contrato	contract
la desventaja	disadvantage
el empleo	job
la empresa	business
ganarse la vida	to earn a living
jubilarse	to retire
el puesto	position
requerir (e→ie)	to require
el requisito	requirement
el sueldo	salary
el seguro médico	health insurance
trabajo a tiempo…	
completo	full-time job
parcial	part-time job
la ventaja	advantage

CONFIRM AND DENY

Affirmative/Negative expressions

a menudo, muchas veces	often
a veces	sometimes
ni…ni	neither…nor
o…o	either…or

♻ **Ya sabes**

algo	something
alguien	someone, somebody
alguno(a)	some
jamás	never
nada	nothing
nadie	no one, nobody
ninguno(a)	no, not any
nunca	never
siempre	always
también	also
tampoco	neither

EXPRESS EMOTIONS

Past perfect subjunctive

Sentía que no me **hubieran ofrecido** el puesto.

HYPOTHESIZE

Conditional perfect

Si hubiera tenido el entrenamiento, me **habrían ofrecido** el puesto.

Juego

Completa las frases con las palabras apropiadas. Luego pon en orden las letras de los círculos para saber qué es lo bueno de envejecer.

Después de trabajar toda la vida, Carlos quiere

◯ __ __ __ ◯ ◯ __ __ .

Él va a recibir muchos

◯ __ __ __ __ ◯ __ __ __ .

La cantidad de dinero que recibe va a

◯ __ __ __ __ __ ◯ ◯ con los años.

BANCO

doscientos noventa y siete
El Cono Sur Etapa 2 **297**

UNIDAD 4 Etapa 2
Review

Interdisciplinary Connection

Social Studies Have students chart the results of the questions they asked their teachers. Create a master list of subjects and possible careers. Have students evaluate which subject(s) they are best in and which related careers sound interesting.

Quick Start Review

♻ Etapa vocabulary

Use OHT 29 or write on the board. Match each word on the left with a corresponding word:

1. puesto	a. compañía
2. sueldo	b. oficina
3. carrera	c. empleo
4. empresa	d. profesión
5. bufete	e. dinero

Answers
1. c   2. e   3. d   4. a   5. b

Teaching Suggestions
Vocabulary Review

- Have students write **Juegos** similar to the one on p. 297, using words from the **Repaso de vocabulario**.
- Have students make their own sentences for the headings "Express Emotions" and "Hypothesize."

Dictation

Dictate the following sentences to review the **Etapa**:

1. La arquitecta ha diseñado muchos edificios.
2. Me gustaría cuidar a los niños. Quiero ser niñero.
3. Susana no está haciendo nada ahora.
4. Esperaba que te hubiera llamado.

Juego

Answers: jubilarse, beneficios, aumentar no trabajar

Block Schedule

Research Have students find out about at least 1 current event from each of the 4 **Southern Cone** countries. (For additional activities, see **Block Scheduling Copymasters.**)

Teaching All Students

Extra Help Have students write 1 question to ask people in 5 different careers. Then have them write a possible answer for each.

Challenge Have students write down a way that Spanish can be used in 5 careers of their choosing.

Multiple Intelligences

Visual Have students make word webs with various professions to show how the careers are related.

Intrapersonal Have students personalize words in the vocabulary by making lists about themselves. For example, they can use **el conocimiento** as a heading for a list about their knowledge.

Planning Guide CLASSROOM MANAGEMENT

OBJECTIVES

Communication
- Learn about Latin American economics *pp. 300–301, 302–303*
- Avoid redundancy *pp. 314–315*
- Express possession *pp. 308–310*
- Express past probability *pp. 316–317*

Grammar
- Review: Use subject and stressed object pronouns *pp. 306–308*
- Review: Use possessive pronouns *pp. 308–310*
- Use the future perfect tense *pp. 310–312*

Culture
- Regional vocabulary *pp. 306, 311*
- Job hunting in Latin America *p. 308*
- Saving money in Latin America *p. 312*
- Isabel Allende, Chilean novelist *pp. 314–315*
- Languages in Spanish-speaking countries *pp. 316–317*

♻ Recycling
- Numbers *p. 305*
- Professions vocabulary *p. 306*
- Clothing and furniture *p. 309*

STRATEGIES

Listening Strategies
- Pre-listening *p. 302*
- Use statistics to evaluate predictions *p. 302*

Speaking Strategies
- Guess cognates *p. 305*
- Speculate about the past *p. 320*

Reading Strategies
- Speculate about the author *p. 314*
- Activate associated knowledge *TE p. 316*

Writing Strategies
- Organize information by category *TE p. 320*
- Use cause and effect to demonstrate ability *pp. 322–323*

Connecting Cultures Strategies
- Recognize variations in vocabulary *pp. 306, 311*
- Understand job hunting in Latin America *p. 308*
- Learn about saving money in Latin America *p. 312*
- Learn about Isabel Allende, Chilean novelist *pp. 314–315*
- Observe how language reflects culture *pp. 316–317*
- Connect and compare what you know about languages in your community to help you learn about languages in a new community *pp. 316–317*

PROGRAM RESOURCES

 Print
- *Más práctica* Workbook PE *pp. 105–112*
- *Actividades para todos* Workbook PE *pp. 121–130*
- Block Scheduling Copymasters *pp. 97–104*
- Unit 4 Resource Book
  - *Más práctica* Workbook TE *pp. 141–148*
  - *Actividades para todos* Workbook TE *pp. 149–158*
  - *Cuaderno para hispanohablantes* TE *pp. 159–166*
  - Information Gap Activities *pp. 167–170*
  - Family Letter *p. 171*
  - Absent Student Copymasters *pp. 172–178*
  - Family Involvement *pp. 179–180*
  - Audioscript *pp. 181–184*
  - Assessment Program, Unit 4 Etapa 3 *pp. 185–234*
  - Answer Keys *pp. 242–246*

Audiovisual
- Audio Program CD 12
- *Canciones* CD
- Overhead Transparencies M1–M5; GO1–GO5; 4, 33–46
- Word Tiles U4E3

 Technology
- eEdition Plus Online/eEdition CD-ROM
- Easy Planner Plus Online/Easy Planner CD-ROM
- eTest Plus Online/Test Generator CD-ROM
- Online Workbook
- Take-Home Tutor CD-ROM
- www.classzone.com

Assessment Program Options
- Unit 4 Resource Book
  - Vocabulary Quizzes
  - Grammar Quizzes
  - Etapa Exam Forms A and B
  - *Examen para hispanohablantes*
  - Portfolio Assessment
  - Unit 4 Comprehensive Test
  - *Prueba comprensiva para hispanohablantes,* Unit 4
  - Multiple Choice Test Questions
- Audio Program CD 20
- eTest Plus Online/Test Generator CD-ROM

Native Speakers
- *Cuaderno para hispanohablantes* PE *pp. 105–112*
- *Cuaderno para hispanohablantes* TE (Unit 4 Resource Book)
- *Examen para hispanohablantes* (Unit 4 Resource Book)
- *Prueba comprensiva para hispanohablantes,* Unit 4 (Unit 4 Resource Book)
- Audio Program *(Para hispanohablantes)* CD 12, 20
- Audioscript (Unit 4 Resource Book)

Student Text
Listening Activity Scripts

 **Situaciones** *pages 302–303*

- CD 12

La producción mundial

Agricultura
En la producción de maíz, Estados Unidos está en primer lugar. Le siguen China, Brasil, México y Argentina. En sexto lugar está la antigua Unión Soviética, seguida por India.

Ganado
La industria ganadera de Argentina es la quinta en el mundo occidental. Alemania está en el cuarto lugar, Brasil en tercer lugar, la antigua Unión Soviética está en segundo y Estados Unidos en primer lugar.

Minería de cobre
Chile es el país que más cobre produce. Luego sigue Estados Unidos, Canadá, Indonesia y finalmente Perú.

Petróleo crudo
Arabia Saudita es el país que produce el más petróleo crudo. Estados Unidos, China, Irak y México le siguen en esta categoría.

Industria pesquera
China es el primer país en la industria pesquera, seguido por Perú, Chile, Japón y Estados Unidos.

Turismo
¿Qué país es el más visitado del mundo? ¡Francia! *¿Parlez vous français?* En segundo lugar, está Estados Unidos. España le sigue en tercer lugar. Italia está en cuarto lugar, seguido por el Reino Unido o Inglaterra.

 **ACTIVIDAD 5 ¿Quién?** *page 306*

Modelo:
Tío:	¿Quién es abogado?
Chico:	Él.
Tío:	¿Quién es médica?
Chico:	Ella.

1. Tío: ¿Estudiaron ustedes ingeniería?
   Chica: Nosotros sí. Ella no.
2. Tío: ¿Quieren ser veterinarios?
   Chico: Él sí. Yo no. Yo quiero ser bombero.
3. Tío: ¿Fueron a la Universidad de Buenos Aires?
   Mujer: Él fue a la Universidad de Buenos Aires pero ella fue a la Universidad de Chile.
4. Tío: ¿Estudiaste para ser arquitecto?
   Hombre: Yo sí, pero ella no. Ella estudió para ser ingeniera.
5. Tío: ¿Les interesa el mercadeo?
   Mujer: A ella le interesa el mercadeo, pero a él le interesa más la publicidad.
6. Tío: ¿Quién de ustedes es bailarina?
   Chica: Yo soy bailarina. Él es deportista.

 **ACTIVIDAD 12 ¡Pobre Carlos!** *page 311*

Modelo:
Chica: Carlos tiene hambre.
Chico: No habrá comido bien.

1. Chica: Carlos está enojado.
   Chico: No le dieron el puesto.
2. Chica: Carlos se siente mal.
   Chico: Habrá comido algo que le hizo daño.
3. Chica: Carlos tiene mucho sueño.
   Chico: Se habrá acostado muy tarde.
4. Chica: Carlos está muy triste.
   Chico: Vio a su ex-novia con otro chico.
5. Chica: Carlos dijo que iba a traer los discos compactos y no los trajo.
   Chico: Se le habrán olvidado.
6. Chica: ¿Dónde está Carlos?
   Chico: Se habrá ido.

Pacing Guide

Sample Lesson Plan - 50 Minute Schedule

DAY 1

Etapa Opener
- Quick Start Review (TE, p. 298) 5 MIN.
- Have students look at the *Etapa* Opener and answer the questions. 5 MIN.

En contexto: Vocabulario
- Quick Start Review (TE, p. 300) 5 MIN.
- Present *Descubre*, p. 300. Have students use context and pictures to learn *Etapa* vocabulary. Use the Situational OHTs for additional practice. 15 MIN.

En vivo: Situaciones
- Quick Start Review (TE, p. 302) 5 MIN.
- Present the Listening Strategy, p. 302. Have students read section 1, p. 302. Play the audio for section 2. Have students work in groups to complete section 3. 15 MIN.

Homework Option:
- Have students write answers to *¿Comprendiste?*, p. 303.

DAY 2

En acción: Vocabulario y gramática
- Check homework. 5 MIN.
- Quick Start Review (TE, p. 304) 5 MIN.
- Have students complete *Actividad* 1 in pairs. 5 MIN.
- Have students do *Actividad* 2 in writing. Go over answers orally. 5 MIN.
- Present the *Vocabulario*, p. 305. Then have students read and do *Actividad* 3 in pairs. 10 MIN.
- Present the Speaking Strategy, p. 305. Then have students do *Actividad* 4 in pairs. 5 MIN.
- Present *Repaso:* Subject and Stressed Object Pronouns and the *Vocabulario*, p. 306. 10 MIN.
- Play the audio; do *Actividad* 5. 5 MIN.

Homework Option:
- *Más práctica* Workbook, pp. 109–110. *Cuaderno para hispanohablantes*, p. 107.

DAY 3

En acción (cont.)
- Check homework. 5 MIN.
- Present the *Vocabulario*, p. 307. Then do *Actividad* 6 in pairs. 10 MIN.
- Have students complete *Actividad* 7 in pairs. Expand using Information Gap Activities, *Más comunicación*, p. R14. 15 MIN.
- Quick Start Review (TE, p. 308) 5 MIN.
- Present *Repaso:* Possessive Pronouns and the *Vocabulario*, p. 308. 10 MIN.
- Have students complete *Actividad* 8 in pairs. 5 MIN.

Homework Option:
- *Más práctica* Workbook, p. 111. *Cuaderno para hispanohablantes*, p. 108.

DAY 4

En acción (cont.)
- Check homework. 5 MIN.
- Do *Actividad* 9 orally. 5 MIN.
- Have students complete *Actividad* 10 in groups. 10 MIN.
- Have students complete *Actividad* 11 in pairs. 5 MIN.
- Present *Gramática:* The Future Perfect Tense, p. 310. 10 MIN.
- Play the audio; do *Actividad* 12. 5 MIN.
- Present the *Vocabulario*, p. 311. Then do *Actividad* 13 orally. 10 MIN.

Homework Option:
- Have students complete *Actividad* 9 in writing. *Más práctica* Workbook, p. 112. *Cuaderno para hispanohablantes*, pp. 109–110.
- *Actividades para todos* Workbook, pp. 121–130.

DAY 5

En acción (cont.)
- Check homework. 5 MIN.
- Do *Actividad* 14 orally. 5 MIN.
- Do *Actividad* 15 in groups. 5 MIN.
- Have students read and complete *Actividad* 16 in writing. Expand using Information Gap Activities, Unit 4 Resource Book, p. 168; *Más comunicación*, p. R14. 15 MIN.

Refrán
- Present the *Refrán*, p. 313. 5 MIN.

En voces: Lectura
- Present the Reading Strategy, p. 314. Call on volunteers to read the *Lectura* aloud. Have students answer the *¿Comprendiste?/ ¿Qué piensas?* questions, p. 315. 15 MIN.

Homework Option:
- Have students complete *Hazlo tú*, p. 315.

DAY 6

En colores: Cultura y comparaciones
- Check homework. 5 MIN.
- Quick Start Review (TE, p. 316) 5 MIN.
- Present the Connecting Cultures Strategy, p. 316. Call on volunteers to read the article aloud. Have students answer the *¿Comprendiste?/¿Qué piensas?* questions, p. 317. 20 MIN.

En uso: Repaso y más comunicación
- Have students do *Actividades* 1 and 3 in pairs and *Actividades* 2 and 4 orally. 20 MIN.

Homework Option:
- Have students complete *Hazlo tú*, p. 317. Review for *Etapa* 3 Exam.

DAY 7

En uso (cont.)
- Check homework. 5 MIN.
- Present the Speaking Strategy, p. 320, and have students do *Actividades* 5 and 6 in groups. 15 MIN.

En tu propia voz: Escritura
- Have students begin their research for *Actividad* 7. 5 MIN.

En resumen: Repaso de vocabulario
- Review grammar questions, etc., as necessary. 5 MIN.
- Complete *Etapa* 3 Exam. 20 MIN.

Homework Option:
- Have students complete their reports for *Actividad* 7, p. 320. Review for Unit 4 Comprehensive Test.

DAY 8

Conexiones
- Check homework. 5 MIN.
- Discuss *Los estudios sociales*, p. 320. 5 MIN.

Unit 4 Comprehensive Test
- Review grammar questions, etc., as necessary. 5 MIN.
- Complete Unit 4 Comprehensive Test. 30 MIN.

En tu propia voz: Escritura
- Present the Writing Strategy, p. 322. Do the writing activity, pp. 322–323. 5 MIN.

Ampliación
- Optional: Use a suggested project, game, or activity. (TE, pp. 253A–253B)

Homework Option:
- Have students complete the assignment for *Conexiones*. Preview *Unidad 5* Opener: Have students read and study pp. 324–325.

Sample Lesson Plan - Block Schedule (90 minutes)

DAY 1

Etapa Opener
- Quick Start Review (TE, p. 298) 5 MIN.
- Have students look at the *Etapa* Opener and answer the questions. 5 MIN.
- Use Block Scheduling Copymasters. 5 MIN.

En contexto: Vocabulario
- Quick Start Review (TE, p. 300) 5 MIN.
- Present *Descubre*, p. 300. Have students use context and pictures to learn *Etapa* vocabulary. Use the Situational OHTs for additional practice. 15 MIN.

En vivo: Situaciones
- Quick Start Review (TE, p. 302) 5 MIN.
- Present the Listening Strategy, p. 302. Have students read section 1, p. 302. Play the audio for section 2. Have students work in groups to complete section 3. 15 MIN.

En acción: Vocabulario y gramática
- Quick Start Review (TE, p. 304) 5 MIN.
- Have students complete *Actividad* 1 in pairs. 5 MIN.
- Have students do *Actividad* 2 in writing. Go over answers orally. 5 MIN.
- Present the *Vocabulario*, p. 305. Then have students read and do *Actividad* 3 in pairs. 10 MIN.
- Present the Speaking Strategy, p. 305. Then have students do *Actividad* 4 in pairs. 10 MIN.

Homework Option:
- Have students write answers to *¿Comprendiste?*, p. 301.

DAY 2

En acción (cont.)
- Check homework. 5 MIN.
- Quick Start Review (TE, p. 306) 5 MIN.
- Present *Repaso:* Subject and Stressed Object Pronouns and the *Vocabulario*, p. 306. 10 MIN.
- Play the audio; do *Actividad* 5. 5 MIN.
- Present the *Vocabulario*, p. 307. Then do *Actividad* 6 in pairs. 10 MIN.
- Have students complete *Actividad* 7 in pairs. Expand using Information Gap Activities, Unit 4 Resource Book, p. 167; *Más comunicación*, p. R14. 20 MIN.
- Quick Start Review (TE, p. 308) 5 MIN.
- Present *Repaso:* Possessive Pronouns and the *Vocabulario*, p. 308. 10 MIN.
- Have students complete *Actividad* 8 in pairs. 5 MIN.
- Do *Actividad* 9 orally. 5 MIN.
- Have students complete *Actividad* 10 in groups. 10 MIN.

Homework Option:
- *Más práctica* Workbook, pp. 109–111. *Cuaderno para hispanohablantes*, pp. 107–108.

DAY 3

En acción (cont.)
- Check homework. 5 MIN.
- Have students complete *Actividad* 11 in pairs. 5 MIN.
- Quick Start Review (TE, p. 310) 5 MIN.
- Present *Gramática:* The Future Perfect Tense, p. 310. 10 MIN.
- Play the audio; do *Actividad* 12. 5 MIN.
- Present the *Vocabulario*, p. 311. Then do *Actividad* 13 orally. 10 MIN.
- Do *Actividad* 14 orally. 5 MIN.
- Do *Actividad* 15 in groups. 5 MIN.
- Have students read and complete *Actividad* 16 in writing. Expand using Information Gap Activities, Unit 4 Resource Book, p. 168; *Más comunicación*, p. R14. 20 MIN.

Ampliación
- Use a suggested project, game, or activity. (TE, pp. 253A–253B) 15 MIN.

Refrán
- Present the *Refrán*, p. 313. 5 MIN.

Homework Option:
- Have students complete *Actividad* 9 in writing. *Más práctica* Workbook, p. 112. *Cuaderno para hispanohablantes*, pp. 109–110.
- *Actividades para todos* Workbook, pp. 121–130.

DAY 4

En voces: Lectura
- Check homework. 5 MIN.
- Quick Start Review (TE, p. 314) 5 MIN.
- Present the Reading Strategy, p. 314. Call on volunteers to read the *Lectura* aloud. Have students answer the *¿Comprendiste?/ ¿Qué piensas?* questions, p. 315. 15 MIN.

En colores: Cultura y comparaciones
- Quick Start Review (TE, p. 316) 5 MIN.
- Present the Connecting Cultures Strategy, p. 316. Call on volunteers to read the article aloud. Have students answer the *¿Comprendiste?/¿Qué piensas?* questions, p. 317. 15 MIN.

En uso: Repaso y más comunicación
- Quick Start Review (TE, p. 318) 5 MIN.
- Do *Actividades* 1–4. 20 MIN.
- Present the Speaking Strategy, p. 320, and do *Actividades* 5 and 6 in groups. 15 MIN.
- Have students begin their research for *Actividad* 7. 5 MIN.

Homework Option:
- Have students complete their reports for *Actividad* 7, p. 320. Review for *Etapa* 3 Exam and Unit 4 Comprehensive Test.

DAY 5

En resumen: Repaso de vocabulario
- Check homework. 5 MIN.
- Quick Start Review (TE, p. 321) 5 MIN.
- Review grammar questions, etc., as necessary. 5 MIN.
- Complete *Etapa* 3 Exam. 20 MIN.

Conexiones
- Discuss *Los estudios sociales*, p. 320. 5 MIN.

Unit 4 Comprehensive Test
- Review grammar questions, etc., as necessary. 5 MIN.
- Complete Unit 4 Comprehensive Test. 30 MIN.

En tu propia voz: Escritura
- Present the Writing Strategy, p. 322. Do the writing activity, pp. 322–323. 15 MIN.

Homework Option:
- Have students complete the assignment for *Conexiones.* Preview *Unidad 5* Opener: Have students read and study pp. 324–325.

▼ Buscar y conseguir trabajo no es fácil.

Etapa Theme

Learning about Latin American economics, expressing and clarifying possession and past probability

Grammar Objectives

- Reviewing the use of subject and stressed object pronouns
- Reviewing the use of possessive pronouns
- Using the future perfect tense

Teaching Resource Options

Print

Block Scheduling Copymasters
Unit 4 Resource Book
  Family Letter, p. 171
  Absent Student Copymasters, p. 172

Audiovisual

OHT 4, 39 (Quick Start)

Quick Start Review

♻ Conditional perfect

Use OHT 39 or write on the board:
Tell what the following people probably would have done if they had had the money.

Modelo: Susana / viajar a Argentina
Habría viajado a Argentina.

1. tú / comprar un carro elegante
2. nosotros / trabajar como voluntarios
3. ustedes / visitar a amigos en España
4. yo / vivir en una mansión

Answers
1. Habrías comprado un carro elegante.
2. Habríamos trabajado como voluntarios.
3. Habrían visitado a amigos en España.
4. Habría vivido en una mansión.

Teaching Suggestions

Previewing the Etapa

- Ask students to study the photo on pp. 298–299 (1 min.).
- Close books; ask students to name the things they recall seeing:
  Nombren las cosas que recuerdan haber visto.
- Reopen books. Have students describe the photo in greater detail, using the Supplementary Vocabulary on TE p. 299.
- Use the **¿Qué ves?** questions to focus the discussion.

UNIDAD 4

ETAPA 3

Un mundo de posibilidades

OBJECTIVES

- Learn about Latin American economics
- Clarify meaning
- Express possession
- Express past probability

¿Qué ves?

Mira la foto. Contesta las preguntas.

1. ¿Qué cosas ves en la foto?
2. ¿Crees que es un lugar divertido o serio? ¿Cómo lo sabes?
3. ¿Por qué iría alguien a un lugar como éste?
4. ¿Cuáles son algunos(as) profesionales que podrían trabajar aquí?

298

Classroom Management

Planning Ahead In preparation for discussing Latin American economics, invite a social studies or economics teacher to come and present basic economic concepts to the class.

Organizing Group Work Set up a station for each **Cono Sur** country. For each station, provide sheets or folders for **agricultura, población, mercadeo internacional,** and other categories that students can research. Students can record the information in the folders as you work through the **Etapa.** At the end of the **Etapa,** divide the class into 4 groups to organize, complete, and present the information on each country.

Cross Cultural Connections

Have students identify major industrial ports in the U.S. What are they like? Are they similar or different from the port in the photo? Have students study port cities on maps to compare the geography (bay areas, rivers, etc.).

Culture Highlights

● **PORTEÑO** A las personas que viven en Buenos Aires se les llama porteños, ya que viven cerca de un puerto. «Porteño» también se usa para referirse a personas de Cortés en Honduras, Valparaíso en Chile y Puerto Barrios en Guatemala.

Supplementary Vocabulary

el barco de carga	cargo ship
el contenedor	container
la grúa	crane
la lancha	launch, small boat
el puerto	port
la zona de descarga	loading zone, dock

Teaching All Students

Extra Help Have students brainstorm a list of items and products that might be handled at a port such as the one shown here. Are students familiar with any large ports?

Multiple Intelligences

Naturalist Have students discuss the effects of large cities on the environment, especially the air and water. What steps can cities take to cut back on pollution?

Block Schedule

Personalizing Discuss what it is like to live in an industrial environment. What are the advantages and disadvantages of living in an industrial city? Make a chart on the board and have students list **ventajas** and **desventajas.** (For additional activities, see **Block Scheduling Copymasters.**)

Teaching Resource Options

Print 📖

Block Scheduling Copymasters
Unit 4 Resource Book
  Absent Student Copymasters, p. 172

Audiovisual 📼

OHT 33, 34, 35, 35A, 36, 36A, 39
(Quick Start)

Technology 💻 CD-ROM

Online Workbook, U4E3
Take-Home Tutor CD-ROM, U4E3

🔔 Quick Start Review

♻ **Stores**

Use OHT 39 or write on the board: **Haz una lista de 5 tipos de tiendas.**

Answers
Answers will vary. Answers could include:
la carnicería, la farmacia, la joyería, la librería, la panadería, la papelería, la tienda de música y videos, la zapatería

Teaching Suggestions
Introducing Vocabulary

- Have students look at pp. 300–301. Use OHT 33 and 34 to present the vocabulary.
- Ask the Comprehension Questions on TE p. 301 in order of yes/no (questions 1–3), either/or (questions 4–6), and simple word or phrase (questions 7–10). Expand by adding similar questions.
- Use the TPR activity to reinforce the meaning of individual words.

Descubre

Answers

A. 1. economic profile 2. petroleum 3. tourism
   4. export 5. import 6. textiles
   7. forestry products 8. principal
B. 1. fishing industry 2. refining
   3. mining industry 4. livestock industry

En contexto VOCABULARIO

Países en conferencia

🔲 Descubre

A. Los cognados Adivina el significado de los cognados.

1. perfil económico
2. petróleo
3. turismo
4. exportación
5. importación
6. textiles
7. productos forestales
8. principal

B. Palabras similares Ya sabes muchas palabras que terminan en -ía: **frutería, heladería, juguetería, carnicería, panadería.** ¿Qué crees que quieren decir las siguientes palabras?

1. industria pesquera
2. refinería

3. minería
4. ganadería

El representante

¡Hola! Soy Ramón Fuentes del Castillo y voy a representar a mi escuela durante una conferencia del Comité de Economía y Desarrollo Social de la NUMAS (Naciones Unidas Modelo de América del Sur). Me enfocaré en Argentina, Chile, Paraguay y Uruguay.

La investigación

Creo que NUMAS va a ser interesante. Puedes conocer a mucha gente... pero antes ¡hay que estudiar mucho! La economía internacional no es un tema de todos los días, al menos que seas un presidente o un experto en el tema. Antes de la conferencia investigué el **perfil económico** de cada país para estar preparado para los debates del comité: las **industrias**, los **productos principales de importación** y **exportación**, las **unidades monetarias...**

Unidades monetarias: Las unidades monetarias de los países que estudiaré son el peso argentino, el peso chileno, el guaraní y el peso uruguayo.

300 trescientos
Unidad 4

Classroom Community

TPR Set up 5 stations: **la minería, la refinería, la ganadería, la industria pesquera, una hacienda.** Then tell a student or a pair of students: **Necesitas (Necesitan) ganado.** The student(s) go to the **ganadería.** Give similar sentences for the other 4 stations (**petróleo, hierro, trigo,** etc.).

Portfolio Have students write a **perfil económico** similar to the ones on p. 301 for their area or state.

Rubric A = 13–15 pts. B = 10–12 pts. C = 7–9 pts. D = 4–6 pts. F = < 4 pts.

Writing criteria	Scale
Clear detail	1 2 3 4 5
Logical organization	1 2 3 4 5
Creativity/appearance	1 2 3 4 5

CD-ROM
Take-Home Tutor

Una vez en la conferencia...

¡Por suerte traje una computadora! Así puedo estudiar la información que aprendimos en la clase de geografía y compararla con los datos que obtenga en esta conferencia. Además, en Internet pude conseguir información importante como ésta:

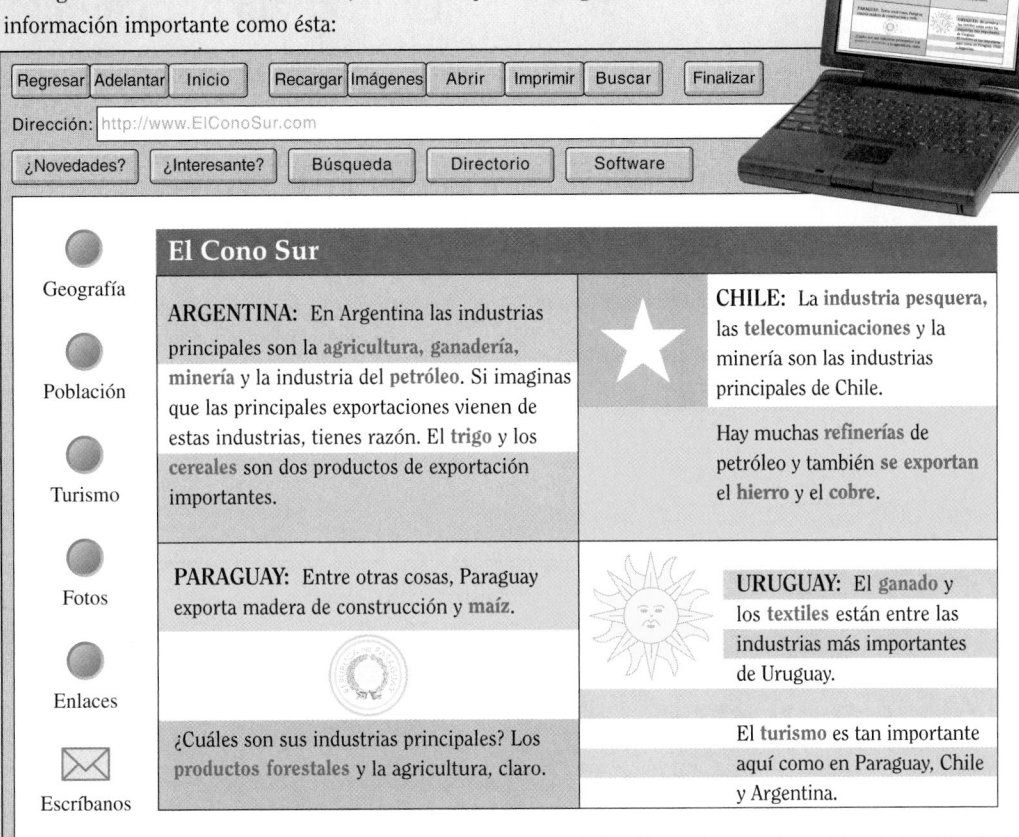

| Regresar | Adelantar | Inicio | Recargar | Imágenes | Abrir | Imprimir | Buscar | Finalizar |

Dirección: http://www.ElConoSur.com

| ¿Novedades? | ¿Interesante? | Búsqueda | Directorio | Software |

- Geografía
- Población
- Turismo
- Fotos
- Enlaces
- Escríbanos

El Cono Sur

ARGENTINA: En Argentina las industrias principales son la **agricultura, ganadería, minería** y la industria del **petróleo**. Si imaginas que las principales exportaciones vienen de estas industrias, tienes razón. El **trigo** y los **cereales** son dos productos de exportación importantes.

CHILE: La **industria pesquera**, las **telecomunicaciones** y la minería son las industrias principales de Chile.

Hay muchas **refinerías** de petróleo y también **se exportan** el **hierro** y el **cobre**.

PARAGUAY: Entre otras cosas, Paraguay exporta madera de construcción y **maíz**.

¿Cuáles son sus industrias principales? Los **productos forestales** y la agricultura, claro.

URUGUAY: El **ganado** y los **textiles** están entre las industrias más importantes de Uruguay.

El **turismo** es tan importante aquí como en Paraguay, Chile y Argentina.

Online Workbook
CLASSZONE.COM

¿Comprendiste?

1. ¿Qué categorías puedes incluir en una descripción del perfil económico de Estados Unidos?
2. Indica dos industrias de cada país mencionado.
3. ¿Han trabajado tú o tu familia en una de estas industrias? Da todos los detalles que puedas.
4. ¿Qué problemas debatirías en un club modelo de las Naciones Unidas? ¿Por qué?

trescientos uno
El Cono Sur Etapa 3
301

UNIDAD 4 Etapa 3
Vocabulary Input

Comprehension Questions

1. ¿Es NUMAS un modelo de las Naciones Unidas? (Sí)
2. ¿Representa Ramón Fuentes a España? (No)
3. ¿Investigó Ramón Fuentes el perfil económico de cada país? (Sí)
4. ¿En Argentina una industria principal es la agricultura o el cine? (la agricultura)
5. ¿En Argentina se exporta el maíz o el trigo? (el trigo)
6. ¿Una industria principal de Paraguay es los productos forestales o el petróleo? (los productos forestales)
7. ¿Cuáles son las industrias principales de Chile? (la industria pesquera, las telecomunicaciones, la minería)
8. ¿Cuáles son los metales que exporta Chile? (el hierro y el cobre)
9. ¿Cuáles son las industrias más importantes de Uruguay? (el ganado y los textiles)
10. ¿Qué industria es importante en todos los países del Cono Sur? (el turismo)

Culture Highlights

● **DATOS SOBRE EL CONO SUR**
Comparta estos datos con sus estudiantes:
- Argentina tiene una base industrial diversa y es uno de los primeros 5 exportadores de grano y carne en el mundo.
- Paraguay exporta mayormente semillas de soja *(soybeans)*, algodón, ganado y madera.
- La industria de Uruguay se orienta en el sector agropecuario, en especial ganadero (carnes, cueros, lanas)
- Chile es el productor más grande de cobre en el mundo. El cobre es la exportación principal de este país.

Block Schedule

Research Using library or Internet resources, have students find 10 economic facts about a **Southern Cone** country of their choosing. Have them present the facts graphically and in writing. Display students' work on the bulletin board. (For additional activities, see **Block Scheduling Copymasters**.)

Teaching All Students

Extra Help Have students draw pictures to illustrate the words from the **En contexto**. Collect the drawings and ask simple yes/no questions. For example: ¿Es trigo? ¿Son las telecomunicaciones?

Multiple Intelligences

Visual Have students design a poster extolling the economy of one of the **Southern Cone** countries.

Naturalist Have students research the geography of the **Southern Cone** countries to show the relationship between the landforms and the industries.

Teaching Resource Options

Print ✎

Block Scheduling Copymasters
Unit 4 Resource Book
  Absent Student Copymasters, p. 173
  Audioscript, p. 181

Audiovisual 📺

OHT 37, 38, 40 (Quick Start)
Audio Program CD 12, Track 1

Technology 💻 CD ROM

Take-Home Tutor CD-ROM, U4E3

🔔 Quick Start Review

♻ **Vocabulary review**

Use OHT 40 or write on the board:
Complete the following sentences:

1. El trigo, el maíz y otros cereales
   son parte de la ___ de EE.UU.
2. En Canadá hay muchos bosques y
   se exportan ___ .
3. En Chile hay mucho cobre y nitrato.
   La ___ es importante.
4. La ___ de Paraguay es el guaraní.

Answers
1. agricultura
2. productos forestales
3. minería
4. unidad monetaria

Teaching Suggestions
Presenting Situations

• Present the Listening Strategy, p. 302,
  and discuss the Pre-listening question.
• Use OHT 37 and 38 to present the
  Leer section. Ask simple yes/no,
  either/or, or short-answer questions.
• Use Audio CD 12 and have students
  do the **Escuchar** section (see Script, TE
  p. 297B). Then have students complete
  the Listening Strategy exercise.
• Have students work in pairs or groups
  to complete the **Hablar/Escribir** section.

AUDIO 🎧 *En vivo*
SITUACIONES

PARA ESCUCHAR
STRATEGY: LISTENING

Pre-listening Predict what countries are the largest
producers of the world's resources. Do you think
these are also favorites with tourists? Think of
countries in each category and write your
predictions.

Use statistics to evaluate predictions Write down the
countries as directed in **Escuchar**, then evaluate your
predictions. How well did you identify the countries
where major world producers and industries are
located? Discuss your insights with your classmates.

Alimentos	Minerales	Turismo
1.		
2.		
3.		

¡Encuéntralo por Internet!

Tienes que escribir un informe sobre la
producción mundial (*worldwide*) de varios
productos. Encuentras información en
Internet. Primero ves la información en
la página-web. Luego escuchas más
información por audio.

❶ Leer

Encontraste esta página en Internet. Lee la página
para saber qué tipo de información tiene.

| Regresar | Adelantar | Inicio | | Recargar | Imágenes | Abrir | Imprimir | Buscar | | Finalizar |

Dirección: http://www.mundial.com

| ¿Novedades? | ¿Interesante? | Búsqueda | Directorio | Software |

LA PRODUCCIÓN MUNDIAL

Agricultura   Minería   Telecomunicaciones

Ganadería   Petróleo   Textiles

Maderas   Industria pesquera   Turismo

302   trescientos dos
            Unidad 4

Classroom Community

Paired Activity Have students work in pairs and
explain to each other the words that appear on the
Web page on p. 302. For example: **Minería: la
industria que tiene que ver con los minerales
como cobre, oro y plata.**

Group Activity Have students work in groups of 3
or 4 and draw 2 items for each of the industries shown
on the Web page on p. 302. They should not label the
drawings. Then have them show their drawings to
another group and ask to what industry each one
belongs.

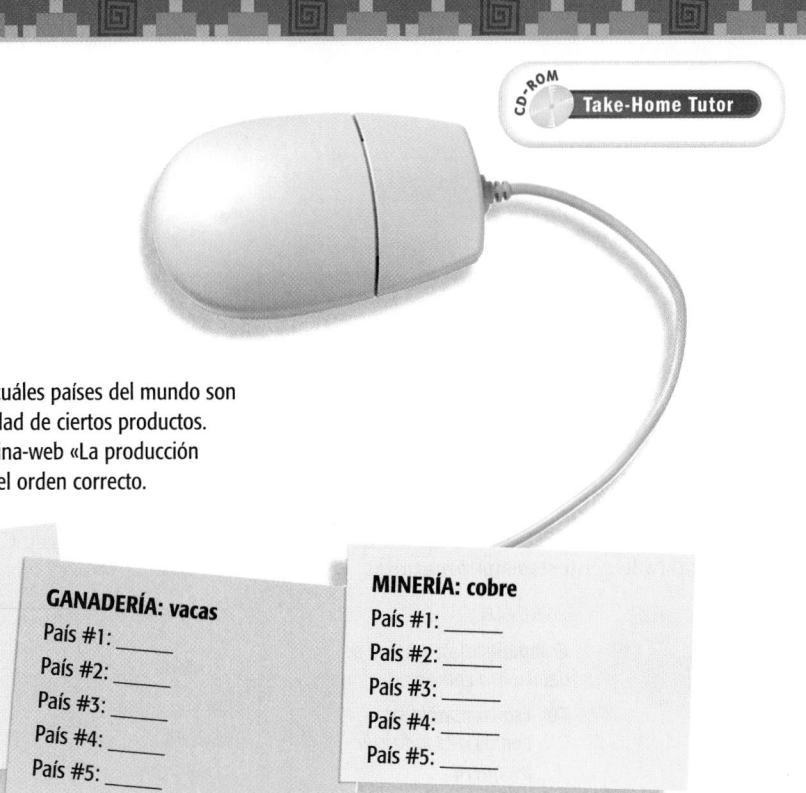

❷ Escuchar 🎧

Tienes que informarle a la clase cuáles países del mundo son los que producen la mayor cantidad de ciertos productos. Escucha la información de la página-web «La producción mundial» y escribe los países en el orden correcto.

AGRICULTURA: maíz
País #1: _____
País #2: _____
País #3: _____
País #4: _____
País #5: _____

GANADERÍA: vacas
País #1: _____
País #2: _____
País #3: _____
País #4: _____
País #5: _____

MINERÍA: cobre
País #1: _____
País #2: _____
País #3: _____
País #4: _____
País #5: _____

PETRÓLEO CRUDO
País #1: _____
País #2: _____
País #3: _____
País #4: _____
País #5: _____

INDUSTRIA PESQUERA
País #1: _____
País #2: _____
País #3: _____
País #4: _____
País #5: _____

TURISMO
País #1: _____
País #2: _____
País #3: _____
País #4: _____
País #5: _____

❸ Hablar/Escribir 👥

En grupos de dos o tres, conversen sobre el perfil económico de su ciudad, estado o país. ¿Cuál es la industria más importante de su estado o región? ¿Conocen a alguien que trabaje en esa industria? Entrevisten a esa persona o busquen datos por Internet o en la biblioteca. Escriban un informe en español que explique la importancia de esa industria en su región. También incluyan ideas sobre el desarrollo futuro de sus regiones.

Teaching All Students

Extra Help After playing the audio CD, read the Script to students (see Listening Activity Scripts, TE p. 297B). Pause after each section. Let students ask questions to clarify what you read. Then have them complete the appropriate chart.

Multiple Intelligences

Verbal Using the notes they took for the **Escuchar**, have students explain in their own words what they wrote about each industry.

Visual Have students make word webs for the industries listed on the Web page on p. 302.

Escuchar (See script, p. 297B.)

Answers

AGRICULTURA: maíz
País #1: Estados Unidos
País #2: China
País #3: Brasil
País #4: México
País #5: Argentina

GANADERÍA: vacas
País #1: Estados Unidos
País #2: Unión Soviética
País #3: Brasil
País #4: Alemania
País #5: Argentina

MINERÍA: cobre
País #1: Chile
País #2: Estados Unidos
País #3: Canadá
País #4: Indonesia
País #5: Perú

PETRÓLEO CRUDO
País #1: Arabia Saudita
País #2: Estados Unidos
País #3: China
País #4: Iraq
País #5: México

INDUSTRIA PESQUERA
País #1: China
País #2: Perú
País #3: Chile
País #4: Japón
País #5: Estados Unidos

TURISMO
País #1: Francia
País #2: Estados Unidos
País #3: España
País #4: Italia
País #5: Reino Unido/Inglaterra

Hablar/Escribir

Answers
Answers will vary.

Critical Thinking

Have students think about how a country's resources might affect its economy and political power. Discuss embargoes. Can students give any specific examples where a country's exports were used politically? ¿Pueden dar ejemplos específicos de usos políticos de las exportaciones de un país?

▣ Block Schedule

Change of Pace Have students imagine that they represent a particular industry in a Spanish-speaking country. Have them prepare a presentation about their industry and present it to the class. For example: **Yo represento la industria del turismo. En mi país tenemos muchas cosas bonitas que ver.** etc. (For additional activities, see **Block Scheduling Copymasters.**)

Teaching Resource Options

Print

Block Scheduling Copymasters
Unit 4 Resource Book
  Absent Student Copymasters, p. 174

Audiovisual

OHT 40 (Quick Start)

Quick Start Review

 Vocabulary review

Use OHT 40 or write on the board:
Write 2 items you associate with each
of the following words:

1. minería
2. telecomunicaciones
3. textiles
4. productos forestales
5. unidad monetaria

Answers

Answers will vary. Answers could include:
1. cobre, hierro, oro, plata
2. televisión, teléfono, computadora
3. ropa, alfombras, seda
4. madera, papel
5. dólares, pesos, guaraní

Teaching Suggestions
Comprehension Check

Use **Actividades 1–4** to assess retention
after the **Vocabulario** and **Situaciones.**
Have students write as many additional
items as possible for the chart in
Actividad 2. Compile everyone's
answers to make a larger chart.

 Objective: Controlled practice
Vocabulary in conversation

Answers
1. Esa compañía se dedica a la ganadería.
2. Esa compañía se dedica a los textiles.
3. Esa compañía se dedica al petróleo.
4. Esa compañía se dedica a la agricultura.
5. Esa compañía se dedica a las
  telecomunicaciones.
6. Esa compañía se dedica a los productos
  forestales.

En acción

PARTE **A**   **Práctica del vocabulario**

Objectives for Activities 1–4
• Learn about Latin America economics

1 Las compañías

Hablar/*Escribir* Tu compañero(a) quiere
saber a qué se dedican varias compañías
de Buenos Aires. Como sabes un poco de
Argentina, tú le contestas sus preguntas.

modelo

Compañero(a): *¿A qué se
dedica esa compañía?*

Tú: *Esa compañía se
dedica a la industria
pesquera.*

1.
2.
3.
4.
5.
6.

2 Los productos

Escribir En tu clase de geografía, tienes que
hacer una tabla que indica los productos que
van bajo cada categoría. Copia la tabla y
complétala.

Agricultura	cereales			
Ganadería				
Minería				
Industria pesquera				
Textiles				

aceitunas	lana
algodón	maíz
arroz	oro
atún	ovejas *(sheep)*
caballos	pieles de cuero
cabras *(goats)*	plata
café	ropa
calamares	seda
cereales	suéteres
cobre	toallas
frutas	trigo
gallinas	trucha *(trout)*
hierro	vacas

304   trescientos cuatro
Unidad 4

Classroom Management

Planning Ahead In preparation for discussing Latin
American economics and statistics, supervise a
volunteer who can help you research a list of Web sites
for the class to refer to when necessary.

Peer Review Have students complete **Actividad 2**
in pairs. Then have them share papers with another
pair and correct their answers.

3 Internet

Leer/Hablar Conversa con tu compañero(a) sobre las estadísticas sobre los visitantes a las páginas web de cada país.

modelo

Tú: *Este año, la página de Paraguay recibió un millón doscientos mil visitantes.*

Compañero(a): *De esos visitantes, casi la mitad fue hispanohablante.*

Estadísticas sobre los visitantes

Paraguay: 1.200.000 visitantes
Edad promedio: 32
Hispanohablantes: 50%
Inglés: 25%
Otros idiomas: 25%

Chile: 1.500.800 visitantes
Edad promedio: 25
Hispanohablantes: 33%
Inglés: 33%
Otros idiomas: 33%

Argentina: 2.350.700 visitantes
Edad promedio: 22
Hispanohablantes: 20%
Inglés: 40%
Otros idiomas: 40%

Uruguay: 850.000 visitantes
Edad promedio: 45
Hispanohablantes: 70%
Inglés: 10%
Otros idiomas: 20%

Vocabulario

Comparaciones numéricas

comparar *to compare*
las estadísticas *statistics*
mil millones *a billion*
un millón de millones *a trillion*
la mitad de *one half of*
el por ciento *percent*
el porcentaje *percentage*
el promedio *average*
el quinto *one fifth*

sumar *to add*
el tercio *one third*

♻ Ya sabes

un cuarto
un décimo
la mayoría
medio(a)

▸ ¿Puedes usar estas palabras para hablar sobre tu ciudad o estado?

4 Tu estado

STRATEGY: SPEAKING

Guess cognates Spanish and English share many words derived from Latin. Try adding a Spanish ending to an English word and it might be a correct word in Spanish. Look at these cognates for discussing your state's industries: **construcción, cinematografía, energía nuclear, radiodifusión, fuerzas armadas**.

Hablar Tú y tu compañero(a) tienen que preparar un reporte sobre tu estado para la clase de estudios sociales. Antes de ir a la biblioteca tienen que decidir qué tipo de información económica necesitan buscar.

modelo

Tú: *La agricultura es muy importante para la economía de Texas.*

Compañero(a): *Tienes razón. También necesitamos información sobre la ganadería.*

Teaching All Students

Extra Help Have students use 3 of the words from the **Vocabulario** on p. 305 in a sentence that relates to the school or to the town/city students live in.

Challenge Have students explore additional cognates related to industries, using a dictionary.

Multiple Intelligences

Logical/Mathematical Using the Internet, have students look up economic statistics for one of the **Southern Cone** countries. They should first prepare a list of words to use as search criteria. After researching, have them talk about the statistics using the **Vocabulario** on p. 305.

Objective: Transitional practice
Vocabulary

Answers *Answers may vary.*

Agricultura
cereales	frutas
aceitunas	gallinas
arroz	maíz
café	trigo

Ganadería
caballos	ovejas
cabras	vacas

Minería
cobre	oro
hierro	plata

Industria Pesquera
atún	trucha
calamares	

Textiles
algodón	seda
lana	suéteres
pieles de cuero	toallas
ropa	

Teaching Suggestions
Presenting Vocabulary

- Present the **Vocabulario** using examples written on the board or on an OHT.
- You may wish to point out that **billón** is the equivalent of a trillion.

Objective: Transitional practice
Vocabulary in conversation
♻ **Numbers**

Answers will vary.

Objective: Open-ended practice
Vocabulary in conversation

Answers will vary.

Block Schedule

Variety Have students complete a chart like the one in **Actividad 2** for **refinería, telecomunicaciones,** and **construcción de edificios**. Make a master chart on the board with students' responses. (For additional activities, see **Block Scheduling Copymasters**.)

UNIDAD 4 Etapa 3
Vocabulary/Grammar

Teaching Resource Options

Print 📖

Más práctica Workbook PE,
  pp. 109–110
Cuaderno para hispanohablantes
  PE, p. 107
Block Scheduling Copymasters
Unit 4 Resource Book
  Más práctica Workbook TE,
    pp. 145–146
  Cuaderno para hispanohablantes
    TE, p. 161
  Absent Student Copymasters, p. 174
  Audioscript, p. 181

Audiovisual 🎛️

OHT 41 (Quick Start), 44 (Grammar)
Audio Program CD 12, Track 2, Activity 5

Technology 💻

Online Workbook, U4E3
Take-Home Tutor CD-ROM, U4E3

Quick Start Review

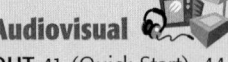 Numbers

Use OHT 41 or write on the board:
Write the Spanish words for these
numbers:

1. 1/5
2. 100%
3. 1/2
4. 1.000.000.000
5. 1/3
6. 1/10

Answers
1. el quinto
2. cien por ciento
3. la mitad
4. mil millones
5. el tercio
6. el décimo

Teaching Suggestions
Reviewing Subject and Stressed Object Pronouns

• Call individual students to the board
and dictate forms of the pronouns as
such: **primera persona singular,
segunda persona plural,** etc.
• Have each student provide a
personalized sentence using a
stressed object pronoun.

PARTE B — Práctica: gramática y vocabulario

Objectives for Activities 5–15
• Clarify meaning • Express possession • Express past probability

REPASO — Subject and Stressed Object pronouns

Most of the time you do not use **subject pronouns** in Spanish, because
the verb ending shows who the subject is. When you do include them it
is because you wish to add emphasis, clarify, or make a contrast.

• to show emphasis

  Yo le di las estadísticas,
  no Roberto.
  I gave him the statistics, not Roberto.

• to make a comparison or clarify

  Él salió. Ella se quedó
  en casa.
  He went out. She stayed home.

You use the prepositional **a** + **subject pronouns** to clarify who
the object of a preposition is, except in the case of **yo** and **tú**. Here
special object pronouns are used (**mí, ti**).

El profesor les dio
el reportaje **a ellos.**
*The teacher gave the report
to them.*

No me lo dio **a mí.**
*He didn't give it **to me.***

Vocabulario

♻️ **Ya sabes**

Subject	a + Pronoun
yo	a mí
tú	a ti
usted	a usted
él	a él
ella	a ella
nosotros	a nosotros
vosotros	a vosotros
ustedes	a ustedes
ellos	a ellos
ellas	a ellas

Practice:
Actividades
5 6 7

Más práctica
cuaderno pp. 109–110
Para hispanohablantes
cuaderno p. 107

🛈 **Online Workbook**
CLASSZONE.COM

---

5 ¿Quién?

Escuchar/*Escribir* Estás en una
reunión familiar. Contesta las
preguntas de tu tío sobre los
intereses de todos.

modelo
¿Quién es abogado? él
¿Quién es médica? ella

1. ¿Quién estudió ingeniería?
   _____

2. ¿Quién quiere ser
   veterinario? _____
   ¿Y bombero? _____

3. ¿Quién fue a la
   Universidad de Buenos
   Aires? _____ ¿Quién fue a
   la Universidad de Chile?
   _____

4. ¿Quién estudió para
   ser arquitecto? _____
   ¿E ingeniera? _____

5. ¿A quién le interesa el
   mercadeo? _____ ¿A quién
   le interesa la publicidad?
   _____

6. ¿Quién es bailarina? _____
   ¿Quién es deportista?

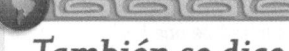

También se dice

Trabajar y **trabajo** son términos
universales en todo el mundo de
habla española. Pero en México y
Colombia se dice también
chambear y **chamba** para
referirse al trabajo. En Argentina
se usa la palabra **changa** y en
Puerto Rico **chiripa** para referirse
a un trabajo pequeño.

Classroom Community

Group Activity Plan ahead: Have each student
bring in at least 5 magazine pictures of people working
at different jobs or doing different activities. Working in
groups of 3–4, have students take turns pointing and
telling who the people are. They should also try to
make a statement about the person's activities using a
stressed object pronoun. For example: **Ella es
arquitecta. A ella le gusta diseñar edificios.**

Paired Activity Have students work in pairs and
write related words for each profession in the
Vocabulario on p. 307. For example: **el (la)
banquero(a)—el banco, dinero, prestar, la cuenta
de ahorros.**

6 Ganándose la vida

Hablar/Escribir Conversa con tu compañero(a) sobre las profesiones de las personas de la lista y de otras personas que conocen. ¿Cómo se ganan la vida?

Buenos días, Buon giorno, Guten Tag

modelo

la Sra. Martínez

Tú: ¿Cómo se gana la vida la Sra. Martínez?

Compañero(a): Ella es intérprete.

1. el Sr. Martínez

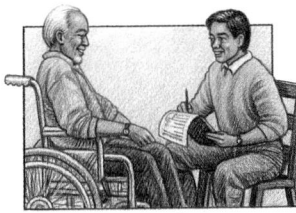

2. Ángel

3. el Sr. Beltrán

4. Susana

5. los Sres. Gutiérrez

6. el Sr. Henares

7. un(a) amigo(a)

8. un(a) pariente

9. un(a) vecino(a)

10. tú

Vocabulario

Carreras con el español

el (la) académico(a) *academic*

el (la) agente de ventas *sales agent*

el (la) banquero(a) *banker*

el (la) bibliotecario(a) *librarian*

el (la) corresponsal *correspondent*

el (la) diplomático(a) *diplomat*

el (la) financiero(a) *financial expert*

el (la) intérprete *interpreter*

el (la) trabajador(a) social
social worker

el (la) traductor(a) *translator*

▶ ¿Conoces a alguien que trabaje en una de estas profesiones?

Objective: Controlled practice
Listening comprehension/subject and stressed object pronouns
♻ **Professions vocabulary**

Answers (See script, p. 289B.)
1. nosotros
2. él / yo
3. él / ella
4. yo / ella
5. a ella / a él
6. yo / él

Teaching Suggestions
Presenting Vocabulary

• Have students provide descriptions of the activities of each professional.

• Ask students how each professional might use Spanish on an everyday basis.

Objective: Transitional practice
Subject and stressed object pronouns/vocabulary in conversation

Answers will vary.

🔔 Quick Wrap-up

Name a famous person or TV character in one of the professions in the **Vocabulario** (or in other professions). Have students name the profession.

▮ Block Schedule

FunBreak Have students work in round-robin format to create a profession chain. For example, the first student begins with a sentence such as, **El banquero le presta dinero a la arquitecta.** The next student replies with a sentence such as, **La arquitecta diseña las oficinas del médico.** The next student says, **El médico cura al intérprete.** Challenge students to include as many professions as possible. (For additional activities, see **Block Scheduling Copymasters.**)

Teaching All Students

Extra Help Ask students which subject pronouns they would use to refer to these people: **una amiga, los profesores, tú mismo(a), una amiga y tú mismo(a), tus padres, un agente de viajes.**

Multiple Intelligences

Musical/Rhythmic Remind students that there are only 2 changes in regards to subject pronouns and object pronouns with **a (yo/a mí, tú/a ti)**. Have students recite these to themselves using a catchy beat. Have volunteers share their "personal musical device" for remembering these pronouns with the class.

Teaching Resource Options

Print

Más práctica Workbook PE, p. 111
Cuaderno para hispanohablantes
PE, p. 108
Block Scheduling Copymasters
Unit 4 Resource Book
Más práctica Workbook TE, p. 147
Cuaderno para hispanohablantes
TE, p. 162
Information Gap Activities, p. 167
Absent Student Copymasters,
pp. 174–175

Audiovisual

OHT 41 (Quick Start), 45 (Grammar)

Technology

Online Workbook, U4E3
Take-Home Tutor CD-ROM, U4E3

Objective: Open-ended practice
Subject and stressed object pronouns
in conversation

Answers will vary.

Quick Start Review

♻ Subject and stressed object
pronouns
Use OHT 41 or write on the board:
Rewrite the sentences to emphasize the
subject and/or object.
Modelo: Es ingeniero. Soy arquitecta.
Él es ingeniero. Yo soy arquitecta.

1. Somos académicas. Son
   financieros.
2. Me gustan los animales. Te gusta
   leer.
3. Mis padres le dieron un carro. Mis
   padres me dieron una bicicleta.
4. Eres profesor. Es ingeniera.

Answers

1. Nosotras somos académicas. Ellos (ustedes)
   son financieros.
2. A mí me gustan los animales. A ti te gusta
   leer.
3. Mis padres le dieron un carro a él (ella).
   Mis padres me dieron una bicicleta a mí.
4. Tú eres profesor. Ella (usted) es ingeniera.

---

7 ¿Los conoces?

Hablar/Escribir Un alumno
nuevo acaba de llegar a tu
escuela. Te toca informarle
sobre la escuela y los otros
alumnos. Están en la clase
de español y él te pregunta
sobre los alumnos y el (la)
maestro(a).

> **modelo**
>
> **Compañero(a):** *¿Quién es él?*
>
> **Tú:** *Él es el maestro de español.*
>
> **Compañero(a):** *¿Y aquellos
> muchachos allí?*
>
> **Tú:** *Él es Toño y ella es Ryoko.*

More Practice:
Más comunicación *p. R14*

Nota cultural

En Latinoamérica, buscar y
conseguir trabajo no es tan
fácil como en Estados Unidos.
Si se encuentra un anuncio
interesante en el periódico,
se debe ir a una entrevista para
presentar el currículum
personalmente. Frecuentemente
hay muchas personas esperando
turno y es necesario esperar
mucho. Luego se espera la
confirmación telefónica y puede
haber otra entrevista antes de
obtener el trabajo.

REPASO **Possessive Pronouns**

You use **possessive** adjectives and **pronouns** to express possession.

Possessive adjective:
Aquí están **mis** datos.
*Here are **my** facts.*

Possessive pronoun:
Los míos están en el libro.
Mine are in the book.

Aquí esta **mi** reportaje.
*Here is **my** report.*

El mío está en la mesa.
Mine is on the table.

Allí está **tu** reportaje.
*There is **your** report.*

Ese reportaje es **el tuyo.**
*That report is **yours**.*

- -

Note that **possessive** adjectives are used with **nouns**, while **possessive** pronouns replace them:

replaced with

Tu carrera es interesante.
Your career is interesting.

Sí, pero **la tuya** es más
interesante que **la mía.**
Yes, but yours is more interesting than mine.

Vocabulario

♻ **Ya sabes**

mi	mío(a)
tu	tuyo(a)
su	suyo(a)
nuestro(a)	nuestro(a)
vuestro(a)	vuestro(a)
su	suyo(a)

Practice:
Actividades
8 9 10 11

Más práctica
cuaderno p. 111
Para hispanohablantes
cuaderno p. 108

 Online Workbook
CLASSZONE.COM

Classroom Community

Group Activity Divide the class into groups of 4.
Have each group use possessive adjectives and
pronouns to talk about things people own and
relationships among people. Each group should write
a summary of the discussion to present to the class.

Learning Scenario Divide the class into groups of
5–6. Have students imagine that they have found a
treasure chest filled with CDs, music videos, money,
jewelry, hats, etc. Tell students to have a discussion
over whose items are whose. For example: **Es mi disco
compacto de Gloria Estefan. No es el tuyo.**

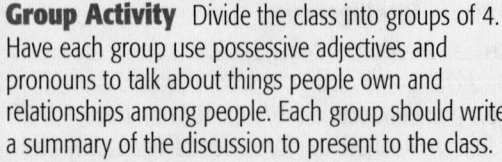

8 Los productos de América Latina

Hablar/Escribir Tú y tu compañero(a) compraron varios productos y comidas de América Latina. Compara tus productos con los de tu compañero(a).

modelo

Tú: *Mi anillo es de oro. ¿Y el tuyo?*

Compañero(a): *El mío es de plata.*

oro/plata

1. Colombia/Oaxaca 2. cuero/lana

3. cobre/plata 4. Perú/México

5. cuero 6. madera

9 ¿De Argentina o de Chile?

Hablar/Escribir Entre tus amigos, todos compraron estas cosas en Argentina o en Chile. ¿De qué país son las cosas que compraron?

modelo

la chaqueta (yo: Argentina; tú: Chile)

La mía es de Argentina.

La tuya es de Chile.

1. los zapatos (yo: Argentina; ella: Chile)
2. el collar (ella: Argentina; tú: Chile)
3. los muebles (nosotros: Argentina; tú: Chile)
4. la camisa (él: Argentina; ella: Chile)
5. las sillas (nosotros: Argentina; ellos: Chile)
6. ¿...?

10 ¿Y el tuyo?

Hablar/Escribir Tú y tus compañeros tienen que hacer un informe sobre la economía latinoamericana, pero nadie puede escoger el mismo tema. En grupos de tres o cuatro, hablen del tema que va a tratar el reporte de cada uno.

modelo

Tú: *El informe de Ricardo es sobre la ganadería en Argentina. ¿Y los suyos?*

Compañero(a): *El mío es sobre el turismo en Chile…*

Teaching All Students

Extra Help Have students expand **Actividades 8** and **9** by comparing what they are wearing or carrying today. For example. **Mi suéter es de Perú. El tuyo es de Estados Unidos.**

Native Speakers Ask students to prepare a simple explanation of possessive pronouns to help students having difficulty. They may also prepare a short worksheet to accompany the explanation.

Multiple Intelligences

Visual Have students draw cartoons to illustrate the possessive pronouns. For example: a scene with 3 or more people–the closest person is pointing to his/her red book; someone next to him/her is pointing to his/her green book; a person in the background is pointing to his/her black book. Display the drawings and have students take turns talking about them.

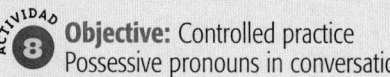
Teaching Suggestions
Reviewing Possessive Pronouns

• Stress that possessive adjectives and pronouns agree in gender and number with the nouns they modify.
• Remind students that possessive pronouns are usually preceded by the definite article.

ACTIVIDAD 8 **Objective:** Controlled practice
Possessive pronouns in conversation

Answers
1. A: Mi café es de Colombia. ¿Y el tuyo?
   B: El mío es de Oaxaca.
2. A: Mis guantes son de cuero. ¿Y los tuyos?
   B: Los míos son de lana.
3. A: Mi pulsera es de cobre. ¿Y la tuya?
   B: La mía es de plata.
4. A: Mi collar es de Perú. ¿Y el tuyo?
   B: El mío es de México.
5. A: Mi chaqueta es de cuero. ¿Y la tuya?
   B: La mía es de cuero también.
6. A: Mi silla es de madera. ¿Y la tuya?
   B: La mía es de madera también.

ACTIVIDAD 9 **Objective:** Transitional practice
Possessive pronouns

 Clothing and furniture

Answers
1. Los míos son de Argentina.
   Los suyos son de Chile.
2. El suyo es de Argentina.
   El tuyo es de Chile.
3. Los nuestros son de Argentina.
   Los tuyos son de Chile.
4. La suya es de Argentina.
   La suya es de Chile.
5. Las nuestras son de Argentina.
   Las suyas son de Chile.
6. *Answers will vary.*

ACTIVIDAD 10 **Objective:** Open-ended practice
Possessive pronouns in conversation

Answers will vary.

Block Schedule

Change of Pace Have students work in groups of 5–6 and play a round robin of "el mío/el tuyo/el suyo." One student turns to another and begins with **Mi cuaderno es [amarillo]. ¿Y el tuyo?** The next student responds as he/she turns to the next student: **El mío es [verde]. El suyo es [amarillo]. ¿Y el tuyo?** The group completes the round robin. Then another student starts the next round with a new item of his/her choosing. (For additional activities, see **Block Scheduling Copymasters.**)

Teaching Resource Options

Print

Más práctica Workbook PE, p. 112
Cuaderno para hispanohablantes
PE, pp. 109–110
Unit 4 Resource Book
  Más práctica Workbook TE, p. 148
  Cuaderno para hispanohablantes
  TE, pp. 163–164
  Absent Student Copymasters,
  pp. 175–176
  Audioscript, p. 181

Audiovisual

OHT 41 (Quick Start), 46 (Grammar)
Audio Program CD 12, Track 3,
  Activity 12
Word Tiles, U4E3

Technology

Online Workbook, U4E3
Take-Home Tutor CD-ROM, U4E3

ACTIVIDAD 11 **Objective:** Open-ended practice
Possessive pronouns in conversation

Answers will vary.

Quick Start Review

♻ Past participles

Use OHT 41 or write on the board:
Write the past participles of the
following verbs:

1. abrir   6. morir
2. decir   7. poner
3. descubrir   8. resolver
4. escribir   9. ver
5. hacer   10. volver

Answers
1. abierto   6. muerto
2. dicho   7. puesto
3. descubierto   8. resuelto
4. escrito   9. visto
5. hecho   10. vuelto

Práctica: gramática y vocabulario continuación

11 Mi favorito(a)

Hablar/*Escribir* Comenta
tus preferencias con tu
compañero(a) mientras él
(ella) te pregunta sobre las
tuyas. Escoge de la lista o
usa tus propias ideas.

modelo

Tú: *Mi clase favorita es el dibujo
técnico. ¿Y la tuya?*

Compañero(a): *La mía es la
informática
porque…*

pasatiempo

poema

estrella de cine

cantante

película

clase

campo de estudio

programa de televisión

libro   ¿…?

GRAMÁTICA   The Future Perfect Tense

You use the **future perfect tense** to express what will have happened
by a certain time. To form this tense use:

future of **haber**   +   **past participle** of the verb

habré terminado	habremos terminado
habrás terminado	habréis terminado
habrá terminado	habrán terminado

—Llegaremos a las dos.
We will arrive at two.

—Pero a esa hora, nosotros
ya **habremos salido.**
*But at that time, we **will have** already **left.***

—Pasaré para recoger
el informe a las tres.
*I'll come by to pick up the report
at three.*

—No sé si **habré terminado.**
*I don't know if **I will have finished** (by then).*

The **future perfect tense** is often used with **dentro de** + **time.**

Dentro de tres años, me **habré graduado.**
*In three years, **I will have graduated.***

....

You also use the **future perfect** to speculate about something that
may have happened in the past.

—Todavía no han llegado
tus primos.
Your cousins haven't arrived yet.

—Se **habrán perdido.**
*They **probably got lost.***

—Miguel está deprimido.
¿Qué le **habrá pasado?**
*Miguel is depressed. What **could
have happened** to him?*

—No sé. No le **habrán dado**
el puesto que quería.
*I don't know. **Perhaps they didn't give
him** the job he wanted.*

Practice:
Actividades
12 13 14 15

Más práctica
cuaderno p. 112
Para hispanohablantes
cuaderno pp. 109–110

 Online Workbook
CLASSZONE.COM

---

310   trescientos diez
Unidad 4

Classroom Community

Paired Activity Working in pairs, one students says
a sentence with the verb in the present tense. The
other student changes the action to the future perfect
tense. For example: **Termino la tarea antes de las 9.**
→ **Habré terminado la tarea antes de las 9.**

Cooperative Learning Students work in groups of
3. Student 1 writes a sentence using the future tense.
Student 2 rewrites the sentence using the future perfect
tense. Student 3 changes the sentence to express
probability or speculation. For example: **Javier hará la
tarea.** → **Javier habrá hecho la tarea antes de salir.**
→ **¿Habrá hecho la tarea Javier?**

12 ¡Pobre Carlos!

Escuchar/*Escribir* Carlos tuvo un día malísimo. Dos de sus amigos comentan sobre lo que le pasó o lo que le habrá pasado. Primero, copia la siguiente tabla. Luego escucha la conversación. Si la persona sabe lo que le pasó a Carlos, marca «sabe». Si la persona está especulando sobre lo que le habrá pasado, marca «no sabe».

sabe	no sabe
1.	
2.	
3.	
4.	
5.	
6.	

También se dice

Para referirse a los distintos tipos de industrias, no siempre se usan las mismas expresiones. Por ejemplo, se habla de **la industria ganadera** o de **la ganadería**; de **la industria petrolera** o de **la industria del petróleo**; de **la industria agrícola** o de **la agricultura**. Además, las fábricas también se conocen como **factorías** y la bolsa de valores se nombra familiarmente como **la bolsa**.

13 La economía chilena

Hablar/*Escribir* Los chilenos miran con optimismo el futuro económico de Chile. ¿Qué habrá pasado antes del año 2015?

> **modelo**
>
> *economía chilena / florecer (to flourish)*
>
> *Antes del año 2015, la economía chilena habrá florecido.*

1. las fábricas / aumentar en número
2. las compañías multinacionales / incorporar el uso de las telecomunicaciones
3. la industria del turismo / aumentar dramáticamente
4. la ganadería / crecer
5. los productos / exportarse en cantidades más grandes
6. los precios / bajar
7. la industria del petróleo / desarrollarse
8. la inflación / controlarse

Vocabulario

Tipos de compañías

la bolsa de valores *stock exchange*

la fábrica *factory*

el laboratorio *laboratory*

la multinacional *multinational business*

la sociedad anónima (S.A.) *corporation (Inc.)*

▶ ¿Puedes usar estas palabras para describir empresas locales?

Teaching Suggestions
Teaching The Future Perfect Tense

- Emphasize that one use of the future perfect is to describe an action that must be completed before another action happens in the future.
- It also expresses a completed possibility. The speaker may have reason to assume that the action has taken place, but is not sure about it.

12 Objective: Controlled practice
Listening comprehension/future perfect tense

Answers (See script, p. 297B.)
1. sabe
2. no sabe
3. no sabe
4. sabe
5. no sabe
6. no sabe

Dictation

Using the Listening Activity Script for **Actividad 12** on TE p. 297B, dictate selected sentences to students. You may want to write answers on the board for students to correct their own work.

13 Objective: Controlled practice
Future perfect tense

Answers
1. Antes del año 2005, las fábricas habrán aumentado en número.
2. Antes del año 2005, las compañías multinacionales habrán incorporado el uso de las telecomunicaciones.
3. Antes del año 2005, la industria del turismo habrá aumentado dramáticamente.
4. Antes del año 2005, la ganadería habrá crecido.
5. Antes del año 2005, los productos se habrán exportado en cantidades más grandes.
6. Antes del año 2005, los precios habrán bajado.
7. Antes del año 2005, la industria del petróleo se habrá desarrollado.
8. Antes del año 2005, la inflación se habrá controlado.

Block Schedule

Variety Have students write and design a job ad or job description using at least one of the words in the **Vocabulario** on p. 311.

Teaching All Students

Extra Help Write the following sentences on the board:
Este trabajo es mi mejor experiencia en Monterrey.
A las nueve, yo salgo para la oficina.
Él regresa a las cuatro.
Have students rewrite the sentences in the future perfect, then explain how the meaning has changed.

Multiple Intelligences

Logical/Mathematical Write several professions on the board and have students speculate about what the people studied. For example: **un contador: Habrá estudiado matemáticas.**

Interpersonal Have students speculate about things that have happened at school. For example: **La profesora no estaba en clase. Habrá estado enferma.**

Teaching Resource Options

Print

Más práctica Workbook PE,
  pp. 105–108
Actividades para todos Workbook PE,
  pp. 121–126
Cuaderno para hispanohablantes
  PE, pp. 105–106
Block Scheduling Copymasters
Unit 4 Resource Book
  Más práctica Workbook TE,
    pp. 141–144
  Actividades para todos Workbook
    TE, pp. 149–154
  Cuaderno para hispanohablantes
    TE, pp. 159–160
  Information Gap Activities, p. 168
  Absent Student Copymasters, p. 176

Technology
Online Workbook, U4E3
Take-Home Tutor CD-ROM, U4E3

ACTIVIDAD 14 Objective: Transitional practice
Future perfect tense

Answers will vary.

ACTIVIDAD 15 Objective: Open-ended practice
Future perfect tense in conversation

Answers will vary.

Quick Wrap-up

Write the following list of expressions on the board or on an OHT. Have students write a sentence for each in which they use possessive pronouns in place of the expressions.

  mi informe
  tu carrera
  nuestra clase
  sus libros

Sentences will vary, but will include:
el mío, la tuya, la nuestra, los suyos

14 ¿Qué habrá pasado?

Hablar/*Escribir* Imagina qué habrá pasado en el mundo económico y profesional al final del día. Contesta las siguientes preguntas.

> **modelo**
>
> *¿Cómo se comunicaron?*
>
> *No sé. ¿Se habrán comunicado por Internet?*

1. ¿Qué pasó hoy con la bolsa de valores?
2. ¿Descubrieron algo los científicos?
3. ¿Cuántos boletos vendió el agente de viajes?
4. ¿Quién tradujo las conversaciones diplomáticas?
5. ¿Qué manejaron los banqueros?
6. ¿A quiénes ayudaron los trabajadores sociales?
7. ¿Qué inventaron en el laboratorio?
8. ¿Qué hicieron en la fábrica?
9. ¿Qué tradujo el traductor del periódico?
10. ¿Qué vendió la compañía multinacional?

15 El año 2025

Hablar/*Escribir* En grupos de tres o cuatro, hablen sobre el futuro. ¿Pueden imaginar cómo será la vida entonces? ¿Cómo será tu rutina diaria? ¿Cómo será tu familia? ¿Tu trabajo?

> **modelo**
>
> **Tú:** *Para el año 2025, habremos construido casas en el planeta Marte.*
>
> **Compañero(a) 1:** *No, yo no lo creo. Para el año 2025, habremos curado todas las enfermedades.*
>
> **Compañero(a) 2:** *No, yo no lo creo. Lo que yo creo es que para el año 2025, habrán inventado carros que pueden volar.*
>
> **Amigo(a) 3:** *No, yo no lo creo. Lo que yo creo es que para el año 2025…*

Nota cultural

En muchos países de Latinoamérica, la gente tiene una forma especial de ahorrar dinero. Van a una casa de cambio o a un banco y compran dólares estadounidenses. Cuando necesitan usar el dinero, cambian los dólares nuevamente.

312 trescientos doce
Unidad 4

Classroom Community

Game Have students play a game of charades in which the class has to guess what might have happened before. For example, a student acts out exhaustion until someone guesses: **Habrá corrido un maratón.**

Storytelling Working in pairs, have students write a short story about what someone they know will have done by the year 2025. Encourage them to use humor and imagination. Have students present their stories to the class, using appropriate gestures and props.

Todo en acción

Activity 16 brings together all concepts presented.

16 Los bosques

Leer/Escribir Lee la tabla sobre los bosques de Latinoamérica (Iberoamérica) y contesta las preguntas.

1. ¿Qué porcentaje de la tierra paraguaya está cubierta de bosques?

2. ¿Cuál es el área de tu país?

3. Tienes un amigo panameño. ¿Cuál es la tasa anual de cambio de su país?

4. ¿Cuántas especies de árboles tiene Paraguay que son comercialmente explotables? ¿Cuántas de ésas se exportan?

5. PNB quiere decir «Producto Nacional Bruto».¿Sabes cómo se dice eso en inglés?

Fuente de divisas

Un tercio de la tierra paraguaya es boscosa. Hasta 1959, la madera fue el principal producto de exportación del país, y aunque actualmente su contribución al PNB es pequeña, representa una fuente importante de divisas. Unas cuarenta y cinco especies de árboles de los bosques de Paraguay son comercialmente explotables y siete se exportan.

BOSQUES DE IBEROAMÉRICA

PAÍS	ÁREA (1000 Ha)	TASA ANUAL DE CAMBIO
Costa Rica	1,456	2.44
El Salvador	127	1.85
Guatemala	4,253	1.58
Honduras	4,608	1.94
México	48,695	1.21
Nicaragua	6,027	1.69
Panamá	3,123	1.70
Cuba	1,960	0.19
Rep. Dominicana	1,084	2.43
Argentina	34,436	0.57
Chile	8,033	0.07
Uruguay	813	0.12
Bolivia	49,345	1.12
Brasil	566,007	0.58
Colombia	54,190	0.62
Ecuador	12,007	1.65
Paraguay	12,868	2.38
Perú	68,090	0.37
Venezuela	45,943	1.13

More Practice: Más comunicación *p. R14*

 Online Workbook CLASSZONE.COM

Refrán

Promete poco y haz mucho.

¿Qué quiere decir el refrán? En tu opinión, ¿por qué es mejor decir poco y dejar que tus acciones muestren tus intenciones?

 «Prometo que lo hago más tarde.»

 «¡Gracias! ¡Qué sorpresa magnífica!»

Teaching All Students

Extra Help Have students take turns guessing what you did at certain times yesterday or earlier today. For example: **A mediodía habrás almorzado.**

Native Speakers Ask students to research the Cuban artist Wifredo Lam and present the information to the class.

Multiple Intelligences

Visual Have students sketch a scene from their past and have the class guess what it might have been. For example: **Habrá sido la celebración de su quinto cumpleaños.**

16 ACTIVIDAD Objective: Transitional practice Etapa review

Answers
1. Un tercio o treinta y tres por ciento.
2. *Answers will vary.*
3. 1.70%
4. 12.868
5. Gross National Product

Interdisciplinary Connections

Math Have students research: (a) the value of the currencies of the **Southern Cone** countries in U.S. dollars, and (b) the **PNB** (GNP) of each **Southern Cone** country.

Social Studies Have students create maps of the **Southern Cone** countries showing the location of the major industries.

Block Schedule

Change of Pace Have students write a description of the painting on p. 312. Then have them draw their own interpretation of a scene from a window. (For additional activities, see **Block Scheduling Copymasters.**)

Teaching Resource Options

Print 📖

Actividades para todos Workbook PE, pp. 127–129
Block Scheduling Copymasters
Unit 4 Resource Book
   Actividades para todos Workbook TE, pp. 155–157
   Absent Student Copymasters, p. 177
   Audioscript, pp. 113–114

Audiovisual 💻

OHT 42 (Quick Start)
Audio Program CD 12, Tracks 4–5

Technology 💻

Online Workbook, U4E3
Take-Home Tutor CD-ROM, U4E3

🔔 Quick Start Review

♻️ **Future perfect tense**

Use OHT 42 or write on the board:
Answer the following questions:

1. ¿Qué habrá hecho en diez años?
2. ¿Dónde habrá estudiado?
3. ¿Con qué compañeros(as) se habrá mantenido en contacto?
4. ¿Dónde habrá viajado?

Answers will vary.

Teaching Suggestions

• **Prereading** Have students look at the pictures on pp. 314–315. What clues do they give about the subject matter of the reading?

• **Strategy: Speculate about the author** Before reading the selection, discuss the questions in the Reading Strategy.

• **Reading** In order to focus students' reading, have them look at the ¿Comprendiste? questions first. Then have volunteers read each paragraph.

AUDIO 🎧

En voces
LECTURA

PARA LEER • STRATEGY: READING

Speculate about the author From your reading, what do you think was the age and professional status of Isabel Allende during her career? What other qualities does she reveal? Do you think it is better to read a piece of literature with or without knowledge about the author? Explain your answer.

EL TRABAJO

a cargo de tener responsabilidad por algo
asomar tras un vidrio verse por un cristal
el canal la compañía de televisión
el guión las palabras de un programa
las orejas una manera de decir "personas"
la pantalla por donde se ve la televisión
puntual a tiempo
el vacío donde no hay nadie

Sobre la autora

Isabel Allende, novelista chilena, nació en Lima, Perú, en 1942. Su familia tuvo que exiliarse de Chile cuando su tío Salvador Allende, el presidente del país, fue vencido por una junta militar en 1973. Isabel Allende empezó a escribir a la edad de diecisiete años y escribió su primera novela, *La casa de los espíritus*, en 1982. También ha trabajado como periodista y en la televisión.

Introducción

Allende comenzó a escribir su libro autobiográfico *Paula* mientras su hija estaba muy enferma. Es una historia que ofrece mucha información y varias anécdotas sobre la familia de Allende y sobre la historia y la política de Chile. En la selección que vas a leer, Allende le habla a su hija sobre su trabajo en Chile.

314 trescientos catorce
Unidad 4

Classroom Community

Learning Scenario Have students work in pairs to carry out an interview. One person plays the role of Isabel Allende and the other plays the role of a reporter from a local television station. The reporter interviews Allende about her life, her work, and her daughter.

Storytelling Have groups of students write the sentences of the reading on index cards, one sentence per card. Have them shuffle the cards and then try to put them back in order. Finally, have students retell the story in their own words, striving for two sentences per paragraph. Advanced students may add imagined details.

Paula

A comienzo de los años sesenta mi trabajo había progresado de las estadísticas forestales a unos tambaleantes inicios[1] en el periodismo, que me condujeron por casualidad a la televisión.

....

Fue así como terminé a cargo de un programa en el cual me tocaba hacer desde el guión hasta los dibujos de los créditos. El trabajo en el Canal consistía en llegar puntual, sentarme ante una luz roja y hablar al vacío; nunca tomé conciencia de que al otro lado de la luz un millón de orejas esperaban mis palabras y de ojos juzgaban mi peinado[2], de ahí mi sorpresa[3] cuando desconocidos[4] me saludaban por la calle. La primera vez que me viste aparecer en la pantalla, Paula, tenías un año y medio y el susto[5] de ver la cabeza decapitada de tu mamá asomando tras un vidrio, te dejó un buen rato[6] en estado catatónico… Me convertí en la persona más conspicua del barrio, los vecinos me saludaban con respeto y los niños me señalaban[7] con el dedo… (Michael y yo) conseguimos un par de becas[8], partimos a Europa y llegamos a Suiza contigo de la mano, tenías casi dos años y eras una mujer en miniatura.

---

[1] shaky beginning   [2] judged my hairdo   [3] surprise
[4] strangers   [5] shock, fright   [6] quite a while
[7] gestured to me   [8] scholarships

Online Workbook
CLASSZONE.COM

¿Comprendiste?

1. ¿En qué campos trabajaba Isabel Allende?
2. ¿En qué consistía su trabajo en la televisión?
3. ¿Por qué se fue la escritora de Chile?
4. ¿De qué se trata el libro *Paula*?

¿Qué piensas?

1. ¿Cómo se explica la reacción de Paula al ver a su madre en la televisión?
2. ¿Por qué crees que Isabel Allende comenzó a escribir su autobiografía en 1992 a la edad de 50 años?

Hazlo tú

¿Te parece interesante trabajar en la televisión? Si pudieras trabajar en la televisión, ¿qué harías — noticias, pronóstico del tiempo, telenovelas, o programas para niños? Explica tu preferencia.

Culture Highlights

● **ISABEL ALLENDE** Isabel Allende nació en Perú, mientras su padre, que era diplomático, trabajaba en ese país.

Ella empezó a escribir el libro *Paula*, mientras Paula, su hija, se encontraba en un estado de coma. Allende empezó a escribir el libro como una carta para informar a su hija de todo lo que ocurría mientras ella estaba inconsciente. La hija de Allende falleció.

Cross Cultural Connections

Strategy Have students research television stations in Spanish-speaking countries. Some have Web sites. What programs do they feature? Have students compare and contrast the stations with stations in the U.S.

¿Comprendiste?

Answers

1. Trabajaba en el periodismo y la televisión.
2. Consistía en llegar puntual, sentarse ante una luz roja y hablar al vacío.
3. Porque ella y su esposo consiguieron un par de becas.
4. Se trata de mucha información y varias anécdotas sobre la familia de Allende.

Teaching All Students

Extra Help Have students read sentences from the selection out loud. As each sentence is read, a volunteer either explains what it says in his/her own words or tries to act out its meaning.

Native Speakers Have students read additional passages from *Paula* and present the information to the class.

Multiple Intelligences

Verbal Have students imagine what little Paula was thinking when she first saw her mother on television. What would she have said?

Kinesthetic Have students recreate facial expressions that Paula may have used upon seeing her mother for the first time on TV. Have them vote on the best facial expression and discuss why they think it is the best one.

Block Schedule

Reference Lists Have students research the names and brief information about other Latin American writers. (For additional activities, see **Block Scheduling Copymasters**.)

Teaching Resource Options

Print

Block Scheduling Copymasters
Unit 4 Resource Book
  Absent Student Copymasters, p. 178

Audiovisual

OHT 42 (Quick Start)

Technology

 www.classzone.com

🔔 Quick Start Review

♻ Languages

Use OHT 42 or write on the board:
Write 2 countries where each of the
following languages is spoken:

1. francés   3. español
2. inglés   4. portugués

Answers
Answers will vary. Answers could include:
1. Francia, Canadá
2. Estados Unidos, Inglaterra
3. España, México
4. Portugal, Brasil

Teaching Suggestions
Presenting Cultura y comparaciones

- Have students read the Connecting
  Cultures Strategy and complete the
  chart.
- Expand the Quick Start Review by
  having students add other languages
  and countries.
- Have students read the passage to
  themselves, listing any words they
  don't know. Go over context clues to
  help them with any they still do not
  know.

Reading Strategy

Tell students to "activate associated
knowledge." In social studies classes, students
may have studied various cultures in Spain
and Latin America, such as the Basques,
the Mayas, the Incas, and the Aztecs. Have
them recall any information they remember
and keep this in mind as they read.

En colores
CULTURA Y
COMPARACIONES

México
NÁHUATL

Algunas
palabras del
náhuatl son:
aguacate
cacahuete
chocolate
nopal

Guatemala
El Salvador

Honduras
Nicaragua

PARA CONOCERNOS
STRATEGY: CONNECTING CULTURES
Observe how language reflects culture Each language reveals
the background of the people who speak it. For example,
arithmetic is derived from Latin and mathematics from
Greek. There is not one English language but several,
including Australian, Canadian, British, and American
versions. Think about these examples and conjecture what
events and experiences cause language to evolve. Organize
your ideas in a chart.

Cosas que cambian un idioma
1.
2.
3.

Which of your ideas are
represented in *Se hablan…
¡muchos idomas!*?

Se hablan... ¡muchos idiomas!

Galicia
GALLEGO

País Vasco
VASCUENCE

Cataluña
CATALÁN

ESPAÑA

El español o castellano es el idioma oficial de los
países hispanohablantes, pero también se hablan
otros idiomas. ¡A ver cuáles son!

España

El castellano, que también se conoce como
español, se originó en España. En el este de
España también se habla el **catalán** y en el
noroeste, el **gallego**. El **euskera**, o **vascuence**, se
habla en el País Vasco desde antes que llegaran
los romanos a España en 202 antes de Cristo[1].

---
[1] before the Christian era

316   trescientos dieciséis
Unidad 4

Classroom Community

Group Activity Have students research the groups
of people who spoke/speak the Latin American
languages mentioned in the reading. Students should
divide up the task into research topics, such as
agriculture, the family unit, etc. Have students prepare
verbal and visual presentations.

Portfolio Have students research and write 2
paragraphs on 1 of the 17 autonomous communities in
Spain. They should include information about the
languages spoken and what distinguishes the community.

Rubric A = 13–15 pts. B = 10–12 pts. C = 7–9 pts. D = 4–6 pts. F = < 4 pts.

Writing criteria	Scale
Grammar/spelling accuracy	1 2 3 4 5
Logical organization	1 2 3 4 5
Clear, accurate details	1 2 3 4 5

TAÍNO

Mar Caribe

Costa Rica
Panamá

Venezuela

Colombia

Ecuador

Río Amazonas

Perú

Brasil

QUECHUA

Bolivia

Paraguay

Río de la Plata

Uruguay

Chile

Argentina

Océano Pacífico

Océano Atlántico

Algunas palabras del taíno son:
canoa
hamaca
huracán
maíz
tiburón

Algunas palabras del quechua son:
cóndor
llama
pampa
papa

Latinoamérica

Huracán, chocolate, pampa: son palabras que nos hablan de la historia y el presente de Latinoamérica. En el mapa, puedes ver éstas y otras palabras que pasaron al español del **taíno**, **náhuatl** y **quechua**, algunos de los idiomas que hablaban los habitantes de América al llegar los españoles. Algunos de estos idiomas todavía se hablan en Latinomérica.

El taíno era el idioma de los indígenas [2] del Caribe, también llamados taínos. En México y en Centroamérica los aztecas hablaban el náhuatl y los mayas el **maya-quiché**. El **miskito** se hablaba en Nicaragua. En la capital del Imperio Inca en Cuzco, Perú, se usaba el quechua.

El náhuatl, el maya-quiché y el quechua todavía se hablan hoy en día en México, Guatemala y Perú respectivamente. El país donde mejor se ha conservado un idioma indígena es el Paraguay, donde el **guaraní** es tan oficial como el español.

---

[2] indigenous, indigenous peoples

CLASSZONE.COM
More About the Southern Cone

¿Comprendiste?

1. ¿Qué otros idiomas se hablan en España?
2. ¿Qué idiomas indígenas se hablaban en las Américas al llegar los españoles? ¿Cuáles se hablan todavía?
3. Da ejemplos de diez palabras indígenas. Menciona el idioma del cual viene cada palabra.

¿Qué piensas?

Observa las palabras que pasaron al español. ¿Qué categorías hay? ¿En qué situaciones crees que los españoles aprendieron estas palabras?

Hazlo tú

Busca palabras de origen español en inglés. ¿Por qué crees que tenemos estas palabras?

trescientos diecisiete
El Cono Sur Etapa 3 | **317**

Culture Highlights

● **INFLUENCIA ÁRABE EN ESPAÑA**
Los árabes vivieron en España por ocho siglos, concentrándose principalmente en el sur. Muchas palabras árabes pasaron al castellano como resultado de esto; por ejemplo: **almirante, arsenal, alcalde, almacén, aduana, quilate, quintal, espinaca, albaricoque, café**.

¿Con qué cosas se relacionan estas palabras? Pida a los estudiantes que las coloquen en categorías. ¿Qué nos dicen sobre la influencia árabe en la vida diaria de España? ¿Pueden reconocer palabras árabes que han pasado al inglés?

Interdisciplinary Connection

English Have students look up various words at random in an English dictionary to find out their origins. Can they find any words of Spanish origin? List these on the board.

¿Comprendiste?

Answers
1. el catalán, el gallego, el euskera o vascuence
2. El taíno, el náhuatl, el quechua, el maya-quiché, el miskito y el guaraní se hablaban al llegar los españoles. El náhuatl, el maya-quiché, el quechua y el guaraní se hablan todavía.
3. *Answers will vary, but may include:*
   del náhuatl: aguacate, cacahuete, chocolate, nopal
   del taíno: canoa, hamaca, huracán, maíz, tiburón
   del quechua: cóndor, llama, pampa, papa

Block Schedule

Variety Have students make illustrated mini-dictionaries with the words from the indigenous languages. They should include a description in Spanish as well as an illustration of each item. Students may want to research other words to add to their dictionaries. (For additional activities, see **Block Scheduling Copymasters**.)

Teaching All Students

Native Speakers Have students find more words in **náhuatl, maya-quiché,** and **quechua** that have become part of the Spanish language.

Multiple Intelligences

Visual Have students create maps of the U.S. that show areas of the country where languages other than English are spoken.

Verbal Have students find Internet Web sites in **catalán, gallego,** and **euskera.** Do they recognize any of the words? How do these languages compare to **castellano**?

Teaching Resource Options

Print

Cuaderno para hispanohablantes PE,
pp. 111–112

Unit 4 Resource Book
Cuaderno para hispanohablantes
TE, pp. 161–162
Information Gap Activities,
pp. 169–170
Family Involvement, pp. 179–180

Audiovisual

OHT 42 (Quick Start)

Technology

eTest Plus Online/Test Generator
CD-ROM

 www.classzone.com

Quick Start Review

♻ Possessive pronouns

Use OHT 42 or write on the board:
Answer the following questions:

Modelo: ¿Es tu mochila? (no, de él)
No, no es mía. Es suya.

1. ¿Es mi carro? (no, de ellos)
2. ¿Son mis libros? (no, de ella)
3. ¿Es el libro de Ana? (no, de
   nosotros)
4. ¿Es la casa de los Sres. Gómez?
   (no, de mí)
5. ¿Son las plumas de Roberto? (no,
   de ti)

Answers
1. No, no es tuyo. Es suyo.
2. No, no son tuyos. Son suyos.
3. No, no es suyo. Es nuestro.
4. No, no es suya. Es mía.
5. No, no son suyas. Son tuyas.

Teaching Suggestions
What Have Students Learned?

Have students look at the "Now you can…" notes listed on the left side of pages 318–319. Remind them to review the material in the "To review" notes before doing the activities or taking the test.

ETAPA 3

Now you can...

• discuss Latin
American economics.

Now you can...

• avoid redundancy.

To review

• subject and stressed
object pronouns
see p. 306.

En uso
REPASO Y MÁS COMUNICACIÓN

OBJECTIVES

• Learn about Latin American economics
• Clarify possession
• Express possession
• Express past probability

1 La población

Estás creando una encuesta para buscar unas estadísticas demográficas. Primero escribe preguntas y luego contéstalas con la información indicada.

modelo

porcentaje de la población (¿habla español?): $\frac{1}{5}$

Compañero(a): ¿Qué porcentaje de la población habla español?

Tú: Un quinto de la población habla español.

1. porcentaje de la población (¿de habla hispana?): $\frac{1}{3}$
2. edad promedio: 25
3. porcentaje de la población (¿vivir en la ciudad?): 50%
4. porcentaje de la población (¿vivir en el campo?): 50%
5. parte de la población (¿graduarse de la universidad?): la mayoría
6. parte de la población (¿trabajar en la ganadería?): la menor parte

2 ¿Él o ella?

Conoces a varias parejas que trabajan en industrias diferentes. Di en qué trabaja él y en qué trabaja ella.

modelo

Los Sres. Mendoza: una compañía multinacional de turismo / una compañía multinacional de petróleo

Él trabaja en una compañía multinacional que se dedica al turismo. Ella trabaja en una compañía multinacional de petróleo.

1. Los Sres. Moré: un laboratorio / una agencia de viajes para ejecutivos
2. Los Sres. Valdés: una fábrica de textiles / una compañía de telecomunicaciones
3. Los Sres. Puente: una compañía de exportaciones / un banco
4. Los Sres. Colón: un taller de artesanías / la bolsa de valores
5. Los Sres. Prado: un laboratorio/ una refinería de petróleo

---

Classroom Community

Paired Activity Have students work in pairs. One student points to an object and says it is his/hers. The other student contradicts him/her and says to whom the object belongs. For example: **Este cuaderno es mío.** → **No, no es tuyo. Es de Inés. Es el suyo.**

Group Activity Have students work in groups of 3–4 to create an international company. They should invent a company name and design a logo, a business card, and a poster promoting the company and the jobs it has to offer. Display students' work in class.

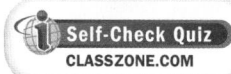

Self-Check Quiz
CLASSZONE.COM

Now you can...
- express possession.
- clarify possession.

To review
- possessive pronouns see p. 308.

3 **¡No!**

Estás en una fiesta y ahora tú y tus amigos se están despidiendo de la anfitriona. Ella trata de devolverte cosas que no son tuyas. También trata de devolverles cosas a tus amigos que no son suyas. ¿Cómo le respondes?

modelo

tu paraguas: *negro*

Anfitriona: *Ten, aquí está tu paraguas.*

Tú: *No, ése no. El mío es negro.*

1. tu abrigo: azul
2. la mochila de Hernán: verde
3. la bolsa de Mariluz: amarilla
4. el sombrero de Juan: rojo
5. los platos de Minerva: nuevos
6. los zapatos de tenis de Arnoldo: viejo
7. tu chaqueta: de cuero

Now you can...
- express past probability.

To review
- the future perfect see p. 310.

4 **Para ese entonces**

Tu abuelo(a) está pensando en el futuro de su familia. ¿Qué cree que va a pasar en veinte años? Sigue el modelo.

modelo

(tú) comprar una casa

Para ese entonces, habrás comprado una casa.

1. (nosotros) viajar a Argentina
2. (tú) empezar tu carrera en la industria del petróleo
3. (Enrique y Elena) casarse
4. (Anilú) graduarse de la universidad
5. (Rudi y Luisa) empezar una familia
6. (Felipe) hacerse banquero
7. (ustedes) ahorrar mucho dinero
8. (tú) realizar tus sueños

trescientos diecinueve
El Cono Sur Etapa 3

319

ACTIVIDAD 1 Answers

1. A: ¿Qué porcentaje de la población es de habla hispana? / B: Un tercio de la población...
2. A: ¿Cuál es la edad promedio? / B: La edad promedio es veinticinco.
3. A: ¿Qué porcentaje de la población vive en la ciudad? / B: Cincuenta por ciento de la población...
4. A: ¿Qué porcentaje de la población vive en el campo? / B: Cincuenta por ciento de la población...
5. A: ¿Cuál parte de la población se graduó de la universidad? / B: La mayoría de la población...
6. A: ¿Cuál parte de la población trabaja en la industria ganadera? / B: La menor parte de la población...

ACTIVIDAD 2 Answers

1. Él trabaja en un laboratorio. Ella trabaja en una agencia de viajes para ejecutivos.
2. Él trabaja en una fábrica de textiles. Ella trabaja en una compañía de telecomunicaciones.
3. Él trabaja en una compañía de exportaciones. Ella trabaja en un banco.
4. Él trabaja en un taller de artesanías. Ella trabaja en la bolsa de valores.
5. Él trabaja en un laboratorio. Ella trabaja en una refinería de petróleo.

ACTIVIDAD 3 Answers

1. No, ése no. El mío es azul.
2. No, ésa no. La suya es verde.
3. No, ésa no. La suya es amarilla.
4. No, ése no. El suyo es rojo.
5. No, ésos no. Los suyos son nuevos.
6. No, ésos no. Los suyos son viejos.
7. No, ésa no. La mía es de cuero.

ACTIVIDAD 4 Answers

1. Para ese entonces, habremos viajado...
2. Para ese entonces, habrás empezado...
3. Para ese entonces, se habrán casado.
4. Para ese entonces, se habrá graduado...
5. Para ese entonces, habrán empezado...
6. Para ese entonces, se habrá hecho banquero.
7. Para ese entonces, habrán ahorrado...
8. Para ese entonces, habrás realizado...

Block Schedule

Variety Have students work in groups to create surveys within the classroom (e.g., **color de ojos, animales/músicos favoritos**). Have them illustrate their findings with charts/graphs and present them using number words. (For additional activities, see **Block Scheduling Copymasters**.)

Teaching All Students

Extra Help Use students and the classroom to model use of pronouns to emphasize and clarify. For example: **Yo llevo zapatos negros, pero tú no. Tú llevas zapatos blancos.** Encourage students to follow your model.

Multiple Intelligences

Logical/Mathematical Have students illustrate the numeric values in **Actividad 1** with pie charts or bar graphs.

Intrapersonal Have students expand **Actividad 4** by writing similar sentences about their family or close friends.

Teaching Resource Options

Print

Unit 4 Resource Book
Audioscript, p. 183–184
Vocabulary Quizzes, pp. 186–188
Grammar Quizzes, pp. 189–190
Etapa Exam, Forms A and B,
  pp. 191–200
Examen para hispanohablantes,
  pp. 201–205
Portfolio Assessment, pp. 206–207
Unit 4 Comprehensive Test,
  pp. 210–217
Prueba comprensiva para
hispanohablantes, Unit 4,
  pp. 218–225
Multiple Choice Test Questions,
  pp. 232–234

Audiovisual

OHT 43 (Quick Start)
Audio Program Cassette 20 / CD 20

Technology

eTest Plus Online/Test Generator
CD-ROM
 www.classzone.com

 **and**

Rubric: Speaking

Criteria	Scale	
Sentence structure	1 2 3	A = 11–12 pts.
Vocabulary use	1 2 3	B = 9–10 pts.
Originality	1 2 3	C = 7–8 pts.
Fluency	1 2 3	D = 4–6 pts.
		F = < 4 pts.

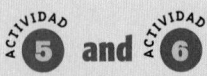 **En tu propia voz**

Rubric: Writing

Criteria	Scale	
Vocabulary use	1 2 3 4 5	A = 14–15 pts.
Accuracy	1 2 3 4 5	B = 12–13 pts.
Creativity, appearance	1 2 3 4 5	C = 10–11 pts.
		D = 8–9 pts.
		F = < 8 pts.

Teaching Note: En tu propia voz

Writing Strategy Suggest that students organize information by category. They should first brainstorm a list of information, then organize it.

---

5 ¿Dónde está Gerardo?

> **STRATEGY: SPEAKING**
>
> **Speculate about the past** When the unexpected occurs, it is natural to express opinions about what may have happened. Your conjecture about Gerardo's absence can be humorous, pleasant, logical or illogical: **¿Por qué no vino Gerardo? Se habrá perdido en el parque zoológico**. Be inventive!

Hablar/*Escribir* Gerardo prometió que iba a venir a la reunión del consejo estudiantil. ¡Pero no llegó! Todos tienen ideas de por qué no vino. Dramaticen esta situación.

modelo

Tú: *¿Pero dónde está Gerardo? Dijo que iba a venir.*

Compañero(a) 1: *Se le habrá olvidado.*

Compañero(a) 2: *Se habrá acostado muy tarde y no se despertó a tiempo.*

Compañero(a) 3: *No, no es eso. Yo creo que…*

---

6 El mío es de...

En grupos de dos o tres, conversen sobre las cosas que tengan y de qué tienda son.

modelo

Tú: *Yo compré mi chaqueta de piel en Ropafina.*

Compañero(a) 1: *¿Ah, sí? La mía es de Ropafina también.*

Compañero(a) 2: *Yo no tengo una chaqueta de piel, pero mi collar de oro es de la tienda en la plaza.*

Tú: *El mío es de la misma tienda.*

---

7 *En tu propia voz*

ESCRITURA Escribe un informe sobre el perfil económico de tu estado. Destaca el producto de más importancia. Las siguientes categorías pueden ayudarte a comenzar. Si quieres, incluye fotos en tu informe.

Mi estado:	El petróleo:
Capital:	Los productos forestales:
Unidad monetaria:	La minería:
Perfil económico:	El turismo:
Productos de exportación:	La industria pesquera:
La agricultura:	Las telecomunicaciones:
La ganadería:	Los textiles:

CONEXIONES

Los estudios sociales ¿Qué sabes de la ONU (Organización de las Naciones Unidas)? ¿Has oído alguna vez de la OEA (Organización de los Estados Americanos)? ¿Cuál es el propósito de estas dos organizaciones internacionales? ¿Quiénes son los miembros? Busca la información por Internet o en la biblioteca y escribe un reporte. Comparte tu reporte con la clase.

320 trescientos veinte
Unidad 4

Classroom Community

Portfolio Have students write poems for professions they have learned. The first line should be a sentence about an activity; the second, 2 adjectives; the third, 3 gerunds; the fourth, identify the subject. For example:

> Vende los textiles.
> Amable, hablador.
> Buscando, viajando, vendiendo.
> Un agente de ventas.

Students should illustrate their work as well.

Rubric A = 13-15 pts. B = 10-12 pts. C = 7-9 pts. D = 4-6 pts. F = < 4 pts.

Writing criteria	Scale
Grammar/spelling accuracy	1 2 3 4 5
Correct poem form	1 2 3 4 5
Creativity/appearance	1 2 3 4 5

En resumen
REPASO DE VOCABULARIO

LEARN ABOUT LATIN AMERICAN ECONOMICS

Careers in Spanish

el (la) **académico(a)**	academic
el (la) **agente de ventas**	sales agent
el (la) **banquero(a)**	banker
el (la) **bibliotecario(a)**	librarian
el (la) **corresponsal**	correspondent
el (la) **diplomático(a)**	diplomat
el (la) **financiero(a)**	financial expert
el (la) **intérprete**	interpreter
el (la) **trabajador(a) social**	social worker
el (la) **traductor(a)**	translator

Industries

la **agricultura**	agriculture
los **cereales**	grains
el **cobre**	copper
la **exportación**	export
exportar	to export
la **ganadería**	livestock industry
el **ganado**	livestock
el **hierro**	iron
la **importación**	import
la **industria**	industry
la **industria pesquera**	fishing industry
el **maíz**	corn
la **minería**	mining
el **perfil económico**	economic profile
el **petróleo**	petroleum
principal	principal
los **productos forestales**	forestry products
la **refinería**	refinery
las **telecomunicaciones**	telecommunications
los **textiles**	textiles
el **trigo**	wheat
el **turismo**	tourism
la **unidad monetaria**	currency

Statistics

comparar	to compare
las **estadísticas**	statistics
mil millones	billion
un **millón de millones**	trillion
la **mitad de**	one half of
por ciento	percent
el **porcentaje**	percentage
el **promedio**	average
el **quinto**	one fifth
sumar	to add
el **tercio**	one third

 Ya sabes

un **cuarto**	one fourth
un **décimo**	one tenth
la **mayoría**	majority
medio(a)	half

Types of companies

la **bolsa de valores**	stock exchange
la **fábrica**	factory
el **laboratorio**	laboratory
multinacional	multinational
la **sociedad anónima (S.A.)**	corporation (Inc.)

AVOID REDUNDANCY

 Ya sabes

a mí	to me
a ti	to you
yo	I
tú	you (fam.)
usted	you (for.)
él	he
ella	she
nosotros(as)	we
vosotros(as)	you (fam. pl.)
ustedes	you (for. pl.)
ellos	they
ellas	they (fem.)

EXPRESS POSSESSION

 Ya sabes

mi/mío(a)	my/mine
tu/tuyo(a)	your (fam.)/yours (fam.)
su/suyo(a)	your (for.), his, her/ yours (for.), his, hers, its
nuestro(a)	our/ours
vuestro(a)	your (pl. fam.)/yours (pl. fam.)
su/suyo(a)	your (pl.), their/ yours (pl.), theirs

EXPRESS PAST PROBABILITY

The future perfect tense

No sé dónde está Élmer. Fue a la oficina. **Habrá encontrado** más trabajo allí.

Juego

¿Cuál es tu profesión?

¿Puedes encontrar en el dibujo dos profesiones cuyos nombres empiecen con la letra **a**?

trescientos veintiuno
El Cono Sur Etapa 3   **321**

Interdisciplinary Connection

Social Studies Ask students to research the U.N. agency UNESCO, and find out what this organization does in Latin American countries.

Quick Start Review

🔄 Vocabulary review

Use OHT 43 or write on the board: Match the words in the 2 columns:

1.	bibliotecario(a)	a.	política
2.	traductor(a)	b.	libros
3.	banquero(a)	c.	universidad
4.	diplomático(a)	d.	idiomas
5.	académico(a)	e.	dinero

Answers
1. b   2. d   3. e   4. a   5. c

Teaching Suggestions
Vocabulary Review

Have students choose 3 related words (**maíz, trigo, cereales**). Have them scramble each word, then exchange papers with a partner. Students must unscramble each other's words, then guess the relationship (**agricultura**).

Dictation

Dictate the following sentences to review the **Etapa**:

1. Mi anillo es de Chile y el tuyo es de Argentina.
2. A las siete, nosotros ya habremos comido.
3. ¿Cómo se gana la vida tu madre? Ella es financiera.
4. Esa compañía se dedica a la ganadería.

Juego

Answers: académico, agente de ventas

Block Schedule

Change of Pace Have students find travel brochures about Argentina, Chile, Uruguay, and Paraguay and present them to the class. They should point out what interests them as well as what students in the class might be interested in.

Teaching All Students

Extra Help Have students study the **Repaso de vocabulario** for 2 minutes, then close their books. Write the headings and subheadings of each section on the board. Call out words from the lists at random. Have students go to the board and write the word/expression under the appropriate heading.

Challenge Have students research a corporation from one of the **Southern Cone** countries. They should find out what kind of industry it is and statistics about it.

Multiple Intelligences

Visual Have students create posters promoting career connections to language study.

Teaching Resource Options

Print
Block Scheduling Copymasters

Audiovisual
OHT GO1–GO5; 43 (Quick Start)

Technology
🌐 www.classzone.com

🔔 Quick Start Review

♻ **Past perfect subjunctive**

Use OHT 43 or write on the board:
Write sentences using the following
verbs to say that you wish things had
happened differently:

Modelo: ir
Ojalá que hubiera ido a la fiesta.

1. ver
2. estudiar
3. escribir
4. aprender
5. escuchar

Answers will vary.

Teaching Strategy
Prewriting

- Lead students in brainstorming a list
  of professions. Then have each
  student choose a profession for the
  assignment.
- Have partners discuss the qualifications
  for the professions they picked, then
  fill out their cause and effect charts.
- Review the function, context, content,
  text type, and structure with the class.
  Be sure students are clear about these
  elements of the assignment.

Post-writing

- Have group members help each
  other clarify the cause and effect
  relationship between the qualifications
  and the ability to do the job.
- Encourage students to use the
  proofreading marks they have learned.

UNIDAD 4

En tu propia voz ✍
ESCRITURA

Una carrera: ¿Dónde empezar?

Una empresa local busca internos para su programa de
entrenamiento. El conocimiento del español es esencial y también
una familiaridad con administración de empresas, economía,
humanidades o matemáticas. Tu carta adjunta (*cover letter*) debe
resumir tus experiencias escolares.

Función: Describirse a sí mismo
Contexto: Informar al Jefe de
personal

Contenido: Relación entre tu educación,
experiencia y habilidad
Tipo de texto: Carta adjunta

PARA ESCRIBIR • STRATEGY: WRITING

Use cause and effect to demonstrate ability A good cover letter highlights
the relationship between your education and experiences (cause) and
your ability to do the job (effect). You must impress the potential
employer and show that you can handle the position by applying
your knowledge to the work.

Modelo del estudiante

> A salutation in a business
> letter is formal, using
> **Estimado(a)** and the person's
> title, and ending with a colon.

> The phrase **por eso** indicates the
> connection between the writer's
> coursework and her ability to
> contribute to the company.

> The expression **así que** points
> out the relationship between the
> writer's previous experience and
> her understanding of the needs
> for the current position.

Estimado Licenciado Ramírez:
   El motivo de la presente es solicitar el puesto de interno en su compañía.
Actualmente estoy tomando cursos en mercadeo y economía en mi escuela
secundaria. También estoy estudiando español y pienso participar en un programa
de estudios en el extranjero el año que viene. Tengo buenas notas en estos cursos
y por eso creo que tengo la educación y las habilidades necesarias para contribuir
al éxito de su distinguida compañía.
   El verano pasado trabajé en el departamento de ventas y mercadeo de una
compañía multinacional. Estaba trabajando directamente con el gerente del
departamento, así que entiendo bien las responsabilidades de un interno
internacional. El gerente me escribió una carta de recomendación diciendo
que siempre desempeñé todos mis cargos de una manera excelente.
   Adjunto mi currículum vitae. Espero que me encuentre bien capacitada
para servirle.

Atentamente,
Karen Willis
Karen Willis

> Typical closings to business
> letters include **Atentamente** and
> **Le saluda muy atentamente.**

322 trescientos veintidós
Unidad 4

Classroom Community

Group Activity Have students work in groups of
3–4. At the end of the prewriting step, have them read
the qualifications from their charts to their fellow group
members. The others must guess what type of job is
being described.

Paired Activity Have pairs role-play interviews of
invented ideal candidates by "internship supervisors."
The "supervisors" should ask questions based on the
cover letters of the "candidates."

Portfolio Have students save their letters for their
portfolios. Subsequent writing projects will show their
progress in Spanish.

Estrategias para escribir

Antes de escribir...

Piensa en las calificaciones que necesita un(a) candidato(a) para un trabajo que conoces. Considera la educación, experiencia y las habilidades que se requieren. Inventa un(a) candidato(a) perfecto(a) y crea su perfil. Crea una tabla como la de la derecha para analizar la calificación del (de la) candidato(a).

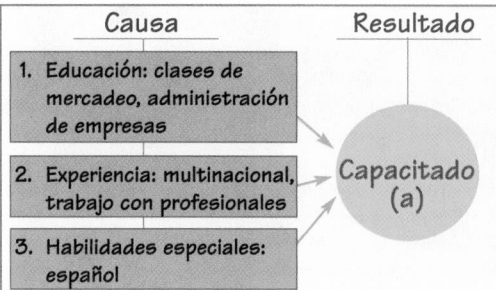

Causa	Resultado
1. Educación: clases de mercadeo, administración de empresas	
2. Experiencia: multinacional, trabajo con profesionales	Capacitado (a)
3. Habilidades especiales: español	

Revisiones

Después de escribir el primer borrador de la carta adjunta, trabajen en grupos de cuatro para intercambiar las cartas y leerlas en voz alta. Decidan qué aspectos de cada carta son más efectivos. Revisen cada carta en grupo para incorporar las técnicas más eficientes y convincentes.

- *¿Qué expresiones usaron para demostrar la conexión entre las calificaciones y la capacidad de hacer el trabajo?*
- *¿Qué datos mencionaron para indicar lo que ha hecho el (la) candidato(a) y lo que está haciendo para desarrollar sus habilidades?*

La versión final

Para completar tu carta, léela de nuevo y repasa los siguientes puntos:

- *¿Usé bien el **presente continuo** (present progressive) o el **presente perfecto** (present perfect)?*

Haz lo siguiente: Subraya los verbos en estos tiempos. ¿Usaste la forma correcta de **estar**? ¿Del presente participio?

- *¿Usé bien el **potencial compuesto** (conditional perfect) o el **pluscuamperfecto de subjuntivo** (past perfect subjunctive)?*

Haz lo siguiente: Repasa las conjugaciones de **haber** en estos tiempos. Haz un círculo alrededor de estos verbos. ¿Está conjugado correctamente **haber** y está seguido por un participio pasado correcto?

> Sr. Gerente:
>
> Le escribo para solicitar un puesto de trabajo en su compañía editorial. Acabo de terminar mis estudios de periodismo y quisiera trabajar para usted. Además, estoy tomando clases de francés e italiano. Habría estudiando alemán si no habría tenido que viajar a Europa a hacer una entrevista. He trabajado en algunos periódicos y revistas y quisiera tener una entrevista con usted para ofrecerle mis servicios.

Let students know ahead of time which elements of their writing you will be evaluating. A global evaluation is more helpful to students than a correction of every mistake made. Consider the following in scoring compositions:

Sentences	
1	Most not logical
2	Somewhat logical
3	In logical order
4	Logical with some flow
5	Flow purposefully

Details	
1	Few details
2	Some basic details
3	Sufficient basic details
4	Substantial details
5	Clear and vivid detail

Organization	
1	Very little organization
2	Poorly organized
3	Some organization
4	Sufficiently organized
5	Strong organization

Accuracy	
1	Errors prevent comprehension
2	Comprehensible, yet many errors
3	Some spelling and agreement errors throughout
4	A few errors
5	Very few errors

Criteria	Scale	
Logical sentence order	1 2 3 4 5	A = 17–20 pts.
Clear and vivid detail	1 2 3 4 5	B = 13–16 pts.
Organization	1 2 3 4 5	C = 9–12 pts.
Accuracy	1 2 3 4 5	D = 5–8 pts.
		F = < 5 pts.

Teaching All Students

Extra Help Review structures with students before writing:
- Present progressive
- Past progressive
- Conditional perfect
- Past perfect subjunctive

Challenge Have students write specific internship announcements to accompany their cover letters. They should include education and experience requirements as well as the duties of the intern.

Block Schedule

Variety Have pairs of students discuss what their ideal internships might be. What abilities do they have that would make them good candidates? (For additional activities, see **Block Scheduling Copymasters**.)

Unit Theme
Discussing the arts (fine arts, crafts, architecture, music, dance, literature, film) in Spain and the Americas

Teaching Resource Options

Print

Block Scheduling Copymasters
Unit 5 Resource Book
  Absent Student Copymasters, p. 33

Audiovisual

OHT M5; 1–3
Canciones CD
Video Program Videotape 39:00 / DVD, Unit 5

Technology

eEdition Plus Online/eEdition CD-ROM
Easy Planner Plus Online/Easy Planner CD-ROM

 www.classzone.com

U N I D A D 5

STANDARDS

Communication
• Discussing and describing art forms and crafts
• Identifying and specifying
• Requesting clarification
• Expressing relationships
• Referring to people and objects
• Making generalizations
• Talking about literature
• Talking about film
• Avoiding redundancy

Cultures
• Art forms in Spain and the Americas
• Well-known authors, artists, architects, and filmmakers from Spain and the Americas
• Pre-Columbian civilizations

Connections
• Social Studies: Creating a time line
• Mathematics: Investigating a mathematical system

Comparisons
• Spanish-speaking authors
• Architecture in Mexico and in the U.S.
• Spanish-language movies and English-language movies

Communities
• Using Spanish in the workplace
• Using Spanish with family and friends

INTERNET Preview
CLASSZONE.COM
• More About Spain and the Americas
• Webquest
• Self-Check Quizzes
• Flashcards
• Writing Center
• Online Workbook
• eEdition Plus Online

324

ARTES EN ESPAÑA Y LAS AMÉRICAS

Océano Atlántico
ESPAÑA
MÉXICO
CUBA
REPÚBLICA DOMINICANA
PUERTO RICO
GUATEMALA HONDURAS
EL SALVADOR NICARAGUA
COSTA RICA PANAMÁ
VENEZUELA
CANARY ISLANDS
COLOMBIA
ECUADOR
PERÚ
BOLIVIA
Océano Pacífico
PARAGUAY
CHILE
URUGUAY
ARGENTINA

ESPAÑA Y LATINOAMÉRICA
CHOCOLATE Y CHURROS
¿Por qué crees que esta combinación es tan popular en el mundo hispanohablante? ¡Muestra la mezcla de sabores entre España y Latinoamérica!

Classroom Community

Paired Activity Divide the class into pairs. Give students a time limit of 5 minutes to discuss what art they have seen in their textbooks up to now. Then have them write a short list of things they would expect to see/experience in relation to arts in Spain and the Americas. They should check off those things that they already know something about.

Learning Scenario Have students imagine they are television reporters for a children's news magazine. Ask them to give a "capsule" report in their own words on one aspect of the information presented on pp. 324–325. Reports should be no longer than one minute.

ALMANAQUE CULTURAL

POBLACIÓN DE ESPAÑA: 40.037.995

ALTURA: 3718 m sobre el nivel del mar (Pico del Teide, Islas Canarias)

TEMPERATURA: 66°F (20°C) Sevilla (temp. promedio más alta); 57°F (25°C) Madrid (temp. promedio más baja)

COMIDA TÍPICA: paella, zarzuela de mariscos, tortilla española, cochinillo

GENTE FAMOSA: Julio Iglesias (cantante), Andrés Segovia (músico), Pablo Casals (músico), Sus Majestades Juan Carlos y Sofía (rey y reina), Adolfo Domínguez (diseñador)

VIDEO   DVD Mira el video para más información.

 CLASSZONE.COM
More About Spain and the Americas

ESPAÑA
LA REINA ISABEL
(1451–1504) fue la esposa de Fernando V. Apoyó el viaje de Cristóbal Colón. ¿Qué argumentos crees que utilizó Colón para convencerla de que apoyara su viaje?

ARGENTINA
TEATRO COLÓN Ecléctico, histórico y super elegante: el Teatro Colón en Buenos Aires impresiona por la calidad de los espectáculos que se han presentado allí desde que se construyó en el siglo XIX. ¿Qué te sugieren los detalles del edificio sobre el intercambio de la cultura europea y latinoamericana?

COLOMBIA
FERNANDO BOTERO
Nació en 1932 en Medellín, Colombia y tal vez sea el artista latinoamericano de más fama internacional. Sorprende cómo utiliza la proporción de las cosas. Al observar la imagen, ¿qué ideas crees que impulsaron los cambios de forma que ves en la pintura?

ESPAÑA
SALVADOR DALÍ
Junto a Pablo Picasso y Joan Miró, Dalí es uno de los artistas españoles más importantes del siglo XX. Es uno de los mayores exponentes del surrealismo. Observa la pintura. ¿Qué crees que la hace surrealista?

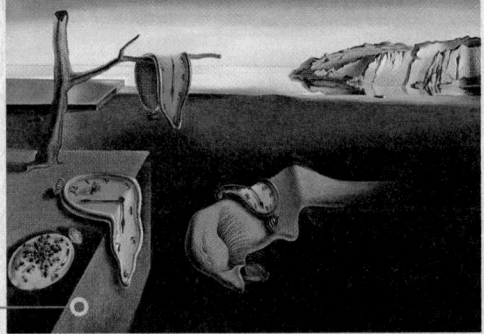

Salvador Dalí, *La persistencia de la memoria,* (1931)

325

Teaching All Students

Extra Help Ask students to reread all the culture notes, jotting down any words they don't understand. Then have students work in pairs to guess the meanings.

Multiple Intelligences

Musical/Rhythmic Have students research Gregorian chants to find out whom they are named after, what they represent, and the styles of Gregorian Chants (**accentus** and **concentus**). Play examples of Gregorian Chants for students to describe the melody.

Teaching Suggestion
Previewing the Unit
Tell students that this unit centers on the arts in Spain and the Americas. Ask students to scan these pages for 15 seconds, then close their books. Have them tell you what they remember. The cultural video is available for expansion.

Culture Highlights

● **FERNANDO BOTERO** El arte de Fernando Botero se caracteriza por su uso de figuras redondas e infladas, y pinceladas (*brushstrokes*) casi invisibles. Las figuras son casi siempre humanas. Botero cambia las proporciones de las figuras de acuerdo a su estilo humorístico y exagerado.

● **CHOCOLATE Y CHURROS** Los churros, una de las comidas más populares en España, están hechos de masa (*batter*) de harina. La masa se echa en unas máquinas que la fríen y le dan su forma espiral. Los churros se acompañan de chocolate caliente o café y generalmente se comen en el desayuno.

● **TEATRO COLÓN** El Teatro Colón en Buenos Aires es un escenario reconocido mundialmente para ballet, ópera y música clásica. El edificio de siete pisos ocupa una cuadra entera y tiene 2.500 asientos. Otras mil personas pueden mirar los espectáculos de pie.

● **SALVADOR DALÍ** Los cuadros de Salvador Dalí (1904–1989) se caracterizan por sus detalles meticulosos. Dalí utilizó barnices (*glazes*) para intensificar la calidad de los colores que utilizaba. La pinturas del período surrealista de Dalí muestran sueños (*dreams*) y objetos comunes con formas extrañas.

Block Schedule

Change of Pace Have students study the paintings of either Botero or Dalí, then discuss each painter's style. What makes it unique? What colors are used? How is light used? After the discussion, have students draw a picture imitating either artist's style. (For additional activities, see **Block Scheduling Copymasters**.)

Standards for Foreign Language Learning

The Comparisons standard is the focus for this unit.

Comparisons

Standard 4.1 Students demonstrate understanding of the nature of language through comparisons of the language studied and their own.

Standard 4.2 Students demonstrate understanding of the concept of culture through comparisons of the cultures studied and their own.

Teaching Resource Options

Print
Block Scheduling Copymasters

Audiovisual
Poster

Technology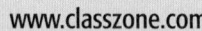

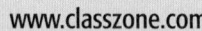 www.classzone.com

Teaching Suggestion
Previewing the Standard

Comparisons encourages students to hypothesize and develop insights into language and culture. As suggested when discussing Cultures, beginning with the similarities between English and Spanish helps students bridge gaps in language learning and acquisition. Focusing on the similarities helps students to hypothesize and test strategies for language learning.

UNIDAD

5

ARTES EN ESPAÑA Y LAS AMÉRICAS

- Comunicación
- Culturas
- Conexiones
- **Comparaciones**
- Comunidades

Webquest
CLASSZONE.COM

Explore comparisons in Spain and in the Americas through guided Web activities.

Comparaciones

La arquitectura de una cultura cambia a través de los años. Muchas veces, sin embargo, los edificios de diferentes épocas tienen estilos similares y es interesante compararlos. ¿En tu comunidad hay edificios modernos o antiguos? ¿Cuáles son las diferencias?

Comparaciones en acción
Compara los dos edificios que se ven en las fotos; ¿Crees que a la gente le gustan más los edificios antiguos o los modernos? ¿Cuál es la importancia de cada uno?

Culturas

Las perspectivas de las culturas hispanas se reflejan en sus artes. Describe las perspectivas reflejadas en este baile español.

Classroom Community

Paired Activity With a partner, have students make a list of similarities between Spanish and English that they have observed over the course of their language study. Have one person write down linguistic similarities (e.g. cognates) and the other student write down cultural similarities (e.g., sports, school, shared holidays, dress).

Class Activity Using the lists of comparisons between Spanish and English generated during the previous pair activity, make a class chart that shows them all. Place the list on the bulletin board and have students continue to add to the list over the course of the school year.

Conexiones

Los mayas usaban un sistema de numeración diferente del nuestro. ¿Qué opinas de su sistema? ¿Te parece más fácil o más difícil?

NUMERACIÓN MAYA

👁	CERO
●	UNO
●●	DOS
●●●	TRES
●●●●	CUATRO
▬	CINCO
▬	SEIS
▬	SIETE
▬	OCHO
▬	NUEVE

La prima Angélica (1973)

Comunicación

En esta unidad comunicaremos información sobre las artes, incluido el cine. ¿Te gustaría ver esta película? Explica tu respuesta.

Comunidades

En esta unidad conocerás a una alumna que usa el español para ayudar a su familia y también en el trabajo. ¿Y tú? ¿Cómo usas el español fuera de la clase? ¿Hablas español con alguien de tu familia?

Fíjate 💡

Identifica las formas de arte que ves representadas en las fotos de estas páginas.

_____ la arquitectura   _____ la escultura

_____ el baile   _____ la literatura

_____ el canto   _____ la música

_____ el cine   _____ la pintura

327

Unit 5 and Comparisons

When beginning Unit 5, **Artes en España y las Américas,** have students brainstorm celebrations in their own culture that typically include music, singing, dance, or other forms of artistic expression. Then have them hypothesize about or share any knowledge they have of how similar occasions or events are celebrated in Spain or Latin America.

Culture Highlights

● **FERNANDO BOTERO** El cuadro que se ve en la parte superior de la página 326 se llama *Los Músicos.* Es de Fernando Botero, un artista colombiano, cuyas figuras humanas redondas son características de su estilo.

● **RICARDO LEGORRETA** Legorreta, un arquitecto mexicano, diseñó la Fábrica de Automóviles Automex en la ciudad de Toluca, México. En la página 326 se ve parte de su moderna estructura.

● **TEOTIHUACÁN** En la página 326 se ve Teotihuacán, una antigua ciudad del Valle Central de México. Esta ciudad estaba dividida por una avenida central, al costado de la cual había dos pirámides enormes.

● **LA SARDANA** La foto que aparece al pie de la página 326 muestra a varias personas bailando la sardana, un baile tradicional de Cataluña, España.

● **CARLOS SAURA** La foto central de la página 327 muestra una escena de *La prima Angélica,* una de las películas del director español Carlos Saura.

Fíjate

All forms of art are represented, with the possible exceptions of *el canto* and *la literatura.*

▮ Block Schedule

Variety Have students look up Velázquez, Goya, or El Greco. Among other questions, have them find answers to the following: When did the artist live? What are considered to be his most important works? Was the artist appreciated during his lifetime? Why or why not? As a class, have them describe, compare, and contrast the individual styles of each artist. (For additional activities, see **Block Scheduling Copymasters**.)

Teaching All Students

Extra Help Have students write three similarities between Spanish and English that they feel have made learning Spanish easy. Then share the lists with the class.

Native Speakers Have students bring in photos or drawings of houses, buildings, or cities reflective of their country of heritage. Have them describe the architecture typical of the region.

Challenge Have students create a chart with three columns, labeled **inglés, español,** and **catalán.** Then have them choose five vocabulary words from a previous unit and fill in the columns with the words in English and Spanish. They should then go to the Internet to find the word in **catalán.** Ask them to use their charts to note similarities and differences among the three languages.

Ampliación

These activities may be used at various points in the Unit 5 sequence.

For Block Schedule, you may find that these projects will provide a welcome change of pace while reviewing and reinforcing the material presented in the unit. See the **Block Scheduling Copymasters.**

PROJECTS

Create a cultural guide to the Spanish-speaking world Have students work in pairs and assign each pair a country or region from the Spanish-speaking world. Have them research artists, authors, dance, music, and other arts from their country or region. Give all students the same size paper or posterboard for their cultural entries. Have them write and illustrate their findings with magazine clippings, photocopies, or drawings. The class will work together to order and bind the reports, and to create a cover for the completed cultural guide. Share the guide with other classes and/or display it in class.

PACING SUGGESTION: Upon completion of Etapa 3.

Film or record an audiovisual report on a cultural center for the arts. Have students work in small groups to select and gather information on a center such as **El Palacio de Bellas Artes** or **El Prado.** Have them present a brief report about the center and about a current or upcoming exhibition or event.

PACING SUGGESTION: Upon completion of Etapa 1.

STORYTELLING

En el Prado After reviewing the vocabulary on art and paintings, model a mini-story (using student actors or photos from the text) that students will revise, retell, and expand:

> Susan es una estudiante norteamericana que estudia español en Madrid. Va con su amigo español, Daniel, al Museo del Prado. Daniel le pregunta: «¿Conoces este cuadro?» Susan contesta: «Ay, sí. Este cuadro es *Las meninas* de Diego de Velázquez. Es muy interesante. Generalmente prefiero cuadros de artistas modernos, pero la perspectiva en los cuadros de Velázquez es muy interesante».

Pause as the story is being told so that students may fill in words and act out gestures. Students then write, narrate, and read aloud a longer main story. This new version should include vocabulary from the previous story.

Vamos al museo o al concierto Have students tell a story about going to the museum or going to a concert. They may plan the excursion, the artists, or musicians they want to see, and who they want to go with.

PACING SUGGESTION: Upon completion of Etapa 1.

BULLETIN BOARD/POSTERS

Bulletin Board **Plan ahead:** Bring in photocopies and magazine clippings of buildings from different regions in Spain. Have students work together to make a bulletin board with images of buildings from the regions of Spain. They should include famous government buildings and cathedrals as well as typical housing. The areas should be labeled by region.

Posters **Have students create** •**Brochures** for different cultural events •**Posters** to promote the arts in a Spanish-speaking country •**A calendar** of events for one month at a museum or performing arts center

GAMES

Los artistas

Prepare ahead: Set up a station of photos and books on the paintings of 20 or more Spanish-speaking artists at the beginning of Unit 5. Use the images to discuss artists from different countries, styles, etc. Make photocopies of 1 of each of the artists' paintings (without identification) and arrange them on the board or on a wall. Write the names of the artists on index cards. Divide the class into teams. Have students take turns drawing cards and matching the artist with his/her painting. The team with the most matches wins.

PACING SUGGESTION: Upon completion of Etapa 1.

En el mapa

Prepare ahead: Draw the outlines of Spain, Mexico, and Central and South America on the board or on large posterboards. Write the names of different cities and regions (**el Cono Sur, Galicia, Bogotá,** etc.) from the Spanish-speaking world on slips of paper and place them in a bag. Divide the class into teams. Have members of the teams take turns drawing a note from the bag. If the student can tape the note in the correct place on the map, the team receives 5 points. If he/she can also give cultural, historical, architectural, or culinary information about that place, the team receives an additional 5 points. The team with the most points when the bag is empty wins.

PACING SUGGESTION: Upon completion of Etapa 3.

MUSIC

Have students work together to make a dictionary of Hispanic music. Have them research musical styles (flamenco, Andean flute music, salsa, etc.) and write brief descriptions of each. Their entries should include special instruments and artists associated with the music they choose. Help them locate sound clips (Internet) or recordings of their musical styles to play in class. More music samples are available on your *Canciones* CD.

HANDS-ON CRAFTS

Have students create torn paper reproductions of Hispanic art. Have each student select a different painting from a magazine or book, trace it using tracing paper and pencil, then transfer the traced line drawing to paper using transfer paper. Have them fill the line drawing with torn or cut pieces of magazine or color paper. Mount the collages on posterboard to give them a framed effect (students can decorate their "frames" as well). Display the reproductions in class.

RECIPE

Gazpacho andaluz Gazpacho is a cold, vegetable soup, especially popular during the summer months. Though it tastes better on a patio in southern Spain, it's becoming a gourmet favorite in the United States. This soup requires no cooking, and it can be considered a cross-continental dish as it was created in the Old World (Spain) and its main ingredient, tomatoes, is from the New World.

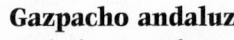

Receta

Gazpacho andaluz

1 pimiento verde	1/2 cucharadita de comino
1 pepino pelado	2 dientes de ajo
1 cebolla pelada	2 cucharaditas de azúcar
1 libra de tomates maduros	1 taza de agua fría
1 lata grande de tomates	sal al gusto
5 cucharadas de vinagre de vino	2 rebanadas de pan cortadas en
4 cucharadas de aceite de oliva	cuadraditos

Pique los vegetales y combínelos con los otros ingredientes, menos el pan, en un procesador de comida. Haga puré de la mezcla. Si quiere, puede añadir más sal o vinagre al gusto. Pase la mezcla por un colador y viértala en una jarra o en una fuente honda. Enfríela en el frigorífico por 3 o 4 horas. Para servirla, adórnela con un poco de pimiento verde. Luego, sírvala con pepino picado y cuadraditos de pan encima.

Planning Guide CLASSROOM MANAGEMENT

OBJECTIVES

Communication
- Identify and specify *pp. 336–338*
- Request clarification *pp. 338–340*
- Express relationships *pp. 341–342*
- Discuss art forms *pp. 330–331, 332–333*

Grammar
- Review the use of demonstrative adjectives and pronouns *pp. 336–338*
- Use **¿qué?** vs. **¿cuál?** *pp. 338–340*
- Use relative pronouns *pp. 341–343*

Culture
- The arts in Spain and the Americas *pp. 324–325*
- The arts in Spain *pp. 330–331, 332–333, 344–345*
- Regional vocabulary *p. 335*
- **El Museo del Prado** *pp. 332–333, 341*
- Miguel de Unamuno *p. 344*
- Ana María Matute *p. 345*

♻ Recycling
- Economy vocabulary *p. 339*
- Demonstratives *p. 342*

STRATEGIES

Listening Strategies
- Use advance knowledge of the topic *p. 332*

Speaking Strategies
- Discuss a painting *p. 340*
- Organize ideas for research *p. 348*

Reading Strategies
- Compare famous authors *p. 344*

Writing Strategies
- Present a thorough and balanced review *TE p. 348*

Connecting Cultures Strategies
- Learn about the arts in Spain and the Americas *pp. 326–327, 330–331, 332–333, 344–345*
- Recognize variations in vocabulary *p. 335*
- Learn about **El Museo del Prado** *pp. 332–333, 341*
- Compare famous authors: Miguel de Unamuno and Ana María Matute *pp. 344–345*
- Connect and compare what you already know about famous authors in your community to help you learn about famous authors in another community *pp. 344–345*

PROGRAM RESOURCES

 Print
- *Más práctica* Workbook PE *pp. 113–120*
- *Actividades para todos* Workbook PE *pp. 131–140*
- Block Scheduling Copymasters *pp. 105–112*
- Unit 5 Resource Book
  Más práctica Workbook TE *pp. 2–9*
  Actividades para todos Workbook TE *pp. 10–19*
  Cuaderno para hispanohablantes TE *pp. 20–27*
  Information Gap Activities *pp. 28–31*
  Family Letter *p. 32*
  Absent Student Copymasters *pp. 33–38*
  Family Involvement *pp. 39–40*
  Video Activities *pp. 235–238*
  Videoscript *pp. 239–241*
  Assessment Program, Unit 5 Etapa 1 *pp. 45–67; 226–228*
  Answer Keys *pp. 242–247*

 Audiovisual
- Audio Program CD 13
- *Canciones* CD
- Video Program Videotape 39:00 / DVD, Unit 5
- Overhead Transparencies M1–M5; 2, 5–18
- Word Tiles U5E1

 Technology
- eEdition Plus Online/eEdition CD-ROM
- Easy Planner Plus Online/Easy Planner CD-ROM
- eTest Plus Online/Test Generator CD-ROM
- Online Workbook
- Take-Home Tutor CD-ROM
- www.classzone.com

Assessment Program Options
- Unit 5 Resource Book
  Vocabulary Quizzes
  Grammar Quizzes
  Etapa Exam Forms A and B
  Examen para hispanohablantes
  Portfolio Assessment
  Multiple Choice Test Questions
- Audio Program CD 20
- eTest Plus Online/Test Generator CD-ROM

Native Speakers
- *Cuaderno para hispanohablantes* PE *pp. 113–120*
- *Cuaderno para hispanohablantes* TE (Unit 5 Resource Book)
- *Examen para hispanohablantes* (Unit 5 Resource Book)
- Audio Program *(Para hispanohablantes)* CD 13, 20
- Audioscript (Unit 5 Resource Book)

Student Text
Listening Activity Scripts

Situaciones *pages 332–333*

• CD 13

Bienvenidos al Museo del Prado. Probablemente ya saben que El Prado es el museo más importante de España y uno de los más famosos del mundo. Les va a encantar nuestra magnífica colección.

Carlos III mandó a construir el edificio, obra del arquitecto Juan de Villanueva. Originalmente, El Prado iba a ser un museo de ciencias naturales. La invasión napoleónica en 1807 interrumpió la construcción, pero se resumió en el año 1811, después de la muerte del arquitecto. El rey Fernando VII inauguró el museo en 1819.

El Prado contiene las colecciones de varios reyes y reinas españoles. Hasta se puede decir que El Prado nació de la pasión por la pintura de once reyes españoles. El Prado posee una colección magnífica de los siglos 12 al 18. Entre las escuelas representadas en El Prado están la flamenca, la italiana y la española.

Los artistas Brueghel, Rubens y Van Dyck representan la escuela flamenca, Botticelli, Tiziano y Tintoretto la italiana y, por supuesto, Velázquez, Goya y el Greco son los grandes maestros de la escuela española.

Sin duda alguna, El Prado posee la colección más comprensiva de pintura española que existe. De las treinta mil pinturas, casi un tercio son de la escuela española. Hay 100 pinturas de Francisco de Goya, unas 50 de Diego de Velázquez, y unas 20 de El Greco.

¿Qué se puede decir de *Las meninas* de Velázquez que todavía no se ha dicho? Es una obra sumamente importante. Nos instruye sobre la perspectiva y el sentido del humor del artista, que se incluye a sí mismo en la pintura. *Las meninas* capta un momento en la vida de la familia real que jamás se había capturado.

La obra de Francisco de Goya presenta una serie de etapas que hacen de este pintor uno de los grandes del mundo. Fue pintor de la corte y sus cuadros muestran lo mucho que disfrutó esa etapa. Pero su trágica experiencia personal en sus últimos años de vida influyó los cuadros que pintó durante ese período, llamado el Período Negro. Éstos expresan su horror y pena ante el sufrimiento humano. Murió aislado en 1828.

Aunque El Greco no sea de origen español, lo consideramos como nuestro. Sus obras contienen toda la espiritualidad de los españoles. Encontramos en su imaginación figuras de grande inspiración religiosa y mística. No se pierdan las secciones del museo dedicadas a las obras de El Greco.

¿Preguntas?

Los turistas *page 336*

Modelo: ¿Ves aquel cuadro de Goya? ¡Qué belleza!

1. Quiero ver aquel cuadro de Velázquez que está en el otro salón.
2. A mí me gusta este cuadro. No quiero irme de aquí.
3. Quisiera ver ese cuadro, pero esa gente no se mueve.
4. Este cuadro de El Greco me encanta. ¡Qué detalle!
5. Ese cuadro no me gusta para nada. No tiene ningún sentido de detalle ni de pasión.

Conversaciones *page 341*

Modelo: Ese cuadro lo pintó mi vecino, el artista.

1. Esa escultura la hizo mi primo, el escultor.
2. Ese museo tiene pinturas de la escuela española.
3. Esa clase de violín la da el profesor gallego.
4. Goya pintó esas obras en sus últimos años de vida. No me gustan.
5. Anoche fuimos a un espectáculo de flamenco. El cantaor tenía una voz increíble.
6. Ayer fuimos al museo y vimos unas pinturas muy bellas.

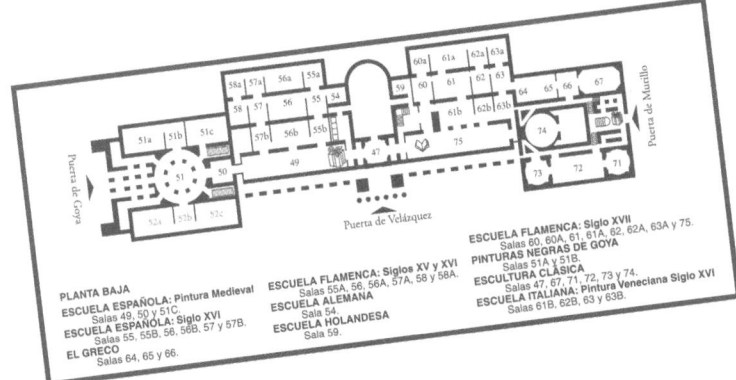

Sample Lesson Plan - 50 Minute Schedule

DAY 1

Unit Opener
• Anticipate/Activate prior knowledge: Present the *Almanaque* and the cultural notes. Use Map OHTs as needed. 15 MIN.

Etapa Opener
• Quick Start Review (TE, p. 328) 5 MIN.
• Have students look at the *Etapa* Opener and answer the questions. 5 MIN.

En contexto: Vocabulario
• Quick Start Review (TE, p. 330) 5 MIN.
• Present *Descubre*, p. 330. 5 MIN.
• Have students use context and pictures to learn *Etapa* vocabulary, then answer the *¿Comprendiste?* questions, p. 331. Use the Situational OHTs for additional practice. 15 MIN.

Homework Option:
• Have students write answers to the *¿Comprendiste?* questions, p. 331.

DAY 2

En vivo: Situaciones
• Check homework. 5 MIN.
• Quick Start Review (TE, p. 332) 5 MIN.
• Present the Listening Strategy, p. 332. 5 MIN.
• Have students look at section 1, p. 332. Play the audio for section 2. Then have students work in pairs or groups to complete section 3. 15 MIN.

En acción: Vocabulario y gramática
• Have students complete *Actividad* 1 in writing. Then have them exchange papers for peer correction. 5 MIN.
• Have students read and complete *Actividad* 2 in pairs. 5 MIN.
• Present the *Vocabulario*, p. 335; then have students do *Actividad* 3 in pairs. 10 MIN.

Homework Option:
• Have students write a description of a painting, using the *Vocabulario*, pp. 330, 325.

DAY 3

En acción (cont.)
• Check homework. 5 MIN.
• Quick Start Review (TE, p. 336) 5 MIN.
• Present *Repaso:* Demonstrative Adjectives and Pronouns, p. 336. 5 MIN.
• Play the audio; do *Actividad* 4. 10 MIN.
• Present the *Vocabulario*, p. 337, then have students do *Actividad* 5 in pairs. 10 MIN.
• Use one or more expansion activities from TE pp. 336–337 for variety and reinforcement. 10 MIN.
• Have students complete *Actividad* 6 in pairs. 5 MIN.

Homework Option:
• *Más práctica* Workbook, pp. 117–118. *Cuaderno para hispanohablantes*, pp. 115–116.

DAY 4

En acción (cont.)
• Check homework. 5 MIN.
• Quick Start Review (TE, p. 338) 5 MIN.
• Present *Gramática: ¿Qué?* vs. *¿Cuál?* p. 338. 10 MIN.
• Do *Actividad* 7 orally. 5 MIN.
• Present the *Vocabulario*, p. 339, then have students do *Actividad* 7 in pairs. 10 MIN.
• Have students do *Actividad* 8 orally 5 MIN.
• Have students read and complete *Actividad* 9 in writing. Go over answers orally. Expand using *Más comunicación*, p. R15. 15 MIN.

Homework Option:
• *Más práctica* Workbook, p. 119. *Cuaderno para hispanohablantes*, p. 117.

DAY 5

En acción (cont.)
• Check homework. 5 MIN.
• Present the Listening Strategy, p. 340. Have students complete *Actividad* 10 in pairs. 10 MIN.
• Present *Gramática:* Relative Pronouns, p. 341. 10 MIN.
• Play the audio; do *Actividad* 11. 5 MIN.
• Present the *Vocabulario*, p. 342, then have students do *Actividad* 12 in pairs. 10 MIN.
• Have students complete *Actividad* 13 in groups. 10 MIN.

Homework Option:
• *Más práctica* Workbook, p. 120. *Cuaderno para hispanohablantes*, p. 118.

DAY 6

En acción (cont.)
• Check homework. 5 MIN.
• Have students complete *Actividad* 14 in groups. Expand using *Más comunicación*, p. R15. 15 MIN.

Refrán
• Present the *Refrán*, p. 343. 5 MIN.

En voces: Lectura
• Quick Start Review (TE, p. 344) 5 MIN.
• Present the Reading Strategy, p. 344. Call on volunteers to read the *Lectura* aloud. Have students answer the *¿Comprendiste?/¿Qué piensas?* questions, p. 345. 20 MIN.

Homework Option:
• Have students complete *Hazlo tú*, p. 345.
• *Actividades para todos*, Workshop, pp. 131–140

DAY 7

En uso: Repaso y más comunicación
• Check homework. 5 MIN.
• Quick Start Review (TE, p. 346) 5 MIN.
• Do *Actividades* 1, 2, and 3 orally. 15 MIN.
• Have students do *Actividad* 4 in pairs. 10 MIN.
• Present the Speaking Strategy, p. 348. Do *Actividad* 5 in groups. 10 MIN.

En tu propia voz: Escritura
• Have students plan their essays for *Actividad* 6. 5 MIN.

Homework Option:
• Have students write their essays for *Actividad* 6. Review for *Etapa* 1 Exam.

DAY 8

En tu propia voz (cont.)
• Have students present their essays. 10 MIN.

Conexiones
• Present and discuss *Los estudios sociales*, p. 348. 5 MIN.

En resumen: Repaso de vocabulario
• Quick Start Review (TE, p. 349) 5 MIN.
• Review grammar questions, etc., as necessary. 10 MIN.
• Complete *Etapa* 1 Exam. 20 MIN.

Ampliación
• Optional: Use a suggested project, game, or activity. (TE, pp. 327A–327B)

Homework Option:
• Have students complete the assignment for *Conexiones*. Preview *Etapa* 2 Opener.

Sample Lesson Plan - Block Schedule (90 minutes)

DAY 1

Unit Opener
- Anticipate/Activate prior knowledge: Present the *Almanaque* and the cultural notes. Use Map OHTs as needed. 15 MIN.

Etapa Opener
- Quick Start Review (TE, p. 328) 5 MIN.
- Have students look at the *Etapa* Opener and answer the questions. 5 MIN.
- Use Block Scheduling Copymasters. 10 MIN.

En contexto: Vocabulario
- Quick Start Review (TE, p. 330) 5 MIN.
- Present *Descubre*, p. 330. 5 MIN.
- Have students use context and pictures to learn *Etapa* vocabulary, then answer the *¿Comprendiste?* questions, p. 331. Use the Situational OHTs for additional practice. 15 MIN.

En vivo: Situaciones
- Quick Start Review (TE, p. 332) 5 MIN.
- Present the Listening Strategy, p. 332. 5 MIN.
- Have students look at section 1, p. 332. Play the audio for section 2. Then have students work in pairs or groups to complete section 3. 20 MIN.

Homework Option:
- Have students write answers to the *¿Comprendiste?* questions, p. 331.

DAY 2

En acción: Vocabulario y gramática
- Check homework. 5 MIN.
- Quick Start Review (TE, p. 334) 5 MIN.
- Have students complete *Actividad* 1 in writing. Then have them exchange papers for peer correction. 5 MIN.
- Have students read and complete *Actividad* 2 in pairs. 5 MIN.
- Present the *Vocabulario*, p. 335; then have students do *Actividad* 3 in pairs. 15 MIN.
- Quick Start Review (TE, p. 336) 5 MIN.
- Present *Repaso:* Demonstrative Adjectives and Pronouns, p. 336. 10 MIN.
- Play the audio; do *Actividad* 4. 10 MIN.
- Present the *Vocabulario*, p. 337, then have students do *Actividad* 5 in pairs. 15 MIN.
- Use one or more expansion activities from TE pp. 336–337 for variety and reinforcement. 10 MIN.
- Have students complete *Actividad* 6 in pairs. 5 MIN.

Homework Option:
- Have students write a description of a painting, using the *Vocabulario*, pp. 320, 325. *Más práctica* Workbook, pp. 117–118. *Cuaderno para hispanohablantes*, pp. 115–116.

DAY 3

En acción (cont.)
- Check homework. 5 MIN.
- Quick Start Review (TE, p. 338) 5 MIN.
- Present *Gramática: ¿Qué?* vs. *¿Cuál?* p. 338. 5 MIN.
- Present the *Vocabulario*, p. 339, then have students do *Actividad* 7 in pairs. 10 MIN.
- Do *Actividad* 8 orally. 5 MIN.
- Have students read and complete *Actividad* 9 in writing. Go over answers orally. Expand using Information Gap Activities, Unit 5 Resource Book, p. 27; *Más comunicación*, p. R15. 20 MIN.
- Present the Listening Strategy, p. 340. Have students complete *Actividad* 10 in pairs. 10 MIN.
- Quick Start Review (TE, p. 341) 5 MIN.
- Present *Gramática:* Relative Pronouns, p. 341. 10 MIN.
- Play the audio; do *Actividad* 11. 5 MIN.
- Present the *Vocabulario*, p. 342, then have students do *Actividad* 12 in pairs. 10 MIN.

Homework Option:
- *Más práctica* Workbook, pp. 119–120. *Cuaderno para hispanohablantes*, pp. 117–118.
- *Actividades para todos* Workbook, pp. 131–140.

DAY 4

En acción (cont.)
- Check homework. 5 MIN.
- Have students complete *Actividad* 13 in groups. 5 MIN.
- Have students do *Actividad* 14 in groups. Expand using Information Gap Activities, Unit 5 Resource Book, p. 28; *Más comunicación*, p. R15. 20 MIN.

Refrán
- Present the *Refrán*, p. 343. 5 MIN.

En voces: Lectura
- Quick Start Review (TE, p. 344) 5 MIN.
- Present the Reading Strategy, p. 344. Call on volunteers to read the *Lectura* aloud. Have students answer the *¿Comprendiste?/¿Qué piensas?* questions, p. 345. 20 MIN.

En uso: Repaso y más comunicación
- Quick Start Review (TE, p. 346) 5 MIN.
- Do *Actividades* 1–3 orally and *Actividad* 4 in pairs. 15 MIN.
- Present the Speaking Strategy, p. 348. Do *Actividad* 5 in groups. 10 MIN.

Homework Option:
- Have students complete *Hazlo tú*, p. 345. Review for *Etapa* 1 Exam.

DAY 5

En tu propia voz: Escritura
- Check homework. 5 MIN.
- Have students write and present their essays for *Actividad* 6. 25 MIN.

Conexiones
- Present and discuss *Los estudios sociales*, p. 348. 5 MIN.

En resumen: Repaso de vocabulario
- Quick Start Review (TE, p. 349) 5 MIN.
- Review grammar questions, etc., as necessary. 10 MIN.
- Complete *Etapa* 1 Exam. 20 MIN.

Ampliación
- Use a suggested project, game, or activity. (TE, pp. 327A–327B) 20 MIN.

Homework Option:
- Have students complete the assignment for *Conexiones*. Preview *Etapa* 2 Opener.

▼ La sardana es el baile tradicional de Cataluña.

Etapa Theme
Learning about Spanish traditions

Grammar Objectives
• Reviewing the use of demonstrative adjectives and pronouns
• Using ¿qué? vs. ¿cuál?
• Using relative pronouns

Teaching Resource Options

Print

Block Scheduling Copymasters
Unit 5 Resource Book
 Family Letter, p. 32
 Absent Student Copymasters, p. 33

Audiovisual

OHT 138, 11 (Quick Start)
Canciones CD
Video Program Videotape 39:00 / DVD, Unit 5

Quick Start Review
 ♻ Celebrations

Use OHT 11 or write on the board:
Haz una lista de 5 cosas que hacen las personas para celebrar un evento especial.

Answers
Answers will vary. Answers could include:
usar fuegos artificiales, bailar, escuchar música, comer comidas especiales, dar la enhorabuena, tener fiestas hasta la madrugada, tener desfiles, tocar campanas

Teaching Suggestion
Previewing the Etapa
• Ask students to study the photo on pp. 328–329 (1 min.).
• Close books; ask students to describe at least 3 things that they noticed.
• Ask students what they notice about the punctuation of the Flamenco brochure: **¿Qué notan acerca de la puntuación del folleto de flamenco?** The opening exclamation points are missing: **Le faltan los signos de exclamación iniciales.** This is an authentic Flamenco brochure. As in English, grammar and punctuation rules are sometimes broken.
• Use the **¿Qué ves?** questions to focus the discussion.

UNIDAD 5
ETAPA 1
Tradiciones españolas

OBJECTIVES

• Identify and specify

• Request clarification

• Express relationships

• Discuss art forms

¿Qué ves?

Mira la foto. Contesta las preguntas.

1. ¿Qué están haciendo las personas en la foto?

2. ¿Cómo puedes describir a las personas que están allí?

3. ¿Crees que es una celebración? ¿Por qué?

4. Mira el póster. ¿Crees que hay una conexión entre el baile mostrado ahí y la foto? ¿Cuál?

328

Classroom Management

Planning Ahead Collect posters/reproductions of works by Spanish painters (Dalí, Miró, Goya, Velázquez, and El Greco). Bring in magazine pictures/photos of Spain and the city of Barcelona, and tapes/CDs of flamenco music or bagpipes from Galicia and popular Spanish music. Music samples are available on the **Canciones** CD.

Peer Review After going over the objectives for the **Etapa,** ask students which art form is pictured in the photo. Ask students what they already know about this art form and other art forms. Have them predict what they can expect to learn about in this **Etapa.**

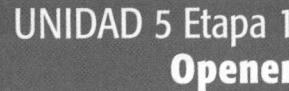

FLAMENCO

ARTIBUS
TEATRO DE MADRID
Del 23 de abril al 10 de mayo

con **Beatriz Martín**
dirección: Ricardo Franco

YSARCA

Taquilla: 740 52 74

TEATRO DE MADRID

329

UNIDAD 5 Etapa 1
Opener

Cross Cultural Connections

Ask students if they have ever seen a scene similar to the one in the photo in their community or in the U.S. Have students describe folk dancing or square dancing in the U.S.

Culture Highlights

● **LA SARDANA** La sardana es el baile típico de Cataluña. Todos los domingos, personas de varias edades se reúnen en una plaza en Barcelona para bailar la sardana. Este baile celebra la identidad de Cataluña y es tan importante para los catalanes que le han dedicado una escultura.

● **CATALÁN** El catalán es una lengua romance que se habla en Cataluña. La mayoría de las siete millones de personas que hablan catalán viven en el este de España. También viven en Aragón, Andorra, el suroeste de Francia y partes de Sardinia.

Supplementary Vocabulary

agarrarse/cogerse de las manos	to hold hands
la sombra	shadow
zapatear	to tap
el zapateo	tapping, stamping

Block Schedule

Setting the Theme Play music and ask students to close their eyes and pretend they are in Spain. Have them describe what they might see and what they might be doing. Would they join the dancers in the photo? (For additional activities, see **Block Scheduling Copymasters.**)

Teaching All Students

Extra Help Ask students about the photo and Flamenco poster using yes/no or either/or questions. For example: ¿Están las personas en un teatro? ¿Cantan las personas? ¿Están en un mercado o una plaza? ¿El espectáculo de flamenco es en un teatro o en un cine? ¿Es el flamenco un baile o una comedia?

Multiple Intelligences

Verbal Have students pick a person from the photo on pp. 328–329 and imagine they are that person's best friend. Then have them present a description of the person and what he/she is doing in the photo.

Etapa Opener • UNIDAD 5 Etapa 1 **329**

Teaching Resource Options

Print

Block Scheduling Copymasters
 Absent Student Copymasters, p. 33

Audiovisual

OHT 4, 5, 6, 7, 7A, 8, 8A, 11
 (Quick Start)

Technology

Online Workbook, U5E1
Take-Home Tutor CD-ROM, U5E1

🔔 Quick Start Review
❖ Art forms
Use OHT 11 or write on the board:
Haz una lista de 5 formas de arte diferentes.

Answers
Answers will vary. Answers could include:
la música, el canto, el baile, la pintura, la escultura, la fotografía, el cine, la escritura, el dibujo

Teaching Suggestions
Introducing Vocabulary
• Have students look at pp. 330–331. Use OHT 5 and 6 to present the vocabulary.
• Ask the Comprehension Questions on TE p. 331 in order of yes/no (questions 1–3), either/or (questions 4–6), and simple word or phrase (questions 7–10). Expand by adding similar questions.
• Use the TPR activity to reinforce the meaning of individual words.

Descubre

Answers
1. century 2. painting 3. self-portrait
4. background; perspective 5. foreground
6. tapestry 7. dancer; tapping of the feet; stamps, strikes; rhythm

Language Note
An explanation of the words **bailaor, tablao,** and **cantaor** is found on p. 335.

En contexto VOCABULARIO

España para jóvenes

MADRID: EL MUSEO DEL PRADO

¡Hola! Soy Miguel Antonio Ramírez Benavente. Bienvenidos al Museo del Prado, uno de mis lugares preferidos. Quiero ser artista y por eso paso muchas horas aquí. Este museo tiene obras de varias escuelas de pintura europea de los siglos XII al XIX.

🔲 Descubre

Lee las siguientes definiciones. ¿Puedes adivinar el significado de las palabras en azul?

1. Un **siglo** es un espacio temporal de cien años.
2. Un **cuadro** es lo mismo que una pintura.
3. Un **autorretrato** es un retrato de una persona hecho por ella misma.
4. Se dice que una imagen está al **fondo** de una pintura cuando ocupa el punto más distante de la **perspectiva**.
5. Una imagen ocupa el **primer plano** cuando ocupa el punto más cercano de la perspectiva.
6. Un **tapiz** es un cuadro grande de lana o seda, hecho algunas veces con oro y plata.
7. El **bailaor** de flamenco ejecuta el **zapateado** – unos ruidos rítmicos – cuando **da golpes** en el suelo con los zapatos rápidamente al **compás** de la música.

Si pasas por El Prado, tienes que ver a Diego de Velázquez. Él es uno de los maestros de la perspectiva. *Las meninas* es su obra más importante. Te recomiendo que vengas temprano para ver este cuadro al óleo. ¡Siempre hay mucha gente!

Diego de Velázquez (1599–1660)

Las figuras del rey Felipe IV y de la reina Mariana se ven en el espejo al fondo, como si posaran para su retrato.

Y por supuesto, el autorretrato de Velázquez es una de las cosas que más me gusta de esta pintura.

La Infanta Margarita está en primer plano con sus cortesanas, las meninas.

Las meninas, 1656, Diego de Velázquez

La familia de Carlos IV (c.1800), Francisco de Goya

Francisco de Goya es otro pintor que yo estudio mucho. Cuando Goya comenzó a pintar se especializó en diseños para tapices y luego en la decoración de iglesias con frescos. En 1799 se hizo el pintor de la corte de Carlos IV y luego de Fernando VII.

Francisco de Goya, 1746–1828

330 trescientos treinta
Unidad 5

Classroom Community

TPR Ask each student to create a drawing for one vocabulary word. Collect the drawings, shuffle them, and hand one out to each student. Then call out various commands. For example: **Levanta la mano si tienes el tapiz. Venga acá la persona que tiene la sardana. La persona que tiene la jota, désela a otro(a) compañero(a). La persona que tiene el cantaor, vaya a la puerta.**

Cooperative Learning Divide the class into groups of 3. Student 1 guesses the meaning of a vocabulary word from the **Descubre**. Student 2 looks up the word to confirm its meaning. Student 3 uses the word in a sentence. Students switch roles with each word they practice.

España para jóvenes

El *flamenco* y otros bailes típicos

¡Saludos! Soy María del Pilar Arriaga Méndez y me dedico al flamenco. Lo he estudiado desde niña.

En un tablao, generalmente hay por lo menos cuatro personas en el tablado:

El flamenco es una expresión artística. Aunque se interpreta por toda España, este baile se asocia con Andalucía, que está en el sur. Hay muchos estilos de cante, el tipo de canción con que se acompaña el flamenco. El cante es una parte integral del flamenco.

el guitarrista
el cantaor
el bailaor o la bailaora
el vestido tradicional de lunares
las que dan palmadas

El cante jondo es el cante más serio y más apasionado. Tiene un compás muy marcado. Otro estilo de cante, la saeta, es el único que no tiene compás fijo. Los bailaores siguen el ritmo de la guitarra y del momento. La coreografía es espontánea. La guitarra, las palmas y el zapateado del bailaor crean el compás del flamenco.

Otros bailes típicos

La jota es un baile de Aragón, pero también se interpreta en otras regiones españolas.

La sardana es el baile tradicional de Cataluña.

Online Workbook
CLASSZONE.COM

¿Comprendiste?

1. ¿Te gustan los museos? ¿Te gusta admirar y analizar las pinturas en los museos? ¿Por qué sí o por qué no?
2. ¿Qué piensas de la pintura *Las meninas* de Velázquez? ¿Por qué crees que el artista se incluyó en el retrato?
3. ¿Alguna vez has visto un espectáculo de flamenco? ¿Qué pensaste? Si nunca lo has visto, ¿crees que te gustaría? ¿Por qué?

trescientos treinta y uno
España y las Américas Etapa 1
331

● **LA PINTURA** La obra maestra de Velázquez, **Las meninas,** es un retrato de la familia real que incluye al artista, a las meninas (las compañeras de la princesa o infanta) y a otros personajes de la corte.

La obra de Goya incluye varios géneros. Hizo arte religioso, tapices, caricaturas y retratos de gente famosa, además de pinturas sobre varios temas cotidianos y mitológicos. Goya retrata las facetas múltiples de la experiencia humana, desde lo sublime hasta lo satírico.

● **EL FLAMENCO** El flamenco, el baile de los gitanos de Andalucía, surgió a través de la combinación de culturas gitanas, andaluzas y árabes durante varios siglos. La música flamenca se puso de moda a principios del siglo diecinueve como espectáculo de café. Las castañuelas utilizadas en el flamenco provienen originalmente de bailes árabes.

Comprehension Questions

1. ¿Es **Las meninas** la obra más importante de Velázquez? (Sí)
2. ¿Siempre hay poca gente viendo **Las meninas**? (No)
3. ¿Se ven las figuras de los reyes en el espejo al fondo de la pintura? (Sí)
4. ¿Qué hay en primer plano, la figura de Velázquez o la de la Infanta Margarita? (la de la Infanta Margarita)
5. ¿Al principio, se especializó Goya en diseños para tapices o autorretratos? (diseños para tapices)
6. ¿Se hizo Goya pintor de la corte de Carlos IV o de Felipe II? (de Carlos IV)
7. ¿Con qué región se asocia el flamenco? (con Andalucía)
8. ¿Qué cante no tiene compás fijo? (la saeta)
9. ¿Qué baile es propio de Aragón? (la jota)
10. ¿Cuál es la danza tradicional de Cataluña? (la sardana)

Teaching All Students

Extra Help Make true/false statements about the information on pp. 330–331. Have students hold up cards showing **Cierto** or **Falso.**

Native Speakers Ask students to describe and/or demonstrate dances from their country of origin. They may also bring in traditional music.

Multiple Intelligences

Musical/Rhythmic Play flamenco music and ask students to clap out as many different rhythms as they can, yet still keep time with the music. If castanets are available, ask volunteers to show how rhythms are made with them.

Visual Have students design posters for museum exhibits of Velázquez and Goya.

Block Schedule

FunBreak Show a clip from a film on flamenco, such as **Bodas de sangre, Carmen,** or **El amor brujo** directed by Carlos Saura and danced by Antonio Gades' company. (For additional activities, see **Block Scheduling Copymasters.**)

Teaching Resource Options

Print

Block Scheduling Copymasters
Unit 5 Resource Book
  Absent Student Copymasters, p. 34
  Audioscript, p. 41

Audiovisual

OHT 9, 10, 12 (Quick Start)
Audio Program CD 13, Track 1

Technology

Take-Home Tutor CD-ROM, U5E1

Quick Start Review

🔄 Vocabulary review

Use OHT 12 or write on the board:
Match the words in the 2 columns:

1. ___ autorretrato
2. ___ tapiz
3. ___ saeta
4. ___ cantaor
5. ___ guitarrista
   a. el que toca la guitarra
   b. cuadro hecho por la misma
      persona
   c. cuadro grande de lana o seda
   d. el que canta
   e. cante sin compás fijo

Answers
1. b 2. c 3. e 4. d 5. a

Teaching Suggestions
Presenting Situations

• Present the Listening Strategy, p. 332, and have students answer the Pre-listening questions.
• Use OHT 9 and 10 to present the **Mirar** section. Ask simple yes/no, either/or, or short-answer questions.
• Use Audio CD 13 and have students do the **Escuchar** section (see Script p. 327D) and complete the Listening Strategy exercise.
• Have students work in pairs or groups to complete the **Hablar** section.

AUDIO
SITUACIONES

PARA ESCUCHAR
STRATEGY: LISTENING

Pre-listening How is a lecture different from a conversation? Think about the information and the rate of speech. Which do you think is easier to understand?

Use advance knowledge of the topic The guide in El Prado will talk about the subjects on the map. First identify what might be said in general. Then, while listening, jot down any note to jog your memory later.

Un paseo por El Prado

Estás en el Museo del Prado en Madrid, España. Como vas a ir por el museo en grupo, primero miras el mapa del museo. Luego escuchas a la guía turística mientras habla del museo y de las obras de arte que se encuentran allí.

① Mirar

Antes de entrar al Museo del Prado, estudia el mapa de la planta baja del museo. ¿Qué tipo de arte vas a ver?

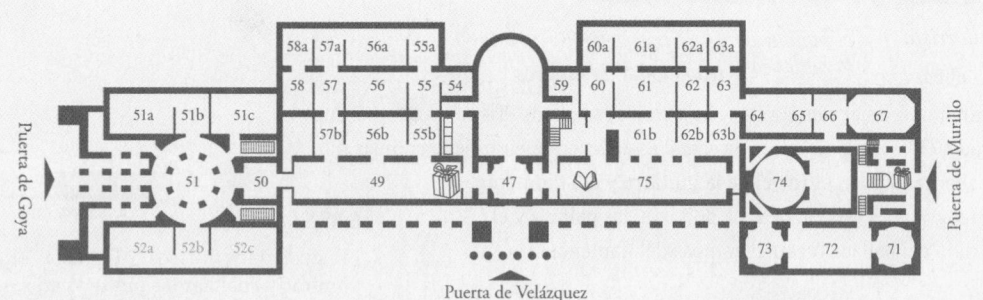

PLANTA BAJA
ESCUELA ESPAÑOLA: Pintura Medieval
  Salas 49, 50 y 51C.
ESCUELA ESPAÑOLA: Siglo XVI
  Salas 55, 55B, 56, 56B, 57 y 57B.
EL GRECO
  Salas 64, 65 y 66.

ESCUELA FLAMENCA: Siglos XV y XVI
  Salas 55A, 56, 56A, 57A, 58 y 58A.
ESCUELA ALEMANA
  Sala 54.
ESCUELA HOLANDESA
  Sala 59.

ESCUELA FLAMENCA: Siglo XVII
  Salas 60, 60A, 61, 61A, 62, 62A, 63A y 75.
PINTURAS NEGRAS DE GOYA
  Salas 51A y 51B.
ESCULTURA CLÁSICA
  Salas 47, 67, 71, 72, 73 y 74.
ESCUELA ITALIANA: Pintura Veneciana Siglo XVI
  Salas 61B, 62B, 63 y 63B.

Classroom Community

Game Divide the class into groups of 3–4. Have groups write 6 statements about the Prado: 3 that are true and 3 that are false. Group members take turns reading the statements aloud, and the other groups try to guess which statements are false. Students should correct the false statements.

Paired Activity Looking at the map of the Prado, students take turns calling out a room number. The partner then states the school of painting or sculpture found there as well as the century or centuries represented.

CD-ROM
Take-Home Tutor

MUSEO DEL PRADO

② Escuchar

La guía española les da una breve introducción al museo y las obras que se encuentran allí. Escucha su narración y decide si las oraciones que siguen son ciertas o falsas. Si la oración es falsa, cámbiala para que sea cierta.

1. El Museo del Prado es el museo más importante de México.
2. Carlos III mandó a construir el museo como Museo de Ciencias Naturales.
3. Napoleón inauguró el museo en el año 1819.
4. Las obras de arte del museo eran de las colecciones de los reyes y reinas de España de los tres siglos anteriores.
5. Las escuelas de arte representadas en el Museo del Prado son la norteamericana, la argentina y la chilena.
6. El Prado posee la colección más grande de pintura española que existe.
7. De las treinta mil pinturas, casi una quinta parte es de la escuela española.
8. Francisco de Goya expresó mucha alegría en las obras de los últimos años de su vida.
9. El Greco es de origen español.
10. Las obras de El Greco tratan de temas religiosos y místicos.

③ Hablar

En grupos de dos o tres, conversen sobre la obra de Velázquez, *Las meninas*. ¿Qué ven en la obra? Nombren todo lo que puedan detalladamente. Vayan a la biblioteca y busquen un libro sobre algún (alguna) artista que les interese. Cada uno debe escoger una obra favorita y compartir con sus compañeros tres observaciones sobre la obra.

MUSEO DEL PRADO
Precio de entrada
2 € : Estudiante

trescientos treinta y tres
España y las Américas Etapa 1
333

Escuchar (See script, p. 327D.)

Answers
1. Falso. Es el museo más importante de España.
2. Cierto
3. Falso. El rey Fernando VII inauguró el museo en el año 1819.
4. Falso. Eran las colecciones de los reyes y reinas de España de los seis siglos anteriores.
5. Falso. Las escuelas de arte representadas en el Museo del Prado son la flamenca, la italiana y la española.
6. Cierto
7. Falso. De las treinta mil pinturas, casi un tercio son de la escuela española.
8. Falso. Francisco de Goya expresó mucho horror y pena en las obras de sus últimos años de vida.
9. Falso. El Greco no es de origen español.
10. Cierto

Hablar

Answers will vary.

Teaching Note
- **Currency:** On January 1, 2002, the **euro** became the new currency of twelve European countries including Spain, where it replaced the **peseta.**
- **La escuela flamenca** refers to the Flemish school of painting. Context is used to distinguish *Flemish* from the Andalusian dance.

Critical Thinking
Have students discuss the cultural importance of museums. Have them think about some of the original reasons why museums were built. What purposes do they serve? Consider promoting discussion by asking what the world would be like without museums.

Block Schedule
Research Have students work in groups to research the history of the Prado museum and specific paintings found there. Have them use this information to create a museum information brochure. (For additional activities, see **Block Scheduling Copymasters.**)

Teaching All Students

Extra Help Have students read the statements on p. 333 before listening to **Escuchar.** Then have them write down key words/concepts to listen for. As you play **Escuchar,** have students take notes. Then do the activity.

Native Speakers Ask students to supply additional vocabulary pertaining to painting. Have them model the pronunciation. Have the class add these words to their Supplementary Vocabulary Lists.

Multiple Intelligences

Naturalist Have students research the role nature plays in Spanish painting. What kind of natural settings are used? Are the settings allegorical or real? What kind of plants and trees can be found in them? Where can these settings be found in Spain?

Teaching Resource Options

Print

Block Scheduling Copymasters
Unit 5 Resource Book
  Absent Student Copymasters, p. 35

Audiovisual

OHT 12 (Quick Start)

🔔 Quick Start Review

 Vocabulary review

Use OHT 12 or write on the board:
Identify the following:

1. un cuadro
2. *Las meninas*
3. un bailaor
4. el compás
5. un siglo

Answers

Answers will vary. Answers could include:
1. una pintura
2. una pintura famosa de Velázquez
3. un hombre que baila el flamenco
4. el ritmo de la música
5. un espacio temporal de cien años

Teaching Suggestions
Comprehension Check

Use **Actividades 1–4** to assess retention after the **Vocabulario** and **Situaciones**. After completing **Actividad 1**, read items 1, 3, 5, and 7 aloud as a dictation exercise. Have volunteers write the sentences on the board for class review and student self-check.

1 Objective: Transitional practice
Vocabulary in writing

Answers
1. escuela
2. siglo
3. al óleo
4. en primer plano
5. fondo
6. figura
7. perspectiva, retrato

2 Objective: Transitional practice
Vocabulary in reading

Answers
1. interpreta
2. tablao
3. bailaores
4. cantaor
5. cante jondo
6. golpes
7. zapateado
8. palmadas

En acción

PARTE A Práctica del vocabulario

Objectives for Activities 1-3
• Identify and specify • Request clarification

1 Las meninas

Escribir Acabas de estudiar la pintura más famosa de Velázquez. Completa las oraciones con estas palabras.

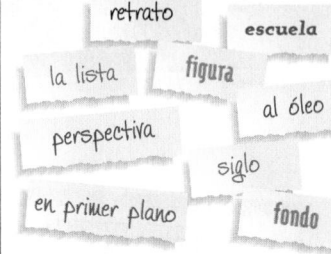

retrato
escuela
la lista
figura
al óleo
perspectiva
siglo
en primer plano
fondo

1. Diego de Velázquez es un pintor de la _____ española.

2. Las pinturas de Velázquez son del _____ XVII.

3. *Las meninas* es una pintura _____.

4. En *Las meninas*, Velázquez pintó a la Infanta Margarita _____.

5. El rey y la reina se pueden ver reflejados en el espejo al _____ de la pintura.

6. La _____ de Velázquez también se puede ver en el cuadro.

7. La _____ de la pintura parece ser del rey y la reina, donde posan para su _____.

2 El flamenco

Leer/Escribir Querías saber más sobre el flamenco y le pediste a Isabel, tu amiga andaluza, que te lo explicara. Ella te escribió una carta para contestar tus preguntas. Completa su carta con las palabras de la lista.

cantaor   golpes   interpreta   tablao
bailaores   palmadas   zapateado   cante jondo

Querido(a) amigo(a):

Para contestarte, el flamenco es el baile tradicional de Andalucía que se __1__ de muchas maneras. Hoy en día puedes ver el espectáculo de flamenco en un __2__ flamenco en muchas partes de España, incluso en Madrid, donde lo bailan unos de los mejores __3__ del mundo.

El __4__ tiene que cantar con una voz dura y vibrante. El __5__ es el cante más serio y más apasionado de todos los cantes flamencos.

Los bailaores, al darle __6__ al tablado con los zapatos, ejecutan lo que se llama el __7__. Las personas que dan __8__ también contribuyen al compás del zapateado. ¡Tienes que venir a España a disfrutar de este espectáculo magnífico!

Abrazos,

Isabel

Classroom Management

Planning Ahead Find prints of 5 different historical paintings. Describe a painting based on the questions in **Actividad 3**, then have the class pick out the painting you are describing.

Peer Review Have students brainstorm/research historical moments in Spanish or Latin American history that deserve to be depicted in a painting. Then divide the class into groups of 3. Assign each group an historical moment. Have each group discuss what their painting of this event would look like, turning in a description of it when they're finished.

3 En el museo

Hablar Pasaste el día en El Prado donde viste la obra a la derecha. Al otro día le explicas a tu compañero(a) por qué te gustó.

modelo

Compañero(a): *¿Hay figuras en la pintura?*

Tú: *Sí, hay seis figuras en la pintura.*

- ¿De qué siglo es el cuadro?
- ¿Dónde están las figuras? ¿En el fondo o en primer plano?
- ¿Qué hacen las figuras?
- ¿Qué tipo de cuadro es?
- ¿De quién es la perspectiva?
- ¿Qué pasa en el cuadro?
- ¿…?

La defensa de Cádiz contra los ingleses, Francisco de Zurbarán, 1634

Vocabulario

La pintura

el cuadro histórico *historical painting*
el paisaje *landscape*
la naturaleza muerta *still-life*

Ya sabes

el bote	el ejército	luchar contra
el océano	el opresor	la orilla

¿Cuál es tu estilo de pintura preferido?

También se dice

Cuando se habla de flamenco, se usa la palabra **bailaor** o **bailaora** en vez de **bailador** o **bailadora.** Esto se debe a un modo de hablar en Andalucía, España, donde el flamenco tiene su origen. Cuando pronuncian una palabra que contiene una **d** entre dos vocales, quitan la **d;** entonces, **bailador** se convierte en **bailaor.**

Teaching Suggestions
Teaching Vocabulary

Plan ahead: Find examples of paintings to which these terms apply. Use the pictures to introduce and practice the vocabulary.

Actividad 3 Objective: Transitional practice Vocabulary in conversation

Answers

Questions and answers will vary in some cases.
Es del siglo XVII.
Las figuras están en primer plano.
Hablan y miran la escena.
Es un cuadro histórico.
La perspectiva es de las figuras.
Los botes están luchando en el océano y en la orilla, mientras las figuras observan la lucha y hablan.

Culture Highlights

FRANCISCO DE ZURBARÁN
Francisco de Zurbarán (1598–1664) se hizo pintor de la corte española en 1634. Pintó varias escenas de batalla. Su obra tiene una mezcla de realismo y misticismo que todavía impresiona. Esta mezcla se ve reflejada en la sencillez de sus líneas y los colores vivos de sus composiciones originales.

Teaching All Students

Extra Help Have students work in groups of 3 to review vocabulary related to art presented in this and other **Etapas.** As the group brainstorms, one student writes down the words. The group then checks the list and writes it on the board. All students make complete lists in their notebooks to refer to throughout the **Etapa.**

Multiple Intelligences

Interpersonal After completing **Actividad 3** with a partner, have pairs discuss their personal impressions of the painting by Zurbarán. Do they like this painting? Why or why not?

Logical/Mathematical Have students choose one of the men from the painting on p. 335 and come up with a logical elimination game—for example, **No estoy sentado,** etc.—until there is only the one man left. Students exchange games.

Block Schedule

Variety Have students work in groups to make up and present a story about the Zurbarán painting. It does not have to be factual. Students should make up names for the main characters, tell what they did and felt, and what happened after the battle.. (For additional activities, see **Block Scheduling Copymasters.**)

Quick Start Review

♻ Culture/vocabulary review

Use OHT 13 or write on the board:
Answer the following questions:

1. ¿Quién es un pintor surrealista?
2. ¿Qué son churros?
3. ¿Cuál es un museo famoso en España?
4. ¿Cuáles son algunos bailes folklóricos de España?
5. ¿Cómo se llama el tipo de canción que acompaña al flamenco?

Answers

1. Salvador Dalí 2. algo que se come con chocolate 3. el Prado 4. el flamenco, la jota, la sardana 5. el cante

Teaching Suggestions
Reviewing Demonstrative Adjectives and Pronouns

• Use gestures and demonstrative adjectives as you point to items around the room and tell to whom they belong.

PARTE B
Práctica: gramática y vocabulario

Objectives for Activities 4–13
• Identify and specify • Request clarification • Express relationships • Discuss art forms

REPASO **Demonstrative Adjectives and Pronouns**

▶ You use demonstrative adjectives to point out specific things and to show the distance between the speaker and the item.

▶ Demonstrative pronouns are used in place of the adjective and noun. Their forms are the same as demonstrative adjectives, but they have an accent over the first **e**.

	masculine singular	masculine plural	feminine singular	feminine plural
this, these *near the speaker*	este / éste	estos / éstos	esta / ésta	estas / éstas — adjectives / pronouns
that, those *near the person spoken to*	ese / ése	esos / ésos	esa / ésa	esas / ésas
that, those *not associated with either the speaker or the person spoken to*	aquel / aquél	aquellos / aquéllos	aquella / aquélla	aquellas / aquéllas

▶ Remember that **demonstrative** adjectives and pronouns agree in gender and number with the nouns to which they refer.

agrees
Regina: Est**a** novela me gustó mucho.
*I liked **this** novel very much.*

agrees
Carolina: Sí, es**e** libro es excelente.
*Yes, **that** book is excellent.*

▶ Remember that there are also **demonstrative pronouns** that refer to ideas or unidentified things that do not have a specific gender.

> Don't put an **accent** mark on these words.

esto   eso   aquello

—Marcos faltó otra vez.
Marcos was absent again.

—**Esto** me preocupa.
This worries me.

Practice: Actividades ④⑤⑥ | **Más práctica** *cuaderno* pp. 117–118
Para hispanohablantes *cuaderno* pp. 115–116 | **Online Workbook** CLASSZONE.COM

---

④ Los turistas

Escuchar/*Escribir* En el museo, oyes si los cuadros están próximos, cerca o lejos. Escribe **este** si está próximo; **ese** si está cerca o **aquel** si está lejos.

modelo

«¿Ves el cuadro de Goya? ¡Qué belleza!»

  aquel cuadro

1. el cuadro de Velázquez
2. el cuadro que quiero ver
3. el cuadro detrás de la gente
4. el cuadro de El Greco
5. el cuadro sin detalle

Vista de Toledo, El Greco

Classroom Community

Learning Scenario Have students imagine they are guides in the Prado. They need to describe works of art to visitors to the museum. Have students choose at least 3 nouns from the **Vocabulario**, p. 330. Students then write a sentence for each of their chosen nouns, using the correct demonstrative adjective for those nouns. For example: **las figuras → Estas figuras son del rey Felipe IV y de la reina Mariana.**

Portfolio Have students write a description of El Greco's painting on p. 336 and tell why they like/don't like the painting. They must use at least 3 demonstrative adjectives/pronouns in their essay.

Rubric A = 13–15 pts. B = 10–12 pts. C = 7–9 pts. D = 4–6 pts. F = < 4 pts.

Writing criteria	Scale
Vocabulary use	1 2 3 4 5
Clear and vivid details	1 2 3 4 5
Grammar/spelling accuracy	1 2 3 4 5

5 Los instrumentos musicales

Hablar/*Escribir* Tú y tu amigo(a) están en una tienda de música. Le dices a tu amigo(a) qué instrumento te gustaría comprar. Usa **este** si está próximo, **ese** si está cerca y **aquel** si está lejos. Luego cambien de papel.

modelo

Tú: *Creo que voy a comprar este violín.*

Compañero(a): *Yo prefiero aquel violín.*

Vocabulario

La música

el arpa (fem.) *harp*	**las maracas** *maracas*	**el tambor** *drum*
las castañuelas *castanets*	**la pandereta** *tambourine*	**la trompeta** *trumpet*
		el violín *violin*

▶ ¿Sabes tocar alguno de estos instrumentos?

Teaching All Students

Extra Help Have students identify items in the classroom, using demonstrative adjectives and brief descriptions. For example: **ventana → Esa ventana está abierta.** Objects might include: **mesa, lápices, puerta, papeles, libro, mochilas.**

Multiple Intelligences

Kinesthetic Plan ahead: Make a large vocabulary card for each of the nouns from the **Vocabulario** on pp. 330–331. Also make cards for each of the demonstrative adjectives (several cards of each adjective). Tape them to the board in two categories: nouns and demonstrative adjectives. Call on students to come to the board and choose a noun card. They then find a matching demonstrative adjective card. Students then place the two cards next to each other on the board.

Teaching Note

• The **Real Academia Española** has ruled that accents on demonstrative pronouns are no longer required unless the meaning of the pronoun is ambiguous. However, demonstrative pronouns are traditionally taught with accents.

ACTIVIDAD 4 **Objective:** Controlled practice Listening comprehension/ demonstrative adjectives

Answers (See script, p. 327D.)
1. aquel 2. este 3. ese 4. este 5. ese

Dictation

Using the Listening Activity Script for **Actividad 4** on TE p. 327D, dictate selected sentences to students. You may want to use this dictation for a quiz grade.

Teaching Suggestions
Teaching Vocabulary

Plan ahead: Bring in toy or real instruments (or pictures of instruments). Use the items to teach and practice the vocabulary. Have students name musicians they know who play these instruments. They may also name well-known musical pieces where the instruments figure prominently.

ACTIVIDAD 5 **Objective:** Transitional practice Demonstrative adjectives/vocabulary in conversation

Answers will vary.

Block Schedule

Change of Pace Have students who are band members bring their instruments to class. Have each instrument played, then played again while students' eyes are closed. Ask students to name the instrument they hear. Then play a recorded piece of classical music by Manuel de Falla, or another Spanish composer, and have students name the instruments they hear. (For additional activities, see **Block Scheduling Copymasters.**)

Teaching Resource Options

Print

Más práctica Workbook PE, p. 119
Cuaderno para hispanohablantes PE,
p. 117
Block Scheduling Copymasters
Unit 5 Resource Book
  Más práctica Workbook TE, p. 8
  Cuaderno para hispanohablantes
  TE, p. 24
  Absent Student Copymasters,
  pp. 35–36

Audiovisual

OHT 13 (Quick Start), 17 (Grammar)

Technology

Online Workbook, U5E1
Take-Home Tutor CD-ROM, U5E1

Objective: Open-ended practice
Demonstrative adjectives and
pronouns in conversation

Answers
*Following are the questions. Student responses
will vary.*
1. A: ¿Qué te parece aquel autorretrato?
2. A: ¿Qué te parece ese paisaje?
3. A: ¿Qué te parecen estos cuadros al óleo?
4. A: ¿Qué te parecen aquellas figuras?
5. A: ¿Qué te parece esta naturaleza muerta?

Quick Start Review
♻ Musical instruments

Use OHT 13 or write on the board:
Sketch a picture of each of the
following instruments:

1. el arpa   4. el tambor
2. la pandereta 5. el violín
3. la trompeta

Answers
*Drawings should be of the following
instruments:* harp, tambourine, trumpet,
drum, violin

Teaching Suggestions
Teaching ¿Qué? vs. ¿Cuál?

• Write on the board: ¿Qué es su
hermana? ¿Cuál es su hermana?
Ask students to tell you the
difference. Point out that the first
sentence asks what is the sister's
profession. The second asks which
one she is from among a group.

---

6 **¿Qué te parece?**

Hablar/*Escribir* Tú y tu
compañero tienen opiniones
sobre varias obras de arte.
Conversen sobre sus opiniones.

modelo

Tú: *¿Qué te parece aquel cuadro
histórico?*

Compañero(a): *¿Aquél? Me parece
que es demasiado
serio y le falta luz.*

1. el autorretrato
2. el paisaje
3. los cuadros al óleo
4. las figuras
5. la naturaleza muerta

GRAMÁTICA   **¿Qué? vs. ¿Cuál?**

▸ Both **qué** and **cuál** can be used to express *what* in English. **Cuál** is also used to express *which*.

¿Qué quieres ver en el museo?   **¿Cuál** de los cuadros te interesa más?
***What** do you want to see in the museum?*   ***Which** of the paintings are you more interested in?*

....

▸ You use **qué** to ask someone to **define** or **describe** something. Use **cuál** if you are asking
someone to **select** or **make a choice,** and to **identify** or **name** something.

¿Qué es un fresco?   **¿Cuál es el nombre** de la obra que
***What** is a fresco?*   vamos a ver?
                                            ***What is the name** of the play that we are going to see?*

Practice: **Actividades** ⑦⑧⑨⑩   **Más práctica** *cuaderno p. 119*   **Online Workbook**
                                         Para hispanohablantes *cuaderno p. 117*   CLASSZONE.COM

338   trescientos treinta y ocho
          Unidad 5

Classroom Community

Learning Scenario Have students work in pairs
and interview each other about their free-time activities.
First, students write a list of 8–10 basic questions, of
which at least 5 must use **qué** or **cuál.** Then have
students complete the interviews and take notes.
Finally, have them summarize their partners' activities
for the class.

Paired Activity Have students work in pairs to
brainstorm a list of all the different kinds of music they
can think of. Then have them compare and contrast the
music in terms of lyrics, instruments, beats, melodies,
and themes.

7 ¡Viva la música!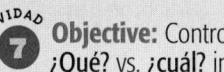

Hablar/Escribir A tu compañero(a) le fascina la música contemporánea y ustedes hablan mucho de ella. Él (Ella) te hace una pregunta con **¿qué?** Tú contestas la pregunta y le haces otra pregunta con **¿cuál?** Sigue el modelo.

modelo

la guitarra / el tambor

Compañero(a): *¿Qué instrumento prefieres, la guitarra o el tambor?*

Tú: *Pues, yo prefiero el tambor. Y a ti, ¿cuál te gusta más?*

1. la letra de una canción de rock /
   la letra de una canción de hip-hop
2. un concierto de rock /
   un recital de música clásica
3. el repertorio de un conjunto de rock /
   el repertorio de una orquesta
4. los conjuntos de salsa /
   los conjuntos de rock
5. el son del piano /
   el son de la trompeta
6. el ritmo de la música rock /
   el ritmo de la rap
7. una canción en inglés /
   una canción en español
8. las cantantes mujeres /
   los cantantes hombres

Vocabulario

La música

la letra *lyrics*	**el recital** *recital*	**el son** *sound*
la melodía *melody*	**el repertorio** *repertoire*	

▶ ¿Qué te importa más, la melodía o la letra? ¿Por qué?

8 Las respuestas

Hablar/Escribir Arturo estudia para el examen de geografía. Tú le haces preguntas para ayudarlo a estudiar. Usa **¿qué?** y **¿cuál?**

modelo

La Pampa es una región de Argentina donde hay mucha agricultura.

Tú: *¿Qué es La Pampa?*

1. La industria más importante para la economía de Argentina es la industria ganadera.
2. 9,7% de las exportaciones de Argentina van destino a Estados Unidos.
3. El sector más rico de la economía chilena es el minero.
4. La unidad monetaria de Paraguay es el guaraní.
5. En Chile se producen muchas frutas como las guayabas, uvas, manzanas, peras y papayas.
6. Paraguay tiene más bosques que los otros países sudamericanos.
7. Los uruguayos toman mucho mate.
8. La Paz y Sucre son las capitales de Bolivia.

trescientos treinta y nueve
España y las Américas Etapa 1
339

Answers

1. A: ¿Qué letra prefieres, la letra de una canción de rock o la letra de una canción de hip-hop?
   B: Pues, yo prefiero... Y a ti, ¿cuál te gusta más?
2. A: ¿Qué prefieres, un concierto de rock o un recital de música clásica?
3. A: ¿Qué repertorio prefieres, el repertorio de un conjunto de rock o el repertorio de una orquesta?
4. A: ¿Qué conjuntos prefieres, los conjuntos de salsa o los conjuntos de rock?
5. A: ¿Qué son prefieres, el son del piano o el son de la trompeta?
6. A: ¿Qué ritmo prefieres, el ritmo de la música rock o el ritmo de la rap?
7. A: ¿Qué canción prefieres, una canción en inglés o una canción en español?
8. A: ¿Qué cantantes prefieres, los hombres o las mujeres?

Teaching Suggestions
Presenting Vocabulary

Present the vocabulary words using definitions and examples. Then have students answer the question at the bottom of the box.

Answers *Answers may vary.*

1. ¿Cuál es la industria más importante para la economía de Argentina?
2. ¿Qué porcentaje de las exportaciones de Argentina van destino a los Estados Unidos?
3. ¿Cuál es el sector más rico de la economía chilena?
4. ¿Cuál es la unidad monetaria de Paraguay?
5. ¿Qué frutas se producen en Chile?
6. ¿Qué país sudamericano tiene más bosques que los otros países sudamericanos?
7. ¿Qué toman los uruguayos?
8. ¿Cuáles son las capitales de Bolivia?

Teaching All Students

Extra Help Have students go back to the reading **El flamenco y otros bailes típicos** on p. 331 and make up study questions using **¿qué?** and **¿cuál?** Then have pairs exchange questions and answer them orally.

Multiple Intelligences

Intrapersonal Ask students to write about whether the music they listen to reflects the mood they are in. What do they listen to when they're sad? Excited? Happy? Angry? Feeling lonely?

Block Schedule

Project Have students pick a type of Spanish music or art movement/school, research its roots and history, and write a short report about how it came to be and who were its most renowned practitioners. (For additional activities, see **Block Scheduling Copymasters**.)

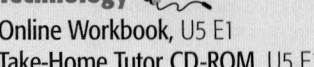

Objective: Transitional practice
Use of ¿qué? in reading

Answers
1. El Museo de Bellas Artes de Valencia.
2. Se presenta Cinco Siglos de Pintura Valenciana.
3. Las obras más representativas de los artistas de esta región.
4. Las pinturas son de los siglos XIV a XIX.
5. 70 pinturas
6. 30 dibujos
7. Sorolla, Pinazo, Degrain y Agrasot
8. Termina el 30 de septiembre.

Objective: Open-ended practice
¿Qué? vs. ¿cuál? in conversation

Answers
Answers will vary. Sample questions:
¿Cuál es la diferencia entre un tapiz y un cuadro?
¿Qué escuela de arte es más reconocida en el mundo, la flamenca o la española?
¿Qué es una naturaleza muerta?
¿Qué hace la figura del artista en *Las meninas*?
¿Qué es un autorretrato?
¿Cuál es la obra más famosa de Goya?

Quick Wrap-up

Have 1 student ask another student a question with ¿qué? or ¿cuál? using the following information:
- tu dirección
- tu música favorita
- tus pasatiempos favoritos
- un bailaor
- la perspectiva

---

9 Cinco siglos

Leer/Hablar/*Escribir* Estás en Valencia y ves este artículo en una revista. Contesta las preguntas.

Aquellos maravillosos años

CINCO SIGLOS DE PINTURA VALENCIANA

El Museo de Bellas Artes de Valencia ha organizado una de sus muestras más ambiciosas de los últimos meses. Su objetivo: ofrecer al visitante un pausado recorrido por más de Cinco Siglos de Pintura Valenciana a través de las obras más representativas de los artistas que han configurado el panorama cultural de esta región entre los siglos XIV y XIX. Un total de 70 pinturas y 30 dibujos ilustran esta brillante exposición antológica, que arranca en el Gótico y concluye en el XIX, con el panorama cultural de grandes artistas como Sorolla, Pinazo, Degrain y Agrasot. *Valencia: Museo de Bellas Artes. Hasta el 30 de septiembre.*

Museo de Bellas Artes de Valencia

1. ¿Qué institución está al centro del artículo?
2. ¿Qué se presenta en ese museo?
3. ¿Qué obras se presentan?
4. ¿De qué siglos son las pinturas?
5. ¿Cuántas pinturas se muestran en esta exposición?
6. ¿Cuántos dibujos se muestran?
7. ¿Qué artistas se mencionan en el artículo?
8. ¿En qué fecha termina la exposición?

More Practice: **Más comunicación** *p. R15*

---

10 En el Prado

STRATEGY: SPEAKING
Discuss a painting For a discussion about a painting, you can talk about **lo que veo, lo que siento, pienso que significa…** and artistic elements that support your ideas: **color, luz y sombra, figuras, perspectiva,** etc.

Hablar/*Escribir* Usa la siguiente lista y escribe seis preguntas para el guía turístico del Museo del Prado. Usa **¿qué?** o **¿cuál(es)?** Luego, discute las preguntas con un(a) compañero(a).

modelo
aspecto de las figuras de El Greco

Tú: *¿Qué aspectos te gustan más de la obra de El Greco?*

Compañero(a): *Me gustan sus figuras largas y también sus colores intensos.*

- **diferencia entre un tapiz y un cuadro**
- **escuela de arte más reconocida**
- **la definición de naturaleza muerta**
- **la figura del artista en** *Las meninas* **(¿hacer?)**
- **la definición de autorretrato**
- **la obra más famosa de Goya**

---

340 | trescientos cuarenta
Unidad 5

Classroom Community

Group Activity Have students work in groups of 4. Each student takes a turn asking the other group members a question using **¿qué?** or **¿cuál?** and the following categories: **bebidas, comida, películas, deportes, música.**

Paired Activity Give each pair of students a print of a painting. After reading the Speaking Strategy on p. 340, have students ask their partner about the painting. When pairs finish discussing their painting, have them trade paintings with another pair and change roles.

GRAMÁTICA — Relative Pronouns

 ¿RECUERDAS? *p. 136* When you learned the subjunctive, you combined two sentences using the relative pronoun **que.**

Relative pronouns are used to link information found in different parts of a sentence. The **relative clause** provides additional information about the person or thing mentioned in the first part of the sentence.

relative pronoun   *relative clause*

Quiero ir al **museo que está cerca del centro**.

*I want to go to the museum **that** is near the center of town.*

You introduce a **relative clause** with a **relative pronoun**. The most common **relative pronoun** in Spanish is **que**. You can use it to refer to both people and things.

refers to a person, the artist

el **artista que pintó este cuadro**

*the artist **who** painted this painting*

refers to a thing, a play

una **obra** teatral **que divierte a todo el mundo**

*a theater play **that** entertains everyone*

Quien (and the plural **quienes**) is the relative pronoun that is used to refer to people. It is usually used after a preposition.

la **cantante con quien** hablé
*the singer **with whom** I spoke*

los **pintores de quienes** te hablé
*the painters **of whom** I spoke*

> There is no accent mark on **quien/quienes** when you use them as **relative pronouns**.

Practice:
Actividades
11 12 13

Más práctica
cuaderno p. 120
Para hispanohablantes
cuaderno p. 118

 Online Workbook
CLASSZONE.COM

11 Conversaciones

Escuchar/Escribir Estás en un museo y te sientas a descansar. Oyes varias conversaciones. Escribe de nuevo lo que dicen las personas en una oración que use **que**.

> **modelo**
>
> **Escuchas:** *Ese cuadro lo pintó mi vecino, el artista.*
>
> **Escribes:** *El artista que pintó ese cuadro es mi vecino.*

1. El escultor _____.
2. Las pinturas _____.
3. El profesor _____.
4. No me gustan las obras _____.
5. El cantaor _____.
6. Las pinturas _____.

Nota cultural

El Museo del Prado tiene un origen curioso. Cuando el rey Fernando VII decidió cambia, las decoraciones del Palacio Real en 1818, puso papel tapiz (*wallpaper*) francés, que no hacía juego con los cuadros de Velázquez y Tiziano que había en las paredes. Entonces el rey integró estos cuadros con los de las colecciones de Carlos III, Carlos V, Felipe II, Felipe IV y Felipe V y creó, en un edificio aparte lo que hoy es el Museo del Prado.

Teaching All Students

Extra Help Working in pairs, have students take turns beginning a sentence by saying the name of a person or thing. The partner must complete the sentence using **que** or preposition + **quien(es)** followed by a clause that describes the person or thing. For example: Luisa... → **Luisa es la compañera con quien practico el zapateado.**

Multiple Intelligences

Kinesthetic Have pairs of students create 5 sentences with relative clauses, then cut their sentences up so that only 1 clause appears on each slip of paper. After they've placed the pieces in an envelope, have them exchange with another pair, who will put the pieces back together again.

Use OHT 14 or write on the board:
Escribe cuantas palabras de preguntar que recuerdes.

Answers
Answers will vary. Answers could include:
¿qué?, ¿cuál(es)?, ¿quién(es)?, ¿dónde?, ¿adónde?, ¿cuándo?, ¿por qué?, ¿cómo?

Teaching Suggestions
Teaching Relative Pronouns

- Point out that the relative pronoun is often omitted in English, but can never be omitted in Spanish.
- Explain that the relative pronouns **que** and **quien** can both be used to speak of a person. After a preposition, **quien** is used.

 11 Objective: Controlled practice Listening comprehension/relative pronouns

Answers (See script, p. 327D.)
1. El escultor que hizo esa escultura es mi primo.
2. Las pinturas que tiene ese museo son de la escuela española.
3. El profesor que da esa clase de violín es el profesor Gallego.
4. No me gustan las obras que pintó Goya en sus últimos años de vida.
5. El cantaor que vimos en el espectáculo de flamenco tenía una voz increíble.
6. Las pinturas que vimos ayer en el museo eran muy bellas.

Teaching Note

The art in the **Nota cultural** is **Las hilanderas** by Velázquez from the Prado.

Block Schedule

Retention Divide the class into groups of 4. Have each group write 10 simple sentences (for example, **El artista tiene mucho talento.**), then exchange their sentences with another group who adds a relative clause to each sentence (for example, **El artista que pintó este cuadro tiene mucho talento.**). Ask groups to present their best sentences to the class. (For additional activities, see **Block Scheduling Copymasters**.)

Teaching Resource Options

Print

Más práctica Workbook PE,
  pp. 113–116; 120
Actividades para todos Workbook PE,
  pp. 131–136
Cuaderno para hispanohablantes
  PE, pp. 113–114; 118
Block Scheduling Copymasters
Unit 5 Resource Book
  Más práctica Workbook TE,
    pp. 2–5; 9
  Cuaderno para hispanohablantes
    TE, pp. 20–21; 25
  Actividades para todos Workbook
  TE, pp. 10–15
  Information Gap Activities, p. 29
  Absent Student Copymasters, p. 37

Technology

Online Workbook, U5E1
Take-Home Tutor CD-ROM, U5E1

Teaching Suggestions
Presenting Vocabulary

Use books and/or the names of literary works of the various types to present the vocabulary. Give the names of additional literary works and have students give the type. Discuss students' reading preferences.

Objective: Controlled practice
Relative pronouns/vocabulary
in conversation

Answers

1. A: ¿Qué es eso? B: Es el cuento que leí en la clase de literatura. 2. A: ¿Quién es él? B: Es el actor con quien hablé después de la producción. 3. A: ¿Qué es eso? B: Es el cuadro que pinté en la clase de arte. 4. A: ¿Qué es eso? B: Es la obra de teatro que estamos leyendo en la clase de drama. 5. A: ¿Quién es él? B: Es el pintor a quien más admiro. 6. A: ¿Qué es eso? B: Es la novela que compré el otro día. 7. A: ¿Qué es eso? B: Es la autobiografía que quiero leer. 8. A: ¿Qué es eso? B: Es la biografía de que te hablé el otro día. 9. A: ¿Qué es eso? B: El la poesía que escribió me padre. 10. A: ¿Quién es él? B: Es el actor que trabaja en la producción de la obra de teatro.

---

12 ¿Qué es eso?

Hablar/Escribir Le preguntas a tu amigo(a) español(a) sobre varias cosas y personas. Cuando trate de una persona, usa **quien** y no **que**. ¿Cómo te responde?

> **modelo**
>
> escritora (estudié)
>
> **Tú:** ¿Quién es ella?
>
> **Compañero(a):** *Es la escritora con quien estudié.*

1. cuento (leí en la clase de literatura)
2. actor (hablé después de la producción)
3. cuadro (pinté en la clase de arte)
4. obra de teatro (estamos leyendo en la clase de drama)
5. pintor (más admiro)
6. novela (compré el otro día)
7. autobiografía (quiero leer)
8. biografía (te hablé el otro día)
9. poesía (escribió mi padre)
10. actor (trabaja en la producción de la obra de teatro)

Vocabulario

La literatura

la autobiografía *autobiography*	**la ficción** *fiction*
la biografía *biography*	**la poesía** *poetry*
el cuento *short story*	**la producción** *production*
el drama *drama*	

♻️ **Ya sabes:**   el ensayo   la novela   la obra de teatro   el poema

¿Qué tipo de literatura disfrutas más?

---

13 Los artistas ♻️

Hablar/Escribir En grupos de tres o cuatro, escojan una identidad artística: uno(a) puede ser un(a) pintor(a), otro(a) un(a) bailador(a), un(a) escritor(a), un(a) actor (actriz), etc. Imaginen que están en una fiesta hablando de su trabajo, sus obras o las obras de los demás.

> **modelo**
>
> escritor
>
> **Tú:** ¿Quién es ese señor?
>
> **Compañero(a): 1:** *¿Ése? Es el escritor que escribió* El mundo del artista.
>
> **Compañero(a): 2:** *¿No te acuerdas de esa novela? Es la novela de la que te hablé el otro día.*
>
> **Compañero(a): 3:** …

1. escritor(a)		5. novela
2. pintor(a)		6. drama
3. bailador(a)		7. cuento
4. actor (actriz)		8. producción

Classroom Community

Paired Activity Write a list of people students know on the board. Have pairs of students work together to write descriptions of the people, using relative pronouns. For example: **El señor Green → El señor Green es el profesor que enseña matemáticas.** Have pairs present their descriptions to the class.

Portfolio Have students imagine they are art critics. Their job is to review an imaginary exhibit of Spanish art that has come to town. Have students pick the artist(s) they want to review and explain why they do or don't like the works in the exhibit.

Rubric   A = 13–15 pts. B = 10–12 pts. C = 7–9 pts. D = 4–6 pts. F = < 4 pts.

Writing criteria	Scale
Vocabulary use	1 2 3 4 5
Grammar/spelling accuracy	1 2 3 4 5
Creativity/appearance	1 2 3 4 5

PARTE C
Todo en acción

Activity 14 brings together all concepts presented.

14 Mi colección privada

Hablar En grupos de tres o cuatro, conversen sobre la colección que se ofrece en este anuncio. Hablen sobre las pinturas que les gustan o que no les gustan, por qué, si les interesa la oferta, etc.

Los más bellos cuadros del arte tradicional de España

Ahora las obras de los grandes pintores españoles están reunidas en una colección única: «*Obras Maestras de los Grandes Pintores Españoles*». Admirará retratos, paisajes, naturalezas muertas... todos en reproducciones de alta calidad.

modelo

Tú: *¿Cuál de estos pinturas te gusta más?*

Compañero(a): 1: *¿A mí? Me gusta la de El Greco.*

Compañero(a): 2: *Yo prefiero la de Goya. No hay nadie que pinte como él.*

More Practice: Más comunicación *p. R15*   **Online Workbook** CLASSZONE.COM

 **Refrán**

De músico, poeta y loco, todos tenemos un poco.

¿Qué quiere decir el refrán? ¿Crees que es verdad? ¿Cuál de las características que se mencionan te parece más importante? ¿Por qué?

trescientos cuarenta y tres
España y las Américas Etapa I **343**

---

13 Objective: Transitional practice
Relative pronouns in conversation
♻ **Demonstratives**

Answers will vary.

14 Objective: Open-ended practice
Relative pronouns in conversation

Answers will vary.

Quick Wrap-up

Have students say what the following people were doing when they saw them yesterday: **¿Qué estaban haciendo las siguientes personas cuando las viste ayer?** For example: un pintor → Ayer vi un pintor que pintaba al óleo.
• una bailaora
• un músico
• una niña
• dos muchachas
• un señor

Teaching All Students

Extra Help Have students complete the following sentences: **No me gustó la pintura que... Ayer conocimos al hombre que... El novio de mi amiga es el actor que... Éstas son las esculturas que...**

Challenge Ask students to give an oral synopsis of their favorite piece of literature. They should include the title, author, theme(s), and a brief summary of the plot.

Multiple Intelligences

Intrapersonal Ask students to pick a work of art, piece of music, or piece of literature that has had a profound effect on them and explain why it moved them.

Block Schedule

Variety Have pairs of students write definitions for the following words, using a relative pronoun in each definition: un arpa, el cante jondo, un cuadro histórico, el fresco, una trompeta, el flamenco, una autobiografía, una naturaleza muerta. (For additional activities, see **Block Scheduling Copymasters**.)

Teaching Resource Options

Print

Actividades para todos Workbook PE,
  pp. 137–139
Block Scheduling Copymasters
Unit 5 Resource Book
  Actividades para todos Workbook
    TE, pp. 16–18
  Audioscript, p. 42
  Video Activities, pp. 235–238
  Absent Student Copymasters, p. 38
  Audioscript, pp. 239–241

Audiovisual

OHT 14 (Quick Start)
Audio Program CD 13, Tracks 4–5
Video Program Videotape 39:00 / DVD,
  Unit 5

Technology

Online Workbook, U5E1
Take-Home Tutor CD-ROM, U5E1

Quick Start Review

♻ Literature vocabulary
Use OHT 14 or write on the board:
Escribe 3 tipos de no-ficción y 3 tipos
de ficción.

Answers
biografía, autobiografía, ensayo
novela, drama, cuento

Teaching Suggestions

- **Prereading** Provide students with
  the information in the Culture
  Highlights on TE p. 345.
- **Strategy: Compare famous authors**
  Present the Reading Strategy and
  have students prepare their charts.
- **Reading** Ask students to skip over
  any unknown words as they read.
  Then have students check their
  comprehension by summarizing each
  paragraph to themselves after they
  read it.
- **Post-reading** Have students
  complete their Reading Strategy
  charts. Then ask them which U.S.
  writers have been influenced by their
  wartime experience?

AUDIO
En voces
LECTURA

PARA LEER

STRATEGY: READING
Compare famous authors Unamuno
and Matute share a love of Spain.
How else are they alike or
different? Use this chart to make
your comparisons:

	Unamuno	Matute
fechas importantes		
eventos influyentes		
preocupaciones		
¿?		

What emotions does each express
in the excerpts you read?

LA IDENTIDAD ESPAÑOLA

la guerra	lucha entre dos fuerzas
derechista	conservador en extremo
posguerra	después de la guerra
vencer	conquistar

Miguel de Unamuno

Miguel de Unamuno, escritor español, nació en Bilbao en
1864 y fue uno de los autores más importantes del siglo XIX.
Tuvo una gran conciencia social y se preocupó mucho por la
identidad y el futuro de España, como otros autores de su
generación, que se llama «La Generación del '98».

Unamuno además pensaba mucho sobre cuestiones filosóficas
de la vida y de la inmortalidad. Cultivó todos los géneros
literarios, pero sus ensayos y novelas son los más famosos.

Unamuno escribió sobre su amor a España y los problemas
políticos del país durante un período de cambio violento. De
él es la cita conocida:

❝ ¡Me duele España! ❞

Durante esa época, una guerra civil empezó en España.
Unamuno se opuso a Francisco Franco, el general derechista.
Por esto, las fuerzas de Franco mantuvieron a Unamuno bajo
arresto a domicilio. Unamuno murió el último día de 1936—el
primer año de la guerra—sin cambiar su opinión política. Dijo:

❝ Venceréis pero no convenceréis. ❞

344 doscientos cuarenta y cuatro
     Unidad 5

Classroom Community

Paired Activity Provide students with the
information in the Culture Highlights on TE p. 345.
Then have partners pretend that one of them is Miguel
de Unamuno or Ana María Matute and the other is a
magazine reporter. Have students write an interview
between the reporter and the writer. Then have them
dramatize their interview for the class.

Storytelling Ask students to work with a partner to
tell a coming-of-age story about a girl or boy who
grows up during a time of war. Have them focus on the
child's experiences, what he/she sees, and how it
changes him/her into a different person.

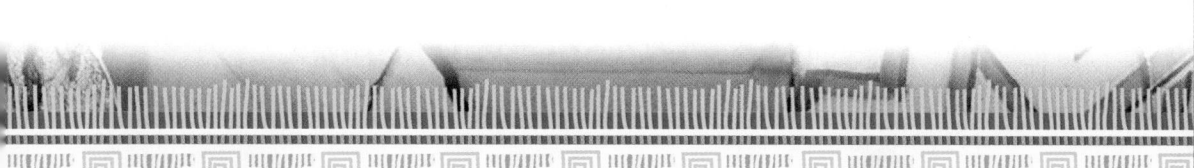

Ana María Matute

Ana María Matute, novelista española contemporánea, nació en Barcelona en 1926. Tenía diez años cuando comenzó la guerra civil y su familia se mudaba de Madrid a Barcelona para escaparse de la violencia. El punto de vista triste de sus novelas refleja[1] la desilusión que ella sintió durante la guerra civil y los años de represión que la siguieron. Ella dice:

> 66 Todo era injusto e incomprensible. El mundo no era tal y como nos lo habían explicado. Yo creo que nuestra generación dio tantos grandes escritores porque fuimos víctimas de un trauma muy fuerte. No se podía hacer ni decir nada. De ahí nació un sentimiento de rebeldía que creo aún mantengo. 99

A pesar de sus experiencias traumáticas de niña, Matute ha tenido un éxito extraordinario con su producción literaria. Además de ser una de los autores más importantes de la narrativa de posguerra española, es la única mujer en la Real

[1] reflects

Academia de España. Entre sus novelas más conocidas están *Los Abel, Los hijos muertos, La trampa, El río* y *Olvidado Rey Gudú*.

Ella reconoce la dificultad de escribir novelas. Dice:

> 66 Quien diga lo contrario o miente[2], ¡o es un genio[3] o es un desastre! 99

[2] is lying
[3] genius

Online Workbook
CLASSZONE.COM

¿Comprendiste?

1. ¿A qué generación literaria pertenece Unamuno?
2. ¿Cuál es la actitud de Unamuno hacia Francisco Franco y sus fuerzas?
3. ¿Cómo influyó la guerra civil de España en el pensamiento y la vida de Matute?
4. Según Matute, ¿por qué hay tantos escritores buenos en su generación?

¿Qué piensas?

1. ¿Qué quiere decir el comentario famoso de Unamuno: «¡Me duele España!»?
2. En tu opinión, ¿qué significa el comentario de Matute sobre la dificultad de escribir novelas?

Hazlo tú

Haz una investigación sobre la guerra civil española y escribe un ensayo breve sobre ella. Explica sus causas, quiénes participaron, etc. O escoge un cuento, una película o un libro que tenga una guerra como tema y escribe un ensayo sobre éste.

trescientos cuarenta y cinco
España y las Américas Etapa 1
345

Teaching Resource Options

Print

Cuaderno para hispanohablantes
PE, pp. 119–120
Unit 5 Resource Book
Cuaderno para hispanohablantes
TE, pp. 26–27
Information Gap Activities, pp. 30–31
Family Involvement, pp. 39–40

Audiovisual

OHT 15 (Quick Start)

Technology

eTest Plus Online/Test Generator
CD-ROM

www.classzone.com

Quick Start Review

 Demonstrative adjectives

Use OHT 15 or write on the board:
Make the necessary changes in the
following sentences:

1. Este / melodía es muy bonita.
2. Ese / cuadros / son interesantes.
3. Aquel / mujeres son cantadoras.
4. Este / figuras son pequeñas.
5. Aquel / ensayo es de Unamuno.

Answers
1. Esta...
2. Esos...
3. Aquellas...
4. Estas...
5. Aquel...

Teaching Suggestions
What Have Students Learned?

Have students look at the "Now you
can…" notes and give examples of
each category. Have them spend extra
time reviewing categories they feel they
are weak in by consulting the "To
review" notes.

 **Answers**

1. esa	6. este
2. Esa	7. Aquellos
3. ésa	8. Aquéllos
4. Este	9. Aquel
5. Éste	

ETAPA 1

En uso
REPASO Y MÁS COMUNICACIÓN

OBJECTIVES
- Identify and specify
- Request clarification
- Express relationships
- Discuss art forms

Now you can...
- discuss art forms.
- identify and specify.

To review
- demonstrative adjectives and pronouns see p. 336.

1 Hoy

Completa varias conversaciones que escuchaste hoy con las
formas correctas de las palabras entre paréntesis.

Conversación No. 1 (ese)

José: ¿Ves __1__ guitarra?

María: ¿__2__ guitarra en la mesa?

José: Sí, __3__ ¡La acabo de comprar!

Conversación No. 2 (este)

Ana: __4__ cuadro es muy interesante.

Irma: ¿__5__? No me gusta.

Ana: ¿De veras? Yo pienso que __6__ cuadro es el mejor en el museo.

Conversación No. 3 (aquel)

Andrés: __7__ muchachos son artistas.

Beto: ¿Estás seguro? ¿__8__?

Andrés: Sí. El muchacho de la camisa azul pintó __9__ cuadro.

Now you can...
- request clarification.

To review
- ¿qué? vs. ¿cuál? see p. 338.

2 La clase de arte

Estás en la clase de arte. Durante la clase, tu compañero(a) te
pregunta varias cosas. Primero, escribe preguntas para cada
tema y luego contéstalas.

modelo

autorretrato
¿Qué es un autorretrato?
Un autorretrato es un retrato de una persona hecho por ella misma.

tapiz o pintura al óleo
¿Cuál te gusta más: el tapiz o la pintura al óleo?
A mí me gusta más el tapiz.

1. naturaleza muerta o paisaje
2. tapiz
3. escuela española o escuela flamenca
4. naturaleza muerta
5. los cuadros de Goya o los cuadros de Velázquez
6. el primer plano

346 trescientos cuarenta y seis
Unidad 5

Classroom Community

Game Call on a volunteer to pick out something in
the classroom to describe. The student begins with a
demonstrative pronoun, then proceeds to describe the
item. The class has to guess what the object is.

Cooperative Learning Have students work in
groups of 4. Groups do the activities on pp. 346–347
orally, while members write the answers. Student 1
writes **Actividad 1,** Student 2 writes **Actividad 2,**
Student 3 writes **Actividad 3,** and Student 4 writes
Actividad 4. Then the group checks the papers before
submitting them for a class grade.

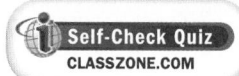

Now you can...
- request clarification.

To review
- ¿qué? vs. ¿cuál?
see p. 338.

③ La profesora de música

Tomas una clase de música y tu profesora quiere saber más sobre tus intereses. Completa sus preguntas con **¿qué?** o **¿cuál(es)?**

modelo

¿ <u>Qué</u> instrumento quieres aprender a tocar?

1. ¿_____ crees es más fácil de aprender, la guitarra o el violín?
2. ¿_____ clase de música quieres aprender?
3. ¿_____ de las canciones quieres aprender primero?
4. ¿_____ son tus grupos musicales favoritos?
5. ¿_____ estudiaste en el colegio?
6. ¿_____ entrenamiento musical has tenido?

Now you can...
- express relationships.

To review
- relative pronouns
see p. 341.

④ La reunión

Estás en una reunión estudiantil en Madrid con tu amigo(a) madrileño(a). Pregúntale a tu compañero(a) quiénes son las personas que ves, basándote en los dibujos y las siguientes palabras.

modelo

¿él?

Tú: *¿Quién es él?*

Compañero(a): *¿Él? Es el estudiante que toca la trompeta.*

pintar   tocar   bailar jota   escribir   marcar el compás

Mi autobiografía

1. ¿ella?   2. ¿él?   3. ¿ella?   4. ¿ella?   5. ¿él?   6. ¿él?

trescientos cuarenta y siete
España y las Américas Etapa 1

347

---

② Answers

1. ¿Cuál te gusta más: la naturaleza muerta o el paisaje? / *Responses will vary.*
2. ¿Qué es un tapiz? / Un tapiz es un cuadro hecho de lana, seda o algodón decorado con un imagen de lana o seda.
3. ¿Cuál te gusta más: la escuela española o la escuela flamenca? / *Responses will vary.*
4. ¿Qué es una naturaleza muerta? / Una naturaleza muerta es un cuadro que representa cosas inanimadas.
5. ¿Cuáles te gustan más: los cuadros de Goya o los cuadros de Velázquez? / *Responses will vary.*
6. ¿Qué es el primer plano? / Es la parte del cuadro más cerca de la persona que lo está mirando.

③ Answers

1. Cuál	4. Cuáles
2. Qué	5. Qué
3. Cuál *o* Cuáles	6. Qué

④ Answers

1. A: ¿Quién es ella?
   B: Es la estudiante que baila la jota.
2. A: ¿Quién es él?
   B: Es el estudiante que toca el arpa.
3. A: ¿Quién es ella?
   B: Es la estudiante que escribió su autobiografía.
4. A: ¿Quién es ella?
   B: Es la estudiante que pintó el paisaje.
5. A: ¿Quién es él?
   B: Es el estudiante que pintó la naturaleza muerta.
6. A: ¿Quién es él?
   B: Es el estudiante que marca el compás con el zapateado.

■ Block Schedule

Retention Divide students into groups of 4. Have students go around the group stating who their favorite singer is and why. For example: **El cantante a quien prefiero es.... Tiene una voz muy buena y original.** Once they've gone around once, have them repeat the activity with their favorite **escritor(a), artista,** and **bailarín(a).** (For additional activities, see **Block Scheduling Copymasters.**)

Teaching All Students

Extra Help Before doing **Actividad 3,** have students determine if each item calls for a choice or if the question is general. Remind them that **¿cuál?** implies choice. Do the activity as a class. Make up similar items if students require additional practice.

Multiple Intelligences

Visual Hold up a picture of a famous person. Tell students they can't use the person's name, but must tell who it is. For example: **Es el pintor que pintó** *Guernica.*

Verbal Have students respond to the following statements with either **¡Es horrible!** or **¡Es una maravilla!:** Hay un accidente en el tablado de flamenco. / Te regalo una pintura de naturaleza muerta. / Aquí hay una pintura de Goya. / Te invitan a bailar la sardana. / Acabas de leer un libro muy interesante.

Teaching Resource Options

Print 📖

Block Scheduling Copymasters
Unit 5 Resource Book
  Audioscript, p. 44
  Vocabulary Quizzes, pp. 46–48
  Grammar Quizzes, pp. 49–50
  Etapa Exam, Forms A and B,
    pp. 51–60
  Examen para hispanohablantes,
    pp. 61–65
  Portfolio Assessment, pp. 66–67
  Multiple Choice Test Questions,
    pp. 226–228

Audiovisual 🎧

OHT 15 (Quick Start)
Audio Program CD 20, Track 8

Technology 💻

eTest Plus Online/Test Generator
CD-ROM

  ⓘ www.classzone.com

Rubric: Speaking

Criteria	Scale	
Sentence structure	1 2 3	A = 11–12 pts.
Vocabulary use	1 2 3	B = 9–10 pts.
Originality	1 2 3	C = 7–8 pts.
Fluency	1 2 3	D = 4–6 pts.
		F = < 4 pts.

En tu propia voz

Rubric: Writing

Criteria	Scale	
Vocabulary use	1 2 3 4 5	A = 13–15 pts.
Accuracy	1 2 3 4 5	B = 10–12 pts.
Creativity, appearance	1 2 3 4 5	C = 7–9 pts.
		D = 4–6 pts.
		F = < 4 pts.

Teaching Note: En tu propia voz

Writing Strategy Suggest that students present a thorough and balanced review. In order to write an informative review, they should discuss positive and negative attributes of the painting.

---

⑤ Investigación

STRATEGY: SPEAKING

Organize ideas for research Good research begins with good questions, but first categorize the areas to investigate. Where do you want to begin? Use the following chart to ask questions that will direct your research.

Francisco de Goya
¿Cuándo empezó a pintar?
¿Dónde vivía?
¿Cuántos años vivió?
¿Cuántos cuadros pintó?
¿A quiénes conocía?

En grupos de dos o tres, escriban seis preguntas sobre los grandes pintores españoles. Busquen las respuestas en una enciclopedia o en Internet.

modelo

Tú: *Yo quiero saber cuándo y por qué empezó a pintar Francisco de Goya.*

Compañero(a) 1: *Yo quiero saber cuántas obras pintó Goya durante su vida y cuántos años vivió.*

Compañero(a) 2: …

---

⑥ En tu propia voz

ESCRITURA Trabajas como crítico(a) de arte para el periódico estudiantil. Usa la pintura aquí o busca otra pintura de uno de los grandes pintores españoles y escribe un breve ensayo. Incluye observaciones sobre lo siguiente:

Pablo Picasso, Las meninas, 1957

- cómo te hace sentir
- colores
- figuras
- escuela
- tipo de pintura
- algún detalle de la vida del pintor
- ¿…?

modelo

Usando Las meninas *de Velázquez como modelo, Picasso rehace el cuadro en su propio estilo, usando técnicas modernas de composición y color.*

CONEXIONES

Los estudios sociales La guerra civil de España fue un evento muy importante en la vida de la gente española. Esta tragedia también tuvo una gran influencia sobre algunos de los artistas y autores más conocidos de España. ¿Por qué empezó la guerra civil? ¿Cómo terminó? Crea una cronología *(timeline)* de la época, incluyendo por lo menos diez eventos importantes de la guerra. Describe en una o dos oraciones la importancia de cada evento.

General Primo de Rivera establece una dictadura militar. ○ ——— Elecciones municipales

1923 ——————— **1931**

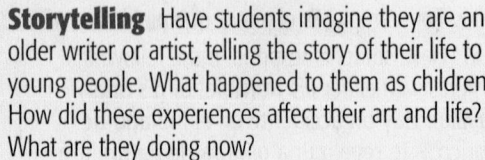

348 trescientos cuarenta y ocho
Unidad 5

Classroom Community

Storytelling Have students imagine they are an older writer or artist, telling the story of their life to young people. What happened to them as children? How did these experiences affect their art and life? What are they doing now?

Learning Scenario Ask students to bring in a print or photocopy of their favorite painting. Students should research the artist, the period, the style, etc. so that they are knowledgeable about the painting. Each student presents his/her painting to the class and answers any questions.

En resumen
REPASO DE VOCABULARIO

 Flashcards
CLASSZONE.COM

DISCUSS ART FORMS

Art and paintings

al óleo	oil (painting)
el autorretrato	self-portrait
el cuadro	painting
el cuadro histórico	historical painting
la escuela	school (of art)
la figura	figure
el fondo	background
el fresco	fresco
la naturaleza muerta	still life
el paisaje	landscape
la perspectiva	perspective
el primer plano	foreground
el retrato	portrait
el siglo	century
el tapiz	tapestry

♻ **Ya sabes**

el bote	boat
el ejército	army
luchar contra	to fight against
el océano	ocean
el (la) opresor(a)	oppressor
la orilla	shore

Dance

el (la) bailaor(a)	flamenco dancer
el (la) cantaor(a)	flamenco singer
el cante	flamenco song
el cante jondo	tragic flamenco song
dar golpes	to stamp
dar palmadas	to clap hands
el flamenco	flamenco dancing
interpretar	to interpret
la jota	Aragonese folk dance
la saeta	Andalusian song
la sardana	Catalan folk dance
el tablado	stage floor
el tablao	flamenco group
el zapateado	rhythmic heel tapping

Literature

la autobiografía	autobiography
la biografía	biography
el cuento	short story
el drama	drama
la ficción	fiction
la poesía	poetry
la producción	production

Music

el compás	rhythm, beat
la letra	lyrics
la melodía	melody
el recital	recital
el repertorio	repertoire
el ritmo	rhythm
el son	sound

Musical instruments

el arpa (fem.)	harp
las castañuelas	castanets
las maracas	maracas
la pandereta	tambourine
el tambor	drum
la trompeta	trumpet
el violín	violin

♻ **Ya sabes**

el ensayo	essay
la novela	novel
la obra teatral	theatrical work, play
el poema	poem

IDENTIFY AND SPECIFY

♻ **Ya sabes**

este, esta, estos, estas
éste, ésta, éstos, éstas
ese, esa, esos, esas
ése, ésa, ésos, ésas
aquel, aquella, aquellos, aquellas
aquél, aquélla, aquéllos, aquéllas
esto, eso, aquello

REQUEST CLARIFICATION

¿Qué? vs. ¿cuál?

¿**Qué** es el cante jondo?
¿**Cuál** prefieres, el flamenco o la jota?

EXPRESS RELATIONSHIPS

Relative pronouns

Ésta es la bailaora **que** vimos anoche.
Aquél es el cantaor con **quien** hablamos.

Juego

Sopa de letras
¡Nunca tuve vida pero ahora estoy
muerta! ¿Qué soy?

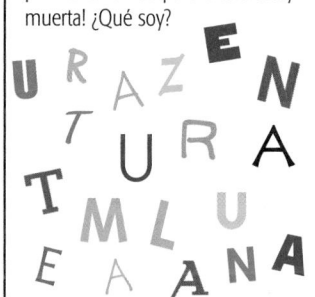

Critical Thinking

Ask students to discuss the reasons behind their art preferences. What influences their preferences? Content? Style? Color? If they were to go to a museum, what type of exhibit would they prefer to see? Why?

Interdisciplinary Connections

Social Studies Have students research one particular event of the Spanish Civil War from the timeline they created for **Conexiones**. What was the event? What led up to it? What were the repercussions?

Quick Start Review

♻ Etapa vocabulary

Use OHT 15 or write on the board:
Escribe 3 tipos de bailes españoles y 2 tipos de canciones españolas.

Answers
el flamenco, la jota, la sardana
el cante jondo, la saeta

Teaching Suggestions
Vocabulary Review

Give a definition, synonym, or example of 15 vocabulary words. Have students write the words. Then have students exchange papers for peer correction.

Dictation

Dictate the following sentences to review the **Etapa**:

1. Esta pintura es de El Greco. Ésta es de Velázquez.
2. ¿Cuál de los tapices te interesa más?
3. ¿Te gustan los bailaores de quienes te hablé?
4. Quiero hablar con el artista que pintó este cuadro.

Juego

Answer: una naturaleza muerta

Block Schedule

Retention Have students create 5 groups of 3 words in which 1 word doesn't fit the group theme. Then have them exchange with a partner to guess which words don't belong. (For additional activities, see **Block Scheduling Copymasters**.)

Teaching All Students

Extra Help Have students work in small groups to create word puzzles using the vocabulary. Distribute the words among the groups. They can create crosswords, word searches, or **sopa de letras** puzzles. Copy and distribute the puzzles for students to solve.

Native Speakers Have students prepare the biography of a well-known Spanish or Latin American composer. Then have them present the biography to the class and play, if possible, an example of his/her music.

Multiple Intelligences

Visual Show students Pablo Picasso's **Las meninas**. Then have students create their own versions of **Las meninas**. They may use stick figures, cubes, paper cut-outs, etc. Display the art work in the room and have students discuss what they see.

Planning Guide CLASSROOM MANAGEMENT

OBJECTIVES

Communication
- Referring to people and objects *pp. 358–361*
- Expressing relationships *pp. 362–363*
- Making generalizations *pp. 364–365*
- Describing arts and crafts *pp. 352–353, 354–355*

Grammar
- Reviewing the use of direct object pronouns *pp. 358–359*
- Reviewing the use of indirect object pronouns *pp. 360–361*
- Using relative pronouns *pp. 362–363*
- Using **lo que** *pp. 364–365*

Culture
- Pre-Columbian civilizations *p. 352–353, 354–355, 360–364*
- Regional vocabulary *p. 356*
- Traditional regional dances *p. 359*
- The Mexican architect Ricardo Legorreta *pp. 366–367*

♻ Recycling
- Arts vocabulary *p. 358*
- Workplace vocabulary *p. 360*
- Verbs like **gustar** *p. 361*

STRATEGIES

Listening Strategies
- Improve your auditory memory *p. 354*

Speaking Strategies
- Maintain a discussion *p. 356*
- Discuss Latin American dance *p. 370*

Reading Strategies
- Gather and sort information *TE p. 366*

Writing Strategies
- Tell who, what, where, when, why, and how *TE p. 370*

Connecting Cultures Strategies
- Learn about pre-Columbian civilizations *p. 352–353, 354–355, 360, 364*
- Recognize variations in vocabulary *p. 356*
- Discover traditional regional dances *p. 359*
- Use architecture as a cultural text *p. 366*
- Connect and compare what you know about architecture in your community to help you learn about architecture in a new community *pp. 366–367*

PROGRAM RESOURCES

Print
- *Más práctica* Workbook PE *pp. 121–128*
- *Actividades para todos* Workbook PE *pp. 141–150*
- Block Scheduling Copymasters *pp. 113–120*
- Unit 5 Resource Book
  Más práctica Workbook TE *pp. 71–78*
  Actividades para todos Workbook TE *pp. 79–88*
  Cuaderno para hispanohablantes TE *pp. 89–96*
  Information Gap Activities *pp. 97–100*
  Family Letter *p. 101*
  Absent Student Copymasters *pp. 102–108*
  Family Involvement *pp. 109–110*
  Audioscript *pp. 111–113*
  Assessment Program, Unit 5, Etapa 2 *pp. 115–138; 229–231*
  Answer Keys *pp. 242–247*

Audiovisual
- Audio Program CD 14
- *Canciones* CD
- Overhead Transparencies M1–M5; 19–33
- Word Tiles U5E2

Technology
- eEdition Plus Online/eEdition CD-ROM
- Easy Planner Plus Online/Easy Planner CD-ROM
- eTest Plus Online/Test Generator CD-ROM
- Online Workbook
- Take-Home Tutor CD-ROM
- ⓘ www.classzone.com

✔ Assessment Program Options
- Unit 5 Resource Book
  Vocabulary Quizzes
  Grammar Quizzes
  Etapa Exam Forms A and B
  Examen para hispanohablantes
  Portfolio Assessment
  Multiple Choice Test Questions
- Audio Program CD 20
- eTest Plus Online/Test Generator CD-ROM

Native Speakers
- *Cuaderno para hispanohablantes* PE *pp. 121–128*
- *Cuaderno para hispanohablantes* TE (Unit 5 Resource Book)
- *Examen para hispanohablantes* (Unit 5 Resource Book)
- Audio Program *(Para hispanohablantes)* CD 14, 20
- Audioscript (Unit 5 Resource Book)

Student Text
Listening Activity Scripts

 **Situaciones** *pages 354–355*

• CD 14

Álvaro: ¿Adónde fuiste con tu familia este verano?

Marta: Bueno, mamá siempre ha querido conocer México, así que pasamos un mes en la Ciudad de México.

Iván: ¿Qué te pareció?

Marta: Pues, increíble. ¡Hubieras visto las pirámides de Teotihuacán! ¡Enormes!

Isabel: Sí, he leído un poco sobre esas pirámides. Son una obra de arquitectura sin igual en el mundo.

Marta: Sin duda. Pero lo que más me impresionó es que esa civilización existió siglos antes de que Colón haya llegado a las Américas.

Iván: Es verdad. Había civilizaciones muy avanzadas en partes de México y Guatemala cuando París y Madrid se construían.

Isabel: Difícil de creer. Como papá es arqueólogo, desde niños nos ha contado mucho sobre la escritura jeroglífica de los mayas, y de los descubrimientos más recientes en México y Guatemala.

Álvaro: ¿Sabías que en los Altos de Chiapas y en Guatemala todavía hay muchos indígenas de descendencia maya?

Marta: Sí, claro. Las mujeres mayas de Chiapas hacen unos tejidos preciosos. Papá me trajo uno en uno de sus viajes.

Isabel: ¡Las técnicas que usan hoy día para hacer los tejidos son las mismas que usaban los mayas hace siglos!

Iván: Y tú, ¡que no te puedes acordar de lo que te enseñó tu madre ayer!

Isabel: ¡No seas bárbaro!

Álvaro: La verdad es que todos los países latinoamericanos tienen una historia precolombina fascinante. Piensa en los incas de Machu Picchu; o los chibchas en partes de Colombia.

Marta: ¿Sabéis que? Me gustaría estudiar más sobre la historia precolombina.

Iván: Como yo quiero ser artista, prefiero estudiar el arte precolombino.

Isabel: Pero, Iván, los artistas registraban la historia en el arte; interesante, ¿no? No sólo estaban creando piezas de belleza, también estaban documentando la historia de su pueblo.

Álvaro: ¡Dios mío! Hay mucho que aprender. Pero por el momento tengo mucha hambre. ¿Por qué no vamos al café?

 **4 ¿Lo conoces?** *page 358*

Modelo:

    Chica: ¿Conoces las pirámides de Teotihuacán?

    Chico: No, no las conozco. Nunca he viajado a México.

1. **Chica:** ¿Conoces las ruinas de Tenochtitlán?

    Chico: Fíjate que las conozco. Fuimos a México hace dos años.

2. **Chica:** ¿Conoces el Templo del Gran Jaguar?

    Chico: Claro. Viví en Guatemala por un año.

3. **Chica:** ¿Conoces el Templo Mayor?

    Chico: ¿El Templo Mayor? ¿Dónde está?

4. **Chica:** ¿Conoces el Museo del Prado en Madrid?

    Chico: ¡Es un museo increíble! Puedes pasar horas allí.

5. **Chica:** ¿Conoces las pinturas de El Greco?

    Chico: No, no las conozco, pero he leído un poco sobre su vida.

6. **Chica:** ¿Conoces la obra maestra de Velázquez, *Las meninas?*

    Chico: Ay, sí, claro. Es una gran obra.

 **13 Efraín** *page 364*

Te voy a decir todo lo que vi en mi viaje a Guatemala. Aprendí mucho sobre el período clásico de los mayas. Lo que más me inspiró fueron las pirámides enormes en Tikal. Vine aquí a estudiar la historia maya. Lo más fascinante tiene que ser la escritura jeroglífica en la cerámica y también en las piedras de los templos. ¡Vi unos objetos de arte bellísimos! No me explico cómo sabían hacer obras tan delicadas y tan finas. Lo que descubrí es que me fascina la historia maya. Ay, antes de que se me olvide, te compré unos tejidos hechos por las mujeres mayas. Son increíbles. Te los mando cuando pueda. Abrazos de tu amigo Efraín.

Sample Lesson Plan - 50 Minute Schedule

DAY 1

Etapa Opener
• Quick Start Review (TE, p. 350) 5 MIN.
• Have students look at the *Etapa* Opener and answer the questions. 5 MIN.
• Use an expansion activity from TE p. 351 for variety and reinforcement. 5 MIN.

En contexto: Vocabulario
• Quick Start Review (TE, p. 352) 5 MIN.
• Present *Descubre*, p. 352. 5 MIN.
• Have students use context and pictures to learn *Etapa* vocabulary, then answer the *¿Comprendiste?* questions, p. 353. Use the Situational OHTs for additional practice. 25 MIN.

Homework Option:
• Have students write answers to the *¿Comprendiste?* questions, p. 353.

DAY 2

En vivo: Situaciones
• Check homework. 5 MIN.
• Quick Start Review (TE, p. 354) 5 MIN.
• Present the Listening Strategy, p. 354. 5 MIN.
• Have students read section 1, p. 354. Play the audio for section 2. Then have students work in groups to begin section 3. 20 MIN.

En acción: Vocabulario y gramática
• Have students complete *Actividad* 1 in writing, then exchange papers for peer correction. 5 MIN.
• Present the Speaking Strategy, p. 356. Then have students do *Actividad* 2 in pairs. 5 MIN.
• Have students complete *Actividad* 3 in pairs. 5 MIN.

Homework Option:
• Have students do research for *Situaciones*, section 3, p. 355.

DAY 3

En acción (cont.)
• Check homework. 5 MIN.
• Quick Start Review (TE, p. 358) 5 MIN.
• Present *Repaso:* Direct Object Pronouns, p. 348. 10 MIN.
• Play the audio; do *Actividad* 4. 10 MIN.
• Present the *Vocabulario*, p. 359. Then do *Actividad* 5 in pairs. 10 MIN.
• Have students do *Actividad* 6 in pairs. Expand using *Más comunicación*, p. R16. 10 MIN.

Homework Option:
• *Más práctica* Workbook, p. 125. *Cuaderno para hispanohablantes*, p. 123.

DAY 4

En acción (cont.)
• Check homework. 5 MIN.
• Quick Start Review (TE, p. 360) 5 MIN.
• Present *Repaso:* Indirect Object Pronouns, p. 360. 10 MIN.
• Have students complete *Actividad* 7 in pairs. 5 MIN.
• Present the *Vocabulario*, p. 361. Then do *Actividad* 8 in pairs. 5 MIN.
• Have students complete *Actividad* 9 in pairs. 5 MIN.
• Quick Start Review (TE, p. 362) 5 MIN.
• Present *Gramática:* More on Relative Pronouns, p. 362. 10 MIN.

Homework Option:
• *Más práctica* Workbook, p. 126. *Cuaderno para hispanohablantes*, p. 124.

DAY 5

En acción (cont.)
• Check homework. 5 MIN.
• Have students complete *Actividad* 10 in writing. Go over answers orally. 5 MIN.
• Do *Actividad* 11 orally. 5 MIN.
• Have students read and do *Actividad* 12 in pairs. Expand using *Más comunicación*, p. R16. 15 MIN.
• Quick Start Review (TE, p. 364) 5 MIN.
• Present *Gramática: Lo que*, p. 364. 5 MIN.
• Play the audio; do *Actividad* 13. 10 MIN.

Homework Option:
• *Más práctica* Workbook, pp. 127–128. *Cuaderno para hispanohablantes*, pp. 125–126
• *Actividades para todos* Workbook, pp. 141–150.

DAY 6

En acción (cont.)
• Check homework. 5 MIN.
• Have students complete *Actividad* 14 in pairs. 5 MIN.
• Have students complete *Actividad* 15 in groups. 10 MIN.

Refrán
• Present the *Refrán*, p. 365. 5 MIN.

En colores: Cultura y comparaciones
• Present the Connecting Cultures Strategy, p. 366. Call on volunteers to read the selection aloud. Have students answer the *¿Comprendiste?/¿Qué piensas?* questions, p. 367. 25 MIN.

Homework Option:
• Have students complete *Hazlo tú*, p. 367.

DAY 7

En uso: Repaso y más comunicación
• Check homework. 5 MIN.
• Have students do *Actividades* 1 and 2 in pairs. 10 MIN.
• Do *Actividades* 3 and 4 orally. 5 MIN.
• Present the Speaking Strategy, p. 370, and have students do *Actividad* 5 in groups. 10 MIN.

En tu propia voz: Escritura
• Have students do *Actividad* 6 in writing. 20 MIN.

Homework Option:
• Review for *Etapa* 2 Exam.

DAY 8

Conexiones
• Present *Las matemáticas*, p. 370, and have students complete the assignment for homework. 5 MIN.

En resumen: Repaso de vocabulario
• Quick Start Review (TE, p. 371) 5 MIN.
• Review grammar questions, etc., as necessary. 10 MIN.
• Complete *Etapa* 2 Exam. 20 MIN.

Ampliación
• Use a suggested project, game, or activity. (TE, pp. 327A–327B) 10 MIN.

Homework Option:
• Have students complete the assignment for *Conexiones*. Preview *Etapa* 3 Opener.

Sample Lesson Plan - Block Schedule (90 minutes)

DAY 1

Etapa Opener
- Quick Start Review (TE, p. 350) 5 MIN.
- Have students look at the *Etapa* Opener and answer the questions. 5 MIN.
- Use Block Scheduling Copymasters. 10 MIN.

En contexto: Vocabulario
- Quick Start Review (TE, p. 352) 5 MIN.
- Present *Descubre*, p. 352. 5 MIN.
- Have students use context and pictures to learn *Etapa* vocabulary, then answer the *¿Comprendiste?* questions, p. 353. Use the Situational OHTs for additional practice. 25 MIN.

En vivo: Situaciones
- Quick Start Review (TE, p. 354) 5 MIN.
- Present the Listening Strategy, p. 354. 5 MIN.
- Have students read section 1, p. 354. Play the audio for section 2. Then have students work in groups to begin section 3. 25 MIN.

Homework Option:
- Have students write answers to the *¿Comprendiste?* questions, p. 353. Have students do research for *Situaciones,* section 3, p. 355.

DAY 2

En acción: Vocabulario y gramática
- Check homework. 5 MIN.
- Quick Start Review (TE, p. 356) 5 MIN.
- Have students complete *Actividad* 1 in writing, then exchange papers for peer correction. 5 MIN.
- Present the Speaking Strategy, p. 356. Then have students do *Actividad* 2 in pairs. 5 MIN.
- Have students complete *Actividad* 3 in pairs. 5 MIN.
- Quick Start Review (TE, p. 358) 5 MIN.
- Present *Repaso:* Direct Object Pronouns, p. 358. 10 MIN.
- Play the audio; do *Actividad* 4. 5 MIN.
- Present the *Vocabulario,* p. 359. Then do *Actividad* 5 in pairs. 10 MIN.
- Have students do *Actividad* 6 in pairs. Expand using Information Gap Activities, Unit 5 Resource Book, p. 97; *Más comunicación,* p. R16. 15 MIN.
- Quick Start Review (TE, p. 360) 5 MIN.
- Present *Repaso:* Indirect Object Pronouns, p. 360. 10 MIN.
- Have students complete *Actividad* 7 in pairs. 5 MIN.

Homework Option:
- *Más práctica* Workbook, pp. 125–126. *Cuaderno para hispanohablantes,* pp. 123–124.

DAY 3

En acción (cont.)
- Check homework. 10 MIN.
- Present the *Vocabulario,* p. 361. Then do *Actividad* 8 in pairs. 10 MIN.
- Have students complete *Actividad* 9 in pairs. 5 MIN.
- Quick Start Review (TE, p. 362) 5 MIN.
- Present *Gramática:* More on Relative Pronouns, p. 362. 10 MIN.
- Have students complete *Actividad* 10 in writing. Go over answers orally. 5 MIN.
- Do *Actividad* 11 orally. 5 MIN.
- Have students read and do *Actividad* 12 in pairs. Expand using Information Gap Activities, Unit 5 Resource Book, p. 98; *Más comunicación,* p. R16. 20 MIN.
- Quick Start Review (TE, p. 364) 5 MIN.
- Present *Gramática: Lo que,* p. 364. 5 MIN.
- Play the audio; do *Actividad* 13. 10 MIN.

Homework Option:
- *Más práctica* Workbook, pp. 127–128. *Cuaderno para hispanohablantes,* pp. 125–126.
- *Actividades para todos* Workbook, pp. 141–150.

DAY 4

En acción (cont.)
- Check homework. 10 MIN.
- Have students complete *Actividad* 14 in pairs. 10 MIN.
- Have students complete *Actividad* 15 in groups. 10 MIN.

Refrán
- Present the *Refrán,* p. 365. 5 MIN.

En colores: Cultura y comparaciones
- Quick Start Review (TE, p. 366) 5 MIN.
- Present the Connecting Cultures Strategy, p. 366. Call on volunteers to read the selection aloud. Have students answer the *¿Comprendiste?/¿Qué piensas?* questions, p. 367. 25 MIN.

En uso: Repaso y más comunicación
- Quick Start Review (TE, p. 368) 5 MIN.
- Have students do *Actividades* 1 and 2 in pairs. 10 MIN.
- Do *Actividades* 3 and 4 orally. 10 MIN.

Homework Option:
- Have students complete *Hazlo tú,* p. 367. Review for *Etapa* 2 Exam.

DAY 5

En uso (cont.)
- Check homework. 10 MIN.
- Present the Speaking Strategy, p. 370, and have students do *Actividad* 5 in groups. 10 MIN.

En tu propia voz: Escritura
- Have students do *Actividad* 6 in writing. 20 MIN.

Conexiones
- Present *Las matemáticas,* p. 370, and have students complete the assignment for homework. 5 MIN.

En resumen: Repaso de vocabulario
- Quick Start Review (TE, p. 371) 5 MIN.
- Review grammar questions, etc., as necessary. 10 MIN.
- Complete *Etapa* 2 Exam. 20 MIN.

Ampliación
- Use a suggested project, game, or activity. (TE, pp. 327A–327B) 10 MIN.

Homework Option:
- Have students complete the assignment for *Conexiones.* Preview *Etapa* 3 Opener.

▼ Las pirámides de Teotihuacán–una obra de arquitectura sin igual en el mundo.

Etapa Theme
Discovering pre-Columbian civilizations and learning about arts and crafts in Latin America

Grammar Objectives
- Reviewing the use of direct object pronouns
- Reviewing the use of indirect object pronouns
- Using relative pronouns
- Using **lo que**

Teaching Resource Options

Print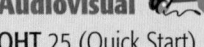
Block Scheduling Copymasters
Unit 5 Resource Book
  Family Letter, p. 101
  Absent Student Copymasters, p. 102

Audiovisual
OHT 25 (Quick Start)

🔔 Quick Start Review
♻ **¿Qué?** vs. **¿cuál?**

Use OHT 25 or write on the board:
Complete each question with **Qué** or **Cuál**:

1. ¿ ____ es tu baile favorito?
2. ¿ ____ de los cuadros prefieres?
3. ¿ ____ es la bamba?
4. ¿ ____ música usa arpa?
5. ¿ ____ son sus autorretratos?

Answers
1. Cuál	4. Qué
2. Cuál	5. Cuáles
3. Qué	

Teaching Suggestions
Previewing the Etapa
- Ask students to study the photo on pp. 350–351 (1 min.).
- Have them talk about their impressions of the setting. Ask: **¿Cuáles son sus impresiones iniciales del ambiente de la foto—el tiempo, los edificios, las actividades, etc.?**
- Use the **¿Qué ves?** questions to focus the discussion.

UNIDAD 5

ETAPA 2

El Nuevo Mundo

OBJECTIVES

- Refer to people and objects
- Express relationships
- Make generalizations
- Describe arts and crafts

¿Qué ves?

Mira la foto. Contesta las preguntas.

1. ¿En qué lugar de América Latina se encuentran los estudiantes?
2. ¿Cómo puedes describir la escena?
3. ¿Qué crees que existía en este lugar? ¿Por qué?

350

Classroom Management

Planning Ahead Set up stations for different kinds of indigenous contributions: woven goods, ceramics and pottery, architectural wonders, foods and recipes, language. Include 1 or 2 images with information at each station. The information should identify the indigenous group, country of origin, significance of the item featured, etc. As you work through the **Etapa**, have students add information to each station. The information can also be used for discussions and projects.

Organizing Paired/Group Work Take a poll to find out what interests each student regarding arts and crafts in the Spanish-speaking world (clothing, pottery, musical instruments, etc.), architecture, and/or language. Use the results of the poll to group students according to interests when doing activities.

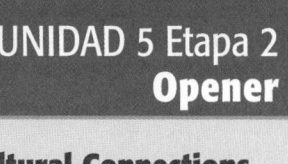

Cross Cultural Connections

Have students research pictures of the ancient homes of indigenous groups in the U.S. Then have them note similarities and differences with the photo of Teotihuacán.

Culture Highlights

● **LAS PIRÁMIDES** Las primeras pirámides se construyeron en Egipto, entre los años 2700 y 2500 antes de Cristo. Los egipcios construyeron pirámides sobre las tumbas *(tombs)* de reyes y nobles. En México y América Central, las pirámides se construyeron como centros religiosos. Los toltecas, los zapotecas y los aztecas construyeron esas pirámides.

● **LA PIRÁMIDE DEL SOL** La Pirámide del Sol en Teotihuacán es la más conocida de todas las pirámides en México. Está ubicada al noreste de la Ciudad de México y mide alrededor de 213 pies de altura. Tiene una base de casi 700 pies en cada lado y cinco terrazas que demarcan los niveles principales de ésta.

Supplementary Vocabulary

la pirámide	pyramid
la plataforma	platform
el escalón	step

351

Block Schedule

Change of Pace Have students draw a map of Mexico and Guatemala on a posterboard. Then have them research known pyramid sites in those countries, identify the sites by name on the map, and list the civilization that built the pyramid. Display the map in class. (For additional activities, see **Block Scheduling Copymasters**.)

Teaching All Students

Extra Help Have students write 3 questions about the photo. Then have them exchange papers with a partner and answer each other's questions.

Native Speakers Ask students if there are pyramids in their countries of origin. If so, where? Have them point out the locations on a map.

Multiple Intelligences

Logical/Mathematical Have students research the size of some of the best-known pyramids in Egypt and compare the size to the ones in Mexico and Central America. The largest known pyramid in the Western hemisphere is in Cholula, Mexico.

Teaching Resource Options

Teaching Resource Options

Print

Block Scheduling Copymasters

Unit 5 Resource Book
  Absent Student Copymasters, p. 102

Audiovisual

OHT 19, 20, 21, 21A, 22, 22A, 25
  (Quick Start)

Technology

Online Workbook, U5E2
Take-Home Tutor CD-ROM, U5E2

🔔 Quick Start Review

♻ **Cristóbal Colón**

Use OHT 25 or write on the board:
Complete the following sentences with
appropriate words:

1. Cristóbal Colón descubrió a
   América en el año ___ .
2. Los reyes ___ y ___ ayudaron a
   Colón.
3. Colón venía en busca de las ___ .
4. Él no encontró las riquezas que
   buscaba, como ___ y ___ .
5. Colón murió sin saber que había
   encontrado un nuevo ___ .

Answers

1. 1492   4. oro, plata
2. Isabel, Fernando   5. continente
3. India

Teaching Suggestions
Introducing Vocabulary

• Have students look at pp. 352–353.
  Use OHT 19 and 20 to present the
  vocabulary.
• Ask the Comprehension Questions
  on TE p. 353 in order of yes/no
  (questions 1–3), either/or (questions
  4–6), and simple word or phrase
  (questions 7–10).
• Use the TPR activity to reinforce the
  meaning of individual words.

Descubre

Answers

1. to civilize; civilization 2. to believe; belief
3. to descend; descent 4. to decipher or
decode; code 5. to reflect; reflection

En contexto VOCABULARIO

Las civilizaciones precolombinas

🔲 Descubre

En español, como en inglés, hay verbos
que tienen la misma raíz que el sustantivo
que les corresponde. Si sabes qué quiere
decir el verbo, puedes adivinar qué quiere
decir el sustantivo. Primero decide cuál es
el significado del verbo, y luego da el
significado del sustantivo.

construir → construcción

to construct → construction

1. civilizar → **civilización**
2. creer → **creencia**
3. descender → **descendencia**
4. descifrar → **cifra**
5. reflejar → **reflejo**

Se encuentran dos mundos

El año es 1518 en el calendario europeo. Barcos misteriosos
llegan a la costa atlántica de México. Un indio sale para dar las
noticias a su emperador, Moctezuma. Él gobierna al imperio
azteca, una de las civilizaciones precolombinas de América.

Ha llegado a México Hernán Cortés
(1485–1547), un conquistador español.
Él sigue el ejemplo de Cristóbal Colón,
quien abrió el paso entre Europa y
América en 1492. Bernal Díaz del
Castillo (1492–1584), un conquistador
joven, viene con Cortés. Para Bernal y
los demás europeos, están en un Nuevo
Mundo. Éste es el nombre que los
europeos le dan a América.

Hernán Cortés (centro)

Tenochtitlán

Bernal, que también es cronista, escribe:
*«Que por una parte había grandes ciudades…
Y en la laguna otras muchas, y veíamoslo todo
lleno de canoas… Y por delante estaba la gran
Ciudad de México».*
Los españoles quedaron impresionados al ver la
ciudad azteca de Tenochtitlán. Cuando Moctezuma
y los aztecas recibieron a los españoles, los llevaron
al Templo Mayor. El Templo tenía varias pirámides
grandes. Pero la amistad entre los españoles y los aztecas no duró mucho.
Pronto hubo una guerra y los españoles conquistaron a los aztecas. Después
de la conquista española, Tenochtitlán desapareció debajo de los edificios
europeos. En 1978, se encontraron las ruinas del Templo Mayor, que hoy
se pueden ver en la Ciudad de México.

352 trescientos cincuenta y dos
Unidad 5

Classroom Community

TPR In pairs or small groups, have students act out
something from the vocabulary readings. For instance,
they can act out the arrival of Cortés, the writing of
hieroglyphics, making textiles, etc. The rest of the class
guesses which action or scene is being depicted.

Paired Activity Have students work in pairs to read
the paragraphs on pp. 352–353 together. Then have
them take turns summarizing each paragraph in their
own words in Spanish, preferably with their books
closed.

Los libros mayas

Al mismo tiempo, en la península de Yucatán y por Centroamérica, los hombres religiosos de los mayas escribieron los libros *Chilam Balam* y *Popol Vuh*. Utilizaron jeroglíficos, un sistema complicado de escritura. Con los jeroglíficos narraron la historia de casi tres mil años del pueblo maya y también sus creencias. Hoy, los arqueólogos continúan descifrando la escritura jeroglífica con sus cifras misteriosas.

Las tejedoras de Los Altos de Chiapas

Los textiles son una tradición indígena. Las mujeres de descendencia maya han mantenido viva esta tradición. Ellas aprenden las técnicas para hacer los textiles de sus madres y las enseñan a sus hijas. Las imágenes en sus tejidos reflejan diseños mayas de casi 1200 años.

Los incas

Los incas, otra civilización indígena avanzada, establecieron un imperio en la costa del Pacífico de América del Sur. En la década de 1530, Atahualpa era el Inca, el título del gobernante que significa «hijo del sol». Francisco Pizarro (c.1478–1541) y otros conquistadores llegaron hasta Cuzco. Ellos lucharon por el oro y objetos prehispánicos preciosos, que los incas hicieron antes de la llegada de los españoles. Los incas construyeron ciudades como Machu Picchu, una obra maestra de arquitectura precolombina.

Online Workbook
CLASSZONE.COM

¿Comprendiste?

1. ¿Te interesan la historia y el arte precolombino? ¿Qué te interesa más, la arquitectura, el arte o los textiles? ¿Por qué?
2. ¿Qué piensas de las ruinas de Tenochtitlán?
3. La escritura jeroglífica de los mayas no se ha descifrado por completo. ¿Qué te parece la invención de una forma de escribir tan complicada?
4. Las pirámides en México y en Perú son obras de arquitectura que no se pueden reproducir hoy. ¿Cómo crees que se construyeron estos edificios enormes sin la ayuda de máquinas?

Teaching All Students

Extra Help Give students copies of the Comprehension Questions on TE p. 353. Have them write the answers for homework.

Multiple Intelligences

Logical/Mathematical Create or have students create a timeline on the board as a display of the pre-Columbian civilizations, especially the Maya, Aztec, and the Inca. Mark the beginning, the height, and the disintegration of these civilizations, as well as other recorded or estimated dates of feats and confrontations.

Culture Highlights

● **LA CIVILIZACIÓN MAYA** Los mayas establecieron una civilización que prosperó desde el 250 hasta el 900 después de Cristo. Construyeron campos de juego, hogares y templos monumentales. También desarrollaron un sistema jeroglífico conocido como «stalae», con el cual escribieron mitos, historia y ritos. Alrededor del año 900, los mayas abandonaron sus ciudades y migraron a la Península de Yucatán, que se convirtió en el centro de la cultura maya hasta el siglo XVI. La cronología maya está basada en un calendario elaborado. Aunque es muy complejo, éste fue el calendario humano más exacto hasta que el calendario Gregoriano se introdujo en el siglo XVI.

Comprehension Questions

1. ¿Llegan barcos misteriosos a la costa atlántica de México en 1518? (Sí)
2. ¿Hernán Cortés es el emperador de México? (No)
3. ¿Bernal Díaz del Castillo es un joven cronista azteca? (No)
4. ¿La capital del imperio azteca es la Ciudad de México o Tenochtitlán? (Tenochtitlán)
5. ¿En 1978, se encontraron las ruinas del Templo Mayor o del Templo Menor? (del Templo Mayor)
6. ¿Los mayas estaban en la península de Yucatán o en Cuba cuando llegaron los españoles a México? (en la península de Yucatán)
7. ¿Cómo escribían los mayas? (con jeroglíficos)
8. ¿A qué se dedican muchas mujeres indígenas en Chiapas? (a hacer tejidos)
9. ¿Quién era el gobernante de los incas? (Atahualpa)
10. ¿Cómo se llama la ciudad inca que es una obra maestra de arquitectura precolombina? (Machu Picchu)

Block Schedule

Research Have students define **civilización**, then work in groups to research the Mayan, Aztec, and Incan governmental and social structures. (For additional activities, see **Block Scheduling Copymasters**.)

Teaching Resource Options

Print

Block Scheduling Copymasters
Unit 5 Resource Book
  Absent Student Copymasters, p. 103
  Audioscript, p. 111

Audiovisual

OHT 23, 24, 26 (Quick Start)
Audio Program CD 14, Track 1

Technology

Take-Home Tutor CD-ROM, U5E2

Quick Start Review

♻ Vocabulary review

Use OHT 26 or write on the board:
Complete the sentences with the
following words:

precioso / precolombino / Templo /
Nuevo Mundo / cronista / jeroglíficos

1. El ____ Mayor estaba en
   Tenochtitlán.
2. América es el ____ .
3. Un ____ cuenta lo que pasó.
4. Los ____ se usan para escribir.
5. El arte ____ es arte indígena.

Answers
1. Templo   4. jeroglíficos
2. Nuevo Mundo 5. precolombino
3. cronista

Teaching Suggestions
Presenting Situations

• Present the Listening Strategy, p. 354,
  and have students complete the
  Pre-listening exercise.
• Use OHT 23 and 24 to present the
  Leer section. Ask simple yes/no,
  either/or, or short-answer questions.
• Use Audio CD 14 and have students
  do the **Escuchar** section (see Script
  p. 349B) and complete the Listening
  Strategy exercise.
• Have students work in groups to
  complete the **Hablar/Escribir** section.

AUDIO *En vivo*
SITUACIONES

PARA ESCUCHAR
STRATEGIES: LISTENING

Pre-listening Most people can remember about
seven items briefly. Read the phrases under
Escuchar three times. Then close your eyes
and say as many as you can. How many can
you recall?

Improve your auditory memory To help you
remember what is mentioned in the
conversation, (a) re-read the list, (b) close your
eyes to shut out distractions, (c) when you hear
one of the phrases, say it and check it on the
list. Did your auditory memory improve?

Una visita virtual

Estás en la biblioteca buscando información
para tu curso sobre el arte y la historia
precolombina de las Américas. Mientras lees,
oyes cuatro estudiantes españoles conversando.
Por casualidad, hablan del mismo tema — las
contribuciones artísticas de las civilizaciones
indígenas precolombinas.

❶ Leer

Has encontrado una página-web que ofrece «una visita
virtual» al mundo del arte y de la historia precolombina
de América Latina.

trescientos cincuenta y cuatro
Unidad 5

Classroom Community

Cooperative Learning Have students work in
groups of 4 to find other examples of pre-Columbian
art like that featured on p. 354. Two students focus on
finding and writing information, and the other two look
for images to complement the information. Have
groups present the information and images they collect
to the class.

Paired Activity Working in pairs, have students
locate the places mentioned on pp. 354–355 on a map
and review the material together. Then have them work
individually to write short true/false or multiple choice
quizzes. Partners then exchange and take each other's
quiz. You might want to collect and correct the quizzes.

② Escuchar

Mientras estudias, escuchas la conversación de cuatro estudiantes españoles que están sentados en la mesa junto a la tuya. Decide si mencionan cada objeto, tema o concepto en la siguiente lista.

1. la escritura jeroglífica
   ❏ La mencionan.
   ❏ No la mencionan.

2. los chibchas
   ❏ Los mencionan.
   ❏ No los mencionan.

3. las creencias mayas sobre el cosmos
   ❏ Las mencionan.
   ❏ No las mencionan.

4. las tejedoras mayas
   ❏ Las mencionan.
   ❏ No las mencionan.

5. Tenochtitlán
   ❏ La mencionan.
   ❏ No la mencionan.

6. las pirámides de Teotihuacán
   ❏ Las mencionan.
   ❏ No las mencionan.

7. la joyería de oro precolombina
   ❏ La mencionan.
   ❏ No la mencionan.

8. el descubrimiento del Nuevo Mundo
   ❏ Lo mencionan.
   ❏ No lo mencionan.

9. las molas
   ❏ Las mencionan.
   ❏ No las mencionan.

10. los incas
    ❏ Los mencionan.
    ❏ No los mencionan.

arqueología
MEXICANA

LOS MAYAS
VIDA COTIDIANA

VOL. V · NÚM. 28 $ 35

③ Hablar/Escribir

Escoge una de las culturas precolombinas mencionadas en esta lección y haz una investigación sobre la arquitectura, el arte o los textiles de esa cultura. Escribe tres cosas que no sabías antes de hacer la investigación. Trae tus observaciones a la clase. En grupos de tres o cuatro, comparen los resultados de sus investigaciones. Hagan una lista de los aspectos de las culturas que son similares y los aspectos que son diferentes.

trescientos cincuenta y cinco
España y las Américas Etapa 2
355

Culture Highlights

● **LAS MOLAS** Los indios cuna (conocidos también como Kuna) comenzaron a crear molas a mediados del siglo XIX, bordando los diseños de su tribu en telas de algodón. Las molas son usualmente moradas y generalmente se utilizan tres capas de tela.

● **LOS MAYAS** Los mayas han vivido en México y Centroamérica por más de dos mil años. La tribu maya, según la cual se nombra la civilización, ocupa la Península de Yucatán. Todas las tribus formaban parte de una civilización común, que en muchos aspectos realizaron los logros más notables de las civilizaciones indígenas de las Américas.

Escuchar (See script, p. 349B.)

Answers
1. la escritura jeroglífica
   La mencionan.
2. los chibchas
   Los mencionan.
3. las creencias mayas sobre el cosmos
   No las mencionan.
4. las tejedoras mayas
   Las mencionan.
5. Tenochtitlán
   No la mencionan.
6. las pirámides de Teotihuacán
   Las mencionan.
7. la joyería de oro precolombina
   No la mencionan.
8. el descubrimiento del Nuevo Mundo
   Lo mencionan.
9. las molas
   No las mencionan.
10. los incas
    Los mencionan.

Hablar/Escribir

Answers will vary.

Teaching All Students

Extra Help Have students look at the images on p. 354 before reading and write down what they think they already know about what they see. Then have them scan the text for familiar words.

Multiple Intelligences

Visual Have students create icons to represent the different kinds of pre-Columbian art presented on pp. 354-355. If you have a display map of Latin America, they can tack the icons to the corresponding areas. If not, have students make their own maps and use the icons to indicate the areas of origin.

Naturalist Have students discuss what might have inspired the images that people used in their **tejidos, molas,** and **quimbayas.** They should consider the flora and fauna of the regions of origin.

Block Schedule

Process Time Before students listen to the **Escuchar** on p. 355, allow them 2–3 minutes to review items 1–10. Encourage them to try to guess what they might hear on the audio. (For additional activities, see **Block Scheduling Copymasters.**)

Teaching Resource Options

Print

Block Scheduling Copymasters
Unit 5 Resource Book
  Absent Student Copymasters, p. 104

Audiovisual

OHT 26 (Quick Start)

Quick Start Review

♻ Pre-Columbian art

Use OHT 26 or write on the board:
Match the words in the 2 columns:

1. ___ la mola
2. ___ el Templo del Jaguar
3. ___ Machu Picchu
4. ___ la Pirámide del Sol
5. ___ el arte «quimbaya»
   a. Tikal
   b. Teotihuacán
   c. ciudad inca
   d. los indígenas Kuna Yala
   e. Colombia

Answers
1. d   2. a   3. c   4. b   5. e

Teaching Suggestions
Comprehension Check

Use **Actividades 1–4** to assess retention after the **Vocabulario** and **Situaciones**. After completing **Actividad 1**, have students give definitions of the lettered words.

Actividad 1 Objective: Controlled practice
Vocabulary

Answers
1. b, d   4. c
2. f   5. g
3. a   6. e

Actividad 2 Objective: Transitional practice
Vocabulary in conversation

Answers will vary.

En acción

PARTE A

Práctica del vocabulario

Objectives for Activities 1-3
• Refer to people and objects • Express relationships

1 El examen

Escribir Mario tuvo un examen sobre la historia precolombina de las Américas. Completa las oraciones que él tuvo que completar para su examen.

a. descendencia   e. precolombinos
b. ruinas   f. cronista
c. pirámides   g. escritura jeroglífica
d. civilización

1. En la Ciudad de México, encontraron las _____ de una _____ muy avanzada.

2. Bernal Díaz de Castillo era un conquistador y _____ español.

3. Las tejedoras de los Altos de Chiapas son de _____ maya.

4. En el centro de Tikal se encuentran dos _____; la primera se llama El Templo del Gran Jaguar.

5. La _____ de los mayas narra la historia del pueblo.

6. En las excavaciones del Templo Mayor, se encontraron objetos _____ de mucho valor.

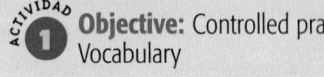

Nota cultural

Cuando los españoles llegaron al Nuevo Mundo adoptaron muchas palabras indígenas, como las siguientes.

• **huracán** (taíno) • **tomate** (náhuatl) • **papa** (quechua)

2 Comentarios

STRATEGY: SPEAKING

Maintain a discussion In a serious discussion, words may be used that are not known to everyone. Ask for a definition or be prepared to give one. Example: **¿Qué es precolombina? — La cultura que existía en América antes de los viajes de Colón.**

Hablar/*Escribir* Tú y tu compañero(a) comentan sobre las civilizaciones precolombinas de las Américas. Conversen sobre los siguientes temas.

modelo

el sistema de escritura de los mayas: escritura jeroglífica

Tú: *El sistema de escritura de los mayas era muy complicado.*

Compañero(a): *Sí, la escritura jeroglífica de los mayas es tan complicada que los arqueólogos siguen tratando de descifrarla.*

los cronistas españoles: crónicas

las técnicas para construir pirámides: olvidarse

los mayas: extenso conocimiento de ingeniería y matemáticas

los tejidos: expresión artística

las tradiciones de los mayas: pasar siglo tras siglo

las civilizaciones precolombinas: avanzadas

las pirámides: obras de arquitectura

356 trescientos cincuenta y seis
Unidad 5

Classroom Management

Planning Ahead Have students prepare and practice the dialogs for **Actividad 3** outside of class. Then have them act out the scene for the class. You might also videotape/record the scene.

Organizing Paired Work For **Actividad 2**, pair students who have trouble maintaining a conversation in Spanish with stronger students/native speakers.

3 Teotihuacán

Hablar/*Escribir* Elena y Enrique fueron a Teotihuacán, «la ciudad de los dioses». Imagina y escribe la conversación que tienen los dos compañeros. Luego, léela en voz alta.

1.
2.
3.
4.
5.
6.

Culture Highlights

● **TEOTIHUACÁN** El nombre **Teotihuacán** significa «el lugar donde nacieron los dioses» en náhuatl, la lengua de los aztecas. La Pirámide del Sol fue comenzada alrededor del año 100 antes de Cristo, a la vez que al otro lado del mundo se construían los grandes monumentos de la Grecia antigua.

Se sabe muy poco de los habitantes de este lugar, de dónde venían, qué idioma hablaban y porqué abandonaron la ciudad en el año 700 después de Cristo. Solamente se ha establecido que ese año hubo un fuego que destruyó la ciudad.

La ubicación de los edificios puede considerarse como un plano cósmico. La Pirámide del Sol cuadra exactamente con el punto donde el sol se pone el día que éste pasa por su punto más alto. Si ese día se dibujara una línea desde la pirámide del sol al mediodía hasta el punto más alto, y luego otra desde la pirámide hasta el punto donde el sol se pone en el horizonte, la pirámide cuadraría exactamente con las dos líneas. El resto de los edificios ceremoniales están ubicados en ángulos rectos con relación a la

ACTIVIDAD 3 Objective: Open-ended practice Vocabulary in conversation

Answers will vary.

Teaching All Students

Extra Help Before completing **Actividad 3,** point to the pictures of Teotihuacán and ask simple questions. For example: ¿Dónde están Elena y Enrique? ¿Qué hacen? ¿Por qué toman agua?

Native Speakers Have students work with others to generate a list of vocabulary words that would be helpful in developing the dialog in **Actividad 3.** These words can be written on the board as an aid to students.

Multiple Intelligences
Kinesthetic Have students work in pairs to make 3–4 drawings and write the conversation of 2 students visiting 1 of the places mentioned so far in this **Etapa.** Have them display their drawings and captions in the classroom. Have pairs act out their scenes.

Block Schedule

Process Time Students may need to organize their thoughts for commenting on the themes of **Actividad 2.** Have them organize their ideas before class or allow them a few minutes in class to prepare. (For additional activities, see **Block Scheduling Copymasters.**)

Teaching Resource Options

Print

Más práctica Workbook PE, p. 125
Cuaderno para hispanohablantes
  PE, p. 123
Block Scheduling Copymasters
Unit 5 Resource Book
  Más práctica Workbook TE, p. 75
  Cuaderno para hispanohablantes
    TE, p. 91
  Information Gap Activities, p. 97
  Absent Student Copymasters, p. 104
  Audioscript, p. 111

Audiovisual

OHT 26 (Quick Start), 30 (Grammar)
Audio Program CD 14, Track 2, Activity 4

Technology

Online Workbook, U5E2
Take-Home Tutor CD-ROM, U5E2

Quick Start Review

♻ Vocabulary review

Use OHT 26 or write on the board:
Write a vocabulary word that
corresponds to each of the following:

1. creer	4. conquistar
2. reflejo	5. descifrar
3. avanzar	6. descender

Answers
1. creencia 2. reflejar 3. avanzado
4. conquistador 5. cifra 6. descendencia

Teaching Suggestions
Reviewing Direct Object Pronouns

• Hold up or point to props/photos
  and ask questions to which students
  answer affirmatively or negatively. For
  example, point to a piece of paper:
  ¿Ves el papel? → Sí, lo veo./No, no
  lo veo.
• Remind students that the personal **a**
  is used before a direct object that
  refers to a person.

Objectives for Activities 4-14
• Refer to people and objects • Express relationships • Make generalizations • Describe arts and crafts

REPASO **Direct Object Pronouns**

▶ You use **direct object pronouns** in Spanish to refer to items or people that have already been mentioned.

Direct Object Pronouns

me	nos
te	os
lo/la	los/las

becomes

—¿Has visto **las ruinas** en Chichén Itzá?
*Have you seen **the ruins** at Chichén Itzá?*

—Sí, **las** vi el verano pasado.
*Yes, I saw **them** last summer.*

▶ Third-person direct object pronouns (**lo, la, los, las**) refer to **usted** and **ustedes** as well as to **él, ella, ellos,** and **ellas.**

Perdón señora. No **la** vi.
*I'm sorry ma'am. I didn't see **you.***

▶ **Direct object pronouns** go before the conjugated verb except in **affirmative commands**, where you attach them.

Alfredo y Marta no saben que Uds. van a la exhibición de máscaras. **Invíten**los. *attaches*
*Alfredo y Marta don't know that you are going to the mask exhibit. **Invite them.***

▶ **Direct object pronouns** come before **conjugated verbs** or attached to **infinitives** and **-ndo forms**.

attaches

—Esta novela es muy buena. ¿Quieres **leer**la?
*This novel is very good. Do you want to read **it?***

¿**La quieres** leer?
*Do you want to read **it?***

attaches

—Mira. Estoy **leyéndo**la.
*Look. I'm reading **it.***

La estoy leyendo.
*I'm reading **it.***

Practice: Actividades 4 5 6

Más práctica *cuaderno* p. 125
Para hispanohablantes *cuaderno* p. 123

Online Workbook CLASSZONE.COM

---

4 ¿Lo conoces?

Escuchar/Escribir Escucha las conversaciones de varias personas. Di si la persona que contesta conoce o no las cosas mencionadas.

modelo
No las conoce.

1. _____
2. _____
3. _____
4. _____
5. _____
6. _____

Figura precolombina de un hombre. Cultura quimbayá.

Classroom Community

Paired Activity Working in pairs, one student gives a command to the other. The partner changes the command to the negative. For example: **Cierra el libro.** → **No lo cierres.** Have partners take turns and give at least 5 commands.

Group Activity Divide the class into groups of 3. First, students each write a list of 5 questions that contain direct object nouns. Then they take turns asking and answering the questions, replacing the direct object nouns with direct object pronouns. For example: **¿Compro las molas?** → **Sí, cómpralas.**

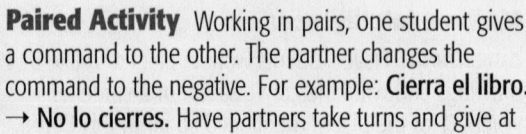

5 Los bailes

Hablar/Escribir Tú y tu compañero(a) quieren saber si el otro (la otra) sabe bailar varios bailes. Pregúntale a tu compañero(a) si sabe bailarlos y luego, él (ella) te pregunta a ti.

modelo

Tú: *¿Sabes bailar la sardana?*

Compañero(a): *Sí, (No, no) sé bailarla.*

1. el mambo
2. la cumbia
3. el merengue
4. la habanera
5. el tango
6. el jarabe tapatío
7. la bamba
8. ¿…?

Vocabulario

Bailes típicos

el jarabe tapatío

el baile folklórico *folk dance*

la bamba *Mexican dance from Veracruz*

la danza *dance*

la habanera *habanera*

el mambo *mambo*

el merengue *merengue*

el tango

▶ ¿Conoces a algunos músicos que toquen este tipo de música?

6 Mi primo(a) panameño(a)

Hablar/Escribir Tu primo(a) de Panamá vino a visitarte y quieres hacerle muchas preguntas. Primero tu compañero(a) hace el papel del (de la) primo(a). Luego, cambien de papel. Usen las ideas de la lista o inventen otras.

modelo

Tú: *¿Viste la nueva película de Benicio del Toro?*

Compañero(a): *No, no la he visto.*

More Practice: **Más comunicación** *p. R16*

> ver (la película nueva de…)
> leer (la última novela de…)
> escribir (la tarjeta postal para tu…)
> escuchar (el nuevo disco compacto de…)
> limpiar (tu cuarto)
> hacer (los quehaceres)
> visitar (a tu familia)
> mandar (la carta por Internet)

Nota cultural

Parece que cada región de América Latina tiene su propio baile típico. Estos bailes muestran una mezcla de tradiciones precolombinas, africanas y europeas. Además de los mencionados a la izquierda, aquí hay otros muy conocidos:

- **el candombe** (Uruguay)
- **la cueca** (Chile)
- **la marinera** (Perú)
- **la cumbia** (Colombia)
- **la bachata** (República Dominicana)

trescientos cincuenta y nueve
España y las Américas Etapa 2 `359`

ACTIVIDAD 4 Objective: Controlled practice Listening comprehension/direct object pronouns

♻ Arts vocabulary

Answers (See script, p. 349B.)
1. Sí, las conoce.
2. Sí, lo conoce.
3. No lo conoce.
4. Sí, lo conoce.
5. No las conoce.
6. Sí, la conoce.

Dictation

Using the Listening Activity Script for **Actividad 4** on TE p. 349B, dictate selected sentences to students. You may want to have students peer correct the sentences.

Teaching Suggestions
Presenting Vocabulary

If possible, play videoclips demonstrating these and other Hispanic dances. Some dance scenes can be found in **Evita** (tango) and **Mambo Kings** (mambo).

ACTIVIDAD 5 Objective: Transitional practice Direct object pronouns/vocabulary in conversation

Answers
1. Compañero(a): Sí, (No, no) sé bailarlo.
2. Compañero(a): Sí, (No, no) sé bailarla.
3. Compañero(a): Sí, (No, no) sé bailarlo.
4. Compañero(a): Sí, (No, no) sé bailarla.
5. Compañero(a): Sí, (No, no) sé bailarlo.
6. Compañero(a): Sí, (No, no) sé bailarlo.
7. Compañero(a): Sí, (No, no) sé bailarla.
8. *Questions and answers will vary.*

ACTIVIDAD 6 Objective: Open-ended practice Direct object pronouns in conversation

Answers will vary.

Block Schedule

Reference Lists Have students create a table for each Spanish-speaking country and/or specific regions or cities with columns for categories such as **baile típico, comida típica/popular, artesanía, arquitectura,** etc. (For additional activities, see **Block Scheduling Copymasters**.)

Vocabulary/Grammar • UNIDAD 5 Etapa 2 **359**

Teaching Resource Options

Print

Más práctica Workbook PE, p. 126
Cuaderno para hispanohablantes
  PE, p. 124
Block Scheduling Copymasters
Unit 5 Resource Book
  Más práctica Workbook TE, p. 76
  Cuaderno para hispanohablantes
  TE, p. 92
  Absent Student Copymasters, p. 105

Audiovisual

OHT 27 (Quick Start), 31 (Grammar)

Technology

Online Workbook, U5E2
Take-Home Tutor CD-ROM, U5E2

Quick Start Review

♻ **Direct object pronouns**

Use OHT 27 or write on the board:
Use direct object pronouns to rewrite
the sentences so that they are not so
repetitive:

1. La turista mira la mola y compra
   la mola.
2. Elena y Enrique van a las
   pirámides y suben las pirámides.
3. Los europeos vinieron al nuevo
   mundo y conquistaron el nuevo
   mundo.
4. Los arqueólogos descubren los
   jeroglíficos y tratan de descifrar
   los jeroglíficos.

Answers
1. La turista mira la mola y la compra.
2. Elena y Enrique van a las pirámides y las
   suben.
3. Los europeos vinieron al nuevo mundo y
   lo conquistaron.
4. Los arqueólogos descubren los jeroglíficos
   y tratan de descifrarlos.

Teaching Suggestions
Indirect Object Pronouns

Point out that indirect object pronouns
answer the questions *to whom/
what?* or *for whom/what?* Also say that
there must be an indirect object
pronoun in a sentence with an indirect
object.

Práctica: gramática y vocabulario continuación

REPASO   Indirect Object Pronouns

You use indirect object pronouns in
Spanish to refer to the person who is
receiving the action of the verb.

Indirect Object Pronouns	
me	nos
te	os
le	les

Mandé las fotos a María.
I sent the photos to María.

Le mandé las fotos.
*I sent **her** the pictures.*

Indirect object pronouns, like the direct object pronouns, precede the
conjugated verbs.

—¿Qué le **regalaste**?
*What (gift) did you give **her**?*

—Le **regalé** una pulsera
de jade.
*I gave **her** a jade bracelet.*

Remember that sometimes you use **a + person** to clarify to whom
the indirect object pronouns le and les are referring.

—¿Les **escribes** a tus
amigos?
Do you write to your friends?

—A Magdalena le **escribo**
mucho.
I write to Magdalena a lot.

You attach indirect object pronouns to **affirmative commands**
just like you do with direct object pronouns.

Préstame tu libro de arquitectura.
Lend me your architecture book.

You can attach indirect object pronouns to **infinitives** and
progressive tenses or you can put them before the **conjugated verbs**.

¿Puedes **prestar**le tu
libro a José también?
Can you lend your book to José also?

¿Le **puedes** prestar tu
libro a José también?

¿Estás **prestándo**le tu
libro a Luisa?
Are you lending your book to Luisa?

¿Le **estás** prestando tu
libro a Luisa?

Practice:
Actividades
7 8 9

Más práctica
cuaderno p. 126
Para hispanohablantes
cuaderno p. 124

Online Workbook
CLASSZONE.COM

360   trescientos sesenta
Unidad 5

---

7 Después de la entrevista ♻

Hablar/*Escribir* Tu
compañero(a) hace el papel
de supervisor(a) y tú le
hablas sobre una entrevista
que hiciste. Luego, cambien
de papel.

modelo

pedir los datos

Tú: *¿Le pediste los datos?*

Compañero(a): *Sí, señor(a), le
pedí los datos.*

1. pedir la solicitud
2. explicar el puesto
3. explicar los beneficios
4. contestar sus preguntas
5. informar del sueldo
6. pedir tres
   recomendaciones

Nota cultural

El Inca Garcilaso de la Vega, hijo
del español Garcilaso de la Vega
y la princesa india Isabel Chimpu
Ocllo, escribió sus *Comentarios
reales del Perú* dando los detalles
de la vida diaria de los incas. Se
considera uno de los textos claves
para entender la sociedad inca
precolombina, ya que describe
la conquista desde la perspectiva
indígena.

Classroom Community

Paired Activity Have each partner write his/her
name on a slip of paper, then the names of 3 other
classmates. Put the names in a "name" bag. On 4 more
slips of paper, each student writes the names of items
he/she might give or get as gifts (**un llavero, un disco
compacto,** etc.). These go in a "gift" bag. One student
holds the "name" bag and the other the "gift" bag. The
student with the "gift" bag draws a slip of paper, then
asks the partner a question; for example, **¿A quién le
das el llavero?** The partner draws a name and
answers; for example, **Le doy el llavero a Jaime.** When
the bags are empty, students change roles.

Learning Scenario What would people want to
know about a muralist? Have pairs of students write
and present an interview between a magazine reporter
and **un(a) muralista.**

8 El viaje (primera parte)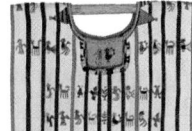

Hablar/*Escribir* Vas de viaje a México y Guatemala con tu familia. Piensan visitar las ruinas de algunas civilizaciones precolombinas. Conversa con tu compañero(a) sobre lo que quieres ver. Usa ideas de la lista si es necesario.

modelo

Compañero(a): *¿Te interesan las ruinas de Tenochtitlán?*

Tú: *Sí, hombre, ¡me fascinan! Me gustaría pasar más tiempo estudiando las civilizaciones precolombinas.*

interesar
fascinar
gustar
parecer
explicar
¿…?

la escritura jeroglífica
los tejidos de las mujeres mayas
las ruinas de Tenochtitlán
las pirámides de Tikal
el Templo Mayor
los objetos precolombinos de jade
las blusas bordadas de Guatemala
las tradiciones de los mayas
las creencias sobre el cosmos
los objetos de piedra labrada
¿…?

Vocabulario

Las artesanías

bordado(a)   **el mural**   **tallado(a)**

decorado(a) *decorated*   **labrado(a)** *worked, cut*
el jade *jade*   **el (la) muralista** *muralist*

▶ ¿Comprarías algún objeto así? ¿Por qué?

9 El viaje (segunda parte)

Hablar Sigues hablando con tu compañero(a) sobre tu viaje a México y Guatemala. Él (Ella) te hace muchas preguntas sobre lo que compraste, lo que viste, lo que le preguntaste al guía turístico, etc. Usen los verbos de la lista si quieren.

modelo

Compañero(a): *¿Qué le compraste a tu mamá?*

Tú: *Le compré una blusa bordada muy bonita de Guatemala.*

Compañero(a): *¿Qué le preguntaste al guía turístico?*

Tú: *Le pregunté en qué año se habían descubierto las pirámides de Teotihuacán.*

comprar	leer
contestar	llevar
dar	mandar
decir	pedir
escribir	preguntar
prestar	preguntar
hablar	traer
	servir

Teaching All Students

Extra Help Write **la hora, el problema, la verdad, el dinero, una carta.** Then ask questions that solicit those answers; for example, **¿Qué me preguntas?** Have a student respond; for example, **Te pregunto la hora.** Other verbs: **explicar, decir, pedir, escribir.** Do the same, or have pairs of students do the same, for other verb-object series.

Multiple Intelligences

Intrapersonal Have students write to whom they gave gifts this year. Also have them write who gave them gifts this year. Students may invent gifts if they prefer.

Objective: Controlled practice
Indirect object pronouns in conversation

 Workplace vocabulary

Answers
1. A: ¿Le pediste la solicitud?
   B: Sí, señor(a), le pedí la solicitud.
2. A: ¿Le explicaste el puesto?
   B: Sí, señor(a), le expliqué el puesto.
3. A: ¿Le explicaste los beneficios?
   B: Sí, señor(a), le expliqué los beneficios.
4. A: ¿Le contestaste sus preguntas?
   B: Sí, señor(a), le contesté sus preguntas.
5. A: ¿Le informaste del sueldo?
   B: Sí, señor(a), le informé del sueldo.
6. A: ¿Le pediste tres recomendaciones?
   B: Sí, señor(a), le pedí tres recomendaciones.

Teaching Suggestions
Presenting Vocabulary

- **Plan ahead:** Bring in illustrations or the items in the **Vocabulario.** Place them around the classroom and use them to introduce the new words.
- Using commands, tell students to go to where items are located. Have them repeat the words.

ACTIVIDAD **8**
Objective: Transitional practice
Indirect object pronouns in conversation

 Verbs like **gustar**

Answers will vary.

ACTIVIDAD **9**
Objective: Open-ended practice
Indirect object pronouns in conversation

Answers will vary.

🔲 Block Schedule

Change of Pace Have students work in pairs to create a comic strip in which indirect object pronouns are part of the dialog. Elicit scenes about giving/receiving gifts or information, asking for something, etc. Display the comics in the classroom. (For additional activities, see **Block Scheduling Copymasters.**)

Teaching Resource Options

Print

Más práctica Workbook PE, p. 127
Cuaderno para hispanohablantes
PE, p. 125
Block Scheduling Copymasters
Unit 5 Resource Book
Más práctica Workbook TE, p. 77
Cuaderno para hispanohablantes
TE, p. 93
Information Gap Activities, p. 98
Absent Student Copymasters, p. 106

Audiovisual

OHT 27 (Quick Start), 32 (Grammar)

Technology

Online Workbook, U5E2
Take-Home Tutor CD-ROM, U5E2

Quick Start Review

♻ Relative pronouns

Use OHT 27 or write on the board:
Complete the following sentences with
que or **quien**:

1. Este es el libro ___ te compré.
2. Ese es el muchacho de ___ te hablé.
3. Es la muralista a ___ más admiro.
4. Es el mural ___ compró ayer.
5. Es el cuadro ___ pintó Velázquez.
6. Es la cantante con ___ hablé.

Answers
1. que 2. quien 3. quien
4. que 5. que 6. quien

Teaching Suggestions
More on Relative Pronouns

• Point out to students that **el cual** and **el que** are used more frequently in formal writing and speech.
• Emphasize that relative pronouns do not have accents.

Objective: Controlled practice
Relative pronouns in writing

Answers
1. el que 2. las que 3. los que 4. la que
5. el que 6. las que 7. la que 8. el que
9. la que 10. los que

GRAMÁTICA More on Relative Pronouns

♻ **¿RECUERDAS?** *p. 341* You have already learned to use the **relative pronouns** **que** or **quien** to provide additional information.

You can also use the **relative pronouns**, **el que** and **el cual**, in the same way, but to show a stronger relationship or provide greater emphasis.

	singular		plural	
masculine	el cual	el que	los cuales	los que
feminine	la cual	la que	las cuales	las que

You will often use **el que**, **el cual**, etc. after **prepositions** where you wish to show a stronger relationship or greater emphasis than **que** or **quien** would provide.

agrees
un templo **en el que** hay jeroglíficos
*a temple **in which** there are hieroglyphics*

agrees
la guitarrista **sin la cual** no podemos tocar
*the guitarist **without whom** we can't play*

> Notice that these forms agree in gender and number with the noun to which they refer.

Note that in formal uses, such as writing, it is more common to use **el cual** instead of **el que**.

informal
Hablé con **el que** llegó tarde.
*I spoke with **the one who** arrived late.*

formal
Cristóbal Colón fue un explorador famoso, **el cual** llegó las Américas.
*Christopher Columbus was a famous explorer **who** arrived in the Americas.*

The **relative pronoun** **cuyo(a)** means *whose*. Remember to make it agree in gender and number with the noun that follows:

agrees
el pintor **cuyos** cuadros nos gustaron
*the painter **whose** paintings we liked*

Practice:
⑩ ⑪ ⑫

Más práctica
cuaderno p. 127
Para hispanohablantes
cuaderno p. 125

Online Workbook
CLASSZONE.COM

362 trescientos sesenta y dos
Unidad 5

---

⑩ México

Escribir Tu amigo(a) te escribe y te cuenta todo lo que hizo y vio en sus viajes a México. Completa sus oraciones con la forma correcta de **el que**.

1. Vimos un templo en _____ hay jeroglíficos.
2. Entramos a las pirámides en _____ enterraban (*buried*) a los reyes mayas.
3. Visitamos los templos en _____ encontraron los objetos de arte precolombino.
4. Leí la crónica de Colón en _____ escribió sobre el descubrimiento de las Indias.
5. Caminamos por el centro en _____ encontraron las ruinas del Templo Mayor.
6. Vi unas piedras en _____ están escritas las historias de los reyes mayas.
7. Hicimos una excursión en _____ vimos muchas ruinas.
8. Compré un libro en _____ explican el significado de palabras mayas.
9. Entramos a una tienda en _____ había artesanías muy bellas.
10. Observamos unos lugares en _____ se hacían ceremonias.

Classroom Community

Storytelling Working in pairs, have students write and present a travel story similar to the one in **Actividad 10**. The story may describe a trip to an interesting site in Latin America or to an imaginary place. Remind students that they must use relative pronouns.

Portfolio Have students make a list of 10 people and items. Next to each person/item, they should write a definition, using relative pronouns.

Rubric A = 13–15 pts. B = 10–12 pts. C = 7–9 pts. D = 4–6 pts. F = < 4 pts.

Writing criteria	Scale				
Accuracy of information	1	2	3	4	5
Vocabulary use	1	2	3	4	5
Grammar/spelling accuracy	1	2	3	4	5

11 Revisiones

Hablar/Escribir Escribiste un ensayo pero hay unas oraciones que quieres cambiar para decirlas en clase. Sigue el modelo.

modelo

La escritura jeroglífica es un sistema de escritura pictórica. Todavía no se ha descifrado por completo.

La escritura jeroglífica, la cual todavía no se ha descifrado por completo, es un sistema de escritura pictórica.

1. Las composiciones jeroglíficas también contenían sus creencias sobre el cosmos. Narraban la historia del pueblo.

2. Bernal Díaz del Castillo escribió una descripción de Tenochtitlán en su crónica. Era cronista español.

3. Cristóbal Colón murió sin saber qué había descubierto. Abrió el paso entre Europa y las Américas.

4. Los mayas construyeron grandes pirámides. Tenían un conocimiento de ingeniería extenso.

5. La cultura mexica no desapareció. Dejó su influencia en el mundo del arte y de la arquitectura.

12 El Templo Mayor

Leer/Hablar Lee la información de un folleto del Templo Mayor. Hazle tres preguntas a tu compañero(a). Luego cambien de papel.

modelo

Tú: *¿Qué se encuentra en 1790?*

Compañero(a): *En 1790 se encuentran la Coatlicue y la Piedra del Sol, las cuales actualmente pueden verse en el Museo Nacional.*

Principales excavaciones realizadas en el Templo Mayor

1790 El 13 de agosto y el 17 de diciembre se encuentran la Coatlicue y la Piedra del Sol, respectivamente. Actualmente pueden verse en el Museo Nacional de Antropología.

1901 Se encuentran escalinatas, una gran cabeza de serpiente y el *ocelotl-cuauxicalli*, una enorme escultura que representa a un jaguar que actualmente está a la entrada de la sala Mexica del Museo Nacional de Antropología.

1913–1914 Don Manuel Gamio excava y encuentra restos de la esquina suroeste del Templo Mayor, así como una de las cabezas de serpiente del extremo sur de la escalinata de Huitzilopochtli.

1964 Eduardo Matos Moctezuma realiza el rescate de un adoratorio decorado con mascarones del dios Tlaloc, al norte de la calle de Justo Sierra.

1978–1982 Desde el 20 de marzo de 1978 hasta noviembre de 1982, un equipo de especialistas realizan el Proyecto Templo Mayor, que da por resultado el descubrimiento del principal templo de los mexicas y de edificios aledaños al mismo.

trescientos sesenta y tres
España y las Américas Etapa 2
363

ACTIVIDAD 11 **Objective:** Transitional practice Relative pronouns

Answers

1. Las composiciones jeroglíficas, en las cuales narraban la historia del pueblo, también contenían sus creencias sobre el cosmos.
2. Bernal Díaz del Castillo, el cual era cronista español, escribió una descripción de Tenochtitlán en su crónica.
3. Cristóbal Colón, el cual abrió el paso entre Europa y las Américas, murió sin saber qué había descubierto.
4. Los mayas, los cuales tenían un conocimiento de ingeniería extenso, construyeron grandes pirámides.
5. La cultura mexica, la cual dejó su influencia en el mundo del arte y de la arquitectura, no desapareció.

ACTIVIDAD 12 **Objective:** Open-ended practice Relative pronouns in conversation

Answers will vary.

Quick Wrap-up

Have students identify the relative pronouns in the entries for **Actividad 12: Identifiquen los pronombres relativos en las entradas para la Actividad 12.**

Culture Highlights

● **PIEDRA DEL SOL** Así se conoce al calendario azteca, un símbolo de México. Está hecho en piedra, pesa 25 toneladas y mide 12 pies. Los aztecas lo hicieron en el siglo XV.

Teaching All Students

Extra Help Ask students to complete the following sentences using relative pronouns: **El explorador... , El conquistador... , Las ruinas... , El jade... , Los muralistas... , Los bailes...** Have several students write their answers on the board for the class to correct.

Native Speakers Have students read aloud the information about the **Principales excavaciones**, pronouncing any long or difficult words slowly.

Multiple Intelligences

Interpersonal Working in pairs, have each student make a list of 5 friends. Partners then take turns describing the friends. For example: **Gabi es una amiga la cual es muy inteligente. Ella es la que me ayuda a hacer la tarea de la clase de español.**

Block Schedule

Peer Teaching Have stronger students work with weaker students to read and form questions for **Actividad 12.** (For additional activities, see **Block Scheduling Copymasters.**)

Teaching Resource Options

Print

Más práctica Workbook PE, pp. 121–124; 128

Actividades para todos Workbook PE, pp. 141–146

Cuaderno para hispanohablantes PE, pp. 121–122; 126

Block Scheduling Copymasters

Unit 5 Resource Book

  Más práctica Workbook TE, pp. 71–74; 78

  Actividades para todos Workbook TE, pp. 79–85

  Cuaderno para hispanohablantes TE, pp. 89–90; 94

  Absent Student Copymasters, p. 107

  Audioscript, p. 111

Audiovisual

OHT 28 (Quick Start), 33 (Grammar)

Audio Program CD 14, Track 3, Activity 13

Technology

Online Workbook, U5E2

Take-Home Tutor CD-ROM, U5E2

Quick Start Review

🔄 Relative pronouns

Use OHT 28 or write on the board: Complete the sentences with the appropriate forms of **el cual, el que,** or **cuyo:**

1. Es un edificio en ___ hay jeroglíficos.
2. Eran unos cantaores sin ___ no se podía cantar cante jondo.
3. Ésta es la mujer de ___ te hablé.
4. Francisco Pizarro fue un conquistador ___ estuvo en Perú.
5. La cantante ___ canciones nos gustaron no canta hoy.

Answers

1. el que 2. los cuales 3. la cual
4. el cual 5. cuyas

Teaching Suggestions
Teaching Lo que

- Emphasize that **lo que** is invariable in form and have students provide personalized sentences with **lo que.**

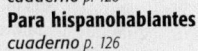 **Lo que**

The relative phrase **lo que** means *what* or *that which.* You use it when there is no direct person, place or thing in the main clause to which you are referring. It refers to a more generalized idea or concept.

No comprendo **lo que** quieres decir.
*I don't understand **what** you mean.*

¿Por qué no me dices **lo que** piensas?
*Why don't you tell me **what** you think?*

When you use **lo que** after **todo** it means *all that, everything that.*

Tienes que decirme **todo lo que** sabes.
*You have to tell me **everything that** you know.*

Nos dieron **todo lo que** tenían.
*They gave us **everything that** they had.*

Practice: Actividades 13 14

Más práctica *cuaderno p. 128*
Para hispanohablantes *cuaderno p. 126*

Online Workbook CLASSZONE.COM

 **13 Efraín**

Escuchar/*Escribir* Efraín hizo un viaje educativo a Guatemala para estudiar la historia maya del período clásico. Escucha lo que dice de su viaje y escribe una oración que haga un resumen de cada cosa mencionada. Sigue el modelo.

modelo

el período clásico de los mayas

Lo que aprendió fue sobre el período clásico de los mayas.

1. las pirámides de Tikal
2. la historia maya
3. la escritura jeroglífica
4. los objetos de arte
5. la historia maya
6. unos tejidos

Nota cultural

Uno de los lugares más importantes para visitar son las ruinas de Tikal, en Guatemala. En ese sitio se levantaba la antigua ciudad maya del mismo nombre. Tikal está considerado como uno de los sitios arqueológicos más importantes de Mesoamérica. Esta imagen nos muestra el Templo del Jaguar, animal que representaba la sabiduría maya.

364 trescientos sesenta y cuatro
Unidad 5

Classroom Community

Learning Scenario Divide the class into 6 groups and assign one of the topics from the items in **Actividad 13** to each group. Each group researches their topic and presents the information to the class. They then administer a short quiz to see how well the class understood the material.

Game Have students work in groups to play "Twenty Questions." Each student takes a turn thinking of a Spanish-speaking country/historical site/dance/type of music/famous person, etc. The rest of the group asks questions about the person, place, or thing. They can ask up to 20 questions.

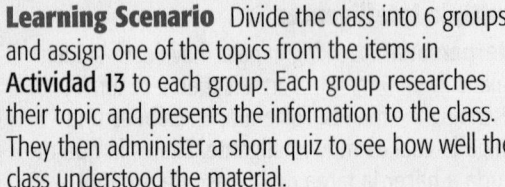

Activity **15** brings together all concepts presented.

14 Lo que quieren

Hablar/*Escribir* Estás de viaje con tu clase de español. Todo el mundo quiere hacer algo diferente. Hablas con tu compañero(a) sobre lo que quieren hacer todos.

modelo

Ernesto prefiere ver el Templo Mayor.

Lo que Ernesto prefiere es ver el Templo Mayor.

1. Javier necesita más tiempo para ver las ruinas.
2. Elena quiere comprar una camisa bordada.
3. El Sr. Quintana quiere descifrar los jeroglíficos.
4. A Daniela le gustaría subir las pirámides.
5. Juan Felipe prefiere ir a Teotihuacán.
6. Amalia quiere ver los murales en el museo.

15 Un viaje ideal

Hablar En grupos de tres o cuatro, conversen sobre un viaje imaginario que hicieron. ¿Qué vieron? ¿Qué les gustó? Mencionen algunos elementos que aparecen en las fotos y otros que ustedes escojan.

modelo

Tú: *Cuéntenme sobre su viaje a Mesoamérica.*

Compañero(a) 1: *Vimos muchas artesanías, las cuales estaban hechas por los indígenas.*

Compañero(a) 2: *Sí, y les mandamos fotos de las pirámides a nuestros amigos.*

More Practice: **Más comunicación** *p. R16* **Online Workbook** CLASSZONE.COM

Refrán

Lo que fue y no es ya, menos es que lo que será.

¿Qué quiere decir el refrán? ¿Estás de acuerdo o no? ¿Por qué? ¿Piensas que el futuro siempre es mejor que el pasado? ¿Crees que nuestras civilizaciones van mejorándose?

Teaching All Students

Extra Help Have each student write 2 more items for **Actividad 14**. Call on volunteers to write their items on the board for the class to complete.

Native Speakers Based on the photos and information presented in this **Etapa**, have students present a short oral presentation of the important aspects of the Maya and Aztec civilizations.

Multiple Intelligences

Logical/Mathematical Have students research the dimensions, then compare the size and shape, of the Tikal ruins to the ruins of the **Pirámide del Sol**.

Visual Have students make models of a Mayan or an Aztec pyramid. Variation: Have students draw a city in which all of the buildings are pyramids.

---

 13 Objective: Controlled practice Listening comprehension/**lo que**

Answers (See script, p. 349B.)
1. Lo que más le inspiró fueron las pirámides de Tikal.
2. Lo que estudió fue la historia maya.
3. Lo que más le fascinó fue la escritura jeroglífica.
4. Lo que vio fueron los objetos de arte.
5. Lo que descubrió fue que le fascina la historia maya.
6. Lo que compró fueron unos tejidos.

14 Objective: Transitional practice **Lo que**

Answers
1. Lo que Javier necesita es más tiempo para ver las ruinas.
2. Lo que Elena quiere es comprar una camisa bordada.
3. Lo que el Sr. Quintana quiere es descifrar los jeroglíficos.
4. Lo que a Daniela le gustaría es subir las pirámides.
5. Lo que Juan Felipe prefiere es ir a Teotihuacán.
6. Lo que Amalia quiere es ver los murales en el museo.

15 Objective: Open-ended practice **Lo que** in conversation

Answers will vary.

Quick Wrap-up

Give students commands using **lo que** to carry out. For example: **Tráeme lo que se usa para escribir. Dale a (Miguel) lo que se usa para borrar. Ve al pizarrón y escribe con lo que se escribe en él. Abre lo que te explica la lección.**

Critical Thinking

Discuss the importance of studying ruins with students. What other ancient civilizations do we know about because of their ruins? What have these ruins taught us about these civilizations?

Block Schedule

Personalizing Have students work in round robin format to create sentences using phrases such as **Lo que me gusta es...** or **Lo que me interesa es...** (For additional activities, see **Block Scheduling Copymasters**.)

Teaching Resource Options

Print 📖

Actividades para todos Workbook PE, pp. 147–149

Block Scheduling Copymasters

Unit 5 Resource Book
Actividades para todos Workbook TE, pp. 85–87
Absent Student Copymasters, p. 108

Audiovisual 🎧

OHT 28 (Quick Start)
Canciones CD

Technology 💻

ℹ️ www.classzone.com

🔔 Quick Start Review

♻️ **Lo que**

Use OHT 28 or write on the board:
Complete the following sentences with
your own ideas:

1. Lo que quiero hacer esta tarde es...
2. Lo que me gusta hacer los sábados es...
3. Lo que necesito estudiar esta semana es...
4. Lo que prefiero almorzar es...

Answers

Answers will vary. Answers could include:
1. tomar una siesta 2. visitar con amigos
3. biología 4. un sándwich con papas fritas

Teaching Suggestions
Presenting Cultura y comparaciones

• Begin by asking students to look at
the pictures and tell if they have seen
buildings like the ones here: **¿Alguna
vez han visto edificios como los
que aparecen aquí?** Which buildings
appeal to them? **¿Qué edificios les
gustan?** Do they prefer modern or
traditional architecture? **¿Prefieren la
arquitectura moderna o tradicional?**

• Have students complete the Strategy
task. Have students sketch a building
for their town/city. What would they
try to achieve with their buildings?

En colores

CULTURA Y COMPARACIONES

UN ARQUITECTO Y SUS OBRAS

PARA CONOCERNOS
STRATEGY: CONNECTING CULTURES

Use architecture as a cultural text Look at
important buildings in your community.
Are there any that reflect an earlier time
or culture? Are there any that reflect the
present or represent the future? Categorize
them in the chart below. Be sure to name
the buildings.

Edificios del pasado	Edificios del presente	Edificios del futuro
1.	1.	1.
2.	2.	2.
3.	3.	3.

After reading and learning more about
Barragán and Legorreta, which one would
you choose to design a major building for
your town? Why?

Instituto Salk, Luis Barragán
(La Jolla, California)

*La vegetación y el agua son componentes
esenciales de la arquitectura de Barragán.
La presencia del agua es especialmente
expresiva en La Jolla, California. Allí, la
contribución de Barragán al Instituto Salk de
Louis Kahn fue la plaza creada entre las dos
grandes alas[3] de hormigón[4] y separada por
un canal de agua, que simboliza el límite
entre el continente y el océano.*

Un estilo cultural: Ricardo Legorreta

¿Qué espacios ves cuando piensas en los edificios
de México? ¿Pirámides? ¿Plazas? ¿Espacios de
colores vivos? El arquitecto Ricardo Legorreta usa
elementos arquitectónicos[1] de éstos para crear
estructuras como las que ves a la derecha.

Legorreta fue alumno de Luis Barragán
(1902–1988), sin duda el arquitecto
mexicano más importante del
siglo XX. Barragán buscó
las huellas[2] de su propia
cultura para dar lugar
a una obra muy
personal en la que la
tradición combina con
la modernidad.

[1] architectural [3] wings
[2] footprints, impressions [4] concrete

366 trescientos sesenta y seis
Unidad 5

Classroom Community

Group Activity Have students work in small groups
to research works of Barragán and Legorreta. They can
organize their information and images in the form of a
visual report with captions, an illustrated written report,
or oral presentations.

Portfolio Have students write a paragraph reacting
to the architectural styles of Barragán and/or Legorreta.

Rubric A = 13–15 pts. B = 10–12 pts. C = 7–9 pts. D = 4–6 pts. F = < 4 pts.

Writing criteria	Scale
Vocabulary use	1 2 3 4 5
Grammar/spelling accuracy	1 2 3 4 5
Details and organization	1 2 3 4 5

Ricardo Legorreta es el arquitecto más importante de México hoy en día. Su padre apoyó el interés que sintió desde niño por los pueblos y las ciudades de México. En oposición a Barragán, Legorreta da énfasis a la belleza de las cosas ordinarias, que tras el proceso de la arquitectura se convierten en extraordinarias.

AUTOMEX, Ricardo Legorreta
(Toluca, México)
El primer gran proyecto de Legorreta fue la Fábrica de Automóviles Automex. «Cuando diseñé Automex fue como un gran grito[7]: ¡Viva México! ¡Viva Automex!»

Hotel Camino Real, Ricardo Legorreta
(Cancún, México)
En los hoteles que ha construido Legorreta, el agua parece fluir [5] a través de estos edificios y la luz solar proyecta sombras espectaculares sobre las baldosas [6]. Los tonos azulados, rosas y el amarillo tostado nos recuerdan al sol, al cielo y a las buganvillas, invitándonos a disfrutar y relajarnos.

CLASSZONE.COM
More About Spain and the Americas

¿Comprendiste?
1. ¿Qué distingue la obra de Luis Barragán?
2. ¿Qué elementos son esenciales en la arquitectura de Barragán? Da un ejemplo de un edificio donde los utiliza.
3. ¿Quén es el arquitecto más importante de México hoy en día?
4. ¿Qué sugieren los colores de Legorreta?

¿Qué piensas?
¿Qué elementos crees que comparten los edificios de Barragán y Legorreta? ¿Cuáles crees que son distintos?

Hazlo tú
¡Diseña tu casa ideal! Al pensar en el diseño, piensa en el lugar donde la construirás, si utilizarás colores vivos u oscuros, cuánta luz quieres, la forma de las habitaciones, cuántas tendrá, y si pondrás árboles y agua en los jardines. Puedes dibujar la casa o describirla. Usa estas imágenes o revistas para inspirarte.

[5] to flow
[6] paving stones, tiles
[7] shout

trescientos sesenta y siete
España y las Américas Etapa 2

367

Teaching All Students

Extra Help Assign each paragraph/photo caption from the reading to a group of students, and have them rewrite it in simpler sentences. Go through the reading by having the groups read their sentences in turn.

Multiple Intelligences
Visual Point out that some pyramids were built in relation to sun and shadow, so that at certain times, the light and shadow patterns across one side of the pyramid resembled a slithering snake. Have students build a pyramid of blocks, and play with light and shadow to see what patterns they can make.

Logical/Mathematical Have students list and describe the elements that make modern architecture like pre-Columbian architecture.

Teaching Resource Options

Print 📖

Cuaderno para hispanohablantes PE,
  pp. 127–128
Block Scheduling Copymasters
Unit 5 Resource Book
  Cuaderno para hispanohablantes
    TE, pp. 95–96
  Information Gap Activities,
    pp. 99–100
  Family Involvement, pp. 109–110

Audiovisual 🎧

OHT 29 (Quick Start)

Technology 💻

eTest Plus Online/Test Generator
CD-ROM
🌐 www.classzone.com

🔔 Quick Start Review

♻️ **Direct object pronouns**

Use OHT 29 or write on the board:
Complete the conversations with a
direct object pronoun:

1. –¿Tienes mi blusa bordada?
   –Sí, ____ tengo.
2. –¿Tienes la olla decorada?
   –Sí, ____ tengo.
3. –¿Tienes las joyas de jade?
   –Sí, ____ tengo.
4. –¿Tienes el tejido de Chiapas?
   –Sí, ____ tengo.
5. –¿Tienes los tallados de piedra?
   –Sí, ____ tengo.

Answers
1. la   2. la   3. las   4. lo   5. los

✓ Teaching Suggestions
What Have Students Learned?

Have students look at the "Now you
can…" notes listed on the left side of
pp. 368–369. Tell students to think
about which areas they might not be
sure of. For those areas, they should
consult the "To review" notes.

ETAPA **2**

En uso
REPASO Y MÁS COMUNICACIÓN

OBJECTIVES
• Refer to people and objects
• Express relationships
• Make generalizations
• Describe arts and crafts

Now you can...
• describe arts and crafts.

To review
• direct object pronouns see p. 358.

① ¿Qué viste?

Acabas de regresar de un viaje a
México donde viste cosas muy
interesantes. Tu compañero(a)
quiere saber qué viste. Contéstale.

modelo

las ruinas

Compañero(a): *¿Viste las ruinas?*

Tú: *Sí, sí las vi.*   **o** *No, no las vi.*

1. el Templo Mayor
2. los jeroglíficos en el Templo de las Inscripciones
3. la Pirámide del Sol
4. un mural de Diego Rivera
5. los tejidos de las mujeres mayas
6. las ollas prehispánicas en el Museo de Antropología

Now you can...
• refer to people and objects.

To review
• indirect object pronouns see p. 360.

② Mi amiga española

Tu compañero(a) fue a España y se hizo amigo(a) de una joven
española. Tú le haces muchas preguntas. Sigue el modelo.

modelo

¿regalar / a ella?

Tú: *¿Qué le regalaste?*

Compañero(a): *Le regalé una pulsera de jade.*

1. ¿traer de España / a mí?

2. ¿mandar / a ustedes?

3. ¿pedir / a ella?

4. ¿llevar / a ella?

5. ¿dar / a ti?

6. ¿prestar / a ti?

368   trescientos sesenta y ocho
Unidad 5

Classroom Community

Storytelling Have students tell a real or imagined
story about the things they bought and sent to other
people while they were on a vacation. Tell students to
be sure and use direct and indirect object pronouns in
their stories.

Cooperative Learning Have students work in
groups of 4 to string sentences together. Student 1 says
a noun, such as **el niño.** Student 2 follows up with a
relative clause, such as **el cual vive en la casa vecina.**
Student 3 finishes the sentence with the main clause,
such as **es de México.** Student 4 records the sentences.
Student 2 begins the next round. Finally, the group
checks the 4 sentences and submits them for a grade.

Now you can...

- express relationships.

To review

- relative pronouns see p. 362.

③ Natalia

Tu amiga mexicana Natalia te escribió esta carta. Complétala con las formas correctas de **el que**, **el (la) cual** o **cuyo** para aprender más sobre los mayas.

> Hola,
>
> Como me fascina la historia maya, es el tema sobre ___1___ escribí para la clase de cultura. Te voy a contar algunas de las cosas que aprendí. La civilización maya, ___2___ era muy avanzada, tenía un calendario muy preciso. También entendían el concepto del cero, ___3___ nos sorprende porque en esos tiempos el cero todavía no se usaba en el sistema europeo. Muchas de las técnicas de los mayas se han perdido, pero la tradición de los textiles es una de ___4___ no ha desaparecido. Linda Schiele, una arqueóloga ___5___ estudios de los mayas son mundialmente reconocidos, ha descubierto muchas cosas fascinantes sobre esta cultura precolombina. Sin embargo, los arqueólogos no saben por completo las condiciones bajo ___6___ desapareció el pueblo de los mayas. Te escribo después.
>
> Abrazos,
>
> Natalia

Now you can...

- make generalizations.

To review

- uses of **lo que** see p. 364.

④ Lo que...

Tienes un(a) amigo(a) que acaba de volver de Centroamérica. Le preguntas lo que hizo. Tu amigo(a) te contesta con muchos detalles.

modelo

¿hacer?

Tú: *¿Hiciste lo que querías hacer?*

Tú amigo(a): *Sí. Hice muchas excursiones y visité templos mayas.*

1. ¿ver?
2. ¿comprar?
3. ¿aprender?
4. ¿visitar?
5. ¿traer?
6. ¿llevar?

1. A: ¿Viste el Templo Mayor?
   B: Sí, sí lo vi./No, no lo vi.
2. A: ¿Viste los jeroglíficos en el Templo de las Incripciones?
   B: Sí, sí los vi./No, no los vi.
3. A: ¿Viste la Pirámide del Sol?
   B: Sí, sí la vi./No, no la vi.
4. A: ¿Viste el mural de Diego Rivera?
   B: Sí, sí lo vi./No, no lo vi.
5. A: ¿Viste los tejidos de las mujeres mayas?
   B: Sí, sí los vi./No, no los vi.
6. A: ¿Viste las ollas prehispánicas en el Museo de Antropología?
   B: Sí, sí las vi./No, no las vi.

 ② **Answers**

1. A: ¿Qué me trajiste de España?
   B: Te traje un disco compacto.
2. A: ¿Qué les mandó?
   B: Nos mandó una tarjeta postal.
3. A: ¿Qué le pediste?
   B: Le pedí su dirección.
4. A: ¿Qué le llevaste?
   B: Le llevé una camiseta de Nueva York.
5. A: ¿Qué te dio?
   B: Me dio su numero de teléfono.
6. A: ¿Qué te prestó?
   B: Me prestó su libro sobre los pintores españoles.

ACTIVIDAD
③ **Answers**

1. el que	4. las que, las cuales
2. la cual	5. cuyos
3. lo cual	6. las que, las cuales

 ④ **Answers**

1. ¿Viste lo que querías ver?
2. ¿Compraste lo que querías comprar?
3. ¿Aprendiste lo que querías aprender?
4. ¿Visitaste lo que querías visitar?
5. ¿Trajiste lo que querías traer?
6. ¿Llevaste lo que querías llevar?

Teaching All Students

Extra Help Write sentences on the board that can be joined using relative pronouns. For example: **Mis padres quieren comprar la casa de los Jiménez. La casa de los Jiménez tiene piscina.** → **Mis padres quieren comprar la casa de los Jiménez, la cual tiene piscina.**

Multiple Intelligences

Verbal Have students talk about what they want to do and what they need to do this weekend or this summer, using **lo que**. For example, **Lo que quiero hacer es descansar, pero lo que tengo que hacer es trabajar.**

▪ Block Schedule

Variety Have students write what gifts they are going to give and to whom in the upcoming months or year. Then have them write what gifts they are going to ask for. (For additional activities, see **Block Scheduling Copymasters**.)

Teaching Resource Options

Print

Unit 5 Resource Book
  Audioscript, p. 113
  Vocabulary Quizzes, pp. 117–119
  Grammar Quizzes, pp. 120–121
  Etapa Exam, Forms A and B,
    pp. 122–131
  Examen para hispanohablantes,
    pp. 132–136
  Portfolio Assessment, pp. 137–138
  Multiple Choice Test Questions,
    pp. 229–231

Audiovisual

OHT 29 (Quick Start)
Audio Program CD 20, Track 9

Technology

eTest Plus Online/Test Generator
  CD-ROM
  www.classzone.com

ACTIVIDAD **5**

Rubric: Speaking

Criteria	Scale	
Sentence structure	1 2 3	A = 11–12 pts.
Vocabulary use	1 2 3	B = 9–10 pts.
Originality	1 2 3	C = 7–8 pts.
Fluency	1 2 3	D = 4–6 pts.
		F = < 4 pts.

ACTIVIDAD **6**

En tu propia voz

Rubric: Writing

Criteria	Scale	
Vocabulary use	1 2 3 4 5	A = 13–15 pts.
Accuracy	1 2 3 4 5	B = 10–12 pts.
Creativity, appearance	1 2 3 4 5	C = 7–9 pts.
		D = 4–6 pts.
		F = < 4 pts.

Teaching Note: En tu propia voz

Writing Strategy Suggest that students cover all details by answering the interrogatives who, what, where, when, why, and how.

---

5 ## Los bailes latinoamericanos

STRATEGY: SPEAKING

Discuss Latin American dance Dance is an important part of Latin culture. But how do you discuss and demonstrate musical and physical events? You can tell the place of origin (**origen**), musical terms (**compás, ritmo, melodía**), steps (**pasos**). If you can dance it, teach it to others.

En grupos de tres o cuatro, escojan el baile latinoamericano que más les interesa. Busquen información sobre el baile por Internet o en la biblioteca. Traigan un casete o un CD de música y traten de aprender a bailarlo. Cuando sepan más, hagan una presentación para la clase. Expliquen qué van a presentar y por qué lo escogieron.

modelo

Vamos a hacer una presentación sobre el merengue. Escucharemos una canción de Juan Luis Guerra. Buscamos el CD en la tienda de música. El merengue es la música de la República Dominicana.

6 ## En tu propia voz

ESCRITURA Escoge una civilización precolombina que te interese (los mayas, los incas, los aztecas u otra). Prepara una gráfica para organizar tus ideas en una hoja grande de papel. Escribe el nombre de la civilización en el centro. Luego añade palabras que se asocian con la primera. Estudia el modelo antes de empezar. Después de acabar con la gráfica, escribe un párrafo breve que describa la civilización que investigaste.

modelo

LOS MAYAS
1. Período Clásico: 300 - 900 d.C.
2. escritura
3. textiles
4. pirámides
5. ¿…?

CONEXIONES

Las matemáticas Los mayas tenían un sistema de matemática diferente al nuestro. Busca información sobre su sistema en la biblioteca o por Internet. Crea un póster con los «números» entre 0 y 20. Incluye también algunos números más grandes como tu fecha de nacimiento y cualquier otro número que tenga importancia para ti.

NUMERACIÓN MAYA

🥟	CERO
●	UNO
●●	DOS
●●●	TRES
●●●●	CUATRO
▬	CINCO
●	SEIS
●●	SIETE
●●●	OCHO
●●●●	NUEVE

370 trescientos setenta
Unidad 5

Classroom Community

Portfolio Have students expand the paragraph they wrote for **Actividad 6** into a more focused essay. They can study an aspect of that civilization in more detail; for example, Mayan numbers and calendars. Have them also illustrate the essay with original drawings, clippings, or photocopies.

Rubric A = 13–15 pts. B = 10–12 pts. C = 7–9 pts. D = 4–6 pts. F = < 4 pts.

Writing criteria	Scale
Grammar/spelling accuracy	1 2 3 4 5
Details	1 2 3 4 5
Logical organization	1 2 3 4 5

En resumen
REPASO DE VOCABULARIO

DESCRIBE ARTS AND CRAFTS

Crafts

bordado(a)	embroidered
decorado(a)	decorated
el jade	jade
labrado(a)	worked, cut
el mural	mural
el (la) muralista	muralist
precioso(a)	precious, valuable
tallado(a)	carved
el tejido	weaving

Dances

el baile folklórico	folk dance
la bamba	dance from Veracruz
la cumbia	cumbia
la danza	dance
la habanera	habanera
el jarabe tapatío	dance from Guadalajara
el mambo	mambo
el merengue	merengue
el tango	tango

The New World

abrir el paso	to open the way
avanzado(a)	advanced
la cifra	statistic, code
la civilización	civilization
el conquistador	conqueror
la creencia	belief
el cronista	chronicler
la descendencia	descent
descifrar	to decipher
los jeroglíficos	hieroglyphics
el Nuevo Mundo	the New World
la pirámide	pyramid
precolombino(a)	pre-Columbian
reflejar	to reflect
las ruinas	ruins
la técnica	technique
el templo	temple
la tradición	tradition

REFER TO PEOPLE AND OBJECTS

Direct objects

—¿Viste el Templo Mayor cuando fuiste a México?
—Sí, **lo** vi.

Indirect objects

—¿Qué **te** puedo traer de Chiapas?
—¿**Me** puedes traer un tejido tradicional?

EXPRESS RELATIONSHIPS

Relative pronouns

Ésta es la Pirámide del Sol, **la que** visitamos cuando fuimos a México.

MAKE GENERALIZATIONS

Lo que

Para las culturas precolombinas, **lo que** consideramos el «descubrimiento» del Nuevo Mundo no fue un descubrimiento verdadero.

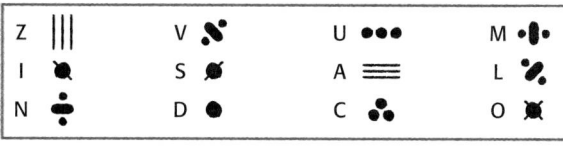

Juego

Los jeroglíficos

Usa la siguiente clave *(key)* para descifrar este mensaje de cuatro palabras que está escrito en jeroglíficos de una civilización desconocida.

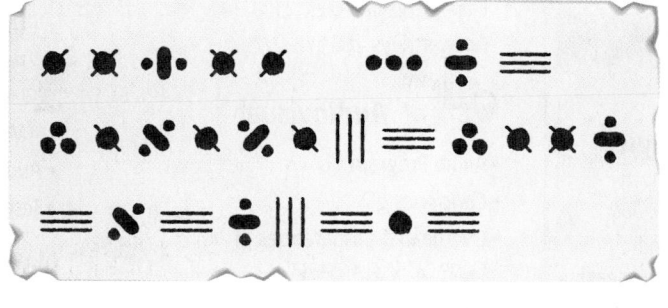

Teaching All Students

Extra Help Have students illustrate and label drawings for as many words from the **Repaso de vocabulario** as possible.

Multiple Intelligences

Musical/Rhythmic Help students find information about dances for **Actividad 5.** Locate videos and descriptions of the dances as well as music. Point out that encyclopedias often describe the **pasos** of dances under the entry *Dance.*

Interdisciplinary Connection

Mathematics Have students research how math is taught in one Spanish-speaking country. For example, do they write subtraction formulas as we do in the U.S.? Do they do the subtraction steps the same way?

Quick Start Review

♻ Etapa vocabulary

Use OHT 29 or write on the board: Write a personalized sentence for each of the following categories:
• Describing arts and crafts
• Referring to people and objects
• Expressing relationships
• Making generalizations
Answers will vary.

Teaching Suggestions
Vocabulary Review

Have students create clues for at least 10 words. Then have them work in pairs to take turns giving clues and guessing the words without their books.

Dictation

Dictate the following sentences to review the **Etapa:**

1. Las pirámides del Templo Mayor son enormes. ¿Quieres visitarlas?
2. Le di las fotos de Teotihuacán a mi profesor de español.
3. Entramos al templo en el que hay jeroglíficos.
4. ¡Dime todo lo que viste en México!

Juego

Answer: Somos una civilización avanzada.

Block Schedule

Change of Pace Have students work in pairs to create mini-dialogs to model the vocabulary category "Refer to people and objects." Have volunteers role play their dialogs for the class.

Planning Guide CLASSROOM MANAGEMENT

OBJECTIVES

Communication
- Talk about literature *pp. 374–375, 388–389*
- Talk about film *pp. 376–377, 390–391*
- Avoid redundancy *pp. 380–386*

Grammar
- Review the use of double object pronouns *pp. 380–382*
- Use nominalization *pp. 382–386*

Culture
- Regional vocabulary *pp. 374, 380*
- Film and television in Spanish-speaking countries *p. 381*
- Rosario Ferré *p. 386*
- Federico García Lorca and **La casa de Bernarda Alba** *pp. 388–389*
- Spanish and Latin American film directors *pp. 390–391*

♻ Recycling
- Preterite tense *p. 381*
- Clothing and colors *p. 383*
- Arts and crafts vocabulary *p. 385*

STRATEGIES

Listening Strategies
- Evaluate discussions *p. 376*

Speaking Strategies
- Discuss a novel *p. 379*
- Critique a film *p. 394*

Reading Strategies
- Interpret a drama *p. 388*
- Categorize details *TE p. 390*

Writing Strategies
- Present a thorough and balanced review *TE p. 394*
- Support an opinion with facts and examples *p. 396*

Connecting Cultures Strategies
- Recognize variations in vocabulary *pp. 374, 380*
- Learn about film and television in Spanish-speaking countries *p. 381*
- Learn about Rosario Ferré *p. 386*
- Learn about Federico García Lorca and **La casa de Bernarda Alba** *pp. 388–389*
- Reflect on the international appeal of movies *p. 390*
- Connect and compare what you know about movie directors in your community to help you learn about movie directors in a new community *pp. 390–391*

PROGRAM RESOURCES

 Print
- *Más práctica* Workbook PE *pp. 129–136*
  Actividades para todos Workbook PE *pp. 151–160*
- Block Scheduling Copymasters *pp. 121–128*
- Unit 5 Resource Book
  Más práctica Workbook TE *pp. 141–148*
  Actividades para todos Workbook TE *pp. 149–158*
  Cuaderno para hispanohablantes TE *pp. 159–166*
  Information Gap Activities *pp. 167–170*
  Family Letter *pp. 171*
  Absent Student Copymasters *pp. 172–178*
  Family Involvement *pp. 179–180*
  Audioscript *pp. 181–184*
  Assessment Program, Unit 5 Etapa 3 *pp. 185–225, 232–234*
  Answer Keys *pp. 242–247*

 Audiovisual
- Audio Program CD 15
- *Canciones* CD
- Overhead Transparencies M1–M5; GO1–GO5; 3, 4, 34-48
- Word Tiles U5E3

 Technology
- eEdition Plus Online/eEdition CD-ROM
- Easy Planner Plus Online/Easy Planner CD-ROM
- eTest Plus Online/Test Generator CD-ROM
- Online Workbook
- Take-Home Tutor CD-ROM
- www.classzone.com

Assessment Program Options
- Unit 5 Resource Book
  Vocabulary Quizzes
  Grammar Quizzes
  Etapa Exam Forms A and B
  Examen para hispanohablantes
  Portfolio Assessment
  Unit 5 Comprehensive Test
  Prueba comprensiva para hispanohablantes, Unit 5
  Multiple Choice Test Questions
- Audio Program CD 20
- Test Plus On Line/Test Generator CD-ROM

Native Speakers
- *Cuaderno para hispanohablantes* PE *pp. 129–136*
- *Cuaderno para hispanohablantes* TE (Unit 5 Resource Book)
- *Examen para hispanohablantes* (Unit 5 Resource Book)
- *Prueba comprensiva para hispanohablantes,* Unit 5 (Unit 5 Resource Book)
- Audio Program *(Para hispanohablantes)* CD 15, 20
- Audioscript (Unit 5 Resource Book)

Student Text
Listening Activity Scripts

🎧 Situaciones *pages 376–377*

• CD 15

Paco: Creo que todos nuestros contemporáneos disfrutarían de una película basada en la novela deslumbrante *Bajo otro cielo*.

Carlota: Estoy de acuerdo. Pero creo que debemos crear una protagonista inteligente que represente la poeta, cuentista y novelista que la escribió. Una chica innovadora como Josefina.

Sra. Pérez: Yo pienso que debemos utilizar imágenes cargadas de simbolismo profundo: los aereopuertos para representar la carrera de la vida moderna que no le permite a la gente detenerse a disfrutar...

Paco: Definitivamente no. Ese simbolismo no me parece lo suficientemente emocionante. Los aeropuertos pertenencen a directores de un estilo predecible. Todos sabemos que la gran escena va a suceder en el aeropuerto.

Carlota: ¿Qué sugieres entonces?

Sr. Zavala: Lo que creo que quiere decir Paco es que para que la sátira sea cómica, debemos usar elementos distintos.

Sra. Pérez: ¿Algo así como en el género del realismo mágico?

Sr. Zavala: Exacto.

Paco: El simbolismo de la computadora me pareció un poco absurdo.

Sra. Pérez: ¡No! La computadora como símbolo de nuestra obsesión con el futuro es un concepto profundo.

Carlota: ¿Crees tú? Lo que a mí me dio mucha gracia fue la sátira de la tecnología y de las personas enamoradas de ella. Fue muy cómica.

Sr. Zavala: Estoy de acuerdo. Es una sátira deliciosa, ¿no creen?, de la vida de los ciber-fanáticos que nunca ponen pie en la calle ni saben cómo jugar en el mar.

Sra. Pérez: La autora tiene mucho talento. Me gustaría leer más de lo que ha escrito.

Carlota: Creo que podemos convertir la novela de Josefina en una película con un final profundo y emocionante. ¡Manos a la obra! Amelia, tú escribes...

🎧 ACTIVIDAD 9 Ana y Manuel *page 383*

Modelo:
Ana: ¡Vamos a ver una película!
Manuel: Sí claro. Yo tengo ganas de ver una película cómica.
Ana: ¡Ay, no! Prefiero ver una romántica.

1. **Ana:** A mí me encanta ir al cine.
Manuel: A mí también. Pero, cuál prefieres, ¿el cine mexicano o el cine español?
Ana: Yo prefiero el cine español.
Manuel: ¡Uy, no! Yo prefiero el mexicano.

2. **Ana:** ¿Te gusta el autor Gabriel García Márquez?
Manuel: Sí, claro, ¿a quién no le gusta?
Ana: ¿Prefieres su nuevo libro o su primero?
Manuel: El primero, por supuesto.
Ana: ¿Por qué «por supuesto»? Para mí, el nuevo es mucho mejor.

3. **Ana:** ¿Te gusta leer cuentos?
Manuel: Sí, bastante. Me fascinan los cuentos contemporáneos.
Ana: ¿Contemporáneos? ¿No te parecen un poco predecibles?
Manuel: No, para nada.
Ana: Pues yo prefiero los cuentos viejos.

4. **Ana:** ¿Dónde vamos a cenar?
Manuel: Pues hay un restaurante dominicano y uno puertorriqueño cerca de aquí.
Ana: ¿Prefieres la comida dominicana o la puertorriqueña?
Manuel: ¿Yo? La comida puertorriqueña es mi favorita.
Ana: Tuvo que ser. A mí me encanta la dominicana.

5. **Ana:** Quiero comprarme una blusa. ¿Te gusta esta azul?
Manuel: ¿Quieres que te diga la verdad?
Ana: Pues, sí claro.
Manuel: La verdad es que prefiero la verde.
Ana: ¡Es un color horrible! Me voy a comprar la azul.
Manuel: ¡Parece que no estamos de acuerdo en nada!

🎧 ACTIVIDAD 13 Lo contemporáneo *page 386*

Buenos días, clase. Hoy tenemos que tomar varias decisiones sobre lo que vamos a estudiar este semestre. Ustedes me van a ayudar con las decisiones. Simplemente escriban sus preferencias en una hoja de papel mientras yo les hago varias preguntas.

Modelo: En el género de cuentos, ¿prefieren leer los cuentos del argentino Jorge Luis Borges, o los cuentos de la chilena Isabel Allende?

1. ¿Prefieren estudiar la novela *Eva Luna* de Isabel Allende o la novela *Como agua para chocolate* de Laura Esquivel?

2. De los poetas, podemos leer los poemas de Pablo Neruda o podemos leer los de Nicolás Guillén.

3. En el mundo del arte, podemos leer una biografía sobre ese gran pintor español, Pablo Picasso, o, si gustan, podemos leer sobre la vida del pintor colombiano, Fernando Botero.

4. Vamos a estudiar un guión cinemático. Tienen que escoger entre el guión de Laura Esquivel para la película *Como agua para chocolate,* o el guión de Antonio Skármeta para *Eva Luna.*

5. Muy bien, tenemos que leer algunos ensayos. En este género hay unos muy buenos escritos por Jorge Luis Borges y también unos de Gabriel García Márquez.

6. Para terminar, díganme si prefieren estudiar la película *Bodas de Sangre* de Carlos Saura o *Mujeres al borde de un ataque de nervios* de Pedro Almodóvar.

Muy bien. Pásenme los papeles y veré qué prefieren.

Sample Lesson Plan - 50 Minute Schedule

DAY 1

Etapa Opener
- Quick Start Review (TE, p. 372) 5 MIN.
- Have students look at the *Etapa* Opener and answer the questions. 5 MIN.

En contexto: Vocabulario
- Quick Start Review (TE, p. 374) 5 MIN.
- Present *Descubre*, p. 374. Have students use context and pictures to learn *Etapa* vocabulary. Use the Situational OHTs for additional practice. 15 MIN.

En vivo: Situaciones
- Quick Start Review (TE, p. 376) 5 MIN.
- Present the Listening Strategy, p. 376. Have students read section 1, p. 376. Play the audio for section 2. Have students work in groups to complete section 3. 15 MIN.

Homework Option:
- Have students write answers to *¿Comprendiste?*, p. 375.

DAY 2

En acción: Vocabulario y gramática
- Check homework. 5 MIN.
- Quick Start Review (TE, p. 378) 5 MIN.
- Have students complete *Actividad* 1 orally. 5 MIN.
- Have students do *Actividad* 2 in writing. Go over answers orally. 5 MIN.
- Present the *Vocabulario,* p. 379. Then have students do *Actividad* 3 in pairs. 10 MIN.
- Present the Speaking Strategy, p. 379. Then have students do *Actividad* 4 in pairs. 5 MIN.
- Quick Start Review (TE, p. 380) 5 MIN.
- Present *Repaso:* Double Object Pronouns, p. 380. 5 MIN.
- Do *Actividad* 5 orally. 5 MIN.

Homework Option:
- Have students complete *Actividad* 5 in writing. *Más práctica* Workbook, pp. 133–134. *Cuaderno para hispanohablantes*, pp. 131–132.

DAY 3

En acción (cont.)
- Check homework. 5 MIN.
- Have students complete *Actividades* 6 and 7 in pairs. 10 MIN.
- Quick Start Review (TE, p. 382) 5 MIN.
- Present *Gramática:* Nominalization, p. 382. 10 MIN.
- Do *Actividad* 8 orally. 5 MIN.
- Play the audio; do *Actividad* 9. 10 MIN.
- Use an expansion activity from TE pp. 382–383 for variety and reinforcement. 5 MIN.

Homework Option:
- *Más práctica* Workbook, p. 135. *Cuaderno para hispanohablantes,* p. 133.

DAY 4

En acción (cont.)
- Check homework. 5 MIN.
- Have students complete *Actividad* 10 in pairs. 5 MIN.
- Present the *Vocabulario,* p. 384. Then have students read and complete *Actividad* 11 in groups. Expand using *Más comunicación*, p. R17. 15 MIN.
- Quick Start Review (TE, p. 385) 5 MIN.
- Present *Gramática:* More on Nominalization, p. 384. 10 MIN.
- Have students complete *Actividad* 12 in pairs. 5 MIN.
- Play the audio; do *Actividad* 13. 5 MIN.

Homework Option:
- *Más práctica* Workbook, p. 136. *Cuaderno para hispanohablantes,* p. 134.
- *Actividades para todos* Workbook, p. 151–160.

DAY 5

En acción (cont.)
- Check homework. 5 MIN.
- Do *Actividad* 14 in pairs. 5 MIN.
- Have students read and complete *Actividad* 15 in groups. Expand using *Más comunicación,* p. R17. 10 MIN.

Refrán
- Present the *Refrán*, p. 387. 5 MIN.

En voces: Lectura
- Quick Start Review (TE, p. 388) 5 MIN.
- Present the Reading Strategy, p. 388. Call on volunteers to read the *Lectura* aloud. Have students answer the *¿Comprendiste?/ ¿Qué piensas?* questions, p. 389. 20 MIN.

Homework Option:
- Have students complete *Hazlo tú*, p. 389.

DAY 6

En colores: Cultura y comparaciones
- Check homework. 5 MIN.
- Quick Start Review (TE, p. 390) 5 MIN.
- Present the Connecting Cultures Strategy, p. 390. Call on volunteers to read the article aloud. Have students answer the *¿Comprendiste?/¿Qué piensas?* questions, p. 391. 15 MIN.

En uso: Repaso y más comunicación
- Quick Start Review (TE, p. 392) 5 MIN.
- Have students do *Actividad* 1 in pairs, *Actividades* 2 and 3 orally, and *Actividad* 4 in pairs. 20 MIN.

Homework Option:
- Have students complete *Hazlo tú,* p. 391. Review for *Etapa* 3 Exam.

DAY 7

En uso (cont.)
- Check homework. 5 MIN.
- Present the Speaking Strategy, p. 394, and have students do *Actividad* 5 in groups. 10 MIN.

En tu propia voz: Escritura
- Have students write *Actividad* 6. 10 MIN.

En resumen: Repaso de vocabulario
- Review grammar questions, etc., as necessary. 5 MIN.
- Complete *Etapa* 3 Exam. 20 MIN.

Homework Option:
- Review for Unit 5 Comprehensive Test.

DAY 8

Tú en la comunidad
- Discuss *Laura,* p. 394. 5 MIN.

Unit 5 Comprehensive Test
- Review grammar questions, etc., as necessary. 5 MIN.
- Complete Unit 5 Comprehensive Test. 30 MIN.

En tu propia voz: Escritura
- Present the Writing Strategy, p. 396. Do the writing activity, pp. 396–397. 10 MIN.

Ampliación
- Optional: Use a suggested project, game, or activity. (TE, pp. 327A–327B)

Homework Option:
- Preview *Unidad 6* Opener: Have students read and study pp. 398–399.

Sample Lesson Plan - Block Schedule (90 minutes)

DAY 1

Etapa Opener
- Quick Start Review (TE, p. 372) 5 MIN.
- Have students look at the *Etapa* Opener and answer the questions. 5 MIN.
- Use Block Scheduling Copymasters. 10 MIN.

En contexto: Vocabulario
- Quick Start Review (TE, p. 374) 5 MIN.
- Present *Descubre*, p. 374. Have students use context and pictures to learn *Etapa* vocabulary. Use the Situational OHTs for additional practice. 15 MIN.

En vivo: Situaciones
- Quick Start Review (TE, p. 376) 5 MIN.
- Present the Listening Strategy, p. 376. Have students read section 1, p. 376. Play the audio for section 2. Have students work in groups to complete section 3. 15 MIN.

En acción: Vocabulario y gramática
- Quick Start Review (TE, p. 378) 5 MIN.
- Have students complete *Actividad* 1 orally. 5 MIN.
- Have students do *Actividad* 2 in writing. Go over answers orally. 5 MIN.
- Present the *Vocabulario*, p. 379. Then have students do *Actividad* 3 in pairs. 10 MIN.
- Present the Speaking Strategy, p. 379. Then have students do *Actividad* 4 in pairs. 5 MIN.

Homework Option:
- Have students write answers to *¿Comprendiste?*, p. 375.

DAY 2

En acción (cont.)
- Check homework. 5 MIN.
- Quick Start Review (TE, p. 380) 5 MIN.
- Present *Repaso:* Double Object Pronouns, p. 380. 10 MIN.
- Do *Actividad* 5 orally. 5 MIN.
- Have students complete *Actividades* 6 and 7 in pairs. 10 MIN.
- Quick Start Review (TE, p. 382) 5 MIN.
- Present *Gramática:* Nominalization, p. 382. 10 MIN.
- Do *Actividad* 8 orally. 5 MIN.
- Play the audio; do *Actividad* 9. 10 MIN.
- Have students complete *Actividad* 10 in pairs. 5 MIN.
- Present the *Vocabulario*, p. 384. Then have students read and complete *Actividad* 11 in groups. Expand using Information Gap Activities, Unit 5 Resource Book, p. 167; *Más comunicación*, p. R17. 20 MIN.

Homework Option:
- Have students complete *Actividad* 5 in writing. *Más práctica* Workbook, pp. 133–135. *Cuaderno para hispanohablantes*, pp. 131–133.

DAY 3

En acción (cont.)
- Check homework. 5 MIN.
- Quick Start Review (TE, p. 385) 5 MIN.
- Present *Gramática:* More on Nominalization, p. 385. 10 MIN.
- Have students complete *Actividad* 12 in pairs. 5 MIN.
- Play the audio; do *Actividad* 13. 10 MIN.
- Do *Actividad* 14 in pairs. 5 MIN.
- Have students read and complete *Actividad* 15 in groups. Expand using Information Gap Activities, Unit 5 Resource Book, p. 168; *Más comunicación*, p. R17. 20 MIN.
- Use an expansion activity from TE pp. 386–387 for variety and reinforcement. 10 MIN.

Ampliación
- Use a suggested project, game, or activity. (TE, pp. 327A–327B) 15 MIN.

Refrán
- Present the *Refrán*, p. 387. 5 MIN.

Homework Option:
- *Más práctica* Workbook, p. 136. *Cuaderno para hispanohablantes*, p. 134.
- *Actividades para todos* Workbook, p. 151–160.

DAY 4

En voces: Lectura
- Check homework. 5 MIN.
- Quick Start Review (TE, p. 388) 5 MIN.
- Present the Reading Strategy, p. 388. Call on volunteers to read the *Lectura* aloud. Have students answer the *¿Comprendiste?/¿Qué piensas?* questions, p. 389. 15 MIN.

En colores: Cultura y comparaciones
- Quick Start Review (TE, p. 390) 5 MIN.
- Present the Connecting Cultures Strategy, p. 390. Call on volunteers to read the article aloud. Have students answer the *¿Comprendiste?/¿Qué piensas?* questions, p. 391. 20 MIN.

En uso: Repaso y más comunicación
- Quick Start Review (TE, p. 392) 5 MIN.
- Do *Actividad* 1 in pairs, *Actividades* 2 and 3 orally, and *Actividad* 4 in pairs. 15 MIN.
- Present the Speaking Strategy, p. 394, and do *Actividad* 5 in groups. 10 MIN.
- Have students write *Actividad* 6. 10 MIN.

Homework Option:
- Have students complete *Hazlo tú*, pp. 389, 391. Review for *Etapa* 3 Exam and Unit 5 Comprehensive Test.

DAY 5

En resumen: Repaso de vocabulario
- Check homework. 5 MIN.
- Quick Start Review (TE, p. 395) 5 MIN.
- Review grammar questions, etc., as necessary. 5 MIN.
- Complete *Etapa* 3 Exam. 20 MIN.

Tú en la comunidad
- Discuss *Laura*, p. 394. 5 MIN.

Unit 5 Comprehensive Test
- Review grammar questions, etc., as necessary. 5 MIN.
- Complete Unit 5 Comprehensive Test. 30 MIN.

En tu propia voz: Escritura
- Present the Writing Strategy, p. 396. Do the writing activity, pp. 396–397. 15 MIN.

Homework Option:
- Preview *Unidad 6* Opener: Have students read and study pp. 398–399.

▼ Las ferias de libros son muy populares a través del mundo hispanohablante.

Etapa Theme
Talking about literature and film and avoiding redundancy

Grammar Objectives
- Reviewing the use of double object pronouns
- Using nominalization

Teaching Resource Options
Print

Block Scheduling Copymasters
Unit 5 Resource Book
Family Letter p. 171
Absent Student Copymasters, p. 172

Audiovisual

OHT 40 (Quick Start)
Canciones CD

Quick Start Review
🔄 **Reading vocabulary**
Use OHT 40 or write on the board:
Answer the following questions:
1. ¿Qué puedes comprar en una librería?
2. ¿Qué libros compraste este año?
3. ¿Qué novela o libro leíste recientemente?
4. ¿Dónde compras libros?
5. ¿Quién es tu autor(a) favorito(a)?
Answers will vary.

Teaching Suggestions
Previewing the Etapa
- Ask students to study the picture on pp. 372–373 (1 min.).
- Close books; ask various students to name 1 thing they noticed: **Nombra una cosa que notaste acerca de la foto.**
- Reopen books and look at the picture again. Have students describe the people and the setting: **Describe a las personas y el ambiente de la foto.**
- Use the ¿Qué ves? questions to focus the discussion.

UNIDAD 5

ETAPA 3

Lo mejor de dos mundos

OBJECTIVES
- Talk about literature
- Talk about film
- Avoid redundancy

¿Qué ves?

Mira la foto. Contesta las preguntas.
1. ¿Dónde están estas personas?
2. ¿Qué cosas están mirando?
3. ¿Quiénes de la foto se ven más interesados? ¿Por qué?
4. Mira el folleto. ¿Qué anuncia? ¿Has visto folletos así en tu ciudad?

372

Classroom Management

Planning Ahead To prepare to present the theme of literature, bring in examples of various types of Spanish literature. To prepare to present the theme of movies, bring in the following: photos or movie posters of Spanish or Latin American movies; magazines such as **TeleNovela, Vanidades, Hola, Eres;** photos of Spanish-speaking actors from the U.S., Spain, and Latin America.

Peer Review Have students work in pairs to list words or make word webs related to books, reading, and film. Then have them organize the words and use some in sample sentences.

LIBROS
de
MADRID

EDICIONES LA LIBRERÍA
MAYOR, 80 · 28013 MADRID
Telf.: (91) 541 71 70 · Fax: (91) 559 42 49

373

Cross Cultural Connections

Ask students if they have ever been to a book fair in the U.S. (Book publishers often hold book fairs in schools for students.) Is it common to see books displayed on tables on the sidewalk in a town/city? Why or why not?

✷ Culture Highlights

● **LAS FERIAS DE LIBROS** Las ferias de libros son muy populares a través del mundo hispanohablante. Casi todos los domingos hay una en el Parque del Buen Retiro en Madrid, España. La más grande se lleva a cabo en Guadalajara, México, en noviembre. Muchas casas editoriales *(publishers)* del mundo hispanohablante y de Estados Unidos acuden a esta feria.

Supplementary Vocabulary

la feria de libros	book fair
el libro de bolsillo	paperback book
el libro de tapa	hardcover book
la portada	front cover (book or magazine)
el puesto	stall

Teaching All Students

Extra Help Ask students yes/no or simple answer questions about the photo. For example: **¿Están las personas en una feria de libros? ¿Hay muchos libros en la mesa? ¿Qué tiene en la mano el hombre a la derecha?** Then ask them to describe the picture in greater detail by calling on various students to supply one sentence at a time.

Multiple Intelligences

Verbal Have students talk about the different ways of buying books today: super bookstores, online, independent book dealers, etc. Have them name advantages and disadvantages of each. List these on the board.

◼ Block Schedule

Setting the Theme Ask students to bring in copies of their 2 favorite books. Then ask them to explain why they are their favorite books and why other students should read them. (For additional activities, see **Block Scheduling Copymasters**.)

Teaching Resource Options

Print

Block Scheduling Copymasters
Unit 5 Resource Book
Absent Student Copymasters, p. 172

Audiovisual

OHT 34, 35, 36, 36A, 37, 37A, 40
(Quick Start)

Technology

Online Workbook, U5E3
Take-Home Tutor CD-ROM, U5E3

Quick Start Review

♻ Reading vocabulary

Use OHT 40 or write on the board:
Tell what the following people write:

1. un(a) ensayista 4. un(a) cuentista
2. un(a) novelista 5. un(a) reportero(a)
3. un(a) poeta 6. un(a) biógrafo(a)

Answers
1. ensayos   4. cuentos
2. novelas   5. artículos
3. poemas   6. biografías

Teaching Suggestions
Introducing Vocabulary

• Have students look at pages 374–375.
Use OHT 34 and 35 to present the
vocabulary.
• Ask the Comprehension Questions
on TE p. 375 in order of yes/no
(questions 1–3), either/or (questions
4–6), and simple word or phrase
(questions 7–10). Expand by adding
similar questions.
• Use the TPR activity to reinforce the
meaning of individual words.

Descubre

Answers

A. poeta: *poet;* novelista: *novelist;* críticos: *critics;*
culminado: *culminated;* irónico: *ironic;* género:
genre; estilos: *style;* final: *finale, ending;*
contemporáneo: *contemporary;* protagonista:
protagonist; simbolismo: *symbolism;*
innovadora: *innovative;* sátira: *satire;*
romanticismo: *romanticism;* clímax: *climax;*
realismo mágico: *magic realism;* Premio
Nóbel: *Nobel Prize;* prosa: *prose*

B. 1. d   3. e   5. g   7. h   9. j
   2. c   4. a   6. b   8. f   10. i

En contexto VOCABULARIO

mayo

Trayendo a los chicos y chicas
contemporáneos lo mejor de su mundo

Un talento deslumbrante **por Pepe A. Álvarez Gómez**

LECTORES DE LA ONDA: En esta edición, les traigo
una entrevista con Josefina Teresa Almodóvar
Pérez, la joven **poeta, cuentista** y más
recientemente **novelista** de 17 años que ha
causado una sensación increíble entre los
críticos literarios al publicar su novela *Bajo
otro cielo*.
Encontré a Josefina en el balcón de su
casa, descansando después del trabajo que
ha **culminado** en un éxito absoluto. Josefina
se ha hecho famosa de la noche a la mañana;
sin embargo, se mantiene amistosa y no se olvida
de sus compañeros de clase.

▣ Descubre

A. Los cognados De todas las palabras
en azul en el artículo, haz una lista de
cognados y sus equivalentes en inglés.
B. Palabras en contexto Ahora lee el
artículo. Trata de decidir el significado
de las palabras que no son cognados
según el contexto.

1. trama	a. praise
2. personaje	b. dazzling
3. cibernético	c. character
4. elogian	d. plot
5. dentro del alcance	e. relating to cyberspace
6. deslumbrante	f. predictable
7. amenazadores	g. within reach
8. predecible	h. threatening
9. sin embargo	i. blind
10. ciega	j. nevertheless

También se dice

Un dos por tres Josefina dice
que los protagonistas no se
enamoraronen **un dos por
tres.** Es una manera de decir
que no se enamoraron muy
rápido.

La Onda: Josefina, es un placer
conocerte. ¿Te gusta ser famosa?
Josefina: Pues Pepe, es
emocionante, pero también estoy
muy ocupada con las ventas de mi
novela y pensando en la próxima.
La Onda: ¡En la próxima! ¿No es
demasiado pronto?
Josefina: (ríe) Parece **irónico,** ¿no?
Cuando escribo algo, siempre estoy
pensando en otra cosa. Aunque *Bajo
otro cielo* ha tenido mucho éxito y
sé que los críticos la **elogian** en la
prensa, estoy lista para intentar
otros **géneros** y **estilos.** Además
quiero seguir mejorando mi **prosa.**

La Onda: ¿Qué puedes decirnos
sobre *Bajo otro cielo*?
Josefina: Es una novela
contemporánea de **personajes** que
luchan por sus vidas respectivas
en lugares distintos del planeta.
Margarita Buscasueños y Joaquín
Esperanzado—los **protagonistas**—
viven en Europa y en Estados
Unidos. Parte de la **trama** se
desarrolla en aeropuertos, cuando
Joaquín se lleva por equivocación
las maletas de Margarita y regresa
a España. Al abrir las maletas,
encuentra el libro de direcciones
de Margarita y le escribe por
correo electrónico…

374 trescientos setenta y cuatro
Unidad 5

Classroom Community

TPR Plan ahead: Make 2 sets of cards. One set has
the Spanish words in the **Descubre** box (if necessary,
make duplicates so that you have enough for half the
class). The other set has the English words. Distribute a
card to each student, then have them stand up. Call out a
Spanish word. Those students have to stand next to the
students holding the correct English translations.
Continue until all students are paired up.

Portfolio Have students write an expository article
about Josefina based on what she says. They may want
to select and rearrange information from the interview.

Rubric A = 13–15 pts. B = 10–12 pts. C = 7–9 pts. D = 4–6 pts. F = < 4 pts.

Writing criteria	Scale
Details	1 2 3 4 5
Logical organization	1 2 3 4 5
Grammar/spelling accuracy	1 2 3 4 5

La Onda: Eso de las maletas me parece muy interesante. ¿Hay algún **simbolismo** en esa confusión?

Josefina: Puede ser. Hay objetos en la vida de uno que tienen un significado especial, que llegan a ser un símbolo.

La Onda: Volvamos a Margarita, Joaquín y a los aeropuertos. ¿Le das una interpretación **innovadora** a eso de que el amor es **ciego**?

Josefina: No, Pepe. Eso sería bastante **predecible.** No, el encuentro de Joaquín y Margarita es hasta cierto punto una **sátira** de las novelas de amor populares durante el **romanticismo,** y también populares ahora, donde un chico y una chica se conocen y en un dos por tres se enamoran. Esto es un poco más complicado. Cuando Joaquín comienza a escribirle a Margarita, ella lo encuentra **amenazador;** él, al ver la reacción que ella tiene, cree que ella es paranoica.

La Onda: El **clímax** de la novela es mucho más emocionante. ¿Cómo es que Joaquín y Margarita descubren a los terroristas?

Josefina: Me gusta mucho esa parte también, pero mejor es que los lectores la lean.

La Onda: *Bajo otro cielo* es una historia que sin duda está **dentro del alcance** de muchos gustos. ¿Tienes un título para tu próxima novela?

Josefina: No sé cómo se llamará, pero tratará algún tema **cibernético** siguiendo el estilo del **realismo mágico,** que mezcla la realidad y la fantasía.

La Onda: Te acabas de ganar el Premio del Escritor Joven del Año. ¿Quisieras ganarte el **Premio Nóbel** alguna vez?

Bajo otro cielo

Josefina Teresa Almodóvar Pérez

Josefina: ¡Qué pregunta, Pepe! Pero no escribo porque quiero ganarme premios. Escribo porque me gusta, porque no me imagino la vida sin escribir.

La Onda: Creo que nuestra entrevista está llegando a su **final.** ¿Tienes algún consejo para nuestros lectores?

Josefina: Bueno, que disfruten la vida y que lean, claro.

La Onda: Te deseamos mucho éxito y será hasta la próxima.

Online Workbook
CLASSZONE.COM

¿Comprendiste?

1. ¿Has pensado alguna vez en hacerte famoso(a) haciendo algo creativo? ¿Qué has querido hacer?
2. ¿Cuál es el (la) cuentista, novelista o poeta que más te gusta? ¿Por qué?
3. ¿Qué preguntas le harías tú a un(a) escritor(a) famoso(a)?
4. ¿Qué clase de libros te gusta leer? ¿Cuál es tu estilo preferido?
5. ¿Crees que los temas cibernéticos van a ser más o menos importantes en el futuro? ¿Por qué?

trescientos setenta y cinco
España y las Américas Etapa 3   **375**

Culture Highlights

● **LA INDUSTRIA EDITORIAL** La industria editorial es muy importante en España, Argentina y México. Las casas editoriales en Estados Unidos han descubierto la importancia del mercado hispanohablante en su propio país. En los últimos 20 años se han hecho famosos escritores como Jorge Luis Borges, Isabel Allende, Laura Esquivel, Carlos Fuentes, Rosario Ferré y Gabriel García Márquez.

Comprehension Questions

1. ¿Es Josefina una joven escritora? (Sí)
2. ¿Piensa Josefina en su próxima novela? (Sí)
3. ¿Cuenta Josefina toda la trama de su novela? (No)
4. ¿Está basada la novela en la vida real o es una sátira? (Es una sátira.)
5. ¿Encuentra Margarita a Joaquín amenazador o romántico? (amenazador)
6. ¿El clímax de la novela es emocionante o aburrido? (emocionante)
7. ¿Cuál es el título de la próxima novela de Josefina? (No se sabe.)
8. ¿De qué se tratará? (de algún tema cibernético)
9. ¿Qué premio se acaba de ganar Josefina? (el Premio del Escritor Joven del Año)
10. ¿Qué les aconseja Josefina a los lectores? (que disfruten la vida y que lean)

Block Schedule

Expansion Have students work in pairs to brainstorm and write additional questions they would ask Josefina, especially about her personal life, favorite writers, activities, etc. Then have pairs act out this expanded interview. (For additional activities, see **Block Scheduling Copymasters.**)

Teaching All Students

Extra Help Have 9 pairs of students each read 1 of the 9 question/answer exchanges of the interview. Stop after each section and ask students for a 1-sentence summary.

Native Speakers Have students research the names of popular Spanish-language magazines and what their main topics are. Have them point out which ones are teen-oriented.

Multiple Intelligences

Visual Have students design their own version of a book jacket for **Bajo otro cielo.**

Intrapersonal Have students talk about the kinds of novels they prefer to read and why.

Teaching Resource Options

Print 🕮

Block Scheduling Copymasters
Unit 5 Resource Book
  About Student Copymasters, p. 173
  Audioscript, p. 181

Audiovisual 📼

OHT 38-39, 41 (Quick Start)
Audio Program CD 15, Track 1

Technology 💻

Take-Home Tutor CD-ROM, U5E3

🔔 Quick Start Review

♻ Vocabulary review

Use OHT 41 or write on the board:
Write a brief definition of the following
words:

1. un(a) novelista
2. contemporáneo
3. el realismo mágico
4. la trama
5. el (la) protagonista

Answers
Answers will vary. Answers could include:
1. persona que escribe novelas
2. que tiene que ver con el presente
3. que mezcla la realidad y la fantasía
4. de lo que se trata la novela
5. el personaje principal

Teaching Suggestions
Presenting Situations

• Present the Listening Strategy, p. 376,
  and have students complete the
  Pre-listening exercise.

• Use OHT 165 and 166 to present the
  Leer section. Ask simple yes/no,
  either/or, or short-answer questions.

• Use Audio CD 15 and have students
  do the **Escuchar** section (see Script
  p. 371B) and complete the Listening
  Strategy exercise.

• Have students work in groups to
  complete the **Hablar/Escribir** section.

AUDIO 🎧 *En vivo*
SITUACIONES

PARA ESCUCHAR
STRATEGY: LISTENING

Pre-listening Write down terms you use in
English class to discuss literature. Then scan
the seven words listed under **Escuchar.** What
words on your list mean the same? Finally,
define each of the Spanish words not found
on your list.

Evaluate discussions Group discussions cover
many topics. Here four people are discussing
a new novel. After listening, decide:

1. About what do they agree?
2. About what do they disagree?
3. What do you consider is the value of a
   discussion like this?

376 trescientos setenta y seis
Unidad 5

El club de cine

Estás en el club de cine de la escuela, donde
un grupo de estudiantes se reúne para discutir
ideas para la próxima película que van a hacer.

① Leer

En esta reunión, hablan de hacer una película sobre la
novela de Josefina Teresa Almodóvar Pérez. Lee la cubierta
(*cover*) del libro.

> Margarita Buscasueños es una muchacha luchadora y
> Joaquín Esperanzado vive para un mundo mejor. Su
> amistad virtual comienza a través de una equivocación,
> cuando Joaquín se lleva las maletas de Margarita. Al
> principio ella cree que él es un tipo amenazador, pero
> luego llega a saber la verdad. Lo que comienza como
> conflicto termina en una gran amistad *Bajo otro cielo*.
>
> «Drámatico. Alucinante. No me pude acostar hasta que
> leí la última página de *Bajo otro cielo*». Arturo Costas,
> *Nuestro País*
>
> «¡Qué delicia! Por fin, una novela sin trama predecible.
> Cada página es una sorpresa y una lección inolvidable
> sobre la psicología de los ciber-fanáticos». Alma Reyes,
> *Ser es Leer*
>
> «¿Qué pasa cuando el
> realismo mágico se une con
> el romanticismo? *Bajo otro
> cielo*, ¡por supuesto! Si lee
> sólo un libro este año, tiene
> que ser éste». Rosalinda
> Salinas, *Opiniones
> Literarias*

Josefina Teresa Almodóvar Pérez

ISBN 0-386-47137-8

Classroom Community

Paired Activity Give students copies of the
Listening Script on TE p. 371B. Have students work in
pairs to write 6 comprehension questions. Then have
them exchange papers with another pair and answer
each other's questions.

Cooperative Learning Have students work in
groups of 5 to write the first chapter of a novel. They
should work together to come up with a protagonist

and other characters, a general theme, a plot, and the
title. Have 1 student design the novel cover, 2 students
work on the text of the chapter, and 2 students work
on a general review of the novel (similar to what
Josefina gives on pp. 375–376). Have groups take turns
presenting their covers, reading their first chapters, and
giving a general overview of the plot. Students can vote
on the most interesting novel.

2 Escuchar

Escucha la disusión del club de cine. Decide cuál(es) de estas palabras se usa(n) para describir el concepto en **negrilla**. ¡OJO! A veces se menciona más de una palabra.

1. **la protagonista:** ❏ inocente ❏ inteligente ❏ cómica

2. **el simbolismo:** ❏ profundo ❏ emocionante ❏ absurdo

3. **la sátira:** ❏ deslumbrante ❏ cómica ❏ emocionante

4. **la autora:** ❏ talento ❏ Premio Nóbel ❏ innovadora

5. **el estilo:** ❏ complicado ❏ predecible ❏ claro

6. **el género:** ❏ simbolismo ❏ romanticismo ❏ realismo mágico

7. **el final:** ❏ irónico ❏ profundo ❏ emocionante

3 Hablar/Escribir

En grupos de tres o cuatro, hagan una lista de cinco novelas favoritas del grupo. Hagan una tabla con los cinco títulos de las novelas. Bajo cada título, escriban el nombre del autor y el género. Luego, para cada novela, escriban una oración sobre una de las siguientes cosas.

- la trama
- la sátira
- el protagonista
- el estilo
- el simbolismo
- el final

Hablen entre sí sobre sus opiniones antes de escribir las oraciones finales. Compartan sus tablas con la clase.

Teaching All Students

Extra Help Have students work in pairs to make sure they understand the meaning of the words in the chart in **Actividad 2** before listening to the conversation.

Challenge Have students work in small groups and choose a book they all have read. Then have them write a discussion similar to the one in the **Escuchar.**

Multiple Intelligences

Interpersonal Have students work in pairs to discuss what they consider to be the central ideas of the discussion in **Escuchar.** Have them write a summary of the discussion. Then have them exchange summaries with another pair for peer correction. Pairs then make the necessary corrections and present them to the class.

Escuchar (See script, p. 371B.)

Answers

la protagonista: inteligente
el simbolismo: profundo / emocionante / absurdo
la sátira: cómica
la autora: talento / innovadora
el estilo: predecible
el género: realismo mágico
el final: profundo / emocionante

Hablar/Escribir

Answers will vary.

Language Note

Another word for *plot* is **el argumento.**

Block Schedule

Change of Pace Have students work in pairs or small groups to write a short scene from the book **Bajo otro cielo.** Then have them read and act out the scene for the class. (For additional activities, see **Block Scheduling Copymasters.**)

Teaching Resource Options

Print

Block Scheduling Copymasters
Unit 5 Resource Book
  Absent Student Copymasters, p. 174

Audiovisual

OHT 41 (Quick Start)

Quick Start Review

♻ Vocabulary review

Use OHT 41 or write on the board:
Make sentences from the following
elements:

1. trama / novela / interesante
2. novelista / crear / personajes /
   romanticismo / convertirse /
   sátira
3. escribir / libro / estilo sencillo
4. crítico / decir / uso / realismo
   mágico / ser / sensacional
5. protagonistas / odiarse / hasta /
   final

Answers
Answers will vary. Answers could include:
1. La trama de la novela es interesante.
2. La novelista crea personajes cuyo
   romanticismo se convierte en sátira.
3. Escribió el libro en un estilo sencillo.
4. Los críticos dicen que su uso de realismo
   mágico es sensacional.
5. Los protagonistas se odian hasta el final.

Teaching Suggestions
Comprehension Check

Use **Actividades 1–4** to assess retention
after the **Vocabulario** and **Situaciones**.
After completing **Actividad 1**, have
students write similar descriptions of 2
additional books. After completing
Actividad 2, dictate the sentences to
students for a quiz grade.

En acción

PARTE A — **Práctica del vocabulario**

Objetives for Activities 1-4
• Talk about literature

1 La librería

Hablar/Escribir Vas a la librería a comprar varios libros.
Le pides ayuda al dependiente. ¿Qué le dices?

modelo

Balance total *por Aída Estrada*

¡La mejor novela del año!

Busco una novela que se titula Balance total.
La novelista se llama Aída Estrada.

I. *Avenida nueve de julio*
   por Marcos Ybarra
   ¡Una colección de cuentos
   inolvidable!

2. *El jaguar en mi corazón*
   por Sonia Cisneros
   Una colección de poemas
   para el romántico

3. *Siete años en Costa Rica*
   por Andrés Gutiérrez
   Con esta colección de
   ensayos, conozca Costa Rica
   por dentro y por fuera.

4. *Una vida artística:*
   La vida de Pablo Pérez
   por Amalia de la Rosa
   La biografía de un artista
   sin límites

2 Los críticos

Escribir Cada semana lees las
opiniones de los críticos en el
periódico. Escoge la palabra
de la lista que mejor define o
explica lo que dice cada crítico.

modelo

*«Es un tema que trata de la vida
moderna.»*

f. *contemporáneo*

a. estilo
b. romanticismo
c. realismo mágico
d. sátira
e. clímax
f. contemporáneo
g. personaje

I. «La trama se concentra en
   un romance misterioso.»

2. «Hay escenas que
   convierten la realidad
   en algo mágico.»

3. «La protagonista es una
   persona muy inteligente.»

4. «La novela pone en
   ridículo a los cibernéticos.»

5. «La autora escribe
   oraciones muy claras
   y sencillas.»

6. «La novela culmina en una
   escena muy explosiva.»

378 trescientos setenta y ocho
Unidad 5

Classroom Management

Time Saver Assign **Actividades** 1 and 2 for
homework. Have copies of the answers ready the next
day so that students can check their own work.

Peer Review Have students brainstorm a list of
novels, poetry collections, etc., that they have read.
Write the list on the board for students to refer to when
doing **Actividades** 3 and 4.

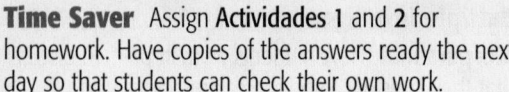

③ El grupo de lectores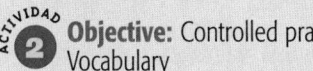

Hablar/*Escribir* Tú y tu compañero(a) son miembros de un grupo de lectores que analiza una novela cada mes. Háganse preguntas y expresen sus opiniones sobre alguna novela que hayan leído recientemente.

modelo

Tú: *¿Qué pensaste de la trama de Mi doble vida?*

Compañero(a): *Pensé que la trama era predecible.*

---

trama (complicada, innovadora, formulista…)

estilo del autor (claro, expresivo, creativo…)

final (emocionante, irónico, predecible…)

protagonista (inocente, inteligente, valiente…)

novela (dramática, deslumbrante, contemporánea, inolvidable, impresionante…)

Vocabulario

La literatura

creativo(a) *creative*

derivado(a) *derivative, unoriginal*

dramático(a) *dramatic*

expresivo(a) *expressive*

formulista *formulaic*

impresionante *impressive*

original *original*

simbólico(a) *symbolic*

titularse *to be titled*

el título *title*

tratarse de (*¿De qué se trata?*) *to be about*

▶ ¿Puedes usar algunas de estas palabras para describir algo que has leído recientemente?

④ La clase de literatura

> **STRATEGY: SPEAKING**
>
> **Discuss a novel** Sharing and discussing a book can be as rewarding as reading it. Here are some topics for the discussion: **lo que me gustó más, lo que me molestó, lo que no comprendí, el personaje más interesante, el mensaje del autor, cómo se compara con otras novelas del mismo autor, el valor de la novela**. Encourage others to talk by asking their opinions.

Hablar En la clase de literatura, tú y tu compañero(a) tienen que analizar su novela favorita. Escriban cinco opiniones sobre varios aspectos de la novela: el tema, la trama, el protagonista, el clímax y el estilo.

modelo

Tú: *¿Cuál es tu novela favorita?*

Compañero(a): *Pues, me gustan muchas, pero creo que la que más me gusta es* The Great Gatsby, *de F. Scott Fitzgerald.*

Tú: *¿De qué se trata?*

Compañero(a): *Pues, el protagonista, Jay Gatsby, es un hombre muy rico pero misterioso…*

trescientos setenta y nueve
España y las Américas Etapa 3
379

Teaching All Students

Extra Help Review the meanings of literary terms for students who are less familiar with them.

Native Speakers Have students write a 1-page book report, using at least 6 of the words from the **Vocabulario** on p. 379.

Multiple Intelligences

Kinesthetic Have students relate the novel types (romantic, melodramatic, dramatic, etc.) to facial expressions.

Musical/Rhythmic Have students choose or create music to accompany a brief reading from a novel. How does the music relate to the text?

ACTIVIDAD ① Objective: Controlled practice
Vocabulary

Answers
1. Busco una colección de cuentos que se titula *Avenida nueve de julio.* El cuentista se llama Marcos Ybarra.
2. Busco una colección de poemas que se titula *El jaguar en mi corazón.* La poeta se llama Sonia Cisneros.
3. Busco una colección de ensayos que se titula *Siete años en Costa Rica.* El autor se llama Andrés Gutiérrez.
4. Busco una biografía que se titula *Una vida artística: La vida de Pablo Pérez.* La autora se llama Amalia de la Rosa.

ACTIVIDAD ② Objective: Controlled practice
Vocabulary

Answers
1. b. romanticismo
2. c. realismo mágico
3. g. personaje
4. d. sátira
5. a. estilo
6. e. clímax

Teaching Suggestions
Presenting Vocabulary

• After presenting the **Vocabulario**, have students use the words in original sentences about literary selections.

• Have students find different parts of speech that correspond to these **Vocabulario** words; for example, **creativo(a) → crear.**

ACTIVIDAD ③ Objective: Transitional practice
Vocabulary in conversation

Answers will vary.

ACTIVIDAD ④ Objective: Open-ended practice
Vocabulary in conversation

Answers will vary.

🔔 Quick Wrap-up

Have students describe the climax of a well-known novel or movie without identifying it, then have the class guess the title.

▮ Block Schedule

Variety Have students extend **Actividad 3** by using the same or similar terms to talk about movies they have seen. (For additional activities, see **Block Scheduling Copymasters.**)

Teaching Resource Options

Print 📖

Más práctica Workbook PE,
  pp. 133–134
Cuaderno para hispanohablantes
  PE, pp. 131–132
Block Scheduling Copymasters
Unit 5 Resource Book
  Más práctica Workbook TE,
  pp. 145–146
  Cuaderno para hispanohablantes
  TE, pp. 161–162
  Absent Student Copymasters, p. 174

Audiovisual 🎧

OHT 42 (Quick Start), 46 (Grammar)

Technology 💻

Online Workbook, U5E3
Take-Home Tutor CD-ROM, U5E3

Quick Start Review

♻️ Object nouns and pronouns

Use OHT 42 or write on the board:
Identify the object(s) in each sentence.
If it's a direct object, underline it.
If it's an indirect object, circle it.

1. Compré una novela.
2. Le regalé un libro a mi amiga.
3. Nos escribieron una carta.
4. ¿Me describes la trama?
5. Te traemos las revistas.

Answers
1. Compré <u>una novela</u>. 2. (Le)regalé <u>un libro</u> a (mi amiga.) 3. (Nos)escribieron <u>una carta</u>. 4. ¿(Me)describes <u>la trama</u>? 5. (Te) traemos <u>las revistas</u>.

Teaching Suggestions
Reviewing Double Object Pronouns

Point out that in sentences with both direct and indirect third person object pronouns, students only need to focus on the gender of the direct object pronoun. The indirect object pronoun will always be **se**.

Objectives for Activities 5-14
• Talk about literature • Talk about film • Avoid redundancy

REPASO   Double Object Pronouns

♻️ **¿RECUERDAS?** *pp. 358, 360* You have already learned to use **direct** and **indirect object pronouns** to avoid redundancy. You can also use these two kinds of object pronouns together. When you do, you put the **indirect** object **before** the **direct** object.

Ya tengo el libro de cuentos. **Me lo** prestó mi amiga Julia.
*I already have the book of short stories. My friend Julia lent **it** to **me**.*

Comprendemos los poemas porque **nos los** explicó el profesor.
*We understand the poems because the teacher explained **them** to **us**.*

There is a special rule for verbs with two pronouns when both are **third person**: change the **indirect** object pronoun to **se**.

le + lo = se lo

¿**Le** mostraste el dibujo a Carlos?   Sí, **se lo** mostré.
Did you show the drawing to Carlos?   *Yes, I showed **it** to **him**.*

¿**Les** diste el guión a las actrices?   Sí, **se lo** di.
Did you give the script to the actresses?   *Yes, I gave **it** to **them**.*

Don't forget to put **object pronouns** before all **conjugated verbs** except **affirmative commands**, where you attach them. When you attach them, put an accent mark on the verb.

Mauricio quiere usar nuestro carro.   **Présten**selo.
Mauricio wants to use our car.   *Lend **it** to **him**.*

Remember that when you use **object pronouns** with **infinitives** and the **-ndo forms**, you can put the pronouns either before or after the verb.

Me gusta esa computadora.   Me gusta esa computadora.
Me la quiero comprar.   Quiero **comprár**mela.
*I like that computer. I want to buy **it*** *I like that computer. I want to buy **it***
*for **myself**.*   *for **myself**.*

Mamá **nos los está**   Mamá está
preparando.   **preparándo**noslos.
*Mom is preparing **them** for **us**.* *Mom is preparing **them** for **us**.*

Practice:
Actividades
5 6 7

Más práctica
cuaderno pp. 133-134
Para hispanohablantes
cuaderno pp. 131-132

🌐 **Online Workbook**
CLASSZONE.COM

También se dice

Hay muchas maneras de decir que algo no es interesante o que… ¡es aburrido!

• ¡Qué lata!
  (la mayoría de los países hispanohablantes)

• ¡Qué plomo!
  (España, Argentina)

• ¡Qué denso!
  (Argentina)

• ¡Qué barro! / ¡Qué charro!
  (Colombia)

• ¡Qué pejiguera! /
  ¡Qué hartero!
  (Puerto Rico)

• ¡Qué palo! / ¡Qué rollo!
  (España)

Classroom Community

Paired Activity Have students work in pairs to ask and answer questions about things they want, using verbs like **dar, regalar, traer, explicar,** and **prestar**. For example, ¿Me prestas tu lápiz? → Sí, te lo presto.

Group Activity Have students work in groups of 4–5. Students pass around a ball or other small object until you say stop. The student holding the object has to give a command or a sentence about what someone must do with the object. For example: **Dásela a Pedro. Llévasela a Inés.** Continue for a few minutes.

5 El (La) presidente(a) ♻

Hablar/Escribir Tú eres el (la) secretario(a) del club literario. El (la) presidente(a) te pregunta si has hecho varias cosas que te había pedido. ¿Cómo le respondes?

modelo

¿Compraste el libro de poemas para Marta?

Sí, yo se lo compré. **o** No, no se lo compré.

1. ¿Prestaste la colección de ensayos a Miguel?
2. ¿Regalaste la biografía de Pablo Neruda a Carlos?
3. ¿Devolviste el guión a Anilú?
4. ¿Diste el libro de cuentos a Marcelo?
5. ¿Recomendaste esa novela a Juan?
6. ¿Mandaste la colección de obras teatrales a Lisa?

Nota cultural

Muchas de las películas y programas de televisión producidos en Estados Unidos son populares en los países de habla española. En algunas ocasiones, los títulos en inglés pueden ser traducidos literalmente al español. Pero en otras ocasiones las traducciones al español no son tan exactas, y a veces completamente diferentes. Por ejemplo, la película americana *It Could Happen to You*, con Nicolas Cage, Bridget Fonda y Rosie Pérez, en español se llama «La lotería del amor». Otros títulos diferentes son:

- *Ghost*: «La sombra del amor»
- *Star Trek:* «Viaje a las estrellas»
- *A River Runs Through It:* «Nada es para siempre»

6 En la cafetería

Hablar/Escribir Estás hablando con tu mejor amigo(a) en la cafetería. Usando elementos de las tres columnas, hazle preguntas sobre varias acciones. Sigue el modelo.

modelo

Tú: ¿Le diste el disco compacto a Mireya?

Compañero(a): Sí, se lo di ayer.

Tú: ¿Le comentaste el simbolismo del poema a Martín?

Compañero(a): Sí, se lo comenté anoche.

Acción	Objetos/Conceptos	Persona
dar	novela(s)	¿a quién?
mostrar	colección de poemas	
prestar	disco(s) compacto(s)	
comentar	juego(s) electrónico(s)	
mandar	película(s)	
recomendar	video(s)	
hablar de	carta(s)	
devolver	tarjeta(s)	
	postal(es)	
	poema	
	trama	
	sátira	
	simbolismo	
	...	

Teaching All Students

Extra Help Have students imagine that they are at the dinner table and are still hungry. They ask their brother/sister if there is any more of certain items and to pass them to him/her. For example: carne → ¿Hay más carne? ¿Me la pasas? Provide the following list: **frutas, ensalada, pollo, pan, arroz, tomates, frijoles.**

Multiple Intelligences

Visual Have students create a newspaper ad for an international best seller. Remind students to use the **Ud.** form in their ads. They must use commands with object pronouns. For example: ¡Cómprelo! ¡No se lo pierda!

Objetivo ACTIVIDAD 5 Objective: Controlled practice Double object pronouns

♻ Preterite tense

Answers

1. Sí, se la presté.
   o:
   No, no se la presté.
2. Sí, se la regalé.
   o:
   No, no se la regalé.
3. Sí, se lo devolví.
   o:
   No, no se lo devolví.
4. Sí, se lo di.
   o:
   No, no se lo di.
5. Sí, se la recomendé.
   o:
   No, no se la recomendé.
6. Sí, se la mandé.
   o:
   No, no se la mandé.

ACTIVIDAD 6 Objective: Transitional practice Double object pronouns in conversation

Answers will vary.

🔔 Quick Wrap-up

Have students change these sentences so that the object pronouns come after the verb. Can students come up with possible nouns that were replaced by the object pronouns?

Carlos se lo compra.

Me la quiero leer.

Los primos de Laura se las están mandando.

Block Schedule

FunBreak Have students read the Nota cultural. Then have them guess which U.S. movies these Spanish titles are for: **La dama y el vagabundo** *(Lady and the Tramp),* **El extraterrestre** *(E.T.),* **Tiburón** *(Jaws),* **Cazadores del arca perdida** *(Raiders of the Lost Ark),* **La guerra de las galaxias** *(Star Wars),* **Los reyes del mambo** *(Mambo Kings).* (For additional activities, see **Block Scheduling Copymasters.**)

Teaching Resource Options

Print

Más práctica Workbook PE, p. 135
Cuaderno para hispanohablantes PE, p. 133
Block Scheduling Copymasters
Unit 5 Resource Book
  Más práctica Workbook TE, p. 147
  Cuaderno para hispanohablantes TE, p. 163
  Absent Student Copymasters, pp. 174–175
  Audioscript, p. 181

Audiovisual

OHT 42 (Quick Start), 47 (Grammar)
Audio Program CD 15, Track 2

Technology

Online Workbook, U5E3
Take-Home Tutor CD-ROM, U5E3

Objective: Open-ended practice Double object pronouns in conversation

Answers will vary.

Quick Start Review

♻ Double object pronouns

Use OHT 42 or write on the board:
Match the columns:

1. ___ ¿Nos explican Uds. la lección?
2. ___ ¿No hace Ud. la tarea?
3. ___ ¿Me sirves la limonada?
4. ___ ¿Me muestras las fotos?
5. ___ ¿Te sirven ellas el té?
6. ___ ¿Me explicas la geometría?
  a. La hago ahora mismo.
  b. Te las muestro esta tarde.
  c. Te la explico esta noche.
  d. Te la sirvo más tarde.
  e. Se la explicamos el martes.
  f. Me lo sirven a las cuatro.

Answers
1. e 2. a 3. d 4. b 5. f 6. c

---

7 El cumpleaños

Hablar Muchos de tus amigos y parientes cumplen años este mes. Conversa con tu compañero(a) sobre tus ideas para varios regalos. Menciona cinco regalos para cinco personas. Luego, cambien de papel.

modelo

Tú: *Quiero comprarle una novela latinoamericana a mi novio(a) para su cumpleaños.*

Compañero(a): *Pues, ¡cómprasela!*

 **Apoyo para estudiar**

Negative command

Remember that in a negative command, object pronouns precede the verb. So you can advise against an action (¡No se la compre!), but you should give a reason why (porque ella prefiere la poesía).

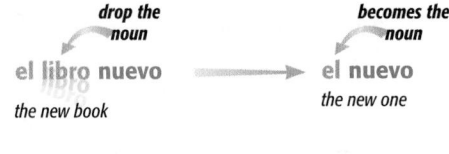 **GRAMÁTICA**   **Nominalization**

▸ If you want to avoid repeating the same word over again in a sentence, you can use **nominalization.**

▸ You can **drop the noun** if it's used with an **adjective** and use just the **adjective** and **article** instead.

drop the noun → *becomes the noun*

el libro nuevo → **el nuevo**
the new book — *the new one*

las películas cómicas → **las cómicas**
the comic films — *the comic ones*

Me gusta **la camisa amarilla.** No me pondría **la roja.**
I like the yellow shirt. I wouldn't wear the red one.

> You know that the **red** one is referring to the **red** shirt.

▸ This structure also works with **indefinite articles**, **demonstrative adjectives**, and **numbers.**

No quiero un carro viejo. Quiero **uno nuevo.**
I don't want an old car. I want a new one.

Esas novelas realistas no son muy buenas. **Estas simbólicas** son mejores.
Those realist novels aren't very good. These symbolic ones are better.

Necesito cajas para enviar regalos. Quiero **tres cuadradas** y **dos redondas.**
I need boxes to send gifts. I want three square ones and two round ones.

Practice: **Actividades** 8 9 10 11   **Más práctica** *cuaderno p. 135*   **Para hispanohablantes** *cuaderno p. 133*   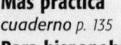 **Online Workbook** CLASSZONE.COM

---

382   trescientos ochenta y dos
Unidad 5

Classroom Community

TPR **Plan ahead:** Bring in sets of 3 objects, such as pens that have different attributes, e.g., size or color. For each set, have students take turns holding an object and stating their preference. For example:
  STUDENT 1: **Yo prefiero la pluma negra.**
  STUDENT 2: **Yo prefiero la verde.**

Learning Scenario Divide the class into groups of 4. Each group is a family that is buying a new car. Have them role-play a car-shopping scene, using nominalization. For example: MAMÁ: **A mí me gusta el carro negro.** HIJO: **Yo prefiero el blanco.**

8 Los actores

Hablar/*Escribir* Paco y Elena son dos actores que se están vistiendo para una obra. Eligen ropa distinta para sus personajes. ¿Qué dice cada uno sobre las piezas de ropa?

modelo

Elena (jeans azules); yo (jeans negros)

Elena se puso los jeans azules.

Yo me puse los negros.

1. Elena (zapatos marrones);
yo (zapatos blancos)

2. Paco (bufanda a cuadros);
yo (bufanda verde)

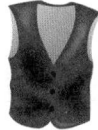

3. Paco (chaqueta
anaranjada); yo
(chaqueta amarilla)

4. Elena (blusa púrpura);
yo (camisa roja)

5. Paco (chaleco de piel);
yo (chaleco blanco)

6. Elena (sandalias cafés);
yo (sandalias negras)

9 Ana y Manuel

Escuchar/*Escribir* Ana y Manuel han sido novios por muy poco tiempo, por eso no conocen los gustos del otro muy bien todavía. Escucha su conversación y di cuál de las cosas mencionadas prefiere cada uno.

modelo

Ana: Prefiere la romántica.

Manuel: Prefiere la cómica.

1. Ana:
Manuel:

2. Ana:
Manuel:

3. Ana:
Manuel:

4. Ana:
Manuel:

5. Ana:
Manuel:

Teaching All Students

Extra Help Before having students complete **Actividad 8**, have them write the definite articles for each of the nouns.

Native Speakers Ask students to look through Spanish children's books or song lyrics in Spanish that have examples of nominalization. Have them bring in what they find to present to the class.

Multiple Intelligences

Kinesthetic Plan ahead: Have students bring in catalog pictures of contrasting objects (a black dress and a red dress, cowboy boots and dress boots, etc.). Have students take turns pointing to their objects and comparing them; for example, **El negro es más elegante que el rojo.** Then have students elicit responses from the class: **¿Prefieres el rojo o el negro?**

Teaching Suggestions
Presenting Nominalization

Offer students examples in English to help them understand why nominalization is used. For example: *I want to buy a sweater. I don't want to buy the red sweater. I want to buy the blue sweater. The red sweater is more expensive than the blue sweater.* Have students explain how they would use nominalization in English to avoid this repetition.

ACTIVIDAD 8
Objective: Controlled practice
Nominalization

 Clothing and colors

Answers
1. Elena se puso los zapatos marrones.
   Yo me puse los blancos.
2. Paco se puso la bufanda a cuadros.
   Yo me puse la verde.
3. Paco se puso la chaqueta anaranjada.
   Yo me puse la amarilla.
4. Elena se puso la blusa púrpura.
   Yo me puse la roja.
5. Paco se puso el chaleco de piel.
   Yo me puse el blanco.
6. Elena se puso las sandalias cafés.
   Yo me puse las negras.

ACTIVIDAD 9
Objective: Controlled practice
Listening comprehension/
nominalization

Answers (See script, p. 371B.)
1. Ana: Prefiere el español.
   Manuel: Prefiere el mexicano.
2. Ana: Prefiere el nuevo.
   Manuel: Prefiere el primero.
3. Ana: Prefiere los viejos.
   Manuel: Prefiere los contemporáneos.
4. Ana: Prefiere la dominicana.
   Manuel: Prefiere la puertorriqueña.
5. Ana: Prefiere la azul.
   Manuel: Prefiere la verde.

Block Schedule

Variety Have one student refer to a thing that several people have without naming the object; for example, **la negra es de Juan y la roja es de María.** The class tries to guess what the object is; for example, **la mochila.** (For additional activities, see **Block Scheduling Copymasters.**)

Teaching Resource Options

Print

Block Scheduling Copymasters
Unit 5 Resource Book
  Information Gap Activities, p. 167
  Absent Student Copymasters,
  pp. 175–176

Audiovisual

OHT 43 (Quick Start), 48 (Grammar)

Technology

Online Workbook, U5E3
Take-Home Tutor CD-ROM, U5E3

 Objective: Transitional practice Nominalization in conversation

Answers will vary.

Objective: Open-ended practice Nominalization/vocabulary in reading and conversation

Answers will vary.

Quick Start Review

♻ Nominalization

Use OHT 43 or write on the board: Rewrite the sentences using nominalization to avoid repetition:

1. Los zapatos grises son bonitos, pero los zapatos negros son más elegantes.
2. La actriz rubia es bonita, pero la actriz morena tiene más talento.
3. Las películas formulistas son menos originales que las películas innovadoras.
4. El primer guión fue muy difícil. El segundo guión es mejor.

Answers
1. Los zapatos grises son bonitos, pero los negros son más elegantes.
2. La actriz rubia es bonita, pero la morena tiene más talento.
3. Las películas formulistas son menos originales que las innovadoras.
4. El primer guión fue muy difícil. El segundo es mejor.

10 Los gustos

Hablar/*Escribir* Acabas de conocer a un(a) amigo(a) nuevo(a). Quieres saber más sobre sus gustos. Hazle cinco preguntas a tu nuevo(a) amigo(a), y él (ella) te hace cinco preguntas a ti. Usa ideas de las dos columnas. Estudia los modelos.

modelo

Tú: *¿Cuáles botas te gustan más?*

Compañero(a): *Me gustan las negras.*

Tú: *¿Cuál película te gustó más, la de Argentina o la de España?*

Compañero(a): *Me gustó más la española.*

> ropa
> accesorios
> persona
> objeto
> obra de arte
> color
> nacionalidad
> número

11 Eva Luna

Leer/Hablar/*Escribir* Con tu compañero(a), lee el artículo sobre la novela *Eva Luna* de Isabel Allende. Juntos escriban cinco preguntas sobre el director, el cineasta, la novela, la novelista, la protagonista, el guión o el guionista. Usando sus preguntas, conversen sobre el artículo.

modelo

Tú: *¿Quién va a ser el director de Eva Luna?*

Compañero(a): *El británico Michael Radford.*

Tú: *¿Qué otras películas ha dirigido?*

Compañero(a): …

Radford adapta novela de Allende

EFE. Santiago de Chile.

El británico Michael Radford, director de *Il Postino*, basado en una novela del escritor chileno Antonio Skármeta, se encuentra en Chile trabajando en la adaptación de una novela de Isabel Allende al cine.

Eva Luna, la obra de la chilena Isabel Allende que relata la vida de una huérfana que de la miseria pasa a la fama y fortuna, es el proyecto del director.

«Originalmente el guión lo escribiría Laura Esquivel, pero ella no estaba disponible y yo sugerí que lo hiciera Antonio».

La cinta sobre *Eva Luna* será en inglés, «con un presupuesto de Hollywood»

y tendrá ciertas licencias sobre el escrito original a fin de «rejuvenecerlo» y «rescatar la riqueza de sus personajes distintivamente sudamericanos».

Radford sostuvo que la adaptación de la obra implica «un enorme reto por la envergadura de la historia» y anticipó que su filmación no será en Chile, debido a requerimientos del libro, que exigen paisajes selváticos que no se encuentran en el país.

More Practice: **Más comunicación** p. R17

Vocabulario

Las películas

el (la) cineasta *filmmaker*

el (la) cinematógrafo(a) *cinematographer*

el (la) director(a) *director*

dirigir *to direct*

el guión *script*

el (la) guionista *scriptwriter*

hacer el papel *to play the role*

Classroom Community

Group Activity Have students brainstorm or research the names of Spanish-speaking filmmakers, actors, and actresses, such as Rosie Pérez, Antonio Banderas, and Edward James Olmos. Have them identify as many of their films as possible and have them discuss how the Spanish-speaking characters they play are portrayed.

Paired Activity Have pairs work together to practice nominalization. One student provides a short phrase that will then be "reduced" by the other student, using nominalization. Students should have 2 examples with possessives, 2 examples with phrases beginning with **de,** and 2 examples that shorten a clause. Pairs should then write their examples on the board for the class to evaluate.

GRAMÁTICA More on Nominalization

 ¿RECUERDAS? *p. 382* You have already learned some ways to use **nominalization** in order to shorten sentences and reduce redundancy. Here are some other uses of nominalization.

▶ With possessives:

la fiesta **de Ana María**	**la** de Ana María
los cuentos **de este autor**	**los** de este autor

Me interesan las películas de Saura, pero me gustan más **las** de Almodóvar.
*I'm interested in Saura's films, but I like **Almodóvar's** better.*

El bordado de tu mamá es más bonito que **el de la señora Vélez.**
*Your mother's embroidery is prettier than **Mrs. Vélez's.***

▶ With other phrases beginning with **de**:

Hay muchos abrigos en esta tienda. **Los de cuero** son más caros que **los de lana.**
*There are many coats in this store. The leather **ones** are more expensive than the woolen **ones**.*

▶ To shorten clauses:

la fiesta **que vimos**	**la** que vimos
el programa **que mencioné**	**el** que mencioné

Vimos dos películas la semana pasada. **La que vimos** el lunes era mucho mejor que **la que vimos** el martes.
*We saw two movies last week. **The one** we saw on Monday was much better than **the one** we saw on Tuesday.*

▶ **Lo de** is a phrase that doesn't refer to any specific noun. You use it to mean "the matter of," "the news about," etc.

Lo del Premio Nóbel es muy interesante.
That business about the Nobel Prize is very interesting.

Practice: Actividades ⑫ ⑬ ⑭	**Más práctica** *cuaderno pp. 135–136* **Para hispanohablantes** *cuaderno pp. 133–134*	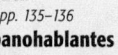 **Online Workbook** CLASSZONE.COM

⑫ Clarificaciones

Hablar/*Escribir* Tu compañero(a) acaba de regresar de un viaje a México. Tú le haces muchas preguntas sobre su viaje y él (ella) te pide clarificaciones. Sigue el modelo.

modelo
subir (pirámide: está al sur / está al norte)

Tú: *¿Subiste la pirámide?*

Compañero(a): *¿Cuál? ¿La que está al sur o la que está al norte?*

1. ver (objeto de arte precolombino: está hecho de jade / está hecho de oro)

2. gustar (mural: pintó Diego Rivera / pintó David Alfaro Siqueiros)

3. visitar (ruinas: están en el centro de la ciudad / están más lejos del centro)

4. interesar (tradiciones: de los mayas / de los mexica)

5. gustar (blusa: está bordada / tiene diseños mayas)

6. gustar (CD: de música mariachi / de salsa)

trescientos ochenta y cinco
España y las Américas Etapa 3
385

Teaching Suggestions
Presenting More on Nominalization

You may want to explain to students that nominalization is sometimes used to refer to a person. However, this construction is less formal and usually only used among friends.

—¿Conoces a esas dos chicas?
—Conozco a la rubia. Nunca he visto a la morena.

Conozco a la muchacha rubia would be considered more polite.

 Objective: Controlled practice Nominalization in conversation
♻ Arts and crafts vocabulary

Answers
1. A: ¿Viste el objeto de arte precolombino?
   B: ¿Cuál? ¿El que está hecho de jade o el que está hecho de oro?
2. A: ¿Te gustó el mural?
   B: ¿Cuál? ¿El que pintó Diego Rivera o el que pintó David Alfaro Siqueiros?
3. A: ¿Visitaste las ruinas?
   B: ¿Cuáles? ¿Las que están en el centro de la ciudad o las que están más lejos del centro?
4. A: ¿Te interesaron las tradiciones?
   B: ¿Cuáles? ¿Las de los mayas o las de los mexica?
5. A: ¿Te gustó la blusa?
   B: ¿Cuál? ¿La que está bordada o la que tiene diseños mayas?
6. A: ¿Te gustó el CD?
   B: ¿Cuál? ¿El de música mariachi o el de salsa?

Critical Thinking

Have students imagine and discuss the process and difficulties of adapting a novel to the cinema. Do they know of any novels that have been well adapted or poorly adapted? What made the adaptation successful or unsuccessful?

Teaching All Students

Extra Help Have students tell what homework they have in different classes. For example, **En la clase de biología tengo que... En la de matemáticas...**, etc.

Native Speakers Ask students to provide 5 more vocabulary words they can think of that would fit the movie theme of the **Vocabulario** box on p. 384. Use these extra words as a source of bonus points on future quizzes and tests.

Multiple Intelligences

Logical/Mathematical Have students research the history of cinema and create a timeline that marks important dates.

Visual Have students cut out movie ads from the newspaper and write 2–3 sentence descriptions of them.

Block Schedule

Extension Have each student write and model with another student his/her own item for **Actividad 12**. Students should give an infinitive, the object, and 2 different phrases referring to the object. (For additional activities, see **Block Scheduling Copymasters**.)

Teaching Resource Options

Print 📖

Más práctica Workbook PE,
  pp. 129–132; 136
Actividades para todos Workbook PE,
  pp. 151–156
Cuaderno para hispanohablantes
  PE, pp. 129–130; 134
Block Scheduling Copymasters
Unit 5 Resource Book
  Más práctica Workbook TE,
    pp. 141–144; 148
  Actividades para todos Workbook
    TE, pp. 149–154
  Cuaderno para hispanohablantes
    TE, pp. 159–160; 164
  Information Gap Activities, p. 168
  Absent Student Copymasters, p. 176
  Audioscript, p. 181

Audiovisual

Audio Program CD 15, Track 3, Activity 13

Technology

Online Workbook, U5E3
Take-Home Tutor CD-ROM, U5E3

ACTIVIDAD 13 **Objective:** Controlled practice
Listening comprehension/
nominalization

Answers (See script, p. 371B.)
1. la novela de Allende o la de Esquivel
2. los poemas de Neruda o los de Guillén
3. la biografía sobre Picasso o la de Botero
4. el guión de Esquivel o el de Skármeta
5. los ensayos de Borges o los de García Márquez
6. la película de Saura o la de Almodóvar

ACTIVIDAD 14 **Objective:** Transitional practice
Nominalization in conversation

Answers will vary.

---

13 **Lo contemporáneo**

Escuchar/*Escribir* Estás en una clase en la cual
van a estudiar la literatura y el cine
contemporáneo de España y Latinoamérica.
Escucha y escribe lo que pregunta el profesor
a los estudiantes.

> **modelo**
>
> *El profesor les pregunta a los estudiantes si prefieren
> estudiar* los cuentos de Borges o los de
> Allende.

1. El profesor les pregunta a los estudiantes
   si prefieren estudiar _____.
2. El profesor les pregunta a los estudiantes
   si prefieren estudiar _____.
3. El profesor les pregunta a los estudiantes
   si prefieren estudiar _____.
4. El profesor les pregunta a los estudiantes
   si prefieren estudiar _____.
5. El profesor les pregunta a los estudiantes
   si prefieren estudiar _____.
6. El profesor les pregunta a los estudiantes
   si prefieren estudiar _____.

14 **¿Cuál?**

Hablar/*Escribir* Pregúntale a tu compañero(a)
sobre varios libros que ha leído y sobre
algunas películas que ha visto. Luego,
cambien de papel. Traten de expresar de una
forma clara y precisa por qué les gustó alguna
obra más que otra.

> **modelo**
>
> **Tú:** *¿Cuál te gustó más, la novela de García Márquez
> o la de Esquivel?*
>
> **Compañero(a):** *Me gustó más la de Esquivel.*
>
> **Tú:** *¿Por qué?*
>
> **Compañero(a):** …

Ideas:

	✓
1 la colección de cuentos de …	
2 la colección de poemas de …	
3 la colección de ensayos de …	
4 la novela de …	
5 la autobiografía de …	
6 la biografía de …	
7 la película de …	

Nota cultural

La casa de la laguna (1997) es una de las obras más famosas de la
escritora puertorriqueña Rosario Ferré (1942). En su obra, Rosario
Ferré observa el impacto que han tenido las relaciones de Puerto
Rico con España y con Estados Unidos. Como otros escritores
latinoamericanos, ella utiliza la historia y las tradiciones de Puerto
Rico para darles un contexto a sus personajes.

386 trescientos ochenta y seis
Unidad 5

Classroom Community

Group Activity After students have read the
summary of **Como agua para chocolate**, have
groups of 3 write an imaginary scene. Each student is
responsible for one of the following characters: Tita,
Mamá Elena, Pedro. Encourage any students who may
have read the book or seen the film to bring that
knowledge to their group. Then, have groups present
their scenes to the class.

Portfolio Have students write a brief review of a novel
or story they have read. They can use the passage in
Actividad 15 as a model, but should be briefer.

Rubric A = 13–15 pts. B = 10–12 pts. C = 7–9 pts. D = 4–6 pts. F = < 4 pts.

Writing criteria	Scale
Details	1 2 3 4 5
Logical organization	1 2 3 4 5
Grammar/spelling accuracy	1 2 3 4 5

Todo en acción

Activity 15 brings together all concepts presented.

15 Comentarios literarios

Hablar/*Escribir* En grupos de tres o cuatro, lean la información que viene de la cubierta de la novela *Como agua para chocolate.* Luego, conversen sobre la autora, la novela o la película según lo que aprendieron.

modelo

Tú: *¿Leíste la novela Como agua para chocolate?*

Compañero(a) 1: *No, pero vi la película.*

Compañero(a) 2: *¿Quién es la protagonista?*

Compañero(a) 3: *Tita, la tía de la narradora.*

Tú: *¿Qué sabes de Laura Esquivel, la autora?*

More Practice:

Más comunicación *p. R17*

 Online Workbook
CLASSZONE.COM

Como agua para chocolate

Como agua para chocolate, el libro de mayor venta en México en 1990, es una novela romántica e intensa, condimentada con momentos dulces y agrios. Parecida en su estructura a *How To Make An American Quilt,* a «Tampopo» en su celebración de la comida, y a «Heartburn» en su ironía y agudeza, *Como agua para chocolate* es una historia animada y divertida sobre la vida familiar en México a principios de siglo.

Tita, la tía de la narradora, es la más joven de las hijas de Mamá Elena, la tiránica dueña del rancho de la familia De la Garza. Al crecer, Tita se convirtió en una cocinera extraordinaria. Cada capítulo comienza con una receta de Tita y sus esmeradas instrucciones de preparación.

En ciertas familias mexicanas la tradición determina que la hija menor no puede casarse ya que debe permanecer en el hogar al cuidado de su madre. Tita se enamora de Pedro, pero Mamá Elena decide respetar la tradición y arregla que Pedro se case con la hermana mayor.

La voz de Laura Esquivel es directa, simple y fascinante. Ella ha escrito una novela fresca e innovadora, brindando su inimitable talento a una clásica historia de amor.

Laura Esquivel se inició como guionista. Su guión *Chido One* fue nominado al premio «Ariel» que otorga la Academia Mexicana de Ciencias y Artes Cinematográficas. Este año, la versión fílmica de *Como agua para chocolate,* arrasó con los premios ganando un total de diez «Arieles,» incluyendo el mejor guión para Laura Esquivel, quien vive en la Ciudad de México acompañada de su esposo e hija.

ISBN 0-385-47137-8

9 780385 471374

Dictation

Using the Listening Activity Script for **Actividad 13** on TE p. 371B, dictate selected sentences to students. You may want to write answers on the board for students to correct their own work.

Culture Highlights

● **LAURA ESQUIVEL** Laura Esquivel nació en la ciudad de México el 30 de septiembre de 1950. **Como agua para chocolate** es su primera novela. Ella también escribió el guión de la película del mismo nombre. Al principio, el lector no sabe si el libro es una memoria, una colección de recetas o una novela. Esquivel ha mezclado elementos de cada género para producir una narrativa colorida e interesante.

ACTIVIDAD
15 **Objective:** Open-ended practice Nominalization in reading and conversation

Answers will vary.

Refrán

La imaginación hace cuerpo de lo que es visión.

¿Qué quiere decir el refrán? En tu opinión, si tienes una idea, ¿qué más necesitas para realizarla? ¿Cuál es más importante — la visión original o la imaginación para darle vida?

Teaching All Students

Extra Help For **Actividad 15,** have students read one paragraph at a time, then provide a 1-sentence summary of each one.

Multiple Intelligences

Verbal Have students name and describe other novels and movies about family traditions.

Naturalist In small groups, have students write a short film plot with a naturalist theme; for example, the rain forest, a natural disaster, etc. Each group presents its plot. Students act as movie critics and give each plot a 1–4 star rating. The plot with the best rating wins.

Block Schedule

Change of Pace Have students write the information for the book jacket of their favorite book. (For additional activities, see **Block Scheduling Copymasters**.)

Teaching Resource Options

Print

Actividades para todos Workbook PE, pp. 157–159

Block Scheduling Copymasters *Actividades para todos* Workbook TE, pp. 155–157

Unit 5 Resource Book
  Absent Student Copymasters, p. 177
  Audioscript, p. 182

Audiovisual

OHT 43 (Quick Start)
Audio Program CD 15, Tracks 4–5

Technology

Online Workbook, U5E3
Take-Home Tutor CD-ROM, U5E3

🔔 Quick Start Review

♻ **Literature**

Use OHT 43 or write on the board: Give a brief definition of the following in your own words:

1. drama
2. comedia
3. autor(a)

Answers will vary.

Teaching Suggestions

- **Prereading** Have students scan the reading and describe what they see. Ask them to give a general description of a play: ¿Pueden dar una descripción general de la obra de teatro?

- **Strategy: Interpret a drama** Discuss the reading strategy and have students talk about the kinds of things a director tells actors and actresses.

- **Reading** Have volunteers (3 female) role-play the parts of Martirio, Amelia, and Magdalena for the class.

- **Post-reading** Have students complete the Reading Strategy activity.

AUDIO

En voces

LECTURA

PARA LEER

STRATEGY: READING

Interpret a drama Reading a play requires the interpretation of characters, their motivations, even their movements and gestures. In a novel those elements are often described. Imagine yourself as the director of «La casa de Bernarda Alba». First read the entire scene; then read the lines of each character separately, ignoring all others. How would you advise each actress to play her role?

Cómo hacer el papel de...

- Magdalena
- Martirio
- Amelia

EL AMOR Y EL MATRIMONIO

buen mozo	guapo
emisario	representante
pretender	venir en busca de una novia
pretendiente	el que busca una novia
rondar la casa	visitar frecuentemente
soltero	no se ha casado
tener buenas condiciones	ser rico

Sobre el autor

Federico García Lorca nació en Granada en 1898. Vivió durante la Guerra Civil en España, período turbulento, y murió a manos del ejército del General Francisco Franco. García Lorca es famoso por su poesía lírica y sus obras teatrales. Tal vez sea mejor conocido por su gran trilogía de dramas: *Bodas de sangre, Yerma* y *La casa de Bernarda Alba.*

Classroom Community

Storytelling Have students rewrite the scene for 3 brothers objecting to a woman another brother intends to marry. They can use different or similar objections, but encourage them to make the objections "modern." Have volunteers role-play the scene for the class.

Learning Scenario Have students work in pairs to write and act out a brief scene between Angustias, the prospective bride, and Pepe el Romano.

Introducción

La casa de Bernarda Alba, «Drama de mujeres en los pueblos de España», tiene tres actos. Vas a leer unas líneas de una escena del primer acto. Tres hijas de Bernarda Alba discuten sobre el pretendiente de su hermana Angustias. Hablan Magdalena, que tiene 30 años, Martirio, de 24 años y Amelia, de 27 años.

La casa de Bernarda Alba

MAGDALENA ¡Ah! Ya se comenta por el pueblo. Pepe el Romano viene a casarse con Angustias. Anoche estuvo rondando la casa y creo que pronto va a mandar un emisario.

MARTIRIO Yo me alegro. Es buen mozo.

AMELIA Yo también. Angustias tiene buenas condiciones.

MAGDALENA Ninguna de las dos os alegráis.

MARTIRIO ¡Magdalena! ¡Mujer!

MAGDALENA Si viniera por el tipo de Angustias, por Angustias como mujer, yo me alegraría; pero viene por el dinero. Aunque Angustias es nuestra hermana, aquí estamos en familia y reconocemos que está vieja, enfermiza[1], y que siempre ha sido la que ha tenido menos méritos de todas nosotras. Porque si con veinte años parecía un palo[2] vestido, ¡qué será ahora que tiene cuarenta!

MARTIRIO No hables así. La suerte viene a quien menos la aguarda[3].

AMELIA ¡Después de todo dice la verdad! ¡Angustias tiene todo el dinero de su padre, es la única rica de la casa y por eso ahora que nuestro padre ha muerto y ya se harán particiones[4] viene por ella!

MAGDALENA Pepe el Romano tiene veinticinco años y es el mejor tipo de todos estos contornos[5]. Lo natural sería que te pretendiera a ti, Amelia, o a nuestra Adela, que tiene veinte años, pero no que

venga a buscar lo más oscuro[6] de esta casa, a una mujer que, como su padre, habla con las narices.

MARTIRIO ¡Puede que a él le guste!

MAGDALENA ¡Nunca he podido resistir[7] tu hipocresía!

---

[1] sickly
[2] stick
[3] luck comes to he who least expects it
[4] the inheritance will be divided up
[5] surrounding area
[6] the least desirable
[7] to stand, put up with

Online Workbook
CLASSZONE.COM

¿Comprendiste?

1. ¿Cuál es la actitud de cada una de las hermanas en cuanto al novio de Angustias?
2. ¿Quién es Adela? ¿Cuántos años tiene? ¿Quién es Pepe el Romano?
3. ¿Cómo es Angustias, según Magdalena?

¿Qué piensas?

1. ¿A quién se refiere Magdalena cuando habla de la hipocresía?
2. ¿Crees que las hermanas Alba tienen motivos que no se expresan? ¿Qué podrán ser?

Hazlo tú

1. Representen la escena para la clase.
2. Imagina los motivos de Pepe el Romano en pretender a Angustias y escribe una escena entre Pepe el Romano y su mejor amigo en la cual hablan de estos motivos.

The art on these 2 pages is from a sketch drawn by García Lorca for set and costume design.

Cross Cultural Connections

Strategy Have students identify characteristics of a successful play. Ask various students if they have a favorite play and why it is a favorite. How does it compare to this play?

Critical Thinking

Point out that the mother, Bernarda Alba, sustains an iron grip on her 5 daughters for fear of **el qué dirán**. Explain that **el qué dirán** refers to the social stigma of what people will say. Have students discuss how fear of gossip can affect behavior and cause problems.

Culture Highlights

● **FEDERICO GARCÍA LORCA** Federico García Lorca (1898–1936) nació en Fuente Vaqueros, un pueblo pequeño en Andalucía, España, ubicado en un valle junto a la Sierra Nevada. Además de sus obras de teatro, sus colecciones de poemas, **Romancero gitano** (1928) y **Poeta en Nueva York,** son muy conocidas.

¿Comprendiste?

Answers
1. Martirio y Amelia se alegran. Martirio dice que es buen mozo. Pero Magdalena dice que viene por el dinero de Angustias.
2. Adela es la hermana más pequeña. Tiene veinte años. Pepe el Romano es el novio de Angustias.
3. Según Magdalena, Angustias está vieja, enfermiza, y siempre ha sido la que ha tenido menos méritos de las otras hermanas.

Block Schedule

Variety Have students discuss how the conversation between these sisters might or might not be different today. Volunteers can role play a "modern" scene. (For additional activities, see **Block Scheduling Copymasters**.)

Teaching All Students

Extra Help Have students list the objections made against the relationship between Pepe and Angustias; for example, **Pepe sólo busca dinero.**

Native Speakers Have students read the complete play and present a summary to the class.

Multiple Intelligences

Visual Have students work in small groups to sketch what they think the sisters should look like and should be wearing.

Teaching Resource Options

Print

Block Scheduling Copymasters
Unit 5 Resource Book
  Absent Student Copymasters, p. 178

Audiovisual

OHT 44 (Quick Start)
Canciones CD

Technology

  www.classzone.com

Quick Start Review

♻ Film vocabulary

Use OHT 44 or write on the board:
Give the words that match the
descriptions below:

1. la persona que dirige la filmación
de una película
2. la persona que escribe el diálogo
de una película
3. el diálogo y la descripción de
escena de una película
4. el personaje principal

Answers
1. director o cineasta
2. guionista
3. guión
4. protagonista

Teaching Suggestions

Presenting Cultura y comparaciones

• Have students read the Connecting
Cultures Strategy and complete the
chart. Discuss students' answers.

• Have students look at the scenes
from the 3 movies and describe what
they see. When do they think each
movie takes place? **¿Cuándo piensan
que toma lugar cada película?** Ask
them to make a guess at what each
movie might be about: **Adivinen de
qué se trata cada película.**

En colores TRES DIRECTORES

CULTURA Y COMPARACIONES

PARA CONOCERNOS

STRATEGY: CONNECTING CULTURES

Reflect on the international appeal of movies
In many ways the director is the
"author" of a movie using the skill and
art of writers, actors, and camera person
to form a finished work. What film
directors can you name? Here you will
read about directors of international
fame. What aspects of a film help or
hinder its international appeal?

Influencias	Para un interés internacional
Lengua	
Aspectos visuales	
Guión -original -basado en novela	
Renombre -de actores -de director	
¿?	

¡Luces, cámara, acción! ¿Alguna vez has querido actuar o
dirigir una película? ¿Y una película en español? Entonces,
te presentamos a este grupo de directores. Carlos Saura,
Fina Torres y María Luisa Bemberg son tres de los
directores más famosos del mundo hispanohablante. Si te
gusta el cine, ¡estás en buena compañía!

Carlos Saura

Carlos Saura es el director clásico del cine español
moderno. Una de sus primeras películas, *La caza* (1965), se
considera el modelo del «nuevo cine español», un período
entre 1960 y 1975. Otras películas importantes de Saura
son *La prima Angélica* (1973), *Cría cuervos* (1975) y *Mamá
cumple cien años* (1979).

La prima Angélica (1973)

390 trescientos noventa
Unidad 5

Classroom Community

Learning Scenario Have students work in pairs to
role-play a dialog between a movie director and an
actor/actress. The director tells the actor/actress how to
play a dramatic scene. The actor/actress disagrees.
Students should incorporate **Etapa** vocabulary and
grammar.

Game Divide the class into groups. Two groups will
compete against each other. Give each team a list of
the following words: **director(a), cinematógrafo(a),
hacer el papel, escena, trama, pantalla, crítico(a),
personaje, protagonista, guionista.** Members from
each team take turns acting out the words. The other
team has to guess what word it is.

Fina Torres

Fina Torres, directora venezolana de cine, ha vivido en París desde los años '70. *Oriana* (1985), su primera película, ganó el premio la Cámara de Oro en el Festival de Cannes. *Mecánicas celestes* (1996), su segunda película, es una versión moderna y romántica del cuento de la Cenicienta[1]. Fue presentada en el Festival de Sundance en 1996 y premiada como mejor película en el Festival de Cine Venezolano.

[1] Cinderella

Mecánicas celestes (1996)

María Luisa Bemberg

María Luisa Bemberg, directora argentina, escribió obras de teatro y guiones de película. También produjo, escribió y dirigió muchas películas: *Momentos* (1981), *Miss Mary* (1986), *Yo, la peor de todas* (1990), y *De eso no se habla* (1993), su última película. Muchas películas suyas son obras de comentario político y social, como su película más famosa, *Camila* (1984), que fue nominada al Oscar.

Miss Mary (1986)

CLASSZONE.COM
More About Spain and the Americas

¿Comprendiste?

1. ¿Qué importancia tiene *La caza* de Carlos Saura?
2. ¿Cuándo pasó el cine español por un período de transición? ¿Qué director se asocia con esta época?
3. ¿Qué tema trata la película *Mecánicas celestes* de Fina Torres?
4. ¿Qué fama tiene *Camila*? ¿Quién la dirigió?

¿Qué piensas?

1. ¿Crees que las películas deben tratar temas realistas o románticas?¿Por qué?
2. ¿Cuál de estos directores te interesa más? ¿Y de las películas?

Hazlo tú

Escribe un ensayo sobre tu director(a) favorito(a). Di qué películas ha hecho, qué premios ha ganado, cuál película te gusta más y cómo es su estilo.

Reading Strategy

Have students implement the Reading Strategy "Categorize details." First have them determine categories common to 2 or all 3 directors (country of origin, names of movies, types/themes of movies, prizes they've won), and then complete a chart with the details.

Culture Highlights

● **LUIS BUÑUEL** Luis Buñuel (1900–1983) es otro director español muy conocido. Las películas de Buñuel tienen una trama sencilla que presta el armazón necesario para imágenes naturales, dándoles una transparencia única. Varias películas de Buñuel ganaron premios en el festival Cannes. **El discreto encanto de la burguesía** (1972) ganó un Óscar.

Critical Thinking

Many Hispanic films offer acute criticisms of social behavior, customs, and structure of the country of origin, or sometimes of another country such as the U.S. Ask students what aspects of U.S. society and politics might most often come under fire. Have them name U.S. movies that criticize the U.S.

¿Comprendiste?

Answers

1. Se considera el modelo del «nuevo cine español».
2. Pasó por un período de transición entre 1960 y 1975. Carlos Saura se asocia con esta época.
3. Trata de una versión moderna y romántica del cuento de la Cenicienta.
4. *Camila* fue nominada al Óscar. María Luisa Bemberg la dirigió.

Teaching All Students

Extra Help Have students make Venn diagrams to compare the directors.

Challenge Ask students to research and write a more detailed biography of one of the movie directors mentioned here or another Spanish-speaking director.

Multiple Intelligences

Interpersonal Have students work in pairs to talk about a foreign film they have seen. How are foreign films different from Hollywood films?

Intrapersonal Have students write a critique of a movie they have seen recently.

Block Schedule

Change of Pace Have students work in groups to guess what the plots of the movies mentioned on pp. 390–391 might be. Then have volunteers research this information and present it to the class. How close were students' guesses? (For additional activities, see **Block Scheduling Copymasters.**)

Teaching Resource Options

Print

Cuaderno para hispanohablantes
PE, pp. 135–136

Unit 5 Resource Book
  Cuaderno para hispanohablantes
  TE, pp. 165–166
  Information Gap Activities,
  pp. 169–170
  Family Involvement, pp. 179–180

Audiovisual

OHT 44 (Quick Start)

Technology

eTest Plus Online/Test Generator
  CD-ROM

www.classzone.com

Quick Start Review

 Vocabulary review

Use OHT 44 or write on the board:
Write a sentence with each of the
following words:

1. innovador
2. irónico
3. dramático
4. emocionante
5. deslumbrante

Answers will vary.

Teaching Suggestions
What Have Students Learned?

Have students look at the "Now you
can…" notes listed on the left side of
pp. 392–393. Remind them to review
the material in the "To review" notes
before doing the activities or taking the
test.

ETAPA **3**

En uso
REPASO Y MÁS COMUNICACIÓN

OBJECTIVES
• Talk about literature
• Talk about film
• Avoid redundancy

Now you can...

• talk about
  literature.

To review

• double object
  pronouns
  see p. 380.

1 Los regalos

Tu compañero(a) quiere saber qué les regalaste a varias personas
y cuál fue la ocasión. Sigan el modelo.

modelo

Elvira (una colección de poemas / las Navidades)
Compañero(a): *¿Qué le regalaste a Elvira?*
Tú: *Le regalé una colección de poemas.*
Compañero(a): *¿Cuándo se la regalaste?*
Tú: *Se la regalé en las Navidades.*

1. Diana (un libro de cuentos / su cumpleaños)
2. Antonio (unos libros de poemas / las Navidades)
3. Marta (una novela latinoamericana / su cumpleaños)
4. Tomás (una colección de ensayos / el día de la Amistad)
5. Marcos (una biografía / la Hanuka)
6. Inés (una autobiografía / su cumpleaños)

Now you can...

• avoid redundancy.

To review

• double object
  pronouns
  see p. 380.

2 El profesor de literatura

Joaquín describe su clase de literatura. Completa las oraciones
para saber qué piensa Joaquín de la clase y de su profesor.

modelo

«El profesor nos explicó el simbolismo. Nos lo explicó de una manera muy original».

1. «Nos recomendó la última novela de Laura Esquivel. _____ _____
   recomendó enfáticamente».
2. «Nos mostró la cubierta. _____ _____ mostró durante la clase».
3. «Nos devolvió los exámenes. _____ _____ devolvió ayer».
4. «Me dio una nota muy buena. _____ _____ dio porque contesté todas
   las preguntas correctamente».
5. «Me prestó su diccionario. _____ _____ prestó porque no sabía
   algunas palabras».

392 trescientos noventa y dos
Unidad 5

Classroom Community

Paired Activity Have students work in pairs to
extend **Actividad 1** by talking about what they have
given to people.

Modelo: A: ¿Qué le regalaste a tu mamá este año?
        B: Le regalé un bolso.
        A: ¿Cuándo se lo regalaste?
        B: Se lo regalé para el día de las madres.

Game Divide the class into 2 or more teams. Have
teams take turns giving clues using nominalization to
name a type of object. The other team(s) guess what
they are talking about. For example: **La de Laura
Esquivel tiene lugar en México. La de Isabel Allende
tiene lugar en Chile.** → película

Self-Check Quiz
CLASSZONE.COM

Now you can...

- talk about literature.
- talk about film.

To review

- nominalization
- see pp. 382, 385.

③ Preferencias

Tú y tu amigo(a) tienen preferencias diferentes. Explica.

modelo

la novela romántica / la novela cómica

Yo prefiero la novela romántica. Mi amigo(a) prefiere la cómica.

1. la película romántica / la película cómica
2. la pintura realista / la pintura abstracta
3. el último libro de Esquivel / el primer libro de Esquivel
4. los poemas largos de Neruda / los poemas cortos de Neruda
5. los dos murales de Rivera / los dos murales de Orozco
6. el guión dramático / el guión cómico

Now you can...

- avoid redundancy.

To review

- nominalization
- see pp. 382, 385.

④ ¿Cuál compraste?

Fuiste de compras con tu compañero(a), pero tuviste que irte antes de que él (ella) terminara sus compras. Lo (La) ves después y quieres saber qué decidió comprar y por qué. Sigan el modelo.

modelo

¿color claro o color oscuro?

Tú: *¿Compraste el chaleco de color claro o el de color oscuro?*

Compañero(a): *Compré el de color oscuro.*

Tú: *¿Por qué lo compraste?*

Compañero(a): *Lo compré porque es ideal para la fiesta de Susana.*

1. ¿verde o azul? 2. ¿estampado(a) o a rayas? 3. ¿de tacón alto o tacón bajo?

4. ¿azul o gris? 5. ¿oro o plata? 6. ¿de lunares o de un solo color?

trescientos noventa y tres
España y las Américas Etapa 3 **393**

ACTIVIDAD ① Answers

1. A: ¿Qué le regalaste a Diana?
   B: Le regalé un libro de cuentos.
   A: ¿Cuándo se lo regalaste?
   B: Se lo regalé para su cumpleaños.
2. A: ¿Qué le regalaste a Antonio?
   B: Le regalé unos libros de poemas.
   A: ¿Cuándo se los regalaste?
   B: Se los regalé en las Navidades.
3. A: ¿Qué le regalaste a Marta?
   B: Le regalé una novela latinoamericana.
   A: ¿Cuándo se la regalaste?
   B: Se la regalé para su cumpleaños.
4. A: ¿Qué le regalaste a Tomás?
   B: Le regalé una colección de ensayos.
   A: ¿Cuándo se la regalaste?
   B: Se la regalé para el día de la Amistad.
5. A: ¿Qué le regalaste a Marcos?
   B: Le regalé una biografía.
   A: ¿Cuándo se la regalaste?
   B: Se la regalé para la Hanuka.
6. A: ¿Qué le regalaste a Inés?
   B: Le regalé una autobiografía.
   A: ¿Cuándo se la regalaste?
   B: Se la regalé para su cumpleaños.

ACTIVIDAD ② Answers

1. Nos la 4. Me la
2. Nos la 5. Me lo
3. Nos los

ACTIVIDAD ③ Answers

1. Yo prefiero la película romántica. Mi amigo(a) prefiere la cómica.
2. Yo prefiero la pintura realista. Mi amigo(a) prefiere la abstracta.
3. Yo prefiero el último libro de Esquivel. Mi amigo(a) prefiere el primero.
4. Yo prefiero los poemas largos de Neruda. Mi amigo(a) prefiere los cortos.
5. Yo prefiero los dos murales de Rivera. Mi amigo(a) prefiere los dos de Orozco.
6. Yo prefiero el guión dramático. Mi amigo(a) prefiere el cómico.

ACTIVIDAD ④ Answers

1. A: ¿Compraste la camiseta verde o la azul?
   B: Compré la azul.
2. A: ¿Compraste la bufanda estampada o la bufanda con rayas?
   B: Compré la estampada.
3. A: ¿Compraste los zapatos de tacón alto o los de tacón bajo?
   B: Compré los de tacón alto.
4. A: ¿Compraste el traje de color azul o el de color gris?
   B: Compré el gris.
5. A: ¿Compraste los pendientes de oro o los de plata?
   B: Compré los de oro.
6. A: ¿Compraste el vestido de lunares o el de un solo color?
   B: Compré el de lunares.

Teaching All Students

Extra Help Before doing the double object pronoun activities, write a few model sentences on the board showing question-to-answer transformations and/or underscoring and circling the objects in the sentences.

Multiple Intelligences

Verbal Have students talk about what movies are currently showing, what kind of movies they are, and which ones they are interested in seeing. Elicit nominalization to avoid repetition. For example:
La de Spielberg es dramática. Me interesa ver la de Spielberg.

Teaching Resource Options

Print 📖

Block Scheduling Copymasters
Unit 5 Resource Book
  Audioscript, pp. 183–184
  Vocabulary Quizzes, pp. 186–188
  Grammar Quizzes, pp. 189–190
  Etapa Exam, Forms A and B,
    pp. 191–200
  Examen para hispanohablantes,
    pp. 201–205
  Portfolio Assessment, pp. 206–207
  Unit 5 Comprehensive Test,
    pp. 210–217
  *Prueba comprensiva para
    hispanohablantes,* Unit 5,
    pp. 218–225
  Multiple Choice Test Questions,
    pp. 232–234

Audiovisual 🎧

OHT 45 (Quick Start)
Audio Program CD 20, Tracks 10–14

Technology 🎧💻

eTest Plus Online/Test Generator
  CD-ROM
  ℹ️ www.classzone.com

Rubric: Speaking

Criteria	Scale	
Sentence structure	1 2 3	A = 11–12 pts.
Vocabulary use	1 2 3	B = 9–10 pts.
Originality	1 2 3	C = 7–8 pts.
Fluency	1 2 3	D = 4–6 pts.
		F = < 4 pts.

En tu propia voz

Rubric: Writing

Criteria	Scale	
Vocabulary use	1 2 3 4 5	A = 13–15 pts.
Accuracy	1 2 3 4 5	B = 10–12 pts.
Creativity, appearance	1 2 3 4 5	C = 7–9 pts.
		D = 4–6 pts.
		F = < 4 pts.

Teaching Note: En tu propia voz

Writing Strategy Suggest that students implement the writing strategy "Present a thorough and balanced review." An informative review helps the reader decide if the material will be of interest to them.

---

5 Mi película favorita

STRATEGY: SPEAKING

Critique a film In what ways can you share your enthusiasm about a movie with others who may or may not have seen it? Give as much information as possible about the plot, director, actors, and script. Tell what impressed you, and tell just enough to build interest and curiosity. If everyone has seen your favorite, different opinions may be expressed.

En grupos de dos o tres, conversen sobre sus películas favoritas. Hablen sobre el director, la trama, los protagonistas, el clímax, los actores, el guión, etc. Expliquen por qué la película es su favorita.

modelo

Tú: *Mi película favorita es…*

Compañero(a): *¿Quién fue el director?*

---

6 En tu propia voz ✒️

ESCRITURA ¡Tú eres crítico(a) para una revista! Escribe una crítica de un libro o de una película. Antes de empezar a escribir, organiza tus ideas en un esquema. Da por lo menos tres opiniones para cada categoría.

> *Nombre de la película*
> *(o del libro)*
>
> *El (La) director(a) (o el (la) autor(a))*
> *Los actores*
> *Los protagonistas*
> *La trama*
> *El final*
> *¿…?*

TÚ EN LA COMUNIDAD

Laura es alumna en Maryland. Ayuda a su hermano, quien está aprendiendo a hablar español. Laura trabaja en un restaurante y ayuda a los clientes que están aprendiendo inglés a pedir la comida. Laura también traduce para su madre. Su madre es enfermera y frecuentemente trata con hispanohablantes en su trabajo.

394 trescientos noventa y cuatro
Unidad 5

Classroom Community

Learning Scenario Have pairs of students imagine that they are going shopping in a large bookstore to buy books as gifts for several friends. Each student has a different idea as to what kind of book to buy and for whom. Have pairs discuss and resolve the problem, using **Etapa** grammar and vocabulary.

Storytelling Have students use "chain links" to review a movie or TV program. They should refer to the **Repaso de vocabulario** on p. 395. One student begins the review. The next students repeats that sentence and adds another. Students continue adding links until the review is finished.

En resumen
REPASO DE VOCABULARIO

TALK ABOUT LITERATURE

Literature

el clímax	climax
el (la) cuentista	short story writer
el estilo	style
el final	ending
el género	genre
el (la) novelista	novelist
el personaje	character
el (la) poeta	poet
la prosa	prose
el (la) protagonista	protagonist
la sátira	satire
titularse	to be titled
el título	title
la trama	plot
tratarse de	to be about

Literary criticism

amenazador(a)	threatening
cibernético(a)	relating to cyberspace
ciego(a)	blind
contemporáneo(a)	contemporary
creativo(a)	creative
el (la) crítico(a)	critic
culminar	to end, to culminate
dentro del alcance	within reach
derivado(a)	derivative, unoriginal
deslumbrante	dazzling
dramático(a)	dramatic
elogiar	to praise
emocionante	exciting
expresivo(a)	expressive
formulista	formulaic
impresionante	impressive
innovador(a)	innovative
irónico(a)	ironic
original	original
predecible	predictable
el Premio Nóbel	the Nobel Prize
el realismo mágico	magical realism
el romanticismo	romanticism
simbólico(a)	symbolic
el simbolismo	symbolism
sin embargo	nevertheless

TALK ABOUT FILM

Films

el (la) cineasta	filmmaker
el (la) cinematógrafo(a)	cinematographer
el (la) director(a)	director
dirigir	to direct
el guión	script
el (la) guionista	scriptwriter
hacer el papel	to play the role

AVOID REDUNDANCY

Double object pronouns

—¿Tienes la revista de arte para Marisol?
—No, ya **se la** di.

Nominalization

—¿Cuál de los libros prefieres, **el de Matute** o **el de Lorca**?
—Prefiero **el de Lorca**.
—¿Y entre las novelas contemporáneas y **las tradicionales**?
—Me gustan más **las contemporáneas**.

Juego

La creación literaria

¿Cuál de estas palabras no se relaciona con el dibujo?

a. el autor **b.** el crítico **c.** la protagonista **d.** el título

trescientos noventa y cinco
España y las Américas Etapa 3

395

Community Connections

Have students talk to the school Guidance Department to find out what opportunities are available for peer tutors for Spanish-speaking students or for teaching ESL to Spanish speakers in the community.

Quick Start Review

♻ Etapa vocabulary

Use OHT 45 or write on the board: Match the columns:

1. ___ prosa   a. final
2. ___ derivado   b. protagonista
3. ___ dirigir   c. predecible
4. ___ culminarse   d. novela
5. ___ personaje   e. cineasta

Answers
1. d   2. c   3. e   4. a   5. b

Teaching Suggestions
Vocabulary Review

Ask simple questions using some of the vocabulary, especially adjectives. For example: ¿Las películas de Spielberg son derivadas?

Dictation

Dictate the following sentences to review the Etapa:

1. Comprendo el poema porque me lo explicó la profesora.
2. No me gustan las novelas clásicas. Prefiero las contemporáneas.
3. ¿Quieres la camisa verde o azul? Quiero la verde.
4. Juan quiere este libro. Voy a comprárselo.

Juego

Answer: b. el crítico

Block Schedule

Research Have students research one of the following in the Spanish-speaking world: (1) names and brief descriptions of popular movies; (2) brief bios of popular actors and actresses; (3) names and brief descriptions of best seller books. (For additional activities, see **Block Scheduling Copymasters**.)

Teaching All Students

Extra Help Draw 2–3 large word webs on the board. In each middle circle, write the name of a well-known author, book, or film (García Márquez, for example). Call on students to go up and fill in one circle of any web with a "Literary Criticism" word from the **Repaso de vocabulario** that accurately describes the author, book, or film. Continue until all circles are filled.

Multiple Intelligences

Visual Have students work in pairs to imagine they are filmmakers. They should brainstorm ideas for a movie plot, assign a title, then design a poster advertising it. The poster should include quoted critics' comments, a summary of the plot, and perhaps names of featured actors. Display the posters in the classroom and vote on the most original title and plot.

Teaching Resource Options

Print

Block Scheduling Copymasters

Audiovisual

OHT GO1–GO5; 45 (Quick Start)

Technology

 www.classzone.com

🔔 Quick Start Review

♻ Relative clauses

Use OHT 45 or write on the board:
Match each noun with the appropriate
relative clause:

1. el libro
2. la película
3. la canción
4. el sombrero

a. la que oyeron
b. el que te pusiste
c. la que vi
d. el que leí

Answers
1. d   2. c   3. a   4. b

Teaching Strategy
Prewriting

• Have students list the novels they
have read in the past year or two.
They should include books they read
independently as well as those they
read for school. Each student then
chooses a book he/she likes and
remembers well to review.

• Have pairs ask each other what they
liked and didn't like about their
books. Student should record
responses on their charts.

• Review the funtion, context, content,
and structure with the class. Be sure
students are clear about these
elements of the assignment.

Post-writing

• Have partners who have not read
each other's books exchange papers.
Ask them to review the summaries
and confirm that they include key
aspects of the plot. Then have them
check to be sure the thesis
statements are sufficiently and clearly
supported with examples.

• Encourage students to use the
proofreading marks they have learned.

En tu propia voz
ESCRITURA

Mitos, leyendas, ficciones

La Nación, un periódico español, ha organizado un concurso
literario para jóvenes estadounidenses. Tienen que escribir reseñas
breves de sus novelas favoritas. Las mejores reseñas se publicarán
en una edición especial. Piensa en una obra que te guste. Luego
escribe un resumen breve con tu propio punto de vista.

Función: Resumir una novela

Contexto: Informar a los lectores jóvenes

Contenido: Descripción de una novela

Tipo de texto: Una reseña

PARA ESCRIBIR • STRATEGY: WRITING

Support an opinion with facts and examples A good review begins with a
thesis statement that clearly gives your opinion. Support that opinion
with facts and examples from the work reviewed, and supply a brief
plot summary for readers who have not read the work.

Modelo del estudiante

> The writer includes a **clear thesis statement**, identified as personal opinion.

La Casa en Mango Street por Sandra Cisneros

En mi opinión, la historia de Esperanza Cordero es una de las historias
inmigrantes que forman parte de la narrativa nacional de Estados Unidos.
La experiencia de Esperanza en un barrio hispano de Chicago es particular,
también es una con la cual muchos lectores pueden identificarse.

> The writer includes a **brief summary** of the book's content.

La familia de Esperanza llega a vivir a Mango Street cuando Esperanza
tiene doce años. Desde ese momento, Esperanza se ve obligada a analizar
sus sueños en un ambiente nuevo. Se siente decepcionada cuando sus padres
la llevan a la casa. «La casa de Mango Street no es de ningún modo como
ellos la contaron».

Este tono de desilusión continúa durante la primera parte del libro.
Pero, poco a poco, Esperanza descubre que la realidad que la rodea es tan
interesante como su mundo interior. Observa de cerca a su familia, a sus
amigos y a sus vecinos y escribe las historias que los unen a todos.

> The writer **supports his opinion** with a scene from the book.

Sus descripciones tienen un lenguaje detallado y colorido. El retrato de su
casa ideal es un ejemplo: «Nuestra casa sería blanca, rodeada de árboles,
un jardín enorme»… Además de las descripciones detalladas, Esperanza
escribe experiencias, como la vez que se disgusta con su mejor amiga.

Para Esperanza, la casa en Mango Street es un lugar desagradable al
principio. Al final, pasa a ser el lugar donde una familia hace su vida y
trabaja para tener una vida mejor.

Classroom Community

Paired Activity Have students exchange pre-final
versions of their reviews. They should read each other's
work to verify verb agreement, adjective agreement,
and to check for misspellings.

Group Activity In groups of 5, have students
collaborate and create a "literary review" booklet. Final
versions of all members' reviews should be included.
The group decides on a title for their collection and

binds the reviews into booklet format. An appropriate
cover should then be designed. Set up a table in the
front of the classroom with all booklets displayed. Allow
time for groups to look at all booklets.

Portfolio Have students save their summaries for
their portfolios. Subsequent writing projects will show
their progress in Spanish.

Estrategias para escribir

Antes de escribir...

Usa la tabla de la derecha para ayudarte a escoger una tésis. Puedes analizar la novela que escogiste e identificar las cosas que te gustaron (P: positivo), las que no te gustaron (N: negativo) y las interesantes (I: interesante). Así puedes organizar tus reacciones e identificar una opinión que te puede servir de tésis. Luego busca ejemplos y datos específicos del libro que apoyen esta opinión.

Revisiones

Después de escribir el primer borrador de la reseña, pídele a un(a) compañero(a) que la lea y comente sobre la tésis y los ejemplos que la apoyan. Tienes que seleccionar y resumir sólo los ejemplos importantes para apoyar tu perspectiva. Pregúntale:

- *¿Cuál es la tesis? ¿Fue fácil o difícil identificarla?*
- *¿Cuáles son los ejemplos de libro que apoyan la tésis?*
- *¿Cómo la apoyan? ¿Hay otros ejemplos que serían mejores? ¿Cuáles?*

La versión final

Para completar tu reseña, léela de nuevo y repasa los siguientes puntos:

- *¿Usé* **la nominalización** *para hablar de cosas e ideas que mencioné?*

Haz lo siguiente: Subraya todos los ejemplos de la nominalización. Luego busca la idea o cosa a la que se refiere. ¿Usaste correctamente los artículos o pronombres?

- *¿Usé* **lo** + *adjetivo o* **lo que** *para referir a ideas o conceptos abstractos?*

Haz lo siguiente: Repasa el uso de **lo** y **lo que**. Haz un círculo alrededor de la palabra **lo**. ¿Has usado **lo** de una manera apropiada?

Libro: *La Casa en Mango Street* **por Sandra Cisneros**		
P (+)	• La personalidad de Esperanza	
	• La amistad de Esperanza y su mejor amiga	
	• La trama	
N (-)	• Los episodios a veces no dan muchos detalles	
	• Todo se ve a través de los ojos de un personaje	
I (¿ ?)	• La experiencia de cambiar de hogar	
	• Una protagonista de dos culturas	
	• El plan que tiene Esperanza para lograr su casa ideal	
	• Las diferencias y las cosas en común que tiene la familia de Esperanza con otras familias en Estados Unidos	

La casa en Mango St. ~~es un cuento que~~ narra la historia de Esperanza Cordero. (Lo) que me impresionó es que el nombre de Esperanza tiene mucho significado. ~~La chica llamada~~ Esperanza vive con la ilusión de vivir en una casa grande. La que alquilan es pequeña
^ la familia

Let students know ahead of time which elements of their writing you will be evaluating. A global evaluation is more helpful to students than a correction of every mistake made. Consider the following in scoring compositions:

Sentences	
1	Most not logical
2	Somewhat logical
3	In logical order
4	Logical with some flow
5	Flow purposefully

Details	
1	Few details
2	Some basic details
3	Sufficient basic details
4	Substantial details
5	Clear and vivid detail

Organization	
1	Very little organization
2	Poorly organized
3	Some organization
4	Sufficiently organized
5	Strong organization

Accuracy	
1	Errors prevent comprehension
2	Comprehensible, yet many errors
3	Some spelling and agreement errors throughout
4	A few errors
5	Very few errors

Criteria	Scale	
Logical sentence order	1 2 3 4 5	A = 17–20 pts.
Clear and vivid detail	1 2 3 4 5	B = 13–16 pts.
Organization	1 2 3 4 5	C = 9–12 pts.
Accuracy	1 2 3 4 5	D = 5–8 pts.
		F = < 5 pts.

Teaching All Students

Extra Help Review structures with students before writing:
- nominalization
- **lo** + adjective

Native Speakers Encourage students to choose a book they have read in Spanish.

Challenge Have students write a separate paragraph that discusses aspects of the book that they didn't like and suggests means of improvement.

Multiple Intelligences

Verbal Have students include a paragraph or chart explaining why their novels would or would not be successfully adaptable for film.

Block Schedule

Variety Have volunteers read their reviews to the class. After each presentation, have students say whether or not they are motivated to read the book. (For additional activities, see **Block Scheduling Copymasters**.)

Unit Theme
Discussing television, talking about technology, and navigating cyberspace

Teaching Resource Options

Print
Block Scheduling Copymasters
Unit 6 Resource Book
   Absent Student Copymasters, p. 34

Audiovisual
OHT M4; 1, 2
Canciones CD
Video Program Videotape 49:10/DVD
   Unit 6

Technology
eEdition Plus Online/eEdition
   CD-ROM
Easy Planner Plus Online/Easy
   Planner CD-ROM
 www.classzone.com

UNIDAD

¡YA LLEGÓ EL FUTURO!

STANDARDS

Communication
- Narrating in the past
- Expressing doubt and certainty
- Reporting what others say
- Talking about television
- Talking about technology
- Stating locations
- Making contrasts
- Describing unplanned events
- Comparing and evaluating
- Expressing precise relationships
- Navigating cyberspace

Cultures
- The history and culture of Venezuela, Colombia, Ecuador, Peru, and Bolivia
- Television in the Spanish-speaking world
- Technology in the Spanish-speaking world

Connections
- Art: Designing an ad for an electronic device
- Technology: Choosing a computer system

Comparisons
- Television programming in the Spanish-speaking world and in the U.S.
- Technology the Spanish-speaking world and in the U.S.

Communities
- Using Spanish in the workplace
- Using Spanish to help others

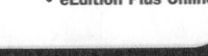

INTERNET Preview
CLASSZONE.COM
- More About Colombia, Venezuela, and the Andean Countries
- Webquest
- Self-Check Quizzes
- Flashcards
- Writing Center
- Online Workbook
- eEdition Plus Online

398

VENEZUELA, COLOMBIA Y ECUADOR PLÁTANOS FRITOS Éste es un plato típico que sirve para acompañar casi todas las comidas de estos países. Es muy sabroso y se destaca por la combinación del sabor dulce de los plátanos con el sabor característico del aceite. ¿Qué otras comidas como ésta conoces?

ECUADOR
EL TELÉFONO CELULAR En la Etapa 2 vas a ver que el teléfono celular tiene una importancia especial para las áreas remotas de América Latina. ¿Puedes adivinar qué tipo de importancia?

Classroom Community

Group Activity Divide the class into groups of 4–5. Give students a time limit of 5 minutes to discuss and write a list of things they know about these 5 countries. Have them also write a list of things they would like to learn. Discuss the lists as a class.

Paired Activity Have students work in pairs to discuss similarities and differences between what they know about these 5 countries and their own region. Have them outline what information they would substitute if they were to write a similar Cultural Opener about their area of the U.S.

ALMANAQUE CULTURAL

POBLACIÓN: Bolivia: 8.300.463, Colombia: 40.349.388, Ecuador: 13.183.978, Perú: 27.483.864, Venezuela: 23.916.810

ALTURA: 6882 m sobre el nivel del mar (Cerro Illimani, Bolivia)

CLIMA: 84°F (29°C) Maracaibo, Venezuela, 46°F (10°C) La Paz, Bolivia

COMIDA TÍPICA: locro, llapingachos, ocopa, carapulcra, chuao, arepa, hallaca, sancocho de sábalo, rendón, asado de llama, chuñia, salteños

GENTE FAMOSA: Gabriel García Márquez (escritor), Jaime Freire (escritor), Simón Bolívar (político), Fina Torres (directora), María Reiche (estudiosa de los misterios de Nazca, Perú)

 VIDEO DVD Mira el video para más información.

 CLASSZONE.COM
More About Colombia, Venezuela, and the Andean Countries

COLOMBIA
PARQUE DE CIENCIA Y TECNOLOGÍA MALOKA
¿Un parque de atracciones dedicado a la ciencia y la tecnología? Lo puedes encontrar en Colombia; es el único parque de este tipo en América Latina. ¿Qué clase de atracciones crees que tiene?

VENEZUELA
SIMÓN BOLÍVAR (1783-1830) nació en Venezuela y se llama «El Libertador de América» por sus esfuerzos para la independencia de América Latina. Se compara con figuras históricas de EE.UU. ¿Quiénes serán?

PERÚ
MACHU PICCHU
Los incas usaron tecnologías nuevas para construir sus templos y ciudades. ¿Puedes pensar en otras tecnologías del pasado que cambiaron la forma de hacer las cosas?

VENEZUELA
ARMANDO REVERÓN Este artista usa la realidad y lo moderno como inspiración para sus obras de arte. En tu opinión, ¿qué comentario hace esta escultura sobre la tecnología?

399

Standards for Foreign Language Learning

The Communities standard is the focus for this unit.

Communities

Standard 5.1 Students use the language both within and beyond the school setting.

Standard 5.2 Students show evidence of becoming lifelong learners by using the language for personal enjoyment and enrichment.

Teaching Resource Options

Print
Block Scheduling Copymasters

Audiovisual
Poster

Technology
 www.classzone.com

Teaching Suggestion
Previewing the Standard

Communities is logically the last C of the national standards 5 Cs. Our goal as teachers is to create lifelong learners of Spanish who will use it in a variety of ways during their adult lives. Whether they use it in their jobs or for pleasure, the goal of Communities is to share with students the possibilities and needs for other languages.

UNIDAD

¡YA LLEGÓ EL FUTURO!

- Comunicación
- Culturas
- Conexiones
- Comparaciones
- Comunidades

Webquest
CLASSZONE.COM

Explore communities in the Andean countries, Colombia, and Venezuela through guided Web activities.

400

Comunidades

Existen muchas oportunidades de usar el español en nuestras comunidades. Piensa en las diferentes situaciones en que podrías usar el español para ayudar a otras personas.

Comunidades en acción Explica cómo usarías el español en estas situaciones:
- con pacientes hispanohablantes en un hospital
- con turistas hispanohablantes en una tienda
- con niños hispanohablantes después de la escuela

Conexiones

¿Es importante la tecnología en tu vida? ¿Cómo la usas para mejorar tu español y para aprender más de las culturas hispanas?

Classroom Community

Paired Activity With a partner, have students list times when they have been able to use Spanish outside of the classroom. What has been most helpful to them in their study of Spanish?

Group Activity Have groups of students make a list of how they could use the Spanish language outside of the classroom, such as making the morning announcements in Spanish, creating a column in the school newspaper in Spanish, or ordering in a local restaurant. Then have each group choose one of their suggestions and prepare a presentation of that idea for the class.

Comparaciones

¿Te gusta mirar la televisión? ¿Ves muchas telenovelas? Las telenovelas latinoamericanas son muy populares. Pero hay una gran diferencia entre las telenovelas latinoamericanas y las estadounidenses. ¿Sabes cuál es?

Comunicación

La comunicación es un elemento esencial de la vida diaria. Frecuentemente usamos Internet para comunicarnos con otras personas y para buscar información nueva. ¿Cómo lo usas tú?

Culturas

El teléfono celular es un medio de comunicación usado en todo el mundo. ¿Crees que se usa mucho o poco en los países andinos? ¿Por qué?

Fíjate

Imagina tu vida en el futuro. ¿Cómo usarás el español? Piensa en tu carrera profesional y en tus pasatiempos. Haz una lista, incorporando ideas de estas páginas.

401

Unit 6 and Communities

Unit 6, **¡Ya llegó el futuro!**, brings together all of the national standards and the weave of curricular elements. Throughout this unit, work to have students communicate regarding the electronic media as it exists both in the Spanish-speaking world and in the United States. Encourage students to explore connections with other disciplines, particularly science and technology, as they apply to the countries studied and the United States. Also have students make comparisons between the Andean countries, the other Spanish-speaking countries studied, and the United States. Additionally, support students as they explore how they will be able to use Spanish in the community now and in the future.

Culture Highlights

● **PARQUE DE CIENCIA Y TECNOLOGÍA MALOKA** Este parque de Colombia (foto superior de la página 400) está dedicado a la ciencia y la tecnología.

Fíjate
Answers
Answers will vary.

Block Schedule

Variety Have students think of people they know in their community who use another language in their job or volunteer work. Encourage students to seek persons that represent a variety of occupations, such as hospital or restaurant workers, government employees, or volunteers who tutor Spanish-speaking children. Have the students prepare five or more interview questions and conduct an interview. Ask them to report their results to the class. They may also wish to share their interviews with the school newspaper or a local paper. (For additional activities, see **Block Scheduling Copymasters**.)

Teaching All Students

Extra Help Have students look at the photograph of the two girls on page 400, read the caption, and describe what they think is happening in the picture.

Native Speakers Have students interview their parents or relatives to answer the question, **¿Por qué es importante saber más de un idioma?**

Challenge Ask students to research their family histories to discover which generations spoke a language other than English. Discover if there are any students who have only English-speaking ancestors.

Ampliación

These activities may be used at various points in the Unit 6 sequence.

For Block Schedule, you may find that these projects will provide a welcome change of pace while reviewing and reinforcing the material presented in the unit. See the **Block Scheduling Copymasters.**

● PROJECTS

Create Web pages Have students work in pairs to design the home page of a Web site for a Spanish-speaking country. Their home page should include an index of other pages covering different topics from government to entertainment. The page might include the flag or colors of the flag, a map image, important areas, statistics about the country, etc. The designs can be drawn on posterboards if computers are not available. If your school has the technology and software to allow students to design pages on a computer, have them include links to other Web sites as well. If your school has its own Web page, these pages can be included on the school Web site.

PACING SUGGESTION: Upon completion of Etapa 3.

Film or record a television program Have students work in small groups to create a scene in a television movie, series, or situation comedy, or to simulate a television news broadcast, talk show, or game show. Encourage creativity and humor.

PACING SUGGESTION: Upon completion of Etapa 1.

● STORYTELLING

Surfea la red por medio de la Onda Cibernética El mejor proveedor de Internet en Caracas

Una casa moderna After reviewing the vocabulary for technology and computers, model a mini-story (using student actors or photos from the text) that students will revise, retell, and expand:

> La familia Torres vive en una casa muy bonita pero vieja. El hijo mayor, César, insiste en que necesitan modernizar la casa. El agente de ElectraCasa, un almacén electrónico, los visita para ayudarlos a modernizar la casa con aparatos electrónicos y con la tecnología disponible. El agente llega y dice: «Buenas tardes a todos. Soy el señor Suárez, representante de ElectraCasa. Estoy a sus órdenes para analizar sus necesidades electrónicas». El padre responde: «Pase usted, señor Suárez. Mi hijo César teme por su futuro porque sin los aparatos ¡ya no puede estudiar!» El señor Suárez le dice: «Bueno, es bastante difícil competir estos días sin la tecnología. ¿Puedo ver la casa?»

As you give your model, be sure to pause as the story is being told so that students may fill in the words and act out gestures. Students should then write, narrate, and read aloud a longer main story.

Un desastre tecnológico Have students tell a story about a technology disaster or mishap. The problem can either be the result of having but misusing or not knowing how to use the technology, or it can be the result of not having the technology needed.

PACING SUGGESTION: Upon completion of Etapa 3.

● BULLETIN BOARD/POSTERS

Bulletin Board Have students work in pairs to collect images and information about the indigenous groups of Venezuela, Colombia, Ecuador, Peru, and Bolivia. The class then arranges the information on the bulletin board, either geographically, alphabetically, or temporally.

Posters Have students create ●**Information brochures** on the use of technology to discover the world ●**Posters** for an international technology fair ●**Time lines** showing the changes in an apparatus, e.g., the telephone

GAMES

Piedra-papel-tijeras

Prepare ahead: Have students work in pairs to create a trio of items similar to the rock-paper-scissors game. They should use technological devices or vocabulary items from this unit; for example, **un beeper le gana a la contestadora automática porque te avisa inmediatamente de un mensaje, pero una pila le gana al beeper porque el beeper no funciona sin pilas, pero la contestadora le gana a la pila porque no le hace falta pila.** The relationship between the 3 can be humorous and a "stretch." Students then create a deck of cards: 20 cards with images or words for each item in the trio. To play, they shuffle and deal all the cards. They each draw and lay down the card from the top of their pile. Whoever has the winning device, takes both cards. The first player to win all cards or to have the most cards when time is up wins.

PACING SUGGESTION: Upon completion of Etapa 2.

Tipo de cambio

Prepare ahead: Have students research and post exchange rates for currencies in all Spanish-speaking countries. Make a deck of cards by writing the name of each currency on an index card. Then make a spinner with a paper clip and cardboard. Divide the spinner into wedges of numeric values in increments of 10 (10–100). Divide the class into teams. Have 1 team member draw a currency card, then spin the wheel. If the student draws **pesos** and spins a 10, record for that team **diez pesos.** Alternate teams until all the cards are drawn. Have students use their calculators and/or math skills to figure out how much money each team has in U.S. dollars. The team with the most money wins.

PACING SUGGESTION: Upon completion of Etapa 3.

MUSIC

Point out that the fusion of old and new music styles has revived many traditional beats and sounds, especially flamenco, salsa, Mexican boleros, and more. Have students research Hispanic musical artists on the Internet and if possible play music clips. Some artists to look for are the Gypsy Kings and Carlos Villalobos (flamenco), Gloria Estefan (salsa), Tish Hinojosa (boleros, cumbia, salsa), and Inti Illimani (Andean). More music samples are available on your *Canciones* CD.

HANDS-ON CRAFTS

Have students create computer art using a painting or drawing software program on the computer (this can be done by hand as well). Have students research art of indigenous groups from Latin America and choose 1 or more images for their art. They can create a message or simply use the images to create an interesting visual composition. Have them use the drawing and painting tools of the computer to create the images (or draw with pencil, crayons, and/or paint on paper).

RECIPE

Llapingachos ecuatorianos The potato was second only to corn in the agriculture and cuisine of the indigenous people of Latin America. **Llapingachos** is a potato dish that also includes the cheese and butter that were made after the Spaniards brought cattle to the New World. This is considered one of the traditional dishes of Ecuador and is especially popular in the Sierra region. **Llapingachos** can be served with dinners of beef steak or stew and green salad, or with a breakfast of eggs and sausage.

Receta

Llapingachos ecuatorianos

2 libras de papas	2 huevos
sal al gusto	2 cucharadas de
1/2 libra de queso fresco o requesón	mantequilla

Pele las papas y hiérvalas en agua con sal. Cuando estén suaves, escúrralas y haga puré. Agregue la mantequilla y el queso desmenuzado, mezcle todo bien. Agregue los huevos y amase bien. Haga bolitas y aplánelas con la mano para darles la forma de tortillas. Déjelas reposar por 15 minutos. Fríalas en un sartén con un poco de manteca o aceite. Los llapingachos salen más sabrosos si los tuesta un poco. Sirve de 6 a 8 personas.

Planning Guide CLASSROOM MANAGEMENT

OBJECTIVES

Communication
- Narrate in the past *pp. 410–411*
- Express doubt and certainty *pp. 412–414*
- Report what others say *pp. 414–415*
- Talk about television *pp. 404–405, 406–407, 418–419*

Grammar
- Review the use of the preterite and the imperfect *pp. 410–411*
- Review the use of the indicative and the subjunctive *pp. 412–414*
- Review the use of reported speech *pp. 414–415*
- Use sequence of tenses *pp. 415–417*

Culture
- History and culture of Venezuela, Colombia, Ecuador, Perú, and Bolivia *pp. 400–401*
- Regional vocabulary *p. 408*
- Television programming in Latin America *pp. 412, 418–419*
- Extending invitations *p. 416*

♻ Recycling
- Demonstratives *p. 408*
- Literature and movie vocabulary *p. 413*
- Commands *p. 416*

STRATEGIES

Listening Strategies
- Keep up with what is said and agreed *p. 406*

Speaking Strategies
- Negotiate *p. 414*
- Retell memories *p. 422*

Reading Strategies
- Distinguish facts from interpretations *pp. 418*

Writing Strategies
- Develop your story *TE p. 422*

Connecting Cultures Strategies
- Learn about Venezuela, Colombia, Ecuador, Perú, and Bolivia *pp. 398–399*
- Recognize regional vocabulary *p. 408*
- Learn about television programming in Latin America *pp. 412, 418–419*
- Understand extending invitations *p. 416*
- Connect and compare what you already know about television programming in your community to help you learn about television programming in a new community *pp. 422–423*

PROGRAM RESOURCES

Print
- *Más práctica* Workbook PE *pp. 137–144*
- *Actividades para todos* Workbook PE *pp. 161–170*
- Block Scheduling Copymasters *pp. 129–136*
- Unit 6 Resource Book
  Más práctica Workbook TE *pp. 3–10*
  Actividades para todos Workbook TE *pp. 11–20*
  Cuaderno para hispanohablantes TE *pp. 21–28*
  Information Gap Activities *pp. 29–32*
  Family Letter *p. 33*
  Absent Student Copymasters *pp. 34–40*
  Family Involvement *pp. 41–42*
  Audioscript *pp. 43–46*
  Assessment Program, Unit 6, Etapa 1 *pp. 47–70; 226–228*
  Answer Keys *pp. 250–254*

Audiovisual
- Audio Program CD 16
- *Canciones* CD
- Overhead Transparencies M1–M5; 2, 5–19
- Word Tiles U6E1

Technology
- eEdition Plus Online/eEdition CD-ROM
- Easy Planner Plus Online/Easy Planner CD-ROM
- eTest Plus Online/Test Generator CD-ROM
- Online Workbook
- Take-Home Tutor CD-ROM
- www.classzone.com

✓ Assessment Program Options
- Unit 6 Resource Book
  Vocabulary Quizzes
  Grammar Quizzes
  Etapa Exam Forms A and B
  Examen para hispanohablantes
  Portfolio Assessment
  Multiple Choice Test Questions
- Audio Program CD 20
- eTest Plus Online/Test Generator CD-ROM

Native Speakers
- *Cuaderno para hispanohablantes* PE *pp. 137–144*
- *Cuaderno para hispanohablantes* TE (Unit 6 Resource Book)
- *Examen para hispanohablantes* (Unit 6 Resource Book)
- Audio Program *(Para hispanohablantes)* CD 16, CD 20
- Audioscript (Unit 6 Resource Book)

Student Text
Listening Activity Scripts

 Situaciones *pages 406–407*

• CD 16

Papá: Mira, a las dos van a pasar un documental sobre las Islas Galápagos. A ver, aquí dice que «Las Islas Galápagos son uno de los pocos laboratorios vivientes a escala natural que existen en el planeta». ¿No les parece interesante?

Hijo: ¡Ay, papá! ¡Un documental! ¡Qué aburrido! ¿Por qué no vemos esta película de acción? También es a las dos.

Mamá: A ver, ¿cuál, hijo?

Hijo: Ésta, «Alarma nuclear».

Mamá: Pero hijo, aquí dice que esa película es prohibida para menores.

Hija: Yo quiero ver este teledrama «El pasado perdido».

Papá: Ése no empieza hasta las tres, así que primero podemos ver el documental de las islas Galápagos, y entonces podemos ver tu teledrama.

Hijo: ¡No es justo! Yo quiero escoger algo también.

Papá: Está bien, Riqui, sigue buscando. Como está lloviendo, creo que vamos a pasar casi todo el día viendo la tele.

Hijo: Bueno, ésta. Es una película de horror «Vino del lago».

Mamá: Ay, Riqui. ¿No ves que dice que «se recomienda discreción»? Busca una película que sea apta para toda la familia, ¿no crees?

Hijo: ¡Uy, qué aburrido!

Mamá: ¡Mira, Riqui! ¿Qué te parece este misterio, «Mí tío, el ladrón»?

Hija: Y empieza a las cuatro, después de que termina el teledrama.

Hijo: Bueno, está bien. Parece interesante.

Papá: Entonces ya estamos de acuerdo. Pongan el documental, ¡que ya va a empezar!

Hijo: Uy, documental. Despiértenme cuando empiece el misterio.

ACTIVIDAD 5  La escritora *page 411*

Modelo: Cuando era niña, siempre iba al cine los domingos por la mañana.

Me encantaban las comedias. Si iba a estrenar una comedia, yo estaba allí. Un día, me enfermé y no pude ir al cine para ver mi actriz favorita en su nueva película. Mientras me perdía le película más importante del año, empecé a escribir un guión. La fiebre le dio vuelo a mi imaginación. Escribí por horas sin parar. Como era muy exagerada, siempre les decía a mis padres que un día iba a ser famosa. Lo que no sabía era que mi talento no estaba en la actuación. Ese día me di cuenta que iba a ser escritora.

ACTIVIDAD 11  Jorge *page 414*

Modelo: Voy a ir al cine esta tarde.

1. Voy a buscar una película de acción.
2. Voy a ver la nueva película de mi actor favorito.
3. Anda, ven conmigo.
4. Bueno, si no quieres ir, voy a invitar a mi hermano.

Sample Lesson Plan - 50 Minute Schedule

DAY 1

Unit Opener
• Anticipate/Activate prior knowledge: Present the *Almanaque* and the cultural notes. Use Map OHTs as needed. 15 MIN.

Etapa Opener
• Quick Start Review (TE, p. 402) 5 MIN.
• Have students look at the *Etapa* Opener and answer the questions. 5 MIN.

En contexto: Vocabulario
• Quick Start Review (TE, p. 404) 5 MIN.
• Present *Descubre,* p. 404. 5 MIN.
• Have students use context and pictures to learn *Etapa* vocabulary, then answer the *¿Comprendiste?* questions, p. 405. Use the Situational OHTs for additional practice. 15 MIN.

Homework Option:
• Have students write answers to the *¿Comprendiste?* questions, p. 405.

DAY 2

En vivo: Situaciones
• Check homework. 5 MIN.
• Quick Start Review (TE, p. 406) 5 MIN.
• Present the Listening Strategy, p. 406. 5 MIN.
• Have students look at section 1, p. 406. Play the audio for section 2. Then have students work in groups to complete section 3. 15 MIN.

En acción: Vocabulario y gramática
• Quick Start Review (TE, p. 408) 5 MIN.
• Have students complete *Actividades* 1–4 in pairs. 15 MIN.

Homework Option:
• Have students write 2 movie reviews for a TV guide, using pp. 404–405 as a model.

DAY 3

En acción (cont.)
• Check homework. 5 MIN.
• Quick Start Review (TE, p. 410) 5 MIN.
• Present *Repaso:* Preterite vs. Imperfect, p. 410. 10 MIN.
• Play the audio; do *Actividad* 5. 5 MIN.
• Have students do *Actividad* 6 in writing. Then have them exchange papers for peer correction. 10 MIN.
• Have students do *Actividad* 7 in writing. Go over answers orally. Expand using *Más comunicación,* p. R18. 15 MIN.

Homework Option:
• *Más práctica* Workbook, p. 141. *Cuaderno para hispanohablantes,* p. 139.

DAY 4

En acción (cont.)
• Check homework. 5 MIN.
• Quick Start Review (TE, p. 412) 5 MIN.
• Present *Repaso:* Indicative vs. Subjunctive, p. 412. 5 MIN.
• Present the *Vocabulario,* p. 413. Then do *Actividad* 8 orally. 10 MIN.
• Have students do *Actividad* 9 in pairs. 5 MIN.
• Present the Speaking Strategy, p. 414. Then have students do *Actividad* 10 in pairs. 5 MIN.
• Quick Start Review (TE, p. 414) 5 MIN.
• Present *Repaso:* Reported Speech, p. 414. 5 MIN.
• Play the audio; do *Actividad* 11. 5 MIN.

Homework Option:
• *Más práctica* Workbook, pp. 142–143. *Cuaderno para hispanohablantes,* pp. 140–141.

DAY 5

En acción (cont.)
• Check homework. 5 MIN.
• Do *Actividad* 12 orally. 5 MIN.
• Have students complete *Actividad* 13 in pairs. 5 MIN.
• Quick Start Review (TE, p. 415) 5 MIN.
• Present *Gramática:* Sequence of Tenses, p. 415. 10 MIN.
• Present the *Vocabulario,* p. 416. Then do *Actividad* 14 orally. 10 MIN.
• Have students complete *Actividad* 15 in pairs. 5 MIN.
• Have students read and complete *Actividad* 16 in groups. 5 MIN.

Homework Option:
• Have students complete *Actividad* 14 in writing. *Más práctica* Workbook, p. 144. *Cuaderno para hispanohablantes,* p. 142.

DAY 6

En acción (cont.)
• Check homework. 5 MIN.
• Have students complete *Actividad* 17 in groups. Expand using *Más comunicación,* p. R18. 15 MIN.

Refrán
• Present the *Refrán,* p. 417. 5 MIN.

En voces: Lectura
• Quick Start Review (TE, p. 418) 5 MIN.
• Present the Reading Strategy, p. 418. Call on volunteers to read the *Lectura* aloud. Have students answer the *¿Comprendiste?/¿Qué piensas?* questions, p. 419. 20 MIN.

Homework Option:
• Have students complete *Hazlo tú,* p. 419.
• *Actividades para todos* Workbook, pp. 161–170

DAY 7

En uso: Repaso y más comunicación
• Check homework. 5 MIN.
• Quick Start Review (TE, p. 420) 5 MIN.
• Do *Actividades* 1 and 2 orally. 10 MIN.
• Have students do *Actividades* 3 and 4 in writing. Go over answers orally. 15 MIN.
• Present the Speaking Strategy, p. 422. Do *Actividad* 5 in groups. 10 MIN.

En tu propia voz: Escritura
• Have students plan their movies/TV series for *Actividad* 6. 5 MIN.

Homework Option:
• Have students write their posters for *Actividad* 6. Review for *Etapa* 1 Exam.

DAY 8

En tu propia voz (cont.)
• Have students present their posters. 10 MIN.

Tú en la comunidad
• Present and discuss *Lucille,* p. 422. 5 MIN.

En resumen: Repaso de vocabulario
• Quick Start Review (TE, p. 423) 5 MIN.
• Review grammar questions, etc., as necessary. 10 MIN.
• Complete *Etapa* 1 Exam. 20 MIN.

Ampliación
• Optional: Use a suggested project, game, or activity. (TE, pp. 401A–401B)

Homework Option:
• Preview *Etapa* 2 Opener.

Sample Lesson Plan - Block Schedule (90 minutes)

DAY 1

Unit Opener
- Anticipate/Activate prior knowledge: Present the *Almanaque* and the cultural notes. Use Map OHTs as needed. 15 MIN.

Etapa Opener
- Quick Start Review (TE, p. 402) 5 MIN.
- Have students look at the *Etapa* Opener and answer the questions. 5 MIN.
- Use Block Scheduling Copymasters. 10 MIN.

En contexto: Vocabulario
- Quick Start Review (TE, p. 404) 5 MIN.
- Present *Descubre*, p. 404. 5 MIN.
- Have students use context and pictures to learn *Etapa* vocabulary, then answer the *¿Comprendiste?* questions, p. 393. Use the Situational OHTs for additional practice. 15 MIN.

En vivo: Situaciones
- Quick Start Review (TE, p. 406) 5 MIN.
- Present the Listening Strategy, p. 406. 5 MIN.
- Have students look at section 1, p. 406. Play the audio for section 2. Then have students work in groups to complete section 3. 20 MIN.

Homework Option:
- Have students write answers to the *¿Comprendiste?* questions, p. 405.

DAY 2

En acción: Vocabulario y gramática
- Check homework. 5 MIN.
- Quick Start Review (TE, p. 408) 5 MIN.
- Have students complete *Actividades* 1–4 in pairs. 20 MIN.
- Quick Start Review (TE, p. 410) 5 MIN.
- Present *Repaso:* Preterite vs. Imperfect, p. 410. 10 MIN.
- Play the audio; do *Actividad* 5. 5 MIN.
- Have students do *Actividad* 6 in writing. Then have them exchange papers for peer correction. 10 MIN.
- Have students do *Actividad* 7 in writing. Go over answers orally. Expand using Information Gap Activities, Unit 6 Resource Book, p. 29; *Más comunicación*, p. R18. 20 MIN.
- Quick Start Review (TE, p. 412) 5 MIN.
- Present *Repaso:* Indicative vs. Subjunctive, p. 412. 5 MIN.

Homework Option:
- Have students write 2 movie reviews for a TV guide, using pp. 404–405 as a model. *Más práctica* Workbook, p. 141. *Cuaderno para hispanohablantes*, p. 139.

DAY 3

En acción (cont.)
- Check homework. 5 MIN.
- Present the *Vocabulario*, p. 413. Then do *Actividad* 8 orally. 10 MIN.
- Have students do *Actividad* 9 in pairs. 5 MIN.
- Present the Speaking Strategy, p. 414. Then have students do *Actividad* 10 in pairs. 10 MIN.
- Quick Start Review (TE, p. 414) 5 MIN.
- Present *Repaso:* Reported Speech, p. 414. 5 MIN.
- Play the audio; do *Actividad* 11. 10 MIN.
- Do *Actividad* 12 orally. 5 MIN.
- Have students complete *Actividad* 13 in pairs. 5 MIN.
- Quick Start Review (TE, p. 415) 5 MIN.
- Present *Gramática:* Sequence of Tenses, p. 415. 10 MIN.
- Present the *Vocabulario*, p. 416. Then do *Actividad* 14 orally. 10 MIN.
- Have students complete *Actividad* 15 in pairs. 5 MIN.

Homework Option:
- Have students complete *Actividad* 14 in writing. *Más práctica* Workbook, pp. 142–144. *Cuaderno para hispanohablantes*, pp. 140–142.
- *Actividades para todos* Workbook, pp. 161–170.

DAY 4

En acción (cont.)
- Check homework. 5 MIN.
- Have students read and complete *Actividad* 16 in groups. 5 MIN.
- Have students complete *Actividad* 17 in groups. Expand using Information Gap Activities, Unit 6 Resource Book, p. 30; *Más comunicación*, p. R18. 20 MIN.

Refrán
- Present the *Refrán*, p. 417. 5 MIN.

En voces: Lectura
- Quick Start Review (TE, p. 418) 5 MIN.
- Present the Reading Strategy, p. 418. Call on volunteers to read the *Lectura* aloud. Have students answer the *¿Comprendiste?/¿Qué piensas?* questions, p. 419. 20 MIN.

En uso: Repaso y más comunicación
- Quick Start Review (TE, p. 420) 5 MIN.
- Do *Actividades* 1–4 orally. 15 MIN.
- Present the Speaking Strategy, p. 422. Do *Actividad* 5 in groups. 10 MIN.

Homework Option:
- Have students complete *Hazlo tú*, p. 419. Review for *Etapa* 1 Exam.

DAY 5

En tu propia voz: Escritura
- Check homework. 5 MIN.
- Have students write and present their posters for *Actividad* 6. 25 MIN.

Tú en la comunidad
- Present and discuss *Lucille*, p. 422. 5 MIN.

En resumen: Repaso de vocabulario
- Quick Start Review (TE, p. 423) 5 MIN.
- Review grammar questions, etc., as necessary. 10 MIN.
- Complete *Etapa* 1 Exam. 20 MIN.

Ampliación
- Use a suggested project, game, or activity. (TE, pp. 401A–401B) 20 MIN.

Homework Option:
- Preview *Etapa* 2 Opener.

▼ ¿Qué programa transmiten?

Etapa Theme

Talking about television; narrating in the past; expressing doubt and certainty; and reporting what others say

Grammar Objectives

- Reviewing the use of the preterite and the imperfect
- Reviewing the use of the indicative and the subjunctive
- Reviewing the use of reported speech
- Using sequence of tenses

Teaching Resource Options

Print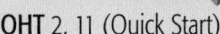

Block Scheduling Copymasters
Unit 6 Resource Book
  Family Letter, p. 33
  Absent Student Copymasters, p. 34

Audiovisual

OHT 2, 11 (Quick Start)

Quick Start Review

♻ House vocabulary

Use OHT 11 or write on the board:
What room(s) do you associate with the following items?

1. el sofá	5. el sillón
2. la estufa	6. la mesa con sillas
3. la almohada	7. la cama
4. el escritorio	8. la lámpara

Answers

Answers will vary. Answers could include:
1. la sala
2. la cocina
3. la habitación, la sala
4. la oficina, la habitación, la cocina
5. la sala
6. la cocina, el comedor
7. la habitación
8. el comedor, la oficina, la habitación

UNIDAD 6

ETAPA 1

¿Qué quieres ver?

OBJECTIVES

- Narrate in the past
- Express doubt and certainty
- Report what others say
- Talk about television

¿Qué ves?

Mira la foto. Contesta las preguntas.

1. ¿Qué cosas en la foto te dicen dónde están los actores?
2. ¿Cuál es la actitud del hombre? ¿Y de la mujer?
3. Mira la revista. ¿De qué crees que se trata? ¿Cómo lo sabes?

402

Classroom Management

Planning Ahead Prepare to introduce the theme of television programming by bringing in Spanish-language and English-language TV guides or TV program listings from newspapers.

Time Saver If time is short, have students write a description of the photo and do the ¿Qué ves? questions as homework.

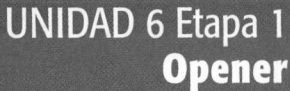

403

Teaching Suggestion
Previewing the Etapa
- Ask students to study the photo on pp. 402–403 (1 min.).
- Close books; ask students to name at least 3 things that they noticed.
- Reopen books and look at the photo again. Ask students: **¿Qué palabras ya saben para describir la foto?**
- Use the **¿Qué ves?** questions to focus the discussion.

Cross Cultural Connections
Have students look through a TV listing from a U.S. TV guide or newspaper listing. Can they find any Spanish-language broadcasts? What type of shows are they?

Culture Highlights

● **LAS TELENOVELAS** La duración de la trama es la diferencia más grande entre las telenovelas producidas en países como Colombia y Venezuela y las producidas en Estados Unidos. Las novelas estadounidenses duran varios años, mientras que las novelas latinoamericanas tienen una trama que se desarrolla y termina dentro de un año.

Supplementary Vocabulary

la cortina	curtain
la escena	scene
el escenario	set, stage
el estudio de televisión	television studio
el galán	(handsome) leading man

Teaching All Students

Extra Help Help students read the cover of **TV y novelas** on p. 403. Have them compare this with what they might find on U.S. soap opera magazine covers.

Challenge Working in pairs, have students write a short dialog for the characters in the photo based on the actors' attitudes. Students can present their dialogs to the class.

Multiple Intelligences
Kinesthetic Have students work in pairs to write a dialog between the 2 people in the photo. Then have students act out their dialogs for the class, using expression and appropriate gestures.

Block Schedule
Setting the Theme Have students discuss the kinds of plots, characters, sets, music, etc., that they associate with **telenovelas.** (For additional activities, see **Block Scheduling Copymasters.**)

Teaching Resource Options

Print 📖

Block Scheduling Copymasters
Unit 6 Resource Book
  Absent Student Copymasters, p. 34

Audiovisual 📺

OHT 5, 6, 7, 7A, 8, 8A, 11 (Quick Start)

Technology 💻

Online Workbook, U6E1
Take-Home Tutor CD-ROM, U6E1

🔔 Quick Start Review

♻️ Television vocabulary

Use OHT 11 or write on the board:
Match the words in the 2 columns:

1. __ película   a. canales
2. __ comediante   b. cine
3. __ telenovela   c. noticias
4. __ televisión   d. melodrama
5. __ reportero   e. reírse

Answers
1. b   2. e   3. d   4. a   5. c

Teaching Suggestions
Introducing Vocabulary

• Have students look at pp. 404–405.
  Use OHT 5 and 6 to present the
  vocabulary.
• Ask the Comprehension Questions
  on TE p. 405 in order of yes/no
  (questions 1–3), either/or (questions
  4–6), and simple word or phrase
  (questions 7–10).
• Use the TPR activity to reinforce the
  meaning of individual words.

Descubre

Answers
A. *Answers will vary.*
B. 1. c   2. a   3. b

En contexto VOCABULARIO

Recomendaciones para la semana

TELE-GUÍA: *PROGRAMACIÓN TV-CABLE UNIVISA*

🔲 Descubre

A. Las películas Las películas se clasifican en categorías como Acción, Comedia, Documental, Misterio, etc. Haz una lista de todas las categorías en la sección **En contexto**. Luego, da dos ejemplos de películas para cada categoría.

B. Índice de audiencia Las películas siempre tienen un índice de audiencia *(ratings)*. Este índice les indica a los padres si es apropiado que sus hijos vean esa película o no. Adivina qué quieren decir los siguientes índices.

  1. apto para toda la familia
  2. se recomienda discreción
  3. prohibido para menores
     a. PG–13
     b. R–rated
     c. G–rated

DOCUMENTAL
Las Islas Galápagos: Paraíso biológico
CANAL 5   DOMINGO 14.00h
Viajen con un científico y una bióloga a las islas que siguen fascinando al mundo científico. **Apto para toda la familia.**

CIENCIA FICCIÓN
CINE: Los robots humanos
CANAL 6   JUEVES 20.00h
Unos robots extraterrestres eligen un pueblo venezolano como su próxima base. **Se recomienda discreción.**

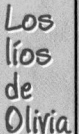

COMEDIA
TELESERIE Los líos de Olivia
CANAL 3   MARTES 18.00h
En este **episodio**, Olivia hace el papel de Cupido y le presenta su mejor amiga a su agente. El instante que se conocen, ¡se odian!, pero Olivia no lo quiere dejar así. Apto para toda la familia.

MISTERIO
CINE: Mi tío, el ladrón
CANAL 3   DOMINGO 16.00h
El tío del narrador tiene una falta pequeña: por las noches es ladrón. Pero no sabe lo que hace –todo ocurre mientras camina dormido. Apto para toda la familia.

MISTERIO
CINE: La vida secreta del gobernador
CANAL 5   VIERNES 22.30h
El gobernador tiene un secreto que sólo su **guardaespaldas** sabe. ¿Qué hace el empleado leal con la información explosiva? **Prohibido para menores.**

404   cuatrocientos cuatro
       Unidad 6

Classroom Community

TPR Write the name of each type of program on a slip of paper and put all the slips in a bag. Groups of 3–4 take turns choosing a slip and acting out the type of show for the class to guess.

Paired Activity Have students work in pairs to list U.S. programs similar to the ones on pp. 404–405. Have them also give a rating to each one.

Take-Home Tutor

HORROR
CINE: Vino del lago
CANAL 6   **DOMINGO 16.30h**
Un animal acuático misterioso sale del lago para aterrorizar un pueblo ecuatoriano. Se recomienda discreción.

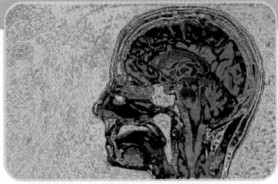

DRAMA
TELEDRAMA: El pasado perdido
CANAL 3   **DOMINGO 15.00h**
El protagonista pierde la memoria en un accidente automovilístico. Cuando sale del coma, no conoce ni a su familia ni a sus amistades.

AVENTURA
Héroe sin hogar
CANAL 5   **DOMINGO 16.30h**
Un agente del gobierno descubre prácticas ilegales. En vez de ser elogiado, huye por su vida. Se recomienda discreción.

ACCIÓN
Alarma nuclear
CANAL 6   **DOMINGO 14.00h**
Dos pilotos norteamericanos tienen que desarmar unos misiles nucleares. Prohibido para menores.

DIBUJOS ANIMADOS
Thumbelina
CANAL 5   **SÁBADO 10.00h**
Este clásico infantil es la historia de una niña que se despierta y encuentra que es tan pequeña como un dedo. Apto para toda la familia.

CONCURSO
Inteligencia
CANAL 3   **LUNES 9.00h**
Tendrás la oportunidad de mostrar tu inteligencia mientras ganas premios valiosos.

PROGRAMA DE ENTREVISTAS
ROSIE O'GORMAN
CANAL 3   **LUNES 11.00h**
En vivo y directo desde Nueva York, Rosie habla con los miembros de la obra teatral «Titanic», la actriz puertorriqueña Rita Moreno y el cantante Luis Miguel.

 Online Workbook
CLASSZONE.COM

¿Comprendiste?

1. ¿Vas al cine a menudo? ¿Cuántas veces al mes? ¿O prefieres ver películas en casa: en la tele o en video? ¿Tienen cable en tu casa?
2. ¿Qué clase de película o programa te interesa más? ¿Por qué? ¿Hay algunos actores que se asocien con ese tipo de película o programa? Nombra dos o tres.
3. ¿Cómo se decide en tu casa qué programa van a poner? ¿Es fácil o difícil que los miembros de tu familia se pongan de acuerdo?
4. Escoge una película o teleserie de la tele-guía en esta sección y convence a tus compañeros que es el programa que deben ver. Explica por qué te parece interesante.

cuatrocientos cinco **405**
Colombia, Venezuela y los países andinos Etapa 1

Teaching Resource Options

Print

Block Scheduling Copymasters
Unit 6 Resource Book
  Absent Student Copymasters, p. 35
  Audioscript, p. 43

Audiovisual

OHT 9, 10, 11 (Quick Start)
Audio Program CD 16, Track 1

Technology

Take-Home Tutor CD-ROM, U6E1

🔔 Quick Start Review

♻ Television programs

Use OHT 11 or write on the board:
Match each program title with the type
of program it might be:

1. __ *La gente y la cultura de los Andes*
2. __ *El monstruo de la selva*
3. __ *Los héroes del cielo*
4. __ *Veinte preguntas*
5. __ *La gatita Fifí*
   a. acción   b. dibujo animado
   c. documental d. horror
   e. concurso

Answers
1. c   2. d   3. a   4. e   5. b

Teaching Suggestions
Presenting Situations

- Present the Listening Strategy, p. 406.
- Use OHT 9 and 10 to present the **Mirar** section. Ask simple yes/no, either/or, or short-answer questions.
- Use Audio CD 16 and have students do the **Escuchar** section (see Script p. 401D).
- Complete the Listening Strategy exercise.
- Have students work in groups to complete the **Hablar** section.

AUDIO

En vivo
SITUACIONES

PARA ESCUCHAR
STRATEGY: LISTENING

Keep up with what is said and agreed Reporting a lively conversation requires accurate listening. What does the Domínguez family finally agree to watch on television? To keep everything straight, focus only on facts:

1. ¿Qué programas discuten?
2. ¿A qué hora empiezan? ¿Hay conflictos?
3. Después de la discusión, ¿qué programa(s) escogen?

¿Qué vamos a ver?

Estás en Quito, Ecuador. Pasas un domingo con los Domínguez, una familia que conoces desde chico(a). Todos quieren ver la tele y miran la Tele-Guía para ver qué programas hay. Luego hablan de lo que quieren ver.

① Mirar

Estudia la siguiente programación que salió en la edición del domingo en la TeleGuía.

TELE– GUÍA domingo   C11

Programas en la tarde   domingo, 13 de marzo

Acción	**Teledrama**	**Documental**	**Horror**	**Misterio**
Alarma nuclear	*El pasado perdido*	*Las Islas Galápagos: Paraíso biológico*	*Vino del lago*	*Mí tío, el ladrón*
14.00h CANAL 6	15.00h CANAL 3	14.00h CANAL 5	16.30h CANAL 6	16.00h CANAL 3

 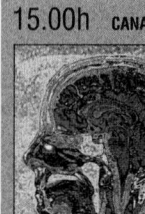   

| Dos pilotos norteamericanos tienen que desarmar unos misiles nucleares. Prohibido para menores. | El protagonista pierde la memoria en un accidente automovilístico. Cuando sale del coma, no conoce ni a su familia ni a sus amistades. | Viajen con un científico y una bióloga a las islas que siguen fascinando al mundo científico. Apto para toda la familia. | Un animal acuático misterioso sale del lago para aterrorizar un pueblo ecuatoriano. Se recomienda discreción. | El tío del narrador tiene una falta pequeña: por las noches es ladrón. Pero no sabe lo que hace –todo ocurre mientras camina dormido. Apto para toda la familia. |

406 cuatrocientos seis
Unidad 6

Classroom Community

Cooperative Learning Divide the class into 7 groups and have students create a week-long TV programming guide. Assign each group a day. Then have each group divide up the day into morning, afternoon, and evening. They can work individually to create a title and brief description of their programs. After each group has put together their section, display or circulate the "guide pages" and have students select the shows they would watch. Additionally, all the pages can be integrated to form a complete guide.

Game Have students describe the plot or a scene from a program they like to watch. The class guesses which program is begin described.

CD-ROM
Take-Home Tutor

② Escuchar 🎧

Escucha la conversación entre los Domínguez. Copia la siguiente tabla y marca **sí** junto a los programas que deciden ver, y **no** junto a los que no deciden ver. Luego, escribe la hora de los programas que van a ver este domingo.

	Sí	No	Hora
acción			
ciencia ficción			
comedia			
dibujos animados			
documental			
teledrama			
horror			
misterio			

③ Hablar 👥

En grupos de tres o cuatro, comenten sobre las decisiones de los Domínguez. Traigan una tele-guía de su periódico a la clase. Comparen los programas de su periódico con los de los Domínguez. Escojan un día de programación y decidan qué verían si estuvieran en la misma situación que los Domínguez.

407

Escuchar (See script, p. 401D.)

Answers

acción	no	
ciencia ficción:	no	
comedia:	no	
dibujos animados	no	
documental:	sí	hora: 14.00 h (las dos de la tarde)
teledrama:	sí	hora: 15.00h (las tres de la tarde)
horror:	no	
misterio:	sí	hora: 16:00 h (las cuatro de le tarde)

Hablar

Answers will vary.

Cross Cultural Connections

Bring to class a TV guide that includes one or more of the Spanish-language networks. Have students compare the programming on those networks to that of the major English-language networks.

🔔 Quick Wrap-up

Villains are often the biggest draw for soap operas and other shows. Have students explain why villainous characters are attractive to television audiences.

■ Block Schedule

Personalizing Have students list the programs they regularly watch during the week, then categorize each; for example, **acción**, **teledrama**, etc. Then have volunteers describe what kind of **televidentes** they are. (For additional activities, see **Block Scheduling Copymasters**.)

Teaching All Students

Extra Help Have students give their own definitions in Spanish of what each program category is. Have them include examples of programs they might watch.

Challenge Following the models on p. 406, have students write a short description of one of their favorite television shows.

Multiple Intelligences

Visual Record short clips of various kinds of television programs in Spanish. Show the clips in class and have students tell what kind of program each clip is from based on what they see and hear.

Teaching Resource Options

Print

Block Scheduling Copymasters
Unit 6 Resource Book
  Absent Student Copymasters, p. 36

Audiovisual

OHT 12 (Quick Start)

Quick Start Review

♻ Television vocabulary review

Use OHT 12 or write on the board:
List 5 of your favorite TV shows and write what kind of program each ones is.

Answers will vary.

Teaching Suggestions
Comprehension Check

Use **Actividades 1–4** to assess retention after the **Vocabulario** and **Situaciones**. After completing **Actividades 1** and **2**, have each pair create 2 items for each one and present them for the class to talk about.

ACTIVIDAD 1 **Objective:** Controlled practice
Vocabulary in conversation

Answers

1. A: ¿Por qué no vemos esa comedia?
   B: Recibió cuatro estrellas. Quiere decir que es una película muy buena.
2. A: ¿Por qué no vemos ese documental?
   B: Recibió tres estrellas. Quiere decir que es una película buena.
3. A: ¿Por qué no vemos ese drama?
   B: Recibió dos estrellas. Quiere decir que es una película interesante.
4. A: ¿Por qué no vemos esa película de horror?
   B: Recibió una estrella. Quiere decir que es una película regular.

En acción

PARTE A **Práctica del vocabulario**

Objectives for Activities 1–4
• Narrate in the past • Talk about television

1 ¿Por qué no...?

Hablar/*Escribir* Estás en Bogotá con tu compañero(a) y quieren ir al cine. Tú le sugieres una película a tu compañero(a) y él (ella) te dice si la película es buena o mala.

¡Escape!
★★★

modelo

Tú: ¿Por qué no vemos esa película de acción?

Compañero(a): *Recibió tres estrellas. Quiere decir que es una película buena.*

1/2★ MALA	★★★ BUENA
★ REGULAR	★★★★ MUY BUENA
★★ INTERESANTE	★★★★★ EXCELENTE

1.

¡Qué confusión!
★★★★

2.

Los mayas
★★★

3.

La familia
★★

4.

LA MANO
★

2 Quiero ver...

Hablar/*Escribir* Tus padres salieron y tú tienes que cuidar a tu hermanito(a) de ocho años. Él (Ella) quiere ver ciertas películas. Tú le tienes que decir si puede verlas, según los índices de audiencia.

modelo

Blancanieves (G)

Compañero(a): *Quiero ver la película Blancanieves.*

Tú: *Está bien. Puedes verla. Es «apta para toda la familia».*

1. *Aladín (G)*
2. *Los robots humanos (PG-13)*
3. *Alarma nuclear (R)*

También se dice

En español se usa la palabra **televisor** para referirse al aparato que transmite programas. La palabra **televisión** se refiere a la programación de los varios canales. Muchos hispanohablantes usan la palabra **tele** para hablar de la televisión: «Voy a ver la tele». o «Vamos a mirar la televisión». Los dos verbos, **mirar** y **ver,** pueden usarse igualmente para hablar de esta actividad.

408 cuatrocientos ocho
Unidad 6

Classroom Management

Planning Ahead Bring programming guides for **Univisión** or **Telemundo** to class. These are available on the Internet or in some Spanish-language newspapers. Use these for discussion and activities.

Peer Review Write the list below on the board. Have students work in pairs. One partner describes a TV program using the words from the list and their own words. The partner guesses the name of the program.

• el programa más chistoso
• el mejor concurso
• una telenovela
• una comedia
• el/la protagonista de un programa popular

3 La tele-guía

Hablar/*Escribir* Tu mejor amigo(a) ha venido a tu casa a pasar unas horas hablando y viendo la tele contigo. Tienen que decidir qué van a ver. Conversen sobre las selecciones en la tele-guía.

modelo

Tú: *¿Qué hay en la tele?*

Compañero(a): *A ver, hay un documental sobre los misterios del universo en el canal 2 a las 9 de la noche.*

Tú: *No quiero ver un documental. ¿Qué más hay?*

Compañero(a): …

4 ¡No! ¡Mejor ésta!

Hablar Con la tele-guía del periódico o la de «En contexto» elige un programa y convence a tu compañero(a) de que deben verlo.

modelo

Tú: *Esta película se ve interesante y recibió cuatro estrellas.*

Compañero(a): *¿A qué hora es?*

Tú: *A las tres de la tarde.*

Compañero(a): *¡Ay, no! Yo quería ver ésta…*

8.05

La historia del béisbol
¡desde los comienzos de este deporte excitante!

9 Muzzik

9.50 Itzhak Perlman: En casa del violinista **10.50** Mozart, por Natalie Dessay **12.30** E. Ansermet dirige la O.S.R.: Overtura op. 115 de Beethoven **12.45** E. Ansermet dirige la O.S.R.: El vals de Ravel **13.25** Cierre

50 Documanía

8.00 Microdocus: Misterios del universo **9.05** Explorer: Rastreadores de tiburones **9.50** Nova: Hawai, nacida del fuego **10.45** Explorer: Carreras de submarinos **11.30** Agencia Capa: Los marinos de Cronstadt/ La ciudad de la alegría **12.25** Explorer: Pirañas **13.20** El siglo del cine: El cine ruso según…**14.15** Explorer: Frailecillo, un pájaro viajero **15.00** Nova: Rescatando crías de ballena **16.20** Explorer: Fotógrafos de acción **17.05** Agencia Capa: Barcelona por Javier Mariscal **20.05** Explorer: Inteligencia animal **21.00** Microdocus: Misterios del universo **21.05** National Geographic **2.10** Cierre

60 Estaciones

13.15 Miles de palomas en el País Vasco 2/2 **13.55** Las crónicas de Walker's Cay: Lo mejor de Walker's Cay **14.15** Pesca mayor: Guadalupe y sus marlines azules **15.35** Terra animae: Arrecifes de coral **16.25** La gran enciclopedia de la caza: Caza y gastronomía **16.50** Temporada no 25 **17.55** El mercado del hurón **18.55** Cazas del mundo: Gansos silvestres de Patagonia **20.20** Cuando despiertan las marmotas **20.50** Serie Brasil: Pesca del tucunare Açu **21.35** La afición de la pesca: El gave se rebela **22.00** Truchas arco iris del lago Washington **22.30** Pez vela de Costa Rica **1.20** Cierre

---

Teaching All Students

Extra Help Using a copy of a TV programming guide, ask questions about it. For example: *¿A qué hora presentan Nova? ¿Cuál es el programa acerca de un violinista famoso?*

Multiple Intelligences

Verbal Have students talk about how much television they watch, how much they should watch, and how a **tele-guía** can be used to make intelligent viewing choices.

Musical/Rhythmic Using well-known tunes, have students create a short theme song for one of the TV program types.

ACTIVIDAD 2 **Objective:** Transitional practice
Vocabulary in conversation

Answers
1. A: Quiero ver la película «Aladín».
   B: Está bien. Puedes verla. Está clasificada «apta para toda la familia».
2. A: Quiero ver la película «Los robots humanos».
   B: No puedes verla. Está clasificada «se recomienda discreción».
3. A: Quiero ver la película «Alarma nuclear».
   B: No puedes verla. Está clasificada «prohibida para menores».

ACTIVIDAD 3 **Objective:** Open-ended practice Vocabulary in conversation

Answers will vary.

ACTIVIDAD 4 **Objective:** Open-ended practice Vocabulary in conversation

Answers will vary.

🔔 **Quick Wrap-up**

Call out the names of various TV shows. Have students give the type of show it is. Then give the types of shows and have students give the names of TV shows in those categories.

Block Schedule

FunBreak Have each student think of one of his/her favorite TV actors/actresses. Without naming the person, have each student describe the various roles the actor/actress has played. Have the class guess the identity. (For additional activities, see **Block Scheduling Copymasters**.)

Teaching Resource Options

Print

Más práctica Workbook PE, p. 141
Cuaderno para hispanohablantes
  PE, p. 139
Block Scheduling Copymasters
Unit 6 Resource Book
  Más práctica Workbook TE, p. 7
  Cuaderno para hispanohablantes
    TE, p. 23
  Information Gap Activities, p. 29
  Absent Student Copymasters, p. 37
  Audioscript, p. 43

Audiovisual

OHT 12 (Quick Start), 16 (Grammar)
Audio Program CD 16, Track 2, Activity 5

Technology

Online Workbook, U6E1
Take-Home Tutor CD-ROM, U6E1

Quick Start Review

♻ Preterite and imperfect review

Use OHT 12 or write on the board:
Conjugate each verb in (a) the preterite
and (b) in the imperfect:

1. ir
2. ver
3. ser

Answers
1. a. fui, fuiste, fue, fuimos, fuisteis, fueron
   b. iba, ibas, iba, íbamos, ibais, iban
2. a. vi, viste, vio, vimos, visteis, vieron
   b. veía, veías, veía, veíamos, veíais, veían
3. a. fui, fuiste, fue, fuimos, fuisteis, fueron
   b. era, eras, era, éramos, erais, eran

Objectives for Activities 5–16
• Narrate in the past • Express doubt and certainty • Report what others say • Talk about television

 **REPASO**   **Preterite vs. Imperfect**

▶ Remember there are two different tenses to speak about the past, the preterite and the imperfect.

Use the preterite: • to describe a past action with a specific beginning and ending.

Encendí la tele, **vi** las noticias y luego la **apagué.**
*I **turned on** the TV, **saw** the news, and then **turned** it **off.***

Use the imperfect: • to talk about past actions without saying when
they began or ended.

Eran las once de la mañana y **llovía.**
*It **was** eleven o'clock in the morning and it **was** raining.*

> You use
> the imperfect to talk
> about time and describe
> weather in the past.

• to describe habitual or repeated, or two
simultaneous actions in the past.

Cuando **éramos** chicos, **mirábamos** los dibujos animados.
*When we **were** children, we **used to watch** cartoons.*

▶ When you use the imperfect and preterite together, use the
imperfect to tell what was going on in the background
and the preterite to express what happened.

Cuando **vi** que **transmitían** un programa que no
me **interesaba, cambié** de canal.
*When I **saw** that they **were broadcasting** a program
that **didn't interest** me, I **changed** channels.*

▶ Some verbs have different
meanings in the preterite
and imperfect.

	preterite	imperfect
saber	supe *I found out*	sabía *I knew*
conocer	conocí *I met*	conocía *I knew, used to know (a person/place)*
querer	quise *I tried to*	quería *I wanted*
no querer	no quise *I refused to*	no quería *I didn't want*
poder	pude *I could (and did)*	podía *I was able to (but didn't necessarily do it)*
tener	tuve *I got*	tenía *I had*

Practice: **Actividades**
5 6 7
   Más práctica *cuaderno p. 141*
   Para hispanohablantes *cuaderno p. 139*
 **Online Workbook**
CLASSZONE.COM

Classroom Community

Group Activity Working in groups of 3, have
student tell each other what TV programs they and
their family members liked to watch when they were
children: **Cuando yo era niño(a), me gustaba ver...**
A mi hermano Carlos, le gustaba ver...

Storytelling Have students work in pairs to write the
story for an episode/scene of a television program or
movie they have seen. Remind them to use the imperfect
to describe the scene, what people are like, and habitual/
repeated actions, and to use the preterite for actions
that were completed at a specified time. Pairs can read
their stories to the class to see if they can guess what
program or movie the episode/scene is from.

5 La escritora

Escuchar/*Escribir* Estás viendo un documental sobre escritores famosos. Escucha la entrevista con la escritora. Decide si ella siempre hacía las cosas indicadas, o si las hizo sólo una vez.

modelo

ir al cine los domingos
Siempre lo hacía.

1. ver una comedia nueva
2. enfermarse
3. escribir un guión
4. escribir por horas
5. decirles a sus padres que iba a ser famosa
6. darse cuenta de que iba a ser escritora

6 Cuando era niño(a)

Escribir Quieres comparar tus hábitos relacionados a la tele cuando eras pequeño(a) con tus hábitos de hoy. Escribe dos oraciones: en la primera, emplea el imperfecto y en la segunda emplea el pretérito. Sigue el modelo.

modelo

Cuando era niño(a), veía los dibujos animados el sábado por la mañana. Este sábado por la mañana vi videos musicales.

ver los dibujos animados

ir al cine a ver películas de horror

pasar horas enfrente de la tele

hacer la tarea antes de encender la tele

participar en los concursos en la tele

pelearse por el control remoto

7 El (La) guionista

Escribir Eres el (la) guionista de un documental sobre una persona que admiras mucho. ¿Sobre quién es el documental? En la primera escena cuenta la historia de su vida. ¿Cómo era cuando era joven? ¿Qué pasó para cambiar su vida? Escribe la narración de la primera escena. Usa tu imaginación.

modelo

Adela Quiñones era una muchacha sencilla, de una familia muy unida. Cuando tenía diez años, pensaba que el mundo era como una película. Pensaba que los finales siempre serían felices. Pero entonces, un día, todo cambió…

More Practice: **Más comunicación** *p. R18*

Teaching Suggestions
Reviewing Preterite vs. Imperfect

Write the following sentences on the board:
Anoche vi un programa muy interesante.
Eran las doce y dormía en frente del televisor.
Veía la tele cuando llegó Arturo.
Cuando yo era chica, me gustaba ver dibujos animados.
Ask students to explain why each verb tense was used.

 Objective: Controlled practice
Listening comprehension/preterite vs. imperfect

Answers (See script, p. 401D.)
1. Siempre lo hacía.
2. Lo hizo.
3. Lo hizo.
4. Lo hizo.
5. Siempre lo hacía.
6. Lo hizo.

 Objective: Transitional practice
Preterite vs. imperfect in writing

Answers will vary.

Objective: Open-ended practice
Preterite vs. imperfect in writing

Answers will vary.

Dictation

Using the Listening Activity Script for **Actividad 5** on TE p. 401D, dictate selected sentences to students. You may want to use this dictation for a quiz grade.

Teaching All Students

Extra Help Have students write about 3 TV programs they wanted to watch last week, but couldn't. They should also explain why. **La semana pasada quería ver... pero no pude porque...**

Multiple Intelligences

Kinesthetic Have students talk about and act out what famous actors/actresses did on shows they watched when they were kids. Encourage creativity and humor.

Block Schedule

Variety Have students write a paragraph describing the plot of a short story/novel that they read a long time ago. **Hace... años yo leí un cuento/ una novela...** (For additional activities, see **Block Scheduling Copymasters**.)

Teaching Resource Options

Print

Más práctica Workbook PE, p. 142
Cuaderno para hispanohablantes
PE, p. 140
Block Scheduling Copymasters
Unit 6 Resource Book
Más práctica Workbook TE, p. 8
Cuaderno para hispanohablantes
TE, p. 24
Absent Student Copymasters, p. 38

Audiovisual

OHT 13 (Quick Start), 17 (Grammar)

Technology

Online Workbook, U6E1
Take-Home Tutor CD-ROM, U6E1

Quick Start Review

 Indicative and subjunctive

Use OHT 13 or write on the board:
Write whether the underlined verb is in
the indicative or the subjunctive:

1. Es importante que <u>venga</u> a las
   ocho.
2. Mamá dice que <u>veo</u> mucha
   televisión.
3. Sé que el programa <u>es</u> largo.
4. Quieren que <u>lleguemos</u>
   temprano.
5. Prefieren que <u>escribas</u> otra carta.

Answers
1. subjunctive
2. indicative
3. indicative
4. subjunctive
5. subjunctive

REPASO **Indicative vs. Subjunctive**

You can use the **indicative** or the **subjunctive** after some conjunctions or verbs, depending
on what you want to express.

Use the **indicative** after these phrases:	Use the **subjunctive** after these phrases:
• when the outcome of the action is **certain**.	• when the outcome of the action is **uncertain** or after a **command**.

cuando   tan pronto como   en cuanto

después (de) que   hasta que

Esperaron hasta que terminó la fiesta.	Te **llamaré cuando** vengan nuestros amigos.
They waited until the party ended.	*I'll call you when (as soon as) our friends come.*
• after verbs and phrases that indicate certainty or opinion.	• after verbs and phrases that indicate **doubt** or **disbelief**.
No dudo que quieren venir.	**Es dudoso que** puedan venir.
I don't doubt that they want to come.	*It's doubtful they'll be able to come.*

You use the **subjunctive** after **aunque,** *although,* if you are **not sure** about whether the
action of the subordinate clause is happening or not.

indicative: I know it's bad.	*subjunctive: I'm not sure if it's bad.*
Tengo que salir **aunque** hace mal tiempo.	Tengo que salir **aunque** haga mal tiempo.
I have to go out even though the weather is bad.	*I have to go out even though the weather may be bad.*

Practice: **Actividades** 8 9 10   **Más práctica** *cuaderno p. 142*   **Para hispanohablantes** *cuaderno p. 140*    **Online Workbook** CLASSZONE.COM

Nota cultural

Las telenovelas son muy populares en Latinoamérica. México, Venezuela y Argentina son
los productores principales de este tipo de programación, que además de verse en su país
de origen, se exporta a otros países. Las de mayor éxito pueden llegar a los canales
hispanos de Estados Unidos, como por ejemplo "La venganza", Vale todo" y "Las vías del
amor". Al contrario de las telenovelas americanas, la mayoría de las telenovelas en español
tienen un comienzo, un desarrollo y un final, ¡generalmente feliz!

412   cuatrocientos doce
Unidad 6

Classroom Community

Group Activity Divide the class into groups of 6.
Students in each group make 2 sets of cards with the
6 conjunctions on this page. One card from each set is
given to each student. The group leader calls on
students to give either an indicative or subjunctive
sentence, using the conjunctions the student has.

Paired Activity First, have each student make a list
of things he/she plans to do in the future. Then,
working in pairs, have students use the expressions
cuando, en cuanto, hasta que, tan pronto como, and
después de que to tell when they will do these things.

8 Mis amigos venezolanos

Hablar/*Escribir* Estás en casa de unos amigos venezolanos. Oyes comentarios sobre varias cosas. Completa las oraciones con el indicativo o el subjuntivo según el contexto.

modelo

yo: *tener el dinero*

Compraré una videocasetera tan pronto como tenga el dinero.

1. nosotros: terminar la cena
   Pondré la tele tan pronto como _____.
2. yo: encontrar el video
   Grabaré el programa tan pronto como _____.
3. nosotros: comprar el televisor
   Tendremos que pedir el servicio de cable después que _____.
4. ellos: encontrar un programa de dibujos animados
   Los niños no estarán felices hasta que _____.
5. sus padres: llegar a casa
   Apagaron el televisor cuando _____.
6. el programa: empezar
   Cambiaré de canal en cuanto _____.

Vocabulario

La televisión

la antena parabólica *satellite dish*
cambiar de canal *to change channels*
grabar *to record*
la televisión por cable *cable television*
la televisión por satélite *satellite television*
la videocasetera *videocassette recorder*
el control remoto *remote control*

▶ ¿Cuáles de estos aparatos tienes en casa?

9 ¡Es dudoso!

Hablar/*Escribir* Tú y tu compañero(a) nunca están de acuerdo en sus opiniones sobre las novelas que han leído o las películas que han visto. Sigan el modelo.

modelo

ser buena novelista

Tú: *Es buena novelista.*

Compañero(a): *Dudo que sea buena novelista. Sus novelas son aburridas.*

1. final ser predecible
2. tener un estilo moderno
3. escribir prosa buena
4. ser su primera película como director
5. tener que filmar esa escena otra vez
6. preparar un guión corto
7. llamar a buenos actores
8. usar música clásica
9. hacer una película de su novela
10. ¿…?

Teaching All Students

Extra Help Have students complete the following sentences:

- Te pido que mañana vengas tan pronto como...
- Puedes tomar vacaciones hasta que...
- Debes encender la televisión cuando...

Multiple Intelligences

Intrapersonal Have students write 5 sentences describing what they doubt will happen at home or at school next week.

Verbal Have students hypothesize about what characters on shows they watch will do, using expressions such as **cuando, en cuanto,** etc.

Teaching Suggestions
Reviewing Indicative vs. Subjunctive

- Have students brainstorm one list of expressions that express doubt (**dudo, es dudoso, no creo,** etc.) and another list of expressions that express certainty (**creo, estoy seguro[a], no dudo, es verdad,** etc.).
- Have students create contrasting models with **aunque** and explain the difference in meaning when they use the indicative vs. the subjunctive.

Teaching Vocabulary

- **Plan ahead:** Bring in ads to illustrate each of the vocabulary words. Use the ads for presentation and practice.
- Challenge students to write sentences with as many of the vocabulary words as possible.

ACTIVIDAD 8 Objective: Controlled practice
Indicative vs. subjunctive/vocabulary

Answers
1. terminemos la cena
2. encuentre el video
3. pedimos el servicio de televisión por cable
4. encuentren un programa de dibujos animados
5. sus padres llegaron a casa
6. empiece el programa

ACTIVIDAD 9 Objective: Transitional practice
Indicative vs. subjunctive in conversation

♻ Literature/movies vocabulary

Answers
1. A: El final es predecible. B: Dudo que el final sea predecible. 2. A: Tiene un estilo moderno. B: Dudo que tenga un estilo moderno. 3. A: Escribe prosa buena. B: Dudo que escriba prosa buena. 4. A: Es su primera película como director. B: Dudo que sea su primera película como director. 5. A: Tienen que filmar esa escena otra vez. B: Dudo que tengan que filmar esa escena otra vez. 6. A: Preparan un guión corto. B: Dudo que preparen un guión corto. 7. A: Llaman a buenos actores. B: Dudo que llamen a buenos actores. 8. A: Usa música clásica. B: Dudo que use música clásica. 9. A: Hace una película de su novela. B: Dudo que haga una película de su novela. 10. *Answers will vary.*

Teaching Resource Options

Print

Más práctica Workbook PE, p. 143
Cuaderno para hispanohablantes
  PE, p. 141
Unit 6 Resource Book
  Más práctica Workbook TE, p. 9
  Cuaderno para hispanohablantes
    TE, p. 25
  Absent Student Copymasters,
    pp. 38–39
  Audioscript, p. 43

Audiovisual

OHT 13 (Quick Start), 18–19 (Grammar)
Audio Program CD 16, Track 3, Activity 11

Technology

Online Workbook, U6E1
Take-Home Tutor CD-ROM, U6E1

 Objective: Open-ended practice
Indicative vs. subjunctive in conversation

Answers will vary.

Quick Start Review

🔄 Conditional

Use OHT 13 or write on the board:
Use the conditional to tell what Jorge
would do if he won the lottery:

1. celebrar con su familia
2. poner dinero en el banco
3. comprar un carro
4. salir de viaje con sus amigos
5. tener un asistente personal

Answers
1. Celebraría con su familia.
2. Pondría dinero en el banco.
3. Compraría un carro.
4. Saldría de viaje con sus amigos.
5. Tendría un asistente personal.

Teaching Suggestions
Reviewing Reported Speech

Give students some sample sentences
and have them tell you if it's a present
tense command, present tense reported
speech, or past tense reported speech.

---

10 Los hermanos Saldívar

STRATEGY: SPEAKING

Negotiate Negotiation is
the art of reaching an
agreement in which
everyone wins. In order
to reach an agreement,
set conditions for doing
something later that both
want: **Te daré el control
remoto tan pronto
como empiece nuestro
programa favorito.**

Hablar Los hermanos Saldívar
se pelean siempre porque cada
uno quiere quedarse con el
control remoto. Con un
compañero(a), haz el papel de
los hermanos. ¡Sean creativos!

modelo

Tú: *Dame el control remoto.*

Compañero(a): *Te daré el control
remoto en cuanto
termines la tarea.*

REPASO Reported Speech

You have learned two ways to indicate what someone is saying:

Direct quote:	Carlos: «No salgo». *Carlos: "I'm not going out."*	**Reported Speech:**	Carlos **dice que** no sale. *Carlos **says** he's not going out.*

You use the **indicative** to summarize what someone said.

- When you report what someone **said** (*dijo*), you use one of the **past tenses** or the **conditional**.

Carlos **dijo que** **no salía**. *Carlos **said** he wasn't going out.*	Carlos **dijo que** **no saldría**. *Carlos **said** he wouldn't go out.*

- When you report what someone **says** or **is saying** (*dice*), you use the **present tense**, **future tense** or **ir + a + infinitive**.

Carlos **dice que** **no saldrá**. *Carlos **says** he won't go out.*	Carlos **dice que** **no va a salir**. *Carlos **says** he is not going out.*

Remember that if you are using **decir** to indicate what someone tells another person to do, you use the **subjunctive** to express that idea.

Carlos **dice que** **no salgas**. *Carlos **is telling you** not to go out.*

Practice: Actividades 12 13	**Más práctica** *cuaderno p. 143* **Para hispanohablantes** *cuaderno p. 141*	 **Online Workbook** CLASSZONE.COM

11 Jorge

Escuchar/Escribir Escuchas la conversación de Jorge.
Mientras escuchas, tu hermanita te pregunta qué dice Jorge.
Más tarde, tu hermanito te pregunta qué dijo Jorge.

modelo

¿Qué dice? Dice que irá al cine esta tarde.

¿Qué dijo? Dijo que iría al cine esta tarde.

1. ¿Qué dice? / ¿Qué dijo?
2. ¿Qué dice? / ¿Qué dijo?
3. ¿Qué dice? / ¿Qué dijo?
4. ¿Qué dice? / ¿Qué dijo?

Classroom Community

Cooperative Learning Have students work in
groups of 3. Student 1 gives a direct quote of
something someone said. Student 2 rephrases it using
reported speech. Student 3 records the answer. Then
the group works together to check grammar and
spelling accuracy of the sentence. Student 2 begins the
next round. Groups continue until they complete 6
sentences.

Paired Activity Have students work in pairs to talk
about what people at school are saying or have said
this week. Have them keep track of what they already
knew by responding **No sabía que dijo eso** or **Ya
sabía que dijo eso.** Then have them make a tally of
what they each knew vs. what they both knew.

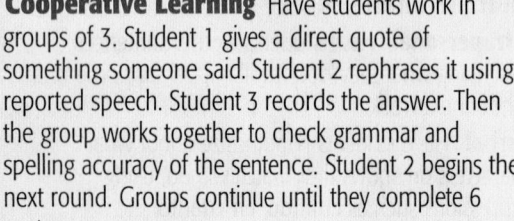

12 Tu papá dijo...

Hablar/*Escribir* Estás cuidando a tu primito(a) de nueve años y le dices las instrucciones que le dijo su papá.

modelo

Tu papá me dijo que te acostaras a las nueve.

hacer la tarea

cepillarte los dientes

(no) hablar por teléfono con tus amigos antes de cenar

(no) navegar por Internet

(no) ver esa película prohibida para menores esta noche

obedecerme todo el tiempo

13 Mi novio(a)

Hablar Hablas por teléfono con tu novio(a). Tu mejor amigo(a) quiere saber lo que te está diciendo. Cuéntale a tu amigo(a) qué te dice tu novio(a).

modelo

Compañero(a): *¿Qué dice? o ¿Qué dijo?*

Tú: *Dice que vendrá a verme esta tarde. o Dijo que vendría a verme esta tarde.*

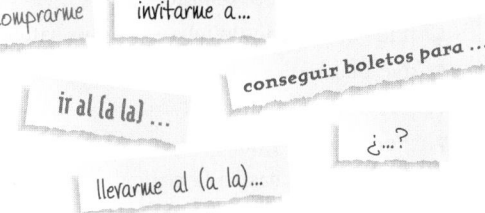

comprarme   invitarme a...

ir al (a la) ...   conseguir boletos para ...

¿...?

llevarme al (a la)...

GRAMÁTICA   Sequence of Tenses

You have already learned a number of indicative and subjunctive tenses in Spanish. Here's a guide to how they work together.

Indicative verb in the main clause: Subjunctive verb in the subordinate clause:

With **present** **present** **perfect**	Quiero que **cambies** de canal. He dicho que no **mires** ese programa. Me alegro de que **hayas grabado** el programa.	use **present subjunctive** or **present perfect subjunctive**
With **preterite** **imperfect** **past perfect** **conditional**	Te dije que **cambiaras** de canal. Quería que **miraras** ese programa. Te había dicho que no **miraras** ese programa. Preferiría que no **hubieras grabado** el programa.	use **imperfect subjunctive** or **past perfect subjunctive**

Practice: **Actividades**    **Más práctica** *cuaderno p. 144*   **Online Workbook** CLASSZONE.COM
Para hispanohablantes *cuaderno p. 142*

Teaching All Students

Extra Help Have each student tell what someone said (especially a parent or sibling) before they came to school today.

Multiple Intelligences

Interpersonal Have students work in pairs. Students take turns playing a movie critic who gives 5 sentences of praise or criticism of a movie. The other student reports what the movie critic said.

Verbal Have students circulate and ask 5 classmates for a direct quote, such as their opinion of a book or movie they have seen. Then have them report the quotes to the class.

---

 11 Objective: Controlled practice Listening comprehension/reported speech

Answers (See script, p. 401D.)
1. Dice que buscará una película de acción. / Dijo que buscaría una película de acción.
2. Dice que verá la nueva película de su actor favorito. / Dijo que vería la nueva película de su actor favorito.
3. Dice que vaya su amigo con él. / Dijo que fuera su amigo con él.
4. Dice que invitará a su hermano. / Dijo que invitaría a su hermano.

12 Objective: Transitional practice Reported speech

Answers
Answers will vary. Sample answers:
Tu papá me dijo que hicieras la tarea.
Tu papá me dijo que te cepillaras los dientes.
Tu papá me dijo que no hablaras por teléfono con tus amigos.
Tu papá me dijo que no navegaras por Internet.
Tu papá me dijo que no vieras esa película prohibida para menores.
Tu papá me dijo que me obedecieras.

 13 Objective: Open-ended practice Reported speech in conversation

Answers will vary.

Quick Start Review

♻ Subjunctive review

Use OHT 13 or write on the board: Give the present subjunctive, the present perfect subjunctive, and the imperfect subjunctive of each verb.

1. yo / saber   4. nosotros / leer
2. tú / decir   5. ella / estudiar
3. Uds. / pedir

Answers
1. yo sepa, yo haya sabido, yo supiera
2. tú digas, tú hayas dicho, tú dijeras
3. Uds. pidan, Uds. hayan pedido, Uds. pidieran
4. nosotros leamos, nosotros hayamos leído, nosotros leyéramos
5. ella estudie, ella haya estudiado, ella estudiara

Teaching Suggestions
Teaching Sequence of Tenses

• Have students make an organized list of expressions that require the subjunctive.
• Have students work in small groups to make models of specific subjunctive patterns. Divide up the task so that all patterns learned are covered.

Teaching Resource Options

Print
Más práctica Workbook PE,
  pp. 137–140, 144
Actividades para todos Workbook PE,
  pp. 161–166
Cuaderno para hispanohablantes
  PE, pp. 137–138, 142
Block Scheduling Copymasters
Unit 6 Resource Book
  Más práctica Workbook TE,
    pp. 3–6, 10
  Actividades para todos Workbook TE,
    pp. 11–16
  Cuaderno para hispanohablantes
    TE, pp. 21–22, 26
  Information Gap Activities, p. 30
  Absent Student Copymasters, p. 39

Technology
Online Workbook, U6E1
Take-Home Tutor CD-ROM, U6E1

Teaching Suggestions
Teaching Vocabulary
Have each student use at least 2 of the words from the **Vocabulario** to describe a show, program, or movie they know.

 **Objective:** Controlled practice
Sequence of tenses/vocabulary

♻ Present perfect

Answers
1. He dicho que apagues la tele.
2. He dicho que no veas ese programa sensacionalista.
3. He dicho que me des el control remoto.
4. He dicho que pidas el servicio de televisión por satélite.
5. He dicho que no manipules a tus hermanos.
6. He dicho que no discutas conmigo.
7. He dicho que pongas otro programa.
8. He dicho que no le hagas caso a la crítica.
9. He dicho que bajes el volumen.
10. He dicho que me traigas palomitas de maíz.

Práctica: gramática y vocabulario continuación

⑭ Abuelo
Hablar/*Escribir* Tu abuelo viene de visita. Cree que no oyes lo que te pide. ¿Qué te dice?

modelo
¡Cambia de canal!
He dicho que cambies de canal.

1. ¡Apaga la tele!
2. ¡No veas ese programa sensacionalista!
3. ¡Dame el control remoto!
4. ¡Pide el servicio de televisión por satélite!
5. ¡No manipules a tus hermanos!
6. ¡No discutas conmigo!
7. ¡Pon otro programa!
8. ¡No le hagas caso a la crítica!
9. ¡Baja el volumen!
10. ¡Tráeme palomitas de maíz!

Vocabulario

La crítica

controlar *to control*
entretenido(a) *entertaining*
influir *to influence*
manipular *to manipulate*
la percepción *perception*
el público *audience*
la reacción crítica *critical response*
sensacionalista *sensationalized*

▶ ¿Crees que la televisión nos influye mucho? ¿Por qué?

⑮ El (La) director(a)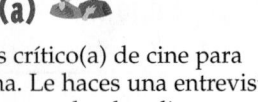
Hablar/*Escribir* Eres crítico(a) de cine para una revista boliviana. Le haces una entrevista a un(a) director(a) que acaba de salir con una película muy bien recibida. Dramatiza la situación con tu compañero(a).

modelo
Tú: *La película le gustó al público.*
Compañero(a): *Me alegro de que la película le haya gustado al público.*

1. La reacción de los críticos ha sido muy positiva.
2. El público ha dicho que la película es entretenida.
3. El público ha comparado su trabajo al de Bergman.
4. Por fin usted ha completado su obra maestra.
5. A usted lo han invitado al festival de cine en Cannes.
6. La película ha recibido diez nominaciones para el premio Óscar.

Nota cultural
Cuando le haces una invitación a otra persona, debes usar la frase «Te invito». Por ejemplo, si haces una fiesta en tu casa, puedes decir «Te invito a mi fiesta». Y si quieres invitar a alguien a comer, debes decir, «Te invito a comer…» Pero… ¡cuidado! En los países de habla hispana, si «invitas» a alguien a comer o a tomar un refresco, tú debes pagar.

Classroom Community

Learning Scenario Have students work in pairs to create and present a skit between a TV talk show host and a movie/television director. The skit should use the grammar and vocabulary in **Actividades** 14 and 15.

Portfolio Have students videotape or record their skits from the "Learning Scenario" to place in their portfolios.

Rubric A = 13–15 pts. B = 10–12 pts. C = 7–9 pts. D = 4–6 pts. F = < 4 pts.

Writing criteria	Scale
Grammar accuracy	1 2 3 4 5
Originality	1 2 3 4 5
Fluency	1 2 3 4 5

16 El documental

Hablar/Leer Están reunidos para estudiar juntos y ven que hay un documental en la televisión. En grupos de tres o cuatro lean la descripción del documental. Hablen de por qué quisieran verlo o no usando frases como **pienso que, dudo que, tan pronto como, en cuanto, hasta que** y **después de que.**

modelo

Tú: *Pienso que si viera el documental de los osos polares, no podría terminar mi trabajo a tiempo. No lo quiero ver.*

Compañero(a) 1: *Yo lo voy a ver en cuanto termine de leer este capítulo.*

Compañero(a) 2: *No creo que puedas terminar tu trabajo sin ver el documental…*

Documentales 3

Osos polares, los señores del Ártico

El mayor carnívoro del mundo tiene su reducto en el Ártico, en las regiones polares del norte del planeta. Durante más de 100 mil años los osos polares han sido los señores supremos de esta tierra de hielo y nieve, pero su señorío acaba donde comienza la aldea de Churchill, en Canadá.

Viernes, 20.00h Canal 3

Activity 17 brings together all concepts presented.

17 Mis reacciones

Hablar En grupos de tres o cuatro, hablen sobre alguna película o teleserie que hayan visto recientemente. Hablen sobre los temas en la lista y los que les interesen.

modelo

Tú: *¿Viste la película Mi tío, el ladrón?*

Compañero(a) 1: *Sí, claro, ¿quién no la ha visto?*

Compañero(a) 2: *Es una comedia muy buena.*

Compañero(a) 3: *¿Qué pensaste de…es más divertida?*

Compañero(a) 4: *¿Creo que la película…?*

el género (acción, drama, etc.)
la reacción crítica (¿cuántas estrellas?)
la percepción del público
los actores
¿…?

More Practice: **Online Workbook**
Más comunicación *p. R18* CLASSZONE.COM

Refrán

Lo futuro aún no ha llegado y lo presente es casi pasado.

¿Qué quiere decir el refrán? En tu opinión, ¿qué comentario hace sobre el tiempo? ¿Crees que el tiempo pasa rápido para personas de todas edades? ¿Pasa más rápido cuando uno es joven o mayor (o adulto)?

cuatrocientos diecisiete
Colombia, Venezuela y los países andinos Etapa 1 **417**

15 Objective: Transitional practice
Sequence of tenses in conversation

Answers
1. Me alegro de que la reacción de los críticos haya sido muy positiva.
2. Me alegro de que el público haya dicho que la película es entretenida.
3. Me alegro de que el público haya comparado mi trabajo al de Bergman.
4. Me alegro de que por fin haya completado mi obra maestra.
5. Me alegro de que me hayan invitado al festival de cine en Cannes.
6. Me alegro de que la película haya recibido diez nominaciones para el premio Óscar.

16 Objective: Open-ended practice
Sequence of tenses in reading and conversation

Answers will vary.

17 Objective: Open-ended practice
Sequence of tenses in conversation

Answers will vary.

Interdisciplinary Connection

Social Studies Have students research the history of television and create a timeline of the important dates. On the timeline they might also include the names of 1–2 popular shows in each 5-year time span.

Block Schedule

Variety Have students work in pairs to role-play 2 parents or 2 teachers. One gives a child or student a command (**Lee la página 10**) and the other repeats the command as if the child or student did not hear well (**Dijo que leyeras la página 10**). (You or another student can play the role of the child/student.) (For additional activities, see **Block Scheduling Copymasters**.)

Teaching All Students

Extra Help Ask yes/no questions that establish a subjunctive pattern. For example, **¿Te alegras de que no haya examen esta semana?** or **¿Querías que viéramos una telenovela en clase?**

Native Speakers Have students imagine they are a movie reviewer and write a 1-page review of their favorite movie. Then have them present their review to the class.

Multiple Intelligences

Kinesthetic Have students use the **Vocabulario** on p. 416 to describe and act out a movie or TV program they have seen.

Logical/Mathematical Have students take a poll to find out what kinds of programs their classmates watch, how many hours per week, etc. Have them translate that information into a bar graph or pie chart.

Teaching Resource Options

Print

Actividades para todos Workbook PE, pp. 167–169

Block Scheduling Copymasters
Unit 6 Resource Book
Actividades para todos Workbook TE, pp. 17–19
Absent Student Copymasters, p. 40
Audioscript, p. 25

Audiovisual

OHT 14 (Quick Start)
Audio Program CD 16, Track 4–5

Technology

Online Workbook, U6E1
Take-Home Tutor CD-ROM, U6E1

Quick Start Review

♻ TV programs

Use OHT 14 or write on the board:
Write 5 sentences describing your favorite TV program.

Answers will vary.

Teaching Suggestions

- **Prereading** Have students discuss the kinds of articles usually found in soap opera magazines.
- **Strategy: Distinguish facts from interpretation** Present the Reading Strategy. Have students look at the list of 6 facts/interpretations and keep them in mind when they read.
- **Reading** Have students read through the article the first time without stopping to look up words. Then have students read a second time and write a 3–5 word description about each paragraph as they read.
- **Post-reading** Have students complete the Reading Strategy exercise.

AUDIO *En voces*
LECTURA

PARA LEER • **STRATEGY: READING**

Distinguish facts from interpretations Magazine articles offer both factual information and the author's interpretations. Based on your reading of *Brillo afuera, oscuridad en casa*, decide which of these statements are fact and which are interpretation.

1. El autor representa una perspectiva venezolana.
2. «Amor mío» es más popular en EE.UU. que en Venezuela.
3. La población hispana en EE.UU. ha aumentado. Por eso, la popularidad de programas hispanos ha aumentado también.
4. Tres programas venezolanos están entre los diez primeros espacios en popularidad.
5. Era inevitable que «Amor mío» tuviera éxito internacional.
6. Es mejor tener éxito internacional que éxito doméstico.

Use the text of the article to justify your choices.

PROGRAMAS DE TELEVISIÓN

actual	en este momento, presente
brillar	iluminar
el brillo	una luz brillante
los creadores del dramático	escritores de guion
creciente	va aumentando
emanar	tener origen en
idolatrados	admirados, populares

Farándula es una revista sobre la programación de televisión en Venezuela. Esta revista también ofrece artículos sobre actores populares de América Latina, Estados Unidos y Europa.

Introducción

Vas a leer un artículo sobre una telenovela que se llama «Amor mío», uno de los programas de origen venezolano más populares en Estados Unidos.

418 cuatrocientos dieciocho
Unidad 6

Classroom Community

Paired Activity Have students work in pairs to write a short comprehension quiz using true/false or multiple choice items. Have pairs exchange and take each other's quizzes.

Portfolio Have students write a summary of what they think the «Amor mío» plot line is.

Rubric A = 13–15 pts. B = 10–12 pts. C = 7–9 pts. D = 4–6 pts. F = < 4 pts.

Criteria	Scale
Vocabulary	1 2 3 4 5
Grammar/spelling accuracy	1 2 3 4 5
Creativity, appearance	1 2 3 4 5

Brillo afuera, oscuridad en casa

«Amor mío»: Si bien en nuestra tierra esta telenovela pasó por debajo de la mesa[1], en los Estados Unidos brilla como un sol, al estar en el primer lugar de los veinte programas más vistos de ese país. Astrid Gruber y Julio Pereira (sus protagonistas) consiguieron fuera el éxito que nunca encontraron en casa….

Los programas de habla hispana son cada vez más populares en Estados Unidos. Al parecer, la creciente población latina de ese país es la razón principal. Pero lo importante de todo esto es que en esta área le llevamos ventaja a muchas naciones, pues nuestra televisión es una de las más vistas.

Es así como en los actuales momentos, según el *ranking* que incluyen los veinte primeros espacios[2] de la televisión emanados de la Nielsen Hispanic Television, tenemos tres muy buenas posiciones. «Sábado sensacional», por su parte, ocupa el puesto número siete, «Maite» está en el puesto tres y, como gran victoria, encontramos a la novela «Amor mío» en el primer lugar.

Sus protagonistas, Astrid Gruber y Julio Pereira, son idolatrados (como nunca aquí) en los Estados Unidos al igual que los creadores del dramático que son Isamar Hernández, Ricardo García y Manuel Manzano.

Ahora sí pueden cantar victoria y no pasar por debajo de la mesa. Por tanto, demostramos que, una vez más, existe brillo afuera y oscuridad en casa.

---
[1] went unnoticed
[2] television programs

Online Workbook CLASSZONE.COM

¿Comprendiste?

1. ¿Por qué son cada vez más populares en Estados Unidos los programas en español?
2. ¿Qué programas venezolanos son más populares entre los televidentes hispanos? ¿Cómo lo sabes?
3. Según el artículo, el éxito de «Amor mío» demuestra que «existe brillo afuera y oscuridad en casa». ¿Qué quiere decir?

¿Qué piensas?

1. ¿Qué clase de programa será «Sábado sensacional»? ¿Y «Maite»?
2. ¿Por qué es «Amor mío» más popular afuera de Venezuela?

Hazlo tú

Tú eres creador(a) de una telenovela. Escribe una escena de la telenovela. Escribe cómo se titula, de qué se trata, cómo se llaman los actores y los personajes, cuál es el tema y dónde y cuándo sucede la acción.

Culture Highlights

● **PROGRAMAS EN ESPAÑOL EN EE.UU.**
Muchos de los programas de televisión en español mostrados en Estados Unidos son importados de México, Venezuela y Argentina. En los últimos años, sin embargo, algunas cadenas de televisión basadas en Miami han comenzado a producir programas en Estados Unidos.
Pregúnteles a los estudiantes qué pueden inferir sobre el uso del español basándose en la información sobre este cambio.

Cross Cultural Connections
Strategy Have students think about the cultural role of television. How does TV programming reflect the values of a culture? What can students interpret about a culture from a list of a country's top 5 shows?

¿Comprendiste?
Answers
1. La creciente población latina de nuestro país es la razón principal. Pero también nuestra televisión es una de las más vistas.
2. «Sábado sensacional», «Maite» y «Amor mío» son programas venezolanos populares. Es así según el *ranking* de la Nilsen Hispanic Televisión.
3. Quiere decir que en su país de origen la telenovela no es popular, pero fuera del país sí lo es.

Teaching All Students

Extra Help Have students work in pairs to ask each other a series of yes/no or simple-answer questions about the reading.

Native Speakers Have students write an article about a different **telenovela** shown on Spanish-language television.

Multiple Intelligences
Interpersonal Have students talk about their favorite kind of soap opera character. As a class, determine which kind of character is most popular among students and why.

Block Schedule
Change of Pace Soap operas normally have several type-cast characters. Have students list the types of characters a soap opera would include. (For additional activities, see **Block Scheduling Copymasters.**)

Teaching Resource Options

Print

Cuaderno para hispanohablantes PE,
  pp. 143–144

Block Scheduling Copymasters

Unit 6 Resource Book
  Cuaderno para hispanohablantes
    TE, pp. 27–28
  Information Gap Activities, pp. 31–32
  Family Involvement, pp. 41–42

Audiovisual

OHT 15 (Quick Start)

Technology

eTest Plus Online/eTest Generator
  CD-ROM

 www.classzone.com

Quick Start Review

♻ **Verb tense review**

Use OHT 15 or write on the board:
Match each verb tense to an
underlined verb in each sentence:

a. present indicative   e. future
b. present subjunctive   f. conditional
c. imperfect indicative g. imperfect
d. preterite   subjunctive

1. __ Ana dice que <u>irá</u> con nosotros.
2. __ Mario <u>llegó</u> a las seis.
3. __ Nos alegramos de que se <u>casaran</u>.
4. __ Creo que los músicos <u>son</u> venezolanos.
5. __ Paloma <u>quería</u> dormir un rato.
6. __ Juan dijo que <u>haría</u> la cama después.
7. __ Dudo que <u>haya</u> suficiente dinero.

Answers
1. e 2. d 3. g 4. a 5. c 6. f 7. b

Teaching Suggestions
What Have Students Learned?

Have students look at the "Now you can…" notes and give examples of each category. Have them spend extra time reviewing categories they feel they are weak in by consulting the "To review" notes.

ETAPA **1**

Now you can...

• narrate in the past.

To review

• preterite vs. imperfect, see p. 410.

Now you can...

• express doubt and certainty.

To review

• indicative vs. subjunctive, see p. 412.

En uso
REPASO Y MÁS COMUNICACIÓN

1 El viaje inolvidable

Viste una película venezolana en la tele titulada *El viaje inolvidable*. Completa la narración de la película para saber cómo se sintió la protagonista de la película. Usa el pretérito o el imperfecto de los verbos entre paréntesis.

Cuando __1__ (ser) chica, mis padres __2__ (decidir) que __3__ (ir) a vivir en Venezuela. ¡Yo __4__ (estar) aterrorizada! No __5__ (saber) hablar español y tampoco __6__ (querer) dejar atrás mis amiguitos de clase.

__7__ (Ser) un día muy bonito cuando nos __8__ (despedir) de los vecinos y de la familia. Yo __9__ (estar) muy triste. No __10__ (poder) imaginar cómo __11__ (ir) a ser mi nueva vida.

Pero en fin, no __12__ (tener) de qué preocuparme. Me __13__ (encantar) Venezuela y ahora como adulta no puedo imaginar cómo hubiera sido mi vida sin ese viaje inolvidable.

2 La conversación telefónica

Hablas con un(a) amigo(a) colombiano(a) por teléfono. Completa sus oraciones para saber qué te dijo. Usa el indicativo o el subjuntivo de los verbos entre paréntesis.

modelo

«Te llamé tan pronto como supe que iban a dar esa película que querías ver. ¿Por qué no hacemos planes para ir a verla?» (yo: saber)

1. «¡Hola! Mis primos van a venir tan pronto como _____ la tarea. ¿Quieres venir?». (terminar)
2. «¡Espera! Primero tenemos que comer así que iremos al cine después de que _____ el almuerzo. ¿Luego te llamo?». (tomar)
3. «¡Hola, Julio! Invita a tus hermanos. No dudo que _____ venir». (querer)
4. «¡Buenas tardes, Sra. Díaz! Nos quedaremos en el centro comercial hasta que (usted) _____ por nosotros». (venir)
5. «Mamá nos llevará a la discoteca después de que nos _____. ¿Te vea a las?». (reunir)
6. «¡Hola, Luis! La semana pasada, fuimos a comer después de que _____ de la discoteca. ¿Quieres ir de nuevo.». (nosotros: salir)

420

cuatrocientos veinte
Unidad 6

Classroom Community

Storytelling Have students work in pairs to create a picture story using simple drawings. They should narrate the story using the imperfect and preterite. Present or display the picture stories in class.

Group Activity Have students work in small groups and imagine they are the principal writers for a TV soap opera. Ask them to write a list of characters and the role each plays in the show.

Self-Check Quiz
CLASSZONE.COM

Now you can...
- talk about television.

To review
- sequence of tenses, see p. 415.

③ Entre hermanos

Mario y Miguel son hermanos. ¡Siempre se pelean! Completa su diálogo con la forma correcta de los verbos entre paréntesis para ver quién se quedó con el control remoto.

Mario: Quiero que ___1___ de canal, por favor. (cambiar)

Miguel: Pero yo quiero ver este programa.

Mario: ¡Te dije que ___2___ de canal! (cambiar)

Miguel: ¡Yo tengo el control remoto y digo que no!

Mario: He dicho que me ___3___ el control remoto. (dar)

Miguel: Preferiría que te ___4___ a tu cuarto. (ir)

Mario: Voy a llamar a papá.

Miguel: Llámalo. He dicho que te ___5___ a tu cuarto. (ir)

Papá: Bien. Denme el control remoto. No va a haber televisión por tres días.

Mario: ¡Te dije que ___6___ caso! (hacerme)

Now you can...
- report what others say.

To review
- reported speech, see p. 414.

④ El (La) hermano(a) mayor

Los padres de Antonio salieron a cenar con unos amigos y lo dejaron a él en casa. Ahora él te cuenta todo lo que dijo su mamá.

modelo

«Mamá dijo que no trabajara en la computadora».

 1.

 2.

 3.

 4.

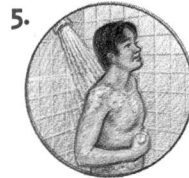 5.

 6.

Answers

Paragraph 1
1. era
2. decidieron
3. íbamos
4. estaba
5. sabía
6. quería

Paragraph 2
7. Era
8. despedimos
9. estaba
10. podía
11. iba

Paragraph 3
12. tenía
13. encantó

Answers

1. terminen
2. tomemos
3. quieren
4. venga
5. reunamos
6. salimos

Answers

1. cambies
2. cambiaras
3. des
4. fueras
5. vayas
6. me hicieras

④ **Answers**

1. Mamá dijo que limpiara mi cuarto.
2. Mamá dijo que lavara la ropa.
3. Mamá dijo que no vieras la televisión.
4. Mamá dijo que hiciera ejercicio.
5. Mamá dijo que me duchara.
6. Mamá dijo que no hablara por teléfono.

Block Schedule

Personalization Have students write 5 sentences about things their parents tell them not to do. Then have students work in groups of 4 and compare their lists with the other students. Have the groups make a list of the things they all have in common. Then pool the lists of all groups and determine which are common to the entire class. (For additional activities, see **Block Scheduling Copymasters**.)

Teaching All Students

Extra Help Before completing **Actividad 3**, work with students to make a list of possible verb tenses and review when and why each is used.

Multiple Intelligences

Verbal Give individual students a direct command or give them a piece of information; for example, **Haz la Actividad 4 para la tarea** or **Voy de compras mañana**. The student should report what you said to the class; for example, **Dijo que hiciera la Actividad 4 para la tarea** or **Dice que irá de compras mañana**.

Teaching Resource Options

Print

Block Scheduling Copymasters
Unit 6 Resource Book
  Audioscript, p. 46
  Vocabulary Quizzes, pp. 49–51
  Grammar Quizzes, pp. 52–53
  Etapa Exam, Forms A and B,
    pp. 54–63
  Examen para hispanohablantes,
    pp. 64–68
  Portfolio Assessment, pp. 69–70
  Multiple Choice Test Questions,
    pp. 229–231

Audiovisual

OHT 15 (Quick Start)
Audio Program CD 20, Track 15

Technology

eTest Plus Online/Test Generator
CD-ROM

  www.classzone.com

ACTIVIDAD 5

Rubric: Speaking

Criteria	Scale	
Sentence structure	1 2 3	A = 11–12 pts.
Vocabulary use	1 2 3	B = 9–10 pts.
Originality	1 2 3	C = 7–8 pts.
Fluency	1 2 3	D = 4–6 pts.
		F = < 4 pts.

ACTIVIDAD 6
En tu propia voz

Rubric: Writing

Criteria	Scale	
Vocabulary use	1 2 3 4 5	A = 13–15 pts.
Accuracy	1 2 3 4 5	B = 10–12 pts.
Creativity, appearance	1 2 3 4 5	C = 7–9 pts.
		D = 4–6 pts.
		F = < 4 pts.

Teaching Note: En tu propia voz

Writing Strategy Suggest that students develop their story. An interesting and well-planned story will hold the viewers attention. Students should remember to thoroughly develop their ideas for characters and plot.

---

5 Programas de ayer y hoy

STRATEGY: SPEAKING

Retell memories Reminiscences are memories of the past relived in the present. Tell about your childhood preferences and experiences relating to television. **(Me encantaban los dibujos animados, pero mis padres me decían que no podría verlos antes de acostarme.)** Then contrast those memories with your current tastes, experiences, and what others say to you about them. **(Anoche los vi otra vez. No me gustaron tanto.)**

En grupos de dos o tres, conversen sobre los tipos de programas que les gustaban cuando eran chicos. Compárenlos con los que les gustan ahora.

modelo

Tú: *Cuando era chico(a), me encantaban los dibujos animados.*

Compañero(a) 1: *Y, ¿ahora?*

Tú: *Ahora prefiero las películas de acción. El otro día vi una película que se titulaba…*

TÚ EN LA COMUNIDAD

Lucille es alumna en Florida. Habla español con su familia. También hablaba español en su trabajo de voluntaria en un hospital. Cuando no había enfermeras que hablaran español, ella traducía. Lucille siempre ofrece su ayuda cuando está en una tienda y ve a turistas hispanohablantes que no hablan inglés.

6 En tu propia voz

ESCRITURA Vas a inventar tu propia película o teleserie. Primero decide las siguientes cosas:

• ¿género? (aventura, acción, etc.)

• ¿título?

• ¿trama?

Ahora escribe una descripción breve de la película o teleserie. Cuando estés satisfecho(a) con tu descripción, haz un póster de tu programa. Usa fotos o dibujos para ilustrar tu concepto. Si quieres, puedes escribir un lema *(slogan)* para el programa o película.

Classroom Community

Learning Scenario Have students work in pairs. Ask them to imagine that they both are in charge of programming for a major television network. Each has a different idea as to what kind of programming should appear for the new season. Have them discuss and resolve the problem, using grammar and vocabulary from the **Etapa.**

Paired Activity Have students work in pairs to rewrite the ending of a popular program or movie. Then have them present their endings. Let the class determine which endings were more effective, the original or the rewritten ones.

En resumen
REPASO DE VOCABULARIO

TALK ABOUT TELEVISION

Equipment

la antena parabólica	satellite dish
cambiar de canal	to change channels
el control remoto	remote control
grabar	to record
la televisión por cable	cable television
la televisión por satélite	satellite television
la videocasetera	video cassette recorder

Programs

los dibujos animados	cartoons
el documental	documentary
en vivo y directo	live programming
el episodio	episode
el (la) guardaespaldas	bodyguard
el programa de acción	action program
el programa de ciencia ficción	science fiction program
el programa de concurso	game show
el programa de entrevistas	talk show
el programa de horror	horror program
el programa de misterio	mystery program
la tele-guía	television guide
el teledrama	mini-series
la teleserie	TV series

Reactions

apto(a) para toda la familia	G-rated
controlar	to control
entretenido(a)	entertaining
influir	to influence
manipular	to manipulate
la percepción	perception
prohibido(a) para menores	R-rated
el público	audience
la reacción crítica	critical response
se recomienda discreción	PG-13 rated
sensacionalista	sensationalized

NARRATE IN THE PAST

Preterite vs. imperfect

Eran las seis de la tarde cuando **nos sentamos** para ver el documental.

EXPRESS DOUBT AND CERTAINTY

Subjunctive vs. indicative

Veremos la teleserie en cuanto **lleguen** los abuelos.
Vimos los dibujos animados tan pronto como **llegaron** los primos.

REPORT WHAT OTHERS SAY

Reported speech

Mamá **nos dijo que** el documental empezaba a las diez.
Mamá **nos dijo que** no miráramos la película prohibida para menores.

Juego

¿Qué vamos a ver?

Completa las frases con las palabras apropiadas. Luego pon en orden las letras de los círculos para saber qué es lo que todo el mundo quiere tener cuando mira la tele.

A Marisol le gustan mucho las sorpresas y lo desconocido. Por eso, siempre mira los ⬜ ⬜ ◯ ⬜ ◯ ⬜
◯ ⬜ ⬜ ⬜ ◯ ⬜
◯ ⬜ ⬜ ⬜ ⬜ ⬜

A Jorge le gusta obtener nueva información. Así que él prefiere ver ⬜ ◯ ◯ ⬜ ⬜ ◯ ◯ ⬜
⬜ ⬜ ◯ ⬜ ⬜.

Respuesta: ___ ___ ___ ___ ___ ___ ___
___ ___ ___ ___ ___

Teaching All Students

Extra Help Have students make word maps for at least 5 words. Encourage them to include as many words from the vocabulary as possible in each map.

Native Speakers Have students find out from a parent, grandparent, or other adult what Spanish-language programs they used to watch, what they were like, etc. Then have them report to the class what that person told him/her.

Multiple Intelligences

Naturalist Have students look at a Spanish-language TV program guide and find the names of TV programs that deal with nature, either directly (documentary) or indirectly (the setting for a movie).

Community Connections

Have students think of 3–5 professions in the entertainment industry in which knowing Spanish would be helpful. Have them explain why.

Quick Start Review

♻ Vocabulary review

Use OHT 15 or write on the board: Unscramble the following words. Then give a definition in Spanish of each.

1. dmteelaar
2. eate-lugí
3. isreeltee

Answers
1. teledrama: un programa de varios episodios
2. tele-guía: una lista de la hora y el día de cada programa
3. teleserie: un programa de televisión

Teaching Suggestions
Vocabulary Review

Have students work in pairs to give each other synonyms of a vocabulary word and have the other guess the word.

Dictation

Dictate the following sentences to review the **Etapa:**

1. Esta película es apta para toda la familia.
2. Cuando era joven, pasaba todos los fines de semana con mis abuelos.
3. Anita me llamará cuando vengan sus primos.
4. José dijo que no saldría con nosotros.

Juego

Answers: programas de misterio, los documentales, el control remoto

Block Schedule

Research Have students research one of the following: (a) which U.S. TV program is popular in one Spanish-speaking country; (b) the name of 3 popular movies in one Spanish-speaking country; (c) how much time teenagers spend watching television in one Spanish-speaking country. (For additional activities, see **Block Scheduling Copymasters.**)

Planning Guide CLASSROOM MANAGEMENT

OBJECTIVES

Communication
- Talk about technology *pp. 426–427, 428–429, 440–441*
- State locations *pp. 433–434*
- Make contrasts *pp. 435–436*
- Describe unplanned events *pp. 437–438*

Grammar
- Review the use of conjunctions *pp. 432–433*
- Review the use of prepositions and adverbs of location *pp. 433–434*
- Use **pero** and **sino** *pp. 435–436*
- Use **se** for unplanned occurrences *pp. 437–438*

Culture
- Regional vocabulary *p. 435*
- Television game shows in Spanish-speaking countries *p. 437*
- Cell phone technology in South America *pp. 440–441*

Recycling
- Extending invitations *p. 440*
- Television vocabulary *p. 424*
- Commands *p. 416*

STRATEGIES

Listening Strategies
- Analyze the appeal in radio ads *p. 428*

Speaking Strategies
- Make excuses *p. 438*
- Consider the factors for or against an electronic purchase *p. 444*

Reading Strategies
- Skim *TE p. 440*

Writing Strategies
- Persuade your reader *TE p. 444*

Connecting Cultures Strategies
- Recognize variations in vocabulary *p. 435*
- Learn about television game shows in Spanish-speaking countries *p. 437*
- Survey technology in daily life *p. 440*
- Connect and compare what you know about technology in your community to help you learn about technology in a new community *pp. 440–441*

PROGRAM RESOURCES

 Print
- *Más práctica* Workbook PE *pp. 145–152*
- *Actividades para todos* Workbook PE *pp. 171, 180*
- Block Scheduling Copymasters *pp. 137–144*
- Unit 6 Resource Book
  - *Más práctica* Workbook TE *pp. 72–79*
  - *Actividades para todos* Workbook TE *pp. 80–89*
  - *Cuaderno para hispanohablantes* TE *pp. 90–97*
  - Information Gap Activities *pp. 98–101*
  - Family Letter *p. 102*
  - Absent Student Copymasters *pp. 103–109*
  - Family Involvement *pp. 110–111*
  - Audioscript *pp. 112–114*
  - Assessment Program, Unit 6 Etapa 2 *pp. 115–138, 232–234*
  - Answer Keys *pp. 250–254*

Audiovisual
- Audio Program CD 17
- *Canciones* CD
- Overhead Transparencies M1–M5; 173, 3, 20–34
- Word Tiles U6E2

Technology
- eEdition Plus Online/eEdition CD-ROM
- Easy Planner Plus Online/Easy Planner CD-ROM
- eTest Plus Online/Test Generator CD-ROM
- Online Workbook
- Take-Home Tutor CD-ROM
- www.classzone.com

✔ Assessment Program Options
- Unit 6 Resource Book
  - Vocabulary Quizzes
  - Grammar Quizzes
  - Etapa Exam Forms A and B
  - *Examen para hispanohablantes*
  - Portfolio Assessment
  - Multiple Choice Test Questions
- Audio Program CD 120
- eTest Plus Online/Test Generator CD-ROM

Native Speakers
- *Cuaderno para hispanohablantes* PE *pp. 145–152*
- *Cuaderno para hispanohablantes* TE (Unit 6 Resource Book)
- *Examen para hispanohablantes* (Unit 6 Resource Book)
- Audio Program *(Para hispanohablantes)* CD 17, 20
- Audioscript (Unit 6 Resource Book)

Student Text
Listening Activity Scripts

 **Situaciones** *pages 428–429*

• CD 17

¡Es sábado! En ElectroMundo, hoy es el día de los súper-descuentos. Si usted está buscando productos electrónicos de calidad a precios accesibles, ¡venga hoy a ElectroMundo!

¿Necesita una computadora portátil? Para trabajar o escribir su correspondencia o navegar por Internet en cualquier sitio, las computadoras portátiles son esenciales. Tenemos una selección muy variada. Compre una hoy y recibirá un descuento de 25 por ciento del precio original.

¿Quién puede existir hoy sin un beeper? Comuníquese cuando quiera con su oficina, su familia, sus amigos. El hombre o la mujer de hoy depende de su beeper. Cómprese uno hoy en ElectroMundo y le daremos un descuento de 10 por ciento del precio original.

¿Necesita tener el número de teléfono de sus amigos, familiares y colegas a la mano? ¡Puedo hacerlo con un asistente electrónico! Si se compra uno hoy, recibirá un descuento de 15 por ciento del precio original.

¿No tiene teléfono celular? ¿Qué espera? Es el implemento más necesario de la vida moderna. Puede hacer llamadas desde el carro, la calle, el aeropuerto, de donde sea. Olvide las largas líneas en los teléfonos públicos, ya no tiene que buscar un teléfono desocupado. Hoy en ElectroMundo el teléfono celular es casi un regalo con un descuento de 30 por ciento del precio original. ¡Sí! ¡Me han escuchado bien! ¡Un descuento del 30 por ciento! No hay razón para no comprarlo hoy.

¡Nos vemos hoy sábado, día de los súper-descuentos en ElectroMundo!

 **ACTIVIDAD 10** **Alma** *page 435*

¡Ay, Ana! ¡No lo vas a creer! Ayer me llamaron Julio y Juan. Los dos querían salir conmigo. Al principio pensé que preferiría salir con Julio. Después de pensarlo un rato, cambié de opinión y decidí salir con Juan. Cuando llegó Juan, eran las seis más o menos, me preguntó si quería ir al cine o al restaurante. Como tenía hambre, le dije que mejor al restaurante. Fuimos a un restaurante muy elegante. ¡Ay, las calorías! En vez de pedir pescado, que me encanta, pedí carne. No sé por qué. Nos tocó un camarero medio tonto. Le pedí un café. ¡No creerás lo que me trajo! ¡Me trajo un refresco de muchas calorías! ¡Y después, pedí un postre, pero ¡qué error! ¡Fue horrible! No me gustó para nada. Por fin llegó la cuenta y Juan decidió pagar en efectivo. No tenía su tarjeta de crédito. El servicio fue muy malo, pero ésa no fue la razón por la cual Juan no dejó propina. ¡No dejó propina porque no tenía lo suficiente! ¡Ay, qué lío! Juan se sintió muy mal así que cuando nos levantamos para salir, él le dio las gracias al camarero aunque había sido el peor camarero del mundo. Allí acaba la historia. ¿Sabes qué? ¡Mejor hubiera salido con Julio!

 **ACTIVIDAD 13** **Las excusas** *page 438*

Modelo: Yo no pude ir a la fiesta porque se me descompuso el coche.
1. Yo no fui a la fiesta porque se me olvidó la fecha.
2. Yo nunca llegué a la fiesta porque se me perdió la dirección.
3. Yo llegué tarde porque se me descompuso el reloj.
4. Yo no fui a la fiesta porque se me olvidó que tenía otra cita.
5. Yo nunca llegué porque se me hizo tarde.

Sample Lesson Plan - 50 Minute Schedule

DAY 1

Etapa Opener
• Quick Start Review (TE, p. 424) 5 MIN.
• Have students look at the *Etapa* Opener and answer the questions. 5 MIN.
• Use an expansion activity from TE p. 425 for variety and reinforcement. 5 MIN.

En contexto: Vocabulario
• Quick Start Review (TE, p. 426) 5 MIN.
• Present *Descubre*, p. 426. 5 MIN.
• Have students use context and pictures to learn *Etapa* vocabulary, then answer the *¿Comprendiste?* questions, p. 427. Use the Situational OHTs for additional practice. 25 MIN.

Homework Option:
• Have students write answers to the *¿Comprendiste?* questions, p. 427.

DAY 2

En vivo: Situaciones
• Check homework. 5 MIN.
• Quick Start Review (TE, p. 428) 5 MIN.
• Present the Listening Strategy, p. 428. 5 MIN.
• Have students read section 1, p. 428. Play the audio for section 2. Then have students work in groups to complete section 3. 15 MIN.

En acción: Vocabulario y gramática
• Quick Start Review (TE, p. 430) 5 MIN.
• Have students complete *Actividad* 1 in writing, then exchange papers for peer correction. 10 MIN.
• Have students do *Actividad* 2 in pairs. 5 MIN.

Homework Option:
• Have students write 5 personalized sentences about electronic products.

DAY 3

En acción (cont.)
• Check homework. 5 MIN.
• Present the *Vocabulario*, p. 431. Then have students read and complete *Actividad* 3 in pairs. 10 MIN.
• Present *Repaso:* Conjunctions and the *Vocabulario*, p. 432. 10 MIN.
• Have students do *Actividad* 4 in pairs. 5 MIN.
• Do *Actividad* 5 orally. 5 MIN.
• Have students do *Actividad* 6 in pairs. Expand using Information Gap Activities, Unit 6 Resource Book, p. 98; *Más comunicación*, p. R19. 15 MIN.

Homework Option:
• Have students complete *Actividad* 5 in writing. *Más práctica* Workbook, p. 149. *Cuaderno para hispanohablantes*, p. 147.

DAY 4

En acción (cont.)
• Check homework. 5 MIN.
• Quick Start Review (TE, p. 433) 5 MIN.
• Present *Repaso:* Prepositions and Adverbs of Location and the *Vocabulario*, p. 433. 10 MIN.
• Do *Actividad* 7 orally. 5 MIN.
• Have students complete *Actividad* 8 in pairs. 5 MIN.
• Have students complete *Actividad* 9 in pairs. Expand using *Más comunicación*, p. R19. 20 MIN.

Homework Option:
• Have students complete *Actividad* 7 in writing. *Más práctica* Workbook, p. 150. *Cuaderno para hispanohablantes*, p. 148.
• *Actividades para todos* Workbook, pp. 171–180.

DAY 5

En acción (cont.)
• Check homework. 5 MIN.
• Quick Start Review (TE, p. 435) 5 MIN.
• Present *Gramática: Pero* vs. *sino*, p. 435. 10 MIN.
• Play the audio; do *Actividad* 10. 5 MIN.
• Do *Actividad* 11 in pairs. 5 MIN.
• Have students write *Actividad* 12. Go over answers orally. 5 MIN.
• Present *Gramática: Se* for Unplanned Occurrences and the *Vocabulario*, p. 437. 5 MIN.
• Play the audio; do *Actividad* 13. 5 MIN.
• Do *Actividad* 14 orally. 5 MIN.

Homework Option:
• *Más práctica* Workbook, pp. 151–152. *Cuaderno para hispanohablantes*, pp. 149–150.

DAY 6

En acción (cont.)
• Check homework. 5 MIN.
• Present the Speaking Strategy, p. 438. Then have students complete *Actividad* 15 in pairs. 5 MIN.
• Have students read and complete *Actividad* 16 in groups. 15 MIN.

Refrán
• Present the *Refrán*, p. 439. 5 MIN.

En colores: Cultura y comparaciones
• Quick Start Review (TE, p. 440) 5 MIN.
• Present the Connecting Cultures Strategy, p. 440. Call on volunteers to read the selection aloud. Have students answer the *¿Comprendiste?/¿Qué piensas?* questions, p. 441. 15 MIN.

Homework Option:
• Have students complete *Hazlo tú*, p. 441.

DAY 7

En uso: Repaso y más comunicación
• Check homework. 5 MIN.
• Quick Start Review (TE, p. 442) 5 MIN.
• Have students do *Actividad* 1 in pairs. 5 MIN.
• Do *Actividades* 2, 3, and 4 orally. 10 MIN.
• Present the Speaking Strategy, p. 444, and have students do *Actividad* 5 in groups. 10 MIN.

En tu propia voz: Escritura
• Have students do *Actividad* 6 in writing. 15 MIN.

Homework Option:
• Review for *Etapa* 2 Exam.

DAY 8

Conexiones
• Present *El arte*, p. 444, and have students complete the assignment for homework. 5 MIN.

En resumen: Repaso de vocabulario
• Quick Start Review (TE, p. 445) 5 MIN.
• Review grammar questions, etc., as necessary. 10 MIN.
• Complete *Etapa* 2 Exam. 20 MIN.

Ampliación
• Use a suggested project, game, or activity. (TE, pp. 401A–401B) 10 MIN.

Homework Option:
• Have students complete the assignment for *Conexiones*. Preview *Etapa* 3 Opener.

Sample Lesson Plan - Block Schedule (90 minutes)

DAY 1

Etapa Opener
- Quick Start Review (TE, p. 424) 5 MIN.
- Have students look at the *Etapa* Opener and answer the questions. 5 MIN.
- Use Block Scheduling Copymasters. 10 MIN.

En contexto: Vocabulario
- Quick Start Review (TE, p. 426) 5 MIN.
- Present *Descubre*, p. 426. 5 MIN.
- Have students use context and pictures to learn *Etapa* vocabulary, then answer the *¿Comprendiste?* questions, p. 427. Use the Situational OHTs for additional practice. 25 MIN.

En vivo: Situaciones
- Quick Start Review (TE, p. 428) 5 MIN.
- Present the Listening Strategy, p. 428. 5 MIN.
- Have students read section 1, p. 428. Play the audio for section 2. Then have students work in groups to complete section 3. 25 MIN.

Homework Option:
- Have students write answers to the *¿Comprendiste?* questions, p. 427. Have students write 5 personalized sentences about electronic products.

DAY 2

En acción: Vocabulario y gramática
- Check homework. 5 MIN.
- Quick Start Review (TE, p. 430) 5 MIN.
- Have students complete *Actividad* 1 in writing, then exchange papers for peer correction. 5 MIN.
- Have students do *Actividad* 2 in pairs. 5 MIN.
- Present the *Vocabulario*, p. 431. Then have students read and complete *Actividad* 3 in pairs. 10 MIN.
- Quick Start Review (TE, p. 432) 5 MIN.
- Present *Repaso:* Conjunctions and the *Vocabulario*, p. 432. 10 MIN.
- Have students do *Actividad* 4 in pairs. 5 MIN.
- Do *Actividad* 5 orally. 5 MIN.
- Have students do *Actividad* 6 in pairs. Expand using Information Gap Activities, Unit 6 Resource Book, p. 98; *Más comunicación*, p. R19. 15 MIN.
- Quick Start Review (TE, p. 433) 5 MIN.
- Present *Repaso:* Prepositions and Adverbs of Location and the *Vocabulario*, p. 433. 10 MIN.
- Do *Actividad* 7 orally. 5 MIN.

Homework Option:
- Have students complete *Actividades* 5 and 7 in writing. *Más práctica* Workbook, pp. 149–150. *Cuaderno para hispanohablantes*, pp. 147–148.

DAY 3

En acción (cont.)
- Check homework. 5 MIN.
- Have students complete *Actividad* 8 in pairs. 5 MIN.
- Have students complete *Actividad* 9 in pairs. Expand using Information Gap Activities, Unit 6 Resource Book, p. 99; *Más comunicación*, p. R19. 20 MIN.
- Quick Start Review (TE, p. 435) 5 MIN.
- Present *Gramática: Pero* vs. *sino*, p. 435. 10 MIN.
- Play the audio; do *Actividad* 10. 5 MIN.
- Do *Actividad* 11 in pairs. 5 MIN.
- Have students write *Actividad* 12. Go over answers orally. 10 MIN.
- Quick Start Review (TE, p. 437) 5 MIN.
- Present *Gramática: Se* for Unplanned Occurrences and the *Vocabulario*, p. 437. 10 MIN.
- Play the audio; do *Actividad* 13. 5 MIN.
- Do *Actividad* 14 orally. 5 MIN.

Homework Option:
- *Más práctica* Workbook, pp. 151–152. *Cuaderno para hispanohablantes*, pp. 149–150.
- *Actividades para todos* Workbook, pp. 171–180.

DAY 4

En acción (cont.)
- Check homework. 5 MIN.
- Present the Speaking Strategy, p. 438. Then have students do *Actividad* 15 in pairs. 10 MIN.
- Have students read and complete *Actividad* 16 in groups. 15 MIN.

Refrán
- Present the *Refrán*, p. 439. 5 MIN.

En colores: Cultura y comparaciones
- Quick Start Review (TE, p. 440) 5 MIN.
- Present the Connecting Cultures Strategy, p. 440. Call on volunteers to read the selection aloud. Have students answer the *¿Comprendiste?/¿Qué piensas?* questions, p. 441. 25 MIN.

En uso: Repaso y más comunicación
- Quick Start Review (TE, p. 442) 5 MIN.
- Have students do *Actividad* 1 in pairs. 5 MIN.
- Do *Actividades* 2, 3, and 4 orally. 15 MIN.

Homework Option:
- Have students complete *Hazlo tú*, p. 441. Review for *Etapa* 2 Exam.

DAY 5

En uso (cont.)
- Check homework. 5 MIN.
- Present the Speaking Strategy, p. 444, and have students do *Actividad* 5 in groups. 10 MIN.

En tu propia voz: Escritura
- Have students do *Actividad* 6 in writing. 20 MIN.

Conexiones
- Present *El arte*, p. 444, and have students complete the assignment for homework. 5 MIN.

En resumen: Repaso de vocabulario
- Quick Start Review (TE, p. 445) 5 MIN.
- Review grammar questions, etc., as necessary. 10 MIN.
- Complete *Etapa* 2 Exam. 20 MIN.

Ampliación
- Use a suggested project, game, or activity. (TE, pp. 401A–401B) 15 MIN.

Homework Option:
- Have students complete the assignment for *Conexiones*. Preview *Etapa* 3 Opener.

▼ ¿Quieres tener a la mano la última tecnología personal? ¡Ven a ElectroMundo!

Etapa Theme

Talking about technology; stating locations; making contrasts; and describing unplanned events

Grammar Objectives

- Reviewing the use of conjunctions
- Reviewing the use of prepositions and adverbs of location
- Using **pero** and **sino**
- Using **se** for unplanned occurrences

Teaching Resource Options

Print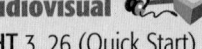

Block Scheduling Copymasters
Unit 6 Resource Book
  Family Letter, p. 102
  Absent Student Copymasters, p. 103

Audiovisual

OHT 3, 26 (Quick Start)

Quick Start Review

♻ Television vocabulary review

Use OHT 26 or write on the board:
Match each description with a word:

1. ___ información de satélites
2. ___ líneas subterráneas
3. ___ grabar programas
4. ___ cambiar de canal
   a. videocasetera
   b. control remoto
   c. antena parabólica
   d. televisión por cable

Answers
1. c   2. d   3. a   4. b

UNIDAD 6

ETAPA 2

Aquí tienes mi número...

OBJECTIVES

- Talk about technology
- State locations
- Make contrasts
- Describe unplanned events

¿Qué ves?

Mira la foto. Contesta las preguntas.

1. ¿En qué lugares puedes encontrar esta clase de tienda?
2. ¿Qué cosas comprarías?
3. ¿Cómo crees que se sienten estos amigos?
4. Mira el anuncio. ¿Conoces otras tiendas que vendan lo mismo?

424

Classroom Management

Planning Ahead Bring in, and ask students to bring in, pictures and ads for electronic devices from Spanish-language and English-language magazines and newspapers. Bring in actual electronic devices or toy items.

Organizing Group Work Set up several stations representing different work places; for example, a hospital, a restaurant, a school, a department store, a police station, etc. Have students work in the stations periodically as you work through this **Etapa** to illustrate technical devices that would be used in each and with explanations about why that device would be important there.

425

Teaching Suggestions
Previewing the Etapa
- Ask students to study the photo on pp. 424–425 (1 min.).
- Have them close their books and ask various students to name 1 thing they noticed: **Nombra una cosa que notaste acerca de la foto.**
- Have students open their books and look at the **Etapa** title. Ask what they think the relationship is between the title and the photo.
- Use the **¿Qué ves?** questions to focus the discussion.

Cross Cultural Connections
Ask students to compare shopping at the the electronics store in the photo with one they have been to. Are there more similarities or more differences? Why do they think so? What about the ad? Is it similar to ads in the U.S.?

Culture Highlights
● **TELECOMUNICACIONES** Muchas compañías estadounidenses trabajan con compañías de telecomunicaciones latinoamericanas para suplir la demanda de tecnología en América Latina. En la Ciudad de México, por ejemplo, estas compañías están reemplazando los cables telefónicos, instalados por primera vez en 1920.

Supplementary Vocabulary
el auricular	telephone receiver
la cuerda	cord
el enchufe	jack, outlet

Block Schedule
Setting the Theme Plan ahead: Record your own ads for electronics stores based on real ads from Spanish-language radio broadcasts. Have students listen to the ads and write a list of words they understand. (For additional activities, see **Block Scheduling Copymasters**.)

Teaching All Students

Extra Help Have students write 5 true/false statements about the photo. Have them take turns reading their statements for the class to respond to.

Challenge Encourage students to give a complete description of the photo using words they already know. One student creates a sentence and others follow in turn. They should elaborate by adding adjectives when possible.

Multiple Intelligences

Intrapersonal Have students tell what items in the photo they have and/or use.

Kinesthetic Set up an electronics store display using either actual electronics items, toy items, or pictures of items. Have groups of 3 students act out a conversation in the store.

Teaching Resource Options

Print

Block Scheduling Copymasters
Unit 6 Resource Book
  Absent Student Copymasters, p. 103

Audiovisual 🎧📺

OHT 20, 21, 22, 22A, 23, 23A, 26

Technology 💻

Online Workbook, U6E2
Take Home Tutor CD-ROM, U6E2

🔔 Quick Start Review

♻ **Professions**

Use OHT 26 or write on the board:
**Make a list in Spanish of 4
professions that depend on the
computer and briefly explain why.**

Answers will vary.

Teaching Suggestions
Introducing Vocabulary

• Have students look at pp. 426–427.
  Use OHT 20 and 21 to present the
  vocabulary.

• Ask the Comprehension Questions
  on TE p. 427 in order of yes/no
  (questions 1–3), either/or (questions
  4–6), and simple word or phrase
  (questions 7–10). Expand by adding
  similar questions.

• Use the TPR activity to reinforce the
  meaning of individual words.

Descubre

Answers

1. c
2. b
3. e
4. a
5. f
6. d

En contexto VOCABULARIO

Descubre

En ElectroMundo Estás en el almacén
ElectroMundo y escuchas estas
conversaciones. ¿Puedes adivinar qué
quieren decir las palabras en azul?

1. Tengo un radio **portátil** y una
   computadora **portátil**. Los puedo
   llevar adondequiera.

2. Es difícil decidir qué **marca** debo
   comprar. ¡Hay tantas **marcas** de
   todos los productos!

3. Dice el anuncio que están ofreciendo
   un **descuento** de 10 por ciento.
   ¡Puedo ahorrar mucho dinero!

4. Quiero un teléfono **inalámbrico**
   porque quiero hacer mis llamadas
   de cualquier sitio.

5. Compré este modelo de fax por su
   durabilidad. Tengo un amigo que ha
   tenido el mismo fax por cinco años.

6. Esta computadora tiene una
   garantía de dos años. Si le pasa
   algo dentro de dos años, me la
   componen gratis.

   a. *cordless*
   b. *brand*
   c. *portable*
   d. *guarantee*
   e. *discount*
   f. *durability*

ELECTROMUNDO

Donde la tecnología existe solamente para ti.
¿Quieres tener a la mano la última tecnología personal? ¡Ven a
ElectroMundo! Puedes contar con la durabilidad de las marcas
más conocidas y los descuentos más bajos. Ofrecemos garantías
de un año para todos los productos electrónicos. ¡Ven hoy a
ElectroMundo! ¡Hay una tienda accesible cerca de ti!

**Radio
portátil**

14.000 B
Ahora 12.790 B

**Equipo
estereofónico**

113.900 B
Ahora 85.390 B

**Walkman™
con
audífonos**

25.600 B
Ahora 20.500 B

Altoparlantes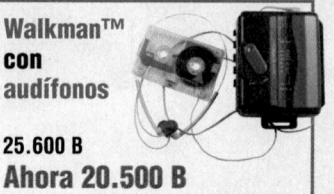

102.500 B
Ahora 82.000 B

¡REBAJA!

Videocámara

284.800 B
Ahora 242.100 B

**Televisor
portátil**

56.900 B
Ahora 48.400 B

Classroom Community

TPR Give students simple commands having to do
with the electronic devices to act out. If possible, give
them props. For example: **Pon las pilas en la radio
portátil. Escucha los mensajes de la contestadora
automática.**

Paired Activity Have students work in pairs to
make 2 lists for the electronic devices on pp. 426–427.
The first list ranks the equipment in order of
importance for themselves. In the second list, students
guess the importance of each piece of equipment for
an adult they know, such as a parent or teacher. Have
them discuss how the lists differ and why.

CD-ROM Take-Home Tutor

Teléfono celular
19.900 B
Ahora 17.900 B

Contestadora automática
(Espacio para dos horas de **telemensajes**)
69.000 B
Ahora 48.400 B

Teléfono con identificador de llamadas
153.800 B
Ahora 115.300 B

Teléfono inalámbrico
22.700 B
Ahora 15.900 B

Pilas/Baterías
2.800-8.500 B
Ahora 2.200-6.800 B

Asistente electrónico
512.600 B
Ahora 435.800 B

Beeper
42.700 B
(servicio17.000 B/mes)
Ahora 36.300 B
(servicio 14.500 B/mes)

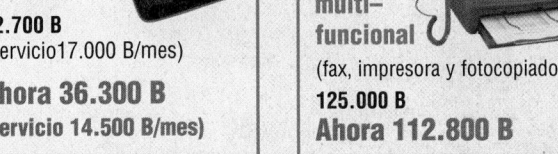
Fax multi–funcional
(fax, impresora y fotocopiadora)
125.000 B
Ahora 112.800 B

Computadora portátil
1.196.000 B
Ahora 957.012 B

¡Todos los sábados, descuentos del 10% al 30% para ciertos modelos! Precios razonables todos los días.

Centro Comercial Chacaíto,
Chuao, Caracas
tel. 02/959-3824

Online Workbook
CLASSZONE.COM

¿Comprendiste?

1. ¿Cuántos de estos productos tienes tú en casa? ¿Cuáles te gustaría tener? ¿Por qué?
2. ¿Tienes una computadora portátil? Si tuvieras una, ¿adónde la llevarías?
3. ¿Qué tres productos electrónicos han cambiado tu vida? Di cómo era tu vida antes de haber comprado cada producto y cómo cambió después de haberlo comprado.
4. ¿Crees que es importante siempre comprar la marca más conocida de un producto? ¿Por qué?
5. Algunos creen que la vida se ha complicado mucho con la tecnología personal. Hay otros que piensan que se ha hecho más sencilla y más fácil. ¿Qué opinas tú? Explica.

Culture Highlights

● **COMUNICACIONES** La demanda por tecnologías de comunicación, como los teléfonos celulares, las máquinas de fax y las computadoras, ha aumentado a través del mundo hispanohablante. Aunque se tiene acceso a estas tecnologías, muchas personas también se comunican por telegrama, un método eficiente y fácil.

Comprehension Questions

1. ¿Venden radios portátiles en ElectroMundo? (Sí)
2. ¿Venden antenas parabólicas? (No)
3. ¿Hay videocaseteras? (No)
4. ¿Venden equipos estereofónicos o controles remotos? (equipos estereofónicos)
5. ¿Hay Walkman™ con audífonos o sin audífonos? (con audífonos)
6. ¿Ofrecen precios bajos o altos? (bajos)
7. ¿Qué clase de teléfonos venden? (celular e inalámbrico)
8. ¿Qué compras si necesitas un calendario electrónico? (un asistente electrónico)
9. ¿Qué clase de teléfono compras si quieres saber quién te llama antes de contestar el teléfono? (teléfono con identificador de llamadas)
10. ¿Qué compras si te hace falta hacer copias y mandar cartas electrónicamente? (un fax multifuncional / con impresora y fotocopiadora)

Block Schedule

Change of Pace Have students write short poems to describe one of the devices. The first line is a sentence about it (without naming it); the second, 4 infinitives associated with it; the third, 3 adjectives describing it; the fourth, 2 adverbs about it, and the fifth line should name the device. (For additional activities, see **Block Scheduling Copymasters**.)

Teaching All Students

Extra Help Have students create word webs using the electronic devices from pp. 426–427.

Native Speakers Ask students to imagine that they already have all kinds of electronic devices. Now they want a robot. Have them write a paragraph explaining exactly why they need a robot.

Multiple Intelligences

Logical/Mathematical Have students come up with different ways of categorizing the items on pp. 426–427. Encourage them to be creative.

Teaching Resource Options

Print

Block Scheduling Copymasters
Unit 6 Resource Book
  Absent Student Copymasters, p. 104
  Audioscript, p. 112

Audiovisual

OHT 24, 25, 27 (Quick Start)
Audio Program CD 17, Track 1

Technology

Take-Home Tutor CD-ROM, U6E2

Quick Start Review

♻ Vocabulary review

Use OHT 27 or write on the board:
Complete the following sentences:

1. Necesito pilas porque...
2. Necesito una videocámara
   porque...
3. Necesito un equipo estereofónico
   porque...

Answers will vary.

Teaching Suggestions
Presenting Situations

• Present the Listening Strategy, p. 428,
  and have students prepare their charts.
• Use OHT 24 and 25 to present the
  Leer section. Ask simple yes/no,
  either/or, or short-answer questions.
• Use Audio CD 17 and have students
  do the **Escuchar** section (see Script
  p. 423B) and complete the Listening
  Strategy exercise.
• Have students work in groups to
  complete the **Hablar** section.

Para escuchar

Answers

Comunicación con otros	sí
Conveniencia personal	sí
Necesidad personal	sí
Personas famosas lo usan	no
Reputación del producto	no

AUDIO
SITUACIONES

PARA ESCUCHAR

STRATEGY: LISTENING

Analyze the appeal in radio ads Commercials
contain a double appeal: one is monetary,
the other psychological. First listen to and
identify what is being sold and at what
discount. Then listen again to determine in
what other ways the ad appeals to potential
customers. Check which elements you believe
are present:

	sí	no
Comunicación con otros		
Conveniencia personal		
Necesidad personal		
Personas famosas lo usan		
Reputación del producto		

Which ad appeals to you most? Why?

¡Grandes rebajas!

Estás en Caracas, Venezuela y ves este anuncio
en el periódico. Luego, escuchas un anuncio de
radio para saber más sobre los descuentos que
se ofrecen.

① Leer

Quieres comprar algunos productos electrónicos, pero
primero quieres saber qué descuentos se ofrecen. Lee
el anuncio de ElectroMundo y haz una lista de todos los
productos en el anuncio.

¡Venga el sábado para ahorrar con nuestros súper
descuentos! Ofrecemos descuentos sensacionales
de ciertos productos populares.

¡Escuche WVZA-109 FM a las diez de la mañana
para saber cuáles son y cuánto va a ahorrar!

428 cuatrocientos veintiocho
Unidad 6

Classroom Community

Group Activity Have students work in small groups
to make a newspaper ad and a radio ad for a specific
electronic device or electronics store. Have the group
devise an ad campaign together, then divide up the
task (art, writing, narration, etc.). Have groups present
their ads to the class.

Game Plan ahead: Make, or have students make,
posters for as many electronic devices as possible using
drawings or magazine clippings. For each poster,
establish a price on a sheet of paper that students don't
see. Divide the class into 4 teams. Team members take
turns being contestants. A member from each team
tries to guess the price of an item as the poster of it is
displayed. The contestant with the price closest to yours
without exceeding it scores. The team with the most
points wins.

CD-ROM Take-Home Tutor

② Escuchar

Pones la radio a las diez de la mañana y escuchas el anuncio del almacén ElectroMundo. Si el anuncio ofrece un descuento para el producto, escribe **sí** y el porcentaje del descuento en la lista que hiciste en la Actividad 1. Si el anuncio no ofrece un descuento para ese producto, escribe **no** junto a ese producto.

③ Hablar

En grupos de tres o cuatro, comenten sobre los productos electrónicos que usan todos los días. ¿Cuánto les costaron? ¿Dónde los compraron? ¿Recibieron un descuento? ¿Hay algunos que siempre han tenido? Inventen un producto electrónico que no existe todavía pero que tendría usos importantes para el estudiante de hoy.

cuatrocientos veintinueve **429**
Colombia, Venezuela y los países andinos Etapa 2

Language Note
In Puerto Rico the word **bocinas** is used instead of **altoparlantes**.

Escuchar (See script, p. 423B.)

Answers

beeper	sí	descuento: 10%
teléfono celular	sí	descuento: 30%
videocámara	no	
computadora portátil	sí	descuento: 25%
equipo estereofónico	no	
radio portátil	no	
asistente electrónico	sí	descuento: 15%
Walkman™	no	

Hablar

Answers will vary.

Critical Thinking
Have students name the modes of communication and services related to communication that are common now, but that were not common or didn't even exist when they were born. Ask them what they think the effect of these new modes and services is on people's lives. Is the world a better place because of them?

Teaching All Students

Extra Help Have students tell you what information they expect to hear in the radio ad in the **Escuchar** section. Then write or say some of the words that might be used before they listen.

Challenge Ask students to complete the following: **El mejor medio de comunicación es... porque...**

Multiple Intelligences

Interpersonal Have students work in pairs to discuss what kinds of ads they are most often exposed to, newspaper/magazine, radio, television, billboard, electronic, etc. Which ads do they think are most effective and why?

Verbal Have students create a short message in Spanish for their answering machine.

Block Schedule

Personalizing Have students talk about the electronic devices they use in their households. Who is the most electronically equipped? (For additional activities, see **Block Scheduling Copymasters**.)

Teaching Resource Options

Print

Block Scheduling Copymasters
Unit 6 Resource Book
  Absent Student Copymasters, p. 105

Audiovisual

OHT 27 (Quick Start)

Quick Start Review

♻ Vocabulary review

Use OHT 27 or write on the board:
Give the word for each of the following
definitions:

1. un televisor que se puede llevar
   a todas partes
2. se usa para escuchar el estéreo o
   el Walkman™ sin molestar a nadie
3. son necesarias para varios
   aparatos electrónicos
   inalámbricos
4. se usa para grabar lo que hacen
   las personas cerca de uno
5. son buenos para comunicarse
   con una persona que no lleva
   teléfono

Answers

1. televisor portátil   4. videocámara
2. audífonos   5. beeper
3. pilas/baterías

Teaching Suggestions
Comprehension Check

Use **Actividades 1–4** to assess retention
after the **Vocabulario** and **Situaciones**.
After completing **Actividad 1**, read
items 2, 4, and 6 aloud as a dictation
exercise. Have volunteers write the
sentences on the board for class
review and student self-check.

Objetive: Controlled practice
Vocabulary

Answers

1. c   4. d
2. e   5. f
3. a   6. b

En acción

PARTE A — Práctica del vocabulario

Objectives for Activities 1–3
• Talk about technology

1 La tecnología personal

Escribir Estás en Colombia
en una fiesta con tus amigos.
Todos comentan las ventajas
de sus productos electrónicos.
Completa sus comentarios.

a. baterías
b. teléfono celular
c. computadora portátil
d. altoparlantes
e. Walkman™
f. grabadora
g. contestadora automática

1. «Viajo mucho y necesito
   trabajar en el avión. Por eso
   compré una _____.»

2. «Cuando hago ejercicio, me
   gusta oír música. Siempre
   llevo mi _____
   al gimnasio.»

3. «El radio no funciona. Creo
   que tengo que comprar unas
   _____.»

4. «Tengo un equipo
   estereofónico pero me faltan
   los _____.»

5. «Para mi proyecto quiero
   entrevistar a los miembros
   de mi familia. ¿Me prestas
   tu _____?»

6. «Viajo mucho por la noche
   en el coche. Por eso quiero
   comprar un _____, en caso
   de emergencia.»

2 ¡Voy a ElectroMundo! ♻ 👥

Hablar/Escribir Quieres ir a ElectroMundo para
aprovechar (*take advantage of*) los descuentos. Invita a tu
compañero(a). Dile qué vas a comprar y por qué necesitas
ese producto. Luego, cambien de papel.

modelo

Tú: *Voy a ElectroMundo. ¿Quieres ir conmigo?*

Compañero(a): *Sí, claro. ¿Qué vas a comprar?*

Tú: *Me gustaría comprar una videocámara.
Quiero grabar mi fiesta de cumpleaños.*

1.

2.

3.

4.

5.

6.

Classroom Management

Peer Review Have students work in pairs to review
the electronic devices on pp. 426–427. Students take
turns pointing to an item and asking questions. For
example: **¿Qué es? ¿Para qué se usa? ¿Cuánto
cuesta?**

Streamlining Combine **Actividades 2** and **3** and
have students work in groups of 3 (2 friends shopping,
1 sales clerk). Both friends can ask the salesclerk
questions.

3 El (La) vendedor(a)

Hablar Estás en un almacén que vende productos electrónicos. Quieres comprar un identificador de llamadas. Tu compañero(a) hace el papel del (de la) vendedor(a) y trata de convencerte de que compres El Óptimo. Luego, cambien de papel.

modelo

Tú: *Quiero comprar un identificador de llamadas.*

Compañero(a): *Déjeme mostrarle El Óptimo de ComSinc.*

Tú: *¿Cuáles son las ventajas de Él Óptimo?*

Compañero(a): ...

Vocabulario

De compras

la **confiabilidad** *reliability, dependability*

convencer *to convince*

devolver *to return something*

distinguir entre *to distinguish between*

equivocarse *to make a mistake*

estar descompuesto(a)/roto(a) *to be broken*

(no) funcionar *to (not) work*

fijarse en *to notice*

inigualable *unequalled*

la **nitidez** *clarity, sharpness*

respaldado(a) *supported (by); backed (by)*

tomar en cuenta *to take into account*

▶ ¿Cuáles de estas palabras puedes usar para decir lo que más te importa al momento de comprar?

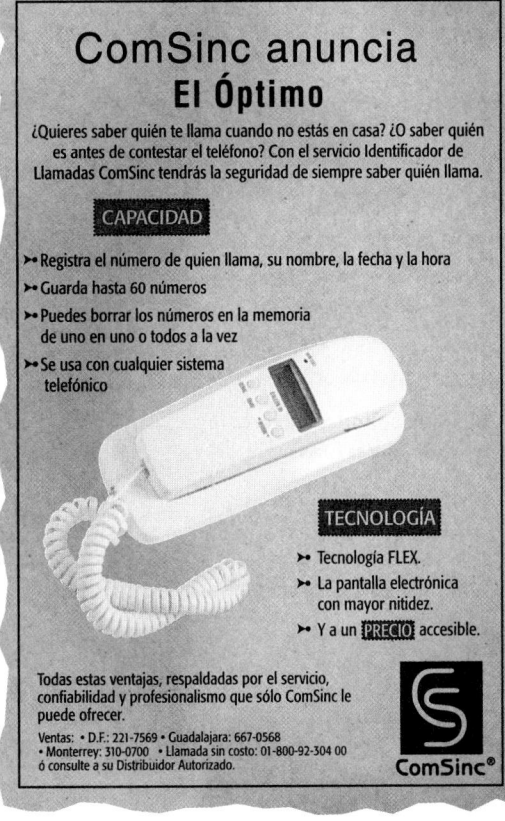

CapSinc anuncia
El Óptimo

¿Quieres saber quién te llama cuando no estás en casa? ¿O saber quién es antes de contestar el teléfono? Con el servicio Identificador de Llamadas ComSinc tendrás la seguridad de siempre saber quién llama.

CAPACIDAD

➤ Registra el número de quien llama, su nombre, la fecha y la hora

➤ Guarda hasta 60 números

➤ Puedes borrar los números en la memoria de uno en uno o todos a la vez

➤ Se usa con cualquier sistema telefónico

TECNOLOGÍA

➤ Tecnología FLEX.
➤ La pantalla electrónica con mayor nitidez.
➤ Y a un **PRECIO** accesible.

Todas estas ventajas, respaldadas por el servicio, confiabilidad y profesionalismo que sólo ComSinc le puede ofrecer.

Ventas: • D.F.: 221-7569 • Guadalajara: 667-0568
• Monterrey: 310-0700 • Llamada sin costo: 01-800-92-304 00
ó consulte a su Distribuidor Autorizado.

ComSinc®

cuatrocientos treinta y uno
Colombia, Venezuela y los países andinos Etapa 2
431

Objective: Transitional practice
Vocabulary in conversation

 Extending invitations

Answers
*Answers will vary. The following are partial responses for **tú**:*
1. Me gustaría comprar un televisor portátil.
2. Me gustaría comprar baterías.
3. Me gustaría comprar un asistente electrónico.
4. Me gustaría comprar un fax multifuncional.
5. Me gustaría comprar una contestadora automática.
6. Me gustaría comprar un teléfono celular.

Teaching Suggestions
Teaching Vocabulary
Have students associate each word with a product or store and explain why.

Objective: Open-ended practice
Vocabulary in reading and conversation

Answers will vary.

🔔 Quick Wrap-up
Have each student name 1 electronic device that he/she would like to own, why, and approximately how much it costs.

Teaching All Students

Extra Help Have students create simple crossword puzzles, using definitions, synonyms, or fill-ins as the clues. Have pairs exchange puzzles and complete them.

Challenge Have students write a sales pitch for one of the items on p. 430, using as many vocabulary words as possible.

Multiple Intelligences
Musical/Rhythmic Have students create a jingle for one of the electronic devices.

Interpersonal Have students work in pairs to act out a short skit between a person trying to return an electronic device and the store clerk.

Block Schedule
Variety Have students create simple ads similar to the one on p. 431. They should be sure to include words from the **Vocabulario**. (For additional activities, see **Block Scheduling Copymasters**.)

Teaching Resource Options

Print

Más práctica Workbook PE, p. 149
Cuaderno para hispanohablantes
  PE, p. 147
Block Scheduling Copymasters
Unit 6 Resource Book
  Más práctica Workbook TE, p. 76
  Cuaderno para hispanohablantes
   TE, p. 92
  Information Gap Activities, p. 98
  Absent Student Copymasters, p. 105

Audiovisual

OHT 27, 28 (Quick Start), 31, 32
(Grammar)

Technology

On-line Workbook, U6E2
Take Home Tutor CD-ROM, U6E2

Quick Start Review

♻ **Shopping vocabulary**

Use OHT 27 or write on the board:
(a) Unscramble each word.
(b) Place the words in the sentence to
complete it:

1. dreevlov
2. coniunfa
3. poemssetudoc

Si un aparato está ___ o no ___ ,
lo puedes ___ .

Answers
1. devolver   2. funciona
3. descompuesto
Si un aparato está descompuesto o no
funciona, lo puedes devolver.

Teaching Suggestions
Reviewing Conjunctions

• Explain that the conjunctions in the
  Vocabulario always require the use
  of the subjunctive because they
  stipulate a condition that does not yet
  exist.
• Point out that compound
  conjunctions must be learned as
  single units, not separate words.

Objectives for Activities 4–15
• Talk about technology • State locations • Make contrasts • Describe unplanned events

REPASO   Conjunctions

♻ **¿RECUERDAS?** *pp. 162, 190, 234* You have already learned some
conjunctions you can use to relate events in time or to express
cause-and-effect relationships.

▶ Always use the subjunctive after these
conjunctions listed in the vocabulary
box at the right.

▶ You can use either the subjunctive or the
indicative after the following **conjunctions**:

   **cuando   en cuanto   hasta que
        tan pronto como**

• Use the subjunctive if the outcome of the
  action is **uncertain** or after a **command**.

   Lo veré cuando entre.
   I'll see him when he comes in.

   Dime cuando entre.
   Tell me whenever he comes in.

• Use the indicative if the outcome of the action is **certain**.

   Lo vi cuando entró.
   I saw him when he came in.

....

▶ You use the indicative after **aunque** (*although, even though, even if*) if the
action of the subordinate clause is a **fact**. Use the subjunctive if it is
just a **possibility**.
                                    *It is a possibility that
                                     it may be expensive.*

Voy a comprar esa computadora **aunque** sea **cara**.
I'm going to buy that computer even if it's expensive.

                          It is a fact that it's expensive.

Voy a comprar esa computadora **aunque** es **cara**.
I'm going to buy that computer although it's expensive.

Vocabulario

♻ **Ya sabes**

a menos que
antes (de) que
con tal (de) que
en caso (de) que
para que
sin que

Practice:
Actividades
4 5 6

Más práctica
cuaderno p. 149
Para hispanohablantes
cuaderno p. 147

 **Online Workbook**
CLASSZONE.COM

---

4 ¿Para qué?

Hablar/*Escribir* Tu
hermanito(a) siempre quiere
saber para qué quieres ciertas
cosas. Dile tus razones.
Primero tu compañero(a) hará
el papel de tu hermanito(a).
Luego, cambien de papel.

   modelo

   *videocámara: grabar la boda de
   nuestro primo*

   Tú: *¿Para qué me das la
        videocámara?*

   Compañero(a): *Para que grabes
             la boda de nuestro
             primo.*

1. Walkman™: escuchar
   música mientras hacer
   ejercicio
2. teléfono celular: llamar
   del carro si hay una
   emergencia
3. contestadora automática:
   recibir mensajes
4. identificador de llamadas:
   saber quién llama sin
   contestar
5. radio portátil: oír música
   en la playa
6. computadora portátil:
   trabajar en el avión
7. baterías: escuchar la
   radio en el parque
8. teléfono: invitar a Diana
   al cine
9. discos compactos: poner
   música alegre
10. disquetes: guardar el
    archivo electrónico

---

432 cuatrocientos treinta y dos
Unidad 6

Classroom Community

Paired Activity Have students work in pairs to
discuss answers to the following questions:
• ¿Qué haces en cuanto llegas a casa después de las
  clases?
• Tan pronto como terminas la tarea, ¿adónde vas?
• Aunque no tengas tarea el fin de semana, ¿estudias?

Game Play "I Spy" by having students say where
something is and providing 1 detail. The class tries to
guess what the object is. The student keeps adding
details until the object is guessed.

5 Aunque

Hablar/*Escribir* Estás seguro(a) de que quieres comprar ciertos productos aunque existan razones para no comprarlos. Di que vas a comprar cuatro productos y menciona la razón contraria. Usa la conjunción **aunque** en tus oraciones.

modelo

Voy a comprar un teléfono celular aunque no lo necesite.

no necesitarlo(la)	no ofrecer descuento
ser caro(a)	no tener garantía
ya tener uno (una)	no ser la marca que
no gustarme	quiero
	¿...?

6 ¿Lo vas a comprar?

Hablar Estás de compras en una tienda de equipo electrónico con un(a) amigo(a). Tu amigo(a) no ha decidido qué va a comprar. Conversen sobre el producto y usen las frases de la lista.

modelo

Tú: *¿Vas a comprar la computadora portátil?*

Compañero(a): *Sí, la voy a comprar a menos que cueste demasiado.*

a menos (de) que	con tal (de) que
antes (de) que	sin que aunque
para que	en caso (de) que

More Practice: Más comunicación *p. R19*

REPASO   **Prepositions and Adverbs of Location**

You can indicate one object's relation to another by using adverbs and prepositions of location.

Use **de** only when the phrase is followed by a specific location.

> *Not clear where, just inside.*

Adverb: Mi hermano salía de la casa mientras yo todavía estaba **dentro.**
*My brother was leaving the house while I was still **inside.***

> *Exact: Inside the house.*

Preposition: El televisor está **dentro de** la casa.
*The television set is **inside** the house.*

Practice: Actividades 7 8 9

Más práctica cuaderno p. 150
Para hispanohablantes cuaderno p. 148

Online Workbook CLASSZONE.COM

Vocabulario

Adverbs/Prepositions of location

afuera *outside*
al lado (de) *next to*
atrás *in back, behind*
detrás (de) *behind*
enfrente (de) *in front of*

♻ **Ya sabes**

abajo	**encima (de)**
debajo (de)	**frente (a)**
delante (de)	**fuera (de)**
dentro (de)	**junto (a)**

cuatrocientos treinta y tres
Colombia, Venezuela y los países andinos Etapa 2
433

Teaching All Students

Extra Help Have students work in pairs to review recycled and new prepositions and adverbs of location. They should use objects in their backpacks and in the classroom and describe location.

Native Speakers Have students write a paragraph about the advantages and disadvantages of personal technology, using at least 4 conjunctions.

Multiple Intelligences

Kinesthetic Have students pantomime to illustrate where certain things are so that students guess the directions; for example, **Está debajo del escritorio del profesor.**

ACTIVIDAD 4 **Objective:** Controlled practice
Conjunctions in conversation

Answers
1. A: ¿Para qué quieres el Walkman™? / B: Lo quiero para que pueda escuchar música mientras hago ejercicio.
2. A: ¿Para qué quieres el teléfono celular? / B: Lo quiero para que pueda llamar del carro si hay una emergencia.
3. A: ¿Para qué quieres la contestadora automática? / B: La quiero para que pueda recibir telemensajes.
4. A: ¿Para qué quieres el identificador de llamadas? / B: Lo quiero para que pueda saber quién llama sin contestar.
5. A: ¿Para qué quieres el radio portátil? / B: Lo quiero para que pueda oír música en la playa.
6. A: ¿Para qué quieres la computadora portátil? B: La quiero para que pueda trabajar en el avión.
7. A: ¿Para qué quieres las baterías? B: Las quiero para escuchar la radio en el parque.
8. A: ¿Para qué quieres el teléfono? B: Lo quiero para invitar a Diana al cine.
9. A: ¿Para qué quieres los discos compactos? B: Los quiero para poner música alegre.
10. A: ¿Para qué quieres los disquetes? B: Los quiero para guardar el archivo electrónico.

ACTIVIDAD 5 **Objective:** Transitional practice
Conjunctions

Answers will vary.

ACTIVIDAD 6 **Objective:** Open-ended practice
Conjunctions in conversation

Answers will vary.

🔔 Quick Start Review

♻ **Prepositions review**

Use OHT 28 or write on the board: Match the following items/places in the home and the prepositions:

1. __ antena   a. junto a
2. __ muebles   b. dentro de
3. __ patio   c. alrededor de
4. __ vecino   d. encima de
5. __ césped   e. detrás de

Answers
1. d   2. b   3. e   4. a   5. c

Teaching Suggestions
Reviewing Prepositions and Adverbs of Location

You may wish to remind students of other prepositions/adverbs of location that they have learned including **hacia, hasta, alrededor (de), entre,** and **sobre.**

Teaching Resource Options

Print

Más práctica Workbook PE,
  pp. 150–151
Cuaderno para hispanohablantes
  PE, pp. 148–149
Block Scheduling Copymasters
Unit 6 Resource Book
  Más práctica Workbook TE,
    pp. 77–78
  Cuaderno para hispanohablantes
    TE, pp. 93–94
  Information Gap Activities, p. 99
  Absent Student Copymasters,
    pp. 106–107
  Audioscript, p. 112

Audiovisual

OHT 28 (Quick Start), 33 (Grammar)
Audio Program CD 17, Track 2,
  Activity 10

Technology

On-line Workbook, U6E2
Take Home Tutor CD-ROM, U6E2

ACTIVIDAD 7 **Objective:** Controlled practice
Prepositions and adverbs of location

Answers
Answers will vary. Answers could include:
El fax multifuncional está detrás de la
  computadora portátil.
Los altoparlantes están al lado de la
  computadora.
El equipo estereofónico está debajo de la mesa.
El radio portátil está encima del televisor.
La computadora portátil está encima de unas
  revistas.

ACTIVIDAD 8 **Objective:** Transitional practice
Prepositions and adverbs of location
in conversation

Answers will vary.

ACTIVIDAD 9 **Objective:** Open-ended practice
Prepositions and adverbs of location
in conversation

Answers will vary.

---

7 En mi cuarto

Hablar/*Escribir* Le vas a prestar varios objetos
a tu mejor amigo(a). Le tienes que decir
dónde están esos objetos porque va a ir a
recogerlos cuando tú no estás. ¿Qué le dices?

modelo

La video cámara está delante del televisor.

8 ¿Dónde está?

Hablar/*Escribir* Tú y tu compañero(a) quieren
saber dónde están varias personas, cosas y
mascotas. Háganse preguntas y contesten
lógicamente.

modelo

Tú: *¿Dónde está tu gato?*
Compañero(a): *Está afuera.*
Tú: *Y tu perro, ¿dónde está?*
Compañero(a): *Está dentro de la casa.*

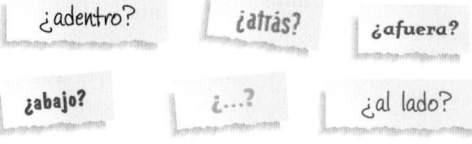

¿adentro?   ¿atrás?   ¿afuera?

¿abajo?   ¿...?   ¿al lado?

9 Perdido

Hablar Nunca puedes encontrar tus cosas. Le
preguntas a tu hermano(a) si ha visto ciertas
cosas. Tu compañero(a) hace el papel de tu
hermano(a). Pregúntale dónde están cuatro
objetos perdidos y luego cambien de papel.

modelo

Tú: *He buscado por dondequiera y no puedo
encontrar mi asistente electrónico. ¿Lo has visto?*
Compañero(a): *Sí, claro, lo vi por la mañana.*
Tú: *¿Dónde lo viste?*
Compañero(a): *Estaba debajo del periódico en la
mesa del comedor.*

Classroom Community

Paired Activity Have students identify people in
the classroom by describing their locations to a partner.
The partner guesses who is being described. Students
should each take at least 3 turns.

Learning Scenario Have students work in pairs to
write and present a "moving day" skit. One student
plays a person who is moving to a new house and the
other plays a mover. As the mover brings the items into
the new house, the homeowner tells him/her where to
place the items. Encourage students to add humor.

GRAMÁTICA Pero vs. Sino

▶ You know that the word **pero** is usually the equivalent of the English conjunction *but*. However, there is another word in Spanish, **sino**, that also means *but*. It is used in situations where the idea being conveyed is *not this*, **but** *rather that*.

No vamos a comer carne, sino pescado.
*We're not going to eat meat, **but** (rather) fish.*

No debes vender la computadora vieja, sino repararla.
*You shouldn't sell the old computer, **but** (rather) fix it.*

▶ You can also use **sino** with:

   no sólo… sino también…
   *not only… **but** also…*

Compró **no sólo** una computadora portátil, **sino también** un teléfono inalámbrico.
*He bought **not only** a laptop, **but** a cordless phone **too**.*

▶ When there is a **conjugated verb** in the second part of the sentence you use **sino que** instead of **sino**.

No sólo escribe cartas **sino que también manda** correo electrónico.
*He doesn't only write letters **but he** also **sends** e-mail.*

No vendí la computadora vieja, **sino que** la **reparé**.
*I didn't sell the old computer, **but** (instead) **I fixed it**.*

Practice:
Actividades
10 11 12

Más práctica
cuaderno p. 151
Para hispanohablantes
cuaderno p. 149

🖥 **Online Workbook**
CLASSZONE.COM

---

10 Alma

Escuchar/*Escribir* Alma salió con Juan anoche. Escucha su descripción de lo que pasó y decide si la palabra que le falta a las oraciones es **pero** o **sino**.

   modelo
   Alma iba a salir con Julio **pero** *cambió de opinión y salió con Juan.*

1. Alma y Juan no fueron al cine _____ al restaurante.
2. Alma no comió pescado _____ carne.
3. Alma pidió un café _____ le trajeron un refresco.
4. Alma pidió un postre _____ no le gustó.
5. Juan no pagó con tarjeta de crédito _____ en efectivo.
6. Juan no dejó propina _____ le dio las gracias al camarero.

También se dice
Hay varias maneras de hablar de las computadoras en los países hispanohablantes.

- **computador** (Latinoamérica)
- **computadora** (Latinoamérica)
- **ordenador** (España)

Teaching All Students

Extra Help Write these sentences on the board and have students explain the use of **pero**, **sino**, and **sino que**.
- Me gustaría comprar la videocámara, pero no puedo.
- No es sólo un fax sino también una fotocopiadora.
- No venden computadoras sino que las alquilan.

Multiple Intelligences

Verbal Have students work in pairs and take turns describing where things are located in their bedrooms. The other student tries to sketch what he/she hears.

Naturalist Have students write a description of a country, seaside, or mountain scene using adverbs/prepositions of location. They should also include at least one use of **pero**, **sino**, and **sino que**.

🔔 **Quick Start Review**
♻ Adverbs/prepositions of location
Use OHT 28 or write on the board: Use adverbs/prepositions of location to write where the following items might be located:
1. el altoparlante
2. la computadora
3. las pilas
4. el identificador de llamadas
5. el teléfono celular
6. el beeper
Answers will vary.

Teaching Suggestions
Presenting Pero vs. Sino
- Point out that **pero** connects two contrasting ideas in a sentence.
- **Sino** is used after a negative clause to set up a contrast. There is no conjugated verb following it.

ACTIVIDAD
10 **Objective:** Controlled practice Listening comprehension/**pero** vs. **sino**

Answers (See script, p. 423B.)
1. sino
2. sino
3. pero
4. pero
5. sino
6. pero

📘 **Block Schedule**

Change of Pace Have students create symbols for each of the adverbs/prepositions of location. Then have them create "sentences" that use only drawing and symbols. For example, a drawing of a book followed by a symbol for **encima de** followed by a drawing of a table would mean **El libro está encima de la mesa.** Have students guess the meanings of each other's sentences in Spanish. (For additional activities, see **Block Scheduling Copymasters**.)

Teaching Resource Options

Print

Block Scheduling Copymasters
Unit 6 Resource Book
  Absent Student Copymasters, p. 107

Audiovisual

OHT 29 (Quick Start), 34 (Grammar)

Technology

On-line Workbook, U6E2
Take Home Tutor CD-ROM, U6E2

ACTIVIDAD 11 **Objective:** Transitional practice
Pero vs. sino in conversation

♻ Television vocabulary

Answers will vary.

ACTIVIDAD 12 **Objective:** Open-ended practice
Pero vs. sino in writing

Answers will vary.

Interdisciplinary Connection

Social Studies Have students research
the history of the telephone and create a
timeline of the important dates. On the
timeline they might also include sketches
of various phone models from different
eras.

---

11 **¿Qué vieron por fin?**

Hablar/*Escribir* Tu amigo(a) te
pregunta qué viste anoche en
la tele. Dramaticen la situación
y cambien de papel.

> **modelo**
>
> **acción**
>
> **Compañero(a):** *¿Viste el programa
> de acción?*
>
> **Tú:** *Sí, lo vi. No, no vi el programa
> de acción sino el de misterio.*

1. misterio / ¿?
2. drama / ¿?
3. comedia / ¿?
4. documental / ¿?
5. ciencia ficción / ¿?
6. concurso / ¿?
7. programa de entrevistas / ¿?
8. dibujos animados / ¿?
9. la telenovela / ¿?
10. ¿...?

12 **¿Qué regalo compraré?**

Escribir Estás tratando de decidir si debes comprarte un
teléfono celular u otro producto electrónico. Lee el anuncio
y decide si lo vas a comprar o no. Escribe cuatro oraciones
explicando por qué no te lo debes comprar.

> **modelo**
>
> *Quiero comprarme un teléfono celular, pero de veras no lo necesito.*
>
> *No quiero comprarme un teléfono celular sino...*

¿Cuál de éstos es tu caso?

¡R-I-I-I-I-I-I-N-G!
—¿Alo?
—¡Asdkf jfald jfalfnk al jutyr CD kf iutncpa tlono celular!
—¿Quééé?

¡Es mejor precaver que tener que remediar!
Si quieres que tu voz se oiga clarita, llama
con un **Celular Supra 1020**.
¡Al activar tu cuenta
también te llevarás
un radio CD!

¡R-I-I-I-I-I-I-N-G!
—¿Alo?
—Soy yo. ¡Me acabo de ganar un radio CD al activar mi Celular Supra 1020!
—¡Qué bueno! Y lo del radio no está nada mal.

Nada como el **Celular Supra 1020**—
para que te oigas bien. Llámanos hoy.

Classroom Community

Paired Activity Extend **Actividad 12** by having
pairs of students write explanations as to why someone
should buy the following items: **un teléfono con
identificador de llamadas, un equipo estereofónico,
una contestadora automática.**

Group Activity In groups of 3–4, have students talk
about how today's phone problems may be different
from those that people had with traditional rotary dial
phones on a cord; for example, charging the battery,
range, etc.

GRAMÁTICA · Se for Unplanned Occurences

You can use a special construction with **se** to indicate that an action was unplanned or unexpected.

Se le cayeron los libros.
She (He, You form.) dropped the books.

Se me rompieron los anteojos.
I (accidentally) broke my glasses.

Se nos acaba la leche.
We're running out of milk.

• Notice that the verb is always in either the third-person singular or third-person plural.

• You use an **indirect object pronoun** to say to whom the action occurred.

• To emphasize this relationship, you can also add a phrase consisting of **a + the person** (noun or pronoun).

A mí se me perdieron los audífonos y a Luisa **se le** perdieron las pilas.
I lost my earphones and Luisa lost her batteries.

Vocabulario

Unplanned events

acabársele (a uno) *to run out of*

caérsele (a uno) *to drop*

descomponérsele (a uno) *to break down, to malfunction*

ocurrírsele (a uno) *to dawn on, to occur to*

olvidársele (a uno) *to forget*

perdérsele (a uno) *to lose*

quedársele (a uno) *to leave something behind*

rompérsele (a uno) *to break*

▶ ¿Te ha pasado alguna de estas cosas recientemente?

Practice:
Actividades 13 14 15
Más práctica *cuaderno p. 152*
Para hispanohablantes *cuaderno p. 150*
 **Online Workbook** CLASSZONE.COM

Nota cultural

En Latinoamérica y España, los programas de concursos son muy populares y cuentan con miles de televidentes. Algunos de los programas más populares son «Sorpresa y media» (Argentina), «La noche del domingo» (Argentina) y «¿Quiere cacao?» (Colombia; «cacao» quiere decir «ayuda».) Generalmente los participantes tienen que cantar, responder a preguntas o participar en diversos concursos para ganar los premios

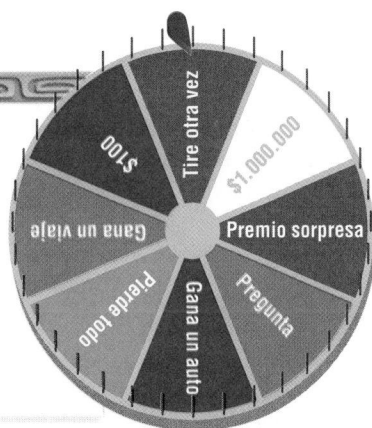

Teaching Resource Options

Print

Más práctica Workbook PE,
pp. 145–148, 152

Actividades para todos Workbook PE,
pp. 171–176

Cuaderno para hispanohablantes
PE, pp. 145–146, 150

Block Scheduling Copymasters

Unit 6 Resource Book

Más práctica Workbook TE,
pp. 72–75, 79

Actividades para todos Workbook
TE, pp. 80–85

Cuaderno para hispanohablantes
TE, pp. 90–91, 95

Audioscript, p. 112

Audiovisual

Audio Program CD 17, Track 3, Activity 13

Technology

Online Workbook, U6E2
Take-Home Tutor CD-ROM, U6E2

 Objective: Controlled practice
Listening comprehension/se for
unplanned occurrences

Answers (See script, p. 423B.)
1. se le olvidó la fecha
2. se le perdió la dirección
3. se le descompuso el reloj
4. se le olvidó que tenía otra cita
5. se le hizo tarde

 **Objective:** Transitional practice
Se for unplanned occurrences

Answers will vary.

 Objective: Open-ended practice
Se for unplanned occurrences
in conversation

Answers will vary.

Dictation

Using the Listening Activity Script for
Actividad 13 on TE p. 423B, dictate
selected sentences to students. You may
want to have students peer correct the
sentences.

---

13 Las excusas

Escuchar/*Escribir* Hubo una fiesta y todos explicaron
luego por qué no pudieron ir. Escribe las excusas de
cada persona.

> **modelo**
>
> *Marcela no pudo ir a la fiesta porque se le descompuso el coche.*

1. Joaquín no fue a la fiesta porque _____.
2. Norma nunca llegó a la fiesta porque _____.
3. Arturo llegó tarde porque _____.
4. Sandra no fue a la fiesta porque _____.
5. Ileana nunca llegó porque _____.

14 Lo inesperado

Hablar/*Escribir* A menudo hay ocasiones en las cuales
ocurren cosas inesperadas y uno tiene que explicar por
qué no ha ocurrido lo que todo el mundo esperaba. Ahora
tú estás en esa situación. Explica qué pasó.

> **modelo**
>
> *¡Ay! ¡No te compré un regalo porque se me olvidó que hoy era tu
> cumpleaños!*

perder	acabar
• las llaves	• la leche
• los libros	• la gasolina
descomponer	**olvidar**
• la computadora portátil	• comprar un regalo
• el equipo estereofónico	• mandar una tarjeta

15 ¡Perdona!

> **STRATEGY: SPEAKING**
>
> **Make excuses** When making
> an apology, you have the
> choice of giving a short
> answer: **Se me olvidó**.
> But consider telling the
> whole story that led up
> to your having forgotten:
> **Todo empezó cuando fui
> al centro.**

Hablar A menudo tenemos
que pedir perdón cuando no
cumplimos nuestras promesas.
Con tu compañero(a), inventa
cuatro situaciones en las cuales
tienes que pedir perdón.

> **modelo**
>
> **Tú:** *¿Por qué no me llamaste
> anoche?*
>
> **Compañero(a):** *¡Se me acabaron
> las baterías del
> teléfono celular!
> Y cuando por fin
> llegué a casa,
> ya era muy tarde.*

438

cuatrocientos treinta y ocho
Unidad 6

Classroom Community

Learning Scenario Have students work in groups
of 3 to role-play the following scene: 2 students have
not done their homework. Each student gives the
teacher 3 excuses as to why the homework is not done.
The teacher accepts or does not accept the excuses.

Portfolio Have students imagine that they lost,
broke, or forgot something very important to their
parents, teacher, or another adult. Have them write a
letter of apology and an excuse for the incident.

Rubric A = 13–15 pts. B = 10–12 pts. C = 7–9 pts. D = 4–6 pts. F = < 4 pts.

Writing criteria	Scale
Organization	1 2 3 4 5
Grammar/spelling accuracy	1 2 3 4 5
Creativity/appearance	1 2 3 4 5

Activity 16 brings together all concepts presented.

16 El fax multifuncional

Hablar/Escribir En grupos de tres o cuatro, conversen sobre los modelos de fax diferentes que se ofrecen en el anuncio. Escojan el fax que comprarían si pudieran. Hagan una lista de las ventajas y desventajas.

modelo

Tú: *Yo creo que debemos comprar el fax que tiene copiadora a color.*

Compañero(a) 1: *¡Eso no importa! Lo que importa es que tenga un centro de mensajes.*

Compañero(a) 2: *En la tienda de enfrente venden muchos.*

Es un tren . . .
Es un avión . . .
¡Es . . . FAX ZIP!

El fax más rápido del mundo

Fax Zip cuenta con todos los avances tecnológicos que harán de su fax un placer

► Impresora de alta resolución–¡no más cartas ilegibles!
► Centro de mensajes–¡ningún recado perdido!
► Escáner–¡imágenes claras!
► Función computarizada de teléfono–¡una conexión asegurada y rápida!

FAX MULTIFUNCIONAL 3X2Y
• Función computarizada de teléfono

FAX MULTIFUNCIONAL 7Z9T
• Impresora/copiadora a colores
• Centro de mensajes

FAX CONTESTADOR 9P3S
• Impresora/copiadora a colores
• Centro de mensajes
• Función computarizada de teléfono

FAX MULTIFUNCIONAL 4J6P
• Impresora/copiadora a colores
• Centro de mensajes

Llame a su distribuidor más cercano para conseguir un catálogo.

More Practice: Más comunicación *p. R19*

Online Workbook
CLASSZONE.COM

Refrán

No hay cosa de más saber que a sí mismo conocer.

¿Qué quiere decir el refrán? En tu opinión, ¿qué es más importante, saber muchos datos o conocerse a sí mismo? ¿Por qué?

cuatrocientos treinta y nueve
Colombia, Venezuela y los países andinos Etapa 2
439

Teaching All Students

Extra Help Have students explain why the **se** for unplanned occurrences expressions are often in the preterite (completed action). Use yes/no questions to practice using the different persons (**se me, se te, se nos,** etc.) with both singular and plural objects (**la tarea, las llaves,** etc.).

Multiple Intelligences

Logical/Mathematical Have students work in groups to survey the class. Each group uses a different unplanned occurrence expression, tallies what is most often forgotten, lost, etc. Have each group illustrate the results of their poll with a bar graph or pie chart. Display and use them in class to practice the expressions; for example, **A muchos estudiantes se les olvida la tarea.**

Objective: Open-ended practice

16 Etapa review in reading and conversation

Answers will vary.

Quick Wrap-up

Give students the following scenarios and have them give an explanation, using an expression for unplanned events.

1. Ana no puede llamar por teléfono a su amiga.
2. Tomás quiere tomar un refresco pero no hay más en casa.
3. Sylvia no puede ver bien.
4. Óscar no puede manejar su carro.

Answers
Answers will vary. Answers could include:

1. Se le olvidó el número.
2. Se le acabó el refresco.
3. Se le rompieron los anteojos.
4. Se le perdieron las llaves.

Critical Thinking

Have students discuss how electronic advancements have helped or hindered the work environment of professions not generally associated with electronic devices; for example, an upholsterer, a farmer, a rock band, etc.

Block Schedule

Personalization Have students tell about when something broke down on them; for example, a car. What did they do, where were they, etc.? (For additional activities, see **Block Scheduling Copymasters.**)

Teaching Resource Options

Print

Actividades para todos Workbook PE, pp. 177–179
Block Scheduling Copymasters
Unit 6 Resource Book
   Actividades para todos Workbook TE, pp. 86–88
   Absent Student Copymasters, p. 109

Audiovisual

OHT 29 (Quick Start)

Quick Start Review

♻ **Se** for unplanned occurrences

Use OHT 29 or write on the board: Write sentences using the following elements:

1. Esteban / perdérsele / altoparlantes
2. Leonardo / descomponérsele / grabadora
3. Estela / olvidársele / teléfono celular
4. Carmen / caérsele / contestadora automática

Answers
1. A Esteban se le perdieron los altoparlantes.
2. A Leonardo se le descompuso la grabadora.
3. A Estela se le olvidó el teléfono celular.
4. A Carmen se le cayó la contestadora automática.

Teaching Suggestions
Presenting Cultura y comparaciones

• Begin by asking students to look at the photos of the woman and the man on pp. 440 and 441. What conclusion can they draw about technology based on these photos? **¿A qué conclusión puedes llegar acerca de la tecnología en base a estas fotos?**
• Present the Connecting Cultures Strategy. Either complete the survey in class and have students make charts or assign the survey as homework.

En colores
CULTURA Y COMPARACIONES

PARA CONOCERNOS

STRATEGY: CONNECTING CULTURES

Survey technology in daily life How common is the use of personal technology in your life? Do an informal survey in your class or school to determine what percentage of those you survey have and use a cellular phone. Document the range of specific uses among those you interview. Show the proportion of users and non-users in a pie chart and rank order the uses from the most common to the least common. How do these uses compare with those mentioned in *¿Un aparato democrático?* Which of the uses would have the most appeal in a commercial ad?

¿Un aparato democrático?

A todas horas y en todo lugar se puede contar con el timbre[1] del más moderno de los aparatos telefónicos— el teléfono celular. En muchos países de Sudamérica, este aparato está convirtiéndose en un elemento esencial de la comunicación… y no hay duda de que el uso del celular aumentará porque los precios están bajando, la competencia está aumentando y los servicios que se ofrecen están multiplicándose.

---

[1] ring

440 cuatrocientos cuarenta
Unidad 6

Classroom Community

Cooperative Learning Have students work in groups of 5 to read and summarize the passage. Student 1 is the recorder and writes down summary sentences as they are given. Student 2 reads the first paragraph. Student 3 provides a 1-sentence summary, then reads the second paragraph. Student 4 provides a 1-sentence summary, then reads the third paragraph. Student 5 provides a 1-sentence summary, then reads the fourth paragraph. Student 2 provides a 1-sentence summary. The group then verifies the information and submits the paper for a grade.

Paired Activity Have students work in pairs to discuss and list the advantages and disadvantages of using cellular telephones. Have pairs share and compare their lists.

Este aparato tiene mucha importancia en Sudamérica, sobre todo en los países andinos, porque el terreno[2] de estas regiones remotas ha dificultado mucho la expansión del sistema tradicional de teléfonos. El servicio telefónico en casa es caro, a veces no muy bueno y difícil de conseguir.

El teléfono celular transmite mensajes por medio de las ondas[3] de radio. Los abonados[4] usan aparatos móviles que les dan la oportunidad de comunicarse con cualquier otro usuario[5] desde cualquier lugar. Así que es posible que el teléfono celular pueda lograr[6] lo que hasta ahora nadie ha podido hacer— ¡democratizar las comunicaciones y unir zonas remotas del continente!

El teléfono celular ofrece muchas posibilidades la participación en la red mundial[7] de comunicaciones. No sorprende que en América Latina el teléfono celular sea un servicio que todo el mundo desea tener.

---

[2] terrain, landscape
[3] waves
[4] subscribers
[5] users
[6] to achieve
[7] worldwide web

CLASSZONE.COM
More About Colombia, Venezuela, and the Andean countries

¿Comprendiste?

1. ¿Por qué está aumentando el uso del teléfono celular en América Latina?
2. ¿Qué ventajas tiene el teléfono celular sobre el teléfono tradicional?
3. ¿Qué es posible que pueda lograr el teléfono celular? ¿Por qué?

¿Qué piensas?

1. ¿Puedes pensar en otros tipos de tecnología que sirven para unir regiones remotas?
2. ¿Cuáles son otros obstáculos físicos que la tecnología tal vez pueda superar (overcome)?

Hazlo tú

Busca información sobre el uso del teléfono celular en Estados Unidos y haz una presentación de lo que descubras.

cuatrocientos cuarenta y uno | **441**
Colombia, Venezuela y los países andinos Etapa 2

Reading Strategy

Skim Remind students that before reading a passage, it is helpful to read quickly to get a general idea of its content. Have them skim the paragraphs, noting clues that indicate the topic.

Culture Highlights

● **INDUSTRIAS Y TELÉFONOS CELULARES** Pida a los estudiantes que recuerden las industrias principales en el Cono Sur: la agricultura, la minería, la industria pesquera y el turismo. Luego, pídales que piensen en situaciones donde tener un teléfono celular puede ayudar a que el trabajo sea más fácil en cada una de estas industrias. Los agricultores, por ejemplo, pueden moverse fácilmente entre el campo y sus oficinas de trabajo.

Interdisciplinary Connections

Science Have students research how cellular phones work and why they would be easier to set up in remote areas. Encourage them to look for cellular phone towers in their area.

¿Comprendiste?

Answers
1. Porque los precios están bajando, la competencia está aumentando y los servicios que se ofrecen están multiplicándose.
2. El servicio telefónico tradicional es más caro, a veces no es muy bueno y es difícil de conseguir.
3. Es posible que el teléfono celular pueda democratizar las comunicaciones y unir zonas remotas de América Latina porque da la oportunidad de comunicarse con cualquier persona desde cualquier lugar.

Teaching All Students

Extra Help Have students write 2 true/false statements for each paragraph. Then have them exchange with a partner to verify the statements and correct those that are false.

Native Speakers Ask students to write a paragraph responding to the following: **Cada año se fabrican muchas cosas que no necesitamos. ¿Cuáles son algunas de las cosas que crees que no necesitamos?**

Multiple Intelligences

Verbal Have students talk about situations in which cell phones would be useful, even critical. Encourage them to relate personal experiences; for example, **Cuando se nos descompuso el carro...**

Naturalist Have students use topography maps to identify possible remote, hard-to-reach cities and towns in South America. In which countries are most located?

Block Schedule

FunBreak Have students play the Piedra–papel–tijeras game in the **Ampliación** section, TE p. 401B. (For additional activities, see **Block Scheduling Copymasters**.)

Teaching Resource Options

Print

Cuaderno para hispanohablantes PE, pp. 151–152

Block Scheduling Copymasters

Unit 6 Resource Book
Cuaderno para hispanohablantes
TE, pp. 96–97
Information Gap Activities, pp. 100–101
Family Involvement, pp. 110–111

Audiovisual

OHT 30 (Quick Start)

Technology

eTest Plus Online/Test Generator
CD-ROM

www.classzone.com

Quick Start Review

♻ Conjunctions

Use OHT 30 or write on the board:
Write whether each of these sentences
expresses something that is **pending,
habitual,** or **past:**

1. Iremos a la tienda en cuanto
   llegue Pedro.
2. Los niños se portan mal cuando
   llega su madre.
3. No puedes jugar con tus amigos
   hasta que termines la tarea.
4. Se me perdieron las llaves
   después de que llamaste.
5. Tomasito no va a dormir hasta
   que apagues la luz.

Answers

1. pending   4. past
2. habitual   5. pending
3. pending

✓ Teaching Suggestions
What Have Students Learned?

Have students look at the "Now you
can…" notes listed on the left side of
pp. 442–443. Tell students to think
about which areas they might not be
sure of. For those areas, they should
consult the "To review" notes.

ETAPA **2**

Now you can...

• talk about
  technology.

To review

• conjunctions,
  see p. 432.

Now you can...

• state location.

To review

• prepositions and
  adverbs of location,
  see p. 433.

En uso
REPASO Y MÁS COMUNICACIÓN

OBJECTIVES
• Talk about technology
• State locations
• Make contrasts
• Describe unplanned
  events

❶ ¡Sí, claro!

Tu compañero(a) quiere saber si vas a comprar varios productos
electrónicos. Tú le dices que sí, bajo ciertas condiciones. ¿Qué
le dices?

modelo

computadora portátil (en cuanto yo tener el dinero)

Compañero(a): *¿Vas a comprar una computadora portátil?*

Tú: *Sí, claro, en cuanto tenga el dinero.*

1. contestadora automática (cuando tener mi propio teléfono)
2. beeper (para que tú poder encontrarme a cualquier hora)
3. asistente electrónico (para que yo no olvidar tu número de teléfono)
4. teléfono celular (en caso de que haber una emergencia)

❷ El cuarto de Gloria

El cuarto de Gloria es un desastre. Su mamá entra a su cuarto
y no puede creer lo que ve. ¿Qué le dice a Gloria?

modelo

las camisetas

*¡Ay, hija! ¡Las camisetas están
encima de la computadora!*

1. los zapatos
2. los periódicos
3. los discos compactos
4. la raqueta de tenis
5. las pelotas de tenis
6. la guitarra

Classroom Community

Paired Activity Have students work in pairs and tell
each other what their parents or another adult might
say if they were to go into the students' bedrooms right
now. For example: **¡Los zapatos están encima de la
cama!** Students might try to sketch what they hear,
then check to see how accurately they understood.

Storytelling Have students do the "Storytelling"
activities in the **Ampliación** section on TE p. 401A.

Group Activity Have students work in groups to
imagine that they are making plans to open an office.
First, they should decide what kind of office (medical,
construction, etc.), then they should make a list of the
electronic equipment they will need. They should justify
each item by explaining its use or benefit. You might
also impose budget restrictions, and have them price
and prioritize the equipment they want.

Now you can...

• make contrasts.

To review

• **pero** vs. **sino**,
see p. 435.

3 CompuVisión

Ricardo fue con su mamá a CompuVisión para hacer unas compras. Completa sus oraciones con **sino**, **pero** o **sino que** para saber cómo les fue.

modelo

No fuimos a ElectroMundo ___sino___ a CompuVisión.

1. No fuimos por la mañana _____ por la tarde.
2. Yo iba a comprar una computadora portátil _____ no lo hice.
3. Mamá quería un televisor portátil _____ no tenían la marca que quería.
4. No compramos el teléfono celular _____ el inalámbrico.
5. Papá no fue con nosotros _____ se quedó en casa.
6. Yo quería comprar muchas cosas _____ no tenía suficiente dinero.

Now you can...

• describe unplanned events.

To review

• **se** for unplanned occurrences,
see p. 437.

4 El aeropuerto

La familia Núñez acaba de llegar al aeropuerto para empezar sus vacaciones en Perú. ¡Pero a todos se les olvidó algo! ¿Qué se les olvidó? Luego, di qué va a pasar.

modelo

señor Núñez

Al señor Núñez se le olvidó el pasaporte. No va a poder viajar.

1.  señores Núñez

2.  señor Núñez

3.  Miguelito

4.  Arturo y Alejandra

5.  señora Núñez

6.  Miguelito

ACTIVIDAD 1  Answers

1. A: ¿Vas a comprar una contestadora automática?
   B: Sí, claro, cuando tenga mi propio teléfono.
2. A: ¿Vas a comprar un beeper?
   B: Sí, claro, para que me puedas encontrar a cualquier hora.
3. A: ¿Vas a comprar un asistente electrónico?
   B: Sí, claro, para que no se me olvide tu número de teléfono.
4. A: ¿Vas a comprar un teléfono celular?
   B: Sí, claro, en caso de que haya una emergencia.

ACTIVIDAD 2 Answers

1. ¡Ay, hija! ¡Los zapatos están debajo de la cama!
2. ¡Ay, hija! ¡Los periódicos están alrededor de la cama!
3. ¡Ay, hija! ¡Los discos compactos están debajo del escritorio!
4. ¡Ay, hija! ¡La raqueta de tenis está detrás del escritorio!
5. ¡Ay, hija! ¡Las pelotas de tenis están dentro del basurero!
6. ¡Ay, hija! ¡¡La guitarra está encima del armario!

ACTIVIDAD 3  Answers

1. sino   4. sino
2. pero   5. sino que
3. pero   6. pero

ACTIVIDAD 4  Answers

1. A los señores Núñez se les olvidaron los zapatos de tenis.
2. Al señor Núñez se le olvidaron los boletos de avión.
3. A Miguelito se le olvidó la maleta.
4. A Arturo y a Alejandra se les olvidó la videocámara.
5. A la señora Núñez se le olvidó la computadora portátil.
6. A Miguelito se le olvidó el Walkman™.

Teaching All Students

Extra Help Have each student expand **Actividades 1–4** by writing one additional item for each. Have volunteers write their items on the board or on OHTs for more practice.

Multiple Intelligences

Logical/Mathematical Point out that there are theories about how to conveniently lay out rooms; for example, the kitchen triangle (refrigerator, sink, stove). Have students design a convenient/efficient work place, and tell where things go; for example, **La computadora debe estar encima del escritorio principal.**

◼ Block Schedule

Variety Have students use the **se** for unplanned occurrences expressions to come up with ads or slogan ideas for electronic devices; for example, **¿Se le descompuso el carro? Con el teléfono celular nunca está solo.**

Teaching Resource Options

Print

Unit 6 Resource Book
  Audioscript, p. 114
  Vocabulary Quizzes, pp. 117–119
  Grammar Quizzes, pp. 120–121
  Etapa Exam, Forms A and B,
    pp. 122–131
  Examen para hispanohablantes,
    pp. 132–136
  Portfolio Assessment, pp. 137–138
  Multiple Choice Test Questions,
    pp. 229–231

Audiovisual

OHT 30 (Quick Start)
Audio Program CD 20, Track 16

Technology

eTest Plus Online/Test Generator
CD-ROM

  www.classzone.com

Rubric: Speaking

Criteria	Scale	
Sentence structure	1 2 3	A = 11–12 pts.
Vocabulary use	1 2 3	B = 9–10 pts.
Originality	1 2 3	C = 7–8 pts.
Fluency	1 2 3	D = 4–6 pts.
		F = < 4 pts.

En tu propia voz

Rubric: Writing

Criteria	Scale	
Vocabulary use	1 2 3 4 5	A = 13–15 pts.
Accuracy	1 2 3 4 5	B = 10–12 pts.
Creativity, appearance	1 2 3 4 5	C = 7–9 pts.
		D = 4–6 pts.
		F = < 4 pts.

Teaching Note: En tu propia voz

Writing Strategy Suggest that students persuade their reader. In their ads, they should offer simple, direct information in an intriguing format to make a lasting impression.

---

5 El almacén

STRATEGY: SPEAKING

Consider the factors for or against an electronic purchase For some purchases, it is useful to plan what you want to know before talking with the salesperson. Think about your personal needs and finances, and ask for information about these: **las mejores marcas, diferencias entre marcas, descuentos, rebajas, garantía, durabilidad, ventajas y desventajas de uso**.

En grupos de tres o cuatro, dramaticen la siguiente situación. Dos o tres amigos van al almacén a comprar varios productos electrónicos. Tienen muchas preguntas sobre los varios modelos y marcas. El (La) dependiente contesta sus preguntas y trata de convencerlos que compren un producto bastante caro.

modelo

Vendedor(a): *¿En qué puedo servirles?*

Compañero(a) 1: *Pues, yo buscaba un televisor.*

Vendedor(a): *Muy bien. Aquí tenemos el modelo Q2010…*

Compañero(a) 2: …

---

6 En tu propia voz

ESCRITURA Escoge un producto electrónico o inventa uno. Luego, escribe un anuncio para el periódico que convenza al público que es el mejor modelo de ese tipo que se vende hoy día. Asegúrate que contestaste las siguientes preguntas en tu anuncio.

- ¿Qué hace el producto?
- ¿Para quién es el producto?
- ¿Por qué es el mejor?
- ¿Cuáles son las ventajas de este modelo?
- ¿Es el precio razonable?
- ¿Se ofrece un descuento?

CONEXIONES

El arte Usando la información que sacaste de la Actividad 6, diseña un anuncio para un producto electrónico. Toma en cuenta que un anuncio debe tener mucho impacto y no puede tener demasiado texto. ¿Cuáles son los puntos más importantes que quieres comunicar? Tal vez tendrás que cortar el texto que escribiste. ¿Necesitas un lema publicitario? ¿Qué tipo de foto o dibujo necesitas para acompañar el texto? Haz un póster o diseña el anuncio en la computadora si prefieres. Piensa bien en la importancia de los colores y el diseño que escoges. Explícale a la clase por qué elegiste los elementos en tu anuncio.

Surfea la red por medio de la **Onda Cibernética**
El mejor proveedor de Internet en Caracas

444   cuatrocientos cuarenta y cuatro
Unidad 6

Classroom Community

Learning Scenario Have students work in pairs to present a skit about an experience in an electronics equipment store. They should talk about what they see, what they want, the price, the discount, the guarantee, etc.

Group Activity Plan ahead: Bring in several ads for electronic devices from newspapers and magazines from a variety of Spanish-speaking countries. Make copies so that groups can receive several examples. Divide the class into groups of 4. Have students scan the ads for items whose names they have learned and make a chart of the items they find. Then have them compare word usage from different countries.

En resumen
REPASO DE VOCABULARIO

Flashcards
CLASSZONE.COM

TALK ABOUT TECHNOLOGY

Equipment

el altoparlante	speaker
el asistente electrónico	electronic assistant
los audífonos	headphones
la batería	battery
el beeper	beeper
la computadora portátil	laptop computer
la contestadora automática	answering machine
el equipo estereofónico	stereo equipment
el fax multifuncional	multifunctional fax machine
el identificador de llamadas	caller identification
la pila	battery
el radio portátil	portable radio
el teléfono celular/ inalámbrico	cellular / cordless telephone
el telemensaje	voice mail
el televisor portátil	portable television
la videocámara	videocamera
el Walkman™	walkman™

Shopping

accesible	available, accessible
la confiabilidad	reliability,
convencer (zo)	to convince
el descuento	discount
devolver (ue)	to return
distinguir entre	to distinguish
la durabilidad	durability
equivocarse	to make a mistake
estar descompuesto(a)	to be broken
estar roto(a)	to be broken
fijarse en	to notice
la garantía	guarantee
inigualable	unequalled
la marca	brand name
la nitidez	clarity, sharpness
(no) funcionar	to (not) work
respaldado(a)	backed (by)
tomar en cuenta	to take into account

MAKE CONTRASTS

♻ **Ya sabes**

a menos que	unless
antes (de) que	before
con tal (de) que	as long as
cuando	when
en caso (de) que	in case (of)
en cuanto	as soon as
hasta que	until
para que	so that
tan pronto como	as soon as

STATE LOCATIONS

Adverbs/prepositions of location

afuera	outside
al lado (de)	beside, next to
atrás	in back, behind
detrás (de)	behind
enfrente (de)	facing

♻ **Ya sabes**

abajo	below
alrededor (de)	around
debajo (de)	underneath
delante (de)	in front of
dentro (de)	inside
encima (de)	on top of
frente (a)	facing
fuera (de)	outside of
junto (a)	next to

DESCRIBE UNPLANNED EVENTS

Accidents

acabársele (a uno)	to run out of
caérsele (a uno)	to drop
descompónersele (a uno)	to break down, to malfunction
ocurrírsele (a uno)	to dawn on, to occur to
olvidársele (a uno)	to forget
perdérsele (a uno)	to lose
quedársele (a uno)	to leave behind
rompérsele (a uno)	to break

Juego

Sopa de letras
¡Tengo mucha energía pero nunca hago ejercicio! ¿Qué soy?

cuatrocientos cuarenta y cinco
Colombia, Venezuela y los países andinos Etapa 2
445

Interdisciplinary Connection

Art Have students research and analyze schematic drawings for electronic devices. Then have them draw the schema for a different device (real or imaginary).

🔔 Quick Start Review

♻ Etapa vocabulary

Use OHT 30 or write on the board: Match the words with the verbs:

1. ___ descompuesto   a. escuchar
2. ___ garantía   b. comprar
3. ___ descuento   c. prometer
4. ___ audífonos   d. apoyar
5. ___ respaldado   e. romper

Answers
1. e   2. c   3. b   4. a   5. d

Teaching Suggestions
Vocabulary Review

Bring a large illustration to class that includes items students know how to say and that can be used to talk about location. Display the illustration for 20 seconds. Put it away and have students write the location of as many things as they can remember in the illustration.

Dictation

Dictate the following sentences to review the **Etapa:**

1. Voy a comprar este televisor portátil aunque sea caro.
2. Las pilas están dentro del asistente electrónico.
3. Compraron no sólo un equipo estereofónico, sino también un teléfono celular.
4. Se me quedó el Walkman™ en casa.

Juego

Answer: una batería

Block Schedule

Research Have students work in groups to research and illustrate development that led to a particular electronic device; for example, the fax machine (from regular messages and mail to fax), the beeper (from messengers to beepers), etc. (For additional activities, see **Block Scheduling Copymasters.**)

Teaching All Students

Extra Help Give each student 4–5 words from the **Repaso de vocabulario,** so that most or all of the words are taken. Have students write sentences for their words, putting a blank for the target word. Have them exchange and complete each other's sentences with the correct words.

Multiple Intelligences

Intrapersonal Have students write about 3 things they forgot, broke, or lost this week.

Verbal Have students create word problems. They list 3 related words and have someone come up with a fourth related word. Variation: Students list 4 words and have someone identify the word that doesn't belong.

Planning Guide CLASSROOM MANAGEMENT

OBJECTIVES

Communication
- Compare and evaluate *pp. 454–456*
- Express precise relationships *pp. 457–461*
- Navigate cyberspace *pp. 448–449, 450–451, 464–465*

Grammar
- Review the use of comparatives and superlatives *pp. 454–456*
- Review the use of prepositions *pp. 457–459*
- Use verbs with prepositions *pp. 459–461*

Culture
- Regional vocabulary *pp. 452, 456*
- Computers in Latin America *p. 453*
- Spanish-language Internet sites *p. 460*
- Gabriel García Márquez *pp. 462–463*
- A visit to Bolivia by Internet *pp. 464–465*

 Recycling
- Electronics vocabulary *p. 455*
- Demonstratives *p. 455*

STRATEGIES

Listening Strategies
- Identify important computer vocabulary *p. 450*

Speaking Strategies
- Compare and evaluate films in a chat group *p. 456*
- Compare and evaluate computer configurations *p. 468*

Reading Strategies
- Monitor comprehension *p. 462*
- Scan for cognates *TE p. 464*

Writing Strategies
- Use different kinds of descriptive words *TE p. 468*
- Prioritize information in order of importance *p. 470*

Connecting Cultures Strategies
- Recognize variations in vocabulary *pp. 452, 456*
- Learn about computers in Latin America *p. 453*
- Visit Spanish-language Internet sites *p. 460*
- Learn about Gabriel García Márquez *pp. 462–463*
- Evaluate the Internet as a means of developing cultural knowledge and understanding *p. 464*
- Connect and compare what you know about the Internet in your community to help you learn about the Internet in a new community *pp. 464–465*

PROGRAM RESOURCES

 Print
- *Más práctica* Workbook PE *pp. 153–160*
- *Actividades para todos* Workbook PE *pp. 181–190*
- Block Scheduling Copymasters *pp. 145–152*
- Unit 6 Resource Book
  - *Más práctica* Workbook TE *pp. 141–148*
  - *Actividades para todos* Workbook TE *pp. 149–158*
  - *Cuaderno para hispanohablantes* TE *pp. 159–166*
  - Information Gap Activities *pp. 167–170*
  - Family Letter *p. 171*
  - Absent Student Copymasters *pp. 172–178*
  - Family Involvement *pp. 179–180*
  - Audioscript *pp. 181–184*
  - Assessment Program, Unit 6, Etapa 3 *pp. 185–225, 232–234*
  - Video Activities *pp. 243–246*
  - Videoscript *pp. 247–249*
  - Answer Keys *pp. 250–254*

Audiovisual
- Audio Program CD 18
- *Canciones* CD
- Video Program Videotape 49:10 / DVD, Unit 6
- Overhead Transparencies M1–M5; GO1–GO5; 4, 35–49
- Word Tiles U6E3

 Technology
- eEdition Plus Online/eEdition CD-ROM
- Easy Planner Plus Online/Easy Planner CD-ROM
- eTest Plus Online/Test Generator CD-ROM
- Online Workbook
- Take-Home Tutor CD-ROM
- www.classzone.com

✓ Assessment Program Options
- Unit 6 Resource Book
  - Vocabulary Quizzes
  - Grammar Quizzes
  - Etapa Exam Forms A and B
  - *Examen para hispanohablantes*
  - Portfolio Assessment
  - Unit 6 Comprehensive Test
  - *Prueba comprensiva para hispanohablantes,* Unit 6
  - Final Test
  - Multiple Choice Test Questions
- Audio Program CD 20
- eTest Plus Online/Test Generator CD-ROM

Native Speakers
- *Cuaderno para hispanohablantes* PE *pp. 153–160*
- *Cuaderno para hispanohablantes* TE (Unit 6 Resource Book)
- *Examen para hispanohablantes* (Unit 6 Resource Book)
- *Prueba comprensiva para hispanohablantes,* Unit 6 (Unit 6 Resource Book)
- Audio Program *(Para hispanohablantes)* CD 18, 20
- Audioscript (Unit 6 Resource Book)

Student Text Listening Activity Scripts

 **Situaciones** *pages 450–451*

• CD 18

1. «El disco duro tiene que tener más de 3.2 GB.»
2. «Quiero que la pantalla del monitor sea muy grande.»
3. «El módem tiene que ser interno.»
4. «Necesitamos una hoja de cálculo muy buena para hacer las cuentas.»
5. «El sistema tiene que tener capacidades de multimedia. El CD-ROM es muy importante para nuestros negocios.»
6. «Quiero una impresora láser de color.»
7. «Necesitamos una base de datos para mantener toda la información sobre nuestros clientes.»
8. «También quiero comprar una computadora portátil para usar cuando viajo.»
9. «Vamos a necesitar un programa anti-virus.»

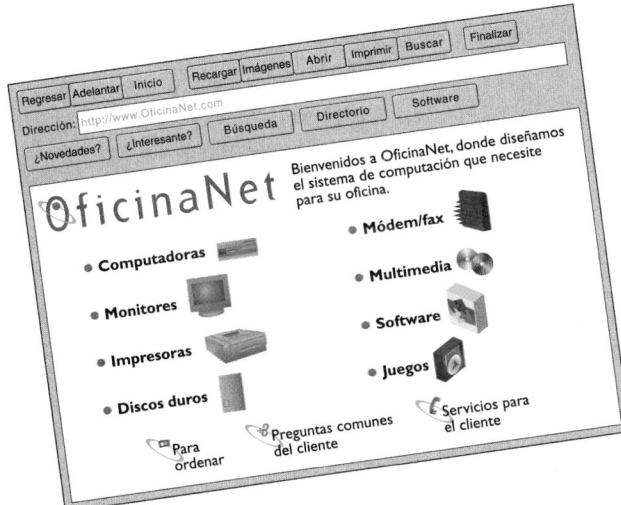

ACTIVIDAD 5  **Marcos** *page 455*

Modelo: Esta computadora tiene mucha memoria. Tiene tanta memoria como ésa.

1. ¿Has jugado este juego interactivo alguna vez? Éste es más divertido que ése.
2. Espero que tengas un programa anti-virus. Si no, te recomiendo éste. Este programa anti-virus es el mejor en el mercado.
3. Tu módem es demasiado lento. Este módem es el más rápido que existe.
4. Nunca compres esta marca de computadora. Es la peor en el mercado.
5. ¿Necesitas una hoja de cálculo? Esta hoja de cálculo es más útil que ésa.
6. Debes comprar la computadora aquí en CompuVisión. En este momento, CompuVisión ofrece el mejor descuento.
7. ¡Mira el precio! Casi no lo puedo creer. ¡Es el mejor precio que he visto por un sistema de computación!

ACTIVIDAD 13  **La página-web** *page 460*

Hoy mis amigos y yo tratamos de crear una página-web. Empezamos a diseñarla a las ocho de la mañana. ¡Son las ocho de la noche y apenas acabamos de terminarla! Ricardo vino a ayudarnos. Hay que saber muchas cosas para crear una página-web interesante. Pero ahora tengo que irme. Mi novia está esperándome para cenar. ¡Me olvidé de la cita! Me acordé de ella cuando vi mi reloj. ¡Caramba! Ella insiste en que yo sea puntual. ¡Me va a matar!

Sample Lesson Plan - 50 Minute Schedule

DAY 1

Etapa Opener
- Quick Start Review (TE, p. 446) 5 MIN.
- Have students look at the *Etapa* Opener and answer the questions. 5 MIN.

En contexto: Vocabulario
- Quick Start Review (TE, p. 448) 5 MIN.
- Present *Descubre*, p. 448. Have students use context and pictures to learn *Etapa* vocabulary. Use the Situational OHTs for additional practice. 15 MIN.

En vivo: Situaciones
- Quick Start Review (TE, p. 450) 5 MIN.
- Present the Listening Strategy, p. 450. Have students read section 1, p. 450. Play the audio for section 2. Have students work in pairs or groups to complete section 3. 15 MIN.

Homework Option:
- Have students write answers to *¿Comprendiste?*, p. 449.

DAY 2

En acción: Vocabulario y gramática
- Check homework. 5 MIN.
- Quick Start Review (TE, p. 452) 5 MIN.
- Have students complete *Actividad* 1 in writing. Go over answers orally. 5 MIN.
- Have students do *Actividad* 2 in pairs. 5 MIN.
- Have students read and complete *Actividad* 3 in pairs. 10 MIN.
- Present *Repaso:* Comparatives and Superlatives, p. 454. 10 MIN.
- Do *Actividad* 4 orally. 5 MIN.
- Play the audio; do *Actividad* 5. 5 MIN.

Homework Option:
- Have students complete *Actividad* 4 in writing. *Más práctica* Workbook, pp. 157–158. *Cuaderno para hispanohablantes*, pp. 155–156.

DAY 3

En acción (cont.)
- Check homework. 5 MIN.
- Present the *Vocabulario*, p. 456. Then have students do *Actividad* 6 in pairs. 5 MIN.
- Present the Speaking Strategy, p. 456. Then have students do *Actividad* 7 in groups. 10 MIN.
- Quick Start Review (TE, p. 457) 5 MIN.
- Present *Repaso:* Prepositions, p. 457. 10 MIN.
- Do *Actividad* 8 orally. 5 MIN.
- Have students do *Actividad* 9 in writing, then exchange papers for peer correction. 5 MIN.
- Have students complete *Actividad* 10 in pairs. 5 MIN.

Homework Option:
- *Más práctica* Workbook, p. 159. *Cuaderno para hispanohablantes*, p. 157.

DAY 4

En acción (cont.)
- Check homework. 5 MIN.
- Have students do *Actividad* 11 in writing. Ask volunteers to present their paragraphs. Expand using *Más comunicación*, p. R20. 15 MIN.
- Quick Start Review (TE, p. 459) 5 MIN.
- Present *Gramática:* Verbs with Prepositions and the *Vocabulario*, p. 459. 10 MIN.
- Have students complete *Actividad* 12 in writing. Go over answers orally. 5 MIN.
- Play the audio; do *Actividad* 13. 5 MIN.
- Have students complete *Actividad* 14 in pairs. 5 MIN.

Homework Option:
- *Más práctica* Workbook, p. 160. *Cuaderno para hispanohablantes*, p. 158.

DAY 5

En acción (cont.)
- Check homework. 5 MIN.
- Have students complete *Actividad* 15 in groups. Expand using *Más comunicación*, p. R20. 15 MIN.

Refrán
- Present the *Refrán*, p. 461. 5 MIN.

En voces: Lectura
- Quick Start Review (TE, p. 462) 5 MIN.
- Present the Reading Strategy, p. 462. Call on volunteers to read the *Lectura* aloud. Have students answer the *¿Comprendiste?/¿Qué piensas?* questions, p. 463. 20 MIN.

Homework Option:
- Have students complete *Hazlo tú*, p. 463.
- *Actividades para todos* Workbook, pp. 181–190

DAY 6

En colores: Cultura y comparaciones
- Check homework. 5 MIN.
- Quick Start Review (TE, p. 464) 5 MIN.
- Present the Connecting Cultures Strategy, p. 464. Call on volunteers to read the article aloud. Have students answer the *¿Comprendiste?/¿Qué piensas?* questions, p. 465. 20 MIN.

En uso: Repaso y más comunicación
- Quick Start Review (TE, p. 466) 5 MIN.
- Have students do *Actividad* 1 orally and *Actividad* 2 in pairs. 5 MIN.
- Have students do *Actividades* 3 and 4 in writing. Go over answers orally. 10 MIN.

Homework Option:
- Have students complete *Hazlo tú*, p. 465. Review for *Etapa* 3 Exam.

DAY 7

En uso (cont.)
- Check homework. 5 MIN.
- Present the Speaking Strategy, p. 468, and have students do *Actividad* 5 in groups. 10 MIN.

En tu propia voz: Escritura
- Have students brainstorm their ideas for *Actividad* 6. 5 MIN.

En resumen: Repaso de vocabulario
- Quick Start Review (TE, p. 469) 5 MIN.
- Review grammar questions, etc., as necessary. 5 MIN.
- Complete *Etapa* 3 Exam. 20 MIN.

Homework Option:
- Have students complete their web pages for *Actividad* 6, p. 468. Review for Unit 6 Comprehensive Test.

DAY 8

Conexiones
- Check homework. 5 MIN.
- Discuss *La tecnología*, p. 468. 5 MIN.

Unit 6 Comprehensive Test
- Complete Unit 6 Comprehensive Test. 30 MIN.

En tu propia voz: Escritura
- Present the Writing Strategy, p. 470. Do the writing activity, pp. 470–471. 10 MIN.

Ampliación
- Optional: Use a suggested project, game, or activity. (TE, pp. 401A–401B)

Homework Option:
- Have students complete the assignment for *Conexiones*. Review for Final Exam.

Sample Lesson Plan - Block Schedule (90 minutes)

DAY 1

Etapa Opener
- Quick Start Review (TE, p. 446) 5 MIN.
- Have students look at the *Etapa* Opener and answer the questions. 5 MIN.
- Use Block Scheduling Copymasters. 10 MIN.

En contexto: Vocabulario
- Quick Start Review (TE, p. 448) 5 MIN.
- Present *Descubre*, p. 448. Have students use context and pictures to learn *Etapa* vocabulary. Use the Situational OHTs for additional practice. 15 MIN.

En vivo: Situaciones
- Quick Start Review (TE, p. 450) 5 MIN.
- Present the Listening Strategy, p. 450. Have students read section 1, p. 450. Play the audio for section 2. Have students work in pairs or groups to complete section 3. 20 MIN.

En acción: Vocabulario y gramática
- Quick Start Review (TE, p. 452) 5 MIN.
- Have students complete *Actividad* 1 in writing. Go over answers orally. 5 MIN.
- Have students do *Actividad* 2 in pairs. 5 MIN.
- Have students read and complete *Actividad* 3 in pairs. 10 MIN.

Homework Option:
- Have students write answers to *¿Comprendiste?*, p. 449.

DAY 2

En acción (cont.)
- Check homework. 5 MIN.
- Quick Start Review (TE, p. 454) 5 MIN.
- Present *Repaso:* Comparatives and Superlatives, p. 454. 10 MIN.
- Do *Actividad* 4 orally. 5 MIN.
- Play the audio; do *Actividad* 5. 5 MIN.
- Do an expansion activity from TE pp. 454–455 for variety and reinforcement. 10 MIN.
- Present the *Vocabulario*, p. 456. Then have students do *Actividad* 6 in pairs. 10 MIN.
- Present the Speaking Strategy, p. 456. Then have students do *Actividad* 7 in groups. 10 MIN.
- Quick Start Review (TE, p. 457) 5 MIN.
- Present *Repaso:* Prepositions, p. 457. 10 MIN.
- Do *Actividad* 8 orally. 5 MIN.
- Have students do *Actividad* 9 in writing, then exchange papers for peer correction. 5 MIN.
- Have students complete *Actividad* 10 in pairs. 5 MIN.

Homework Option:
- Have students complete *Actividad* 4 in writing. *Más práctica* Workbook, pp. 157–159. *Cuaderno para hispanohablantes*, pp. 155–157.

DAY 3

En acción (cont.)
- Check homework. 10 MIN.
- Have students do *Actividad* 11 in writing. Ask volunteers to present their paragraphs. Expand using Information Gap Activities, Unit 6 Resource Book, p. 167; *Más comunicación*, p. R20. 20 MIN.
- Quick Start Review (TE, p. 459) 5 MIN.
- Present *Gramática:* Verbs with Prepositions and the *Vocabulario*, p. 459. 10 MIN.
- Have students complete *Actividad* 12 in writing. Go over answers orally. 5 MIN.
- Play the audio; do *Actividad* 13. 10 MIN.
- Have students complete *Actividad* 14 in pairs. 5 MIN. Have students complete *Actividad* 15 in groups. Expand using Information Gap Activities, Unit 6 Resource Book, p. 168; *Más comunicación*, p. R20. 20 MIN.

Refrán
- Present the *Refrán*, p. 461. 5 MIN.

Homework Option:
- *Más práctica* Workbook, p. 160. *Cuaderno para hispanohablantes*, p. 158.
- *Actividades para todos* Workbook, pp. 181–190

DAY 4

En voces: Lectura
- Check homework. 5 MIN.
- Quick Start Review (TE, p. 462) 5 MIN.
- Present the Reading Strategy, p. 462. Call on volunteers to read the *Lectura* aloud. Have students answer the *¿Comprendiste?/¿Qué piensas?* questions, p. 463. 15 MIN.

En colores: Cultura y comparaciones
- Quick Start Review (TE, p. 464) 5 MIN.
- Present the Connecting Cultures Strategy, p. 464. Call on volunteers to read the article aloud. Have students answer the *¿Comprendiste?/¿Qué piensas?* questions, p. 465. 15 MIN.

En uso: Repaso y más comunicación
- Quick Start Review (TE, p. 466) 5 MIN.
- Do *Actividad* 1 orally, 2 in pairs, and 3 and 4 in writing. 15 MIN.
- Present the Speaking Strategy, p. 468, and have students do *Actividad* 5 in groups. 10 MIN.
- Do *Actividad* 6 in writing. 15 MIN.

Homework Option:
- Have students complete *Hazlo tú*, pp. 463, 465. Review for *Etapa* 3 Exam and Unit 6 Comprehensive Test.

DAY 5

En resumen: Repaso de vocabulario
- Check homework. 5 MIN.
- Quick Start Review (TE, p. 469) 5 MIN.
- Review grammar questions, etc., as necessary. 5 MIN.
- Complete *Etapa* 3 Exam. 20 MIN.

Conexiones
- Discuss *La tecnología*, p. 468. 5 MIN.

Unit 6 Comprehensive Test
- Review grammar questions, etc., as necessary. 5 MIN.
- Complete Unit 6 Comprehensive Test. 30 MIN.

En tu propia voz: Escritura
- Present the Writing Strategy, p. 470. Do the writing activity, pp. 470–471. 15 MIN.

Ampliación
- Optional: Use a suggested project, game, or activity. (TE, pp. 401A–401B) 15 MIN.

Homework Option:
- Have students complete the assignment for *Conexiones*. Review for Final Exam.

▼ ¿Tienes tu propia página-web en la red mundial?

Etapa Theme

Navigating cyberspace, comparing and evaluating, and expressing precise relationships

Grammar Objectives

- Reviewing the use of comparatives and superlatives
- Reviewing the use of prepositions
- Using verbs with prepositions

Teaching Resource Options

Print

Block Scheduling Copymasters
Unit 6 Resource Book
  Family Letter, p. 171
  Absent Student Copymasters, p. 172

Audiovisual

OHT 4, 41 (Quick Start)

Quick Start Review

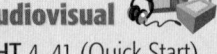 Technology vocabulary

Use OHT 41 or write on board:
Identify the electronic device or service needed:

1. para contestar llamadas
2. para mandar documentos rápidamente
3. para organizar direcciones y números de teléfono
4. para grabar fiestas y bailes en casa
5. para escuchar música mientras hace ejercicio

Answers
1. el telemensaje; la contestadora automática
2. el fax
3. el asistente electrónico
4. la videocámara
5. el Walkman™

Teaching Suggestions
Previewing the Etapa

- Ask students to study the photo on pp. 446–447 (1 min.).
- Close books; ask students to name at least 3 things they remember.
- Reopen books and look at the picture again. Have students describe the people and the setting.
- Use the ¿Qué ves? questions to focus the discussion.

UNIDAD 6

ETAPA 3

¡Un viaje al ciberespacio!

OBJECTIVES

- Compare and evaluate
- Express precise relationships
- Navigate cyberspace

¿Qué ves?

Mira la foto. Contesta las preguntas.

1. ¿Qué tipo de lugar es este?
2. ¿Qué clase de productos crees que tienen?
3. ¿Qué cosas crees que podrá hacer el chico de la mochila roja?
4. ¿Qué te dice la página-web de los servicios que ofrecen en este sitio?

446

Classroom Management

Planning Ahead Prepare to introduce the theme of cyberspace by bringing in computer catalogs and computer ads from newspapers and magazines.

Time Saver Prepare a list of Spanish-language Web sites and Internet chat rooms for students who are learning Spanish or who speak Spanish.

Cross Cultural Connections

Point out to students that they can find addresses, phone numbers, and other information for cyber cafés all over the world on the Internet; for example, at the Curious Cat Web site. In some areas, cyber cafés provide Internet access for people who otherwise could not explore cyberspace because they do not have access to a computer.

Culture Highlights

● **INTERNET EN ESPAÑOL** Internet tiene muchos usuarios en América Latina y España. Muchos servicios de búsqueda tienen secciones exclusivas para España y América Latina. En un cibercafé como Monkey on Line, en Ecuador, los usuarios pueden alquilar una computadora por hora. Pregunte a los estudiantes si creen que los cibercafés son una buena forma de obtener acceso a la red.

● **MONEDA** In 2000, Ecuador changed its currency from the **sucre** to the U.S. dollar.

Block Schedule

Setting the Theme Download from the Internet the home pages of Web sites of several Spanish-speaking countries or have students search for them. Then have students give descriptions of the pages. (For additional activities, see **Block Scheduling Copymasters**.)

Teaching All Students

Extra Help Remind students that Web searches using Spanish words will have different results. To get accent marks and tildes, they might copy and paste the search term from their word processor.

Challenge Have students use the Internet to obtain a list of cyber cafes in Latin America. Can they find at least one in each Spanish-speaking country?

Multiple Intelligences

Interpersonal Have students research and talk about services available at cyber cafes (Internet access, e-mail, travel reservations, etc.).

Naturalist Have students discuss ideal locations for cyber cafes (urban, pedestrian areas, etc.).

Teaching Resource Options

Print 📖

Block Scheduling Copymasters
Unit 6 Resource Book
 Absent Student Copymasters, p. 172

Audiovisual 📽️

OHT 35, 36, 37, 37A, 38, 38A, 41
(Quick Start)

Technology 💻

Online Workbook, U6E3
Take-Home Tutor CD-ROM, U6E3

🔔 Quick Start Review

♻️ Vocabulary

Use OHT 41 or write on the board:
Which word doesn't belong?

1. telemensaje, teleserie, beeper, contestadora automática
2. control remoto, tele-guía, televisor portátil, teléfono inalámbrico
3. videocámara, radio portátil, equipo estereofónico, Walkman™
4. audífonos, altoparlantes, asistente electrónico, radio portátil

Answers
1. teleserie   2. teléfono inalámbrico
3. videocámara   4. asistente electrónico

Teaching Suggestions
Reviewing Vocabulary

• Have students look at pp. 448–449. Use OHT 35 and 36 to present the vocabulary.
• Ask the Comprehension Questions in on TE p. 449 in order of yes/no (questions 1–3), either/or (questions 4–6), and simple word or phrase (questions 7–10).
• Use the TPR activity to reinforce the meaning of individual words.

Descubre

Answers
A. 1. b 2. c 3. d 4. a
B. The World Wide Web

En contexto VOCABULARIO

JOVENET

🔲 Descubre

A. Las relaciones entre palabras
Adivina el significado de las palabras en azul basándote en el significado de los verbos.

1. usar: **usuario**
2. ampliar: **ampliable**
3. configurar: **configuración**
4. calcular: **hoja de cálculo**
   a. spreadsheet
   b. user
   c. expandable
   d. configuration

B. Cognados falsos En español hay palabras que se parecen mucho a palabras en inglés, pero que no tienen el mismo significado. ¿Puedes adivinar qué significa **la red mundial**? ¡No es un color!

Perfil
de nuestros lectores #11:
Jimena Villaroel

Hablamos con Jimena, una joven estudiante peruana, sobre su computadora personal.

¡Hola! Yo soy Jimena Villarroel, una estudiante de colegio en Lima, Perú. Me fascinan las computadoras— ¡mi cuarto es un verdadero laboratorio de computación! Tengo todo ordenado según mi propia configuración. También tengo mi propia página–web en la red mundial. Si quieren, ¡escríbanme para decirme qué piensan de mi sistema! Mi dirección electrónica es jimenav@colcen.edu.

Creo que nosotros, los usuarios, debemos tener los últimos y mejores programas de software disponibles para aprovechar los sistemas. Yo tengo:
• Programas antivirus
• Procesador de texto
• Hojas de cálculo
• Base de datos

HARDWARE
• Doce discos
• 256 MB de memoria, ampliable a 1 GB
• Conexión a Internet de alta velocidad
• Tarjeta de sonido
• Tarjeta gráfica
• Micrófono Multimedia

448 cuatrocientos cuarenta y ocho
Unidad 6

Classroom Community

TPR If you have a computer in your classroom, have volunteers go to it and hold up or point to different parts and name them. If you don't have a computer, use a picture of one from a computer catalog or draw one. Have students point to the various parts and name them.

Learning Scenario Have students prepare a sales presentation of a computer. The presentation should include how the machine can help people in their daily life and work-related tasks.

MARZO

Altoparlantes Multimedia

Disco

Microprocesador

Monitor a color, tamaño 17"

Disco duro de 40 GB

CD-ROM

Impresora a color

Teclado profesional expandido de 105 teclas

Ratón de tres botones

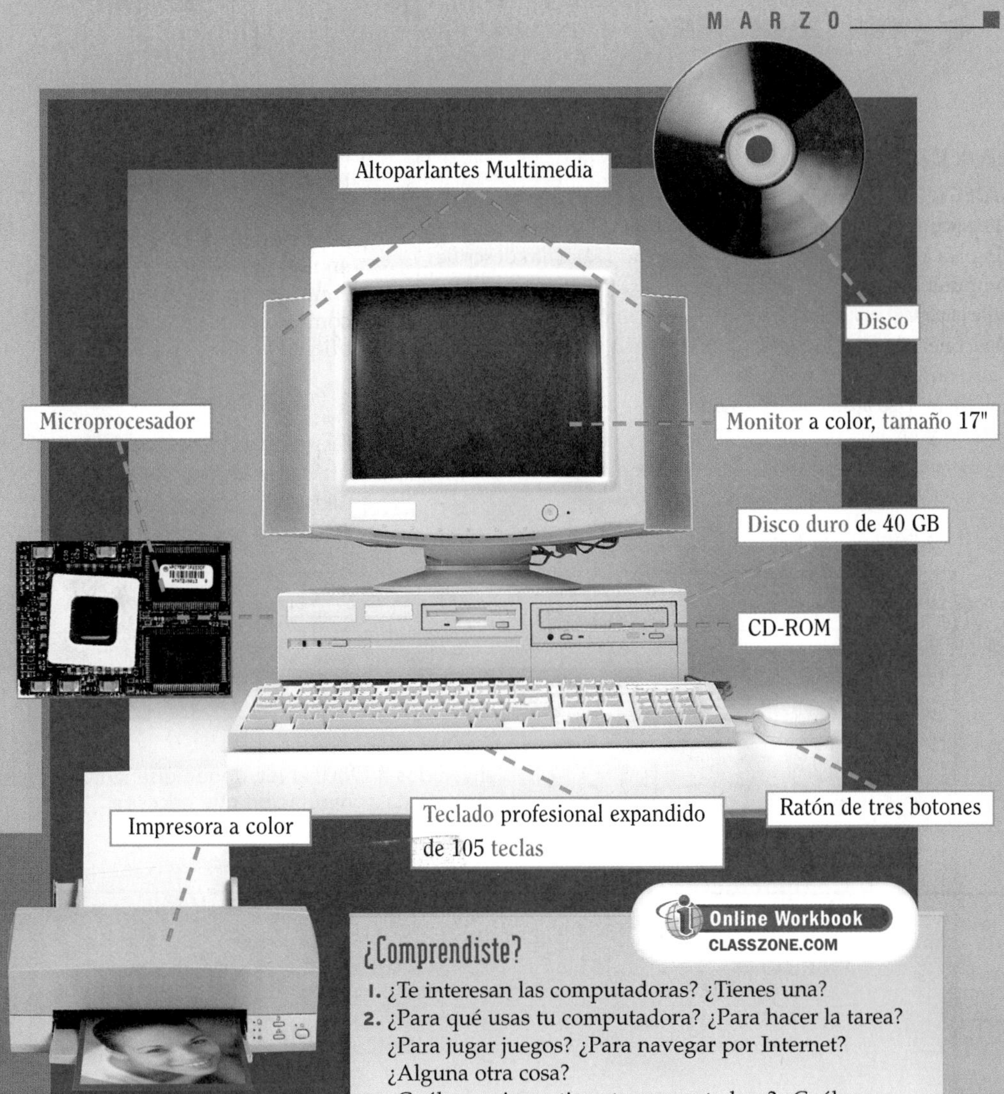

Online Workbook
CLASSZONE.COM

¿Comprendiste?

1. ¿Te interesan las computadoras? ¿Tienes una?
2. ¿Para qué usas tu computadora? ¿Para hacer la tarea? ¿Para jugar juegos? ¿Para navegar por Internet? ¿Alguna otra cosa?
3. ¿Cuáles opciones tiene tu computadora? ¿Cuáles no tiene que quisieras que tuviera?
4. ¿Crees que las computadoras son un implemento importante para los estudios? ¿Para tu carrera? ¿Para el entretenimiento? ¿Para la comunicación entre personas, países y gobiernos? Explica por qué sí o por qué no.

cuatrocientos cuarenta y nueve
Colombia, Venezuela y los países andinos Etapa 3   **449**

Comprehension Questions

1. ¿Es Jimena una estudiante de colegio? (Sí)
2. ¿Vive Jimena en Santiago, Chile? (No)
3. ¿Tiene Jimena su propia computadora? (Sí)
4. ¿Tiene una página-web o tres páginas-web? (una página-web)
5. ¿Tiene su computadora 32 MB de memoria o 128MB de memoria? (32 MB de memoria)
6. ¿Tiene o no tiene tarjeta de sonido? (tiene tarjeta de sonido)
7. ¿Qué clase de monitor tiene? (un monitor a color, tamaño 25")
8. ¿Cómo es la impresora? (Es a color.)
9. ¿Qué tipo de teclado tiene? (teclado profesional expandido de 105 teclas.)
10. ¿Cómo es el fax de la computadora? (Es un fax/módem de 56k.)

Supplementary Vocabulary

La computadora

adjuntar	to attach
almacenar	to store
archivar	to file
el archivo	file
copiar	to copy
el documento	document
el escáner	scanner
la impresora inyección de tinta	ink jet printer
pasar un mensaje a alguien	to send someone a message
el procesador de textos	word processor
responder	to answer

La tecnología

la conferencia por video	video conference
la realidad virtual	virtual reality

Block Schedule

Change of Pace Have students talk about personal computers they own or would like to have, and explain how a specific situation was different or would have been different due to the computer (writing a letter, researching, etc.). (For additional activities, see **Block Scheduling Copymasters.**)

Teaching All Students

Extra Help If you have a computer in the classroom, have students label the parts, and suggest that they label their computers at home. Students may also create drawings of computers to label.

Native Speakers Have students provide additional computer and Internet vocabulary. The rest of the class can add these words to their supplementary vocabulary lists to use in writing assignments.

Multiple Intelligences

Kinesthetic Have students take turns acting out computer components and features for the class to guess.

Teaching Resource Options

Print

Block Scheduling Copymasters
Unit 6 Resource Book
   Absent Student Copymasters, p. 173
   Audioscript, p. 181

Audiovisual

OHT 39, 40, 42 (Quick Start)
Audio Program CD 18, Track 1

Technology

Take-Home Tutor CD-ROM, U6E3

Quick Start Review

♻ Computer vocabulary

Use OHT 42 or write on the board:
Sketch the following items and label
them with the Spanish names:
keyboard, mouse, printer, disk,
microprocessor.

Sketches will vary, but the labels should read:
teclado, ratón, impresora, disco,
microprocesador

Teaching Suggestions
Presenting Situations

• Present the Listening Strategy, p. 450,
  and have students complete the
  Pre-listening exercise.
• Use OHT 39 and 40 to present the
  Leer section. Ask simple yes/no,
  either/or, or short-answer questions.
• Use Audio CD 18 and have students
  do the **Escuchar** section (see Script
  p. 445B) and complete the Listening
  Strategy exercise.
• Have students work in groups to
  complete the **Hablar/Escribir** section.

AUDIO

En vivo
SITUACIONES

PARA ESCUCHAR
STRATEGY: LISTENING

Pre-listening Check your computer vocabulary by making a list
in English and Spanish of terms you already know to describe
a computer system.

Identify important computer vocabulary Listen and note the items that
Sr. Martínez mentions. (See **Escuchar**.) Then verify whether they
are also on your list. If not, add them because you will need to
know them. Use a dictionary to find any remaining English
words on your list.

El mejor sistema

Eres el (la) asistente del señor
Martínez, un hombre de
negocios con una oficina
en La Paz, Bolivia. Él quiere
comprar un sistema de
computación nuevo para la
oficina y quiere tus consejos.

❶ Leer

Para poder darle buenos consejos a tu
jefe, decides visitar la página-web de
OficinaNet, una compañía que se
especializa en sistemas de computación.

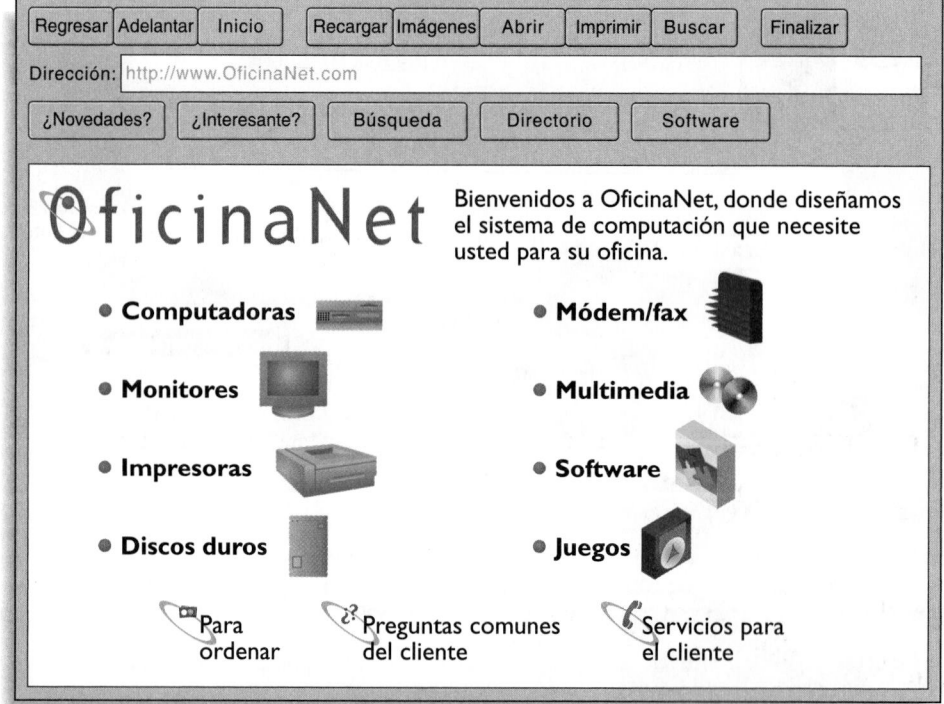

Classroom Community

Paired Activity Have students take turns explaining
the function of each of the items represented on the
Web page and the services represented at the bottom
of the page.

Group Activity Divide the different categories of
items on the Web page on p. 450 among small groups.
Have each group research brands, models, prices, etc.
from computer catalogs and/or online computer stores.
Have groups present the information to the class. Have
the class choose a brand/model of an item from each
category.

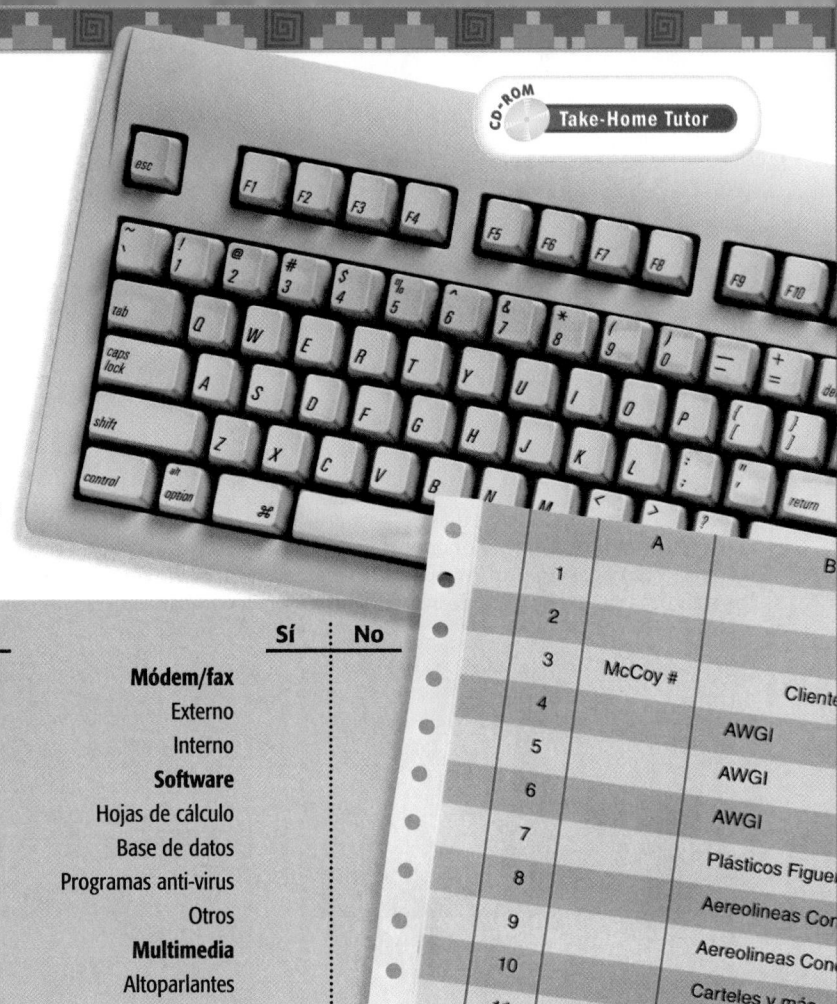

❷ Escuchar

El señor Martínez te describe el sistema de computación que quiere para la oficina. Escucha lo que dice e identifica las categorías que tienes que investigar en la página-web de OficinaNet, según sus necesidades.

	Sí	No		Sí	No
Computadoras			**Módem/fax**		
Marca y modelo			Externo		
Precio			Interno		
Velocidad			**Software**		
Memoria			Hojas de cálculo		
Portátiles			Base de datos		
Monitores			Programas anti-virus		
Tamaño			Otros		
Resolución máxima			**Multimedia**		
Impresoras			Altoparlantes		
Impresoras láser			Tarjeta gráfica		
Tamaño máximo			Tarjeta de sonido		
Resolución máxima			CD-ROM		
Discos duros			**Juegos**		
1.2 GB a 3.2 GB			Edades 8-14		
Más de 3.2 GB			Edades 12-16		
			Juegos para adultos		

❸ Hablar/Escribir

En grupos de dos o tres, diseñen el sistema de computación ideal para los estudiantes. Hagan una lista o un dibujo de todos los accesorios del sistema. Expliquen la función de cada accesorio. Luego, diseñen una página-web para vender el sistema ideal que inventaron.

cuatrocientos cincuenta y uno
Colombia, Venezuela y los países andinos Etapa 3
451

Escuchar (See script, p. 445B.)

Escuchar

Answers
*The following categories should have a check mark under **Sí:***
Computadoras
   Portátiles
Monitores
   Tamaño
Impresoras
   Impresoras láser
Discos duros
   Más de 3.2 GB
Módem/fax
   Interno
Software
   Hojas de cálculo
   Base de datos
   Programas anti-virus
Multimedia
   CD-ROM

Hablar/Escribir

Answers will vary.

Teaching All Students

Extra Help Have students identify the cognates in sections 1 and 2 before doing the listening activity.

Native Speakers Have students tell the class Spanish names (official or translated) of popular computer games. Can the class guess the English names?

Multiple Intelligences

Logical/Mathematical Have students research the prices of different computer components. Then have them "put together" systems based on different budgets.

Intrapersonal After listening to **Escuchar**, have students write a brief description of what kind of computer system they would like.

Block Schedule

Variety Have students list different kinds of software, then associate each with professional needs; for example, a teacher would need a word processor, but perhaps not programming software, etc. (For additional activities, see **Block Scheduling Copymasters**.)

Teaching Resource Options

Print

Block Scheduling Copymasters
Unit 6 Resource Book
  Absent Student Copymasters, p. 174

Audiovisual

OHT 42 (Quick Start)

Quick Start Review

♻ Vocabulary review

Use OHT 42 or write on the board:
Give the name of the item for each of the
following functions:

1. se usa para escribir en la
   computadora
2. se usa para comunicarse con
   otras computadoras
3. se usa para que un virus no
   ataque la computadora
4. se usa para no perder los datos
5. se usa para ver lo que haces en
   la computadora

Answers
1. el teclado
2. el módem
3. el programa anti-virus
4. el disco duro
5. el monitor

Teaching Suggestions
Comprehension Check

Use **Actividades 1–4** to assess retention
after the **Vocabulario** and **Situaciones**.
After completing **Actividad 2** orally,
have students write out 5 of their
exchanges and submit them for a
grade.

Objective: Controlled practice
Vocabulary in writing

Answers
la computadora	el módem
el monitor	los discos
el teclado	el software
el ratón	el usuario

En acción

PARTE A

Práctica del vocabulario

Objectives for Activities 2–3
• Compare and evaluate

1 El cuarto de Esteban

Escribir A Esteban le encanta su
computadora y siempre lo encuentras en
su cuarto navegando por Internet. Escribe
los nombres de los objetos de su escritorio.

También se dice

Hay varias palabras que se usan en vez de
altoparlante, entre las cuales están:

• **bocina** (Colombia)
• **altavoz** (Venezuela)
• **caja acústica** (España)
• **gabinete acústico** (México)
• **bafle** (Argentina)
• **parlante** (general)

2 Quiero comprar...

Hablar/*Escribir* Tú y tu compañero(a) quieren
comprar varios accesorios para su sistema de
computación. Usando palabras de las dos
columnas, pregúntense qué quieren comprar
y por qué.

modelo

Tú: *Necesito comprar un módem externo.*

Compañero(a): *¿No tienes uno?*

Tú: *Sí, pero es muy lento y para navegar por Internet
necesito uno más rápido.*

módem externo	muy lento
monitor	pantalla más grande
computadora	viajar
portátil	más memoria
disco duro	proteger mis programas
programa anti-virus	para las matemáticas
hoja de cálculo	para divertirse
juego interactivo	usar un programa
CD-ROM	de multimedia
tarjeta de sonido	¿...?
tarjeta gráfica	
¿...?	

Classroom Management

Time Saver If time is short, have students do
Actividad 2 as a paired homework assignment. Have
each pair present one mini-exchange to the class.

Organizing Paired/Group Work Find out the
level of computer expertise among your students
through a show of hands or private survey. Form
groups that include 1 student with excellent computer
skills and others with lesser skills. You can have the
computer whiz explain in Spanish the different
components of the computer and/or how to use a
specific program.

Práctica del vocabulario continuación

3 La nueva computadora

Hablar Estás pensando que te quieres comprar la nueva computadora de Xilo. Tu compañero(a) quiere saber por qué. Conversen sobre las ventajas de la computadora según el anuncio.

modelo

Tú: *Me interesa mucho la nueva Xilo.*

Compañero(a): *¿Ah, sí? ¿Por qué?*

Tú: *Pues, mira el anuncio. Es un equipo totalmente multimedia.*

Compañero(a): …

Con la **NUEVA**
computadora

Conecta
a tu familia

$13,999.00*

Porque la nueva computadora de **XILO** es la computadora para el hogar, que ha logrado integrar todo lo que cada miembro de tu familia estaba esperando.

La Computadora de **XILO** es mucho más que una computadora. Es un equipo totalmente multimedia, capaz de reconocer la voz, tomar llamadas y recados con alta fidelidad y consultar información por Internet. Con el microprocesador podrás jugar en tercera dimensión, consultar alguna de sus múltiples enciclopedias o trabajar en su procesador de textos, su hoja de cálculo o cualquiera de sus herramientas de productividad. No le falta nada.

XILO creó esta computadora porque piensa en tu familia.

XILO
Computadoras

*Precio en pesos más I.V.A. Cambios sujetos a la fluctuación del dólar.

Nota cultural

Hace veinte años, solamente las grandes instituciones de gobierno en Latinoamérica tenían computadoras. Éstas se encontraban en grandes cuartos con aire acondicionado y eran del tamaño de máquinas industriales. La revolución de la computadora personal cambió esto. Ahora, no sólo las oficinas de gobierno sino también las empresas privadas, y sobre todo las escuelas, pueden tener una o varias computadoras. Poco a poco se han creado cursos de computación en las escuelas privadas, públicas y más recientemente, en las escuelas primarias.

Objetive: Transitional practice
Vocabulary in conversation

Answers will vary.

Objective: Open-ended practice
Vocabulary in reading and conversation

Answers will vary.

Interdisciplinary Connection
Social Studies Have students research the history of the computer (from the abacus to modern times) and create a timeline of the important dates and people in the industry. On the timeline they might also include sketches of various computer models.

Teaching All Students

Extra Help Have students reread the Xilo ad on p. 453. Then have them work with a partner to write a 3–sentence summary. Have volunteers write their sentences on the board for the class to correct.

Challenge Using a word processing program and clip art, have students prepare a simple ad for a computer, similar to the one on p. 453.

Multiple Intelligences

Logical/Mathematical Have students research the different prices of computer system package deals sold through computer catalogs and online computer stores. Have them vote on the system that gives the consumer the most for the money.

Naturalist Have students research how park/forest rangers use computers in their job.

Block Schedule
Research Have students look up schools in Latin America and in Spain with Web sites. If possible, have them send queries or request information from those schools about computer classes and computer use. (For additional activities, see **Block Scheduling Copymasters**.)

Vocabulary/Grammar • UNIDAD 6 Etapa 3   453

Teaching Resource Options

Print 📖

Más práctica Workbook PE,
 pp. 157–158
Cuaderno para hispanohablantes
 PE, pp. 155–156
Block Scheduling Copymasters
Unit 6 Resource Book
 Más práctica Workbook TE,
 pp. 145–146
 Cuaderno para hispanohablantes
 TE, pp. 161–162
 Absent Student Copymasters, p. 174
 Audioscript, p. 181

Audiovisual 🎧

OHT 43 (Quick Start), 47 (Grammar)
Audio Program CD 18, Track 2, Activity 5

Technology 💻

Online Workbook, U6E3
Take-Home Tutor CD-ROM, U6E3

Quick Start Review

♻ Vocabulary review

Use OHT 43 or write on the board:
Match the words in the 2 columns. Then
use each pair together in a sentence:

1. __ monitor   a. memoria
2. __ disco duro   b. teclado
3. __ botón   c. pantalla
4. __ escribir   d. ratón

Answers
1. c   2. a   3. d   4. b
Sentences will vary.

Objectives for Activities 4–14
• Compare and evaluate • Express precise relationships • Navigate cyberspace

REPASO   Comparatives and Superlatives

You use the words **más, menos,** and **tan** to make comparisons.

- **más** + **adjective** or **adverb** + **que**
  more… than

  Este programa es **más interesante** que el otro.
  *This program is **more interesting than** the other one.*

- **menos** + **adjective** or **adverb** + **que**
  less… than

  Este programa es **menos interesante** que el otro.
  *This program is **less interesting than** the other one.*

- **tan** + **adjective** or **adverb** + **como**
  as… as

  Este programa es **tan interesante** como el otro.
  *This program is **as interesting as** the other one.*

To form the **superlative** in Spanish (*the biggest, the greatest,* etc.), you use:

- **definite article** + **más/menos** + **adjective**

  Este programa es **el más interesante.**
  *This program is **the most interesting** one.*

  Este programa es **el menos interesante.**
  *This program is **the least interesting** one.*

The adjectives **bueno** and **malo** have irregular comparative and superlative forms:

	comparative	superlative
bueno	mejor, mejores	el/la… mejor, los/las… mejores
malo	peor, peores	el/la… peor, los/las… peores

When the comparative word comes before the noun, you use the same constructions except
that **tan** becomes **tanto/tanta/tantos/tantas** to agree with the noun that follows.

Yo preparé **menos documentos** que Pedro.
*I prepared **fewer documents than** Pedro.*

matches

Yo preparé **tantos documentos** como Pedro.
*I prepared **as many documents as** Pedro.*

Practice:
Actividades 4 5 6 7
Más práctica cuaderno pp. 157–158
Para hispanohablantes *cuaderno* pp. 155–156
🌐 **Online Workbook**
CLASSZONE.COM

454
cuatrocientos cincuenta y cuatro
Unidad 6

Classroom Community

Paired Activity Have students work in pairs for
5 minutes to write as many sentences as possible
comparing Spanish-speaking countries/areas; for
example, **Cuba es más grande que Puerto Rico.**
Bolivia es más lejos de Estados Unidos que México.
Have pairs present sample items and check them for
spelling and content accuracy.

Game Have each student write 5 sentences
comparing himself/herself to a well-known person or
cartoon character. Then have them present themselves
and the class guesses who the person/character is.

4 Comparaciones ♻

Hablar/*Escribir* Todos tienen diferentes opiniones sobre el objeto que es más importante o necesario para la vida moderna. Escribe tus opiniones sobre las siguientes cosas. Sigue el modelo.

modelo

«El teléfono celular es más necesario que el asistente electrónico».

(+) necesario

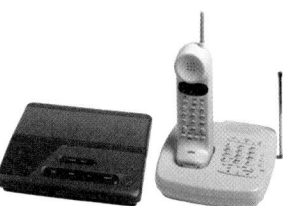

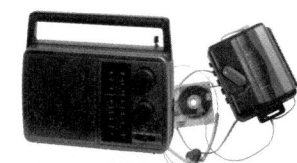

1. (+) importante   **2.** (–) útil

3. (+) necesario   **4.** (+) cara

5. (=) importantes   **6.** (–) divertido

5 Marcos ♻

Escuchar/*Escribir* Estás en CompuVisión, un almacén de productos electrónicos, con tu amigo venezolano Marcos. Él tiene unas opiniones muy fuertes sobre varias cosas que quieres comprar. Escucha a Marcos y escribe su opinión sobre los objetos indicados.

modelo

esta computadora/ésa

Esta computadora tiene tanta memoria como ésa.

1. este juego interactivo/ése
2. este programa anti-virus
3. este módem
4. esta marca de computadora
5. esta hoja de cálculo/ésa
6. el descuento
7. el precio

Teaching Suggestions
Reviewing Comparatives and Superlatives
- Use pictures of trios of items or actual objects to present and practice comparatives and superlatives.
- Have students write a personalized sentence for each form (**más, menos, tan**, superlative, **bueno, malo**). Have volunteers write their sentences on the board for the class to analyze.

ACTIVIDAD 4

Objective: Controlled practice Comparatives

♻ Electronics vocabulary

Answers
1. «La contestadora automática es más importante que el teléfono inalámbrico».
2. «El radio portátil es menos útil que el Walkman™».
3. «El beeper es más necesario que el teléfono celular».
4. «La videocámara es más cara que la grabadora».
5. «Los altoparlantes son tan importantes como los audífonos».
6. «El radio portátil es menos divertido que el televisor portátil».

ACTIVIDAD 5

Objective: Transitional practice Listening comprehension/comparatives and superlatives

♻ Demonstratives

Answers (See script, p. 445B.)
Answers may vary slightly. Sample answers:
1. Este juego interactivo es más divertido que ése.
2. Este programa anti-virus es el mejor del mercado.
3. Este módem es el más rápido que existe.
4. Esta marca de computadora es la peor del mercado.
5. Esta hoja de cálculo es más útil que ésa.
6. Compuvisión ofrece el mejor descuento.
7. Es el mejor precio que ha visto por un sistema de computación.

Teaching All Students

Extra Help Review the forms and meanings of demonstrative adjectives and pronouns before doing **Actividad 5.**

Native Speakers Have students use comparatives and superlatives to write/talk about how life would be different without personal computers.

Multiple Intelligences

Interpersonal Have students talk about how they compare with family and friends in at least 5 different aspects.

Verbal Expand **Actividad 4** by having students tell which items in the entire activity are the most expensive, most useful, most fun, etc.

Block Schedule

Change of Pace Plan ahead: Have students bring in a picture of a personal technology item. Then have them work in small groups to compare their items using various adjectives and adverbs. (For additional activities, see **Block Scheduling Copymasters.**)

Teaching Resource Options

Print 📖

Block Scheduling Copymasters
Unit 6 Resource Book
  Absent Student Copymasters, p. 174

Audiovisual 🎧📽️

OHT 43 (Quick Start), 48 (Grammar)

Technology 🎧💻

Online Workbook, U6E3
Take-Home Tutor CD-ROM, U6E3

Teaching Suggestions
Teaching Vocabulary

Have students use the vocabulary words to give instructions for how to perform tasks on the computer; for example, **Para usar tu correo electrónico, primero escribe tu contraseña, luego haz doble clic en el icono,** etc.

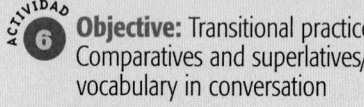
Objective: Transitional practice Comparatives and superlatives/ vocabulary in conversation

Answers will vary.

Objective: Open-ended practice Comparatives and superlatives in conversation

Answers will vary.

🔔 Quick Wrap-up

Call out various adjectives/adverbs. Have students give comparative or superlative statements using the adjectives/adverbs. For example: **inteligente → Ignacio es el más inteligente de la clase.**

---

6 Internet 👥

Hablar/*Escribir* Tú y tu compañero(a) navegan por Internet y ven varias cosas que les gustan y otras que no. Comparen las cosas que encuentran en Internet.

modelo

Tú: *¿Te gusta esta página-web?*

Compañero(a): *Sí, es más interesante que la otra.*

Vocabulario

La red mundial

el buzón electrónico *electronic mailbox*

conectarse a/   *to connect to /*
  desconectarse de   *disconnect from*

la contraseña *password*

el correo electrónico *e-mail*

en línea *online*

el enlace *link*

el grupo de conversación *chat group*

el grupo de noticias *news group*

hacer clic/doble clic *click/double click*

el icono del programa *program icon*

el Localizador Unificador de Recursos (LUR) *URL*

el servicio de búsqueda *search engine*

el sitio *site*

correo electrónico

▶ ¿Cuáles de estas cosas ves con frecuencia cuando navegas por Internet?

---

7 Grupo de conversación 👥

> **STRATEGY: SPEAKING**
>
> **Compare and evaluate films in a chat group** You can compare recent films based on their story (**guión, personajes, trama, clímax, final**), expertise of those involved (**cinematógrafo, director, actores, actrices**), and emotions they create (**emociones, sentimientos**). Can you decide which are the best or the worst (**la mejor, la peor película**)?

Hablar/*Escribir* Participas en un grupo de conversación por Internet. ¿Cuál es el tema principal del grupo? ¿Cuál es la edad promedio de los participantes? Escribe una conversación entre los miembros de tu grupo de conversación.

modelo

Grupo de conversación: Películas recientes

Tú: *A mí me encantan las películas de acción. ¿Has visto la última de Bruce Willis?*

Compañero(a) 1: *No prefiero las películas menos Violentas.*

También se dice

Cuando navegas por Internet puedes ir a muchos sitios. En algunos verás que se habla de **la Internet**, ya que la palabra *net* significa *red* en español, una palabra femenina (la red). En otros casos te encontrarás con **el Internet**, porque se refiere al sistema de comunicación (masculino). Y otras veces verás simplemente **Internet**, sin artículo. ¡No te preocupes! Todas son correctas y puedes usar la que más te guste.

Classroom Community

Cooperative Learning Have students work in groups of 4. Student 1 names a person, place, or thing; student 2 gives an adjective or adverb related to the person/place/thing; student 3 makes a comparative or superlative statement; student 4 writes the sentence down. Student 2 begins the next round. Continue until all students have begun a round. The group reviews the 4 sentences and makes corrections as necessary.

Learning Scenario Have students work in groups of 3 to write and present a skit. One student plays a teenager. The others play the parents. The teenager and the parents disagree on what computer hardware and software to buy. They discuss the problem, using comparatives and superlatives, and come to an agreement at the end.

REPASO   Prepositions

You use **prepositions** to clarify locations and to show relationships among people, places, and things.

Use the preposition **a** to express:

- **motion toward** a **place**

  Vamos **al cine**/**a Venezuela**.
  We're going to the movies/to Venezuela.

- how **far away** something is in space or time

  Adela vive **a tres cuadras del colegio**.
  Adela lives three blocks from the school.

  Caracas está **a tres horas de mi ciudad**.
  Caracas is three hours (away) from my city.

- a **point in time**

  Se fue **a las ocho y media**.
  He left at eight-thirty.

- units of **measurement**

  Viajábamos **a 50 millas por hora**.
  We were traveling at 50 miles per hour.

Use the preposition **en** to express:

- **position** or **location**

  Trabaja **en este edificio**.
  He works in this building.

  Están **en Bogotá**.
  They're in Bogotá.

- a **period of time**
  (as opposed to a specific point of time)

  Vuelvo **en una semana**.
  I'll be back in a week.

  Terminamos **en una hora**.
  We'll finish in an hour.

You have already used **de** to express **possession**. You can also use the preposition **de**:

- to form **compound nouns**

  el banco de datos
  database

  la hoja de cálculo
  spreadsheet

- to mark a **characteristic feature**

  un niño de tres años
  a three-year-old child

Use **con** to express the idea of **accompaniment**.

  Alfredo sale **con Anita**.
  Alfredo is going out with Anita.

  Tomo café **con leche**.
  I have coffee with milk.

Practice: **Actividades** 8 9 10 11   **Más práctica** *cuaderno p. 159*   **Para hispanohablantes** *cuaderno p. 157*    **Online Workbook** CLASSZONE.COM

Teaching All Students

Extra Help Ask questions that use prepositions at the beginning; for example, ¿Adónde vamos? ¿A qué hora se fue? ¿En qué edificio trabaja? ¿Con quién sale?

Multiple Intelligences

Visual Have students draw examples of Web pages to illustrate the words in the **Vocabulario** on p. 456.

Interpersonal Have students discuss the different uses of e-mail; for example, communicating with friends, sending greeting cards, etc. What are some of the drawbacks? (For example, spam, privacy issues, etc.)

Critical Thinking

Have students brainstorm the impact e-mail has had on services like the U.S. Postal Service, telephone companies, and overnight delivery services.

Quick Start Review

Comparatives and superlatives

Use OHT 43 or write on the board: Use comparatives and superlatives to write sentences using the following elements:

1. un monitor grande / un monitor pequeño
2. el correo electrónico / el correo regular
3. el teléfono inalámbrico / el teléfono celular
4. una impresora a color / una impresora de blanco y negro

Answers will vary.

Teaching Suggestions
Reviewing Prepositions

- Point out that prepositions express relationships in time and space.
- Stress that some Spanish prepositions have several English equivalents; for example, **de** can mean *of* (San Juan es la capital de Puerto Rico), *from* (Yo soy de Cuba), or *about* (Hablan de Jimena). Likewise, some English prepositions have more than one Spanish equivalent; for example, *at* can be **a** (Voy a salir a las ocho) or **en** (Hay mucha gente en la playa).

Block Schedule

Variety Challenge students to complete phrases you will provide by using a preposition. Give them a word, for example, **vaso**. They should add to it by saying, **vaso de agua**. (For additional activities, see **Block Scheduling Copymasters**.)

Teaching Resource Options

Print

Más práctica Workbook PE, p. 159
Cuaderno para hispanohablantes
  PE, p. 157
Block Scheduling Copymasters
Unit 6 Resource Book
  Más práctica Workbook TE, p. 147
  Cuaderno para hispanohablantes
   TE, p. 163
  Information Gap Activities, p. 167
  Absent Student Copymasters, p. 175

Audiovisual

OHT 44 (Quick Start), 49 (Grammar)

Technology

Online Workbook, U6E3
Take-Home Tutor CD-ROM, U6E3

8 Objective: Controlled practice
Prepositions

Answers
1. con
2. en
3. Con
4. en
5. a
6. al
7. de
8. a
9. de
10. Con
11. de
12. a

9 Objective: Controlled practice
Prepositions

Answers
1. en
2. de
3. de
4. de
5. en
6. de
7. con
8. a
9. En
10. de
11. con

8 Ana

Hablar/*Escribir* Estás en casa de tu amiga ecuatoriana, Ana. Ella te enseña a navegar por Internet en la computadora de su padre. Para saber lo que te dice, completa sus oraciones con **a**, **con**, **de** o **en**.

> **modelo**
>
> «*La computadora de mi padre es nueva.*»

1. «La computadora vino _____ tarjeta de sonido y tarjeta gráfica.»
2. «Primero voy a hacer doble clic _____ el icono del programa.»
3. «_____ este módem puedes conectarte rápidamente a Internet.»
4. «¡Mira! Tengo seis mensajes _____ mi buzón electrónico.»
5. «Voy a copiar _____ mi amigo en ese mensaje.»
6. «Voy a tratar de responder _____ el correo electrónico de hoy.»
7. «Más tarde podemos ir al grupo _____ conversación para estudiantes de español.»
8. «Este grupo empieza _____ las ocho.»
9. «Quiero ver la página-web _____ OficinaNet.»
10. «_____ el servicio de búsqueda, es fácil encontrar lo que quieras en Internet.»
11. «Ahora me voy a desconectar _____ Internet.»
12. «Voy _____ la tienda de computación a comprar unos disquetes».

9 Entrevista en las noticias

Hablar/*Escribir* Ves las noticias en la tele. Completa lo que dicen la reportera y el chico con las preposiciones **a**, **con**, **de** o **en**.

Reportera:

¡Buenas tardes! Soy Ana de la Cruz y les hablo hoy desde el Café Ciberespacio __1__ el centro de Caracas. Como ya saben, Internet ha cambiado la vida __2__ todos. No podemos salir __3__ la casa sin que alguien nos hable __4__ la red mundial. Hay de todo __5__ la red: juegos, grupos de conversación y páginas-web __6__ muchas compañías e individuos. Estoy aquí __7__ Joaquín. ¿Joaquín, cuánto tiempo navegas por Internet?

Chico:

La verdad es que navego por Internet todos los días __8__ las tres. __9__ mi casa hay tres computadoras: la mía, la __10__ mi hermano y una para mis papás. Los mejores sitios son los grupos de conversación __11__ otros jóvenes.

La verdad es que navego por Internet todos los días.

¡Hola! Soy Ana de la Cruz y les hablo hoy desde el Café Ciberespacio.

Classroom Community

Paired Activity Have students work in pairs to expand on **Actividad 9.** They create and role-play their own scene in a cyber café in which a reporter interviews someone who uses the café to access the Internet.

Portfolio Have students write instructions describing how to do something on the computer. Encourage creativity and humor.

Rubric A = 13–15 pts. B = 10–12 pts. C = 7–9 pts. D = 4–6 pts. F = < 4 pts.

Writing criteria	Scale
Logical sentence order	1 2 3 4 5
Grammar/spelling accuracy	1 2 3 4 5
Creativity/appearance	1 2 3 4 5

10 ¿Adónde vas?

Hablar/*Escribir* Conversa con tu compañero(a) sobre lo que va a hacer después de clases. Usa las ideas de la lista.

modelo

Tú: ¿Adónde vas?

Compañero(a): *Voy al Café Ciberespacio.*

Tú: ¿Con quién vas?

Compañero(a): *Voy con un amigo de la clase de español.*

a (lugar)	de (persona)
a (distancia)	de (edad)
a (tiempo)	con (persona)
en (lugar)	con (objeto)
en (tiempo)	¿...?

11 Mis planes

Escribir Escribe un párrafo describiendo tus planes para el resto de la tarde. Trata de usar las preposiciones **a, con, de** y **en**.

modelo

Voy a la casa de mi amigo Arturo a las cuatro de la tarde. Vamos a navegar por Internet con unos amigos.

More Practice:
Más comunicación *p. R20*

GRAMÁTICA Verbs with Prepositions

▶ Many verbs require the use of a certain **preposition.** With verbs of **motion** such as **entrar, ir, salir, subir, venir, volver,** you use the preposition **a** when the verb is followed by an **infinitive.** The same preposition is used with the verbs in the left column in the box below.

Vinimos a jugar.
We came to play.

Entraron al comedor.
They went into the dining room.

▶ Other verbs like those in the right column in the box below require the use of the preposition **de** as part of their essential meaning.

Tratamos de crear una página-web.
We're trying to create a web page.

Ahora **se acuerdan** de la contraseña.
Now they remember the password.

▶ After **insistir** you use the preposition **en.**

Insisto en que me mandes un mensaje.
I insist that you send me a message.

▶ Remember that **tener que** means *to have to do something* and that **hay que** means *one must, you should.*

Hay que tener correo electrónico.
You should (It's a necessity to) have e-mail.

Entonces, **tengo que** comprarme un módem.
Then I have to buy a modem.

Vocabulario

♻ **Ya sabes**

aprender a	acabar de
ayudar a	acordarse de (ue)
comenzar a (ie)	dejar de
empezar a (ie)	olvidarse de
enseñar a	tener ganas de
invitar a	tratar de
prepararse a	

Practice:
Actividades
12 13 14

Más práctica
cuaderno p. 160
Para hispanohablantes
cuaderno p. 158

(i) **Online Workbook**
CLASSZONE.COM

Teaching All Students

Extra Help Have students write 5 sentences about what they are learning to do in school this year and/or what their teachers are teaching them to do.

Multiple Intelligences
Visual Have students create a comic strip in which the characters use at least 3 of the verbs with prepositions. Display the strips in class.

---

 10 **Objective:** Transitional practice
Prepositions in conversation

Answers will vary.

 11 **Objective:** Open-ended practice
Prepositions in writing

Answers will vary.

🔔 Quick Start Review

♻ **Verb review**
Use OHT 44 or write on the board: Match the words in the 2 columns. :

1. ___ es necesario   a. tratar
2. ___ deber   b. acordarse
3. ___ estudiar   c. insistir
4. ___ no olvidar   d. hay que
5. ___ intentar   e. aprender
6. ___ querer   f. tener que

Answers
1. d 2. f 3. e 4. b 5. a 6. c

Teaching Suggestions
Presenting Verbs with Prepositions

• Have students make their own lists or tables in their notebooks categorizing verbs under prepositions they are used with.
• Ask yes/no questions using the verbs with prepositions.
• Have students give personalized sentences using the verbs in the **Vocabulario.**

Block Schedule

Expansion Have students expand **Actividad 10** by interviewing each other about where they went yesterday afternoon. (For additional activities, see **Block Scheduling Copymasters.**)

UNIDAD 6 Etapa 3
Vocabulary/Grammar

Teaching Resource Options

Print

Más práctica Workbook PE,
  pp. 153–156, 160
Actividades para todos Workbook PE,
  pp. 181–186
Cuaderno para hispanohablantes
  PE, pp. 153–154, 158
Block Scheduling Copymasters
Unit 6 Resource Book
  Más práctica Workbook TE,
    pp. 141–144, 148
  Actividades para todos Workbook TE,
    pp. 149–154
  Cuaderno para hispanohablantes
    TE, pp. 159–160, 164
  Information Gap Activities, p. 168
  Absent Student Copymasters p. 176
  Audioscript, p. 181

Audiovisual

Audio Program CD 18, Track 3, Activity 13

Technology

Online Workbook, U6E3
Take-Home Tutor CD-ROM, U6E3

ACTIVIDAD 12 Objective: Controlled practice
Verbs with prepositions

Answers
1. aprender a
2. enseño a
3. enseñar a
4. acabo de
5. Tengo muchas ganas de
6. voy a
7. invito a
8. Prepárate a

ACTIVIDAD 13 Objective: Controlled practice
Listening comprehension/verbs with
prepositions

Answers (See script, p. 445B.)
1. empezaron a
2. acabaron de
3. vino a
4. hay que
5. tiene que
6. tenía la
7. tiene que
8. se olvidó de
9. se acordó de
10. insiste en que

Dictation

Using the Listening Activity Script for
Actividad 13 on TE p. 445B, dictate
selected sentences to students. You may
want to write answers on the board for
students to correct their own work.

Práctica: gramática y vocabulario continuación

12 Conversación telefónica

Hablar/*Escribir* Alberto y Herlinda son
amigos peruanos. Alberto quiere aprender
más sobre cómo usar la computadora
y navegar por Internet. Completa la
conversación telefónica entre ellos usando
los verbos de la lista y las preposiciones
apropiadas.

preparar   aprender   invitar
tener muchas ganas   ir   acabar
enseñar   ayudar

Alberto: Quiero __1__ usar la hoja de
cálculo.

Herlinda: Yo te __2__ usarla.

Alberto: ¿También me puedes __3__
usar Internet?

Herlinda: ¡Sí, claro! Pero __4__
desconectarme de Internet.

Alberto: ¡Perfecto! __5__ aprender a
navegar por Internet.

Herlinda: Mira, __6__ salir para clases
ahora, pero vuelvo a las cinco.
¿Por qué no vienes a casa a las
siete?

Alberto: ¡Me parece perfecto! Te __7__
tomar un café después de que
acabemos.

Herlinda: ¡De acuerdo! ¡__8__ divertirte
mucho! Internet es muy
divertido.

---

13 La página-web

Escuchar/*Escribir* Escucha lo que le pasó a
Eduardo cuando él y sus amigos decidieron
crear una página-web. Completa las oraciones
para describir su situación.

modelo

Él y sus amigos trataron de crear una página-web.

1. Ellos _____ las ocho de la mañana.
2. Eran las ocho de la noche y apenas
   _____ terminarla.
3. Ricardo _____ ayudarlos.
4. Para crear una página-web interesante,
   _____ saber muchas cosas.
5. Eduardo _____ irse.
6. Eduardo _____ la cita con su novia.
7. Eduardo _____ cenar con su novia.
8. Eduardo _____ la cita.
9. Eduardo _____ ella cuando vio su reloj.
10. Su novia _____ él sea puntual.

Nota cultural

Cuando quieres navegar por Internet y encontrar
sitios en español, debes empezar tu búsqueda
escribiendo lo que quieres encontrar en español.
También será mucho más fácil si incluyes la palabra
«español». Por ejemplo, puedes buscar «música en
español» y encontrarás muchísimos sitios. Muchos de
los servicios de búsqueda te dan la opción de
escoger el idioma que quieres usar.

460 cuatrocientos sesenta
Unidad 6

Classroom Community

Group Activity Have students work in groups to
create a Web page in Spanish for your school. They
should decide on and divide the tasks of creating the
layout, art, information, and links they would like to
include.

Storytelling Have students work in pairs to write
and illustrate a short story with a technology theme
that uses at least 5 examples of verbs with prepositions.
Encourage humor and creativity. Have students present
their stories and have the class award **El premio de
literatura** to the best story.

Activity 15 brings together all concepts presented.

14 ¡Tengo ganas de...!

Hablar/*Escribir* Es el fin de semana. Tú y tu compañero(a) quieren hacer varias cosas, pero también tienen otras obligaciones. Conversen sobre lo que quieren hacer y por qué no pueden. Usen los verbos de la lista.

modelo

Tú: *Tengo ganas de navegar por Internet.*

Compañero(a): *¿No te acuerdas de la tarea para la clase de español?*

Tú: *La haré más tarde.*

> acordarse de
> aprender a
> ayudar a
> dejar de
> enseñar a
> invitar a
> olvidarse de
> tener ganas de
> tratar de
> ¿...?

15 Libros de informática

Hablar/*Escribir* En grupos de tres o cuatro, lean las descripciones de los libros de informática a continuación. Conversen sobre los temas y sobre los libros que les interesarían a todos.

modelo

Tú: *A mí me gustaría saber cómo proteger mi sistema de un virus.*

Compañero(a) 1: *Pues, entonces debes comprar el libro Virus Informático.*

Compañero(a) 2: *Creo que es uno de los mejores.*

Compañero(a) 3: *Hay otro más interesante. Se llama…*

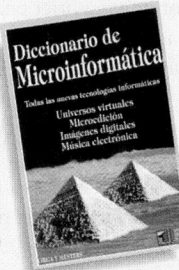

¿Qué es un virus? ¿Cómo funciona? ¿Cómo se protege de ellos? Este libro responde de forma sencilla y completa.

Ayuda al usario a obtener el máximo partido del disco duro de su ordenador y resolver muchos problemas.

Explica con claridad los conceptos utilizados en el ámbito de la microinformática y otras disciplinas afines.

More Practice:
Más comunicación p. R20

Online Workbook
CLASSZONE.COM

Refrán

El que sabe dos lenguas vale por dos.

¿Qué quiere decir el refrán? ¿Por qué crees que es importante hablar más de una lengua? ¿Crees que esta habilidad será más o menos importante en el futuro? ¿Por qué?

cuatrocientos sesenta y uno
Colombia, Venezuela y los países andinos Etapa 3
461

Teaching All Students

Extra Help Before doing **Actividad 14,** call on various students to use each of the verbs in a sentence.

Native Speakers Have students share their responses to the **refrán** with the class. What do they think are the advantages of knowing two languages?

Multiple Intelligences

Interpersonal Many users now have their own Web sites. Have students work in pairs to find Web sites of Spanish-speaking students and send them an e-mail in Spanish.

Objective: Transitional practice Verbs with prepositions in conversation

Answers will vary.

Objective: Open-ended practice Verbs with prepositions in conversation

Answers will vary.

Quick Wrap-up

Call on students to complete the following sentences using verbs with prepositions:

- El viernes por la noche voy…
- Los sábados…
- Nos gusta…
- No recibo mucho correo electrónico…

Interdisciplinary Connection

Computer Science Have students work to create and try out search phrases in Spanish for specific topics. Which searches are the most successful?

Critical Thinking

Have students debate whether knowing a computer language could be considered knowing a second language.

Block Schedule

Variety Have students visit online bookstores to search for books in Spanish. They should select 3 books they might like to buy and write down the name, description, and price. Have students present their selections to the class and explain why the books interest them. (For additional activities, see **Block Scheduling Copymasters.**)

Teaching Resource Options

Print

Actividades para todos Workbook PE,
pp. 187–189

Block Scheduling Copymasters

Unit 6 Resource Book
Actividades para todos Workbook TE,
pp. 155–157
Absent Student Copymasters, p. 177
Audioscript, p. 181

Audiovisual

OHT 44 (Quick Start)
Audio Program CD 18, Tracks 4–5

Technology

Online Workbook, U6E3
Take-Home Tutor CD-ROM, U6E3

♻ Quick Start Review

Events and activities

Use OHT 44 or write on the board:
Classify each of the following activities
as an event—**acontecimiento**—or as
daily activity—**cotidiano:**

1. la boda
2. el desayuno
3. el baño
4. el cumpleaños
5. la fiesta
6. la tarea

Answers
1. acontecimiento
2. cotidiano
3. cotidiano
4. acontecimiento
5. acontecimiento
6. cotidiano

Teaching Suggestions

- **Prereading** Have students think
about life in a small town and how it
differs from life in a city.

- **Strategy: Monitor comprehension**
Discuss the Reading Strategy. Ask if
students have ever used it before
when reading. Point out that they will
carry out the strategy as they read.

- **Reading** Have students read silently
without looking up words. Have them
jot down their paraphrase of each
paragraph. Read a second time
together, eliciting brief summaries of
each paragraph.

- **Post-reading** Have students create
outlines in Spanish that reflect the
organization of the reading.

AUDIO
En voces
LECTURA

PARA LEER
STRATEGY: READING

Monitor comprehension A good
self-check is to restate (paraphrase)
what each paragraph is about with
a phrase or short sentence. If you
can't, then reread, identify what
seems unclear, and ask questions.
Jot down a brief paraphrase of
each paragraph as you read. You
can then use those notes to write
a brief summary about **el autor,
su vida y su obra**. This will help
you start:

1. La lectura empieza con
una cita de una novela
de García Márquez.
2.
3.

LA LITERATURA

los acontecimientos	eventos
cotidiano(a)	diario(a)
entretejer	combinar

Nota cultural

Macondo es el lugar imaginario donde
suceden muchas de las obras de García
Márquez. Los personajes allí viven en un
ambiente misterioso y mágico.
Este pueblo apareció por primera vez en
La hojarasca, luego en *Los funerales de
la Mamá Grande*, y también en la
famosa novela *Cien años de soledad*.

462 cuatrocientos sesenta y dos
Unidad 6

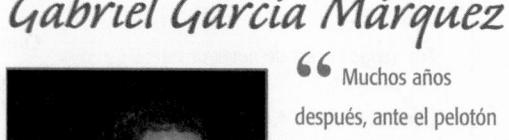

Gabriel García Márquez

" Muchos años
después, ante el pelotón
de fusilamiento[1], el coronel
Aureliano Buendía había
de recordar aquella tarde
remota en que su padre
lo llevó a conocer
el hielo[2] ".

Así comienza *Cien años de soledad* (1967), la novela
más conocida de Gabriel García Márquez, uno de
los escritores principales de las Américas en el
siglo XX. Se ha dicho que dentro de la literatura
latinoamericana, *Cien años de soledad* tiene tanta
importancia como *El Quijote* de Cervantes.

Como en muchas de las obras de García Márquez,
esta novela entreteje las historias de individuos
con la historia de su pueblo. En *Cien años de
soledad*, el pueblo es Macondo y los individuos
son los miembros de la familia Buendía. García
Márquez narra los acontecimientos de la historia
del pueblo y de la familia Buendía utilizando un
estilo conocido como realismo mágico. Este estilo
combina la realidad con elementos fantásticos.

[1] firing squad   [2] ice

Classroom Community

Paired Activity Have students work in pairs to
research additional information about Gabriel García
Márquez. Then have them act out an interview scene
between García Márquez and a book critic.

Portfolio Give students brief examples of **realismo
mágico,** pointing out that it is not science fiction, nor
pure fantasy, but often a realistic setting and plot with
an occasional meaningful element of fantasy such as a
family whose members have tails or a character who at
the end of her life simply floats up into the sky instead
of dying. Have students describe a scenario along those
lines.

Rubric A = 13–15 pts. B = 10–12 pts. C = 7–9 pts. D = 4–6 pts. F = < 4 pts.

Writing criteria	Scale
Accuracy of form	1 2 3 4 5
Grammar/spelling accuracy	1 2 3 4 5
Creativity/appearance	1 2 3 4 5

Culture Highlights

● **CIEN AÑOS DE SOLEDAD** *Cien años de soledad* combina mitos, romance e historia. Hay varias maneras de leer la novela: como una alegoría mitológica, como la historia del pueblo de Macondo y como la historia de la familia Buendía.

El escritor insiste en que el realismo mágico no es una combinación de elementos reales y fantásticos, sino que es la manera en que sucede la vida cotidiana de Colombia. García Márquez nació en ese país en 1928 y se crió [3] con sus abuelos hasta la edad de ocho años. Los cuentos que le hacía su abuela influyeron sus escritos.

Cuando era joven, García Márquez se dedicó al periodismo. Publicó su primera novela, *La hojarasca*, en 1955. En *El coronel no tiene quien le escriba* (1957), García Márquez siguió utilizando la historia de Colombia como marco de referencia para sus protagonistas.

Su fama aumentó con *El otoño del patriarca* (1975) y *Crónica de una muerte anunciada* (1981). En 1982, García Márquez ganó el Premio Nóbel de Literatura. Continúa escribiendo novelas y guiones para películas.

Sin duda, García Márquez es una de las voces más potentes de América Latina. Su visión sugiere que el individuo es protagonista de dos historias: la de su vida y la de su pueblo. Al leer la obra de García Márquez, vemos que a veces no es fácil saber dónde comienza una historia y termina la otra. Nuestra inquietud [4] no es confusión, sin embargo: es el comienzo de la búsqueda [5] intrépida de quiénes somos y seremos en el lugar donde nos ha tocado vivir [6], sea en Macondo o Main Street.

---

[3] was raised   [5] search
[4] uncertainty   [6] where it is our fate to live

Interdisciplinary Connection

English Work with a teacher from the English department to discuss García Márquez and his place in the world of literature.

Online Workbook
CLASSZONE.COM

¿Comprendiste?

1. ¿Quiénes son los protagonistas de *Cien años de soledad*? ¿Dónde sucede?
2. ¿Qué es el realismo mágico? ¿Qué combina?
3. ¿Qué influencia de la niñez de García Márquez aparece en sus obras?
4. ¿Qué papel juega la historia de un pueblo en la obra de García Márquez?

¿Qué piensas?

¿Por qué crees que un escritor como García Márquez puede afectar cómo vemos la historia?

Hazlo tú

Elige un lugar en tu estado o ciudad e investiga algún evento que te llame la atención. Luego, inventa un nombre ficticio para el lugar e imagina qué personajes (tanto reales como ficticios) participaron en ese evento. Si quieres, escribe un cuento corto o dibuja tus personajes y el lugar.

¿Comprendiste?
Answers
1. Los protagonistas son los miembros de la familia Buendía. La novela sucede en Macondo, un pueblo imaginario.
2. El realismo mágico es un estilo literario que combina la realidad con elementos fantásticos.
3. En la obra de García Márquez aparece la influencia de los cuentos que le hacía su abuela.
4. La historia de un pueblo es parte de la historia del individuo.

Teaching All Students

Challenge Have students look up information about Colombia, its people, history, and geography. Can they find anything that indicates why García Márquez believes that daily life in Colombia has an element of **realismo mágico**?

Multiple Intelligences

Interpersonal Have students discuss contemporary fiction they have read. How would they compare the authors they know to García Márquez?

Block Schedule

Reference Lists Have students look up the names of other Latin American writers, especially writers who belong to the *Boom*. They can find information about these writers on the Internet. (For additional activities, see **Block Scheduling Copymasters.**)

Teaching Resource Options

Print

Block Scheduling Copymasters
Unit 6 Resource Book
  Absent Student Copymasters, p. 178
  Video Activities, pp. 243–246
  Videoscript, pp. 247–249

Audiovisual

OHT 45 (Quick Start)
Canciones CD
Video Program Videotape 49:10 /
  DVD, Unit 6

Technology

 www.classzone.com

Quick Start Review

♻ Bolivia

Use OHT 45 or write on the board:
Which of the following things do you
associate with Bolivia?

1. el océano Pacífico
2. los Andes
3. el lago Titicaca
4. el Caribe
5. los aztecas
6. las Amazonas

Answers
2, 3, 6

Teaching Suggestions
Presenting Cultura y comparaciones

• Have students read the Connecting
Cultures Strategy and discuss their
cultural goals. Then have them
complete their charts. Ask volunteers
to present their reasons.
• Have students brainstorm a list of
information they already know about
Bolivia and a list of topics they would
like to know more about.

Reading Strategy

Ask students to use the Reading Strategy
"Scan for cognates," before reading. They
should glance quickly over the selection to
identify words they already know because
of their similarity to English. What do these
words tell them about the content of the
reading selection?

En colores

CULTURA Y COMPARACIONES

Bolivia

PARA CONOCERNOS

STRATEGY: CONNECTING CULTURES

**Evaluate the Internet as a means of developing
cultural knowledge and understanding** You have
learned about Latin cultures through many
media (print, video, conversations,
Internet). These media cover social and
business interactions, traditions, history,
geography, contributions in literature,
fine arts, social, economic, and political
institutions. Out of these general topics,
think of three personal cultural goals.
Then evaluate whether the Internet is high,
medium, or low as a means of helping you
reach those goals. Give reasons. Use
"Bolivia en la red" plus your own
knowledge to guide your thinking.

Metas	Evaluación	Comentario
1.		
2.		
3.		

¡Conoce Bolivia por Internet! Un viaje virtual
puede darte mucha información y ayudarte a
planificar un viaje verdadero.

　　Tú, como usuario(a) de Internet, puedes acceder
a la página-web de Bolnet, el sitio oficial de Bolivia,
y escoger entre las posibilidades del menú. Puedes
explorar varios aspectos de la sociedad boliviana
(educación, gobierno, el mundo de los negocios, etc.)
usando los enlaces de la página. Puedes leer la
prensa[1] del país en tu pantalla, conversar con
abonados[2] de Bolnet o escuchar un cuento.

[1] press　　[2] subscribers

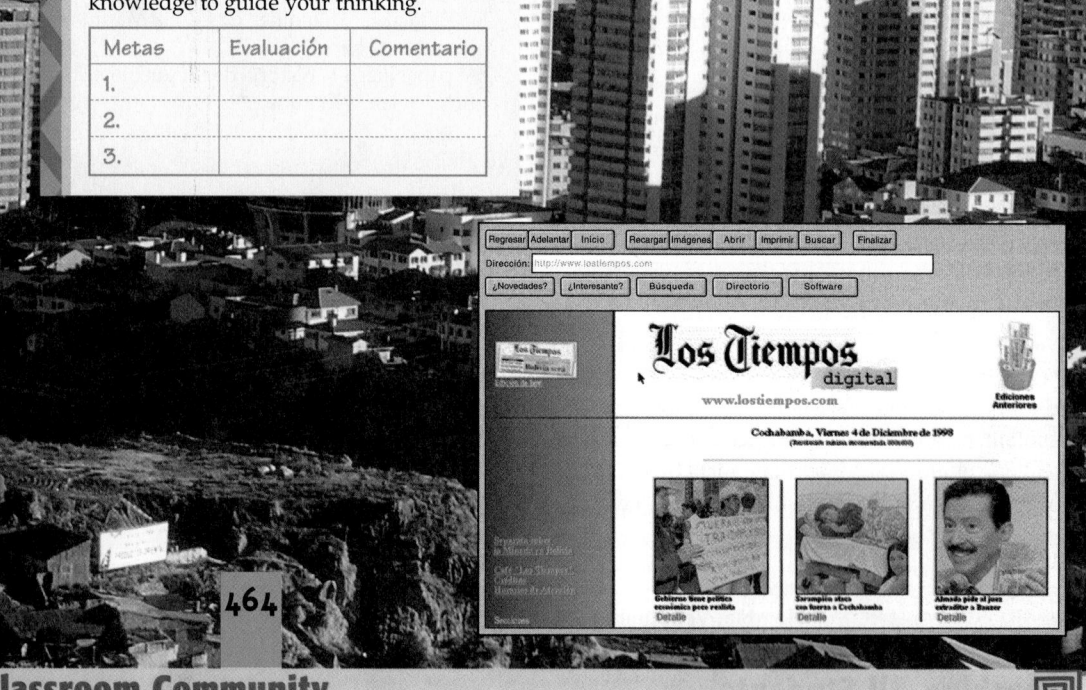

464

Classroom Community

Cooperative Learning Have students work in
groups to create a comprehensive report on Bolivia.
Have them divide the report into categories;
for example, geography, indigenous populations,
languages, foods, arts and crafts, music, history, etc.
Encourage them to include drawings, magazine
clippings, and photocopies of images. Have them
integrate and organize the individual reports and bind
the entire report with an illustrated cover. Display the
reports in class.

Paired Activity Have students work in pairs to
make a list of questions they might ask a teenager from
Bolivia. Have them also make a list of questions a
teenager from Bolivia might ask them.

en la red

Otro servicio boliviano de Internet, Bolivianet, ofrece a sus miembros una guía de correo electrónico, que es una lista de las direcciones electrónicas de casi dos mil personas, bolivianas en su mayoría. Esta guía existe con el fin[3] de unir a los bolivianos a través del mundo. ¡Es una guía telefónica para la época de Internet!

[3] exists with the goal

¿Quisieras hacer un viaje a Bolivia? Toda la información que necesites está disponible[4] en la red mundial. Con una página como ésta puedes conocer las regiones del país, leer una descripción de cada una, ver fotos de los lugares de interés turístico y obtener una lista de hoteles. ¡Incluso puedes reservar tu habitación de hotel por Internet! ¿No ves? Un viaje a Bolivia puede empezar con un viaje por el ciberespacio.

[4] available

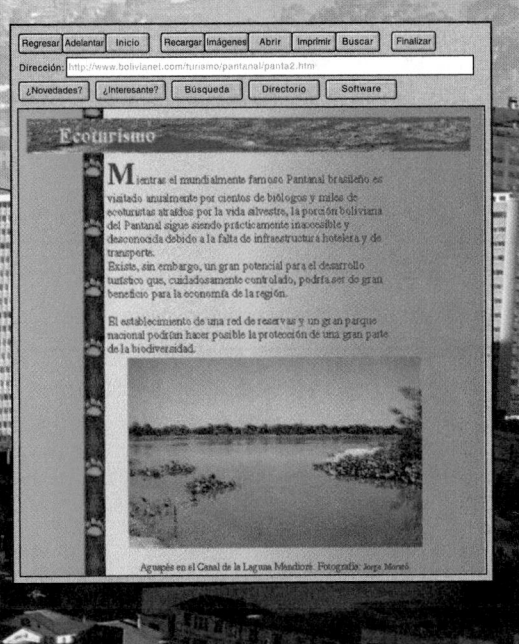

| Regresar | Adelantar | Inicio | Recargar | Imágenes | Abrir | Imprimir | Buscar | Finalizar |

Dirección: http://www.bolivianet.com/turismo/pantanal/panta2.htm

| ¿Novedades? | ¿Interesante? | Búsqueda | Directorio | Software |

Ecoturismo

Mientras el mundialmente famoso Pantanal brasileño es visitado anualmente por cientos de biólogos y miles de ecoturistas atraídos por la vida silvestre, la porción boliviana del Pantanal sigue siendo prácticamente inaccesible y desconocida debido a la falta de infraestructura hotelera y de transporte.

Existe, sin embargo, un gran potencial para el desarrollo turístico que, cuidadosamente controlado, podría ser de gran beneficio para la economía de la región.

El establecimiento de una red de reservas y un gran parque nacional podrían hacer posible la protección de una gran parte de la biodiversidad.

Aguapés en el Canal de la Laguna Mandioré. Fotografía: Jorge Mareso.

CLASSZONE.COM
More About Colombia, Venezuela, and the Andean countries

¿Comprendiste?

1. ¿Qué es Bolnet?
2. ¿Cómo nos ayuda Internet a conocer Bolivia?
3. ¿Qué es la guía de correo electrónico? ¿Para qué sirve?
4. ¿Qué utilidad tiene Internet para el (la) turista que quiere viajar por Bolivia?

¿Qué piensas?

1. Da un ejemplo de cómo Internet facilita el contacto entre personas.
2. ¿Qué aspectos de Internet te parecen más útiles para conocer los países hispanoamericanos?

Hazlo tú

Usa un servicio de búsqueda para encontrar otras páginas sobre Bolivia o los otros países de esta unidad. Explora los enlaces de las páginas que visites y prepara un resumen de lo que se puede aprender sobre el país usando Internet.

cuatrocientos sesenta y cinco

Colombia, Venezuela y los países andinos Etapa 3

465

Teaching Resource Options

Print

Cuaderno para hispanohablantes
  PE, pp. 159–160
Block Scheduling Copymasters
Unit 6 Resource Book
  Cuaderno para hispanohablantes
   TE, pp. 165–166
  Information Gap Activities,
   pp. 169–170
  Family Involvement, pp. 179–180

Audiovisual

OHT 45 (Quick Start)

Technology
eTest Plus Online

 www.classzone.com

Quick Start Review

♻ Verbs with prepositions

Use OHT 45 or write on the board:
Write a sentence for each of the
following verbs with prepositions:

1. tener ganas de
2. aprender a
3. prepararse a
4. olvidarse de
5. tratar de

Answers will vary.

Teaching Suggestions
What Have Students Learned?

Have students look at the "Now you
can…" notes listed on the left side of
pp. 466–467. Remind them to review
the material in the "To review" notes
before doing the activities or taking the
test.

ETAPA 3

En uso
REPASO Y MÁS COMUNICACIÓN

OBJECTIVES
- Compare and evaluate
- Express precise relationships
- Navigate cyberspace

Now you can...
- navigate cyberspace.

To review
- superlatives, see p. 454.

1 El mejor

Tu amigo(a) ecuatoriano(a) pregunta qué piensas sobre cosas que
encuentras en Internet. Escríbele para contestar sus preguntas.

modelo

¿Qué piensas de esta página-web? (interesante)
Esta página-web es la más (la menos) interesante de todas.

1. ¿Qué piensas de este grupo de conversación? (divertido)
2. ¿Qué piensas de este grupo de noticias? (útil)
3. ¿Qué piensas de este servicio de búsqueda? (mejor/peor)
4. ¿Qué piensas de este sitio? (mejor/peor)
5. ¿Qué piensas de este enlace? (mejor/peor)

Now you can...
- compare and evaluate.

To review
- comparatives, see p. 454.

2 Opiniones

Tú y dos compañeros están en CompuVisión y comparan varios
productos. Los tres tienen opiniones diferentes. ¿Qué dicen?

modelo

complicado

Tú: *Este programa de software es más complicado que el otro.*
Compañero(a) 1: *No, no, éste es menos complicado.*
Compañero(a) 2: *Pienso que ése es tan complicado como
el otro.*

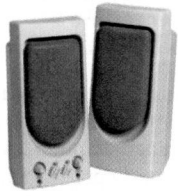   

Classroom Community

Portfolio Using **Actividad 4** as a model, have
students write their own diary entry about using or
trying to use a computer. Encourage humor and
creativity.

Rubric A = 13–15 pts. B = 10–12 pts. C = 7–9 pts. D = 4–6 pts. F = < 4 pts.

Writing criteria	Scale				
Vocabulary use	1	2	3	4	5
Grammar/spelling accuracy	1	2	3	4	5
Creativity/appearance	1	2	3	4	5

Paired Activity Have students work in pairs to
make comparisons of computers and computer
equipment that they have, that the school has, or that
they know about.

Self-Check Quiz
CLASSZONE.COM

Now you can...
- express precise relationships.

To review
- prepositions, see p. 457.

③ La carta

Elena le escribió una carta a su mejor amiga, María. Completa la carta con las preposiciones **a**, **de**, **con** y **en** para saber qué le pasó el otro día.

> Querida María,
>
> El otro día, navegué por Internet ___1___ mi hermano ___2___ quince años. Como él quería comprar una computadora, fuimos ___3___ la página-web ___4___ OficinaNet. En la página-web vimos que la compañía está ___5___ el centro de Caracas. Está ___6___ tres cuadras de mi colegio. ___7___ las dos de la tarde fuimos ___8___ la oficina para ver los sistemas de computación. Hablamos con la señora Villarreal, la dueña ___9___ la compañía. Ella convenció a mi hermano que la computadora que le gustaba era la computadora ___10___ sus sueños. Antes de que decidiera qué iba a hacer, yo le dije a la señora Villarreal «Volvemos ___11___ una semana». Saqué a mi hermano y le dije «¿Qué estabas pensando? No tienes el dinero para comprar esa computadora!».
> Abrazos,
>
> Elena

Now you can...
- express precise relationships.

To review
- verbs with prepositions, see p. 459.

④ El diario

Lee la entrada del 11 de mayo en el diario de Abigail. Completa la entrada con las preposiciones apropiadas.

> 11 de mayo
>
> Por fin aprendí ___1___ navegar por Internet. Empecé ___2___ conectarme cuando me di cuenta de que no podía acordarme ___3___ mi contraseña. En ese momento, mi hermanita entró ___4___ ver qué estaba haciendo. En vez de ayudarme ___5___ recordar mi contraseña, empezó ___6___ reírse. «Deja ___7___ reírte de mí», le dije, enojada. «Estoy tratando ___8___ aprender algo nuevo y tú, ¡burlándote de mí!» Trató ___9___ pedirme perdón pero yo no tenía ganas ___10___ perdonarla. «Insisto ___11___ que salgas de aquí inmediatamente», le grité. «Vas ___12___ quedarte tranquila», me respondió y se fue ___13___ decirles a mis padres que ¡yo la había insultado a ella! ¡Imagínate!

cuatrocientos sesenta y siete
Colombia, Venezuela y los países andinos Etapa 3
467

ACTIVIDAD ① **Answers**

1. Este grupo de conversación es el más (el menos) divertido de todos.
2. Este grupo de noticias es el más (el menos) útil de todos.
3. Este servicio de búsqueda es el mejor (el peor) de todos.
4. Este sitio es el mejor (el peor) de todos.
5. Este enlace es el mejor (el peor) de todos.

ACTIVIDAD ② **Answers**

Answers will vary slightly. Sample answers:
1. A: Estos altoparlantes son más claros que los otros.
   B: Éstos son menos claros que los otros.
   C: Éstos son tan claros como los otros.
2. A: Este teclado es más expandido que el otro.
   B: Éste es menos expandido que el otro.
   C: Éste es tan expandido como el otro.
3. A: Esta impresora es más rápida que la otra.
   B: Ésta es menos rápida que la otra.
   C: Ésta es tan rápida como la otra.
4. A: Este ratón es más útil que el otro.
   B: Éste es menos útil que el otro.
   C: Éste es tan útil como el otro.

ACTIVIDAD ③ **Answers**

1. con	7. A
2. de	8. a
3. a	9. de
4. de	10. de
5. en	11. en
6. a	

ACTIVIDAD ④ **Answers**

1. a	8. de
2. a	9. de
3. de	10. de
4. a	11. en
5. a	12. a
6. a	13. a
7. de	

Teaching All Students

Extra Help Have students write down 5 adjectives/adverbs and build comparative and superlative statements around them. For example: **fuerte: El Pato Donald es fuerte. El Ratón Miguel es más fuerte. Popeye es el más fuerte.**

Multiple Intelligences

Kinesthetic Have pairs of students act out the scene in **Actividad 4.** One student plays Abigaíl (or Arturo) and the other plays the little sister/brother. As students act out the scene, they should also provide the narration, using the verbs with prepositions.

Visual Have students make sketches of the computer of the future, or another technology device.

Block Schedule

Change of Pace Have students write a brief letter about looking at or buying a computer and remove the prepositions **a, de, con,** and **en** from it. Have them exchange and complete each other's letters. (For additional activities, see **Block Scheduling Copymasters.**)

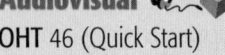

ACTIVIDAD 5

Rubric: Speaking

Criteria	Scale	
Sentence structure	1 2 3	A = 11–12 pts.
Vocabulary use	1 2 3	B = 9–10 pts.
Originality	1 2 3	C = 7–8 pts.
Fluency	1 2 3	D = 4–6 pts.
		F = < 4 pts.

ACTIVIDAD 6

Rubric: Writing

Criteria	Scale	
Vocabulary use	1 2 3 4 5	A = 13–15 pts.
Accuracy	1 2 3 4 5	B = 10–12 pts.
Creativity, appearance	1 2 3 4 5	C = 7–9 pts.
		D = 4–6 pts.
		F = < 4 pts.

---

5 CompuVisión

STRATEGY: SPEAKING

Compare and evaluate computer configurations
Judging the value of technology involves comparing performance in relation to cost. Securing the knowledgeable opinions of others also helps. Consider: **hardware (tamaño, color, memoria, velocidad, resolución); software (usos, resultados); necesidades y preferencias personales; precio, descuento, garantía**

Hablar/Escribir Están en CompuVisión. Examinen todas las configuraciones y hablen sobre ellas. Conversen sobre las ventajas y desventajas de todas las computadoras que ven. Dramaticen esta situación en grupos de dos o tres.

modelo

Tú: *¿Qué te parece esta computadora?*

Compañero(a) 1: *No sé. ¿Cuánta memoria tiene?*

Compañero(a) 2: …

CONEXIONES

La tecnología La escuela piensa comprar una computadora nueva para el salón de tu clase de español. Te toca a ti escribir los requisitos. Habla con el (la) profesor(a) y los otros alumnos y averigua para qué piensan usar la computadora. Tomando en cuenta esta información, decide qué tipo de sistema necesitan. Puedes consultar con el (la) profesor(a) de informática para ver si tienes toda la información que necesitas.

468 cuatrocientos sesenta y ocho
Unidad 6

---

6 *En tu propia voz*

ESCRITURA ¡Diseña tu propia página-web! Primero decide qué quieres incluir en tu página. Luego haz dibujos y escribe narraciones que pondrías en tu página–web.

- Nombre
- Mis actividades
- Mis películas
- Mis deportes
- Mis clases
- ¿…?
- Mis viajes
- Mi familia
- Mis planes para el futuro

Classroom Community

Paired Activity Have students take turns describing a computer component (what it looks like, does, or is used for) so that the partner can guess the item.

Group Activity Have students work in groups to set up a computer store. They should illustrate and/or list items they sell, including the prices. Then have groups take turns opening their stores for other students. Have students evaluate the stores—the best buys, most variety, best quality, etc.

Flashcards
CLASSZONE.COM

En resumen
REPASO DE VOCABULARIO

Computer equipment

ampliable	expandable
la configuración	configuration
el disco	disk
el disco duro	hard drive
disponible	available
externo(a)	external
el fax	fax
el hardware	hardware
interno(a)	internal
la memoria	memory
el micrófono	microphone
el microprocesador	microprocessor
el módem	modem
el monitor	monitor
el tamaño	size
la tarjeta de sonido	sound card
la tarjeta gráfica	graphics card
la tecla	key
el teclado	keyboard
el (la) usuario(a)	user

Cyberspace

el buzón electrónico	electronic mailbox
conectarse a	to connect to
la contraseña	password
el correo electrónico	e-mail
desconectarse de	to disconnect from
la dirección electrónica	e-mail address
en línea	on-line
el enlace	link
el grupo de conversación	chat group
el grupo de noticias	news group
hacer (doble) clic	to (double) click
el icono del programa	program icon

Cyberspace (continued)

el Localizador Unificador de Recursos (LUR)	URL
la página-web	web page
la red mundial	World Wide Web
el servicio de búsqueda	search engine
el sitio	site

Software

la base de datos	database
la hoja de cálculo	spreadsheet
el juego interactivo	interactive game
el programa anti-virus	anti-virus program
el software	software

Comparatives and superlatives

Este juego es **más** interesante **que** el otro.
Aquel programa es **el menos** interesante.
Yo preparé **tantos** documentos **como** Pedro.

Prepositions

Voy **a** comprar un sistema **de** computación.
Quiero uno **con** base de datos.
Pienso comprarlo **en** una semana.

 Ya sabes

acabar de	to have just
acordarse de (ue)	to remember
aprender a	to learn to
ayudar a	to help to
comenzar a (ie)	to begin to
dejar de	to stop doing something
empezar a (ie)	to begin
enseñar a	to teach to
invitar a	to invite
olvidarse de	to forget to
prepararse a	to prepare to
tener ganas de	to feel like to
tratar de	to try to

Juego

¿Quién ganó la computadora?

El premio del concurso de ElectroMundo fue una computadora. Mira esta información para saber quién ganó.

¡CONCURSO!

- Roberto tiene una tarjeta de sonido.
- El (La) ganador(a) es miembro de un grupo de conversación en la red mundial.
- Carmen tiene varios juegos interactivos para su computadora.
- A Carmen le gusta hablar con otras personas usando Internet.
- Roberto quiere comprarse un fax/módem para navegar en Internet.

Teaching All Students

Extra Help **Prepare ahead:** Write 30 computer and cyberspace vocabulary words on slips of paper and put them in a bag. Have volunteers take turns picking a slip and drawing the vocabulary word on the board for the class to guess. You may want to have the class play in teams.

Multiple Intelligences

Visual Have students create crossword puzzles with drawings for horizontal and vertical cues. Encourage them to use as many of the vocabulary words as possible.

Logical/Mathematical Ask students to research the rate of growth of people owning personal computers in 5 Spanish-speaking countries. Compile all the statistics as a class and create a graph.

Teaching Note: En tu propia voz
Writing Strategy Suggest that students use different kinds of descriptive words. They should help their readers get to know them and understand what kind of person they are by giving detailed descriptions.

 Quick Start Review

🔁 Verbs with prepositions

Use OHT 46 or write on the board: Write the prepositions that go with these verbs:

1. olvidarse   5. invitar
2. empezar   6. dejar
3. acabar   7. insistir
4. acordarse   8. enseñar

Answers
1. de 2. a 3. de 4. de
5. a 6. de 7. en 8. a

Teaching Suggestions
Vocabulary Review

Ask questions or have students ask each other questions using the vocabulary words; for example, **¿Qué hardware necesitas si quieres conectarte al Internet? (un módem)**

Dictation

Dictate the following sentences to review the **Etapa:**

1. Esta impresora a color es la más cara.
2. Trato de crear una página-web en la red mundial.
3. ¿Qué servicio de búsqueda te gusta más?
4. ¡Este grupo de conversacíon es el mejor!

Juego

Answers: Carmen

Block Schedule

FunBreak Have students play **Tipo de cambio** in the **Ampliación** on TE p. 401B.

Teaching Resource Options

Print
Block Scheduling Copymasters

Audiovisual
OHT GO1–GO5; 46 (Quick Start)

Technology
www.classzone.com

🔔 Quick Start Review

♻ Technology

Use OHT 46 or write on the board:
Complete the following sentences:

La red mundial es tan...
El correo electrónico es más...
El grupo de noticias es menos...

Answers will vary.

Teaching Strategy
Prewriting

• Have students brainstorm a list of technology-related events. The events could be personal (buying a computer), school-based (new technology equipment), or of general interest (new software or Web site).
• Ask students to choose one event. Then have them fill out their charts.

Post-writing

• Have partners confirm that the most important information is presented first, followed by secondary information and less important details. Partners may suggest that additional information be added.
• Encourage students to use the proofreading marks they have learned.

En tu propia voz

ESCRITURA
La tecnología del mundo de hoy

Tú eres reportero(a) del periódico de tu escuela. Tienes que escribir un artículo para la próxima edición sobre algún evento escolar relacionado con la tecnología. Recuerda que tus lectores son estudiantes como tú, así que escoge un tema que les interese. En tu artículo, escribe un resumen dando detalles del evento y citas de los participantes.

Función: Presentar un resumen   **Contenido:** Visita de estudiantes colombianos
Contexto: Informar a los estudiantes   **Tipo de texto:** Artículo periodístico

PARA ESCRIBIR • STRATEGY: WRITING

Prioritize information in order of importance When writing a journalistic article, identify the most important facts and summarize them first. (These basic facts should answer the "who, what, when, where, why" questions of the reader.) Then present additional facts of secondary importance. Next, give information that is least important to a general understanding of the event, but that provides color or background.

Modelo del estudiante

Visita de estudiantes colombianos

*The first paragraph gives a **complete summary** of the most important aspects of the event.*

El martes pasado un grupo de quince estudiantes colombianos vinieron a nuestra escuela para visitar el nuevo laboratorio de computadoras y conocer la nueva tecnología que ofrece, ya que es la más avanzada de la región.

Primero disfrutaron una recepción en su honor en el auditorio. Después, el maestro Stan Smith, especialista en computadoras y tecnología, hizo una presentación breve sobre el hardware y software que hay en el laboratorio, sus capacidades y los programas que utilizamos más frecuentemente.

*The **secondary facts** provide more details about the information in the first paragraph and break it down into smaller pieces.*

Después de la presentación todos los participantes fueron al laboratorio para que los estudiantes colombianos tuvieran la oportunidad de ver y usar nuestro equipo.

Exploramos juntos en Internet y nos divertimos mucho con los programas de realidad virtual y los videojuegos.

Cuando los estudiantes tuvieron que salir, el maestro Smith propuso una visita de estudiantes de nuestra escuela a la suya, diciendo, «Ojalá que puedan regresar algún día o, aún mejor, que nosotros podamos ir a Colombia y visitarlos a Uds. la próxima vez».

La visita terminó con sonrisas por todas partes. Los estudiantes colombianos no estaban acostumbrados al tiempo de aquí, que es mucho más frío que el de Colombia. Pero todos parecían muy entusiasmados con la visita. Guillermo Díaz, un estudiante de Bogotá, comentó, «Nos alegramos de estar aquí... ¡a pesar del frío increíble que hace!» y todos nos reímos.

*The next level of information includes a **quotation** with a hope about a future related event.*

*The final level of information provides some **colorful information** about the event, focusing on a funny quotation.*

Classroom Community

Group Activity Have the class compile their articles to make a technology newspaper. Divide the class into 3 groups, according to the scope of their article: personal, school-wide, or general. Each group is responsible for organizing their section. Encourage students to compile the articles on the computer.

Paired Activity Have partners help each other choose events for their articles. They can share opinions on what topics would be most interesting to others.

Portfolio Remind students to save their articles for their portfolios. Their collections of writing projects demonstrate their progress in Spanish.

Writing Center
CLASSZONE.COM

Estrategias para escribir

Antes de escribir …

Piensa en un suceso reciente que quieras describir. Para organizar la información según el nivel (level) de importancia, usa una gráfica como la de la derecha. La información más importante va primero; luego la información que da más detalles. Al final escribes datos que presenten información adicional.

el martes pasado, estudiantes colombianos, visita a la escuela, conocer la nueva tecnología

recepción en el auditorio, presentación sobre la tecnología, visita al laboratorio

despedida, sugerencia del maestro Smith sobre una visita a su escuela

todos muy animados, quejas sobre el frío de aquí

Revisiones

Después de escribir el primer borrador de tu artículo, compártelo con un compañero de clase. Pregúntale:

- ¿Cuál es la información más importante del artículo?
- ¿Dónde está la información que amplifica la idea central? ¿Cuál es?
- ¿Qué efecto tienen los comentarios de los participantes sobre el tono del artículo?

La versión final

Antes de crear tu versión final, léela de nuevo y repasa los siguientes puntos:

- ¿Usé bien el **pretérito** y el **imperfecto**?

Haz lo siguiente: Subraya todos los verbos y determina si se debe usar el imperfecto o el pretérito. Repasa el uso del pretérito y del imperfecto.

- ¿Usé **formas comparativas y superlativas** para añadir más información a los datos del artículo?

Haz lo siguiente: Haz un círculo alrededor de las expresiones comparativas o superlativas. ¿Concuerda el artículo definido con el sustantivo relacionado? ¿Concuerdan los adjetivos con los sustantivos?

El mes pasado, ~~hice~~ un proyecto de investigación por Internet. ~~Buscaba~~ Busqué artículos periodísticos y escribí informes sobre ciudades latinoamericanas. ~~Aprendía~~ Aprendí a usar los servicios de búsqueda. ~~Escogía~~ Escogí estudiar la ciudad de Bogotá porque es la ciudad (más poblado) de Colombia. a

cuatrocientos setenta y uno
Colombia, Venezuela y los países andinos Etapa 3
471

Rubric: Writing

Let students know ahead of time which elements of their writing you will be evaluating. A global evaluation is more helpful to students than a correction of every mistake made. Consider the following in scoring compositions:

Sentences	
1	Most not logical
2	Somewhat logical
3	In logical order
4	Logical with some flow
5	Flow purposefully

Details	
1	Few details
2	Some basic details
3	Sufficient basic details
4	Substantial details
5	Clear and vivid detail

Organization	
1	Very little organization
2	Poorly organized
3	Some organization
4	Sufficiently organized
5	Strong organization

Accuracy	
1	Errors prevent comprehension
2	Comprehensible, yet many errors
3	Some spelling and agreement errors throughout
4	A few errors
5	Very few errors

Criteria	Scale	
Logical sentence order	1 2 3 4 5	A = 17–20 pts.
Clear and vivid detail	1 2 3 4 5	B = 13–16 pts.
Organization	1 2 3 4 5	C = 9–12 pts.
Accuracy	1 2 3 4 5	D = 5–8 pts.
		F = < 5 pts.

Teaching All Students

Extra Help Review structures with students before writing:
- preterite vs. imperfect
- comparatives
- superlatives

Challenge Have students summarize their article in a brief speech to the class. They should include "who, what, when, where, why."

Block Schedule

Change of Pace Ask volunteers to read their articles to the class. Then hold a question and answer session with the "reporters." (For additional activities, see **Block Scheduling Copymasters**.)

RECURSOS

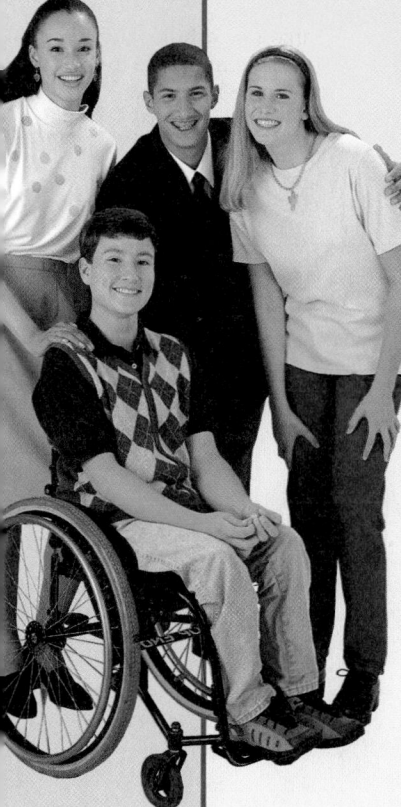

1 Answers

A: ¿Qué hizo a las ocho de la mañana?
B: A las ocho de la mañana se despertó en su cuarto. ¿Qué hizo a las diez de la mañana?
A: A las diez de la mañana planchó la ropa. ¿Qué hizo a las doce?
B: A las doce jugó al fútbol en la escuela. ¿Qué hizo a las dos?
A: A las dos comió con su familia. ¿Qué hizo a las cuatro?
B: A las cuatro compró una blusa nueva en la tienda. ¿Qué hizo a las seis?
A: A las seis vio una película cómica. ¿Qué hizo a las ocho de la noche?
B: A las ocho de la noche visitó a un amigo enfermo en su casa. ¿Qué hizo a las diez de la noche?
A: A las diez de la noche se acostó.

2 Answers

a. A: El mesero les sirvió un pastel.
b. A: El mesero les dio los menús.
c. A: El mesero les sirvió los platos.
d. B: Las dos personas pidieron la comida.
e. B: Las dos personas fueron al restaurante.
f. B: El mesero les dio la cuenta.

En orden
e, b, d, c, a, f

MÁS COMUNICACIÓN

1 Etapa preliminar p. 13
¿Qué hizo ayer?

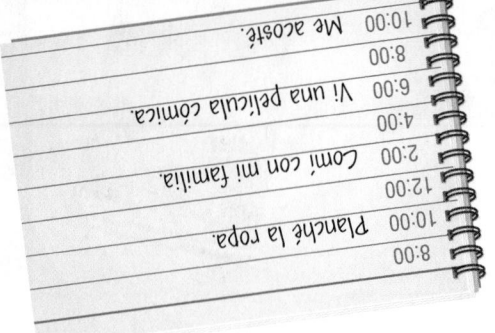

8:00
10:00 Planché la ropa.
12:00
2:00 Comí con mi familia.
4:00
6:00 Vi una película cómica.
8:00
10:00 Me acosté.

modelo

Estudiante A: ¿Qué hizo a las ocho de la mañana?
Estudiante B: A las ocho se despertó en su cuarto.

Estudiante A Marcela escribió todo lo que hizo ayer en su diario. Tú tienes parte de la información y tu compañero(a) tiene la otra parte. Juntos(as) describan las actividades que hizo Marcela ayer y traten de imaginar dónde las hizo.

Estudiante B Marcela escribió todo lo que hizo ayer en su diario. Tú tienes parte de la información y tu compañero(a) tiene la otra parte. Juntos(as) describan las actividades que hizo Marcela ayer y traten de imaginar dónde las hizo.

modelo

Estudiante A: ¿Qué hizo a las ocho de la mañana?
Estudiante B: A las ocho se despertó en su cuarto.

8:00 Me desperté.
10:00
12:00 Jugué al fútbol.
2:00
4:00 Compré una blusa nueva.
6:00
8:00 Visité a un amigo enfermo.
10:00

2 Etapa preliminar p. 25
¡Qué cita!

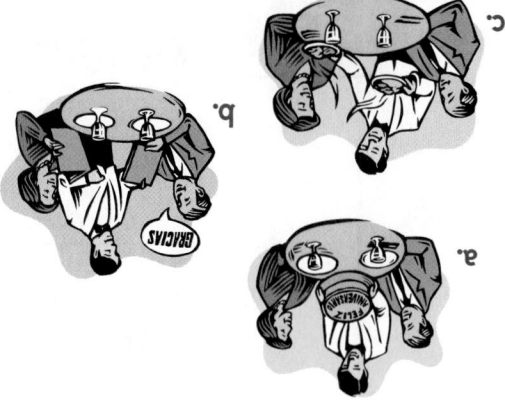

a.
b.
c.

Estudiante A Antonio hizo seis dibujos de lo que le pasó ayer. Tú tienes la mitad de los dibujos y tu compañero(a) tiene los demás. Usa el pretérito para poner los dibujos en orden sin mirar los de tu compañero(a).

Estudiante B Antonio hizo seis dibujos de lo que le pasó ayer. Tú tienes la mitad de los dibujos y tu compañero(a) tiene los demás. Usa el pretérito para poner los dibujos en orden sin mirar los de tu compañero(a).

d.
e.
f.

R2 RECURSOS
Más comunicación

③ Unidad 1 Etapa 1 p. 41 — Cita a ciegas

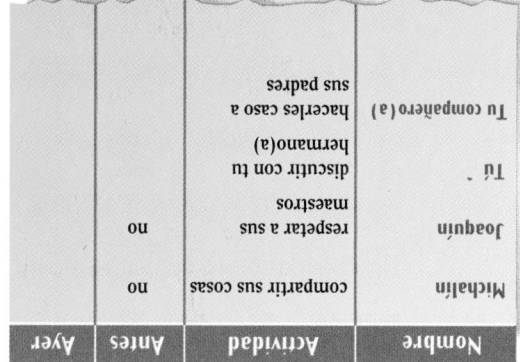

Estudiante A Tu compañero(a) te quiere arreglar una cita a ciegas (blind date). Hazle preguntas para saber más de la cita. Luego cambien de papel y contesta las preguntas de tu compañero(a) con la siguiente información.

modelo
Estudiante A: ¿De dónde es?
Estudiante B: Es de Seattle.

moreno y lacio	una fiesta en casa
grandes y negros	de Carlota
Miami	sociable y atrevido(a)
el 14 de septiembre	a la una de la tarde

Origen: _____ Personalidad: _____
Cabello: _____ Ojos: _____
Fecha y hora de la cita: _____
Lugar de la cita: _____

Estudiante B Tu compañero(a) te pregunta sobre la persona que le buscaste para una cita a ciegas (blind date). Contéstale con la siguiente información. Luego cambien de papel.

modelo
Estudiante A: ¿De dónde es?
Estudiante B: Es de Seattle.

verdes	Seattle
el cine Estrella	rojizo y ondulado
considerado(a)	el 15 de septiembre
y cómico(a)	a las 7 de la tarde

Origen: _____ Personalidad: _____
Cabello: _____ Ojos: _____
Fecha y hora de la cita: _____
Lugar de la cita: _____

④ Unidad 1 Etapa 1 p. 45 — Antes y ayer

Estudiante A Tú y tu compañero(a) quieren saber qué hicieron estas personas ayer y en su niñez (antes). Trabajen juntos(as) para completar la tabla.

modelo
Estudiante B: ¿Michalín compartió sus cosas ayer?
Estudiante A: No, no compartió sus cosas ayer. ¿Compartía sus cosas antes?

Nombre	Actividad	Antes	Ayer
Tu compañero(a)	hacerles caso a sus padres		
Tú	discutir con tu hermano(a)		
Joaquín	respetar a sus maestros	no	
Michalín	compartir sus cosas	no	

Estudiante B Tú y tu compañero(a) quieren saber qué hicieron estas personas ayer y en su niñez (antes). Trabajen juntos(as) para completar la tabla.

modelo
Estudiante B: ¿Michalín compartió sus cosas ayer?
Estudiante A: No, no compartió sus cosas ayer. ¿Compartía sus cosas antes?

Nombre	Actividad	Antes	Ayer
Michalín	compartir sus cosas	no	
Joaquín	respetar a sus maestros	no	
Tú	discutir con tu hermano(a)		
Tu compañero(a)	hacerles caso a sus padres		

③ Answers

A: ¿De dónde es?
B: Es de Seattle.
A: ¿De qué color son los ojos?
B: Los ojos son verdes.
A: ¿Cuál es el lugar de la cita?
B: El lugar es el cine Estrella.
A: Describe su personalidad.
B: Es considerado(a) y cómico(a).
A: Describe el cabello.
B: Él/Ella tiene el cabello rojizo y ondulado.
A: ¿Cuál es la fecha de la cita?
B: La fecha es el quince de septiembre.
A: ¿A qué hora es la cita?
B: Es a las siete de la tarde.

B: ¿De dónde es?
A: Es de Miami.
B: ¿Cómo son los ojos?
A: Los ojos son grandes y negros.
B: ¿Cuál es el lugar de la cita?
A: El lugar es una fiesta en casa de Carlota.
B: Describe su personalidad.
A: Es sociable y atrevido(a).
B: Describe el cabello.
A: El cabello es moreno y lacio.
B: ¿Cuál es la fecha de la cita?
A: La fecha es el catorce de septiembre.
B: ¿A qué hora es la cita?
A: Es a la una de la tarde.

④ Answers

Answers may vary, but should show the correct usage of the preterite and the imperfect.

⑤ Answers

1. A: A Norberto le encantan las montañas.
   B: Hará alpinismo.
2. A: Cristina es descarada.
   B: No les hará caso a sus padres.
3. A: Chalo es atrevido.
   B: Volará en planeador.
4. A: A Francisca le interesan las computadoras.
   B: Navegará por Internet.
5. B: Cecilia es aficionada al béisbol.
   A: Coleccionará tarjetas de los jugadores.
6. B: Virginia es modesta.
   A: No te describirá sus talentos.
7. B: A Andrés le fascinan los deportes de agua.
   A: Navegará en tabla de vela.
8. B: Jaime es mimado.
   A: Podrá hacer todo lo que quiera.

⑥ Answers

1. A: Marta va al gimnasio.
   B: d. Llevará sus sudaderas.
2. A: Marta va a una boda.
   B: a. Llevará su vestido con rayas.
3. A: Marta va a la playa.
   B: c. Llevará sus shorts.
4. A: Marta va a acampar.
   B: b. Llevará su camisa de cuadros.
5. A: Pedro va a la escuela.
   A: b. Llevará sus jeans.
6. B: Pedro va a un restaurante elegante.
   A: a. Llevará su traje.
7. B: Pedro va a una competencia de ciclismo.
   A: c. Llevará sus sudaderas.
8. B: Pedro va a una fiesta de los setenta.
   A: d. Llevará su medalla.

MÁS COMUNICACIÓN

⑤ Unidad 1 Etapa 2 p. 67
¿Qué harán?

(texto para Estudiante A, impreso al revés)

- navegar en tabla de vela
- no describirte sus talentos
- poder hacer todo lo que quiere
- coleccionar tarjetas de los jugadores
4. A Francisca le interesan las computadoras.
3. Chalo es atrevido.
2. Cristina es descarada.
1. A Norberto le encantan las montañas.

Estudiante B: *No pescará en alta mar.*

Estudiante A: *Olivia detesta andar en bote.*

modelo

Estudiante A Descríbele a las siguientes personas a tu compañero(a), usando las oraciones que aparecen a continuación. Entonces tu compañero(a) te dice lo que cada persona hará según sus gustos y personalidad. Luego cambien de papel y contéstale a tu compañero(a), usando las frases de abajo.

Estudiante B Tu compañero(a) va a describir a varias personas. ¿Qué crees que harán las personas mencionadas según sus gustos y personalidad? Escoge actividades lógicas de la lista. Luego cambien de papel y usa las oraciones de abajo para describirle a las personas indicadas a tu compañero(a).

modelo

Estudiante A: *Olivia detesta andar en bote.*

Estudiante B: *No pescará en alta mar.*

- no hacerles caso a sus padres
- navegar por Internet
- volar en planeador
- hacer alpinismo
5. Cecilia es aficionada al béisbol.
6. Virginia es modesta.
7. A Andrés le fascinan los deportes de agua.
8. Jaime es mimado.

---

⑥ Unidad 1 Etapa 2 p. 69
¿Cómo se ve?

(texto para Estudiante A, impreso al revés)

4. a acampar
2. una boda
3. la playa
1. el gimnasio

Estudiante B: *Llevará su blusa de lunares.*

Estudiante A: *Marta va a un concierto.*

modelo

Estudiante A Dile a tu compañero(a) adónde va Marta. Él (Ella) te va a decir qué ropa llevará. Luego cambien de papel y dile que llevará Pedro. Sigan el modelo.

Estudiante B: Tu compañero(a) te dice adónde va Marta. Dile qué ropa llevará. Luego cambien de papel y dile adónde va Pedro. Sigan el modelo.

modelo

Estudiante A: *Marta va a un concierto.*

Estudiante B: *Llevará su blusa de lunares.*

a.

c.

b.

d.

5. la escuela
6. un restaurante elegante
7. una competencia de ciclismo
8. una fiesta de los setenta

R4 RECURSOS
Más comunicación

7 Unidad 1 Etapa 3 p. 88 — ¡Adivinen!

Estudiante A Da pistas (clues) para que tu compañero(a) adivine (guess) el verbo en negrita de cada oración. ¡Ojo! No puedes usar ese verbo en tu descripción. Luego, cambien de papel y trata de adivinar los verbos de tu compañero(a).

modelo

Martina y Bárbara **se conocen** bien.

Estudiante A: Martina y Bárbara se hablan de todo… Hace muchos años que son amigas… Frecuentemente Martina sabe lo que Bárbara va a decir…

Estudiante B: ¿Se llevan bien?… ¿Se saludan?… ¡Se conocen bien!

1. David y su primo **se telefonean.**
2. Elvira y su vecina **se pelean.**
3. Carlos y Anita **se quieren.**
4. Lucí y Ana **se ayudan** con la tarea.

Estudiante B Trata de adivinar las actividades que hacen varias personas según las pistas (clues) de tu compañero(a). Luego, cambien de papel y da pistas para que tu compañero(a) adivine (guess) el verbo en negrita de cada oración de abajo. ¡Ojo! No puedes usar ese verbo en tu descripción.

modelo

Martina y Bárbara **se conocen** bien.

Estudiante A: Martina y Bárbara se hablan de todo… Hace muchos años que son amigas… Frecuentemente Martina sabe lo que Bárbara va a decir…

Estudiante B: ¿Se llevan bien?… ¿Se saludan?… ¡Se conocen bien!

5. David y Lola **se cuentan** chismes.
6. Jovita y su abuela **se escriben.**
7. Los padres de César **se perdonan.**
8. Los estudiantes **se quejan.**

8 Unidad 1 Etapa 3 p. 91 — ¿Cuáles son las diferencias?

Estudiante A Con tu compañero(a), háganse preguntas sobre los diferentes objetos de sus dibujos para identificar siete diferencias entre los dos dibujos. ¡Buena suerte!

modelo

Estudiante A: Veo una bandera de Estados Unidos…

Estudiante B: Aquí se ven dos banderas, una de Estados Unidos y otra de México… ¿A qué hora cierra el…?

Estudiante B Con tu compañero(a), háganse preguntas sobre los diferentes objetos de sus dibujos para identificar siete diferencias entre los dos dibujos. ¡Buena suerte!

modelo

Estudiante A: Veo una bandera de Estados Unidos…

Estudiante B: Aquí se ven dos banderas, una de Estados Unidos y otra de México…¿A qué hora cierra el…?

7 Answers

Answers will vary.

8 Answers

Answers will vary, but should include the following lists of differences:

A: una bandera de Estados Unidos
quiosco de periódicos
una bicicleta
horas del banco: 9–2
dos hombres hablando
anuncio: se habla español

B: dos banderas
quiosco de revistas
un caballo
horas del banco: 10–2
dos hombres con un cartón
no hay anuncio que diga qué idioma se habla

9 Answers

Answers will vary, but should include what follows.
1. A: Voy a sembrar árboles.
2. A: Voy a donar ropa a los pobres.
3. A: Voy a cocinar en el comedor de beneficencia.
4. A: Voy a recoger la basura.
5. B: Voy a juntar fondos.
6. B: Voy a ayudar a los ancianos.

10 Answers

Answers will vary. Suggested answers are given.
1. A: ¿Cómo mejorarías tu escuela?
   B: Sería voluntario(a) en...
2. A: ¿Cómo conservarías el agua?
   B: Educaría el público sobre la conservación.
3. A: ¿Cómo buscarías trabajo después de la graduación?
   B: Buscaría algo que me importe.
4. B: ¿Cómo ayudarías a la gente sin hogar?
   A: Sería voluntario(a) en...
5. B: ¿Cómo escogerías una universidad?
   A: Buscaría una que ofrezca clases de...
6. B: ¿Cómo ayudarías a los ancianos?
   A: Los visitaría.

MÁS COMUNICACIÓN

9 Unidad 2 Etapa 1 p. 118
¿Me puedes ayudar?

Estudiante A Mira los dibujos y pide a tu compañero(a) que te ayude con las actividades. Él (Ella) te puede ayudar o te dará una excusa. Luego, cambien de papel. Sigan el modelo.

modelo

sembrar árboles

Estudiante A: *¿Podrías darme una mano? Voy a sembrar árboles hoy.*

Estudiante B: *Sí, con mucho gusto. ¡Sembremos árboles!* o *Si pudiera, lo haría, pero tengo que ayudar a mi mamá.*

Estudiante B: Tu compañero(a) te pide ayuda con las actividades mostradas en los dibujos. Dile que sí o dale una excusa. Luego, cambien de papel. Sigan el modelo.

modelo

sembrar árboles

Estudiante A: *¿Podrías darme una mano? Voy a sembrar árboles hoy.*

Estudiante B: *Sí, con mucho gusto. ¡Sembremos árboles! o Si pudiera, lo haría, pero tengo que ayudar a mi mamá.*

10 Unidad 2 Etapa 1 p. 121
¿Qué harías?

6. visitarlos / ayudarlos a ir de compras
5. buscar una escuela bilingüe ... / escoger una con un buen programa de deportes

Para responder
4. darle dinero / ser voluntario(a) en...
3. buscar trabajo después de la graduación
2. conservar el agua
1. mejorar tu escuela

Para preguntar

Estudiante B: *Educaría al público.*

Estudiante A: *¿Cómo lucharías contra el racismo?*

luchar contra el racismo

modelo

preguntar y responder. Sigan el modelo.

Estudiante A Conversa con un(a) compañero(a) sobre lo que harían en cada situación. Pueden usar las siguientes ideas para preguntar y responder. Sigan el modelo.

Estudiante B Conversa con un(a) compañero(a) sobre lo que harían en cada situación. Pueden usar las siguientes ideas para preguntar y responder. Sigan el modelo.

modelo

luchar contra el racismo

Estudiante A: *¿Cómo lucharías contra el racismo?*

Estudiante B: *Educaría al público.*

Para responder
1. ser voluntario en...
2. reciclar / educar al público sobre...
3. buscar un trabajo mejor pagado / buscar algo interesante

Para preguntar
4. ayudar a la gente sin hogar
5. escoger una universidad
6. ayudar a los ancianos

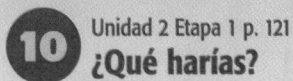

R6 RECURSOS
Más comunicación

11 · Unidad 2 Etapa 2 p. 140 — Treinta segundos

(Estudiante A — texto invertido)

entender	vestirse	**pensar**
ser	pedir	decir	hacer

| estar | empezar | **ir** | **cerrar** | repetir |

2. la escuela
4. el restaurante
1. el centro de la comunidad
3. el parque

modelo

Estudiante A: *Estás en la clase de español.*

Estudiante B: *No es bueno que la maestra les dé mucha tarea a los estudiantes de la clase de español. Es importante que tú no salgas temprano de la clase de español...*

Estudiante A Menciona uno de estos lugares a tu compañero(a). Él (Ella) tiene 30 segundos para hacer todas las oraciones que pueda. Tiene que incluir el lugar, las expresiones impersonales y los verbos de su lista. Luego, cambien de papel.

Estudiante B Tu compañero(a) te menciona un lugar. ¿Cuántas oraciones puedes hacer en 30 segundos? Incluye el lugar, las expresiones impersonales y los verbos de la lista en tu respuesta. Luego, cambien de papel.

modelo

Estudiante A: *Estás en la clase de español.*

Estudiante B: *No es bueno que la maestra les dé mucha tarea a los estudiantes de la clase de español. Es importante que tú no salgas temprano de la clase de español...*

dar	**mentir**	jugar	**saber**	**volver**	seguir
ver	servir	conocer	dormir	**reír**	salir

5. el cine
6. en casa
7. en la clase
8. en una tienda

12 · Unidad 2 Etapa 2 p. 143 — ¿Bueno o malo?

(Estudiante A — texto invertido)

una buena causa
• juntar fondos para voluntario(a)
• trabajar de
• no reciclar
la capa de ozono
• ayudar a proteger

2. echar químicos en el aire
1. haber una sequía (¿dónde?)

ese país.

Estudiante B: *Es bueno que tu maestra haya visitado*

Estudiante A: *Mi maestra de historia fue a España.*

modelo

ir a España

Estudiante A Lee las situaciones en la primera lista. Imagina quién las hizo y dónde ocurrieron. Cuéntasela a tu compañero(a) para saber su opinión. Sigue el modelo. Luego, cambien de papel y opina sobre los comentarios de tu compañero(a) usando las opciones de la segunda lista.

Estudiante B Tu compañero(a) te cuenta unas situaciones. ¿Qué opinas? Usa las ideas de la primera lista para responder. Sigue el modelo. Luego, cambien de papel. Imagina cómo pasaron las situaciones en la segunda lista. ¿Quién las hizo y dónde ocurrieron? Cuéntaselas a tu compañero(a).

modelo

ir a España

Estudiante A: *Mi maestra de historia fue a España.*

Estudiante B: *Es bueno que tu maestra haya visitado ese país.*

- no llover bastante
- embellecer la tierra
- visitar ese país
- contaminar

3. echar botellas y latas en el basurero
4. no usar aerosoles

11 Answers

Answers will vary.

12 Answers

Answers will vary.

13 Answers

Answers will vary.

14 Answers

Answers will vary.

1. A: ¿Voy a alquilar videos?
   B: Dudo que alquiles videos.
2. A: ¿Voy a hacer montañismo?
   B: Dudo que hagas montañismo.
3. A: ¿Voy a navegar en tabla de vela?
   B: Creo que vas a navegar en tabla de vela.
4. A: ¿Voy a esquiar en el agua?
   B: Creo que vas a esquiar en el agua.
5. B: ¿Voy a pescar en alta mar?
   A: Dudo que vayas a pescar en alta mar.
6. B: ¿Voy a esquiar?
   A: Dudo que esquíes.
7. B: ¿Voy a escalar montañas?
   A: Creo que vas a escalar montañas.
8. B: ¿Voy a volar en planeador?
   A: Creo que vas a volar en planeador.

---

13 Unidad 2 Etapa 3 p. 159
Chisme

Estudiante A Dile a tu compañero(a) algo extraordinario que sepas o puedas inventar acerca de las siguientes personas. Él (Ella) te va a dar su opinión. Luego cambien de papel. Tu compañero(a) te va a hacer un comentario. ¿Qué opinas? Responde con una expresión de emoción de la segunda.

modelo

el jugador de béisbol

Estudiante A: ¿Sabes que Barry Bonds tiene el récord de jonrones?

Estudiante B: ¡Me alegro de que él disfrute de ese honor!

- 1. el (la) presidente de…
- 2. el actor…
- 3. la cantante…
- 4. el (la) autor(a)…

- Espero que…
- Me alegro de que…
- Siento que…
- Es triste que…
- Ojalá que…

Estudiante B Tu compañero(a) te va a contar ciertas cosas extraordinarias de varias personas. ¿Qué opinas? Escoge una expresión de emoción de la primera lista para responder. Luego cambien de papel y dile a tu compañero(a) algo extraordinario que sepas o puedas inventar acerca de las personas de la segunda lista. Él (Ella) te va a dar su opinión.

modelo

Me alegro de que…

Estudiante A: ¿Sabes que Barry Bonds tiene el récord de jonrones?

Estudiante B: ¡Me alegro de que él disfrute de ese honor!

- **5.** el (la) cantante…
- **6.** uno(a) de los profesores…
- **7.** la actriz…
- **8.** el (la) deportista…

- Es ridículo que…
- Ojalá que…
- Espero que…
- Es una lástima que…
- Me alegro de que…

---

14 Unidad 2 Etapa 3 p. 165
¡Vacaciones ideales!

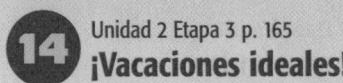

Estudiante A Pregúntale a tu compañero(a) si podrás hacer estas actividades durante tus vacaciones. Él (Ella) te responde después de consultar el folleto turístico. Sigan el modelo. Luego, cambien de papel.

modelo

andar en bicicleta

Estudiante A: ¿Voy a andar en bicicleta?

Estudiante B: Dudo que andes en bicicleta allí. o Creo que vas a andar en bicicleta allí.

- 1. alquilar videos
- 2. hacer montañismo
- 3. navegar en tabla de vela
- 4. esquiar en el agua

Estudiante B Tienes el folleto turístico de las vacaciones de tu compañero(a). Mira el folleto y contesta sus preguntas sobre las actividades que podrá hacer. Sigan el modelo. Luego, cambien de papel.

modelo

andar en bicicleta

Estudiante A: ¿Voy a andar en bicicleta?

Estudiante B: Dudo que andes en bicicleta allí. o Creo que vas a andar en bicicleta allí.

- **5.** pescar en alta mar
- **6.** esquiar
- **7.** escalar montañas
- **8.** volar en planeador

---

15 Unidad 3 Etapa 1 p. 191
Según ciertas condiciones

Estudiante A Pregunta a tu compañero(a) sobre las siguientes actividades. Luego contesta sus preguntas escogiendo una de las opciones de la segunda lista. Sigan el modelo.

modelo

ir al teatro

Estudiante A: ¿Vas al teatro?

Estudiante B: Voy con tal de que vea una comedia. **o** Voy con tal de que vea un musical.

1. hablar en clase
2. ir a fiestas
3. cantar
4. esquiar

• con tal de que (ser por correo electrónico / ¿?)
• con tal de que (ser interesante / ¿?)
• antes de que (salir de casa / ¿?)
• a menos que (ser deportes individuales / ¿?)

Estudiante B Tu compañero(a) te va a hacer preguntas. Contéstalas con oraciones escogiendo una de las opciones de la primera lista. Luego cambien de papel.

modelo

con tal de que (un musical / ¿?)

Estudiante A: ¿Vas al teatro?

Estudiante B: Voy con tal de que vea un musical. **o** Voy con tal de que vea una comedia.

• a menos que (estar cansado(a) / ¿?)
• con tal de que (ir mis amigos / ¿?)
• con tal de que (hacer buen tiempo / ¿?)
• para que (todos saber mis opiniones / ¿?)

5. trabajar
6. practicar deportes
7. hacer la tarea
8. escribir cartas

16 Unidad 3 Etapa 1 p. 195
¿Qué querían?

Estudiante A Las personas que aparecen a continuación querían que otras personas hicieran algo. Pregúntale a tu compañero(a) qué querían. Luego cambien de papel y contesta las preguntas de tu compañero(a), usando la segunda lista.

modelo

los músicos

Estudiante A: ¿Qué querían los músicos?

Estudiante B: Deseaban que la gente bailara la bomba.

1. la madre de Hernán
2. el graduando
3. la mesera
4. el presidente de la compañía

• la profesora no dar un examen difícil
• las fotos salir bien
• a la graduanda gustarle su regalo
• los estudiantes entrenarse todos los días

Estudiante B Contesta las preguntas de tu compañero(a) usando la información de la primera lista. Luego cambien de papel y pregunta a tu compañero(a) qué querían estas personas. Sigan el modelo.

modelo

la gente bailar la bomba

Estudiante A: ¿Qué querían los músicos?

Estudiante B: Deseaban que la gente bailara la bomba.

• los clientes dejar una buena propina
• su hijo hacer la limpieza
• los empleados trabajar más rápidamente
• todos sus parientes y amigos venir a su fiesta

5. los padrinos de la graduanda
6. la profesora de educación física
7. los estudiantes de español
8. el fotógrafo

15 Answers

Answers will vary. Suggested answers are given.

1. A: ¿Hablas en clase?
   B: Hablo en clase para que todos sepan mis opiniones.
2. A: ¿Vas a fiestas?
   B: Voy a fiestas con tal de que vayan mis amigos.
3. A: ¿Cantas?
   B: Canto a menos que esté cansado(a).
4. A: ¿Esquías?
   B: Esquío con tal de que haga buen tiempo.
5. B: ¿Trabajas?
   A: Trabajo con tal de que sea interesante.
6. B: ¿Practicas deportes?
   A: Practico deportes a menos que sean deportes individuales.
7. B: ¿Haces la tarea?
   A: Hago la tarea antes de salir de casa.
8. B: ¿Escribes cartas?
   A: Escribo cartas con tal de que sea por correo electrónico.

16 Answers

1. A: ¿Qué quería la madre de Hernán?
   B: Deseaba que su hijo hiciera la limpieza.
2. A: ¿Qué quería el graduando?
   B: Deseaba que todos sus parientes y amigos vinieran a su fiesta.
3. A: ¿Qué quería la mesera?
   B: Deseaba que los clientes dejaran una buena propina.
4. A: ¿Qué quería el presidente de la compañía?
   B: Deseaba que los empleados trabajaran más rápidamente.
5. B: ¿Qué querían los padrinos de la graduanda?
   A: Deseaban que le gustara su regalo.
6. B: ¿Qué quería la profesora de educación física?
   A: Deseaba que los estudiantes se entrenaran todos los días.
7. B: ¿Qué querían los estudiantes de español?
   A: Deseaban que la profesora no diera un examen difícil.
8. B: ¿Qué quería el fotógrafo?
   A: Deseaba que las fotos salieran bien.

17 Answers

1. A: Manolo busca a alguien que sea intelectual.
   B: Recomiendo que llame al número 3-23-40-68.
   Mensaje: «Paso mucho tiempo leyendo...»
2. A: Perla busca a alguien que sea activo.
   B: Recomiendo que llame al número 8-98-14-15.
   Mensaje: «Mis pasatiempos incluyen volar en planeador...»
3. A: Javier busca a alguien que sea cómica.
   B: Recomiendo que llame al número 6-77-71-52.
   Mensaje: «Conmigo, todo el mundo se ríe...»
4. A: Cristóbal busca a alguien que sea sociable.
   B: Recomiendo que llame al número 5-22-47-34.
   Mensaje: «Me encanta conocer a otra gente...»
5. B: Julieta busca a alguien que sea activo.
   A: Recomiendo que llame al número 2-53-56-52.
   Mensaje: «Trabajo de voluntario después de la escuela...»
6. B: Víctor busca a alguien que sea divertida.
   A: Recomiendo que llame al número 7-74-80-34.
   Mensaje: «Soy una persona positiva y me río mucho...»
7. B: Nadia busca a alguien que sea sincero.
   A: Recomiendo que llame al número 5-35-98-80.
   Mensaje: «Soy una persona muy honesta y fiel...»
8. B: Jesús busca a alguien que sea creativa.
   A: Recomiendo que llame al número 7-74-12-38.
   Mensaje: «En mi tiempo libre, hago esculturas...»

18 Answers

Some answers will vary.

1. A: ¿Qué pedirías si tuvieras mucha hambre?
   B: Pediría una hamburguesa.
2. A: ¿Qué servirías para celebrar la fiesta de Navidad?
   B: *Possible answer:* Serviría pavo.
3. A: ¿Qué tomarías si comieras pastel de chocolate?
   B: *Possible answer:* Tomaría leche.
4. A: ¿Qué comerías si fueran las 10:00 de la noche?
   B: *Answers will vary.*
5. B: ¿Qué pedirías si quisieras ser más delgado(a)?
   A: *Possible answer:* Comería fruta.
6. B: ¿Qué beberías si tuvieras mucha sed?
   A: *Possible answer:* Bebería agua.
7. B: ¿Qué servirías para celebrar una fiesta de graduación?
   A: *Answers will vary.*
8. B: ¿Qué comerías si estuvieras en la casa de mis abuelos?
   A: *Answers will vary.*

---

17 Unidad 3 Etapa 2 p. 213
Anuncios personales

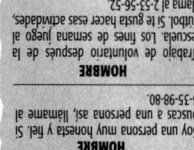
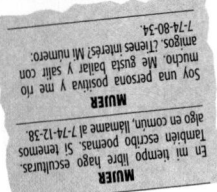

HOMBRE
Soy una persona muy honesta y fiel. Si buscas a una persona así, llámame al 5-35-98-80.

HOMBRE
Trabajo de voluntario después de la escuela. Los fines de semana juego al fútbol. Si te gusta hacer esas actividades, llama al 2-53-56-52.

MUJER
En mi tiempo libre hago esculturas. También escribo poemas. Si tenemos algo en común, llámame al 7-74-12-38.

MUJER
Soy una persona positiva y me río mucho. Me gusta bailar y salir con amigos. ¿Tienes interés? Mi número: 7-74-80-34.

1. Manolo / intelectual
2. Perla / activo
3. Javier / cómica
4. Cristóbal / sociable

modelo

Cristina/atleta

Estudiante A: Cristina busca a alguien que sea atleta.
Estudiante B: Recomiendo que llame al número 3-34-61-57.
Mensaje: «Soy una mujer atleta interesada en una persona a quien le gusta entrenarse».

Estudiante A Busca un(a) amigo(a) para estas personas. Lee las características que busca y tu compañero(a) leerá los anuncios. ¿A qué número debe llamar? Escriban un mensaje para cada una.

Estudiante B Tu compañero(a) te lee las características de personas que buscan amigos. Decide a qué número debe llamar la persona. Escriban un mensaje para cada una.

modelo
Cristina / atleta
Estudiante A: Cristina busca a alguien que sea atleta.
Estudiante B: Recomiendo que llame al número 3–34–61–57.
Mensaje: «Soy una mujer atleta interesada en una persona a quien le gusta entrenarse».

5. Julieta / activo
6. Víctor / divertida
7. Nadia / sincero
8. Jesús / creativa

MUJER.
Me encanta conocer a otra gente. Voy a fiestas y bailes con frecuencia. Si te gusta charlar, me puedes llamar al 5-22-47-34.

MUJER.
Paso mucho tiempo leyendo. Me fascinan las matemáticas y algún día quiero descubrir una fórmula nueva. Si quieres conocerme, llama al 3-23-40-68.

MUJER.
Conmigo, todo el mundo se ríe. Dicen que cuento los mejores chistes...pero siempre son de buen gusto. Llámame al 6-77-71-52.

HOMBRE.
Mis pasatiempos incluyen volar en planeador y escalar montañas. Si te gusta la aventura, soy la persona que buscas. Marca el 8-98-14-15.

---

18 Unidad 3 Etapa 2 p. 217
¡Delicioso!

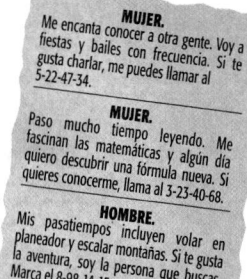

1. pedir / tener mucha hambre
2. servir / celebrar la fiesta de Navidad
3. tomar / comer pastel de chocolate
4. comer / ser las 10:00 de la noche

modelo

comer / querer ser más grande

Estudiante A: ¿Qué comerías si quisieras ser más grande?
Estudiante B: Comería mucho queso y helado.

Estudiante A Pregunta a tu compañero(a) qué comería en estas ocasiones. Luego, cambien de papel y responde a sus preguntas basándote en el dibujo.

Estudiante B Tu compañero(a) quiere saber qué comerías en estas ocasiones. Usa el dibujo para responder a sus preguntas. Luego, cambien de papel.

modelo
comer / querer ser más grande
Estudiante A: ¿Qué comerías si quisieras ser más grande?
Estudiante B: Comería mucho queso y helado.

5. pedir / querer ser más delgado(a)
6. beber / tener mucha sed
7. servir / celebrar una fiesta de graduación
8. comer / estar en la casa de mis abuelos

19 Unidad 3 Etapa 3 p. 237
¡A jugar!

Estudiante A Juega a esto con tu compañero(a). El objeto es que tu compañero(a) adivine quiénes son las personas que tú describes. ¡Ojo! Sólo puedes describir los deseos de la persona. Sigue el modelo. ¿Cuántas personas puede adivinar en cuatro minutos? Luego, cambien de papel y trata de adivinar quiénes son las personas que describe tu compañero(a).

modelo

Estudiante A: Insiste en que los escritores terminen su trabajo a tiempo. Quiere que no haya errores en el libro… Desea que muchas personas compren el libro…

Estudiante B: ¿El maestro?… ¡La editora!

estudiante	actor
novio(a)	reina
piloto	peatón(a)
agente de viajes	policía

Estudiante B

Adivina quiénes son las personas que describe tu compañero(a). Tienes cuatro minutos para adivinarlas. Luego cambien de papel y describe a las personas a continuación. ¡Ojo! Sólo puedes contar a tu compañero(a) los deseos de la persona. Sigue el modelo.

modelo

Estudiante A: *Insiste en que los escritores terminen su trabajo a tiempo. Quiere que no haya errores en el libro… Desea que muchas personas compren el libro…*

Estudiante B: *¿El maestro?… ¡La editora!*

doctor(a)	**bebé**
presidente	maestro(a)
pintor(a)	comediante
mesero(a)	ladrón

20 Unidad 3 Etapa 3 p. 239
¿Verdad o mentira?

Estudiante A Di algo cierto o inventa algo falso sobre las siguientes personas. ¿Lo cree tu compañero(a)? Si no te cree, te va a responder con una expresión de duda. Si te cree, responderá con una expresión positiva. ¿Puedes engañarlo(la)? Luego, cambien de papel.

modelo

tus tíos / verdad

Estudiante A: Mis tíos tienen nueve hijos.

Estudiante B: Dudo que tus tíos tengan nueve hijos. **o:** Pienso que tus tíos tienen nueve hijos.

Estudiante A: ¡Tienes razón! Es verdad que tienen nueve hijos. **o:** ¡Te engañé!

1. tu madre / verdad
2. tu mejor amigo(a) / verdad
3. tu primo(a) / mentira
4. un(a) maestro(a) / mentira

Estudiante B

Tu compañero(a) te va a decir algo cierto o inventar algo falso. Si le crees, responde con una expresión positiva. Si no, responde con una expresión de duda. ¿Puede engañarte? Luego, cambien de papel y usa la siguiente lista.

modelo

tus tíos / verdad

Estudiante A: *Mis tíos tienen nueve hijos.*

Estudiante B: *Dudo que tus tíos tengan nueve hijos. **o**: Pienso que tus tíos tienen nueve hijos.*

Estudiante A: *¡Tienes razón! Es verdad que tienen nueve hijos. **o**: ¡Te engañé!*

5. tu(s) hermano(s) / mentira	**7.** tus padres / verdad
6. un actor (una actriz) / mentira	**8.** tu abuelo(a) / verdad

19 Answers

Answers will vary.

20 Answers

Answers will vary.

Answers 21

A: ¿Cómo se llama?
B: Se llama Juana Aiken.
A: ¿Cuál es su fecha de nacimiento?
B: Su fecha de nacimiento es el veintiuno de marzo de 1978.
A: ¿Cuál es su ciudadanía?
B: Es argentina.
A: ¿Cuál es su campo de estudio?
B: Su campo de estudio es la informática.
A: ¿Cuál es su sueldo?
B: Su sueldo es treinta mil dólares.
B: ¿Cuál es su fecha de solicitud?
A: Su fecha de solicitud es el veinticinco de abril del 2000.
B: ¿Cuál es su teléfono?
A: Su teléfono es nueve-setenta y seis-cuarenta y dos-noventa y ocho.
B: ¿Cuál es su estado civil?
A: Es soltera.
B: ¿Cuál es su educación?
A: Tiene licenciatura.
B: ¿Quién le da una recomendación?
A: José Cruz le da una recomendación.

Answers 22

Answers will vary.

---

21 Unidad 4 Etapa 1 p. 263
Una solicitud

Estudiante A Con tu compañero(a), completa la información en la solicitud. Usa palabras interrogativas para obtener la información necesaria.

modelo

Estudiante A: ¿Cómo se llama?

Estudiante B: …

(solicitud form, rotated:)

Nombre:
Fecha de solicitud: 25-4-05
Teléfono: 9-76-42-98
Fecha de nacimiento:
Ciudadanía
Estado civil: soltera
Educación: licenciatura
Campo de estudio:
Sueldo corriente:
Recomendación: José Cruz

Estudiante B Con tu compañero(a), completa la información en la solicitud. Usa palabras interrogativas para obtener la información necesaria.

modelo

Estudiante A: ¿Cómo se llama?

Estudiante B: Se llama Juana Aiken.

Nombre: Juana Aiken
Fecha de solicitud: _____
Teléfono: _____
Fecha de nacimiento: 21-3-78
Ciudadanía: argentina
Estado civil: _____
Educación: _____
Campo de estudio: informática
Sueldo: $30.000
Recomendación: _____

---

22 Unidad 4 Etapa 1 p. 265
Piccionario

Estudiante A Juega a esto con tu compañero(a). Haz dibujos para comunicar las siguientes acciones y tu compañero(a) va a adivinarlas. Luego cambien de papel y adivina las acciones que dibuja tu compañero(a).

modelo

(Está cantando.)

Estudiante A: (Dibuja a una persona cantando.)

Estudiante B: Está hablando… Está gritando… ¡Está cantando!

Está volando en planeador.
Está buceando.
Está escribiendo.
Está haciendo alpinismo.
Está corriendo.
Está dibujando.

Estudiante B Juega a esto con tu compañero(a). Él (Ella) va a hacer dibujos para representar a varias acciones. Adivina lo que está pasando. Luego cambien de papel y haz dibujos para comunicar las siguientes acciones a tu compañero(a).

modelo

(Está cantando.)

Estudiante A: (Dibuja a una persona cantando.)

Estudiante B: Está hablando… Está gritando… ¡Está cantando!

Está comiendo.
Está bailando.
Está durmiendo.
Está estudiando.
Está lloviendo.
Está graduándose.

23 ¿Qué hay?

Unidad 4 Etapa 2 p. 285

Estudiante A ¿Son iguales los dibujos que tienen tú y tu compañero(a)? Hazle preguntas a tu compañero(a) para saber más de su dibujo. Después contesta sus preguntas sobre la escena que ves. Sigan el modelo.

modelo

Estudiante A: ¿Hay algún anuncio publicitario en la puerta?

Estudiante B: No hay ningún anuncio publicitario en la puerta.

Estudiante B ¿Son iguales los dibujos que tienen tú y tu compañero(a)? Contesta las preguntas de tu compañero(a) sobre la escena que ves. Luego hazle preguntas para saber más sobre su dibujo. Sigan el modelo.

modelo

Estudiante A: ¿Hay algún anuncio publicitario en la puerta?

Estudiante B: No hay ningún anuncio publicitario en la puerta.

---

24 ¿Ideas diferentes?

Unidad 4 Etapa 2 p. 288

5. Chela / arquitecta

7. Miguel / ingeniero

1. Bárbara / maestra
2. Óscar / mecánico
3. Lola / abogada
4. Miguel / ingeniero

modelo

Emilio/artista

Estudiante A: Emilio es artista.

Estudiante B: Sus padres querían que hubiera sido deportista.

Estudiante A Aquí ves las profesiones de varias personas. Pregúntale a tu compañero(a) si son las profesiones que los padres de las personas habían querido para sus hijos. Luego cambien de papel y contesta las preguntas de tu compañero(a), usando la información de abajo.

Estudiante B Tu compañero(a) te va a decir las profesiones que escogieron varias personas. ¿Es lo que querían sus padres? Usa la siguiente información para contestar. Luego cambien de papel y describe a tu compañero(a) las profesiones de las personas de abajo.

modelo

Emilio/artista

Estudiante A: Emilio es artista.

Estudiante B: Sus padres querían que hubiera sido deportista.

5. Chela / arquitecta
6. Paco / intérprete
7. Félix / juez
8. Diana / taxista

1. 2. 3. 4.

---

23 Answers

Answers will vary.

24 Answers

1. A: Bárbara es maestra.
   B: Sus padres querían que hubiera sido veterinaria.
2. A: Óscar es mecánico.
   B: Sus padres querían que hubiera sido bombero.
3. A: Lola es abogada.
   B: Sus padres querían que hubiera sido jueza.
4. A: Miguel es ingeniero.
   B: Sus padres querían que hubiera sido agricultor.
5. B: Chela es arquitecta.
   A: Sus padres querían que hubiera sido maestra.
6. B: Paco es intérprete.
   A: Sus padres querían que hubiera sido mecánico.
7. B: Félix es juez.
   A: Sus padres querían que hubiera sido un hombre de negocios.
8. B: Diana es taxista.
   A: Sus padres querían que hubiera sido ingeniera.

25 Answers

1. A: ¿Cuántos son académicos?
   B: El treinta por ciento de ellos son académicos.
2. A: ¿Cuántos son agentes de viajes?
   B: El veinte por ciento son agentes de viajes.
   o: Un quinto de ellos son agentes de viajes.
3. A: ¿Cuántos son corresponsales?
   B: El veinticinco por ciento de ellos son corresponsales. o: Un cuarto de ellos son corresponsales.
4. A: ¿Cuántos son financieros?
   B: El cinco por ciento de ellos son financieros.
5. B: ¿Cuántos son diplomáticos?
   A: El diez por ciento de ellos son diplomáticos.
6. B: ¿Cuántos son trabajadores sociales?
   A: El cincuenta por ciento de ellos son trabajadores sociales. o: La mitad de ellos son trabajadores sociales.
7. B: ¿Cuántos son traductores?
   A: El veinticinco por ciento de ellos son traductores. o: Un cuarto de ellos son traductores.
8. B: ¿Cuántos son banqueros?
   A: El quince por ciento de ellos son banqueros.

26 Answers

Personal answers will vary.
1. A: ¿Cuándo se habrá casado Estela?
   B: Habrá hecho eso dentro de diez años.
2. A. ¿Cuándo se habrá graduado Estela de la escuela?
   B: Habrá hecho eso dentro de un año.
3. A: ¿Cuándo se habrá jubilado Estela?
   B: Habrá hecho eso dentro de treinta años.
4. A: ¿Cuándo habrá sido Estela diplomática?
   B: Habrá hecho eso dentro de quince años.
5. B: ¿Cuándo habrá hecho Octavio un doctorado?
   A: Habrá hecho eso dentro de diez años.
6. B: ¿Cuándo habrá tenido Octavio dos hijos?
   A: Habrá hecho eso dentro de quince años.
7. B: ¿Cuándo habrá trabajado Octavio para una compañía multinacional?
   A: Habrá hecho eso dentro de veinte años.
8. B: ¿Cuándo habrá trabajado Octavio de voluntario en otro país?
   A: Habrá hecho eso dentro de cinco años.

25 — Unidad 4 Etapa 3 p. 308 — Estadísticas

Estudiante A Tu compañero(a) tiene estadísticas sobre las carreras de varios estudiantes bilingües que acaban de graduarse de la universidad. Pregunta cuáles son los datos para las siguientes carreras. Luego cambien de papel y contesta las preguntas de tu compañero(a), usando los datos de la gráfica de abajo.

modelo

intérprete

Estudiante A: ¿Cuántos son intérpretes?

Estudiante B: Un quinto de ellos son intérpretes. o El veinte por ciento de ellos son intérpretes.

1. académicos
2. agentes de viajes
3. corresponsales
4. financieros

Estudiante B Tu compañero(a) busca estadísticas sobre las carreras de estudiantes bilingües que acaban de graduarse de la universidad. Contesta sus preguntas basándote en la información de la siguiente gráfica. Luego cambien de papel y pregunta cuáles son los datos para las siguientes carreras.

modelo

intérprete

Estudiante A: ¿Cuántos son intérpretes?

Estudiante B: Un quinto de ellos son intérpretes. o El veinte por ciento de ellos son intérpretes.

5. diplomáticos
6. trabajadores sociales
7. traductores
8. banqueros

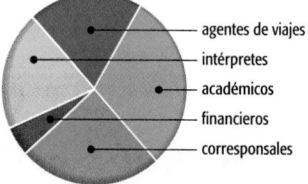

26 — Unidad 4 Etapa 3 p. 313 — ¿Cuándo?

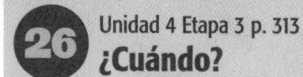

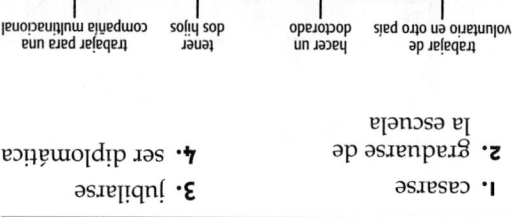

Estudiante A Pregunta a tu compañero(a) cuándo Estela habrá hecho estas cosas. ¿Y él (ella)? Luego, cambien de papel y contesta las preguntas de tu compañero(a) según las metas de Octavio.

modelo

viajar a muchos países

Estudiante A: ¿Cuándo habrá viajado Estela a muchos países?

Estudiante B: Habrá hecho eso dentro de cinco años. ¿Y tú?...

1. casarse
2. graduarse de la escuela
3. jubilarse
4. ser diplomática

Estudiante B Contesta las preguntas de tu compañero(a) sobre Estela. Luego, pregunta cuándo Octavio habrá hecho estas cosas y cuándo las hará tu compañero(a).

modelo

viajar a muchos países

Estudiante A: ¿Cuándo habrá viajado Estela a muchos países?

Estudiante B: Habrá hecho eso dentro de cinco años. ¿Y tú?...

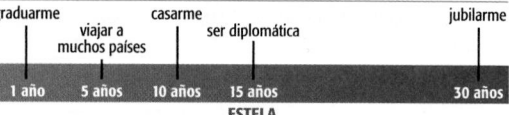

5. hacer un doctorado
6. tener dos hijos
7. trabajar para una compañía multinacional
8. trabajar de voluntario en otro país

27 Unidad 5 Etapa 1 p. 340
¿Cuántas diferencias?

[Estudiante A — texto invertido:]

3. ¿cuál? / diferencia / panderetas

1. ¿qué? / primer plano   5. ¿qué? / instrumentos   7. ¿?

Estudiante B: No sé cuál es su nombre. ¿Cuál es el nombre de la joven?

Estudiante A: ¿Cuál es su nombre?

modelo

¿cuál? / nombre

para determinar cuántas diferencias hay.

Estudiante A Hay algunas diferencias entre tu dibujo y el de tu compañero(a). Hazle preguntas y contesta las preguntas de tu compañero(a)

Estudiante B Hay algunas diferencias entre el dibujo que tienes y el de tu compañero(a). Hazle preguntas usando la siguiente lista y contesta las preguntas de tu compañero(a) para determinar cuántas diferencias hay.

modelo

¿cuál? / nombre

Estudiante A: ¿Cuál es su nombre?

Estudiante B: No sé cuál es su nombre. ¿Cuál es el nombre de la joven?

2. ¿qué? / fondo   6. ¿qué? / tocar
4. ¿qué? / hacer   8. ¿?

28 Unidad 5 Etapa 1 p. 343
Intereses personales

[Listas — texto invertido:]

A
1. música / interesar
2. pintores / admirar
3. bailarines / gustar mirar

B
4. (incluye / no incluye) letra
5. darme (risa / miedo)
6. ser (siglo 17 / siglo 20)

modelo

literatura (cómica / ciencia ficción)

Estudiante A: ¿Qué tipo de literatura te interesa?

Estudiante B: Me interesa la literatura que sea muy cómica.

Estudiante A Pregúntale a tu compañero(a) sobre sus intereses, usando la lista de la parte A. Luego contesta las preguntas de tu compañero(a), basándote en la lista de la parte B. Sigue el modelo.

Estudiante B Tú y tu compañero(a) quieren conocerse mejor. Contesta las preguntas de tu compañero(a) basándote en la información de la lista A. Sigue el modelo. Luego hazle preguntas a tu compañero(a) usando la lista B.

modelo

literatura (cómica / ciencia ficción)

Estudiante A: ¿Qué tipo de literatura te interesa?

Estudiante B: Me interesa la literatura que sea muy cómica.

A
1. darme (ánimo / tranquilidad)
2. pintar (naturalezas muertas / cuadros históricos)
3. bailar (el tango / el flamenco)

B
4. música / escuchar más
5. obras teatrales / preferir ver
6. estilo de cuadros / interesar más

27 Answers

Answers will vary.

1. A: ¿Qué hay en primer plano?
   B: Hay dos jóvenes en primer plano.
2. B: ¿Qué hay al fondo?
   A: Hay un tapiz al fondo.
3. A: ¿Cuál es la diferencia entre las panderetas?
   B: La pandereta a la derecha es más grande que la pandereta a la izquierda.
4. B: ¿Qué hacen los jóvenes?
   A: Bailan y tocan instrumentos.
5. A: ¿Qué instrumentos hay?
   B: Hay una trompeta y dos panderetas.
6. B: ¿Qué tocan los jóvenes?
   A: La chica toca las castañuelas y el chico da palmadas.
7. A and B: *Answers will vary.*
8. A and B: *Answers will vary.*

28 Answers

Answers will vary. Possible answers are given.

1. A: ¿Qué tipo de música te interesa?
   B: Prefiero música que me dé tranquilidad.
2. A: ¿Qué tipo de pintores admiras?
   B: Admiro pintores que pintan naturalezas muertas.
3. A: ¿Qué tipo de bailarines te gusta mirar?
   B: Me gusta mirar bailarines que bailan el tango.
4. B: ¿Qué tipo de música escuchas más?
   A: Escucho música que incluye letra.
5. B: ¿Qué obras de teatro prefieres ver?
   A: Prefiero obras que me den risa.
6. B: ¿Qué estilo de cuadros te interesa más?
   A: Me interesan más los cuadros que son del siglo 20.

29 Answers

1. A: ¿Hiciste los quehaceres?
   B: Sí, los hice.
2. A: ¿Escuchaste salsa?
   B: Sí, la escuché.
3. A: ¿Escribiste el ensayo?
   B: No, no lo escribí.
4. A: ¿Navegaste por Internet para buscar información?
   B: Sí, lo navegué.

1. B: ¿Bañaste los perros?
   A: No, no los bañé.
2. B: ¿Leíste la biografía?
   A: Sí, la leí.
3. B: ¿Practicaste el violín?
   A: Sí, lo practiqué.
4. B: ¿Compraste el tejido?
   A: No, no lo compré.

30 Answers

Answers will vary.

MÁS COMUNICACIÓN

29 Unidad 5 Etapa 2 p. 359
¿Lo hizo?

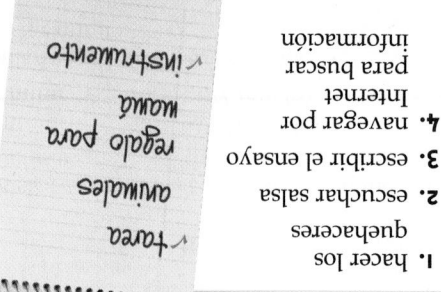

Estudiante A Tu compañero(a) escribió una lista de actividades. Pregúntale si ya las hizo, usando la siguiente información. Luego cambien de papel e imagínate que la lista en el cuaderno es tuya. Una marca indica que cumpliste la actividad. Sigue el modelo.

modelo

pintar la máscara

Estudiante A: ¿Pintaste la máscara?

Estudiante B: Sí, la pinté.

1. hacer los quehaceres
2. escuchar salsa
3. escribir el ensayo
4. navegar por Internet para buscar información

tarea ✓
regalo para mamá ✓
animales
instrumento ✓

Estudiante B Imagínate que la lista en el cuaderno es tuya. Una marca indica que hiciste la actividad indicada. Contesta las preguntas de tu compañero(a) según la lista. Luego cambien de papel y pregúntale a tu compañero(a) si hizo cada una de las siguientes actividades.

modelo

Pintar la máscara

Estudiante A: ¿Pintaste la máscara?

Estudiante B: Sí, la pinté.

1. bañar los perros
2. leer la biografía
3. practicar el violín
4. comprar el tejido

✓ nuevo disco compacto
tarea
✓ limpiar
✓ computadora

---

30 Unidad 5 Etapa 2 p. 363
¿Quién es?

Estudiante A Juega a esto con tu compañero(a). Para cada categoría de la siguiente lista, escoge un ejemplo y escríbelo en una hoja aparte. Dale pistas (clues), usando la forma correcta de **el que** o **el cual**, para que tu compañero(a) lo adivine. Sigue el modelo. Luego, cambien de papel y trata de adivinar los ejemplos de tu compañero(a).

modelo

jueza

Estudiante A: Esta jueza es la que fue la primera mujer en la Corte Suprema de Estados Unidos.

Estudiante B: ¡Sandra Day O'Connor!

1. político
2. actriz
3. conquistador
4. artista
5. monumento
6. película

Estudiante B Juega a esto con tu compañero(a). Tu compañero(a) te va a dar pistas (clues) para ver si puedes adivinar una cosa o una persona que él (ella) ha escrito en otra hoja de papel. Sigue el modelo. Luego cambien de papel. Para cada categoría de la siguiente lista, escoge un ejemplo y escríbelo en una hoja aparte. Dale pistas a tu compañero(a), usando la forma correcta de **el que** o **el cual**, para que tu compañero(a) lo adivine.

modelo

jueza

Estudiante A: Esta jueza es la que fue la primera mujer en la Corte Suprema de Estados Unidos.

Estudiante B: ¡Sandra Day O'Connor!

7. músico o conjunto
8. explorador
9. actor
10. libro
11. país
12. deportista

31 Unidad 5 Etapa 3 p. 384
¡No repitas!

Estudiante A Entrevista a tu compañero(a), usando las siguientes opciones. Luego cambien de papel y contesta las preguntas de tu compañero(a). Cuando contestes, no repitas el sustantivo. Sigan el modelo.

modelo

comer comidas (picantes / blandas)

Estudiante A: ¿Prefieres comer las comidas picantes o las comidas blandas?

Estudiante B: Me gustan más las picantes.

1. comprar un carro (nuevo / usado)
2. tomar una clase (fácil / interesante)
3. ver finales (feliz / irónico)
4. leer novelas (innovador / tradicional)
5. hacer deportes (individuales / en equipo)

Estudiante B Tu compañero(a) te va a entrevistar. Cuando contestes sus preguntas, no repitas el sustantivo. Sigan el modelo. Luego cambien de papel y entrevista a tu compañero(a), usando las opciones de la siguiente lista.

modelo

comer comidas (picantes / blandas)

Estudiante A: ¿Prefieres comer las comidas picantes o las comidas blandas?

Estudiante B: Me gustan más las picantes.

6. ver una película (creativo / dramático)
7. escuchar una canción (expresivo / divertido)
8. mirar a modelos (rubio / pelirrojo)
9. llevar la ropa (clásico / original)
10. hacer los papeles (romántico / cómico)

32 Unidad 5 Etapa 3 p. 387
¿De quién?

| Oprah Winfrey | Elvis Presley |
| Tiger Woods | Laura Esquivel |

1. mirar una película de ciencia ficción
2. leer un libro sobre la esclavitud
3. estudiar el cubismo
4. coleccionar tarjetas de un atleta

modelo

visitar una compañía de tecnología fenomenal

Estudiante A: Visité una compañía de tecnología fenomenal.

Estudiante B: Ah, visitaste la de Bill Gates.

Estudiante A A ti y a tus amigos siempre les fascinan las personas famosas. Dile a tu compañero(a) la actividad que hiciste y él (ella) tiene que identificar a la persona famosa relacionada con la actividad. Sigue el modelo. Luego cambien de papel.

Estudiante B A ti y a tus amigos siempre les fascinan las personas famosas. Tu compañero(a) te dice la actividad que hizo y tienes que identificar a la persona famosa relacionada con la actividad. Sigue el modelo. Luego cambien de papel.

modelo

visitar una compañía de tecnología fenomenal

Estudiante A: Visité una compañía de tecnología fenomenal.

Estudiante B: Ah, visitaste la de Bill Gates.

| Michael Jordan | George Lucas |
| Pablo Picasso | Toni Morrison |

5. visitar una casa famosa llamada «Graceland»
6. leer una novela que en cada capítulo describe cómo preparar comida
7. ver un programa de tele con una anfitriona que también es actriz
8. mirar partidos de golf increíbles

31 Answers

Answers will vary. Suggested answers are given.

1. A: ¿Prefieres comprar un carro nuevo o un carro usado?
   B: Me gusta más uno nuevo.
2. A: ¿Prefieres tomar una clase fácil o una clase interesante?
   B: Me gusta más una interesante.
3. A: ¿Prefieres ver finales felices o finales irónicos?
   B: Me gustan más los irónicos.
4. A: ¿Prefieres leer novelas innovadoras o novelas tradicionales?
   B: Me gustan más las tradicionales.
5. A: ¿Prefieres hacer deportes individuales o deportes en equipo?
   B: Me gustan más los individuales.
6. B: ¿Prefieres ver una película creativa o una película dramática?
   A: Me gusta más una dramática.
7. B: ¿Prefieres escuchar una canción expresiva o una canción divertida?
   A: Me gusta más una expresiva.
8. B: ¿Prefieres mirar a modelos rubios o modelos pelirrojos?
   A: Me gustan más los rubios.
9. B: ¿Prefieres llevar la ropa clásica o la ropa original?
   A: Me gusta más la original.
10. B: ¿Prefieres los papeles románticos o los papeles cómicos?
    A: Me gustan más los románticos.

32 Answers

1. A: Miré una película de ciencia ficción.
   B: Ah, miraste la de George Lucas.
2. A: Leí un libro sobre la esclavitud.
   B: Ah, leíste el de Toni Morrison.
3. A: Estudié el cubismo.
   B: Ah, estudiaste el de Pablo Picasso.
4. A: Coleccioné tarjetas de un atleta.
   B: Ah, coleccionaste las de Michael Jordan.
5. B: Visité una casa famosa llamada «Graceland».
   A: Ah, visitaste la de Elvis Presley.
6. B: Leí una novela que en cada capítulo describe cómo preparar comida.
   A: Ah, leíste la de Laura Esquivel.
7. B: Vi un programa de tele con una anfitriona que también es actriz.
   A: Ah, viste el de Oprah Winfrey.
8. B: Miré partidos de golf increíbles.
   A: Ah, miraste los de Tiger Woods.

33 Answers

Order of pictures: b, d, f, a, e, c.

34 Answers

1. A: ¿Qué dijo el actor?
   B: Dijo que quería hacer el papel de Juan Carlos.
2. A: ¿Qué dijo la crítica?
   B: Dijo que todos deberían ir a ver esta película de cuatro estrellas.
3. A: ¿Qué dijeron los padres?
   B: Dijeron que no miraran la tele antes de hacer la tarea.
4. A: ¿Qué dijo la deportista?
   B: Dijo que ojalá que alguien grabara el partido.
5. B: ¿Qué dijeron los niños?
   A: Dijeron que querían mirar los dibujos animados.
6. B: ¿Qué dijo el guionista?
   A: Dijo que era el mejor guión que había escrito.
7. B: ¿Qué dijeron los padres?
   A: Dijeron que no miraran esa película porque era prohibida para menores.
8. B: ¿Qué dijo la directora?
   A: Dijo que era bastante difícil dirigir un programa en vivo y directo.

33 Unidad 6 Etapa 1 p. 411
El perro, el gato y el ratón

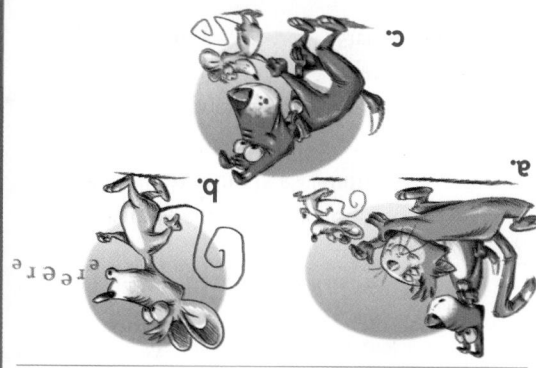

Estudiante A Los dibujos representan lo que pasó en un dibujo animado, pero no aparecen en el orden correcto. Hay seis dibujos en total. Junto a tu compañero(a), determinen el orden lógico de los dibujos.

modelo

Estudiante A: ¿Cuál es el primer dibujo?

Estudiante B: Pues, el gato...

Estudiante B Los dibujos representan lo que pasó en un dibujo animado, pero no aparecen en el orden correcto. Hay seis dibujos en total. Junto a tu compañero(a), determinen el orden lógico de los dibujos.

modelo

Estudiante A: ¿Cuál es el primer dibujo?

Estudiante B: Pues, el gato…

34 Unidad 6 Etapa 1 p. 417
¿Qué dijo?

- «Es el mejor guión que he escrito.»
- «No miren esa película porque es prohibida para menores.»
- «Queremos mirar los dibujos animados.»
- «Es bastante difícil dirigir un programa en vivo y directo.»

1. el actor
2. la crítica
3. los padres
4. la deportista

Estudiante A: ¿Qué dijeron los jóvenes?
Estudiante B: Dijeron que iban a alquilar un video para el sábado.

modelo

los jóvenes   «Vamos a alquilar un video para el sábado.»

Estudiante A Pregúntale a tu compañero(a) qué dijeron las siguientes personas. Luego, cambien de papel y escoge una de las opciones de la derecha para contestar lógicamente las preguntas de tu compañero(a).

Estudiante B Tu compañero(a) quiere saber qué dijeron varias personas. Escoge una de las siguientes opciones para contestar sus preguntas lógicamente. Luego, cambien de papel y pregúntale qué dijeron las personas de la lista de la derecha.

modelo

los jóvenes   «Vamos a alquilar un video para el sábado.»

Estudiante A: ¿Qué dijeron los jóvenes?

Estudiante B: Dijeron que iban a alquilar un video para el sábado.

- «Todos deben ir a ver esta película de cuatro estrellas.»
- «Ojalá que alguien grabe el partido.»
- «Quiero hacer el papel de Juan Carlos.»
- «No miren la tele antes de hacer la tarea.»

5. los niños
6. el guionista
7. los padres
8. la directora

35 Unidad 6 Etapa 2 p. 433
¿Qué quieres?

Estudiante A Pregúntale a tu compañero(a) si quiere las siguientes cosas. Luego, cambien de papel y contéstale sus preguntas, usando las expresiones de la lista a la derecha.

modelo

radio portátil   en cuanto

Estudiante A: ¿Te gustaría comprar un radio portátil?

Estudiante B: Sí, voy a comprar uno en cuanto tenga bastante dinero.

1. videocámara • hasta que
2. contestadora automática • aunque
3. asistente electrónico • para que
4. beeper • con tal que

Estudiante B Cuando tu compañero(a) te pregunte si quieres varias cosas, usa las siguientes expresiones para contestar. Luego, cambien de papel y pregúntale a él (ella) si quiere las cosas de la lista a la derecha.

modelo

radio portátil   en cuanto

Estudiante A: ¿Te gustaría comprar un radio portátil ?

Estudiante B: Sí, voy a comprar uno en cuanto tenga bastante dinero.

• a menos que   5. audífonos
• tan pronto como   6. computadora portátil
• para que   7. telemensaje
• en caso de que   8. equipo estereofónico

36 Unidad 6 Etapa 2 p. 434
Dibujos con acción

Estudiante A Dibuja las siguientes cosas. Tu compañero(a) describe cada objeto y su posición en la escena. Luego, cambien de papel y adivina (describe) lo que dibuja tu compañero(a). ¿Quién adivina más rápido?

1. El teléfono inalámbrico está delante de la computadora portátil.
2. El beeper está encima de la contestadora automática.
3. Los audífonos están alrededor del radio portátil.
4. La grabadora está debajo de la mesa.

Estudiante B Tu compañero(a) te va a dibujar cuatro escenas. ¿Puedes describir cada objeto y su posición en la escena? Luego, cambien de papel y dibuja las siguientes escenas para tu compañero(a). ¿Quién adivina más rápido?

5. La pila está junto a la videocámara.
6. El equipo estereofónico está abajo.
7. El teléfono celular está dentro del carro.
8. El televisor portátil está frente al altoparlante.

35 Answers
Answers will vary.

36 Answers
Answers will vary.

37 Answers

A: ¿Cuál es la distancia que va a viajar Esteban?
B: Esteban va a viajar ochocientos cincuenta millas.
A: ¿Cuál es su hora de salida?
B: Va a salir a las trece y cuarto (la una y cuarto).
A: ¿Cuál es la destinación de Jesús?
B: Su destinación es Mérida.
A: ¿Cuál es la duración de su viaje?
B: La duración es doce días.
A: ¿Cuál es la distancia que va a viajar Emilia?
B: Emilia va a viajar quinientos cuarenta millas.
A: ¿Cuál es su hora de salida?
B: Va a salir a las catorce y media (las dos y media).
A: ¿Cuál es la destinación de Dani?
B: Su destinación es Madrid.
A: ¿Cuál es la duración de su viaje?
B: La duración es cinco días.
A: ¿Cuál es la destinación de Esteban?
A: Su destinación es Cali.
B: ¿Cuál es la duración de su viaje?
A: La duración es siete días.
B: ¿Cuál es la distancia que va a viajar Jesús?
A: Jesús va a viajar seiscientos setenta y cinco millas.
B: ¿Cuál es su hora de salida?
A: Va a salir a las catorce y media.
B: ¿Cuál es la destinación de Emilia?
A: Su destinación es Ponce.
B: ¿Cuál es la duración de su viaje?
A: La duración es quince días.
B: ¿Cuál es la distancia que va a viajar Dani?
A: Dani va a viajar mil ochocientos millas.
A: ¿Cuál es su hora de salida?
B: Va a salir a las nueve menos quince (cuarto).

38 Answers

Answers will vary.

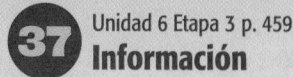

37 Unidad 6 Etapa 3 p. 459
Información

destinación		Cali	Ponce	
	Esteban	**Jesús**	**Emilia**	**Dani**
distancia		675 mi.		1800 mi.
hora de salida		14:30		8:45
duración del viaje	7 días		15 días	

Estudiante A Cuatro de tus amigos van a viajar este verano. Trabajando junto a tu compañero(a), completa la tabla con la información que falta para saber más sobre los viajes.

modelo

Estudiante A: ¿Cuál es la hora de salida de Esteban?

Estudiante B: La hora de salida de Esteban es las 13:15.

Estudiante B Cuatro de tus amigos van a viajar este verano. Trabajando junto a tu compañero(a), completa la tabla con la información que falta para saber más sobre los viajes.

modelo

Estudiante A: ¿Cuál es la hora de salida de Esteban?

Estudiante B: La hora de salida de Esteban es las 13:15.

	Esteban	Jesús	Emilia	Dani
destinación		Mérida		Madrid
distancia	850 mi.		540 mi.	
hora de salida	13:15		14:30	
duración del viaje		12 días		5 días

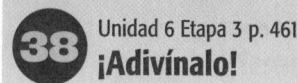

38 Unidad 6 Etapa 3 p. 461
¡Adivínalo!

4. El programador **acaba de** limpiar la pantalla.
3. La secretaria **se olvida de** enviar el fax.
2. El estudiante **aprende a** crear una página-web.
1. La niña **tiene que** comprar un disco.

El niño **viene con** su mamá.

Estudiante B: El niño va con su mamá… sale con su mamá… ¡**Viene con** su mamá!

Estudiante A: El niño acompaña a su mamá… Él llega acompañado por ella… Su mamá lo trae…

El niño **viene con** su mamá.

modelo

de adivinar las expresiones de tu compañero(a).

tu descripción. Luego cambien de papel y trata en negrita de cada una de las siguientes oraciones. ¡Ojo! No puedes usar esas palabras en compañero(a) adivine el verbo y la preposición compañero(a). Da pistas para que tu

Estudiante A Juega a esto con tu compañero(a).

Estudiante B Juega a esto con tu compañero(a). Trata de adivinar las expresiones según las pistas de tu compañero(a). Luego cambien de papel y da pistas para que tu compañero(a) adivine la expresión en negrita de cada una de las siguientes oraciones. ¡Ojo! No puedes usar esas palabras en tu descripción.

modelo

*El niño **viene con** su mamá.*

Estudiante A: *El niño acompaña a su mamá… Él llega acompañado por ella… Su mamá lo trae…*

Estudiante B: *El niño va con su mamá… sale con su mamá… ¡**Viene con** su mamá!*

5. El programa **insiste en** que uses la contraseña.
6. **Hay que** hacer doble clic.
7. La profesora **comienza a** participar en un grupo de conversación.
8. **Tengo ganas de** navegar por Internet.

Juegos—respuestas

UNIDAD 1

Etapa 1   p. 53: c. descarado

Etapa 2   p. 75: monedero

Etapa 3   p. 99: reparar, desyerbar, vaciar, descansar

UNIDAD 2

Etapa 1   p. 127: 1. c, 2. b, 3. a

Etapa 2   p. 149: la capa de ozono

Etapa 3   p. 173: mono, mariposa

UNIDAD 3

Etapa 1   p. 201: b. prohibir

Etapa 2   p. 223: pavo, pastel

Etapa 3   p. 247: faro

UNIDAD 4

Etapa 1   p. 275: 2

Etapa 2   p. 297: jubilarse, beneficios, aumentar, no trabajar

Etapa 3   p. 321: académico, agente de ventas

UNIDAD 5

Etapa 1   p. 349: una naturaleza muerta

Etapa 2   p. 371: Somos una civilización avanzada.

Etapa 3   p. 395: b. el crítico

UNIDAD 6

Etapa 1   p. 423: programas de misterio, los documentales, el control remoto

Etapa 2   p. 445: una batería

Etapa 3   p. 469: Carmen

Gramática-resumen

Grammar Terms

Adjective (p. 336): a word that describes a noun
*A Francisco le gustan las pinturas **modernas.***

Adverb (p. 433): a word that modifies a verb, an adjective, or another adverb
*Puerto Rico es **muy** bonito, **especialmente** la playa.*

Article: a word that identifies the class of a noun: masculine or feminine, singular or plural
***El** Yunque es **un** bosque tropical. **El** perfume de **las** orquídeas es muy agradable.*

Auxiliary Verb (pp. 46, 141): a secondary verb that is used with a main verb
*Nuestra visita al Prado **ha** sido increíble y ya **estamos** pensando ir otra vez.*

Command (pp. 114, 116): a verb form used to tell someone to do something
***Haga** ejercicio para bajar el estrés.*

Comparative (p. 454): a phrase that compares two different things
*El teatro español es **más divertido que** el cine.*

Conditional Tense (pp. 119, 214, 289, 414): a verb form that indicates that the action in a sentence could happen at a future time
*¿Te **gustaría** proteger el medio ambiente?*

Conditional Perfect Tense (p. 289): a verb form that expresses actions that would have been done if something else had been true
***Habríamos trabajado** en finanzas si hubiéramos estudiado economía.*

Conjugated verb (pp. 360, 380): a verb whose endings reflect person and number (as opposed to an infinitive)
*Muchas personas **quieren** prepararse para carreras en tecnología.*

Conjunction (pp. 162, 190, 234, 412, 432, 435): a word that acts as a connector between words, phrases, clauses, or sentences
*También queremos ir al Parque Nacional Volcán Póas, **pero** no pensamos que haya tiempo.*

Demonstrative (pp. 336, 382): an adjective or a pronoun that points out someone or something
*Francisco, ¿escribiste **este** poema?–¿**Éste?** Sí, lo escribí.*

Direct Object (pp. 46, 264, 306, 358, 380): a noun or pronoun that receives the action of the main verb in a sentence
*La mesera puso **la mesa** con cubiertos. **La** puso con cubiertos.*

Future Tense (pp. 65, 68, 119): a tense that indicates that the action in a sentence will happen in the future
*Francisco **escribirá** un artículo sobre la conservación de la naturaleza.*

Future Perfect Tense (p. 310): a verb form that expresses what will have happened by a certain time
*A las dos, ya **habremos salido.***

Gender: a term that categorizes a noun or pronoun as masculine or feminine
*Laura no quiere **el azúcar** en **la sopa.***

Imperfect Tense (pp. 42, 43, 268, 286, 410): a verb form that notes incomplete or repeated actions or states with reference to the past
***Juntábamos** fondos para el centro de la comunidad cuando supimos cuántos servicios **se ofrecían** allí.*

Indicative Mood (pp. 238, 412, 414, 415, 432): the mood of the verb used for statements that report what is/was and for questions (as opposed to the subjunctive mood)
***Voy** a celebrar el día de la Independencia en Puerto Rico. ¿Adónde **vas** tú?*

Indirect Object (pp. 46, 62, 360, 380): a noun or pronoun that tells to or for whom/what the action is done
*Catalina recomendó el libro a sus **amigos.** Catalina **les** recomendó el libro.*

Infinitive: the basic form of a verb that ends in **-ar, -er, -ir.**
*Susana quiere **ser** una estrella.*

Interrogative (pp. 262, 338): a word that asks a question
*¿**Qué** te gusta hacer durante las vacaciones?*

Main Clause (pp. 46, 141, 210, 214, 232, 234, 288, 364, 415): in a sentence with two clauses, the main clause is the one that can function alone as a complete sentence
*Con tal de que haya buen tiempo, **vamos a hacer alpinismo este fin de semana.***

Negative Command (p. 114): a verb form used to tell someone not to do something
*Alejandro, **no vayas** al campamento hasta mañana.*

Nominalization (pp. 382, 385): to use another part of speech (such as an article, an adjective or a pronoun) instead of a noun
*Esta computadora es increíble, pero **la tuya** es mejor. **La suya** es **la más impresionante**.*

Noun: a word that names a person, animal, place, or thing
***Frida Kahlo**, una **pintora** muy famosa, pintó **pinturas** sobre su **vida** en **México**.*

Number: a term that categorizes a noun or pronoun as singular or plural
*Donde hay **una piñata**, hay **una fiesta**. Hay **muchas fiestas** en **México**.*

Past Participle (pp. 46, 141, 286, 289, 310): a verb form that indicates past action but does not specify person or number; used in the present and past perfect tenses; also is used as an adjective
*La impresora está **rota**. La hemos **comprado** hace sólo dos semanas. Hemos **vendido** la otra.*

Past Perfect Tense (p. 46): a verb form that focuses on actions that were completed before others in the past, consisting of an auxiliary verb and the past participle
*Ya **habíamos regado** las plantas cuando empezó a llover.*

Past Progressive Tense (p. 268): a verb form that describes an action that was in progress in the past at a certain point in time
***Estábamos mirando** un espectáculo de flamenco cuando Mario tuvo que irse.*

Possessive (pp. 308, 385): an adjective or a pronoun that tells to whom the noun it describes belongs
*Don Miguel dice que son **sus** marionetas. Son las marionetas*

*suyas. **Las suyas** son muy comunes en México.*

Preposition (pp. 63, 341, 433, 457): a word that shows the relationship between its object and another word
***Por** su segundo álbum Cristian Castro ganó un premio.*

Present Participle (p. 46): the **-ando/-endo/-iendo** form of a verb
*Estamos **regando** las plantas.*

Present Perfect Tense (p. 46): a verb form that indicates that the action in a sentence has been done in the past
*¡Me **ha gustado** tanto Ecuador!*

Present Progressive Tense (pp. 264, 266): a verb form that indicates that an action is in progress at this very moment
*Alicia **está preparándose** para su entrevista.*

Present Tense (pp. 4, 8, 264): a verb form that indicates that the action is happening now, does happen, or will happen in the near future.
*Antonio Banderas **participa** en películas en inglés y español.*

Preterite Tense (pp. 12, 16, 20, 24, 43, 268, 286, 410): a verb form that indicates that the action in a sentence happened at a particular time in the past
*¿Cuándo **se inventó** la guitarra eléctrica?*

Pronoun (pp. 84, 264, 306, 308, 336, 358, 360, 362, 364, 380): a word that takes the place of a noun
*Catalina siempre compra el periódico. **Ella** siempre **lo** compra.*

Reciprocal Verb (p. 86): verb that expresses actions that people do for or to each other
*Marta y Fernanda **se escriben** todos los días y **se hablan** por teléfono una vez a la semana.*

Reflexive Verb (pp. 84, 86, 89): a verb for which the subject receives the action
*Las letras D.F. **se refieren** a la Ciudad de México.*

Relative Clause (p. 341): a subordinate clause that is introduced by a relative pronoun
*Quiero ir al museo **que está cerca del centro**.*

Relative Pronoun (pp. 341, 362, 364): a pronoun that refers to something that has been mentioned previously
*Esa celebración patriótica, **la cual** te describí antes, es famosa por todo el mundo.*

Si Clause (p. 214): a clause that expresses a hypothetical or contrary-to-fact situation
Si tenemos tiempo, vamos a ver una película de Carlos Saura.

Stem (p. 20): the part of the infinitive that remains after the **-ar, -er,** or **-ir** ending is deleted
*Para formar el futuro del verbo **hablar**, hay que añadir las terminaciones a la forma **habl-**.*

Subject: the noun or noun phrase in a sentence that tells who or what does the action
Isabel saltaba la cuerda cuando era niña.

Subjunctive Mood (pp. 136, 138, 139, 141, 158, 160, 162, 188, 190, 192, 210, 212, 214, 232, 234, 238, 286, 412, 414, 415, 432): a verb form in a dependent clause that indicates that a sentence expresses doubt, emotion, opinion or an unlikely happening (as opposed to the indicative mood)
*Francisco no cree que **vaya** a nevar.*

Subordinate Clause (pp. 46, 141, 210, 232, 415, 432, 435): in a sentence with two clauses, this clause is incomplete and cannot function as a sentence on its own
Además de ser atrevida, Manuela también es muy independiente.

Superlative (p. 454): a phrase that describes which item has the most or least of a quality
*¡Isabel y Andrea van a ser **las más elegantes** de todas las chicas en la fiesta!*

Tense: the conjugated form of a verb whose endings follow a pattern
*Soy muy creativo. **Creo** que **puedo** inventar anuncios para la tele.*

Verb: a word that expresses action or a state of being
*Don Miguel **viene** al parque con sus marionetas.*
*Está contento cuando los niños **se sonríen**.*

Nouns, Articles, and Pronouns

Nouns

Nouns identify people, animals, places, or things. Spanish nouns are either **masculine** or **feminine**. They are also either **singular** (identifying one thing) or **plural** (identifying more than one thing). **Masculine nouns** usually end in **-o** and **feminine nouns** usually end in **-a**.

To make a noun **plural,** add **-s** to a word ending in a vowel and **-es** to a word ending in a consonant. When a noun ends in **z,** change the **z** to **ces** to form the plural: *actriz, actrices.* Generally, the same syllable carries the force of pronunciation in plural and in singular forms: *lápiz, lápices; pantalón, pantalones; joven, jóvenes.*

Singular Nouns	
Masculine	**Feminine**
amigo	amiga
chico	chica
hombre	mujer
suéter	blusa
zapato	falda

Plural Nouns	
Masculine	**Feminine**
amigos	amigas
chicos	chicas
hombres	mujeres
suéteres	blusas
zapatos	faldas

Articles

Articles identify the class of a noun: masculine or feminine, singular or plural. **Definite articles** are the equivalent of the English word *the*. **Indefinite articles** are the equivalent of *a, an,* or *some*.

Definite Articles		
	Masculine	**Feminine**
Singular	**el** amigo	**la** amiga
Plural	**los** amigos	**las** amigas

Indefinite Articles		
	Masculine	**Feminine**
Singular	**un** amigo	**una** amiga
Plural	**unos** amigos	**unas** amigas

Pronouns

A **pronoun** can take the place of a noun. The choice of pronoun is determined by how it is used in the sentence.

Subject Pronouns	
yo	nosotros(as)
tú	vosotros(as)
usted	ustedes
él, ella	ellos(as)

Pronouns Used After Prepositions	
de **mí**	de **nosotros(as)**
de **ti**	de **vosotros(as)**
de **usted**	de **ustedes**
de **él**, de **ella**	de **ellos(as)**
After **con, mí** and **ti** become **conmigo, contigo.**	

Direct Object Pronouns	
me	nos
te	os
lo, la	los, las

Indirect Object Pronouns	
me	nos
te	os
le	les

Reflexive Pronouns	
me	nos
te	os
se	se

Demonstrative Pronouns	
éste(a), esto	éstos(as)
ése(a), eso	ésos(as)
aquél(la), aquello	aquéllos(as)

Adjectives

Adjectives describe nouns. In Spanish, adjectives must match the **number** and **gender** of the nouns they describe. When an adjective describes a group with both genders, the masculine form is used. To make an adjective plural, apply the same rules that are used for making a noun plural. Most adjectives are placed after the noun.

Adjectives		
	Masculine	**Feminine**
Singular	el chico **guapo**	la chica **guapa**
	el chico **paciente**	la chica **paciente**
	el chico **fenomenal**	la chica **fenomenal**
	el chico **trabajador**	la chica **trabajadora**
Plural	los chicos guapo**s**	las chicas guapa**s**
	los chicos paciente**s**	las chicas paciente**s**
	los chicos fenomenal**es**	las chicas fenomenal**es**
	los chicos trabajador**es**	las chicas trabajadora**s**

Adjectives cont.

Sometimes adjectives are placed before the noun and **shortened. Grande** is shortened before any singular noun. Several others are shortened before a masculine singular noun.

Shortened Forms			
alguno	**algún** chico	primero	**primer** chico
bueno	**buen** chico	tercero	**tercer** chico
malo	**mal** chico	grande	**gran** chico(a)
ninguno	**ningún** chico		

Possessive adjectives identify to whom something belongs. They agree in gender and number with the possessed item, not with the person who possesses it. These forms always come before nouns.

Possessive Adjectives				
	Masculine		**Feminine**	
Singular	**mi** amigo	**nuestro** amigo	**mi** amiga	**nuestra** amiga
	tu amigo	**vuestro** amigo	**tu** amiga	**vuestra** amiga
	su amigo	**su** amigo	**su** amiga	**su** amiga
Plural	**mis** amigos	**nuestros** amigos	**mis** amigas	**nuestras** amigas
	tus amigos	**vuestros** amigos	**tus** amigas	**vuestras** amigas
	sus amigos	**sus** amigos	**sus** amigas	**sus** amigas

Demonstrative adjectives point out which noun is being referred to. Their English equivalents are *this, that, these,* and *those.*

Demonstrative Adjectives		
	Masculine	**Feminine**
Singular	**este** amigo	**esta** amiga
	ese amigo	**esa** amiga
	aquel amigo	**aquella** amiga
Plural	**estos** amigos	**estas** amigas
	esos amigos	**esas** amigas
	aquellos amigos	**aquellas** amigas

Interrogatives

Interrogatives		
¿Adónde?	¿Cuándo?	¿Por qué?
¿Cómo?	¿Cuánto(a)? ¿Cuántos(as)?	¿Qué?
¿Cuál(es)?	¿Dónde?	¿Quién(es)?

Comparatives and Superlatives

Comparatives

Comparatives are used when comparing two different things.

Comparatives		
más (+) **más** interesante **que…** Me gusta correr **más que** nadar.	menos (−) **menos** interesante **que…** Me gusta nadar **menos que** correr.	tan(to) (=) **tan** interesante **como…** Me gusta leer **tanto como** escribir.

There are a few irregular comparatives:
• When talking about people, use **mayor** and **menor**.

Age	Quality
mayor	mejor
menor	peor

• **Mejor** and **peor** are the comparative forms of **bueno(a)** and **malo(a).**

• When talking about numbers, use **de** instead of **que.**

> **más de** cien…
> **menos de** cien…

Superlatives

Superlatives are used to distinguish one item from a group. They describe which item has the most or least of a quality.

The ending **-ísimo(a)** can be added to an adjective to form a superlative.

Irregular comparatives are also irregular as superlatives.

Use "de" after a superlative:
El más alto de la clase

Superlatives		Masculine	Feminine
Singular		**el** chico **más** alto **el** chico **menos** alto	**la** chica **más** alta **la** chica **menos** alta
Plural		**los** chicos **más** altos **los** chicos **menos** altos	**las** chicas **más** altas **las** chicas **menos** altas
Singular		mole buen**ísimo**	pasta buen**ísima**
Plural		frijoles buen**ísimos**	enchiladas buen**ísimas**

Prepositions and Adverbs of Location

Prepositions and Adverbs of Location					
abajo afuera al lado (de)	alrededor (de) atrás debajo (de)	delante (de) dentro (de) detrás (de)	encima (de) enfrente (de) frente (a)	fuera (de) hacia hasta	junto (a) sobre

Affirmative and Negative Words

Affirmative	Negative
a menudo	jamás
algo	nada
alguien	nadie
algún (alguna)	ningún (ninguna)
alguno(a)	ninguno(a)
muchas veces	rara vez
o… o…	ni… ni…
siempre	nunca
también	tampoco

Adverbs

Adverbs modify a verb, an adjective, or another adverb. Many adverbs in Spanish are made by changing an existing adjective.

Adjective	→	Adverb
reciente	→	reciente**mente**
frecuente	→	frecuente**mente**
fácil	→	fácil**mente**
normal	→	normal**mente**
especial	→	especial**mente**
feliz	→	feliz**mente**
cuidadoso(a)	→	cuidadosa**mente**
rápido(a)	→	rápida**mente**
lento(a)	→	lenta**mente**
tranquilo(a)	→	tranquila**mente**

Verbs

Simple Tenses

		Indicative					Subjunctive	
		Present	**Imperfect**	**Preterite**	**Future**	**Conditional**	**Present**	**Imperative**
Infinitive *Present Participle* *Past Participle*	hablar hablando hablado	hablo hablas habla hablamos habláis hablan	hablaba hablabas hablaba hablábamos hablabais hablaban	hablé hablaste habló hablamos hablasteis hablaron	hablaré hablarás hablará hablaremos hablaréis hablarán	hablaría hablarías hablaría hablaríamos hablaríais hablarían	hable hables hable hablemos habléis hablen	habla no hables hable hablemos hablen
Infinitive *Present Participle* *Past Participle*	comer comiendo comido	como comes come comemos coméis comen	comía comías comía comíamos comíais comían	comí comiste comió comimos comisteis comieron	comeré comerás comerá comeremos comeréis comerán	comería comerías comería comeríamos comeríais comerían	coma comas coma comamos comáis coman	come no comas coma coman
Infinitive *Present Participle* *Past Participle*	vivir viviendo vivido	vivo vives vive vivimos vivís viven	vivía vivías vivía vivíamos vivíais vivían	viví viviste vivió vivimos vivisteis vivieron	viviré vivirás vivirá viviremos viviréis vivirán	viviría vivirías viviría viviríamos viviríais vivirían	viva vivas viva vivamos viváis vivan	vive no vivas viva vivan

Perfect Tenses

Perfect Tenses		
Present Perfect	**Present Perfect Subjunctive**	**Future Perfect**
he has ha hemos habéis han } hablado comido vivido	haya hayas haya hayamos hayáis hayan } hablado comido vivido	habré habrás habrá habremos habréis habrán } hablado comido vivido
Past Perfect	**Past Perfect Subjunctive**	**Conditional Perfect**
había habías había habíamos habíais habían } hablado comido vivido	hubiera hubieras hubiera hubiéramos hubierais hubieran } hablado comido vivido	habría habrías habría habríamos habríais habrían } hablado comido vivido

Progressive Tenses

Progressive Tenses			
Present Progressive	**Present Participle**	**Past Progressive**	**Present Participle**
estoy estás está estamos estáis están	hablando comiendo viviendo	estaba estabas estaba estábamos estabais estaban	hablando comiendo viviendo

Stem-Changing Verbs

Infinitive in -ar	Present Indicative	Present Subjunctive
cerrar **e→ie**	cierro cierras cierra cerramos cerráis cierran	cierre cierres cierre cerremos cerréis cierren
probar **o→ue**	pruebo pruebas prueba probamos probáis prueban	pruebe pruebes pruebe probemos probéis prueben
jugar **u→ue**	juego juegas juega jugamos jugáis juegan	juegue juegues juegue juguemos juguéis jueguen

like **cerrar:** comenzar, despertar(se), empezar, merendar, nevar, pensar, recomendar, regar, sembrar, sentar(se)

like **probar:** acostar(se), almorzar, contar, costar, encontrar(se), mostrar, recordar, rogar, sonar, volar

GRAMÁTICA—RESUMEN

Stem-Changing Verbs cont.

Infinitive in -er	Present Indicative	Present Subjunctive
perder e→ie	pierdo pierdes pierde perdemos perdéis pierden	pierda pierdas pierda perdamos perdáis pierdan
volver o→ue	vuelvo vuelves vuelve volvemos volvéis vuelven	vuelva vuelvas vuelva volvamos volváis vuelvan

like **perder:** atender, entender, querer
like **volver** (past participle: vuelto)**:** devolver (devuelto), doler, encender, llover, mover, poder, resolver (resuelto)

Infinitive in -ir	Indicative		Subjunctive
	Present	**Preterite**	**Present**
pedir e→i pidiendo	pido pides pide pedimos pedís piden	pedí pediste pidió pedimos pedisteis pidieron	pida pidas pida pidamos pidáis pidan
dormir o→ue, u durmiendo	duermo duermes duerme dormimos dormís duermen	dormí dormiste durmió dormimos dormisteis durmieron	duerma duermas duerma durmamos durmáis duerman
sentir e→ie, i sintiendo	siento sientes siente sentimos sentís sienten	sentí sentiste sintió sentimos sentisteis sintieron	sienta sientas sienta sintamos sintáis sientan

like **pedir:** competir, despedir(se), repetir, seguir, servir, vestir(se)
like **dormir(se):** morir (past participle: **muerto**)
like **sentir:** divertir(se), mentir, preferir, requerir, sugerir

Spell-Changing Verbs

buscar

Preterite: bus**qué**, buscaste, buscó, buscamos, buscasteis, buscaron
Present Subjunctive: bus**que**, bus**ques**, bus**que**, bus**que**mos, bus**qué**is, bus**quen**

like **buscar:** marcar, pescar, sacar, secar(se), tocar

conducir

Present Indicative: condu**zco**, conduces, conduce, conducimos, conducís, conducen
Preterite: condu**je**, condu**jiste**, condu**jo**, condu**jimos**, condu**jisteis**, condu**jeron**
Present Subjunctive: condu**zca**, condu**zcas**, condu**zca**, condu**zcamos**, condu**zcáis**, condu**zcan**

like **conducir:** producir, reducir, traducir

conocer

Present Indicative: cono**zco**, conoces, conoce, conocemos, conocéis, conocen
Present Subjunctive: cono**zca**, cono**zcas**, cono**zca**, cono**zcamos**, cono**zcáis**, cono**zcan**

like **conocer:** crecer, nacer, ofrecer, pertenecer

conseguir

Present Indicative: consi**go**, consigues, consigue, conseguimos, conseguís, consiguen
Present Subjunctive: consi**ga**, consi**gas**, consi**ga**, consi**gamos**, consi**gáis**, consi**gan**

like **conseguir:** seguir

construir

Present Indicative: constru**yo**, constru**yes**, constru**ye**, construimos, construís, constru**yen**
Preterite: construí, construiste, constru**yó**, construimos, construisteis, constru**yeron**

creer

Preterite: creí, creíste, cre**yó**, creímos, creísteis, cre**yeron**
Present Participle: cre**yendo**
Past Participle: creído

like **creer:** leer

cruzar

Preterite: cru**cé**, cruzaste, cruzó, cruzamos, cruzasteis, cruzaron
Present Subjunctive: cru**ce**, cru**ces**, cru**ce**, cru**cemos**, cru**céis**, cru**cen**

like **cruzar:** almorzar (o→ue), comenzar (e→ie), empezar (e→ie)

escoger

Present Indicative: esco**jo**, escoges, escoge, escogemos, escogéis, escogen
Present Subjunctive: esco**ja**, esco**jas**, esco**ja**, esco**jamos**, esco**jáis**, esco**jan**

like **escoger:** proteger

esquiar

Present Indicative: esquío, esquías, esquía, esquiamos, esquiáis, esquían
Present Subjunctive: esquíe, esquíes, esquíe, esquiemos, esquiéis, esquíen

llegar

Preterite: lle**gué**, llegaste, llegó, llegamos, llegasteis, llegaron
Present Subjunctive: lle**gue**, lle**gues**, lle**gue**, lle**guemos**, lle**guéis**, lle**guen**

like **llegar:** apagar, jugar, pagar

Irregular Verbs

andar

Preterite: anduve, anduviste, anduvo, anduvimos, anduvisteis, anduvieron

caer

Present Indicative: caigo, caes, cae, caemos, caéis, caen
Preterite: caí, caíste, cayó, caímos, caísteis, cayeron
Present Subjunctive: caiga, caigas, caiga, caigamos, caigáis, caigan
Present Participle: cayendo
Past Participle: caído

dar

Present Indicative: doy, das, da, damos, dais, dan
Preterite: di, diste, dio, dimos, disteis, dieron
Present Subjunctive: dé, des, dé, demos, deis, den
Commands: da (tú), no des (neg. tú), dé (Ud.) den (Uds.)

decir

Present Indicative: digo, dices, dice, decimos, decís, dicen
Preterite: dije, dijiste, dijo, dijimos, dijisteis, dijeron
Future: diré, dirás, dirá, diremos, diréis, dirán
Conditional: diría, dirías, diría, diríamos, diríais, dirían
Present Subjunctive: diga, digas, diga, digamos, digáis, digan
Commands: di (tú), no digas (neg. tú), diga (Ud.), digan (Uds.)
Present Participle: diciendo
Past Participle: dicho

estar

Present Indicative: estoy, estás, está, estamos, estáis, están
Preterite: estuve, estuviste, estuvo, estuvimos, estuvisteis, estuvieron
Present Subjunctive: esté, estés, esté, estemos, estéis, estén

haber

Present Indicative: he, has, ha, hemos, habéis, han
Preterite: hube, hubiste, hubo, hubimos, hubisteis, hubieron
Future: habré, habrás, habrá, habremos, habréis, habrán
Conditional: habría, habrías, habría, habríamos, habríais, habrían
Present Subjunctive: haya, hayas, haya, hayamos, hayáis, hayan

hacer

Present Indicative: hago, haces, hace, hacemos, hacéis, hacen
Preterite: hice, hiciste, hizo, hicimos, hicisteis, hicieron
Future: haré, harás, hará, haremos, haréis, harán
Conditional: haría, harías, haría, haríamos, haríais, harían
Present Subjunctive: haga, hagas, haga, hagamos, hagáis, hagan
Commands: haz (tú), no hagas (neg. tú), haga (Ud.), hagan (Uds.)
Past Participle: hecho

ir

Present Indicative: voy, vas, va, vamos, vais, van
Imperfect: iba, ibas, iba, íbamos, ibais, iban
Preterite: fui, fuiste, fue, fuimos, fuisteis, fueron
Present Subjunctive: vaya, vayas, vaya, vayamos, vayáis, vayan
Commands: ve (tú), no vayas (neg. tú), vaya (Ud.), vayan (Uds.)
Present Participle: yendo

Irregular Verbs cont.

oír

Present Indicative: oigo, oyes, oye, oímos, oís, oyen
Preterite: oí, oíste, oyó, oímos, oísteis, oyeron
Present Subjunctive: oiga, oigas, oiga, oigamos, oigáis, oigan
Present Participle: oyendo
Past Participle: oído

poder

Present Indicative: puedo, puedes, puede, podemos, podéis, pueden
Preterite: pude, pudiste, pudo, pudimos, pudisteis, pudieron
Future: podré, podrás, podrá, podremos, podréis, podrán
Conditional: podría, podrías, podría, podríamos, podríais, podrían
Present Subjunctive: pueda, puedas, pueda, podamos, podáis, puedan
Present Participle: pudiendo

poner

Present Indicative: pongo, pones, pone, ponemos, ponéis, ponen
Preterite: puse, pusiste, puso, pusimos, pusisteis, pusieron
Future: pondré, pondrás, pondrá, pondremos, pondréis, pondrán
Conditional: pondría, pondrías, pondría, pondríamos, pondríais, pondrían
Present Subjunctive: ponga, pongas, ponga, pongamos, pongáis, pongan
Commands: pon (tú), no pongas (neg. tú), ponga (Ud.), pongan (Uds.)
Past Participle: puesto

like **poner:** descomponer(se), imponer, oponer(se)

querer

Present Indicative: quiero, quieres, quiere, queremos, queréis, quieren
Preterite: quise, quisiste, quiso, quisimos, quisisteis, quisieron
Future: querré, querrás, querrá, querremos, querréis, querrán
Conditional: querría, querrías, querría, querríamos, querríais, querrían
Present Subjunctive: quiera, quieras, quiera, queramos, queráis, quieran

saber

Present Indicative: sé, sabes, sabe, sabemos, sabéis, saben
Preterite: supe, supiste, supo, supimos, supisteis, supieron
Future: sabré, sabrás, sabrá, sabremos, sabréis, sabrán
Conditional: sabría, sabrías, sabría, sabríamos, sabríais, sabrían
Present Subjunctive: sepa, sepas, sepa, sepamos, sepáis, sepan
Commands: sabe (tú), no sepas (neg. tú), sepa (Ud.), sepan (Uds.)

salir

Present Indicative: salgo, sales, sale, salimos, salís, salen
Future: saldré, saldrás, saldrá, saldremos, saldréis, saldrán
Conditional: saldría, saldrías, saldría, saldríamos, saldríais, saldrían
Present Subjunctive: salga, salgas, salga, salgamos, salgáis, salgan
Commands: sal (tú), no salgas (neg. tú), salga (Ud.), salgan (Uds.)

ser

Present Indicative: soy, eres, es, somos, sois, son
Imperfect: era, eras, era, éramos, erais, eran
Preterite: fui, fuiste, fue, fuimos, fuisteis, fueron
Present Subjunctive: sea, seas, sea, seamos, seáis, sean
Commands: sé (tú), no seas (neg. tú), sea (Ud.), sean (Uds.)

GRAMÁTICA–RESUMEN

Irregular Verbs cont.

tener

Present Indicative: tengo, tienes, tiene, tenemos, tenéis, tienen
Preterite: tuve, tuviste, tuvo, tuvimos, tuvisteis, tuvieron
Future: tendré, tendrás, tendrá, tendremos, tendréis, tendrán
Conditional: tendría, tendrías, tendría, tendríamos, tendríais, tendrían
Present Subjunctive: tenga, tengas, tenga, tengamos, tengáis, tengan
Commands: ten (tú), no tengas (neg. tú), tenga (Ud.), tengan (Uds.)
like **tener:** mantener, obtener

traer

Present Indicative: traigo, traes, trae, traemos, traéis, traen
Preterite: traje, trajiste, trajo, trajimos, trajisteis, trajeron
Present Subjunctive: traiga, traigas, traiga, traigamos, traigáis, traigan
Present Participle: trayendo
Past Participle: traído

valer

Present Indicative: valgo, vales, vale, valemos, valéis, valen
Preterite: valí, valiste, valió, valimos, valisteis, valieron
Future: valdré, valdrás, valdrá, valdremos, valdréis, valdrán
Conditional: valdría, valdrías, valdría, valdríamos, valdríais, valdrían
Present Subjunctive: valga, valgas, valga, valgamos, valgáis, valgan
Commands: val (tú), no valgas (neg. tú), valga (Ud.), valgas (Uds.)

venir

Present Indicative: vengo, vienes, viene, venimos, venís, vienen
Preterite: vine, viniste, vino, vinimos, vinisteis, vinieron
Future: vendré, vendrás, vendrá, vendremos, vendréis, vendrán
Conditional: vendría, vendrías, vendría, vendríamos, vendríais, vendrían
Present Subjunctive: venga, vengas, venga, vengamos, vengáis, vengan
Commands: ven (tú), no vengas (neg. tú), venga (Ud.), vengan (Uds.)
Present Participle: viniendo

ver

Present Indicative: veo, ves, ve, vemos, veis, ven
Preterite: vi, viste, vio, vimos, visteis, vieron
Imperfect: veía, veías, veía, veíamos, veíais, veían
Past Participle: visto

GLOSARIO
español-inglés

This Spanish-English glossary contains all of the active vocabulary words that appear in the text as well as passive vocabulary from readings and culture sections. Most inactive cognates have been omitted. The active words are accompanied by the number of the unit and etapa in which they are presented. For example, **la autobiografía** can be found in **5.1** *(Unidad 5, Etapa 1)*. The roman numerals I and II indicate words that were taught in Levels 1 and 2.

a to, at I
  a la(s)… at … o'clock I
  a continuación next II
  a gusto comfortable, happy
  a la derecha (de)
    to the right (of) I
  a la izquierda (de)
    to the left (of) I
  a la venta for sale
  a lo largo de throughout
  a menos que unless **3.1**
  a menudo often **4.2**
  a pie on foot I
  ¿A qué hora es…?
    (At) What time is…? I
  a tiempo on time II
  A todos nos toca…
    It is up to all of us… II
  a veces sometimes **I, II, 4.2**
abajo down **I, II**
el abecedario alphabet
abierto(a) open **I, II**
el (la) abogado(a) lawyer **II, 4.2**
el (la) abonado(a) subscriber
abordar to board (a plane) II
el abrazo hug II
el abrelatas can opener **II, 2.3**
el abrigo coat I
abril April I
abrir to open I
abrir el paso to open the way **5.2**

la abuela grandmother I
el abuelo grandfather I
los abuelos grandparents I
aburrido(a) boring I
aburrir(se) to get bored II
acá here I
acabar de to have just I
acabársele (a uno) to run out of **6.2**
el (la) académico(a) academic **4.3**
acampar to camp **II, 1.2**
accesible available, accessible **6.2**
el aceite oil **I, II**
las aceitunas olives I
la acera sidewalk II
acertado(a) right
aconsejar to advise II
acordarse (ue) de to remember **6.3**
acostar (ue) to go to bed, to lie
  down II
el (la) actor/actriz actor/actress II
la actuación performance II
acudir a to attend **3.3**
acuerdo
  estar de acuerdo to agree **I, II**
el acumulador battery
adaptarse to adapt oneself **4.1**
Adiós. Good-bye. I
la administración de empresas
  business administration **4.1**
adónde (to) where I
los adornos decorations II
la aduana customs II
la aerolínea airline II
el aeropuerto airport I

el aerosol aerosol **2.2**
afeitarse to shave oneself **I, II**
afuera outside **6.2**
el (la) agente de ventas sales
  agent **4.3**
el (la) agente de viajes
  travel agent II
agosto August I
agotado
  Estoy agotado(a).
    I'm exhausted. **2.1**
agradecer to thank **3.1**
el (la) agricultor(a) farmer **II, 4.2**
la agricultura agriculture **4.3**
la agronomía agronomy **4.1**
el agua (fem.) water I
  el agua de coco coconut milk II
  el agua dulce fresh water **2.3**
  esquiar en el agua
    to water-ski **1.2**
el aguacero downpour **II, 2.3**
ahora now I
  ¡Ahora mismo! Right now! I
el aire
  al aire libre outdoors I
  la contaminación del aire
    air pollution **I, 2.2**
el aire acondicionado air
  conditioning II
el ajedrez
  jugar al ajedrez to play chess II
al to the I
  al aire libre outdoors I
  al contrario on the contrary II

al lado (de) beside, next to I
al óleo oil painting **5.1**
el ala wing
el (la) alcalde mayor **3.3**
alegrar(se) de que
    to be happy that II
alegre happy I
alemán(ana) German II
la alfabetización literacy
algo something I
el algodón cotton **1.2**
alguien someone I
    conocer a alguien to know, to
        be familiar with someone I
alguno(a) some I
la alimentación nourishment II
el alimento food II
allá there I
allí there I
el alma (fem.) soul
el almirante admiral **3.3**
la almohada pillow **II, 2.3**
almorzar (ue) to eat lunch I, II
el almuerzo lunch I
alquilar to rent I
    alquilar un video
        to rent a video I
alrededor around II
alto(a) tall I
el altoparlante speaker **6.2**
la altura altitude, height **II, 2.2**
    la altura del terreno
        altitude of terrain
el aluminio aluminum II
amable nice II
    Muy amable.
        That's kind of you. **3.2**
el amanecer dawn **2.3**
amanecer to start the day **2.3**
amarillo(a) yellow I
la ambulancia ambulance II
amenazador(a) threatening **5.3**
el (la) amigo(a) friend I
la amistad acquaintance,
    friendship II
el amor love II
ampliable expandable **6.3**
anaranjado(a) orange I
ancho(a) wide I, II
los ancianos the elderly **2.1**
andar to walk II
    andar en bicicleta
        to ride a bike I

andar en patineta
    to skateboard I
el (la) anfitrión(a) host(ess) **3.2**
el anillo ring I
animado(a) animated II
el animal animal I
animarse to get encouraged,
    interested **1.3**
el aniversario anniversary II
anoche last night I, II
anochecer to get dark **2.3**
el anochecer nightfall **2.3**
anteayer day before yesterday I, II
la antena parabólica
    satellite dish **6.1**
los anteojos glasses **1.1**
los antepasados ancestors **I, 3.3**
antes (de) before I
antiguo(a) old, ancient I, II
el anuncio commercial II
el año year I
    el año escolar the school year II
    el Año Nuevo New Year **3.2**
    el año pasado last year I
    ¿Cuántos años tiene…?
        How old is…? I
    ¡Próspero Año Nuevo!
        Happy New Year! **3.2**
    Tiene… años.
        He/She is… years old. I
    apagar la luz
        to turn off the light I
el apartamento apartment I
aparte separate
    Es aparte. Separate checks. I
el apellido last name, surname I
apenas scarcely II
apoyarse to support each other **1.3**
el apoyo support **3.1**
apreciar to appreciate **3.1**
aprender to learn I
apretado(a) tight II
aprovechar to take advantage of
apto(a) para toda la familia
    G-rated (movie) **6.1**
aquel(la) that (over there) **I, 5.1**
aquél(la) that one (over there) **I, 5.1**
aquello that (over there) **I, 5.1**
aquí here I
el árbol tree **I, 2.1**
    trepar a un árbol
        to climb a tree II
la arena sand II

el arete earring I
argentino(a) Argentine II
armar to assemble **1.3**
el armario closet I, II
el arpa (fem.) harp **5.1**
el (la) arquitecto(a)
    architect **I, II, 4.2**
arquitectónico(a) architectural
la arquitectura architecture I
arreglar(se) to get ready; to get
    dressed up II
el arreglo arrangement
arriba up I, II
el arroz rice I
    el arroz con dulce dessert of
        rice, cinnamon, and coconut
        milk **3.2**
    el arroz con gandules
        rice and pigeon peas **3.2**
    el arroz con leche dessert of
        sweet rice and milk **3.2**
el arte art I
la artesanía handicraft I
el (la) artesano(a) artisan **I, II, 4.2**
el artículo article II
los artículos de cuero
    leather goods I
el (la) artista artist II
el ascensor elevator II
así fue que and so it was that II
el asiento seat II
el (la) asistente assistant **II, 402**
    el asistente electrónico
        electronic assistant **6.2**
asistir (a) to attend II
la aspiradora vacuum cleaner I
    pasar la aspiradora
        to vacuum I, II
la aspirina aspirin II
el asta (fem.) flagpole
asustar to frighten
    asustar(se) (de)
        to be scared of II
atardecer to get dark **2.3**
el atardecer late afternoon **2.3**
el atletismo athletics II
atrás in back, behind **6.2**
atrevido(a) daring **1.1**
el atún tuna II
los audífonos headphones **6.2**
el auditorio auditorium I
aumentar to increase **4.2**
aunque even though II

la autobiografía autobiography **5.1**
el autobús bus **I**
el (la) autor(a) author **II**
el autorretrato self-portrait **5.1**
el (la) auxiliar de vuelo
    flight attendant **II**
avanzado(a) advanced **5.2**
avanzar to advance **3.1**
el ave (fem.) bird
la avenida avenue **I**
las aventuras adventures **II**
el avión airplane **I**
    pilotar una avioneta to fly a
      single-engine plane **1.2**
avisar to announce
ayer yesterday **I, II**
ayudar (a) to help **I**
    ¿Cómo puedo ayudarte?
      How can I help you? **2.1**
    ¿Me ayuda a pedir?
      Could you help me order? **I**
ayudarse to help (each other) **1.3**
el azúcar sugar **I**
azul blue **I**

el (la) bailaor(a) flamenco dancer
    5.1
bailar to dance **I**
el bailarín/la bailarina
    dancer **II, 4.2**
el baile folklórico folk dance **5.1**
bajar (por) to go down,
    to descend **II**
    bajar un río en canoa to go
      down a river by canoe **II**
bajo(a) short (height) **I**
balanceado(a) balanced **II**
el balde bucket **II**
la baldosa paving stone, tile
la ballena jorobada
    humpback whale **2.3**
el balón soccer ball **1.1**
el baloncesto basketball **I**
la bamba Mexican dance from
    Veracruz **5.2**
el banco bank **I**
la banda band **3.3**
la bandera flag **3.3**
el (la) banquero(a) banker **4.3**

bañarse to take a bath **I, II**
la bañera bathtub **II**
el baño bathroom **I, II**
barato(a) cheap, inexpensive **I**
la barba beard **1.1**
el barco ship **I**
barrer to sweep **I**
    barrer el piso
      to sweep the floor **II**
la base de datos database **6.3**
bastante enough **II**
la basura trash, garbage **I, 2.1**
    sacar la basura
      to take out the trash **I**
el basurero trash can,
    wastebasket **II, 1.3**
el bate bat **I**
la batería battery **6.2**
el batido milk shake **II**
el bebé baby **II**
beber to drink **I**
    ¿Quieres beber…?
      Do you want to drink…? **I**
    Quiero beber…
      I want to drink… **I**
la bebida beverage, drink **I**
la beca scholarship
el beeper beeper **6.2**
el béisbol baseball **I**
las bellas artes fine arts **II**
la belleza beauty **II**
los beneficios benefits **II, 4.2**
el beso kiss **II**
la biblioteca library **I**
el (la) bibliotecario(a) librarian **4.3**
la bicicleta bike
    andar en bicicleta
      to ride a bike **I**
bien well **I**
    (No muy) Bien, ¿y tú/usted?
      (Not very) Well, and you? **I**
el bienestar well-being **II**
bienvenido(a) welcome **I**
el bigote mustache **1.1**
la billetera wallet **1.2**
la biografía biography **5.1**
el birrete cap **3.1**
el (la) bisabuelo(a)
    great grandfather/
    great grandmother **II**
el bistec steak **I**
blanco(a) white **I**
la blusa blouse **II**

la boa constrictora
    boa constrictor **2.3**
la boca mouth **I**
la boda wedding **II**
la bola ball **I**
el boleto ticket **II**
boliviano(a) Bolivian **II**
la bolsa bag **I**
la bolsa de valores
    stock exchange **4.3**
el bolso shoulder bag **1.2**
la bomba
    Afro-Caribbean dance **3.3**
el bombero
    firefighter, fireman **I, II, 4.2**
la bombilla lightbulb **1.3**
bonito(a) pretty **I**
el bordado embroidery **5.2**
el borrador eraser **I**
el bosque forest **I, 2.2**
las botas boots **I**
el bote boat **II**
la botella bottle **I, II, 2.2**
el brazo arm **I, II**
brindar to make a toast **3.1**
el brindis toast **3.1**
el broche fastener, clip
el bronceador suntan lotion **I**
bucear to scuba-dive **2.3**
el budín pudding **3.2**
bueno(a) good **I**
    ¡Buen provecho!
      Enjoy! (your meal) **3.2**
    Buenas noches.
      Good evening. **I, II**
    Buenas tardes.
      Good afternoon. **I, II**
    Buenos días.
      Good morning. **I, II**
    Es bueno que…
      It's good that… **II**
    Hace buen tiempo.
      It is nice outside. **I**
    lo bueno the good thing **1.1**
la bufanda scarf **I**
el búho owl **2.3**
buscar to look for, to search **I**
la búsqueda search
    el servicio de búsqueda
      search engine **6.3**
el buzón mailbox **II**
    el buzón electrónico
      electronic mailbox **6.3**

el caballo horse I
el cabello hair **1.1**
la cabeza head I, II
   lavarse la cabeza
     to wash one's hair I
cada each, every I
la cadena chain **1.2**
caer(se) (me caigo) to fall down II
   caer bien/mal
     to like/dislike II, **1.2**
   caérsele (a uno) to drop **6.2**
el café café, coffee I
la cafetería cafeteria, coffee shop I
la caja registradora cash register II
el (la) cajero(a) cashier II
el cajero automático
   ATM II
los calamares squid I
el calcetín sock I
la calculadora calculator I
la calefacción heat, heating II
la calidad quality I
caliente hot, warm I
¡Cállate! Be quiet! I
la calle street I
el calor
   Hace calor. It is hot. I
   tener calor to be hot I
la caloría calorie II
calvo(a) bald **1.1**
la cama bed I, II
   hacer la cama to make the bed I
la cámara camera I, II
cambiar to change, to exchange I
   cambiar de canal
     to change channels (TV) **6.1**
el cambio change, money
   exchange I
caminar con el perro
   to walk the dog I
el camino path, road I, **3.1**
la camisa shirt I
la camiseta T-shirt I
el campamento camp II
la campana bell **3.2**
la campanada tolling of the bell **3.2**
la campaña campaign **2.1**
el campo
   field, countryside, country I

el campo de estudio
   field of study **4.1**
canadiense Canadian II
el canal channel II
la cancha court I
el cangrejo crab
cansado(a) tired I
cansarse to get tired II
el (la) cantante singer II
el (la) cantaor(a) flamenco singer
   5.1
cantar to sing I
   cantar en el coro
     to sing in the chorus II
el cante
   el cante jondo
     tragic flamenco song **5.1**
la capa de ozono ozone layer II, **2.2**
capacitado(a) qualified II, **4.1**
la capilla chapel
la cara face I, II
el caracol shell II
la careta mask
la carne meat I
   la carne de res beef I, II
la carnicería butcher's shop I
caro(a) expensive I
   ¡Es muy caro(a)!
     It's very expensive! I
la carrera career II, **4.2**
la carretera road, highway I, **4.1**
el carro car I
la carta letter I
   mandar una carta
     to send a letter I
la cartera wallet I
el (la) cartero(a)
   mail carrier I, II, **4.2**
el cartón cardboard, cardboard
   box, carton II, **2.2**
la casa house I
casarse to get married II
el casco helmet I
el casete cassette I
casi almost II
castaño(a) brown (hair) I
las castañuelas castanets **5.1**
la catarata waterfall
catorce fourteen I
la causa cause II
la cebolla onion I, II
celebrar to celebrate I
la cena supper, dinner I

cenar to eat dinner I, II
Cenicienta Cinderella
el centígrado centigrade II, **2.3**
el centro center, downtown I
   el centro comercial
     shopping center I
   el centro de la comunidad
     community center **2.1**
   el centro de rehabilitación
     rehabilitation center **2.1**
cepillarse el pelo
   to brush one's hair II
el cepillo hairbrush I, II
el cepillo (de dientes)
   brush (toothbrush) I, II
la cerámica ceramics I
cerca (de) near to I
la cerca fence I
el cerdo pig I
el cereal cereal I, II
los cereales grains **4.3**
la ceremonia de graduación
   graduation ceremony **3.1**
la cereza cherry II
cero zero I
cerrado(a) closed I, II
cerrar (ie) to close I
el chaleco vest II
el champú shampoo I, II
Chao. Goodbye. II
la chaqueta jacket I
los cheques checks II
   los cheques de viajero
     travelers' checks II
chévere awesome I
   ¡Qué chévere! How awesome! I
los chicharrones pork rinds I
   comer chicharrones
     to eat pork rinds I
el (la) chico(a) boy/girl I
chileno(a) Chilean II
chino(a) Chinese II
chismoso(a) gossipy **4.2**
el chorizo sausage I
cibernético(a) relating to
   cyberspace **5.3**
el ciclo level of high school
   curriculum
ciego(a) blind **5.3**
el cielo sky **2.2**
cien one hundred I
la ciencia ficción science fiction II
las ciencias science I

cierto(a) certain

    Es cierto. It's certain.

    No es cierto que…

        It is not certain that… I

la cifra number, numeral **5.2**

cinco five I

cincuenta fifty I

el cine movie theater I

    ir al cine to go to the movies I

el (la) cineasta filmmaker **5.3**

el (la) cinematógrafo(a)

    cinematographer **5.3**

el cinturón belt I

la cita appointment I

la ciudad city I

la ciudadanía citizenship II

el (la) ciudadano(a) citizen **2.1**

la civilización civilization **5.2**

claro

    ¡Claro que sí! Of course! I

la clase class, classroom I

el (la) cliente customer II

el clima climate **II, 2.2**

el clímax climax **5.3**

el cobre copper **4.3**

el coche car **4.2**

la cocina kitchen I, II

cocinar to cook I

el codo elbow II

el cofre chest

el cohete firecracker **3.2**

la cola de caballo ponytail **1.1**

colaborar con

    to collaborate with **2.1**

coleccionar to collect **1.2**

el colegio school I

la colina hill **II, 2.2**

el collar necklace I

Colombia Colombia I

colombiano(a) Colombian II

el color color I

    ¿De qué color…?

        What color…? I

    el color brillante bright color **1.2**

    el color claro pastel **1.2**

    el color oscuro dark color **1.2**

    de un solo color solid color **1.2**

el columpio de mimbre

    wicker rocking chair

el combustible fuel **II, 2.2**

el (la) comediante

    comedian/comedienne II

el comedor dining room I, II

el comedor de beneficencia

    soup kitchen **2.1**

comenzar (ie) to begin II

comer to eat I, II

    comer chicharrones

        to eat pork rinds I

    darle(s) de comer to feed I

    ¿Quieres comer…?

        Do you want to eat…? I

    Quiero comer…

        I want to eat… I

el comercio business **4.1**

cómico(a) funny, comical I

la comida food, meal I

cómo how I

    ¿Cómo es?

        What is he/she like? I

    ¿Cómo está usted?

        How are you? (formal) I

    ¿Cómo estás?

        How are you? (familiar) I

    ¿Cómo me veo?

        How do I look? II

    ¡Cómo no! Of course! I

    ¿Cómo se llama?

        What is his/her name? I

    ¿Cómo se va a…?

        How do you get to…? II

    ¿Cómo te llamas?

        What is your name? I

    ¿Cómo te queda?

        How does it look on you? II

    Perdona(e), ¿cómo llego a…?

        Pardon, how do I get to…? I

cómodo(a) comfortable **II, 1.2**

el (la) compañero(a) companion II

la compañía company I

comparar to compare **4.3**

compartir to share **I, 1.1**

el compás rhythm, beat **5.1**

la competencia competition **3.3**

competir (i) to compete II

complicado(a) complicated **II, 2.2**

comprar to buy I

comprender to understand I

comprensivo(a) understanding **1.1**

la computación

    computer science I, II

la computadora computer I

    la computadora portátil

        laptop computer **6.2**

común common II

    tener en común

        to have in common **1.1**

la comunidad community

con with I

    con rayas striped I

    con tal de que

        provided that, as long as **3.1**

el concierto concert I

el concurso contest **I, II, 3.2**

conducir to drive II

el (la) conductor(a) driver II

conectar to connect **1.3**

    conectarse de to connect to **6.3**

la confiabilidad reliability,

    dependability **6.2**

la configuración configuration **6.3**

el congelador freezer I

el conjunto musical group **3.3**

conmemorar to commemorate **3.3**

conmigo with me I

conmovedor(a) moving

conocer to know, to be familiar

    with I, II

    conocer a alguien to know, to

        be familiar with, someone I

    conocerse bien (mal) to know

        each other (not very) well **1.3**

el conocimiento knowledge **4.2**

el conquistador

    conqueror, ladykiller **5.2**

conseguir (i) to obtain II

el consejo advice II

conservador(a) conservative **3.3**

conservar to conserve **II, 2.1**

considerado(a) considerate **1.1**

la constitución constitution **3.3**

construir to construct II

la consulta consultation II

el consultorio office (doctor's) II

consumir to consume **2.1**

la contabilidad accounting **4.1**

el (la) contador(a) accountant I, II,

    4.2

la contaminación pollution II

    la contaminación del aire

        air pollution **I, 2.2**

el contaminante pollutant **2.2**

contaminar to pollute II

contar (ue) to count, to tell or

    retell I

    contar chistes to tell jokes II

    contarse chismes

        to tell each other gossip **1.3**

contarse secretos
to tell each other secrets **1.3**
contemporáneo(a)
contemporary **5.3**
contento(a) content, happy,
pleased **I**
la contestadora automática
answering machine **6.2**
contestar to answer **I**
contigo with you **I**
el contorno surrounding area
la contraseña password **6.3**
el contrato contract **II, 4.2**
el control remoto
remote control **6.1**
controlar to control **6.1**
convencer to convince **6.2**
la conversación
el grupo de conversación
chat group **6.3**
convivir
to live together, to get along **2.1**
el coquito eggnog **3.2**
el corazón heart **I**
el corral corral, pen **I**
el correo post office **I**
el correo electrónico e-mail **6.3**
correr to run **I**
correr riesgos to take risks **4.1**
el (la) corresponsal
correspondent **4.3**
el cortacésped lawnmower **1.3**
cortar el césped to cut the grass **II**
cortarse to cut one's self **II**
corto(a) short (length) **I**
la cosa thing **I**
costar (ue) to cost **I**
a mí me cuesta mucho
it's hard for me
¿Cuánto cuesta(n)…?
How much is (are)…? **I**
costarricense Costa Rican **II**
la costumbre custom **3.3**
crear to create **II, 2.1**
creativo(a) creative **5.3**
crecer to grow up **II**
la creencia belief **5.2**
creer to think, to believe **I, II**
Creo que sí/no.
I think so. I don't think so. **I**
¿Tú crees? Do you think so? **II**
la crema cream **I, II**
criarse to be raised

la crítica criticism **II**
el (la) crítico(a) critic **5.3**
el (la) cronista chronicler **5.2**
el cruce crossing **II**
cruzar to cross **I**
el cuaderno notebook **I**
la cuadra city block **I**
cuadrado(a) square **1.1**
el cuadro painting **5.1**
el cuadro histórico
historical painting **5.1**
cuál(es) which (ones), what **I**
¿Cuál es la fecha?
What is the date? **I**
¿Cuál es tu teléfono? What is
your phone number? **I, II**
cuando when, whenever **I, 2.3**
cuando era niño(a) when
I/he/she was young **II**
cuándo when **I**
cuánto how much **I**
¿A cuánto está(n)…?
How much is (are)…? **I**
¿Cuánto cuesta(n)…?
How much is (are)…? **I**
¿Cuánto es? How much is it? **I**
¿Cuánto le doy de propina?
How much do I tip? **I**
¿Cuánto tiempo hace que…?
How long is it since…? **I**
cuántos(as) how many **I**
¿Cuántos años tiene…?
How old is…? **I**
cuarenta forty **I**
el cuarto room **I**
limpiar el cuarto
to clean the room **I, II**
cuarto(a) quarter, fourth **I, II**
y cuarto quarter past **I**
cuatro four **I**
cuatrocientos four hundred **I**
cubano(a) Cuban **II**
los cubiertos utensils **II**
la cuchara spoon **I**
el cuchillo knife **I**
el cuello neck **II**
la cuenta bill, check **I, II**
la cuenta de ahorros
savings account **II**
La cuenta, por favor.
The check, please. **I**
el (la) cuentista
short-story writer **5.3**

el cuento short story **5.1**
la cuerda rope
saltar la cuerda to jump rope **II**
el cuero leather **I, 1.2**
los artículos de cuero
leather goods **I**
el cuerpo body **I, II**
cuidado
tener cuidado to be careful **I, II**
cuidadosamente carefully **I**
cuidadoso(a) careful **I**
cuidar to take care of **I, 2.1**
culminar to end, to culminate **5.3**
la cumbia cumbia (Latin music) **5.2**
el cumpleaños birthday **I**
el (la) cuñado(a)
brother-in-law/sister-in-law **II**
el currículum résumé, curriculum
vitae **II, 4.1**
cursar to be enrolled in, to take

la danza dance **5.2**
dañino(a) damaging **2.2**
dar (doy) to give **I**
dar palmadas to clap hands **5.1**
dar una vuelta to take a walk,
stroll, or ride **II**
dar(se) cuenta de to realize **II**
darle(s) de comer to feed **I**
los datos facts; information **II, 4.1**
de of, from **I**
de buen humor
in a good mood **I**
de cuadros plaid, checkered **I**
de la mañana in the morning **I**
de la noche at night **I**
de la tarde in the afternoon **I**
de mal humor in a bad mood **I**
de maravilla marvelous **II**
De nada. You're welcome. **I**
¿De veras? Really? **II**
de vez en cuando
once in a while **I**
debajo (de) below, underneath **I, II**
deber should, ought to **I**
decidir to decide **I**
décimo(a) tenth **I, II**
decir (digo) to say, to tell **I, II**

decisiones
   tomar decisiones
      to make decisions **4.1**
decorado(a) decorated **5.2**
dedicarse a to apply oneself to
   (something) **1.3**
los dedos fingers, toes **II**
dejar to leave (behind) **I**;
   to allow **3.1**
   dejar la propina to leave the tip **I**
   dejar un mensaje
      to leave a message **I**
   **Deje un mensaje después del
      tono.** Leave a message after
      the tone. **I**
   Le dejo… en…
      I'll give…to you for… **I**
   **Quiero dejar un mensaje
      para…** I want to leave a
      message for… **I**
dejar de to stop doing something
del from the **I**
delante de in front of **I, II**
delgado(a) thin **I**
delicioso(a) delicious **I**
demasiado(a) too much **I, II**
la democracia democracy **3.3**
democrático(a) democratic **3.3**
dentro (de) inside (of) **I**
   dentro del alcance
      within reach **5.3**
el (la) dependiente(a)
   salesperson **II**
el deporte sport
   practicar deportes
      to play sports **I**
el (la) deportista sportsman,
   sportswoman **II**; athlete **4.2**
deprimido(a) depressed **I**
la derecha right **I**
   a la derecha (de) to the right (of) **I**
derecho straight ahead **I**
el derecho law; right **3.3**
los derechos (humanos) (human)
   rights **2.1**
derivado(a) derivative,
   unoriginal **5.3**
el derrame de petróleo oil spill **2.2**
desafortunadamente
   unfortunately **II**
desagradable unpleasant **1.1**
desanimarse to get discouraged **1.3**
desarmar to take apart **1.3**

desarrollar to develop **2.2**
el desarrollo development **II, 2.1**
desayunar to have breakfast **I, II**
el desayuno breakfast **I**
descansar to rest **I**
descarado(a) insolent, shameless **1.1**
la descendencia descendants **5.2**
descifrar to decipher **5.2**
descomponérsele (a uno)
   to break down, to malfunction
   6.2
descompuesto
   estar descompuesto(a)
      to be broken **6.2**
desconectar to turn off **1.3**
   desconectarse de
      to disconnect from **6.3**
los desconocidos strangers
el descubrimiento discovery **3.3**
descubrir to discover **II, 2.2, 2.3**
el descuento discount **6.2**
desde from **I**
   desde allí from there **II**
desear to desire **II**
desempeñar un cargo
   to carry out a responsibility **4.1**
desenchufar to unplug **1.3**
el desfile parade, procession **I, 3.1**
el desierto desert **I**
deslumbrante dazzling **5.3**
el desodorante deodorant **II**
desorganizado(a) disorganized **1.3**
la despedida good-bye **3.2**
despedirse (i) to say good-bye **II**
el desperdicio waste **2.2**
el despertador alarm clock **I, II**
despertarse (ie) to wake up **I**
después (de) after, afterward **I**
destacarse to stand out **1.2**
la destrucción destruction **II, 2.2**
el desván attic **1.3**
la desventaja disadvantage **II, 4.2**
desyerbar to weed **1.3**
el detalle detail **II**
detestar to hate **1.2**
detrás (de) behind **I**
devolver (ue) to return **I, 6.2**
el día day **I**
   Buenos días. Good morning. **I**
   el Día de Acción de Gracias
      Thanksgiving Day **3.2**
   **el Día de la Abolición de
      Esclavitud** Abolition Day **3.3**

   el Día de la Amistad
      Valentine's Day **3.2**
   el Día de la Independencia
      Independence Day **3.2**
   el Día de la Madre/del Padre
      Mother's/Father's Day **3.2**
   el Día de la Navidad
      Christmas Day **3.2**
   el Día de la Raza
      Columbus Day **3.2**
   ¿Qué día es hoy?
      What day is today? **I**
   Tal vez otro día.
      Maybe another day. **I**
   todos los días every day **I**
diario(a) daily **II**
dibujar to draw **II**
el dibujo drawing
   el dibujo técnico
      technical drawing **4.1**
   los dibujos animados
      cartoons **6.1**
el diccionario dictionary **I**
diciembre December **I**
diecinueve nineteen **I**
dieciocho eighteen **I**
dieciséis sixteen **I**
diecisiete seventeen **I**
el diente tooth **I, II**
   lavarse los dientes
      to brush one's teeth **I, II**
la dieta diet **II**
diez ten **I**
diferencia
   a diferencia de
      as contrasted with **1.1**
difícil difficult, hard **I**
el dinero money **I**
el diploma diploma **3.1**
el (la) diplomático(a) diplomat **4.3**
la dirección address, direction **I**
   la dirección electrónica
      e-mail address **6.3**
el (la) director(a) director **5.3**
dirigir (dirijo) to direct **5.3**
el disco disk **6.3**
   el disco compacto
      compact disc **I**
   el disco duro hard drive **6.3**
la discriminación
   discrimination **2.1**
disculpar(se) to apologize **II**
   disculpe(me) excuse (me) **II**

el discurso speech 3.1
discutir to discuss, to argue 1.1
el (la) diseñador(a) designer 1.2
el diseño design 4.1
el disfraz costume
disfrutar con los amigos
    to enjoy time with friends II
disponible available 6.3
dispuesto
    estar dispuesto(a)
        to be willing to 4.1
la distancia distance II
distinguir entre
    to distinguish between 6.2
diverso(a) diverse II, 2.2
divertido(a) enjoyable, fun,
    entertaining I, II
divertirse (ie) to enjoy oneself II
doblar to turn I
doce twelve I
la docena dozen I
el (la) doctor(a) doctor II
el doctorado doctorate 4.1
el documental documentary 6.1
el dólar dollar I
doler (ue) to hurt II
el dolor pain
    el dolor de cabeza headache II
domingo Sunday
dominicano(a) Dominican II
don/doña Mr./Mrs. I, II
donar to donate 2.1
dónde where I
    ¿De dónde eres?
        Where are you from? I
    ¿De dónde es?
        Where is he/she from? I
    ¿Dónde tiene lugar?
        Where does it take place? II
dormir (ue) to sleep I
    el saco de dormir
        sleeping bag II, 2.3
dormirse (ue) to fall asleep I
dos two I
doscientos(as) two hundred I, II
el drama drama 5.1
dramático(a) dramatic 5.3
ducharse to take a shower I, II
dudar que… to doubt that… II
el (la) dueño(a) owner II, 4.2
dulce sweet I
la durabilidad durability 6.2
durante during I

duro(a) hard, tough I

echar to throw out, away II, 2.2;
    to send out
echar de menos to miss
el ecosistema ecosystem 2.2
el (la) ecoturista ecotourist 2.3
ecuatoriano(a) Ecuadorian II
la edad age I
la edición edition II
el edificio building I
el (la) editor(a) editor I, II
la educación education II, 4.1
    la educación física
        physical education I
educar al público
    to educate the public 2.1
el efectivo cash I
el efecto effect II, 2.2
el ejército army 3.3
él he I
la electricidad electricity II
elegante elegant II
ella she I
ellos(as) they I
elogiar to praise 5.3
embellecer to beautify 2.1
emocionado(a) excited I
emocionante exciting 5.3
empezar (ie) to begin I, II
el (la) empleado(a) employee 4.2
el empleo employment, job I, II, 4.2
emprendedor(a) enterprising 4.1
la empresa
    business, company II, 4.2
empujar to push
en in I
    en caso de que in case 3.1
    en cuanto as soon as 2.3
    en línea on-line 6.3
    en oferta on sale
    en seguida at once I
    en vivo y en directo
        live (programming) 6.1
enamorar(se) de to fall in love II
Encantado(a). Delighted/Pleased
    to meet you. I
encantar to delight II
encargarse de to take charge of 4.1

encender (ie) to turn on 1.3
la enchilada enchilada I
enchufar to plug in 1.3
encima (de) on top (of) I, II
encontrar (ue) to find, to meet I
el encuentro meeting I
la energía energy II
enero January I
la enfermedad sickness II
el (la) enfermero(a) nurse II
enfermizo(a) sickly
enfermo(a) sick I
los enfermos the sick 2.1
enfrentar to confront 3.3
enfrente (de) in front (of) I, 6.2
el engaño trick, deceit
englobar to encompass
enhorabuena congratulations 3.1
el enlace link 6.3
enojado(a) angry I
enojarse con to get angry with II
enorme huge, enormous I, II
la ensalada salad I
el ensayo essay 3.3
enseñar to teach I
entender (ie) to understand I
entonces then, so I
entrar (a, en) to enter I
entre between I
el entrenamiento training II, 4.2
entrenarse to train II
entretenido(a) entertaining 6.1
la entrevista interview I, II
el (la) entrevistador(a)
    interviewer II, 4.2
entusiasmarse to get excited 1.3
envidia
    tener envidia to be envious II
el episodio episode 6.1
el equipaje luggage II
el equipo team I
el equipo estereofónico
    stereo equipment 6.2
equivocarse to make a mistake 6.2
esbelto(a) slender 1.1
escalar montañas
    to mountain climb II, 1.2
la escalera stairs II
la escena scene II
el (la) esclavo(a) slave 3.3
escoger (escojo) to choose II
los escombros rubble, debris
esconder(se) to hide II, 1.3

escribir to write I, II
el (la) escritor(a) writer I, II
el escritorio desk I
escuchar to listen (to) I
la escuela school I, 5.1
el (la) escultor(a) sculptor II
la escultura sculpture II
ese(a) that I, 5.1
ése(a) that one I, 5.1
esencial
    Es esencial que…
        It's essential that… II
el esfuerzo
    hacer un esfuerzo
        to make the effort 2.1
eso that I, 5.1
el espacio de la televisión
    television program
la espada sword
el español Spanish (language) I
el (la) español(a) Spaniard II
especial special I
la especialidad de la casa
    specialty of the house II
especializarse to specialize 4.1
especialmente
    specially, especially I, II
las especies species 2.2
el espejo mirror I, II
esperar to wait for, to expect,
    to hope I, II
    Esperar que… to hope that… I
la esposa wife I
el esposo husband I
esquiar to ski I
    esquiar en el agua
        to water-ski 1.2
la esquina corner II
la estación de autobuses
    bus station I
el estacionamiento
    parking space II
las estaciones seasons I
el estadio stadium I
las estadísticas statistics 4.3
el estado civil civil status
    (married, divorced, or single)
    4.1
estadounidense of the U.S. II
estampado(a) embossed (fabric) 1.2
estar (estoy) to be I, II
    ¿A cuánto está(n)…?
        How much is (are)…? I

¿Cómo está usted?
    How are you? (formal) I
¿Cómo estás?
    How are you? (familiar) I
¿Está incluido(a)…?
    Is… included? I
estar a favor de to be for II, 2.1
estar bien informado(a)
    to be well informed II
estar de acuerdo to agree I, II
estar descompuesto(a)
    to be broken 6.2
estar dispuesto(a) a
    to be willing to 4.1
estar en contra de
    to be against 2.1
estar resfriado to have a cold II
estar roto(a) to be broken 6.2
no estar seguro(a) (de) que
    not to be sure that 3.2
la estatura height II, 4.1
el este east II
este(a) this I, 5.1
éste(a) this one I, 5.1
el estilo style 5.3
estirar(se) to stretch II
esto this I, 5.1
el estómago stomach I, II
estrecho(a) narrow I, II
la estrella star I
el estreno new release II
el estrés stress I, II
el (la) estudiante student II
estudiar to study I
    estudiar las artes marciales
        to study martial arts II
los estudios sociales
    social studies I
la estufa stove I, II
el examen test I
el exceso de equipaje
    excess luggage II
exclamar to exclaim II
exigir (exijo) to demand 3.1
el éxito success I, 3.1
    tener éxito to be successful II
explicar to explain II
la exportación exportation 4.3
exportar to export 4.3
la exposición exhibit II
expresivo(a) expressive 5.3
externo(a) external 6.3
el(la) extranjero(a) foreigner II

extraño(a) strange

la fábrica factory 4.3
fácil easy I
fácilmente easily I, II
la falda skirt I
faltar to lack II
la familia family II
la farmacia pharmacy, drugstore I
el faro lighthouse 3.3
fascinar to fascinate II
la fauna silvestre
    wild animal life 2.2
favorito(a) favorite I
el fax fax 6.3
    el fax multifuncional
        multifunctional
        fax machine 6.2
febrero February I
la fecha date I
    la fecha de nacimiento
        date of birth II, 4.1
    ¿Cuál es la fecha?
        What is the date? I
la felicidad happiness II
felicidades congratulations I
feliz happy I
felizmente happily I
feo(a) ugly I
feroz ferocious II
festejar to celebrate 3.2
la ficción fiction 5.1
la fiebre fever II
fiel faithful 1.1
la fiesta party I, II
    la fiesta continua
        party in stages 3.2
la figura figure 5.1
fijarse en to notice 6.2
el fin de semana weekend I
el final ending 5.3
el (la) financiero(a)
    financial expert 4.3
las finanzas finance 4.1
la firma signature II, 4.1
el flamenco
    flamenco-style dancing 5.1
el flan caramel custard I
el fleco fringe 1.2

el flequillo bangs **1.1**
flojo(a) loose **II**
la flor flower **I**
la flora silvestre wild plant life **2.2**
fluir to flow
la fogata campfire **II**
el fondo background **5.1**
la formación training, education **4.1**
formal formal **I, II**
formidable great **1.2**
formulista formulaic **5.3**
el fósforo match **II, 2.3**
la foto photo, picture
   sacar fotos
     to take pictures **I**
el (la) fotógrafo(a)
   photographer **I, II**
francés(esa) French **II**
frecuente frequent **I**
frecuentemente
   often, frequently **I, II**
frente a in front of, opposite **II**
la fresa strawberry **II**
   Hace fresco. It is cool. **I**
el frigorífico refrigerator **I**
los frijoles beans **II**
frío cold **I**
   Hace frío. It is cold. **I**
   tener frío to be cold **I**
la fruta fruit **I**
fue cuando it was when **II**
el fuego fire **I, 2.3**
la fuente source
fuera (de) outside (of) **I**
fuerte strong **I**
la fuerza motriz
   power, moving force
funcionar to work, to run **II, 6.2**
el fútbol soccer **I**
el fútbol americano football **I**

el gabinete cabinet **1.3**
las gafas de sol sunglasses **I**
la gala big, formal party **3.2**
la galería gallery **II**
la galleta cookie, cracker **I, II**
la gallina hen **I**
el gallo rooster **I**
la ganadería livestock industry **4.3**

el (la) ganadero(a) farmer **I**
el ganado livestock **4.3**
el (la) ganadora winner **I, II**
ganar to win **I**
ganarse la vida
   to earn a living **II, 4.2**
ganas
   tener ganas de… to feel like… **I**
la ganga bargain **II**
el garaje garage **II**
la garantía guarantee **6.2**
la garganta throat **II**
la gasolina gasoline **II**
gastar to spend **II**
los gastos expenses **II**
el (la) gato(a) cat **I**
la gaviota seagull
los (las) gemelos(as) twins **II**
el género genre **5.3**
la generosidad generosity **3.1**
generoso(a) generous **3.1**
genial wonderful **1.2**
el genio genius
la gente people **I**
   la gente sin hogar the homeless
    2.1
el (la) gerente manager **I, II, 4.2**
gestionar to arrange
el gimnasio gymnasium **I**
girar to turn **II**
los globos balloons **II**
el (la) gobernador(a) governor **3.3**
el gobierno government **3.3**
el gol goal **I**
gordo(a) fat **I**
la gorra baseball cap **I**
el gorro cap **I**
gozar de to enjoy, to have
la grabadora tape recorder **I, 6.2**
grabar to record **6.1**
Gracias. Thank you. **I, II**
   Gracias, pero no puedo.
    Thanks, but I can't. **I**
   Mil gracias. Many thanks. **3.1**
el grado degree **I**
el (la) graduando(a) graduate **3.1**
el gramo gram **I, II**
grande big, large **I**
la granja farm **I**
la gripe flu **II**
gritar to scream **II**
el grito shout
grueso(a) heavy **1.1**

el grupo group
   el grupo de conversación
    chat group **6.3**
   el grupo de noticias
    news group **6.3**
el guante glove **I**
guapo(a) good-looking **I**
el (la) guardaespaldas
   bodyguard **6.1**
guardar to hold, to keep **I, II**
guatemalteco(a) Guatemalan **II**
la guerra war
la guía telefónica
   phone directory **I**
los guineítos en escabeche
   small green bananas in garlic
   vinegar, red pepper and oil **3.2**
el guión script **5.3**
el (la) guionista scriptwriter **5.3**
la guitarra guitar **I**
   tocar la guitarra
    to play the guitar **I**
gustar to like **I, II**
   Le gusta… He/She likes… **I**
   Me gusta… I like… **I**
   Me gustaría… I would like… **I**
   Te gusta… You like… **I**
   ¿Te gustaría…?
    Would you like…? **I**
el gusto pleasure **I**
   a gusto comfortable, happy
   El gusto es mío.
    The pleasure is mine. **I**
   Mucho gusto.
    Nice to meet you. **I**
   Sí, con mucho gusto.
    Yes, gladly. **2.1**

la habanera
   habanera (Latin music) **5.2**
había there was, there were **II**
las habichuelas coloradas
   red beans **II**
las habilidades capabilities **II, 4.2**
la habitación bedroom, room **I, II**
hablar to talk, to speak **I, II**
   ¿Puedo hablar con…?
    May I speak with… **I**
hacer (hago) to make, to do **I, II**

¿Hace… que? How long has it been since…? **II**
Hace buen tiempo.
It is nice outside. **I**
Hace calor. It is hot. **I**
Hace fresco. It is cool. **I**
Hace frío. It is cold. **I**
Hace mal tiempo.
It is bad outside. **I**
Hace sol. It is sunny. **I**
Hace viento. It is windy. **I**
hacer alpinismo to go hiking **1.2**
hacer clic/doble clic
to click/to double click **6.3**
hacer ejercicio to exercise **I**
hacer el papel to play the role **5.3**
hacer juego con…
to match with…
hacer la cama to make the bed **I**
hacer la limpieza
to do the cleaning
hacer montañismo
to go mountaineering **1.2**
hacerle caso a uno
to pay attention to **1.1**
hacer un esfuerzo
to make the effort **2.1**
¿Qué tiempo hace?
What is the weather like? **I**
hacerse pedazos to fall apart
hacia toward **II**
el halcón falcon **2.3**
el hambre (fem.) hunger
tener hambre to be hungry **I**
la hamburguesa hamburger **I**
el hardware hardware **6.3**
la harina flour **I, II**
la harina de trigo wheat flour
hasta until, as far as **I, II**
Hasta luego. See you later. **I**
Hasta mañana.
See you tomorrow. **I**
hasta que until **2.3**
hay there is, there are **I**
hay que one has to, one must **I**
Hay sol. It's sunny. **I**
Hay viento. It's windy. **I**
No hay de qué. It's nothing. **3.2**
el hecho fact **II**
la heladería ice cream parlor **II**
el helado ice cream **I, II**
el (la) hermanastro(a)
stepbrother/stepsister **II**

el(la) hermano(a) brother/sister **I**
los hermanos brother(s) and
sister(s) **I**
el héroe hero **II**
la heroína heroine **II**
el hielo ice **I**
sobre hielo on ice **I**
el hierro iron **4.3**
la hija daughter **I**
el hijo son **I**
los hijos son(s) and daughter(s),
children **I**
hincharse to swell
la historia history, story **I, II**
el hockey hockey **I**
la hoja leaf **II**
la hoja de cálculo spreadsheet **6.3**
Hola. Hello. **I**
el hombre man **I**
el (la) hombre/mujer de
negocios businessman
businesswoman **I, II**
el hombro shoulder **II**
hondureño(a) Honduran **II**
honrar to honor **3.3**
la hora hour
¿A qué hora es…?
(At) What time is…? **I**
¿Qué hora es? What time is it? **I**
el horario schedule **I**
el hormigón concrete
el horno oven **I, II**
el horno microondas
microwave oven **II**
horrible horrible **1.2**
el horror horror **II**
hospedarse to stay at **II**
el hotel hotel **I**
hoy today **I**
Hoy es… Today is… **I**
¿Qué día es hoy?
What day is it? **I**
hubo there was, there were **II**
el (la) huésped(a) guest **II**
el huevo egg **I, II**
las humanidades humanities **4.1**
húmedo(a) humid **II, 2.3**
el huracán hurricane **II, 2.3**

I

el icono del programa
program icon **6.3**
la ida y vuelta round trip **II**
la identificación identification **II**
el identificador de llamadas caller
identification **6.2**
la ideología ideology **3.3**
la iglesia church **I**
Igualmente. Same here. **I**
la iguana iguana **2.3**
impaciente impatient **II**
el impermeable raincoat **I**
implicar to mean
imponer (impongo) to impose **3.1**
importar to be important **II**
Es importante que…
It's important that… **II**
imposible
Me es imposible. It's just not
possible for me. **2.1**
impresionante impressive **5.3**
la impresora printer **I**
incluido(a) included **I**
¿Está incluido(a)…?
Is … included? **I**
incómodo(a) uncomfortable **1.2**
increíble incredible **II, 2.2**
los (las) indígenas indigenous,
indigenous peoples
la industria industry **4.3**
la industria pesquera fishing
industry **4.3**
la infección infection **II**
influir to influence **1.1**
informal informal **I**
la informática
computer science **4.1**
la ingeniería engineering
la ingeniería mecánica
mechanical engineering **4.1**
el (la) ingeniero(a) engineer **II**
el inglés English (language) **I**
inglés(esa) English **II**
el ingreso entrance, admission
el inicio beginning
los tambaleantes inicios
shaky beginnings
inigualable unequalled **6.2**
la injusticia injustice **3.3**

inmediatamente immediately **II**
innovador(a) innovative **5.3**
inolvidable unforgettable **3.2**
la inquietud uncertainty
insistir en (que) to insist (on) **II, 3.1**
instituir to institute **2.2**
inteligente intelligent **I**
interesante interesting **I**
interesar to interest **II**
internacional international **II**
Internet
    navegar por Internet
       to surf the Internet **1.2**
interno(a) internal **6.3**
interpretar to interpret **5.1**
el (la) intérprete interpreter **4.3**
inútil useless **II, 2.2**
el invierno winter **I**
la invitación invitation **I, II**
invitar to invite
    Te invito.
       I'll treat you. I invite you. **I**
la inyección injection **II**
ir (voy) to go **I, II**
    ir a… to be going to… **I**
    ir al cine to go to the movies **I**
    ir al supermercado
       to go to the supermarket **I**
    ir de compras to go shopping **I**
    Vamos a… Let's… **I**
irónico(a) ironic **5.3**
irse (me voy) to leave, to go away **I**
italiano Italian **II**
la isla island **II**
la izquierda left
    a la izquierda (de)
       to the left (of) **I**

el jabalí wild boar
el jabón soap **I, II**
el jade jade **5.2**
el jaguar jaguar **II, 2.3**
jamás never
el jamón ham **I, II**
japonés(esa) Japanese **II**
el jarabe tapatío Mexican dance
    from Guadalajara **5.2**
el jardín garden **I, II**
el (la) jardinero(a) gardener **4.2**

la jarra pitcher **I**
los jeans jeans **I**
el (la) jefe(a) boss **I, II**
los jeroglíficos hieroglyphics **5.2**
la jota Aragonesa folk dance **5.1**
joven young **I**
los jóvenes young people **2.1**
las joyas jewelry **I**
la joyería jewelry store **I**
jubilarse to retire **4.2**
el juego interactivo
    interactive game **6.3**
jueves Thursday **I**
el (la) juez(a) judge **II, 4.2**
jugar (ue) to play **I, II**
    jugar al ajedrez to play chess **II**
el jugo juice **II**
el juguete toy **II**
la juguetería toy store **II**
julio July **I**
junio June **I**
juntar fondos to fundraise **2.1**
junto a next to **II**
juntos together **I**
justo(a) just, fair **3.3**
juzgar to judge

el kilo kilogram **I, II**

L

el laboratorio laboratory **4.3**
labrado(a) worked, cut **5.2**
lacio straight (hair) **II**
el lado side
    al lado (de) beside, next to **I, 6.2**
    por otro lado
       on the other hand **1.1**
    por un lado on the one hand **1.1**
el (la) ladrón(a) thief **II**
el lago lake **I**
la lámpara lamp **I, II**
la lana wool **I, 1.2**
el lápiz pencil **I**
largo(a) long **I**
    a lo largo de throughtout
la lástima

Es una lástima que…
    It's a shame that… **II**
    ¡Qué lástima! What a shame! **I**
lastimarse to hurt oneself **II**
la lata can **I, II, 2.2**
el lavabo washbowl **II**
el lavaplatos dishwasher **I, II**
lavar to wash **I**
    lavar los platos
       to wash the dishes **I, II**
lavarse to wash oneself **I, II**
    lavarse la cabeza
       to wash one's hair **I**
    lavarse los dientes
       to brush one's teeth **I, II**
la lección lesson **I**
la leche milk **I, II**
el lechón asado
    roast suckling pig **3.2**
la lechuga lettuce **I**
leer to read **I**
lejos (de) far (from) **I**
    ¿Queda lejos? Is it far? **I**
la lengua language **I**
lentamente slowly **I, II**
la lentejuela sequin **1.2**
los lentes de contacto
    contact lenses **1.1**
lento(a) slow **I**
la leña firewood **II, 2.3**
el león lion **II**
la letra lyrics **5.1**
el letrero sign **II**
levantar pesas to lift weights **I**
levantarse to get up **I, II**
la ley law **3.3**
liberal liberal **3.3**
la librería bookstore **I**
el libro book **I**
la licenciatura university degree **4.1**
el (la) líder leader **3.3**
la limonada lemonade **I**
limpiar el cuarto to clean the
    room **I, II**
la limpieza
    hacer la limpieza
       to do the cleaning **II**
limpio(a) clean **I, II**
    mantener (mantengo) limpio(a)
       to keep clean **II**
la línea line
    en línea on-line **6.3**
la linterna flashlight **II, 2.3**

listo(a) ready **I**
la literatura literature **I**
el litro liter **I, II**
la llama llama **I**
la llamada call **I**
llamar to call **I**
    ¿Cómo se llama?
      What is his/her name? **I**
    ¿Cómo te llamas?
      What is your name? **I**
    Dile/Dígale que me llame.
      Tell (familiar/formal) him or
      her to call me. **I**
    Me llamo… My name is… **I**
    Se llama…
      His/Her name is… **I**
la llave key **I, II**
el llavero keychain **1.2**
la llegada arrival **II**
llegar to arrive **I, II**
llenar to fill up **II**
lleno(a) full **II**
llevar
    to wear, to carry; to take along **I**
    llevar a cabo to accomplish **3.1**
    llevar(se) bien
      to get along with **II**
    llevarse bien/mal
      to get along well/badly with
      each other **1.3**
llorar to cry **II**
llover (ue) to rain **I**
la llovizna drizzle **II, 2.3**
la lluvia rain **I**
el lobo wolf **II**
local local **II**
el Localizador Unificador de
    Rescursos (LUR) URL **6.3**
la loción aftershave **II**
la loción protectora
    sunscreen **II**
loco(a) crazy **I**
lógico
    Es lógico que…
      It's logical that… **II**
lograr to achieve
el loro parrot **II, 2.3**
la lucha fight **3.3**
luchar contra to fight against **2.1**
lucir to appear
luego later **I**
    Hasta luego. See you later. **I**
el lugar place **I**

lujoso(a) luxurious **I, II**
la lumbre light
el lunar beauty mark **1.1**
los lunares polka dots **1.2**
lunes Monday **I**
la luz light **I, II, 2.3**
    apagar la luz
      to turn off the light **I**

la madrastra stepmother **II**
la madre mother **I**
    el Día de las Madres
      Mother's Day **3.2**
la madrugada
    early morning, dawn **3.2**
la maestría master's degree **4.1**
el (la) maestro(a) teacher **I**
el maíz corn **4.3**
las malas hierbas weeds **1.3**
el malecón boardwalk
la maleta suitcase **II**
el (la) maletero(a) porter **II**
malo(a) bad **I**
    Es malo que… It's bad that… **II**
    Hace mal tiempo.
      It is bad outside. **I**
    lo malo the bad thing **1.1**
    Lo malo es que…
      The trouble is that… **II**
el mambo mambo
    (Latin music) **5.2**
mandar una carta
    to send a letter **I**
manejar to drive **I**
manipular to manipulate **6.1**
la mano hand **I, II**
la manta blanket **I, II, 2.3**
el mantel tablecloth **II**
mantener (mantengo)
    mantener limpio to keep clean **II**
mantenerse sano(a)
    to be healthy **II**
la mantequilla butter **I, II**
la mantequilla de cacahuate
    peanut butter **II**
la manzana apple **II**
mañana tomorrow **I**
la mañana morning **I**
    Mañana es… Tomorrow is… **I**

    de la mañana in the morning **I**
    Hasta mañana.
      See you tomorrow. **I**
    por la mañana
      during the morning **I**
el mapa map **I**
el maquillaje makeup **II**
maquillarse to put on makeup **I, II**
la máquina contestadora
    answering machine **I**
el mar sea **I**
de maravilla marvelous **II**
la marca brand **6.2**
marcar to dial **I**
la marina navy
la marioneta marionette **II**
la mariposa butterfly **II, 2.3**
marrón brown **I**
martes Tuesday **I**
marzo March **I**
más more **I**
    más de more than **I**
    lo más the most **1.1**
    más… que more… than **I, 6.3**
la máscara mask
el mascarero maskmaker
las matemáticas mathematics **I**
la materia subject **I**
mayo May **I**
mayor older **I**
    mayor que older than **II**
la mayoría majority **II**
el (la) mecánico(a) mechanic **II, 4.2**
la medalla medallion **1.2**
la media hermana half-sister
la medianoche midnight **I, II**
mediante by means of
la medicina medicine **II**
medio(a) half **I, II**
el medio means, medium
el medio ambiente
    environment **II, 2.2**
el medio hermano half-brother **I**
el mediodía noon **I**
la mejilla cheek
mejor better **I**
    Es mejor que…
      It's better that… **II**
    lo mejor the best **1.1**
    mejor que better than **II**
la melodía melody **5.1**
el melón melon **II**
la memoria memory **6.3**

menor younger **I**
  menor que younger than **II**
menos to, before; less **I**
  menos de less than **I**
  lo menos the least **1.1**
  menos… que less…than **I**
el mensaje message **I**
  dejar un mensaje
    to leave a message **I**
  Deje un mensaje después del
    tono. Leave a message after
    the tone. **I**
  Quiero dejar un mensaje
    para… I want to leave a
    message for… **I**
mentir (ie) to lie
la mentira lie **II**
el menú menu **I**
el mercadeo marketing **4.1**
el mercado market **I**
merendar (ie) to have a snack **I**
el merengue
  merengue (Latin music) **5.2**
la merienda snack **I**
el mes month **I**
  el mes pasado last month **I**
la mesa table **I, II**
  poner la mesa to set the table **I**
  quitar la mesa to clear the table **I**
el (la) mesero(a) waiter (waitress) **I**
la meta goal **II**
meterse en to get into
el metro subway **I**
mexicano(a) Mexican **II**
mezclar to mix
la mezclilla denim **1.2**
mi my **I**
el micrófono microphone **6.3**
el microondas microwave **I**
el microprocesador
  microprocessor **6.3**
el miedo fear **I**
  tener miedo to be afraid **I, II**
mientras while **II**
miércoles Wednesday **I**
mil millones billion **4.3**
mil one thousand **I, II**
millón de millones trillion **4.3**
millón million **II**
mimado(a) spoiled **1.1**
la minería mining **4.3**
los minusválidos

the physically challenged **2.1**
mío(a) mine
mirar to watch, to look at **I**
mismo(a) same **I**
la mitad de one half of **4.3**
la mochila backpack **I**
la moda fashion, style **1.2**
el módem modem **6.3**
moderno(a) modern **I, II**
modesto(a) modest **1.1**
mojado(a) wet **II**
molestar to bother **II**
el momento moment **I**
  Un momento. One moment. **I**
la monarquía monarchy **3.3**
el monedero change purse **1.2**
el monitor monitor **6.3**
la monja nun
el mono monkey **II**
  el mono araña
    spider monkey **2.3**
la montaña mountain **I**
  escalar montañas
    to mountain climb **II, 1.2**
el montañismo mountaineering **II**
  hacer montañismo
    to go mountaineering **1.2**
morado(a) purple **I**
moreno(a) dark hair and skin **I**
morir (ue) to die **II**
el mostrador counter **II**
mostrar (ue) to show **II**
el motivo purpose **3.2**
la moto(cicleta) motorcycle **I**
mover los muebles
  to move the furniture **I**
la muchacha girl **I**
el muchacho boy **I**
muchas veces often **4.2**
mucho often **I**
mucho(a) much, many **I**
los muebles furniture **I, II**
la mujer woman **I**
  la mujer de negocios
    businesswoman **I, II**
multinacional multinational **4.3**
el mundo world
la muñeca doll; wrist **II**
el muñeco de peluche
  stuffed animal **II**
el mural mural **5.2**
el (la) muralista muralist **5.2**

el museo museum **I**
la música music **I**
el musical musical **II**
el (la) músico(a) musician **II, 3.2**
muy very **I**

nacer to be born
el nacimiento
  la fecha de nacimiento
    date of birth **II, 4.1**
nada nothing **I**
  De nada. You're welcome.
nadar to swim **I**
  nadar con tubo de respiración
    to snorkel **2.3**
nadie no one **I**
la nariz nose **I, II**
la naturaleza nature **II, 2.2**
  la naturaleza muerta still life **5.1**
la navaja jackknife **II, 2.3**
navegar to navigate, sail
  navegar en tabla de vela
    to windsurf **1.2**
  navegar por Internet
    to surf the Internet **1.2**
  navegar por rápidos to go
    whitewater rafting **2.3**
la Navidad Christmas **3.2**
la neblina mist, fog **II, 2.3**
necesitar to need **I**
  Es necesario que…
    It's necessary that… **II**
negro(a) black **I**
nervioso(a) nervous **I**
  ponerse nervioso(a)
    to get nervous **1.3**
nevar (ie) to snow **I**
la neverita cooler **II**
ni nor, neither, not even **II**
ni… ni neither…nor **4.2**
nicaragüense Nicaraguan **II**
la nieta granddaughter
el nieto grandson
los nietos grandchildren
la nieve snow
la niña girl
el (la) niñero(a) babysitter **II, 4.2**
ninguno(a) none, not any **I**
el niño boy

la **nitidez** clarity, sharpness **6.2**
el **nivel** level
no no, not **I**
  ¡No digas eso! Don't say that! **I**
  ¡No me digas! Don't tell me! **I**
  ¡No te preocupes! Don't worry! **I**
la **noche** night, evening **I**
  Buenas noches. Good evening. **I**
  de la noche at night **I**
  por la noche
    during the evening **I**
el **nombre** name, first name **I**
normal normal **I**
normalmente normally **I, II**
el **norte** north **II**
nosotros(as) we **I**
la **nota** grade
  sacar una buena nota
    to get a good grade **I**
las **noticias** news **II**
  el grupo de noticias
    news group **6.3**
el **noticiero** news program **II**
novecientos nine hundred **I**
la **novela** novel **I**
el (la) **novelista** novelist **5.3**
noveno(a) ninth **I, II**
noventa ninety **I**
noviembre November **I**
el (la) **novio(a)**
  boyfriend/girlfriend **II**
la **nube** cloud **II, 2.3**
nublado cloudy **I**
  Está nublado. It is cloudy. **I**
nuestro(a) our **I**, ours **II**
nueve nine **I**
nuevo(a) new **I**
  el Año Nuevo New Year **3.2**
  el Nuevo Mundo New World **5.2**
el **número** number **I**; shoe size **II**
nunca never **I**
nutritivo(a) nutritious **II**

o or **I**
o…o either…or **4.2**
obediente obedient **II**
la **obra** work **I**; work of art **II**
  la obra de teatro

theatrical production **II**
el (la) **obrero(a)** worker **II**
obtener (obtengo)
  to obtain, to get **II**
el **océano** ocean **II**
el **ocelote** ocelot **2.3**
ochenta eighty **I, II**
ocho eight **I, II**
ochocientos eight hundred **I, II**
octavo(a) eighth **I, II**
octubre October **I**
ocupado(a) busy **I**
ocurrir to occur **II**
  ocurrírsele (a uno)
    to dawn on, to occur to **6.2**
odiarse to hate each other **1.3**
el **oeste** west **II**
la **oficina** office **I**
ofrecer to offer **I, II**
  Le puedo ofrecer…
    I can offer you… **I**
  ¿Se le(s) ofrece algo más? May
    I offer you anything more? **I**
el **oído** inner ear **II**
oír (oigo) to hear **I**
ojalá que I hope that, hopefully **II**
el **ojo** eye **I, II**
la **ola** wave **I, II**
al óleo oil painting **5.1**
oler (huelo) (ue) a to smell
la **olla** pot **I**
el **olmo** elm
olvidar to forget **I**
  olvidársele (a uno) to forget **6.2**
once eleven **I**
la **onda** trendy thing to do; wave
ondulado(a) wavy **1.1**
el (la) **operador(a)** operator **I, II, 4.2**
opinar
  no opinar que
    not to be of the opinion that
oponerse a (me opongo)
  to oppose **1.3**
el (la) **opresor(a)** oppressor **3.3**
opuesto(a) opposite **1.1**
ordenar (las flores, los libros)
  to arrange (flowers, books) **I**
ordinario(a) ordinary **I**
la **oreja** ear **I, II**
el **orfelinato** orphanage
el **orgullo** pride **3.1**
orgulloso(a) proud **3.1**

original original **5.3**
la **orilla** edge; shore **II**
el **oro** gold **I**
la **orquesta** orchestra **3.2**
oscurecer to get dark **2.3**
la **oscuridad** darkness **2.3**
oscuro(a) dark **II**
  lo más oscuro
    the most incomprehensible,
    the least desirable
el **oso hormiguero** anteater **2.3**
el **otoño** fall **I**
otro(a) other, another **I**
ovalado(a) oval **1.1**

paciente patient **I**
el **padrastro** stepfather **II**
el **padre** father **I**
  el día de los Padres
    Father's Day **3.2**
los **padres** parents **I**
los **padrinos** godparents **3.1**
pagar to pay **I**
la **página-web** Web page **6.3**
el **país** country **I**
el **paisaje** landscape **5.1**
el **pájaro** bird **I**
la **palma** palm tree **II**
el **palmar** palm tree grove **II**
el **palo** stick
el **pan** bread **I, II**
  el pan dulce sweet roll **I**
la **panadería** bread bakery **I**
panameño(a) Panamanian **II**
la **pandereta** tambourine **5.1**
la **pantalla** screen **I**
los **pantalones** pants **I**
  los pantalones cortos shorts **I**
el **pañuelo** scarf **II**
la **papa** potato **II**
  las papas fritas French fries **I**
el **papel** paper **I**; role **II**
  hacer el papel to play the role **5.3**
la **papelería** stationery store **I**
el **paquete** package **I, 4.1**
el **par**
  un par de a pair of
para for, in order to **I**

para empezar to begin with I
para que so that 3.1
¿Para qué? For what purpose?
la parada stop, stand II
el paraguas umbrella I
paraguayo(a) Paraguayan II
parar to stop II
la pared wall I, II
el (la) pariente relative II
el parque park I
la partición
    se harán particiones the
        inheritance will be divided up
participar to participate 2.1
el partido game I
el (la) pasajero(a) passenger II
el pasaporte passport II
pasar to happen, to pass,
    to pass by I
    pasar la aspiradora
        to vacuum I, II
    pasar por debajo de la mesa
        to go unnoticed
    pasar un rato con los amigos
        to spend time with friends I
    pasarlo bien
        to have a good time 3.2
las Pascuas Easter 3.2
pasear to go for a walk I
el pasillo aisle II
el paso the way 5.2
la pasta pasta I, II
la pasta de dientes toothpaste I
el pastel cake I; tamale-like mixture
    of plantain, yuca and meat 3.2
la pastelería pastry shop I
la pastilla pill II
el pastor shepherd I
la patata potato I
patinar to skate I
los patines skates I
la patineta skateboard I
    andar en patineta
        to skateboard I
la patria mother country 3.3
el (la) patriota patriot 3.3
patriótico(a) patriotic 3.3
el patriotismo patriotism 3.3
patrocinar to sponsor 3.2
el pavo turkey 3.2
el payaso clown
la paz peace

el peatón (la peatona) pedestrian II
las pecas freckles 1.1
el pedazo piece I
pedir (i) to ask for, to order I, II
    ¿Me ayuda a pedir?
        Could you help me order? I
el peinado hairdo
peinarse to comb one's hair I
el peine comb I
pelearse to fight II, 1.3
el pelícano pelican 2.3
la película movie I
peligroso(a) dangerous I, II, 2.3
    Es peligroso que…
        It's dangerous that… II
pelirrojo(a) redhead I
el pelo hair I
la pelota baseball I
el pelotón de fusilamiento firing
    squad
el (la) peluquero(a)
    hairstylist II, 4.2
los pendientes
    dangling earrings 1.2
pensar (ie) to think, to plan I
la pensión pension; boarding
    house II
peor worse I
    lo peor the worst 1.1
    peor que worse than II
pequeño(a) small I
la pera pear II
la percepción perception 6.1
perder (ie) to lose I
perdérsele (a uno)
    to lose (something) 6.2
Perdona(e)… Pardon…
    Perdona(e), ¿cómo llego a…?
        Pardon, how do I get to…? I
perdonarse
    to forgive each other 1.3
perezoso(a) lazy I
perfecto(a) perfect I
el perfil económico
    economic profile 4.3
el perfume perfume II
el periódico newspaper I
el periodismo journalism II
el (la) periodista journalist I, II
el permiso permission II, 2.2
permitir to permit II, 2.1
pero but I

el (la) perro(a) dog I
    caminar con el perro
        to walk the dog I
el personaje character 5.3
la perspectiva perspective 5.1
pertenecer
    to belong, to pertain II, 2.1
peruano(a) Peruvian II
pesado(a) boring, heavy 1.2
    el pesado lecho heavy bed
el pescado fish I, II
el (la) pescador(a) fisherman II
pescar to fish II
    pescar en alta mar
        to go deep-sea fishing 1.2
pese a in spite of
el petróleo petroleum 4.3
el pez fish I, 2.3
el piano piano I
    tocar el piano
        to play the piano I
el picaflor hummingbird 2.3
picante spicy I
el pie foot I, II
    a pie on foot I
la piedra stone, rock II, 2.2
la piel skin II
la pierna leg I, II
la pila battery 6.2
pilotar una avioneta to fly a
    single-engine plane 1.2
el piloto pilot II
la pimienta pepper I, II
pintar to paint I
el (la) pintor(a) painter II
la pintura
    painting, picture II; paint
la pirámide pyramid 5.2
la piscina swimming pool I
el piso floor, story II
el pizarrón chalkboard I
el placer pleasure
    Es un placer. It's a pleasure. I
planchar (la ropa)
    to iron (the clothes) I
el planeta planet II, 2.2
la planta plant I
    la planta silvestre wild plant II
la planta baja ground floor II
el plástico plastic 2.2
la plata silver I
el plátano verde plantain II

el plato plate **I**
  lavar los platos
    to wash the dishes **I, II**
la playa beach **I**
la plaza town square **I**
la plena Afro-Caribbean dance **3.3**
la pluma pen **I**
la población population **II, 2.2**
pobre poor **II**
la pobreza poverty **II, 2.1**
poco a little **I**
poder (ue) to be able, can **I, II**
  Gracias, pero no puedo.
    Thanks, but I can't. **I**
  Le puedo ofrecer…
    I can offer you… **I**
  No, de veras, no puedo.
    No, really, I can't. **2.1**
  Si pudiera, lo haría.
    If I could, I would. **2.1**
  ¿Podría(s) darme una mano?
    Could you give me a hand?
    2.1
  ¿Me puede atender? Can you
    help (wait on) me? **II**
  ¿Me puede(s) ayudar?
    Can you help me? **2.1**
  ¿Me puede(s) hacer un favor?
    Can you do me a favor? **2.1**
  ¿Puedes (Puede usted) decirme
    dónde queda…? Could you
    tell me where… is? **I**
  ¿Puedo hablar con…?
    May I speak with…? **I**
el poder power **3.3**
el poema poem **I**
la poesía poetry **I, 5.1**
el (la) poeta poet **5.3**
el (la) policía police officer **II**
el poliéster polyester **1.2**
el pollo chicken **I**
  el pollo asado
    barbecued chicken **II**
el polvo dust **I**
  quitar el polvo to dust **I, II**
poner (pongo) to put **I, II**
  poner la mesa to set the table **I**
  ponerse (me pongo)
    to put on (clothes) **I**
  ponerse la ropa
    to get dressed **I, II**
  ponerse nervioso(a)
    to get nervous **1.3**

el por ciento percent **4.3**
por for, by, around **I**
  por favor please **I**
  por fin finally **I**
  por la mañana
    during the morning **I**
  por la noche
    during the evening **I**
  por la tarde
    during the afternoon **I**
  por otro lado
    on the other hand **1.1**
  por todas partes
    everywhere **I, 2.2**
  por un lado on the one hand **1.1**
¿Por qué? Why? **I**
  ¿Por qué no? Why not? **2.1**
el porcentaje percentage **4.3**
porque because **I**
portarse bien/mal
  to behave well/badly **II**
posible
  Es posible que…
    It's possible that… **II**
el postre dessert **I**
practicar to play, to practice **I, II**
  practicar deportes
    to play sports **I**
el precio price **I**
precioso(a) precious, valuable **5.2**
precolombino(a)
  pre-Columbian **5.2**
predecible predictable **5.3**
preferir (ie) to prefer **I, II**
el prejuicio prejudice **2.1**
el Premio Nóbel Nobel Prize **5.3**
el prendedor pin **1.2**
la prensa press
preocupado(a) worried **I**
preocuparse (por)
  to be worried about **II**
  ¡No te preocupes!
    Don't worry! **I**
preparar to prepare **I**
la preparatoria preparatory school
presentar to introduce
  Te/Le presento a…
    Let me introduce you
    (familiar/formal) to… **I**
preservar to preserve **II, 2.1**
el (la) presidente(a) president **3.3**
el préstamo loan **II**
prestar to lend **II**

prevalecer to prevail
la primavera spring **I**
el primer plano foreground **5.1**
primero first **I**
primero(a) first **I, II**
el (la) primo(a) cousin **I**
principal principal **4.3**
prisa
  tener prisa to be in a hurry **I**
probable
  Es probable que…
    It's probable that… **II**
el problema problem **I, II**
la procesión procession **3.3**
la producción production **5.1**
producir to produce **II**
los productos forestales
  forestry products **4.3**
la profesión profession **I, II**
el programa program **II**
  el ícono del programa
    program icon **6.3**
  el programa anti-virus
    anti-virus program **6.3**
  el programa de acción
    action program **6.1**
  el programa de ciencia ficción
    science fiction program **6.1**
  el programa de concurso
    game show **6.1**
  el programa de entrevistas
    talk show **6.1**
  el programa de horror
    horror program **6.1**
  el programa de misterio
    mystery program **6.1**
  el programa de reciclaje
    recycling program **2.2**
prohibido(a) para menores
  R-rated (movie) **6.1**
prohibir to prohibit **2.2**
el promedio average **4.3**
el pronóstico forecast **II**
pronto soon **I, II**
la propina tip **I**
  ¿Cuánto le doy de propina?
    How much do I tip? **I**
  dejar la propina
    to leave the tip **I**
el (la) proponente supporter **3.3**
la prosa prose **5.3**
¡Próspero Año Nuevo!
  Happy New Year! **3.2**

el (la) protagonista protagonist 5.3
proteger to protect II, 2.2
    proteger las especies
      to protect the species I
la prueba quiz I
la publicidad publicity 4.1
el público audience 6.1
el pueblo town, village I
el puente bridge II
el puerco pork I
la puerta door I, II
puertorriqueño(a) Puerto Rican II
pues well I
el puesto position II, 4.2
la pulsera bracelet I
la puntualidad punctuality II, 4.2

qué what? I
    ¿A qué hora es…?
      (At) What time is… ? I
    ¿Qué desea(n)?
      What would you like? I
    ¿Qué día es hoy?
      What day is today? I
    ¡Qué (divertido)! What (fun)! I
    ¿Qué hora es? What time is it? I
    ¡Qué lástima! What a shame! I
    ¡Qué lío! What a mess! II, 2.2
    ¿Qué lleva? What is he/she
      wearing? I
    ¿Qué me (nos) recomienda?
      What do you recommend? II
    ¿Qué tal? How is it going? I
    ¿Qué tiempo hace?
      What is the weather like? I
quedar (en) to stay, to be (in a
    specific place), to agree on I
    ¿Puedes (Puede usted) decirme
      dónde queda…? Could you
      tell me where…is? I
    ¿Queda lejos? Is it far? I
quedársele (a uno)
    to leave something behind 6.2
los quehaceres chores I, II
quejarse to complain 1.3
la quemadura burn II
quemar to burn II
querer (ie) to want, to love I, II
    ¿Quieres beber…?
      Do you want to drink…? I

¿Quieres comer…?
    Do you want to eat…? I
Quiero beber…
    I want to drink… I
Quiero comer…
    I want to eat… I
Quiero dejar un mensaje
    para… I want to leave a
    message for… I
el queso cheese I
quién who I
    ¿De quién es…?
      Whose is…? I
    ¿Quién es? Who is it? I
    ¿Quiénes son? Who are they? I
el químico chemical II, 2.2
quince fifteen I
la quinceañera
    fifteenth birthday 3.2
quinientos(as) five hundred I
el quinto one fifth 4.3
quinto(a) fifth I, II, 4.3
el quiosco kiosk; newstand II
Quisiera… I would like… I
quitar
    quitar el polvo to dust I, II
    quitar la mesa
      to clear the table I
    quitarse la ropa
      to take off your clothes II
quizás perhaps II

el radio radio I
    el radio portátil
      portable radio 6.2
el radiocasete radio-tape player I
la radioemisora radio station 3.2
la radiografía X-ray II
la rana frog II
rápidamente quickly I, II
rápido(a) fast, quick I
la raqueta racket I
rara vez rarely I
raro(a) rare, strange II
    Es raro que… It's rare that… II
el rato
    un buen rato quite a while
el ratón mouse I
las rayas stripes II

el rayo thunderbolt, flash of
    lightning II, 2.3
la raza race I
la razón reason I
    Con razón. That's why. I
    tener razón to be right I
la reacción crítica
    critical response 6.1
real royal
el realismo mágico
    magical realism 5.3
la rebaja sale II
rebosante overflowing
la recepción
    reception/front desk II
el (la) recepcionista receptionist I
el receso break I
la receta prescription II
recibir to receive I
el reciclaje recycling II
reciclar to recycle II
reciente recent I
recientemente lately, recently I, II
el recital recital 5.1
recoger to collect; to pick up 2.1
las recomendaciones
    recommendations II
recomendar (ie) to recommend II
recordar (ue) to remember I
recuperar(se) to get better II
los recursos naturales
    natural resources II, 2.2
la red mundial World Wide Web 6.3
redondo(a) round 1.1
reducir to reduce II, 2.2
la refinería oil refinery 4.3
reflejar to reflect 5.2
el reflejo reflection
el refresco soft drink I
el refrigerador refrigerator II
el refugio de vida silvestre
    wildlife refuge 2.3
el regalo gift I
regar (ie) to water 1.3
regatear to bargain I
regresar to return, to go back I, II
    Regresa más tarde.
      He/She will return later. I
Regular. So-so. I
la reina queen 3.3
reír(se) (i) to laugh II
las relaciones públicas
    public relations 4.1

relajarse (i) to relax II
el relámpago lightning II, 2.3
el reloj clock, watch I
remar to row II
reparar to repair 1.3
el repertorio repertoire 5.1
repetir (i) to repeat II
el reportaje report II
el (la) reportero(a) reporter II
requerir (ie) to require II, 4.2
el requisito requirement II, 4.2
rescatar to rescue II
el rescate rescue II
la reserva reservation II
resfriado
    estar resfriado(a) to have a cold II
resistir to stand, to put up with 2.1
resolver (ue) to resolve II, 1.1
respaldado(a)
    supported by; backed by 6.2
respectivamente respectively
respetar to respect 1.1
respirar to breathe II
el restaurante restaurant I
el retrato portrait II
la reunión gathering II
reunir(se) to get together II
revisar to review, to check II
la revista magazine I
el rey king 3.3
rico(a) tasty I; rich II
ridículo
    Es ridículo que…
        It's ridiculous that… II
el riesgo
    correr riesgos to take risks 4.1
el río river I
riquísimo(a) very tasty I
la risa laugh, laughter II
el ritmo rhythm 5.1
rizado curly (hair) II
robar to steal II
el robo robbery II
rodeado(a) surrounded
la rodilla knee II
rogar (ue) to beg 3.1
rojizo(a) reddish 1.1
rojo(a) red I
el romanticismo romanticism 5.3
romántico(a) romantic II
romperromper la piñata
    to break the piñata II

rompérsele (a uno) to break 6.2
la ropa clothing
    ponerse la ropa
        to get dressed I, II
    quitar(se) la ropa
        to take off one's clothes II
rosado(a) pink I
roto(a)
    estar roto(a) to be broken 6.2
rubio(a) blond I
el ruido noise 3.2
las ruinas ruins 5.2

sábado Saturday I
la sábana sheet II
saber (sé) to know I, II
el sabor taste II
sabroso(a) tasty I, II
sacar to take II
    sacar fotos
        to take pictures I
    sacar la basura
        to take out the trash I
    sacar una buena nota
        to get a good grade I
el saco de dormir
    sleeping bag II, 2.3
le saeta Andalusian song 5.1
la sal salt I, II
la sala living room I, II
la sala de emergencia
    emergency room II
la salchicha sausage I; hot dog II
la salida departure II
salir (salgo) to go out, to leave I
saltar
    saltar la cuerda to jump rope II
¡Salud! Cheers! II
saludable healthy II
saludarse
    to greet (each other) II, 1.3
salvadoreño(a) Salvadoran II
salvaje wild II, 2.3
las sandalias sandals II
la sangre blood II
sano(a)
    mantenerse sano(a)
        to be healthy II
la sardana Catalan folk dance 5.1

la sátira satire 5.3
se recomienda discreción
    PG-13 rated (movie) 6.1
el secador de pelo hair dryer I, II
secarse to dry oneself I
seco(a) dry II
el (la) secretario(a)
    secretary I, II, 4.2
sed
    tener sed to be thirsty I
la seda silk 1.2
seguir (i) to follow, to continue II
segundo(a) second I, II
la seguridad security II
el seguro insurance II
    el seguro médico
        medical insurance 4.2
seguro(a) sure
    (No) es seguro que… It is (not) certain that… II
    (No) estoy seguro(a).
        I'm (not) sure. 3.3
    no estar seguro (de) que
        not to be sure that 3.2
seis six I, II
seiscientos six hundred I, II
la selva forest, jungle I, II, 2.2
el semáforo traffic light/signal II
la semana week I
    el fin de semana weekend I
    la semana pasada last week I
sembrar (ie) to plant 2.1
semejante a similar to 1.1
el semestre semester I
sencillo(a) simple, plain I, II
el sendero path, trail II, 2.3
sensacionalista sensationalized 6.1
sentar(se) (ie) to sit II
sentir (ie)
    sentir que to be sorry that II
    sentirse to feel II
    Lo siento mucho, pero…
        I'm sorry, but… 2.1
    Lo siento. I'm sorry. I
    sentirse frustrado(a)
        to feel frustrated 1.3
señalar to gesture
el señor Mr. I
la señora Mrs. I
la señorita Miss I
separar to separate II, 2.2
septiembre September I
séptimo(a) seventh I, II

la sequía drought **2.2**
ser (soy) to be **I, II**
    Es la…/Son las…
      It is… o'clock. **I**
    ser de… to be from… **I**
el ser humano human being **II, 2.1**
la serie series **II**
serio(a) serious **I**
la serpiente snake **II, 2.3**
el servicio service
    el servicio de búsqueda
      search engine **6.3**
    el servicio social
      social service **2.1**
los servicios bathrooms **II**
la servilleta napkin **II**
servir (i) to serve **I, II**
    servir de to be used as
sesenta sixty **I**
setecientos seven hundred **I, II**
setenta seventy **I**
sexto(a) sixth **I**
los shorts shorts **I**
si if **I, II**
sí yes **I**
    ¡Claro que sí! Of course! **I**
    Sí, con mucho gusto.
      Yes, gladly. **2.1**
    Sí, me encantaría.
      Yes, I would love to. **I**
siempre always **I**
siete seven **I**
el siglo century **5.1**
siguiente next **II**
la silla chair **I, II**
el sillón armchair **I, II**
simbólico(a) symbolic **5.3**
el simbolismo symbolism **5.3**
simpático(a) nice **I**
sin without **I**
sin embargo nevertheless **5.3**
el sitio site **6.3**
la situación situation **II**
el smog smog **II, 2.2**
sobrante leftover, surplus
sobre on **II**
    sobre hielo on ice **I**
el sobre envelope **4.1**
el (la) sobrino(a) nephew/niece **II**
sociable sociable **II**
la sociedad anónima (S.A.)
    corporation (Inc.) **4.3**
¡Socorro! Help! **II**

el sofá sofa, couch **I, II**
el software software **6.3**
el sol sun **I**
    las gafas de sol sunglasses **I**
    Hay sol./Hace sol. It's sunny. **I**
    tomar el sol to sunbathe **I**
soleado(a) sunny **II, 2.3**
solemne solemn **3.3**
solicitar to request, to apply for **II, 4.1**
la solicitud application **II, 4.1**
sólo only **I**
solo(a) alone **I**
la solución solution **2.1**
la sombra shade, shadow **II**
el sombrero hat **I**
la sombrilla de playa
    beach umbrella **II**
el son sound, rhythm **5.1**
sonar (ue) to sound, ring **3.3**
soñar (ue) to dream about
el sonido sound **I**
sonreír(se) (i) to smile **II**
la sopa soup **I**
sorprender to surprise **I, II**
la sorpresa surprise **I, II**
el sótano basement **1.3**
su your, his, her, its, their **I**
subir por to go up/to climb **II**
sucio(a) dirty **I, II**
las sudaderas sweats **1.2**
sudar to sweat **II**
el sueldo salary **II, 4.2**
suelen acercarse
    they often come up to
el suelo floor **I, II**
    barrer el suelo
      to sweep the floor **I**
suelto(a) loose **1.2**
el sueño sleep; dream
    tener sueño to be sleepy **I**
la suerte luck
    La suerte viene a quien menos la aguarda. Luck comes to he who least expects it.
    tener suerte to be lucky **I**
el suéter sweater **I**
suficiente enough **II**
sugerir (ie) to suggest **II**
sumar to add **4.3**
superarse to get ahead, to excel **4.1**
la superficie surface
el supermercado supermarket **I**

    ir al supermercado
      to go to the supermarket **I**
suplicar to ask, to plead **3.1**
el sur south **II**
el surfing surfing **I**
el susto shock, fright
suyo(a)
    yours (formal), his, hers, theirs

T

el tablado stage floor **5.1**
el tablao flamenco group **5.1**
tacaño(a) stingy **II**
el taco taco **II**
tal vez maybe **I**
    Tal vez otro día.
      Maybe another day. **I**
el talento talent **II**
la talla size (clothing) **II**
tallado(a) carved **5.2**
el taller workshop **I**
el tamaño size **6.3**
también also, too **I**
el tambor drum **5.1**
tampoco neither, either **I**
tan as **I**
    tan pronto como as soon as **2.3**
    tan… como as…as **I, II, 6.3**
el tango tango (Latin music) **5.2**
tanto as much **I**
    tanto como as much as **I**
    tantos… como as many…as **II, 6.3**
las tapas appetizers **I**
el tapiz tapestry **5.1**
la taquería taco restaurant **II**
la taquilla box office **II**
tarde late **I**
    Regresa más tarde.
      He/She will return later. **I**
la tarde afternoon **I**
    Buenas tardes. Good afternoon. **I**
    de la tarde in the afternoon **I**
    por la tarde during the afternoon **I**
la tarea homework **I**
la tarjeta card
    la tarjeta de crédito credit card **I**
    la tarjeta de sonido
      sound card **6.3**

la tarjeta gráfica
graphics card **6.3**
el **taxi** taxi, cab I
el (la) **taxista** taxi driver I, II, **4.2**
la **taza** cup I
el **té** tea I
el **teatro** theater I
la **obra de teatro**
theatrical production II
el **techo** roof
la **tecla** key **6.3**
el **teclado** keyboard I, **6.3**
la **técnica** technique **5.2**
el **técnico** technician II, **4.2**
el **tejido** textile, weaving **5.2**
las **telecomunicaciones**
telecommunications **4.3**
el **teledrama** TV mini-series **6.1**
telefonearse
to telephone each other **1.3**
el **teléfono** telephone I
el **teléfono celular**
cellular telephone **6.2**
el **teléfono inalámbrico**
cordless telephone **6.2**
¿**Cuál es tu teléfono?** What is
your phone number? I, II
la **teleguía** television guide **6.1**
el **telemensaje** voice mail **6.2**
la **telenovela** soap opera II
la **teleserie** TV series **6.1**
el (la) **televidente** viewer II
la **televisión** television I
el **espacio de la televisión**
television program
la **televisión por cable**
cable television **6.1**
la **televisión por satélite**
satellite television **6.1**
ver la televisión
to watch television I
el **televisor** television set I
el **televisor portátil**
portable television **6.2**
el **tema** theme, subject II
el **tembleque**
coconut-milk custard **3.2**
la **temperatura** temperature I
el **templo** temple **5.2**
la **temporada**
season, period of time **1.2**
temprano early I
el **tenedor** fork I

tener (tengo) to have I
¿**Cuántos años tiene…?**
How old is…? I
tener calor to be hot I
tener cuidado to be careful I, II
tener en común
to have in common **1.1**
tener envidia to be envious II
tener éxito to be successful II
tener frío to be cold I
tener ganas de… to feel like… I
tener hambre to be hungry I
tener miedo to be afraid I, II
tener prisa to be in a hurry I
tener que to have to I
tener razón to be right I
tener sed to be thirsty I
tener sueño to be sleepy I
tener suerte to be lucky I
tener vergüenza
to be ashamed II
Tiene… años.
He/She is…years old. I
el **tenis** tennis I
teñido(a) dyed **1.1**
tercero(a) third I, II
el **tercio** third **4.3**
terminar to finish I
el **terreno** terrain, landscape
la **altura del terreno**
altitude of terrain
terrible terrible, awful I
los **textiles** textiles **4.3**
la **tía** aunt I
el **tiburón** shark **2.3**
el **tiempo** time; weather I
a tiempo on time II
Hace buen tiempo.
It is nice outside. I
Hace mal tiempo.
It is bad outside. I
¿**Qué tiempo hace?**
What is the weather like? I
tiempo completo full time
el **tiempo libre** free time I
la **tienda** store I
la **tienda de deportes**
sporting goods store I
la **tienda de música y videos**
music and video store I
la **tienda de campaña** tent II, **2.3**
la **tierra** land I, II, **2.2**
las **tijeras** scissors I, II

el **timbre** ring
tímido(a) shy II
la **tintorería** dry cleaner II
el **tío** uncle I
los **tíos** uncle(s) and aunt(s) I
típicamente typically II
típico(a) typical, regional **3.2**
la **tira cómica** comic strip II
el **titular** headline II
titularse to be called **5.3**
el **título** title **5.3**
la **tiza** chalk I
la **toalla** towel I, II
el **tobillo** ankle II
tocar to play (an instrument);
to touch I, II
¡**A todos nos toca!**
It's up to all of us! **2.2**
tocar el piano
to play the piano I
tocar la guitarra to play the
guitar I
todavía still, yet I
todo(a) all I
todo el mundo everyone II
todos los días every day I
la **toga** gown **3.1**
tomar to take, to eat or drink I
tomar decisiones
to make decisions **4.1**
tomar el sol to sunbathe I
tomar en cuenta
to take into account **6.2**
tomar un curso de natación
to take a swimming class II
el **tomate** tomato I, II
tonto(a) silly
la **tormenta** storm I
el **toro** bull I
la **torta** sandwich I, II
la **tortilla española** potato omelet I
la **tortuga** turtle II, **2.3**
la **tos** cough II
los **tostones** fried plantains II
trabajador(a) hard-working I
el (la) **trabajador(a) social**
social worker **4.3**
trabajar to work
trabajar de voluntario(a)
to volunteer **2.1**
el **trabajo** job, work
el **trabajo a tiempo completo**
full-time job **4.2**

el trabajo a tiempo parcial
part-time job **4.2**
la tradición tradition **5.2**
tradicional traditional I, II
traducir to translate II
el (la) traductor(a) translator **4.3**
traer (traigo) to bring I
¿Me trae...?
Could you bring me...? I
el tráfico traffic I
el traje suit II
el traje de baño bathing suit I
la trama plot **5.3**
tranquilamente calmly I, II
tranquilo(a) calm I
trasladarse to move I
tratar to treat II
tratar de to try to
tratarsede to be about **5.3**
trece thirteen I
treinta thirty I
el tren train I
trepar a un árbol to climb a tree II
tres three I, II
trescientos three hundred I
triangular triangular **1.1**
el trigo wheat **4.3**
triste sad I
Es triste que... It's sad that... II
la tristeza sadness II
la trompeta trumpet **5.1**
el tropiezo setback **3.1**
el trueno thunder II, **2.3**
tu your (familiar) I
tú you (familiar singular) I
el tucán toucan II, **2.3**
el turismo tourism II
tuyo(a) yours (familiar) II

ubicado(a) located
último(a) last I
único(a) unique, only **1.2**
la unidad monetaria currency **4.3**
unir to unite
la universidad university II
uno one I, II
Uruguay Uruguay I
uruguayo(a) Uruguayan II
usar to use, to wear, to take
a size I, II

usted you (formal singular) I
ustedes you (formal, plural) I
el (la) usuario(a) user **6.3**
útil useful II
la uva grape I, II

la vaca cow I
vaciar to empty **1.3**
vacío(a) empty II
valer (valgo)
to value, to be worth II
valer la pena
to be worthwhile **3.1**
el valle valley II, **2.2**
valorar
to appreciate, to value II, **2.1**
vanidoso(a) vain **1.1**
el vaso glass I
el vaso de glass of I
el vecindario neighborhood II
el (la) vecino(a) neighbor I
vegetariano(a) vegetarian I
veinte twenty I
veintiuno twenty-one I
las velas candles II
el venado deer II, **2.3**
vencer (venzo)
to defeat, to overcome **3.1**
vender to sell I
venezolano(a) Venezuelan II
venir (vengo) to come I, II
la ventaja advantage II, **4.2**
la ventana window I, II
la ventanilla window II
las ventas sales **4.1**
a la venta for sale
ver (veo) to see I, II
¿Me deja ver...? May I see...? I
Nos vemos. See you later. I
ver la televisión
to watch television I
verse to look, to appear **1.1**
el verano summer I
la verdad truth I
Es verdad. It's true. I
No es verdad que...
It's not true that... II
verde green I
la verdura vegetable I, II
la vergüenza

tener vergüenza
to be ashamed II
el vestido dress I
vestir(se) (i) to dress oneself II
el vestuario wardrobe **1.2**
el (la) veterinario(a)
veterinarian II, **4.2**
viajar to travel I
el viaje trip I
la victoria victory **3.3**
la vida life I
el video video I
alquilar un video
to rent a video I
la videocámara videocamera **6.2**
la videocasetera
videocassette recorder **6.1**
la videograbadora VCR I
el videojuego video game I
el vidrio glass II, **2.2**
viejo(a) old I
el viento wind I
Hace viento. It's windy. I
Hay viento. It's windy. I
viernes Friday I
violento(a) violent II
el violín violin **5.1**
visitar to visit I
vivir to live I
Vive en... He/She lives in... I
Vivo en... I live in... I
volar (ue) to fly II
volar en planeador
to hang-glide **1.2**
el voleibol volleyball I
el (la) voluntario(a) volunteer II
volver (ue)
to return, to come back I
vosotros(as) you (familiar plural) I
votar to vote **2.1**
el vuelo flight II
vuestro(a) your (familiar plural) I,
yours II

y and I
y cuarto quarter past I
y media half past I
ya already, now II
¡Ya lo sé! I already know! I
ya no no longer I

el yeso cast **II**
yo I **I**
el yogur yogurt **I, II**

la zanahoria carrot **I, II**
el zapateado
   rhythmic heel tapping **5.1**
la zapatería shoe store **I**
el zapato shoe **I**
   el zapato de tacón
      high-heeled shoe **II**
las zonas de reserva ecológica
   conservation lands **2.2**
el zorrillo skunk **2.3**
el zumo juice **I**

GLOSARIO
inglés-español

This English–Spanish glossary contains all of the active vocabulary words that appear in the text as well as passive vocabulary from readings and culture sections. It contains all words listed in the Spanish–English Glossary.

abilities las habilidades **4.2**
to be able poder (ue) **I, II**
Abolition Day el día de la Abolición de Esclavitud **3.3**
to be about tratarse de **5.3**
academic el (la) académico(a) **4.3**
accessible accesible **6.2**
to accomplish llevar a cabo **3.1**
accountant el (la) contador(a) **I, II, 4.2**
accounting la contabilidad **4.1**
to achieve lograr
acquaintance la amistad **II**
actor/actress el (la) actor/actriz **II**
to adapt oneself adaptarse **4.1**
to add sumar **4.3**
address la dirección **I**
admiral el (la) almirante **3.3**
admission el ingreso
to advance avanzar **3.1**
advanced avanzado(a) **5.2**
advantage la ventaja **II, 4.2**
adventures las aventuras **II**
advice el consejo **II**
to advise aconsejar **II**
aerosol el aerosol **2.2**
afraid
to be afraid tener miedo **I, II**
  I'm afraid that…
    Tengo miedo de que… **2.3**

after después (de) **I**
afternoon la tarde **I**
  during the afternoon
    por la tarde **I**
  Good afternoon.
    Buenas tardes. **I, II**
  in the afternoon de la tarde **I**
after-shave lotion la loción **II**
afterward después **I**
against
  to be against
    estar en contra de **II, 2.1**
age la edad **I**
ago hace…que **II**
to agree estar de acuerdo **I, II**
to agree (on) quedar (en) **I**
agriculture la agricultura **4.3**
agronomy la agronomía **4.1**
air el aire **I**
  air conditioning
    el aire acondicionado **II**
  air pollution
    la contaminación del aire **I, 2.2**
airline la aerolínea **II**
airplane el avión **I**
airport el aeropuerto **I**
aisle el pasillo **II**
alarm clock el despertador **I, II**
all todo(a) **I**
  all around por todas partes **2.2**
  It is up to all of us…
    A todos nos toca… **II, 2.2**
to allow dejar **3.1**

almost casi **II**
alone solo(a) **I**
alphabet el abecedario
already ya **II**
also también **I**
altitude la altura **II, 2.2**
  altitude of terrain
    la altura del terreno
aluminum el aluminio **II**
always siempre **I**
ambulance la ambulancia **II**
ancestors los antepasados **3.3**
ancient antiguo(a) **I**
and y **I**
and so it was that así fue que **II**
anger la ira
angry enojado(a) **I**
  to get angry with enojarse con **II**
animal el animal **I**
animated animado(a) **II**
ankle el tobillo **II**
anniversary el aniversario **II**
to announce avisar
another otro(a) **I**
to answer contestar **I**
answering machine
    la máquina contestadora **I**; la contestadora automática **6.2**
anteater el oso hormiguero **2.3**
apartment el apartamento **I**
to apologize disculparse **II**
to appear lucir; verse **1.1**
appetizers las tapas **I**
apple la manzana **II**

application la solicitud II, **4.1**
to apply for solicitar II, **4.1**
to apply oneself to dedicarse a **1.3**
appointment la cita I
to appreciate
    valorar II; apreciar **3.1**
April abril I
architect
    el (la) arquitecto(a) I, II, **4.2**
architectural arquitectónico(a)
architecture la arquitectura I
Argentine argentino(a) II
to argue discutir **1.1**
arm el brazo I, II
armchair el sillón I, II
army el ejército
around alrededorde II; por I
to arrange ordenar I; gestionar
arrangement el arreglo
arrival la llegada II
to arrive llegar I, II
art el arte I
article el artículo II
artisan el (la) artesano(a) I, II, **4.2**
artist el (la) artista II
as como
    as…as tan…como I, II
    as contrasted with
        a diferencia de **1.1**
    as far as hasta I
    as long as con tal de que **3.1**
    as many…as tantos… como II, **6.3**
    as much as tanto como I
    as soon as en cuanto, tan pronto como **2.3**
ashamed
    to be ashamed
        tener vergüenza II
to ask suplicar **3.1**
to ask for pedir (i) I, II
aspirin la aspirina II
to assemble armar **1.3**
assistant el (la) asistente II, **4.2**
at a
    At…o'clock A la(s)… I
    at once en seguida II
athlete el (la) deportista II, **4.2**
athletics el atletismo II
ATM machine
    el cajero automático II
to attend asistir a II; acudir a **3.3**
attic el desván **1.3**

audience el público **6.1**
auditorium el auditorio I
August agosto I
aunt la tía I
author el (la) autor(a) II
autobiography la autobiografía **5.1**
available disponible **6.3**, accesible **6.2**
avenue la avenida I
average el promedio **4.3**
award el premio I, II
awesome
    How awesome! ¡Qué chévere! I
awful terrible I

baby el bebé II
babysitter el (la) niñero(a) II, **4.2**
backed by respaldado(a) **6.2**
background el fondo **5.1**
backpack la mochila I
bad malo(a) I
    the bad thing lo malo **1.1**
    It is bad (weather) outside. Hace mal tiempo. I
    It's bad that… Es malo que… II
bag la bolsa I
balanced balanceado(a) II
bald calvo(a) **1.1**
ball la bola, la pelota I
ballet el ballet **5.1**
balloons los globos II
bananas
    small green bananas in garlic vinegar, red pepper and oil los guineítos en escabeche **3.2**
band la banda **3.3**
bangs el flequillo **1.1**
bank el banco I
banker el (la) banquero(a) **4.3**
barber
    el (la) peluquero(a) II
bargain la ganga II
to bargain regatear I
baseball el béisbol I
baseball cap la gorra I
basement el sótano **1.3**
basketball el baloncesto I
bat el bate I
bath

to take a bath bañarse I, II
bathing suit el traje de baño I
bathroom el baño, el servicio I, II
bathtub la bañera II
battery storage el acumulador; la batería, la pila **6.2**
to be estar I, II; ser I, II
    to be enrolled in cursar
    to be against
        estar en contra de **2.1**
    to be for estar a favor de **2.1**
    to be raised criarse
    to be thrilled, touched
        emocionarse **3.1**
    to be willing to
        estar dispuesto(a) **4.1**
    to be worth valer II
    to be worthwhile valer la pena **3.1**
beach la playa I
beach umbrella
    la sombrilla de playa II
beans los frijoles II
beard la barba **1.1**
beat el compás **5.1**
to beautify embellecer **2.1**
beauty la belleza II
beauty mark el lunar **1.1**
because porque I
bed la cama I, II
    to go to bed acostarse (ue) I
    to make the bed hacer la cama I
bedroom la habitación I, II
beef la carne de res I, II
beeper el beeper **6.2**
before antes (de) I
to beg rogar (ue) **3.1**
to begin comenzar (ie) II; empezar (ie) I, II
to begin with para empezar II
beginning el inicio
    shaky beginnings los tambaleantes inicios
to behave well/badly portarse bien/mal II
behind detrás (de) I; atrás **6.2**
belief la creencia **5.2**
to believe creer I, **3.3**
    not to believe that… no creer que… II
bell la campana **3.2**
to belong pertenecer II, **2.1**
below debajo de I, II

belt el cinturón **I**
benefits los beneficios **II, 4.2**
beside al lado (de) **I**
best lo mejor **1.1**
better mejor **I**
   better than mejor que **II**
   to get better recuperarse **II**
   It's better that…
      Es mejor que… **II**
between entre **I**
beverage la bebida **I**
big grande **I**
bike la bicicleta
   to ride a bike
      andar en bicicleta **I**
bill la cuenta **I, II**
billion mil millones **4.3**
biography la biografía **5.1**
bird el pájaro **I**; el ave (fem.)
birth
   date of birth la fecha de
      nacimiento **II, 4.1**
birthday el cumpleaños **I**
black negro(a) **I**
blanket la manta **I, II, 2.3**
blind ciego(a) **5.3**
blond rubio(a) **I**
blood la sangre **II**
blouse la blusa **I**
blue azul **I**
boa constrictor
   la boa constrictora **2.3**
to board (a plane) abordar **II**
boarding house la pensión **II**
boardwalk el malecón
boat el bote **II**
body el cuerpo **I, II**
bodyguard
   el (la) guardaespaldas **6.1**
Bolivian boliviano(a) **II**
book el libro **I**
bookstore la librería **I**
boots las botas **I**
bored
   to get bored aburrirse **II**
boring aburrido(a) **I**;
   pesado(a) **1.2**
born
   to be born nacer
boss el (la) jefe(a) **I, II**
to bother molestar **II**
bottle la botella **I, II, 2.2**
box office la taquilla **II**

boy el chico; el muchacho;
   el niño **I**
boyfriend
   el (la) novio(a) **II**
bracelet la pulsera **I**
brand la marca **6.2**
bread el pan **I, II**
bread bakery la panadería **I**
break el receso **I**
to break rompérsele (a uno) **6.2**
   to break down
      descomponérsele (a uno) **6.2**
   to break the piñata
      romper la piñata **II**
breakfast el desayuno **I**
   to have breakfast desayunar **I**
to breathe respirar **II**
bridge el puente **II**
to bring traer **I**
   Could you bring me …?
      ¿Me trae…? **I**
broken
   to be broken
      estar descompuesto(a),
      estar roto(a) **6.2**
brother el hermano **I**
brother(s) and sister(s)
   los hermanos **I**
brother-in-law el cuñado **II**
brown marrón **I**
brown (hair) castaño(a) **I**
brush el cepillo **I**
to brush one's hair cepillarse el
   pelo **II**
to brush one's teeth
   lavarse los dientes **I, II**
bucket el balde **II**
building el edificio **I**
bull el toro **I**
burn la quemadura **II**
to burn quemar **II**
bus el autobús **I**
bus station
   la estación de autobuses **I**
business el comercio **4.1**;
   la empresa **II, 4.2**
business administration la
   administración de empresas **4.1**
businessman
   el hombre de negocios **I, II**
businesswoman
   la mujer de negocios **I, II**
busy ocupado(a) **I**

but pero **I**
butcher's shop la carnicería
butter la mantequilla **I, II**
butterfly la mariposa **II, 2.3**
to buy comprar **I**
by por **I**
by means of mediante

C

cab el taxi **I**
cabinet el gabinete **1.3**
café el café **I**
cafeteria la cafetería **I**
cake el pastel **I**
calculator la calculadora **I**
call la llamada **I**
to call llamar **I**
   to be called titularse **5.3**
   Tell him or her to call me.
      Dile/Dígale que me llame. **I**
caller identification el
   identificador de llamadas **6.2**
calm tranquilo(a) **I**
calmly tranquilamente **I, II**
calorie la caloría **II**
camera la cámara **I, II**
camp el campamento **II, 2.3**
to camp acampar **1.2**
   to camp in the mountains
      acampar en las montañas **II**
campaign la campaña **2.1**
campfire la fogata **II**
can la lata **I, II, 2.2**
can poder (ue) **I, II**
   Can (May) I offer you anything
      more? ¿Se les ofrece algo
      más? **II**
   Can you do me a favor? ¿Me
      puede(s) hacer un favor? **2.1**
   Can you give me a hand?
      ¿Podría(s) darme una mano?
      2.1
   Can you help me? ¿Me
      puede(s) ayudar? **2.1**
   Can you help (wait on) me?
      ¿Me puede atender? **II**
   I can offer you… Le puedo
      ofrecer… **I**
   No, really, I can't. No, de veras,
      no puedo. **2.1**

Thanks, but I can't. Gracias, pero no puedo. I
can opener el abrelatas II, 2.3
Canadian canadiense II
candles las velas II
cap el gorro I; el birrete 3.1
   baseball cap la gorra I
capabilities las habilidades II
car el carro I, el coche 4.2
card la tarjeta
   graphics card la tarjeta gráfica 6.3
   sound card la tarjeta de sonido 6.3
cardboard, cardboard box el cartón II, 2.2
career la carrera II, 4.2
careful cuidadoso(a) I
   to be careful tener cuidado I, II
carefully cuidadosamente I
carrot la zanahoria I, II
to carry llevar I
to carry out a responsibility desempeñar un cargo 4.1
cartoons los dibujos animados 6.1
carved tallado(a) 5.2
cash el efectivo I
cash register la caja registradora II
cashier el (la) cajero(a) II
cassette el casete I
cast el yeso II
castanets las castañuelas 5.1
cat el (la) gato(a) I
cause la causa II
to celebrate celebrar, festejar 3.2
center el centro I
   community center el centro de la comunidad 2.1
   rehabilitation center el centro de rehabilitación 2.1
   shopping center el centro comercial I
centigrade el centígrado II, 2.3
century el siglo 5.1
ceramics la cerámica I
cereal el cereal I, II
certain
   It is not certain that… No es cierto que… II
      No es seguro que… II
chain la cadena 1.2
chair la silla I, II

chalk la tiza I
chalkboard el pizarrón I
change el cambio I
to change cambiar I
change purse el monedero 1.2
channel el canal II
   to change channels (TV) cambiar de canal 6.1
chapel la capilla
character el personaje 5.3
chat group el grupo de conversación 6.3
cheap barato(a) I
check la cuenta I
   Separate checks. Es aparte. I
   The check, please. La cuenta, por favor. I
to check revisar II
checked de cuadros I
checks los cheques II
cheek la mejilla
Cheers! ¡Salud! II
cheese el queso I
chemical el químico II, 2.2
cherry la cereza II
chess
   to play chess jugar al ajedrez II
chest el cofre
chicken el pollo I
   barbecued chicken el pollo asado II
Chilean chileno(a) II
Chinese chino(a) II
to choose escoger II
chores los quehaceres I, II
Christmas la Navidad 3.2
chronicler el (la) cronista 5.2
church la iglesia I
Cinderella Cenicienta
cinematographer el (la) cinematógrafo(a) 5.3
citizen el (la) ciudadano(a) 2.1
citizenship la ciudadanía II
city la ciudad I
city block la cuadra I
civil engineer el (la) ingeniero(a) civil 4.2
civil status el estado civil 4.1
civilization la civilización 5.2
to clap hands dar palmadas 5.1
clarity la nitidez 6.2
class la clase I
classroom la clase I

clean limpio(a) I, II
to clean hacer la limpieza II
to clean the room limpiar el cuarto I, II
to click hacer clic 6.3
   to double click hacer doble clic 6.3
climate el clima II, 2.2
climax el clímax 5.3
to climb a tree trepar a un árbol II
to climb mountains escalar montañas II
clip el broche
clock el reloj I
to close cerrar (ie) I
closed cerrado(a) I, II
closet el armario I, II
clothing la ropa II
cloud la nube II, 2.3
cloudy
   It is cloudy. Está nublado. I
clown el payaso
coat el abrigo I
coconut milk el agua de coco II
coconut-milk custard el tembleque 3.2
coffee el café I
coffee shop la cafetería I
cold
   to be cold tener frío I
   to have a cold estar resfriado(a) II
   It is cold. Hace frío. I
to collaborate with colaborar con 2.1
to collect coleccionar 1.2
Colombian colombiano(a) II
color el color I
   bright color el color brillante 1.2
   dark color el color oscuro 1.2
   solid color de un solo color 1.2
   What color…? ¿De qué color…? I
Columbus Day el día de la Raza 3.2
comb el peine I
to comb one's hair peinarse I
to come venir I, II
to come back volver (ue) I
comedy la comedia II
comedian, comedienne el (la) comediante II

comfortable cómodo(a) **II**; a gusto **1.2**
comic strip la tira cómica **II**
comical cómico(a) **I**
to commemorate conmemorar **3.3**
commercial el anuncio **II**
common común **II**
   to have in common tener en común **1.1**
community la comunidad **I**
compact disc el disco compacto **I**
companion el (la) compañero(a) **II**
company (business) la empresa **II**
company la compañía **I**
to compare comparar **4.3**
to compete competir (i) **II**
competition la competencia **3.3**
to complain quejarse **1.3**
complicated complicado(a) **II, 2.2**
computer la computadora **I**
computer science la computación **I**; la informática **4.1**
concert el concierto **I**
concrete el hormigón
configuration la configuración **6.3**
to confront enfrentar **3.3**
to congratulate felicitar **3.1**
congratulations felicidades **I**; enhorabuena **3.1**
to connect conectar **1.3**
   to connect to conectarse a **6.3**
conqueror el(la) conquistador(a) **5.2**
conservation land las zonas de reserva ecológica **2.2**
conservative conservador(a) **3.3**
to conserve conservar **II, 2.1**
considerate considerado(a) **1.1**
constitution la constitución **3.3**
to construct construir **II**
consultation la consulta **II**
to consume less consumir menos **2.1**
contact lenses los lentes de contacto **1.1**
contemporary contemporáneo(a) **5.3**
content contento(a) **I**
contest el concurso **I, 3.2**
contract el contrato **II, 4.2**
contrary
   on the contrary al contrario **II**
to control controlar **6.1**
to convince convencer **6.2**

to cook cocinar **I**
cookie la galleta **I, II**
cool
   It is cool. Hace fresco. **I**
cooler la neverita **II**
copper el cobre **4.3**
corn el maíz **4.3**
corner la esquina **I**
corporation (Inc.) la sociedad anónima (S.A.) **4.3**
corral el corral **I**
correspondent el (la) corresponsal **4.3**
cost costar (ue) **I**
Costa Rican costarricense **II**
costume el disfraz
cotton el algodón **1.2**
couch el sofá **I**
cough la tos **II**
to count contar (ue) **I**
counter el mostrador **II**
country el país, el campo **I**
   mother country la patria **3.3**
countryside el campo **I**
court la cancha **I**
cousin el (la) primo(a) **I**
cow la vaca **I**
crab el cangrejo
cracker la galleta **I**
crazy loco(a) **I**
cream la crema **I, II**
to create crear **II, 2.1**
creative creativo(a) **5.3**
credit card la tarjeta de crédito **I**
critic el (la) crítico(a) **5.3**
critical response la reacción crítica **6.1**
criticism la crítica **II**
to cross cruzar **I**
crossing el cruce **II**
to cry llorar **II**
Cuban cubano(a) **II**
to culminate culminar **5.3**
cumbia la cumbia (Latin music) **5.2**
cup la taza **I**
curly (hair) rizado **II**
currency la unidad monetaria **4.3**
custom la costumbre **3.3**
customer el (la) cliente(a) **II**
customs la aduana **II**
cut labrado(a) **5.2**
to cut cortar
   to cut oneself cortarse **II**

to cut the grass cortar el césped **II**
cyberspace relating to cyberspace **5.3**

daily diario(a) **II**
damaging dañino(a) **2.2**
dance la danza **5.2**
   Afro-Caribbean dance la bomba, la plena **3.3**
   Aragonese folk dance la jota **5.1**
   Catalan folk dance la sardana **5.1**
   Mexican dance from Guadalajara el jarabe tapatío **5.2**
   Mexican dance from Veracruz la bamba **5.2**
to dance bailar **I**
dancer el (la) bailarín/bailarina **II, 4.2**; **of flamenco** el (la) bailaor(a) **5.1**
dangerous peligroso(a) **I, II, 2.3**
   It's dangerous that… Es peligroso que… **II**
daring atrevido(a) **1.1**
dark oscuro **II**
   dark hair and skin moreno(a) **I**
   to get dark anochecer, oscurecer, atardecer **2.3**
darkness la oscuridad **2.3**
database la base de datos **6.3**
date la fecha **I**
   date of birth la fecha de nacimiento **II, 4.1**
   What is the date? ¿Cuál es la fecha? **I**
daughter la hija **I**
dawn el amanecer **2.3**; la madrugada **3.2**
to dawn on ocurrírsele (a uno) **6.2**
day el día **I**
   day before yesterday anteayer **I, II**
   What day is today? ¿Qué día es hoy?
dazzling deslumbrante **5.3**

debris los escombros
deceit el engaño
December diciembre I
to decide decidir I
to decipher descifrar **5.2**
decisions
  to make decisions
    tomar decisiones **4.1**
decorated decorado(a) **5.2**
decorations los adornos II
deer el venado II, **2.3**
to defeat vencer **3.1**
degree el grado I
delicious delicioso(a) I
to delight encantar II
to demand exigir **3.1**
democracy la democracia **3.3**
democratic democrático(a) **3.3**
denim la mezclilla **1.2**
deodorant el desodorante II
departure la salida II
dependability la confiabilidad **6.2**
depressed deprimido(a) I
derivative derivado(a) **5.3**
descent la descendencia **5.2**
desert el desierto I
design el diseño **4.1**
designer el (la) diseñador(a) **1.2**
to desire desear II
desk el escritorio I
dessert el postre I
destruction la destrucción II, **2.2**
detail el detalle II
to develop desarrollar **2.2**
development el desarrollo II, **2.1**
to dial marcar I
dictionary el diccionario I
to die morir (ue) II
diet la dieta II
difficult difícil I
dining room el comedor I, II
dinner la cena I, II
  to eat dinner cenar I, II
diploma el diploma **3.1**
diplomat el (la) diplomático(a) **4.3**
to direct dirigir **5.3**
direction la dirección I
director el (la) director(a) **5.3**
dirty sucio(a) I, II
disadvantage la desventaja II, **4.2**
to disconnect desconectar **1.3**
to disconnect from
  desconectarse de **6.3**

discount el descuento **6.2**
to discover descubrir II, **2.2**
discovery el descubrimiento **3.3**
discrimination
  la discriminación **2.1**
to discuss discutir **1.1**
disk el disco **6.3**
dishwasher el lavaplatos I, II
to dislike caer mal **1.2**
disorganized desorganizado(a) **1.3**
distance la distancia II
to distinguish between
  distinguir entre **6.2**
diverse diverso(a) II, **2.2**
to divide
  the inheritance will be divided
    up se harán particiones
to do hacer I, II
doctor el (la) doctor(a) I
doctorate el doctorado **4.1**
documentary el documental **6.1**
dog el (la) perro(a) I
  to walk the dog
    caminar con el perro I
doll la muñeca II
dollar el dólar I
Dominican dominicano(a) II
to donate donar **2.1**
door la puerta I, II
to doubt that dudar que II
  It's doubtful that…
    Es dudoso que…
down abajo I, II
downpour el aguacero II, **2.3**
downtown el centro I
dozen la docena I
drama el drama **5.1**
dramatic dramático(a) **5.3**
to draw dibujar II
drawing
technical drawing
  el dibujo técnico **4.1**
dream el sueño
to dream about soñar (ue)
dress el vestido I
to dress oneself vestirse (i) II
  to get dressed
    ponerse la ropa I, II
  to get dressed up arreglarse II
drink la bebida I
to drink beber; tomar I
  Do you want to drink…?
    ¿Quieres beber…? I

  I want to drink…
    Quiero beber… I
to drive conducir II; manejar I
driver el (la) conductor(a) II
drizzle la llovizna II, **2.3**
to drop caérsele (a uno) **6.2**
drought la sequía **2.2**
drugstore la farmacia I
drum el tambor **5.1**
dry seco(a) II
dry cleaner la tintorería II
to dry oneself secarse I
durability la durabilidad **6.2**
during durante I
to dust quitar el polvo I, II
dyed teñido(a) **1.1**

e-mail el correo electrónico **6.3**
  e-mail address
    la dirección electrónica **6.3**
each cada I
ear la oreja I, II
early temprano I
early morning la madrugada **3.2**
to earn a living
  ganarse la vida II, **4.2**
earring el arete I
  earrings (dangling)
    los pendientes **1.2**
easily fácilmente I, II
east el este II
Easter las Pascuas **3.2**
easy fácil I
to eat comer I, II; tomar I
  Do you want to eat…?
    ¿Quieres comer…? I
  to eat breakfast desayunar I
  to eat dinner cenar I, II
  to eat lunch almorzar (ue) I, II
  I want to eat…
    Quiero comer… I
economic profile
  el perfil económico **4.3**
ecosystem el ecosistema **2.2**
ecotourist el (la) ecoturista **2.3**
Ecuadorian ecuatoriano(a) II
edge la orilla II
edition la edición II
editor el (la) editor(a) I, II

to educate the public
educar al público **2.1**
education la educación **II, 4.1;**
la formación **4.1**
effects los efectos **II, 2.2**
effort
to make an effort
hacer el esfuerzo **2.1**
egg el huevo **I, II**
eggnog el coquito **3.2**
eight ocho **I, II**
eight hundred ochocientos(as) **I**
eighteen dieciocho **I**
eighth octavo(a) **I, II**
eighty ochenta **I**
either…or o… o **4.2**
elbow el codo **II**
the elderly los ancianos **2.1**
electricity la electricidad **II**
electronic electrónico(a)
electronic assistant
el asistente electrónico **6.2**
electronic mailbox
el buzón electrónico **6.3**
elegant elegante **II**
elevator el ascensor **II**
eleven once **I**
elm el olmo **I**
embroidery el bordado **5.2**
emergency room
la sala de emergencia **II**
employee el (la) empleado(a) **4.2**
employment el empleo **II**
to empty vaciar **1.3**
empty vacío(a) **II**
enchilada la enchilada **I**
to encompass englobar
to end culminar **5.3**
ending el final **5.3**
energy la energía **II**
engineer el (la) ingeniero(a) **II**
engineering la ingeniería
civil engineering
la ingeniería civil **4.1**
mechanical engineering
la ingeniería mecánica **4.1**
English inglés(esa) **II;** (lang.) el
inglés **I**
to enjoy gozar de; disfrutar de
to enjoy oneself divertirse **II**
to enjoy time with friends
disfrutar con los amigos **II**

Enjoy! (your meal)
¡Buen provecho! **3.2**
enjoyable divertido(a) **I**
enormous enorme **I, II**
enough bastante; suficiente **II**
to enroll in cursar
to enter entrar (a, en) **I**
enterprising emprendedor(a) **4.1**
entertaining divertido(a) **II;**
entretenido(a) **6.1**
entrance el ingreso
envelope el sobre **4.1**
environment
el medio ambiente **II, 2.2**
envious
to be envious tener envidia **II**
episode el episodio **6.1**
eraser el borrador **I**
especially especialmente **I, II**
essay el ensayo **3.3**
even though aunque **II**
evening la noche **I**
during the evening
por la noche **I**
Good evening. Buenas noches. **I**
every cada **I**
every day todos los días **I**
everyone todo el mundo **II**
everywhere por todas partes **II**
to excel superarse **4.1**
excess luggage
el exceso de equipaje **II**
to exchange cambiar **I**
excited emocionado(a) **I**
to get excited entusiasmarse **1.3**
exciting emocionante **5.3**
to exclaim exclamar **II**
to exercise hacer ejercicio **I**
exhausted
I'm exhausted.
Estoy agotado(a). **2.1**
exhibit la exposición **II**
expandable ampliable **6.3**
to expect esperar **I**
expenses los gastos **II**
expensive caro(a) **I**
It's very expensive!
¡Es muy caro(a)! **I**
to explain explicar **II**
to export exportar **4.3**
exportation la exportación **4.3**
expressive expresivo(a) **5.3**

external externo(a) **6.3**
eye el ojo **I, II**
eyeglasses los anteojos **1.1**

face la cara **I, II**
facing enfrente (de) **I**
fact el hecho **II**
factory la fábrica **4.3**
facts los datos **II, 4.1**
fair justo(a) **3.3**
faithful fiel **1.1**
falcon el halcón **2.3**
fall el otoño **I**
to fall apart hacerse pedazos
to fall asleep dormirse (ue) **I**
to fall down caerse **II**
to fall in love with
enamorarse de **II**
to be familiar with conocer **I**
to be familiar with someone
conocer a alguien **I**
family la familia **I**
far (from) lejos (de) **I**
Is it far? ¿Queda lejos? **I**
farm la granja **I**
farmer el (la) ganadero(a) **I;** el (la)
agricultor(a) **II, 4.2**
to fascinate fascinar **II**
fashion la moda **1.2**
fast rápido(a) **I**
fastener el broche
fat gordo(a) **I**
father el padre **I**
Father's Day
el día de los Padres **3.2**
favor
to be in favor of
estar a favor de **II, 2.1**
favorite favorito(a) **I**
fax el fax **6.3**
multifunctional fax machine
el fax multifuncional **6.2**
February febrero **I**
to feed darle(s) de comer **I**
to feel sentirse (ie) **II**
to feel frustrated
sentirse frustrado(a) **1.3**
to feel like tener ganas de **I**
fence la cerca **I**

ferocious feroz **II**
fever la fiebre **II**
fiction la ficción **5.1**
field el campo **I**
  field of study
    el campo de estudio **4.1**
fifteen quince **I**
fifteenth birthday
  la quinceañera **3.2**
fifth quinto(a) **I, II**
fifty cincuenta **I**
fight la lucha **3.3**
to fight pelearse **II, 1.3**
to fight against luchar contra **2.1**
figure la figura **5.1**
to fill llenar **II**
filmmaker el (la) cineasta **5.3**
finally por fin **I, II**
finance las finanzas **4.1**
financial expert
  el (la) financiero(a) **4.3**
to find encontrar (ue) **I**
fine arts las bellas artes **II**
fingers los dedos **II**
to finish terminar **I**
fire el fuego **II, 2.3**
firecracker el cohete **3.2**
firefighter el bombero **I, II, 4.2**
firewood la leña **II, 2.3**
firing squad el pelotón de
  fusilamiento
first primero(a) **I, II**
first name el nombre **I**
fish el pescado **I, II**; el pez **I, 2.3**
to fish pescar **II**
fisherman el (la) pescador(a) **II**
fishing industry la industria
  pesquera **4.3**
five cinco **I, II**
five hundred quinientos(as) **I**
flag la bandera **3.3**
flagpole el asta (fem.)
flamenco group el tablao **5.1**
  flamenco song el cante **5.1**
  tragic flamenco song
    el cante jondo **5.1**
  flamenco-style dancing
    el flamenco **5.1**
flash (of lightning) el rayo **II**
flashlight la linterna **II, 2.3**
flavor el sabor **I**
flight el vuelo **II**
flight attendant
  el (la) auxiliar de vuelo **II**

floor el suelo **1, II**; el piso **II**
flour la harina **I, II**
to flow fluir
flower la flor **I**
flu la gripe **II**
to fly volar (ue) **II**
  to fly a single-engine plane
    pilotar una avioneta **1.2**
fog la neblina **II, 2.3**
folk dance el baile folklórico **5.2**
to follow seguir (i) **II**
food el alimento **II**; la comida **I**
foot el pie **I, II**
  on foot a pie **I**
football el fútbol americano **I**
footprint la huella
for por; para **I**
  For what purpose? ¿Para qué?
  for sale a la venta
forecast el pronóstico
foreground el primer plano **5.1**
foreigner el (la) extranjero(a) **II**
forest el bosque **I, 2.2**;
  la selva **II, 2.2**
forestry products
  los productos forestales **4.3**
to forget olvidar **I, II**; olvidársele
  a uno, **6.2**
to forgive each other
  perdonarse **1.3**
fork el tenedor **I**
formal formal **I, II**
formulaic formulista **5.3**
forty cuarenta **I**
four cuatro **I, II**
four hundred cuatrocientos(as) **I**
fourteen catorce **I**
fourth cuarto(a) **I, II**
freckles las pecas **1.1**
free time el tiempo libre **I**
freezer el congelador **I, II**
French francés(esa) **II**
French fries las papas fritas **I**
frequent frecuente **I**
frequently frecuentemente **I, II**
fresco (art) el fresco **5.1**
fresh water el agua dulce **2.3**
Friday viernes **I**
friend el (la) amigo(a) **I**
  to spend time with friends
    pasar un rato con los amigos **I**
friendship la amistad **II**
fright el susto
to frighten asustar

fringe el fleco **1.2**
frog la rana **II**
from de; desde **I**
  from there desde allí **II**
front frente
  in front of delante de **II**; frente
    a **II**
front desk la recepción **II**
fruit la fruta **I**
frying pan la sartén **I**
fuel el combustible **II, 2.2**
full lleno(a) **II**
full time tiempo completo
full-time job
  el trabajo a tiempo completo **4.2**
fun divertido(a) **I**
to fundraise juntar fondos **2.1**
funny cómico(a) **I**
furniture los muebles **I, II**

G-rated (movie)
  apto(a) para toda la familia **6.1**
gallery la galería **II**
game el partido **I**
  interactive game
    el juego interactivo **6.3**
garage el garaje **II**
garbage la basura **2.1**
garden el jardín **I, II**
gardener el (la) jardinero(a) **4.2**
gathering la reunión **II**
generosity la generosidad **3.1**
generous generoso(a) **3.1**
genius el genio
genre el género **5.3**
German alemán(ana) **II**
to gesture señalar
to get conseguir **II**; obtener **II**
  to get ahead superarse **4.1**
  to get along convivir **2.1**
  to get along well/badly llevarse
    bien/mal **II, 1.3**
  to get better recuperarse **II**
  to get dark anochecer,
    oscurecer, atardecer **2.3**
  to get discouraged
    desanimarse **1.3**
  to get encouraged animarse **1.3**
  to get excited entusiasmarse **1.3**
  to get interested animarse **1.3**

INGLÉS-ESPAÑOL

to get into meter en
to get nervous
  ponerse nervioso(a) **1.3**
to get together reunirse II
to get up levantarse I, II
gift el regalo I
girl la chica; la muchacha; la niña I
girlfriend la novia II
to give dar I
  I'll give… to you for…
    Le dejo… en… I
glad
  to be glad that alegrarse de
  que II
glass el vaso I; el vidrio II, **2.2**
  glass of el vaso de I
glasses los anteojos **1.1**
glove el guante I
to go ir I, II
  to be going to… ir a… I
  to go away irse I
  to go back regresar II
  to go deep-sea fishing
    pescar en alta mar **1.2**
  to go down bajar por II
  to go down a river by canoe
    bajar un río en canoa II
  to go for a walk pasear I
  to go hiking hacer alpinismo **1.2**
  to go mountaineering
    hacer montañismo **1.2**
  to go out salir I
  to go shopping ir de compras I
  to go to bed acostarse (ue) I
  to go to the movies ir al cine I
  to go to the supermarket
    ir al supermercado I
  to go unnoticed
    pasar por debajo de la mesa
  to go up subir por II
  to go whitewater rafting
    navegar por rápidos **2.3**
goal el gol I; la meta II
godparents los padrinos **3.1**
gold el oro I
good bueno(a) I
  Good afternoon.
    Buenas tardes. I, II
  Good evening.
    Buenas noches. I, II
  Good morning.
    Buenos días. I, II
  the good thing lo bueno **1.1**

It's good that…
  Es bueno que… II
Good-bye. Adiós.
good-looking guapo(a) I
gossipy chismoso(a) **4.2**
government el gobierno **3.3**
governor el (la) gobernador(a) **3.3**
gown la toga **3.1**
grade la nota
  to get a good grade
    sacar una buena nota I
graduate el (la) graduando(a) **3.1**
to graduate graduarse **3.1**
graduation ceremony
  la ceremonia de graduación **3.1**
grains los cereales **4.3**
gram el gramo I
grandchildren los nietos I
granddaughter la nieta I
grandfather el abuelo I
grandmother la abuela I
grandparents los abuelos I
grandson el nieto
grape la uva II
gray gris I
great grande I, formidable **1.2**
great grandfather el bisabuelo II
great grandmother la bisabuela II
green verde I
to greet saludar
to greet each other saludarse **1.3**
ground floor la planta baja II
group el grupo
  chat group
    el grupo de conversación **6.3**
  news group
    el grupo de noticias **6.3**
to grow crecer II
guarantee la garantía **6.2**
Guatemalan guatemalteco(a) II
guest el (la) huésped(a) II
guitar la guitarra I
  to play the guitar
    tocar la guitarra I
gymnasium el gimnasio I

habanera
  la habanera (Latin music) **5.2**
hair el pelo I; el cabello **1.1**

hair dryer el secador de pelo I, II
hairbrush el cepillo II
hairdo el peinado
hairstylist el (la) peluquero(a) II,
  4.2
half medio(a) I, II
  half past y media I
half-brother el medio hermano I
half-sister la media hermana I
ham el jamón I, II
hamburger la hamburguesa I
hand la mano I, II
handbag la bolsa I
handicraft la artesanía I
to hang–glide
  volar en planeador **1.2**
to happen pasar I
happily felizmente I
happiness la felicidad II
happy alegre; contento(a); feliz I;
  a gusto
  to be happy that
    alegrarse de que II
  Happy New Year!
    ¡Próspero Año Nuevo! **3.2**
hard difícil; duro(a) I
  It's hard for me
    A mí me cuesta mucho
hard drive el disco duro **6.3**
hard-working trabajador(a) I
hardware el hardware **6.3**
harp el arpa (fem.) **5.1**
hat el sombrero I
to hate detestar **1.2**
  to hate each other odiarse **1.3**
to have tener I, II
  to have a cold estar resfriado(a)
    II
  to have a good time
    pasarlo bien **3.2**
  to have a snack merendar (ie) I
  to have breakfast desayunar I
  to have dinner, supper cenar I
  to have in common
    tener en común **1.1**
  to have just… acabar de… I, II
  to have to tener que I
he él I
head la cabeza I, II
headache el dolor de cabeza II
headline el titular II
headphones los audífonos **6.2**
healthy saludable II

to be healthy
mantenerse sano(a) **II**
to hear oír **I**
heart el corazón **I**
heat la calefacción **II**
heating la calefacción **II**
heavy grueso(a) **1.1**; pesado(a) **1.2**
heavy bed el lecho pesado
height la altura **II, 2.2;**
la estatura **4.1**
Hello. Hola. **I**
helmet el casco **I**
Help! ¡Socorro! **II**
to help ayudarse **I, 1.3**
to help each other ayudarse **1.3**
Could you help me order?
¿Me ayuda a pedir? **I**
How can I help you?
¿Cómo puedo ayudarte? **2.1**
hen la gallina **I**
her su, ella **I**
here acá; aquí **I**
hero el héroe **II**
heroine la heroína **II**
hers suyo(a)
to hide esconderse **II, 1.3**
hieroglyphics los jeroglíficos **5.2**
highway la carretera **4.1**
to hike
to go hiking hacer alpinismo **1.2**
hill la colina **II, 2.2**
his su **I**; suyo(a) **II**
history la historia **I**
hockey el hockey **I**
to hold guardar **II**
homeless la gente sin hogar **2.1**
homework la tarea **I**
Honduran hondureño(a) **II**
to honor honrar **3.3**
to hope esperar **I, II**
I hope that ojalá que **II**
to hope that esperar que **II**
hopefully ojalá que **II**
horrible horrible **1.2**
horror el horror **II**
horse el caballo **I**
host(ess) el (la) anfitrión(a) **3.2**
hot caliente **I**; caluroso(a) **II**
to be hot tener calor **I**
It is hot. Hace calor. **I**
hot dog la salchicha **II**
hotel el hotel **I**
house la casa **I**

how cómo **I**
How are you? (familiar)
¿Cómo estás? **I**
How are you? (formal)
¿Cómo está usted? **I**
How awesome! ¡Qué chévere! **I**
How can I help you? ¿Cómo
puedo ayudarte(lo, la)? **2.1**
How do I look?
¿Cómo me veo? **II**
How does it look on you?
¿Cómo te queda? **II**
How is it going? **II** ¿Qué tal? **I**
How long has it been since…?
¿Cuánto tiempo hace que…?
II
How old is…?
¿Cuántos años tiene...? **I**
Pardon, how do I get to…?
Perdona(e), ¿cómo llego
a…? **I**
how much cuánto **I**
How much do I tip?
¿Cuánto le doy de propina? **I**
How much is (are)…?
¿Cuánto cuesta(n)…? **I**
¿A cuánto está(n)…? **I**
hug el abrazo **II**
huge enorme **I**
human being el ser humano **II, 2.1**
human rights los derechos
humanos **2.1**
humanities las humanidades **4.1**
humid húmedo(a) **II, 2.3**
hummingbird el picaflor **2.3**
humpback whale
la ballena jorobada **2.3**
hungry
to be hungry tener hambre **I**
hurricane el huracán **II, 2.3**
to hurry
to be in a hurry tener prisa **I**
to hurt doler (ue) **II**
to get hurt lastimarse **II**
husband el esposo **I**

I

I yo **I**
ice el hielo **I**
on ice sobre hielo **I**

ice cream el helado **I, II**
ice cream store la heladería **II**
identification la identificación **II**
ideology la ideología **3.3**
if si **I**
iguana la iguana **2.3**
immediately inmediatamente **II**
impatient impaciente **II**
important
to be important importar **II**
It's important that…
Es importante que… **II**
to impose imponer **3.1**
impossible
It's impossible that…
Es imposible que…
impression
**make a good (bad) impression
on someone**
caerle bien (mal) a alguien **II**
impressive impresionante **5.3**
improbable
It's improbable that…
Es improbable que…
in en **I**
in a bad mood de mal humor **II**
in a good mood
de buen humor **II**
in back atrás **6.2**
in case en caso de que **3.1**
in front of
delante de **I, II**; frente a **II**
in order (to) para **I**
in spite of pese a
included incluido(a)
Is…included?
¿Está incluido(a)…? **I**
to increase aumentar **4.2**
incredible increíble **II, 2.2**
Independence Day
el Día de la Independencia **3.2**
indigenous, indigenous peoples
los (las) indígenas
industry la industria **4.3**
inexpensive barato(a) **I**
infection la infección **II**
to influence influir **1.1**
informed
to be well informed
estar bien informado(a) **II**
informal informal **I**
information los datos **II, 4.1**
injection la inyección **II**

INGLÉS–ESPAÑOL

injustice la injusticia **3.3**
inner ear el oído **II**
innovative innovador(a) **5.3**
inside (of) dentro (de) **I, II**
to insist insistir (en) **II**
to insist on insistir en que **3.1**
insolent descarado(a) **1.1**
to institute instituir **2.2**
insurance el seguro **II**
   health insurance
      el seguro médico **4.2**
intelligent inteligente **I**
to interest interesar **II**
interested
   to get interested animarse **1.3**
interesting interesante **I**
internal interno(a) **6.3**
international internacional **II**
Internet
   to surf the Internet
      navegar por Internet **1.2**
to interpret interpretar **5.1**
interpreter el (la) intérprete **4.3**
interview la entrevista **I, II**
interviewer
   el (la) entrevistador(a) **II, 4.2**
to introduce presentar
   Let me introduce you
      (familiar/formal) to…
      Te/Le presento a… **I**
invitation la invitación **I, II**
to invite invitar
   I invite you. Te invito. **I**
iron el hierro **4.3**
to iron (the clothes)
   planchar (la ropa) **I**
ironic irónico(a) **5.3**
island la isla **II**
Italian italiano(a) **II**
its su **I**

jacket la chaqueta **I**
jackknife la navaja **II, 2.3**
jade el jade **5.2**
jaguar el jaguar **II, 2.3**
January enero **I**
Japanese japonés(esa) **II**
jeans los jeans **I**
jewelry las joyas **I**

jewelry store la joyería **I**
job el empleo **II, 4.2**
   full-time job
      el trabajo a tiempo completo
      4.2
   part-time job
      el trabajo a tiempo parcial **4.2**
journalism el periodismo **II**
journalist el (la) periodista **I, II**
judge el (la) juez(a) **II, 4.2**
to judge juzgar
juice el jugo **II**; el zumo **I**
July julio **I**
to jump rope saltar la cuerda **II**
June junio **I**
jungle la selva **I, II, 2.2**
just justo(a) **3.3**

to keep guardar **II**
to keep clean mantener limpio(a) **II**
key la llave **I, II**; **(of an**
   instrument) la tecla **6.3**
keyboard el teclado **I, 6.3**
keychain el llavero **1.2**
kilogram el kilo **I**
kind
   That's kind of you.
      Muy amable. **3.2**
king el rey **3.3**
kiosk el quiosco **II**
kiss el beso **II**
kitchen la cocina **I, II**
knee la rodilla **II**
knife el cuchillo **I**
to know conocer **I, II**; saber **I, II**
   to know each other well/not
      very well conocerse
      bien/mal **1.3**
   to know someone
      conocer a alguien **I**
knowledge el conocimiento **4.2**

laboratory el laboratorio **4.3**
to lack faltar **II**
lake el lago **I**
lamp la lámpara **I, II**

land la tierra **I, II, 2.2**
landscape
   el paisaje **I, 5.1**; el terreno
language la lengua **I, II**
laptop computer
   la computadora portátil **6.2**
large grande **I**
last último(a) **I**
   last month el mes pasado **I**
   last name el apellido
   last night anoche **I, II**
   last week la semana pasada **I**
   last year el año pasado **I, II**
late tarde **I**
   late afternoon el atardecer **2.3**
lately recientemente **I**
later luego **I**
   See you later.
      Hasta luego; Nos vemos. **I**
laugh la risa **II**
to laugh reírse **II**
laughter la risa **II**
law el derecho; la ley **3.3**
law office el bufete **4.2**
lawnmower el cortacésped **1.3**
lawyer el (la) abogado(a) **II, 4.2**
lazy perezoso(a) **I**
leader el (la) líder **3.3**
leaf la hoja **II**
to learn aprender **I**
least
   the least
      lo menos **1.1**
   the least desirable
      lo más oscuro **1.1**
leather el cuero **1.2**
   leather goods
      los artículos de cuero **I**
to leave salir; irse **I**
   to leave a message
      dejar un mensaje **I**
   Leave a message after the tone.
      Deje un mensaje después del
      tono. **I**
   to leave behind dejar **I**;
      quedársele (a uno) **6.2**
   to leave the tip
      dejar la propina **II**
left la izquierda
   to the left (of)
      a la izquierda (de) **I**
leftover sobrante
leg la pierna **I, II**

lemonade la limonada I
to lend prestar II
less menos
   less than menos de I
   less… than
      menos… que I, II
lesson la lección I
Let's… Vamos a…
letter la carta I
   to send a letter
      mandar una carta I
lettuce la lechuga I
level of high school curriculum
   el ciclo
liberal liberal 3.3
librarian el (la) bibliotecario(a) 4.3
library la biblioteca I
lie la mentira II
to lie mentir (ie)
to lie down acostarse (ue) II
life la vida I
to lift weights levantar pesas I
light la luz II, 2.3; lumbre
lightbulb la bombilla 1.3
lighthouse el faro 3.3
lightning el relámpago II, 2.3
   lightning flash el rayo 2.3
like como
to like gustar II; caerle bien 1.2
   He/She likes… Le gusta… I
   I like… Me gusta… I
   I would like… Me gustaría… I
   Would you like… ?
      ¿Te gustaría…? I
   You like… Te gusta… I
link el enlace 6.3
lion el león II
to listen (to) escuchar I
liter el litro I
literacy la alfabetización
literature la literatura I
to live vivir I
to live together convivir 2.1
lively animado(a) II
livestock el ganado 4.3
living room la sala I, II
llama la llama I
loan el préstamo II
local local II
located ubicado(a)
logical
   It's logical that…
      Es lógico que… II

long largo(a) I
to look verse 1.1
to look at mirar I
to look for buscar I
loose flojo(a) II; suelto(a) 1.2
to lose perder (ie) I
   to lose something
      perdérsele (a uno) 6.2
love el amor II
to love querer (ie) II
luck la suerte I
   Luck comes to him who least
      expects it. La suerte viene a
         quien menos la aguarda.
lucky
   to be lucky tener suerte I
luggage el equipaje II
lunch el almuerzo I
   to eat lunch almorzar (ue) I
luxurious lujoso(a) I, II
lyrics la letra 5.1

magazine la revista I
magical realism
   el realismo mágico 5.3
mail carrier
   el (la) cartero(a) I, II, 4.2
mailbox el buzón II
majority
   la mayoría II
to make hacer I, II
   to make a mistake
      equivocarse 6.2
   to make a toast brindar 3.1
   to make an effort
      hacer un esfuerzo 2.1
   to make decisions
      tomar decisiones 4.1
   to make the bed hacer la cama I
makeup el maquillaje II
   to put on makeup
      maquillarse I, II
to malfunction
   descomponérsele (a uno) 6.2
mambo (Latin music)
   el mambo 5.2
man el hombre I
manager el (la) gerente I, II, 4.2
to manipulate manipular 6.1

many mucho(a) I
map el mapa I
March marzo I
marionette la marioneta II
market el mercado I
marketing el mercadeo 4.1
to marry
   to get married (to) casarse (con)
      II
marvelous de maravilla II
mask la careta, la máscara
maskmaker el mascarero
Master's degree la maestría 4.1
masterpiece la obra maestra I
masthead el titular II
match el fósforo II, 2.3
to match with
   hacer juego con II, 1.2
mathematics las matemáticas I
to matter importar II
May mayo I
maybe tal vez I
   Maybe another day.
      Tal vez otro día. I
mayor el (la) alcalde(sa) 3.3
meal la comida I
to mean implicar
means el medio
meat la carne I
mechanic el (la) mecánico(a) II, 4.2
medallion la medalla 1.2
medicine la medicina II
medium medio
to meet encontrar (ue) I
melody la melodía 5.1
melon el melón II
memory la memoria 6.3
menu el menú I
merengue (Latin music)
   el merengue 5.2
message el mensaje
   I want to leave a message for…
      Quiero dejar un mensaje
      para… I
   to leave a message
      dejar un mensaje I
   Leave a message after the tone.
      Deje un mensaje después del
      tono. I
Mexican mexicano(a) II
microphone el micrófono 6.3
microprocessor
   el microprocesador 6.3

microwave el microondas **I**
  el horno microondas **II**
midnight la medianoche **I**
milk la leche **I, II**
milk shake el batido **II**
million millón **I**
mine mío(a) **II**
mining la minería **4.3**
miniseries teledrama **6.1**
mirror el espejo **I, II**
Miss (la) señorita **I**
to miss echar de menos
mist la neblina **II, 2.3**
mistake
  to make a mistake
    equivocarse **6.2**
to mix mezclar
modem el módem **6.3**
modern moderno(a) **I, II**
modest modesto(a) **1.1**
moment el momento **I**
One moment. Un momento. **I**
monarchy la monarquía **3.3**
Monday lunes **I**
money el dinero **I**
  money exchange el cambio **I**
monitor el monitor **6.3**
monkey el mono **II**
month el mes **I**
more más **I**
  more or less más o menos **II**
  more… than
    más… que **I, II, 6.3**
  more than más de **I**
morning la mañana **I**
  during the morning por la
    mañana **I**
  Good morning. Buenos días. **I**
  in the morning de la mañana **I**
the most lo más **1.1**
mother la madre **I**
Mother's Day
  el Día de las Madres **3.2**
motorcycle la moto(cicleta) **I**
mountain la montaña **I**
  to mountain climb
    escalar montañas **1.2**
mountaineering el montañismo **II**
  to go mountaineering
    hacer montañismo **1.2**
mouse el ratón **I**
mouth la boca **I, II**
to move mover (ue) **I**; trasladarse

to move the furniture
  mover los muebles **I**
movie la película **I**
  to go to the movies
    ir al cine **I**
moving conmovedor(a)
moving force la fuerza motriz
Mr. (el) señor **I**
Mrs. (la) señora **I**
much mucho(a) **I**
  as much as tanto como **I**
multinational multinacional **4.3**
mural el mural **5.2**
muralist el (la) muralista **5.2**
museum el museo **I**
music la música **I**
  music and video store la tienda
    de música y videos **I**
musical el musical **II**
musical group el conjunto **3.3**
musician el (la) músico(a) **II, 3.2**
must
  one must hay que **I**
mustache el bigote **1.1**
my mi **I**

name el nombre **I**
  His/Her name is…
    Se llama… **I**
  My name is… Me llamo… **I**
  What is his/her name?
    ¿Cómo se llama? **I**
  What is your name?
    ¿Cómo te llamas? **I**
napkin la servilleta **II**
narrow estrecho(a) **I, II**
natural resources
  los recursos naturales **II, 2.2**
nature la naturaleza **II, 2.2**
navy la marina
near (to) cerca (de) **I**
necessary
  It's necessary that…
    Es necesario que… **II**
neck el cuello **II**
necklace el collar **I**
to need necesitar **I**
neighbor el (la) vecino(a)
neighborhood el vecindario **II**

neither tampoco **I**; ni **II**
  neither… nor ni… ni **4.2**
nephew el sobrino **II**
nervous nervioso(a) **I**
  to get nervous
    ponerse nervioso(a) **1.3**
never nunca **I**
nevertheless sin embargo **5.3**
new nuevo(a) **I**
  new release el estreno **II**
  New World el Nuevo Mundo
    5.2
  New Year el Año Nuevo **3.2**
  New Year's Eve la despedida
    del año **3.2**
news las noticias **II**
  news group
    el grupo de noticias **6.3**
  news program el noticiero **II**
newspaper el periódico **I**
newstand el quiosco **II**
next siguiente **II**
  next to
    al lado de **I, 6.2**; junto (a) **II**
Nicaraguan nicaragüense **II**
nice amable **II**; simpático(a) **I**
  It's nice outside.
    Hace buen tiempo. **I**
  Nice to meet you.
    Mucho gusto. **I**
niece la sobrina **II**
night la noche **I**
  at night de la noche **I**
nightfall el anochecer **2.3**
nine nueve **I**
nine hundred novecientos(as) **I**
nineteen diecinueve **I**
ninety noventa **I**
ninth noveno(a) **I, II**
no no **I**
no longer ya no **I**
no one nadie **I**
Nobel Prize el Premio Nóbel **5.3**
noise el ruido **3.2**
none ninguno(a) **I**
noon el mediodía **I**
nor ni **II**
normal normal **I**
normally normalmente **I, II**
north el norte **II**
nose la nariz **I, II**
not no **I**
not even ni **II**

notebook el cuaderno I
nothing nada I
 It's nothing. No hay de qué. 3.2
to notice fijarse en 6.2
nourishment la alimentación II
novel la novela I
novelist el (la) novelista 5.3
November noviembre I
now ahora I
 Right now! ¡Ahora mismo! I
number, numeral la cifra 5.2
 What is your phone number?
  ¿Cuál es tu teléfono? I
nun la monja
nurse el (la) enfermero(a) II
nutritious nutritivo(a) II

obedient obediente II
to obtain obtener II
to occur ocurrir II
 to occur to
  ocurrírsele (a uno) 6.2
ocean el océano II
ocelot el ocelote 2.3
October octubre I
of de
 Of course!
  ¡Claro que sí!; ¡Cómo no! I
to offer ofrecer I, II
office la oficina I
law office el bufete 4.2
doctor's office el consultorio II
often mucho; frecuentemente I;
 a menudo, muchas veces 4.2
oil el aceite I, II
oil painting al óleo 5.1
oil spill el derrame de petróleo 2.2
old antiguo I, II; viejo(a) I
 How old is…?
  ¿Cuántos años tiene…? I
older mayor I
 older than mayor que II
olives las aceitunas I
on en I, sobre II
 on ice sobre hielo I
 on sale en oferta
 on the one hand
  por un lado 1.1
 on the other hand
  por otro lado 1.1

on top (of) encima (de) I, II
once in a while
 de vez en cuando I
one uno I, II
one fifth el quinto 4.3
one half of la mitad de 4.3
one hundred cien I
one third el tercio 4.3
onion la cebolla I, II
on-line en línea 6.3
only sólo I, único(a) 1.2
open abierto(a) I, II
to open abrir I
 to open the way
  abrir el paso 5.2
operator
 el (la) operador(a) I, II, 4.2
opinion
 not to be of the opinion that
  no opinar que
to oppose oponerse a 1.3
opposite frente a II; opuesto 1.1
oppressor el (la) opresor(a) 3.3
or o I
orange anaranjado(a) I
orchestra la orquesta 3.2
to order pedir (i) I, II
 Could you help me order?
  ¿Me ayuda a pedir? I
ordinary ordinario(a) I
organized organizado(a) 1.3
original original 5.3
orphanage el orfelinato
other otro(a) I
ought to deber I, II
our nuestro(a) I
ours nuestro(a) II
outdoors al aire libre I
outside afuera II, 6.2
 outside (of) fuera (de) I, II
oval ovalado(a) 1.1
oven el horno I, II
to overcome vencer 3.1
overflowing rebosante
owl el búho 2.3
owner el (la) dueño(a) II, 4.2
ozone layer
 la capa de ozono II, 2.2

package el paquete I, 4.1

pain el dolor
paint la pintura
to paint pintar I
painter el (la) pintor(a) II
painting el cuadro 5.1, la pintura
 II
 historical painting
  el cuadro histórico 5.1
pair
 a pair of un par de II
palm tree la palma II
palm tree grove el palmar II
Panamanian panameño(a) II
pants los pantalones I
paper el papel I
parade el desfile 3.1
Paraguayan paraguayo(a) II
Pardon, how do I get to…?
 Perdona(e), ¿cómo llego
 a…? I
parents los padres I
park el parque I
parking space
 el estacionamiento II
parrot el loro II, 2.3
to participate participar 2.1
party la fiesta I, II
 big, formal party la gala 3.2
 party in stages
  la fiesta continua 3.2
to pass (by) pasar I
passenger el (la) pasajero(a) II
passport el pasaporte II
password la contraseña 6.3
pasta la pasta I, II
pastel el color claro 1.2
pastry shop la pastelería I
path el sendero II, 2.3;
 el camino 3.1
patient paciente I
patriot el (la) patriota 3.3
patriotic patriótico(a) 3.3
patriotism el patriotismo 3.3
paving stone la baldosa
to pay pagar I
 to pay attention to
  hacerle caso 1.1
peace la paz
peanut butter
 la mantequilla de cacahuate II
pear la pera II
pedestrian el peatón II
pelican el pelícano 2.3

pen la pluma I; (animal) el corral I
pencil el lápiz I
pension la pensión II
people la gente I
pepper la pimienta I, II
percent el por ciento 4.3
percentage el porcentaje 4.3
perception la percepción 6.1
perfect perfecto(a) I
perfume el perfume II
perhaps quizás II
period la época I
period of time la temporada 1.2
permission el permiso II, 2.2
to permit permitir II, 2.1
perspective la perspectiva 5.1
Peruvian peruano(a) II
petroleum el petróleo 4.3
PG-13 rated (movie)
   se recomienda discreción 6.1
pharmacy la farmacia I
phone directory la guía telefónica I
   to phone each other
      telefonearse 1.3
photographer el (la)
   fotógrafo(a) I, II
physical education
   la educación física I
physically challenged
   los (las) minusválidos 2.1
piano el piano I
   to play the piano
      tocar el piano I
to pick up recoger 2.1
picture
   to take pictures
      sacar fotos I
piece el pedazo I, II
pig el cerdo I
pill la pastilla II
pillow la almohada II, 2.3
pilot el piloto II
pin el prendedor 1.2
pink rosado(a) I
pitcher la jarra I
pity
   It's a pity that…
      Es una lástima que… II
place el lugar I
plaid de cuadros I
plain sencillo(a) I
to plan pensar (ie) en + *infinitive* I
planet el planeta II, 2.2

plant la planta I
to plant sembrar (ie) 2.1
plantain el plátano verde II
   fried plantains los tostones II
plastic el plástico 2.2
plate el plato I
play la obra de teatro 5.1
   to play jugar (ue) I, II; practicar
      I; (an instrument) tocar I, II
   to play chess jugar al ajedrez II
   to play sports
      practicar deportes I
   to play the guitar
      tocar la guitarra I
   to play the piano
      tocar el piano I
   to play the role
      hacer el papel 5.3
to plead suplicar 3.1
please por favor I
pleased contento(a) I
   Pleased to meet you.
      Encantado(a). I
   It's a pleasure. Es un placer. I
   The pleasure is mine.
      El gusto es mío. I
plot la trama 5.3
to plug in enchufar 1.3
poem el poema I
poet el (la) poeta 5.3
poetry la poesía I, 5.1
police officer el (la) policía I
polka dots los lunares 1.2
pollutant el contaminante 2.2
to pollute contaminar II
pollution la contaminación II
polyester el poliéster 1.2
ponytail la cola de caballo 1.1
poor pobre II
population la población II, 2.2
pork el puerco I
   pork rinds los chicharrones I
   to eat pork rinds
      comer chicharrones I
porter el (la) maletero(a) II
portrait el retrato II
position el puesto II, 4.2
possible
   It's just not possible for me
      Me es imposible 2.1
   It's possible that…
      Es posible que… II
post office el correo I

pot la olla I
potato la patata I; la papa II
poverty la pobreza II, 2.1
power
   la fuerza motriz; el poder 3.3
to practice practicar I, II
to praise elogiar 5.3
pre-Columbian
   precolombino(a) 5.2
precious precioso(a) 5.2
predictable predecible 5.3
to prefer preferir (ie) I, II
prejudice el prejuicio 2.1
preparatory school la preparatoria
to prepare preparar I
prescription la receta II
to preserve preservar II, 2.1
president el (la) presidente(a) 3.3
press la prensa
pretty bonito(a) I
to prevail prevalecer
price el precio I
pride el orgullo 3.1
principal principal 4.3
print estampado(a) 1.2
printer la impresora I
prize el premio
probable
   It's probable that…
      Es probable que… II
problem el problema I, II
procession
   el desfile 3.1; la procesión 3.3
to produce producir II
production la producción 5.1
profession la profesión I, II
program el programa I, II
   action program
      el programa de acción 6.1
   anti-virus program
      el programa anti-virus 6.3
   horror program
      el programa de horror 6.1
   mystery program
      el programa de misterio 6.1
   program icon
      el icono del programa 6.3
   science fiction program
      el programa de ciencia
      ficción 6.1
to prohibit prohibir 2.2
prose la prosa 5.3
protagonist el (la) protagonista 5.3

to protect proteger **II, 2.2**
  to protect the species
    proteger las especies **II**
proud orgulloso(a) **3.1**
provided that con tal de que **3.1**
public relations
  las relaciones públicas **4.1**
publicity la publicidad **4.1**
pudding el budín **3.2**
Puerto Rican puertorriqueño(a) **II**
punctuality la puntualidad **II, 4.2**
purple morado(a) **I**
purpose el motivo **3.2**
to push empujar
to put poner **I, II**
  to put on (clothes) ponerse **I**
  to put on makeup maquillarse **I**
  to put up with resistir
pyramid la pirámide **5.2**

qualified capacitado(a) **II, 4.1**
quality la calidad **I**
quarter cuarto(a) **I, II**
  quarter past y cuarto **I**
queen la reina **3.3**
quick rápido(a) **I**
quickly rápidamente **I, II**
quiet
  Be quiet! ¡Cállate! **I**
quiz la prueba **I**

R-rated (movie)
  prohibido(a) para menores **6.1**
racket la raqueta **I**
radio el radio **I**
  portable radio
    el radio portátil **6.2**
  radio station la radioemisora
    3.2
  radio-tape player
    el radiocasete **I**
rain la lluvia **I**
to rain llover (ue) **I**

raincoat el impermeable **I**
to raise criar
rare raro(a) **II**
  It's rare that… Es raro que… **II**
rarely rara vez **I**
reach
  within reach
    dentro del alcance **5.3**
to read leer **I**
ready listo(a) **I**
  to get ready (dressed)
    arreglarse **II**
to realize darse cuenta de **II**
Really? ¿De veras? **II**
reason la razón **I**
to receive recibir **I**
recent reciente **I**
recently recientemente **I, II**
reception desk la recepción **II**
receptionist el (la) recepcionista **I**
recital el recital **5.1**
to recommend recomendar (ie) **II**
recommendations
  las recomendaciones **II**
to record grabar **6.1**
to recycle reciclar **II**
recycling el reciclaje **II**
  recycling program
    el programa de reciclaje **2.2**
red rojo(a) **I**
red beans
  las habichuelas coloradas **II**
reddish rojizo(a) **1.1**
redhead pelirrojo(a) **I**
to reduce reducir **II, 2.2**
to reflect reflejar **5.2**
reflection el reflejo
refrigerator
  el frigorífico **I**; el refrigerador **II**
regional típico(a) **3.2**
rehabilitation center
  el centro de rehabilitación **2.1**
relative el (la) pariente **II**
to relax relajarse **II**
reliability la confiabilidad **6.2**
to remember recordar (ue) **I**;
  acordarse (ue) de
remote control el control remoto
  6.1
to rent a video
  alquilar un video **I**
to repair reparar **1.3**
to repeat repetir (i) **II**

repertoire el repertorio **5.1**
report el reportaje **II**
reporter el (la) reportero(a) **II**
to request solicitar **II, 4.1**
to require requerir (ie) **II, 4.2**
requirement el requisito **II, 4.2**
rescue el rescate **II**
to rescue rescatar **II**
reservation la reserva **II**
to resolve resolver (ue) **II, 1.1**
to respect respetar **1.1**
respectively respectivamente
to rest descansar **I**
the rest of the people los demás **II**
restaurant el restaurante **I**
résumé el currículum **II**;
  el currículum vitae **4.1**
to retell contar (ue) **I**
to retire jubilarse **4.2**
to return regresar **II**; volver (ue) **I**
  He/She will return later.
    Regresa más tarde. **I**
  to return (an item)
    devolver (ue) **I, 6.2**
review la crítica **II**
to review revisar **II**
rhythm el ritmo **5.1**; el compás **5.1**
rhythmic heel tapping
  el zapateado **5.1**
rice el arroz **I**
  dessert of rice, cinnamon,
    and coconut milk
    el arroz con dulce **3.2**
  dessert of sweet rice and milk
    el arroz con leche **3.2**
  rice and pigeon peas
    el arroz con gandules **3.2**
rich rico(a) **II**
ridiculous
  It's ridiculous that…
    Es ridículo que… **II**
right el derecho **3.3**
  to the right (of)
    a la derecha (de) **I**
  (human) rights
    los derechos (humanos) **2.1**
  right, correct acertado(a)
  to be right tener razón **I**
ring el anillo **I**; **(of telephone)** el
  timbre
to ring sonar (ue) **3.3**
risk
  to take risks correr riesgos **4.1**

river el río **I**
road el camino **I, 3.1;**
   la carretera **4.1**
roast suckling pig
   el lechón asado **3.2**
robbery el robo **II**
rock la piedra **2.2**
role el papel **II**
   to play the role
      hacer el papel **5.3**
romantic romántico(a) **II**
romanticism el romanticismo **5.3**
roof el techo
room el cuarto **I;** la habitación **II**
rooster el gallo **I**
round redondo(a) **1.1**
to row remar **II**
royal real
rubble los escombros
ruins las ruinas **5.2**
rule la regla **I**
to run correr **I**
to run out of
   acabársele (a uno) **6.2**

sad triste **I**
   It's sad that… Es triste que… **II**
sadness la tristeza **II**
salad la ensalada **I**
salary el sueldo **II, 4.2**
sale la rebaja **II**
sales las ventas **4.1**
sales agent el (la) agente de ventas **4.3**
salesperson el (la) dependiente **II**
salsa la salsa **I**
salt la sal **I, II**
Salvadoran salvadoreño(a) **II**
same mismo(a) **I**
sand la arena **II**
sandals las sandalias **II**
sandwich (sub) la torta **I, II**
satellite dish la antena parabólica **6.1**
satire la sátira **5.3**
Saturday sábado **I**
sausage el chorizo; la salchicha **I, II**
to save ahorrar **II**

savings account
   la cuenta de ahorros **II**
saxophone el saxofón **I**
to say decir **I**
   Don't say that! ¡No digas eso! **I**
   to say goodbye despedirse **I, II**
   to say hello to each other
      saludarse **1.3**
scarcely apenas **II**
scared
   to be scared of asustarse de **II**
scarf la bufanda **I;** el pañuelo **II**
scene la escena **II**
schedule el horario **I**
scholarship la beca
school la escuela **I, 5.1;** el colegio
science las ciencias **I**
   science fiction
      la ciencia ficción **II**
scissors las tijeras **I, II**
to scream gritar **II**
screen la pantalla **I**
script el guión **5.3**
scriptwriter el (la) guionista **5.3**
to scuba-dive bucear **2.3**
sculptor el (la) escultor(a) **II**
sculpture la escultura **II**
sea el mar **I**
seagull la gaviota
search la búsqueda
   search engine
      el servicio de búsqueda **6.3**
to search buscar **I**
season la temporada **1.2**
seasons las estaciones **I**
seat el asiento **II**
second segundo(a) **I, II**
secretary
   el (la) secretario(a) **I, II, 4.2**
security la seguridad **II**
to see ver **I, II**
   May I see…? ¿Me deja ver…? **I**
self-portrait el autorretrato **5.1**
to sell vender **I**
semester el semestre **I**
to send mandar
   to send a letter
      mandar una carta **I**
   to send out echar
sensationalized sensacionalista **6.1**
to separate separar **II, 2.2**
September septiembre **I**
sequin la lentejuela **1.2**

series la serie **II**
serious serio(a) **I**
to serve servir (i) **I, II**
to set the table poner la mesa **I**
setback el tropiezo **3.1**
seven siete **I, II**
seven hundred setecientos(as) **I**
seventeen diecisiete **I**
seventh séptimo(a) **I, II**
seventy setenta **I**
shade la sombra **II**
shadow la sombra **II**
shame la lástima
   What a shame! ¡Qué lástima! **I**
shameless descarado(a) **1.1**
shampoo el champú **I, II**
to share compartir **I, 1.1**
shark el tiburón **2.3**
sharpness la nitidez **6.2**
to shave afeitarse **I**
she ella **I**
sheet la sábana **II**
shell el caracol **II**
shepherd(ess) el (la) pastor(a) **I**
ship el barco **I**
shirt la camisa **I**
shock el susto
shoe el zapato **I**
   high-heeled shoe
      el zapato de tacón **II**
   shoe size el número **II**
   shoe store la zapatería **I**
shopping
   to go shopping ir de compras **I**
   shopping center
      el centro comercial **I**
   shore la orilla, **II**
short (height)
   bajo(a) **I; (length)** corto(a) **I**
shorts los shorts; los pantalones cortos
should deber **I**
shoulder el hombro **II**
shoulder bag el bolso **1.2**
shout el grito
show
   game show
      el programa de concurso **6.1**
   talk show
      el programa de entrevistas **6.1**
to show mostrar (ue) **II**
shower

to take a shower ducharse **I, II**
sick enfermo(a) **I**
   the sick los enfermos **2.1**
sickly enfermizo(a)
sickness la enfermedad **II**
sidewalk la acera **II**
sign el letrero **II**
signature la firma **II, 4.1**
silk la seda **1.2**
silly tonto(a)
silver la plata **I**
silverware los cubiertos **II**
similar to semejante a **1.1**
simple sencillo(a) **I, II**
to sing cantar **I**
   to sing in the chorus
      cantar en el coro **II**
singer el (la) cantante **II;**
   (of flamenco) el (la) cantaor(a)
   5.1
sink (bathroom) el lavabo **II**
sister la hermana **I**
   sister-in-law la cuñada **II**
to sit down sentarse(ie) **II**
site el sitio **6.3**
situation la situación **II**
six seis **I**
six hundred seiscientos(as) **I**
sixteen dieciséis **I**
sixth sexto(a) **I, II**
sixty sesenta **I**
size (clothing) la talla **II; (shoe)** el
   número **II**
el tamaño **6.3**
to skate patinar **I**
skateboard la patineta **I**
to skateboard andar en patineta **I**
skates los patines **I**
to ski esquiar **I**
skin la piel **II**
skirt la falda **I**
skunk el zorrillo **2.3**
sky el cielo **2.2**
slave el (la) esclavo(a) **3.3**
to sleep dormir (ue) **I**
sleeping bag
   el saco de dormir **II, 2.3**
sleepy
   to be sleepy tener sueño **I**
slender esbelto(a) **1.1**
slow lento(a) **I**
slowly lentamente **I, II**
small pequeño(a) **I**

to smell of oler (ue) a
to smile sonreírse (i) **II**
smog el smog **II, 2.2**
snack la merienda **I**
to snack merendar (ie) **I**
snake la serpiente **II, 2.3**
to snorkel nadar con tubo de
   respiración **2.3**
snow la nieve **I**
to snow nevar (ie) **I**
so entonces **I**
So-so. Regular. **I**
so that para que **3.1**
soap el jabón **I**
soap opera la telenovela **II**
soccer el fútbol **I**
   soccer ball el balón **1.1**
sociable sociable **II**
social sciences
   las ciencias sociales **2.1**
social service
   el servicio social **2.1**
social studies
   los estudios sociales **I**
social worker
   el (la) trabajadora social **4.3**
sock el calcetín **I**
sofa el sofá **I, II**
soft drink el refresco **I**
software el software **6.3**
solemn solemne **3.3**
solution la solución **2.1**
some alguno(a) **I**
someone alguien **I**
   to know (be familiar with)
      someone conocer a alguien **I**
something algo **I**
sometimes a veces **I, II, 4.2**
son el hijo **I**
son(s) and daughter(s) los hijos **I**
soon pronto **I**
sorry
   to be sorry that sentir (ie) que **II**
   I'm sorry. Lo siento. **I**
   I'm sorry, but…
      Lo siento mucho, pero… **2.1**
soul el alma (fem.)
sound el sonido **I;** el son **5.1**
to sound sonar (ue) **3.3**
soup la sopa **I**
soup kitchen
   el comedor de beneficencia **2.1**
source la fuente

south el sur **II**
Spaniard el (la) español(a) **II**
Spanish el español **I**
to speak hablar **I, II**
   May I speak with…?
      ¿Puedo hablar con…? **I**
speaker el altoparlante **6.2**
special especial **I**
to specialize especializarse **4.1**
specially especialmente **I**
specialty of the house la
   especialidad de la casa **II**
species las especies **2.2**
speech el discurso **3.1**
to spend gastar **II**
spicy picante **I**
spider monkey el mono araña **2.3**
spoiled mimado(a) **1.1**
to sponsor patrocinar **3.2**
spoon la cuchara **I**
sport el deporte **I**
   to play sports
      practicar deportes **I**
sporting goods store
   la tienda de deportes **I**
spreadsheet la hoja de cálculo **6.3**
spring la primavera **I**
square cuadrado(a) **1.1**
squid los calamares **I**
stadium el estadio **I**
stage floor el tablado **5.1**
staircase las escaleras **II**
stairs las escaleras **II**
stand la parada **II**
to stand (endure) resistir
to stand out destacarse **1.2**
star la estrella **I**
to start comenzar (ie) **II**
   to start the day amanecer **2.3**
station el canal **II**
stationery store la papelería **I**
statistics las estadísticas **4.3**
to stay (at) hospedarse (en) **II**
steak el bistec **I**
to steal robar **II**
stepbrother el hermanastro **II**
stepfather el padrastro **I**
stepmother la madrastra **II**
stepsister la hermanastra **II**
stereo equipment
   el equipo estereofónico **6.2**
stick el palo
still todavía **I**

still life la naturaleza muerta **5.1**
stingy tacaño(a) **II**
stock exchange
    la bolsa de valores **4.3**
stomach el estómago **I, II**
stone la piedra **II**
stop la parada **II**
to stop parar **II**
    to stop doing something
      dejar de
storage battery el acumulador **I**
store la tienda **I**
storm la tormenta **I**
story la historia **II; (of building)** el
    piso **II**
    short story el cuento **5.1**
    short story writer
      el (la) cuentista **5.3**
stove la estufa **I, II**
straight (hair) lacio **II**
straight ahead derecho **I**
strange raro(a) **II;** extraño(a)
strangers los desconocidos
strawberry la fresa **II**
street la calle **I**
stress el estrés **II**
to stretch estirarse **II**
striped con rayas **I**
stripes las rayas **II**
strong fuerte **I**
student el (la) estudiante **I**
to study estudiar **I**
    to study martial arts
      estudiar las artes marciales **II**
stuffed animal
    el muñeco de peluche **II**
style la moda **1.2;** el estilo **5.3**
subject
    la materia **I;** el tema **II**
subscriber el (la) abonado(a)
subway el metro **I**
success el éxito **3.1**
successful
    to be successful tener éxito **II**
suddenly de repente **II**
sugar el azúcar **I**
to suggest sugerir (ie) **II**
suit el traje **II**
suitcase la maleta **II**
summer el verano **I**
sun el sol **I**
to sunbathe tomar el sol **I**
Sunday domingo **I, II**

sunglasses las gafas de sol **I**
sunny soleado(a) **II, 2.3**
    It is sunny. Hace sol.; Hay sol. **I**
sunscreen la loción protectora **II**
suntan lotion el bronceador **I**
supermarket el supermercado **I**
    to go to the supermarket
      ir al supermercado **I**
supper la cena **I**
    to have supper cenar **I**
support el apoyo **3.1**
    to support each other
      apoyarse **1.3**
supported (by) respaldado(a) **6.2**
supporter el (la) proponente **3.3**
sure seguro(a)
    I'm (not) sure.
      (No) Estoy seguro(a). **3.3**
    not to be sure that
      no estar seguro (de) que **3.2**
to surf the Internet
    navegar por Internet **1.2**
surface la superficie
surfing el surfing **I**
surname el apellido **I**
surplus sobrante
surprise la sorpresa **I, II**
to surprise sorprender **I, II**
surrounded rodeado(a)
surrounding area el contorno
to sweat sudar **II**
sweater el suéter **I**
sweats las sudaderas **1.2**
to sweep the floor barrer el suelo
    I; barrer el piso **II**
sweet dulce **I**
    sweet roll el pan dulce **I**
to swell hincharse
to swim nadar **I**
swimming pool la piscina **I**
sword espada
symbolic simbólico(a) **5.3**
symbolism el simbolismo **5.3**

T-shirt la camiseta **I**
table la mesa **I, II**
    to clear the table quitar la mesa **I**
    to set the table poner la mesa **I**
tablecloth el mantel **II**
taco el taco **II**

taco restaurant la taquería **II**
to take tomar **I;** sacar **II;** cursar
    to take a bath bañarse **I**
    to take a shower ducharse **I**
    to take a swimming class
      tomar un curso de natación **II**
    to take a walk, stroll, or ride
      dar una vuelta **II**
    to take advantage of aprovechar
    to take along llevar **I**
    to take apart desarmar **1.3**
    to take care of cuidar de **I, 2.1**
    to take charge of
      encargarse de **4.1**
    to take into account
      tomar en cuenta **6.2**
    to take off one's clothes
      quitarse la ropa **II**
    to take out the trash
      sacar la basura **I**
    to take pictures
      sacar fotos **I**
    to take risks correr riesgos **4.1**
talent el talento **II**
to talk hablar **I, II**
talk show el programa de
    entrevistas
tall alto(a) **I**
tamale-like mixture of plantain,
    yuca and meat el pastel **3.2**
tambourine la pandereta **5.1**
tango (Latin music) el tango **5.2**
tape recorder la grabadora **I, 6.2**
tapestry el tapiz **5.1**
taste el sabor **II**
tasty rico(a); sabroso(a) **I, II**
taxi el taxi **I**
taxi driver el (la) taxista **I, II 4.2**
tea el té **I**
to teach enseñar **I**
teacher el (la) maestro(a) **I**
team el equipo **I**
technician el (la) técnico **II, 4.2**
technique la técnica **5.2**
telecommunications
    las telecomunicaciones **4.3**
telephone el teléfono **I**
    cellular telephone
      el teléfono celular **6.2**
    cordless telephone
      el teléfono inalámbrico **6.2**
    to telephone each other
      telefonearse **1.3**

television
  cable television
    la televisión por cable **6.1**
  portable television
    el televisor portátil **6.2**
  satellite television
    la televisión por satélite **6.1**
  television guide la teleguía **6.1**
  television mini-series
    el teledrama **6.1**
  television program
    el espacio de la televisión
  television series la teleserie **6.1**
  television set el televisor **I**
  to watch television
    ver la televisión **I**
to tell decir (i) **I, II**; contar (ue) **I**
  Don't tell me! ¡No me digas! **II**
  to tell each other gossip
    contarse (ue) chismes **1.3**
  to tell each other secrets
    contarse (ue) secretos **1.3**
  Tell him or her to call me.
    Dile/Dígale que me llame. **I**
  to tell jokes
    contar (ue) chistes **II**
temperature la temperatura **I**
temple el templo **5.2**
ten diez **I**
tennis el tenis **I**
tent la tienda de campaña **II, 2.3**
tenth décimo(a) **I, II**
terrain el terreno
  altitude of terrain
    la altura del terrano
terrible terrible **I**
test el examen **I**
textiles los textiles **4.3**
to thank agradecer **3.1**
  Many thanks. Mil gracias. **3.1**
  Thank you. Gracias. **I**
Thanksgiving el Día de Acción, de Gracias **3.2**
that aquello, eso **I, 5.1**
that ese(a) **I, 5.1**
that (over there)
  aquel(la); aquello **I, 5.1**
that one ése(a) **I, 5.1**
that one (over there) aquél(la) **I, 5.1**
theater el teatro **I**
theatrical production
  la obra de teatro **II**
their su **I**
theirs suyo(a) **II**

theme el tema **II**
then entonces **I**
there allá/allí **I**
there is/are hay **I**
there was/were había **II**; hubo **II**
they ellos(as) **I**
thief el ladrón (la ladrona) **II**
thin delgado(a) **I**
thing la cosa **I**
to think pensar (ie) **I**; creer **I**
  Do you think so? ¿Tú crees? **II**
  I don't think that…
    No creo que… **2.3**
  I think so. / I don't think so.
    Creo que sí/no. **I**
third tercero(a) **I, II**; tercio **4.3**
thirsty
  to be thirsty tener sed **I**
thirteen trece **I**
thirty treinta **I**
this este(a); esto **I, 5.1**
this one éste(a) **I, 5.1**
thousand mil **I**
threatening amenazador(a) **5.3**
three tres **I**
three hundred trescientos(as) **I**
throat la garganta **II**
throughout a lo largo de
to throw out, away echar **II, 2.2**
thunder el trueno **II, 2.3**
thunderbolt el rayo **II, 2.3**
Thursday jueves **I, II**
ticket el boleto **II**
tight apretado(a) **II**
tile la baldosa
time el tiempo **I**
  (At) What time is…?
    ¿A qué hora es…? **I**
  free time el tiempo libre **I**
  on time a tiempo **II**
  to spend time with friends
    pasar un rato con los amigos **I**
  What time is it? ¿Qué hora es? **I**
tip la propina **I**
  How much do I tip?
    ¿Cuánto le doy de propina? **I**
  to leave the tip
    dejar la propina **I**
tired cansado(a) **I**
  to get tired cansarse de **II**
title el título **5.3**
to a
  to the left (of)
    a la izquierda (de) **I**

  to the right (of)
    a la derecha (de) **I**
toast el brindis **3.1**
  to make a toast brindar **3.1**
today hoy **I, II**
  Today is… Hoy es… **I**
  What day is today?
    ¿Qué día es hoy? **I, II**
together juntos **I**
  to get together reunirse **II**
tolling of the bell
  la campanada **3.2**
tomato el tomate **I**
tomorrow mañana **I**
  See you tomorrow.
    Hasta mañana. **I**
  Tomorrow is… Mañana es… **I**
too también **I**
too much demasiado(a) **I, II**
tooth el diente **I, II**
toothbrush
  el cepillo de dientes **I, II**
toothpaste la pasta de dientes **I, II**
toucan el tucán **II, 2.3**
to touch tocar
tough duro(a) **I**
tourism el turismo **II**
toward hacia **II**
towel la toalla **I**
town el pueblo **I**
town square la plaza **I**
toy el juguete **I, II**
toy store la juguetería **II**
tradition la tradición **5.2**
traditional tradicional **I, II**
traffic el tráfico **I**
traffic light/signal el semáforo **II**
trail el sendero **II**
train el tren **I**
to train entrenarse **II**
training la capacitación **II**, la formación **4.1**; el entrenamiento **4.2**
to translate traducir **II**
translator el (la) traductor(a) **4.3**
trash la basura **I**
trash can el basurero **II, 1.3**
to travel viajar **I**
travel agent
  el (la) agente de viajes **II**
traveler's checks
  los cheques de viajero **II**
to treat tratar **II**
  I'll treat you. Te invito. **I**

tree el árbol **I, 2.1**
trendy thing to do la onda
triangular triangular **1.1**
trick el engaño
trillion billón **4.3**
trip el viaje **I**
trouble
    The trouble is that…
        Lo malo es que… **II**
trumpet la trompeta **5.1**
truth la verdad **I**
    It's not true that…
        No es verdad que… **II**
    It's true. Es verdad. I
to try to tratar de
Tuesday martes **I**
tuna el atún **II**
turkey el pavo **3.2**
to turn doblar **I;** girar **II**
    to turn off desconectar **1.3**
    to turn off the light
        apagar la luz **I**
    to turn on encender (ie) **1.3**
turtle la tortuga **I, 2.3**
twelve doce **I**
twenty-one veintiuno **I**
twenty veinte **I**
twins los (las) gemelos(as) **II**
two dos **I**
two hundred doscientos(as) **I**
typical típico(a) **3.2**
typically típicamente **II**

ugly feo(a) **I**
umbrella el paraguas **I**
    beach umbrella
        la sombrilla de playa **II**
uncertainty unquietud
uncle el tío **I**
uncle(s) and aunt(s) los tíos **I**
uncomfortable incómodo(a) **1.2**
under(neath) debajo (de) **I, II**
to understand
    comprender; entender (ie) **I**
understanding comprensivo(a) **1.1**
unequalled inigualable **6.2**
unforgettable inolvidable **3.2**
unfortunately
    desafortunadamente **II**

unique único(a) **1.2**
to unite unir
university la universidad **II**
university degree
    la licenciatura **4.1**
unless a menos que **3.1**
unoriginal derivado(a) **5.3**
unpleasant desagradable **1.1**
to unplug desenchufar **1.3**
until hasta (que) **I, II, 2.3**
up arriba **I, II**
URL el Localizador Unificador
    de Recursos (LUR) **6.3**
Uruguayan uruguayo(a) **II**
to use usar **I, II**
    to be used as servir (i) de
useful útil **II**
useless inútil **II, 2.2**
user el (la) usuario(a) **6.3**

to vacuum pasar la aspiradora **I, II**
vacuum cleaner la aspiradora **I**
vain vanidoso(a) **1.1**
Valentine's Day
    el día de la Amistad **3.2**
valley el valle **II, 2.2**
valuable precioso(a) **5.2**
to value valorar **2.1**
VCR la videograbadora **I**
vegetable la verdura **I, II**
vegetarian vegetariano(a) **I**
Venezuelan venezolano(a) **II**
very muy **I**
vest el chaleco **II**
veterinarian
    el (la) veterinario(a) **II, 4.2**
victory la victoria **3.3**
video el video **I**
    video game el videojuego **I**
    to rent a video
        alquilar un video **I**
    videocamera la videocámara **6.2**
    videocassette recorder
        la videocasetera **6.1**
viewer el (la) televidente **II**
village el pueblo **I**
violent violento(a) **II**
violin el violín **5.1**
to visit visitar **I**

voice mail el telemensaje **6.2**
volleyball el voleibol **I**
volunteer el (la) voluntario(a) **II**
to volunteer
    trabajar de voluntario(a) **2.1**
to vote votar **2.1**

to wait for esperar **I**
waiter el mesero **I**
waitress la mesera **I**
to wake up despertarse (ie) **I**
to walk andar **II**
    to walk the dog
        caminar con el perro **I**
wall la pared **I, II**
wallet la cartera **I,** la billetera **1.2**
to want querer (ie) **I, II, 3.1**
    Do you want to drink…?
        ¿Quieres beber…? **I**
    Do you want to eat…?
        ¿Quieres comer…? **I**
    I want to drink…
        Quiero beber… **I**
    I want to eat…
        Quiero comer… **I**
    I want to leave a message for…
        Quiero dejar un mensaje
        para… **I**
war la guerra
wardrobe el vestuario **1.2**
warm caliente **I**
to wash lavar **I**
    to wash one's hair
        lavarse la cabeza **I**
    to wash oneself lavarse **I, II**
    to wash the dishes
        lavar los platos **I, II**
waste el desperdicio **2.2**
wastebasket el basurero **1.3**
watch el reloj **I**
to watch mirar **I**
    to watch television
        ver la televisión **I**
water el agua (fem.) **I**
to water regar (ie) **1.3**
waterfall la catarata
to water-ski esquiar en el agua **1.2**
wave la ola **I, II;** la onda
wavy ondulado(a) **1.1**

way el paso **5.2**
   to open the way abrir el paso
we nosotros(as) **I**
to wear llevar **I**
   What is he/she wearing?
      ¿Qué lleva? **I**
weather el tiempo **I**
   What is the weather like?
      ¿Qué tiempo hace? **I**
weaving el tejido **5.2**
Web page la página-web **6.3**
wedding la boda **II**
Wednesday miércoles **I, II**
to weed desyerbar **1.3**
weeds las malas hierbas **1.3**
week la semana **I**
weekend el fin de semana
weights
   to lift weights levantar pesas **I**
welcome bienvenido(a) **I**
   You're welcome. De nada. **I**
well bien; pues **I**
well-being el bienestar **II**
west el oeste **II**
wet mojado(a) **II**, húmedo(a) **2.3**
what cuál(es); qué **I**
   What (fun)! ¡Qué (divertido)! **I**
   What a mess! ¡Qué lío! **II, 2.2**
   What a shame! ¡Qué lástima! **I**
   What day is today?
      ¿Qué día es hoy? **I**
   What do you recommend?
      ¿Qué me recomienda? **II**
   What is he/she like?
      ¿Cómo es? **I**
   What is your phone number?
      ¿Cuál es tu teléfono? **I**
   What would you like?
      ¿Qué desea(n)? **II**
wheat el trigo **4.3**
wheat flour la harina de trigo
when cuando; cuándo **I, 2.3**
   when I/he/she was young
      cuando era niño(a) **II**
whenever cuando **I**
where dónde; adónde **I**
   Could you tell me where… is?
      ¿Puedes (Puede usted)
      decirme dónde queda…? **I**
   Where are you from?
      ¿De dónde eres? **I**
   Where is he/she from?
      ¿De dónde es?

Where will it take place?
   ¿Dónde tiene lugar?
which (ones) cuál(es) **I**
while mientras **II**
   quite a while un buen rato
white blanco(a) **I**
who quién(es) **I**
   Who are they? ¿Quiénes son? **I**
   Who is it? ¿Quién es? **I**
   Whose is…? ¿De quién es…? **I**
why por qué **I**
   That's why. Con razón. **I**
   Why not? ¿Por qué no? **2.1**
wicker rocking chair
   el columpio de mimbre
wide ancho(a) **I, II**
wife la esposa **I**
wild salvaje **II, 2.3**
   wild animal life
      la fauna silvestre **2.2**
   wild boar el jabalí
   wild plant la planta silvestre **II**
   wild plant life
      la flora silvestre **2.2**
   wildlife refuge el refugio de
      vida silvestre **2.3**
willing
   to be willing to
      estar dispuesto(a) a **4.1**
to win ganar **I**
wind el viento **I**
window
   la ventana **I, II**; la ventanilla **II**
to windsurf
   navegar en tabla de vela **1.2**
windy
   It is windy.
      Hace viento; Hay viento. **I**
wing el ala (fem.)
winner el (la) ganador(a) **I, II**
winter el invierno **I**
with con **I**
   with me conmigo **I**
   with you contigo **I**
without sin **I**
wolf el lobo **II**
woman la mujer **I**
wonderful genial **1.2**
wonderfully a las mil maravillas
wool la lana **I, 1.2**
work of art la obra **II**
to work trabajar **I**; funcionar **II, 6.2**
worked labrado(a) **5.2**

worker el (la) obrero(a) **II**
workshop el taller **I**
world el mundo **I**
World Wide Web
   la red mundial **6.3**
worried preocupado(a) **I**
   to be worried about
      preocuparse por **II**
to worry preocuparse **II**
   Don't worry!
      ¡No te preocupes! **I**
worse peor **I**
   worse than peor que **II, 6.3**
the worst lo peor **1.1**
worthwhile
   to be worthwhile
      valer la pena **3.1**
wrist la muñeca **II**
to write escribir **I**
writer el (la) escritor(a) **I, II**
   short story writer el (la)
   cuentista

x-ray la radiografía **II**

year el año **I**
   He/She is… years old.
      Tiene… años. **I**
   school year el año escolar **II**
yellow amarillo(a) **I**
yes sí **I**
   Yes, gladly.
      Sí, con mucho gusto. **2.1**
   Yes, I would love to.
      Sí, me encantaría. **I**
yesterday ayer **I, II**
yet todavía **I**
yogurt el yogur **I, II**
you tú **(familiar singular)**,
   usted **(formal singular)**,
   ustedes **(plural)**,
   vosotros(as) **(familiar plural) I**
young joven **I**
young people los jóvenes **2.1**

younger menor **I**
   younger than menor que **II**
your su **(formal)**, tu **(familiar)**,
   vuestro(a) **(plural familiar) I**
yours tuyo **(familiar)**, suyo(a)
   (formal), vuestro(a) **(plural**
   familiar) II

zero cero **I, II**

Índice

Créditos

Acknowledgments

91 Excerpt from *La casa en Mango Street* by Sandra Cisneros. Copyright © 1984 by Sandra Cisneros. Published by Vintage Español, a division of Random House, Inc. Translation copyright © 1994 by Elena Poniatowska. Reprinted by permission of Susan Bergholz Literary Services, New York. All rights reserved. **94–95** Excerpts and adapted material from "El Legendario Rey del Mambo" by Mark Holston, from *Américas* magazine, volume 42, no. 6, 1990-91. Courtesy of *Américas* magazine, a bimonthly magazine published in English and Spanish by the General Secretariat of the Organization of American States. **95** Cover of *The Best of Tito Puente, el Rey del Timbal* CD, by Tito Puente. Copyright © 1997. Reprinted by courtesy of RCA, Beverly Hills, U.S.A. **167** Excerpts from "Baby H.P." by Juan José Arreola, from *Confabulario*. Copyright © 1952 by Fondo de Cultura Económica. Reprinted by permission of Fondo de Cultura Económica. **176** Cover of *Live in New York* CD, by Los Muñequitos de Matanzas. Copyright © 1992. Reprinted by courtesy of QBADISC, New York, U.S.A. **197** "Ébano real" by Nicolás Guillén, from *Antología Mayor*. Copyright © 1972. Reprinted by permission of Editorial Letras Cubanas, Havana, Cuba. **207** Cover of *Gilberto Santa Rosa... de corazón* CD, by Gilberto Santa Rosa. Copyright © 1997. Reprinted by courtesy of Sony Discos, Inc, Miami, U.S.A. **211** Cover of *Hecho en Puerto Rico* CD, by Willie Colón. Copyright © 1993. Reprinted by courtesy of Sony Discos, Inc, Miami, U.S.A. **300** Cover for *Américas*. Copyright © 1998. Reprinted by courtesy of OAS, Washington, U.S.A. **313** Material for statistics on Paraguay from *Almanaque Mundial 1998*. Used with the permission of Andrés Jorge González Ortega, Editorial Director of *Almanaque Mundial*. **325** Cover of *Chant* CD, by The Benedictine Monks of Santo Domingo de Silos. Copyright © 1994. Reprinted by courtesy of EMI Odeon, Madrid, Spain. **329** *Flamenco*. Copyright © Teatro de Madrid, Spain. **332** Map of Museo del Prado. Reprinted by courtesy of Museo del Prado, Madrid, Spain. **342** *Pajarico.* Copyright © P.C. Filmart, Madrid, Spain. *Mensaka.* Copyright © Tornasol Films, Madrid, Spain. Reprinted by courtesy of Filmart and Tornasol Films. **355** *Arqueología Mexicana*. Copyright © 1998. Reprinted by courtesy of Editorial Raíces, Mexico City, Mexico. **363** Excerpt from *Guía Oficial, Templo Mayor*. Copyright © 1996. Reprinted by courtesy of INAH-JGH Editores, Mexico City. **373** *Libros de Madrid*. Copyright © Ediciones La Librería, Madrid, Spain. **384** *La Nación*. Copyright © 1998. Reprinted by courtesy of La Nación, Santiago, Chile. **389** Excerpt from *La casa de Bernarda Alba* by Federico García Lorca. Copyright © Herederos de Federico García Lorca. Reprinted by permission of Mercedes Casanovas Agencia Literaria, Barcelona. **403** Cover of *TV y Novelas* magazine. Copyright © 1998. Reprinted by courtesy of Editorial América, S.A., Virginia Gardens, U.S.A. **407** *El Comercio*. Copyright © 1996. Reprinted by permission of C.A. *El Comercio*, Quito, Ecuador. **419** Excerpts from "Amor mío: Brillo afuera, oscuridad en casa..." by Friné Sánchez Brandt, from *Venezuela Farándula* No. 1039. Copyright © Revista Ronda C.A. **425** *La Nación*. Copyright © 1998. Reprinted by courtesy of La Nación, Santiago, Chile. **447** *Monkey On Line*. Copyright © 1998. Reprinted by permission of Monkey On Line, Quito, Ecuador. **461** *Virus informático, Diccionario de Microinformática, Disco Duro*. Copyright © 1998. Reprinted by courtesy of Hobby Post, Madrid, Spain. **464** *Tiempos Digital*. Copyright © 1998. Reprinted by permission of *Los Tiempos Digital*, Cochabamba, Bolivia. **465** *Bolivia Net*. Copyright © 1998. Reprinted by permission of Bolivia Net, Bolivia.

Photography

1 *top* Jean-Leo Dugast/ Panos Pictures; *bottom right* Tony Morrison/South American Pictures; *center right* Getty Images/ Picturequest; *center left* Robert Frerck/ Odyssey/Chicago; **3** *top left* Sophie Dauwe / Robert Fried Photography; *top right, top center* Richard B. Levine; *center* Courtesy of Kiwanis Club of Little Havana, Miami; *bottom left* Randy Taylor/ Getty Images; *bottom right* RMIP/ Richard Haynes; **7** *top left* Tropix/ C. Moulds; *top right* Corbis Sygma; *bottom right* Barrett & MacKay Photo; *bottom left* Gerald & Buff Corsi; **11** top left, top right Suzanne Murphy-Larronde; bottom left Jan Buchovsky / Dave Houser; bottom right David Simson / Stock Boston; **15** *top left* DDB Stock Photo; *top right* Gordon Gahanngs / National Geographic Image Collection; *center* George Mobley/ National Geographic Image Collection; *bottom left* Robert Frerck / Odyssey /Chicago; *bottom right* Image State; *bottom center* Ned Gillette / Image State; **16** Bob Daemmrich / Stock Boston/ Picturequest; **19** top left Walter Bibikow / Viesti Associates, Inc.; *top right* Joe Viesti/ Viesti Associates, Inc.; *bottom right* Paul A. Hein / Unicorn Stock Photo; *bottom left* Eric Vandeville / Getty Images; **23** *top right* R. E. Barber / Visuals Unlimited; *top left* David R. Frazier Photolibrary / Photo Researchers, Inc.; *center right* David Matherly/ Visuals Unlimited; *bottom left* Wolfgang Kaehler; *bottom right* Tony Morrison/ South American Pictures; **26** *top* David Young-Wolff/PhotoEdit; *bottom* Joe Viesti/ Viesti Associates, Inc.; **28** *right* Courtesy of La Prensa; **29** *top left* Kevork Djansezian/AP Wide World Photos, *top right* Ken O'Donoghue, *bottom right* Courtesy of Repertorio Español, NYC, *bottom left* Courtesy of NASA; **32-33** Tom Stack & Associates; **30** *top* Spencer Grant/PhotoEdit, *center* Frank Siteman/Stock Boston, *bottom* Nova Online/Getty Images **31** *top right* Bob Daemmrich/The Image Works **33** *inset* Courtesy of Miami Mensual; **34-35** RMIP/Richard Haynes; **37** School Division, Houghton Mifflin Co.; **38** RMIP/Richard Haynes; **43** Bob Daemmrich/Stock Boston; **51** School Division, Houghton Mifflin Co.; **52** Bob Daemmrich/The Image Works; **54-55** Bob Daemmrich Photography; **56-57** RMIP/Richard Haynes; **58** left School Division, Houghton Mifflin Co., *right* Robert Burke/Getty Images; **59** *top left* H. Martin, *top right* Claude Poulet/Getty Images; *bottom right* Telegraph Colour Library/Getty Images, *center* Paul Howell/Getty Images; **60** RMIP/Richard Haynes; **65** Frank Siteman/Stock Boston; **67** *bottom* NOVA Online/Getty Images; **68** Myrleen Ferguson/PhotoEdit; **70** *left* Gerardo Somoza/Corbis Outline, **70** *right*, **71** *top left* Courtesy of Oscar de la Renta; **71** *center* Bill Davila/Retna Ltd., *bottom right* Ted Mehieu/Corbis; **76-77** RMIP/Richard Haynes; **78-79** *background* Ken O'Donoghue; **80-81** RMIP/Richard Haynes; **87** Nancy Sheehan; **88** Elsa Hasch/Allsport; **89** W.B. Spunburg/PhotoEdit/PictureQuest; **94** *top* Dan Dion/Getty Images, *bottom* Spencer Grant/PhotoEdit; **95** *top* PPI Entertainment Group; **102** *right* "Family Portrait," María Izquierdo. Museo de Arte Moderno, Mexico City/Schalkwijk/Art Resource, NY; **103** *top left* Bill Cardoni/Getty Images, *top center* Suzanne Murphy-Larronde/Getty Images, *top right* Mes Beveridge/Visuals Unlimited, *center* J. Becker, *bottom right* Ken O'Donoghue, *bottom left* Gianni Vechiatto; **104** *top right* Gianni Vecchiatto, *center left* RMIP Richard haynes, *bottom left* Alyx Kellington/DDB Stock Photo, *bottom right* Unicorn Stock Photos **105** *center left* María Izquierdo, Family Portrait. Museo de Arte Moderno, Mexico City, Schalkwijk/Art Resource, New York, *center* Jay Ireland & Georgienne E. Bradley, *center right* Gary Payne/Getty Images, *bottom* Patricia A. Eynon **106-107** Daniel Aguilar/Hulton Archive/Getty Images; **108** RMIP/Richard Haynes; **109** *left* Michael Newman/PhotoEdit, *right* PhotoEdit; **110-111** *balloons* PhotoDisc, *all others* RMIP/Richard Haynes; **115** PhotoEdit; **118** Jeff Greenberg/Photo Researchers; **120** Bob Daemmrich; **122** *top inset* Sipa Press, **122-123** *background* RMIP/Richard Haynes; **123** *top inset* Gary Payne/Getty Images; **125** Unicorn Stock Photos; **126** *bottom right* Bob Daemmrich/Stock Boston; **127** *top left* Skjold/The Image Works, *top right* Patricia A. Eynon; **128-129** Ulrike Welsch; **130** *top* Courtesy of NASA, *center* Steve Winter/Black Star/PictureQuest; **131** *top left* Robert Frerck/Woodfin Camp, *center left* Rob Crandall/Stock Boston/PictureQuest, *bottom left* School Division, Houghton Mifflin Co., *top right* Visuals Unlimited, *center right & bottom right* Jay Ireland & Georgienne E. Bradley/Earth Images; **140** School Division, Houghton Mifflin Co.; **141** Patricia A. Eynon; **144** Patricia Ramsy/eStock; **145** pen School Division, Houghton Mifflin Co., *background* Alyx Kellington/DDB Stock Photo, *bottom left inset* Michelle Bridwell/PhotoEdit; **147** Chris R. Sharp/DDB Stock Photo; **152** *toucan* Gail Shumway/Getty Images, *butterfly* Leroy Simon/Visuals Unlimited, *anteater* Claus Meyer/Black Star/PictureQuest, *skunk* Renee Lynn, *falcon* John S. Dunning/Animals Animals, *deer* Robert A. Luback/Animals Animals, *monkey* Richard K. LaVal/Animals Animals, *others* Jay Ireland & Georgienne E. Bradley/Earth Images; **153** *snorklers & tropical fish* Jay Ireland & Georgienne E. Bradley/Earth Images, *whale* W. Ober/Visuals Unlimited, *jaguar* Mes Beveridge/Visuals Unlimited, *snake* Merli/Visuals Unlimited, *pelican* Lynn M. Stone/Animals Animals, *shark* Stuart Westmorland/Getty Images; **155** top School Division, Houghton Mifflin Co.; **157** *monkey* Richard K. LaVal, *whale* W. Ober/Visuals Unlimited, *hummingbird & tortoise* Jay Ireland & Georgienne E. Bradley/Earth Images, *skunk* Renee Lynn, *snake* Jim Merli/Visuals Unlimited, *pelican* Lynn M. Stone/Animals Animals; **158** Kim Exterberg; **165** *left* Fian Arroyo, *right* La Finca de Mariposa, Frente Club Campestre Los Reyes, Costa Rica; **168** *top right* PictureQuest, *bottom left* Richard K. LaVal, *bottom right* Gail Shumway/Getty Images; **168-169** *background* Jay Ireland & Georgienne E. Bradley; **169** *bottom left* Leroy Simon/Visuals Unlimited, *bottom right* Roy Morsch/Corbis; **171** Bob Firth/eStock; **172** Patricia A. Eynon; **177** *top left* Richardo Figueroa/AP Wide World Photos, *top right* School Division, Houghton Mifflin Co., *center* Gerardo Somoza/Corbis Outline, *bottom right* Robert Frerck/Odyssey Productions, *bottom left* Tom & Therisa Stack; **178** *top right* Robert Frerck/Odyssey Productions, *center left* Joe Viesti/The Viesti Collection, *center* School Division, Houghton Mifflin Co., *center right & bottom* Tom & Therisa Stack **179** *top left* Andre Jenny/Stock South/Atlanta/PictureQuest, *center left* Suzanne Murphy-Larronde, *center* Raffi Trelles, *center right* Tom Bean/DRK Photo **180-181** Tom & Therisa Stack; **181** *inset* School Division, Houghton Mifflin Co.; **182** *bottom left* School Division, Houghton Mifflin Co., *others* Tom & Therisa Stack; **182-183** *background* School Division, Hougton Mifflin Co.; **183** *top left & center left* Tom & Therisa Stack, *top right & bottom left* School Division, Houghton Mifflin

Lockwood/DRK Photo; **365** *top left* Peter Purchia/Viesti Associates, Inc., *center* Eastfoto, *top right* Joe Viesti/Viest Associates, Inc., *bottom left* Barry Barker/Odyssey Productions; **366** Marc Liberman/the Salk Institute; **367** *top* Courtesy of Ricardo Legorreta, *bottom* Courtesy of Camino Real, Cancun; **373-373** Erica Lananan/Black Star/PictureQuest; **374, 376** Michael Newman/PhotoEdit/PictureQuest; **377** School Division, Houghton Mifflin Co., **380** *center* Photofest **384** credit unavailable; **386** Emece Editores S.A. Argentina; **390** Photofest; **391** *top left* Photofest, *top center* Robin Holland/Corbis Outline, *center left* Jane Brown/Camera Press/Retna, Ltd. USA, *center right* Carrion/Corbis Sygma; **394** *bottom right* The Granger Collection, New York; **398** *bottom* PhotoDisc, Inc.; **399** *top left* Courtesy, Maloka Park, Columbia; *center* Bettman-Corbis; *bottom left* Robert Frerck/Odyssey Productions; *bottom right* Courtesy, Colección Museo Armando Reveron; **400** *top right* Courtesy of Maloka Park, Colombia, *center left* Myrleen Ferguson/PhotoEdit **401** *top right* Eduardo Gil/Black Star **402-403** Eduardo Gil/Black Star; **404** *top left* Wolfgang Kaehler; *center* Owen Franken/Stock Boston; *bottom* Getty Images; *top right* Bud Gray/Motion Picture & Television Archive; **405** *top left* Photofest; *top center* Getty Images; *top right* ©1993 Warner Bros. Inc/Photofest; *center left* Guido A. Rossi/Getty Images; *center* ©1994 Warner Bros. Animation/Motion Picture & Television Archive; *center right* Nubar Alexanian/Stock Boston; *bottom* David Young-Wolff/PhotoEdit; **406** *From left to right:* Guido A. Rossi/Getty Images; Getty Images; Wolfgang Kaehler; Photofest; **407** School Division, Houghton Mifflin Company; **409** Al Bello/Allsport/Getty Images; **416** José Peláez Photography; **417** Randy Green/Getty Images; **418** Courtesy Venevisión; **422** *left* Merleen Ferguson/PhotoEdit; **424-425** RMIP/Richard Haynes; **426** *top left, center left* School Division, Houghton Mifflin Company; *bottom left, top right, center right, bottom right* PhotoDisc, Inc.; **427** *top left, bottom left to bottom right* PhotoDisc, Inc.; *top center, top right, center left to center right* School Division, Houghton Mifflin Company; **428** *Clockwise from top left:* School Division, Houghton Mifflin Company; PhotoDisc, Inc.; Spencer Jones/Getty Images; School Division, Houghton Mifflin Company; **429** School Division, Houghton Mifflin Company; **430** *top left, top center left, center right, bottom right* PhotoDisc, Inc.; *top right, bottom left* School Division, Houghton Mifflin Company; **419** School Division, Houghton Mifflin Company; **435** Jeff Greenberg/Index Stock; **439** PhotoDisc, Inc.; **440-441** *background* Telegraphy Color Library/Getty Images; **440** *bottom left* J. Carini/The Image Works; **429** *bottom left* Mark E. Gibson/Visuals Unlimited; *top center* Degas-Parra/Ask Images/The Viesti Collection, Inc.; **444** All PhotoDisc, Inc. except *top right*; **447** Courtesy, Monkey Online; **448** Tony Anderson/Getty Images; **449** Mark M. Lawrence/Corbis; **451** School Division, Houghton Mifflin Company; **453** Jeff Greenberg/Index Stock; **455** *Answering machine, white telephone, portable personal stereo* School Division, Houghton Mifflin Company; all others PhotoDisc, Inc. ; **462** Francoise de Mulder/Corbis; **463** UPI/Bettman-Corbis; **464-465** *background* Vera Lentz/Black Star/PictureQuest; **464** *bottom right* Editorial Canas S.A. Bolivia; **465** *left* HighINFO, creaters of Bolivianet; **466** School Division, Houghton Mifflin Company; **468** *top left, top center* PhotoDisc, Inc.; *top right* Mark M. Lawrence/Corbis; *bottom right* Jeff Greenberg/Index Stock; **470** David Young-Wolff/PhotoEdit.

All other photography by Martha Granger/EDGE Productions

Illustration Credits

5, 13, 17 Donna Ruff; **21** Nikki Middendorf; **36** Donna Ruff; **47** Bryan Leister; **48** *top* Kent A. Barton; **48-49** *bottom spread* Rubén de Anda; **50** Rick Powell; **53** Fian Arroyo; **69** Mike Deitz; **72** Rick Powell; **78-79** Fian Arroyo; **82** Jim Nuttle; **83** Matthew Pippin; **85** Fian Arroyo; **91** Randy Verougstraete; **92** *top* Kent A. Barton, *bottom* Neverne Covington; **93** Neverne Covington; **99, 112** Jim Nuttle; **121** Fian Arroyo; **135** Randy Verougstraete; **143** Frian Arroyo; **154, 156, 157** Gary Antonetti; **166** *top* Kent A. Barton, **166** *bottom,* **167** Catherine Leary; **173** Fian Arroyo; **186, 187, 194** Donna Ruff; **195** Nikki Middendorf; **196** *top* Kent A. Barton; **196-197** Fabricio Vanden Broeck; **201** Mike Deitz; **204** Mike Reed; **209** Rick Powell; **216** Susan Blubaugh; **217** Mike Deitz; **223** Fian Arroyo; **228-229** Neverne Covington; **235** Susan Blubaugh; **238** Neverne Covington; **239** Susan Blubaugh; **240** Kent A. Barton; **240-241** Enrique O. Sánchez; **247** Jim Nuttle; **255** Fian Arroyo; **265** Matthew Pippin; **269** Susan Blubaugh; **275** Fian Arroyo; **291** *left two columns* Fian Arroyo, *bottom right* Mike Reed; **297** Fian Arroyo; **304** Jim Nuttle; **307** Rick Powell; **313** Catherine Leary; **314** *top* Kent A. Barton; **314-315** Mike Reagan; **319** Stacey Schuett; **321** Catherine Leary; **337, 338** Stacey Schuett; **343** Fian Arroyo; **357** Patrick O'Brien; **365, 387** Fian Arroyo; **388** *top* Kent A. Barton, *bottom* Fundacion Federico García Lorca; **395** Fian Arroyo; **408** Patrick O'Brien; **417** Neverne Covington, Inc.; **421** Rick Powell; **423** Catherine Leary; **434** Stacey Schuett; **439, 442** Nikki Middendor; **443** Bryan Leister; **449** Fian Arroyo; **452** Patrick O'Brien; **458, 469** Neverne Covington, Inc.

Graphic Organizers and Hooks

Graphic Organizers and Hooks help students organize their thinking and learning. Listed below is a quick guide to those referenced in your Teacher's Edition.

Venn Diagram Two intersecting circles are used to compare and contrast ideas, concepts, cultures, stories, etc. Students write the similarities in the space where the circles intersect; the differences are in the non-intersecting areas.

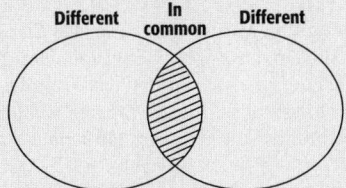

Fishbone Diagram Using the main topic as the "backbone" of the fish, students list related information on slanting lines off the horizontal main idea. This diagram can also be used to identify cause-and-effect relationships, by listing a sequence of events along the horizontal, and indicating causes or effects on the slanting lines.

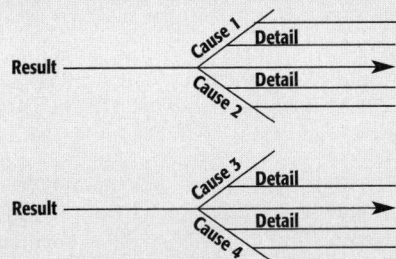

Spider or Web Diagram Students start with a main topic, the "spider," in the center, then branch off that into more and more related ideas, forming a web. Webs use this visual pattern to show connections between words, concepts, strategies, etc.

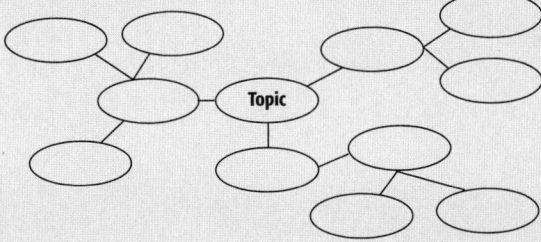

Mind Map Mind maps combine the graphical patterns of spider or web diagrams (see above) with colors, symbols, pictures, and shapes to stimulate right brain activity and retention. Then students add colors, symbols, pictures, etc. to the main topic and branches, for instance, varying word size and color to indicate relative importance of ideas.

Pie Chart Pie charts are used to show the relative importance, size, and proportion of ideas, concepts, quantities, etc. Students draw a circle, then indicate each idea's relative importance by designating how big a piece of the "pie" belongs to that idea.

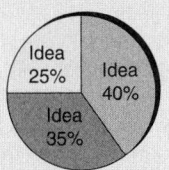

Cluster Diagram Students write down three or four main ideas relevant to their topic, each in its own circle, then write related concepts in bubbles around each main idea, forming clusters. They use each cluster to flush out each main idea as they progress from one to the next in their writing.

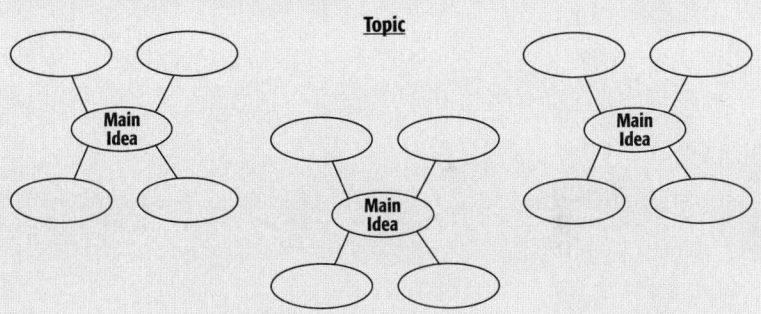

Visual Hook Visual Hooks serve to elicit previously learned material when a teacher wishes to build upon that knowledge. A Hook is a visual aid, such as a family tree or the layout of a house, that helps students make visual relationships while learning a new concept or vocabulary, thereby reinforcing the new material.

Verbal Hook Verbal Hooks are previously learned vocabulary words that are relevant to the new material the teacher is presenting. The words serve to hook the student back into their knowledge of vocabulary in order to expand upon it. An example would be to recall the word for "letter" when the teacher is presenting new vocabulary about the post office.